Praise for Bill May's *Tourney Time*

"High school basketball fans will find Tourney Time *to be extremely interesting and informative, since it contains the experiences of one who officiated basketball in Indiana for twenty-three years, including the state finals in 1972, '73, and '74, plus his thoughts and opinions on the game today.*
"Also, it is believed to be the only one book that has the score of every boys state tournament game from 1911 through 2005. That alone makes the book a valuable reference source for every fan."
—Roger Dickinson, Executive Director, Indiana Basketball Hall of Fame

"Bill May has recorded his personal memories of a long list of events as an Indiana basketball official. It will be an opportunity for reflection by anyone who has officiated."
—Herb Schwomeyer, former coach, administrator, official, author of *Hoosier Hysteria*, and foremost historian of Indiana basketball

"Bill May was one of the premier officials in Indiana high school basketball. He always had control of the game and was respected by his peers. It was my pleasure to work with him on his last high school game in the 1974 state finals."
—Gary Muncy, retired teacher, sales executive, and Mid-American, Ohio Valley, and Big Ten Conference official, who officiated the 1979 NCAA final game

"I traveled many miles and worked many games with Bill May over the years. Although he could have moved into the college leagues and worked several more years, he decided to retire at an early age. However, he is still interested and attends many high school and small college games."
—Bob Showalter, retired school administrator and Mid-American and Big Ten Conference official

Tourney Time

The Indiana High School Athletic Association
Boys Basketball Tournament
1911–2005

Scores, History, and a Referee's Memories,
Thoughts and Opinions

Bill May

IHSAA Official, 1951–1974

Copyright © 2005 by Bill May
All rights reserved. No portion of this book may be reproduced in any fashion, print, facsimile, or electronic, or by any method yet to be developed, without express permission of the copyright holder.

For further information, contact the publisher at

Emmis Books
1700 Madison Road
Cincinnati, OH 45206
www.emmisbooks.com

Library of Congress Cataloging-in-Publication Data

May, Bill (William)
  Tourney time : the Indiana High School Athletic Association Boys Basketball Tournament 1911-2005 / by Bill May.-- 2nd ed.
    p. cm.
  ISBN-13: 978-1-57860-194-3
  ISBN-10: 1-57860-194-0
  1. Basketball--Tournaments--Indiana--History. 2. Indiana High School Athletic Association. 3. School sports--Indiana--History. I. Title.
  GV885.72.I6M39 2005
  796.323'62'09772--dc22
                              2005021791

Cover designed by Pat Prather
Interior designed by Andrea Kupper

PERMISSIONS
Indiana High School Basketball, New and Old, Silver and Gold, Vol. 2; pages 232, 233, 234. "Muncie Central-Martinsville in 1928" by Thomas R. Cox (one of three authors).
  The Hammond Times, March 1, 1970. "Roosevelt Gets By Washington" by William E. Nangle, Executive Editor.
  Indianapolis Star Magazine, March 12, 1972. Exterior and interior of the Hinkle Fieldhouse, by *The Indianapolis Star*. *The Indianapolis Star*, March 31 and April 1, 1993. Obituary of Ward Hampton Smith by *The Indianapolis Star*.
  Bearcats, A History of Basketball at Muncie Central High School, 1901–1988. "Muncie Central, Some Explanations" by Dick and Jackie Stodghill, authors.
  Indiana Hall of Fame Classic program in 1979–80. Exterior picture of Muncie Fieldhouse, "Storm Over Stinesville" written by Wendell Trogdon, 1995, approved by Indiana Basketball Hall of Fame, Roger Dickinson, Executive Director.
  The Richmond Palladium Item, February 5, 1985, "Lone Loss for Oscar, Attucks." August 15, 1996, "Our View Column" by *The Richmond Palladium-Item*.

Preface

This book has been on my mind for nearly forty years. I finally got started after a happenstance visit with strangers at the Indiana Basketball Hall of Fame in New Castle, where I do volunteer work. When Mildred Booth Mitchell of Independence, Missouri, asked for information and memorabilia about Jasper High School's state championship team of 1949, it got my attention. She was a senior at Jasper that year. Fortunately, she asked the right person. There are a few years in my lifetime of interest in the game that stand out above others, and 1949 is one of them. Jasper lost nine regular season games but ended up state champions. Only Anderson's championship team of 1935 had lost that many games before becoming state champion.

When Mildred's husband, Jim, a native of Huntington County, asked several questions, I had the answers and added comments of my own. As Mildred and Jim were leaving the Hall of Fame, Jim said, "Bill, you are a walking encyclopedia of Indiana high school basketball history." I said, "I have been told that," although I could not remember by whom.

This chance meeting and visit reminded me that I have too many memories and too much knowledge of Indiana high school basketball history not to share them with others. It gave me the impetus to get started on this book. I am grateful to Jim and Mildred Mitchell.

Introduction

It has been said that the residents of Indiana have more interest in and dedication to high school basketball than those of any other state. Every year, the interest peaks in late February and early March, when the boys state championship tournament is played. Although the interest, dedication, and attendance at high school games, and especially the tourneys, have declined in the last forty years, particularly in the last eight years, many fans have long, strong memories.

To ensure that the history of 95 years of tournaments will not be lost, this list of scores is being published. From 1911 through 2005, exactly 50,386 boys state tournament games have been played or forfeited in Indiana. The scores have always been available in various publications, most notably the annual handbooks and, in recent years, the website of the Indiana High School Athletic Association (IHSAA), but to my knowledge, no one book has them in their entirety. Indiana high school basketball fans have wanted these records for many years, and now here they are.

Preceding the scores are "The Indiana High School Athletic Association (IHSAA) Boys Basketball Tournament History," a brief account of Hoosier Basketball and its teams, and "A Referee's Memories," an introductory essay in which I recall important personal events from my twenty-three years of officiating. Following the memories are my observations of the numerous historic and notable high school arenas in Indiana, and my insights into other aspects of Hoosier basketball.

There have been other books written about referees, but to my knowledge, this is the only one written by a referee. Enjoy.

Dedication

Without a doubt, my interest in basketball came from my parents, Wilbur (Bill) and Thelma Franklin May, two of the greatest basketball fans, especially of Indiana high school basketball. Although they always rooted for our hometown Hagerstown Tigers and Indiana University, from which my sister, Linda May French, graduated, they simply liked to watch good basketball, no matter who was playing, when, or where. Many times we drove many miles to see a good game.

No man can spend eighteen years (after marriage) traveling from one end of Indiana to the other, and all points in between, without having a loving and understanding wife, which Carolyn has been. Sons John and Paul, of whom I am very proud, were at home with her many nights and days when I was absent. Some or all of them accompanied me occasionally on officiating trips.

There were countless school personnel, coaches included, and fans who tolerated my oversights and bad calls.

To all of you, I dedicate this book.

—William B. (Bill) May

Acknowledgements

The names, numbers, experiences, and stories herein were obtained from many sources. The disadvantage of listing those who provided them is that inevitably I will forget someone. Hopefully not, however.

Carolyn's computer knowledge and assistance have been invaluable. Without her, this undertaking would have been much more difficult.

My parents, both deceased, kept newspapers, clippings, letters, programs, and other memorabilia, some from the 1920s. They had no idea that I would write this book. They would have been proud of my efforts.

I didn't get into this project until the visit with the previously mentioned Jim and Mildred Mitchell, and I would not have met them if I had not signed on as a volunteer at the Indiana Basketball Hall of Fame. Moreover, I would not have signed on as a volunteer if not for the encouragement and coaxing of the late John Jordan, a family friend and long-time Hall of Fame volunteer.

The staff at the Hall of Fame have been very helpful: Roger Dickinson, Executive Director; Sharon Roberts, Assistant Director; Ruth Coffey, Administrative Assistant; Lesley Vulgan, Artifacts and Collections; Pat Harding, Weekend Manager; the late Roddy Miller, Research and Records; and Jack Riggs, Facility Maintenance.

My brother-in-law, Ron Emmons, made several helpful suggestions.

Emmis Books personnel have been very supportive: Richard Hunt, President and Publisher; Jack Heffron, Editorial Director; Howard Cohen, Director of Publicity; Katie Parker, Library and Bookstore Sales; Andrea Kupper, Designer, and most of all, Don Prues, Project Manager and Editor of this book.

I would also like to thank Frank Wilmot at the Indiana State Library for his assistance.

The vast majority of the scores were obtained from the annual handbooks of the IHSAA.

Richard Maurer of Creative Publishing Concepts of Carmel did most of the rough entry of scores. I am responsible for all the corrections, revisions, and final formatting of the scores.

Others who provided leads, information, and suggestions: Harry Brandley, Connersville; Richard Butt, Ft. Wayne; Rex Cox, Farmland; Ray Craft, Associate Commissioner of the IHSAA; Rick Dawson, Rochester; Ron Divjak, Dyer; Mr. And Mrs. Jules Elzey, Knightstown; Hetty Gray, Fairland; Harold Lakeman, Madison; Grayson Mahin, Rushville; Gary McCann, Rock Hill, South Carolina; John Molodet, Crown Point; Jerry Moore, Muncie; Art Phenis, Liberty; Bobby Plump, Indianapolis; Jim Rayl, Kokomo; Bob Straight, Huntington; Wendell Trogdon, Mooresville; former Athletic Director Rae Woolpy, Athletic Director Chris Rodal, and Secretary Becky Carr of Richmond High School; and Al Dillon, Dick Reynolds, Ed Burkart, Don Crist, and Bill Upchurch, all of Richmond.

Public librarians from these cities were very accommodating: Bluffton, Connersville, Hammond, Jeffersonville, Kokomo, Logansport, Madison, Muncie, New Albany, New Castle, Richmond, Seymour, South Bend, and Warsaw.

Other essential information was obtained from the following: *Hoosier Hysteria* by Herb Schwomeyer, the foremost authority on Indiana high school basketball history; the Butler University sports information department; *Bearcats, a History of Basketball at Muncie Central High School; Indiana Basketball History,* published by the Hall of Fame; the *Membership History Handbook of the IHSAA; Indiana High School Basketball, New and Old, Silver and Gold, '28, '53, '78*; the Hammond Historical Society; and the Northern Indiana Historical Society. Walden Studio of New Castle produced the excellent photo of New Castle Field House. Ron Gary of Richmond shot the author photo.

Much information was obtained from these newspapers: *Bluffton News-Banner; Connersville News-Examiner; Ft. Wayne Journal Gazette; The Graphic; Greensboro, North Carolina, News & Record; The Hammond Times; The Indianapolis News; The Indianapolis Star; The Indianapolis Times; Jeffersonville Evening News; Marion Chronicle-Tribune; The Muncie Evening Press; The Muncie Star; The New Albany Ledger-Tribune; New Castle Courier-Times; Richmond Palladium-Item;* and *Seymour Daily Tribune.*

 **Contents**

IHSAA Boys Basketball Tournament History................... 12

A Referee's Memories........................... 13

Scores by Decade

1911–1919.. 73
1920–1929.. 88
1930–1939.. 148
1940–1949.. 224
1950–1959.. 303
1960–1969.. 383
1970–1979.. 456
1980–1989.. 519
1990–1999.. 581
2000–2005.. 646

IHSAA Boys Basketball Tournament History

1911–2005

Basketball was invented in 1891 by Dr. James Naismith at what is now Springfield College in Springfield, Massachusetts. The game was brought to Indiana by the Reverend Nicholas McKay, who was in Springfield at the time training to be the General Secretary of the Crawfordsville YMCA. When he returned to Indiana, he brought the new game with him.

The first official basketball game in Indiana was played at the Crawfordsville YMCA in 1894, but the first state-wide tournament involving high school teams didn't occur until 1911, when twelve teams entered, each representing a congressional district. Interest in the game increased rapidly, and by 1921 an impressive 394 high schools teams entered the tournament. The peak number of teams was 787 in 1938. It then decreased steadily until the mid 1990s, due to the school reorganization act of 1959, resulting in the consolidation of schools. There were 388 teams in the 2005 tournament. Although few, if anyone, knew it at the time, the 1950s was the last era of great Indiana high school basketball, in terms of interest and enthusiasm.

The rapid increase in the number of teams after 1911 required three more levels, called sectionals, regionals, and semi-finals (later renamed semi-states) being added.

Except in the large metropolitan areas, through the first fifty years a typical sectional tournament involved a county seat school serving as host to several smaller schools from nearby. Naturally, the smaller schools took on the challenge of beating the bigger schools and did so more often than one would imagine. The smaller schools sided with one another when the host school was involved, and when one of the smaller schools did win, all of them were happy. Usually, a small school winning a sectional did not have great hopes of winning a regional tournament. The mission for that year had been accomplished simply by winning the sectional. Such thinking prevailed until the 1960s. After the school reorganization act of 1959 was implemented, things changed greatly.

Scores of all tournament games from 1911 through 2005 are in the last section, but first are the memories, thoughts, and opinions of one who officiated from 1951 through 1974.

A Referee's Memories

The Beginning

I got an early start in officiating since my father was an official from 1926 through 1955.

Growing up in that environment created my addiction to officiate, and I learned things early on that others don't learn until much later. My career began when I was in the tenth grade at Hagerstown High School. Our eighth grade team was challenged by the team from Dalton Township, five miles away. A classmate and I volunteered to officiate. Hagerstown won and the Dalton people weren't happy, a typical expectation in basketball everywhere, even today.

Dad officiated seventeen sectional and nine regional tournaments. He was one of the best never chosen to work the state finals. Why, I do not know, except that when he worked, and even when I worked, except for my last season, tournament officials were chosen by a system involving politics. Dad was not a politician. He simply did his job every night, receiving many compliments and few complaints. He did not ask for political favors, and as a result, got none. His last sectional was in 1955, at Hartford City, the same year as my first, at Bluffton. Our careers overlapped by four years. We worked seven games together.

After graduating from Hagerstown High School, I entered what was then Ball State Teachers College. There were five junior high schools in Muncie and many others nearby, so there was always a need for junior high and ninth grade officials. That was advantageous for me, because I got a fast start in officiating and was able to earn money to help with college expenses.

First Game

My first game as an IHSAA licensed official was in November, 1951, a junior varsity (JV) game between Richmond and Liberty in Civic Hall, Richmond. The other official was Brooks Baynes, a well-respected teacher and coach, later a junior high school principal. Coaching Richmond's JV's team was Hub Etchison, later the very successful football coach. At one point he jumped-up and boomed "No" to one of his players. I thought he was yelling at me. It got my attention since he was an intimidating person and it was my first game.

An Early Lesson

I learned a lesson and learned it well: the lesson of organization and punctuality. Dad and John Hilligoss of Richmond had the Kokomo at Marion game in the 1951–52 season. They left earlier than usual so I could ride along and officiate the JV game. I was in Ball State and didn't yet have a car so I was to meet them at a bus stop in downtown Muncie, before we would proceed to Marion. I forgot that the busses ran on their schedule, not mine. I missed the one that I should have taken and didn't get to the meeting place until one hour before game time in Marion, forty miles away. Hilligoss said, "Hold on; we'll make a fast trip to Marion!" I walked into the Marion Memorial Coliseum five minutes before game time. Afterwards, as we started to drive away, Hilligoss said, "Let's have a slower trip going home than we had coming up!"

Another official, whose name I don't remember, said, "It's better to arrive at a game thirty minutes early than thirty seconds late." There is not an efficient athletic director today who does not breath a sigh of relief when he sees the officials for that night walk in the door.

Veterans' Philosophies

Dad, Marvin Todd of Ft. Wayne, and Don McBride of Richmond, were the only three officials I worked with that seemed to have the play called before it happened. Their judgment and officiating in general were excellent.

McBride often expounded that a good official must read the rule book forward and backward, memorize it, therefore knowing what to do in any situation, then throw the book away and officiate using common sense. In other words: (1) know the rules; (2) have the fortitude to enforce them; (3) have the common sense to know when to enforce them.

I will add that an official will encounter situations, plays, mix-ups, disputes, etc., in grade school, junior high, and junior varsity games that will rarely occur in varsity games, since the players, coaches, scorers and timers are less experienced. That is why it is best for an official to start at the bottom and work his way up.

Hilligoss recommended keeping a tight rein on a game early. As it progressed and the official could see that the players were trying to play good basketball, he could ease up and let the insignificant things, like incidental contact and borderline violations, slide.

My dad said, "You'll have fewer complaints by calling a game a little too tightly than by calling it not tightly enough."

They'll Always Like You

Hilligoss believed that if a coach liked an official the first time they met, he would always like him, and vice versa. I found that to be true generally, but not always. Early in my career, I had a New Castle JV game in the Church Street gymnasium, predecessor to the present New Castle Field House. New Castle was playing another North Central Conference school and near the end of the third quarter, New Castle was awarded the ball under its basket. According to the rules at that time, officials did not have to hand the ball to the thrower-in unless it was from the team's frontcourt. If the throw-in was to be from the backcourt, the team could grab the ball, step out of bounds, and throw it in.

In this case, knowing that time was about to expire, the New Castle player got the ball, threw it in without the other official handling it, and a teammate scored just before the buzzer, ending the third quarter. It was an error by the other official, an older, local man, who made a career out of working JV games. After a discussion, with strong input from both coaches plus the visiting team's head coach, he allowed the basket to count. The visiting head coach, in a heated manner, said, "Don't either of you ever work another game for us!" As luck would have it, I was already scheduled to have their JV game a few weeks later at another NCC school, and things went well that night. A few seasons later, that head coach unexpectedly asked me to work a varsity game, one of my first in the NCC. We got along well, after that rocky start at New Castle. I have fond memories of those experiences, both the JV and first varsity games.

First Varsity Game

After officiating grade school, junior high, and junior varsity games, I moved-up to officiating varsity games in the 1952–53 season. While attending a pre-season rules meeting, I learned that Whitewater High School, in Wayne County, needed two officials for their first game, two weeks away. I remember the look on Ben Rhoades's face when I introduced myself; he certainly was not expecting to see someone that young. He had to have two officials, to work both the JV and varsity games, so he agreed to use me and a college friend, Don Potter.

The Whitewater gymnasium was very small, as were most at that time. It had four or five rows of wooden permanent bleachers that came to within inches of the sideline on one side of the court. There was a stage on the other side, with the teams seated below, their feet on the sideline. The out-of-bounds lines on the ends were painted into the walls. The wooden backboards hung from the walls and the ten-second lines were the foul lines at the opposite end.

There was no public address system, so invariably officials would be asked to announce to the crowd that chili, hamburgers, or whatever would be served in the cafeteria after the game. I performed that task at Whitewater.

Whitewater rallied to win 54–51 over Lewisville. It was a coach vs. former player match-up, as Rhoades had once played for Lewisville coach Beryl (Bud) Bosstick.

Younger people watching professional, college, or even high school games today would have a hard time believing this. Yet, this gymnasium was very common for that era. Probably ninety percent of the small school gymnasiums were in the school building itself. We officials usually used a classroom as our dressing room and would shower with one of the teams afterward, normally the winning team since they would be in a better mood.

I have occasionally driven past the site of the Whitewater school. It has been demolished, but once I stopped and picked up a small piece of brick as a memento of my first varsity game.

Tourney Time

More Schools Then

It was easier to get started in varsity officiating then than now, since there were so many more schools, and therefore more games. In the early 1950s in my immediate five-county area there were sixty-four high schools. Today, there are twenty-six.

We'll Pay $10

A pleasant surprise happened in October, 1952. Potter and I tried to work as many games as we could and we looked at schedules in newspapers looking for "off night" games when many schools weren't playing. We noticed that Kokomo would be playing East Chicago Washington on Monday, December 22, so I wrote to Chester Hill, Athletic Director, and asked if he needed JV officials for that night. Incidentally, Chester Hill was coach of the 1915 state championship team of Thorntown. His reply:

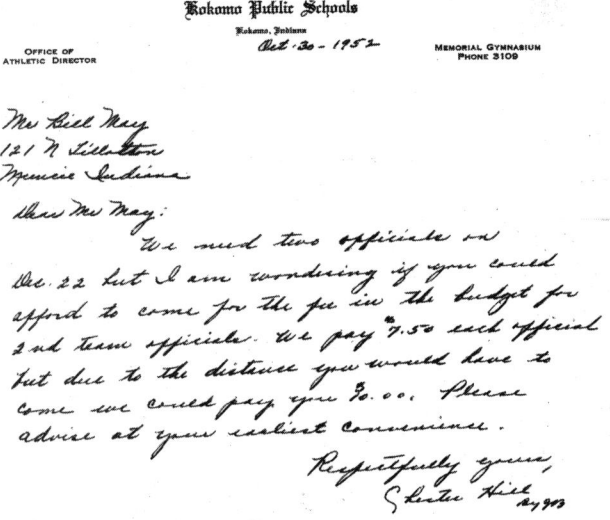

Five Games in One Day

In January, 1953, Potter and I worked a ninth grade, four-team tournament at New Castle: two games in the morning and two in the afternoon. After walking a block to the Plaza Hotel (now demolished) for dinner, we returned and worked the JV game that night. The New Castle players were astonished when we reappeared to officiate the night game. I imagine that five games in one day was common up through the 1930s, but not in the 1950s.

I Almost Waited Too Long

On January 30, 1953, Selma, a small school near Muncie, played Stoney Creek of Randolph County, also a small school. Stoney Creek scored ten points *in the final minute* to win by one. The Stoney coach, Calvin Kitchel, who had graduated from Ball State the previous year, came in the dressing room and said, "Whew, I almost waited too long to tell them to turn it on!"

I Remembered Him

In February, 1953, I heard from another official that the Ridgeville coach had gotten out of hand in a game and gotten a technical foul or two. It doesn't take long for that information to get around among officials. I was interested because I was scheduled to work the Ridgeville game at Spartanburg the next week. I received a card from the Spartanburg coach reminding me of the date, and he closed with "P. S. Bring your best whistle!" We had no trouble. But that's not the end of the story, which didn't come until 1987, thirty-four years later.

The Ridgeville coach had moved several times, had since retired from coaching, and was visiting one of his former players, who lived in Richmond. They happened to sit two seats from us at the Richmond regional tournament. The former player, also a friend of mine, reintroduced us, mentioning that his visitor was an ex-coach. I asked where he coached and he named several schools, but never mentioned Ridgeville. I finally said, "I could swear that you once coached in Randolph County." "Oh yes, I did coach one year at Ridgeville." I don't know whether he remembered me or not, but I remembered him.

Just One Game

The first highlight of the 1954 season for me was the Mt. Summit–New Lisbon game, which was to have been played at New Lisbon on December 23. I was to work both the JV and varsity games, as was the custom then. However, it was decided to play the game as part of a double-header at the Church Street gymnasium in New Castle, instead of at New Lisbon. I would work just one game instead of two, and the other game was between old rivals: Cadiz and Kennard.

That was the biggest crowd that I had worked in front of at that time and getting to work just one game, instead of two, and collecting the same amount of pay was a treat. The Church Street gymnasium, with a seating capacity of 2,000, was home of the New Castle Trojans at that time. There were no other games nearby on that December 23, so practically every fan in Henry County was there.

Nobody Knows Them

Bringing in officials that no one knew previously to work a game between strong rivals is symbolic of the importance of basketball and officiating in the 1950s. The Howard County schools of Northwestern and Western were rivals, of course, and for their game in 1954 they wanted to use officials that no one in the county knew. So, I

Tourney Time

was asked to work the game along with an official from Anderson. They played at the Kokomo Armory, which had been the home gymnasium of Kokomo High School after their gym burned in the mid 1940s.

We Kept The Game Moving

The 1955 season was to have started on November 2 with Geneva hosting Jefferson Township of Adams County. It didn't start then because the Jefferson coach had gotten into a hassle with a baseball umpire that fall, so the school and the coach were put on probation by the IHSAA and were not allowed to play basketball until December 1. The game was rescheduled for a Saturday in January. I was called to work two games as a substitute in the Wayne County tournament that afternoon, after which I drove to Geneva and worked two more games that night. I didn't feel real sharp that night, but the Geneva coach evidently thought so because he commented, "I liked the way you hustled and kept the game moving." I worked for him many times after that and we always got along fine, an example of Hilligoss's theory about first impressions being so important between an official and a coach.

Confine Your Activities

It was nice to know that if you tried to do the right thing in officiating, you had the support of the IHSAA. In February, 1955, I worked a game between Parker and Selma, close rivals, three miles apart. My fellow official ejected the Selma timer for making inappropriate gestures in his disagreement with some calls. A few weeks later I received a copy of a letter from L.V. Phillips, Commissioner of the IHSAA, to the Principal of Selma. Here it is:

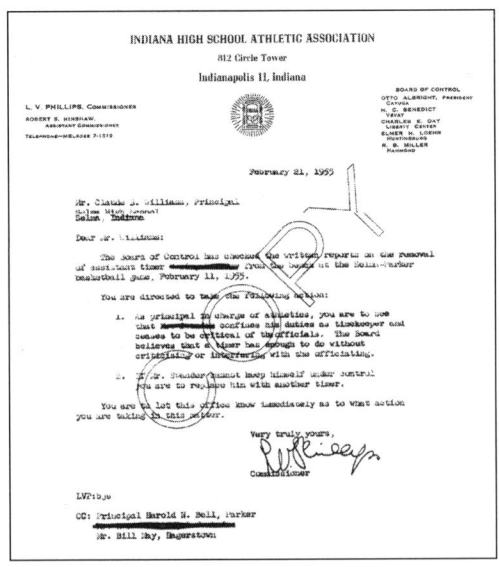

Oops!

Some officials, despite their overall competency, did not always use the correct mechanics of officiating. I worked a game at Fairland in the 1950s with such an official, and near the end, the visitors, Whiteland, had the ball when the other official stopped the game to wipe the floor. A Whiteland player stood holding the ball through the delay. When ready to resume, the other official said to the player holding the ball, "Go ahead," instead of giving it to him out-of-bounds for a throw-in. This created a furor among the Fairland fans since they thought it should have been a double-dribble violation. Shortly thereafter, that official worked two state final tournaments, in spite of mechanical shortcomings like that. As mentioned previously, politics played a big part in tournament assignments. That official had a strong political ally in a high position.

If I Ever See Him, I'll Ask Him

In the 1955 season, I worked the Harrisburg at Brookville game. The old gymnasium, which has been demolished, was below ground level and had a dark tile floor so it could also be used for community activities. It held few people and was very crowded. I was not as alert as I should have been at the end of the JV game and didn't know whether a Brookville shot at the horn should count or not. I guessed and said, "It counts." It was the winning basket, and needless to say the Harrisburg coach and fans weren't very happy the rest of the night, as Brookville won the varsity game handily.

The next fall, official Dan Mitrione, of Richmond, asked if I would like to work a game with him that season at Harrisburg. I said, "It's OK with me, but you'd better check with Harrisburg because they probably won't want me." A few days later I received a contract from Harrisburg. They would be playing Brookville, as luck would have it. The game would be played at the Connersville gymnasium, a precursor to the present 5,800 seat bowl-type arena.

On game night, I picked-up my wife-to-be, Carolyn, then got Dan, and when I told him that we had just become engaged, he insisted that we stop so he could buy us a celebratory dinner.

After the beating from Brookville the previous year, Harrisburg was up for the game. They had kept most of their players from the previous year and Brookville had lost theirs. It was no contest, as Harrisburg won easily. The Brookville coach was unhappy with everything, of course, including my officiating. That's when I called my first technical foul on a coach.

As we were showering after the game, the Harrisburg coach congratulated us on a good game, which is always taken with a grain of salt when coming from a winner. "Bob's pretty upset with your officiating, Bill. He's not upset with you though, Dan. If he thinks you were bad, he evidently doesn't remember the two we had down there last year." One of those two was yours truly. I said nothing, and to this day

I don't know if he was just getting back at me for the previous year or was being honest and didn't remember me. I worked for him eight years later when he was at a bigger school, in an away game. He lost that game but later asked me to work at his school. He lost again, a close one on a call that I made near the end. Again, he was complimentary. If I ever see him again, I'll probably ask about the remark at Connersville, but if I never see him again, it will always be good for a laugh.

Dan Mitrione later became Chief of Police in Richmond, and did police consulting work for the federal government. While on an assignment in Uruguay, he unfortunately was kidnapped and then murdered. I later worked with his younger brother, Ray, who was also a fine official.

The Same Coat

In 1956, I worked a game between Frankton, coached by Muff Davis, and Yorktown, coached by Earl Snider; both coaches were of the "old school." However, Earl had a reputation for taking every advantage he could—switching jumpers, foul shooters, or whatever. The custom then, and now, is for coaches to exchange lineup cards before games.

A split second before tip-off, Muff jumped-up and yelled, "Hold it, hold it. Don't start the game. Snider, what are you trying to pull? Look at this lineup card you gave me. None of these names and numbers are out there on the floor!!" Earl walked-up, looked at the card for a second, grinned, and said, "Muff, you must be wearing the same sport coat you wore last week. These names and numbers are for Northwestern; that's who you played last week!" Muff said nothing and just quietly retreated to his seat. An unusual way to start a game.

One of the Frankton players was Roger Dickinson, later a coach, athletic director, principal, superintendent, even an official, and now Executive Director of the Indiana Basketball Hall of Fame.

Coach's Request Backfired

One of my early sectionals involved a host school and several smaller county schools, very common at that time. One of those county schools had been a perennial challenger for several years. Before the challenger and the host played, the coach of the host school talked to me and the other official and in similar words said, "We've played these guys several years now, and last year they got kind of rough; some of our players got hurt. Just stay on top of it and don't let it get rough." We called 41 fouls; 13 on one, 28 on the other. Guess who had the 28 and guess who won?

That left four county teams in the tournament. Each of the semi-final games had an "unpleasant" (I euphemize) coach, and a "nice guy" coach. Both games went into overtime. And both "unpleasant" coaches ended up winning, so we then had to tolerate them in the championship game.

Rip Van Winkle

In 1953, my dad officiated the sectional at Danville. The winner was one of the smaller schools—the Amo Aces. In 1958, the sectional was moved to Brownsburg and I was assigned there to officiate. The winner—Amo! There were thirteen teams in that tournament, and afterward I thought that any of five teams could have won.

Fifteen years later, in 1973, I was again sent to Brownsburg. I had not worked there or for any of the schools involved in those fifteen years. I felt like Rip Van Winkle. Instead of thirteen schools, there were seven, but we had four officials, instead of three.

Not there in 1973 were Stilesville, Lizton, Plainfield Charlton, New Winchester, Clayton, North Salem, and yes, Amo. Speedway had been assigned to the sectional at Ben Davis, but Monrovia and Mooresville had been transferred in from Bloomington.

Shin Splints

The most exhausting tournament I officiated was the sectional at Winchester in 1959. The hardwood floor evidently was laid directly onto concrete, causing it to be so hard that I, along with others through the years, developed shin splints. They caused so much discomfort that the only relief I got was to keep walking or running, even during time outs. I never had that trouble, before or after. I understand the floor was replaced in later years.

First Game at Butler (Hinkle) Fieldhouse

Although I had watched many games at Butler (later renamed Hinkle) Fieldhouse, I had never worked a game there until I was assigned to work the 1960 sectional, with Hilligoss, Homer Owens of Carlos City, and Bob Showalter, then of Hagerstown.

In the field were seventh-ranked Crispus Attucks, the defending state champion, plus unranked Indianapolis Shortridge and Indianapolis Tech. Shortridge had beaten Attucks by one point in January, but Attucks was still considered the tournament favorite. They had won the 1959 state championship, defeating Shortridge, 63–62, in the sectional semi-final, after losing to them two times in the regular season, by fourteen and three points. When Shortridge beat Attucks again by one point earlier in the 1960 season, the stage was set for a classic rematch.

As luck would have it, they were drawn to play the third game on the first night of the sectional. The four of us officiating naturally rode together, and as we approached the Fieldhouse on 49th Street, Hilligoss drove on past the driveway to the parking lot and proceeded to the Butler University Student Union Building. "I'm going to buy some cigars," he said. Owens, Showalter, and I followed suit since he was the veteran. I said, "I didn't realize you smoke cigars, John." "Oh yeah," he answered.

We returned to the Fieldhouse and while we were dressing, Commissioner Phillips

Tourney Time

walked in. "Hi, L.V. Have a cigar," was Hilligoss's greeting. We then realized why he had bought the cigars. We all gave Mr. Phillips a cigar before the night was over. When he visited the dressing room, he sat down, lit a cigar, and told a few stories—it was a memorable and entertaining experience.

There were fourteen teams in that tournament which necessitated three games on Wednesday and Thursday nights, two on Friday afternoon and night, two on Saturday afternoon, and the final game on Saturday night. On the first night, Hilligoss and I worked the first and third games; Owens and Showalter the second.

With Attucks and Shortridge scheduled for the third game, the first two were almost like JV games. One of my most memorable moments in officiating came when we started the game. I was the referee, which meant I would toss the ball for the opening tip. As I waited for the teams at the center circle, I looked all around the Fieldhouse. It was completely filled. Not an empty seat. According to *The Indianapolis Times*, the attendance was 14,943, which at that time was capacity. Shortridge won 69–56, eliminating the defending state champions.

The Indianapolis Times commented on a Friday afternoon game between Broad Ripple and Washington (see photo).

Ripple won the roughly played game, 67–53, committing 18 of the 38 errors made by both teams, plus some inconsistencies by the harassed officials (Hilligoss and me). About 8,000 fans saw the two-game Friday afternoon session and nobody saw everything alike. Had officials blown whistles on all fouls committed, fans would have seen little basketball.

Caught in the Act?
Referee John Hilligoss (left) apparently caught Shortridge's Paul Henry (30) in the act of hanging to the arm of Whit Warman of North Central during last night's rugged battle between the Blue Devils and the Panthers. There was some controversy whether Henry was guilty of holding Warman or the ball.—Times photo by Lloyd B. Walton.

The winning coach, Gene Beaman, asked Hilligoss, "How can you call a foul and count a basket when the other official is calling traveling?" Hilligoss answered, "It was such a pretty play that I didn't want to spoil it by calling traveling."

These comments, under the picture of John Hilligoss, sound like a major, drawn-out controversy occurred. Actually, there was just a smattering of boos.

The sectional drew 8,000 people to watch four high school teams on a weekday afternoon. Those days are gone, unfortunately, as are the strong inner city and big city—small town rivalries, along with one class basketball, which created great interest and excitement.

New Year's Eve
In 23 years, I officiated on New Year's Eve just once: December 31, 1960. Anderson Highland had a four-team tournament and Dick Tiernan (for whom Richmond's present multi-purpose gymnasium is named) and I worked the second night. I had worked the Lafayette Jefferson tournament on Tuesday and Wednesday, the Elkhart tournament on Thursday and Friday, and was finishing the week at Highland. Middletown was playing Parker in the final game and as we returned to the floor after halftime, I remarked to the Parker coach, "This is a fine way to spend New Year's Eve, isn't it?"

Changes
Although few, if any, people realized it in 1960, change was imminent in Indiana high school basketball and it would never be the same, largely due to two factors:

The increase in other things for people to do, such as more television (including televised basketball), shopping malls, etc.

The school reorganization act of 1959, resulting in the majority of small high schools being reorganized into larger ones, causing a loss of loyalty to small local schools; and more sports being offered by the resulting larger high schools.

The Big Blizzard
There were significant snowstorms at sectional tournament time in six of eight years from 1960 through 1967. Few Hoosiers age fifty or older will forget the blizzard that struck at sectional time in 1961. It happened late Friday night and Saturday, and by afternoon many fans were stranded in gymnasiums.

McBride and I were assigned to the Bluffton sectional, and on our way there on Friday afternoon, I noticed how different the sky looked, very gray and overcast, almost white. As planned, we stayed overnight in Ft. Wayne, and after arising on Saturday morning knew why the sky had looked the way it did. The ground was covered with snow and ice and it was still coming down.

We got to Bluffton with some difficulty. The two tournament favorites, Bluffton and Ossian, played the first afternoon game. According to the officials scheduling rotation system, I worked the first game with Bob Henne, with McBride not scheduled. Knowing that that game would be very competitive, with possibly a close outcome, McBride dressed for the second game so he would be able to see the end of the first game.

Bluffton was one of the first schools to use the spotlight in a darkened gymnasium method of introducing the players. When the lights went off and the spotlight came on, shining on the entrance where the players would enter the court, the announcer said, "Introducing the players for the first game." Who walked into the spotlight on the way to his seat—McBride. He was never known for being inconspicuous anyway.

We completed the two games, after which Fred Park, principal of Bluffton and tournament manager, said that since both winning teams and their fans were there, we would play the final game as scheduled, in spite of the weather. By evening, several sectionals in the state had been postponed until Monday, but many fans and teams spent that Saturday night in gymnasiums. We were fortunate to finish on Saturday.

Four other things come to mind about that tournament:

While working on the first night, I had a severe back spasm but managed to hobble through. However, after sitting down I couldn't stand up straight for several minutes, giving my back muscles time to relax. At halftime, I had to remain standing. It was the same way riding in a car. I walked into restaurants hunched-over. McBride would say, "Straighten-up; you embarrass me," and, "That's the first time I ever refereed with the Hunchback of Notre Dame." It's hard to imagine McBride being embarrassed by anything.

After the final game, several Bluffton people invited us to stay overnight and if I had been driving we would have stayed. However, McBride was driving and he said, "When you've got warm weather at home, you get home to it."

It was the worst night on which I traveled in my twenty-three years of officiating. The snow and ice were deep and drifted, but somehow we made it to Richmond, after a stop to eat and then a visit in Winchester to see a fellow official. McBride drove the same way he officiated—full speed ahead. Several times, with drifts ahead, he hit the accelerator and we plowed on through even in his non-four-wheel car.

The official friend in Winchester had an overnight guest, Cecil Tague, freshman coach and later head coach at New Castle. He had scouted the Winchester sectional because that winner would play New Castle in the regional the next week, they thought. After a series of upsets, Ward-Jackson was a surprise winner at Winchester, but Cecil had few notes on them. The New Castle sectional final game was postponed until Monday. Cecil's scouting was in vain, though, as Lewisville, led by Marion Pierce, beat New Castle.

When we got to Richmond, police officers told us the road we had just come down was closed. To finish the night, when I walked into our house, Carolyn had just gotten up to give our two-week-old son his 2 A.M. bottle, so I handled that duty.

One final note, which didn't come to light until two years ago while I was doing my volunteer work at the Indiana Basketball Hall of Fame, is that we had two visitors at the Hall of Fame: Ray Miller, who had coached Hartford Center in Adams County; and Jerry Augsberger, who played for him in 1953. In a game against Decatur, Augsberger shot 39 free throws and made 24. They were wondering if that's a record.

Although unable to answer the question about the record, Sharon Roberts, Assistant Director of the Hall of Fame, produced the official scorebook with the record of the game. Augsberger mentioned that he had coached at Petroleum, near Bluffton, in the early 1960s. I asked if he was there in 1961 and he said, "Yes, we lost in the final game of the sectional." I asked if he remembered who officiated that tournament. When he said he didn't, I identified myself. Small world!

Things Change, Sometimes

In keeping with Hilligoss's theory about the first meeting between a coach and an official, I worked a game in which the losing coach wasn't very happy with me. I didn't work for him again for a few years. After one call, he remarked, "You haven't changed a bit." "You haven't either," was my reply. A few years later I had him in a sectional. He lost, but was complimentary, so sometimes things do change.

Snow Again

1963 was the fourth straight year that we had snow at sectional time. I wasn't in the mood to fight it on the way to my assignment at Carmel. I rode the train from Richmond to Indianapolis and got a ride to Carmel with Nick Jones, who was covering the tournament for *The Indianapolis News*. On Saturday night, I rode home with Showalter, who had worked at Brownsburg.

Nine Overtimes

John Thomas of Shelbyville and I officiated the longest game in Indiana high school history: nine overtimes in a regional game between Liberty Center and Swayzee in the Marion Memorial Coliseum in 1964. The following newspaper accounts describe it well, but I will add my opinion that Liberty Center probably would have won in regulation time if their best player, 6–5 Dick Harris, hadn't fouled-out with 48 seconds remaining. He had scored 26 points despite sitting-out a large portion of the game in foul trouble.

Could Only Happen In Indiana: Swayzee Wins In 9 Overtimes

MARION, Ind. (AP)—Swayzee and little Liberty Center set a longevity record for Indiana high school basketball Saturday afternoon, playing nine overtime periods before Swayzee finally won 65-61 in the Marion regional tourney.

The previous record was the seven-overtime marathon in which Camden defeated Delphi 22-19 in a 1938 sectional tourney game.

Swayzee, headed for consolidation next year with Oak Hill, now has played more than the equivalent of three games to win its last two. It needed three overtimes to get past Oak Hill in last Saturday's Marion sectional championship game 38-37.

Liberty Center, a Wells County school whose 70 pupils made the smallest sectional winner, was tied 52-52 with Swayzee at the end of regular time. Neither scored in the first five overtimes as they held for last-second shots and missed.

Swayzee gambled by fouling Liberty Center on the seventh overtime tipoff. Bill Day dropped in two free throws for Liberty Center but Lennie Boswell matched the points with a Swayzee field goal and the count was 54-54 going into the eighth overtime.

Both teams gave up caution in the eighth extra period and scored five points apiece for a 59-59 tie.

Burl Turner scored a quick basket for Swayzee after the ninth overtime tipoff. Liberty Center missed a shot and Boswell hit another for Swayzee. Bruce Stanton came back with one for Liberty Center but Rex Woodmansee tossed in two free throws for Swayzee to wind up the game.

The marathon affair delayed the start of the second game between Huntington and Portland for more than an hour. The overtimes ran 55 minutes.

Liberty Center, the Bluffton sectional champion, led at the first three regular stops, 19-15, 31-26 and 38-34 before the 52-52 tie at the end of the fourth quarter.

Dick Harris of Liberty Center was high scorer of the game with 26 points but fouled out shortly before the end of regulation play. Sophomore Jack Saylors led Swayzee with 20.

The weary Swayzee team was no match for Huntington in the final game and bowed to the Vikings 58-33.

Tourney Time

    Liberty Center still controlled the tip and got the ball to start the overtime periods. Through the first five overtimes, they held the ball for the last shot before expiration of time, but never connected. There was some activity from the sixth overtime on, before Swayzee pulled away in the ninth. The Huntington and Portland teams, waiting to play the second game, got a little impatient, to say the least. Fred Park, principal of Bluffton, and a great friend, was seated in the first row directly behind the official bench. Between two of the overtimes, he offered me popcorn and a drink.

In January, 2004, the game was commemorated at a reunion at the Swayzee Public Library. Six of the players, the assistant coach, the cheerleaders, and approximately 65 citizens attended. Carolyn and I were there in addition to John Thomas, the other official, and Roger Dickinson, Executive Director of the Hall of Fame; Herb Schwomeyer, the premier historian; and Dee Compton, a former coach and Hall of Fame member. Carolyn and I also attended a game at Oak Hill High School that night and I threw out the game ball. Swayzee pupils began attending Oak Hill in 1965.

Snow Again

1965 was another year in which snow interfered at sectional time, and I believe that mine, at Milan, was one of the few that went off as scheduled.

While driving home afterward, I thought back to the games and the teams, and decided that any of five teams of the eight entered could have won. Four of the five were in one bracket, meaning only one could get to the championship game. The fifth best was in the bracket with the three weakest, and they won, thanks largely to their lucky draw.

One sequence well describes the tournament. In the final game, the ball went from one end of the court to the other and back in less than ten seconds. The rapid exchange resulted in the team that didn't have the ball in the beginning scoring a lay-up as the horn sounded to end the third quarter. There was a court length pass, a deflection, two saves, and a ricochet off a knee before the player scoring the lay-up got possession at mid-court. The scoring team's crowd, the eventual winner, loved it.

Milan lost by one point in the first game. It was eleven years after their state championship, and I got the impression their fans thought they should win it every year.

Did the Horn Sound?

In 1966, as I officiated the sectional at Lawrenceburg, the host school was very much the underdog in the championship game against close neighbor and rival Aurora.

Aurora led by as much as fourteen points early, but Lawrenceburg came back and with twenty-two seconds remaining, the score was tied. At that time, the rules stated that if a player with the ball was closely guarded for five seconds, a held ball was to be called, which I did. As luck would have it, the tip went directly behind me to the sideline where it was impossible for me or the other official to see whether or not the Aurora player who had possession was out of bounds.

Since nothing was called, Aurora kept possession, scored, and was fouled with four seconds remaining. The free throw was missed. Lawrenceburg got the rebound and called time-out. The clock showed 0:00, but because of the crowd noise neither I nor the other official knew whether the horn had sounded. Upon asking the official timer, I could tell that he didn't know either. After several seconds of confusion on

Tourney Time

his part, with much verbal input from others nearby, he finally shook his head and said that it had counted, but he was not the least bit authoritative. At that point, I declared that time had expired and that Aurora was the winner.

Adding to the timer's confusion was the fact that his son played for Lawrenceburg, had played probably the best game of his life, and it appeared that his team had lost. If I had it to do over, I would have handled it differently, by operating the clock myself to determine if the horn had sounded. If it had sounded, the game was indeed over. If it had not sounded, I would have reset the clock with a split-second remaining and Lawrenceburg would have had possession with a very slim chance to get off a shot. It was unfortunate for everyone, except Aurora.

I Should Have Gotten A Letter

After working five of their ten games in a ten week period in the 1966–67 season, Kokomo High School should have given me a school letter. The last game was in their regional, and afterward I was able to name their first ten players and their numbers.

The author in action in a Marion at Kokomo game, this one on December 8, 1967, with the Kokomo girls cheer block in the background.

My Best Work
I felt that I did the best work of my career in the 1967–68 season. I worked the Southport sectional. The coaches who rated us gave me a perfect score.

I Finally Got Him
One coach for whom I had worked many times was a consistent pest. Whenever any decision, whatever it was, that could have gone either way but did not go his way, he politely told me. He never did anything to warrant a technical foul, though, until 1969.

The opposing team had a fast break, and the player receiving a pass batted and bobbled it, not getting control, but covering ten to fifteen feet in the process. He finally got control, scored a lay-up and was fouled. I called the foul, counted the basket, and my momentum took me toward the official bench and his team bench. He was standing up, giving the traveling signal in a manner conspicuous to the 3,000 plus fans. All in one uninterrupted sequence, I gave the foul signal, the basket good signal, and called a technical foul on him. I don't recall any call ever feeling better.

Things Change Fast
For some reason, I worked the Kokomo–Marion game six times, on both home courts. One time was in the Marion Memorial Coliseum with an official who shall remain unnamed. Whenever I worked at Marion, I was invited to the home of Jim and Imogene Hook, natives of our area, for post-game refreshments. A Marion local TV station taped the games live, then replayed them at around 10 P.M. On this occasion, the announcer commented, "The officials are Bill May of Richmond and _____, two of the finest in Indiana." The game wasn't two minutes old when my partner called a foul on Marion for an illegal screen. The crowd loudly disagreed. The announcer said, "For some reason, _____ has never been too popular in Marion!"

Up the Ladder
When I was working, almost any competent official who wanted to, applied and would be assigned to a sectional. Like teams, though, they got weeded-out fast after that.

Starting in 1967, four officials were used on each of the 64 sectionals, a total of 256. The 16 regionals required 96. The four semi-states needed only 24. Few officials assigned to a semi-state did not move on to officiate the state finals. Therefore, from a numbers standpoint, the toughest jump for an official was from a regional to a semi-state. After having fourteen sectionals and eight regionals, I was very happy to receive a semi-state assignment in 1969. I felt that I had earned it.

Tourney Time

A clue of what was to come came when I was assigned to the sectional at Hinkle Fieldhouse. In the field were the Number 1-rated and undefeated Indianapolis Washington and the Number 3-ranked Crispus Attucks, whose only loss came when their best player was injured. They met in the final game, and the final score was not as close as expected, Washington winning, 90–64. Still, there were so many athletic and talented players that it also brought out the best in the officials. Offensive and defensive goal-tending were always a possibility.

One play in particular stands out. Washington had a two-on-one fast break, with George McGinnis, later an NBA star, dribbling on the right side. When he reached the foul line, he used a fake of some kind, like a head fake or a stutter step, without losing his dribble, then passed behind his back to a teammate coming in from the left who scored the layup. The Attucks defender was completely faked-out and wasn't a factor. I was glad that I wasn't faked-out and didn't anticipate and call something that didn't happen.

The game was intense and remained so even with the score 80–58 with 2:58 remaining. A scuffle broke-out in the north balcony, and after a minute or so delay, we finished the game. The last 2:58 was very uneventful, like the calm after the storm. Three weeks later, Washington won the school's second state championship.

McGinnis shoots; I watch.

McGinnis goes over Lester for one of his many baskets.

Marion Crawley

I officiated the Lafayette Jefferson holiday tournament four times, one of which was 1970. Marion Crawley, coach of four state championship teams and one of the legends of Indiana basketball, had retired from coaching and was Athletic Director. It was the first year for their arena and it had been named in honor of him.

He had been in Florida for Christmas but had flown back for the tournament in case anything went awry. He was returning to Florida after the final game and asked if I would mind if he and his granddaughter rode to the Indianapolis airport with me so someone from Lafayette would not have to take them. It was very little out of my way and I was glad to do it. He talked about historical happenings in his career and Indiana basketball in general, and I kept him going with timely questions. I was glad he asked for the ride.

The author in 1970.

The Laughs

Through the years I worked more games with Bob Showalter than anyone else. He, like me, was a native of Wayne County, but he now lives in Florida, in retirement.

There is more to officiating than meets the eye of fans or casual observers: the scheduling, the travel, the rules and officials associations meetings, the friendships, the good and bad times, etc. Some officials take it very seriously, like a job; others do it for the exercise, or the money (which isn't that great); others as an excuse to get out of the house. I had many jokes, pranks, and laughs, many involving Showalter.

The Quick Changer: One official was well known for being a quick change artist after the game; quick in undressing, showering, getting dressed and leaving. I imagine that sometimes he beat fans out of the parking lot. It seemed that that was his primary objective.

I once worked with him at Portland, where we dressed in a classroom but showered with the Portland team on the other side of the gymnasium. After the game, I went to the classroom to partially undress before going to the shower. He was nowhere to be found because he had gone directly from the playing floor to the shower. He was finished and heading for the classroom before I got to the shower, and was dressed and gone before I returned.

A few years later, Showalter and I worked a holiday tournament at Kokomo, and I worked the first game of the night with our quick-changing friend. Showalter was working the second game and we previously made it up that I would beat our friend to the only shower, lock the door, then take my time therein. He saw me rushing as we got into the dressing room. "What are you trying to do May, beat me to the shower?" I got there first, took my time, and asked Showalter to hand me my shampoo. Our friend was so frantic that when Showalter handed me the shampoo, he reached into the shower, got water in his hands and took his version of a shower while standing outside. He was then dressed and gone before I got out of the shower.

He was also well known for packing a cooler with food and drinks to enjoy on his way home. The last time I saw him, we shook hands and visited so he evidently didn't hold a grudge. I was sorry to read that he died in the summer of 2001.

The Popcorn was Good: Showalter and I worked a holiday tournament at Huntingburg in 1970. Because of our long trip home, we worked the first game of the evening. While preparing to leave, we noticed that the two working the second game, Lowell Smith and Ray (Friday) Robison had bought boxes of popcorn to enjoy on their way home. We enjoyed the popcorn instead. They never mentioned it.

An Important Job: In one of my last sectionals, after working the first game of the evening, I went to get a post game snack—popcorn. An older, scholarly-looking gentleman was operating the machine. "I should introduce myself; I'm the Principal." He evidently felt that popcorn was of such importance that the job could not be delegated.

Rating the Popcorn: Now, as a spectator, I'm aware that nothing adds more to the enjoyment of a game than good popcorn, especially when it is being popped continuously and the aroma is drifting temptingly throughout the arena.

Friend William (Pete) Prosser and I even developed a numerical system for rating popcorn. We use a system from one to seven, seven being the best. Anything less than perfect detracts from the score, such as excessive unpopped kernels, not salty enough or too salty, cold, not fresh. The worse ratings are the ones where the corn has been popped ahead of time, then not hot, or even warm, when sold. An extra point is awarded for those who have heated containers to maintain the heat until the corn is sold. Although Carolyn and Pete's wife, Sue, don't participate in the rating, they enjoy our evaluations.

Turn on the Heat: Another prank was pulled-off at sectional time in 1970. In our travels, Showalter and I liked our vehicle to be warm, or, in fact, almost hot. Another Richmond official, Troy Ingram, didn't like it so warm and always commented to that effect. Showalter and I decided that we should take him with us some night so we could "roast" him.

The opportunity came when Ingram, Bob Beeson of Connersville, and I were assigned to the sectional at Madison. We were going to see riverboat basketball, I said. That year, no sectional games were played on Friday night. The semi-final games were on Saturday afternoon; the finals that night. Because of the distance, Ingram, Beeson, and I went to Madison on Friday night. Showalter was working the sectional at Martinsville and would be at his home in Rushville on Friday night. We would pass through there on our way to Madison. It was my turn to drive on Friday night, so I warmed up the car before leaving home, the heat and blower on high. After it was HOT, I picked-up Ingram, then Beeson. Ingram took off his coat even before getting in the car and Beeson did, too, after Ingram said, "He's got the heat cranked-up again, Bees!"

They both roasted all the way to Rushville, where, instead of turning to go to Madison, I went straight. "I need to stop and see Showalter for a minute. It won't take long." I had my coat fastened, the collar turned up, gloves on, hat pulled down as far as possible, as if I was freezing. All three of us went to the door, and when Showalter opened it he said, "Are they freezing you out, Bill? I'll get you a hot cup of coffee." I took off my coat and under it, above the waist, I was wearing only a sleeveless undershirt. Showalter and I cracked-up. Ingram and Beeson were dumbfounded, but finally laughed. One of Showalter's daughters came downstairs and said "What's wrong with Daddy," in response to his howling in laughter.

In 2000, one of the younger Richmond officials told me he had just heard the story. Guess it was still good after thirty years.

Two New Arenas

The 1971 season had several interesting events, starting with the first game in Seymour's new gymnasium, the fourth largest in Indiana. Showalter was driving, and on the way there he was stopped and given a warning ticket by a state policeman for following another vehicle too closely while passing through a village. This delayed us and we arrived with no time to spare. In jest, Seymour coach Barney Scott told us he wanted a technical foul called on the visiting team for dunking during warm-ups, which we could not have seen because of our late arrival. However, we had played no more than two minutes when Showalter called a technical on the visiting team's coach. A nice way to initiate a new gym.

A week later, I threw the opening tip in Marion's new arena, but we didn't have the extra activities. That arena has now housed six state championship teams.

Out of Action

In mid-January of 1971, I pulled a leg muscle and was out of action until mid-February. That necessitated canceling several games and helping schools find replacements. Several younger officials benefited from this and got to work at schools where they had not worked before. Beeson got several of the games. Fortunately, I was back to nearly full speed by tournament time.

It's Good

My 1971 sectional was at Greencastle, a beautiful facility but with sub-par lights. The final game was decided by a shot in the air when the final horn sounded. I waved it good.

A Long Day

My 1971 regional was at Huntingburg, and it was a long day since I went there the night before due to the distance. I was assigned to the final game and naturally had to sit through the two afternoon games. The first game was an overtime; the second was a blowout, won by the tournament favorite. Guess who won the championship game? The 200-mile trip home on icy roads was no picnic.

Official Scores Two Points

In 1972, Showalter and I worked the Logansport at Kokomo game, won by Kokomo, 74–40. With time winding down, a Kokomo substitute retrieved a loose ball near Logansport's basket. I was a few feet from him and he and I both saw one of his teammates heading for their basket at the opposite end, ahead of any Logansport defenders. I also saw Showalter leading the play. The Kokomo player threw a football type pass and I could tell that it was thrown too far for his teammate to catch it. I also saw Showalter "eyeing" it and, for some reason, knew what was going to happen. He caught it, took one dribble and a perfect two steps and laid the ball in the basket as the final horn sounded. He continued to the dressing room, which was at that end of the court, without breaking stride. I wish I had thought to have given the "good basket" signal, but was too absorbed in the hilarity of the moment.

Needless to say, we both laughed so hard in the dressing room that we couldn't do anything for several minutes. Russ Fiedler, a Logansport administrator and friend, said, "Well Showalter, you called them in their favor all night, you might as well score for them too!" Kokomo coach Carl McNulty was somewhat perplexed, but still humored.

Showalter called IHSAA Commissioner Phil Eskew the next morning, knowing that he would hear about it eventually. Eskew just laughed, and I still laugh when I think about it. The Kokomo and Logansport sports writers must not have been impressed. Neither mentioned it in his account of the game.

Oral Roberts 118, Butler 107

Showalter and I had an interesting game at Hinkle Fieldhouse in 1972. The 225 points were scored, all without the benefit of the three-point shot, and only two of us worked the game, instead of three, as there would be now. *The Indianapolis News* reported on the game the following evening:

IHSAA History: A Referee's Memories

Run, Shoot Game Toughest

A run and shoot game is toughest on officials.

Richmond's Bill May and Rushville's Bob Showalter, who referreed that 118-107 blazer between Oral Roberts and Butler at Hinkle Fieldhouse last night, agreed whole-heartedly on this point.

"It's the most difficult," said Showalter as he changed from his sweat-soaked striped shirt.

Showalter is 36 and May 38. Last night they had to switch ends of the floor at least 200 times and call 51 fouls. Not once did either coach question a decision or lack of one because the two officials kept up with the pace.

"Just remember, we only go half-court and we did not have to play defense," said Showalter, who is in his 18th year of officiating. "I wasn't tired."

"It's usually like running the quarter mile," added May, in his 21st season of whistle-tooting. "You get a second wind. The first four minutes are the hardest."

Showalter says they both get in shape in the fall by running. He works football, too, and at 168 pounds weighs only four more than he did when he got out of high school.

"We are required to get a physical exam every year and do it; an EKG (heart) and a shot at the lungs," he explained.

Showalter doesn't smoke and May only puffs on an occasional cigar.

"This was one of the highest scoring games we've ever had," they both concurred.

Unloading the Bag

The same year, 1972, I'm shown with my wife Carolyn, showcasing her bouffant hairdo of the era, and sons Paul (left) and John unloading the bag at Hinkle Fieldhouse prior to the semi-state tournament. That's a Richmond Red Devil button she's wearing since they were playing in that tournament, where they were upset by Center Grove, still one of the darkest days in Richmond basketball history. Needless to say, the author did not officiate that game.

Tourney Time

The Biggest Highlight

In any official's career, a few things stand out above all others. The biggest in my case was in 1972 when I received my first assignment to the state finals, which had been moved from Hinkle Fieldhouse to the new Assembly Hall at Indiana University, Bloomington. The state finals are naturally the biggest event in Indiana high school boys basketball—only four teams remaining out of over 400 at that time.

Players, coaches, and officials feel they're being watched by every fan in Indiana. I recall hearing older officials who had worked the finals say, "After you finally get there after working so long, you wonder if you can handle it." I did not feel that way since I had worked my way up, had "paid my dues," and was ready. I worked with Dr. Darrell McFall, with whom I had worked previously and with whom I was comfortable. The teams were Gary West Side and Anderson Madison Heights. I felt that we handled the game well.

Getting the call to officiate the state finals is every official's dream, and waiting for that call is every official's nightmare. As officials nervously wait, the Commissioner of the IHSAA calls on Sunday afternoon after the semi-state game. In 1972, I was among the select. All sorts of speculation and rumors fly around the pipeline and rumor mill of officials throughout the state all season. One can't be sure of anything until the call comes. After that, there is a lot to be done: hotel reservations, tickets from the IHSAA, calls to friends, and in this case to a sports writer friend who wanted an exclusive story to be printed a week later after the finals. In spite of all of this, it is a long week from Sunday until Saturday. Still, there is no experience for an Indiana high school official like officiating the state finals, especially in the days of one-class basketball.

Two Fouls on One Play

In a 1973 county tournament game, the other official and I called 52 fouls, 31 on one team. Most games in those days averaged 25 to 40 fouls total. At one point in this game, though, the other official evidently backed-off a call that he intended to make, unbeknownst to me, and let my call be the one we administered. The coach of the team that got the 31 fouls saw his initial signal and wise-cracked, "What are you doing now, calling two on us on the same play?" That brings up one of my pet peeves —teams that play aggressively and get an advantage by committing ticky-tack fouls that on an isolated basis get no advantage. However, by playing that way throughout the game they do get an advantage, if the fouls aren't called. That's what happened to the team with the 31 fouls. Good riddance!

South Bend Adams 99, Anderson 95

The highest scoring game in state finals history was in 1973, and I worked the game with Bob Laird of Shelbyville. Five things that I remember: the high score (and that was before the three-point shot!); only two officials; many of Adams' field goals were open jump shots from the foul line; a defensive goal-tending call against Anderson in the closing seconds by my partner, that I understand was a good call (I was working under the basket and rightfully wasn't watching for it); the number of positive comments from friends, officials, and coaches afterward.

20 or 47 Points

The final game of the Logansport holiday tournament in December, 1973, involved the host Berries and neighboring Peru. Playing for Peru was Kyle Macy, who was named Mr. Basketball in 1975, and coaching was his father, Bob. Both are now members of the Indiana Basketball Hall of Fame.

Logansport won, 90–77. Being aware of Kyle's reputation as a high scorer, I remarked in the dressing room afterward that Logansport had done a good defensive job on him and "I don't think he got more than 20 points." The scorer came in with the official book for us to sign. Macy scored 47 points!! He was so smooth that I didn't realize how much he was accomplishing.

A Good Prediction

While I was standing near the court at Assembly Hall after the 1974 finals, a young man approached me and said, "Mr. May, I'm Dave Colescott of Marion." I had worked their regional final game loss to Logansport. I remarked, "Thanks for stopping, Dave; you have a lot to look forward to the next two years."

Marion won the next two state championships, in 1975 and '76. Dave won the Arthur L. Trester Mental Attitude Award and was named Mr. Basketball in 1976.

Tourney Time

He played in the 1976 NCAA championship game with the University of North Carolina. In 2002, he was inducted into the Indiana Basketball Hall of Fame. Good prediction by me!

The author, second from right, with Hall of Fame members Jack Colescott, left; Bob Straight, second from left; and Dave Colescott, right. Jack Colescott, father of Dave, coached at Swayzee and Marion. His Marion teams made state finals appearances in 1968 and '69, losing in the final seconds both times. The 1969 team was undefeated until losing to eventual champion Indianapolis Washington, 61–60. Straight had a successful coaching career at four schools and led Huntington to the final game of the state tournament in 1964, losing to Lafayette Jefferson, 58–55.

Retirement

After fulfilling my ambition and working 20 sectionals, thirteen regionals, six semi-states, and the state finals in 1972, '73, and '74, there was no where to move up to in high school officiating. My last game was between Franklin and Jeffersonville in the 1974 finals, working with Gary Muncy, a fine official with whom I always enjoyed working. I had offers of political help if I wanted to move further into college basketball, but not having the desire to do so, and not having a job that would permit it if I did, I retired. I served as Supervisor of Officials for the Hoosier-Buckeye Collegiate Conference, comprised of nine small colleges, for five years.

It doesn't seem like it has been 31 years since I last officiated. People ask if I miss it. My reply is still "Yes, pleasantly."

The Night Before

A highlight of every season, from the mid 1960s until the mid 1980s, occurred the night before the state finals. Aptly named by John Hilligoss and continued by me, it was known as "The Night Before." A group of us from the Richmond area hosted a get-together for ourselves, our wives, other officials from throughout the state, plus a few other selectively invited guests. For many years we gathered at the Marott Hotel, which gave us favorable rates for 15 to 20 rooms, plus a suite, which served as the party room. We had appropriate refreshments. Verbal invitations were issued throughout the season and most of those invited showed-up, plus others who somehow got the word. We kept a list one year and over sixty came.

One year I had been ill and in bed for two days, but dressed long enough to ride to Indianapolis. Upon arriving, I put on my pajamas and robe and socialized, forgetting how badly I had felt.

At some point in the mid 1980s, "The Night Before" got to be too much trouble. We had all gotten older, some members of our group saw fit to invite some unwanted visitors, etc., so, like all good things, it came to an end. However, I occasionally have the desire to do it again, on a smaller scale.

This 'n That

These thoughts come to mind when recapping my career:

There are few towns of any size in Indiana in which I don't know, or didn't know at some time, a resident that I met through officiating.

The five schools for which I officiated the most number of games, both home and away, were, in order: Kokomo, Marion, Logansport, Bluffton, Hartford City.

One of my favorite calls was traveling, due to dragging the rear foot. I liked to demonstrate by excessively dragging my rear foot. I left black marks on many floors. One custodian disgustedly pointed one out to me as I was leaving his gymnasium.

Many things happen during games that the average person doesn't understand: Why did the official call this? Why did he not call that? Similar questions come up in every game. To understand many of these, one has to be or have been an official. Officials are human and make mistakes just like players and coaches. All they can do is try to be in position to see what is happening, then "call them as they see them." One administrator from our area, who served on the IHSAA Board of Control and was influential in officiating matters, liked to say, "You've got to call them right down the middle."

Officials have an advantage over coaches. If they have a bad night, they leave town after the game. If a coach has a bad night, he must still live there.

It is unfortunate when an official works for years, finally gets a state finals assignment, then gets a poor game to try to officiate: teams shoot poorly or commit many errors or fouls. Of course, some games become hard to officiate because the officials let them get that way.

Simply said, the three attributes that the best officials have are judgment, common sense, and dedication.

It seemed that every year I would have one game when I would do a sub-par job of officiating and would have been better off to have stayed home. I imagine the players, coaches, and fans thought so, too.

If I were eighteen years old again and knew what I know now, I question if I would become an official. However, if I had chosen not to, I probably would have always wondered how things would have turned out. Since I did officiate, I sometimes wish I had worked longer. At other times, I regret having done it at all.

I told both sons that if they wanted to officiate, I would help them get started. Neither did. I am glad they did not.

Several times during my career I thought that when I retired I would compile a list of "all-time nice guys" whom I had met, worked with and worked for. I'm not going to do it. I'm afraid I would forget someone, and there are so few in the opposite category that it's not worthwhile to mention them.

Basketball is a lot more enjoyable if one doesn't care who wins. Since I am no longer officiating, I have a problem in that now I nearly always do care who wins.

The longer an official has been retired, the better he is reputed to have been, because there are fewer and fewer people still around who remember him.

The Arenas

Not only is Indiana known for its support of high school boys basketball, even though it is not now what it once was, but also for its large high school gymnasiums. Fifteen of the largest sixteen largest in the United States are here. I officiated in eleven of the fifteen, and, as nearly as I recall, worked in 145 different arenas/gymnasiums in my twenty-three years.

From the first game in Indiana in 1894 at the Crawfordsville YMCA, until about the mid 1960s, most gymnasiums were a product of imagination, usually with the goal of squeezing as many seats as possible into the space available, with the amount of money available. Many were probably not designed by professional architects as we know them today, but by engineers and construction tradesmen who wanted the job of building them. Thus each gymnasium had its own characteristics and was built with basketball first in mind, since that was "the only game in town." Since the 1960s or so, and school reorganization, and the addition of more boys sports and now girls sports, the gymnasiums of today have to be more accommodating. As a result, many of them look alike, or so it seems: all rollaway bleachers, no seats on the ends of the court, no angling seats, multiple sets of lines all over the court, and barely passable lighting systems. They have a plain look with no distinguishing characteristics, unlike those of earlier eras.

But this state still has some gems, which I'll now comment on.

The Best of The Best Arenas

Butler/Hinkle Fieldhouse: Opened in March, 1928 and it was the largest basketball facility in the country at that time. It was renamed in honor of Paul D. (Tony) Hinkle, Butler University's highly respected coach from 1926 through 1970, and Athletic Director from 1931 through 1970. He also coached baseball and football at various times. He is a member of the Indiana Basketball Hall of Fame, and the Naismith Memorial Basketball Hall of Fame in Springfield, Massachusetts.

The Fieldhouse has been called "The Cathedral of Indiana Basketball" and is listed in the National Register of Historic Places. The site of the boys state finals tournament from 1928 through 1971, except for 1943, '44, and '45, when it was being used as a military training facility, it is still a great place to play, officiate, or watch basketball. The portable floor has a definite spring to it and the building has a distinct smell. The lighting on the court formerly was perfect, but on a recent visit it seemed to have deteriorated somewhat. Or perhaps it is my eyes that have deteriorated.

Semi-circular steel girders block views from some seats, but those tickets are sold anyway and stamped "Undesirable." With those tickets it is necessary to stand in order to see the entire court. I watched several state finals from "undesirable" locations and was thankful to be there. I remember where I was standing when Bobby Plump hit the winning shot as Milan won the 1954 state championship. The original capacity was 15,000, but in recent years remodeling and the installation of individual chair seats has reduced it to approximately 11,000.

It is often said that the home court is worth ten points to a team. I feel that I was a ten-points better official there than anywhere else. I worked three sectionals, two semi-states, one Marion County tournament, and two Butler games there. I wish I had asked to work one more sectional there, which would have been my fourth, more than any other official, to the best of my knowledge. I'm sorry that I did not get to officiate the state finals there at least once.

Some of the more historic high school games there:

Muncie Central 13, Martinsville 12; state championship game, 1928, less than a month after the building opened. The winning points were on a long shot by Charlie Secrist in the last half-minute. Knowledge of a rule and alert usage thereof assisted Muncie Central. In 1928, a team receiving a free throw for a technical foul did not retain possession and play was resumed by a jump ball at the center circle. Muncie had used its allotted three time-outs, two to tape Secrist's injured ankle. When behind 12–11, Secrist called another time-out, giving Martinsville a free throw which John Wooden unexpectedly missed. Secrist then controlled the jump ball at center and recovered the ball himself, which was legal then. Then seeing that all of his teammates were covered by a sagging Martinsville defense, fired a shot from near mid court that went in. Martinsville was unable to score in the remaining time and Muncie Central had won its first championship.

Jasper 62, Madison 61—state championship game, 1949; **Indianapolis Crispus Attucks 81, Anderson 80**—regional championship game, 1951; **Milan 32,**

Tourney Time

Muncie Central 30—state championship game, 1954, still the most historic game in Indiana history, because of Milan's enrollment of 161, versus Muncie Central's 1400-plus, in addition to the eight teams Milan had beaten previously, including Indianapolis Crispus Attucks and Terre Haute Gerstmeyer. **Crispus Attucks 71, Muncie Central 70**—semi-state championship, 1955; **Crispus Attucks 79, Lafayette Jefferson 57**—state championship game, 1956, first undefeated state championship team; **Crispus Attucks 64, Muncie Central 62**—semi-state championship, 1959; **East Chicago Washington 75, Muncie Central 59**—state championship game, 1960; **Ben Davis 79, Indianapolis Washington 77**—regional first round, 1995; was thought to be the last game ever for Washington, a two-time state champion, but the school is now being phased-back-in as a high school.

Undefeated state championship teams besides Crispus Attucks in 1956 were South Bend Central in 1957, Indianapolis Washington in 1969, East Chicago Roosevelt in 1970, and East Chicago Washington in 1971. Marion became the sixth undefeated state champion in 1985, at Market Square Arena, and Pike became the seventh in 2003, at Conseco Fieldhouse.

BUTLER UN VERSITY FIELDHOUSE

Hinkle Fieldhouse, which has been the site of the state finals every year except three in the last 40, didn't always look as it does now (below). Back in 1932 the floor faced east and west (above) instead of north and south. It was changed, among other reasons, to permit reorganization to increase seating.

IHSAA History: A Referee's Memories

Muncie Fieldhouse: Opened in December, 1928. It is second only to Hinkle Fieldhouse in historical significance. The story by Bob Barnet, Sports Editor of *The Muncie Star*, was in the program for the Indiana Basketball Hall of Fame classic tournament in the 1980 season.

By Bob Barnet
Sports Editor, Muncie Star

A Tradition Since 1928—The Muncie Fieldhouse

Muncie Central dedicated the Muncie Fieldhouse in a manner guaranteed to warm the hearts of all who cheered for the purple and white.

The Bearcats, coached by Raymond (Pete) Jolly, whipped Anderson in that first game in the brand new goalhouse, 35-24, and the pesky redskins were subdued in the fourth game of the 1928-29 season. Date was Dec. 7, 1928.

Central was the defending state champion, having beaten Martinsville the previous March, 13-12, on Charley Secrist's mile-long fielder in the closing seconds of the final game at new Butler Fieldhouse.

The Muncie Fieldhouse, said to be the largest high school gym in the world when completed, seated 7,523 and cost about $200,000, which would buy about a dwelling-house and a half on the present market.

Building of the Fieldhouse was a community project. Central was the only team in town, as Burris had not yet been built and the Golden Owls, who were to become state contenders a few years later, were problems that other Bearcat teams would encounter at other times.

Frank E. Allen, then superintendent of Muncie schools, and Pete Jolly are among the few still living in Muncie who were prominent in the building of the big gymnasium and school building at the north end of the business district. The entire business community joined in making the project successful.

With that first state basketball championship safely stowed away, Muncie folks were ready to accept any challenge.

The Ball family gave the land, which had formerly been used as a baseball diamond and football field used by Shad Cunningham's Muncie Athletics and Cooney Checkayes Muncie Flyers and Congerville Flyers.

A holding company was formed and 10-year season tickets were sold as part of the fund-raising campaign. Allen discovered that rental could be obtained from the school city if school rooms were built around the perimeter of the basketball court. The rooms were built. It was agreed that a part of the receipts from Bearcat games would be steered toward retirement of the debt.

George A. Ball wrote a check for $30,000 to cover cost of the permanent seats that made up the balconies. The project was completed at no cost to Muncie or Delaware County taxpayers. Capacity was reduced several years ago to its present 6,900 at the request of the state fire marshal's office.

Central teams had played previously in the school gymnasium in the building on South High Street, in Campbell Auditorium opposite McCulloch Park and in Ball Gymnasium.

Pete Jolly, who was to win the state crown again in 1931 and become and inductee into the Indiana Basketball Hall of Fame in 1970, had a good team when he opened that 1928-29 season. Bob Yohler, Glen Wolfe, and Bob Parr, who had started the championship game in the 1928 tourney against Martinsville, still were available and so were Ralph Satterlee, Coxie Walsh and Francis Reed, who had been a first-line reserves.

Other squad members were Marion Swift, Earl Sargent, George Maple, Herbert Haskett, Gène Teal, Bill Wulff, Joe Greene, John King and Mattox.

Jolly had still another ace up his sleeve but was a little reluctant to lay it on the table.

The Bearcats beat Hartford City, 19-16, lost to Burl Friddle's Washington Hatchets in overtime, 36-32, and whipped Huntington, 29-23, in the three games prior to the Fieldhouse dedication game with Anderson.

Jolly had been hearing from his veterans that there was a kid named Jimmy Wallace who had been playing over at the "Y" and who was a good one. He was also a Central student.

The Bearcat coach did some checking and learned that Wallace, who was perhaps 5-10 and 160 pounds, had been an all-sectional player at his native Veedersburg, Ind., the previous year. He had come to Muncie for his senior high school year because his sister was moving here to enroll at Ball State. Jimmy's father was a lawyer at Veedersburg.

In an era in which IHSAA commissioner A. L. Trester watched Hoosier high school coaches like farmers watched hawks circling over their chicken-yards, Pete Jolly was fearful that one of his business ad-

versaries who coached somewhere else in Indiana would raise a fearful holler if he used Wallace. But when the game came up with ancient enemy Anderson and it was time to dedicate the Fieldhouse, Pete had Jimmy in the starting lineup at forward. He scored nine points, second only to Bob Yohler's 19 as the Bearcats won their ball game.

Wallace, now a lawyer in Covington, Ind., played through the remainder of a season in which Central won 24 and lost five, with one of their victories a super-sweet 29-21 proposition over Glenn Curtis and Martinsville in the new gym.

The Bearcats won the North Central conference championship with a 9-1 record and the season came to an end when Burl Friddle and his pestiferous Washington Hatches beat the purplecads again, this time in the first round of the 16-team State Finals. Score was 31-24. Yohler led the scoring that season with 355 points with Glen Wolfe second with 181 and Marion Swift third with 165. Wallace followed with 113.

The fieldhouse has been the scene of IHSAA sectional, regional, and semi-state tournaments and has hosted big-time tennis exhibitions, professional boxing and wrestling shows, Christmas dances, and, for 26 years, The Muncie Star's district Golden Gloves tournament. Joe Louis was there, and Max Schmeling and Jack Dempsey. It brought thousands through the doors for Central's wonderful Community Christmas Sing programs and other public events including some dedicated to politics. Church programs have been held in the big arena, and some of the world's greatest musicians have played or sung in a house built primarily for high school basketball.

The Fieldhouse is now the home gym, when requested, for Muncie North and South teams as well as Central. It housed McKinley Junior High School from its opening until 1939, when a new McKinley was built to the north. Some McKinley classes still are being held in the Fieldhouse.

If the old gym could talk it could tell many great stories. It would probably be content with a single sentence:

"Throw up the doggone ball and let's get started."

Tourney Time

The lower picture, taken during the 1948 sectional tournament, shows a sellout. There were three games that Friday afternoon, and the average enrollment of the six schools involved was 150. Muncie Central was not involved. The person standing by the X is my father, official Wilbur May.

Thousands of people! The Muncie Field House was jammed to the rafters yesterday afternoon when Press ʾotographer Bill Jamison took this wide-angle picture during the Burris-Desoto game of the sectional tourna- it. Some 10 per cent of Delaware County population was present.

Seven of Muncie Central's eight state championship teams have played in the Muncie Fieldhouse. The first championship team played in Ball Gymnasium, at what was then Ball State Teachers College. Eight large purple banners hang from the rafters, similar to the Celtics banners in Boston Garden and the Fleet Center, which was recently renamed TD BankNorth Garden. The Fieldhouse was the site of 31 regionals, the last in 1959, and 16 semi-states, the last in 1952. Its original capacity was 7,500, but the state Fire Marshall's regulation reduced it to 6,500. At one time there was a very noticeable sag in the playing floor in the southwest corner, but that was remedied at some point.

Memorable games there: **Muncie Central 23, New Castle 21**—regional first round game, 1931. **New Castle led 21–17** with 2:45 left, but Muncie rallied and went on to win its second state championship the next week.

March 10, 1931, *New Castle Courier-Times* article points out the attention given to officiating in that era:

"An effort was to be made to reach Commissioner A.L. Trester to transfer officials for the tournament. The ability of Johnnie Schramm is not questioned by local school officials, but it was believed that some trouble might arise since the Bloomington man was one of the referees in the New Castle sectional meet.

All sorts of rumors concerning the officials were being winded about New Castle today."

Officiating is not subject to that much interest now.

New Castle 20, Muncie Central 19—regional first round game, 1932. Many predicted that whoever won this game would become state champion. A last second shot from half court won for New Castle, but whether it was before or after the final gun was controversial.

Confusion reigned and the matter wasn't settled until after a phone conversation with Commissioner Arthur L. Trester. My parents were eye-witnesses and they did not know who would play Winchester in the championship game until the New Castle team came onto the court. New Castle won its only state championship a week later. Here's the article that appeared in *The New Castle Courier-Times*:

Greens Fork 25, Muncie Central 22—regional first round game, 1936. The Black Demons had won their only Richmond sectional championship. One of their players took a long shot that was deflected; the ball hit the floor, bounced and went in the basket.

Sectionals, 1939–1944. Muncie Burris won six consecutive sectionals, beating Central in five of them. Center, of Perry Township, beat Central in 1943, 29–27.

Tourney Time

One of the Bearcats was so frustrated that he rammed his hand through a door window on his way to the dressing room and required hospital treatment.

Ft. Wayne South 39, New Castle 37—semi-finals championship, 1940. New Castle had an eight-point lead in the third quarter when a blown fuse caused part of the lights to go out. After a thirty-four minute delay, South rallied to win. Because of their rivalry with Muncie, New Castle fans doubted the actuality of the blown fuse.

Muncie Central 62, Kokomo 60—semi-state championship, 1952. Kokomo was rated No. 1, Central, No. 2. Classic battle. I never saw a more devastated and disconsolate crowd than the Kokomo people. Central won its fourth state championship a week later.

Richmond 54, Muncie Central 52—regional championship, 1953. Central was trying for its third consecutive state championship, which had not been done since the Wonder Five of Franklin did it in 1920, '21, and '22. I was enrolled at Ball State at the time, as were many Central graduates. They boasted that Central was going to be state champions again. I warned, "Don't count your chickens before they hatch." "Who's going to beat us?" was the reply. "I don't know that anyone is, but there are several that could, Richmond for one." "That'll never happen," was their slighting remark. There was not much conversation afterward though, as Richmond won in double overtime.

I was quite popular with some of my Ball State friends that night. I had a ticket, but the others didn't. The Fieldhouse was sold out. As luck would have it, one of my high school teachers was teaching in Muncie by that time and was working as a ticket taker. I asked if he would let some of my friends in through his door. "Sure, bring 'em around." I'm not sure now how many got in that way, but my teacher friend finally said, "Is that it, Bill, or do you have more?"

Muncie Central 49, Yorktown 41 (three overtimes)—sectional first round, 1978. Yorktown had late shots to win at the end of regulation time and the first two overtimes. With :04 to play in the first overtime, they had two free throws, but missed both. Central won its sixth state championship six weeks later, the tournament games having been postponed due to winter storms and an energy shortage, caused by a coal miners strike.

New Castle Field House: The world's largest high school gymnasium with 9,325 seats when all are in use. Normal capacity is 7,500.

In the mid 1950s, the New Castle school board announced plans to build a new high school building, but it would not include a gymnasium, for financial reasons. This was not well received by many of the basketball fans of the city so they took action and formed what became known as the "Gym Now" organization. Citizens and students got behind the project and conducted fundraisers of many kinds: car washes, grass-cutting, trash-hauling, shoe-shining, door-to-door solicitations, and pledges. The group incorporated with the sole purpose of raising enough money to get a mortgage to finance construction of the Field House. After it was built, adjacent to the high school, the school corporation paid leasing fees to enable the corporation to pay off the mortgage. The New Castle Field House was dedicated in November, 1959. By chance, I was present when the mortgage was burned in December, 1979. The Field House is a tribute to the enthusiasm for basketball of the citizens of New Castle. That enthusiasm is also one of the reasons that the Indiana Basketball Hall of Fame is next door to the Field House.

The Field House replaced what was commonly known as the Church Street Gymnasium in downtown New Castle. The school played there from the mid 1920s through the 1959 season. Originally owned by the adjoining YMCA, with a capacity of just 2,000, it was very crowded and gave the Trojans a decided home court advantage. There was a stage at one end, and the band sat in a section above the main entrance at the other end, with a small over-hanging platform for the director. The last regular season game was played in February, 1959, a shootout between Ray Pavy of New Castle with 51 points and Jimmy Rayl of Kokomo with 49. New Castle won, 92-81. It was later used as a recreational and fitness facility by the YMCA, but a new YMCA has opened, so its future use is unknown.

The interior of The New Castle Field House.

The Rest of the Best Arenas

There are other arenas that deserve mention, most of which I officiated in and am glad that I did. A few are still in use and some are not. Some have been demolished. I will now comment on "the rest of the best."

Hartford City: I called it "The Snake Pit." I had one sectional and several season games there. Fans were always in an uproar, from the start of the JV game until the end of the varsity game. It has been demolished, but whenever I pass by the site, I think I hear boos from the past. The fans were the most vociferously critical of officials.

Bluffton: Original gym was in City Hall. A newer one opened in the 1955 season.

It appeared to be in good condition, but was replaced in the 2001 season, causing controversy in the city.

Logansport: The old Berry Bowl was named after the team nickname—Berries. Opened in 1926, before either Butler/Hinkle or Muncie Fieldhouses. I didn't know until recently that the playing floor was actually on the second story of the building; vocational shops and other rooms were on the ground level. It had a wide steep ramp from the entrance to the playing floor, necessitating a net at that end of the floor to keep balls and players (and officials) from falling down the ramp. Due to a shortage of space, one corner of the floor was cut off about three feet. It was a regional tournament site off and on for forty years, ending in 1968. It and the adjoining high school building have been replaced by a supermarket, but the wrought iron fence that surrounded them remains. The last time I was in Logansport, in January, 2004, the donut shop across the street was still there.

Bluffton and Logansport fans tie for second, behind Hartford City, as the most vocal critics of officials. Maybe they weren't that way with other officials, just me.

Marion Memorial Coliseum: Built in 1927 at the north end of the business district, it had a stage at one end, with an organ for religious services and other programs. Broadcasters sat in overhanging boxes at stage end. It had more room from out-of-bounds lines to the bleachers than 99% of others and the floor had a nice spring to it, similar to that of Hinkle Fieldhouse. The lights were not the best. It was the site of the 1964 regional game between Swayzee and Liberty Center that went nine overtimes. The timer shot a gun at the end of each quarter—it sounded more like a cannon. The officials' room was at the end of the stage and was obviously used as a dressing room for performers in theatrical presentations as well. There was a bed therein; I don't know if it was for actors and actresses or exhausted officials. It was the first dressing room that had a bell to signal officials when to come onto court. I have the bell as a souvenir. The building has been used for an Easter pageant and was available for rent, but its future is now indefinite.

Wabash: The gymnasium was in the Honeywell Center, downtown. It is a wonderful facility, compliments of Mr. Honeywell. Wabash High School played there because their gymnasium was too small. It was not the best basketball facility but I am pleased to have worked there. It is now used for community activities only. Wabash High School now has a larger facility.

Delphi: In the city hall, but now replaced.

Portland: The floors were on the stage of an auditorium with theatre seats and balconies. Similar set ups were found in Montpelier, Lewisville, Fountain City, Greens Fork, Milton, and Manchester College. All have been replaced, but the last time I was there, Portland's is still in its original state.

Knightstown: Now known as "The Hoosier Gym" because it was the gymnasium of the Hickory Huskers of "Hoosiers," the movie based on the Milan team that won the 1954 state championship. It is the only gymnasium I've seen with this totally different type of seating arrangement. There are four separate sections of permanent wood seats each enclosed by an outside wall, two sidewalls, and a front wall adjacent to the playing floor.

There are others still in existence that are similar to the Milan gym, which no longer exists. Mays, now a grade school, and Union City and Fort Recovery, both in Ohio, would have been better choices to portray the Milan gym, in my opinion. They had permanent seats on one side of the floor and a stage on the opposite side where temporary bleachers were available. Note: The championship game in the movie takes place in Butler/Hinkle Fieldhouse.

Shelbyville: The Paul Cross gymnasium was the site of ten regionals between 1942 and 1954. It was the home of the 1947 state champions, the Shelbyville Golden Bears. Reconfigured, it is now used as a community center.

Madison: Brown Gymnasium, home of the 1950 state champions, has a prominent sign on the front stating that fact. Downtown, within a block of the Ohio River. Official McBride once had to park on the riverbank, then got wet up to his knees, caused by a swill in the river, caused by passing barges. 1960 was the last year the Madison Cubs played there. It is now used as a community fitness center. I'm sorry I never worked there.

New Albany: One end of the school building was renovated and remodeled in the 1970s, resulting in the floor running in the opposite direction.

Jeffersonville: The Fieldhouse has been renamed Charles Nachand Fieldhouse, and reminds me of Hinkle Fieldhouse, in that the floor runs in the opposite direction of the building. Ramps lead to the balcony, as at Hinkle. Wherever there could be a seat, there was a seat, and many of them would have been undesirable with no view of one of the baskets. It was a regional site off and on for seventeen years, from 1934 through 1966. The last sectional there was in 1971. The Floyd Central Highlanders, affectionately called "The Super Hicks," won three games by a total of six points. They trailed New Albany by eleven points, but rallied to win by four; they were behind Jeffersonville but won by one; then hit two free throws after a wild sequence in the final seconds to beat Clarksville Providence by one. They pulled more heroics the next week. I never officiated there, but wish I had. Other officials have said I should be glad I didn't.

Vincennes: Adams Coliseum was named for the coach of the 1923 state champions, John Adams. It was the home of the 1981 state champions. It has been used as a junior high gymnasium, although varsity games with rival Washington have been played there on occasion.

Center: Team defeated Muncie Central in 1943. Officials have told me it was the smallest of all of the small gymnasiums. I'm sorry I never worked there.

Ft. Wayne North Side: It was symmetrical with seats surrounding the floor behind a wall approximately six feet high. The permanent wooden bleacher seats had backrests. It was in the school building, with the floor running southeast to northwest. The clock malfunctioned one time and the PA announcer said, "The clock at the west end is official." Someone else said, "That's the north end!" The comments almost became confrontational. I settled the disagreement by saying, "Gentlemen, calm down; that's the northwest end." I knew I was right because I had previously checked a city map. I once worked their game with a county rival, who won a close one. The rival coach complimented us and said, "I would have said the same thing if we had lost." The same two teams played two years later but his team lost. We did not see him after the game. We must not have worked as well in that game. The gym was built in 1927 and was a regional site until 1953. It was the home of the Ft. Wayne Zollner Pistons, predecessor of the Detroit Pistons. The 2004 season was its last, since it was converted into a media center. Carolyn and I attended a game there in February, for old times' sake, and had a chance reunion and visit with long-time coach, By Hey. A smaller gymnasium was built nearby.

Ft. Wayne South Side: Was very similar to North Side, but not as large. It was a regional site in 1923 when Richmond's undefeated team, one of the favorites for the state championship, won there to qualify for the state finals. However, their star player, Jack Mattox, was still in the one-sided final game late when he was injured, greatly hampering his effectiveness in the state finals. As a result they lost to Muncie Central, 33–30. This letter from a Hagerstown fan is significant as Hagerstown people have never been great supporters of Richmond. The South Side gym was converted into classrooms in 1995.

Kokomo Memorial Gymnasium: Opened in 1950. One semi-state was played there, 1951. It is still a good place to play, officiate, or spectate, and ties with Seymour for having the best lighting, at least the last time I was there. Official Showalter scored two points there.

Seymour Lloyd E. Scott Gymnasium: Opened in 1970 and has been a tournament site ever since. Named in honor of their long-time successful coach, Barney Scott. One of the more practical buildings for all of the sports it must accommodate. It has very

> **Hagerstown Fan Declares Richmond Best Team in Indiana For 1922-23; Injury to Mattox Upsets Chances**
>
> A fan from Hagerstown declared in a letter that Richmond had the best team in Indiana for the season of 1922-23. He believes that Richmond would have gone to the finals and probably would have won this game if Mattox, backguard, had been in good shape. The letter follows:
>
> Hagerstown, March 20, 1923.
>
> Dear Sir:
>
> "While basketball for 1923 is a closed incident, I could not help but add one word at this late date. Remember what I am going to state is not from prejudice, for I have always had a grudge toward Richmond, probably due to the fact that they always seemed to favor all other basketball teams over us. But, I was at Indianapolis, saw all teams play, and will say that they lost the most heartbreaking game to Muncie I ever witnessed.
>
> "Will further say and the majority of Indianapolis fans are with me, with Mattox in shape, Richmond is at least an eight point better team than Muncie. I surely sympathize with all my heart for I know how they felt in their unfortunne, losing in the last few seconds to a team that they were superior to.
>
> **Attributes to One Factor**
>
> "Of course with that game, they would have cinched their way to the finals and I may be going far, but I believe with Mattox, the best in the country in his position, in form, I really believe Vincennes would not be state champions today.
>
> "Muncie broke through Vincennes' defense time and again, but could not hit the basket. We all know about Richmond's accuracy on hitting the old net. Some people would hollow and call you cheap sports for an alibi, but this is one time where there were good grounds for one. While they did not win, I, as well as all Hagerstown fans at the game, still believe Richmond, with all men in good shape, was best, looking from all angles was best team in Indiana in 1923.
>
> "Our congratulations in going high as you did, and also our sympathy in your misfortune of one of your players, which we think cost you the state championship. We would like for you to extend this to Coach Little and the team."
>
> A Fan.

adequate space between the out-of-bounds lines and the bleachers, and its lights tie with those at Kokomo. Showalter and I worked the first game there. It was the site of more heroics by Floyd Central in 1971.

Civic Hall, Richmond: It was a sectional tournament site from 1940 through 1979, and where I officiated my first high school game. For many years, Morton High School, which was the name of the Richmond high school until 1939, played in the Coliseum, a public building downtown. In 1932, the North Central Conference, of which it is a member, put Richmond on probation for one year and told authorities to improve playing conditions or face expulsion. Thus, they began playing at Trueblood Fieldhouse at Earlham College. Also, they were told that their team needed to improve in order to attract more fans to their out-of-town games. Seven years later, they built a new high school and Civic Hall. Seating capacity was 3,500 and it had an impressive, although excessively spacious, main entrance and lobby. A wall surrounded the court on both sides and one end, and at that end there was a smaller second balcony section referred to as "Peanut Heaven." There was a stage at the other end. After one season it was obvious that 3,500 seats were not enough, so bleachers were added all around the main floor and on the stage. This made for crowded conditions and also gave the Red Devils a distinct home court advantage. Even 4,500 seats were not enough so season tickets were sold as A and B books, with each being good for half of the games, for several years.

Finally, forty years later, when the need for a more accommodating facility was obvious, as the high school changed from a three to a four-year high school, and also lost its role as a sectional host, plans for the present Tiernan Center were announced. A group of taxpayers filed a remonstrance, citing the cost. This action was quite a contrast to the manner in which funds were raised to build New Castle Field House. The remonstrators lost their case and Tiernan Center opened in the fall of 1984.

Richmond then hosted sectional and regional tournaments from 1985 through 1991, and just sectionals from 1992 through 1997, the last year of one-class basketball. Amid cries of gerrymandering, the IHSAA realigned the tournaments in 1992, resulting in the Richmond sectional winner being sent to the New Castle regional. Coincidentally, Richmond won its first state championship that year, George Griffith's team accomplishing something that other Red Devil teams through the years might have been good enough to do, but did not accomplish.

It is interesting that Richmond lost two of the last four one-class sectionals on its home court, to Randolph Southern in 1994 and Winchester in 1997.

Historic and Unique: Although Butler/Hinkle and Muncie Fieldhouses have had the most historically significant events, I believe that the Jeffersonville Fieldhouse and Ft. Wayne North Side gymnasium were the two most unique. They best symbolize the theory of putting as many seats as possible in the space available and using the architect's imagination.

OTHER THOUGHTS AND OPINIONS
The North Central Conference (NCC)
No discussion would be complete without looking at the North Central Conference and its history. It was founded in 1926 to promote athletic competition between schools of similar size. Thirteen schools have been members at one time or another, but there have been eight since 1966. Lafayette Jefferson had planned to withdraw after the 2005 season, but they were removed two years earlier. Huntington North joined the conference in the 2004–05 season.

The record of the schools in the state tournament is impressive:

	State Finals Tournament, through 2005		
	Champions	Runner-up	Final Four
Present members:			
Muncie Central	8	6	4
Marion	7	1	7
Anderson	3	7	7
Kokomo	1	4	3
Richmond	1	2	2
New Castle	1	0	3
Logansport	1	0	3
Huntington/Huntington North	0	1	3
Former members:			
Frankfort	4	1	3
Lafayette Jefferson	3	6	8
Lebanon	3	2	2
Indianapolis Tech	0	4	4
Rochester	0	0	3

To clarify, Muncie Central has been in the final four eighteen times (8 plus 6 plus 4); Logansport and New Castle, each four times. Among the present members, the 75 final four appearances average out to one every 1.3 years. The 22 championships average out to one every 4.3 years. On four occasions since 1978, two NCC members have played in the final game.

It must be pointed out, without going into laborious detail, that for many years most of the schools hosted sectionals and regionals, which was a big advantage in progressing through the tournament. However, Muncie Central, New Castle, and Richmond were in the same regional for 32 years. Other various tournament realignments through the years have minimized final four appearances, as has the advent of class basketball.

Richmond was the last present member of the North Central Conference to win its first state championship, as mentioned previously, in 1992, Only Marion has won since, in 2000.

Muncie Central's Success

The numbers in the table indicate that Muncie Central is the most successful team of all-time. Actually, no other school in Indiana can match its record. In addition to their championships in 1928, '31, '51, '52, '63, '78, '79, and '88, by looking at comparative scores one could say they could have also won in '53, '54, '55, and '59. But, this is speculation and an example of "what might have been." And, in spite of a sixteen-point margin, Central's loss in the 1960 championship game is still considered one of the biggest upsets in tournament history.

Why has Muncie Central been so successful?

In *Bearcats—A History of Muncie Central Basketball from 1901 through 1988*, authors Dick and Jackie Stodghill state that in 1927 Muncie's home games were played in Ball State's Ball Gymnasium and that Ball State sometimes played the preliminary game. After seeing a game there in February, IHSAA Permanent Secretary (later Commissioner) Arthur L. Trester said, "Muncie will have quite a bit of trouble in the tournaments unless their fans act differently."

Those were prophetic words but they weren't realized until January, 1964, when Central was suspended from the IHSAA until January, 1965, because of unruly conduct by fans after a loss to Anderson in a holiday tournament at Frankfort. They were ineligible to defend their 1963 state championship.

When I was officiating seventh, eighth, and ninth grade games in Muncie in the early 1950s, Bearcat coach Jay McCreary would often be there, looking over his prospective players. Some of his varsity players would be with him, as an encouragement to the younger players.

In 1958, his first year as coach, prior to his team's playing in the state finals, Coach John H. Longfellow remarked, "Muncie spirit and tradition were all new to me, but I'm learning, and it's a great experience. These people like to win and somehow they keep winning. Being a new basketball coach in Muncie is like being thrown into a deep surf at high tide. The waves just carry you along; you have no control of yourself."

The late Bill Harrell, coach of the last three state championship teams, once said, "I could coach at Ball State and not have the pressure that I have at Central."

One final explanation came in a remark from friend Kathy Harlan. Carolyn and I have attended many games, both in Richmond and away, with Kathy and husband Ken. In the mid 1990s, we attended a game between Central and Muncie Southside, knowing that it would be a competitive contest. Kathy remarked, "I've never seen as many mothers carrying babies in their arms at a game as I have tonight." We saw ten or so. I commented that that is probably another reason for Central's success over the years. Most of those mothers were probably carried into games by their mothers, and the interest and tradition have carried on from generation to generation. The next night we attended a home game in Richmond. I think we saw two babies.

In the 1976 season, I rode to Kokomo with some Richmond officials who worked a holiday tournament there. It was Harrell's second year as coach of Muncie Central and one of their players was Jack Moore, a sophomore. They lost two games that day, both by twenty-five points, and I thought they didn't have much hope for the future. A few days later I was talking with Jack Moore's dad, Jerry, a fellow native of Wayne County. I asked him, "What are you going to do? Jack has a lot of talent; are you going to stay there and have him play under those conditions?" He replied, "I've looked it over and things look a lot better for the next two years, so I think we'll stay." Two years later they were state champions and Jack won the Arthur L. Trester Mental Attitude Award.

New Castle and Indiana University

It is well known that Indiana University has won five NCAA championships. I don't imagine it is well known that there was a player from New Castle on four of the five teams: Marvin Huffman in 1940, Jack Wright in 1953, Kent Benson in 1976, and Steve Alford in 1987.

Revenge

Eddie Harter and Mac Parker began the 1944–45 season as members of the Mooreland Bobcats, a sometimes thorn-in-the-side of New Castle in sectional play. By the end of the season, both players and their families had moved to New Castle, so the two were then playing for New Castle. The teams met in the semi-finals of the sectional. Guess who won!

Damn You, Ref!

Many years later, New Castle was eliminated in the semi-finals of the sectional by one of the smaller schools. According to an eyewitness, who was neutral, several questionable calls, by one official, went against New Castle in the closing minutes. The next night, several New Castle fans went to the game just to harass the controversial official. I was an eyewitness, but not as an official.

Never a State Champion

Unless I have overlooked something, Evansville Central is the school that has beaten the eventual state champion the most times during the regular season—eight—in 1923, '41, '42, '44 (twice), '45, '48, and '49, but has never won a championship itself.

Questions from Ft. Wayne
In 1939, in a public opinion poll, a Ft. Wayne newspaper asked:

Do you think local officials should be permitted to referee city series games? What do you think would happen to Indiana basketball if the tournaments were eliminated?

Those aren't the type of questions people care about today. It's too bad we no longer have that kind of interest.

Different Schedules
In the 1940s and 50s, the smaller schools played most of their games on Tuesdays and Fridays, rather than Fridays and Saturdays, as they do now. The larger schools played many Saturdays though, often because they were playing opponents from further away. Often the varsity games were not scheduled to start until 9:00 PM in order to give Saturday night shoppers and merchants time to attend after stores closed. That was before the shopping mall craze.

When the visiting team came from a long distance, they often would bring only their varsity team, to save on travel costs. The home school's JVs would often play a nearby small school's varsity team in the preliminary game. When Jeffersonville played at Muncie Central in 1937, Muncie JVs played the varsity of Wayne Township of Randolph County. Later, Wayne won its sectional and in the regional played Muncie's varsity.

They Beat 'Em Both
I believe there are only five years in state tournament history when a team beat both of the final game participants in the regular season: 1946—Richmond beat both Anderson and Ft. Wayne Central; '54—Frankfort beat both Milan and Muncie Central; '64—Tipton beat both Lafayette Jefferson and Huntington; '89—Marion beat both Lawrence North and Kokomo; and '92—Anderson beat both Richmond and Lafayette Jefferson.

What an Oversight
The following article by Wendell Trogdon appeared in *Indiana Basketball History Magazine*, published by the Indiana Basketball Hall of Fame, and it describes the incident when Stinesville High School's principal failed to mail in before the deadline the school's entry form for the state championship tournament:

Tourney Time

> ## STORM OVER STINESVILLE
>
> Fans around Stinesville looked forward to the 1946 state basketball tournament with great expectations, their beloved Quarry Lads having finished the season with a 12-6 record.
>
> A few dared believe that the team from the small school with only 12 students in the senior class had an outside chance of winning the Bloomington sectional. University School of Bloomington and Ellettsville were the favorites, but upsets came often when schools from Monroe and Morgan Counties met.
>
> The Quarry Lads were led by four seniors. The "Quarrian," the school yearbook, listed them as William "Willie" Acuff, "a good shot from any position"; Junior "Whacker" Barr, "a good standby for his rebound work"; Hollis "Mort" Bales, cited for his "determination to win" and Donald "Hunchy" Swafford, "whose long shots kept us in games."
>
> Underclassmen were Marion "Big Butch" Butcher, Freddie "Pete" LaShure, David Rush, Donald "Little Butch" Butcher, Wayne "Tiny" Goble, and Dan "Danny" Jacobs, the lone freshman who sometimes saw action in varsity games.
>
> Other characters in the drama that was about to unfold included the coach, Robert W. Bingham, who still lives in Bloomington; the late A. E. "Archie" Breeden, the school principal, and their boss, Bean Blossom Township trustee Charles Franklin.
>
> The team and school officials did not know it at the time, but an ill wind that had blown a few days earlier was about to continue. The wind storm had broken power lines at Paragon, giving the Quarry Lads an abbreviated 54-29 victory over the host school.
>
> It was Feb. 15 when Principal Breeden met with Bingham and his team, a session that would break hearts and open wounds that would take years to heal. Breeden told them they would not be a contender in the tournament, that due to his oversight he had failed to send an official entry form to the Indiana High School Athletic Association.
>
> He explained: "I had it filled out and it had been on my desk for some time, but I was under the impression that the deadline was later."
>
> Once he learned the deadline had been Feb. 8, he called Commissioner L. V. Phillips and asked for an exception to the rule. His plea to the IHSAA board was turned down. Stinesville was out of the tournament before it started.
>
> Breeden accepted the blame in what sports columnist Grady Bennett called "a clean-cut manner." Fans divided into groups, some recognizing that Breeden had made an honest mistake, others calling for his ouster. One businessman remained about the fray lest he lose customers. "I'm not getting mixed up in this affair," he told a reporter.
>
> A letter to the Bloomington World-Telephone claimed Trustee Franklin had told a crowd at the Stinesville barbershop that Breeden should resign. "After spending $250 for new uniforms, this is the last straw," the writer said.
>
> Franklin, however, set the record straight the next day. He would not, he explained, take any action to dismiss Breeden. There had been demands, he said, that Breeden be fired. "But I had about an equal number asking that he be kept on the job. I don't plan to take any action in any way."
>
> Despite their disappointment most of the Stinesville players attended the sectional as spectators, watching small town teams Smithville, Unionville, Paragon, Eminence, Monrovia and Morgantown and bigger schools Bloomington, University, Mooresville, Martinsville and Ellettsville.
>
> Those 11 schools would each receive checks ranging from $229 to $993 for participating. Stinesville would receive no payment to help fund its athletic program for another year.
>
> • • •
>
> Stinesville players still remember that awful afternoon when "Archie" Breeden broke the news.
>
> "Willie" Acuff will never forget it. "I recall being very sad; very, very let down. It was one of our better teams. University School (the sectional winner) probably had the best team, but we had stayed with the Univees for most of the game a year earlier and felt we could have played with them. Deep down, it really hurt. It was not a good feeling."
>
> Time he says has tempered his disappointment. "Breeden was a good principal, a good guy and we respected him a lot. But we didn't like that part about not getting to play in the sectional." Acuff, who would later serve with the Army in Korea, now lives at Ellettsville.
>
> Danny Jacobs, who would become a basketball official and referee in the 1980 state finals, recalls when Breeden told the team the bad news: "Big tears came into his eyes. None of the players said much at the time, but some might have commented later."
>
> He still believes that 1945-46 team could have competed with Bloomington and Martinsville and, perhaps, even University School. Despite those lost opportunities, Jacobs didn't criticize his principal. "He (Breeden) was a good disciplinarian. A lot of his students went on to college. He was good for the Stinesville community.
>
> "Fans didn't like it. But we had gone through the depression and World War II and people were accustomed to dealing with hardships. It was a different era. If a principal did that now, he might be shot. But 'Archie' was a great guy. You can't be mad at good people," he adds poignantly.
>
> • • •
>
> "Archie" Breeden, who had been at Stinesville for eight years, soon took a job elsewhere, then returned to Stinesville for another tenure as principal. The community agreed with Jacobs. It's hard to stay mad a good people.
>
> Time had blown away those dark clouds of that February in 1946.
>
> Winter 1995

Milan—It Probably Wouldn't Have Happened If...

Few would disagree that Milan's state championship in 1954 is the single greatest happening in Indiana high school basketball history, both because of their small enrollment and the teams they had to beat en route to the championship. I, though, like many others, believe that they would not have won in '54 if they had not been in the final four in 1953. Their getting that experience in '53 is a story in itself. So I'll tell it to you.

Playing Morton Memorial of Knightstown in a regional first round game at Rushville, Milan trailed by nine points with two minutes remaining. At some point thereafter, the official clock did not run for about thirty seconds because the electrical connection from the control panel to the scoreboard was accidentally disconnected. Given the additional time, Milan tied the score and went on to win in two overtimes, 53–51.

They beat Connersville, 24–22 in the regional championship game, and then beat Montezuma and Crispus Attucks in the semi-finals to get to the final four, where they lost to eventual champion South Bend Central, 56–37. Without this extraordinary tournament experience in 1953, I doubt Milan would have won the state championship the following year.

One Loss in Two Years

Led by the incomparable Oscar Robertson, Crispus Attucks lost only one game in the 1955 and '56 seasons, that on February 5, 1955, at Connersville, 58–57. Indianapolis newspaper reports said that Attucks' superior speed and quickness were hampered by the floor's being slippery, due to moisture, but one participant and other eye-witnesses have other versions. A 1985 newspaper article from the *Richmond Palladium-Item* gives its account.

Lone loss for Oscar, Attucks in 2 years came at Connersville 30 years ago today

Thirty years ago today, Indianapolis Crispus Attucks lost a high school basketball game at Connersville, 58-57.

The incident wasn't chronicled in Ripley's Believe It Or Not. It should have been, however, because the defeat turned out to be the only one sustained by the Tigers of Hall of Fame Coach Ray Crowe in two seasons.

The Attucks teams of 1954-55 and 1955-56, led by the incomparable Oscar Robertson, won back-to-back state championships.

But, on this Saturday evening three decades ago, the Tigers were, for a change, second best. Bob Powers, sports editor of the Connersville News Examiner, remembers the game well.

"It was the first time Connersville had played Attucks since the early 1930s and it was one of those odd February nights," he said. "It was extremely humid inside the gymnasium, which caused moisture to come up through the playing surface. Players from both teams were falling down all over the place."

The game was played in the old Connersville gym on Indiana Avenue, which is now referred to as the Junior High North girls gym. The old structure, built in the 1920s, seated only 1,800 "and they were packed in to the rafters that night," Powers said.

Bob Williams, who covered Indiana high school basketball for more than 40 years, was also on hand.

"I RODE down to Connersville on the Attucks team bus and I spent the entire trip telling Coach Crowe what a terrible place that old gym was to play in," Williams said.

Williams, who saw the Big O play 40 times during those two years, gives a description (reprinted with permission) of the game in his "Hoosier Hysteria" book:

"Connersville's small gym couldn't begin to hold the huge overflow crowd, so the school's auditorium was equipped with loud speakers, and the radio play-by-play was piped in for those fans.

"Connersville, coached by Kenny Gunning, was primed for the big upset and played a near perfect first half to take an unexpected 13-point lead. It became clear in the opening seconds of the second half that the Spartans aimed to put the ball in the deep freeze to hang onto that lead.

"Crispus Attucks nevertheless made up most of that deficit, led by the amazing Big O. Connersville took only four shots in the fourth quarter and hit all four, playing its stall game to perfection; but Crispus Attucks was threatening. Oscar had been held to three points in the first half, but he would get 19 in the second.

"Robertson hit one from the side with just five seconds on the clock to cut the Connersville lead to one point, but that was the end of the story. Attucks stood helpless for five seconds as Connersville held the ball safely out of bounds until the final gun sounded."

CONNERSVILLE'S VICTORY over Attucks was completely unexpected, since the Spartans had lost on the road to Shelbyville the night before, 55-53, while the Tigers were steamrolling city rival Washington 75-45. The Spartans rebounded, however, with 60 percent shooting against Attucks the following night (24 of 40) while the Tigers were a bit flat at 49 percent (23 of 47). The score was tied at the end of the first quarter 10-10, Connersville led at the half 34-21 and by 47-37 at the end of the third stanza.

"Connersville took it to the Tigers inside and led the guards drive," Powers said. And the Spartan backcourt tandem of Bob Masters and Larry Alexander responded with 36 of the team's 58 points.

Connersville was not ranked at the time, but climbed all the way to No. 10 the following week. Muncie Central was No. 1 and Attucks, barely escaping Hammond Noll earlier in the week 72-71, was No. 2. The Bearcats lost at Kokomo 65-63 the night before Attucks fell at Connersville, but both kept their 1-2 positions in the AP poll the next week.

The Connersville team of 1954-55, which won 17 and lost seven, lost to Milan in regional play that year but the following season captured the school's first regional crown in two decades. Coach Gunning is now retired and living in Arizona.

Only six players were used by the two coaches. For Connersville it was forwards Ronnie Petty and Gary O'Neal, center John Entner, guards Larry Alexander and Bob Masters and substitute Eddie Masters. Bob Masters scored 19, Alexander 17 and Petty 10.

For Attucks it was the Big O (who, as a junior in that game, led the way with his 22), along with Willie Merriweather, Sheddrick Mitchell, Willie Hampton, Bill Brown and Bill Scott.

Jan Clark, former Palladium-Item sports editor, writes weekly columns of area interest

The Way It Happened

Many upsets have occurred in the ninety-five year history of the state tournament. There are many reasons: injuries, a tough draw, a surprise or gimmick defense, a stall offense, or an extraordinarily good shooting game, etc. In my memory, the biggest upset of all, considering how it was accomplished, was East Chicago Washington's win over previously undefeated Muncie Central in 1960.

Tourney Time

Central had a front line of 6–4 Ron Bonham, 6–2 John Dampier, and 6–7 Jim Davis. Their only close games were a four-point win over Indianapolis Tech, followed by an eight-point win over also undefeated Madison in the semi-state. Some thought that Bloomington, with a record of 26–1, would present a challenge in the afternoon game of the state finals, but that was no contest, Central winning, 102–66. When Washington, with a strong, bulky front line, struggled to get past Ft. Wayne Central by one point in the second afternoon game, Muncie appeared to be a cinch to win the championship game.

Rebounding of Bakos In Second Half Was Key to Upset, Longfellow Says

By BOB WILLIAMS

"If there was a turning point, it was the rebounding of Bakos (6-5 senior center Jim Bakos) in the second half."

This was the observation of disappointed Coach John Longfellow following previously-unbeaten Muncie Central's shocking 75-59 loss against inspired East Chicago Washington in last night's state title at Butler Fieldhouse.

BAKOS GOT ONLY four points, and four rebounds in the unimpressive 62-61 win over Fort Wayne Central yesterday afternoon and he didn't even start the Muncie game.

But big Jim came on strong in the second half to score 17 points and top both teams with 15 rebounds, to pick up the slack created by the subpar shooting of 6-4 senior team captain Ron Divjak, who suffered through his worse slump all year.

Divjak, who got 47 points in two Layfayette Semistate games the preceding week, hit only six of is 35 field attempts on Washington's first trip to the state finals sin ce 1947.

LONGFELLOW, the 34-year-old owner of a 28-0 record going into the final game and a 53-2 record the last two years at Muncie, shed some tears along with the Muncie boys who were favored to become only the third team in the 50-year state tourney to go the route with a perfect record.

But he had no alibis.

"I haven't seen the figures, yet" he said in the dressing room, "but they outshot us and overboarded us. When they pulled away, we were getting the shots. But we didn't quite have it," he continued.

"We thought the zone would slow 'em down a little in the second," Longfellow explained. "It did. But then our offense stalled, too."

LONGFELLOW congratulated rival Coach John Baratto at floorside after the game and he also made a special trip to the Washington dressing room to shake hands.

"You made us look bad on a couple of things ," the Muncie coach told Baratto. It was "a well-coached team and you deserve a lot of credit."

Ron Bonham, the magnificent Muncie forward who set a 40-point single game record for the finals in the afternoon, added 29 last night to come within eight of the 114 point record for four games, although he fouled out in the last four minutes.

It marked the first time in 85 games over the last three years that Bonham had fouled out.

BONHAM, DAMPIER and the rest of the No. 1-ranked team in the state were much too disappointed to talk. But Bonham and Davis had time to congratulate some of their elated opponents between showers.

The 41-year-old Baratto, head coach at Washington for 16 years, was a good winner. His Washington team lost but twice this year and was one of the top-ranking teams in the state all year. But few had rated Washington a chance against Muncie on the strength of what took place in the afternoon.

"We didn't look so good in the afternoon," Baratto confessed. "Muncie did."

Baratto took a good-natured dig from commissioner, L. V. Phillips of the IHSAA. "I saw you jumping up and down a few times there," Phillips told him referring to Baratto's nervous conduct on the bench. "But I see you finally got them straightened out all right."

DISAPPOINTED many times in the Sweet Sixteen, Baratto felt that his Washington team had a psychological edge this time.

"We had everything to gain, if we were going to lose, we would lose to the best."

Concerning the rebounding of Bakos, Coach Baratto said he always looks better against a big team. Ruben Rodriguez, a surprise starter in the championship tilt, also came in for praise from Baratto. Rodriguez had started only one or two games all year.

Was this the most time Divjak ever spent on the bench? Baratto said it was. He had no idea Washington would be able to turn the trick with Divjak "on the bum."

It took an exceptional effort on part of Trester Award winner Bob Cantrell, Phil Dawkins, Bakos, and Williams.

A sign posted in the dressing room told the Washington story best: "When the going gets tough, the tough get going."

This article appeared in *The Indianapolis Star* the day after the game.

I remarked to some Muncie junior high coaches that they could spot Washington twenty points and still win by twenty. They were skeptical, almost apprehensive. The teams were about the same size overall, but Central's quickness and polish were more impressive. However, 6–5, 200 lb. Jim Bakos, who had been replaced in the starting lineup for the championship game, unexpectedly, came off the bench to score 17 points and grab 15 rebounds. They also got eight points each from two usual non-starters. Washington coach John Baratto fussed, fumed, ranted, and raved from the sidelines, and surprisingly, they overpowered Central in the front court. When Central's two big men, Mr. Basketball-to-be Bonham, and Davis left the game on personal fouls, the game was decided.

East Chicago's Years

Ten years later, the city was in the spotlight again. Roosevelt High School became the fourth team to be an undefeated state champion. The next year, Washington duplicated the feat. That brought up several questions. I know that Roosevelt won when the two played in the 1970 sectional, but what was the score? What kind of game was it? Was it close throughout? Was it one-sided, etc., etc.? This newspaper write-up describes it:

Roosevelt Gets by Washington

Roosevelt and Washington high schools were closed in 1986 and a new school, East Chicago Central, opened the same year. When the new school opened, authorities wanted to establish a new identity for Central and did not see fit to keep the trophies, pictures, and other memorabilia of the two old schools. However, one Washington supporter was able to save some of their items.

41 Points in One Quarter

In the final game of the first regional at Seymour in 1971, previously mentioned Floyd Central made another comeback, scoring 41 points in the fourth quarter to beat Seymour, 93–86. They had trailed by 17 points with only 6:50 remaining. They won two more games in the semi-state the next week and moved on to the state finals, where they lost to East Chicago Washington, 102–88. After their semi-state win, their coach, Joe Hinton, was quoted, "It seems that spirit and desire mean more in the south. They seem more grim and mechanical about the game in the north." I agree.

One would think that 41 points in one quarter, especially in tournament play, is

59

a record that would never be surpassed. However, in 2003, in a sectional semi-final game at Columbus North, Columbus East trailed Bloomington South, 51–32, after three quarters. They then scored 46 points in the fourth quarter, but South scored 37 and hung-on to win, 88–78. Eighty-three points by two teams in one quarter, or the equivalent of 332 total for a game!

How Things Change

Two changes have been made in tournament administration over the years and have probably been noticed by only a few people:

1. One of the most important days of the year to anyone connected with high school basketball was the day of the tournament draw, conducted in the offices of the IHSAA, then announced moments later on radio. At one time, the drawing was conducted on a Saturday morning. Later, it was held on a week day morning and some schools played the broadcast on their PA systems. In some schools, coaches and players stayed out of class to listen. Later still, it was held at noon Sunday and televised throughout the state. Now, it's announced on the IHSAA's computer website approximately an hour after the draw is made.

2. Prior to the 1960s, all tournament officials learned of their sectional assignments by special delivery letter on the morning of the draw. Later, special delivery was abandoned and regular delivery was used. Regional and semi-state officials still got their assignments by special delivery on Sunday night. Those assigned to work the state finals got a telephone call from the Commissioner early Sunday afternoon, after the semi-state.

14 of 15 Ain't Bad

Like many businesses, in the office of the Dana Corporation plant where I worked, we had a pool involving picking the winners of the final fifteen games of the 1978 tournament. Coincidentally, an official from our area was assigned to officiate the game between No. 1 ranked Ft. Wayne North and Elkhart, at the South Bend semi-state, and asked me to go along for the ride. Elkhart upset North. As it worked out, I picked the winner in fourteen of the final fifteen games, including that one.

Naturally, I won the pool. One of the other participants asked, "How did you know that Elkhart Central would beat Ft. Wayne North?" I answered, "Why do you think I rode all the way to South Bend with one of the officials?"

A Coach's Memories

Ward Smith coached for over forty years in at least eleven schools and won 692 games, according to his obituary in *The Indianapolis Star* in 1993.

One season at South Central, the father of one of his players was killed in an explosion at Louisville, Kentucky, and the funeral was scheduled for the same night as a game. Mr. Smith said the opposing coach refused a request to postpone the game. "I couldn't believe it," he told Tom Keating, a columnist for *The Star*. "Our players had to come directly to the gym, and they were in no frame of mind to play basketball. Neither was I. We got beat, very, very bad."

South Central did not have a good season and was rated eighth in an eight-team sectional. But during the tournament, it was one upset after another until South Central found itself in the final against the team that had refused to postpone the regular season game.

"On paper, we should have been beaten by forty points, but somehow we won. During the last few minutes of the game, our players were crying on the floor. It was the school's first sectional championship, and the whole town lined the road for miles to greet us. I remember looking ahead through the southern Indiana hills and seeing lights all along the way, and I remember the faces of those kids."

"And people wonder why I'm still a high school coach after all these years."

One to Two to Three Officials

When basketball first started in Indiana, only one official was used in most games. Soon two were used, and now 109 years later, three are used on some regular season games. And, it was recently announced that three will be used on all IHSAA tournament games, starting in 2007.

Who Selects the Officials?

This process has had a similar amount of change. Until the 1974 season, officials were chosen by the IHSAA personnel, namely the Commissioner and Assistant Commissioner, with input, both positive and negative, from the Board of Control, and from school personnel. The IHSAA did welcome recommendations from schools, and officials often asked school personnel and board members to recommend them. To some extent, it was a good-ole-boy and/or buddy system, but what isn't that way today? On behalf of the IHSAA, seldom did they assign an official to a tournament for which he was not qualified.

When Charlie Maas, former coach at Indianapolis Tech and athletic director at Indianapolis Arlington, became assistant commissioner in 1973, he installed a rating system. It involved a rules test, ratings from schools on tournament games, a yes or no vote from schools on whether or not the official was competent to officiate tournaments, and ratings from hopefully knowledgeable and impartial observers at both tournaments and regular season games.

With this system, an official's tournament assignments for Year Two were based on his total rating from Year One. If he was fortunate to have worked an easy to officiate tournament in Year One, and been rated by a lenient observer and got a good rating, he might move up a notch the next year. If he was unfortunate and worked a tournament with a tough observer or the caliber of play was such that no official could do a good job, he was unlucky and very well have been moved down the next year.

I do not know what type of system is used now.

Three Games in One Night

Prior to 1955, only two officials were assigned to many sectionals. Sectionals with nine teams required three games the first night, two the second night, two Saturday afternoon, and one Saturday night. Thus, on the first night, the two officials worked three games, consecutively. Someone evidently realized this was too much, so they assigned a third official to those sectionals for the first night only. Such was my first sectional, at Bluffton, in 1955. I was glad to be that third official.

Welcome Changes

Coinciding with Herman Keller becoming assistant commissioner prior to the 1961–62 season, it was decided to use six officials on regionals, only four having been used previously. I and thirty-one others were the beneficiaries, although I felt like I should have had one in 1960 and '61.

From the late 1940s through 1961, officials got to work the state finals two consecutive years, then were dropped back to the semi-state level, with few exceptions, where they could work indefinitely. In 1962, however, nine of the veterans were cut back to the regional level, opening spots for younger men to move up. Another system is in use now.

Officials' Records

Because he was interested in officiating IHSAA tournaments, in 1937 my dad set up a card file of officials. There is a card for every man who officiated a tournament from 1937 through 1997, listing his assignment(s) for every year. While gathering scores and other facts for this book, I noticed names of several men remembered mostly for their playing or coaching careers, or in other fields, but who also officiated IHSAA tournaments at one time or another. Examples:

Homer Stonebraker, star of Wingate's state championship teams of 1913 and '14; Ward (Piggy) Lambert, coach of Purdue University; Birch Bayh, father of our former United States senator, and grandfather of former governor and present senator Evan Bayh; Paul (Billy) Williams, former athletic director of Ball State Teachers College (now university); Elder Eberhart, coach of Richmond High School from the mid

1930s to 40s; Paul Garrison, long-time superintendent of Richmond schools; John Gant, one of only two players on all three of Franklin' state champions of 1920, '21, and '22; Philip G. (Whitey) Kessler, member of Richmond's final eight teams of 1923 and '24, winner of Gimbel Award for mental attitude (predecessor of the present Arthur L. Trester Award) and founder of the well-known Kessler's Sports Shop.

Also in Dad's file were Dale Morey, four-time winner of both the Indiana Open and Amateur golf championships; Phil N. Eskew, later Commissioner of the IHSAA; Arad McCutcheon, coach of the University of Evansville; Herb Schwomeyer, author of the popular and informative book, Hoosier Hysteria, and foremost basketball historian, officiated the state finals in 1955 and '56; and Blake Ress, present Commissioner of the IHSAA.

I maintained the file from 1992 through 1997. I estimate that the records are 98 percent accurate. The card file is now at the Hall of Fame at New Castle.

Sometimes an Idea Never Dies

In 1988, the *Bearcats* authors wrote the following about an idea that arose in 1924: "For the first time, but not the last, the IHSAA considered class basketball, with small schools having a tourney of their own. The idea never took hold." Well, the *Bearcats* authors didn't know what was coming. Class basketball did take hold less than a decade later, in 1996, when twelve of seventeen members of the IHSAA's Board of Directors voted to use the class system not only in basketball but in four other sports as well.

Class Basketball

The first boys state tournament was in 1911, and all high schools that had teams, from the smallest to the largest, competed in one tournament. For the first forty years, or so, that was the accepted method with little thought about changing it, except in a few instances, as described previously, in 1924. Most small high schools had a baseball team in the fall, basketball in the winter, and some had track and field in the spring. The larger schools may have had cross country and football in the fall, wrestling and swimming in the winter, then baseball, golf, tennis, and track and field in the spring. Thus, in the smaller schools, boys had a choice of only three sports and some took part in two or all three. Any boy with any interest or ability at least tried to play basketball. This contributed to small schools having better basketball teams than they would have had if some of those boys had participated in another winter sport.

Basketball was the main sports interest of most Hoosiers, especially those in villages, small towns, and townships where there was no town but where there was a high school. Because of the nature of Indiana winters, uncomfortable but tolerable, high school basketball took center stage because it was an indoor sport. It was the most popular indoor activity, whether one played on a team or not, and competed only with interest in girls, homework, reading, playing cards, or listening to the radio. Intense rivalries developed between schools, towns, and townships because of basketball. Yearly bragging rights were of the utmost importance and they carried over, not only from year to year, but also from generation to generation.

However, things began to change in the early 1950s. First was a new mode of entertainment—television. Its popularity increased rapidly, especially when college basketball was shown. I was officiating the Shelby County tournament one year in the mid 1950s, and the Shelbyville coach was there, scouting potential sectional opponents, but he left at halftime to go home and watch Indiana University on television. I remember scorers, timers, and other dressing room visitors saying they would rather be at home watching television.

Also, in the early 1950s, many of the small towns and townships still had one school building for all twelve grades. Some townships even had more than one high school, many with fewer than twenty-five boys. Most of these schools had a very limited offering of classes, just the basic reading, writing, and arithmetic. Many school buildings were in bad physical condition. Educators and the population in general began thinking that more diversification in education was necessary. If more subjects and courses were to be offered, then more space, specialized classrooms, and other facilities were needed. Most of the old buildings, especially the smaller ones, would need to be replaced. With this thinking, a school reorganization plan throughout Indiana was adopted in 1959, resulting in many schools being combined. Counties that formerly had eighteen high schools then had five; fifteen combined into one, etc.

Number of teams entered in the state tournament:
787 in 1938
766 in 1950
694 in 1960
443 in 1970
397 in 1980
388 in 2005

The biggest decrease was forty-two, from 1964 to 1965.

Many factors brought the demise of one-class basketball. As the smaller schools were reorganized and consolidated, enrollments at the new or remaining schools were naturally increased. With more pupils in fewer schools, more sports and extra-curricular activities were added. The newly formed schools adopted football, cross-country, swimming, wrestling, tennis, and golf. With these available, boys who formerly would have played basketball decided to participate in others, since only ten or so could play on the varsity basketball team anyway.

With the new schools, pupils might live up to twenty miles from their school, whereas they formerly lived two or three miles, or two or three blocks away. Transportation to and from practice was a problem. Other problems which worked against basketball developed. If a boy dated a classmate who lived ten miles away, he needed a car. So, he bought a car, then needed to work at Wal-Mart or McDonald's to pay for it. Then, because he was working, he couldn't play basketball or any other sport. In addition to television, other things have come along—computers, video games, shopping malls, etc.

Adult basketball fans, who would never have missed a game involving the Alquina Blue Arrows, the Bentonville Trojans, the Everton Bearcats, the Fairview Yellow Jackets, the Harrisburg Hornets, or the Orange Tigers, then had less interest in supporting the surviving Connersville Spartans, who previously had been the despised biggest school in the county.

With all of the above mentioned reasons for the decline in interest, especially among the surviving smaller schools, the quality of the basketball teams declined. With this decline, the smaller schools were more often and more soundly beaten by the surviving larger schools.

This caused people associated with schools other than the top one-fourth or so in enrollment to begin thinking that athletics could be conducted more equitably if they competed only against schools with similar enrollments, especially in basketball. From the mid 1960s until the mid 1990s this thinking became more prevalent. Many of the coaches and administrators were not old enough to remember the small schools' successes in earlier years. And, many were not native Hoosiers and were not aware of those successes. I believe despair and spite also affected their thinking. More and more people who supported class basketball got elected to the IHSAA Board of Control, now called the Board of Directors, over a period of time, so on April 29, 1996, they voted 12–5 to adopt the class system for basketball, plus four other sports. Following the IHSAA's by-laws, some principals throughout the state called for a referendum vote in September, 1996, but in the subsequent vote, the Board's 12–5 vote was upheld, 220–157. Thus, the 1997 tournament was the last one class tournament, and 1998 was the first four-class tournament.

The record for total attendance at all tournaments was in 1962, when school reorganization was in its early stages. Total attendance at all four levels of the tournament:

1962—1,554,454 (record for total attendance at all tournaments)
1990—981,395
1997—786,024 (last year of one class tournament)
1998— 616,170 (first year of four class tournaments)
2000—387,710
2004—448,036

Tourney Time

I have tried to explain why we now have class basketball. Although I understand why the 1A, 2A, and 3A schools want class basketball, it does not mean that I like it. I miss the history, tradition, and big school—small school rivalries.

Following is a copy of a letter that I wrote to the Principal of Hagerstown High School, from which I graduated. It didn't help. He voted for class sports.

```
August 26, 1996


Mr. Mark Childs, Principal
Hagerstown High School
700 Baker Road
Hagerstown, IN 47346

Dear Mr. Childs:

As a graduate of H.H.S. (1951) I am writing to ask you
to not support the amendments to rule 2 of the bylaws of
the Indiana High School Athletic Association, which
would establish multiple classes in team sports.

I cannot express my feelings more clearly than what was
done in our local newspaper's "Our Opinion" column
recently, a copy of which is attached.

Thinking back to when I was in school, a one-class
sectional championship would have been more satisfying
than a state championship in the smallest school
category, especially if we could have beaten Richmond in
the process. And, I take pride in the fact that the
Hagerstown Tigers have won more sectionals than any
other Wayne County school except Richmond.

Sincerely,


William B. May
115 Lin-Kay Place
Richmond, IN 47374
```

Citizens should lobby principals

Single class basketball will get another shot—albeit a long shot—when principals vote again in September.

While it is the principal of each high school who will vote, it will be up to the citizens who want to keep the winner-take-all tournament to convince them that it is best for this Indiana tradition to continue.

There are good arguments on both sides. Those who want class basketball believe it will give students at small schools a better chance of winning a state title. With more titles to go around that obviously will be true. But winning the smaller divisions will be like being the bridesmaid or bestman at a wedding. Smaller schools will get to share the stage, but not the spotlight.

Opponents of class basketball also point out that smaller schools will never again have the thrill of upsetting — or even almost upsetting — a bigger school. This is the true tradition of high school basketball in Indiana.

This is also the single most important thing making the Indiana high school boys tournament the best attended and most envied around the nation.

It also must not be overlooked that this interest in Indiana boys basketball brings money to all athletic departments of all size schools and makes it possible for schools to offer other sports that do not generate revenue.

Athletics are an important part of education. They can be used to create interest in school in general no matter how the basketball and other tournaments are conducted.

But when school boards have to make difficult choices between sports and other activities during budget crunches, sports opportunities are likely to be cut.

In a perfect world, there would be money for any program that benefits students. But this is far from a perfect world.

Principals who believe that athletics for as many students as possible are an important part of their instructional program should think twice about doing anything that might mean less money for athletics, especially for so-called minor sports that do not attract paying spectators.

Those who oppose class basketball should let their high school principal know how they feel before he or she votes on the issue next month.

Our view
■ Remember, single class boys basketball has financed many minor sports.

This is the column referred to in the letter, which appeared in *The Richmond Palladium-Item* in 1996.

Tournament Attendance—A Different Thought

Indiana was well known throughout the country for the number of people attending the tournament. Attendance began to slide in 1963 and has continued, as described above, dropping even more since the beginning of class basketball. Prior to 1963, there were two factors that contributed to the great attendance, in addition to the popularity of and devotion to basketball by our residents.

One was that sectional tournament games were played on the home court of one of the participating teams the majority of the time. Naturally, the home court would attract a good delegation of fans.

Second, during most years, in addition to the semi-finals and finals of the sectionals, the three games of the regionals, the semi-states, and the state finals were played in one day, meaning that the two teams playing in the championship games were playing two games in one day. Most fans would buy a ticket for the entire tournament, even knowing they might not use the second session ticket if their team lost its first game. They would have to make only one trip to the tournament site. This was the case most years after 1936. Prior to that, teams sometimes played three games in one day, when the pace of play was much slower.

I think those two things contributed heavily to the attendance records.

However, I do not believe teams should play two games in one day, especially at the present pace of play. Too many tournament games have been won or lost because of the "luck of the draw," when teams play two games in one day. Now, two games in one day schedules have been eliminated, except at the regional level. I think it should be eliminated there also.

There are ways to improve the present tournament system. I don't want to be critical of the way tournaments are conducted without presenting a suggestion, nor do I want to offend IHSAA personnel. Some suggestions:

Reclassify, with three instead of four classes. The present 388 schools would break down to slightly more than 129 per class. In each class, there would be fifteen sectionals with eight teams each, and one with nine teams. This would eliminate first round byes, except in the nine team sectionals. A team would have to win at least three games to win a sectional.

I believe the IHSAA's policy of allowing teams to move-up in classification is good, if they want to, but I understand that few have done it.

Select tourney sites in the same manner as at present.

Using 2007 dates, the three class sectionals would start on February 9; the state finals would be on March 24. Presently, all sectional games, in all classes, are played on the same days—Tuesday, Friday, and Saturday. Fans are limited as to how many games they can attend. Under my suggestion, 1A schools would play on certain days, 2As another set of days, and 3As another. This would allow more fans to attend more games. It would necessitate the regular season ending three weeks earlier, which would eliminate the one-to-three week layoff that most teams now have around the Christmas—New Year's holiday break. That's too long for teams to be off anyway, when the season is not even half over. This format would still have some teams playing on their home court, but we have too many excellent high school facilities to justify renting college or municipal facilities, except Hinkle and Conseco Fieldhouses, in order to have neutral courts. Some tournament games should always be played at Hinkle Fieldhouse, in respect of its history. Also, with this format, teams would never play two games in one day and would always have at least one whole day's rest between games.

I'm probably overly optimistic about this. There probably aren't as many enthusiastic fans as formerly who would attend as many games as I would. Also, this would probably not counteract all of the other reasons for the decline in interest. I have submitted my suggestion in writing, in detail, to the IHSAA.

The Rules

I like the three-point shot because it maximizes the most basic basketball skill—shooting, although I think too many teams attempt too many of them.

I'd like to come up with a way to prevent the last two or three minutes of a game from taking twenty or so minutes to play.

Other than to begin the game or overtimes, there are now no "jump balls." I would like to see the opening tip-off eliminated also. Give the ball to the visiting team, or toss a coin as is done in football. Use this method or alternating possession to start overtimes. It is difficult for an official to be a very proficient or consistent tosser when he may go several games or a week and not toss one.

I understand that the rules are being changed to stipulate that the home team must wear white jerseys, beginning with the 2007–08 season. That is good. I also think that gold and gray uniforms should be illegal. They do not create enough contrast with other colors, and some teams use them as home uniforms, while others use them as visiting uniforms. I've heard of two instances where teams played on a neutral court and both wore gold uniforms.

The rules should state that home (white) uniforms have even numbers and visiting uniforms have odd numbers. Having identical numbers on opposing teams increases the possibility of an error by a scorer or official. One scorer tried to convince me that I called a foul on blue 50 when it really was on white 50.

I hope a shot clock is never adopted for high school basketball. Proponents say they want action. An underdog team holding or controlling the ball in a close contest may be using the only strategy that it can to stay in the game. To me, it is exciting when an underdog team holds the ball with the score tied while the clock ticks away toward the end of the game.

Formerly, a player had to be in control of the ball with no imminent change of possession in order for him or a teammate to call time-out. Now, if a player has possession, no matter if he's about to be tied-up in a held ball situation or in mid-air and about to go out-of-bounds, he can call time-out. I haven't heard any official or coach say they like the rule. I don't either, and I'm not even involved any more.

Three Concerns

As I watch games today, three aspects of officiating trouble me.

1. I think the most frequent error by officials is improper administration of throw-ins after violations. Unless I'm seriously behind in my knowledge of the rules,

such throw-ins are to be at the spot nearest the violation. Now, more often than not, officials give it to the player for the throw-in at the spot most convenient for themselves. Not often does it make any difference, but near the end of a close contest, it very well could.

2. Often, near the end of a game, the team that is behind will score and call time-out. Almost invariably they will claim that the clock wasn't stopped soon enough and request that the clock be reset. And, almost invariably, the officials go along with the request and add time to the clock. If this happened in the first thirty minutes or so, probably nothing would be said or done. I do not know why officials feel compelled to do so in the last few seconds.

3. In the past few seasons, through 2004, one of the newest and most popular moves was when a player dribbled toward the basket, picked up the ball, then hopped, coming to a landing on both feet, covering ten feet or so in the process. I have concluded that whether it was legal or not depended upon the position of his feet when the ball was picked-up. In the 2005 season though, it seemed to have occurred much less frequently, fortunately for officials who had to judge whether each case was legal or not. Perhaps the officials started calling the players for traveling violations, so the players did not do it as often.

Out of Retirement

Several times I have been tempted to unretire and contract to work one more game. A week before, I would send a letter to both schools:

1. My contract calls for the game to start at 8:00 P.M. If it doesn't, for any reason, we'll start the game with a technical foul on whoever is responsible, usually the home school. In IHSAA tournaments, teams are given a twenty-minute warm-up. However, in regular season games there is no limit, so they take from twenty to thirty minutes to warm-up, then go to the dressing room, then a band presentation takes fifteen minutes, then more festivities preceding our national anthem, then introductions. Finally, at about 8:30, the game starts. If I were a coach, I would want to simulate tournament conditions as much as possible.

2. We officials won't come onto the court until the moment before our national anthem is played. We will not observe warm-ups. We will have an observer in the stands to tell us if anyone dunks the ball so we can penalize that.

3. Any player who deliberately plants himself in position to create contact and draw a foul ("take a charge" as the coaches call it) without trying to play legitimate defense,

will be called for blocking and/or will have to suffer the consequences of whatever happens to him as a result of the contact.

4. The legality or illegality of each case of the "hop stop" move, described above, will be determined as it occurs.

The Pros, Major Colleges, and Division III

In my view, there are several undesirable things happening in basketball:

Professional
1. Multimillion dollar contracts for players and coaches.
2. Overpriced tickets, parking, concessions, souvenirs.
3. Immoral and/or unlawful conduct by players and coaches.
4. Use of taxpayer funded facilities free or at ultra cheap rates.
5. Moving of franchises unless demands for new facilities, at public expense, are met.

Major Colleges
1. High six-figure and million dollar contracts for coaches.
2. Same as No. 2 above.
3. Same as No. 3 above.
4. Same as No. 4 above.
5. Changing of conference memberships, under the belief that "the grass is always greener elsewhere."
6. Schedules requiring extensive and unnecessarily long travel.
7. The myriad NCAA rules.
8. Admitting athletes who are not bona-fide students.
9. Athletes leaving college before graduation to turn professional, in effect making the colleges the farm system for professional teams.

All of these things have lessened my interest in both professional and major college basketball. I have become a fan of NCAA Division III basketball, where there are not supposed to be financial grants based on athletic ability. The chances are greater that the majority of athletes are bona fide students.

North Carolina Should Thank Indiana

In spite of the present state of major college basketball, I must point out one significant fact. The popularity and success of major college basketball in North Carolina, evidenced by national championships by the University of North Carolina (four), Duke University (three), and North Carolina State University (two) in the past forty-nine years, can be traced to a Hoosier, Everett Case.

A native of Anderson, he never played the game, believe it or not, but began coaching a church team while still in high school and continued coaching in several locations for forty-six years. He won four state championships at Frankfort High School, the first school to win that many, and served in the military in World War II.

Through the World War II years, college basketball in North Carolina was an insignificant winter pastime. But, officials at North Carolina State University wanted to have a better team, and to do that, they needed a better coach. They decided that the best place to look for a better coach was in Indiana. One of Case's former players, Chuck Taylor, of Converse shoe fame, suggested that he apply for the job.

In thirty-six years, through the 1946 season, North Carolina State's record had been 328–272, nearly 55 percent. But Case saw potential there, especially since a large building had been under construction since 1942, but not finished. Plans were for it to seat 8,000. He took the job with the understanding that games would be played in that building, to be named William Neal Reynolds Coliseum. Previously, games were played in a 3,000 seat campus gymnasium and in a municipal auditorium in downtown Raleigh.

In Case's first three years, their record was 26–5, 29–3, and 25–8. Interest in basketball in North Carolina and the entire southeast was jump-started. The other schools had to improve or be left behind. Case used his influence to have the capacity of Reynolds Coliseum increased to 12,400, the largest in the south at that time.

Case heavily recruited players from Indiana because they knew the game and were fundamentally sound. At least twelve went there to play for him and others went, even after he retired. Among the first was Dick Dickey, who had played for Pendleton High School. Case installed the Hoosier tradition of cutting down the nets after tournament championships. In the interest of being factual, it must be said that his ethics and tactics were questioned and he was penalized by authorities on several occasions.

Case's record in eighteen seasons was 376–133, nearly 74 percent. He coached two games into the 1964–65 season, then retired because of ill health. He died April 10, 1966. A plaque honoring him is mounted inside the main entrance to Reynolds Coliseum. Since 2000, N. C. State has played in the RBC Center, which seats 21,000 and is near the campus on the outskirts of Raleigh.

To get the full effect of Indiana on college basketball as a whole, consider that UCLA, with Hoosier John Wooden coaching, is the most successful program of all time, winning ten championships in twelve years, including one string of seven straight. The team that broke the seven straight was N. C. State in 1974, with Hoosier and former N. C. State player Norm Sloan coaching and two others, Tim Stoddard, and Monte Towe, in the starting lineup.

The Future

Since basketball has been such a big part of my life, I still attend many boys regular season high school games, plus NCAA Division III games. In the high school state tournament series, I have attended only 4A games, with the exception of five state championship games in which I wanted to watch a particular team. I have been fortunate to attend the finals tournament for the past fifty-eight years. I first attended in 1946, but did not go in 1947, a decision that I still regret. In 2001, my attending necessitated a plane trip from North Carolina.

I have served as a volunteer guide at the Indiana Basketball Hall of Fame, at New Castle, since December, 2000. It was fitting that the first day I worked was the first snowfall of that winter. It reminded me of the many similar trips I made while officiating. I learn something every time I am there. Anyone, Hoosier or not, with interest in basketball, should visit this fine center for Hoosier basketball.

In March, 2005, I was given the Center Circle Officials Award by the Hall of Fame, at its annual banquet. It signifies exemplary service as an official. I was happy to receive it after having been retired for thirty-one years.

Scores by Decade

IHSAA Tournament Scores 1911–2005

Surveying the names of schools is a good lesson in Indiana geography, history, and nostalgia. Some of the more interesting names are Brushy Prairie, Gladdens Corner, Hanging Grove (glad I never officiated there), Rykers Ridge, and Zenas. None of those schools is still in existence.

Generally, the names and scores are listed as published by the IHSAA, with exceptions to provide clarity or to avoid repetition. Many different arenas have been used for tournament games, so basically, with the exception of state finals sites and a few others, only the names of towns and cities hosting tournaments are used. To identify which specific arena was used for every tournament would be nearly impossible.

Officials' names are listed in most cases, except for some of the early years. The number of officials assigned to tournaments has varied from two in 1911, to one in 1912, to eight presently. To find out specifically which officials worked which games it would be necessary to see a tournament program or newspaper box score, if possible. Several numbering rotation systems for officials have been used. I would be glad to assist anyone with a specific question.

Much of the information came from documents and copies of such age that they were difficult to read. Every effort was made to be 100 percent accurate, but, like officiating, it isn't perfect, especially when considering the volume of names and scores involved. I apologize, in advance, for any oversights, errors, or name inconsistencies.

The Format of the Tournaments

1911—One team from each of twelve congressional districts played in the tournament at Indiana University. No team from Indianapolis played, as a result of a decision by the school board.

1912—Thirteen teams played in four district tournaments, with the winners playing in the finals tournament.

1913–1914—All teams played in the finals tournament.

1915–1920—Sectional tournaments were played, with each winner advancing to the finals.

1921–1935—Sectional winners advanced to regional tournaments, with sixteen regional winners advancing to the finals.

1936–1997—Semi–final tournaments were adopted for the sixteen regional winners. The four semi–final winners advanced to the finals. The semi–finals were renamed semi–states in 1957.

From 1911 through 1997, all schools, from the smallest to the largest, played in one open, unclassified tournament.

Since 1998, four different tournaments have been played, with each school classified by enrollment, the smallest in 1A, the largest 4A. The format has remained unchanged since 2002.

In the 1940s and 50s, when the interest and attendance were greater, but the gymnasiums were smaller, the first and second round games of a few of the sectionals were played at two different sites in order to accommodate more spectators. After the final two at each site were determined, the final four then played at one of the sites on Saturday. The majority of the tickets throughout were distributed to only the schools that were participating. The general public usually could not be accommodated.

Also, a few sectionals were played in a two–bracket arrangement. For example, half of the schools played on Wednesday afternoon and night, the other half on Thursday afternoon and night. After the final four were determined, tickets for Saturday's games were distributed on Friday, thereby permitting more of their fans to see the games.

Some sectionals necessitated games being played on Friday morning and afternoon, on which most schools were dismissed for the entire day, much to the joy of most students.

Since 2000, in a few of the sectionals, the two first round games have been played in the participating schools' gymnasiums, rather than at the tournament hosts' gymnasiums. The final three games have been played at the tournament hosts' gymnasiums.

In 1998 and '99, the winner of each of the four classes played in a Tournament of Champions, but that was discontinued. Those results, as well as those for Slam Dunk and Three-Point shooting are not being listed.

1911 STATE FINALS—March 10, 11

BLOOMINGTON (Indiana University): Crawfordsville 36–16 Anderson; Walton 31–23 Morristown; Bluffton 38–22 Evansville; Lafayette 31–14 Oaktown; Lebanon 23–10 Valparaiso; New Albany 19–18 Rochester; Crawfordsville 31–12 Walton; Bluffton 34–20 Lafayette; Lebanon 28–10 New Albany; Crawfordsville 42–16 Bluffton; Crawfordsville 24–17 Lebanon. Officials: Robert Harris, Bert Westover.

Tourney Time

1912 DISTRICT TOURNEYS
MUNCIE: Lebanon 42–14 Portland; Lebanon 36–10 Marion.
VINCENNES: Orleans 25–18 Evansville; Orleans 26–8 Bicknell.
INDIANAPOLIS (YMCA): Richmond 31–14 Oaklandon; Franklin 16–14 Clinton; Franklin 17–13 Richmond.
SOUTH BEND (Notre Dame): Whiting 21–14 Wolf Lake; Whiting 15–12 Culver.

1912 FINALS—March 16
BLOOMINGTON (Indiana University): Lebanon 28–13 Orleans; Franklin 29–21 Whiting; Lebanon 51–11 Franklin. Officials: Dr. A. E. Guedel.

1913 FINALS—March 14, 15
BLOOMINGTON (Indiana University): Thorntown 43–9 Nappanee; South Bend 26–6 Seymour; Gary 28–18 Marco; Clinton 30–28 Cutler; Lafayette 17–6 Petroleum; Indianapolis Manual 15–14 Orleans; South Bend 29–11 Shortridge; Lebanon 26–13 Shelbyville; Gary 18–10 Clinton; Crawfordsville 20–12 Bloomington; Wingate 19–17 Rochester; South Bend 16–8 Gary; Wingate 16–11 Manual; Lafayette 30–8 Thorntown; Crawfordsville 27–14 Lebanon; South Bend 19–11 Crawfordsville; Wingate 23–19 Lafayette; Wingate 15–14 South Bend (5ot). Officials: Dr. A. E. Guedel, Merle Abbett, Arthur Powell.

1914 FINALS—March 13, 14
BLOOMINGTON (Indiana University and Armory): Rochester 17–6 Decatur; Tipton 19–12 Sharpsville; Whiting 33–6 Southport; New Richmond 17–9 Brazil; North Manchester 28–14 Nappanee; Roanoke 8–5 West Lafayette; Anderson 20–12 Marion; Lafayette 31–11 Seymour; Mishawaka 36–15 Swayzee; Crawfordsville 65–9 Plainfield; Manual 31–17 Orleans; Lebanon 32–13 Amboy; Albion 61–8 Milroy; Wingate 42–14 Milan; New Bethel 17–15 Decker; Whiteland 30–13 New London; Rockville 19–14 Liberty Center; Pendleton 21–19 Monrovia; Westport 21–15 Interlaken; Marco 34–10 Connersville; Cutler 77–4 Jasper; Richmond 20–19 Edinburgh; Wolcott 2–0 Gary; Thorntown 35–26 Oaklandon; Kokomo 26–15 Burlington; Clinton 18–17 Bloomington; Franklin 2–0 Wawaka; Brookville 22–19 Rensselaer; Rossville 43–6 LaCrosse; Centerville 17–15 Vincennes; New Castle 34–0 Vevay; New Albany 35–17 New Winchester; New Augusta 22–18 Martinsville; Shortridge 23–11 Amo; Culver 53–17 Ligonier; Bluffton 50–5 Smithville; Akron 32–8 Broad Ripple; Bedford 23–19 Paoli; Lebanon 43–11 Darlington; Rochester 23–15 North Manchester; Manual 18–9 New Bethel; Rockville 16–13 Roanoke; New Richmond 28–9 Whiteland; Anderson; 22–15 Tipton; Crawfordsville 23–17 Lafayette; Wingate 42–18 Westport; Mishawaka 29–23 Albion; Marco 39–23 Pendleton; Whiting 62–8 Wolcott; Lebanon 45–16 Bedford; Akron 25–24 Shortridge; New Augusta 8–6 New Castle; Centerville 15–14 Bluffton; Rossville 11–8 Culver; Franklin 11–5 Cutler; Rochester 19–6 Richmond; Thorntown 9–7 Kokomo; Clinton 20–12 Brookville; New Albany 13–5 Mishawaka; Wingate 24–1 Crawfordsville; Lebanon 17–15 Whiting; New Richmond 19–12 Akron; Anderson 18–12 Manual; Marco 15–6 Rockville; Rochester 31–10 New Augusta; Centerville 17–6 Franklin;

Rossville 21–15 Thorntown; Clinton 14–9 New Albany; Wingate 17–13 Clinton; Anderson 19–9 Rochester; Lebanon 34–21 Marco; New Richmond 14–6 Rossville; Anderson 11–10 Centerville; Lebanon 17–9 New Richmond; Wingate 14–8 Lebanon; Wingate 36–8 Anderson. Officials: Dr. A. E. Guedel, Merle Abbett, Bert Westover, James Kase, Maurice Judd.

1915 SECTIONALS

ANDERSON: Pendleton 40–16 Lapel; Anderson 42–15 Muncie; Hartford City 52–11 Pennville; Arcadia 62–9 Mt. Comfort; Cicero 68–13 Westland; Hartford City 42–5 Greenfield; Cicero 31–30 Anderson; Pendleton 31–24 Arcadia; Pendleton 31–22 Cicero; Hartford City 27–25 Pendleton. Officials: Harrington, Spruce.

BEDFORD: Spencer 32–21 Smithville; Orleans 23–22 Newberry; Switz City 35–15 Bedford; Mooresville 30–7 Paoli; Martinsville 39–15 Salem; Bloomington 44–15 Spencer; Switz City 30–15 Orleans; Martinsville 20–17 Mooresville; Bloomington 24–22 Switz City; Bloomington 33–29 Martinsville. Officials: Jared, Montgomery.

CRAWFORDSVILLE: Attica 28–16 Newton; New Richmond 59–6 Williamsport; Wingate 48–11 Mellott; New Market 27–15 Darlington; Crawfordsville 30–10 Waynetown; Crawfordsville 60–14 Veedersburg; Wingate 28–14 New Market; New Richmond 40–9 Attica; Crawfordsville 26–20 Wingate; Crawfordsville 32–22 New Richmond. Officials: Masters, Stayton.

BRAZIL: Wiley 66–16 Perrysville; Brazil 72–13 Stanton; Clinton 20–14 Garfield; Glenn 24–11 Newport; Bloomingdale 35–16 Normal; Bloomingdale 22–18 Glenn; Wiley 25–19 Brazil; Bloomingdale 19–16 Clinton; Bloomingdale 25–21 Wiley. Officials: Thomas, Smith.

BLUFFTON: Liberty Center 57–9 Auburn; Petroleum 26–15 Pleasant Lake; Huntington 40–16 Albion; Washington 87–18 South Whitley; Hamilton 20–17 Wolf Lake; Bluffton 50–5 Geneva; Decatur 21–19 Ossian; Craigville 32–19 Hamilton; Liberty Center 26–14 Washington; Huntington 38–18 Petroleum; Bluffton 69–16 Decatur; Huntington 29–20 Craigville; Bluffton 38–23 Liberty Center; Bluffton 34–17 Huntington. Officials: Thurman, Bishop.

EVANSVILLE: Princeton 39–16 Newburgh; Washington 66–7 Richland; Mt. Vernon 40–34 Jasper; Oaktown 29–19 Carlisle; Washington 25–14 Vincennes; Princeton 28–15 Mt. Vernon; Evansville 68–28 Oaktown; Evansville 49–20 Washington; Evansville 71–24 Princeton. Officials: Jamison, McCormick.

FRANKLIN: New Augusta 28–18 Edinburg; Shelbyville 37–19 Tech; Southport 54–24 Morristown; Shortridge 30–17 Broad Ripple; New Bethel 31–18 Fairland; Hopewell 18–14 Franklin; Manual 34–17 Whiteland; Manual 19–15 New Bethel; Southport 60–19 Shortridge; Hopewell 45–11 New Augusta; Shelbyville 20–18 Hopewell; Manual 37–23 Southport; Manual 43–27 Shelbyville. Officials: Berndt, Kase.

HAMMOND: South Bend 30–24 Gary; Valparaiso 71–11 Wheeler; LaPorte 38–12 Hammond; Whiting 39–21 Lowell; East Chicago 36–22 Crown Point; Whiting 23–20 LaPorte; Valparaiso 21–16 South Bend; East Chicago 29–19 Valparaiso; East Chicago 27–22 Whiting. Officials: Westover, Mowe.

KOKOMO: Kokomo 24–17 Fairmount; Fairmount Academy 61–19 New London; Bunker Hill 36–17 Sharpsville; Converse 37–19 North Manchester; Swayzee 25–23 Tipton; Fairmount Academy 48–20 Bunker Hill; Kokomo 32–22 Swayzee; Kokomo 27–21 Converse; Fairmount Academy 31–16 Kokomo. Officials: Wicks, Dorste.

Tourney Time

LAFAYETTE: Montmorenci 44–20 Reynolds; Boswell 17–16 Wolcott; Monticello 30–19 West Point; Lafayette 2–0 Wea; Burnetts Creek 17–16 West Lafayette; Monticello 17–9 Lafayette; Montmorenci 22–12 Boswell; Burnetts Creek 14–10 Monticello; Montmorenci 56–14 Burnetts Creek. Officials: Thurber, McGeath.

LEBANON: Thorntown 40–7 Wheeling; Rossville 48–29 Deer Creek; Jamestown 43–24 Zionsville; Plainfield 35–27 Frankfort; Advance 29–22 Cutler; Delphi 34–29 Amo; Lebanon 42–27 Burlington; Flora 34–22 Clayton; Advance 22–20 Flora; Lebanon 49–26 Jamestown; Rossville 49–26 Delphi; Thorntown 43–14 Plainfield; Rossville 25–19 Advance; Thorntown 23–15 Lebanon; Thorntown 28–22 Rossville. Officials: Robinson, Maloney.

RICHMOND: Rushville 37–15 Moreland; New Castle 33–11 Connersville; Richmond 43–14 Cadiz; Brookville 20–16 Hagerstown; Richmond 35–22 Rushville; New Castle 23–18 Brookville; New Castle 23–21 Richmond. Officials: Swaim, Jones.

ROCHESTER: Plymouth 2–0 Warsaw; Medaryville 30–27 Winamac; Akron 44–10 Etna Green; Bremen 56–24 Bourbon; Rochester 37–24 Akron; Medaryville 37–18 Bremen; Rochester 29–17 Plymouth; Rochester 55–15 Medaryville. Officials: Bravy, Miller.

SEYMOUR: Westport 39–19 Austin; Hope 2–0 Moorefield; Crothersville 26–22 Aurora; Seymour 27–17 Milan; Hope 34–24 Seymour; Westport 54–29 Crothersville; Westport 36–20 Hope. Officials: Cook, Regan.

1915 FINALS—March 12, 13

BLOOMINGTON (Indiana University): Rochester 20–17 Crawfordsville; Thorntown 46–20 Hartford City; Bluffton 28–18 Westport; Montmorenci 23–18 Bloomingdale Academy; Evansville 31–22 New Castle; Fairmount Academy 28–27 Bloomington; Indianapolis Manual 21–7 East Chicago; Thorntown 17–14 Rochester; Montmorenci 22–21 Bluffton; Fairmount 37–27 Evansville; Thorntown 30–16 Manual; Montmorenci 35–32 Fairmount; Thorntown 33–10 Montmorenci. Officials: Merle Abbett, Bert Westover.

1916 SECTIONALS

ANDERSON: Pennville 27–16 Sheridan; Atlanta 38–8 Portland; Anderson 28–15 Hartford City; Arcadia 40–12 Walnut Grove; Yorktown 67–18 Westland; Cicero 73–9 Mt. Comfort; Muncie 26–15 Pendleton; Lapel 31–18 McCordsville; Pennville 23–13 Atlanta; Anderson 35–9 Arcadia; Cicero 45–15 Yorktown; Muncie 44–17 Lapel; Anderson 20–5 Pennville; Cicero 23–19 Muncie; Cicero 18–12 Anderson. Officials: Harrington, Spruce.

BEDFORD: Owensburg 23–18 Paoli; Salem 19–18 Orleans; Oolitic 27–8 Springville; New Albany 24–23 Smithville; Linton 43–21 Freedom; Bloomington 29–13 Bedford; Owensburg 25–24 Spencer; Salem 26–25 Oolitic; New Albany 28–26 Lipton; Bloomington 33–9 Owensburg; Salem 15–14 New Albany; Bloomington 25–14 Salem. Officials: Montgomery, Jared.

BLUFFTON: Pleasant Lake 44–21 Waterloo; South Milford 41–22 Albion; Liberty Center 44–15 Hudson; Bluffton 31–23 Auburn; Huntington 46–20 Angola; Craigville 39–26 Geneva; Pleasant Lake 35–31 South Milford; Liberty Center 30–29 Bluffton; Huntington 45–26 Craigville; Liberty Center 42–31 Pleasant Lake; Liberty Center 32–19 Huntington. Officials: Thurman, Bishop.

IHSAA Scores | 1911–1919

CRAWFORDSVILLE: Wingate 98–12 Mellott; Ladoga 18–15 Darlington; Crawfordsville 39–16 New Market; Pine Village 44–7 Williamsport; New Richmond 25–16 Newton; Veedersburg 35–14 Roachdale; Waynetown 25–12 Bowers; Wingate 48–17 Ladoga; Crawfordsville 62–27 Pine Village; New Richmond 23–20 Veedersburg; Wingate 30–21 Waynetown; Crawfordsville 61–18 New Richmond; Crawfordsville 53–9 Wingate. Officials: Stayton, Robinson.

FRANKLIN: Hopewell 17–16 Morristown; Shelbyville 42–15 Whiteland; Fairland 28–19 Waldron; Trafalgar 26–17 Westport; Edinburgh 36–35 Greensburg; Hopewell 28–11 Franklin; Shelbyville 26–11 Fairland; Trafalgar 25–24 Edinburg; Hopewell 33–17 Shelbyville; Hopewell 36–19 Trafalgar. Officials: Smith, Barnhart.

GARY: LaPorte 2–0 Interlaken; South Bend 54–14 Hammond; East Chicago 32–13 Lowell; Whiting 2–0 Brook; Froebel 26–17 Emerson; Valparaiso 39–10 Crown Point; LaPorte 54–14 Rensselaer; South Bend 49–23 East Chicago; Froebel 28–16 Whiting; Valparaiso 30–29 LaPorte; Froebel 31–30 South Bend; Valparaiso 25–15 Froebel. Officials: Mowe, Westover.

KOKOMO: Fairmount 33–21 Gas City; Fairmount Academy 49–17 New London; Tipton 44–22 North Manchester; Windfall 28–25 Russiaville; Kokomo 63–16 Sharpsville; Fairmount 2–0 Swayzee; Fairmount Academy 40–22 Tipton; Kokomo 45–19 Windfall; Fairmount Academy 25–24 Fairmount; Kokomo 25–21 Fairmount Academy. Officials: Brown, Craigle.

LAFAYETTE: Chalmers 36–12 Fowler; Lafayette 80–11 Boswell; Monticello 51–26 Jackson Twp.; Montmorenci 24–18 Otterbein; Oxford 30–11 Reynolds; West Lafayette 19–14 West Point; Lafayette 48–13 Chalmers; Monticello 36–32 Montmorenci; West Lafayette 22–8 Oxford; Lafayette 29–22 Monticello; Lafayette 55–12 West Lafayette. Officials: Thurber, McGeath.

LEBANON: Frankfort 35–34 Danville; Amo 38–31 Clayton; Thorntown 23–9 Zionsville; Lebanon 29–16 Rossville; Advance 34–19 Plainfield; Amo 38–14 Frankfort; Lebanon 15–12 Thorntown; Amo 19–17 Advance; Lebanon 41–11 Amo. Officials: Thomas, Palmer.

LOGANSPORT: Washington C.C. 69–6 Walton; Peru 36–18 Onward; Logansport 25–22 Flora; Cutler 40–13 Deer Creek; Young America 29–23 Bunker Hill; Columbia City 29–28 Amboy; Bringhurst 49–38 Delphi; Washington C.C. 34–13 Peru; Logansport 22–21 Cutler; Young America 20–19 Columbia City; Washington C.C. 31–25 Bringhurst; Logansport 21–17 Young America; Washington C.C. 29–16 Logansport. Officials: Hipskind, Wicks.

MARTINSVILLE: Castleton 36–26 Monrovia; Indianapolis Tech 22–12 Oakland; Southport 48–12 New Augusta; Broad Ripple 28–27 West Newton; New Bethel 31–27 Mooresville; Martinsville 29–19 Manual ; Tech 27–25 Castleton; Southport 33–20 Broad Ripple; Martinsville 33–13 New Bethel; Southport 37–15 Tech; Martinsville 49–17 Southport. Officials: Berndt, Kase.

RICHMOND: Union City 29–15 Lewisville; Carthage 22–21 Rushville; Spiceland Ac. 30–24 Cambridge City; Liberty 37–21 Milroy; Brookville 35–12 Mt. Summit; New Castle 31–9 Cadiz; Richmond 63–7 Union City; Carthage 30–31 Spiceland Ac.; Brookville 46–20 Liberty; Richmond 22–15 New Castle; Brookville 31–30 Carthage; Brookville 19–17 Richmond. Officials: Swaim, Jones.

ROCHESTER: Akron 28–18 Etna Green; Elkhart 27–17 Plymouth; Nappanee 47–19 Richland Center; Winamac 34–22 Bourbon; Culver 43–21 Argos; Medaryville 2–0 Warsaw; Akron 2–0 Rochester; Elkhart 20–16 Nappanee; Culver 34–26 Winamac; Medaryville 35–18 Akron; Elkhart 20–15 Culver; Elkhart 19–16 Medaryville. Officials: Bravy, Miller.

SEYMOUR: Vevay 24–20 Scottsburg; Seymour 53–13 North Vernon; Moorefield 35–29

79

Tourney Time

Osgood; Milan 23–22 Madison; Austin 31–11 Freetown; Vevay 49–28 Crothersville; Seymour 50–18 Moorefield; Milan 36–9 Austin; Seymour 53–12 Vevay; Seymour 37–19 Milan. Officials: Cooke, Thurber.

TERRE HAUTE: Rockville 45–18 Perrysville; Sullivan 22–17 Bloomingdale; Carlisle 32–20 Coalmont; Glenn 43–11 Staunton; Clinton 26–24 Brazil; Garfield 36–21 Normal; Rockville 47–33 Wiley; Sullivan 24–18 Carlisle; Clinton 44–8 Glenn; Rockville 28–17 Garfield; Clinton 30–11 Sullivan; Clinton 24–16 Rockville. Officials: Maloney, Masters.

VINCENNES: Evansville 51–12 Newburgh; Princeton 56–16 Odon; Sandborn 39–27 Mt. Vernon; Washington 50–18 Wheatland; Vincennes 93–9 Jasper; Evansville 34–24 Princeton; Washington 52–17 Sandborn; Vincennes 47–27 Evansville; Vincennes 33–23 Washington. Officials: Jamison, McCormick.

1916 FINALS—March 17, 18

BLOOMINGTON (Indiana University): Lebanon 25–15 Bloomington; Martinsville 53–22 Washington Center; Liberty Center 28–25 Elkhart; Lafayette 39–27 Hopewell; Valparaiso 34–23 Cicero; Vincennes 18–16 Brookville; Kokomo 37–13 Seymour; Crawfordsville 40–17 Clinton; Martinsville 16–13 Lebanon; Lafayette 60–19 Liberty Center; Vincennes 22–16 Valparaiso; Crawfordsville 36–21 Kokomo; Lafayette 29–17 Martinsville; Crawfordsville 33–17 Vincennes; Lafayette 27–26 Crawfordsville (ot). Officials: Merle Abbett, Bert Westover.

1917 SECTIONALS

ANDERSON: Fortville 54–4 McCordsville; Atlanta 37–17 Mt. Comfort; Pendleton 35–19 Arcadia; Anderson 52–5 Walnut Grove; Carmel 51–11 Summitville; Elwood 38–18 Boxley; Cicero 39–24 New Palestine; Lapel 45–7 Westland; Atlanta 22–12 Fortville; Pendleton 33–15 Anderson; Carmel 46–20 Elwood; Cicero 28–22 Lapel; Pendleton 34–20 Atlanta; Carmel 32–21 Cicero; Pendleton 48–21 Carmel. Officials: Harrington, Craigle.

BLOOMINGTON: Smithville 32–9 Springville; Orleans 40–8 Heltonville; Bloomington 54–14 Spencer; Oolitic 38–25 Paoli; Salem 18–13 Bedford; Freedom 24–20 Mitchell; Orleans 25–17 Smithville; Bloomington 39–15 Oolitic; Salem 29–8 Freedom; Bloomington 27–16 Orleans; Bloomington 30–13 Salem. Officials: Jared, Montgomery.

BLUFFTON: Liberty Center 37–14 Markle; Geneva 50–2 Craigville; Huntington 50–25 Berne; Pennville 20–18 Warren; Hartford City 34–26 Decatur; Bluffton 40–21 Liberty Center; Huntington 76–33 Geneva; Hartford City 19–12 Pennville; Bluffton 36–22 Huntington; Bluffton 33–13 Hartford City. Officials: Hipskind, Ritter.

BRAZIL: Wiley 23–14 Garfield; Normal 18–9 Bloomingdale; Glenn 39–11 Fon–tanet; Rockville 25–16 Clinton; Brazil 24–17 Perrysville; Wiley 34–21 Staunton; Normal 27–13 Glenn; Rockville 29–13 Brazil; Wiley 19–15 Normal; Rockville 35–20 Wiley; Officials: Feezle, Pitcher.

COLUMBUS: North Vernon 37–22 Napoleon; Vallonia 22–10 Osgood; Madison 30–27 Vernon; Columbus 52–13 Charleston; Vevay 35–21 Milan; Seymour 43–15 Moorefield; Scottsburg 32–19 New Albany; North Vernon 30–12 Vallonia; Columbus 50–10 Madison; Vevay 34–16 Seymour; Scottsburg 34–16 North Vernon; Columbus 34–14 Vevay; Columbus 27–20 Scottsburg. Officials: Thurber, Cooke.

IHSAA Scores | 1911–1919

CRAWFORDSVILLE: Bowers 43–25 Hillsboro; Crawfordsville 39–12 Ladoga; Veedersburg 2–0 Attica; Wingate 36–21 Covington; New Market 51–9 New Ross; Waynetown 22–21 New Richmond; Newtown 23–10 Mace; Darlington 38–16 Waveland; Crawfordsville 46–12 Bowers; Wingate 31–21 Veedersburg; New Market 14–13 Waynetown; Newtown 25–22 Darlington; Wingate 29–21 Crawfordsville; Newtown 23–14 New Market; Wingate 20–18 Newtown. Officials: Brown, Mattingly.

FRANKLIN: Franklin 25–19 Edinburg; Trafalgar 22–21 Hopewell; Shelbyville 34–22 Whiteland; Union 54–2 Mt. Auburn; Morristown 46–25 Waldron; Fairland 57–6 Boggstown; Trafalgar 34–27 Franklin; Shelbyville 42–25 Union; Morristown 56–30 Fairland; Trafalgar 38–23 Shelbyville; Trafalgar 47–19 Morristown. Officials: Smith, Webb

GREENCASTLE: Danville 26–11 Avon; New Winchester 29–22 Cloverdale; Lizton 39–5 Fillmore; Plainfield 25–17 North Salem; Brownsburg 28–21 Greencastle; Clayton 21–8 Roachdale; Bainbridge 28–9 Pittsboro; Amo 27–8 Danville; Lizton 24–9 New Winchester; Plainfield 15–13 Brownsburg; Bainbridge 36–19 Clayton; Lizton 20–16 Amo; Plainfield 20–17 Bainbridge; Lizton 17–11 Plainfield. Officials: Robinson, McGeath.

KENDALLVILLE: Pleasant Lake 25–20 Auburn; South Milford 39–22 South Whitley; Kendallville 62–15 Ligonier; Garrett 42–25 Butler; Angola 54–26 Monroeville; Fort Wayne 55–19 Waterloo; Pleasant Lake 30–27 South Milford; Kendallville 61–16 Garrett; Angola 26–19 Fort Wayne; Kendallville 28–27 Pleasant Lake; Kendallville 33–25 Angola. Officials: Swaim, Bravy.

KOKOMO: Sharpsville 20–17 Deedsville; N. Manchester 38–11 Swayzee; Kokomo 51–10 New London; Windfall 22–16 Peru; Russiaville 24–21 West Middleton; Amboy 30–19 Bunker Hill; Tipton 25–15 Fairmount Ac.; Sharpsville 27–25 Fairmount; Kokomo 55–28 N. Manchester; Russiaville 18–16 Windfall; Tipton 30–23 Amboy; Kokomo 24–9 Sharpsville; Tipton 40–24 Russiaville; Kokomo 32–20 Tipton. Officials: Thomas, Gorman.

LAFAYETTE: Dayton 29–8 Otterbein; Jackson Twp. 25–24 Oxford; Montmorenci 54–6 Buck Creek; Romney 35–11 Pine Village; West Lafayette 34–14 West Point; Lafayette 56–2 Williamsport; Fowler 29–6 Battle Ground; Jackson Twp. 32–28 Dayton; Montmorenci 33–12 Romney; Lafayette 16–9 West Lafayette; Jackson 27–12 Fowler; Lafayette 35–11 Montmorenci; Lafayette 52–13 Jackson Twp. Officials: Thurber, Kase.

LEBANON: Lebanon 81–12 Cutler; Bringhurst 23–16 Burlington; Frankfort 32–19 Flora; Advance 47–14 Jamestown; Kirklin 21–20 Colfax; Thorntown 41–6 Zionsville; Lebanon 56–7 Delphi; Bringhurst 25–20 Frankfort; Advance 50–17 Kirklin; Lebanon 23–19 Thorntown; Advance 30–19 Bringhurst; Lebanon 37–18 Advance. Officials: Maloney, Sheeks.

LOGANSPORT: Rochester 45–17 Walton; Chalmers 40–20 Akron; Brookston 14–13 Young America; Monon 38–18 Onward; Logansport 40–17 Wolcott; Reynolds 74–11 Galveston; Rochester 58–18 Winamac; Chalmers 41–20 Brookston; Logansport 29–16 Monon; Rochester 66–13 Reynolds; Chalmers 29–23 Logansport; Rochester 63–20. Chalmers Officials: Regan, Haugh.

MARTINSVILLE: West Newton 23–20 New Bethel; Martinsville 33–18 Castleton; Tech 25–22 Broad Ripple; Monrovia 37–19 New Augusta; Paragon 26–19 Mooresville; Ben Davis 37–19 Lawrence; West Newton 35–25 Manual; Martinsville 27–16 Tech; Monrovia 51–12 Paragon; West Newton 47–31 Ben Davis; Martinsville 29–15 Monrovia; Martinsville 39–35 West Newton. Officials: Westover, Spruce.

NEW CASTLE: New Castle 35–11 Spiceland; Mooreland 42–14 Middletown; Lewisville

Tourney Time

25–21 Mt. Summit; Muncie 77–5 Cowan; Yorktown 34–21 Royerton; Moreland 21–13 New Castle; Muncie 85–7 Lewisville; Mooreland 24–21 Yorktown; Muncie 59–7 Mooreland. Officials: Stayton, Palmer

RICHMOND: Richmond 50–20 Rushville; Sandusky 48–15 Cambridge City; Modoc 31–24 Monroe; Greensburg 35–24 Clarksburg; Liberty 20–19 Hagerstown; Westport 29–25 Milroy; Richmond 59–10 Union City; Sandusky 36–27 Modoc; Liberty 27–19 Greensburg; Richmond 99–13 Westport; Liberty 32–18 Sandusky; Richmond 64–14 Liberty. Officials: Bishop, Thurman.

SOUTH BEND: South Bend 37–17 Interlaken; Mishawaka 68–5 Lakeville; Michigan City 16–15 LaPorte; Nappanee 32–12 Union Mills; Syracuse 33–15 New Carlisle; Goshen 40–10 Atwood; Milford 28–23 Etna; South Bend 44–18 Mishawaka; Michigan City 33–13 Nappanee; Syracuse 15–11 Goshen; South Bend 55–18 Milford; Michigan City 47–9 Syracuse; South Bend 34–8 Michigan City. Officials: Mead, Rockwood.

VALPARAISO: Gary Emerson 20–12 Valparaiso; Whiting 38–15 Brook; East Chicago 43–23 Bourbon; Gary Froebel 41–18 Hammond; Crown Point 55–9 Wheatfield; Emerson 37–21 Plymouth; East Chicago 34–19 Whiting; Froebel 27–9 Crown Point; Emerson 33–23 East Chicago; Emerson 26–19 Froebel. Officials not listed.

VINCENNES: Vincennes 55–21 Farmersburg; Sullivan 24–12 Fritchton; Sandborn 67–13 Mt. Vernon; Otwell 20–15 Winslow; Princeton 29–26 Wheatland; Vincennes 48–32 Edwardsport; Sandborn 24–22 Sullivan; Otwell 23–21 Princeton; Vincennes 104–15 Sandborn; Vincennes 122–14 Otwell. Officials: Krause, Lammers.

WASHINGTON: Newberry 18–3 Linton; Loogootee 23–11 Epsom; Lyons; 11–6 Marco; Washington 15–14 Switz City; Newberry 34–17 Montgomery; Lyons 34–29 Loogootee; Washington 43–9 Newberry; Washington 89–13 Lyons. Officials: McCormick, Wiltse.

1917 FINALS—March 16, 17

BLOOMINGTON (Indiana University): Muncie 31–8 Lizton; Kokomo 19–16 South Bend; Bloomington 23–14 Lafayette; Martinsville 27–23 Washington; Rochester 36–15 Wingate; Richmond 29–20 Columbus; Vincennes 42–18 Bluffton; Gary 53–16 Rockville; Lebanon 34–14 Trafalgar; Kendallville 31–24 Pendleton; Kokomo 22–16 Muncie; Martinsville 18–16 Bloomington; Rochester 26–21 Richmond; Gary 19–9 Vincennes; Lebanon 43–8 Kendallville; Martinsville 26–21 Kokomo; Gary 27–17 Rochester; Lebanon 36–12 Martinsville; Lebanon 36–26 Gary. Officials: Bert Westover, Ray Mowe, Merle Abbett.

1918 SECTIONALS

ANDERSON: Anderson 39–21 Fortville; Arcadia 49–8 Cicero; New Palestine 26–12 Markleville; Summitville 38–12 McCordsville; Westfield 33–14 Boxley; Pendleton 48–14 Walnut Grove; Atlanta 22–8 Sheridan; Lapel 41–29 Carmel; Anderson 60–12 Arcadia; New Palestine 32–19 Summitville; Pendleton 55–11 Westfield; Lapel 24–10 Atlanta; Anderson 74–7 New Palestine; Pendleton 19–16 Lapel; Anderson 37–15 Pendleton. Officials: Harrington, Berry.

BEDFORD: Spencer 24–15 West Baden; Mitchell 38–8 Paoli; Orleans 2–0 Salem; Scottsburg 50–10 Stinesville; Charlestown 28–21 Williams; Bloomington 51–4 Needmore; Smithville 46–

IHSAA Scores | 1911–1919

10 Oolitic; Bedford 36–11 Spencer; Mitchell 28–16 Orleans; Scottsburg 38–11 Charlestown; Bloomington 30–25 Smithville; Bedford 65–14 Mitchell; Bloomington 35–17 Scottsburg; Bloomington 27–19 Bedford. Officials: Wiley, Overman.

BRAZIL: Prairie Creek 31–8 Bloomingdale; Brazil 35–13 Tangier; Normal 25–12 Perrysville; Clinton 36–18 Mecca; Rockville 28–18 Wiley; Glenn 18–15 Staunton; Garfield 40–12 Fontanet; Prairie Creek 23–19 Brazil; Normal 27–21 Clinton; Rockville 35–29 Glenn; Garfield 19–12 Prairie Creek; Rockville 29–15 Normal; Rockville 20–16 Garfield. Officials: Thomas, Gorman.

COLUMBUS: Patriot 59–28 Vernon; Columbus 53–7 Milan; North Vernon 61–6 Osgood; Vallonia 28–21 Seymour; Aurora 59–17 Moorefield; Napoleon 25–23 Hayden; Brownstown 19–16 Hanover; Vevay 37–10 Patriot; Columbus 27–5 North Vernon; Aurora 48–22 Vallonia; Brownstown 16–14 Napoleon; Columbus 17–16 Vevay; Aurora 44–10 Brownstown; Columbus 31–13 Aurora. Officials: Cook, Craigle.

CRAWFORDSVILLE: Veedersburg 45–5 Mace; New Richmond 39–15 Waveland; Bowers 25–21 Hillsboro; Wingate 35–10 New Ross; Crawfordsville 38–12 Linden; Ladoga 32–29 Darlington; New Market 18–16 Newton; Veedersburg 30–14 Attica; New Richmond 28–10 Bowers; Wingate 36–16 Crawfordsville; New Market 33–21 Ladoga; Veedersburg 19–13 New Richmond; Wingate 41–20 New Market; Wingate 23–18 Veedersburg. Officials: Brown, Horner.

FRANKLIN: Hopewell 43–12 Edinburg; Morristown 24–16 Nineveh; Shelbyville 33–8 Whiteland; Franklin 44–18 Fairland; Waldron 26–9 Mt. Auburn; Union Twp. 27–15 Trafalgar; Hopewell 33–10 Boggstown Shelbyville 46–15 Morristown; Franklin 44–7 Waldron; Hopewell 32–23 Union Twp.; Franklin 38–17 Shelbyville; Franklin 25–18 Hopewell. Officials: Smith, Palmer.

GREENCASTLE: Greencastle 28–12 Roachdale; Amo 31–27 Bainbridge; Plainfield Academy 11–6 Ben Davis; Lizton 27–3 Danville; Brownsburg 28–17 North Salem; Russellville 37–6 Avon; Plainfield 22–13 Clayton; Cloverdale 22–16 Greencastle; Amo 29–5 Plainfield Academy; Lizton 17–16 Brownsburg; Plainfield 20–16 Russellville; Amo 44–10 Cloverdale; Plainfield 20–16 Lizton; Plainfield 24–20 Amo. Officials: Mowe, Westover.

HAMMOND: Morocco 15–10 Fair Oaks; Medaryville 18–12 Francesville; Crown Point 30–25 Rensselaer; Valparaiso 22–15 Whiting; Brook 18–16 Hammond; Gary Emerson 46–16 East Chicago; Winamac 26–11 Kentland; Lowell 34–11 Morocco; Crown Point 22–5 Medaryville; Valparaiso 21–8 Brook; Emerson 28–18 Winamac; Crown Point 24–17 Lowell; Emerson 26–21 Valparaiso; Emerson 57–23 Crown Point. Officials not listed.

HARTFORD CITY: Huntington 83–19 Tocsin; Markle 44–14 Lynn Grove; Geneva 32–17 Pennville; Andrews 37–19 Keystone; Hartford City 26–21 Rock Creek Twp.; Bluffton 29–26 Monroe; Petroleum 62–11 Kirkland Twp.; Warren 23–17 Montpelier; Huntington 65–33 Markle; Geneva 46–18 Andrews; Bluffton 32–24 Hartford City; Warren 24–20 Petroleum; Huntington 72–30 Geneva; Bluffton 38–27 Warren; Huntington 82–17 Bluffton. Officials: Parker, Schmitz.

KENDALLVILLE: Washington Center 2–0 Churubusco; Fort Wayne 28–20 Angola; Pleasant Lake 42–22 Hudson; Albion 24–17 Waterloo; Kendallville 53–11 Monroeville; Butler 30–29 South Whitley; Auburn 33–16 St. Joe; Washington Center 20–18 Ligonier; Pleasant Lake 24–21 Fort Wayne; Kendallville 47–14 Albion; Auburn 42–17 Butler; Pleasant Lake 41–22 Washington Center; Kendallville 49–30 Auburn; Kendallville 34–18 Pleasant Lake. Officials: Abbett, Hart.

KOKOMO: Bunker Hill 41–8 Swayzee; Kokomo 25–10 Fairmount; Tipton 22–13 Sharpsville;

Fairmount Academy 25–14 Windfall; Laketon 22–21 Roann; Greentown 22–14 New London; Amboy 32–8 Chili; Lagro 19–11 West Middleton; Kokomo 20–16 Bunker Hill; Tipton 24–20 Fairmount Academy; Laketon 31–6 Greentown; Amboy 22–16 Lagro; Kokomo 23–10 Tipton; Amboy 36–20 Laketon; Kokomo 27–12 Amboy. Officials: Johnson, Feezle.

LAFAYETTE: West Point 26–18 Romney; Montmorenci 38–12 Oxford; Lafayette 32–16 Dayton; Delphi 28–12 Buck Creek; Otterbein 24–9 Ambia; West Lafayette 56–2 Monitor; Pine Twp. 2–0 Boswell; Montmorenci 31–11 West Point; Lafayette 34–13 Delphi; West Lafayette 36–7 Otterbein; Montmorenci 86–4 Pine Twp.; Lafayette 27–20 West Lafayette; Montmorenci 17–16 Lafayette. Officials: Maloney, McGeath.

MARTINSVILLE: Morgantown 21–17 Broad Ripple; Shortridge 27–9 New Bethel; Castleton 24–21 Fisher; Valley Mills 28–12 West Newton; Mooresville 17–9 Tech; New Augusta 34–2 Acton; Southport 21–11 Cumberland; Martinsville 19–8 Manual; Morgantown 20–15 Shortridge; Castleton 31–20 Valley Mills; New Augusta 23–9 Mooresville; Martinsville 30–3 Southport; Castleton 17–16 Morgantown; Martinsville 47–12 New Augusta; Martinsville 62–10 Castleton. Officials: Stonebraker, Regan.

NEW CASTLE: Mooreland 16–13 Knightstown; Cowan 33–4 Wilkinson; Cadiz 18–13 Spiceland Academy; Mt. Comfort 32–12 Middletown; New Castle 57–11 Straughn; Kennard 20–19 New Lisbon; Lewisville 23–15 Maxwell; Muncie 20–8 Mooreland; Cowan 27–7 Cadiz; New Castle 35–11 Mt. Comfort; Lewisville 14–10 Kennard; Muncie 26–17 Cowan; New Castle 27–16 Lewisville; Muncie 26–24 New Castle. Officials: Haugh, Wiley.

RICHMOND: Richmond 21–16 Rushville; Milroy 2–0 St. Paul; Liberty 36–20 Cambridge City; Fountain City 48–10 Burney; Green 30–18 Modoc; Manilla 41–11 Connersville; Moscow 52–10 Union City; Sandusky 34–10 Hagerstown; Richmond 22–20 Milroy; Fountain City 19–15 Liberty; Manilla 30–11 Green; Sandusky 22–20 Moscow; Richmond 27–15 Fountain City; Manilla 25–16 Sandusky; Richmond 47–12 Manilla. Officials: Roy Thurman, William Webb.

ROCHESTER: Logansport 34–10 Young America; Rochester 82–5 Reynolds; Monticello 27–26 Deedsville; Kewanna 37–7 Leiters Ford; Chalmers 33–16 Montgomery; Akron 62–8 Macy; Walton 36–6 Twelve Mile; Brookston 34–11 Onward; Rochester 18–12 Logansport; Monticello 47–9 Kewanna; Akron 35–22 Chalmers; Walton 27–14 Brookston; Rochester 47–9 Monticello; Akron 36–12 Walton; Rochester 60–3 Akron. Officials: Mattingly, Thurber.

SOUTH BEND: New Carlisle 23–6 Bourbon; Wanatah 13–12 Etna Green; Interlaken 29–27 Elkhart; Plymouth 20–14 LaPorte; Nappanee 15–14 Goshen; South Bend 29–10 Michigan City; Mishawaka 58–11 Milford; Atwood 18–15 Wakarusa; New Carlisle 18–11 Wanatah; Plymouth 37–9 Interlaken; South Bend 38–9 Nappanee; Mishawaka 63–6 Atwood; Plymouth 32–4 New Carlisle; South Bend 28–16 Mishawaka; South Bend 18–7 Plymouth. Officials not listed.

THORNTOWN: Central 22–19 Deer Creek; Burlington 20–15 Cutler; Bringhurst 38–13 Flora; Thorntown 38–12 Frankfort; Advance 29–25 Jamestown; Lebanon 56–1 Kirklin; Colfax 21–17 Rossville; Zionsville 46–14 Scircleville; Burlington 19–14 Central; Thorntown 41–16 Bringhurst; Lebanon 32–18 Advance; Colfax 21–20 Zionsville; Thorntown 20–12 Burlington; Lebanon 38–10 Colfax; Lebanon 43–14 Thorntown. Officials: Maloney, Sheeks.

VINCENNES: Farmersburg 2–0 Mt. Vernon; Edwardsport 14–6 Decker; Sandborn 17–12 Sullivan; Vincennes 42–7 Fairbanks; Evansville 25–8 Freelandville; Carlisle 18–11 Princeton; Fritchton 33–19 Wheatland; Edwardsport 18–10 Farmersburg; Vincennes 26–21 Sandborn; Evansville 23–16 Carlisle; Edwardsport 20–16 Fritchton; Vincennes 39–13 Evansville; Vincennes

19–10 Edwardsport. Officials: Kase, Robinson

WASHINGTON: Winslow 20–17 Lynnville; Washington 47–12 Linton; Montgomery 36–14 Union; Otwell 27–18 Plainville; Lyons 42–19 Odon; Epsom 15–14 Shoals; Winslow 29–18 Owensburg; Washington 30–11 Montgomery; Lyons 35–17 Otwell; Winslow 20–16 Epsom; Washington 36–18 Lyons; Washington 30–5 Winslow. Officials: Wiltse, Graham.

1918 FINALS—March 15, 16

BLOOMINGTON (Indiana University): Martinsville 33–20 Rockville; Bloomington 39–12 Richmond; Montmorenci 24–16 Muncie; Columbus 2–0 Franklin; Rochester 18–15 Plainfield; Anderson 30–9 Gary Emerson; Vincennes 30–15 Kokomo; Huntington 32–21 Washington; Lebanon 15–6 Wingate; South Bend 15–13 Kendallville; Bloomington 24–22 Martinsville; Montmorenci 16–13 Columbus; Anderson 23–12 Rochester; Huntington 24–12 Vincennes; Lebanon 30–3 South Bend; Bloomington 23–11 Montmorenci; Anderson 29–24 Huntington; Lebanon 17–4 Bloomington; Lebanon 24–20 Anderson. Officials: Chester Regan, Merle Abbett, Bert Westover, Justin Maloney.

1919 SECTIONALS

ANDERSON: Pendleton 30–11 Summitville; Lapel 16–13 Elwood; Atlanta 19–16 Noblesville; Sheridan 18–14 Fishers; Fortville 26–11 Carmel; Westfield 19–7 McCordsville; Anderson 69–1 Markleville; Boxley 27–7 Walnut Grove; Lapel 14–11 Pendleton; Atlanta 16–12 Sheridan; Fortville 14–12 Westfield; Anderson 94–7 Boxley; Lapel 19–14 Atlanta; Anderson 54–10 Fortville; Anderson 26–10 Lapel. Officials: Cooke, Evans.

BEDFORD: Orleans 38–8 Williams; Paoli 19–5 West Baden; Smithville 42–7 Oolitic; Bloomington 36–14 Mitchell; Bedford 40–8 Heltonville; Scottsburg 31–8 French Lick; Orleans 40–6 Spencer; Smithville 26–6 Paoli; Bloomington 53–5 Bedford; Scottsburg 15–12 Orleans; Bloomington 36–10 Smithville; Bloomington 21–9 Scottsburg. Officials: Overman, Wiley.

BLOOMFIELD: Plainville 17–12 Carlisle; Bloomfield 26–11 Montgomery; Washington 40–8 Farmersburg; Pleasantville 2–0 Newberry; Loogootee 16–15 Epsom; Sullivan 16–15 Lyons; Plainville 16–9 Elnora; Washington 42–7 Bloomfield; Pleasantville 29–17 Loogootee; Sullivan 19–13 Plainville; Washington 33–9 Pleasantville; Washington 33–14 Sullivan. Officials: Graham, Gilbert.

BRAZIL: Brazil 31–1 Cayuga; Perrysville 13–6 Bloomingdale; Normal 25–13 Staunton; Glenn 22–9 Coalmont; Fontanet 15–8 Washington Twp.; Garfield 31–3 Clinton; Prairie Creek 26–3 Rosedale; Brazil 13–6 Perrysville; Normal 21–12 Glenn; Garfield 38–15 Fontanet; Brazil 26–7 Prairie Creek; Normal 20–14 Garfield; Brazil 18–13 Normal. Officials: Thomas, Gorman.

COLUMBUS: Vallonia 30–7 Versailles; Burney 29–16 Clearspring; Brownstown 17–8 Crothersville; Seymour 26–13 Aurora; Hope 22–10 Flatrock Twp.; Columbus 61–13 Vernon; North Vernon 40–6 Osgood; Vallonia 28–8 Holton; Brownstown 15–11 Burney; Seymour 32–7 Hope; Columbus 40–8 North Vernon; Brownstown 13–9 Vallonia; Columbus 19–10 Seymour; Columbus 42–8 Brownstown. Officials: Rathbun, Steward.

CRAWFORDSVILLE: Darlington 30–6 Attica; Ladoga 26–16 New Market; Veedersburg 17–13 Waynetown; Romney 32–0 Linden; New Richmond 26–8 New Ross; Kingman 17–8 Mace;

Tourney Time

Crawfordsville 24–6 Wingate; Bowers 20–17 Pine Village; Darlington 14–9 Ladoga; Veedersburg 19–12 Romney; New Richmond 23–7 Kingman; Crawfordsville 52–4 Bowers; Darlington 16–9 Veedersburg; Crawfordsville 38–1 New Richmond; Crawfordsville 16–7 Darlington. Officials: Brown, Horner.

FRANKFORT: Frankfort 15–13 Flora; Lebanon 54–3 Kirklin; Rossville 20–10 Delphi; Thorntown 48–4 Burlington; Advance 34–4 Colfax; Bringhurst 15–7 Cutler; Zionsville 30–8 Scircleville; Lebanon 31–6 Frankfort; Thorntown 53–7 Rossville; Advance 30–7 Bringhurst; Zionsville 14–13 Lebanon; Thorntown 20–6 Advance; Thorntown 22–9 Zionsville. Officials: Townsend, Schoeneman.

FRANKLIN: Franklin 35–3 Southport; Manilla 35–19 Fairland; Whiteland 62–6 Mt. Auburn; Hopewell 28–12 Edinburg; Union 23–16 Center Grove; Shelbyville 15–9 Morristown; Rushville 25–12 Nineveh; Boggstown 19–10 Arlington; Franklin 32–9 Manilla; Hopewell 25–17 Whiteland; Union 17–16 Shelbyville; Rushville 22–13 Boggstown; Franklin 26–14 Hopewell; Rushville 27–18 Union; Franklin 30–8 Rushville. Officials: Palmer, Smith.

GARY: Rensselaer 36–9 Francesville; Emerson 49–5 Monterey; Brook 42–7 Lowell; Whiting 24–21 Crown Point; Kentland 14–8 Fair Oaks; Medaryville 18–12 Froebel; Valparaiso 28–4 Morocco; East Chicago 32–11 Hammond; Emerson 44–15 Rensselaer; Whiting 23–14 Brook; Medaryville 16–12 Kentland; East Chicago 16–11 Valparaiso; Emerson 26–7 Whiting; East Chicago 24–15 Medaryville; Emerson 30–15 East Chicago. Officials: Barr, Sheeks.

GREENCASTLE: Greencastle 39–0 Belle Union; Roachdale 17–3 Cloverdale; Amo 36–8 Stilesville; Clayton 37–20 Plainfield; Clinton Twp. 2–0 Russellville; Bainbridge 17–11 Russellville; Greencastle 24–3 Roachdale; Amo 26–14 Clayton; Bainbridge 28–12 Clinton Twp. Greencastle 18–9 Amo; Greencastle 18–6 Bainbridge. Officials: Jenson, Humke.

HUNTINGTON: Rock Creek 25–21 Markle; Monroe 26–10 Hartford Twp.; Fort Wayne 22–15 Berne; Geneva 30–23 Bluffton; Huntington 45–6 Ossian; Kirkland 18–12 Liberty Center; Petroleum 22–20 Tocsin; Decatur 26–17 Clear Creek; Monroe 23–14 Rock Creek; Geneva 21–10 Fort Wayne; Huntington 53–13 Kirkland; Decatur 31–29 Petroleum; Geneva 29–16 Monroe; Huntington 53–12 Decatur; Huntington 40–16 Geneva. Officials: Palmer, Smith.

INDIANAPOLIS: New Augusta 11–9 New Bethel; Mt. Comfort 12–5 Oaklandon; Shortridge 46–4 Greenfield; Tech 29–3 Fishers; Castleton 40–4 Westland; Acton 29–5 Green Twp.; Manual 28–3 Broad Ripple; Cumberland 17–5 Maxwell; New Augusta 18–11 Mt. Comfort; Shortridge 15–14 Tech; Castleton 22–4 Acton; Manual 53–1 Cumberland; Shortridge 19–13 New Augusta; Manual 32–14 Castleton; Manual 27–8 Shortridge. Officials: Miller, Berry.

KENDALLVILLE: St. Joe 33–20 Hudson; Angola 25–9 Salem Center; Waterloo 37–18 Fremont; Ashley 2–0 Spencerville; Auburn 19–14 Cromwell; Kendallville 48–2 Flint; Churubusco 21–16 Butler; Wolf Lake 21–12 Pleasant Lake; Angola 16–15 St. Joe; Waterloo 24–7 Ashley; Kendallville 19–12 Auburn; Wolf Lake 28–15 Churubusco; Angola 34–14 Waterloo; Kendallville 33–14 Wolf Lake; Kendallville 30–3 Angola. Officials: Abbett, Binford.

KOKOMO: Montpelier 27–21 Marion; Hartford City 11–10 Fairmount Academy; Kokomo 66–11 Howard Twp.; Windfall 16–10 Swayzee; New London 58–6 Upland; Tipton 37–5 Dunkirk; Fairmount 38–11 Greentown; Hartford City 18–15 Montpelier; Kokomo 23–3 Windfall; Tipton 28–11 New London; Fairmount 19–17 Hartford City; Kokomo 23–14 Tipton; Kokomo 21–15 Fairmount. Officials: Ritter, Feezle.

LAFAYETTE: Dayton 39–5 Monitor; Boswell 24–10 Pine Twp.; West Lafayette 52–3

Stockwell; Otterbein 22–8 Buck Creek; Jackson Twp. 36–25 Montmorenci; Wea 22–12 Clarks Hill; Oxford 44–15 Ambia; Lafayette 39–16 West Point; Dayton 57–4 Boswell; West Lafayette 33–5 Otterbein; Jackson Twp. 42–17 Wea; Lafayette 26–15 Oxford; West Lafayette 24–14 Dayton; Lafayette 42–8 Jackson Twp.; Lafayette 22–16 West Lafayette. Officials: Maloney, Johnson.

LOGANSPORT: Deedsville 29–18 Macy; Chalmers 33–12 Reynolds; Amboy 20–7 Twelve Mile; Young America 50–4 Winamac; LaFontaine 22–18 Chili; Converse 18–12 Bunker Hill; Brookston 24–13 Monon; Logansport 16–11 Walton; Chalmers 24–12 Deedsville; Young America 31–14 Amboy; Converse 35–19 LaFontaine; Logansport 19–18 Brookston; Young America 27–23 Chalmers; Logansport 28–20 Converse; Logansport 26–22 Young America. Officials: Babb, Miller.

MARTINSVILLE: North Salem 25–11 Avon; Martinsville 53–4 Pittsboro; West Newton 23–7 Ben Davis; Mooresville 18–17 Valley Mills; Lizton 16–9 Danville; Brownsburg 18–5 Paragon; Eminence 20–10 Monrovia; Martinsville 34–9 North Salem; Mooresville 18–14 West Newton; Brownsburg 10–9 Lizton; Martinsville 44–7 Eminence; Brownsburg 16–5 Mooresville; Martinsville 33–11 Brownsburg. Officials: Mowe, Wright.

NEW CASTLE: Mt. Summit 29–21 Cadiz; Lewisville 24–23 New Lisbon; Muncie 36–9 Gaston; Kennard 27–12 Straughn; New Castle 35–1 Wilkinson; Mooreland 22–16 Middletown; Royerton 15–4 Cowan; Spiceland 29–5 Selma; Mt. Summit 30–17 Lewisville; Muncie 28–6 Kennard; New Castle 26–5 Mooreland; Spiceland 14–6 Royerton; Muncie 30–8 Mt. Summit; Spiceland 18–4 New Castle; Spiceland 18–16 Muncie. Officials: Edwards, Thurber.

RICHMOND: Hagerstown 27–18 Green; Richmond 63–5 Farmland; Connersville 20–13 Cambridge City; Economy 16–12 Modoc; Fountain City 36–14 Stoney Creek; Milroy 30–24 Brookville; Moscow 23–20 Whitewater; Liberty 35–15 Ridgeville; Richmond 32–10 Hagerstown; Connersville 15–7 Economy; Milroy 27–13 Fountain City; Liberty 30–14 Moscow; Richmond 29–15 Connersville; Liberty 18–16 Milroy; Richmond 26–4 Liberty. Officials: Thurman, Webb.

ROCHESTER: Atwood 2–0 Leiters Ford; Argos 22–15 Kewanna; North Manchester 12–9 Culver; Pierceton 20–9 Fulton; Wabash 20–13 Bourbon; Akron 24–8 Talma; Rochester 33–7 Plymouth; Etna Green 21–12 Lagro; Argos 16–12 Atwood; Pierceton 31–12 North Manchester; Akron 23–19 Wabash; Rochester 21–10 Etna Green; Argos 18–11 Pierceton; Rochester 59–10 Akron; Rochester 62–10 Argos. Officials: Mattingly, Arbuckle.

SOUTH BEND: Nappanee 41–24 Leesburg; Michigan City 16–6 New Carlisle; Syracuse 48–24 Ligonier; South Bend 20–10 Mishawaka; LaCrosse 23–22 Goshen; LaPorte 20–17 Rolling Prairie; Milford 24–16 Elkhart; Wanatah 20–9 Wakarusa; Michigan City 15–5 Nappanee; South Bend 21–12 Syracuse; LaPorte 35–14 LaCrosse; Elkhart 21–19 Wanatah; South Bend 23–12 Michigan City; LaPorte 34–18 Elkhart; South Bend 17–11 LaPorte. Officials: Quant, Veenker.

VINCENNES: Winslow 19–13 Decker; Princeton 14–13 Oaktown; Union 29–14 Fritchton; Otwell 47–7 Jasper; Vincennes 28–18 Wheatland; Patoka 22–13 Boonville; Freelandville 48–7 Luce Twp.; Winslow 39–9 Edwardsport; Union 16–9 Princeton; Vincennes 46–13 Otwell; Freelandville 32–15 Patoka; Union 26–25 Winslow; Vincennes 37–9 Freelandville; Vincennes 31–6 Union. Officials: Stiehm, Gilbert.

1919 FINALS—March 13, 14, 15

WEST LAFAYETTE (Purdue University): Bloomington 16–13 Richmond; Indianapolis Manual 19–13 Vincennes; Thorntown 26–23 Anderson; Huntington 24–13 Washington;

Tourney Time

Columbus 24–3 South Bend; Rochester 16–8 Greencastle; Lafayette 22–16 Martinsville; Gary Emerson 33–13 Kendallville; Crawfordsville 18–14 Franklin; Logansport 9–5 Spiceland Academy; Kokomo 11–6 Brazil; Bloomington 23–12 Manual; Thorntown 23–14 Huntington; Columbus 11–5 Rochester; Lafayette 21–18 Emerson; Crawfordsville 20–1 Logansport; Bloomington 23–14 Kokomo; Thorntown 20–16 Columbus; Lafayette 18–15 Crawfordsville; Bloomington 27–17 Thorntown; Bloomington 18–15 Lafayette. Officials: Justin Maloney, Merle Abbett, L.I. Mattingly, Ray Mowe.

1920–1929

1920 SECTIONALS

ANDERSON: Westfield 18–17 Fishers; Arcadia 14–11 Pendleton; Summitville 34–4 Markleville; Anderson 63–8 Noblesville; Lapel 50–4 Sheridan; Carmel 12–8 Cicero; Boxley 27–19 Walnut Grove; Elwood 29–16 Atlanta; Westfield 22–21 Arcadia; Anderson 23–17 Summitville; Lapel 43–7 Carmel; Boxley 21–18 Elwood; Anderson 51–27 Westfield; Lapel 50–9 Boxley; Anderson 41–16 Lapel. Officials: H. Dale Miller, Floyd Wright.

AUBURN: Angola 45–2 Spencerville; Auburn 60–9 Orland; Hamilton 2–0 Garrett; Butler 18–16 Flint; Hudson 40–9 Harlan; Ashley 22–11 St. Joe; Waterloo 20–15 Pleasant Lake; Fremont 18–15 Salem; Angola 21–16 Auburn; Butler 43–8 Hamilton; Hudson 39–15 Ashley; Waterloo 26–20 Fremont; Angola 48–4 Butler; Hudson 26–9 Waterloo; Angola 25–9 Hudson. Officials: Roscoe Abbett, Virgil Binford.

BEDFORD: Seymour 30–12 Loogootee; Williams 20–19 Heltonville; Oolitic 29–15 Mitchell; Bedford 50–12 Courtland; Paoli 54–5 Crothersville; Salem 30–11 Pershing Twp.; Orleans 35–9 Clear Spring; West Baden 58–9 Shoals; Vallonia 20–16 Needmore; Seymour 22–12 Williams; Bedford 30–4 Oolitic; Paoli 25–11 Salem; West Baden 19–18 Orleans; Seymour 33–16 Vallonia; Bedford 42–9 Paoli; Seymour 40–11 West Baden; Bedford 39–13 Seymour. Officials: D.H. Overman, H. McLain.

BLOOMINGTON: Farmersburg 18–15 Stinesville; Pleasantville 23–12 Fairbanks; Lyons 14–5 Carlisle; Smithville 21–1 Bloomfield; Sullivan 36–7 Owensburg; Bloomington 60–4 Ellettsville; Spencer 16–8 Scotland; Farmersburg 41–11 Marco; Lyons 29–18 Pleasantville; Smithville 36–4 Sullivan; Bloomington 40–2 Spencer; Lyons 26–18 Farmersburg; Bloomington 14–13 Smithville; Bloomington 23–17 Lyons. Officials: R. E. Lammers, M. P. Wilder.

BLUFFTON: Liberty Center 28–15 Geneva; Pennville 34–16 Gray; Bryant 18–15 Portland; Ossian 19–11 Tocsin; Dunkirk 13–12 Petroleum; Bluffton 43–23 Hartford Twp.; Monroe 25–19 Kirkland Twp.; Hartford City 49–22 Decatur; Pennville 20–18 Liberty Center; Ossian 22–18 Bryant; Bluffton 39–14 Dunkirk; Hartford City 39–21 Monroe; Ossian; 36–20 Pennville; Hartford City 52–19 Bluffton; Hartford City 39–15 Ossian. Officials: J.J. Ritter, L. Kulcinski.

CLINTON: Rosedale 15–13 Helt Twp.; Normal High 22–12 Prairie Creek; Garfield 30–8 Perrysville; Tangier 15–13 Bellmore; Mecca 42–5 Bridgeton; Washington Twp. 27–22 Wiley; Bloomingdale 12–8 Dana; Rockville 28–9 Cayuga; Glenn 30–21 Newport; Clinton 28–10

Fontanet; Normal High 26–15 Rosedale; Garfield 19–6 Tangier; Washington Twp. 26–12 Mecca; Rockville 12–8 Bloomingdale; Glenn 20–18 Clinton; Normal High 17–10 Garfield; Rockville 23–14 Washington Twp.; Normal High 28–12 Glenn; Normal High 14–4 Rockville. Officials: O.M. Berry, H. Wiltse.

COLUMBUS: Vernon 11–6 Scipio; Sandusky 36–13 Versailles; Letts 28–4 Osgood; Madison 42–5 Clifford; Greensburg 14–9 Holton; Scottsburg 33–8 Hanover; Aurora 26–7 Vevay; Burney 15–6 North Vernon; Newbern 11–4 Milan; Columbus 68–4 Vernon; Sandusky 28–13 Letts; Madison 17–10 Greensburg; Scottsburg 24–6 Aurora; Burney 45–10 Newbern; Columbus 37–9 Sandusky; Scottsburg 31–9 Madison; Columbus 27–8 Burney; Columbus 12–8 Scottsburg. Officials: H.L. Humke, F.V. Ragsdale

EVANSVILLE: Spurgeon 22–12 Mt. Vernon; Jasper 12–8 Milltown; Jeffersonville 19–10 New Harmony; New Albany did not appear, forfeited to Boonville; Evansville Central 54–6 Elberfeld; Otwell 19–11 Union; Petersburg 10–9 Huntingburg; Poseyville 26–3 Cynthiana; Dale 7–6 Velpen; Winslow 15–5 English; Spurgeon 18–10 Jasper; Jeffersonville 25–16 Boonville; Central 47–12 Otwell; Poseyville 20–7 Petersburg; Winslow 7–5 Dale; Spurgeon 24–8 Jeffersonville; Central 32–11 Poseyville; Spurgeon 37–8 Winslow; Central 40–9 Spurgeon. Officials: George Graham, Ivan Zaring.

FRANKLIN: Shelbyville 60–9 Fairland; Franklin 57–14 Nineveh; Morristown 19–12 Center Grove; Hopewell 32–11 Greenwood; Whiteland 37–5 Union; Waldron 21–17 Clark Twp.; Mt. Auburn 26–8 Boggstown; Edinburg 23–13 Trafalgar; Franklin 32–5 Shelbyville; Hopewell 26–6 Morristown; Whiteland 27–21 Waldron; Edinburg 13–11 Mt. Auburn; Franklin 36–17 Hopewell; Whiteland 44–14 Edinburg; Franklin 49–14 Whiteland. Officials: John Craigle, Heze Clark.

GREENCASTLE: Waynetown 28–14 New Market; Alamo 19–14 Mace; Cloverdale 19–5 New Ross; Ladoga 28–18 Bowers; Brazil 17–10 Bainbridge; Darlington 44–5 Staunton; Roachdale 23–6 Waveland; Russellville 50–8 Clinton Twp.; Greencastle 50–2 Fillmore; Waynetown 33–8 Alamo; Ladoga 16–13 Cloverdale; Darlington 19–16 Brazil; Russellville 16–6 Roachdale; Greencastle 33–9 Waynetown; Ladoga 15–13 Darlington; Greencastle 15–13 Russellville; Greencastle 18–13 Ladoga. Officials: Charles Jenson, B.E. Bayh.

HUNTINGTON: Rock Creek 36–25 Roann; Fort Wayne 17–16 Roanoke; Bippus 41–9 Linlawn; Wabash 20–8 Clear Creek; Markle 24–4 LaFontaine; Huntington 39–10 Monroeville; Laketon 21–20 Lagro; Warren 22–14 North Manchester; Fort Wayne 29–15 Rock Creek; Bippus 15–13 Wabash; Huntington 28–10 Markle; Laketon 27–21 Warren; Fort Wayne 20–19 Bippus; Huntington 33–16 Laketon; Huntington 22–14 Fort Wayne. Officials: H.A. Barnhart, Harry Coolman.

INDIANAPOLIS: West Newton 13–12 Valley Mills; Ben Davis 23–15 Fishers; Tech 20–9 Manual; Cumberland 63–2 Beech Grove; Broad Ripple 23–13 New Augusta; Castleton 22–10 Lawrence; Shortridge 29–2 Southport; Oaklandon 15–9 Acton; Ben Davis 16–12 West Newton; Tech 22–9 Cumberland; Broad Ripple 13–7 Castleton; Shortridge 35–22 Oaklandon; Tech 14–11 Ben Davis; Shortridge 13–10 Broad Ripple; Tech 27–16 Shortridge. Officials: D.J. Arbuckle, W.E. Dekyne.

KENDALLVILLE: Washington Center 29–18 North Webster; Silver Lake 68–18 Avilla; Columbia City 21–4 Syracuse; Wolf Lake 40–18 Ligonier; Warsaw 27–6 Churubusco; South Whitley 35–4 Milford; Atwood 52–6 Cromwell; Kendallville 27–5 Etna Green; Washington Center 57–3 Silver Lake; Wolf Lake 16–15 Columbia City; Warsaw 26–13 South Whitley;

Tourney Time

Kendallville 26–8 Atwood; Washington Center 39–10 Wolf Lake; Kendallville 17–7 Warsaw; Kendallville 15–9 Washington Center. Officials: H. Hipskind, R. Gilbert.

KOKOMO: Russiaville 20–16 Swayzee; Kokomo 25–10 Tipton; Windfall 14–12 Howard Twp.; Fairmount 35–4 Union Twp.; Fairmount Academy 32–11 Marion; New London 19–10 Greentown; Upland; 34–5 West Middletown; Kokomo 23–6 Russiaville; Windfall 18–5 Fairmount; Fairmount Academy 22–4 New London; Kokomo 54–1 Upland; Windfall 12–10 Fairmount Academy; Kokomo 36–7 Windfall. Officials: John Miller, C.E. Stewart.

LAFAYETTE: Lafayette Jefferson 30–12 West Lafayette; New Richmond 22–4 Stockwell; Pine Village 20–6 Buck Creek; Romney 12–2 Dayton; Montmorenci 13–8 Jackson Twp.; Battle Ground 38–14 Clarks Hill; Linden 18–4 West Point; Jefferson 35–1 Monitor; New Richmond 23–6 Pine Village; Romney 15–13 Montmorenci; West Point 18–14 Battle Ground; Jefferson 22–10 New Richmond; Romney 14–12 West Point; Jefferson 37–1 Romney. Officials: Harry Schoeneman, J.R. Townsend.

LEBANON: Lebanon 19–12 Colfax; Rossville 23–15 Zionsville; Thorntown 24–11 Scircleville; Jamestown 33–9 Michigantown; Jefferson 37–12 Forest; Frankfort 17–15 Advance; Mulberry 11–6 Kirklin; Lebanon 36–25 Rossville; Jamestown 4–2 Thorntown; Frankfort 19–7 Jefferson; Lebanon 18–4 Mulberry; Frankfort 21–11 Jamestown; Lebanon 22–18 Frankfort. Officials: E.R. Brown, J.M. Horner.

LOGANSPORT: Brookston 36–17 Flora; Young America 50–13 Delphi; Amboy 26–16 Bringhurst; Logansport 23–20 Converse; Burlington 16–13 Monon; Cutler 23–14 Deer Creek; Walton 29–17 Twelve Mile; Wolcott 23–12 Reynolds; Young America 29–13 Brookston; Logansport 28–12 Amboy; Cutler 20–12 Monon; Walton 19–6 Wolcott; Young America 24–18 Logansport; Walton 31–10 Cutler; Young America 18–7 Walton. Officials: Stanley Feezle, Billy Webb.

MARTINSVILLE: Amo 14–13 Plainfield; Pittsboro 16–8 North Salem; Martinsville 31–9 Paragon; Danville 27–8 Avon; Eminence 8–7 Monrovia; Mooresville 31–11 Clayton; Brownsburg 17–5 Stilesville; Lizton 16–9 Amo; Martinsville 25–7 Pittsboro; Danville 15–7 Eminence. Mooresville 15–9 Brownsburg; Martinsville 28–5 Lizton; Mooresville 22–15 Danville; Martinsville 45–10 Mooresville. Officials: Ray Mowe, Nash Higgins.

MUNCIE: Muncie 42–6 Yorktown; Gaston 26–14 DeSoto; Monroe 19–8 Stoney Creek; Eaton 27–7 Winchester; Cowan 28–11 Selma; Ridgeville 42–13 Saratoga; Royerton 21–7 Spartanburg; Losantville 17–12 Green Twp. Jefferson 22–20 Farmland; Modoc 26–8 Union City; Muncie 29–5 Gaston; Eaton 30–19 Monroe; Ridgeville 32–18 Cowan; Royerton 24–7 Losantville; Modoc 30–13 Jefferson; Muncie 26–7 Eaton; Ridgeville 14–9 Royerton; Muncie 33–9 Modoc; Ridgeville 16–15 Muncie. Officials: W.E. Babb, E.B. Palmer.

NEW CASTLE: Middletown 24–10 Cadiz; Richmond 24–15 Kennard; Cambridge City 25–8 Economy; Hagerstown 24–16 Mooreland; Spiceland Academy 22–9 Whitewater; Williamsburg 15–10 Boston; Fountain City 19–10 Centerville; Knightstown 20–19 Lewisville; New Castle 65–8 New Lisbon; Richmond 27–4 Middletown; Hagerstown 17–1 Cambridge City; Spiceland Academy 55–1 Williamsburg; Fountain City 18–14 Knightstown; New Castle 25–11 Richmond; Spiceland Academy 31–9 Hagerstown; New Castle 37–23 Fountain City; Spiceland Academy 19–17 New Castle. Officials: Ross Smith, J.C. Edwards

ROCHESTER: Rochester 40–3 Bourbon; Kewanna 20–9 Talma; Bunker Hill 2–0 Francesville (forfeit); Medaryville 33–9 Macy; Culver 27–15 Winamac; Argos 26–15 Monterey; Chili 14–

13 Deedsville; Rochester 30–8 Kewanna; Bunker Hill 23–14 Medaryville; Culver 15–6 Argos; Rochester 65–4 Chili; Bunker Hill 16–14 Culver; Rochester 34–7 Bunker Hill. Officials: H.H. Rockenbach, L.I. Mattingly.

RUSHVILLE: Connersville 34–17 Arlington; Fortville 47–6 Wilkinson; Milroy 38–21 Fairview Twp.; New Palestine 31–12 Maxwell; Liberty 18–12 Raleigh; Greenfield 29–6 Westland; Manila 70–6 Green Twp.; Rushville 23–21 Carthage; Charlottesville 11–8 McCordsville; Mt. Comfort 26–13 Brooksville; Connersville 36–13 Moscow; Milroy 27–17 Fortville; Liberty 22–12 New Palestine; Manila 33–16 Greenfield; Rushville 29–4 Charlottesville; Connersville 25–9 Mt. Comfort; Milroy 19–9 Liberty; Rushville 19–10 Manila; Milroy 22–17 Connersville; Milroy 21–19 Rushville. Officials: Horace Parker, W.F. Smith.

SOUTH BEND: South Bend 62–1 Bristol; Mishawaka 49–6 North Liberty; Millersburg 17–13 Middlebury; Nappanee 18–10 Rolling Prairie; Elkhart 46–9 Lakeville; Goshen 35–6 West Twp.; Plymouth 17–11 Wakarusa; LaPorte 20–15 Michigan City; South Bend 23–11 Mishawaka; Nappanee 28–10 Millersburg; Elkhart 25–12 Goshen; LaPorte 30–12 Plymouth; South Bend 25–13 Nappanee; Elkhart 23–10 LaPorte; South Bend 12–4 Elkhart. Officials: J.E. Gilroy, Justin Maloney.

VALPARAISO: Kentland 15–11 Goodland; North Judson 20–11 Crown Point; Whiting 32–14 Lowell; Brook 28–15 Hammond; Valparaiso 36–21 Gary Froebel; Wheeler 21–12 Fair Oaks; Gary Emerson 22–9 East Chicago; Rensselaer 33–17 Morocco; North Judson 19–18 Kentland; Whiting 24–13 Brook; Valparaiso 44–14 Wheeler; Emerson 33–11 Rensselaer; Whiting 31–12 North Judson; Emerson 36–18 Valparaiso; Emerson 20–17 Whiting. Officials: M.C. Darnel, L.W. Sinclair.

VEEDERSBURG: Hillsboro 12–4 Covington; Veedersburg 24–7 Freeland Park; Newtown 16–3 Wallace; Oxford 13–8 Boswell; Otterbein 17–6 Attica; Kingman 15–12 Pine Twp.; Ambia 11–4 Fowler; Veedersburg 31–10 Hillsboro; Oxford 13–12 Newtown; Otterbein 28–9 Kingman; Veedersburg 27–8 Ambia; Otterbein 25–16 Oxford; Veedersburg 25–9 Otterbein. Officials: F. McGeath, E.M. Morgan.

VINCENNES: Oakland City 25–23 Plainville; Vincennes 24–5 Fritchton; Washington 27–3 Oaktown; Mt. Olympus 25–11 Decker; Edwardsport 19–3 Monroe City; Elnora 31–11 Epsom; Freelandville 10–8 Sandborn; Odon 27–8 Montgomery; Owensville 19–17 Patoka; Vincennes 22–13 Oakland City; Washington 25–16 Mt. Olympus; Edwardsport 20–10 Elnora; Odon 22–5 Freelandville; Vincennes 34–11 Owensville; Washington 16–14 Edwardsport; Vincennes 28–6 Odon; Washington 19–17 Vincennes. Officials: G.L. Rathbun, J.E. Wakefield.

1920 FINALS—March 11, 12, 13

BLOOMINGTON (Indiana University): Lafayette Jefferson 25–15 Bloomington; Columbus 18–6 Kokomo; Greencastle 20–16 Martinsville; South Bend 27–12 Angola; Spiceland Academy 31–14 Evansville; Anderson 18–16 Rochester; Franklin 43–15 Young America; Terre Haute Normal 20–12 Huntington; Bedford 25–13 Lebanon; Gary Emerson 35–13 Veedersburg; Hartford City 33–29 Washington; Milroy 36–13 Ridgeville; Indianapolis Tech 30–17 Kendallville; Lafayette 17–8 Columbus; Greencastle 17–12 South Bend; Anderson 26–4 Spiceland Academy; Franklin 30–8 Normal; Bedford 23–12 Gary; Hartford City 34–24 Milroy; Lafayette 18–9 Tech; Anderson 24–21 Greencastle; Franklin 28–12 Bedford; Lafayette 21–16 Hartford City; Franklin

Tourney Time

14–12 Anderson; Franklin 31–13 Lafayette. Officials: Justin Maloney, E.B. Palmer, Ross Smith, George Veenker, Ward Lambert.

1921 SECTIONALS

ANDERSON: Anderson 38–13 Pendleton; Summitville 23–7 Westland; Greenfield 22–14 Maxwell; Lapel 38–11 Mt. Comfort; Fortville 22–10 Markleville; Elwood 64–10 Eden; New Palestine 22–13 Noblesville; Charlottesville 14–8 McCordsville; Anderson 41–11 Summitville; Lapel 43–6 Greenfield; Elwood 19–16 Fortville (ot); New Palestine 16–13 Charlottesville; Anderson 37–4 Lapel; New Palestine 29–21 Elwood; Anderson 60–10 New Palestine. Officials not listed.

ATTICA: Covington 13–8 Freeland Park; Ambia 24–4 Pine Twp. (Fowler); Fowler 13–12 Kingman; Attica 12–11 Boswell; Hillsboro 21–6 Williamsport; Pine Village 28–7 Newtown; Oxford 27–8 Wallace; Veedersburg 30–10 Mellott; Covington 15–13 Ambia; Attica 14–7 Fowler; Pine Village 20–12 Hillsboro; Oxford 27–8 Veedersburg; Covington 15–10 Attica; Pine Village 14–12 Oxford; Pine Village 18–17 Covington. Officials: Lee Sinclair, Walter Skemp.

AUBURN: Angola 22–15 Auburn; South Milford 28–14 Metz; Pleasant Lake 21–11 Topeka; Flint 26–23 Garnett; Hudson 2–0 Salem; Butler 24–12 Fremont; Ashley 20–9 Hamilton; Waterloo 24–14 Lima; Angola 74–10 South Milford; Pleasant Lake 15–14 Flint; Hudson 31–17 Butler; Waterloo 13–10 Ashley; Angola 21–4 Pleasant Lake; Hudson 17–7 Waterloo; Angola 38–16 Hudson. Officials not listed.

BEDFORD: Heltonville 13–6 Needmore; Mitchell 10–9 Paoli; West Baden 16–12 Williams; Loogootee 42–5 Huron; Orleans 57–0 Shoals; Bedford 51–8 Jasper; Oolitic 24–8 Fayetteville; Heltonville 14–12 Mitchell; West Baden 11–8 Loogootee; Bedford 18–7 Orleans; Oolitic 24–8 Heltonville; Bedford 26–9 West Baden; Bedford 15–12 Oolitic. Officials not listed.

BLOOMINGTON: Owensburg 18–15 Van Buren; Scotland 11–3 Switz City; Smithville 71–9 Marco; Freedom 21–8 Midland; Lyons 20–8 Stinesville; Spencer 21–14 Ellettsville; Bloomington 56–7 Linton; Scotland 8–7 Owensburg; Smithville 29–5 Freedom; Lyons 26–8 Spencer; Bloomington 54–6 Scotland; Smithville 21–5 Lyons Bloomington 11–9 Smithville. Officials not listed.

BLUFFTON: Hartford Twp. 19–11 Gray (Jay Co.); Bluffton 14–7 Tocsin; Kirkland Twp. 39–8 Berne; Pennville 25–19 Decatur; Geneva 18–6 Dunkirk; Monroe 2–0 Warren; Bryant 45–7 Poling; Liberty Center 19–8 Petroleum; Bluffton 28–8 Hartford Twp.; Pennville 31–20 Kirkland Twp.; Monroe 20–9 Geneva; Liberty Center 25–24 Bryant; Bluffton 42–19 Pennville; Monroe 17–16 Liberty Center; Monroe 22–13 Bluffton. Officials: R. Braesemele, R. Gilbert.

COLUMBUS: North Vernon 14–10 Osgood; Patriot 15–14 Scipio; Newbern 20–15 Batesville; Milan 17–15 Moores Hill; Versailles 35–9 Holton; Madison 26–3 Vernon; Columbus 48–4 Haw Creek Twp.; Aurora 17–15 Vevay; North Vernon 24–16 Patriot; Milan 10–6 Newbern; Madison 14–12 Versailles; Columbus 15–8 Aurora; North Vernon 17–10 Milan; Columbus 39–17 Madison; Columbus 56–14 North Vernon. Officials: Joseph Edwards, C.E. Steward.

CRAWFORDSVILLE: Bowers 13–9 Darlington; Ladoga 25–16 Linden; Crawfordsville 2–0 Mace (forfeit); New Richmond 15–10 New Ross; Wingate 31–18 Waveland; Bowers 17–8 Alamo; Crawfordsville 21–11 Ladoga; Wingate 24–11 New Richmond; Crawfordsville 23–12 Bowers; Crawfordsville 17–9 Wingate. Officials not listed.

IHSAA Scores | 1920–1929

FORT WAYNE: Ligonier 15–14 Churubusco; Wolf Lake 52–6 Avilla; Columbia City 21–9 Harlan; South Whitley 26–2 Cromwell; Monroeville 15–12 Washington Center; Kendallville 44–6 Larwill; Fort Wayne 38–4 Woodburn; Albion 25–9 St. Joe; Wolf Lake 23–15 Ligonier; South Whitley 19–11 Columbia City; Kendallville 18–11 Monroeville; Fort Wayne 59–10 Albion; Wolf Lake 24–15 South Whitley; Kendallville 27–12 Fort Wayne; Kendallville 18–9 Wolf Lake. Officials not listed.

FRANKLIN: Nineveh 38–8 Flat Rock; Morristown 26–25 Hopewell; Clark Twp. 25–21 Greenwood; Center Grove 29–21 Fairland; Franklin 38–5 Waldron; Shelbyville 36–9 Boggstown; Whiteland 23–14 Union Twp.; Trafalgar 23–16 Edinburg; Nineveh 28–6 Fountaintown; Morristown 34–23 Clark Twp.; Franklin 32–12 Center Grove; Shelbyville 28–8 Whiteland; Trafalgar 32–10 Nineveh; Franklin 38–7 Morristown; Shelbyville 20–15 Trafalgar; Franklin 20–14 Shelbyville. Officials: Craigle, Clark.

GARY: Lowell 18–10 Valparaiso; Rensselaer 12–6 Kentland; Emerson 45–15 Hebron; Brook 31–14 East Chicago; Froebel 13–7 Crown Point; Fair Oaks 12–6 Goodland; Whiting 19–12 Lowell; Emerson 15–11 Rensselaer; Brook 13–11 Froebel (ot); Whiting 63–9 Fair Oaks; Emerson 27–6 Brook; Whiting 22–8 Emerson. Officials not listed.

GREENCASTLE: Fillmore 25–13 Bridgeton; Russellville 29–7 Clinton Center; Rockville 28–9 Rosedale; Greencastle 45–11 Mecca; Roachdale 47–11 Montezuma; Cloverdale 17–16 Marshall; Bainbridge 17–8 Bloomingdale; Russellville 26–9 Fillmore; Rockville 17–16 Greencastle; Roachdale 24–11 Cloverdale; Russellville 20–9 Bainbridge; Rockville 19–14 Roachdale; Russellville 23–14 Rockville. Officials not listed.

HUNTINGTON: Bippus 15–13 Lancaster; Linlawn 18–14 Lincolnville; Lagro 21–5 North Manchester; Markle 14–4 Andrews; Clear Creek 47–5 Chippewa; Wabash 27–11 Rock Creek; Roann 24–21 Roanoke; Huntington 42–10 Laketon; Bippus 25–18 Linlawn; Markle 26–7 Lagro; Clear Creek 13–11 Wabash; Huntington 28–4 Roann; Bippus 16–10 Markle; Huntington 29–12 Clear Creek; Huntington 52–6 Bippus. Officials not listed.

INDIANAPOLIS: Tech 32–11 Beech Grove; Valley Mills 30–13 Castleton; Ben Davis 17–5 Southport; Broad Ripple 45–6 New Bethel; Manual 23–12 Shortridge; Oaklandon 26–8 Acton; West Newton 35–12 Shadeland; Cumberland 38–20 New Augusta; Tech 18–14 Valley Mills; Broad Ripple 12–9 Ben Davis; Manual 26–9 Oaklandon; West Newton 18–16 Cumberland; Tech 26–13 Broad Ripple; Manual 38–20 West Newton; Tech 19–14 Manual. Officials not listed.

KOKOMO: Sheridan 30–12 Cicero; Windfall 15–6 Kempton; Carmel 42–10 West Middleton; Kokomo 43–10 Walnut Grove; Tipton 20–15 Fishers; Arcadia 39–5 Russiaville; Howard Twp. 17–9 Sharpsville; Boxley 22–10 Atlanta; Windfall 27–13 Sheridan; Kokomo 38–8 Carmel; Arcadia 23–10 Tipton; Howard Twp. 23–17 Boxley; Windfall 30–11 Kokomo; Arcadia 26–8 Howard Twp. Arcadia 24–13 Windfall. Officials not listed.

LAFAYETTE: Dayton 33–6 Clarks Hill; Montmorenci 21–7 Otterbein; Stockwell 19–16 Reynolds; Brookston 22–14 Romney; Jackson Twp. 24–6 Chalmers; West Point 48–6 Wea; Lafayette 37–20 Battle Ground; Dayton 35–7 Buck Creek; Montmorenci 49–10 Stockwell; Brookston 29–16 Jackson Twp.; Lafayette 38–11 West Point; Montmorenci 27–13 Dayton; Lafayette 23–8 Brookston; Lafayette 29–12 Montmorenci. Officials: Lambert, Townsend.

LEBANON: Thorntown 22–18 Scircleville; Westfield 25–23 Whitestown; Jefferson 23–15 Michigantown; Colfax 14–5 Central; Advance 23–22 Zionsville; Lebanon 53–8 Forest; Frankfort 18–9 Mulberry; Rossville 30–9 Jamestown; Westfield 16–15 Thorntown; Colfax 19–7 Jefferson;

Tourney Time

Lebanon 23–12 Advance; Frankfort 18–14 Rossville; Westfield 17–10 Colfax; Frankfort 22–19 Lebanon; Frankfort 24–12 Westfield. Officials: Overman, Brown.

LOGANSPORT: Flora 16–10 Lucerne; Cutler 41–9 Galveston; Young America 55–11 Royal Center; Camden 40–12 Burnettsville; Wolcott 38–22 Deer Creek; Burlington 17–13 Monon; Walton 51–16 Bringhurst; Logansport 65–10 Twelve Mile; Cutler 30–17 Flora; Young America 41–13 Camden; Wolcott 20–18 Burlington; Walton 22–18 Logansport; Young America 35–16 Cutler; Walton 16–6 Wolcott; Young America 34–24 Walton. Officials: Day, Donlin.

MARION: Montpelier 24–4 Roll; Somerset 7–5 LaFontaine; Gaston 30–4 Gas City; Hartford City 25–4 Matthews; Marion 35–8 Greentown; Fairmount Academy 12–11 Eaton (ot); Union Twp. 13–8 Sweetser; Fairmount 18–6 Montpelier; Gaston 40–5 Somerset; Marion 17–6 Hartford City; Fairmount Academy 24–6 Union Twp.; Gaston 21–15 Fairmount; Marion 14–13 Fairmount Academy (ot); Marion 61–7 Gaston. Officials not listed.

MARTINSVILLE: Plainfield 16–9 Pittsboro; Martinsville 41–11 Monrovia; Paragon 8–6 Stilesville; Lizton 27–9 Mooresville; Morgantown 16–4 North Salem; Amo 23–14 Danville; Eminence 27–19 Brownsburg; Avon 25–11 Clayton; Martinsville 34–8 Plainfield; Lizton 24–19 Paragon; Morgantown 16–6 Amo; Eminence 27–7 Avon; Martinsville 60–12 Lizton; Eminence 17–14 Morgantown; Martinsville 31–9 Eminence. Officials: Archie Erehart, Wyatt May.

NEW CASTLE: Spiceland Academy 17–10 Lewisville; Sulphur Springs 20–17 Yorktown; Knightstown 17–11 Mt. Summit; Daleville 17–5 Middletown; New Castle 31–10 Cadiz; New Lisbon 13–9 Mooreland; Muncie 46–5 Cowan; Spiceland Academy 14–12 Kennard; Knightstown 19–7 Sulphur Springs; New Castle 30–10 Daleville; Muncie 54–8 New Lisbon; Spiceland Academy 24–12 Knightstown; Muncie 18–15 New Castle; Muncie 22–15 Spiceland Academy. Officials not listed.

OWENSVILLE: Boonville 10–6 Evansville Reitz; Francisco 15–12 Cynthiana; Owensville 24–4 Stewartsville; Poseyville 2–0 Rockport (forfeit); Princeton 28–6 Dale; Evansville Central 66–7 Fort Branch; Mount Vernon 33–8 Patoka; New Harmony 17–13 Lynnville; Boonville 24–7 Francisco; Owensville 21–8 Poseyville; Central 27–11 Princeton; Mount Vernon 23–15 New Harmony; Owensville 18–15 Boonville; Central 40–14 Mount Vernon; Central 18–12 Owensville. Officials: George Graham, W.E. Wakefield.

RICHMOND: Fairview 20–16 Brownsville; Brookville 23–15 Boston; Hagerstown 30–7 Liberty; Greensfork 29–17 Orange; Richmond 66–2 Bentonville; Economy 28–26 Connersville; Whitewater 26–19 Cambridge City; Centerville 15–12 Fountain City; Fairview 33–9 Brookville; Hagerstown 29–9 Greensfork; Richmond 43–17 Economy; Whitewater 22–7 Centerville; Hagerstown 21–17 Fairview; Richmond 27–16 Whitewater; Richmond 33–13 Hagerstown. Officials not listed.

ROCHESTER: North Judson 34–5 Monterey; Kewanna 22–10 Bunker Hill; Converse 23–11 Medaryville; Winamac 15–11 Chili; Talma 15–7 Richland Center; Fulton 11–8 Macy; Leiters Ford 20–11 Amboy; Rochester 47–0 Argos; Kewanna 27–17 North Judson; Converse 23–6 Winamac; Talma 12–8 Fulton; Rochester 38–5 Leiters Ford; Converse 23–14 Kewanna; Rochester 50–10 Talma; Rochester 30–3 Converse. Officials: L.I. Mattingly, D.J. Arbuckle.

RUSHVILLE: Rushville 52–4 New Salem; Milroy 44–0 Laurel; Greensburg 20–4 Letts; Sandusky 36–7 Moscow; Arlington 16–13 Webb; Carthage 24–13 Clarksburg; Raleigh 26–10 Glenwood; Manilla 13–11 Burney; Rushville 18–16 Milroy; Sandusky 24–12 Greensburg; Carthage 29–20 Arlington; Manilla 38–12 Raleigh; Sandusky 24–14 Rushville; Manilla 16–13

Carthage; Sandusky 18–12 Manilla. Officials not listed.

SCOTTSBURG: Salem 30–3 Palmyra; Seymour 25–18 Brownstown; Hardinsburg 19–12 Clear Spring; Corydon 2–0 Milltown (forfeit); Jeffersonville 30–5 Cortland; Scottsburg 32–9 Crothersville; Hanover 23–18 Vallonia; Salem 22–9 Freetown; Seymour 21–8 Hardinsburg; Jeffersonville 22–6 Corydon; Scottsburg 25–5 Hanover; Seymour 41–8 Salem; Scottsburg 24–15 Jeffersonville; Scottsburg 14–11 Seymour. Officials: Ivan Zaring, Harlan Craig.

SOUTH BEND: Goshen 37–5 Kingsbury; South Bend 44–7 La Crosse; Nappanee 19–18 Michigan City; LaPorte 55–11 Union Mills; Millersburg 21–18 North Liberty; Elkhart 23–11 Bremen; Mishawaka 25–11 Lakeville; Bristol 21–15 New Paris; South Bend 39–15 Goshen; LaPorte 17–15 Nappanee; Elkhart 22–2 Millersburg; Mishawaka 40–4 Bristol; South Bend 29–16 LaPorte; Mishawaka 16–13 Elkhart; South Bend 24–8 Mishawaka. Officials not listed.

SULLIVAN: New Lebanon 25–19 Plainville; Fairbanks 40–13 Hymera; Washington 83–6 Paxton; Pleasantville 40–5 Montgomery; Epsom 23–8 Dugger; Elnora 17–13 Farmersburg; Sullivan 42–0 Carlisle; New Lebanon 20–14 Fairbanks; Washington 43–4 Pleasantville; Elnora 32–16 Epsom; Sullivan 30–17 New Lebanon; Washington 20–9 Elnora; Sullivan 15–14 Washington. Officials not listed.

TERRE HAUTE: Cayuga 40–1 Riley; West Terre Haute 12–3 Ashboro; Cory 34–11 Clay City; Terre Haute Normal 34–7 Helt Twp.; Terre Haute Garfield 36–14 Perrysville; Glenn 45–19 Staunton; Brazil 19–6 Prairie Creek; Cayuga 19–11 Terre Haute Wiley; Cory 19–14 West Terre Haute; Garfield 25–19 Normal; Glenn 23–10 Brazil; Cayuga 27–16 Cory; Garfield 22–13 Glenn; Garfield 42–17 Cayuga. Officials: Wiltze, Feezle.

VINCENNES: Vincennes 54–4 Bicknell; Spurgeon 31–17 Otwell; Hazelton 24–15 Edwardsport; Oaktown 21–14 Sandborn; Winslow 15–11 Mount Olympus; Velpen 42–4 Freelandville; Union 35–10 Emison; Fritchton 12–10 Decker; Vincennes 46–5 Monroe City; Hazelton 24–15 Spurgeon; Winslow 17–14 Oaktown; Freelandville 25–20 Union; Vincennes 31–8 Fritchton; Oaktown 14–13 Hazelton; Vincennes 42–15 Freelandville; Vincennes 48–6 Oaktown. Officials: Carson, Posey.

WARSAW: Etna Twp. Etna Green 34–16 West Twp. (Plymouth); Pierceton 18–17 Plymouth; Warsaw 17–10 Claypool; Tippecanoe 18–9 Silver Lake; Syracuse 27–8 Inwood; North Webster 21–15 Milford; Bourbon 20–3 Beaver Dam; Atwood 27–12 Burkett; Culver 30–8 Etna Green; Warsaw 26–10 Pierceton; Syracuse 39–14 Tippecanoe; Bourbon 16–14 North Webster; Culver 14–11 Atwood; Syracuse 14–9 Warsaw; Culver 21–5 Bourbon; Syracuse 19–13 Culver. Officials: J.J. Ritter, G.E. Koegan.

WINCHESTER: Jefferson 29–24 Modoc; Huntsville 24–18 Losantville; Union City 20–15 Green Twp.; Stoney Creek 14–12 Winchester; Saratoga 24–15 DeSoto; Ridgeville 39–15 Farmland; Selma 40–10 Parker; Spartanburg 31–8 Jackson; Jefferson 26–24 Huntsville; Stoney Creek 29–25 Union City; Ridgeville 29–18 Saratoga; Selma 27–24 Spartanburg; Jefferson 27–21 Stoney Creek; Ridgeville 46–23 Selma; Ridgeville 36–17 Jefferson. Officials not listed.

1921 REGIONALS

Each regional game winner advanced to state finals.

WEST LAFAYETTE (Purdue University): Frankfort 35–18 Pine Village; Huntington 19–15 Kendallville; Lafayette Jefferson 20–16 Monroe; Walton 24–21 Arcadia; Anderson 32–13 Marion;

Tourney Time

Rochester 33–16 Whiting; South Bend 31–16 Angola; Syracuse 20–17 Crawfordsville. Officials not listed.

BLOOMINGTON (Indiana University): Sandusky 29–22 Evansville; Muncie 18–2 Richmond; Franklin 43–9 Sullivan; Ridgeville 22–15 Scottsburg; Russellville 22–13 Bedford; Martinsville 38–19 Terre Haute Garfield; Bloomington 20–18 Columbus; Vincennes 29–8 Indianapolis Tech. Officials not listed.

1921 FINALS—March 18, 19

INDIANAPOLIS (Old Coliseum): Franklin 27–24 Martinsville; Rochester 31–10 Walton; Huntington 20–16 Syracuse; Lafayette Jefferson 29–23 Frankfort; Russellville 27–22 Bloomington; Muncie 39–4 Ridgeville; Anderson 29–21 South Bend; Vincennes 26–19 Sandusky; Franklin 19–18 Rochester; Jefferson 15–14 Huntington; Muncie 21–15 Russellville; Anderson 37–18 Vincennes; Franklin 17–12 Jefferson; Anderson 26–18 Muncie; Franklin 35–22 Anderson. Officials: Ross Smith, Dale Miller, Merle Abbett, Ward Lambert.

1922 SECTIONALS

ANDERSON: Anderson 76–6 Alexandria; Greenfield 20–14 Maxwell; Frankton 28–14 Wilkinson; Pendleton 15–10 Fortville; Elwood 35–21 McCordsville; Eden 25–11 Charlottesville; Summitville 22–6 Mount Comfort; Daleville 16–14 New Palestine; Lapel 28–16 Westland; Anderson 47–7 Greenfield; Pendleton 21–12 Frankton; Elwood 20–8 Eden; Summitville 18–11 Daleville; Anderson 37–15 Lapel; Elwood 22–18 Pendleton; Anderson 49–14 Summitville; Anderson 42–18 Elwood. Officials: Nash Higgins, Ray Mowe.

ANGOLA: Salem 10–9 South Milford; Lima 19–14 Butler; Hudson 9–5 Shipshewana; Ashley 9–8 Flint; LaGrange 24–10 Fremont; Hamilton 27–8 Mongo; Angola 34–4 Orland; Brighton 16–15 Brushy Prairie; Auburn 24–5 Garrett; Pleasant Lake 16–14 Waterloo; Salem 26–7 Topeka; Hudson 12–5 Lima; LaGrange 28–6 Ashley; Angola 28–16 Hamilton; Auburn 56–4 Brighton; Pleasant Lake 12–5 Salem; Hudson 10–9 LaGrange; Angola 13–7 Auburn; Hudson 17–6 Pleasant Lake; Angola 32–7 Hudson. Officials: F.K. Ferguson, D.C. Johnson.

ATTICA: Pine Village 33–8 Pine Twp.; Boswell 28–8 West Lebanon; Oxford 19–16 Fowler; Mellott 25–4 Raub; Attica 27–4 Freeland Park; Ambia 25–3 Earl Park; Newtown 16–12 Covington; Veedersburg 29–3 Williamsport; Pine Village 17–11 Otterbein; Oxford 17–16 Boswell; Attica 29–8 Mellott; Newtown 36–7 Ambia; Pine Village 12–11 Veedersburg; Oxford 17–12 Attica; Pine Village 24–10 Newtown; Pine Village 15–13 Oxford. Officials: Billy Webb, E.E. Reid.

BEFORD: Mitchell 28–5 French Lick; Shoals 44–7 Huron; Heltonville 35–7 Burns City; Plainville 16–15 Needmore; Williams 23–16 Epsom; Fayetteville 30–11 Tunnelton; Bedford 35–5 Orleans; Oolitic 26–17 Elnora; Paoli 26–15 Loogootee; Mitchell 16–4 West Baden; Heltonville 32–11 Shoals; Williams 20–14 Plainville; Bedford 30–10 Fayetteville; Paoli 15–13 Oolitic; Mitchell 18–16 Heltonville; Bedford 41–10 Williams; Mitchell 23–13 Paoli; Bedford 41–12 Mitchell. Officials: Harry Shoeneman, Archie Erehart.

BLOOMINGTON: Smithville 25–5 Scotland; Spencer 9–4 Midland; Lyons 23–12 Freedom; Quincy 13–5 Ellettsville; Owensburg 18–17 Coal City; Bloomington 39–9 Newberry; Gosport 15–6 Van Buren Twp.; Stinesville 23–9 Patricksburg; Smithville 26–15 Linton; Lyons 23–8

Spencer; Owensburg 18–17 Quincy; Bloomington 33–1 Gosport; Smithville 23–6 Stinesville; Lyons 33–4 Owensburg; Bloomington 35–9 Smithville; Bloomington 25–11 Lyons. Officials: Stanley Morse, Paul Carson.

BRAZIL: Prairie Creek 45–5 Pimento; Clay City 28–6 West Terre Haute; Wiley 14–11 Fontanet; Glenn 16–15 Brazil; Normal (Terre Haute) 49–11 Dana; Clinton 21–16 Ashboro; Garfield (Terre Haute) 32–5 Staunton; Cayuga 33–7 Riley; Cory 30–3 Newport; Perrysville 26–18 Prairie Creek; Clay City 14–12 Wiley; Normal (Terre Haute) 21–8 Glenn; Garfield (Terre Haute) 21–11 Clinton; Cory 20–16 Cayuga; Perrysville 26–10 Clay City; Garfield 17–15 Normal; Perrysville 25–10 Cory; Garfield 15–11 Perrysville. Officials: J.E. Wakefield, Wyatt May.

COLUMBUS: Aurora 41–1 Napoleon; Columbus 67–24 Butlerville; Versailles 39–14 Scipio; North Vernon 35–13 Batesville; Vernon 26–5 Milan; Osgood 32–12 Patriot; Vevay 14–12 Hope; Moores Hill 17–12 Hayden; Columbus 36–15 Aurora; North Vernon 28–27 Versailles; Osgood 19–10 Vernon; Vevay 44–10 Moores Hill; Columbus 30–10 North Vernon; Osgood 27–10 Vevay; Columbus 43–8 Osgood. Officials: R.B. Morrison, E. W. Jamison.

CRAWFORDSVILLE: Waynetown 37–12 Bowers; Waveland 15–9 New Ross; New Richmond 16–14 Darlington; Crawfordsville 43–1 Wallace; Wingate 35–10 New Market; Ladoga 31–8 Alamo; Hillsboro 22–14 Mace; Kingman 28–22 Linden; Waynetown 12–10 Waveland; Crawfordsville 22–6 New Richmond; Wingate 31–15 Ladoga; Hillsboro 20–11 Kingman; Crawfordsville 25–17 Waynetown; Wingate 15–10 Hillsboro; Wingate 21–17 Crawfordsville. Officials: E.R. Brown, Homer Wiltse.

DECATUR: Petroleum 15–7 Dunkirk; Pennville 28–21 Gray (Jay Co.); Bluffton 29–20 Portland; Bryant 34–15 Craigsville; Liberty Center 20–9 Union Center; Decatur 29–16 Berne; Monroe 34–6 Poling; Hartford Twp. 26–11 Kirkland Twp.; Redkey 13–11 Geneva; Pennville 26–15 Petroleum; Bluffton 36–17 Bryant; Decatur 25–14 Liberty Center; Monroe 32–13 Hartford; Pennville 28–6 Redkey; Decatur 16–14 Bluffton; Monroe 28–17 Pennville; Decatur 20–17 Monroe. Officials: Jasper W. Hale, Homer L. Humke.

EVANSVILLE: Lynnville 24–13 Boonville; New Harmony 18–15 Rockport; Yankeetown 28–7 Cynthiana; Wadesville 2–0 Milltown (forfeit); Mount Vernon 23–11 Elberfeld; Central 41–16 Washington; Newburgh 11–9 Poseyville; Reitz 29–10 Stewartsville; Lynnville 43–2 New Harmony; Yankeetown 26–9 Wadesville; Central 39–10 Mount Vernon; Reitz 18–7 Newburgh; Lynnville 23–11 Yankeetown; Central 45–8 Reitz; Central 29–13 Lynnville. Officials: Charles A. Jensen, Elmer Posey.

FORT WAYNE: Churubusco 53–11 Huntertown; Kendallville 28–11 Columbia City; Ligonier 37–6 Avilla; Washington Center 29–20 Spencerville; St. Joe 32–2 LaOtto; South Whitley 19–16 Monroeville; Wawaka 13–9 Harlan; Wolf Lake 43–11 Etna Twp.; Fort Wayne 37–3 Woodburn; Churubusco 26–10 New Haven; Kendallville 30–12 Ligonier; Washington Center 13–7 St. Joe; South Whitley 22–11 Wawaka; Wolf Lake 15–12 Fort Wayne; Kendallville 42–22 Churubusco; South Whitley 16–6 Washington Center; Kendallville 22–10 Wolf Lake; South Whitley 16–13 Kendallville. Officials: Barnhart, Evans.

FRANKLIN: Whiteland 16–13 Boggstown; Hopewell 14–10 Fairland; Shelbyville 43–6 Flat Rock; Edinburg 40–12 Clark Twp. Mount Auburn 24–6 Fountaintown; Center Grove 16–13 Greenwood; Waldron 27–10 Nineveh; Franklin 76–9 Geneva; Union Twp. 41–10 Morristown; Whiteland 17–15 Hopewell; Shelbyville 37–21 Edinburg; Mt. Auburn 16–11 Greenwood; Franklin 60–6 Waldron; Whiteland 21–18 Union Twp.; Shelbyville 55–17 Mt. Auburn; Franklin

Tourney Time

52–3 Whiteland; Franklin 33–20 Shelbyville. Officials: Clark, Wegener.

GREENCASTLE: Clinton Center 15–13 Mecca; Bloomingdale 39–11 Reelsville; Greencastle 29–11 Rosedale; Marshall 37–7 Bridgeton; Russellville 14–10 Tangier; Bainbridge 29–9 Montezuma; Fillmore 16–13 Rockville; Cloverdale 35–4 Bellmore; Roachdale 33–6 Clinton Center; Greencastle 40–7 Bloomingdale; Russellville 22–4 Marshall; Bainbridge 30–6 Fillmore; Cloverdale 40–8 Roachdale; Greencastle 27–9 Russellville; Cloverdale 27–18 Bainbridge; Greencastle 19–11 Cloverdale. Officials: H.O. Page, H.H. Bacon.

HUNTINGTON: Wabash 30–8 Linlawn; Warren 25–20 Clear Creek; Monument City 30–13 Laketon; Chippewa 13–10 Banquo; Lincolnville 25–11 Chester; Andrews 11–7 Somerset; Huntington 21–20 Lagro; Lancaster 24–12 LaFontaine; Bippus 20–12 North Manchester; Roann 25–19 Roanoke; Wabash 19–11 Union Center; Warren 32–18 Monument City; Chippewa 16–15 Lincolnville; Huntington 34–7 Andrews; Bippus 23–6 Lancaster Center; Wabash 16–5 Roann; Warren 28–8 Chippewa; Huntington 29–15 Bippus; Wabash 21–18 Warren; Huntington 18–6 Wabash. Officials: Archie Heller, D.J. Arbuckle.

INDIANAPOLIS: Ben Davis 15–12 Oaklandon; Broad Ripple 37–24 Castleton; New Augusta 23–10 Beech Grove; Manual 48–16 Acton; West Newton 31–20 Cumberland; Tech 26–11 Southport; Valley Mills 24–22 Shortridge; Brownsburg 19–14 Shadeland; Ben Davis 19–18 Broad Ripple; Manual 43–8 New Augusta; Tech 15–9 West Newton; Valley Mills 12–10 Brownsburg; Manual 35–15 Ben Davis; Tech 15–10 Valley Mills; Manual 31–25 Tech. Officials: Claude Draper, Forrest Ragsdale.

KOKOMO: Howard Twp. 14–13 Carmel; New London 39–6 Cicero; Atlanta 13–7 Goldsmith; Arcadia 30–10 Russiaville; Boxley 15–14 Sharpsville; Greentown 25–17 Sheridan; Fishers 21–13 Windfall; Noblesville 14–11 Walnut Grove; Tipton 22–8 West Middleton; Kokomo 34–9 Union Twp.; Howard Twp. 32–15 New London; Arcadia 22–19 Atlanta; Greentown 19–17 Boxley; Fishers 25–9 Noblesville; Kokomo 19–11 Tipton; Howard Twp. 17–16 Arcadia; Fishers 31–13 Greentown; Howard Twp. 19–15 Kokomo; Fishers 20–12 Howard Twp. Officials: Dr. W.E. Deakyne, W.E. Babb.

LAFAYETTE: West Lafayette 34–9 Chalmers; Lafayette Jefferson 57–5 Buck Creek; Dayton 14–13 West Point; Battle Ground 14–9 Monitor; Romney 33–4 Wea; Jackson Twp. (West Point) 21–7 Montmorenci; Reynolds 21–11 Stockwell; Clarks Hill 17–13 Brookston; Jefferson 19–15 West Lafayette; Dayton 20–13 Battle Ground; Jackson Twp. 15–12 Romney; Clarks Hill 22–13 Reynolds; Jefferson 20–16 Dayton; Jackson Twp. 17–13 Clarks Hill; Jefferson 10–7 Jackson Twp. Officials: Townsend, Steward.

LEBANON: Zionsville 18–14 Perry Central; Rossville 17–16 Jefferson; Jamestown 17–15 Advance; Colfax 16–15 Thorntown; Whitestown 23–18 Mulberry; Forest 11–5 Michigantown; Frankfort 19–14 Westfield; Lebanon 42–8 Scircleville; Rossville 38–16 Zionsville; Colfax 26–4 Jamestown; Frankfort 21–9 Lebanon; Whitestown 42–9 Forest; Colfax 24–21 Rossville; Frankfort 25–7 Whitestown; Frankfort 26–22 Colfax. Officials: Skemp, Kenzler.

LOGANSPORT: Young America 28–15 Royal Center; Lucerne 16–10 Deer Creek; Walton 26–8 Flora; Logansport 30–6 Camden; Wolcott 17–6 Galveston; Cutler 32–19 Delphi; Burlington 33–4 Metea; Idaville 15–11 Burnettsville; Bringhurst 22–3 New Waverly; Twelve Mile 15–13 Onward; Young America 27–9 Monon; Walton 42–5 Lucerne; Logansport 25–17 Wolcott; Cutler 28–20 Burlington; Bringhurst 17–9 Idaville; Young America 41–15 Twelve Mile; Logansport 17–11 Walton; Cutler 28–13 Bringhurst; Young America 21–12 Logansport; Cutler 20–17 Young

America. Officials: Donlin, Day.

MARION: Bunker Hill 15–10 Peru; Fairmount Academy 20–4 Butler Twp.; Fairmount High School 22–21 Sweetser; Marion 29–10 Hartford City; Amboy 33–4 Jonesboro; Gas City 20–4 Matthews; Montpelier 31–6 Swayzee; Converse 21–13 Roll; Fairmount Academy 21–10 Bunker Hill; Marion 22–7 Fairmount High School; Amboy 13–6 Gas City; Converse 22–20 Montpelier; Marion 34–16 Fairmount Academy; Amboy 10–5 Converse; Marion 41–2 Amboy. Officials: L.I. Mattingly, Joe C. Edwards.

MOORESVILLE: North Salem 29–26 Mooresville; Pittsboro 23–18 Monrovia; Clayton 21–18 Morgantown; Plainfield 32–11 Avon; Paragon 22–17 Stilesville; Martinsville 30–20 Eminence; Lizton 57–3 New Winchester; Danville 31–23 Amo; Pittsboro 40–10 North Salem; Clayton 28–15 Plainfield; Martinsville 24–13 Paragon; Danville 36–29 Lizton; Pittsboro 29–12 Clayton; Martinsville 30–12 Danville; Pittsboro 23–22 Martinsville. Officials: J.E. Craigle, Lee Sinclair.

NEW CASTLE: New Castle 53–2 Straughn; Eaton 24–11 Kennard; Selma 49–3 DeSoto; Muncie 53–0 Albany; Lewisville 19–8 Cadiz; Middletown 28–14 Yorktown; New Lisbon 15–11 Cowan; Knightstown 24–16 Gaston; Royerton 22–14 Center; Spiceland 23–9 Sulphur Springs; Mount Summit 30–21 Eaton; Muncie 29–17 Selma; Lewisville 26–13 Middletown; Knightstown 21–16 New Lisbon; Spiceland 13–10 Royerton; New Castle 50–22 Mount Summit; Muncie 28–13 Lewisville; Knightstown 14–9 Spiceland; New Castle 15–12 Muncie; New Castle 26–8 Knightstown. Officials: Palmer, Miller.

OWENSVILLE: Owensville 36–13 Winslow; Hazelton 2–0 Otwell (forfeit); Spurgeon 33–4 Haubstadt; Fort Branch 13–12 Patoka; Velpen 21–9 Stendal; Jasper 43–13 Francisco; Mount Olympus 16–10 Huntingburg; Princeton 17–13 Union; Hazelton 16–14 Owensville; Spurgeon 19–13 Fort Branch; Jasper 20–17 Velpen; Mount Olympus 61–14 Princeton; Spurgeon 15–12 Hazelton; Jasper 17–11 Mount Olympus; Jasper 20–17 Spurgeon. Officials: George C. Graham, Ivan A. Zaring.

RICHMOND: Hagerstown 26–10 Alquina; Whitewater 21–7 Boston; Webster 16–3 Milton; Orange 15–4 Everton; Fountain City 22–19 Economy; Richmond 28–12 Liberty; Brownsville 27–24 Fairview; Connersville 43–12 Centerville; Cambridge City 40–10 Bentonville; Hagerstown 82–1 Williamsburg; Webster 31–13 Whitewater; Fountain City 25–16 Orange; Richmond 31–11 Brownsville; Connersville 36–15 Cambridge City; Hagerstown 50–4 Webster; Connersville 28–14 Richmond; Hagerstown 34–15 Fountain City; Connersville 32–10 Hagerstown. Officials: Don Wyrick, J. A. Swope.

ROCHESTER: North Judson 23–20 Knox; Francesville 18–8 San Pierre; Kewanna 43–10 Macy; Rochester 28–14 Monterey; Talma 30–23 Chili; Leiters Ford 30–20 Deedsville; Winamac 51–20 Mexico; Akron 17–7 Fulton; Francesville 23–19 North Judson; Rochester 23–13 Kewanna; Leiters Ford 25–14 Talma; Akron 17–15 Winamac; Rochester 41–19 Francesville; Leiters Ford 21–11 Akron; Rochester 23–15 Leiters Ford. Officials: Kulcinski, Crown.

RUSHVILLE: Letts 25–6 St. Paul; Raleigh 25–10 Laurel; Manilla 49–14 New Salem; Rushville 37–12 Moscow; Greensburg 17–13 Glenwood; Milroy 31–17 Carthage; Webb 38–11 Clarksburg; Arlington 27–20 Brookville; Burney 11–9 Letts; Manilla 27–12 Raleigh; Rushville 26–12 Greensburg; Milroy 30–20 Webb; Arlington 21–19 Burney; Rushville 31–12 Manilla; Milroy 21–18 Arlington; Rushville 29–13 Milroy. Officials: G.W. Trickey, F.L. Busenburg.

SCOTTSBURG: Crothersville 56–15 Medora; Vallonia 19–10 Salem; Scottsburg 61–3 Deputy; Seymour 2–0 Dupont (forfeit); Madison 20–9 Clear Spring; Hardinsburg 30–17 Saluda;

Tourney Time

Little York 19–6 Corydon; Hanover 2–0 Jeffersonville (forfeit); Cortland 38–15 Charlestown; Vallonia 20–17 Crothersville; Scottsburg 17–10 Seymour; Madison 22–11 Hardinsburg; Hanover 13–10 Little York; Vallonia 26–9 Cortland; Scottsburg 18–9 Madison; Vallonia 31–11 Hanover; Scottsburg 8–7 Vallonia. Officials: Allen, Abbett.

SOUTH BEND: Stillwell 15–10 North Liberty; Bristol 20–5 Wanatah; Michigan City 51–4 Mill Creek; Mishawaka 17–7 LaCrosse; Elkhart 14–12 Nappanee; New Paris 27–11 Millersburg; La Porte 35–8 Lakeville; Goshen 32–5 Union Mills; Stillwell 12–10 Bristol; Mishawaka 19–16 Michigan City; Elkhart 21–13 New Paris; Goshen 18–17 LaPorte; Mishawaka 37–12 Stillwell; Goshen 33–10 Elkhart; Goshen 19–6 Mishawaka. Officials: Ralph Braesemle, L.A. Schwan.

UNION CITY: Jefferson (Ridgeville) 17–9 Farmland; Jackson (Union City) 19–18 Winchester; Ridgeville 37–7 Lynn; Huntsville 19–10 Green Twp. (Ridgeville); Spartanburg 27–7 Wayne (Union City); Saratoga 29–19 Modoc; Union City 24–16 Parker; Stoney Creek 28–10 Losantville; Jefferson 21–10 Jackson; Ridgeville 25–9 Huntsville; Spartanburg 23–17 Saratoga; Stoney Creek 18–15 Union City; Jefferson 19–12 Ridgeville; Stoney Creek 21–14 Spartanburg; Stoney Creek 18–17 Jefferson. Officials: W.F. Smith, H.H. Parker.

VALPARAISO: Lowell 9–8 Hebron; Valparaiso 19–14 Hammond; Rensselaer 15–14 East Chicago; Crown Point 25–12 Hobart; Brook 34–5 Remington; Whiting 12–11 Gary Emerson; Kentland 26–2 Boone Grove; Gary Froebel 27–4 Goodland; Valparaiso 19–9 Lowell; Rensselaer 19–16 Crown Point; Whiting 15–11 Brook; Froebel 14–8 Kentland; Rensselaer 7–5 Valparaiso; Whiting 18–14 Froebel; Whiting 25–9 Rensselaer. Officials: Stephenson, Singer.

VINCENNES: Decker 18–10 Wheatland; Sandborn 23–12 New Lebanon; Oaktown 24–19 Pleasantville; Sullivan 23–12 Carlisle; Bruceville 19–16 Farmersburg; Fritchton 23–17 Edwardsport; Freelandville 28–24 Monroe City; Vincennes 74–10 Graysville; Dugger 28–11 Decker; Oaktown 17–14 Sandborn; Sullivan 40–13 Bruceville; Freelandville; 16–15 Fritchton; Vincennes 54–6 Dugger; Sullivan 25–19 Oaktown; Vincennes 40–24 Freelandville; Vincennes 55–4 Sullivan. Officials: B.E. Bayh, D.H. Overman.

WARSAW: Syracuse 19–18 Pierceton; Atwood 25–12 Milford; North Webster 28–12 Bremen; Warsaw 41–7 West Twp.; Tippecanoe 15–10 Plymouth; Claypool 22–11 Sidney; Culver 36–5 Mentone; Bourbon 12–8 Burket; Etna Green 22–8 Leesburg; Syracuse 26–3 Argos; Atwood 19–6 North Webster; Warsaw 38–6 Tippecanoe; Culver 22–20 Claypool; Etna Green 13–9 Bourbon; Atwood 17–12 Syracuse; Culver 7–5 Warsaw; Atwood 21–8 Etna Green; Atwood 13–10 Culver. Officials: Frank McGeath, M.J. Cleary.

1922 REGIONALS

BLOOMINGTON (Indiana University): Bedford 35–7 Stoney Creek; Franklin 51–6 Scottsburg; Vincennes 28–8 New Castle; Indianapolis Manual 34–13 Pittsboro; Terre Haute Garfield 41–11 Jasper; Rushville 21–13 Columbus; Evansville Central 19–18 Connersville; Bloomington 21–7 Greencastle. Officials not listed.

WEST LAFAYETTE (Purdue University): Goshen 16–10 Angola; Anderson 28–10 Pine Village; Atwood 30–10 South Whitley; Marion 22–12 Huntington; Frankfort 16–14 Lafayette; Cutler 45–11 Rochester; Whiting 26–6 Decatur; Fishers 2–0 Wingate (forfeit). Officials not listed.

IHSAA Scores | 1920–1929

1922 FINALS—March 17, 18

INDIANAPOLIS (Old Coliseum): Franklin 27–16 Evansville Central; Bedford 40–14 Atwood; Vincennes 31–22 Cutler; Bloomington 21–7 Manual; Terre Haute Garfield 24–12 Whiting; Fishers 18–9 Goshen; Marion 19–18 Rushville; Anderson 24–16 Frankfort; Franklin 32–15 Bedford; Bloomington 21–15 Vincennes; Garfield 30–16 Fishers; Marion 20–16 Anderson; Garfield 31–15 Marion; Franklin 33–17 Bloomington; Franklin 31–15 Garfield. Officials: G.W. Levis, Ward Lambert, Dale Miller, Ray Mowe.

1923 SECTIONALS

ANDERSON: Elwood 57–4 Markleville; Anderson 39–13 Sharpsville; Pendleton 29–26 Windfall; Alexandria 22–21 Summitville; Tipton 28–16 Lapel; Kempton 21–20 Frankton; Anderson 41–10 Elwood; Pendleton 23–15 Alexandria; Tipton 24–19 Kempton; Anderson 39–17 Pendleton; Anderson 32–22 Tipton. Officials: Don Arbuckle, Watson Deakyne.

ANGOLA: Brighton 11–8 Corunna; Pleasant Lake 22–3 Brushy Prairie; Fremont 10–5 Waterloo; Garrett 29–12 Butler; Angola 15–9 Auburn; Ashley 19–2 Salem; Orland 15–5 Mongo; Hamilton 24–15 Spencerville; Pleasant Lake 20–8 Brighton; Garrett 23–7 Fremont; Ashley 15–11 Angola; Hamilton 25–14 Orland; Garrett 15–8 Pleasant Lake; Hamilton 15–13 Ashley; Garrett 22–17 Hamilton. Officials: Heller, Reid

AURORA: Moores Hill 19–14 Holton; Milan 20–19 Aurora; Brookville 18–8 Osgood; Rising Sun 42–2 New Alsace; Versailles 34–9 Napoleon; Lawrenceburg 15–8 Batesville; Laurel 20–9 Sunman; Dillsboro 22–18 Moores Hill; Brookville 16–15 Milan; Versailles 15–6 Rising Sun; Lawrenceburg 15–10 Laurel; Brookville 32–12 Dillsboro; Versailles 21–15 Lawrenceburg; Brookville 31–14 Versailles. Officials: Paul Hurley, Leroy Cook.

BEDFORD: Orleans 17–8 Needmore; Heltonville 16–15 Paoli; Bedford 35–11 Mitchell; Oolitic 19–8 West Baden; Tunnelton 18–11 Hardinsburg; Little York 16–14 Pekin; Fayetteville 10–7 Orleans; Bedford 56–18 Heltonville; Oolitic 53–8 Tunnelton; Little York 18–13 Fayetteville; Bedford 25–14 Oolitic; Bedford 101–10 Little York. Officials: R.W. Gipson, Don Wyrick.

BLOOMINGTON: Coal City 8–5 Unionville; Spencer 10–7 Ellettsville; Bloomington 50–2 Patricksburg; Freedom 31–23 Stinesville; Smithville 16–5 Coal City; Bloomington 36–9 Spencer; Smithville 38–7 Freedom; Bloomington 32–12 Smithville. Officials: Walter Keller, E.S. Krantz.

BRAZIL: Perry Twp. 28–8 Fayette; Brazil 32–7 Ashboro; Posey Twp. 20–19 Bowling Green; Normal 15–9 Van Buren Twp.; Garfield 27–10 Prairie Creek; Clay City 35–21 Pimento; Concannon 24–17 Glenn; Brazil 30–6 Perry Twp.; Normal 26–10 Posey Twp.; Garfield 23–10 Clay City; Brazil 27–20 Concannon; Garfield 27–23 Normal; Brazil 18–10 Garfield. Officials: Stanley Feezle, Jerry Wakefield.

BROOK: Boswell 16–9 Pine Twp.; Fowler 19–16 Morocco; Rensselaer 20–17 Oxford; Freeland Park 17–12 Otterbein; Goodland 15–10 Ambia; Raub 52–19 Earl Park; Brook 39–11 Boswell; Rensselaer 16–11 Fowler; Freeland Park 16–12 Goodland; Brook 27–9 Raub; Rensselaer 14–10 Freeland Park; Brook 15–14 Rensselaer. Officials: Russell Vaughn, Lee Sinclair.

CLINTON: Cayuga 26–8 Bridgeton; Rockville 27–3 Mecca; Perryville 30–19 Bloomingdale; Washington Twp. 14–13 Bellmore; Tangier 19–10 Newport; Montezuma 22–8 Dana; Rosedale 24–6 Helt Twp.; Cayuga 14–13 Clinton; Perrysville 37–8 Rockville; Tangier 14–11 Washington

Tourney Time

Twp.; Rosedale 14–6 Dana; Perrysville 21–19 Cayuga; Tangier 19–18 Rosedale; Perrysville 25–12 Tangier. Officials: M.P. Wilder, Homer Wiltse.

COLUMBUS: St. Paul 18–14 Hawcreek Twp.; Burney 20–11 Newbern; Columbus 29–5 Greensburg; Westport 47–7 Sandusky; Newpoint 15–9 Flatrock Twp.; Letts 11–10 Van Buren Twp.; St. Paul 21–7 Burney; Columbus 41–11 Westport; Letts 18–14 Newpoint; Columbus 30–7 St. Paul; Columbus 45–14 Letts. Officials: R.B. Morrison, E.C. Auerswald.

CRAWFORDSVILLE: Crawfordsville 23–4 Alamo; New Richmond 18–14 New Ross; Wingate 14–4 Mace; Linden 15–10 Waveland; Darlington 14–11 New Market; Ladoga 30–20 Bowers; Crawfordsville 23–13 Waynetown; Wingate 16–14 New Richmond; Linden 23–12 Darlington; Crawfordsville 30–18 Ladoga; Linden 19–17 Wingate; Crawfordsville 39–4 Linden. Officials: Frank Glenn, C.E. Steward.

CULVER: North Judson 17–9 Tippecanoe; West Twp. 21–16 Knox; Culver 26–4 Argos; Plymouth 15–9 Bremen; Bourbon 20–7 Teegarden; West Twp. 15–14 North Judson; Culver 2–0 Plymouth (forfeit); West Twp. 19–16 Bourbon; Culver 22–11 West Twp. Officials: L.J. Yoder, Don White.

DECATUR: Liberty Center 24–5 Berne; Ossian 24–6 Rock Creek; Decatur 14–13 Monroe; Lancaster 24–20 Bluffton; Union Center 33–12 Geneva; Liberty Center 31–10 Petroleum; Ossian 16–14 Decatur; Union Center 29–19 Lancaster; Liberty Center 22–9 Ossian; Liberty Center 21–9 Union Center. Officials: Walter Geller, Harley Murray.

EVANSVILLE: Yankeetown 24–21 Stewartsville; Poseyville 28–9 New Harmony; Newburgh 20–5 Rockport; Reitz 18–15 Tennyson; Mount Vernon 26–23 Union Twp.; Lynnville 17–10 Elberfeld; Wadesville 13–10 Cynthiana; Central 29–17 Boonville; Poseyville 32–16 Yankeetown; Newburgh 17–16 Reitz; Lynnville 24–19 Mount Vernon; Central 63–7 Wadesville; Poseyville 20–11 Newburgh; Central 28–7 Lynnville; Central 42–11 Poseyville. Officials: Elmer Posey, Charles Jensen.

FORT WAYNE: New Haven 12–6 Churubusco; South Side 58–3 Huntertown; Central 2–0 Etna Twp. (forfeit); Monroeville 17–15 South Whitley; Leo 31–5 Maumee; Harlan 22–5 Larwill; Columbia City 24–12 Washington Center; South Side 39–8 New Haven; Central 22–13 Monroeville; South Side 22–12 Columbia City; Central 38–3 Harlan; South Side 17–15 Central. Officials: Dean Barnhart, George Lewis.

FRANKLIN: Greenwood 29–9 Clark Twp.; Franklin 21–15 Union Twp.; Hopewell 38–7 Nineveh; Edinburg 27–8 Whiteland; Center Grove 38–13 Trafalgar; Franklin 24–19 Greenwood; Hopewell 24–19 Edinburg; Franklin 48–6 Center Grove; Franklin 26–15 Hopewell. Officials: Everett Babb, John Craigle.

FRANKFORT: Delphi 17–11 Bringhurst; Flora 20–15 Burlington; Cutler 27–7 Deer Creek; Scircleville 38–7 Forest; Rossville 25–19 Camden; Jefferson 65–8 Rockfield; Colfax 41–8 Mulberry; Frankfort 27–11 Michigantown; Flora 16–14 Delphi; Scircleville 23–15 Cutler; Jefferson 23–17 Rossville; Frankfort 29–6 Colfax; Scircleville 22–12 Flora; Frankfort 29–22 Jefferson; Frankfort 24–15 Scircleville. Officials: Vedder Gard, George Kenzler.

GREENCASTLE: North Salem 19–16 Fillmore; Lizton 56–6 New Winchester; Greencastle 37–13 Cloverdale; Roachdale 30–22 Danville; Bainbridge 40–10 Russellville; Amo 37–6 Clinton Center; North Salem 17–15 Lizton; Greencastle 26–4 Roachdale; Bainbridge 30–16 Amo; Greencastle 27–10 North Salem; Bainbridge 17–16 Greencastle. Officials: Winston Ashley, Myron Tatlock.

IHSAA Scores | 1920–1929

GREENFIELD: Greenfield 14–11 New Palestine; McCordsville 20–15 Maxwell; Westland 25–19 Charlottesville; Fortville 13–10 Wilkinson; Mount Comfort 27–21 Eden; McCordsville 25–24 Greenfield; Fortville 14–11 Westland; Mount Comfort 24–20 McCordsville; Mount Comfort 19–10 Fortville. Officials: Ross Smith, R.V. Copple.

HAMMOND: Gary Emerson 28–6 East Chicago; Gary Froebel 21–11 Lowell; Fair Oaks 32–13 Wheatfield; Crown Point 22–16 Hobart; Whiting 44–7 DeMotte; Emerson 27–15 Hammond; Froebel 33–12 Fair Oaks; Whiting 14–11 Crown Point; Emerson 15–10 Froebel; Emerson 28–14 Whiting. Officials: Walter Halos, Clarence Grogan.

HANOVER: Saluda 19–18 Deputy; Madison 29–12 New Albany; Dupont 15–11 North Madison; Austin 2–0 Palmyra; Scottsburg 15–12 Corydon; Hanover 25–23 Jeffersonville; Vevay 20–18 Saluda; Madison 21–11 Dupont; Scottsburg 17–8 Austin; Hanover 27–15 Vevay; Scottsburg 12–11 Madison; Hanover 17–11 Scottsburg. Officials: Ivan Zaring, Stanley Moore.

HUNTINGTON: Roanoke 16–15 Union Center; Huntington 54–4 Monument Center; Rock Creek 6–4 Andrews; Warren 23–11 Clear Creek; Bippus 23–18 Roanoke; Huntington 47–3 Rock Creek; Warren 18–14 Bippus; Huntington 27–13 Warren. Officials: Ford Griffith, Jacob McClure.

INDIANAPOLIS: Oaklandon 22–14 New Bethel; Broad Ripple 41–17 Shadeland; Manual 33–8 Lawrence; Shortridge 28–7 New Augusta; Cumberland 18–17 Southport; Ben Davis 48–8 Beech Grove; Tech 25–21 West Newton; Valley Mills 27–20 Castleton; Broad Ripple 34–13 Oaklandon; Manual 33–20 Shortridge; Ben Davis 15–10 Cumberland; Valley Mills 19–14 Tech; Manual 19–12 Broad Ripple; Ben Davis 30–16 Valley Mills; Manual 28–20 Ben Davis. Officials: Newell Day, Claude Draper.

KENDALLVILLE: Avilla 10–8 Cromwell; Kendallville 57–4 Rome City; South Milford 13–10 Lima; LaGrange 28–13 Albion; Wolf Lake 24–9 Shipshewana; Wawaka 11–10 LaOtto; Ligonier 18–14 Topeka; Kendallville 39–7 Avilla; LaGrange 28–9 South Milford; Wolf Lake 34–9 Wawaka; Kendallville 40–11 Ligonier; LaGrange 27–25 Wolf Lake; Kendallville 27–10 LaGrange. Officials: Ralph Gilbert, Floyd Merriman.

KOKOMO: Peru 13–11 Jackson Twp.; Clay Twp. 22–20 Bunker Hill; Butler Twp. 20–7 New London; West Middleton 29–13 Russiaville; Howard Twp. 21–7 Clay Twp. Greentown 21–16 Kokomo; Peru 16–15 Union Twp.; Clay Twp. 22–14 Butler Twp.; Howard Twp. 22–18 West Middleton; Greentown 25–9 Peru; Clay Twp. 19–16 Howard Twp.; Greentown 57–11 Clay Twp. Officials: L.J. Mattingly, Dale Miller.

LAFAYETTE: West Lafayette 37–15 Wea; Jefferson 34–9 Dayton; Battle Ground 38–8 Romney; Jackson Twp. 25–7 Buck Creek; Clarks Hill 18–5 Stockwell; Montmorenci 21–14 West Point; West Lafayette 20–17 Monitor; Jefferson 26–18 Battle Ground; Clarks Hill 24–11 Jackson Twp.; Montmorenci 18–10 West Lafayette; Jefferson 28–14 Clarks Hill; Jefferson 30–23 Montmorenci. Officials: H.H. Bacon, Ward Lambert.

LEBANON: Advance 25–19 Whitestown; Arcadia 32–17 Central; Carmel 33–12 Westfield; Walnut Grove 33–9 Cicero; Fishers 20–7 Boxley; Atlanta 16–12 Sheridan; Lebanon 40–11 Zionsville; Advance 26–24 Thorntown; Carmel 24–21 Arcadia; Fishers 21–14 Walnut Grove; Lebanon 27–9 Atlanta; Advance 31–29 Carmel; Lebanon 30–9 Fishers; Lebanon 35–19 Advance. Officials: Asher Cox, Dan Overman.

LOGANSPORT: Young America 33–8 Royal Center; Washington Twp. 24–14 Mexico; Galveston 25–6 Metea; Logansport 53–8 Lucerne; Gilead 11–7 Chili; Onward 19–7 Twelve Mile;

Tourney Time

Macy 17–14 Deedsville; Young America 20–6 Washington Twp. Logansport 19–11 Galveston; Onward 11–3 Gilead; Young America 21–14 Macy; Logansport 47–10 Onward; Logansport 11–10 Young America. Officials: Billy Webb, Lloyd Etter.

LYONS: Bloomfield 20–9 Owensburg; Lyons 29–7 Switz City; Midland 24–13 Newberry; Loogootee 51–4 Burns City; Shoals 2–0 Scotland; Linton 22–9 Bloomfield; Lyons 24–9 Midland; Loogootee 22–12 Shoals; Lyons 14–4 Linton; Lyons 15–4 Loogootee. Officials: Ben Watt, Wyatt May.

MARION: Jonesboro 14–8 Swayzee; Sweetser 12–10 Fairmount; Marion 36–3 Fairmount Academy; Amboy 14–9 Gas City; Converse 16–8 Jonesboro; Marion 32–16 Fairmount High School; Converse 21–13 Amboy; Marion 35–14 Converse. Officials: Fred Pitcher, Harry Schoeneman.

MOORESVILLE: Pittsboro 31–25 Plainfield; Monrovia 16–10 Avon; Stilesville 26–21 Morgantown; Brownsburg 24–11 Eminence; Martinsville 38–18 Clayton; Mooresville 24–17 Paragon; Monrovia 24–19 Pittsboro; Brownsburg 28–18 Stilesville; Martinsville 37–27 Mooresville; Brownsburg 27–18 Monrovia; Martinsville 36–19 Brownsburg. Officials: M.J. Poland, Glenn Maple.

MUNCIE: Daleville 21–14 Royerton; Muncie 60–7 Albany; Selma 23–14 Eaton; Center 29–14 Yorktown; Cowan 22–12 DeSoto; Muncie 41–16 Daleville; Selma 12–8 Center; Muncie 59–5 Cowan; Muncie 40–6 Selma. Officials: Donald Hobbs, E.D. Palmer.

NEW CASTLE: Cadiz 50–0 Sulphur Springs; Mount Summit 36–13 Kennard; Spiceland 27–20 Middletown; Knightstown 28–14 Lewisville; New Castle 52–4 New Lisbon; Mooreland 43–19 Cadiz; Mount Summit 17–12 Spiceland; New Castle 16–15 Knightstown; Mooreland 40–20 Mount Summit; Mooreland 24–21 New Castle. Officials: Homer Stonebraker, Horace Parker.

NORTH MANCHESTER: LaFontaine 24–10 Lagro; Chippewa 22–6 Linlawn; Roann 49–0 Urbana; Laketon 23–13 Somerset; Wabash 34–16 Chester; North Manchester 36–17 Lincolnville; LaFontaine 16–5 Chippewa; Laketon 18–14 Roann; Wabash 22–10 North Manchester; LaFontaine 14–13 Laketon; Wabash 15–11 LaFontaine. Officials: Don Stephenson, D.C. Johnson.

OWENSVILLE: Union 21–18 Spurgeon; Jasper 28–11 Haubstadt; Patoka 37–19 Velpen; Stendal 19–14 Francisco; Winslow 60–5 Petersburg; Fort Branch 15–9 Oakland City; Owensville 21–7 Princeton; Otwell 32–21 Huntingburg; Union 18–9 Jasper; Patoka 41–13 Meyers; Winslow 23–12 Fort Branch; Owensville 22–9 Otwell; Union 23–21 Patoka; Winslow 17–9 Owensville; Winslow 24–18 Union. Officials: George Graham, Roscoe Meyer.

PORTLAND: Redkey 14–12 Dunkirk; Pennville 26–9 Montpelier; Bryant 18–16 Portland; Hartford City 33–17 Gray; Pennville 23–0 Redkey; Hartford City 24–10 Bryant; Hartford City 16–14 Pennville. Officials: Pat Page, Harry Coolman.

RICHMOND: Liberty 30–13 Whitewater; Richmond 38–13 Brownsville; Centerville 13–8 Cambridge City; Boston 15–6 Economy; Fountain City 27–16 Milton; Hagerstown 32–9 Liberty; Richmond 34–5 Centerville; Fountain City 24–11 Boston; Richmond 42–14 Hagerstown; Richmond 44–25 Fountain City. Officials: Hale, Miller.

ROCHESTER: Fulton 24–6 Grass Creek; Medaryville 11–9 Winamac; Akron 20–17 Talma; Rochester 24–11 Francesville; Kewanna 31–8 Monterey; Fulton 22–4 Pulaski; Akron 18–12 Medaryville; Rochester 16–10 Kewanna; Akron 11–6 Fulton; Rochester 15–12 Akron. Officials: Virgil Binford, Ralph Parker.

RUSHVILLE: Arlington 23–21 Raleigh; Connersville 60–9 Center; New Salem 16–12

Bentonville; Carthage 23–15 Manilla; Webb 24–14 Milroy; Rushville 41–12 Everton; Alquina 41–11 Orange; Connersville 33–23 Arlington; Carthage 30–17 New Salem; Rushville 24–14 Webb; Connersville 41–19 Alquina; Rushville 25–22 Carthage; Connersville 31–29 Rushville. Officials: F.A. Bills, Gilbert Best.

SEYMOUR: Cortland 19–12 Brownstown; Seymour 21–9 Crothersville; North Vernon 27–17 Freetown; Butlerville 36–13 Hayden; Vernon 23–16 Vallonia; Cortland 44–10 Scipio; Seymour 26–11 North Vernon; Butlerville 16–15 Vernon; Seymour 26–14 Cortland; Seymour 43–14 Butlerville. Officials: Harold E. Berges, U.S. Abbott.

SHELBYVILLE: Acton 27–13 Flat Rock; Shelbyville 36–14 Boggstown; Morristown 16–11 Mount Auburn; Waldron 17–8 Fairland; Acton 36–12 Geneva; Shelbyville 55–14 Morristown; Waldron 26–16 Acton; Shelbyville 34–20 Waldron. Officials: F.L. Busenbury, Ray Frohman.

SOUTH BEND: Lakeville 22–20 Goshen; Mishawaka 45–7 Wakarusa; Elkhart 19–18 Nappanee; New Paris 24–7 Millersburg; North Liberty 13–7 Bristol; South Bend 43–7 Walkerton; Lakeville 22–11 Mishawaka; Elkhart 20–14 New Paris; South Bend 59–5 North Liberty; Lakeville 23–14 Elkhart; South Bend 38–15 Lakeville. Officials: Keith Crown, John Kyle.

SULLIVAN: Carlisle 25–9 New Lebanon; Graysville 18–14 Dugger; Sullivan 30–17 Hymera; Farmersburg 29–14 Shelburn; Carlisle 20–13 Pleasantville; Sullivan 26–25 Graysville; Farmersburg 17–15 Carlisle; Sullivan 35–7 Farmersburg. Officials: Lavern Litherland, J. Ora Fortner.

UNION CITY: Parker 36–12 Ridgeville; Modoc 19–12 Wayne; Union City 23–13 Farmland; Stoney Creek 36–23 Jackson; Spartanburg 43–15 Huntsville; Losantville 38–11 Winchester; Saratoga 26–13 Jefferson; Modoc 25–18 Parker; Stoney Creek 31–18 Union City; Losantville 29–16 Spartanburg; Saratoga 22–9 Modoc; Losantville 24–20 Stoney Creek; Losantville 32–20 Saratoga. Officials: Owen Floyd, Ray Mowe.

VALPARAISO: Stillwell 27–2 Boone Grove; LaCrosse 26–5 Mill Creek; Westville 19–10 Rolling Prairie; Valparaiso 25–8 Kouts; LaPorte 52–5 Wanatah; Michigan City 36–7 Hebron; Hanna 26–10 Kingsbury; Stillwell 25–4 Clinton; LaCrosse 30–8 Westville; Valparaiso 18–15 LaPorte; Michigan City 30–8 Hanna; LaCrosse 23–15 Stillwell; Michigan City 20–10 Valparaiso; Michigan City 24–19 LaCrosse. Officials: M.J. Cleary, F.K. Ferguson.

VEEDERSBURG: Veedersburg 15–7 Newton; Hillsboro 21–8 Attica; Pine Village 24–12 Wallace; Covington 22–10 Mellott; West Lebanon 22–9 Judyville; Kingman 19–10 Williamsport; Hillsboro 29–2 Veedersburg; Covington 15–7 Pine Village; Kingman 18–12 West Lebanon; Covington 18–14 Hillsboro; Covington 21–16 Kingman. Officials: E.R. Brown, E.C. Rowe.

VINCENNES: Washington 26–20 Sandborn; Bicknell 23–18 Monroe City; Plainville 31–18 Bruceville; Hazelton 34–11 Decker; Elnora 24–19 Mount Olympus; Edwardsport 37–14 Freelandville; Fritchton 31–13 Odon; Vincennes 63–6 Oaktown; Washington 41–17 Bicknell; Plainville 28–16 Hazelton; Edwardsport 28–22 Elnora; Vincennes 28–5 Fritchton; Washington 21–16 Plainville; Vincennes 58–9 Edwardsport; Vincennes 38–17 Washington. Officials: B.E. Bayh, Ralph Esarey.

WARSAW: Milford 15–9 North Webster; Claypool 20–8 Beaver Dam; Burket 39–16 Silver Lake; Pierceton 29–6 Etna Green; Leesburg 25–8 Sidney; Warsaw 32–3 Mentone; Atwood 12–9 Syracuse; Milford 25–5 Claypool; Pierceton 15–12 Burket; Warsaw 13–9 Leesburg; Milford 25–19 Atwood; Warsaw 36–8 Pierceton; Warsaw 23–9 Milford. Officials: L.A. Schwan, Ben Dubois.

WOLCOTT: Wolcott 26–12 Remington; Brookston 23–15 Burnettsville; Chalmers 21–15 Liberty Twp.; Monticello 15–14 Idaville; Reynolds 18–13 Monon; Wolcott 28–17 Brookston;

Tourney Time

Monticello 16–10 Chalmers; Wolcott 39–22 Reynolds; Wolcott 27–16 Monticello. Officials: Clement Malon, Everett Wiley.

1923 REGIONALS

Five teams from the West Lafayette and Fort Wayne tournaments and six from the Bloomington tournament qualified for the finals.

WEST LAFAYETTE (Purdue University): Crawfordsville 28–23 Logansport; Lebanon 26–23 Jefferson; Bainbridge 42–21 Brook; Martinsville 21–17 Manual; Greentown 32–20 Wolcott; Frankfort 17–11 Emerson; Perrysville 21–11 Brazil; Mount Comfort 30–21 Covington; Anderson 35–14 Michigan City; Crawfordsville 24–12 Lebanon; Martinsville 30–23 Bainbridge; Frankfort 21–16 Greentown; Perrysville 39–19 Mount Comfort. Officials not reported.

BLOOMINGTON (Indiana University): Franklin 15–12 Seymour; Bedford 21–13 Bloomington; Sullivan 28–7 Brookville; Columbus 27–20 Central; Vincennes 59–8 Hanover; Lyons 15–12 Winslow. Officials not reported.

FORT WAYNE (South Side High School): Kendallville 30–16 Liberty Center; Muncie 35–6 Rochester; Warsaw 37–16 Losantville; South Side 29–21 Garrett; South Bend 35–8 Culver; Mooreland 30–25 Shelbyville; Richmond 31–12 Marion; Wabash 23–20 Hartford City; Huntington 33–16 Connersville; Muncie 28–24 Kendallville; Warsaw 19–16 South Side; South Bend 30–14 Mooreland; Richmond 34–6 Wabash. Officials not reported.

1923 FINALS—March 16, 17

INDIANAPOLIS (Old Coliseum): Muncie 29–25 Frankfort; Richmond 28–19 Columbus; Bedford 38–27 Warsaw; Crawfordsville 25–23 Martinsville; South Bend 25–13 Huntington; Anderson 53–13 Sullivan; Franklin 33–25 Perrysville; Vincennes 38–10 Lyons; Muncie 33–30 Richmond; Crawfordsville 23–21 Bedford; Anderson 35–22 South Bend; Vincennes 22–18 Franklin; Muncie 26–19 Crawfordsville; Vincennes 29–27 Anderson; Vincennes 27–18 Muncie. Officials: Ray Mowe, Chester Reagan, Dale Miller, Charles Jensen.

1924 SECTIONALS

ANDERSON: Pendleton 31–18 Summitville; Anderson 44–18 Lapel; Elwood 29–10 Markleville; Windfall 40–26 Frankton; Alexandria 23–20 Tipton; Anderson 42–21 Pendleton; Elwood 26–12 Windfall; Anderson 62–15 Alexandria; Anderson 34–26 Elwood. Officials: R.B. Morrison, Dan Overman.

ANGOLA: Ashley 9–8 Orland; Salem 22–17 Butler; Angola 26–10 Auburn; Waterloo 18–11 Corunna; Garrett 58–5 Flint; Hamilton 26–4 Spencerville; Pleasant Lake 24–0 Scott Center; Fremont 36–8 Metz; Ashley 12–9 Salem; Angola 29–10 Waterloo; Garrett 31–15 Hamilton; Fremont 16–12 Pleasant Lake; Angola 25–7 Ashley; Garrett 23–10 Fremont; Angola 15–7 Garrett. Officials: Homer Stonebraker, Don Stephenson.

AURORA: Milan 24–12 Osgood; Aurora 13–7 Brookville; Laurel 15–13 Dillsboro; Moores Hill 73–8 Guilford; Lawrenceburg 21–19 Batesville; Sunman 17–15 Napoleon; Versailles 36–13 Holton; Milan 12–8 Springfield Twp.; Aurora 14–9 Laurel; Lawrenceburg 18–16 Moores Hill;

Versailles 35–11 Sunman; Aurora 18–12 Milan; Versailles 12–8 Lawrenceburg; Versailles 19–17 Aurora. Officials: P.O. Hurley, J.A. Mohler.

BAINBRIDGE: Roachdale 14–5 New Maysville; Russellville 19–5 Clinton Center; Greencastle 29–16 Reelsville; Bainbridge 33–11 Cloverdale; Fillmore 22–20 Putnamville; Russellville 28–17 Roachdale; Bainbridge 18–15 Greencastle; Russellville 23–19 Fillmore; Bainbridge 35–19 Russellville. Officials: M.P. Wilder, E.E. Reid.

BEDFORD: Burns City 16–10 Williams; West Baden 30–6 Pekin; Heltonville 27–11 Needmore; Bedford 2–0 Oolitic; Huron 18–17 Hardinsburg; Orleans 18–12 Paoli; Salem 38–9 Tunnelton; Mitchell 14–13 Loogootee; West Baden 33–6 Burns City; Bedford 69–12 Heltonville; Orleans 25–7 Huron; Salem 16–14 Mitchell; Bedford 46–14 West Baden; Orleans 15–10 Salem; Bedford 38–12 Orleans. Officials: Bryng Bryngleson, R.W. Gipson.

BRAZIL: Ashboro 17–11 Tangier; Cory 19–16 Clay City; Brazil 38–8 Posey Twp.; Bellmore 30–14 Coalmont; Van Buren Twp. 35–15 Bloomingdale; Montezuma 26–14 Bridgeton; Bowling Green 28–18 Marshall; Rockville 32–12 Mecca; Cory 16–12 Ashboro; Brazil 27–15 Bellmore; Montezuma 10–7 Van Buren; Rockville 25–18 Bowling Green; Brazil 24–10 Cory; Rockville 22–18 Montezuma; Brazil 45–20 Rockville. Officials: F.L. Busenburg, Homer Wiltse.

BROOK: Otterbein 27–14 Boswell; Fowler 19–16 Morocco; Pine Twp. 17–8 Freeland Park; Raub 28–14 Gilboa; Brook 80–4 Earl Park; Goodland 24–15 Kentland; Francesville 36–13 Mount Ayr; Oxford 18–14 Ambia; Otterbein 27–22 Fowler; Raub 23–11 Pine Twp.; Brook 25–10 Goodland; Oxford 28–23 Francesville; Otterbein 28–12 Raub; Brook 33–10 Oxford; Otterbein 18–6 Brook. Officials: F.K. Ferguson, J.B. McBride.

COLUMBUS: Scipio 16–11 Van Buren Twp.; North Vernon 30–15 Butlerville; Newbern 18–17 Hawk Creek Twp.; Columbus 56–7 Flat Rock; Vernon 20–15 Scipio; North Vernon 27–17 Newbern; Columbus 76–14 Vernon; Columbus 48–11 North Vernon. Officials: H.H. Bacon, Gilbert P. Best.

COVINGTON: Mellott 20–12 Kingman; Pine Village 14–11 Wallace; Covington 11–7 Attica; Dana 11–8 West Lebanon; Hillsboro 21–15 Newport; Perrysville 41–19 Williamsport; Veedersburg 27–12 Cayuga; Pine Village 14–10 Mellott; Covington 35–11 Dana; Hillsboro 18–10 Perrysville; Veedersburg 17–16 Pine Village; Covington 17–9 Hillsboro; Veedersburg 13–11 Covington. Officials: E.R. Brown, Vaughn Russell.

CRAWFORDSVILLE: Waynetown 14–11 Darlington; Linden 18–8 New Ross; Bowers 26–21 Wingate; New Market 20–8 Alamo; Crawfordsville 20–16 Waveland; New Richmond 34–10 Mace; Waynetown 28–8 Ladoga; Bowers 17–12 Linden; Crawfordsville 29–8 New Market; Waynetown 24–17 New Richmond; Crawfordsville 23–13 Bowers; Crawfordsville 30–14 Waynetown. Officials: George S. Kenzler, G.W. Trickey.

EVANSVILLE: New Harmony 16–15 Newburgh; Poseyville 34–9 Wadesville; Mount Vernon 15–10 Tennyson; Boonville 19–14 Bosse; Stewartsville 40–10 Griffin; Cynthiana 26–9 Yankeetown; Reitz 20–19 Lynnville; Central 36–13 Elberfeld; Poseyville 35–17 New Harmony; Boonville 14–8 Mount Vernon; Stewartsville 18–16 Cynthiana; Central 33–9 Reitz; Poseyville 26–23 Boonville; Central 34–20 Stewartsville; Central 26–10 Poseyville. Officials: Charles Jensen, Elmer Posey.

FLORA: Camden 22–19 Burlington; Delphi 63–4 Wheeling; Flora 24–22 Monroe Twp. Cutler 37–3 Rockfield; Deer Creek 18–16 Camden; Delphi 28–17 Flora; Cutler 37–8 Deer Creek; Delphi 26–20 Cutler. Officials: Everett Wiley, Fitzhugh Traylor.

Tourney Time

FRANKFORT: Jefferson 33–15 Michigantown; Kempton 17–12 Goldsmith; Frankfort 52–5 Colfax; Scircleville 35–15 Forest; Rossville 21–7 Mulberry; Jefferson 32–12 Kempton; Frankfort 27–16 Scircleville; Jefferson 20–16 Rossville; Frankfort 32–29 Jefferson. Officials: B.J. Westover, Everett Babb.

FORT WAYNE: Central 63–12 Coesse; Churubusco 17–10 Monroeville; Harlan 24–18 Arcola; South Side 56–13 New Haven; Washington Center 22–8 Jefferson Center; Etna 14–9 Huntertown; South Whitley 32–16 Maumee Twp. Columbia City 38–2 Larwill; Central 37–6 Churubusco; South Side 29–14 Harlan; Washington Center 19–15 Etna; Columbia City 25–18 South Whitley; South Side 24–18 Central; Columbia City 22–15 Washington Center; Columbia City 22–20 South Side. Officials: Horace Parker, Will Smith.

FRANKLIN: Edinburg 30–28 Greenwood; Whiteland 20–19 Nineveh; Franklin 34–15 Hopewell; Center Grove 28–13 Clarke Twp.; Union 44–10 Trafalgar; Whiteland 22–19 Edinburg; Franklin 40–9 Center Grove; Union 21–18 Whiteland; Franklin 39–20 Union. Officials: John E. Graigle, Harry Schoeneman.

GARY: Whiting 20–16 Froebel; Valparaiso 48–8 Hobart; Hammond 29–8 Hebron; Boone Grove 18–13 Chesterton; Lowell 35–6 Kouts; Crown Point 40–8 Miller; East Chicago 28–21 Emerson; Whiting 30–25 Valparaiso; Hammond 27–6 Boone Grove; Crown Point 20–13 Lowell; Whiting 30–29 East Chicago; Crown Point 32–26 Hammond; Whiting 19–17 Crown Point. Officials: C.R. Grogan, M.J. Cleary.

GOSHEN: Elkhart 42–6 Brighton; Washington Twp. 16–9 Middlebury; Lima 35–7 Wolcottville; LaGrange 31–15 Shipshewana; Goshen 43–13 Topeka; New Paris 29–6 Wakarusa; Nappanee 14–7 Millersburg; Elkhart 52–7 South Milford; Lima 31–9 Washington Twp.; LaGrange 2–0 Goshen; New Paris 18–12 Nappanee; Elkhart 27–10 Lima; New Paris 18–16 LaGrange; Elkhart 25–17 New Paris. Officials: L.A. Schwan, Ford L. Griffith.

GREENFIELD: Mount Comfort 31–27 Westland; Eden 26–23 Fortville; Maxwell 19–18 Charlottesville; New Palestine 19–14 McCordsville; Wilkinson 34–22 Greenfield; Mount Comfort 18–17 Eden; New Palestine 23–13 Maxwell; Mount Comfort 32–29 Wilkinson; Mount Comfort 27–23 New Palestine. Officials: Guy Ogle, Sidney Peters.

HANOVER: Deputy 16–15 New Albany; Corydon 2–0 New Salisbury; Georgetown 19–18 North Madison; Scottsburg 24–4 Rykers Ridge; Jeffersonville 31–18 Madison; Patriot 25–12 Charlestown; Henryville 14–8 Saluda; Vevay 25–21 Hanover; Corydon 21–17 Deputy; Scottsburg 23–7 Georgetown; Jeffersonville 34–14 Patriot; Vevay 40–4 Henryville; Scottsburg 17–9 Corydon; Jeffersonville 15–8 Vevay; Jeffersonville 37–21 Scottsburg. Officials: Stanley Morse, Ivan Zaring.

HARTFORD CITY: Liberty Center 22–12 Lancaster Center; Union Center 27–14 Montpelier; Bluffton 48–12 Chester Center; Hartford City 44–25 Rock Creek Center; Ossian 27–13 Petroleum; Liberty Center 23–13 Union Center; Bluffton 20–19 Hartford City; Liberty City 26–12 Ossian; Liberty Center 27–13 Bluffton. Officials: Walter Geller, Vedder Gard.

HUNTINGTON: Bippus 13–9 Banquo; Huntington 31–13 Warren; Roanoke 26–17 Union Center; Andrews 53–11 Huntington Twp.; Rock Creek Twp. 22–20 Monroe City; Clear Creek 26–15 Bippus; Huntington 24–15 Roanoke; Andrews 19–10 Rock Creek Twp.; Huntington 32–22 Clear Creek; Huntington 35–18 Andrews. Officials: Ralph Parker, Ralph Eades.

INDIANAPOLIS: Tech 20–14 Cumberland; West Newton 20–18 Shortridge; Ben Davis 23–13 Valley Mills; Manual 20–11 Shadeland; Acton 29–12 Oaklandon; Beech Grove 15–8 Castleton; Southport 49–14 New Bethel; Broad Ripple 25–17 Lawrence; Tech 32–16 West

Newton; Manual 22–18 Ben Davis; Beech Grove 13–12 Acton; Southport 26–20 Broad Ripple; Tech 27–23 Manual; Southport 26–19 Beech Grove; Southport 37–35 Tech (ot). Officials: John D. Miller, James Hale.

KENDALLVILLE: Kendallville 17–13 Wolf Lake; Wawaka 23–7 Cromwell; Ligonier 16–13 Albion; LaOtto 19–15 Rome City; Kendallville 33–16 Wawaka; Ligonier 35–9 LaOtto; Kendallville 25–23 Ligonier. Officials: Ralph Gilbert, Archie Heller.

KOKOMO: Union Twp. 28–15 Clay Twp.; Howard Twp. 20–18 New London; West Middleton 31–17 Prairie Twp.; Kokomo 25–13 Greentown; Russiaville 37–9 Jackson Twp.; Sharpsville 37–19 Union Twp.; West Middleton 26–21 Howard Twp.; Kokomo 32–15 Russiaville; West Middleton 29–21 Sharpsville; Kokomo 34–27 West Middleton. Officials: Watson Deakyne, Lee Sinclair.

LAFAYETTE: West Lafayette 29–5 Wea; Stockwell 16–12 Romney; West Point 34–4 Gladdens Corner; Jefferson 52–6 Monitor; Montmorenci 36–5 Buck Creek; Clarks Hill 18–8 Jackson Twp.; Dayton 22–21 Battle Ground; West Lafayette 26–9 Stockwell; West Point 25–22 Jefferson; West Lafayette 24–16 Dayton; Montmorenci 27–22 West Point; West Lafayette 21–14 Montmorenci. Officials: Russell Hochstetler, E.S. Krantz.

LEBANON: Lebanon 23–14 Central; Thorntown 20–15 Zionsville; Advance 29–28 Jamestown; Whitestown 28–13 New Augusta; Lebanon 23–12 Thorntown; Advance 29–17 Whitestown; Lebanon 27–23 Advance. Officials: Leroy Cook, R.V. Copple.

LOGANSPORT: Onward 18–16 Washington Twp.; New Waverly 16–11 Deacon; Logansport 42–12 Walton; Young America 24–12 Galveston; Lucerne 37–6 Metea; Royal Center 31–8 Lincoln; Onward 41–8 Twelve Mile; Logansport 55–15 New Waverly; Young America 39–5 Lucerne; Onward 20–17 Royal Center; Logansport 31–17 Young America; Logansport 41–6 Onward. Officials: Claude Draper, Edwin H. Miller.

LYONS: Bloomfield 19–8 Owensburg; Midland 42–10 Odon; Washington 40–15 Elnora; Lyons 52–1 Montgomery; Scotland 20–14 Raglesville; Plainville 14–9 Newberry; Midland 16–13 Bloomfield; Lyons 14–13 Washington; Scotland 17–13 Plainville; Midland 17–13 Lyons; Midland 31–5 Scotland. Officials: Gosnell Layman, B.H. Watt.

MARION: Jonesboro 19–9 Upland; Van Buren 21–19 Fairmount; Swayzee 15–7 Matthews; Sweetser 37–15 Gas City; Marion 21–11 Jonesboro; Swayzee 20–15 Van Buren; Marion 30–19 Sweetser; Marion 20–15 Swayzee. Officials: Don Arbuckle, Newell Day.

MARTINSVILLE: Monrovia 42–13 Coal City; Gosport 13–8 Ellettsville; Smithville 23–22 Morgantown; Paragon 48–11 Unionville; Mooresville 26–22 Freedom; Martinsville 34–28 Bloomingdale; Spencer 19–16 Eminence; Gosport 19–14 Stinesville; Monrovia 31–18 Smithville; Paragon 32–20 Mooresville; Martinsville 35–17 Spencer; Monrovia 48–13 Gosport; Martinsville 30–15 Paragon; Martinsville 36–24 Monrovia. Officials: Dale Miller, B.E. Bayh.

MICHIGAN CITY: Union Mills 13–10 Union Twp.; Stillwell 18–11 Hanna; Westville 36–7 Mill Creek; Michigan City 19–14 LaPorte; Wanatah 30–22 Kingsbury; Stillwell 15–12 Union Mills; Michigan City 29–11 Westville; Stillwell 22–13 Wanatah; Michigan City 43–11 Stillwell. Officials: Carl Olson, Floyd Merriman.

MONTICELLO: Wolcott 29–16 DeMotte; Reynolds 20–11 Burnettsville; Wheatfield 29–8 Buffalo; Chalmers 15–11 Remington; Monticello 22–13 Brookston; Monon 37–14 Fair Oaks; Rensselaer 43–14 Idaville; Wolcott 24–11 Reynolds; Wheatfield 25–24 Chalmers; Monticello 16–13 Monon; Wolcott 32–17 Rensselaer; Monticello 29–12 Wheatfield; Monticello 20–12 Wolcott.

Tourney Time

Officials: Clayton Hughes, R.R. Merrell.

MUNCIE: Yorktown 22–13 Albany; Selma 44–11 Royerton; Muncie 33–12 Daleville; Cowan 29–28 Gaston; Eaton 39–22 DeSoto; Yorktown 25–12 Center; Muncie 35–18 Selma; Easton 22–16 Cowan; Muncie 36–7 Yorktown; Muncie 37–21 Eaton. Officials: Howard Hill, F.A. Bills.

NEW CASTLE: New Lisbon 17–9 Straughn; Cadiz 15–9 Middletown; Fairview 25–6 Sulphur Springs; Knightstown 19–10 Kennard; Mooreland 43–5 Lewisville; New Castle 35–7 Mount Summit; Spiceland 30–4 Bentonville; Cadiz 43–10 New Lisbon; Knightstown 28–19 Fairview; Mooreland 19–8 New Castle; Spiceland 20–13 Cadiz; Mooreland 21–13 Knightstown; Mooreland 20–12 Spiceland. Officials: Harrison W. Davis, John Wertz.

NOBLESVILLE: Atlanta 29–12 Boxley; Westfield 17–16 Walnut Grove; Noblesville 29–24 Cicero; Arcadia 23–21 Sheridan; Carmel 28–16 Fishers; Westfield 25–17 Atlanta; Arcadia 24–14 Noblesville; Carmel 23–14 Westfield; Arcadia 21–18 Carmel. Officials: Stanley Feezle, John George.

NORTH MANCHESTER: Roann 27–22 LaFontaine; Laketon 28–4 Linlawn; North Manchester 28–13 Lincolnville; Lagro 14–11 Chippewa; Somerset 25–18 Wabash; Chester 45–3 Urbana; Laketon 16–10 Roann; North Manchester 51–3 Lagro; Chester 17–11 Somerset; North Manchester 44–15 Laketon; North Manchester 57–8 Chester. Officials: E.C. Rowe, P.S. Mason.

OAKLAND CITY: Owensville 26–16 Otwell; Union 23–13 Velpen; Oakland City 38–11 Petersburg; Hazelton 33–24 Francisco; Winslow 33–10 Fort Branch; Patoka 30–12 Spurgeon; Princeton 36–20 Haubstadt; Mount Olympus 51–7 Mackey; Owensville 20–15 Union; Hazelton 31–19 Oakland City; Winslow 33–10 Patoka; Mount Olympus 23–21 Princeton; Hazelton 17–16 Owensville; Winslow 26–21 Hazelton. Officials: J.E. Wakefield, H.R. Henderson.

PERU: Amboy 16–15 Deedsville; Clay Twp. 34–15 Macy; Jefferson Twp. 30–11 Butler Twp.; Peru 55–13 Gilead; Bunker Hill 32–12 Chili; Converse 20–13 Amboy; Clay Twp. 20–9 Jefferson Twp.; Bunker Hill 21–20 Peru; Clay Twp. 24–18 Converse; Bunker Hill 23–17 Clay Twp. Officials: Donald Hobbs, Lloyd Etter.

PITTSBORO: Lizton 22–20 Stilesville; Plainfield 32–9 Avon; Brownsburg 83–10 New Winchester; Pittsboro 48–14 Amo; Clayton 37–17 North Salem; Danville 14–11 Lizton; Brownsburg 45–10 Plainfield; Clayton 30–25 Pittsboro; Brownsburg 36–11 Danville; Clayton 35–33 Brownsburg. Officials: Walter Keller, C.E. Steward.

PORTLAND: Pennville 53–6 Redkey; Kirkland 27–1 Poling; Decatur 29–10 Portland; Berne 21–8 Jefferson Center; Geneva 19–11 Bryant; Salamonia 22–9 Gray; Dunkirk 26–17 Jefferson; Pennville 52–6 Hartford Twp.; Kirkland 14–12 Decatur; Geneva 19–13 Berne; Dunkirk 30–11 Salamonia; Pennville 17–13 Kirkland; Dunkirk 22–18 Geneva; Pennville 28–11 Dunkirk. Officials: Wayne Gill, Paul Williams.

RICHMOND: Whitewater 24–14 Greensfork; Boston 24–13 Brownsville; Richmond Morton 42–11 Lincoln; Centerville 35–26 Williamsburg; Economy 25–20 Milton; Hagerstown 30–11 Liberty; Boston 27–26 Fountain City; Morton 36–14 Centerville; Hagerstown 40–12 Economy; Boston 24–14 Whitewater; Morton 30–18 Hagerstown; Morton 56–15 Boston. Officials: M.W. Tatlock, E.B. Palmer.

ROCHESTER: Monterey 19–13 Fulton; Rochester 43–1 San Pierre; Medaryville 50–15 Richland Center; Grass Creek 25–14 Pulaski; Talma 32–9 Grovertown; Kewanna 32–10 Knox; Winamac 31–8 Star City; Leiters Ford 32–13 North Judson; Rochester 22–19 Monterey; Medaryville 38–21 Grass Creek; Kewanna 36–20 Talma; Leiters Ford 21–12 Winamac; Rochester

IHSAA Scores | 1920–1929

33–16 Medaryville; Kewanna 24–10 Leiters Ford; Rochester 23–4 Kewanna. Officials: Benjamin DuBois, L.I. Mattingly.

RUSHVILLE: Milroy 2–0 New Salem; Moscow 8–6 Carthage; Manilla 16–15 Rushville; Webb 55–8 Everton; Connersville 86–4 Ging; Raleigh 30–11 Glenwood; Alquina 20–16 Orange; Arlington 2–0 Center; Milroy 20–14 Moscow; Manilla 24–18 Webb; Connersville 27–17 Raleigh; Arlington 25–11 Alquina; Milroy 25–19 Manilla; Connersville 42–26 Arlington; Connersville 26–20 Milroy. Officials: E.C. Auerswald, William E. Campbell.

SEYMOUR: Freetown 18–11 Clear Springs; Brownstown 45–24 Austin; Cortland 35–23 Little York; Seymour 20–18 Crothersville; Medora 26–24 Vallonia; Brownstown 22–16 Freetown; Seymour 29–15 Cortland; Brownstown 31–19 Medora; Seymour 19–9 Brownstown. Officials: W.S. Fellmy, H.E. Berges.

SHELBYVILLE: Shelbyville 68–7 Sandusky; St. Paul 16–14 Clarksburg; Waldron 23–22 Morristown; New Point 19–17 Geneva; Greensburg 19–18 Jackson; Letts 18–14 Mt. Auburn; Westport 18–13 Burney; Moral 11–10 Boggstown; Shelbyville 57–10 St. Paul; Waldron 23–19 New Point; Greensburg 36–10 Letts; Moral 14–13 Westport; Shelbyville 58–11 Waldron; Greensburg 23–17 Moral; Shelbyville 34–22 Greensburg. Officials: Ray Frohman, Horace McClain.

SOUTH BEND: Plymouth 32–18 New Carlisle; Argos 21–17 West; Culver 50–12 Walkerton; Lakeville 40–13 Bremen; South Bend 28–5 North Liberty; Mishawaka 28–24 Bourbon; Plymouth 39–14 Tippecanoe; Culver 33–11 Argos; Lakeville 26–17 South Bend; Mishawaka 26–22 Plymouth; Lakeville 29–18 Culver; Lakeville 39–24 Mishawaka. Officials: Keith Crown, John W. Kyle.

SULLIVAN: Carlisle 13–12 New Lebanon; Graysville 27–17 Pleasantville; Shelburn 22–20 Hymera; Dugger 15–11 Fairbanks; Sullivan 30–18 Farmersburg; Graysville 21–15 Carlisle; Dugger 25–10 Shelburn; Sullivan 29–12 Graysville; Sullivan 20–15 Dugger. Officials: J. Ord Fortner, J.H. Hendrickson.

TELL CITY: Oil Twp. 20–8 Cannelton; Troy 21–18 Birdseye; Stendal 37–13 Tobinsport; Rockport 34–24 Dale; Anderson Twp. 30–12 Huntingburg; Tell City 44–15 Bristow; Jasper 33–14 Union Twp.; Troy 25–13 Oil Twp.; Stendal 32–12 Rockport; Tell City 31–20 Anderson Twp.; Jasper 32–12 Troy; Tell City 29–27 Stendal; Tell City 15–13 Jasper. Officials: U.S. Abbott, G.C. Ashcraft.

TERRE HAUTE: Blackhawk 14–11 Fontanet; Concannon 27–8 North Terre Haute; Wiley 30–3 Fayette; Clinton 19–13 Gerstmeyer; Glenn 14–11 Prairie Creek; Pimento 17–8 Otter Creek; Normal 38–14 Prairieton; Garfield 35–4 Helt Twp.; Concannon 32–15 Blackhawk; Wiley 22–13 Clinton; Glenn 16–13 Pimento; Garfield 14–11 Normal; Wiley 36–13 Concannon; Garfield 24–13 Glenn; Wiley 44–5 Garfield. Officials: William Webb, George Graham.

VINCENNES: Freelandville 17–11 Decker; Vincennes 34–19 Bicknell; Sandborn 23–16 Bruceville; Fritchton 26–16 Monroe City; Edwardsport 28–14 Oaktown; Vincennes 57–10 Freelandville; Fritchton 27–12 Sandborn; Vincennes 65–16 Edwardsport; Vincennes 49–12 Fritchton. Officials: Ross Smith, John Schram.

WARSAW: Milford 20–8 Pierceton; Syracuse 26–14 Mentone; Claypool 22–6 Beaver Dam; Etna Green 21–2 Silver Lake; Warsaw 29–22 North Webster; Sidney 18–13 Burket; Leesburg 10–8 Milford; Claypool 22–15 Syracuse; Warsaw 34–11 Etna Green; Leesburg 12–11 Sidney; Warsaw 28–10 Claypool; Warsaw 41–7 Leesburg. Officials: Harry Coolman, Dean Barnhart.

WINCHESTER: Winchester 29–5 Farmland; Losantville 21–17 Spartanburg; Stoney Creek

Tourney Time

36–18 Parker; Huntsville 24–17 Saratoga; Union City 26–20 Modoc; McKinley 25–11 Wayne; Jackson 21–15 Lynn; Ridgeville 20–9 Green; Losantville 25–13 Winchester; Stoney Creek 41–14 Huntsville; Union City 41–8 McKinley; Ridgeville 23–17 Jackson; Stoney Creek 28–19 Losantville; Ridgeville 14–10 Union City; Stoney Creek 33–30 Ridgeville. Officials: Ray Mowe, H.L. Murray.

1924 REGIONALS

Four teams from each regional qualified for the finals.

WEST LAFAYETTE (Purdue University): Frankfort 30–16 Bainbridge; Michigan City 25–17 Whiting; Veedersburg 28–21 Delphi; Otterbein 18–12 Crawfordsville; Lebanon 33–31 Kokomo; Logansport 31–19 West Lafayette; Frankfort 42–14 Monticello; Michigan City 24–16 Veedersburg; Otterbein 18–16 Lebanon. Officials: Clarence Crogan, Charles Jensen, John D. Miller.

RICHMOND (Earlham College): Anderson 45–14 Stoney Creek; Shelbyville 62–25 Arcadia; Muncie 39–16 Mooreland; Connersville 38–24 Versailles; Clayton 21–20 Jeffersonville; Richmond 37–14 Southport; Anderson 28–12 Mt. Comfort; Shelbyville 22–21 Muncie; Connersville 29–27 Clayton. Officials: Dale Miller, Chester Reagan, Hugh Vandivier.

FORT WAYNE: Rochester 34–14 Lakeville; Marion 22–17 Warsaw; North Manchester 28–16 Kendallville; South Side 32–25 Angola; Huntington 35–15 Elkhart; Rochester 28–19 Pennville; North Manchester 27–22 Marion; South Side 34–18 Huntington; Liberty Center 25–13 Bunker Hill. Officials: Keith Crown, Carl Olson, Paul Williams.

BLOOMINGTON (Indiana University): Seymour 24–19 Midland; Sullivan 22–17 Tell City; Bedford 31–23 Columbus; Franklin 31–15 Brazil; Vincennes 32–19 Evansville Central; Martinsville 30–18 Winslow; Terre Haute Wiley 35–20 Seymour; Bedford 25–16 Sullivan; Franklin 23–17 Vincennes. Officials: R.B. Morrison, Birch Bayh, Ray Mowe.

1924 FINALS—March 14, 15

INDIANAPOLIS (Old Coliseum): Frankfort 24–18 Franklin; Richmond 41–22 South Side; Wiley 35–21 Michigan City; Rochester 30–26 Shelbyville; Bedford 35–24 Anderson; North Manchester 34–26 Logansport; Connersville 35–21 Otterbein; Martinsville 39–23 Liberty Center; Frankfort 29–24 Richmond; Wiley 18–14 Rochester; Bedford 37–27 North Manchester; Martinsville 36–33 Connersville; Frankfort 19–6 Wiley; Martinsville 31–15 Bedford; Martinsville 36–30 Frankfort. Officials: Chester Reagan, Ray Mowe. Dale Miller, John Miller.

1925 SECTIONALS

ANDERSON: Alexandria 33–22 Markleville; Anderson 41–20 Pendleton; Lapel 31–14 Summitville; Elwood 37–14 Windfall; Alexandria 21–12 Frankton; Lapel 25–23 Anderson; Elwood 24–23 Alexandria; Lapel 49–32 Elwood. Officials: Leroy Cook, Dale Miller.

ANGOLA: Brighton 16–13 Springfield Twp.; Shipshewana 24–15 Salem Center; Fremont 23–12 Pleasant Lake; Angola 16–8 Hamilton; Lima 11–10 Orland; LaGrange 27–18 Brighton; Fremont 22–18 Shipshewana; Angola 41–12 Lima; Fremont 27–11 LaGrange; Fremont 16–15

Angola. Officials: Don Stephenson, Archie Heller.

ATTICA: Wallace 33–9 Pine Village; Williamsport 34–3 West Lebanon; Attica 48–4 Judyville; Hillsboro 26–24 Veedersburg; Wallace 31–15 Williamsport; Hillsboro 20–17 Attica; Wallace 25–18 Hillsboro. Officials: E.E. Reid, S.C. Davis.

AUBURN: Waterloo 21–8 Spencerville; Butler 37–9 South Milford; Auburn 23–3 Topeka; Garrett 26–18 Corunna; Ashley 13–7 Wolcottville; Butler 37–19 Waterloo; Auburn 18–11 Garrett; Butler 22–15 Ashley; Auburn 23–10 Butler. Officials: Newell Day, Homer Stonebraker.

BAINBRIDGE: Greencastle 41–19 Reelsville; Russellville 24–22 Roachdale; Bainbridge 26–13 Cloverdale; Fillmore 29–17 Clinton Center; Greencastle 32–16 Belle Union; Bainbridge 18–13 Russellville; Greencastle 26–20 Fillmore; Bainbridge 19–16 Greencastle. Officials: Perry Larmore, John Craigle.

BEDFORD: Heltonville 31–15 Huron; Bedford 44–16 Williams; Tunnelton 31–11 Alfordsville; Mitchell 76–2 Montgomery; Washington 51–24 Oolitic; Loogootee 26–14 Needmore; Bedford 41–15 Heltonville; Mitchell 60–4 Tunnelton; Washington 71–8 Loogootee; Bedford 11–9 Mitchell; Washington 34–25 Bedford. Officials: R.W. Gipson, Lee Sinclair.

BRAZIL: Clay City 40–12 Coal City; Posey Twp. 29–20 Cory; Coalmont 18–15 Van Buren Twp.; Bowling Green 24–23 Patricksburg; Brazil 44–21 Ashboro; Posey Twp. 22–21 Clay City; Bowling Green 27–16 Coalmont; Brazil 48–17 Posey Twp. Brazil 37–9 Bowling Green. Officials: Ellsworth Krantz, P.M. Isenbarger.

CLINTON: Bellmore 32–22 Rockville; Clinton 17–11 Cayuga; Rosedale 25–22 Green Twp.; Marshall 30–24 Newport; Montezuma 39–14 Bloomingdale; Helt Twp. 18–14 Dana; Mecca 24–13 Tangier; Clinton 24–21 Bellmore; Marshall 31–28 Rosedale; Montezuma 24–17 Helt Twp.; Clinton 21–18 Mecca; Marshall 31–25 Montezuma; Clinton 21–20 Marshall. Officials: Donald Hobbs, Orville Jones.

COLUMBIA CITY: South Whitley 45–14 Coesse; Columbia City 17–16 Washington Center; Larwill 22–14 Jefferson Center; South Whitley 43–8 Churubusco; Columbia City 28–18 Larwill; South Whitley 22–15 Columbia City. Officials: Lundy Welborn, Ora Davis.

COLUMBUS: North Vernon 29–8 Butlerville; Columbus 54–2 Vernon; Scipio 22–2 Paris Crossing; Hope 23–19 Newbern; Flat Rock 20–8 Van Buren; Columbus 28–16 North Vernon; Hawcreek 28–22 Scipio; Columbus 60–11 Flat Rock; Columbus 53–15 Hope. Officials: John George, Forest Ragsdale.

CONNERSVILLE: Bentonville 23–20 Springfield Twp.; Connersville 63–3 Fairview; Brookville 27–12 Whitewater; Everton 2–0 Waterloo; Orange 17–14 Alquina; Laurel 18–17 Bentonville; Connersville 41–16 Brookville; Orange 26–20 Everton; Connersville 34–17 Laurel; Connersville 36–17 Orange. Officials: Paul Hurley, R.B. Morrison.

CRAWFORDSVILLE: Ladoga 32–12 Waveland; New Richmond 17–12 New Ross; Waynetown 31–14 Darlington; Crawfordsville 18–10 Bowers; Wingate 28–10 Alamo; New Market 14–13 Linden; New Richmond 20–10 Ladoga; Waynetown 26–14 Crawfordsville; Wingate 29–24 New Market; Waynetown 37–19 New Richmond; Wingate 28–22 Waynetown. Officials: L.I. Mattingly, Winston Ashley.

DANVILLE: Brownsburg 37–19 Avon; Lizton 15–14 Amo; Danville 28–16 North Salem; Clayton 31–9 Pittsboro; Plainfield 31–9 New Winchester; Brownsburg 52–20 Stilesville; Danville 30–19 Lizton; Clayton 24–11 Plainfield; Brownsburg 28–17 Danville; Clayton 30–26 Brownsburg. Officials: F.L. Busenburg, Cleon Davies.

Tourney Time

DECATUR: Ossian 25–13 Jefferson Twp. Decatur 33–5 Monmouth; Lancaster Center 25–8 Monroe; Hartford Twp. 19–14 Kirkland Twp.; Berne 31–4 Pleasant Mills; Decatur 23–15 Ossian; Lancaster Center 39–21 Hartford Twp.; Decatur 27–17 Berne; Lancaster Center 25–21 Decatur. Officials: Ford Griffith, H.L. Murray.

EAST CHICAGO: Gary Froebel 29–17 Whiting; Hammond 22–18 Lowell; Gary Emerson 40–4 Hobart; East Chicago 45–5 Griffith; Froebel 41–16 Hammond; Emerson 23–20 East Chicago; Froebel 31–18 Emerson. Officials: L.A. Schwan, C.O. Fulwider.

ELKHART: Millersburg 22–6 Bango Twp.; Goshen 46–20 Middlebury; New Paris 14–13 Washington Twp.; Nappanee 39–8 Wakarusa; Elkhart 26–7 Millersburg; Goshen 20–16 New Paris; Elkhart 34–21 Nappanee; Elkhart 35–19 Goshen. Officials: Walter Geller, George Russell.

EVANSVILLE: Reitz 44–15 Rockport; Central 37–8 Tennyson; Yankeetown 31–10 Dale; Boonville 22–19 Chandler; Bosse 43–8 Lynnville; Elberfeld 32–19 Newburgh; Central 48–10 Reitz; Boonville 32–12 Yankeetown; Bosse 51–6 Elberfeld; Central 40–4 Boonville; Central 39–13 Bosse. Officials: C.D. Manhart, L.A. Schram.

FLORA: Democrat Twp. 38–18 Burlington; Bringhurst 34–14 Wheeling; Flora 36–15 Camden; Delphi 42–13 Rockfield; Flora 29–20 Bringhurst; Delphi 27–24 Cutler; Delphi 19–18 Flora. Officials: Lloyd Etter, Bert Westover.

FORT WAYNE: Central 57–17 Arcola; New Haven 27–17 Maumee Twp.; South Side 57–10 Lafayette Central; Monroeville 21–13 Leo; Harlan 23–22 Huntertown; Central 36–7 New Haven; South Side 36–10 Monroeville; Central 88–5 Harlan; Central 31–15 South Side. Officials: Will Smith, Horace Parker.

FRANKFORT: Frankfort 40–4 Colfax; Rossville 32–13 Jefferson; Michigantown 17–9 Forest; Scircleville 28–7 Kempton; Frankfort 46–23 Rossville; Michigantown 33–31 Scircleville; Frankfort 58–10 Michigantown. Officials: John Miller, James Hale.

FRANKLIN: Hopewell 44–22 Clark Twp.; Greenwood 32–10 Edinburg; Center Grove 39–17 Nineveh; Union Twp. 23–9 Masonic Home; Trafalgar 29–21 Whiteland; Franklin 26–18 Hopewell; Greenwood 21–19 Center Grove; Trafalgar 23–20 Union Twp.; Franklin 38–22 Greenwood; Franklin 60–17 Trafalgar. Officials: Ray Frohman, Laverne Litherland.

GREENFIELD: Eden 22–18 Fortville; Greenfield 26–22 McCordsville; Wilkinson 43–15 Maxwell; Mt. Comfort 19–18 New Palestine; Charlottesville 31–12 Westland; Greenfield 41–20 Eden; Wilkinson 29–14 Mt. Comfort; Greenfield 38–8 Charlottesville; Greenfield 24–23 Wilkinson. Officials: Beryl Black, Benny Evans.

HUNTINGTON: Banquo 24–11 Huntington Twp.; Warren 23–4 Andrews; Clear Creek 53–12 Monument City; Union Center 15–14 Rock Creek; Bippus 23–14 Roanoke; Huntington 75–5 Jefferson Center; Warren 21–13 Banquo; Clear Creek 34–17 Union Center; Huntington 17–6 Bippus; Clear Creek 20–17 Warren; Huntington 32–17 Clear Creek. Officials: M.J. Cleary, Ralph Parker.

INDIANAPOLIS: Tech 28–16 Lawrence; Shortridge 35–9 Valley Mills; Warren Twp. 26–17 Acton; Ben Davis 42–16 Castleton; Manual 37–19 Oaklandon; Broad Ripple 17–15 Southport; West Newton 25–21 Beech Grove; New Augusta 35–20 New Bethel; Shortridge 22–19 Tech; Ben Davis 30–22 Warren Twp.; Manual 21–19 Broad Ripple; West Newton 29–27 New Augusta; Shortridge 24–21 Ben Davis; Manual 33–20 West Newton; Shortridge 22–20 Manual. Officials: Birch Bayh, Paul Williams.

JASPER: Paoli 27–19 French Lick; Huntingburg 24–14 Birdseye; Orleans 42–10 Holland;

West Baden 23–14 Jasper; Orleans 20–17 Cuzco; Huntingburg 27–25 Paoli; Orleans 20–15 West Baden; Huntingburg 37–22 Ireland; Huntingburg 23–21 Orleans. Officials: Ben Watt, William S. Porter.

KENDALLVILLE: Wawaka 31–9 LaOtto; Albion 20–13 Kendallville; Wolf Lake 27–15 Cromwell; Wawaka 28–13 Ligonier; Albion 24–22 Wolf Lake; Wawaka 27–15 Albion. Officials: Leslie Beall, Harry Coolman.

KENTLAND: Goodland 33–22 Francesville; Brook 16–15 Morocco; Medaryville 39–29 Rensselaer; Kentland 33–13 Mt. Ayr; Remington 34–19 Goodland; Brook 24–22 Medaryville; Remington 36–9 Kentland; Brook 33–28 Remington. Officials: Floyd Merriman, Edgar Haffner.

KOKOMO: Howard Twp. 22–17 Russiaville; Sharpsville 40–8 Union Twp.; Kokomo 41–24 West Middleton; Clay Twp.; 61–14 Jackson Twp.; Prairie Twp. 25–20 New London; Greentown 31–24 Howard Twp.; Kokomo 39–20 Sharpsville; Prairie Twp. 23–13 Clay Twp.; Kokomo 57–8 Greentown; Kokomo 39–22 Prairie Twp. Officials: Watson Deakyne, Guy Ogle.

LAFAYETTE: Jefferson 48–12 Monitor; Montmorenci 33–6 Buck Creek; Stockwell 26–7 Dayton; Battle Ground 34–15 Jackson Twp.; Romney 46–11 Gladdens Corner; West Lafayette 29–15 Wea; West Point 30–28 Jefferson; Montmorenci 25–14 Stockwell; Battle Ground 28–11 Romney; West Point 31–22 West Lafayette; Montmorenci 20–15 Battle Ground; West Point 18–16 Montmorenci. Officials: Jerry Wakefield, Alonzo Goldsberry.

LAPORTE: Michigan City 26–9 Union Mills; Union Twp. 25–14 Springfield Twp.; LaPorte 64–2 Kingsbury; Stillwell 35–21 Wanatah; Michigan City 21–11 Westville; LaPorte 60–9 Union Twp.; Michigan City 21–16 Stillwell; LaPorte 27–24 Michigan City. Officials: Clarence Grogan, E.C. Rowe.

LEBANON: Zionsville 25–22 Thorntown; Advance 23–9 Whitestown; Jamestown 40–20 Goldsmith; Lebanon 34–7 Central; Advance 21–13 Zionsville; Lebanon 23–14 Jamestown; Advance 24–20 Lebanon. Officials: Joseph Albert, E.R. Brown.

LINTON: Lyons 41–20 Odon; Jasonville 15–14 Midland; Elnora 34–6 Scotland; Bloomfield 24–15 Switz City; Owensburg 12–8 Marco; Plainville 34–9 Raglesville; Linton 31–27 Newberry; Lyons 50–8 Jasonville; Bloomfield 14–9 Elnora; Plainville 33–12 Owensburg; Lyons 25–22 Linton; Bloomfield 34–22 Plainville; Lyons 35–28 Bloomfield. Officials: Ralph Esary, Leonard Kincade.

MADISON: Deputy 55–8 Saluda; Vevay 37–11 Rykers Ridge; Hanover 17–10 Austin; Scottsburg 40–8 North Madison; Madison 45–6 Dupont; Deputy 27–17 Vevay; Scottsburg 23–15 Hanover; Deputy 31–15 Madison; Deputy 19–15 Scottsburg. Officials: Lloyd Wells, H. C. Henderson.

MARION: Sweetser 20–16 Jonesboro; Marion 34–19 Gas City; Van Buren 22–8 Upland; Fairmount 27–21 Swayzee; Sweetser 23–21 Matthews; Marion 61–15 Van Buren; Sweetser 20–12 Fairmount; Marion 39–17 Sweetser. Officials: H.H. Baconfi, Almon Gerrard.

MARTINSVILLE: Spencer 58–14 Quincy; Paragon 22–21 Morgantown; Monrovia 41–20 Smithville; Martinsville 47–15 Mooresville; Unionville 26–22 Ellettsville; Gosport 31–12 Freedom; Bloomington 56–5 Stinesville; Spencer 37–19 Eminence; Monrovia 47–4 Paragon; Martinsville 73–9 Unionville; Bloomington 41–20 Gosport; Monrovia 31–23 Spencer; Martinsville 36–20 Bloomington; Martinsville 28–23 Monrovia. Officials: Vedder Gard, Charles Jensen.

MISHAWAKA: Mishawaka 24–14 Knox; Lakeville 22–10 Hamlet; North Liberty 31–13 New Carlisle; South Bend 34–10 Walkerton; Mishawaka 61–3 Madison Twp.; Lakeville 14–8 North

Tourney Time

Liberty; Mishawaka 17–15 South Bend; Mishawaka 39–7 Lakeville. Officials: Ralph Worley, Dean Barnhart.

MONTICELLO: Monticello 21–7 Burnettsville; Monon 23–12 Wolcott; Reynolds 49–8 Round Grove; Brookston 28–17 Chalmers; Monon 37–20 Monticello; Brookston 20–14 Reynolds; Brookston 25–24 Monon. Officials: Elder Eberhart, R. R. Merrell.

MONTPELIER: Union Center 33–22 Rock Creek; Chester Center 28–15 Petroleum; Montpelier 25–21 Hartford City; Liberty Center 28–23 Bluffton; Union Center 32–24 Chester Center; Liberty Center 29–12 Montpelier; Liberty Center 23–15 Union Center. Officials: Byron Deakyne, John Wertz.

MUNCIE: Cowan 15–12 Royerton; Daleville 23–12 Center; Selma 29–22 DeSoto; Muncie 67–11 Harrison; Eaton 29–19 Yorktown; Gaston 24–10 Albany; Daleville 24–17 Cowan; Muncie 30–12 Selma; Eaton 25–12 Gaston; Muncie 44–8 Daleville; Muncie 40–12 Eaton. Officials: Harry Schoeneman, Don Arbuckle.

NEW ALBANY: Little York 24–13 New Salisbury; New Albany 35–11 Hardinburg; Jeffersonville 27–6 Pekin; Campbellsburg 19–15 Morgan Twp.; Corydon 40–7 Laconia; Salem 34–12 Franklin Twp.; New Albany 30–9 Little York; Jeffersonville 45–20 Campbellsburg; Salem 29–15 Corydon; New Albany 21–20 Jeffersonville; New Albany 26–17 Salem. Officials: William S. Fellmy, Roy Hunter.

NEW CASTLE: Middletown 28–14 New Lisbon; Straughn 15–11 Mt. Summit; Knightstown 25–19 Spiceland; Mooreland 40–4 Harrison Twp.; New Castle 56–10 Sulphur Springs; Middletown 18–11 Kennard; Knightstown 83–3 Straughn; New Castle 28–19 Mooreland; Knightstown 31–28 Middletown; New Castle 21–18 Knightstown. Officials: Edwin Miller, Oris Vandivier.

NEW HARMONY: Poseyville 14–13 Cynthiana; New Harmony 34–15 Griffin; Stewartsville 30–15 Mt. Vernon; Poseyville 27–9 New Harmony; Poseyville 27–8 Stewartsville. Officials: H.R. Henderson, H. Kilburn Rogers.

NOBLESVILLE: Noblesville 28–21 Sheridan; Walnut Grove 30–20 Boxley; Cicero 42–17 Westfield; Arcadia 25–15 Fishers; Tipton 25–11 Atlanta; Carmel 23–18 Noblesville; Cicero 32–18 Walnut Grove; Tipton 15–5 Arcadia; Carmel 28–13 Cicero; Carmel 19–18 Tipton. Officials: E.B. Palmer, R.V. Copple.

NORTH MANCHESTER: North Manchester 44–10 Somerset; Lincolnville 27–10 Chippewa; Linlawn 31–30; Laketon 39–24 LaFontaine; Chester Twp. 42–4 Lagro; Roann 30–20 Wabash; North Manchester 49–10 Lincolnville; Laketon 14–11 Linlawn; Chester Twp. 30–16 Roann; North Manchester 28–24 Laketon; North Manchester 22–15 Chester Twp. Officials: B.G. Dubois, Robert Lambert.

OXFORD: Otterbein 30–10 Fowler; Ambia 36–18 Freeland Park; Wadena 23–18 Pine Twp.; Boswell 39–11 Gilboa; Oxford 19–17 Raub; Otterbein 28–24 Ambia; Boswell 35–3 Wadena; Oxford 26–16 Otterbein; Boswell 27–13 Oxford. Officials: Homer Wiltse, Donald Reel.

PERU: Chili 19–16 Deedsville; Jefferson Twp. 20–16 Peru; Clay Twp. 23–14 Amboy; Bunker Hill 17–14 Butler Twp.; Converse 26–20 Chili; Clay Twp. 18–14 Jefferson Twp. Converse 25–19 Bunker Hill; Clay Twp. 31–19 Converse. Officials: Ross Smith, Claude Sims.

PLYMOUTH: San Pierre 30–6 North Bend; Plymouth 71–6 West; Bremen 20–12 North Judson; Culver 40–15 Bourbon; San Pierre 14–9 Argos; Plymouth 31–15 Bremen; Culver 15–13 San Pierre; Plymouth 16–14 Culver. Officials: O.F. Helvie, J.C. McBride.

PORTLAND: Dunkirk 31–5 Gray; Pennville 21–11 Madison; Redkey 28–20 Poling;

Dunkirk 18–13 Portland; Pennville 27–13 Redkey; Dunkirk 24–23 Pennville. Officials: C.B. Stemen, Arthur Norris.

PRINCETON: Fort Branch 28–10 Patoka; Francisco 25–11 Hazelton; Mt. Olympus 18–9 Princeton; Oakland City 57–24 Haubstadt; Owensville 61–7 Mackey; Francisco 26–18 Fort Branch; Mt. Olympus 43–20 Oakland City; Owensville 33–20 Francisco; Owensville 31–19 Mt. Olympus. Officials: Frank Hochstetler, Vaughn Russell.

RICHMOND: Richmond Morton 23–12 Hagerstown; Fountain City 25–10 Economy; Cambridge City 25–24 Milton; Centerville 22–17 Boston; Williamsburg 41–12 Kitchel; Whitewater 39–10 Liberty; Morton 67–4 Greensfork; Fountain City 11–8 Cambridge City; Centerville 25–6 Williamsburg; Morton 27–9 Whitewater; Fountain City 17–14 Centerville; Morton 40–14 Fountain City. Officials: M.W. Tatlock, William Webb.

ROCHESTER: Rochester 30–15 Talma; Leiter's Ford 17–9 Grass Creek; Star City 10–7 Fulton; Winamac 19–12 Pulaski; Monterey 28–9 Richland Center; Rochester 39–11 Kewanna; Leiter's Ford 17–16 Star City; Monterey 32–15 Winamac; Rochester 27–13 Leiter's Ford; Rochester 40–7 Monterey. Officials: Carl Olson, Keith Crown.

ROYAL CENTER: Walton 29–16 Lucerne; Royal Center 33–16 Lincoln; New Waverly 31–22 Twelve Mile; Logansport 25–23 Galveston (5 minute OT); Washington Twp. 27–13 Metea; Young America 37–10 Deacon; Walton 26–23 Royal Center; Logansport 32–23 New Waverly; Young America 39–7 Washington Twp.; Logansport 25–15 Walton; Logansport 23–19 Young America. Officials: Claude Draper, George Kenzler.

RUSHVILLE: Arlington 26–17 Orphans Home; Manilla 21–14 Raleigh; Moscow 2–0 Center; Carthage 39–5 Webb; Milroy 45–23 New Salem; Rushville 45–10 Arlington; Manilla 26–24 Moscow; Milroy 30–23 Carthage; Rushville 45–18 Manilla; Rushville 44–29 Milroy. Officials: F.A. Bills, Gilbert Best.

SEYMOUR: Medora 45–12 Tampico; Cortland 29–18 Seymour; Crothersville 26–9 Clearspring; Brownstown 30–15 Vallonia; Freetown 24–12 Houston; Cortland 24–11 Medora; Brownstown 23–14 Crothersville; Freetown 28–18 Cortland; Freetown 20–18 Brownstown. Officials: Everett Babb, Stanley Morse

SHELBYVILLE: Greensburg 24–13 New Point; Moral Twp. 35–25 Jackson Twp.; Boggstown 52–22 Burney; Letts 30–22 West Point; Waldron 32–15 Sandusky; Mt. Auburn 33–21 St. Paul; Shelbyville 34–17 Geneva; Greensburg 26–24 Morristown; Moral Twp. 28–26 Boggstown; Letts 23–21 Waldron; Shelbyville 28–15 Mt. Auburn; Greensburg 26–15 Moral Twp.; Shelbyville 51–16 Letts; Shelbyville 29–24 Greensburg. Officials: Carl Porter, Ray Harrington.

SULLIVAN: Shelburn 38–20 Fairbanks; Carlisle 21–20 Dugger; Sullivan 34–15 Jackson Twp.; Graysville 27–17 Merom; New Lebanon 42–21 Farmersburg; Carlisle 23–20 Shelburn; Sullivan 31–16 Graysville; Carlisle 24–20 New Lebanon; Sullivan 30–29 Carlisle. Officials: J.H. Hendrickson, Harold Berges.

TELL CITY: Bristow 23–9 Union Twp.; Marengo 30–29 Troy; Leavenworth 23–19 Milltown; Tell City 30–14 Anderson Twp.; Bristow 20–13 Marengo; Leavenworth 35–19 Tell City; Tell City 36–15 Bristow. Officials: J.A. Mohler, G.S. Rust.

TERRE HAUTE: Garfield 13–10 Gerstmeyer; Otter Creek 18–16 Fayette; Normal 38–7 Glenn; Concannon 36–22 Blackhawk; Wiley 23–7 Prairie Creek; Pimento 20–18 West Terre Haute; Garfield 50–3 Prairieton; Normal 17–8 Otter Creek; Wiley 29–18 Concannon; Garfield 30–5 Pimento; Wiley 18–13 Normal; Garfield 23–20 Wiley. Officials: Clayton Hughes, Gilbert Rhea.

Tourney Time

VALPARAISO: Wheatfield 25–9 Chesterton; Washington Twp. 15–11 Crisman; Wheeler 28–11 DeMotte; Valparaiso 37–15 Union Twp.; Morgan Twp. 21–17 Kouts; Boone Grove 11–7 Hebron; Wheatfield 11–10 Washington Twp.; Valparaiso 37–19 Wheeler; Boone Grove 17–11 Morgan Twp.; Valparaiso 58–12 Wheatfield; Valparaiso 33–7 Boone Grove. Officials: John Kyle, Harry Warren.

VERSAILLES: Holton 22–19 Batesville; Aurora 63–9 Guilford; Rising Sun 29–24 Sunman; Dillsboro 38–16 Milan; Bright 19–12 New Alsace; Lawrenceburg 75–3 New Marion; Versailles 17–12 Moores Hill; Holton 28–4 Napoleon; Aurora 44–8 Rising Sun; Dillsboro 66–13 Bright; Lawrenceburg 28–20 Versailles; Aurora 28–12 Holton; Dillsboro 27–20 Lawrenceburg; Aurora 34–17 Dillsboro. Officials: Nate Kaufman, Ivan Zaring.

VINCENNES: Freelandville 41–12 Emison; Vincennes 70–14 Monroe City; Decker 16–1 Wheatland; Sandborn 25–16 Oaktown; Bruceville 38–22 Fritchton; Freelandville 15–12 Bicknell; Vincennes 61–13 Decker; Sandborn 23–13 Bruceville; Vincennes 67–10 Freelandville; Vincennes 66–11 Sandborn. Officials: F.K. Ferguson, Elmer Posey.

WARSAW: Atwood 21–14 Atwood; Sidney 24–20 North Webster; Milford 28–13 Leesburg; Syracuse 22–16 Claypool; Beaver Dam 16–11 Mentone; Warsaw 34–13 Silver Lake; Pierceton 40–12 Burket; Atwood 27–18 Sidney; Milford 27–16 Syracuse; Warsaw 29–10 Beaver Dam; Pierceton 21–13 Atwood; Milford 26–21 Warsaw; Milford 33–19 Pierceton. Officials: George Yarnell, O.J. Yoder.

WINCHESTER: Ridgeville 24–11 Winchester; Union City 26–21 Jackson Twp.; Parker 28–12 Losantville; Stoney Creek 27–13 McKinley; Green Twp. 20–15 Saratoga; Modoc 25–12 Huntsville; Wayne 30–24 Jefferson; Spartanburg 36–10 Farmland; Union City 23–12 Ridgeville; Stoney Creek 48–11 Parker; Modoc 18–16 Green Twp.; Spartanburg 25–18 Wayne; Stoney Creek 18–11 Union City; Spartanburg 29–14 Modoc; Stoney Creek 22–9 Spartanburg. Officials: Ralph Gilbert, O.C. York.

WINSLOW: Stendal 27–14 Otwell; Spurgeon 24–18 Petersburg; Winslow 2–0 Stendal; Winslow 30–23 Spurgeon. Officials: Carl Painter, Roy Tate.

1925 REGIONALS

Two teams from each regional qualified for the finals.

ANDERSON: New Castle 26–23 Dunkirk; Carmel 26–22 Stoney Creek; Shortridge 34–26 Greenfield; Muncie 23–21 Lapel; Carmel 26–24 New Castle; Muncie 37–19 Shortridge. Officials: Stanley Feezle, Birch Bayh, Hugh Vandivier.

BLOOMINGTON: Martinsville 40–13 Garfield; Franklin 45–30 Lyons; Washington 41–24 Bainbridge; Brazil 47–20 Sullivan; Martinsville 35–21 Franklin; Washington 38–34 Brazil. Officials: C.A. Jensen, Dale Miller, Paul Williams.

EVANSVILLE: Central 21–14 Winslow; Huntingburg 18–17 Poseyville; Owensville 56–25 New Albany; Vincennes 35–11 Tell City; Central 34–17 Huntingburg; Vincennes 38–22 Owensville. Officials: Elmer Posey, LeRoy Cook, Paul Hurley.

FORT WAYNE: Auburn 20–16 Fremont; Elkhart 32–18 South Whitley; Milford 39–19 Wawaka; Central 27–17 Lancaster; Elkhart 30–18 Auburn; Milford 29–22 Central. Officials: R.B. Mowe, Guy Ogle, James Hale.

FRANKFORT: West Point 41–21 Boswell; Wallace 23–19 Wingate; Clayton 43–26 Advance;

Frankfort 49–11 Clinton; West Point 32–16 Wallace; Frankfort 38–12 Clayton. Officials: M.J. Cleary, Ralph Esarey, John Miller.

GARY: Froebel 35–18 Brook; Plymouth 48–21 Valparaiso; Rochester 20–5 Brookston; LaPorte 35–31 Mishawaka; Froebel 45–25 Plymouth; LaPorte 33–23 Rochester. Officials: Ford Griffith, Benjamin DuBois, D.J. Arbuckle.

KOKOMO: Marion 45–23 Delphi; Huntington 22–20 Liberty Center; Kokomo 34–9 Clay Twp.; Logansport 29–20 North Manchester; Marion 50–25 Huntington; Kokomo 19–16 Logansport. Officials: Keith Crown, Carl Olson, Bert Westover.

RICHMOND: Morton 37–26 Aurora; Connersville 33–17 Deputy; Shelbyville 19–17 Columbus; Rushville 43–15 Freetown; Connersville 18–17 Morton; Rushville 26–23 Shelbyville. Officials: F.A. Bills, R.B. Morrison, Vedder Gard.

1925 FINALS—March 20, 21

INDIANAPOLIS (State Fairgrounds, Exposition Building): Vincennes 45–23 Milford; Marion 33–31 Rushville; Kokomo 34–28 Connersville; West Point 26–21 LaPorte; Washington 28–17 Carmel; Evansville Central 20–14 Elkhart; Frankfort 25–23 Gary Froebel; Muncie 26–22 Martinsville; Vincennes 29–22 Marion; Kokomo 33–29 West Point; Washington 26–15 Evansville Central; Frankfort 24–16 Muncie; Kokomo 39–29 Vin–cennes; Frankfort 30–25 Washington; Frankfort 34–20 Kokomo. Officials: Ray Mowe, Birch Bayh, Stanley Feezle, Dale Miller.

1926 SECTIONALS

ANDERSON: Pendleton 33–14 Markleville; Summitville 23–4 Elwood; Alexandria 32–20 Frankton; Lapel 27–25 Anderson; Summitville 20–19 Pendleton; Alexandria 32–28 Lapel; Summitville 28–22 Alexandria. Officials: Paul Hurley, Bennie Evans.

AUBURN: Orland 18–16 Corunna; Spencerville 31–15 Waterloo; Angola 21–15 Fremont; Garrett 26–12 Ashley; Auburn 33–11 Butler; Pleasant Lake 17–14 Orland; Angola 21–12 Spencerville; Auburn 11–10 Garrett; Angola 27–10 Pleasant Lake; Angola 29–19 Auburn. Officials: Archie Heller, Don Stephenson.

AURORA: Lawrenceburg 60–15 Guilford; Aurora 71–7 Bright; Dillsboro 31–16 New Alsace; Moores Hill 20–19 Rising Sun; Aurora 38–28 Lawrenceburg; Moores Hill 28–16 Dillsboro; Aurora 39–18 Moores Hill. Officials: H. C. Henderson; Martin Luther.

BEDFORD: Heltonville 31–9 Tunnelton; West Baden 28–24 Oolitic; Bedford 61–0 Fayetteville; Mitchell 47–6 Huron; Williams 35–14 French Lick; Orleans 43–16 Shawswick; Paoli 20–12 Needmore; West Baden 26–18 Heltonville; Bedford 21–12 Mitchell; Orleans 40–21 Williams; Paoli 16–10 West Baden; Bedford 42–22 Orleans; Bedford 48–11 Paoli. Officials: Carl Porter, John Wertz.

BLUFFTON: Liberty Center 39–16 Chester Center; Lancaster Center 22–17 Ossian; Union Center 31–29 Rockcreek Center; Bluffton 54–7 Petroleum; Liberty Center 29–18 Lancaster Center; Bluffton 27–26 Union Center; Bluffton 25–22 Liberty Center. Officials: Paul Parker, Harley Murray.

BROOK: Brook 39–14 Medaryville; Remington 33–5 Mt. Ayr; Morocco 29–7 Goodland; Kentland 19–9 Francesville; Brook 30–16 Rensselaer; Morocco 26–21 Remington; Brook 22–17

Tourney Time

Kentland; Brook 22–9 Morocco. Officials: Clarence Fauber, Edwin Miller.

CHARLOTTESVILLE: Wilkinson 28–18 Fortville; Westland 23–20 McCordsville; Charlottesville 34–15 Maxwell; Greenfield 41–7 New Palestine; Mt. Comfort 47–17 Eden; Wilkinson 28–18 Westland; Greenfield 36–20 Charlottesville; Mt. Comfort 35–19 Wilkinson; Greenfield 34–24 Mt. Comfort. Officials: W. S. Porter, Norman Wann.

CLINTON: Rockville 24–22 Cayuga; Green Twp. 38–14 Helt Twp.; Rosedale 40–14 Newport; Vinton 33–15 Bridgeton; Mecca 29–21 Perrysville; Montezuma 37–33 Tangier; Marshall 26–19 Bellmore; Bloomingdale 33–32 Rockville; Rosedale 29–10 Green Twp.; Clinton 33–18 Mecca; Montezuma 36–16 Marshall; Rosedale 28–23 Bloomingdale; Clinton 31–17 Montezuma; Rosedale 26–18 Clinton. Officials: E. R. Carman, Jerry Wakefield.

COLUMBIA CITY: Washington Center 30–10 Etna; Columbia City 49–8 Churubusco; Coesse 19–17 South Whitley; Jefferson Center 11–8 Larwill; Columbia City 28–21 Washington Center; Coesse 20–16 Jefferson Center; Columbia City 39–4 Coesse. Officials: John Bowman, Almon Gerard.

CONNERSVILLE: Connersville 85–8 Whitewater; Brookville 18–15 Laurel; Everton 25–11 Fairview; Bentonville 27–15 Alquina; Springfield 23–9 Orange; Connersville 34–16 Brookville; Bentonville 22–16 Everton; Connersville 50–9 Springfield; Connersville 45–14 Bentonville. Officials: H. B. Metcalf, E.E. Reid.

CRAWFORDSVILLE: Crawfordsville 25–24 Waynetown; Wingate 30–16 New Richmond; Waveland 26–14 Alamo; Linden 37–32 Ladoga; Bowers 31–21 Darlington; New Market 45–2 New Ross; Crawfordsville 27–20 Wingate; Linden 21–12 Waveland; Bowers 20–19 New Market; Crawfordsville 31–11 Linden; Crawfordsville 31–21 Bowers. Officials: Vaughn Russell, John Schram.

DANVILLE: Pittsboro 29–8 New Winchester; Brownsburg 27–21 Stilesville; Danville 32–25 Clayton; Amo 29–18 North Salem; Plainfield 39–20 Avon; Pittsboro 25–20 Lizton; Danville 25–19 Brownsburg; Plainfield 18–17 Amo; Pittsboro 28–21 Danville; Pittsboro 22–18 Plainfield. Officials: Gilbert Rhea, Lee Sinclair.

DECATUR: Berne 18–13 Monmouth; Jefferson Twp. 25–22 Monroe; Kirkland Twp. 19–7 Geneva; Hartford Twp. 8–6 Pleasant Mills; Berne 22–17 Decatur; Kirkland Twp. 26–11 Jefferson Twp.; Berne 31–20 Hartford Twp.; Berne 35–18 Kirkland Twp. Officials: Ford Griffith, J. R. Clark.

EAST CHICAGO: Whiting 38–13 Hammond; Hobart 23–22 Hammond Tech; Roosevelt 29–27 Crown Point; East Chicago 36–11 Lowell; Gary Emerson 28–25 Gary Froebel; Whiting 43–17 Griffith; Roosevelt 16–15 Hobart; East Chicago 26–19 Emerson; Whiting 46–6 Roosevelt; East Chicago 17–13 Whiting. Officials: H. C Warren, Benjamin DuBois.

EVANSVILLE: Poseyville 47–14 Griffin; Boonville 13–7 Lynnville; Central 60–11 Chandler; New Harmony 28–12 Yankeetown; Mt. Vernon 40–21 Tennyson; Cynthiana 61–4 Elberfeld; Reitz 36–35 Bosse; Stewartsville 19–15 Newburgh; Poseyville 33–25 Boonville; Central 38–10 New Harmony; Mt. Vernon 31–24 Cynthiana; Reitz 26–12 Stewartsville; Central 22–17 Poseyville; Reitz 34–23 Mt. Vernon; Central 40–14 Reitz. Officials: George Graham, W.E. Heller.

FLORA: Cutler 37–11 Camden; Flora 26–14 Carrollton; Burlington 51–12 Adams Twp.; Delphi 26–12 Deer Creek; Bringhurst 37–9 Rockfield; Flora 35–20 Cutler; Burlington 25–23 Delphi; Flora 40–19 Bringhurst; Flora 34–25 Burlington. Officials: C. N. Meitzler, Donald Reel.

FORT WAYNE: Central 31–5 Maumee Twp.; New Haven 28–4 Arcola; Harlan 16–9

Huntertown; Leo 17–15 Monroeville; South Side 48–18 Lafayette Twp.; Central 25–13 New Haven; Harlan 39–18 Leo; Central 62–26 Harlan; Central 32–23 South Side. Officials: D. J. Arbuckle, Guy Ogle.

FRANKFORT: Colfax 30–23 Michigantown; Rossville 35–24 Mulberry; Forest 23–20; Jefferson; Frankfort 83–5 Kirklin; Scircleville 41–14 Jackson Twp.; Rossville 29–18 Colfax; Frankfort 58–18 Forest; Rossville 26–15 Scircleville; Frankfort 57–19 Rossville. Officials: R. V. Copple, John Craigle.

FRANKLIN: Greenwood 44–23 Edinburg; Masonic Home 32–11 Jackson Twp.; Trafalgar 32–26 Union Twp.; Hopewell 28–19 Nineveh; Franklin 44–25 Clark Twp.; Center Grove 48–10 Needham; Whiteland 60–8 Van Buren Twp.; Greenwood 28–26 Masonic Home; Trafalgar 24–15 Hopewell; Franklin 33–18 Center Grove; Whiteland 33–31 Greenwood; Franklin 27–20 Trafalgar; Franklin 40–10 Whiteland. Officials: P. H. Larmore, Ray Harrington.

GOSHEN: Nappanee 44–11 Millersburg; Goshen 35–22 Middlebury; Elkhart 16–12 Washington Twp.; New Paris 16–13 Jamestown; Nappanee 47–9 Wakarusa; Goshen 24–22 Elkhart; Nappanee 29–23 New Paris; Nappanee 30–11 Goshen. Officials: Ora M. Davis, George Russell.

GREENCASTLE: Greencastle 28–12 Reelsville; Clinton Center 26–25 Belle Union; Russellville 13–12 Roachdale; Bainbridge 21–13 Fillmore; Greencastle 28–12 Cloverdale; Russellville 23–17 Clinton Center; Bainbridge 18–9 Greencastle; Bainbridge 34–18 Russellville. Officials: Winston Ashley, Orville Jones.

GREENSBURG: Scipio 16–7 Vernon; Letts 28–24 Westport; Newpoint 24–22 Sandusky; Greensburg 34–13 St. Paul; North Vernon 55–7 Burney; Jackson Twp. 43–12 Zenas; Clarksburg 33–3 San Jacinto; Scipio 49–8 Paris Crossing; Letts 40–22 Newpoint; North Vernon 29–23 Greensburg; Clarksburg 15–14 Jackson Twp.; Letts 27–26 Scipio; North Vernon 24–23 Clarksburg; North Vernon 48–24 Letts. Officials: Forrest Ragsdale, Wyatt May.

HUNTINGTON: Monument City 23–12 Banquo; Andrews 19–15 Jefferson; Bippus. 29–15 Huntington Twp.; Clear Creek 29–21 Union Center; Huntington 19–12 Roanoke; Warren 34–21 Lancaster Center; Rock Creek 22–20 Monument City; Bippus 20–17 Andrews; Huntington 18–17 Clear Creek; Warren 33–19 Rock Creek; Huntington 19–17 Bippus; Huntington 20–13 Warren. Officials: Ralph Parker, M. J. Cleary.

HYMERA: Hymera 33–12 Fairbanks; Dugger 41–22 Pleasantville; Carlisle 44–23: Shelburn; Sullivan 23–11 Merom; Farmersburg 26–24 New Lebanon; Hymera 28–23 Graysville; Dugger 23–17 Carlisle; Farmersburg 30–21 Sullivan; Dugger 24–15 Hymera; Dugger 30–23 Farmersburg. Officials: Clyde Cunningham, Jack Hannah.

INDIANAPOLIS: Manual 21–13 Castleton; Shortridge 31–27 Southport; West Newton 22–6 New Bethel; Lawrence 37–21 Oaklandon; Valley Mills 33–14 Acton; Beech Grove 24–23 Warren Central; Tech 28–20 Broad Ripple; New Augusta 24–17 Ben Davis; Shortridge 21–19 Manual; Lawrence 33–24 West Newton; Beech Grove 23–21 Valley Mills; Tech 40–13 New Augusta; Shortridge 37–14 West Newton; Tech 33–21 Beech. Grove; Shortridge 25–16 Tech. Officials: Horace Parker, L. A. Schwan. Stanley Feezle officiated Shortridge–Manual Game.

JASPER: Holland 23–19 Ireland; Winslow 40–13 Clay Twp.; Spurgeon 25–12 Birdseye; Petersburg 29–11 Otwell; Huntingburg 32–14 Jasper; Stendal 30–9 Cuzco; Winslow 39–11 Holland; Spurgeon 19–9 Petersburg; Huntingburg 29–15 Stendal; Winslow 19–18 Spurgeon; Huntingburg 23–14 Winslow. Officials: U. S. Abbott, Elder Eberhart.

Tourney Time

KENDALLVILLE: LaOtto 14–9 Wolf Lake; Wawaka 26–11 Cromwell; Kendallville 19–16 Ligonier; Albion 25–18 Rome City; LaOtto 35–6 Avilla; Kendallville 30–13 Wawaka; Albion 34–8 LaOtto; Kendallville 23–12 Albion. Officials: Dale Kreigh, Lundy Welborn.

KOKOMO: Howard Twp. 17–14 West Middleton; Clay Twp. 35–18 New London; Kokomo 75–17 Jackson Twp.; Greentown 29–16 Union Twp.; Russiaville 27–16 Howard Twp.; Kokomo 66–12 Clay Twp.; Russiaville 22–16 Greentown; Kokomo 49–15 Russiaville. Officials: J. W. Hale, J. D. Miller.

LAFAYETTE: Battle Ground 23–15 West Lafayette; Jackson Twp. 39–21 Monitor; Jefferson 30–19 Wea; Stockwell 29–6 Buck Creek; Dayton 21–15 Clarks Hill; Romney 31–14 Gladdens Corner; West Point 16–14 Montmorenci; Battle Ground 41–14 Jackson Twp.; Jefferson 24–18 Stockwell; Dayton 19–18 Romney; West Point 13–10 Battle Ground; Dayton 25–4 Jefferson; West Point 24–14 Dayton. Officials: Ross Smith, Bert Westover.

LAGRANGE: South Milford 27–7 Scott; LaGrange 28–13 Lima; Topeka 15–13 Shipshewana; Springfield Twp. 13–11 Brighton; LaGrange 16–14 South Milford; Mongo 22–18 Topeka; LaGrange 37–21 Springfield Twp. Officials: Floyd Merriman, Harry Hatcher.

LAPORTE: Westville 33–10 Springfield Twp.; Michigan City 27–15 Hanna; Wanatah 35–20 Stillwell; Union Mills 23–14 LaCrosse; Union Twp. 22–12 Rolling Prairie; LaPorte 76–9 Kingsbury; Michigan City 24–17 Westville; Wanatah 13–11 Union Mills; LaPorte 38–8 Union Twp.; Michigan City 49–9 Wanatah; LaPorte 25–21 Michigan City. Officials: William Thompson, Carl Burt.

LEBANON: Lebanon 31–5 Fishers; Zionsville 29–22 Central; Noblesville 25–9 Whitestown; Advance 19–9 Thorntown; Carmel 16–15 Westfield; Jamestown 22–19 Lebanon; Noblesville 26–18 Zionsville; Carmel 19–14 Advance; Noblesville 23–21 Jamestown; Noblesville 27–26 Carmel. Officials: John W. George, George W. Kenzler.

LYONS: Linton 59–9 Jasonville; Newberry 39–12 Marco; Switz City 25–23 Owensburg; Midland 17–15 Lyons; Linton 22–18 Newberry; Switz City 14–7 Midland; Linton 29–21 Switz City. Officials: J. H. Hendrickson, Elmer Posey.

MADISON: Vevay 18–5 North Madison; Deputy 31–11 Dupont; Patriot 18–13 Hanover; Scottsburg 36–6 Madison; Austin 25–17 Rykers Ridge; Deputy 25–21 Vevay; Patriot 16–13 Scottsburg; Deputy 27–15 Austin; Patriot 32–14 Deputy. Officials: Ivan Zaring, LaVerne Litherland.

MARION: Sweetser 28–13 Swayzee; Marion 61–12 Van Buren; Fairmount 43–21 Upland; Gas City 22–11 Matthews; Sweetser 24–20 Jonesboro; Marion 37–22 Fairmount; Gas City 17–16 Sweetser; Marion 65–19 Gas City. Officials: Will Smith, Vedder Gard.

MARTINSVILLE: Monrovia 43–24 Paragon; Smithville 29–26 Mooresville; Unionville 35–23 Stinesville; Bloomington 53–11 Ellettsville; Morgantown 31–14 Eminence; Martinsville 36–20 Monrovia; Smithville 34–19 Unionville; Bloomington 37–20 Morgantown; Martinsville 44–22 Smithville; Martinsville 25–14 Bloomington. Officials: Dale Miller, F. A. Bills.

MISHAWAKA: Walkerton 32–11 New Carlisle; Knox 35–16 North Liberty; Mishawaka 106–4 Center Twp.; Madison Twp. 38–32 Hamlet; South Bend 28–12 Lakeville; Walkerton 29–21 Knox; Mishawaka 51–3 Madison Twp.; South Bend 34–16 Walkerton; South Bend 26–25 Mishawaka. Officials: Keith Crown, Carl Olson.

MONTICELLO: Monon 28–15 Reynolds; Monticello 20–15 Idaville; Brookston 52–7 Round Grove; Wolcott 26–19 Chalmers; Monon 27–15 Burnettsville; Brookston 23–19 Monticello;

IHSAA Scores | 1920–1929

Monon 20–13 Wolcott; Monon 35–25 Brookston. Officials: Lloyd Etter, J. W. Albert.

MUNCIE: Albany 21–13 DeSoto; Muncie 54–11 Harrison; Daleville 28–18 Eaton; Cowan 33–9 Selma; Yorktown 25–23 Royerton; Center 21–18 Gaston; Muncie 35–13 Albany; Cowan 16–13 Daleville; Center 24–17 Yorktown; Muncie 31–23 Cowan; Muncie 40–9 Center. Officials: LeRoy Cook, R. B. Morrison.

NEW ALBANY: Borden 22–12 New Salisbury; Corydon 20–9 Hardinsburg; Henryville 44–8 New Middletown; New Albany 32–19 Salem; Silver Creek 20–17 Campbellsburg; Little York 31–7 Georgetown; Jeffersonville 42–7 Franklin Twp.; Corydon 49–15 Borden; New Albany 31–16 Henryville; Little York 26–16 Silver Creek; Jeffersonville 31–16 Corydon; New Albany 25–9 Little York; New Albany 22–20 Jeffersonville. Officials: E. P. Brown, M. J. Lorber.

NEW CASTLE: New Castle 47–17 Harrison Twp.; Spiceland 45–15 Mt. Summit; Middletown 24–6 Blue River Twp.; Kennard 28–15 Jefferson Twp.; New Lisbon 20–12 Straughn; New Castle 37–23 Knightstown; Spiceland 28–23 Middletown; Kennard 46–5 New Lisbon; New Castle 41–18 Spiceland; New Castle 36–17 Kennard. Officials: Vern Ruble, Harry Schoeneman.

NORTH MANCHESTER: Laketon 27–15 Roann; Chippewa 30–26 Urbana; Wabash 33–15 Lincolnville; Linlawn 34–23 Chester; North Manchester 32–14 Lagro; Laketon 39–16 Somerset; Wabash 32–15 Chippewa; North Manchester 30–19 Linlawn; Laketon 21–16 Wabash; Laketon 24–15 North Manchester. Officials: Paul Williams, Mode Cranor.

OWENSVILLE: Fort Branch 7–6 Francisco; Oakland City 31–27 Haubstadt; Hazleton 32–8 Wabash; Owensville 72–18 Patoka; Mt. Olympus 41–18 Mackey; Princeton 21–13 Ft. Branch; Oakland City 26–22 Hazleton; Owensville 44–28 Mt. Olympus; Oakland City 33–29 Princeton; Owensville 53–20 Oakland City. Officials: R. R. Miller, F. R. Hochstetler.

PERU: Bunker Hill 19–9 Butler Twp.; Amboy 41–18 Macy; Deedsville 25–18 Peru; Clay Twp. 23–19 Jefferson Twp.; Bunker Hill 19–16 Chili; Deedsville 44–27 Amboy; Clay Twp. 26–18 Bunker Hill; Deedsville 43–22 Clay Twp. Officials: L. L Mattingly, Fitzhugh Traylor.

PLYMOUTH: Bremen 34–12 Culver; Plymouth 75–4 LaPaz; Argos 32–11 West Twp.; Bourbon 27–16 North Judson; San Pierre 48–19 North Bend; Bremen 50–14 Tippecanoe; Plymouth 36–14 Argos; San Pierre 22–21 Bourbon; Plymouth 33–14 Bremen; Plymouth 62–24 San Pierre. Officials: Oris DeVol, J. B. McBride.

PORTLAND: Montpelier 35–18 Pennville; Madison Twp. 21–18 Hartford City; Portland 33–12 Jackson Twp.; Redkey 13–12 Dunkirk; Madison Twp. 19–18 Montpelier; Portland 48–10 Redkey; Portland 35–27 Madison Twp. Officials: Leslie Beall, E. C. Rowe.

RAUB: Boswell 32–10 Wadena; Oxford 33–18 Ambia; Fowler 25–23 Freeland Park; Gilboa 20–19 Raub; Otterbein 33–11 Pine Twp.; Boswell 19–14 Earl Park; Oxford 40–20 Fowler; Otterbein 38–17 Gilboa; Oxford 27–18 Boswell; Oxford 25–18 Otterbein. Officials: John R. Beasley, Earl Boyd.

RICHMOND: Centerville 38–23 Kitchel; Hagerstown 49–12 Boston; Whitewater 30–15 Cambridge; Milton 26–22 Fountain City; Williamsburg 40–18 Greensfork; Liberty 44–19 Economy; Richmond 39–18 Brownsville; Hagerstown 33–27 Centerville; Whitewater 24–23 Milton; Williamsburg 22–21 Liberty; Richmond 31–23 Hagerstown; Whitewater 25–18 Williamsburg; Richmond 37–16 Whitewater. Officials: Watson Deakyne, Guy Woods.

ROCHESTER: Akron 18–14 Winamac; Kewanna 17–14 Grass Creek; Rochester 47–9 Fulton; Leiters Ford 15–11 Richland Center; Talma 21–16 Monterey; Akron 31–19 Pulaski; Rochester 37–16 Kewanna; Leiters Ford 25–7 Talma; Rochester 30–13 Akron; Rochester 34–16

Tourney Time

Leiters Ford. Officials: O. F. Helvie, Daniel Guild.

ROYAL CENTER: Lincoln 16–14 Miami Twp.; Galveston 48–11 Deacon; Logansport 45–17 Twelve Mile; Onward 38–14 Lucerne; Young America 39–25 Washington Twp.; Walton 19–13 Royal Center; Lincoln 33–9 Metea; Logansport 40–25 Galveston; Young America 33–10 Onward; Lincoln 19–16 Walton; Logansport 35–16 Young America; Logansport 36–15 Lincoln. Officials: Claude Draper, T. R. Smith.

RUSHVILLE: Milroy 20–11 New Salem; Moscow 37–6 Glenwood; Orphans' Home 27–20 Webb; Rushville 35–15 Carthage; Manilla 25–14 Arlington; Milroy 25–14 Raleigh; Moscow 22–21 Orphans' Home; Rushville 24–14 Manilla; Milroy 26–23 Moscow; Rushville 35–15 Milroy. Officials: J. Ord Fortner, H. H. Bacon.

SEYMOUR: Freetown 28–14 Clearspring; Brownstown 26–20 Vallonia; Cortland 22–21 Crothersville; Seymour 53–11 Houston; Medora 44–20 Tampico; Freetown 27–22 Brownstown; Seymour 35–22 Cortland; Freetown 26–16 Medora; Seymour 42–30 Freetown. Officials: M.W. Tatlock, Harley Jurgens.

SHELBYVILLE: Shelbyville 24–18 Columbus; Waldron 68–3 Burnsville; Boggstown 29–17 Flat Rock; Moral 15–13 Flat Rock Twp.; Geneva 24–22 Mt. Auburn; Hawcreek Twp. 47–13 Fairland; Morristown 44–30 Cliffy Twp.; Shelbyville 33–18 Waldron; Moral 26–23 Boggstown; Hawcreek Twp. 51–11 Geneva; Shelbyville 37–21 Morristown; Moral 27–21 Hawcreek Twp.; Shelbyville 53–16 Moral. Officials: Alonzo Goldsberry, Arthur Norris.

SPENCER: Posey Twp. 35–17 Coalmont; Sugar Ridge 25–20 Gosport; Spencer 23–19 Van Buren Twp.; Clay City 39–13 Bowling Green; Brazil 42–17 Quincy; Patricksburg 26–17 Freedom; Posey Twp. 51–35 Sugar Ridge; Clay Twp. 45–11 Spencer; Brazil 47–15 Patricksburg; Clay City 32–13 Posey Twp.; Brazil 31–26 Clay City. Officials: Birch Bayh, A. E. Botkin.

TELL CITY: Union Twp. 17–11 Rockport; Anderson Twp. 24–22 Cannelton; Oriole 44–13 Gentryville; Bristow 56–12 Dale; Leavenworth 24–14 English; Tell City 35–10 Troy; Milltown 19–12 Marengo; Union Twp. 21–14 Anderson Twp.; Bristow 16–13 Oriole; Tell City 38–16 Leavenworth; Milltown 21–18 Union Twp; Bristow 21–16 Tell City; Bristow 26–20 Milltown. Officials: W.S. Fellmy, H. R. Henderson.

TERRE HAUTE: W. Terre Haute 33–15 Blackhawk; Gerstmeyer 49–5 Riley; Glenn 35–6 Prairieton; Wiley 33–15 Fayette; Garfield 17–14 Normal; Prairie Creek 20–15 Otter Creek; Honey Creek 24–10 Fontanet; Pimento 35–16 Concannon; Gerstmeyer 26–5 W. Terre Haute; Wiley 17–15 Glenn; Garfield 22–9 Prairie Creek; Pimento 22–18 Honey Creek; Gerstmeyer 20–13 Wiley; Garfield 23–14 Pimento; Garfield 23–16 Gerstmeyer. Officials: H. Kilburn Rogers, Ralph Esarey.

TIPTON: Cicero 30–13 Boxley; Prairie Twp. 20–11 Arcadia; Sharpsville 38–12 Kempton; Tipton 29–16 Goldsmith; Sheridan 27–12 Windfall; Atlanta 22–15 Walnut Grove; Cicero 27–12 Prairie Twp.; Sharpsville 35–20 Tipton; Sheridan 22–14 Atlanta; Sharpsville 32–14 Cicero; Sheridan 17–14 Sharpsville. Officials: Beryl Black, Everett Babb.

VALPARAISO: Valparaiso 45–13 Chesterton; Wheatfield 30–24 Boone Grove; Hebron 2–0 Crisman; Wheeler 57–5 Kniman; Tefft 20–10 Washington Twp.; Morgan Twp. 21–18 Kouts; Valparaiso 58–8 Fair Oaks; Hebron 25–20 Wheatfield; Wheeler 52–14 Tefft. Valparaiso 38–13 Morgan Twp.; Wheeler 29–14 Hebron; Valparaiso 29–9 Wheeler. Officials: R. R. Merrell, Harry Holt.

VEEDERSBURG: Attica 26–10 Newtown; Pine Village 23–20 Covington; Wallace 32–

15 West Lebanon; Veedersburg 25–16 Kingman; Hillsboro 21–13 Attica; Pine Village 39–20 Wallace; Hillsboro 24–20 Veedersburg; Hillsboro 31–23 Pine Village. Officials: George Vaulk, Claude Sams.

VERSAILLES: Holton 41–20 New Marion; Batesville 32–8 Napoleon; Butlerville 21–19 Versailles; Milan 48–17; Sunman; Osgood 32–24 Holton; Butlerville 17–15 Batesville; Osgood 37–16 Milan; Butlerville 21–19 Osgood. Officials: J. A. Mohler, Robert Romberger.

VINCENNES: Bruceville 29–18 Emison; Decker Chapel 24–16 Bicknell; Vincennes 38–22 Freelandville; Oaktown 19–18 Decker; Wheatland 21–13 Edwardsport; Sandborn 22–20 Fritchton; Bruceville 25–13 Monroe City; Vincennes 51–17 Decker Chapel; Oaktown 23–18 Wheatland; Bruceville 24–13 Sandborn; Vincennes 40–9 Oak–town; Vincennes 28–18 Bruceville. Officials: Charles Jensen, C.D. Martin.

WARSAW: Warsaw 32–17 Etna Green; Silver Lake 14–10 Mentone; Atwood 57–15 Burket; Syracuse 44–11 Beaver Dam; North Webster 33–20 Claypool; Pierceton 32–27 Milford; Sidney 28–17 Leesburg; Warsaw 24–18 Silver Lake; Syracuse 32–14 Atwood; North Webster 27–22 Pierceton; Warsaw 43–18 Sidney; Syracuse 32–19 North Webster; Syracuse 27–11 Warsaw. Officials: Walter Geller, Byron Deakyne.

WASHINGTON: Plainville 21–7 Epsom; Washington 60–7 Glendale; Shoals 31–15 Alfordsville; Odon 28–18 Montgomery; Raglesville 24–17 Loogootee; Plainville 47–17 Burns City; Washington 58–6 Shoals; Odon 19–11 Raglesville; Washington 36–10 Plainville; Washington 39–11 Odon. Officials: Harold Berges, G. C. Rust.

WINCHESTER: Modoc 24–22 Jackson Twp.; Green Twp. 28–24 Wayne; Parker 35–20 Losantville; Winchester 35–24 Huntsville; Jefferson 31–21 Farmland; Ridgeville 19–18 McKinley; Union City 46–29 Stoney Creek; Saratoga 17–14 Spartanburg; Green Twp. 23–18 Modoc; Winchester 29–24 Parker; Ridgeville 25–22 Jefferson; Union City 29–17 Saratoga; Winchester 28–25 Green Twp.; Ridgeville 24–23 Union City; Ridgeville 30–15 Winchester. Officials: P.M. Isenbarger, Harry Coolman.

1926 REGIONALS

BEDFORD: Bedford 27–15 New Albany; Huntingburg 24–19 Bristow; Vincennes 14–12 Washington; Evansville Central 23–22 Owensville; Bedford 48–12 Huntingburg; Central 23–15 Vincennes. Officials: Vedder Gard, Charles Jensen, Paul Hurley.

FORT WAYNE: Bluffton 37–18 Kendallville; Central 37–18 Berne; Syracuse 34–13 LaGrange; Columbia City 31–15 Angola; Central 31–19 Bluffton; Syracuse 26–17 Columbia City. Officials: B. G. DuBois, Benny Evans, Paul Williams.

GREENCASTLE: Monon 26–22 Greencastle; Hillsboro 47–30 Oxford; Frankfort 56–22 West Point; Bainbridge 38–22 Pittsboro; Hillsboro 27–23 Monon; Frankfort 48–26 Bainbridge. Officials: R. B. Morrison B.E. Bayh, John Miller.

KOKOMO: Flora 27–26 Deedsville; Logansport 28–13 Huntington; Kokomo 35–14 Portland; Marion 47–20 Laketon; Logansport 42–13 Flora; Marion 24–8 Kokomo. Officials: Keith Crown, Carl Olson, Guy Ogle.

MARTINSVILLE: Franklin 24–18 Garfield; Dugger 38–30 Brazil; Seymour 47–32 Rosedale; Martinsville 44–14 Linton; Franklin 30–21 Dugger; Martinsville 48–31 Seymour. Officials: Winston Ashley, J.W. Hale, George Graham.

Tourney Time

MUNCIE: Summitville 18–16 Shortridge; Noblesville 16–9 Sheridan; Greenfield 28–19 Muncie; New Castle 41–20 Ridgeville; Summitville 12–10 Noblesville; New Castle 38–24 Greenfield. Officials: Gilbert Best, Ralph Esarey, Dale Miller.

RUSHVILLE: North Vernon 51–23 Patriot; Rushville 22–17 Shelbyville; Connersville 28–19 Butlerville; Aurora 35–20 Richmond; North Vernon 27–21 Rushville; Aurora 31–26 Connersville. Officials: F. A. Bills, J. Hendrickson, Elmer Posey.

SOUTH BEND: LaPorte 30–27 Valparaiso; Rochester 31–21 East Chicago; Plymouth 28–18 South Bend; Nappanee 26–25 Brook; LaPorte 28–27 Rochester; Nappanee 26–24 Plymouth. Officials: D. J. Arbuckle, M.J. Cleary, Ford Griffith.

1926 FINALS—March 19, 20

INDIANAPOLIS (State Fairgrounds, Exposition Building): Logansport 33–29 LaPorte; Martinsville 50–24 Summitville; Bedford 33–22 Hillsboro; North Vernon 34–23 Syracuse; Frankfort 48–9 Aurora; Evansville Central 35–29 New Castle; Fort Wayne Central 33–26 Franklin; Marion 49–26 Nappanee; Martinsville 24–20 Logansport; Bedford 36–22 North Vernon; Evansville Central 32–25 Frankfort; Marion 51–26 Fort Wayne Central; Martinsville 28–25 Bedford; Marion 29–22 Evansville Central. Marion 30–23 Martinsville. Officials: B.E. Bayh, Keith Crown, Paul Hurley, Dale Miller.

1927 SECTIONALS

ANDERSON: Pendleton 29–10 Summitville; Anderson 45–15 Frankton; Lapel 21–18 Elwood; Markleville 23–18 Alexandria; Anderson 35–19 Pendleton; Lapel 27–21 Markleville; Anderson 17–12 Lapel. Officials: D.J. Arbuckle, Lee Sinclair.

ANGOLA: Auburn 78–7 Flint; Waterloo 36–20; Butler; Angola 33–13 Fremont; Ashley 41–14 Corunna; Spencerville 41–12 Scott; Pleasant Lake 11–8 Salem; Garrett 21–9 Orland; Hamilton 40–13 Metz; Auburn 37–16 Waterloo; Angola 50–17 Ashley; Spencerville 18–11 Pleasant Lake; Garrett 23–21 Hamilton; Auburn 29–26 Angola; Garrett 31–18 Spencerville; Auburn 35–18 Garrett. Officials: La Verne Litherland, Ervin Doty, Ward Gilbert.

BEDFORD: Bedford 46–14 Shawswick; West Baden 22–16 Paoli; Oolitic 30–20 Williams; Orleans 48–14 Huron; Heltonville 28–17 French Lick; Mitchell 27–12 Needmore; Bedford 53–8 Tunnelton; West Baden 20–16 Oolitic; Heltonville 27–13 Orleans; Bedford 48–18 Mitchell; Heltonville 28–20 West Baden; Bedford 49–19 Heltonville. Officials: Harold Metcalf, John Schram.

BLOOMINGTON: Smithville 30–19 Paragon; Bloomington 66–13 Stinesville; Monrovia 30–19 Mooresville; Martinsville 52–22 Morgantown; Eminence 24–15 Unionville; Smithville 37–9 Ellettsville; Bloomington 27–17 Monrovia; Martinsville 68–27; Eminence; Bloomington 31–8 Smithville; Martinsville 25–21 Bloomington. Officials: B.E. Bayh, Alonzo Goldsberry.

BLUFFTON: Bluffton 47–30 Union; Lancaster 42–19 Chester; Rockcreek 22–18 Petroleum; Ossian 22–9 Liberty Center; Lancaster 19–10 Bluffton; Rockcreek 31–22 Ossian; Rockcreek 33–29 Lancaster (2ot). Officials: Guy Woods, Lundy Welborn.

CLINTON: Montezuma 30–24 Marshall; Mecca 58–5 Hillsdale; Green Twp 40–17 Helt Twp; Newport 18–15 Dana; Clinton 23–19 Perrysville (ot); Cayuga 31–23 Rockville; Rosedale

35–11 Bridgton; Bloomingdale 36–26 Tangier; Montezuma 30–22 Mecca; Green Twp. 34–14 Newport; Clinton 20–17 Cayuga; Rosedale 20–15 Bloomingdale; Montezuma 44–22 Green Twp.; Clinton 17–16 Rosedale; Montezuma 21–18 Clinton. Officials: W.E. Heller, John L. Grose, Russell Newgent.

COLUMBIA CITY: Columbia City 22–20 Jefferson Center; Coesse 25–13 St. Joe; Churubusco 27–12 Washington Center; South Whitley 25–22 Larwill; Columbia City 29–12 Coesse; South Whitley 28–26 Churubusco; Columbia City 40–30 South Whitley. Officials: Dale Kreigh, Don Stephenson.

CONNERSVILLE: Springfield 22–16 Alquina; Connersville 55–14 Bentonville; Brookville 20–5 Orange; Fairview 36–26 Everton; Connersville 43–37 Springfield; Brookville 39–19 Fairview; Connersville 29–15 Brookville. Officials: Ross Smith, Henry Goett.

COVINGTON: Attica 30–16 Pine Village; Wallace 35–23 Newtown; Veedersburg 39–9 Kingman; Hillsboro 2–0 Williamsport (forfeit); Covington 27–10 West Lebanon; Attica 27–16 Wallace; Hillsboro 20–12 Veedersburg; Attica 23–15 Covington; Attica 29–15 Hillsboro. Officials: J.R. Beasley, Vaughn Russell.

CRAWFORDSVILLE: Waveland 30–21 Linden; Crawfordsville 15–14 New Market; Wingate 25–22 Darlington; Waynetown 21–20 New Richmond; Bowers 17–12 Ladoga; New Ross 36–9 Alamo; Waveland 21–17 Crawfordsville; Wingate 21–16 Waynetown; Bowers 34–16 New Ross; Wingate 31–25 Waveland; Bowers 20–10 Wingate. Officials: Orville Jones, Donald Reel.

DANVILLE: North Salem 30–10 New Winchester; Brownsburg 26–25 Pittsboro; Plainfield 41–31 Avon; Clayton 36–18 Stilesville; Amo 43–19 Lizton; Danville 24–23 North Salem; Brownsburg 26–16 Plainfield; Amo 22–15 Clayton; Brownsburg 39–34 Danville; Brownsburg 24–19 Amo. Officials: W.H. Herbst, Byron Deakyne.

DECATUR: Decatur 55–9 Pleasant Mills; Hartford Twp. 49–13 Monroe; Berne 15–13 Geneva; Kirkland 38–12 Jefferson; Decatur; 52–6 Monmouth; Berne 29–17 Hartford; Decatur 31–12 Kirkland; Decatur 42–17 Berne. Officials: J.R. Clark, Ford Griffith.

EAST CHICAGO: Roosevelt 28–20 Hammond; Emerson 38–14 Whiting; Froebel 41–8 Horace Mann; Lowell 38–21 Griffith; Hobart 51–1 Merrillville; Roosevelt 29–22 East Chicago; Emerson 26–16 Froebel; Hobart 34–13 Lowell; Emerson 37–12 Roosevelt; Emerson 32–20 Hobart. Officials: R.R. Merrell, H.C. Warren.

ELKHART: New Paris 27–23 Elkhart; Wakarusa 18–14 Middlebury; Nappanee 28–15 Goshen; Millersburg 25–20 Bristol; New Paris 27–16 Jamestown; Nappanee 30–18 Wakarusa; New Paris 31–28 Millersburg; New Paris 23–21 Nappanee. Officials: O.F. Helvie, E.C. Rowe.

EVANSVILLE: Central 22–17 Reitz; Bosse 19–15 Boonville; Poseyville 33–4 Tennyson; Yankeetown 31–4 Stewartsville; Cynthiana 32–13 New Harmony; Newburgh 23–19 Folsomville; Lynnville 14–12 Mt; Vernon; Elberfeld 27–13 Chandler; Central 25–21 Bosse; Poseyville 23–14 Yankeetown; Cynthiana 56–12 Newburgh; Elberfeld 20–18 Lynnville; Central 49–10 Poseyville; Cynthiana 44–4 Elberfeld; Central 30–26 Cynthiana. Officials: U.S. Abbott, George Graham, Elwood Adams.

FLORA: Flora 34–15 Deer Creek; Camden 16–11 Cutler; Burlington 32–18 Bringhurst; Carrollton 59–10 Adams Twp.; Delphi 50–7 Rockfield; Flora 51–18 Camden; Burlington 25–18 Carrollton; Flora 21–19 Delphi; Burlington 20–15 Flora. Officials: Lloyd Etter, Edwin Miller.

FOUNTAIN CITY: Hagerstown 25–15 Kitchel; Lynn 42–15 Webster; Richmond 37–20 Greens Fork; Liberty 38–20 Economy; Whitewater 37–31 Fountain City; Brownsville 50–37

Tourney Time

Milton; Cambridge City 53–33 Boston; Centerville 34–18 Williamsburg; Hagerstown 44–14 Lynn; Richmond 25–22 Liberty; Whitewater 35–17 Brownsville; Cambridge City 47–31 Centerville; Richmond 30–29 Hagerstown (ot); Whitewater 30–16 Cambridge City; Whitewater 29–18 Richmond. Officials: F.A. Bills, Earl Moomaw, P.M. Isenbarger.

FORT WAYNE: New Haven 29–2 Arcola; Central 63–17 Lafayette Center; Maumee Twp. 18–17 Huntertown; Harlan 38–12 Leo; New Haven 31–11 Monroeville; Central 43–18 Maumee Twp.; New Haven 16–14 Harlan; Central 44–10 New Haven. Officials: George S. Kenzler, Paul Parker.

FOWLER: Ambia 28–12 Oxford; Otterbein 27–17 Raub; Earl Park 34–14 Gilboa; Boswell 44–19 Pine Twp.; Fowler 22–19 Wadena; Freeland Park 34–20 Ambia; Earl Park 21–20 Otterbein; Boswell 42–9 Fowler; Freeland Park 21–15 Earl Park; Boswell 29–27 Freeland Park. Officials: Claude Sams, George Vaulk.

FRANKFORT: Colfax 25–17 Forest; Rossville 40–8 Mulberry; Frankfort 76–8 Kirklin; Michigantown 22–18 Scircleville; Jefferson 36–21 Jackson Twp.; Colfax 21–16 Rossville; Frankfort 43–6 Michigantown; Jefferson 36–24 Colfax; Frankfort 60–10 Jefferson. Officials: Winston Ashley, M.W. Tatlock.

FRANKLIN: Franklin 36–13 Nineveh; Whiteland 41–30 Edinburg; Union 28–13 Trafalgar; Masonic Home 24–22 Greenwood; Franklin 43–11 Clark Twp.; Union 47–9 Whiteland; Franklin 29–22 Masonic Home; Franklin 28–27 Union. Officials: Martin Luther, B.B. Evans.

GOODLAND: Rensselaer 32–7 Tefft; Remington 25–11 Fair Oaks; Brook 22–19 Morocco; Wheatfield 25–15 Hanging Grove; Kentland 41–17 Kniman; Goodland 29–19 Rensselaer; Brook 24–15 Remington; Kentland 29–11 Wheatfield; Goodland 25–20 Brook; Kentland 25–24 Goodland. Officials: Clarence Fauber, Clyde Cunningham.

GREENCASTLE: Greencastle 42–16 Russellville; Bainbridge 20–10 Roachdale; Bellmore 26–25 Belle Union; Cloverdale 36–23 Clinton Center; Putnamville 13–6 Reelsville; Greencastle 42–11 Fillmore; Bainbridge 53–14 Bellmore; Cloverdale 26–10 Putnamville; Greencastle 27–13 Bainbridge; Greencastle 32–12 Cloverdale. Officials: Vedder Gard, Raymond McClure.

GREENFIELD: New Palestine 36–13 Eden; Greenfield 24–21 McCordsville; Fortville 31–30 Mt. Comfort; Westland 46–10 Maxwell; Wilkinson 29–28 Charlottesville; Greenfield 20–19 New Palestine; Fortville 33–23 Westland; Greenfield 25–20 Wilkinson; Greenfield 28–21 Fortville. Officials: John W. George, J.W. Hale.

GREENSBURG: Jackson 20–12 Westport; Clarksburg 34–8 Paris Crossing; Greensburg 49–5 Vernon; Letts 38–20 Butlerville; Zenas 53–10 San Jacinto; New Point 59–8 Hayden; Scipio 20–14 North Vernon; St. Paul 31–13 Burney; Jackson 18–17 Clarksburg; Greensburg 36–24 Letts; New Point 32–26 Zenas; Scipio 32–12; St. Paul; Greensburg 33–23 Jackson; Scipio 27–24 New Point; Greensburg 32–13 Scipio. Officials: R.C. Frohman, Houston Meyer, Kenneth Beckner.

HUNTINGBURG: Spurgeon 36–21 Birdseye; Holland 44–14 Union; Ireland 27–12 Cuzco; Winslow 29–18 Otwell; Jasper 23–21 Petersburg; Huntingburg 48–16 Stendal; Spurgeon 23–19 Holland; Winslow 33–19 Ireland; Huntingburg 28–16 Jasper; Winslow 32–24 Spurgeon; Huntingburg 37–29 Winslow. Officials: George Leavitt, Fred Alwood.

HYMERA: Dugger 45–31 Pleasantville; Fairbanks 19–15 Merom; Sullivan 31–16 Jackson Twp.; Farmersburg 37–20 Shelburn; Carlisle 32–22 Graysville; Dugger 32–30 New Lebanon; Sullivan 39–16 Fairbanks; Carlisle 18–16 Farmersburg; Dugger 27–23 Sullivan; Carlisle 20–15 Dugger. Officials: J. Ord Fortner, D.A. Glascock.

IHSAA Scores | 1920–1929

INDIANAPOLIS: New Bethel 24–19 Castleton; Valley Mills 30–19 Lawrence; Oaklandon 20–5 Broad Ripple; Tech 18–12 Manual Training; Shortridge 30–28 New Augusta (ot); Warren Central 26–13 Ben Davis; Beech Grove 33–11 West Newton; Southport 39–15 Acton; Valley Mills 24–14 New Bethel; Tech 36–30 Oaklandon; Warren Central 20–14 Shortridge; Southport 32–7 Beech Grove; Tech 45–18 Valley Mills; Warren Central 24–17 Southport; Tech 30–14 Warren Central. Officials: C.A. Jensen, W.S. Porter, M.J. Cleary.

JEFFERSONVILLE: Morgan Twp. 24–20 New Salisbury; Hardinsburg 29–12 DePauw; New Albany 29–8 Georgetown; Jeffersonville 30–16 Campbellsburg; Franklin Twp. 22–20 Borden; Salem 19–5 Silver Creek; Corydon 41–5 Posey Twp.; Henryville 26–19 Pekin; Hardinsburg 31–8 Morgan Twp.; Jeffersonville 21–17 New Albany; Salem 42–16 Franklin Twp.; Corydon 20–19 Henryville; Jeffersonville 43–15 Hardinsburg; Salem 29–16 Corydon; Jeffersonville 17–10 Salem. Officials: R.B. Morrison, W.S. Fellmy, Nate Kaufman.

KENDALVILE: Kendallville 44–7 Orange Twp.; LaOtto 24–19 Ligonier; Wawaka 22–17 Cromwell; Albion 17–15 Wolf Lake (ot); Kendallville 31–18 LaOtto; Albion 15–8 Wawaka; Kendallville 39–7 Albion. Officials: Harry Hatcher, Archie Heller.

KOKOMO: Howard Twp. 27–24 Union Twp.; Kokomo 52–16 Greentown; Russiaville 31–12 West Middletown; Jackson Twp. 33–13 New London; Howard Twp. 26–24 Clay Twp.; Kokomo 41–23 Russiaville; Jackson Twp. 41–16 Howard Twp.; Kokomo 49–20 Jackson Twp. Officials: Orbie Branham, P.H. Larmore;

LAFAYETTE (Dayton): Romney 26–22 West Lafayette; Lafayette 25–14 Wea; Dayton 19–17 Klondike; Monitor 34–18 Buck Creek; Montmorenci 50–6 Clarks Hill; Battle Ground 23–13 West Point; Jackson 36–27 Gladdens Corner; Romney 30–15 Stockwell; Lafayette 29–20 Dayton; Montmorenci 34–8 Monitor; Battle Ground 28–14 Jackson Twp.; Lafayette 31–19 Romney; Montmorenci 22–21 Battle Ground; Montmorenci 12–10 Lafayette. Officials: Russell Cook, Bert Westover, Maurice Tudor.

LAGRANGE: LaGrange 30–14 Shipshewana; Lima 12–6 Mongo; South Milford 31–20 Scott; LaGrange 31–18 Topeka; South Milford 26–16 Lima; LaGrange 29–14 Brighton; LaGrange 26–21 South Milford. Officials: B.G. DuBois, F.V. Merriman.

LAPORTE: Union Twp. 26–18 Wanatah; Michigan City 35–18 Union Mills; Stillwell 28–9 LaCrosse; LaPorte 29–17 Hanna; Michigan City 26–10 Union Twp.; LaPorte 22–16 Stilwell; LaPorte 29–24 Michigan City. Officials: George L. Russell, Ralph Eades.

LAWRENCEBURG: Lawrenceburg 72–9 Guilford; Moores Hill 28–11 Dillsboro; Bright 26–20 Aurora; Rising Sun 41–28 New Alsace; Lawrenceburg 37–10 Moores Hill; Rising Sun 28–18 Bright; Lawrenceburg 37–21 Rising Sun. Officials: Elden T. Summers, Howard Henderson.

LINTON: Midland 22–18 Lyons; Scotland 31–12 Marco; Solsberry 39–8 Owensburg; Linton 36–11 Jasonville; Bloomfield 21–18 Switz City; Midland 30–10 Worthington; Scotland 24–20 Solsberry; Linton 30–16 Bloomfield; Midland 24–10 Scotland; Linton 28–11 Midland. Officials: H. Hendrickson, J.C. Hannah.

LOGANSPORT: Onward 30–26 Lucerne; Logansport 56–16 Walton; Royal Center 25–21 Lincoln; Washington Twp. 30–17 Galveston; Deacon 26–18 New Waverly; Young America 53–23 Metea; Logansport 61–8 Onward; Royal Center 34–17 Washington Twp.; Young America 24–17 Deacon; Logansport 43–23 Royal Center; Logansport 50–14 Young America. Officials: Claude Draper, John Miller.

MARION: Sweetser 24–19 Matthews; Fairmount 34–17 Jonesboro; Gas City 24–22 Van

Tourney Time

Buren; Upland 26–18 Swayzee; Marion 27–16 Sweetser; Fairmount 31–21 Gas City; Marion 41–26 Upland; Marion 23–22 Fairmount. Officials: Walter Geller, John Bowman.

MILFORD: Atwood 31–24 Burket; Silver Lake 26–14 Beaver Dam; Syracuse 38–25 Pierceton; Sidney 26–14 Etna Green; North Webster 26–11 Claypool; Milford 29–14 Leesburg; Warsaw 29–16 Mentone; Atwood 27–18 Silver Lake; Syracuse 34–24 Sidney; Milford 23–17 North Webster; Warsaw 33–30 Atwood (ot); Syracuse 24–19 Milford; Syracuse 26–22 Warsaw. Officials: W.M. Thompson, George Yarnelle, P.C. Rhodes.

MISHAWAKA: Lakeville 19–16 Madison Twp.; Hamlet 30–16 Center Twp.; Mishawaka 39–11 Walkerton; Knox 71–10 Grovertown; South Bend 30–11 North Liberty; Lakeville 27–25 Hamlet; Mishawaka 41–21 Knox; South Bend 46–13 Lakeville; Mishawaka 29–10 South Bend. Officials: D.D. Guild, John W. Kyle.

MONTICELLO: Monon 22–18 Burnettsville (ot); Brookston 38–14 Round Grove; Wolcott 29–9 Chalmers; Monticello 44–18 Reynolds; Idaville 25–10 Liberty Twp.; Brookston 36–21 Motion; Monticello 36–15 Walcott; Brookston 25–24 Idaville; Monticello 34–33 Brookston. Officials: E.R. Brown, Virgil Hickman.

MONTPELIER: Montpelier 37–9 Pennville; Redkey 26–19 Dunkirk; Jackson Twp. 2–0 Gray (forfeit); Hartford City 50–19 Madison Twp.; Montpelier 30–29 Portland; Jackson Twp. 37–18 Redkey; Montpelier 23–22 Hartford City; Montpelier 33–14 Jackson Twp. Officials: Guy Ogle, W.E. Deakyne.

MUNCIE: DeSoto 37–17; Royerton; Yorktown 20–15 Eaton; Center 21–10 Albany; Daleville 23–22 Cowan; Gaston 31–23 Selma; Muncie 72–12 Harrison; DeSoto 19–11 Yorktown; Center 21–19 Daleville; Muncie 28–7 Gaston; Center 21–19 DeSoto; Muncie 52–6 Center. Officials: Will Smith, H.E. Vandivier.

NEW CASTLE: Mooreland 26–14 Mt. Summit; New Castle 17–9 Spiceland; Straughn 35–13 Lewisville; Jefferson Twp. 19–11 Knightstown; Kennard 23–18 Middletown; Mooreland 27–20 Harrison Twp.; New Castle 24–18 Straughn; Kennard 42–17 Jefferson Twp.; New Castle 33–11 Mooreland; New Castle 17–10 Kennard. Officials: John Craigle, Horace Parker.

NOBLESVILLE: Cicero 19–15 Carmel; Boxley 23–19 Westfield; Arcadia 26–25 Atlanta; Noblesville 31–15 Walnut Grove; Cicero 30–17 Fishers; Arcadia 26–19 Boxley; Noblesville 26–14 Cicero; Noblesville 34–22 Arcadia. Officials: H.H. Bacon, Arthur Norris.

NORTH MANCHESTER: Chippewa 34–14 Linlawn; Lincolnville 33–27 Urbana; Somerset 26–21 Lagro; Laketon 23–17 Chester; Wabash 22–12 Roann; North Manchester 45–16 Chippewa; Somerset 23–17 Lincolnville; Laketon 25–17 Wabash; North Manchester 27–12 Somerset; North Manchester 46–19 Laketon. Officials: R.P. Chambers, Mode Cranor.

OAKLAND CITY: Wabash 18–13 Francisco; Hazleton 21–17 Ft. Branch; Oakland City 23–18 Haubstadt; Mt. Olympus 47–28 Mackey; Owensville 48–24 Patoka; Princeton 29–26 Wabash; Oakland City 38–23 Hazleton; Owensville 41–35 Mt. Olympus; Oakland City 22–20 Princeton; Owensville 24–22 Oakland City. Officials: Elder J. Eberhart, F. Russell Hochstetler.

PERU: Bunker Hill 23–8 Clay Twp.; Amboy 22–20 Converse; Deedsville 22–9 Chili; Butler Twp. 23–9 Allen Twp.; Peru 20–9 Jefferson Twp.; Bunker Hill 20–8 Amboy; Deedsville 19–17 Butler; Peru 26–17 Bunker Hill; Peru 31–19 Deedsville. Officials: Carl Burt, Carl Porter.

PLYMOUTH: San Pierre 35–15 North Judson; Tippecanoe 10–5 LaPaz; Culver 60–6 North Bend; Plymouth 18–6 Argos; Bremen 31–12 Tyner; Bourbon 16–6 West High; San Pierre 44–8 Tippecanoe; Plymouth 21–16 Culver; Bremen 17–10 Bourbon; San Pierre 33–27 Plymouth;

Bremen 21–20 San Pierre. Officials: Carl Olson, Almon Gerard.

ROCHESTER: Medaryville 28–13 Leiters Ford; Monterey 33–13 Pulaski; Kewanna 24–13 Richland Center; Akron 29–14 Francesville; Rochester 22–11 Fulton; (Star City drew a bye because of error in schedule); Winamac 35–12 Grass Creek; Medaryville 33–21 Talma; Kewanna 32–16 Monterey; Rochester 27–11 Akron; Winamac 50–15 Star City; Kewanna 34–18 Medaryville; Rochester 29–21 Winamac; Kewanna 17–16 Rochester. Officials: John B. McBride, L.I. Mattingly, R.R. Miller.

ROCKPORT: Tobinsport 37–36 Union Twp. (3 OT); Rockport 29–12 Grandview; Leavenworth 25–16 Marengo; Troy 35–20 Cannelton; Tell City 49–16 Milltown; Bristow 36–11 Anderson Twp.; Derby 25–11 Dale; Rockport 26–18 Tobinsport; Troy 29–20 Leavenworth; Tell City 37–15 Bristow; Rockport 27–14 Derby; Tell City 27–21 Troy (ot); Tell City 31–13 Rockport. Officials: V.H. Bosse, G.S. Rust.

RUSHVILLE: Webb 27–10 Center; Orphans Home 22–16 Moscow; Manilla 25–17 Carthage; New Salem 49–10 Ging; Rushville 24–19 Milroy; Arlington 38–17 Raleigh; Webb 22–13 Orphans Home; New Salem 22– 15 Manilla; Rushville 23–19 Arlington; Webb 20–17 New Salem; Rushville 22–17 Webb. Officials: E.C. Auerswald, R.V. Copple.

SCOTTSBURG: Scottsburg 31–27 Dupont; Madison 33–8 Patriot; Austin 37–13 Little York; Rykers Ridge 18–14 Deputy; North Madison 23–16 Hanover; Vevay 15–14 Scottsburg; Madison 15–14 Austin; North Madison 21–19 Rykers Ridge; Vevay 31–21 Madison; Vevay 20–19 North Madison. Officials: Roy Hunter, Vern Ruble.

SEYMOUR: Seymour 41–30 Freetown; Vallonia 32–24 Houston; Cortland 43–25 Medora; Brownstown 36–4 Crothersville; Seymour 48–21 Clearspring; Cortland 42–12 Vallonia; Seymour 34–31 Brownstown; Cortland 32–31 Seymour. Officials: Wyatt E. May, M.F. Poland.

SHELBYVILLE: Clifford 22–10 Newbern; Columbus 51–12 Boggstown; Mt. Auburn 21–19 Hope; Shelbyville 35–18 Flat Rock; Fairland 26–1 Rockcreek Twp.; Waldron 53–14 Moral; Clifford 27–21 Morristown; Columbus 52–17 Mt. Auburn; Shelbyville 55–9 Fairland; Waldron 45–25 Clifford; Shelbyville 28–22 Columbus; Waldron 20–17 Shelbyville. Officials: Horace McClain, LeRoy Cook.

SPENCER: Brazil 31–18 Van Buren; Spencer 23–14 Gosport; Cory 20–11 Freedom; Clay City 48–9 Quincy; Bowling Green 19–17 Posey Twp.; Patricksburg 33–8 Ashboro; Spencer 19–16 Brazil; Clay City 40–8 Cory; Patricksburg 30–22 Bowling Green; Spencer 25–18 Clay City; Spencer 29–23 Patricksburg. Officials: E.C. Boyd, Ralph Esarey.

TERRE HAUTE: Prairie Creek 40–9 West Terre Haute; Riley 17–9 Fayette; Wiley 22–11 Garfield; Pimento 23–5 Fontanet; Honey Creek 22–17 Concannon; Glenn 20–19 Normal (ot); Tech 34–17 Otter Creek; Prairie Creek 16–7 Blackhawk; Wiley 28–16 Riley; Pimento 31–14 Honey Creek; Tech 26–17 Glenn; Wiley 27–13 Prairie Creek; Tech 29–19 Pimento; Wiley 13–12 Tech. Officials: T.R. Smith, Lavon Carey.

TIPTON: Prairie 28–17 Zionsville; Lebanon 36–15 Thorntown; Jamestown 45–13 Kempton; Tipton 33–6 Whitestown; Windfall 35–23 Goldsmith; Sharpsville 62–13 Perry Central; Advance 25–18 Prairie; Jamestown 30–22 Lebanon; Tipton 17–11 Windfall; Sharpsville 30–28 Advance; Tipton 34–28 Jamestown; Sharpsville 31–20 Tipton. Officials: Gilbert Rhea, Harry Schoeneman.

VALPARAISO: Kouts 27–20 Hebron; Morgan Twp. 26–20 Boone Grove; Crisman 15–13 Chesterton; Valparaiso 78–9 Washington Twp.; Wheeler 31–14 Kouts; Crisman 28–13 Morgan

Tourney Time

Twp.; Valparaiso 34–22 Wheeler; Valparaiso 36–9 Crisman. Officials: Robert W. Bain, A.E. Botkin.

VERSAILLES: Milan 37–17 Napoleon; Holton 28–26 New Marion (4ot); Batesville 31–28 Versailles; Sunman 23–22 Osgood (ot); Holton 21–16 Milan; Batesville 31–20 Sunman; Batesville 25–13 Holton. Officials: Ivan Zaring, Russell Pickett.

VINCENNES: Freelandville 44–6 Vincennes Twp.; Bicknell 24–16 Emison; Vincennes 36–20 Fritchton; Monroe City 42–12 Westphalia; Wheatland 21–10 Oaktown; Edwardsport 29–20 Sandborn; Bruceville 33–18 Decker; Freelandville; Bruceville 34–18 Monroe City; Vincennes 38–12 Bruceville; 29–7 Wheatland; Bruceville 26–17 Edwardsport; Vincennes 32–19 Freelandville; Bruceville 34–18 Monroe City; Vincennes 38–12 Bruceville. Officials: Elmer Posey, H. Kilburn Rogers, George Seidensticker.

WARREN: Roanoke 34–31 Polk Twp.; Huntington 27–20 Union Twp.; Rock Creek 17–15 Lancaster Center; Warren 24–21 Jefferson Twp.; Clear Creek 35–15 Andrews; Bippus 12–11 Huntington Twp.; Banquo 47–13 Markle; Huntington 45–16 Roanoke; Rock Creek 26–10 Warren; Clear Creek 30–15 Bippus; Huntington 46–16 Banquo; Clear Creek 26–16 Rock Creek; Clear Creek 28–25 Huntington. Officials: Ralph Parker, Fitzhugh Traylor.

WASHINGTON: Shoals 21–14 Raglesville; Washington 62–6 Glendale; Epsom 49–2 Trinity Springs; Elnora 23–20 Plainville; Alfordsville 38–15 Burns City; Loogootee 22–21 Barr Twp.; Odon 30–18 Shoals; Washington 46–8 Epsom; Elnora 41–17 Alfordsville; Odon 29–19 Loogootee; Washington 49–4 Elnora; Washington 40–13 Odon. Officials: Leo Quillen, C.D. Manhart.

WINCHESTER: Losantville 36–24 Winchester; Saratoga 20–12 Green; Jefferson 25–21 Spartanburg; Stoney Creek 46–25 Farmland; Union City 76–21 Wayne; Jackson 22–17 Modoc; Huntsville 30–28 McKinley; Ridgeville 26–24 Parker; Losantville 28–26 Saratoga; Stoney Creek 38–23 Jefferson; Union City 31–16 Jackson; Ridgeville 31–20 Huntsville; Stoney Creek 26–24 Losantville; Union City 23–19 Ridgeville; Union City 29–17 Stoney Creek. Officials: Harry Coolman, Norman G. Wann, Merle Swanger

1927 REGIONALS

Each regional winner qualified for the finals.

ANDERSON: Sharpsville 20–12 Noblesville; Tech 28–17 Anderson; Sharpsville 31–22 Tech. Officials: J.H. Hendrickson, R.B. Mowe.

AUBURN: Kendallville 26–21 Syracuse; Auburn 27–17 LaGrange; Kendallville 28–15 Auburn. Officials: Carl Olson, Keith Crown.

BEDFORD: Jeffersonville 28–19 Vevay; Bedford 38–11 Cortland; Bedford 59–12 Jeffersonville. Officials: Elmer Posey, Orville Jones.

COLUMBUS: Greensburg 34–22 Batesville; Waldron 21–19 Valparaiso; Waldron 34–25 Greensburg. Officials: R.B. Morrison, Dale Miller.

EAST CHICAGO: LaPorte 45–29 Kentland; Emerson 31–16 Valparaiso; Emerson 30–19 LaPorte. Officials: Gilbert Best, Mode Cranor.

EVANSVILLE: Central 31–19 Tell City; Huntingburg 34–21 Owensville; Central 45–20 Huntingburg. Officials: B.E. Bayh, Ralph Esarey.

FORT WAYNE: Central 21–12 Decatur; Columbia City 20–19 Rockcreek; Central 34–17

Columbia City. Officials: Hugh Vandivier, Benjamin DuBois.

FRANKFORT: Frankfort 42–16 Boswell; Montmorenci 27–22 Monticello; Frankfort 29–11 Montmorenci. Officials: J.W. Hale, Donald Reel.

GREENCASTLE: Greencastle 30–28 Attica; Bowers 23–19 Montezuma; Greencastle 24–15 Bowers. Officials: C.A. Jensen, George Graham.

KOKOMO: Marion 22–15 Montpelier; Kokomo 38–27 Burlington; Kokomo 26–19 Marion. Officials: Winston Ashley, Bert Westover.

LOGANSPORT: Logansport 48–15 Peru; Clear Creek 26–24 North Manchester; Logansport 52–11 Clear Creek. Officials: W.E. Deakyne, B.B. Evans.

MARTINSVILLE: Martinsville 39–14 Brownsburg; Spencer 24–17 Wiley; Martinsville 40–12 Spencer. Officials: F.A. Bills, John Miller.

MUNCIE: Muncie 48–22 Union City; New Castle 31–23 Greenfield; Muncie 24–18 New Castle. Officials: M.J. Cleary, F.R. Gorman.

RUSHVILLE: Connersville 34–14 Lawrenceburg; Whitewater 25–22 Rushville; Connersville 36–14 Whitewater. Officials: Vedder Gard, Guy Woods.

SOUTH BEND: Mishawaka 26–15 New Paris; Kewanna 24–17 Bremen; Misha–waka 38–15 Kewanna. Officials: Ford Griffith, Don Arbuckle.

VINCENNES: Washington 16–6 Linton; Vincennes 44–18 Carlisle; Washington 10–9 Vincennes. Officials: P.O. Hurley, Vaughn Russell.

1927 FINALS—March 18, 19

INDIANAPOLIS (State Fairgrounds, Exposition Building): Bedford 26–25 Evansville Central; Fort Wayne Central 22–19 Washington; Muncie 29–22 Sharpsville; Kendallville 22–19 Greencastle; Frankfort 37–31 Waldron; Connersville 34–27 Kokomo; Gary Emerson 28–21 Mishawaka; Martinsville 27–14 Logansport; Bedford 30–24 Fort Wayne Central; Muncie 44–28 Kendallville; Connersville 31–22 Frankfort; Martinsville 26–14 Gary Emerson; Muncie 25–21 Bedford; Martinsville 32–21 Connersville; Martinsville 26–23 Muncie. Officials: Dale Miller. B.E. Bayh, Ford Griffith, Ray Mowe.

1928 SECTIONALS

ANDERSON: Anderson 34–11 Lapel; Frankton 33–19 Summitville; Alexandria 29–21 Pendleton; Elwood 30–25 Markleville; Anderson 35–19 Frankton; Elwood 30–14 Alexandria; Anderson 29–17 Elwood. Officials: B.B. Evans, Winston Ashley.

ANGOLA: Salem Twp. 22–13 Scott Twp.; Angola 49–36 Orland; Pleasant Lake 15–12 Hamilton; Fremont 2–0 Flint (forfeit); Angola 104–21 Salem Twp.; Pleasant Lake 27–20 Fremont; Angola 35–21 Pleasant Lake. Officials: Ora M. Davis, Laverne Litherland.

AURORA: Aurora 41–17 Dillsboro; Whitewater 19–13 New Alsace; Bright 36–14 Rising Sun; Lawrenceburg 51–18 Springfield Twp.; Aurora 34–10 Whitewater; Lawrenceburg 22–18 Bright; Lawrenceburg 23–13 Aurora. Officials: J.A. Mohler, Russell Pickett.

BEDFORD: Paoli 56–9 Fayetteville; French Lick 28–24 Orleans; Heltonville 30–29 Williams; West Baden 12–11 Needmore; Shawswick 41–15 Tunnelton; Oolitic 47–26 Campbellsburg; Bedford 28–25 Mitchell; French Lick 23–22 Paoli; Heltonville 22–15 West Baden; Shawswick

Tourney Time

35–17 Oolitic; Bedford 57–10 French Lick; Heltonville 18–17 Shawswick; Bedford 49–11 Heltonville. Officials: John Schram, Harold Metcalf.

BLOOMFIELD: Bloomfield 32–29 Switz City; Solsberry 43–19 Lyons; Jasonville 34–16 Worthington; Linton 35–19 Scotland; Bloomfield 25–23 Solsberry; Linton 27–10 Jasonville; Bloomfield 31–28 Linton. Officials: J. Ord Fortner, Ivan Zaring.

BLUFFTON: Union Center 28–19 Ossian; Lancaster 72Center 23–22 Liberty Center; Rockcreek 38–25 Chester Center; Bluffton 24–12 Petroleum; Union Center 22–10 Lancaster; Bluffton 28–25 Rockcreek; Bluffton 25–21 Union Center. Officials: Norman Wann, Virgil Hickman.

CANNELTON: Milltown 18–16 Tobinsport; Tell City 35–17 English; Derby 37–13 Union; Marengo 17–11 Anderson Twp.; Troy 28–16 Rockport; Oil Twp. 26–17 Luce Twp.; Bristow 29–13 Cannelton; Dale 21–16 Leavenworth; Tell City 27–18 Milltown; Derby 27–8 Marengo; Troy 38–21 Oil Twp.; Bristow 25–13 Dale; Derby 23–21 Tell City; Bristow 25–18 Troy; Bristow 19–11 Derby. Officials: Harley Jurgens, Leonard Mayhugh.

CLINTON: Green Twp. 27–24 Bloomingdale; Newport 44–21 Bridgeton; Montezuma 46–17 Dana; Clinton 50–8 Marshall; Rosedale 23–20 Cayuga; Perrysville 33–13 Tangier; Rockville 44–17 Hillsdale; Mecca 26–24 Green Twp.; Montezuma 25–19 Newport; Clinton 35–22 Rosedale; Rockville 22–21 Perrysville; Montezuma 44–18 Mecca; Clinton 36–20 Rockville; Clinton 34–28 Montezuma. Officials: J.C. Hannah, C.A. Jensen.

CONNERSVILLE: Brookville 18–9 Alquina; Liberty 22–11 Brownsville; Orange 27–16 Fairview; Connersville 33–15 Kitchel; Bentonville 37–20 Everton; Brookville 18–9 Laurel; Orange 25–17 Liberty; Connersville 23–15 Bentonville; Brookville 19–16 Orange; Connersville 44–10 Brookville. Officials: Leroy Cook, Henry Goett.

CRAWFORDSVILLE: Crawfordsville 38–17 New Richmond; Waynetown 23–20 Bowers; Wingate 29–11 Waveland; New Ross 22–18 Alamo; New Market 55–13 Ladoga; Linden 19–14 Darlington; Crawfordsville 22–7 Waynetown; Wingate 20–14 New Ross; New Market 39–23 Linden; Crawfordsville 37–15 Wingate; Crawfordsville 44–23 New Market. Officials: R.B. Morrison, Glen Stanbaugh.

DANVILLE: Avon 36–18 Plainfield; New Winchester 20–19 Clayton; Pittsboro 38–12 North Salem; Amo 26–25 Lizton; Brownsburg 26–20 Danville; Avon 32–19 Stilesville; Pittsboro 39–16 New Winchester; Amo 19–15 Brownsburg; Pittsboro 33–23 Avon; Amo 27–25 Pittsboro. Officials: John W. George, Dillon Geiger.

DECATUR: Monmouth 21–15 Jefferson Twp.; Geneva 27–12 Monroe; Kirkland Twp. 24–19 Berne; Hartford Twp. 25–20 Decatur; Geneva 18–10 Monmouth; Kirkland Twp. 36–30 Hartford Twp.; Kirkland Twp. 30–19 Geneva. Officials: Dale Kreigh, J.R. Clark.

EVANSVILLE: Griffin 44–14 Millersburg; Chandler 26–10 Yankeetown; Lynnville 41–22 Tennyson; Stewartsville 18–14 Poseyville; Central 26–6 Folsomville; Bosse 29–17 Mt. Vernon; Boonville 20–7 Newburgh; New Harmony 32–21 Elberfeld; Griffin 38–19 Chandler; Lynnville 18–7 Stewartsville; Central 18–5 Bosse; New. Harmony 28–19 Boonville; Lynnville 19–17 Griffin; Central 29–7 New Harmony; Central 25–7 Lynnville. Officials: George Graham, Donald Wilder.

FLORA: Delphi 34–25 Flora; Deer Creek 16–10 Cutler; Carrollton 32–20 Camden; Burlington 38–16 Rockfield; Delphi 30–17 Deer Creek; Burlington 24–11 Carrollton; Delphi 22–18 Burlington. Officials: T.R. Smith, Red Hughes.

IHSAA Scores | 1920–1929

FORT WAYNE: Lafayette Center 23–21 Woodburn; Huntertown 34–12 Madison Twp.; Harlan 26–19 Arcola; North Side 49–24 Monroeville; South Side 73–7 Leo; Central 27–13 New Haven; Lafayette Center 32–18 Huntertown; North Side 52–16 Harlan; Central 21–17 South Side; North Side 17–15 Lafayette Center; Central 28–11 North Side. Officials: Ralph Parker, Harry Warren.

FOWLER: Gilboa 32–21 Earl Park; Fowler 20–14 Oxford; Otterbein 30–29 Raub; Ambia 32–16 Pine; Freeland 44–17 Wadena; Boswell 37–10 Gilboa; Otterbein 17–12 Fowler; Ambia 20–12 Freeland; Boswell 38–6 Otterbein; Boswell 21–20 Ambia. Officials: Lee Sinclair, George Vaulk.

FRANKFORT: Scircleville 16–15 Forest; Jackson Twp. 33–32 Rossville; Jefferson 34–11 Sugar Creek Twp.; Frankfort 57–21 Mulberry; Colfax 28–27 Michigantown; Scircleville 30–4 Kirklin; Jefferson 37–19 Jackson Twp.; Frankfort 25–15 Colfax; Jefferson 31–20 Scircleville; Frankfort 55–13 Jefferson. Officials: Houston Meyer, Horace Parker.

FRANKLIN: Center Grove 26–24 Nineveh; Edinburg 61–9 Nashville; Greenwood 32–22 Union Twp.; Clark Twp. 36–14 Trafalgar; Masonic Home 25–20 Whiteland; Franklin 40–16 Hopewell; Center Grove 36–7 Jackson Twp.; Greenwood 29–27 Edinburg; Clark Twp. 29–28 Masonic Home; Franklin 37–19 Center Grove; Greenwood 34–26 Clark Twp.; Franklin 43–14 Greenwood. Officials: George Seidensticker, Martin Luther.

GARRETT: Butler 35–25 Waterloo; Columbia City 34–19 Washington Center; Spencerville 33–29 Coesse; St. Joe 33–13 South Whitley; Larwill 43–28 Churubusco; Corunna 2–0 Etna Twp. (forfeit); Auburn 17–15 Garrett; Ashley 27–8 Jefferson Center; Butler 20–17 Columbia City; Spencerville 17–11 St. Joe; Larwill 40–10 Corunna; Auburn 1.8–16 Ashley; Butler 22–9 Spencerville; Auburn 31–23 Larwill; Auburn 27–26 Butler. Officials: Don Stephenson, George Yarnelle.

GARY: Emerson 64–3 Merrillville; Horace Mann 29–16 Whiting; East Chicago Washington 82–2; Calumet Twp.; Hobart 41–21 Hammond Tech; East Chicago Roosevelt 30–19 Griffith; Hammond 35–4 Lowell; Froebel 28–6 Crown Point; Emerson 26–16 Horace Mann; Washington 34–15 Hobart; Hammond 21–19 Roosevelt; Froebel 15–12 Emerson; Washington 31–16 Hammond; Washington 20–12 Froebel. Officials: John Stahr, P.M. Isenbarger.

GOSHEN: Bristol 20–19 New Paris; Nappanee 40–15 Middlebury; Elkhart 30–9 Baugo Twp.; Wakarusa 18–17 Millersburg; Goshen 35–13 Bristol; Elkhart 19–18 Nappanee; Goshen 39–10 Wakarusa; Goshen 22–12 Elkhart. Officials: Carl Olson, George Russell.

GREENCASTLE: Roachdale 50–21 Reelsville; Russellville 58–9 Clinton Center; Belle Union 41–15 Putnamville; Cloverdale 30–20 Bellmore; Greencastle 23–20 Bainbridge; Roachdale 34–32 Fillmore; Russellville 36–23 Belle Union; Greencastle 29–16 Cloverdale; Russellville 44–22 Roachdale; Greencastle 28–19 Russellville. Officials: D. D. Guild, Alonzo Goldsberry.

GREENFIELD: Mt. Comfort 54–18 Eden; Fortville 23–18 Maxwell; Charlottesville 29–14 McCordsville; Greenfield 38–17 Westland; Wilkinson 24–22 New Palestine; Mt. Comfort 31–21 Fortville; Greenfield 22–15 Charlottesville; Mt. Comfort 36–31 Wilkinson; Mt. Comfort 33–22 Greenfield. Officials: W.E. Heller, Will Smith.

GREENSBURG: Greensburg 57–16 Paris Crossing; St. Paul 22–17 North Vernon; New Point 29–13 Hayden; Westport 54–12 Sandusky; Butlerville 38–17 Letts; Scipio 32–21 Clarksburg; Burney 46–8 Zenas; Vernon 34–15 San Jacinto; Greensburg 33–11 St. Paul; Westport 29–24 New Point; Scipio 24–23 Butlerville; Burney 36–18 Vernon; Westport 27–25 Greensburg; Scipio

Tourney Time

22–18 Burney; Scipio 31–18 Westport. Officials: F.A. Bills, Ray Frohman.

INDIANAPOLIS: New Bethel 17–12 Castleton; Valley Mills 34–23 West Newton; Manual 23–20 Washington; Warren 20–17 Oaklandon; Broad Ripple 30–25 Ben Davis; Tech 40–16 Lawrence; Southport 34–14 New Augusta; Shortridge 40–12 Acton; New Bethel 33–23 Valley Mills; Warren 27–19 Manual; Broad Ripple 14–13 Tech; Southport 25–12 Shortridge; Warren 29–18 New Bethel; Broad Ripple 22–11 Southport; Broad Ripple 21–19 Warren. Officials: Vaughn Russell, Harry Conover.

KENDALLVILLE: Wawaka 33–15 Ligonier; Cromwell 46–14 Orange Twp.; Albion 65–13 Avilla; Wolf Lake 29–21 LaOtto; Kendallville 54–12 Wawaka; Albion 32–25 Cromwell; Kendallville 42–21 Wolf Lake; Kendallville 27–10 Albion. Officials: B.G. DuBois, E.C. Rowe.

KOKOMO: Greentown 29–20 Prairie Twp.; New London 33–21 Union Twp.; Sharpsville 49–25 Jackson Twp.; Clay Twp. 23–11 Ervin Twp.; Kokomo 31–26 Windfall; Russiaville 23–19 West Middleton; Greentown 37–26 Howard Twp.; Sharpsville 46–19 New London; Kokomo 40–14 Clay Twp.; Russiaville 19–18 Greentown; Sharpsville 20–18 Kokomo; Sharpsville 35–22 Russiaville. Officials: Claude Draper, Vedder Gard.

LAFAYETTE: Romney 21–15 Wea; Klondike 28–19 Montmorenci; Jefferson 26–11 Clarks Hill; West Point 31–21 Jackson Twp.; Dayton 29–12 Monitor; W. Lafayette 32–30 Battle Ground (ot); Buck Creek 25–15 Stockwell; Romney 40–22 Klondike; Jefferson 38–13 West Point; Dayton 27–20 W. Lafayette; Romney 25–19 Buck Creek; Jefferson 32–7 Dayton; Jefferson 26–16 Romney. Officials: Russell Cook, Ralph Eades.

LAGRANGE: Shipshewana 32–25 Scott; LaGrange 39–21 Springfield Twp.; South Milford 23–20 Brighton; Lima 41–27 Topeka; Shipshewana 31–24 Wolcottville; LaGrange 32–22 South Milford; Shipshewana 15–14 Lima; LaGrange 30–19 Shipshewana. Officials: Clifford Risk, George Allesee.

LAPORTE: Union Twp. 21–19 Stillwell; LaPorte 50–14 Union Mills; Westville 29–24 Rolling Prairie; LaCrosse 21–4 Mill Creek; Michigan City 31–19 Hanna; LaPorte 33–14 Union Twp.; Westville 38–7 LaCrosse; LaPorte 20–17 Michigan City; LaPorte 29–14 Westville. Officials: R.P. Chambers, Clayton Hughes.

LEBANON: Zionsville 36–34 Jamestown; Goldsmith 30–26 Whitestown; Advance 26–24 Thorntown; Tipton 53–16 Central; Lebanon 48–22 Kempton; Zionsville 29–24 Goldsmith; Tipton 19–17 Advance; Lebanon 27–17 Zionsville; Tipton 23–18 Lebanon. Officials: Byron Deakyne, Arthur Norris.

LOGANSPORT: Galveston 21–12 Lucerne; Onward 21–14 Deacon; Twelve Mile 44–16 Metea; New Waverley 26–22 Lincoln; Royal Center 49–16 Washington Twp.; Logansport 37–11 Walton; Young America 24–19 Galveston; Twelve Mile 27–18 Onward; Royal Center 30–28 New Waverly; Logansport 41–10 Young America; Twelve Mile 20–19 Royal Center; Logansport 36–9 Twelve Mile. Officials: John Miller, Don Arbuckle.

MADISON: Austin 26–19 Vevay; Madison 25–16 Central; Deputy 29–10 Hanover; Dupont 13–11 N. Madison; Scottsburg 67–5 Saluda; Austin 33–30 Madison; Dupont 23–20 Deputy; Austin 33–16 Scottsburg; Austin 24–17 Dupont. Officials: Howard Henderson, Roy Hunter.

MARION: Fairmount 60–10 Van Buren; Marion 30–21 Matthews; Jonesboro 23–21 Upland; Gas City 26–18 Swayzee; Fairmount 21–16 Sweetser; Marion 34–21 Jonesboro; Gas City 18–16 Fairmount; Marion 28–12 Gas City. Officials: Dale Miller, Gordon Wise.

MARTINSVILLE: Mooresville 39–12 Ellettsville; Martinsville 56–20 Morgantown;

IHSAA Scores | 1920–1929

Bloomington 38–19 Smithville; Paragon 31–30 Monrovia; Unionville 19–18 Stinesville; Mooresville 36–29 Eminence; Martinsville 28–21 Bloomington; Paragon 39–20 Unionville; Martinsville 43–16 Mooresville; Martinsville 55–20 Paragon. Officials: W.H. Herbst, Paul Hurley.

MISHAWAKA: Mishawaka 21–8 South Bend; Bremen 16–12 West Twp.; Walkerton 43–11 Madison Twp.; Tyner 22–21 LaPaz; Plymouth 45–6 North Liberty; Lakeville 22–20 New Carlisle; Mishawaka 28–15 Bremen; Walkerton 46–13 Tyner; Plymouth 29–15 Lakeville; Mishawaka 37–24 Walkerton; Mishawaka 34–20 Plymouth. Officials: F.V. Merriman, Joe D. Wilt.

MONON: Brookston 40–13 Burnettsville; Wolcott 27–22 Reynolds; Round Grove 19–14 Liberty Twp.; Idaville 16–12 Chalmers; Monon 22–12 Monticello; Brookston 21–20 Wolcott; Round Grove 26–22 Idaville; Monon 34–25 Brookston; Monon 40–27 Round Grove. Officials: Claude Sams, George Kenzler.

MUNCIE: Muncie 69–16 Cowan; Eaton 95–2 Lincoln; Albany 23–20 Harrison; Gaston 36–32 DeSoto; Daleville 39–14 Center; Royerton 22–14 Selma; Muncie 51–19 Yorktown; Eaton 40–13 Albany; Gaston 18–16 Daleville; Muncie 33–11 Royerton; Eaton 43–18 Gaston; Muncie 35–14 Eaton. Officials: Walter Geller, W.S. Porter.

NEW ALBANY: New Albany 47–6 Borden; Henryville 23–20 Silver Creek (ot); Pekin 24–16 Hardinsburg (ot); Salem 39–18 Georgetown; Palmyra 29–17 Franklin Twp.; Charlestown 28–24 New Salisbury; Jeffersonville 64–19 Elizabeth; Corydon 56–8 DePauw; New Albany 58—14 Henryville; Salem 27–13 Pekin; Charlestown 31–26 Palmyra; Jeffersonville 31–22 Corydon; Salem 31–16 New Albany; Jeffersonville 58–36 Charlestown; Salem 27–19 Jeffersonville. Officials: U.S. Abbott, Kenneth Beckner.

NEW CASTLE: New Castle 37–13 Mooreland; Harrison Twp. 38–15 Lewisville; Straughn 30–7 New Lisbon; Middletown 24–13 Knightstown; Spiceland 38–10 Mt. Summit; Jefferson Twp. 21–16 Kennard; New Castle 55–15 Harrison Twp.; Middletown 25–20 Straughn; Spiceland 10–6 Jefferson Twp.; New Castle 15–13 Middletown; New Castle 18–16 Spiceland. Officials: Earl Moomaw, Leo Quillen.

NOBLESVILLE: Noblesville 28–18 Atlanta; Westfield 32–13 Fishers; Cicero 31–7 Walnut Grove; Carmel 18–16 Boxley; Noblesville 24–20 Arcadia; Cicero 31–19 Westfield; Noblesville 17–14 Carmel; Cicero 18–13 Noblesville. Officials: Lavon Carey, Watson Deakyne.

PERU: Mexico 20–14 Butler Twp.; Deedsville 26–14 Gilead; Peru 27–18 Converse; Clay Twp. 21–20 Macy; Chili 18–16 Bunker Hill; Mexico 26–22 Deedsville; Peru 26–10 Clay Twp.; Mexico 22–20 Chili; Peru 27–7 Mexico. Officials: Orbie Branham, Harry Coolman.

PETERSBURG: Winslow 37–15 Cuzco; Otwell 47–5 DuBois; Holland 19–16 Stendal; Huntingburg 26–19 Clay Twp.; Spurgeon 24–9 Birdseye; Petersburg 28–22 Ireland; Winslow 13–12 Jasper (ot); Holland 26–13 Otwell; Spurgeon 18–16 Huntingburg; Petersburg 18–15 Winslow; Spurgeon 23–22 Holland; Spurgeon 24–15 Petersburg. Officials: Fred Alwood, Elder Eberhart.

PORTLAND: Bryant 22–19 Poling; Montpelier 25–7 Redkey; Roll 32–14 Pennville; Portland 18–17 Hartford City; Madison 38–16 Gray; Dunkirk 25–22 Bryant; Roll 27–18 Montpelier; Madison 30–25 Portland; Dunkirk 28–18 Roll; Dunkirk 25–21 Madison. Officials: Mode Cranor, Ervin Doty.

PRINCETON: Patoka 28–17 Branch; Francisco 27–24 Haubstadt; Princeton 34–24 Cynthiana; Mt. Olympus 40–21 Hazleton; Patoka 22–20 Owensville; Princeton 36–16 Francisco; Mt. Olympus

Tourney Time

36–29 Patoka; Princeton 31–29 Mt. Olympus. Officials: G.S. Rust , Kilburn Rogers.

REMINGTON: Tefft 22–18 Wheatfield; Goodland 24–21 Rensselaer; Kniman 30–22 Hanging Grove; Fair Oaks 31–11 DeMotte; Brook 27–15 Kentland; Remington 28–25 Morocco (ot); Goodland 71–14 Tefft; Fair Oaks 27–7 Kniman; Remington 21–20 Brook; Goodland 22–10 Fair Oaks; Goodland 28–26 Remington (2ot). Officials: J.B. McBride, Earl Pike.

RICHMOND: Boston 51–8 Webster; Richmond 24–19 Williamsburg; Hagerstown 39–22 Milton; Whitewater 17–16 Greensfork; Centerville 17–16 Economy; Cambridge City 28–20 Fountain City; Richmond 26–12 Boston; Hagerstown 24–22 Whitewater; Cambridge City 20–12 Centerville; Hagerstown 20–18 Richmond; Hagerstown 30–29 Cambridge City (ot). Officials: Ross Smith, Guy Woods.

ROCHESTER: Grass Creek 34–7 Tippecanoe; Fulton 24–14 Bourbon; Culver 19–18 Richland Center; Kewanna 36–18 Argos; Rochester 44–7 Leiters Ford; Akron 23–14 Talma; Fulton 35–16 Grass Creek; Kewanna 22–15 Culver; Rochester 36–21 Akron; Fulton 30–27 Kewanna; Rochester 32–16 Fulton. Officials: O.F. Helvie, Carl Porter.

RUSHVILLE: Orphans Home 24–17 Arlington; Milroy 35–16 Webb; Rushville 39–19 New Salem; Center 18–15 Gings; Moscow 32–26 Manilla; Carthage 36–23 Raleigh; Milroy 31–18 Orphans Home; Rushville 58–8 Center; Moscow 22–19 Carthage; Rushville 44–28 Milroy; Rushville 38–19 Moscow. Officials: Gilbert Rhea, Norman Durham.

SEYMOUR: Little York 31–22 Crothersville; Vallonia 35–21 Medora; Tampico 39–12 Houston; Seymour 40–15 Cortland; Freetown 37–26 Clearspring; Brownstown 26–20 Little York; Tampico 23–15 Vallonia; Seymour 34–15 Freetown; Brownstown 23–21 Tampico; Seymour 33–8 Brownstown. Officials: Nate Kaufman, Vern Ruble.

SHELBYVILLE: Columbus 56–22 Waldron; Flat Rock 19–18 Shelbyville; Morristown 49–20 Flat Rock Twp.; Hope 26–17 Mt. Auburn; Moral 20–15 Fairland; Columbus 26–8 Boggstown; Flat Rock 20–19 Morristown; Moral 37–30 Hope; Columbus 34–21 Flat Rock; Columbus 60–23 Moral. Officials: Harry Schoeneman, Gerhard Schumacher.

SPENCER: Van Buren 42–14 Posey Twp.; Clay City 24–18 Gosport; Brazil 44–16 Sugar Ridge; Spencer 33–14 Freedom; Patricksburg 24–23 Cory; Quincy 21–15 Bowling Green; Clay City 30–28 Van Buren; Brazil 24–15 Spencer; Patricksburg 24–14 Quincy; Brazil 30–17 Clay City; Brazil 34–8 Patricksburg. Officials: Ralph Esarey, Loyal Duncan.

SULLIVAN: Sullivan 28–16 Fairbanks; Graysville 29–13 New Lebanon; Dugger 36–19 Merom; Pleasantville 18–12 Hymera; Carlisle 28–20 Sullivan; Graysville 27–25 Dugger; Carlisle 25–10 Pleasantville; Carlisle 27–25 Graysville (ot). Officials: Orville Jones, Wyatt May.

TERRE HAUTE: Wiley 21–17 Glenn; Gerstmeyer 19–13 Prairie Creek; Garfield 20–16 Riley; Otter Creek 19–13 Normal; W. Terre Haute 31–15 Fontanet; Honey Creek 20–14 Pimento; Blackhawk 13–8 Fayette; Gerstmeyer 17–16 Wiley; Garfield 18–11 Otter Creek; W. Terre Haute 28–23 Honey Creek; Gerstmeyer 31–8 Blackhawk; Garfield 21–4 W. Terre Haute; Garfield 23–16 Gerstmeyer. Officials: Clyde Cunningham, V. H. Bosse.

VALPARAISO: Morgan Twp. 18–16 Boone Grove; Hebron 45–12 Washington; Valparaiso 48–6 Crisman; Kouts 16–15 Chesterton; Hebron 24–15 Morgan Twp.; Valparaiso 29–8 Kouts; Valparaiso 64–16 Hebron. Officials: Clarence Fauber, Harry Hatcher.

VEEDERSBURG: Attica 44–22 Williamsport; Newtown 27–26 Covington; Mellott 33–10 West Lebanon; Kingman 23–20 Wallace; Veedersburg 20–16 Hillsboro; Attica 24–15 Pine Village; Mellott 31–18 Newtown; Kingman 26–25 Veedersburg; Mellott 18–17 Attica; Mellott

34–29 Kingman. Officials: E.C. Boyd, Lloyd Etter.

VERSAILLES: Versailles 36–10 Napoleon; New Marion 35–33 Batesville; Sunman 20–19 Osgood; Holton 28–13 Milan; Versailles 28–18 New Marion; Holton 22–12 Sunman; Versailles 13–11 Holton. Officials: Lloyd Wells, E.C. Auerswald.

VINCENNES: Wheatland 27–12 Fritchton; Monroe City 39–12 Vincennes Twp.; Freelandville 37–25 Oaktown; Decker 37–16 Emison; Vincennes 37–20 Bruceville; Bicknell 21–19 Sandborn; Decker Chapel 30–27 Edwardsport; Monroe City 26–21 Wheatland; Freelandville 36–22 Decker; Vincennes 41–16 Bicknell; Decker Chapel 33–23 Monroe City; Vincennes 39–18 Freelandville; Vincennes 53–18 Decker Chapel. Officials: B.E. Bayh, Donald Reel.

WABASH: Wabash 41–11 Lincolnville; North Manchester 31–12 Roann; Urbana 19–14 LaFontaine; Laketon 28–11 Somerset; Lagro 31–17 Linlawn; Chippewa 51–1 Chester; North Manchester 19–14 Wabash; Laketon 18–17 Urbana; Lagro 28–11 Chippewa; North Manchester 26–24 Laketon (ot); North Manchester 10–9 Lagro. Officials: Guy Ogle, H.E. Vandivier.

WARREN: Polk Twp. 23–20 Jefferson; Clear Creek 43–21 Andrews; Banquo 18–13 Warren; Huntington 34–24 Rock Creek; Union 35–23 Lancaster Center; Bippus 26–17 Roanoke; Huntington Twp. 53–11 Markle; Clear Creek 57–33 Monument City; Huntington 26–22 Banquo; Union 26–19 Bippus; Clear Creek 43–29 Huntington Twp.; Huntington 34–17 Union; Huntington 24–22 Clear Creek. Officials: Ward Gilbert, Archie Heller.

WARSAW: Warsaw 36–16 Claypool; Atwood 20–19 Sidney; Syracuse 41–19 Burket; Pierceton 40–11 Beaver Dam; Leesburg 36–12 Etna Green; Silver Lake 29–24 North Webster; Mentone 29–23 Warsaw; Syracuse 27–11 Atwood; Pierceton 20–17 Leesburg; Silver Lake 24–19 Mentone; Pierceton 27–22 Syracuse; Pierceton 27–19 Silver Lake. Officials: Ford Griffith, Homer Orsborn.

WASHINGTON: Montgomery 14–12 Burns City; Washington 42–18 Odon; Loogootee 50–16 Trinity Springs; Plainville 48–10 Glendale; Epsom 20–18 Shoals; Elnora 35–13 Raglesville; Alfordsville 11–8 Montgomery; Washington 52–17 Loogootee; Plainville 26–11 Epsom; Elnora 25–12 Alfordsville; Washington 24–14 Plainville; Washington 58–13 Elnora. Officials: W.S. Fellmy, Elmer Posey.

WINAMAC: Winamac 26–22 North Judson; Monterey 52–18 North Bend; Medaryville 35–16 Star City; Pulaski 25–24 Knox; San Pierre 30–14 Center Twp.; Francesville 32–22 Hamlet; Winamac 48–4 Grovertown; Medaryville 27–22 Monterey; San Pierre 40–32 Pulaski; Winamac 22–16 Francesville; Medaryville 42–31 San Pierre; Winamac 22–20 Medaryville. Officials: Carl Burt, R.R. Merrell.

WINCHESTER: Winchester 52–22 Huntsville; Modoc 28–22 Parker; Farmland 32–26 McKinley; Wayne 35–22 Lynn; Union City 37–11 Losantville; Stoney Creek 21–19 Jefferson; Spartanburg 41–30 Ridgeville; Jackson 36–28 Saratoga; Winchester 34–11 Modoc; Wayne 34–20 Farmland; Union City 34–25 Stoney Creek; Spartanburg 36–22 Jackson; Winchester 29–11 Wayne; Spartanburg 32–30 Union City; Winchester 29–25 Spartanburg. Officials: Paul Williams, Paul Parker.

1928 REGIONALS

ANDERSON: Anderson 31–18 Tipton; Broad Ripple 25–15 Cicero; Anderson 28–20 Broad Ripple. Officials: Hugh Vandivier, Paul Williams.

Tourney Time

AUBURN: Angola 21–18 LaGrange (ot); Kendallville 21–12 Auburn; Kendallville 27–20 Angola. Officials: Don Arbuckle, Benjamin DuBois.
BLOOMINGTON: Brazil 29–20 Garfield; Martinsville 44–12 Amo; Martinsville 22–21 Brazil. Officials: Dale Miller, B.B. Evans.
COLUMBUS: Columbus 58–10 Versailles; Franklin 37–7 Scipio; Columbus 20–18 Franklin. Officials: F.A. Bills, Elmer Posey.
EVANSVILLE: Princeton 31–15 Spurgeon; Central 39–15 Bristow; Central 22–17 Princeton. Officials: Vaughn Russell, Orville Jones.
FORT WAYNE: Kirkland Twp. 25–23 Pierceton; Central 18–13 Bluffton; Central 32–24 Kirkland Twp. Officials: Will Smith, J.W. Hale.
FRANKFORT: Jefferson 43–16 Monon; Frankfort 33–19 Boswell; Frankfort 25–19 Jefferson. Officials: John D. Miller, Winston Ashley.
GARY: East Chicago Washington 29–20 Valparaiso; LaPorte 30–21 Goodland; Washington 30–14 LaPorte. Officials: M.J. Cleary, Daniel Guild.
GREENCASTLE: Clinton 32–29 Crawfordsville; Greencastle 47–19 Mellott; Clinton 25–24 Greencastle. Officials: B.E. Bayh, R.B. Morrison.
LOGANSPORT: Peru 36–21 North Manchester; Logansport 38–18 Huntington; Logansport 33–17 Peru. Officials: Guy Woods, O.F. Helvie.
MARION: Delphi 33–11 Marion; Sharpsville 41–16 Dunkirk; Delphi 21–20 Sharpsville. Officials: F.L. Griffith, Gilbert Rhea.
MISHAWAKA: Rochester 26–22 Mishawaka (ot); Goshen 41–32 Winamac; Rochester 27–15 Goshen. Officials: Carl Olson, Keith Crown.
MUNCIE: Mt. Comfort 28–17 Winchester; Muncie 23–17 New Castle; Muncie 33–28 Mt. Comfort. Officials: Vedder Gard, Mode Cranor.
NEW ALBANY: Salem 23–20 Seymour; Bedford 62–9 Austin; Bedford 50–13 Salem. Officials: John Schram, Paul Hurley.
RUSHVILLE: Rushville 42–16 Hagerstown; Connersville 25–18 Lawrenceburg; Rushville 21–19 Connersville. Officials: John Craigle, W.E. Deakyne.
VINCENNES: Washington 34–12 Carlisle; Vincennes 32–26 Bloomfield; Washington 28–19 Vincennes. Officials: Ralph Esarey, J.C. Hannah.

1928 FINALS—March 16, 17

INDIANAPOLIS (Butler Fieldhouse): Clinton 22–21 Fort Wayne Central; Bedford 34–17 Kendallville; Anderson 27–19 Delphi; Muncie 18–10 Evansville Central; Martinsville 21–20 Rochester; Washington 22–20 Columbus; Frankfort 23–20 East Chicago; Logansport 34–17 Rushville; Bedford 32–18 Clinton; Muncie 38–37 Anderson; Martinsville 19–13 Washington; Frankfort 15–11 Logansport; Muncie 40–20 Bedford; Martinsville 30–13 Frankfort; Muncie 13–12 Martinsville. Officials: B.E. Bayh, Dale Miller, Ford Griffith, M.J. Cleary, Paul Williams.

1929 SECTIONALS

ANDERSON: Anderson 30–15 Markleville; Lapel 31–26 Elwood; Alexandria 30–21 Summitville; Pendleton 21–20 Frankton; Anderson 37–24 Lapel; Alexandria 40–19 Pendleton;

IHSAA Scores | 1920–1929

Anderson 51–26 Alexandria. Officials: H.E. Vandiver, H. C. Warren.

ANGOLA: Hamilton 44–5 Scott Center; Pleasant Lake 21–7 Orland; Angola 51–6 Flint; Fremont 25–18 Salem Twp.; Hamilton 13–12 Pleasant Lake; Angola 38–13 Fremont; Angola 44–21 Hamilton. Officials: Ora Davis, C.L. Litherland.

ATTICA: Wallace 49–20 Judyville; Attica 26–16 Covington; Veedersburg 28–25 Hillsboro; Pine Village 29–19 Williamsport; Newton 45–16 West Lebanon; Kingman 20–14 Mellott; Attica 19–17 Wallace; Pine Village 21–20 Veedersburg; Kingman 41–11 Newton; Attica 27–25 Pine Village; Attica 31–25 Kingman. Officials: Charles Jensen, George Vaulk.

BLUFFTON: Petroleum 25–22 Rockcreek; Lancaster Central 32–17 Union Center; Bluffton 22–11 Liberty Center; Chester Center 26–22 Ossian; Petroleum 21–14 Lancaster Central; Bluffton 36–16 Chester Center; Bluffton 25–13 Petroleum. Officials: George Lambert, L.R. Lenon.

CLINTON: Rockville 30–8 Greene Twp.; Dana 31–5 Bellmore; Clinton 34–16 Newport; Cayuga 30–12 Bridgeton Perrysville 20–19 Rosedale; Tangier 28–16 Hillsdale; Montezuma 30–24 Bloomingdale; St. Bernice 26–23 Marshall; Rockville 18–13 Dana; Cayuga 26–24 Clinton; Tangier 17–15 Perrysville; Montezuma 18–14 St. Bernice; Cayuga 35–21 Rockville; Montezuma 34–24 Tangier; Cayuga 22–10 Montezuma. Officials: J.C. Hannah, Glen Adams, Harry Conover.

CONNERSVILLE: Everton 26–15 Whitewater; Fairview 35–15 Waterloo; Connersville 62–9 Springfield; Brownsville 19–13 College Corner; Liberty 43–6 Harrisburg; Harrison Twp. 29–18 Brookville; Alquina 23–20 Bentonville; Orange 24–20 Everton; Connersville 83–19 Fairview; Brownsville 26–21 Liberty; Harrison Twp. 27–24 Alquina; Connersville 68–11 Orange; Brownsville 21–20 Harrison Twp.; Connersville 33–19 Brownsville. Officials: Henri Goett, Russell Pickett, W. S. Porter.

CRAWFORDSVILLE: Waynetown 25–20 New Ross; New Richmond 35–23 Waveland; Linden 24–23 New Market; Ladoga 27–20 Wingate; Bowers 34–15 Darlington; Crawfordsville 27–6 Alamo; Waynetown 22–16 New Richmond; Ladoga 24–15 Linden; Crawfordsville 21–19 Bowers; Waynetown 26–9 Ladoga; Crawfordsville 30–15 Waynetown. Officials: Daniel Guild, Byron Deakyne.

DANVILLE: Clayton 28–26 Plainfield (ot); Danville 35–15 New Winchester; Pittsboro 42–12 Lizton; North Salem 22–18 Avon; Amo 35–21 Brownsburg; Stilesville 31–22 Clayton; Danville 15–13 Pittsboro; Amo 18–8 North Salem; Danville 24–13 Stilesville; Danville 22–18 Amo. Officials: Lee Sinclair, Virgil Hickman.

DECATUR: Hartford 20–16 Monroe; Geneva 21–8 Monmouth; Kirkland 26–20 Jefferson; Berne 21–19 Decatur; Geneva 19–15 Hartford; Berne 26–15 Kirkland; Berne 44–16 Geneva. Officials: Dale Kreigh, Clive Markley.

DELPHI: Carrollton 28–18 Camden; Flora 25–15 Burlington; Delphi 43–2 Adams Twp.; Rockfield 19–14 Cutler; Carrollton 24–15 Deer Creek; Delphi 24–17 Flora; Carrollton 37–18 Rockfield; Delphi 21–12 Carrollton. Officials: Ralph Eades, Mode Cranor.

ELKHART: New Paris 33–19 Wakarusa; Nappanee 71–4 Concord Twp.; Goshen 50–26 Millersburg; Bristol 58–1 Jefferson Twp.; Elkhart 58–17 Clinton Community; New Paris 34–16 Middlebury; Goshen 28–26 Nappanee; Elkhart 28–26 Bristol; Goshen 26–15 New Paris; Goshen 32–23 Elkhart. Officials: J.B. McBride, Homer Orsborn.

FORT WAYNE: South Side 31–26 New Haven; Huntertown 40–22 Arcola; North Side 42–7 Harlan; Central 59–13 Madison Twp.; Lafayette Central 34–19 Monroeville; Leo 31–13 Maumee Twp.; South Side 38–11 Huntertown; Central 27–22 North Side; Lafayette Central 36–14 Leo; South

141

Tourney Time

Side 42–23 Central; South Side 55–26 Lafayette Central. Officials: Horace Parker, Clayton Hughes.

FOWLER: Boswell 47–9 Oxford; Ambia 26–25 Raub; Pine Twp. 26–15 Wadena; Freeland Park 33–23 Gilboa; Otterbein 30–23 Earl Park; Boswell 25–18 Fowler; Ambia 26–24 Pine Twp.; Freeland Park 21–19 Otterbein; Boswell 28–24 Ambia; Freeland Park 16–15 Boswell. Officials: Claude Draper, Paul Hurley.

FRANKFORT: Michigantown 29–27 Rossville; Forest 29–20 Jefferson; Mulberry 31–20 Jackson Twp.; Frankfort 59–10 Sugar Creek; Scircleville 20–17 Colfax; Michigantown 39–17 Forest; Frankfort 55–15 Mulberry; Michigantown 30–20 Scircleville; Frankfort 54–16 Michigantown. Officials: Don Arbuckle, George Kneeler.

FRANKLIN: Masonic Home 16–15 Whiteland; Union Twp. 47–7 Nashville; Hopewell 30–20 Center Grove; Franklin 40–12 Greenwood; Edinburg 20–16 Nineveh; Clark Twp. 19–17 Trafalgar; Masonic Home 35–21 Union Twp.; Franklin 32–13 Hopewell; Clark Twp. 28–26 Edinburg; Franklin 39–19 Masonic Home; Franklin 32–10 Clark Twp. Officials: W.H. Herbst, W.P. McFatridge.

GARRETT: Auburn 39–13 Jefferson Center; Ashley 19–16 Butler; Garrett 55–13 Washington Center; Larwill 37–17 Churubusco; Spencerville 27–18 Etna Twp.; South Whitley 24–21 Coesse; Columbia City 47–12 Concord; Auburn 27–26 Ashley; Garrett 34–14 Larwill; South Whitley 16–12 Spencerville; Columbia City 27–25 Auburn; Garrett 41–13 South Whitley; Columbia City 32–28 Garrett (2ot). Officials: Don Stephenson; Guy Ogle, Chas. Rouch.

GARY: Horace Mann 20–13 Crown Point; Wallace 18–17 Hammond Tech.; Emerson 45–5 Gary Roosevelt; East Chicago Roosevelt 18–12 Whiting; Hammond 67–5 Dyer; Washington 26–19 Griffith; Froebel 36–19 Lowell; Horace Mann 18–10 Hobart; Emerson 53–9 Wallace; East Chicago Roosevelt 22–20 Hammond; Froebel 22–10 Washington; Horace Mann 13–5 Emerson; Froebel 24–21 East Chicago Roosevelt; Horace Mann 20–18 Froebel. Officials: R.W. Aldridge, Paul Isenbarger, Homer Stonebraker.

GREENCASTLE: Roachdale 25–12 Russellville; Bainbridge 28–20 Reelsville; Fillmore 16–15 Greencastle; Cloverdale 33–15 Clinton Center; Roachdale 30–16 Belle Union; Bainbridge 31–16 Fillmore; Roachdale 27–19 Cloverdale; Roachdale 18–14 Bainbridge. Officials: George Seidensticker, J. Ord Fortner.

GREENFIELD: Fortville 18–15 Wilkinson; Eden 33–27 Westland; New Palestine 20–19 Warren Central; Charlottesville 30–15 Maxwell; Mt. Comfort 19–16 McCordsville; New Palestine 38–17 Eden; Mt. Comfort 22–17 Charlottesville; New Palestine 19–17 Greenfield; Mt. Comfort 22–18 New Palestine. Officials: Ross Smith, W. E. Deakyne.

GREENSBURG: St. Paul 28–13 Westport; Scipio 33–31 Sandusky; Greensburg 42–7 Clarksburg; Burney 25–21 Paris Crossing; Butlerville 42–19 New Point; Jackson 40–20 Lovett; Letts 18–14 Hayden; North Vernon 81–3 Zenas; Scipio 26–18 St. Paul; Greensburg 21–19 Burney; Butlerville 39–20 Jackson; North Vernon 49–20 Letts; Greensburg 26–19 Scipio; Butlerville 21–19 North Vernon; Greensburg 32–29 Butlerville. Officials: Nate Kaufman, H.C. Henderson, Gilbert Rhea.

HUNTINGTON: Lancaster 22–5 Markle; Warren 28–9 Jefferson; Roanoke 24–23 Monument City; Bippus 14–10 Rockcreek; Andrews 28–21 Clear Creek; Union Center 21–17 Banquo; Huntington 60–5 Huntington Twp.; Lancaster 25–23 Warren; Bippus 14–12 Roanoke; Union 22–10 Andrews; Huntington 40–14 Lancaster; Union 12–8 Bippus; Huntington 42–13 Union Center. Officials: Ward Gilbert, Archie Heller, Walter Wissard.

IHSAA Scores | 1920–1929

HYMERA: Sullivan 28–9 Fairbanks; Carlisle 28–26 Union Twp.; Jackson Twp. 36–24 Merom; Graysville 27–22 Pleasantville; Sullivan 18–12 New Lebanon; Jackson Twp. 29–24 Carlisle; Graysville 19–14 Sullivan; Graysville 46–39 Jackson Twp. Officials: Wayne Watson, Clyde Cunningham.

INDIANAPOLIS: Manual 22–14 Lawrence; Broad Ripple 39–20 Castleton; Ben Davis 29–24 Beech Grove; Acton 17–13 West Newton; Washington 46–27 Oaklandon; Tech 45–13 Valley Mills; Southport 22–20 New Bethel; Shortridge 28–16 New Augusta; Broad Ripple 21–20 Manual; Ben Davis 32–17 Acton; Tech 24–10 Washington; Southport 22–8 Shortridge; Broad Ripple 18–16 Ben Davis; Tech 30–13 Southport; Tech 23–11 Broad Ripple. Officials: Earl Pike; Karl Kashner, Orville Barnes.

JASPER: Cuzco 19–15 English; Petersburg 24–23 Stendal (ot); Spurgeon 40–13 Milltown; Marengo 54–5 Clay Twp; Jasper 15–11 Birdseye; Winslow 25–18 Ireland; Holland 20–16 Velpen; Otwell 26–6 DuBois; Petersburg 21–14 Cuzco; Spurgeon 25–17 Marengo (ot); Jasper 13–12 Winslow (ot); Holland 26–21 Otwell; Spurgeon 19–18 Petersburg; Holland 17–14 Jasper; Spurgeon 20–13 Holland; Officials: Paul Garrison, Ivan Zaring, Leonard Mayhugh.

KENDALLVILLE: Wolf Lake 25–12 Ligonier; Kendallville 31–9 LaOtto; Albion 28–22 Cromwell; Wawaka 38–11 Avilla; Wolf Lake 45–17 Orange Twp.; Albion 15–14 Kendallville; Wawaka 27–22 Wolf Lake; Wawaka 25–20 Albion. Officials: B.J. DuBois, George Yarnelle.

KOKOMO: West Middleton 30–23 Greentown; Kokomo 24–14 Ervin Twp.; Jackson Twp. 24–15 Clay Twp.; Russiaville 34–23 Union Twp.; Howard Twp. 23–17 New London; Kokomo 41–18 West Middleton; Jackson Twp. 43–20 Russiaville; Kokomo 40–16 Howard Twp.; Kokomo 34–27 Jackson Twp. Officials: Houston Meyer, Charles Garrett.

LAFAYETTE: West Point 23–19 Buck Creek; Clarks Hill 24–20 Wea; Romney 12–5 Stockwell; Monitor 32–15 Montmorenci; Jefferson 25–18 Klondike; Dayton 27–13 Jackson Twp.; West Lafayette 32–12 Battle Ground; West Point 19–15 Clarks Hill; Monitor 22–14 Romney; Jefferson 23–17 Dayton; West Point 16–4 West Lafayette; Jefferson 23–21 Monitor; West Point 29–23 Jefferson. Officials: Vaughn Russell, Dillon Geiger, Russell Cook.

LAGRANGE: Lima 28–22 Topeka; Shipshewana 34–22 Springfield Twp.; La–Grange 77–5 Scott; Wolcottville 22–18 Brighton; Lima 31–20 Shipshewana; LaGrange 64–22 Wolcottville; LaGrange 32–11 Lima. Officials: George Allessee, Clifford Risk.

LAWRENCEBURG: Rising Sun 29–13 Patriot; Aurora 26–21 Dillsboro; Law–renceburg 22–16 Vevay; Bright 44–22 Alsace; Rising Sun 25–21 Moores Hill; Aurora 23–21 Lawrenceburg; Rising Sun 29–21 Bright; Aurora 21–18 Rising Sun. Officials: Harry Blume, Blair Gullion.

LEBANON: Boxley 30–22 Pinnell; Lebanon 27–13 Thorntown; Westfield 38–24 Zionsville; Whitestown 21–12 Central; Advance 25–22 Jamestown; Carmel 21–17 Boxley; Lebanon 30–10 Westfield; Advance 33–10 Whitestown; Lebanon 30–19 Carmel; Lebanon 18–14 Advance. Officials: T.R. Smith, Ralph Parker.

LOGANSPORT: Deacon 19–14 New Waverly; Twelve Mile 45–13 Metea; Young America 25–18 Onward; Logansport 48–4 Lucerne; Walton 51–5 Royal Center; Galveston 44–7 Washington Twp.; Lincoln 14–12 Deacon; Young America 29–16 Twelve Mile; Logansport 20–19 Walton; Galveston 15–12 Lincoln; Logansport 59–15 Young America; Logansport 22–9 Galveston. Officials: E.C. Rowe, Winston Ashley, Ralph Worley.

LYONS: Linton 37–17 Solsberry; Jasonville 41–21 Scotland; Switz City 25–10 Owensburg; Bloomfield 30–19 Newberry; Linton 22–17 Lyons; Switz City 29–20 Jasonville; Linton 37–31

143

Tourney Time

Bloomfield (ot); Linton 37–32 Switz City. Officials: Glen Stanbaugh, Elmer Posey.

MARION: Jonesboro 41–10 Upland; Swayzee 31–20 Matthews; Fairmount 31–19 Gas City; Marion 38–19 Van Buren; Jonesboro 32–23 Sweetser; Fairmount 23–19 Swayzee; Marion 21–17 Jonesboro; Fairmount 17–15 Marion. Officials: M.J. Cleary, Otto Strohmeier.

MARTINSVILLE: Mooresville 51–12 Unionville; Martinsville 33–5 Stinesville; Bloomington 24–18 Monrovia; Smithville 44–18 Eminence; Paragon 33–20 Ellettsville; Mooresville 46–21 Morgantown; Martinsville 38–17 Bloomington; Smithville 23–20 Paragon; Martinsville 32–16 Mooresville; Martinsville 46–4 Smithville. Officials: Thomas Baker, Harold Metcalf

MICHIGAN CITY: Union Twp. 23–16 LaCrosse; Hanna 37–10 Kingsbury; Westville 27–21 Union Mills; Michigan City 20–19 Stilwell; Rolling Prairie 40–12 Mill Creek; LaPorte 35–16 Union Twp.; Westville 14–12 Hanna; Michigan City 24–22 Rolling Prairie; LaPorte 27–7 Westville; LaPorte 33–9 Michigan City. Officials: Carl Porter, Floyd Merriman.

MISHAWAKA: New Carlisle 28–25 Tyner; Mishawaka 15–10 West Twp.; South Bend 47–10 Madison Twp.; Plymouth 26–14 Riley; North Liberty 36–10 LaPaz; Bremen 26–20 Lakeville; Walkerton 20–13 New Carlisle; South Bend 12–10 Mishawaka; Plymouth 22–16 North Liberty; Bremen 21–17 Walkerton; South Bend 43–17 Plymouth; South Bend 29–15 Bremen. Officials: Joe Wilt, D H. Hostetter, J.H. Hendrickson.

MITCHELL: Mitchell 17–16 Oolitic; Marshall Twp. 22–8 Heltonville; Shawswick 50–18 Huron; Williams 24–23 Paoli; Orleans 21–19 West Baden; French Lick 28–21 Tunnelton; Bedford 66–7 Fayetteville; Mitchell 33–20 Marshall Twp.; Shawswick 16–15 Williams; French Lick 44–20 Orleans; Bedford 22–17 Mitchell; French Lick 22–17 Shawswick; Bedford 46–17 French Lick. Officials: John Schram, Judson Deer, Gerald Bottorff.

MONTICELLO: Brookston 50–24 Burnettsville; Monticello 60–14 Chalmers; Monon 27–20 Buffalo; Reynolds 28–15 Idaville; Wolcott 22–17 Round Grove; Monticello 33–17 Brookston; Reynolds 34–33 Monon; Monticello 17–16 Wolcott; Monticello 52–22 Reynolds. Officials: Gordon Wise, F.C. Ritenour.

MUNCIE: Yorktown 22–17 Albany; Royerton 25–12 Selma; Muncie 68–23 Harrison; Eaton 20–5 Gaston; DeSoto 30–19 Daleville; Center 36–20 Cowan; Royerton 22–21 Yorktown; Muncie 25–l8 Eaton; DeSoto 28–27 Center; Muncie 64–7 Royerton; Muncie 66–18 DeSoto. Officials: Guy Woods, Walter Geller.

NEW ALBANY: Silver Creek 20–12 Hardinsburg; Henryville 30–16 Posey Twp.; Pekin 28–25 Georgetown; DePauw 21–13 Franklin Twp.; Jeffersonville 33–14 Corydon; New Washington 35–10 Borden; New Salisbury 35–19 New Middletown; New Albany 53–10 Morgan Twp.; Henryville 15–14 Silver Creek; Pekin 24–16 DePauw; Jeffersonville 68–10 New Washington; New Albany 72–13 New Salisbury; Pekin 31–19 Henryville; New Albany 45–21 Jeffersonville; New Albany 21–20 Pekin. Officials: Ray Frohman, Donald Wilder, W.S. Fellmy.

NEW CASTLE: Mooreland 25–13 Knightstown; Middletown 29–15 Kennard; Sulphur Springs 30–26 Lewisville; Cadiz 28–24 Spiceland; New Castle 34–9 Mt. Summit; Mooreland 41–13 New Lisbon; Middletown 37–18 Sulphur Springs; New Castle 35–23 Cadiz; Middletown 28–22 Mooreland; Middletown 19–18 New Castle. Officials: Allen Klinck, Paul Williams.

NORTH JUDSON: Center Twp. 16–15 Monterey; Francesville 39–15 Grovertown; Medaryville 32–26 San Pierre; Winamac 29–21 Knox; Pulaski 18–17 Star City; North Judson 104–1 North Bend; Hamlet 29–11 Center Twp.; Medaryville 27–24 Francesville; Winamac 31–18 Pulaski; North Judson 36–12 Hamlet; Winamac 33–21 Medaryville; Winamac 25–16 North

IHSAA Scores | 1920–1929

Judson. Officials: G.L. Russell, Charles Link, Carl Burt.

OAKLAND CITY: Reitz 31–11 Newburgh; Millersburg 32–9 Gentryville; Lynn–ville 23–13 Folsomville; Central 35–10 Dale; Bosse 45–18 Yankeetown; Tennyson 31–25 Boonville; Oakland City 35–3 Elberfeld; Reitz 31–24 Chandler; Lynnville 47–14 Millers–burg; Central 16–10 Bosse; Tennyson 28–26 Oakland City; Reitz 31–16 Lynnville; Central 38–10 Tennyson; Central 17–8 Reitz. Officials: George Graham, Kenneth Beckner, J.M. Martin.

OWENSVILLE: Hazleton 22–18 Stewartsville; Poseyville 21–14 Princeton; Haubstadt 29–25 Cynthiana (2ot); Griffin 43–29 Patoka; Owensville 40–14 Francisco; Fort Branch 27–22 New Harmony; Mt. Olympus 22–13 Mt. Vernon; Hazleton 20–18 Poseyville; Griffin 20–18 Haubstadt; Owensville 50–29 Fort Branch; Mt. Olympus 18–12 Hazleton; Owensville 31–12 Griffin; Mt. Olympus 19–12 Owensville. Officials: Ralph Esarey, Clinton Dougherty, John Hoffman.

PERU: Peru 45–18 Bunker Hill; Macy 23–20 Amboy; Deedsville 26–18 Gilead; Jefferson Twp. 25–16 Butler; Clay Twp. 37–34 Converse; Peru 21–11 Chili; Macy 23–14 Deedsville; Clay Twp. 33–21 Jefferson Twp.; Peru 42–14 Macy; Peru 56–23 Clay Twp. Officials: Orbie Branham, Lavon Carey.

PORTLAND: Portland 41–25 Jefferson Twp.; Roll 24–12 Dunkirk; Bryant 34–14 Redkey; Hartford City 50–14 Gray; Madison Twp. 16–15 Poling; Montpelier 43–17 Pennville; Portland 25–12 Roll; Hartford City 28–11 Bryant; Montpelier 15–10 Madison; Portland 28–24 Hartford City; Portland 23–19 Montpelier. Officials: Frederick Shroyer, Leslie Beall.

RENSSELAER: Brook 21–18 Remington; Wheatfield 26–13 Kniman; Kentland 37–15 Tefft; Hanging Grove 16–9 DeMotte; Rensselaer 23–20 Morocco; Goodland 28–11 Fair Oaks; Brook 63–17 Wheatfield; Kentland 36–5 Hanging Grove; Goodland 17–16 Rensselaer; Brook 37–18 Kentland; Brook 24–12 Goodland. Officials: C.E. Fauber, Glenn Farrell.

RICHMOND: Williamsburg 27–19 Boston; Milton 33–21 Economy; Richmond 43–18 Greensfork; Hagerstown 25–21 Fountain City; Centerville 30–7 Whitewater; Cambridge City 31–23 Williamsburg; Richmond 28–19 Milton; Hagerstown 18–11 Centerville; Cambridge City 27–23 Richmond; Hagerstown 28–24 Cambridge City (ot). Officials: Frank Porter, R.P. Chambers.

ROCHESTER: Fulton 33–10 Tippecanoe; Culver 31–9 Talma; Rochester 35–16 Bourbon; Richland Center 25–6 Argos; Akron 23–18 Leiters Ford; Grass Creek 2–0 Kewanna (forfeit); Culver 27–20 Fulton; Rochester 33–16 Richland Center; Akron 30–13 Grass Creek; Rochester 17–16 Culver; Akron 25–19 Rochester. Officials: John Stahr, Robert Bain.

RUSHVILLE: Rushville 42–16 Raleigh; New Salem 31–14 Moscow; Milroy 28–19 Morton Memorial; Manilla 37–22 Center; Arlington 22–18 Carthage; Rushville 15–11 New Salem; Milroy 26–19 Manilla; Rushville 59–21 Arlington; Rushville 28–20 Milroy. Officials: Leo Quillen, Norman Durham.

SCOTTSBURG: Salem 37–19 North Madison; Austin 32–12 Deputy; Campbells–burg 12–11 Central; Scottsburg; 53–6 Saluda; Madison 60–11 Monroe Twp.; Hanover 24–21 Little York; Salem 29–25 Dupont; Austin 35–20 Campbellsburg; Scottsburg 30–21 Madison; Salem 36–6 Hanover; Scottsburg 26–16 Austin; Salem 13–12 Scottsburg. Officials: William Campbell, H.N. McClain, Robert Lambert.

SEYMOUR: Vallonia 44–24 Cortland; Freetown 47–22 Houston; Tampico 38–37 Crothersville; Seymour 58–11 Medora; Brownstown 31–19 Clearspring; Vallonia 37–26 Freetown; Seymour 32–9 Tampico; Vallonia 35–27 Brownstown; Seymour 55–20 Vallonia. Officials: Everett Babb, Roy Hunter.

Tourney Time

SHELBYVILLE: Columbus 60–13 Waldron; Shelbyville 35–15 Hawcreek Twp.; Morristown 34–28 Flat Rock; Flat Rock 24–23 Moral; Fairland 29–18 Mt. Auburn; Columbus 68–22 Boggstown; Shelbyville 32–10 Morristown; Flat Rock 27–22 Fairland (ot); Columbus 15–14 Shelbyville; Columbus 44–17 Flat Rock. Officials: John George, F.A. Bills.

SPENCER: Spencer 22–8 Van Buren; Brazil 33–11 Cory; Posey Twp. 24–22 Quincy; Patricksburg 41–6 Gosport; Clay City 32–10 Freedom; Bowling Green 14–8 Ashboro; Spencer 28–20 Brazil; Patricksburg 31–14 Posey Twp.; Clay City 21–18 Bowling Green; Spencer 37–15 Patricksburg; Clay City 24–20 Spencer. Officials: Donald Reel, Leonard Kincade.

TELL CITY: Tell City 28–9 Grandview; Luce Twp. 16–3 Rome; Rockport 23–14 Troy; Tobinsport 30–15 Oil Twp.; Leopold 30–12 Leavenworth; Derby 22–11 Union Twp.; Cannelton 39–8 Chrisney; Bristow 17–12 Anderson Twp.; Tell City 30–17 Luce Twp.; Rockport 16–9 Tobinsport; Derby 30–18 Leopold; Bristow 26–13 Cannelton; Tell City 24–19 Rockport; Bristow 18–9 Derby; Tell City 34–13 Bristow. Officials: Irvin Springer, Dallas Garland, Harley Jurgens.

TERRE HAUTE: Riley 38–23 Fontanet; Otter Creek 22–17 Prairie Creek; Normal 25–12 Pimento; Glenn 21–19 Honey Creek; Garfield 30–16 Gerstmeyer; Blackhawk 23–21 Concannon; Wiley 58–10 West Terre Haute; Otter Creek 18–16 Riley; Normal 20–16 Glenn; Garfield 30–6 Blackhawk; Wiley 18–16 Otter Creek; Garfield 26–15 Normal; Wiley 26–24 Garfield. Officials: Frank Jerrell, Earl Boyd.

TIPTON: Tipton 34–21 Walnut Grove; Sharpsville 28–9 Goldsmith; Prairie Twp. 25–22 Fishers; Cicero 27–12 Atlanta; Noblesville 29–13 Kempton; Windfall 34–20 Arcadia; Tipton 26–21 Sharpsville; Cicero 30–23 Prairie Twp.; Noblesville 20–18 Windfall; Cicero 26–21 Tipton; Noblesville 25–10 Cicero. Officials: Dale Miller, Harry Champ.

VALPARAISO: Washington 30–18 Boone Twp.; Wanatah 14–12 Boone Grove, Valparaiso 46–11 Wheeler; Chesterton 45–9 Morgan Twp.; Washington 28–17 Wanatah; Valparaiso 35–18 Chesterton; Valparaiso 70–15 Washington. Officials: R.R. Merrell, C.A. Smith.

VERSAILLES: Holton 16–14 Osgood; New Marion 15–8 Versailles; Batesville 23–18 Napoleon; Milan 22–20 Sunman; Holton 26–16 New Marion; Milan 21–11 Batesville; Holton 26–16 Milan. Officials: Harry Vandivier, Martin Luther.

VINCENNES: Vincennes 64–7 Edwardsport; Oaktown 41–13 Sandborn; Fritchton 28–26 Decker Chapel; Decker 25–23 Freelandville; Bruceville 26–17 Wheatland; Bicknell 20–15 Vincennes Twp.; Vincennes 81–12 Monroe City; Oaktown 34–16 Fritchton; Bruceville 35–23 Decker; Vincennes 54–13 Bicknell; Bruceville 29–19 Oaktown; Vincennes 25–11 Bruceville. Officials: Vern Ruble, Crawford Baganz, B.E. Bayh.

WABASH: Lagro 19–14 Laketon; Chippewa 28–17 Chester; Wabash 30–13 Urbana; LaFontaine 26–13 Somerset; North Manchester 52–14 Roann; Linlawn 43–27 Lincolnville; Lagro 24–16 Chippewa; Wabash 23–17 LaFontaine; North Manchester 25–18 Linlawn; Wabash 16–13 Lagro; Wabash 17–9 North Manchester. Officials: Paul Parker, Harry Hatcher.

WARSAW: Van Buren Twp. 35–25 Warsaw; North Webster 30–20 Pierceton; Leesburg 29–10 Mentone; Syracuse 18–13 Silver Lake; Sidney 29–24 Etna Green; Claypool 38–9 Burket; Atwood 21–12 Beaver Dam; Milford 18–11 North Webster; Leesburg 27–19 Syracuse; Sidney 24–23 Claypool; Milford 30–17 Atwood; Leesburg 29–23 Sidney; Milford 25–20 Leesburg. Officials: Will Smith, Harry Coolman, O.F. Helvie.

WASHINGTON: Washington 98–9 Burns City; Barr Twp. 19–13 Shoals; Alfordsville 18–4 Raglesville; Odon 19–13 Plainville; Epsom 19–13 Loogootee; Elnora 56–7 Glendale; Washington

37–18 Montgomery; Odon 35–19 Alfordsville; Elnora 23–16 Epsom; Washington 31–19 Odon; Washington 38–10 Elnora. Officials: G.S. Rust, C.D. Manhart.

WINCHESTER: McKinley 17–13 Losantville; Lincoln 18–17 Jackson; Farmland 25–24 Huntsville; Winchester 56–4 Wayne; Union City 37–10 Lynn; Stoney Creek 29–25 Spartanburg; Ridgeville 26–8 Saratoga; Parker 40–15 Modoc; McKinley 18–15 Lincoln; Winchester 53–16 Farmland; Stoney Creek 28–20 Union City; Parker 24–16 Ridgeville; Winchester 36–6 McKinley; Stoney Creek 32–20 Parker; Winchester 30–25 Stoney Creek. Officials: Lloyd Miller, Maurice Tudor, Fernie Trigalet.

1929 REGIONALS

ANDERSON: Indianapolis Tech 35–16 Lebanon; Anderson 33–22 Noblesville; Tech 27–21 Anderson. Officials: Homer Orsborn, Vaughn Russell.

ATTICA: Roachdale 15–14 Crawfordsville; Attica 20–16 Cayuga; Attica 22–19 Roachdale. Officials: Harry Conover, Donald Arbuckle.

AUBURN: LaGrange 25–24 Wawaka; Columbia City 23–22 Angola; Columbia City 37–32 LaGrange. Officials: O.F. Helvie, Carl Olson.

BEDFORD: Bedford 31–14 Salem; Seymour 24–20 New Albany; Bedford 20–19 Seymour. Officials: B.E. Bayh, Guy Woods.

BRAZIL: Wiley 20–14 Danville; Martinsville 36–23 Clay City; Martinsville 36–13 Wiley. Officials: B.B. Evans, W.S. Porter.

COLUMBUS: Columbus 43–27 Greensburg; Franklin 20–16 Holton; Columbus 29–17 Franklin. Officials: Leroy Cook, Vedder Gard.

FORT WAYNE: South Side 37–17 Bluffton; Berne 28–27 Milford; South Side 40–17 Berne. Officials: Hugh Vandivier, Mode Cranor.

GARY: Horace Mann 24–13 Valparaiso; Brook 23–16 LaPorte; Horace Mann 31–16 Brook. Officials: John Stahr, Paul Hurley.

LAFAYETTE: Frankfort 51–17 Freeland Park; West Point 24–13 Monticello; Frankfort 19–16 West Point. Officials: Paul Williams, Watson Deakyne.

LOGANSPORT: Logansport 42–15 Wabash; Peru 24–19 Delphi; Logansport 35–26 Peru. Officials: Dale Miller, Will Smith.

MARION: Huntington 27–13 Huntington; Kokomo 19–17 Fairmount; Kokomo 27–19 Huntington. Officials: J.E. Craigle, Bruce Morrison.

MISHAWAKA: Winamac 25–21 Goshen; Akron 23–16 South Bend; Winamac 32–18 Goshen. Officials: Daniel Guild, George Vaulk.

MUNCIE: Muncie 26–20 Winchester; Middletown 35–24 Mt. Comfort; Muncie 30–19 Middletown. Officials: M.J. Cleary, Gilbert Rhea.

RUSHVILLE: Rushville 28–14 Aurora; Connersville 32–22 Hagerstown; Rushville 27–23 Connersville. Officials: Winston Ashley, Robert Lambert.

VINCENNES: Linton 27–26 Graysville; Vincennes 26–12 Mt. Olympus; Vincennes 17–12 Linton. Officials: Orville Jones, John Schram.

WASHINGTON: Tell City 21–20 Spurgeon; Washington 13–6 Evansville Central; Washington 37–11 Tell City. Officials: Charles Jensen, Ralph Esarey.

Tourney Time

1929 FINALS—March 15, 16

INDIANAPOLIS (Butler Fieldhouse): Horace Mann 29–22 Kokomo; Bedford 31–29 Martinsville; Frankfort 43–18 Columbia City; Columbus 32–20 Logansport; Indianapolis Tech 23–17 Vincennes; Fort Wayne South Side 44–19 Attica; Washington 31–24 Muncie; Horace Mann 23–18 Bedford; Frankfort 28–21 Columbus; Tech 23–18 South Side; Washington 26–22 Rushville; Frankfort 22–17 Horace Mann; Tech 31–18 Washington; Frankfort 29–23 Tech. Officials: Dale Miller, Vaughn Russell, B. E. Bayh, Paul Williams, Hugh Vandivier.

1930–1939

1930 SECTIONALS

ANDERSON: Summitville 31–25 Elwood. Lapel 21–16 Frankton; Anderson 51–14 Pendleton; Alexandria 29–17 Markleville; Lapel 26–24 Summitville; Anderson 39–37 Alexandria; Anderson 35–18 Lapel. Officials: P. O. Hurley, Harold Metcalf.

ATTICA: Covington 27–21 Kingman; Pine Village 22–10 Hillsboro. Wallace 22–18 Newtown; Williamsport 32–20 Mellott; Veedersburg 33–29 West Lebanon; Attica 20–14 Covington; Pine Village 24–23 Wallace; Veedersburg 21–7 Williamsport; Attica 33–29 Pine Village (2ot); Attica 23–21 Veedersburg. Officials: Glenn Farrell, Gordon Wise.

BLOOMINGTON: Bloomington 19–13 Smithville. Unionville 16–15 Paragon; Monrovia 34–24 Mooresville; Ellettsville 18–17 Morgantown; Martinsville 46–13 Stilesville; Eminence 22–16 Bloomington; Monrovia 13–12 Unionville; Martinsville 57–14 Ellettsville; Monrovia 33–26 Eminence; Martinsville 43–8 Monrovia. Officials: B. E. Bayh, John W. George.

BLUFFTON: Rock Creek 52–7 Pleasant Mills; Berne 30–16 Lancaster; Liberty Center 29–19 Bluffton; Union Center 31–30 Jefferson; Chester Center 36–14 Monroe; Petroleum 43–21 Geneva; Ossian 35–16 Hartford Twp.; Rockcreek 27–23 Kirkland; Liberty Center 36–32 Berne; Chester Center 32–28 Union Center; Ossian 42–23 Petroleum; Liberty Center 23–14 Rockcreek; Ossian 23–10 Chester Center; Liberty Center 20–18 Ossian. Officials: Clifford Risk, Ford Griffith, T. R. Smith.

BOONVILLE: Rockport 27–19 Gentryville; Newburgh 26–25 Luce Twp.; Lynnville 23–18 Grandview; Carter Twp. 23–14 Folsomville; Yankeetown 31–12 Chrisney; Chandler 33–17 Elberfeld; Tennyson 19–6 Boonville; Rockport 27–25 Millersburg; Lynnville 17–15 Newburgh; Yankeetown 30–24 Carter Twp.; Tennyson 31–17 Chandler; Rockport 18–7 Lynnville; Tennyson 24–15 Yankeetown; Tennyson 28–13 Rockport. Officials: C. D. Manhart, Leonard Mayhugh, Hulett Crecelius.

BRAZIL: Spencer 29–12 Freedom; Clay City 26–9 Cory; Brazil 23–11 Van Buren; Quincy 19–11 Bowling Green; Staunton 13–10 Ashboro; Patricksburg 19–12 Gosport; Spencer 20–18 Clay City; Brazil 29–9 Quincy; Staunton 23–9 Patricksburg; Brazil 31–12 Spencer; Brazil 37–18 Staunton. Officials: Harry Champ, Orville Jones.

CLINTON: Green Twp. 24–13 Tangier; Mecca 38–26 St. Bernice; Newport 17–16 Hillsdale;

IHSAA Scores | 1930–1939

Montezuma 41–14 Marshall; Rockville 21–12 Rosedale; Perrysville 55–15 Bellmore; Clinton 27–9 Dana; Cayuga 31–28 Bloomingdale; Green Twp. 26–25 Mecca; Newport 26–13 Montezuma; Rockville 31–18 Perrysville; Clinton 51–8 Cayuga; Newport 36–28 Green Twp.; Clinton 28–16 Rockville; Clinton 22–14 Newport. Officials: Frank Jarrell, Ralph Worley, Norman Dunlap.

COLUMBIA CITY: Wolf Lake 32–15 Washington Center; Jefferson Center 31–25 Larwill; Columbia City 23–20 South Whitley; Etna Twp. 29–24 Churubusco; Jefferson Center 26–16 Wolf Lake; Columbia City 30–9 Etna Twp.; Columbia City 36–22 Jefferson Center. Officials: Ora Davis, Benjamin DuBois.

CONNERSVILLE: Connersville 58–7 Harrisburg; Everton 22–21 Fairview; Alquina 23–15 Brookville; Kitchel 23–21 Brownsville; Laurel 23–22 Orange; Liberty 38–16 Bentonville; Springfield 47–14 College Corner; Connersville 104–12 Whitewater Twp.; Everton 26–16 Alquina; Kitchel 24–20 Laurel; Liberty 40–30 Springfield; Connersville 46–13 Everton; Liberty 39–17 Kitchel; Connersville 54–25 Liberty. Officials: Guy Ogle, Harry Vandiver, Layall Fisher.

CRAWFORDSVILLE: Bowers 29–24 Alamo; Linden 22–12 New Market; Wingate 22–11 Waynetown; Darlington 46–19 Waveland; Crawfordsville 28–27 Ladoga; New Richmond 36–13 Now Ross; Linden 16–9 Bowers; Wingate 28–15 Darlington; Crawfordsville 16–11 New Richmond. Linden 11–9 Wingate; Crawfordsville 14–12 Linden. Officials: Otto Strohmeier, Walter Ross.

DANVILLE: Danville 24–22 Plainfield; Lizton 15–14 Amo; Clayton 21–19 Pittsboro; Brownsburg 37–10 New Winchester; North Salem 19–16 Stilesville; Avon 13–11 Danville; Lizton 33–9 Clayton; North Salem 29–27 Brownsburg; Avon 21–20 Lizton; North Salem 23–22 Avon. Officials: Dale Miller, Virgil Hickman.

DELPHI: Carrollton 19–11 Otter Creek; Camden 42–6 Adams Twp.; Flora 32–14 Cutter; Delphi 29–11 Rockfield; Burlington 28–6 Carrollton; Flora 19–11 Camden; Delphi 26–14 Burlington; Delphi 27–17 Flora. Officials: Charles Garrett, George Kenzler.

EVANSVILLE: Central 18–12 New Harmony; Bosse 54–17 Stewartsville; Reitz 22–21 Griffin; Cynthiana 19–17 Mt. Vernon; Central 19–18 Poseyville; Bosse 40–8 Reitz; Central 14–13 Cynthiana; Bosse 15–14 Central. Officials: Dallas Garland, Paul Lovell.

FORT WAYNE: North Side 28–15 Maumee Twp.; Monroeville 29–13 Lafayette Central; New Haven 35–10 Monmouth; South Side 36–8 Arcola; Central 19–16 Decatur; Leo 40–12 Harlan; Huntertown 22–14 Hoagland; North Side 24–14 Monroeville; South Side 26–16 New Haven; Central 49–25 Leo; North Side 15–8 Huntertown; Central 17–16 South Side; Central 32–16 North Side. Officials: Homer Stonebraker, Allen Klinck, George Lambert.

FOWLER: Otterbein 34–6 Freeland Park; Boswell 22–21 Fowler. Pine Twp. 32–21 Raub; Gilboa 21–20 Ambia; Earl Park 28–22 Oxford; Otterbein 45–13 Wadena; Pine Twp. 17–12 Boswell; Earl Park 20–17 Gilboa; Otterbein 36–17 Pine Twp.; Otterbein 31–10 Earl Park. Officials: Lee Sinclair, Earl Pike.

FRANKFORT: Frankfort 36–9 Jefferson; Colfax 30–16 Mulberry; Rossville 17–12 Sugar Creek; Jackson Twp. 18–16 Forest; Frankfort 56–20 Michigantown; Colfax 31–26 Rossville. Frankfort 71–12 Jackson Twp.; Frankfort 42–23 Colfax. Officials: Dillon Geiger, Walter McFatridge.

FRANKLIN: Clark Twp. 18–17 Union Twp.; Franklin 46–12 Nineveh; Edinburg 27–13 Hopewell; Nashville 13–7 Trafalgar; Center Grove 33–18 Whiteland; Masonic Home 28–15 Greenwood; Franklin 29–20 Clark Twp.; Edinburg 19–11 Nashville; Center Grove 28–27

Tourney Time

Masonic Rome; Franklin 22–16 Edinburg; Franklin 45–17 Center Grove. Officials: Byron J. Deakyne, George Bair.

GARRETT: Spencerville 36–29 Salem Center; Auburn 16–14 Butler; Hamilton 27–22 Pleasant Lake; Scott Center 16–6 Flint; Concord Twp. 11–8 Waterloo; Angola 45–6 Orland; Garrett 41–16 Fremont; Auburn 25–14 Spencerville; Hamilton 32–23 Scott Center; Angola 33–9 Concord Twp.; Auburn 20–15 Garrett; Angola 35–26 Hamilton; Auburn 25–23 Angola (ot). Officials: Carl Porter, Don Stephenson, Joel Wilt.

GARY: Horace Mann 21–4 Gary Roosevelt; Hobart 37–13 Griffith; East Chicago Washington 14–10 East Chicago Roosevelt; Lowell 26–20 Whiting; Emerson 17–16 Hammond; Froebel 17–14 Wallace; Dyer 30–19 Merrillville; Crown Point 48–13 Calumet Twp.; Horace Mann 28–10 Hobart; Washington 20–14 Lowell; Froebel 13–12 Emerson; Crown Point 40–9 Dyer; Washington 16–14 Horace Mann; Froebel 24–21 Crown Point; Washington 20–12 Froebel. Officials: Clayton Hughes, Charles Link, Clarence Grogan.

GOODLAND: Brook 17–14 Rensselaer; Fair Oaks; 21–11 Wheatfield; Morocco 46–1 Hanging Grove; Remington 47–12 DeMotte; Goodland 47–7 Tefft; Kentland 29–11 Mt. Ayr; Brook 32–9 Fair Oaks; Remington 19–17 Morocco (ot); Goodland 25–13 Kentland; Brook 20–17 Remington; Brook 18–11 Goodland. Officials: Alvin Taylor, Floyd Merrman.

GOSHEN: Goshen 24–20 Wakarusa; Elkhart 15–14 Baugo Twp.; Millersburg 31–20 Middlebury; New Paris 46–4 Clinton Twp.; Nappanee 51–21 Washington Twp.; Concord Twp. 40–14 Jefferson Twp.; Goshen 24–22 Elkhart; Millersburg 16–11 New Paris. Nappanee 42–11 Concord Twp.; Goshen 28–17 Millersburg; Goshen 30–20 Nappanee. Officials: O. F. Helvie, Charles Litherland.

GREENCASTLE: Greencastle 42–13 Cloverdale; Fillmore 33–21 Reelsville; Roachdale 50–19 Putnamville; Bainbridge 27–24 Russellville; Greencastle 33–18 Fillmore; Bainbridge 14–13 Roachdale; Greencastle 27–14 Bainbridge. Officials: Leo Quillen, Glenn Adams.

GREENFIELD: Eden 23–15 McCordsville; Fortville 21–20 Maxwell; Mt. Comfort 21–12 Warren Central; New Palestine 17–13 Charlottesville; Greenfield 25–12 Westland; Wilkinson 26–20 Eden; Mt. Comfort 27–20 Fortville; Greenfield 17–15 New Palestine; Mt. Comfort 34–19 Wilkinson; Mt. Comfort 14–9 Greenfield. Officials: Paul Williams, Nate Kaufman.

GREENSBURG: Greensburg 41–10 Clarksburg. St. Paul 27–24 Jackson; New Point 28–10 Zenas; Butlerville 37–14 Letts; North Vernon 33–30 Burney; Westport 24–20 Scipio; Greensburg 41–15 Sandusky; St. Paul 28–16 New Point; Butlerville 21–18 North Vernon; Greensburg 60–7 Westport; St. Paul 24–22 Butlerville; Greensburg 31–14 St. Paul. Officials: Ray Frohman, W. H. Herbst, Roy Hunter.

HOWE: Wolcottville 21–20 Brighton. Lima 34–7 Springfield; Topeka 31–28 Shipshewana; LaGrange 42–10 Scott; Lima 47–13 Wolcottville; LaGrange 26–20 Topeka; Lima 29–26 LaGrange. Officials: Dale Kreigh, Frank Reid.

HUNTINGBURG: Spurgeon 36–20 Cuzco; Holland 33–8 Dubois; Huntingburg 40–15 Union; Petersburg 21–20 Jasper (3ot); Stendal 32–14 Velpen; Winslow 23–19 Otwell; Birdseye 29–20 Ireland; Holland 15–13 Spurgeon; Huntingburg 18–13 Petersburg; Stendal 18–15 Winslow; Holland 32–30 Birdseye (3ot); Huntingburg 31–25 Stendal; Huntingburg 21–12 Holland. Officials: Fred Alwood, John Hoffman, Harlie Jurgens.

HUNTINGTON: Warren 18–17 Roanoke. Huntington Twp. 21–18 Lancaster Center; Monument City 16–12 Markle; Clear Creek 39–19 Banquo; Huntington 43–18 Andrews; Union

IHSAA Scores / 1930–1939

23–10 Rock Creek; Jefferson 25–19 Bippus; Warren 24–22 Huntington Twp.; Clear Creek 26–17 Monument City; Huntington 34–25 Union Center; Warren 28–25 Jefferson Center; Huntington 36–21 Clear Creek; Huntington 22–13 Warren. Officials: Ward Gilbert, L. R. Lenon, Frederick Shroyer.

INDIANAPOLIS: Shortridge 26–19 Ben Davis. Manual 33–19 Castleton; Lawrence 13–8 Broad Ripple; Southport 23–10 New Augusta; Valley Mills 22–16 Oaklandon; Washington 24–10 West Newton; Tech 36–12 New Bethel; Acton 31–30 Beech Grove (4ot); Manual 15–14 Shortridge; Southport 20–18 Lawrence. Washington 28–18 Valley Mills; Tech 30–3 Acton; Manual 15–14 Southport; Tech 20–2 Washington; Tech 38–5 Manual. Officials: Claude Draper, Earl Boyd, Mode Cranor.

KENDALLVILLE: Albion 33 –25 Avilla; Kendallville 49–11 Orange Twp.; Ligonier 17–14 Wawaka; LaOtto 16–14 Cromwell; Kendallville 24–9 Albion; LaOtto 26–21 Ligonier; Kendallville 30–14 LaOtto. Officials: Carl Burt, George Yarnelle.

KOKOMO: New London 32–30 Howard Twp. (ot); Kokomo 72–2 Union Twp.; Jackson Twp. 21–14 Russiaville; Greentown 26–24 Ervin; West Middleton 40–29 New London; Kokomo 29–27 Jackson Twp.; Greentown 45–12 West Middleton; Kokomo 14–12 Greentown. Officials: Orbie Branham, Harry Coolman.

LAFAYETTE: Jefferson 16–15 West Lafayette; Romney 21–16 Monitor; Dayton 21–20 Battle Ground; Clarks Hill 31–19 Jackson Twp.; Klondike 22–21 West Point; Buck Creek 26–21 Stockwell; Wea 34–18 Montmorenci; Jefferson 39–6 Romney; Dayton 20–10 Clarks Hill; Buck Creek 21–13 Klondike; Jefferson 31–11 Wea; Dayton 23–14 Buck Creek; Jefferson 23–18 Dayton. Officials: Henry Goett, Will Smith, Louis Means.

LAPORTE: Kingsbury 24–22 Wanatah; Mill Creek 19–15 Union Twp.; Rolling Prairie 23–16 Hanna (ot); Michigan City 23–18 Westville; LaPorte 14–13 Union Mills; Stillwell 19–16 LaCrosse; Kingsbury 19–18 Mill Creek; Michigan City 24–20 Rolling Prairie; LaPorte 27–10 Stillwell. Michigan City 25–22 Kingsbury (ot); LaPorte 23–18 Michigan City. Officials: John Stahr, C. E. Fauber.

LEBANON: Lebanon 39–16 Whitestown; Zionsville 18–6 Central; Advance 25–10 Jefferson Twp.; Jamestown 31–15 Pinnell; Lebanon 34–16 Thorntown; Advance 14–11 Zionsville; Lebanon 27–17; Jamestown; Advance 27–26 Lebanon. Officials: Ralph Eades, Houston Meyer

LINTON: Bloomfield 27–19 Newberry; Lyons 27–17; Owensburg; Jasonville 21–12 Midland; Switz City 27–17; Solsberry; Linton 55–9 Scotland; Bloomfield 34–27 Lyons; Switz City 30–15 Jasonville; Linton 34–9 Bloomfield; Linton 23–20 Switz City. Officials: Wayne Watson, J. C. Hannah.

LOGANSPORT: Galveston 23–17 Washington Twp.; Onward 20–8 Metea; Lucerne 20–19 Lincoln; Logansport 84–30 Deacon; Twelve Mile 108–8 Noble Twp.; Walton 41–23 Royal Center; Young America 18–16 New Waverly; Onward 27–21 Galveston; Logansport 41–15 Lucerne; Walton 26–18 Twelve Mile; Onward 29–20 Young America; Logansport 38–16 Walton; Logansport 41–20 Onward. Officials: Don Arbuckle, Daniel Guild, Walter Geller.

MADISON: Dupont 31–17 Saluda; Lovett 33–3 Lexington; Deputy 29–15 San Jacinto; Madison 23–20 Austin; Vevay 32–21 Hanover; Paris Crossing 21–14 Patriot; Scottsburg 11–8 North Madison. Dupont 31–13 Central; Deputy 32–7 Lovett; Vevay 27–21 Madison; Scottsburg 21–10 Paris Crossing; Dupont 29–11 Deputy; Scottsburg 25–17 Vevay; Scottsburg 24–8 Dupont. Officials: Martin Luther, Ivan Zaring, Hermon Phillips.

Tourney Time

MARION: Gas City 42–22 Matthews; Jonesboro 17–16 Upland; Swayzee 20–15 Sweetser; Fairmount 38–15 Van Buren; Marion 24–17 Gas City; Swayzee 26–14 Jonesboro; Marion 17–10 Fairmount; Marion 48–31 Swayzee. Officials: Winston Ashley, LeRoy Cook.

MILAN: Rising Sun 15–8 Versailles. Batesville 27–21 Sunman; Center Twp. 27–12 Bright; Lawrenceburg 19–12 Milan; Marion 27–26 New Marion; Napoleon 33–25 Moores Hill. Aurora 48–24 Dillsboro; Rising Sun 34–13 Guilford; Batesville 24–19 Center Twp.; Lawrenceburg 29–19 Holton; Aurora 32–19 Napoleon; Rising Run 29–12 Batesville; Aurora 22–18 Lawrenceburg; Rising Sun 22–17 Aurora. Officials: Blair Gullion, Richard Miller, Hobert Potter.

MISHAWAKA: Mishawaka 37–4 LaPaz; New Carlisle 19–17 Walkerton; Lakeville 22–11 Madison Twp.; Riley 29–22 Plymouth; South Bend 37–21 Tyner; North Liberty 27–7 West Twp.; Mishawaka 24–20 Bremen; Lakeville 23–15 New Carlisle; South Bend 34–10 Riley; North Liberty 22–21 Mishawaka; South Bend 31–12 Lakeville; South Bend 33–5 North Liberty. Officials: Lavon Carey, Condict A. Smith, Maurice Tudor.

MITCHELL: Fayetteville 23–16 Huron; Bedford 17–11 Mitchell; Needmore 22–17 Williams; Shawswick 26–11 Heltonville; Oolitic 35–15 Tunnelton; Bedford 18–6 Fayetteville; Needmore 24–19 Shawswick; Bedford 23–14 Oolitic; Bedford 31–14 Need–more. Officials: Vaughn Russell, Harry Conover.

MONON: Reynolds 26–18 Buffalo; Monon 20–19 Burnettsville; Brookston 24–4 Round Grove; Chalmers 25–16 Idaville; Wolcott 12–10 Monticello; Monon 25–16 Reynolds; Brookston 14–13 Chalmers; Wolcott 20–18 Monon; Brookston 18–6 Wolcott. Officials: George Vaulk, Andrew Gill.

MONTPELIER: Dunkirk 47–10 Bryant. Portland 32–25 Pennville; Redkey 37–23 Green Twp.; Roll 29–16 Poling; Hartford City 34–6 Gray; Madison 23–20 Montpelier; Dunkirk 24–19 Portland; Roll 35–25 Redkey; Hartford City 23–16 Madison; Dunkirk 25–11 Roll; Hartford City 42–9 Dunkirk. Officials: Robert Lambert, Elmer Rowe.

MUNCIE: Harrison Twp. 33–30 Gaston; Royerton 29–12 Albany; Yorktown 48–24 Cowan; Center 37–23 DeSoto; Eaton 46–17 Daleville; Muncie 53–27 Selma; Harrison Twp. 34–24 Royerton; Center 35–28 Yorktown; Muncie 29–15 Eaton; Harrison Twp. 32–25 Center; Muncie 50–23 Harrison Twp. Officials: H. E. Vandiver, John Schram.

NEW ALBANY: Charlestown 42–6 Washington Twp.; Posey Twp. 17–15 New Middletown; Henryville 30–20 Franklin Twp.; New Albany 30–12 Jeffersonville; Georgetown 45–37 New Washington; New Salisbury 40–9 DePauw; Corydon 41–17 Silver Creek; Morgan Twp. 39–12 Borden; Charlestown 19–14 Posey Twp.; New Albany 46–15 Henryville; New Salisbury 33–24 Georgetown; Corydon 34–20 Morgan Twp.; New Albany 18–17 Charlestown; Corydon 54–26 New Salisbury; New Albany 35–19 Corydon. Officials: Elmer Posey, Harry Blume, Gerald Bottorff.

NEW CASTLE: Sulphur Springs 21–13 Kennard; Middletown 12–10 Knightstown (ot); New Castle 24–6 Cadiz; Mt. Summit 20–5 Lewisville; Straughn 25–20 Spiceland; Mooreland 40–10 New Lisbon; Middletown 22–14 Sulphur Springs; New Castle 14–10 Mt. Summit; Mooreland 40–27 Straughn. New Castle 15–11 Middletown; New Castle 16–14 Mooreland (ot). Officials: Elder Eberhart, George Seidensticker.

PAOLI: West Baden 22–15 Paoli; Orleans 32–9 Little York; Hardinsburg 24–12 Campbellsburg; Salem 31–12 French Lick; Pekin 33–15 Monroe Twp.; West Baden 22–13 Orleans; Salem 36–8 Hardinsburg; West Baden 18–7 Pekin; Salem 15–12 West Baden. Officials: George Goerlitz, Elmer Weber.

PERU: Peru 29–13 Bunker Hill; Jefferson Twp. 27–25 Butler Twp.; Gilead 15–13 Macy; Clay Twp. 60–22 Deedsville; Converse 30–15 Amboy; Peru 28–20 Chili; Gilead 34–21 Jefferson Twp.; Clay Twp. 31–23 Converse; Peru 52–12 Gilead; Peru 25–24 Clay Twp. Officials: Walter Bussard, Charles Rouch.

PRINCETON: Francisco 28–25 Ft. Branch; Mt. Olympus 24–22 Owensville; Oakland City 30–15 Hazleton; Princeton 47–10 Patoka; Francisco 22–21 Haubstadt; Oakland City 14–7 Mt. Olympus; Princeton 34–26 Francisco; Princeton 16–8 Oakland City. Officials: Kilburn Rogers, J. E. Wakefield.

RICHMOND: Lynn 36–26 Fountain City; Richmond 41–15 Milton; Cambridge City 22–18 Williamsburg; Boston 19–13 Economy; Hagerstown 45–22 Greensfork; Centerville 42–17 Whitewater; Richmond 28–12 Lynn; Cambridge City 17–15 Boston; Centerville 27–15 Hagerstown; Richmond 35–12 Cambridge City; Richmond 22–18 Centerville. Officials: Everett Babb, D. H. Hostetter.

ROCHESTER: Culver 30–7 Leiters Ford; Akron 32–9 Kewanna; Talma 19–17 Bourbon; Rochester 25–10 Argos; Richland Center 30–22 Tippecanoe (ot); Fulton 24–11 Grass Creek; Akron 18–9 Culver; Rochester 21–11 Talma; Fulton 22–13 Richland Center; Rochester 25–11 Akron; Rochester 21–19 Fulton (ot). Officials: George Allessee, Harry Hatcher.

RUSHVILLE: Milroy 44–4 Mays; Carthage 25–7 Ging; Morton Memorial 20–12 New Salem; Raleigh 27–25 Arlington; Rushville 31–17 Manilla; Milroy 18–14 Carthage; Morton Memorial 24–19 Raleigh; Rushville 24–14 Milroy; Rushville 20–15 Morton Memorial. Officials: William E. Campbell, Forrest Ballinger.

SEYMOUR: Cortland 47–8 Houston; Seymour 33–14 Freetown; Vallonia 21–20 Crothersville (ot); Clearspring 29–21 Medora; Brownstown 25–20 Tampico; Seymour 30–20 Cortland; Clearspring 15–14 Vallonia. Seymour 18–14 Brownstown; Seymour 30–8 Clearspring. Officials: Thomas Baker, F. A. Bills.

SHELBYVILLE: Waldron 32–21 Hawcreek; Mt. Auburn 41–21 Boggstown; Moral 20–17 Flat Rock; Columbus 49–15 Flat Rock Twp.; Shelbyville 34–23 Morristown; Waldron 24–21 Fairland; Moral 40–39 Mt. Auburn; Shelbyville 25–22 Columbus; Waldron 19–18 Moral; Shelbyville 40–12 Waldron. Officials: Charles Jensen, Guy Woods.

SULLIVAN: Pleasantville 30–23 Farmersburg; Sullivan 22–20 New Lebanon; Graysville 30–19 Carlisle; Union (Dugger) 17–12 Jackson Twp.; Fairbanks 28–16 Merom; Sullivan 30–24 Pleasantville; Union 20–14 Graysville; Sullivan 28–9 Fairbanks; Union 21–20 Sullivan. Officials: J. Ord Fortner, Will Kinkaid.

TELL CITY: Union Twp. 23–8 Rome; Tobinsport 25–14 Leavenworth; Troy 17–11 Cannelton; Marengo 44–16 Oil Twp.; Tell City 30–14 English; Leopold 27–26 Anderson Twp.; Derby 39–18 Milltown; Bristow 37–19 Union Twp.; Troy 29–27 Tobinsport; Tell City 15–14 Marengo; Derby 17–13 Leopold; Bristow 17–15 Troy; Tell City 14–11 Derby; Bristow 16–14 Tell City. Officials: Donald Wilder, Paul Garrison, G. S. Rust.

TERRE HAUTE: Wiley 32–11 Honey Creek; Glenn 23–14 West Terre Haute; Concannon 23–22 Normal; Prairie Creek 27–10 Fontanet; Garfield 22–11 Otter Creek; Riley 29–19 Blackhawk; Pimento 25–19 Gerstmeyer; Wiley 42–16 Glenn; Concannon 35–23 Prairie Creek; Garfield 28–8 Riley; Wiley 30–10 Pimento; Concannon 18–17 Garfield; Wiley 37–13 Concannon. Officials: Crawford Baganz, Clinton Dougherty, Mel Puett.

TIPTON: Tipton 25–21 Kempton; Prairie Twp. 37–21 Carmel; Fishers 24–23 Goldsmith;

Tourney Time

Arcadia 19–18 Atlanta; Sharpsville 49–10 Westfield; Windfall 19–10 Noblesville; Cicero 47–7 Boxley; Walnut Grove 14–9 Sheridan; Tipton 29–25 Prairie Twp.; Fishers 20–16 Arcadia; Windfall 16–12 Sharpsville; Cicero 15–14 Walnut Grove; Tipton 42–19 Fishers; Windfall 20–18 Cicero; Tipton 21–20 Windfall. Officials: John Miller, R. B. Morrison, Fernie Trigalet.

VALPARAISO: Crisman 16–12 Liberty Center; Chesterton 29–22 Morgan Twp.; Valparaiso 57–15 Washington Twp.; Wheeler 22–20 Hebron; Chesterton 27–13 Crisman; Valparaiso 42–6 Wheeler; Valparaiso 12–9 Chesterton. Officials: Homer Orsborn, G. L. Russell.

VINCENNES: Oaktown 20–16 Bicknell; Monroe City 28–18 Edwardsport; Decker Chapel 22–13 Decker; Bruceville 47–4 Sandborn; Vincennes 18–16 Fritchton; Freelandville 30–19 Wheatland; Oaktown 29–19 Monroe City; Bruceville 12–8 Decker Chapel; Vincennes 20–16 Freelandville; Bruceville 26–22 Oaktown; Vincennes 14–11 Bruceville. Officials: D. C. Moffett, Irvin Springer.

WABASH: Wabash 25–14 Lincolnville; Lafontaine 27–19 Roann; Laketon 29–15 Linlawn; Chippewa 23–21 Urbana; Lagro 18–11 Chester Twp.; North Manchester 23–21 Somerset; Lafontaine 35–23 Wabash; Chippewa 29–23 Laketon; North Manchester 21–15 Lagro; Chippewa 27–25 Lafontaine; North Manchester 20–12 Chippewa. Officials: R. P. Chambers, Archie Heller.

WARSAW: Van Buren Twp. (Milford) 21–7 Claypool; Burket 24–15 Beaver Dam; Syracuse 12–9 Silver Lake. Mentone 32–15 Warsaw; Atwood 18–13 Pierceton; Etna Green 35–26 Sidney; Leesburg 22–19 North Webster; Van Buren Twp. 42–10 Burket; Syracuse 18–16 Mentone; Etna Green 16–14 Atwood; Van Buren Twp. 22–17 Leesburg; Syracuse 22–16 Etna Green; Van Buren Twp. 14–13 Syracuse. Officials: Lloyd Miller, Ralph Parker, Lundy Welborn.

WASHINGTON: Elnora 15–8 Loogootee; Plainville 37–20 Burns City; Epsom 34–15 Alfordsville; Odon 27–17 Barr Twp.; Shoals 35–10 Raglesville; Washington 45–9 Elnora; Plainville 17–12 Epsom; Odon 36–9 Shoals; Washington 16–9 Plainville; Washington 38–10 Odon. Officials: W. S. Fellmy, H. C. Henderson.

WINAMAC: Winamac 48–8 Center Twp.; Star City 16–14 Monterey; Pulaski 31–12 Grovertown; Knox 33–21 Hamlet; North Judson 55–6 Medaryville; Winamac 62–5 North Bend; Pulaski 19–3 Star City; North Judson 36–27 Knox; Winamac 28–15 Pulaski; Winamac 29–18 North Judson. Officials: Paul Isenbarger, Phocian Rhoads.

WINCHESTER: Jefferson 28–19 Huntsville; Losantville 24–5 Modoc; Stoney Creek 41–4 Lincoln; Union City 40–10 Jackson; Spartanburg 28–19 Ridgeville; Wayne 23–12 McKinley; Winchester 25–11 Farmland; Parker 29–15 Saratoga; Losantville 21–15 Jefferson; Union City 34–29 Stoney Creek; Spartanburg 59–20 Wayne; Parker 30–24 Winchester; Union City 26–9 Losantville; Spartanburg 33–13 Parker; Union City 38–28 Spartanburg. Officials: Norman Durham, Jesse Cage, Clive Markley.

1930 REGIONALS

ATTICA: Greencastle 30–19 Attica; Crawfordsville 19–14 Clinton; Greencastle 37–20 Crawfordsville. Officials: Dale Miller, Will Smith.

AUBURN: Auburn 21–19 Milford; Kendallville 34–25 Lima (ot); Kendallville 23–16 Auburn. Officials: Ralph Eades, Mode Cranor.

BEDFORD: New Albany 22–20 Seymour; Salem 12–9 Bedford; Salem 20–16 New Albany.

Officials: Irvin Springer, H. Kilburn Rogers.

COLUMBUS: Shelbyville 19–6 Scottsburg; Franklin 30–16 Greensburg; Franklin 19–15 Shelbyville. Officials: Winston Ashley, Paul Williams.

FORT WAYNE: Liberty Center 36–22 Columbia City; Central 25–20 Huntington; Central 30–13 Liberty Center. Officials: Carl Burt, Don Arbuckle.

FRANKFORT: Frankfort 39–20 Advance; Lafayette Jefferson 22–18 Otterbein; Frankfort 24–14 Jefferson. Officials: B. B. Evans, Charles Jensen.

GARY: LaPorte 23–13 Brook; Valparaiso 25–22 East Chicago Washington; LaPorte 39–20 Valparaiso; Officials: Homer Stonebraker, Hugh Vandivier.

INDIANAPOLIS: Tipton 45–23 North Salem; Anderson 20–13 Tech; Anderson 43–17 Tipton. Officials: B. E. Bayh, Orville Jones.

LOGANSPORT: Delphi 24–23 Brookston; Logansport 32–16 Peru; Delphi 24–23 Logansport. Officials: John Stahr, Bruce Morrison.

MARION: Marion 23–19 North Manchester; Kokomo 24–19 Hartford City; Kokomo 23–21 Marion. Officials: Homer Orsborn, Gilbert Best.

MARTINSVILLE: Wiley 26–18 Brazil; Martinsville 37–27 Linton; Martinsville 31–20 Wiley. Officials: John Miller, John Schram.

MISHAWAKA: Winamac 14–11 South Bend; Goshen 25–11 Rochester; Goshen 23–15 Winamac. Officials: O.F. Helvie, Carl Olson.

MUNCIE: Mt. Comfort 25–19 Union City; Muncie 31–22 New Castle; Muncie 28–22 Mt. Comfort. Officials: Ford Griffith, George Vaulk.

RUSHVILLE: Connersville 18–15 Richmond; Rushville 36–7 Rising Sun; Connersville 41–20 Rushville; Officials: P. O. Hurley, Guy Woods.

VINCENNES: Union (Dugger) 29–16 Princeton; Evansville Bosse 29–26 Vincennes; Union 33–19 Bosse. Officials: Harry Conover, Vaughn Russell.

WASHINGTON: Washington 26–18 Huntingburg; Tennyson 29–16 Bristow; Washington 47–14 Tennyson. Officials: Henry Goett, W. S. Porter.

1930 FINALS—March 14, 15

INDIANAPOLIS (Butler Fieldhouse): Washington 20–14 Martinsville; Franklin 34–19 Union (Dugger); Delphi 28–17 Kokomo; Connersville 25–18 Salem; LaPorte 21–19 Kendallville; Muncie 30–28 Goshen; Frankfort 31–19 Fort Wayne Central; Anderson 27–23 Greencastle; Washington 31–11 Franklin; Connersville 40–13 Delphi; Muncie 43–25 LaPorte; Frankfort 22–17 Anderson; Washington 35–17 Connersville; Muncie 18–13 Frankfort; Washington 32–21 Muncie. Officials: B. E. Bayh, Dale Miller, Carl Olson, Vaughn Russell, Hugh Vandivier.

1931 SECTIONALS

ANDERSON: Alexandria 19–11 Markleville; Anderson 54–17 Frankton; Pendleton 27–23 Lapel; Summitville 31–24 Elwood; Alexandria 32–30 Anderson (3ot); Summitville 32–27 Pendleton; Alexandria 35–21 Summitville. Officials: Walter Geller, Harry Coolman.

ATTICA: Attica 25–15 Pine Village; West Lebanon 43–18 Covington; Kingman 20–18 Hillsboro; Veedersburg 31–23 Williamsport; Attica 35–26 West Lebanon; Veedersburg 31–25

Tourney Time

Kingman; Veedersburg 19–16 Attica. Officials: Norman Dunlap, Walter Moss.

BLOOMFIELD: Lyons 48–10 Scotland; Linton 26–9 Jasonville. Midland 29–21 Newberry; Switz City 18–16 Owensburg; Solsberry 32–27 Bloomfield; Linton 22–10 Lyons; Switz City 30–25 Midland; Linton 22–17 Solsberry; Switz City 17–8 Linton. Officials: Walter Ringer, Harry Conover.

BLUFFTON: Petroleum 29–24 Lancaster Center; Chester Center 23–20 Ossian; Bluffton 39–19 Rockcreek Center; Liberty Center 30–25 Union Center; Petroleum 27–20 Chester Center; Bluffton 23–11 Liberty Center; Bluffton 39–24 Petroleum. Officials: Leo Quillen Frederick Shroyer.

BOSWELL: Fowler 26–13 Earl Park; Otterbein 28–17 Freeland Park; Gilboa 37–17 Wadena; Boswell 38–17 Oxford; Ambia 22–15 Pine Twp.; Fowler 14–11 Raub; Otterbein 25–15 Gilboa; Boswell 21–6 Ambia. Otterbein 16–15 Fowler; Boswell 24–21 Otterbein. Officials: Will Kinkaid, Myron Moore.

CANNELTON: Troy 26–17 Leopold; Marengo 35–13 Oriole; Bristow 37–30 Union Twp.; Derby 20–10 Cannelton; Tell City 42–13 Rome; Tobinsport 23–12 Leavenworth; Marengo 27–22 Troy; Derby 29–26 Bristow; Tell City 33–14 Tobinsport; Derby 20–18 Marengo; Tell City 43–11 Derby. Officials: Elmer Weber, Ivan Zaring.

CLINTON: Newport 19–14 Montezuma; Cayuga 25–17 Tangier; Clinton 43–10 Dana; St. Bernice 33–22 Mecca; Hillsdale 27–8 Perrysville; Rosedale 17–15 Bloomingdale; Newport 23–19 Cayuga; Clinton 46–12 St. Bernice, Rosedale 15–11 Hillsdale; Clinton 19–15 Newport; Clinton 41–17 Rosedale. Officials: Glenn Adams, Raleigh Phillips.

CONNERSVILLE: Union 20–10 Orange; Brownsville 31–8 Whitewater; Connersville 98–9 Fairview; Everton 19–15 Brookville; Bentonville 19–18 Alquina; Harrison 60–12 Laurel; Liberty 86–6 Harrisburg; Springfield Twp. 21–20 Union; Connersville 42–11 Brownsville; Everton 28–26 Bentonville; Liberty 46–25 Harrison; Connersville 48–23 Springfield; Liberty 41–25 Everton; Connersville 40–21 Liberty. Officials: Gerald Huey, Nate Kaufman, Blair Gullion.

CRAWFORDSVILLE: Crawfordsville 16–9 Linden; Wingate 27–15 Bowers; New Ross 24–23 Alamo; New Market 39–14 Waveland; Waynetown 24–10 Darlington; Ladoga 20–17 New Richmond; Wingate 19–15 Crawfordsville; New Market 27–16 New Ross; Ladoga 17–15 Waynetown; Wingate 26–11 New Market; Wingate 24–14 Ladoga. Officials: Wayne Watson, Harold Metcalf.

DANVILLE: Lizton 26–19 Stilesville; Pittsboro 23–19 Plainfield; Danville 50–7 New Winchester; North Salem 20–12 Clayton; Brownsburg 53–16 Avon; Amo 23–19 Lizton; Danville 23–11 Pittsboro; North Salem 35–34 Brownsburg; Danville 26–21 Amo; Danville 20–11 North Salem. Officials: Thomas Baker, Orville Jones.

DECATUR: Monroe 26–16 Monmouth; Geneva 29–9 Pleasant Mills; Berne 22–19 Hartford Twp.; Kirkland 44–18 Jefferson Twp.; Decatur 44–12 Monroe; Berne 13–12 Geneva; Decatur 23–17 Kirkland; Decatur 17–14 Berne. Officials: George Lambert, Ora Davis.

ELKHART: Nappanee 38–22 Millersburg; New Paris 38–17 Concord Twp.; Goshen 27–18 Middlebury; Elkhart 35–17 Bristol; Wakarusa 32–13 Jefferson Twp.; Nappanee 35–9 Baugo Twp.; Goshen 16–15 New Paris; Elkhart 14–13 Wakarusa; Nappanee 22–15 Goshen; Elkhart 25–20 Nappanee. Officials: Lloyd Miller, O. F. Helvie.

EVANSVILLE: Mt. Vernon 20–19 Stewartsville; Central 9–6 Bosse; Cynthiana 37–24 Chandler; New Harmony 14–12 Poseyville; Griffin 21–17 Millersburg; Elberfeld 18–17 Newburgh;

Reitz 34–20 Mt. Vernon; Central 33–19 Cynthiana; New Harmony 27–5 Griffin; Reitz 23–17 Elberfeld; Central 31–17 New Harmony; Central 30–22 Reitz. Officials: Paul Garrison, George Graham, John Hoffman.

FLORA: Camden 19–17 Cutler; Flora 35–19 Carrollton; Deer Creek 27–6 Rock–field; Delphi 35–15 Burlington; Camden 33–14 Adams Twp.; Flora 22–17 Deer Creek. Delphi 17–13 Camden; Delphi 23–10 Flora. Officials: Will Smith, Ralph Worley.

FORT WAYNE: Huntertown 25–19 Arcola; Woodburn 14–12 Monroeville; South Side 39–5 Leo; North Side 23–9 Lafayette Center; New Haven 29–15 Madison Twp.; Central 54–16 Harlan; Huntertown 16–14 Woodburn; North Side 14–13 South Side; New Haven 19–17 Central; North Side 16–11 Huntertown; North Side 23–19 New Haven. Officials: Paul Williams, Carl Burt.

FRANKFORT: Scircleville 31–28 Mulberry; Colfax 34–15 Sugar Creek Twp.; Rossville 38–15 Jackson Twp.; Frankfort 81–9 Kirklin. Michigantown 45–10 Jefferson; Scircleville 25–11 Forest; Colfax 19–17 Rossville; Frankfort 34–17 Michigantown; Scir–cleville 24–13 Colfax; Frankfort 37–9 Scircleville. Officials: Mode Cranor, Dillon Geiger.

FRANKLIN: Nashville 38–21 Trafalgar; Franklin 16–9 Hopewell; Edinburg 38–22 Center Grove; Masonic Home 41–20 Clark Twp.; Greenwood 17–16 Union; Whiteland 18–16 Nineveh; Franklin 58–12 Nashville; Masonic Home 25–24 Edinburg; Greenwood 32–21 Whiteland; Franklin 21–16 Masonic Home; Franklin 31–10 Greenwood. Officials: Frank Jarrell, Hermon Phillips.

GARRETT: Ashley 2–0 Hamilton (forfeit); Auburn 40–17 Fremont; Concord Twp. 28–23 Orland (ot); Churubusco 30–21 Waterloo; Scott Center 24–14 Flint; Salem Center 33–19 Pleasant Lake; Angola 40–11 Spencerville; Garrett 22–19 Butler; Auburn 48–24 Ashley; Churubusco 28–26 Concord Twp.; Salem Center 40–8 Scott Center; Garrett 18–17 Angola; Auburn 55–17 Churubusco; Garrett 24–18 Salem Center; Auburn 48–28 Garrett. Officials: Carl Porter, Raymond Yoos, L. E. Fink.

GARY: Froebel 25–11 Hammond; Hobart 24–18 Dyer; Whiting 21–20 Hammond Tech; Horace Mann 59–11 East Gary Central; East Chicago Roosevelt 47–14 Calumet Twp.; Wallace 36–14 Merrillville; East Chicago Washington 57–5 Gary Roosevelt; Emerson 53–12 Griffith; Froebel 18–13 Hobart; Horace Mann 27–12 Whiting; East Chicago Roosevelt 27–24 Wallace; East Chicago Washington 28–25 Emerson; Horace Mann 26–13 Froebel; East Chicago Roosevelt 23–20 Washington; Horace Mann 41–17 East Chicago Roosevelt. Officials: Clayton Hughes, Forrest Wood, Paul Hurley.

GREENCASTLE: Cloverdale 22–13 Fillmore. Bridgeton 43–12 Bellmore; Green–castle 21–7 Bainbridge; Rockville 45–4 Reelsville. Belle Union 25–14 Green Twp.; Russellville 29–18 Marshall; Roachdale 31–10 Putnamville; Cloverdale 32–17 Bridgeton; Greencastle 40–17 Rockville. Belle Union 22–7 Russellville; Cloverdale 25–16 Roachdale; Greencastle 20–6 Belle Union; Greencastle 25–18 Cloverdale. Officials: Lavon Carey, Earl Pike, H. D. Williamson.

GREENFIELD: Mt. Comfort 35–19 Fortville; Greenfield 39–22 Westland; Eden 34–16 Charlottesville; Wilkinson 30–16 Maxwell; New Palestine 28–19 Warren Central; Mt. Comfort 32–27 McCordsville; Eden 23–21 Greenfield (4ot); Wilkinson 32–25 New Palestine; Mt. Comfort 34–19 Eden; Wilkinson 24–22 Mt. Comfort. Officials: Layall Fisher, Harry Vandivier.

GREENSBURG: Jackson 26–4 Sandusky; Batesville 27–22 New Point (ot); Letts 39–18 New Marion; Greensburg 33–21 Burney; Holton 27–11 Napoleon; St. Paul 30–14 Clarksburg; Center Twp. 30–16 Westport; Jackson 36–22 Batesville; Greensburg 32–20 Letts; St. Paul 27–20 Holton;

Tourney Time

Jackson 27–11 Osgood; Greensburg 36–16 St. Paul; Greensburg 29–10 Jackson. Officials: Custer Baker, Charles Brehm, Robert Nipper.

HARTFORD CITY: Bryant 35–15 Redkey; Dunkirk 25–17 Poling; Hartford City 31–16 Madison Twp.; Pennville 16–12 Gray; Roll 21–14 Montpelier; Portland 33–22 Bryant; Hartford City 43–13 Dunkirk; Pennville 20–19 Roll; Hartford City 28–20 Portland; Hartford City 17–12 Pennville. Officials: Norman Durham, Virgil Hickman.

HUNTINGTON: Bippus 26–20 Lancaster; Banquo 37–17 Markle; Clear Creek 31–14 Jefferson; Union Center 25–12 Andrews; Warren 32–30 Monument City; Rockcreek 30–28 Huntington Twp.; Huntington 36–21 Roanoke; Banquo 20–9 Bippus; Union 15–14 Clear Creek; Warren 26–13 Rockcreek; Huntington 27–5 Banquo; Union 20–16 Warren; Huntington 13–11 Union. Officials: T. R. Smith, Orbie Branham, Don Jordan.

INDIANAPOLIS: Tech 44–13 Oaklandon; Washington 45–15 Castleton; West Newton 17–16 Lawrence; Southport; 23–15 Valley Mills; Shortridge 14–12 Broad Ripple; New Bethel 31–16 New Augusta; Ben Davis 36–29 Beech Grove; Manual 43–14 Acton; Tech 31–17 Washington; Southport 28–22 West Newton; Shortridge 24–15 New Bethel; Manual 45–20 Ben Davis; Southport 21–16 Tech; Shortridge 25–22 Manual; Shortridge 37–23 Southport. Officials: Clarence Grogan, Ralph Parker, Charles Jensen.

KENDALLVILLE: Kendallville 37–14 LaOtto; Jefferson City 30–22 Washington Center; South Whitley 20–19 Wolf Lake; Cromwell 27–10 Coesse; Wawaka 46–8 Etna; Larwill 27–20 Ligonier; Albion 28–21 Avilla; Columbia City 55–5 Orange Twp.; Kendallville 39–19 Jefferson Center; Cromwell 29–21 South Whitley; Wawaka 31–22 Larwill; Columbia City 19–17 Albion; Kendallville 37–7 Cromwell; Columbia City 34–15 Wawaka; Kendallville 33–15 Columbia City. Officials: Phocian Rhoads, L. B. Hart, Fernie Trigalet.

KOKOMO: Russiaville 42–13 Ervin Twp.; Howard Twp. 22–18 Clay Twp.; New London 37–19 Union Twp.; Kokomo 44–12 Jackson Twp.; West Middleton 16–12 Greentown; Russiaville 27–16 Howard Twp; Kokomo 31–11 New London; West Middleton 18–16 Russiaville; Kokomo 46–23 West Middleton. Officials: Daniel Guild, Byron Deakyne.

LAFAYETTE: Romney 25–17 West Point; Dayton 22–20 Wea; Clarks Hill 27–15 Montmorenci; Jackson Twp. 39–14 Klondike; West Lafayette 33–14 Battle Ground; Lafayette 32–11 Monitor; West Point 23–21 Romney; Clarks Hill 28–16 Stockwell; West Lafayette 26–25 Jackson Twp.; Jefferson 23–12 Dayton; West Lafayette 29–17 Clarks Hill; Jefferson 17–11 West Lafayette. Officials: Reid McLain, S. S. Shake, Charles Garrett.

LAGRANGE: Shipshewana 27–16 Topeka. Lima 35–21 Brighton; LaGrange 28–15 Springfield Twp.; Wolcottville 20–18 Scott; Lima 33–13 Shipshewana; LaGrange 29–17 Wolcottville; Lima 33–22 LaGrange. Officials: Andrew Gill, Charles Link.

LAPORTE: Rolling Prairie 18–11 Stillwell; LaCrosse 21–13 Mill Creek; LaPorte 40–10 Clinton Twp.; Union Mills 23–6 Hanna; Michigan City 27–11 Union Twp.; Kingsbury 29–17 Westville; Wanatah 24–20 Rolling Prairie; LaPorte 38–24 LaCrosse; Union Mills 29–19 Michigan City; Wanatah 26–19 Kingsbury; LaPorte 23–17 Union Mills; LaPorte 39–18 Wanatah. Officials: William E. Campbell, Joel Wilt, Wayne Cunningham.

LAWRENCEBURG: Milan 37–24 Guilford; Versailles 29–23 Sunman; Lawrenceburg 25–21 Rising Sun; Aurora 36–22 Moores Hill; Dillsboro 27–24 Bright; Milan 28–21 Versailles; Lawrenceburg 32–31 Aurora; Milan 29–24 Dillsboro; Lawrenceburg 42–25 Milan. Officials: Robert Potter, Ray Frohman.

IHSAA Scores | 1930–1939

LEBANON: Jamestown 25–18 Union Twp.; Advance 44–19 Central; Thorntown 27–17 Pinnell; Zionsville 23–16 Whitestown; Lebanon 35–17 Jamestown; Advance 30–13 Thorntown; Lebanon 36–23 Zionsville; Lebanon 20–15 Advance. Officials: Jesse Cage, George Kenzler.

LOGANSPORT: Logansport 33–18 Galveston; Metea 54–6 Noble Twp.; Royal Center 14–13 New Waverly; Young America 14–11 Lucerne; Onward 22–21 Twelve Mile; Washington Twp. 24–20 Lincoln; Logansport 28–18 Walton; Metea 18–17 Royal Center; Young America 23 –21 Onward; Logansport 57–15 Washington Twp.; Young America 20–16 Metea; Logansport 13–7 Young America. Officials: George Vaulk, Claude Draper, Charlie Rouch.

MADISON: Madison 20–19 Scottsburg; North Madison 29–17 Saluda; Austin 60–16 Lexington; Vevay 35–25 Central; Dupont 47–20 Lovett; Deputy 17–10 Paris Crossing; Hanover 36–25 Patriot. Madison 41–15 San Jacinto; Austin 31–18 North Madison; Vevay 32–16 Dupont; Hanover 23–20 Deputy; Madison 16–12 Austin; Vevay 26–16 Hanover; Vevay 19–12 Madison. Officials: Gerald Bottorff; Martin Luther, Ray McKinley.

MARION: Sweetser 38–17 Van Buren; Marion 30–22 Jonesboro; Gas City 29–28 Fairmount; Swayzee 33–23 Matthews; Sweetser 46–11 Upland; Marion 35–15 Gas City; Sweetser 38–25 Swayzee; Marion 23–14 Sweetser. Officials: Forrest Ballinger, Homer Stonebraker.

MARTINSVILLE: Monrovia 44–24 Eminence; Martinsville 39–26 Paragon; Ellettsville 22–20 Mooresville; Stinesville 32–19 Unionville; Bloomington 29–23 Smithville; Monrovia 40–19 Morgantown; Martinsville 45–15 Ellettsville; Stinesville 34–29 Bloomington; Martinsville 26–18 Monrovia; Martinsville 43–19 Stinesville. Officials: Gale Robinson, W. H. Herbst.

MISHAWAKA: Plymouth 24–22 Bremen; Mishawaka 20–14 Riley (South Bend); Central (South Bend) 40–16 West Twp.; New Carlisle 35–27 Tyner; North Liberty 41–14 LaPaz; Lakeville 19–14 Walkerton; Plymouth 24–14 Madison Twp.; Central 27–15 Mishawaka; North Liberty 15–7 New Carlisle; Plymouth 30–19 Lakeville; Central 40–14 North Liberty; Central 24–12 Plymouth. Officials: L. R. Lenon, Frank Reid, Allen Klinck.

MITCHELL: Mitchell 46–10 Springville; Fayetteville 20–10 Heltonville; Tunnelton 27–21 Williams; Bedford 48–9 Huron; Oolitic 30–17 Shawswick; Mitchell 31–14 Needmore; Tunnelton 25–18 Fayetteville; Oolitic 19–18 Bedford; Mitchell 19–14 Tunnelton; Mitchell 11–7 Oolitic. Officials: Donald Wilder, Gilbert Rhea.

MONTICELLO: Monon 20–11 Idaville; Wolcott 21–19 Monticello; Chalmers 27–20 Reynolds; Brookston 32–30 Burnettsville; Buffalo 24–18 Round Grove, Monon 26–24 Wolcott; Brookston 24–21 Chalmers; Monon 37–22 Buffalo; Brookston 22–21 Monon. Officials: George Russell, Lee Sinclair.

MUNCIE: Cowan 32–24 Daleville; Royerton 26–25 Center; Eaton 36–20 Albany; Yorktown 32–20 DeSoto; Gaston 22–10 Selma; Muncie 33–18 Harrison Twp.; Cowan 35–21 Royerton; Eaton 25–19 Yorktown; Muncie 43–14 Gaston; Eaton 42–27 Cowan; Muncie 43–16 Eaton. Officials: Hugh Vandivier, George Yarnelle.

NEW ALBANY: Georgetown. 35–10 Webster Twp.; Franklin Twp. 29–22 New Washington; Henryville 29–21 Posey Twp.; New Salisbury 30–15 Heth Twp.; New Albany 31–7 Charlestown. Morgan Twp. 22–21 Borden; Corydon 44–8 Depauw; Silver Creek 31–9 Georgetown; Henryville 26–24 Franklin Twp.; New Albany 26–19 New Salisbury; Corydon 23–17 Morgan Twp.; Silver Creek 19–18 Henryville; Corydon 16–13; New Albany; Corydon 27–15 Silver Creek. Officials: Harry Blume, Elmer Posey, W. S. Fellmy.

NEW CASTLE: Straughn 30–14 Lewisville; New Castle 25–10 Knightstown; Spiceland

Tourney Time

35–16 New Lisbon; Middletown 35–21 Mooreland. Sulphur Springs 29–21 Cadiz; Mt. Summit 19–16 Kennard; New Castle 33–13 Straughn; Spiceland 20–18 Middletown (ot); Mt. Summit 20–16 Sulphur Springs; New Castle 31–13 Spiceland; New Castle 30–21 Mt. Summit. Officials: John Schram, Joe Dienhart.

NORTH JUDSON: Hamlet 25–19 Star City; Monterey 21–18 Medaryville; North Judson 59–6 North Bend; Winamac 48–18 Grovertown; Knox 23–11 Center Twp.; San Pierre 21–9 Francesville. Hamlet 36–28 Pulaski; North Judson 47–6 Monterey; Winamac 34–8 Knox; Hamlet 31–25 San Pierre; Winamac 23–13 North Judson; Winamac 38–16 Hamlet. Officials: George Allesee, R.G. Campbell, Edmund Tully.

OWENSVILLE: Oakland City 40–22 Patoka; Fort Branch 20–19 Francisco; Owensville 16–15 Princeton; Mt. Olympus 17–14 Hazleton; Oakland City 35–15 Haubstadt; Owensville 40–25 Fort Branch; Mt. Olympus 23–19 Oakland City; Owensville 21–16 Olympus. Officials: Fred Alwood, George Bair.

PAOLI: Paoli 30–18 Orleans; French Lick 61–11 Little York; West Baden 38–11 Hardinsburg; Salem 71–9 Monroe Twp.; Pekin 25–15 Campbellsburg; Paoli 29–22 French Lick; Salem 38–20 West Baden; Paoli 45–15. Pekin; Paoli 33–21 Salem. Officials: George Goerlitz, John Harmon.

PERU: Macy 35–20 Butler Twp.; Clay Twp. 21–13 Amboy; Jefferson Twp. 38–10 Deedsville; Converse 33–19 Bunker Hill; Peru 46–21 Chili; Gilead 23–21 Macy; Clay Twp. 32–21 Mexico; Peru 49–19 Converse; Clay Twp. 31–18 Gilead; Peru 34–21 Clay Twp. Officials: C. E. Fauber, Maurice Tudor.

PETERSBURG: Velpen 45–11 Dubois; Petersburg 31–11 Birdseye; Stendal 35–14 Ireland; Winslow 32–17 Cuzco; Huntingburg 27–7 Holland; Spurgeon 33–23 Union; Jasper 27–17 Otwell; Petersburg 26–16 Velpen; Stendal 28–20 Winslow; Spurgeon 18–14 Huntingburg; Jasper 24–18 Petersburg; Stendal 32–20 Spurgeon; Stendal 45–30 Jasper. Officials: Harlie Jurgens, Vaughn Russell, Harold McSwane.

REMINGTON: Rensselaer 20–16 Remington; Tefft 40–27 Wheatfield; Brook 24–18 Kentland; Goodland 40–26 Fair Oaks; Mt. Ayr 32–11 Kniman; DeMotte 27–19 Hanging Grove; Morocco 18–13 Rensselaer; Brook 30–16 Tefft; Goodland 40–15 Mt. Ayr; Morocco 23–15 DeMotte; Brook 22–19 Goodland. Brook 28–27 Morocco. Officials: Condict Smith, Norman McCallum, Ralph Eades.

RICHMOND: Lynn 22–13 Greensfork; Cambridge City 34–17; Economy; Centerville 26–10 Whitewater; Fountain City 26–16 Williamsburg; Spartanburg 33–19 Boston; Hagerstown 18–15 Milton; Richmond 39–26 Lynn; Centerville 25–20 Cambridge City; Fountain City 27–18 Spartanburg; Richmond 14–12 Hagerstown; Centerville 22–11 Fountain City; Richmond 22–6 Centerville. Officials: Guy Ogle, Lundy Welborn, Harrell Parr.

ROCHESTER: Akron 57–19 Richland Center; Tippecanoe 24–19 Talma; Leiters Ford 19–15 Argos (ot); Kewanna 52–23 Grass Creek; Rochester 34–10 Bourbon; Culver 52–11 Fulton; Akron 55–13 Tippecanoe; Kewanna 46–24 Leiters Ford; Culver 24–21 Rochester; Akron 31–22 Kewanna; Culver 27–21 Akron. Officials: Walter Bussard, R. P. Chambers.

ROCKPORT: Chrisney 25–11 Yankeetown; Luce Twp. 36–25 Folsomville; Tennyson 18–11 Boonville (ot); Rockport 36–12 Grandview; Lynnville 25–21 Dale; Gentryville 23–21 Chrisney; Tennyson 37–20 Luce Twp.; Rockport 22–13 Lynnville; Tennyson 34–23 Gentryville; Tennyson 30–10 Rockport. Officials: H. Kilburn Rogers, G. S. Rust.

RUSHVILLE: New Salem 35–9 Arlington; Rushville 21–13 Morton Memorial; Milroy 27–

24 Manilla; Raleigh 29–21 Center; New Salem 39–8 Carthage; Rushville 31–17 Milroy; New Salem 20–17 Raleigh; Rushville 34–23 New Salem. Officials: Albert Harker, Guy Woods.

SEYMOUR: Freetown 19–18 Tampico; Cortland 27–13 Vallonia; Medora 18–10 Hayden; Butlerville 31–8 Crothersville; Brownstown 31–6 Clearspring; Seymour 44–17 Scipio; North Vernon 43–0 Vernon; Freetown 49–19 Zenas; Cortland 31–11 Medora; Brownstown 31–25 Butlerville; Seymour 20–17 North Vernon; Cortland 20–18 Freetown; Brownstown 16–11 Seymour; Brownstown 25–16 Cortland. Officials: Richard Miller, Vern Ruble, Richard Baxter.

SHELBYVILLE: Columbus 41–26 Clifford; Shelbyville 43–23 Hawcreek Twp.; Moral 39–20 Waldron; Washington Twp.; 34–31 Mt. Auburn; Morristown 31–17 Fairland; Columbus 55–20 Boggstown; Shelbyville 35–12 Waldron; Washington Twp. 19–17 Morristown; Columbus 24–22 Shelbyville; Columbus 42–24 Flat Rock. Officials: R. B. Morrison, Winston Ashley.

SPENCER: Posey Twp. 20–13 Gosport; Van Buren 25–15 Bowling Green; Clay City 32–11 Sugar Ridge; Spencer 42–6 Jefferson Twp.; Quincy 22–20 Cory; Brazil 35–24 Patricksburg; Posey Twp. 22–8 Freedom; Clay City 31–18 Van Buren; Spencer 43–19 Quincy; Brazil 19–16 Posey Twp.; Clay City 24–12 Spencer; Clay City 16–15 Brazil. Officials: Raymond Meier, Otto Strohmeier, H.A. Gottfried.

SULLIVAN: Carlisle 28–19 Merom; Sullivan 38–19 Farmersburg; Union (Dugger) 21–18 Graysville; New Lebanon 36–18 Fairbanks; Pleasantville 27–17 Hymera; Sullivan 26–15 Carlisle; Dugger 40–19 New Lebanon; Sullivan 28–18 Pleasantville; Dugger 32–17 Sullivan. Officials: Paul Lovell, B.E. Bayh.

TERRE HAUTE: Fontanet 26–19 Otter Creek; State Training 24–13 Garfield; Pimento 18–17 Gerstmeyer; Glenn 24–14 West Terre Haute; Wiley 37–14 Riley; Honey Creek 14–13 Prairie Creek; Blackhawk 29–13 Fontanet; State Training 19–11 Pimento; Wiley 30–16 Glenn; Blackhawk 28–26 Honey Creek (2ot); Wiley 27–19 State Training; Wiley 37–23 Blackhawk. Officials: Clinton Dougherty, J. E. Wakefield, Everett Babb.

TIPTON: Sharpsville 63–9 Kempton; Sheridan 21–19 Westfield; Prairie Twp.; 39–26 Arcadia; Boxley 30–12 Goldsmith; Cicero 16–13 Noblesville; Atlanta 24–21 Windfall; Fishers 16–14 Carmel; Tipton 44–8 Walnut Grove; Sharpsville 45–13 Sheridan; Prairie Twp. 35–16 Boxley; Atlanta 27–22 Cicero; Tipton 38–21 Fishers; Sharpsville 33–23 Prairie Twp.; Tipton 22–21 Atlanta; Tipton 30–25 Sharpsville. Officials: C. F. Barrett, Von Crowe, Clyde Gentry.

VALPARAISO: Valparaiso 35–3 Hebron; Lowell 36–10 Boone Grove; Chesterton 20–18 Morgan Twp; Crisman 21–18 Wheeler; Crown Point 48–27 Washington Twp.; Valparaiso 31–8 Liberty Center. Lowell 20–18 Chesterton; Crown Point 37–25 Crisman; Valparaiso 35–21 Lowell; Valparaiso 31–29 Crown Point. Officials: Alvin Taylor, William Lucas.

VINCENNES: Decker Chapel 25–9 Edwardsport; Decker 25–24 Sandborn; Bruceville 28–17 Monroe City; Freelandville 31–14 Wheatland; Oaktown 21–19 Fritchton; Vincennes 42–7 Bicknell; Decker 17–16 Decker Chapel; Freelandville 23–14 Bruceville; Vincennes 37–6 Oaktown; Freelandville 26–12 Decker; Vincennes 43–19 Freelandville. Officials: Irvin Springer, Leonard Mayhugh.

WABASH: Central 22–13 Linlawn; Chippewa 30–13 Lincolnville; Laketon 26–21 Urbana (ot); Roann 19–16 Lafontaine; Lagro 22–15 Somerset, Wabash 40–18 Chester Twp.; Chippewa 27–17 Central; Laketon 31–23 Roann; Wabash 21–13 Lagro; Chippewa 35–26 Laketon; Wabash 31–19 Chippewa. Officials: John Miller, Walter McFatridge.

WARSAW: Syracuse 29–18 North Webster; Mentone 17–16 Leesburg; Claypool 29–18 Silver

Tourney Time

Lake; Atwood 16–15 Warsaw; Milford 35–16 Sidney; Etna Green 16–13 Pierceton; Burket 27–14 Beaver Dam; Mentone 26–25 Syracuse; Claypool 15–8 Atwood; Milford 39–13 Etna Green; Mentone 23–19 Burket; Milford 28–20 Claypool; Mentone 29–22 Milford. Officials: Harry Hatcher; Dale Kreight, Elmer Rowe.

WASHINGTON: Alfordsville 22–20 Raglesville; Loogootee 19–15 Elnora; Washington 29–17 Odon; Epsom 39–7 Burns City; Plainville 26–13 Montgomery; Shoals 19–16 Alfordsville; Washington 51–16 Loogootee; Plainville 19–18 Epsom; Washington 64–12 Shoals; Washington 34–12 Plainville. Officials: Hulett Crecelius, William Kingsolver.

WINCHESTER: Saratoga 27–17 Wayne; Stoney Creek; 34–11 Modoc; Ridgeville 27–17 Lincoln; Winchester 27–14 Losantville; Parker 26–23 Jackson; Union City 35–16 McKinley; Farmland 22–13 Green; Jefferson 31–19 Huntsville; Stoney Creek 23–19 Saratoga; Winchester 24–17 Ridgeville; Union City 35–22 Parker; Jefferson 40–21 Farmland; Winchester 33–13 Stoney Creek; Union City 41–22 Jefferson; Union City 31–17 Winchester. Officials: Clive Markley, I.W. Carnes, George Williams.

1931 REGIONALS

ANDERSON: Indianapolis Shortridge 29–18 Danville; Alexandria 18–15 Tipton; Shortridge 22–18 Alexandria. Officials: W. S. Porter, Homer Stonebraker.

AUBURN: Mentone 31–19 Lima; Kendallville 29–21 Auburn; Kendallville 41–15 Mentone. Officials: Will Smith, Carl Burt.

BEDFORD: Brownstown 32–18 Corydon; Mitchell 31–29 Paoli (ot), Brownstown 26–24 Mitchell. Officials: Vaughn Russell, Harry Conover.

BLOOMINGTON: Martinsville 43–17 Clay City; Terre Haute Wiley 27–25 Switz City; Wiley 29–14 Martinsville. Officials: Irvin Springer, Henry Goett.

COLUMBUS: Greensburg 31–27 Vevay; Columbus 25–24 Franklin; Greensburg 34–25 Columbus. Officials: P. O. Hurley, Orville Jones.

EVANSVILLE: Tennyson 25–12 Tell City; Central 19–18 Owensville; Central 15–14 Tennyson. Officials: B. E. Bayh, C. D. Manhart.

FORT WAYNE: Bluffton 18–8 North Side; Decatur 19–14 Huntington; Bluffton 24–15 Decatur; Officials: Winston Ashley, George Yarnelle.

GREENCASTLE: Greencastle 19–16 Wingate; Clinton 23–17 Veedersburg; Greencastle 37–16 Clinton. Officials: George Vaulk, Gilbert Best.

LAFAYETTE: Frankfort 31–16 Boswell; Jefferson 24–21 Lebanon; Frankfort 29–12 Jefferson. Officials: Hugh Vandivier, O.F. Helvie.

LOGANSPORT: Logansport 35–16 Brookston; Delphi 21–18 Peru; Logansport 23–13 Delphi. Officials: George Russell, R. P. Chambers.

MARION: Wabash 22–16 Kokomo; Marion 23–21 Hartford City; Marion 28–16 Wabash. Officials: Paul Williams, Lundy Welborn.

MUNCIE: Muncie 23–21 New Castle; Union City 35–28 Wilkinson; Muncie 31–24 Union City. Officials: J. A. Schram, C. A. Jensen.

ROCHESTER: Central (South Bend) 43–25 Culver; Elkhart 22–20 Winamac (ot); Elkhart 21–20 Central. Officials: Carl Olson, Mode Cranor.

RUSHVILLE: Richmond 25–22 Connersville; Rushville 20–19 Lawrenceburg; Rushville

27–19 Richmond. Officials: Guy Woods, Glenn Adams.
   VALPARAISO: Horace Mann 35–16 Brook; Valparaiso 16–14 LaPorte; Horace Mann 20–12. Officials: M. J. Cleary, John Miller.
   VINCENNES: Washington 34–18 Stendal; Vincennes 33–19 Union (Dugger); Washington 22–19 Vincennes. Officials: Otto Strohmeier, Gerald Bottorff.

1931 FINALS—March 20, 21
   INDIANAPOLIS (Butler Fieldhouse): Muncie 37–16 Kendallville; Washington 23–22 Shortridge; Logansport 23–19 Brownstown; Frankfort 28–19 Bluffton; Greencastle 20–15 Evansville Central; Elkhart 26–22 Marion; Rushville 21–20 Gary Horace Mann; Terre Haute Wiley 31–18 Greensburg; Muncie 21–19 Washington; Logansport 25–21 Frankfort; Greencastle 29–18 Elkhart; Wiley 31–15 Rushville; Muncie 23–17 Logansport; Greencastle 15–10 Wiley; Muncie 31–23 Greencastle. Officials: B. E. Bayh, O. F. Helvie, Paul Williams, Hugh Vandivier, Vaughn Russell.

1932 SECTIONALS
   ANDERSON: Anderson 28–14 Pendleton; Alexandria 29–20 Elwood; Lapel 29–17 Frankton; Markleville 20–11 Summitville; Alexandria 14–13 Anderson; Lapel 29–11 Markleville; Alexandria 19–15 Lapel. Officials: Hugh Vandivier, Lloyd Messersmith.
   ANGOLA: Auburn 30–12 Butler; Garrett 52–6 Flint; Waterloo 39–18 Concord; Hamilton 27–20 Orland; Ashley 23–14 Pleasant Lake; Salem 38–11 Spencerville; Angola 18–12 Scott; Garrett 31–27 Auburn; Hamilton 27–24 Waterloo; Salem 27–23 Ashley; Garrett 21–17 Angola; Hamilton 26–19 Salem; Garrett 33–20 Hamilton. Officials: Joel Wilt, Elmer Rowe, Raymond Yoos.
   ATTICA: Covington 27–24 West Lebanon; Hillsboro 54–15 Kingman; Attica 18–13 Pine Village; Veedersburg 38–15 Wallace; Covington 28–16 Williamsport; Hillsboro 36–15 Attica; Veedersburg 39–9 Covington; Hillsboro 32–23 Veedersburg. Officials: Norman McCallum, Paul Lovell.
   BLOOMINGTON: Martinsville 59–19 Eminence; Ellettsville 24–16 Unionville; Bloomington 23–18 Smithville; Monrovia 22–20 Mooresville; Morgantown 28–19 Paragon; Martinsville 26–15 Stinesville; Bloomington 28–21 Ellettsville; Monrovia 29–17 Morgantown; Bloomington 17–13 Martinsville; Monrovia 23–18 Bloomington. Officials: Layall Fisher, Orville Jones.
   BLUFFTON: Ossian 32–22 Union Center; Rock Creek Center 29–24 Petroleum; Bluffton 44–5 Monroe; Lancaster Central 38–30 Geneva; Hartford Twp. 39–7 Pleasant Mills; Berne 26–19 Chester Center; Kirkland 39–20 Jefferson; Ossian 18–13 Liberty Center; Bluffton 34–22 Rock Creek; Lancaster Central 21–19 Hartford Twp.; Kirkland 27–22 Berne; Bluffton 24–23 Ossian; Lancaster 31–23 Kirkland; Bluffton 33–25 Lancaster Central. Officials: Fernie Trigalet, Lundy Welborn, Guy Ogle.
   BOONVILLE: Selvin 32–19 Yankeetown; Boonville 32–12 Grandview; Tennyson 36–14 Rockport; Dale 16–13 Gentryville; Lynnville 27–12 Folsomville; Richland 38–17 Chrisney; Boonville 20–6 Selvin; Tennyson 31–20 Dale; Lynnville 27–21 Richland; Tennyson 32–17 Boonville; Tennyson 24–9 Lynnville. Officials: W. S. Fellmy, C. D. Manhart.
   BRAZIL: Clay City 41–17 Cory; Gosport 17–12 Freedom; Brazil 46–12 Coal City; Staunton 30–15 Patricksburg; Bowling Green 23–19 Van Buren; Spencer 41–7 Quincy; Gosport 28–26

Tourney Time

Clay City; Brazil 28–20 Staunton; Spencer 39 –17 Bowling Green; Brazil 38–21 Gosport; Brazil 27–12 Spencer. Officials: W.H. Herbst, Will Kinkaid.

BROOK: Wheatfield 45–18 Kankakee Twp.; Goodland 24–22 Kentland; Fair Oaks 32–21 DeMotte; Rensselaer 51–20 Hanging Grove; Remington 47–15 Kniman; Morocco 34–21 Mt. Ayr; Brook 64–16 Wheatfield; Goodland 50–20 Fair Oaks; Rensselaer 35–20 Remington; Brook 20–18 Morocco; Goodland 34–24 Rensselaer; Brook 24–13 Goodland. Officials: Elmer Posey, Ralph Eades, C. E. Fauber.

CLINTON: Montezuma 37–23 Dana; Perrysville 21–6 St. Bernice; Clinton 25–19 Newport; Rosedale 34–21 Cayuga; Mecca 26–10 Hillsdale; Rockville 52–27 Tangier; Montezuma 31–17 Perrysville; Clinton 27–18 Rosedale; Rockville 16–12 Mecca; Clinton 20–16 Montezuma; Clinton 20–17 Rockville. Officials: George Vaulk, Herbert Vaulk.

CONNERSVILLE: Springfield Twp. 25–17 Everton; Bentonville 49–20 Whitewater; Liberty 31–27 Brookville; Harrison Twp. 37–14 Harrisburg; Connersville 68–9 Laurel; Brownsville 40–26 Orange; Fairview 27–5 Alquina; Springfield 39–25 Bentonville; Liberty 23–22 Harrison Twp.; Connersville 48–26 Brownsville; Springfield 28–25 Alquina; Connersville 40–16 Liberty; Connersville 41–14 Springfield. Officials: Byron Deakyne, C. O. Walls, Frederick Shroyer.

CRAWFORDSVILLE: New Ross 22–13 Alamo; Crawfordsville 27–22 Ladoga; Waynetown 37–14 Bowers; New Market 48–14 Linden; Darlington 32–21 Waveland; Wingate 21–15 New Richmond; Crawfordsville 39–19 New Ross; New Market 23–21 Waynetown; Wingate 30–15 Darlington; Crawfordsville 29–27 New Market (ot); Crawfordsville 25–8 Wingate. Officials: B. E. Bayh, Thomas Baker.

CULVER: Lakeville 18–15 LaPaz; Madison Twp. 20–12 North Liberty; Plymouth 34–10 West; Tyner 35–7 Green Twp.; Argos 22–13 Walkerton; Bourbon 24–22 Bremen; Culver 22–15 Lakeville; Plymouth 30–19 Madison Twp.; Tyner 22–18 Argos; Culver 23–16 Bourbon; Plymouth 28–18 Tyner; Plymouth 45–25 Culver. Officials: Kenneth Barr, Wayne Cunningham, Joe Brown.

DANVILLE: Amo 29–25 Clayton; North Salem 33–16 Avon; Danville 29–22 Pittsboro; Brownsburg 24–17 Lizton; Plainfield 41–18 New Winchester; Amo 30–20 Stilesville; Danville 46–19 North Salem; Plainfield 23–17 Brownsburg; Danville 40–13 Amo; Danville 35–25 Plainfield. Officials: Frank Jarrell, Custer Baker.

DELPHI: Carrollton 21–20 Rockfield (ot); Flora 44–9 Adams Twp.; Delphi 27–15 Camden; Burlington 19–18 Deer Creek; Flora 30–20 Carrollton; Delphi 33–18 Burlington; Delphi 35–27 Flora. Officials: Virgil Hickman, Carl Porter.

EVANSVILLE: New Harmony 18–17 Griffin; Reitz 26–24 Cynthiana; Newburgh 23–20 Wadesville; Mt. Vernon 22–16 Stewartsville; Poseyville 27–13 Chandler; Central 52–8 Elberfeld; Bosse 34–23 New Harmony; Reitz 49–12 Newburgh; Mt. Vernon 23–22 Poseyville; Bosse 17–16 Central; Reitz 42–18 Mt. Vernon; Bosse 34–22 Reitz. Officials: Norman Dunlap, H. A. Gottfried, Fred Alwood.

FORT WAYNE: New Haven 27–21 Lafayette Center; Jefferson Center 39–26 Leo; Huntertown 25–14 Woodburn; Decatur 19–12 Monroeville; North Side 40–20 Arcola; Central 43–23 Harlan; Monmouth 27–17 Hoagland; South Side 21–13 Elmhurst; New Haven 24–20 Jefferson Center; Decatur 27–19 Huntertown; Central 19–15 North Side; South Side 39–13 Monmouth; Decatur 27–15 New Haven; South Side 21–20 (ot); Decatur 21–15 South Side. Officials: Clayton Hughes, Lawrence Gaunt, Paul Williams.

IHSAA Scores | 1930–1939

FRANKFORT: Jefferson 31–23 Sugar Creek Twp.; Frankfort 29–22 Michigantown; Jackson Twp. 17–12 Kirklin; Mulberry 37–14 Forest; Scircleville 32–16 Rossville; Colfax 22–11 Jefferson; Frankfort 28–10 Jackson Twp.; Mulberry 25–23 Scircleville; Frankfort 27–17 Colfax; Frankfort 43–13 Mulberry. Officials: Clyde Gentry, Will Smith.

FRANKLIN: Whiteland 31–14 Hopewell; Nashville 36–22 Clark Twp.; Center Grove 22–20 Masonic Home; Greenwood 29–18 Trafalgar; Edinburg 30–27 Union; Franklin 52–7 Jackson; Nineveh 29–15 Van Buren; Whiteland 27–26 Nashville; Center Grove 27–20 Greenwood; Franklin 46–31 Edinburg; Whiteland 36–16 Nineveh; Franklin 31–18 Center Grove; Franklin 32–20 Whiteland. Officials: Dillon Geiger; Forrest Ballinger, Harry Blume.

GARY: Emerson 37–17 Merrillville; Whiting 49–16 Dyer; Horace Mann 51–17 Longfellow; Hammond Tech 16–13 Hammond; Hobart 32–10 East Gary Central; Wallace 44–11 Calumet Twp.; East Chicago Washington 21–20 East Chicago Roosevelt; Froebel 50–14 Griffith; Emerson 33–22 Whiting; Tech 23–14 Horace Mann; Wallace 32–15 Hobart; Froebel 19–15 Washington; Emerson 23–10 Tech.; Froebel 29–26 Wallace; Emerson 20–16 Froebel. Officials: Daniel Guild, Edmund Tully, John Stahr.

GOSHEN: New Paris 20–17 Bristol; Baugo Twp. 15–10 Bristol; Middlebury 25–10 Jefferson; Riley (South Bend) 25–20 Wakarusa; Elkhart 43–16 Millersburg; Goshen 21–19 Central (South Bend); Nappanee 24–20 Mishawaka; New Paris 22–18 Baugo Twp.; Middlebury 18–11 Riley (South Bend); Goshen 13–10 Elkhart; Nappanee 40–25 New Paris; Goshen 27–11 Middlebury; Nappanee 27–23 Goshen. Officials: Carl Burt, Maurice Tudor, Lloyd Miller.

GREENCASTLE: Greene Twp. 15–12 Bloomingdale (ot); Bainbridge 27–21 Belle Union; Roachdale 58–7 Union Twp.; Greencastle 41–22 Russellville; Cloverdale 32–13 Bridgeton; Marshall 27–16 Fillmore; Bainbridge 43–13 Greene Twp.; Greencastle 33–21 Roachdale; Cloverdale 33–21 Marshall; Greencastle 25–21 Bainbridge; Greencastle 30–27 Cloverdale. Officials: Clarence Grogan, Walter Moss.

GREENFIELD: Greenfield 25–20 McCordsville; Mt. Comfort 31–15 New Palestine; Westland 29–16 Eden; Fortville 25–17 Wilkinson; Charlottesville 34–25 Maxwell; Greenfield 26–25 Mt. Comfort; Westland 16–15 Fortville; Greenfield 45–25 Charlottesville; Westland 23–21 Greenfield. Officials: Houston Meyer, R. B. Morrison.

GREENSBURG: Butlerville 27–19 Clarksburg; Sandusky 18–17 Scipio; Jackson 24–11 Zenas; Burney 31–10 Hayden; Greensburg 31–17 North Vernon; St. Paul 37–16 Letts; Westport 36–10 Vernon; Butlerville 44–20 New Point; Jackson 31–11 Sandusky; Greensburg 33–18 Burney; St. Paul 24–15 Westport; Jackson 46–28 Butlerville; Greensburg 23–18 St. Paul; Greensburg 40–16. Jackson. Officials: Hermon Phillips, Blair Gullion, A. E. Abshire.

HARTFORD CITY: Hartford City 27–25 Madison Twp.; Roll 28–25 Redkey; Gray 24–23 Portland; Montpelier 24–22 Pennville; Dunkirk 26–19 Poling; Hartford City 53–17 Bryant; Gray 30–16 Roll; Montpelier 28–20 Dunkirk; Hartford City 26–17 Gray; Hartford City 52–22 Montpelier. Officials: Leon Fadely, M. J. Cleary.

HUNTINGTON: Clear Creek 32–21 Dallas Twp.; Huntington 20–18 Union; Salamonie Twp. 45–18 Rockcreek Twp.; Jefferson Twp. 35–24 Markle; Banquo 29–25 Bippus; Huntington Twp. 42–27 Roanoke; Lancaster Central 30–15 Monument City; Huntington 36–23 Clear Creek; Jefferson 20–19 Salamonie Twp.; Huntington Twp. 31–29 Banquo; Huntington 37–26 Lancaster Central; Huntington Twp. 31–19 Jefferson; Huntington 45–21 Huntington Twp. Officials: Ward Gilbert, Orbie Branham, Condict Smith.

Tourney Time

INDIANAPOLIS: New Augusta 36–23 Acton; Tech 29–15 Shortridge; Oaklandon 12–10 Beech Grove; New Bethel 24–21 Lawrence; Manual Training 19–13 Broad Ripple; Washington 24–15 Southport; Decatur Central 27–16 Castleton; Ben Davis 31–22 Warren Central; Tech 51–20 New Augusta; New Bethel 23–12 Oaklandon; Washington 21–19 Manual Training; Decatur Central 23 –17 Ben Davis; Tech 37–18 New Bethel; Washington 31–20 Decatur Central; Tech 28–14 Washington. Officials: Harry Briggs, Ralph Parker, Winston Ashley.

JASPER: Otwell 19–6 Velpen; Stendal 21–20 Spurgeon; Winslow 24–12 Union; Holland 39–19 Birdseye; Huntington 25–24 Petersburg; Jasper 30–20 Ireland; Cuzco 30–9 Dubois; Stendal 26–16 Otwell; Winslow 24–20 Holland; Jasper 22–20 Huntingburg (ot); Stendal 29–19 Cuzco; Jasper 28–20 Winslow; Stendal 24–20 Jasper. Officials: Harley Jurgens, U.S. Abbott, Borden Purcell.

KENDALLVILLE: Wawaka 36–4 Washington Center; Kendallville 39–16 LaOtto; Larwill 38–22 Orange Twp.; Wolf Lake 24–9 Avilla; Albion 30–15 Churubusco; South Whitley 41–17 Etna Twp.; Columbia City 28–14 Ligonier; Cromwell 24–10 Coesse; Kendallville 36–13 Wawaka; Wolf Lake 20–13 Larwill; Albion 34–16 South Whitley; Columbia City 26–17 Cromwell; Kendallville 29–20 Wolf Lake; Columbia City 36–21 Albion; Columbia 17–16 Kendallville. Officials: George Allesee, George Yarnelle, Forest Wood.

KOKOMO: Greentown 14–11 Ervin Twp.; Jackson Twp. 23–9 Clay Twp.; Kokomo 57–10 New London; Russiaville 33–13 Union Twp.; West Middleton 26–15 Howard Twp.; Jackson Twp. 22–20 Greentown; Russiaville 22–20 Kokomo; Jackson Twp 26–20 West Middleton; Jackson Twp. 13–8 Russiaville. Officials: Myron Moore, T. R. Smith.

LAFAYETTE: Montmorenci 18–15 Monitor; Buck Creek 21–20 Jackson; Dayton 29–19 Klondike; West Point 28–19 Wea; West Lafayette 26–25 Stockwell; Lafayette 45–12 Battle Ground; Clarks Hill 22–11 Romney; Montmorenci 21–18 Buck Creek; Dayton 24–17 West Point; Lafayette 34–15 West Lafayette; Montmorenci 37–15 Clarks Hill; Lafayette 30–23 Dayton; Lafayette 55–13 Montmorenci. Officials: Vaughn Russell, Wayne Watson, George Kerr.

LAGRANGE: Springfield Twp. 41–22 Wolcottville; Topeka 34–15 Brighton; Lima 27–13 Shipshewana; Scott 36–24 LaGrange; Topeka 27–19 Mongo; Lima 40–17 Scott; Lima 45–24 Topeka. Officials: Thomas Fields, A. T. Krider.

LAPORTE: Michigan City 69–2 Lydick; Union Twp. 31–29 Hanna; Union Mills 34–23 New Carlisle; LaPorte 47–23 Stillwell; LaCrosse 22–21 Westville; Springfield Twp. 24–21 Mill Creek; Wanatah 36–20 Kingsbury; Clinton 24–13 Washington Twp.; Michigan City 50–13 Union Twp.; LaPorte 23–17 Union Mills; LaCrosse 22–16 Springfield Twp.; Wanatah 40–9 Clinton; Michigan City 27–23 LaPorte; Wanatah 42–12 LaCrosse; Michigan City 24–19 Wanatah. Officials: Charles Garrett, L. E. Fink, George Russell.

LEBANON: Jefferson Twp. 22–20 Whitestown; Jamestown 14–11 Thorntown; Zionsville 21–11 Pinnell; Lebanon 58–11 Central; Advance 15–12 Jefferson Twp.; Zionsville 27–21 Jamestown; Lebanon 51–20 Advance; Lebanon 40–16 Zionsville. Officials: Walter McFatridge, Lavon Carey.

LYONS: Switz City 27–25 Owensburg; Newberry 20–12 Scotland; Bloomfield 21–14 Midland; Jasonville 33–31 Linton; Switz City 18–15 Lyons (ot); Bloomfield 25–21 Newberry; Switz City 26–23 Jasonville (ot); Bloomfield 19–17 Switz City. Officials: Clyde Walters, John Hoffman.

MARION: Jonesboro 10–9 Swayzee; Marion 29–15 Matthews; Fairmount 26–21 Gas City; Sweetser 36–23 Upland; Jonesboro 31–22 Van Buren; Marion 27–18 Fairmount; Jonesboro 21–

20 Sweetser; Marion 34–22 Jonesboro. Officials: Walter Keller, R. P. Chambers.

MILAN: Batesville 28–17 Versailles; Milan 24–21 Holton; Osgood 43–4 Cross Plains; Napoleon 37–14 New Marion; Batesville 45–15 Sunman; Milan 23–11 Osgood; Batesville 36–30 Napoleon; Milan 32–26 Batesville. Officials: Gale Robinson, Leo Quillen.

MITCHELL: Shawswick 32–11 Huron; Heltonville 26–18 Fayetteville; Tunnelton 21–17 Oolitic; Marshall Twp. (Needmore) 38–27 Williams; Bedford 65–12 Springville; Mitchell 35–14 Shawswick; Tunnelton 21–9 Heltonville; Bedford 26–15 Marshall Twp.; Mitchell 30–25 Tunnelton; Bedford 23–21 Mitchell (ot). Officials: Charles Jensen, Harry Conover.

MONON: Monon 17–16 Brookston; Chalmers 28–19 Burnettsville; Wolcott 24–7 Boone Grove; Monticello 31–4 Reynolds; Idaville 23–16 Liberty Twp.; Chalmers 40–32 Monon; Monticello 23–16 Wolcott; Idaville 22–20 Chalmers; Monticello 24–17 Idaville. Officials: Fletcher Kerr, Dean Malaska.

MUNCIE: Yorktown 24–13 Daleville; Selma 17–16 Royerton; Muncie 24–20 Harrison; Cowan 40–25 Gaston; Eaton 25–21 Center; Albany 32–19 DeSoto; Yorktown 20–6 Selma; Muncie 53–15 Cowan; Eaton 34–14 Albany; Muncie 29–17 Yorktown. Officials: John Schram, C. T. Brehm.

NEW ALBANY: New Washington 19–13 New Middleton; New Albany 22–8 Borden; New Salisbury 20–17 Henryville; Jeffersonville 55–6 Laconia; Silver Creek 26–11 Washington Twp.; Charlestown 36–10 Heth Twp.; Georgetown 29–13 Posey Twp.; Franklin Twp. 21–17 Corydon; New Albany 24–8 New Washington; Jeffersonville 71–17 New Salisbury; Silver Greek 19–10 Charlestown; Franklin Twp.19–14 Georgetown; New Albany 14–9 Jeffersonville; Silver Creek 29–17 Franklin Twp.; New Albany 23–17 Silver Creek. Officials: Nate Kaufman, George Bair, Ray Frohman.

NEW CASTLE: Straughn 28–14 Sulphur Springs; Kennard 18–11 Cadiz; Knightstown 20–17 Mt. Summit; New Castle 23–11 Middletown; Mooreland 30–18 New Lisbon; Spiceland 10–9 Lewisville; Kennard 29–14 Straughn; New Castle 25–14 Knightstown; Spiceland 21–20 Mooreland; New Castle 31–22 Kennard; New Castle 54–9 Spiceland. Officials: R.F. Breedlove, George Seidensticker.

OXFORD: Freeland Park 24–18 Oxford; Fowler 28–15 Pine Twp.; Raub 16–13 Wadena; Earl Park 35–14 Gilboa Twp.; Otterbein 32–23 Ambia; Freeland Park 37–22 Boswell; Fowler 28–14 Raub; Otterbein 36–19 Earl Park; Fowler 25–13 Freeland Park; Fowler 22–20 Otterbein. Officials: Andrew Gill, O. F. Helvie.

PAOLI: Paoli 35–21 Campbellsburg; French Lick 27–12 Pekin; Hardinsburg 32–17 Monroe Twp.; Orleans 30–14 Little York; Paoli 31–21 Salem; French Lich 25–12 Hardinsburg; Orleans 22–18 Paoli; French Lick 23–18 Orleans. Officials: R. Lowell Todd, Ralph Esarey.

PERU: Peru 50–23 Chili; Converse 38–26 Gilead; Butler Twp. 28–7 Deedsville; Mexico 33–31 Bunker Hill; Amboy 33–16 Allen Twp.; Peru 42–20 Converse; Butler Twp. 33–22 Mexico; Peru 30–9 Amboy; Peru 48–17 Butler Twp. Officials: Harry Coolman, R. G. Campbell.

PRINCETON: Patoka 26–24 Mackey; Hazleton 21–14 Princeton; Haubstadt 17–16 Francisco; Owensville 28–17 Mt. Olympus; Oakland City 24–16 Ft. Branch; Hazleton 27–15 Patoka; Owensville 39–18 Haubstadt; Hazleton 19–11 Oakland City; Owensville 21–17 Hazleton. Officials: Elmer Weber, George Goerlitz.

RICHMOND: Richmond 24–19 Cambridge City; Boston 20–18 Williamsburg; Economy 23–16 Whitewater; Hagerstown 24–17 Centerville; Milton 22–20 Fountain City; Lynn 26–22

Tourney Time

Greensfork; Richmond 26–15 Spartanburg; Economy 36–14 Boston; Milton 22–19 Hagerstown; Richmond 19–17 Lynn; Milton 31–19 Economy; Richmond 21–17 Milton. Officials: Hulett Crecelius, George Lambert, Glen Adams.

RISING SUN: Aurora 34–19 Guilford; Lawrenceburg 17–14 Rising Sun; Vevay 40–22 Bright; Moores Hill 31–20 Patriot; Aurora 35–21 Dillsboro; Lawrenceburg 24–17 Vevay; Aurora 37–12 Moores Hill; Lawrenceburg 27–16 Aurora. Officials: Richard Miller, Lawrence Maplesden.

ROCHESTER: Akron 31–13 Talma; Fulton 29–18 Leiters Ford; Rochester 51–25 Grass Creek; Richland Center 26–25 Kewanna; Akron 20–18 Fulton; Rochester 54–23 Richland Center; Rochester 17–9 Akron. Officials: Mode Cranor, L. E. Hart.

ROYAL CENTER: Twelve Mile 27–23 Onward; Royal Center 30–17 New Waverly; Metea 34–20 Walton; Young America 56–20 Noble Twp.; Washington Twp. 28–24 Lucerne; Logansport 46–12 Lincoln; Twelve Mile 44–26 Galveston; Royal Center 22–15 Metea; Young America 22–11 Washington Twp.; Logansport 46–16 Twelve Mile; Young America 16–15 Royal Center; Logansport 15–14 Young America. Officials: George Kenzler, Glenn Farrell, Carl Olson.

RUSHVILLE: Morton Memorial 21–15 New Salem; Milroy 47–18 Gings; Arlington 34–24 Manilla; Raleigh 31–19 Carthage; Rushville 53–15 Mays; Morton Memorial 15–14 Milroy; Arlington 25–22 Raleigh; Rushville 26–12 Morton Memorial; Rushville 23–18 Arlington. Officials: Guy Woods, Reid McLain.

SCOTTSBURG: Paris Crossing 21–12 Lovett; Central 19–12 Dupont; Saluda 23–15 Austin; San Jacinto 36–16 Lexington; Hanover 25–23 Deputy; Scottsburg 40–17 Madison; North Madison 46–25 Paris Crossing; Saluda 31–17 Central; Hanover 33–17 San Jacinto; Scottsburg 51–23 North Madison; Hanover 28–14 Saluda; Scottsburg 38–13 Hanover. Officials: Gerald Bottorff, Ray McKinley, Russell Pickett.

SEYMOUR: Seymour 41–17 Freetown; Clearspring 22–16 Vallonia; Tampico 42–13 Houston; Medora 19–13 Crothersville; Brownstown 20–16 Cortland; Seymour 28–12 Clearspring; Tampico 26–21 Medora; Seymour 35–12 Brownstown; Seymour 28–13 Tampico. Officials: Harry Vandivier, Robert Potter.

SHELBYVILLE: Mt. Auburn 20–13 Hope; Columbus 40–27 Waldron; Clifford 49–23 Morristown; Shelbyville 24–18 Flat Rock; Fairland 33–22 Moral; Mt. Auburn 35–13 Boggstown; Columbus 38–22 Clifford; Shelbyville 31–11 Fairland; Columbus 54–25 Mt. Auburn; Columbus 39–26 Shelbyville. Officials: George Williams, Paul Hurley.

SHERIDAN: Cicero 23–12 Walnut Grove; Kempton 17–9 Westfield; Prairie Twp. 39–18 Noblesville; Sheridan 23–10 Goldsmith; Sharpsville 48–18 Fishers; Tipton 30–23 Windfall; Carmel 34–15 Arcadia; Cicero 24–16 Atlanta; Prairie Twp. 17–5 Kempton; Sharpsville 36–12 Sheridan; Carmel 27–25 Tipton; Cicero 21–20 Prairie Twp.; Sharpsville 43–36 Carmel; Cicero 28–21 Sharpsville. Officials: Clarence Barrett, Norman Durham, Von Crowe.

SULLIVAN: Hymera 13–9 New Lebanon; Carlisle 28–26 Pleasantville; Dugger 27–14 Graysville; Farmersburg 26–21 Shelburn; Merom 18–16 Fairbanks; Sullivan 15–10 Hymera; Dugger 22–14 Carlisle; Farmersburg 22–6 Merom; Dugger 26–16 Sullivan; Dugger 28–19 Farmersburg. Officials: George Graham, Raleigh Phillips.

TELL CITY: Troy 35–10 Leopold; Tell City 90–5 Union; Bristow 25–9 Leavenworth; Tobinsport 34–10 Oriole; Marengo 23–18 Rome; Derby 25–13 Cannelton; Tell City 38–32 Troy; Bristow 28–13 Tobinsport; Marengo 23–18 Derby; Tell City 33–21 Bristow; Tell City 24–19 Marengo. Officials: John Lyskowinski, Herbert Robinson.

TERRE HAUTE: Riley 15–12 Fontanet; State Training 16–11 Glenn; Wiley 44–12 Prairie Creek; Gerstmeyer 12–10 Concannon; Pimento 24–16 Otter Creek; Garfield 21–8 Blackhawk; Honey Creek 17–16 Riley; Wiley 26–14 State Training; Gerstmeyer 19–18 Pimento; Garfield 23–15 Honey Creek; Wiley 27–10 State Training; Wiley 21–7 Garfield. Officials: Hal Harris, J.H. Hendrickson, Irvin Springer.

VALPARAISO: Chesterton 20–18 Wheeler; Valparaiso 35–14 Boone Grove; Lowell 31–18 Washington Twp.; Crown Point 33–14 Kouts; Liberty Center 11–10 Hebron; Chesterton 28–15 Crisman; Valparaiso 15–13 Lowell; Crown Point 20–14 Liberty Center; Valparaiso 23–15 Chesterton; Valparaiso 16–11 Crown Point. Officials: William E. Campbell, L. R. Lenon.

VINCENNES: Vincennes 26–9 Bruceville; Decker 25–10 Wheatland; Oaktown 27–13 Bicknell; Decker Chapel 22–20 Monroe City (ot); Edwardsport 32–26 Sandborn; Freelandville 27–18 Fritchton; Vincennes 26–17 Decker; Oaktown 28–25 Decker Chapel (2ot); Freelandville 27–10 Edwardsport; Vincennes 35–16 Oaktown; Vincennes 38–17 Freelandville. Officials: Vern Ruble, G.S. Rust.

WABASH: Laketon 15–14 Chester; Central 33–7 Lincolnville; Lagro 25–14 Urbana; Somerset 42–14 Roann; Chippewa 39–17 Linlawn; Wabash 27–13 Lafontaine; Laketon 20–15 Central; Somerset 21–18 Lagro; Wabash 25–11 Chippewa; Somerset 24–18 Laketon; Somerset 17–15 Wabash. Officials: Allen Klinck, Jesse Cage.

WARSAW: Beaver Dam 19–17; Leesburg; Pierceton 20–18 Etna Green; Warsaw 28–18 Claypool; Sidney 27–24 Syracuse; North Webster 25–24 Silver Lake; Mentone 28–18 Atwood; Burket 23–22 Milford; Beaver Dam 26–16 Pierceton; Warsaw 29–14 Sidney; Mentone 33–26 North Webster; Beaver Darn 24–12 Burket; Warsaw 23–18 Mentone; Beaver Dam 13–9 Warsaw. Officials: Ora Davis, Phocian Rhoads, Clive Markley.

WASHINGTON: Washington 31–16 Montgomery; Odon 50–9 Trinity; Plainville; 45–8 Raglesville; Alfordsville 16–12 Shoals; Loogootee 42–19 Burns City; Epsom 19–6 Elnora; Washington 23–21 Odon; Plainville 28–9 Alfordsville; Epsom 18–13 Loogootee; Washington 23–13 Plainville; Washington 11–7 Epsom. Officials: Leonard Mayhugh, Paul Garrison.

WINAMAC: North Judson 41–4 Medaryville; Francesville 23–21 Grovertown (ot); Winamac 28–11 Pulaski; Star City 37–6 San Pierre; Hamlet 27–24 Center (ot); North Judson 24–18 Knox; Winamac 48–12 Francesville; Star City 25–7 Hamlet; Winamac 35–12 North Judson; Winamac 38–7 Star City. Officials: Frank Reid, Charles Link.

WINCHESTER: Winchester 26–11 Huntsville; Ridgeville 19–17 Saratoga; Union City 46–26 Losantville; Farmland 26–20 Parker; Stoney Creek 34–15 Modoc; McKinley 22–12 Wayne; Jefferson 33–4 Lincoln; Jackson 15–8 Green Twp.; Winchester 20–19 Ridgeville (ot); Farmland 22–20 Union City; McKinley 19–18 Stoney Creek; Jackson 23–17 Jefferson; Winchester 26–23 Farmland (ot); McKinley 23–13 Jackson; Winchester 38–17 McKinley. Officials: Mark Williams, Gerald Huey, Elder Eberhart.

1932 REGIONALS

ATTICA: Clinton 31–16 Hillsboro; Greencastle 13–12 Crawfordsville; Greencastle 26–20 Clinton; Officials: Orville Jones, J. H. Hendrickson.

AUBURN: Garrett 18–14 Lima; Columbia City 20–19 Beaver Dam; Columbia City 21–20 Garrett. Officials: Carl Burt, Will Smith.

Tourney Time

BEDFORD: Seymour 36–23 French Lick; New Albany 18–16 Bedford; Seymour 27–17 New Albany. Officials: C. D. Manhart, Ray Frohman.
COLUMBUS: Greensburg 30–29 Scottsburg; Columbus 24–18 Franklin; Columbus 24–19 Greensburg. Officials: Winston Ashley, Dillon Geiger.
EVANSVILLE: Owensville 25–20 Tennyson; Bosse 17–16 Tell City; Bosse 30–4 Owensville. Officials: Vaughn Russell, Harry Conover.
FORT WAYNE: Decatur 21–19 Hartford City (2ot); Bluffton 28–23 Huntington; Bluffton 27–23 Decatur. Officials: John Schram, George Vaulk.
FRANKFORT: Lebanon 22–16 Frankfort; Lafayette 34–18 Fowler; Lebanon 39–32 Lafayette. Officials: Carl Olson, R.P. Chambers.
INDIANAPOLIS: Tech 16–14 Alexandria; Danville 34–17 Westland; Tech 32–25 Danville. Officials: Paul Williams, Lundy Welborn.
LAPORTE: Valparaiso 26–11 Brook; Michigan City 19–18 Emerson; Michigan City 26–23 Valparaiso. Officials: Hugh Vandivier, Joel Wilt.
LOGANSPORT: Delphi 31–28 Logansport; Peru 35–25 Monticello; Delphi 17–14 Peru. Officials: O.F. Helvie, Walter Geller.
MARION: Cicero 23–22 Marion; Somerset 24–22 Jackson Twp.; Cicero 31–21 Somerset. Officials: W.S. Porter, Henry Goett.
MARTINSVILLE: Brazil 27–16 Monrovia; Terre Haute 38–19 Bloomfield; Wiley 22–19 Brazil. Officials: P. O. Hurley, Lowell Lenon.
MISHAWAKA: Rochester 24–19 Plymouth; Winamac 37–27 Nappanee; Winamac 23–12 Rochester. Officials: Gilbert Best, Mode Cranor.
MUNCIE: Winchester 27–22 Richmond; New Castle 20–19 Muncie; New Castle 15–13 Winchester. Officials: Ward Gilbert, Clayton Hughes.
RUSHVILLE: Rushville 22–18 Milan; Connersville 25–22 Lawrenceburg; Connersville 14–13 Rushville. Officials: Glenn Adams, Nate Kaufman.
SULLIVAN: Vincennes 28–19 Washington; Union (Dugger) 28–24 Stendal; Vincennes 22–17 Union (Dugger). Officials: B.E. Bayh, Irvin Springer.

1932 FINALS—March 18, 19

INDIANAPOLIS (Butler Fieldhouse): Cicero 17–15 Vincennes; New Castle 25–20 Seymour; Connersville 20–17 Terre Haute Wiley; Greencastle 32–19 Columbia City; Lebanon 31–29 Delphi; Winamac 48–30 Bluffton; Evansville Bosse 25–21 Michigan City; Indianapolis Tech 33–21 Columbus; New Castle 25–13 Cicero; Greencastle 24–23 Connersville; Winamac 34–31 Lebanon; Bosse 27–15 Tech; New Castle 26–18 Greencastle; Winamac 27–23 Bosse; New Castle 24–17 Winamac. Officials: B.E. Bayh, Winston Ashley, H.E. Vandivier, Carl Burt, Vaughn Russell.

1933 SECTIONALS

ALEXANDRIA: Summitville 17–8 Pendleton; Alexandria 33–21 Lapel; Markleville 21–15 Frankton; Elwood 23–20 Summitville; Markleville 25–19 Alexandria; Markleville 30–25 Elwood. Officials: George Bair, Dale Miller.
ANGOLA: Scott 27–13 Scott Center; Mongo 31–10 Shipshewana; Topeka 36–20 Salem;

Brighton 23–15 Wolcottville; Angola 51–13 Pleasant Lake; Fremont 29–16 Flint; Hamilton 33–14 Lima; LaGrange 35–18 Orland; Mongo 38–14 Scott; Topeka 32–28 Brighton; Angola 61–7 Fremont; LaGrange 22–18 Hamilton; Mongo 27–17 Topeka; LaGrange 20–19 Angola; LaGrange 35–17 Mongo. Officials: Charles Link, Clive Markley, Condict Smith.

ATTICA: Williamsport 27–25 Veedersburg; Covington 23–13 West Lebanon; Pine Village 29–28 Attica; Kingman 39–25 Wallace; Hillsboro 38–22 Williamsport; Covington 21–19 Pine Village; Hillsboro 41–21 Kingman; Hillsboro 20–19 Covington. Officials: Russell Newgent, Elmer Posey.

BEDFORD: Heltonville 24–12 Springville; Bedford 32–16 Oolitic; Shawswick 31–25 Mitchell; Needmore 49–20 Williams; Huron 33–28 Fayetteville; Tunnelton 34–19 Heltonville; Bedford 37–17 Shawswick; Needmore 35–28 Huron; Bedford 51–19 Tunnelton; Bedford 44–20 Needmore. Officials: Vaughn Russell, Raleigh Phillips.

BLUFFTON: Berne 23–12 Chester; Geneva 30–13 Monroe; Ossian 54–12 Hartford Twp.; Jefferson 22–20 Petroleum; Lancaster 32–13 Pleasant Mills; Rockcreek 31–26 Liberty Center; Bluffton 26–22 Union; Berne 45–19 Geneva; Ossian 37–29 Jefferson; Rockcreek 31–19 Lancaster; Bluffton 22–17 Berne; Rockcreek 24–23 Ossian; Bluffton 31–20 Rockcreek. Officials: Lundy Welborn, George Yarnelle, Donald Coar.

BRAZIL: Spencer 33–12 Freedom; Van Buren 16–14 Gosport; Posey Twp. 36–19 Jefferson Twp.; Patricksburg 33–20 Quincy; Cory 27–25 Ashboro; Brazil 36–17 Bowling Green; Spencer 29–17 Clay City; Van Buren 25–17 Staunton; Patricksburg 23–20 Cory; Brazil 21–19 Spencer; Van Buren 28–14 Patricksburg; Brazil 30–8 Van Buren. Officials: Lloyd Messersmith, Leo Quillen, Hermon Phillips.

BROWNSBURG: Danville 37–18 Stilesville; Plainfield 30–13 Amo; Brownsburg 50–15 Avon; Clayton 42–9 New Winchester; Pittsboro 32–28 Lizton; Danville 35–18 North Salem; Brownsburg 32–24 Plainfield; Pittsboro 38–31 Clayton; Danville 24–19 Brownsburg; Pittsboro 25–13 Danville. Officials: Will Kinkaid, Will Smith.

CANNELTON: Rome 40–7 Oil Twp.; Marengo 37–27 Troy; Tobinsport 34–16 Milltown; Tell City 29–27 Derby; Cannelton 29–18 Union Twp.; Leavenworth 30–28 Leopold; Bristow 28–23 Rome; Tobinsport 24–22 Marengo; Cannelton 24–22 Tell City; Bristow 32–9 Leopold; Cannelton 26–18 Tobinsport; Cannelton 23–18 Bristow. Officials: U. S. Abbott, Paul Garrison, Harley Jurgens.

CLINTON: Clinton 29–22 Cayuga; Tangier 28–19 Bloomingdale; Hillsdale 37–22 Mecca; Montezuma 25–24 Dana; Rosedale 37–17 St. Bernice; Newport 33–17 Perrysville; Clinton 41–15 Tangier; Hillsdale 33–15 Montezuma; Rosedale 35–18 Newport; Clinton 47–19 Hillsdale; Clinton 33–25 Rosedale. Officials: Fletcher Kerr, Wayne Watson.

CONNERSVILLE: Brownsville 41–25 Laurel; Connersville 50–20 Brookville; Springfield Twp. 45–21 Whitewater Twp.; Liberty 45–13 Orange; Everton 33–21 Fairview Twp.; Harrisburg 26–19 Bentonville; Harrison Twp. 35–20 Alquina; Connersville 49–21 Brownsville; Springfield Twp. 30–21 Liberty; Everton 35–13 Harrisburg; Connersville 67–18 Harrison Twp.; Springfield Twp. 41–31 Everton; Connersville 43–14 Springfield Twp. Officials: Otto Crosley, C. O. Walls, Guy Woods.

CRAWFORDSVILLE: Ladoga 30–23 Wingate; New Market 31–26 Waynetown; Darlington 37–23 New Ross; New Richmond 47–12 Alamo; Waveland 30–16 Bowers; Crawfordsville 24–13 Ladoga; New Market 25–21 Darlington; New Richmond 32–18 Waveland; Crawfordsville 38–7

Tourney Time

New Market; Crawfordsville 29–12 New Richmond. Officials: Frank Jarrell, Harry Conover.

ELKHART: Wakarusa 47–8 Jefferson Twp.; Elkhart 26–20 Nappanee; Concord Twp. 32–20 Millersburg; Goshen 24–12 Middlebury; New Paris 33–6 Baugo Twp.; Wakarusa 33–24 Bristol; Elkhart 41–12 Concord Twp.; New Paris 13–10 Goshen; Wakarusa 33–23 Elkhart; Wakarusa 27–20 New Paris. Officials: Walter Geller, R. Wayne Cunningham.

EVANSVILLE: New Harmony 21–18 Cynthiana; Central 31–14 Stewartsville; Newburgh 27–15 Poseyville; Millersburg 24–17 Chandler; Reitz 21–16 Mt. Vernon; Bosse 38–16 Elberfeld; Griffin 43–17 Wadesville; Central 46–14 New Harmony; Millersburg 24–20 Newburgh; Bosse 25–23 Reitz; Central 37–16 Griffin; Bosse 50–15 Millersburg; Central 17–12 Bosse. Officials: Ralph Esarey, B. E. Bayh, Raymond Sparks.

FLORA: Delphi 63–17 Adams Twp.; Burlington 36–12 Carrollton; Deer Creek 33–16 Rockville; Monroe Twp. 25–8 Cutler; Delphi 43–15 Camden; Burlington 35–18 Deer Creek; Delphi 23–9 Monroe Twp.; Delphi 26–18 Burlington. Officials: Clarence Barrett, George Vaulk.

FORT WAYNE: Arcola 24–19 Monroeville; South Side 26–14 New Haven; North Side 32–11 Woodburn; Central 29–26 Hoagland; Lafayette Central 20–17 Leo; Huntertown 33–14 Monmouth; Decatur 23–15 Elmhurst; Arcola 23–22 Harlan; North Side 28–26 South Side; Lafayette Central 32–23 Central; Decatur 27–24 Huntertown; North Side 34–10 Arcola; Decatur 26–24 Lafayette Central; North Side 40–12 Decatur. Officials: Leon Fadely, Winston Ashley, G. M. Kinzel.

FOWLER: Fowler 33–20 Freeland Park; Gilboa 29–25 Pine; Oxford 27–19 Wadena; Earl Park 42–26 Ambia; Raub 28–21 Boswell; Otterbein 23–22 Fowler; Oxford 26–14 Gilboa; Earl Park 30–27 Raub; Otterbein 15–11 Oxford; Earl Park 28–25 Otterbein. Officials: Herbert Vaulk, Orbie Branham.

FRANKFORT: Colfax 23–21 Sugar Creek Twp.; Scircleville 27–22 Forest; Jefferson 48–25 Mulberry; Michigantown 53–9 Kirklin; Frankfort 35–11 Jackson Twp.; Rossville 32–17 Colfax; Jefferson 35–17 Scircleville; Michigantown 16–10 Frankfort; Jefferson 29–22 Rossville; Michigantown 27–26 Jefferson. Officials: Glenn Adams, Reid McLain.

FRANKLIN: Trafalgar 32–17 Nashville; Greenwood 29–25 Union Twp.; Whiteland 29–21 Nineveh; Edinburg 33–14 Center Grove; Hopewell 42–26 Clark Twp.; Masonic Home 54–34 Jackson Twp.; Franklin 59–22 Van Buren Twp.; Trafalgar 25–24 Greenwood; Edinburg 28–22 Whiteland (ot); Masonic Home 28–13 Hopewell; Franklin 45–17 Trafalgar; Masonic Home 23–21 Edinburg; Franklin 21–20 Masonic Home. Officials: Harry Briggs, Byron Deakyne, Harold Shannon.

GARRETT: Coesse 43–11 Etna Twp.; Churubusco 22–17 Washington Center; Columbia City 28–16 Butler; Ashley 31–20 Concord Twp.; Larwill 30–23 Waterloo; Jefferson Center 30–19 South Whitley; Garrett 23–20 Auburn; Coesse 29–20 Spencerville; Columbia City 35–13 Churubusco; Larwill 25–23; Ashley (ot); Garrett 21–20 Jefferson Center; Columbia City 40–14 Goesse; Garrett 30–14 Larwill; Columbia City 34–23 Garrett. Officials: Ralph Parker, Ora Davis, Carl Porter.

GARY: Froebel 57–19 Gary Longfellow; Hammond Tech 41–11 East Chicago Garfield; Whiting 35–26 Crown Point; Lew Wallace 29–25 Calumet Twp. East Chicago Roosevelt 27–23 Hobart; Emerson 31–11 Lowell; Horace Mann 25–17 East Chicago Washington; Hammond 41–16 Clark; Froebel 22–19 Hammond Tech; Whiting 31–29 Lew Wallace; Emerson 29–27 Roosevelt; Hammond 27–20 Horace Mann; Whiting 27–20 Froebel; Hammond 23–14 Emerson;

Hammond 25–24 Whiting. Officials: Joel Wilt, Carl Burt, O. F. Helvie.

GREENCASTLE: Roachdale 27–26 Rockville; Bainbridge 54–13 Greene Twp.; Bridgeton 29–24 Union Twp.; Belle Union 22–20 Marshall; Greencastle 40–27 Cloverdale; Roachdale 29–27 Fillmore; Bainbridge 48–18 Bridgeton; Greencastle 39–18 Belle Union; Bainbridge 34–16 Roachdale; Greencastle 35–23 Bainbridge. Officials: George Seidensticker, Walter Moss.

GREENFIELD: Wilkinson 23–20 Mt. Comfort; Greenfield 23–20 Westland (ot); New Palestine 30–20 McCordsville; Eden 30–17 Maxwell; Charlottesville 28–27 Fortville; Greenfield 23–17 Wilkinson; New Palestine 22–21 Eden; Greenfield 35–34 Charlottesville; Greenfield 26–24 New Palestine. Officials: Mark Williams, W. H. Herbst.

GREENSBURG: Clarksburg 25–9 Sandusky; Greensburg 61–16 Burney; Butlerville 33–26 Jackson; St. Paul 30–17 New Point; North Vernon 41–20 Vernon; Westport 35–24 Zenas; Clarksburg 37–23 Letts; Greensburg 29–19 Butlerville; North Vernon 35–26 St. Paul; Clarksburg 37–21 Westport; Greensburg 21–18 North Vernon; Greensburg 39–23 Clarksburg. Officials: Hal Harris, William McCorkle, Harry Vandivier.

HUNTINGBURG: Petersburg 38–19 Holland; Ireland 47–12 Birdseye; Jasper 28–24 Huntingburg; Stendal 30–28 Otwell; Winslow 34–8 Velpen; Dubois 33–23 Union; Spurgeon 32–23 Cuzco; Ireland 30–25 Petersburg; Jasper 28–13 Stendal; Winslow 46–28 Dubois; Ireland 21–17 Spurgeon; Jasper 47–18 Winslow; Jasper 41–20 Ireland. Officials: Herbert Robinson, Joe Armstrong, John Lyskowinski.

HUNTINGTON: Union Twp. 33–22 Rock Creek; Clear Creek 36–15 Markle; Andrews 36–24 Jefferson Twp.; Salamonie Twp. 38–19 Huntington Twp.; Roanoke 26–25 Monument City; Huntington 40–19 Bippus; Union Twp. 18–16 Banquo; Clear Creek 31–24 Andrews; Salamonie Twp. 25–23 Roanoke; Huntington 34–20 Union Twp.; Salamonie Twp. 29–18 Clear Creek; Huntington 15–7 Salamonie Twp. Officials: L. E. Fink, George Lambert, George Kenzler.

INDIANAPOLIS: Broad Ripple 22–20; New Augusta; Washington 33–22 Castleton; Shortridge 47–11 Acton; Decatur Central 36–12 Oaklandon; Southport 30–22 Manual Training; Tech 55–16 Lawrence; Warren Central 30–6 New Bethel; Beech Grove 23–20 Ben Davis; Washington 21–14 Broad Ripple; Shortridge 40–15 Decatur Central; Tech 20–17 Southport; Warren Central 19–13 Beech Grove; Shortridge 19–15 Washington; Tech 35–18 Warren Central; Shortridge 25–20 Tech. Officials: Norman Dunlap, W. P. McFatridge, Orville Jones.

JEFFERSONVILLE: Borden 28–19 Franklin Twp.; Washington Twp. 27–25 Georgetown; Corydon 29–7 Henryville; Charlestown 60–12 New Middletown; New Salisbury 28–13 Mauckport; Jeffersonville 21–20 New Albany; New Washington 33–11 Laconia; Silver Creek 33–20 Posey Twp.; Borden 28–23 Washington Twp.; Corydon 38–26 Charlestown; Jeffersonville 41–8 New Salisbury; New Washington 17–16 Silver Creek; Corydon 35–8 Borden; Jeffersonville 69–13 New Washington; Jeffersonville 39–17 Corydon. Officials: Herbert Gottfried, Irvin Springer, Wendell Heath.

KENDALLVILLE: Orange Twp. 28–14 Wolf Lake; Kendallville 36–15 Wawaka; Cromwell 20–19 LaOtto; Ligonier 26–19 Avilla; Albion 44–21 Orange Twp.; Kendallville 24–7 Cromwell; Albion 35–21 Ligonier; Kendallville 26–24 Albion. Officials: W. E. Thurston, Harry Coolman.

KOKOMO: Howard Twp. 23–20 Greentown; Jackson Twp. 22–20 Russiaville; Kokomo 62–14 Union Twp.; West Middleton 65–19 New London; Clay Twp. 23–20 Ervin Twp.; Howard Twp. 21–17 Jackson Twp.; Kokomo 37–15 West Middleton; Clay Twp. 31–23 Howard Twp.; Kokomo 44–27 Clay Twp.. Officials: R. P. Chambers, Layall Fisher.

Tourney Time

LAFAYETTE: West Lafayette 24–18 Clarks Hill; West Point 33–18 Montmorenci; Lafayette 29–12 Dayton; Battle Ground 21–18 Klondike; Buck Creek 34–21 Monitor; Romney 27–24 Stockwell; Jackson Twp. 20–8 Wea; West Point 23–18 West Lafayette; Lafayette 32–16 Battle Ground; Buck Greek 46–19 Romney; West Point 28–19 Jackson Twp.; Lafayette 38–21 Buck Creek; Lafayette 54–25 West Point. Officials: Allen Klinck, Ward Gilbert, Daniel Guild.

LAPORTE: Westville 39–13 LaCrosse; LaPorte 38–17 Union Twp.; Wanatah 49–14 Kingsbury; Union Mills 27–22 Rolling Prairie; Hanna 32–16 Mill Creek; Michigan City 38–16 Clinton Twp.; Stillwell 24–11 Springfield Twp.; LaPorte 22–14 Westville; Wanatah 29–22 Union Mills; Michigan City 41–19 Hanna; LaPorte 39–14 Stillwell; Michigan City 39–21 Wanatah; LaPorte 25–17 Michigan City. Officials: J. L. Campbell, Lawrence Rahbar, George Russell.

LAWRENCEBURG: Rising Sun 35–22 Guilford; Patriot 35–19 Moores Hill; Aurora 41–12 Vevay; Lawrenceburg 29–19 Bright; Dillsboro 22–21 Rising Sun; Aurora 50–17 Patriot; Lawrenceburg 39–27 Dillsboro; Aurora 40–17 Lawrenceburg. Officials: Richard Miller, Thomas Baker.

LEBANON: Eagle Twp. 27–25 Jamestown; Advance 30–29 Central; Dover 30–28 Whitestown; Thorntown 48–31 Pinnell; Lebanon 39–30 Eagle Twp. Advance 33–30 Dover; Lebanon 52–28 Thorntown; Lebanon 65–24 Advance. Officials: Doxie Reeves, Clarence Grogan.

LOGANSPORT: Onward 53–12 Noble Twp.; Washington Twp. 33–23 New Waverly; Metea 24–16 Walton; Twelve Mile 45–24 Galveston; Logansport 48–9 Lucerne; Royal Center 68–7 Deacon; Onward 29–26 Young America; Metea 24–15 Washington Twp.; Logansport 24–21 Twelve Mile; Royal Center 41–30 Onward; Logansport 51–7 Metea; Logansport 44—23 Royal Center. Officials: William Campbell, Jesse Cage, Mode Cranor.

LYNN: Winchester 40–16 Modoc; Lynn 27–10 Wayne; Parker 41–20 Losantville; Jackson Twp. 30–13 Huntsville; Spartanburg 27–21 Farmland; Saratoga 24–23 Stoney Creek; Lincoln 22–21 McKinley; Union City 28–26 Winchester; Lynn 23–21 Parker; Jackson Twp. 33–23 Spartanburg; Saratoga 24–19 Lincoln; Union City 21–15 Lynn; Jackson Twp. 37–24 Saratoga; Union City 37–22 Jackson Twp.. Officials: L. A. Briner, Raymond Yoos, Alfred Jackson.

MARION: Van Buren 22–19 Sims Twp.; Upland 29–13 Sweetser, Jonesboro 31–18 Matthews; Marion 24–17 Gas City; Fairmount 33–25 Van Buren; Jonesboro 31–23 Upland; Marion 21–14 Fairmount; Marion 29–17 Jonesboro. Officials: Clayton Hughes, George Williams.

MARTINSVILLE: Bloomington 56–15 Unionville; Eminence 35–20 Stinesville; Martinsville 41–7 Smithville; Ellettsville 25–19 Paragon; Mooresville 26–24 Morgantown; Bloomington 20–14 Eminence; Martinsville 22–11 Ellettsville; Bloomington 46–22 Mooresville; Martinsville 26–14 Bloomington. Officials: Gale Robinson, Houston Meyer.

MILAN: Center Twp. 29–27 Milan; Versailles 33–25 New Marion; Batesville 36–15 Holton; Napoleon 59–6 Cross Plains; Versailles 39–28 Center Twp.; Batesville 46–26 Napoleon; Batesville 30–23 Versailles. Officials: Palmer Sponsler, A.L. Bruce.

MISHAWAKA: Walkerton 29–25 Bremen; Washington Clay 41–9 Warren; Riley 52–0 West Twp.; Plymouth 35–25 Mishawaka; New Carlisle 24–17 LaPaz; North Liberty 27–19; Madison Twp.; Central (South Bend) 37–13 Green Twp.; Walkerton 27–26 Tyner; Riley 55–13 Washington Clay; Plymouth 47–24 New Carlisle; Central (South Bend) 32–20 North Liberty; Riley 44–14 Walkerton; Plymouth 31–20 Central (South Bend); Riley 34–32 Plymouth. Officials: Paul Hurley, Maurice Tudor, Ralph Eades.

MONTICELLO: Idaville 25–22 Liberty Twp.; Monon 30–15 Round Grove; Wolcott 30–29 Burnettsville; Chalmers 39–26 Monticello; Brookston 30–21 Reynolds; Monon 51–25 Idaville;

Chalmers 35–20 Walcott; Monon 40–27 Brookston; Chalmers 45–21 Monon. Officials: William Lucus, Joe Brown.

MUNCIE: Eaton 39–15 DeSoto; Yorktown 29–21 Center; Cowan 25–21 Burris; Daleville 36–14 Albany; Harrison 18–15 Gaston; Muncie 37–19 Royerton; Eaton 37–12 Selma; Yorktown 20–14 Cowan; Daleville 34–17 Harrison; Muncie 26–19 Eaton; Daleville 24–16 Yorktown; Muncie 33–17 Daleville. Officials: Nate Kaufman, T. R. Smith, John Gant.

NEW CASTLE: Kennard 29–11 Lewisville; New Lisbon 31–17 Sulphur Springs; New Castle 39–23 Middletown; Straughn 24–22 Knightstown; Mooreland 33–12 Mt. Summit; Kennard 28–18 Cadiz; New Castle 47–13 New Lisbon; Straughn 23–21 Mooreland; New Castle 28–15 Kennard; New Castle 45–9 Straughn. Officials: Lawrence Maplesden, Paul Williams.

NORTH JUDSON: Knox 37–30 Pulaski; Grovertown 43–27 Star City; San Pierre 34–23 Medaryville; North Judson 37–22 Hamlet; Winamac 48–8 Center Twp.; Francesville 25–20 Knox; Grovertown 35–19 San Pierre; Winamac 29–21 North Judson; Francesville 30–28 Grovertown; Winamac 40–14 Francesville. Officials: Andy Gill, Edmund Tully.

OWENSVILLE: Haubstadt 25–22 Ft. Branch; Hazleton 20–12 Francisco; Princeton 24–20 Mackey; Owensville 19–18 Patoka; Oakland City 23–17 Mt. Olympus; Hazleton 18–14 Haubstadt; Princeton 27–21 Owensville; Hazleton 38–17 Oakland City; Hazleton 38–17 Princeton. Officials: John Hoffman, Borden Purcell.

PERU: Amboy 35–12 Deedsville; Butler 44–22 Macy; Chili 40–29 Jefferson Twp.; Converse 36–23 Gilead; Bunker Hill 36–23 Clay Twp.; Peru 31–19 Amboy; Butler 34–21 Chili; Bunker Hill 31–29 Converse; Peru 36–16 Butler; Peru 39–18 Bunker Hill. Officials: Norman Durham, Charles Garrett.

PORTLAND: Jefferson 29–18 Green Twp.; Dunkirk 37–23 Roll; Ridgeville 33–17 Bryant; Redkey 31–22 Pennville; Montpelier 29–28 Portland; Madison Twp. 18–14 Poling; Hartford City 26–17 Gray; Jefferson 31–29 Dunkirk; Ridgeville 21–17 Redkey; Madison 39–27 Montpelier; Hartford City 31–15 Jefferson; Madison Twp. 35–18 Ridgeville; Hartford City 36–31 Madison Twp.. Officials: Fernie Trigalet, M. J. Cleary, A. H. Cornwell.

RENSSELAER: Goodland 48–27 Rensselaer; Kentland 28–26 Morocco; Wheatfield 55–12 Kniman; Hanging Grove 2–0 Fair Oaks; Remington 50–23 Demotte; Brook 56–21 Mt. Ayr; Goodland 27–13 Kentland; Wheatfield 28–21 Hanging Grove; Brook 50–20 Remington; Goodland 42–19 Wheatfield; Brook 45–30 Goodland. Officials: R. G. Campbell, Kenneth Barr.

RICHMOND: Richmond 58–18 Economy; Williamsburg 27–24 Boston; Centerville 33–17 Whitewater; Cambridge City 35–7 Webster; Milton 19–18 Fountain City; Greensfork 27–25 Hagerstown; Richmond 20–13 Williamsburg; Centerville 22–20 Cambridge City; Milton 35–18 Greensfork; Richmond 33–14 Centerville; Richmond 33–29 Milton. Officials: Forrest Ballinger, Myron Moore.

ROCHESTER: Talma 23–16 Grass Creek; Tippecanoe 35–30 Fulton; Culver 23–18 Akron; Bourbon 40–19 Leiters Ford; Argos 19–18 Kewanna; Rochester 22–13 Richland Center; Tippecanoe 32–9 Talma; Culver 26–18 Bourbon; Rochester 35–19 Argos; Tippecanoe 21–11 Culver; Rochester 17–15 Tippecanoe. Officials: Frank Reid, George Allesee.

ROCKPORT: Grandview 31–23 Yankeetown; Lynnville 37–21 Gentryville; Richland 39–19 Folsomville; Dale 28–20 Rockport; Chrisney 25–21 Tennyson; Boonville 32–20 Selvin; Lynnville 36–14 Grandview; Dale 31–24 Richland; Boonville 28–15 Chrisney; Dale 30–21 Lynnville; Boonville 28–27 Dale. Officials: W. S. Fellmy, C. D. Manhart.

Tourney Time

RUSHVILLE: Morton Memorial 39–24 Arlington; Rushville 43–30 Raleigh; New Salem 33–18 Carthage; Manilla 36–7 Gings; Milroy 46–6 Glenwood; Morton Memorial 31–21 Mays; Rushville 34–19 New Salem; Manilla 30–16 Milroy; Rushville 26–20 Morton Memorial; Rushville 37–20 Manilla. Officials: Gerald Huey, C. T. Brehm.

SALEM: Paoli 40–22 French Lick; West Baden 24–23 Hardinsburg; Orleans 22–21 Campbellsburg; Salem 43–12 Little York; Pekin 23–14 Monroe Twp.; Paoli 20–17 West Baden; Salem 26–21 Orleans; Paoli 34–27 Pekin; Paoli 21–10 Salem; Officials: Custer Baker, James Adams.

SCOTTSBURG: Central 33–30 Saluda; San Jacinto 22–21 Austin; Madison 73–12 Paris Crossing; Scottsburg 47–9 North Madison; Lovett 32–12 Marion Twp.; Dupont 31–19 Deputy; Hanover 25–15 Lexington; Central 40–10 San Jacinto; Madison 30–20 Scottsburg; Dupont 32–10 Lovett; Hanover 33–23 Central; Madison 43–27 Dupont; Madison 25–14 Hanover. Officials: Russell Pickett, Gerald Bottorff, Ray McKinley.

SEYMOUR: Vallonia 36–29 Freetown; Tampico 29–13 Houston; Medora 44–11 Hayden; Cortland 36–14 Scipio; Seymour 43–5 Clearspring; Brownstown 32–23 Crothersville; Vallonia 27–21 Tampico; Cortland 36–23 Medora; Seymour 31–25 Brownstown; Vallonia 25–18 Cortland; Seymour 46–9 Vallonia. Officials: Ray Frohman, Harry Blume.

SHELBYVILLE: Shelbyville 48–30 Boggstown; Hope 32–23 Fairland; Columbus 47–17 Waldron; Mt. Auburn 25–23 Clifford; Moral 36–20 Morristown; Shelbyville 30–22 Flat Rock; Columbus 46–21 Hope; Moral 40–34 Mt. Auburn; Columbus 38–36 Shelbyville; Columbus 37–21 Moral. Officials: Dillon Geiger, Blair Gullion.

SULLIVAN: Dugger 26–17 New Lebanon; Fairbanks 25–21 Shelburn; Sullivan 30–16 Farmersburg; Graysville 23–21 Hymera; Carlisle 40–11 Merom; Pleasantville 24–17 Dugger; Sullivan 23–13 Fairbanks; Graysville 18–10 Carlisle; Sullivan 18–10 Pleasantville; Sullivan 22–9 Graysville. Officials: James Watts, George Kerr.

SWITZ CITY: Jasonville 27–17 Newberry; Bloomfield 54–22 Scotland; Linton 40–20 Owensburg; Lyons 41–20 Solsberry; Switz City 31–14 Midland; Bloomfield 27–20 Jasonville; Lyons 28–24 Linton; Switz City 29–20 Bloomfield; Lyons 34–19 Switz City. Officials: Robert Green, Fred Alwood.

TERRE HAUTE: Riley 18–12 Garfield; Otter Creek 23–20 Concannon; Blackhawk 30–14 West Terre Haute; Wiley 30–16 State High; Gerstmeyer 22–20 Glenn; Fontanet 31–29 Prairie Creek; Riley 37–21 Pimento; Black Hawk 28–20 Otter Creek; Wiley 31–22 Gerstmeyer; Fontanet 16–12 Riley; Wiley 28—13 Blackhawk; Fontanet 25–23 Wiley. Officials: Charles Jensen, Karl Dickerson, Glenn Farrell.

TIPTON: Windfall 24–17 Sheridan; Tipton 36–16 Kempton; Walnut Grove 26–18 Fishers; Noblesville 18–16 Westfield; Arcadia 29–20 Sharpsville; Prairie Twp. 24–9 Atlanta; Carmel 19–11 Goldsmith; Windfall 25–23 Cicero; Tipton 38–25 Walnut Grove; Noblesville 33–21 Arcadia; Prairie Twp. 22–14 Carmel; Tipton 28–21 Windfall; Noblesville 20–19 Prairie Twp.; Tipton 31–19 Noblesville. Officials: Lavon Carey, Dean Malaska, Frederick Mackey.

VALPARAISO: Valparaiso 34–16 East Gary; Chesterton 23–17 Wheeler; Griffith 25–16 Washington Twp.; Portage 21–17 Hebron; Morgan Twp. 29–14 Dyer; Liberty Center 23–14 Merrillville; Valparaiso 42–8 Boone Grove; Chesterton 17–16 Griffith; Morgan Twp. 24–13 Portage; Valparaiso 28–10 Liberty Center; Morgan 17–16 Chesterton; Valparaiso 72–8 Morgan Twp.. Officials: Forrest Wood, L. R. Lenon, Winston Robbins.

VINCENNES: Sandborn 27–18 Fritchton; Vincennes 50–10 Wheatland; Bruceville 29–19 Bicknell; Oaktown 24–22 Edwardsport; Decker 24–17 Monroe City; Freelandville 35–16 Decker Chapel; Vincennes 58–24 Sandborn; Bruceville 26–21 Oaktown; Freelandville 35–14 Decker; Vincennes 35–19 Bruceville; Vincennes 32–14 Freelandville. Officials: Leonard Mayhugh, Lowell Todd.

WABASH: Manchester 28–18 Somerset; Lafontaine 41–13 Lincolnville; Roann 30–28 Lagro; Wabash 18–13 Laketon; Linlawn 44–33 Chippewa; Chester 22–20 Manchester (ot); Roann 38–22 Lafontaine; Wabash 30–19 Linlawn; Roann 23–22 Chester; Wabash 46–18 Roann. Officials: Thomas Fields, Lloyd Miller.

WARSAW: Leesburg 32–31 Pierceton; Syracuse 40–12 Silver Lake; Claypool 33–14 North Webster; Warsaw 48–22 Burket; Atwood 29–27 Sidney; Mentone 17–9 Etna Green; Beaver Dam 44–18 Milford; Syracuse 30–27 Leesburg; Warsaw 34–11 Claypool; Mentone 24–21 Atwood; Beaver Dam 31–28 Syracuse; Warsaw 26–19 Mentone; Beaver Dam 42–26 Warsaw. Officials: Von Crowe, L. B. Moore, H. E. Vandivier.

WASHINGTON: Elnora 36–22 Raglesville; Epsom 33–11 Trinity; Barr Twp. 29–19 Loogootee; Plainville 31–12 Shoals; Washington 36–18 Odon; Alfordsville 29–10 Elnora; Epsom 16–15 Barr Twp.; Washington 27–16 Plainville; Epsom 26–5 Alfordsville; Washington 33–32 Epsom. Officials: H. M. Crecelius, J. F. Eckensberger.

1933 REGIONALS

AUBURN: Columbia City 29–23 LaGrange; Beaver Dam 29–22 Kendallville; Beaver Dam 38–22 Columbia City. Officials: Ward Gilbert, O. F. Helvie.

BLOOMINGTON: Martinsville 33–20 Brazil; Lyons 32–20 Fontanet; Martinsville 18–11 Lyons. Officials: Winston Ashley, Nate Kaufman.

COLUMBUS: Franklin 26–25 Greensburg; Columbus 30–12 Madison; Franklin 27–21 Columbus. Officials: Will Smith, Irvin Springer.

CRAWFORDSVILLE: Greencastle 32–18 Clinton; Crawfordsville 36–24 Hills-boro; Greencastle 33–15 Crawfordsville. Officials: George Vaulk, B. E. Bayh.

EVANSVILLE: Boonville 30–11 Cannelton; Hazleton 15–11 Central; Hazleton 25–13 Boonville. Officials: C. D. Manhart, George Bair.

FORT WAYNE: Hartford City 23–14 Huntington; North Side 31–24 Bluffton; North Side 40–35 Hartford City. Officials: P. O. Hurley, George Williams.

GARY: Brook 28–25 Hammond; Valparaiso 30–26 LaPorte; Valparaiso 28–26 Brook. Officials: Vaughn Russell, Lowell Lenon.

INDIANAPOLIS: Pittsboro 22–19 Markleville; Shortridge 27–15 Greenfield; Shortridge 41–25 Pittsboro. Officials: W. S. Porter, H. E. Vandivier.

KOKOMO: Tipton 29–20 Marion; Kokomo 37–19 Wabash; Kokomo 30–24 Tipton. Officials: Dillon Geiger, Lundy Welborn.

LEBANON: Lebanon 44–34 Jefferson; Michigantown 35–17 Earl Park; Michigantown 42–30 Lebanon. Officials: Carl Burt, Clayton Hughes.

LOGANSPORT: Logansport 26–22 Chalmers; Delphi 40–26 Peru; Logansport 16–14 Delphi. Officials: Joel Wilt, Walter Geller.

MISHAWAKA: Winamac 24–20 Rochester; Wakarusa 29–23 South Bend Riley; Wakarusa

Tourney Time

31–21 Winamac. Officials: Mode Cranor, George Russell.

MUNCIE: Muncie 19–14 New Castle; Richmond 35–16 Union City; Muncie 39–20 Richmond. Officials: Dale Miller, R. P. Chambers.

NEW ALBANY: Bedford 25–19 Salem; Jeffersonville 33–30 Seymour; Bedford 23–22 Jeffersonville. Officials: Glenn Adams, Charles Jensen.

RUSHVILLE: Rushville 29–16 Aurora; Connersville 36–17 Batesville; Connersville 35–25 Rushville. Officials: Paul Williams, Blair Gullion.

WASHINGTON: Jasper 31–19 Washington; Vincennes 29–12 Sullivan; Vincennes 25–17 Jasper. Officials: Orville Jones, Harry Conover.

1933 FINALS—March 17, 18

INDIANAPOLIS (Butler Fieldhouse): Logansport 22–12 Michigantown; Greencastle 47–25 Wakarusa; Vincennes 40–32 Connersville; Indianapolis Shortridge 36–15 Kokomo; Martinsville 23–20 Valparaiso; Bedford 26–24 Hazleton; Muncie 38–14 Franklin; Fort Wayne North Side 37–25 Beaver Dam; Greencastle 24–21 Logansport; Shortridge 38–26 Vincennes; Martinsville 22–18 Bedford; North Side 28–24 Muncie; Greencastle 31–28 Shortridge; Martinsville 23–14 North Side; Martinsville 27–24 Greencastle. Officials: B. E. Bayh, O. F. Helvie, Carl Burt, W. S. Porter, Vaughn Russell.

1934 SECTIONALS

ANDERSON: Elwood 28–21 Frankton; Lapel 22–18 Alexandria; Anderson 22–7 Pendleton; Markleville 33–26 Summitville; Elwood 21–14 Lapel; Anderson 26–23 Markleville; Anderson 14–11 Elwood. Officials: Maurice Tudor, Dale Miller.

ANGOLA: Angola 29–12 Brighton; Fremont 24–23 Pleasant Lake; Orland 26–20 Scott; Lima 22–18 Scott Center; LaGrange 37–15 Shipshewana; Salem Center 23–16 Hamilton; Springfield 27–16 Topeka; Angola 46–21 Wolcottville; Fremont 31–17 Orland; LaGrange 27–14 Lima; Springfield 17–13 Salem Center; Angola 46–20 Fremont; Springfield 23–16 LaGrange; Angola 41–13 Springfield. Officials: George Allessee, Von Crowe, Thomas Fields.

ATTICA: Kingman 37–19 West Lebanon; Williamsport 35–11 Wallace; Pine Village 26–17 Veedersburg; Hillsboro 48–14 Covington; Attica 23–13 Kingman; Pine Village 34–27 Williamsport; Hillsboro 35–33 Attica; Pine Village 31–28 Hillsboro. Officials: Ralph Eades, Paul Lovell.

BEDFORD: Marshall Twp. 39–20 Fayetteville; Oolitic 26–19 Heltonville; Huron 28–23 Springville; Shawswick 27–15 Tunnelton; Mitchell 46–19 Williams; Bedford 57–30 Needmore; Oolitic 39–20 Huron; Mitchell 31–20 Shawswick; Bedford 32–18 Oolitic; Mitchell 28–23 Bedford. Officials: Dillon Geiger, Frank Jarrell.

BLOOMINGTON: Smithville 19–18 Mooresville; Paragon 24–22 Ellettsville; Unionville 29–18 Morgantown; Stinesville 28–17 Eminence; Bloomington 24–23 Martinsville; Paragon 24–19 Smithville; Unionville 30–20 Stinesville Bloomington 35–29 Paragon; Bloomington 30–20 Unionville. Officials: Vaughn Russell, Charles Jensen.

BLUFFTON: Lancaster 30–13 Liberty Center; Chester Center 34–27 Pleasant Mills; Ossian 24–17 Monroe; Bluffton 31–19 Rockcreek; Jefferson 34–33 Petroleum; Union Center 44–10 Hartford Twp.; Kirkland 32–14 Geneva; Lancaster 27–25 Berne; Ossian 47–21 Chester Center; Bluffton

IHSAA Scores | 1930–1939

29–22 Jefferson; Union Center 34–24 Kirkland; Ossian 35–23 Lancaster; Union Center 24–17 Bluffton; Ossian 43–32 Union Center. Officials: Charles Link, Ralph Parker, Richard Roberts.

BOONVILLE: Rockport 34–28 Luce Twp.; Selvin 47–22 Yankeetown; Boonville 28–17 Tennyson; Folsomville 26–21 Grandview; Dale 30–17 Gentryville; Lynnville 35–18 Chrisney; Rockport 39–30 Selvin; Folsomville 20–18 Boonville; Dale 34–28 Lynnville; Rockport 40–31 Folsomville; Dale 38–20 Rockport. Officials: John Wilson, Raymond Meier.

BOSWELL: Earl Park 26–19 Boswell; Fowler 32–7 Oxford; Wadena 36–32 Pine Twp. (ot); Otterbein 34–30 Gilboa; Ambia 26–19 York Twp.; Earl Park 36–22 Freeland Park; Fowler 33–14 Wadena; Otterbein 35–21 Ambia; Fowler 23–22 Earl Park; Fowler 22–15 Otterbein. Officials: Andrew Gill, George Vaulk.

BRAZIL: Posey Twp. 19–16 Quincy; Gosport 23–10 Patricksburg; Bowling Green 29–19 Jefferson Twp.; Brazil 41–15 Van Buren; Clay City 21–19 Ashboro; Freedom 28–17 Staunton; Gosport 33–25 Bowling Green; Brazil 34–25 Clay City; Gosport 14–7 Freedom; Brazil 26–5 Gosport. Officials: Thomas Baker, Karl Dickerson.

CLINTON: Clinton 25–19 Perrysville; Cayuga 28–16 Tangier; Hillsdale 25–14 Newport; Rosedale 29–14 Mecca; Dana 29–15 Prairie Creek; Bloomingdale 31–14 Montezuma; Clinton 43–15 St. Bernice; Hillsdale 16–13 Cayuga; Rosedale 22–13 Dana; Clinton 28–21 Bloomingdale; Rosedale 24–18 Hillsdale; Clinton 28–24 Rosedale. Officials: C. O. Walls, James Watts, Doxie Reeves.

CONNERSVILLE: Harrisburg 54–9 Orange; Connersville 47–18 Laurel; Alquina 19–18 Harrison Twp.; Everton 16–13 Brownsville; Liberty 48–11 Whitewater Twp.; Brookville 32–24 Fairview; Posey Twp. 34–22 Springfield Twp.; Connersville 53–14 Harrisburg; Everton 27–9 Alquina; Brookville 26–16 Liberty; Connersville 37–12 Posey Twp.; Everton 30–20 Brookville; Connersville 49–28 Everton. Officials: Leon Fadely, Alfred Jackson, Leonard Moore.

CRAWFORDSVILLE: Crawfordsville 28–20 Wingate; Waynetown 33–14 Ladoga; Waveland 29–10 Bowers; Darlington 32–19 Alamo; New Richmond 23–17 Linden; New Market 33–13 New Ross; Waynetown 24–19 Crawfordsville; Darlington 22–15 Waveland; New Richmond 28–20 New Market; Darlington 38–21 Waynetown; New Richmond 35–24 Darlington. Officials: Clarence Grogan, Walter Moss.

DANVILLE: Pittsboro 47–17 Winchester; North Salem 25–19 Amo; Avon 27–21 Danville; Plainfield 34–13 Lizton; Clayton 42–10 Stilesville; Brownsburg 26–24 Pittsboro; Avon 23–18 North Salem; Plainfield 25–17 Clayton; Brownsburg 36–20 Avon; Plainfield 27–22 Brownsburg. Officials: Winston Ashley, Russell Newgent.

DELPHI: Burlington 17–15 Delphi; Cutler 28–14 Deer Creek; Carrollton 24–19 Rockfield; Camden 17–10 Monroe Twp.; Cutler 28–19 Burlington; Camden 24–16 Carrollton; Camden 26–17 Cutler. Officials: Carl Burt, Glenn Farrell.

EVANSVILLE: Newburgh 24–14 Griffin; Millersburg 48–19 Wadesville; Reitz 38–17 Chandler; Central 17–15 Bosse; Elberfeld 20–17 Mt. Vernon; Cynthiana 32–27 New Harmony; Newburgh 23–21 Millersburg; Reitz 27–9 Central; Elberfeld 28–26 Cynthiana; Reitz 38–23 Newburgh; Reitz 42–21 Elberfeld. Officials: Hulett Crecelius, Orville Jones.

FORT WAYNE: Elmhurst 21–18 Huntertown; Central 40–29 Leo; New Haven 31–24 Decatur; Arcola 22–19 Harlan; Monroeville 22–18 Hoagland; Lafayette Central 36–22 Woodburn; North Side 39–8 Monmouth; South Side 33–20 Elmhurst; Central 43–13 New Haven; Monroeville 16–9 Arcola; Lafayette Central 19–14 North Side; South Side 23–21 Central; Monroeville 33–24

179

Tourney Time

Lafayette Central; South Side 22–19 Monroeville (ot). Officials: S. E. Wagner; George Williams, Harry Coolman.

FRANKFORT: Mulberry 28–22 Washington Twp.; Rossville 32–24 Colfax; Kirklin 33–15 Jackson Twp.; Frankfort 30–16 Michigantown; Scircleville 28–26 Forest; Mulberry 46–14 Sugar Creek; Rossville 32–20 Kirklin; Frankfort 33–17 Scircleville; Rossville 40–18 Mulberry; Frankfort 37–13 Rossville. Officials: George Kenzler, Condict Smith.

FRANKLIN: Whiteland 29–13 Clark Twp.; Greenwood 36–26 Edinburg; Masonic Home 43–12 Van Buren Twp.; Center Grove 35–23 Union Twp.; Franklin 36–7 Nashville; Hopewell 37–24 Jackson Twp.; Nineveh 23–13 Trafalgar; Greenwood 26–24 Whiteland; Center Grove 27–20 Masonic Home; Franklin 37–16 Hopewell; Greenwood 35–25 Nineveh; Franklin 28–25 Center Grove; Franklin 32–12 Greenwood. Officials: Russell Pickett, Gale Robinson, Myron Moore.

GARRETT: Spencerville 27–14 Concord Twp.; Washington Center 18–17 Ashley; Garrett 28–15 Coesse; Butler 69–6 Etna Twp.; Auburn 20–10 Churubusco; Larwill 36–25 Jefferson Center; South Whitley 25–24 Waterloo (ot); Columbia City 48–12 Spencerville; Garrett 27–12 Washington Center; Butler 32–19 Auburn; South Whitley 38–26 Larwill; Columbia City 38–21 Garrett; Butler 43–36 South Whitley; Columbia City 34–14 Butler. Officials: Walter Thurston, A. H. Cornwell, Walter Fisher.

GARY: Wallace 35–20 Clark;; Whiting 14–13 Froebel Calumet Twp. 49–14 Longfellow; Hammond 30–27 Hobart; Hammond Tech 28–21 East Gary Edison; Emerson 38–12 Griffith; Horace Mann 50–30 East Chicago Garfield; East Chicago Roosevelt 20–19 East Chicago Washington; Whiting 22–12 Wallace; Hammond 32–14 Calumet Twp.; Tech 32–27 Emerson; Roosevelt 16–12 Horace Mann; Hammond 32–18 Whiting; Tech 21–20 Roosevelt; Hammond 41–26 Tech. Officials: L. R. Lenon; H. C. Warren, Joel Wilt.

GREENCASTLE: Bainbridge 30–15 Union Twp.; Cloverdale 32–17 Bridgeton; Rockville 46–30 Marshall; Belle Union 33–12 Russellville; Fillmore 40–20 Greene Twp.; Greencastle 30–22 Roachdale; Bainbridge 22–17 Cloverdale; Rockville 21–17 Belle Union; Greencastle 34–22 Fillmore; Bainbridge 35–16 Rockville; Greencastle 27–21 Bainbridge (ot). Officials: Norman Dunlap, Hal Harris.

GREENFIELD: Maxwell 28–12 Wilkinson; Greenfield 21–19 Fortville; Mt. Comfort 40–25 McCordsville; Charlottesville 29–21 New Palestine; Eden 27–25 Westland; Maxwell 30–22 Greenfield; Mt. Comfort 42–15 Charlottesville; Maxwell 37–29 Eden; Mt. Comfort 17–11 Maxwell. Officials: Custer Baker, Will Kinkaid.

GREENSBURG: Greensburg 28–20 New Point; Clarksburg 25–8 Zenas; North Vernon 34–17 Butlerville; Westport 34–29 Vernon; Jackson 30–16 Sandusky; St. Paul 37–22 Letts; Greensburg 35–18 Burney; North Vernon 43–20 Clarksburg; Westport 19–14 Jackson; Greensburg 21–18 St. Paul; North Vernon 45–17 Westport; North Vernon 25–21 Greensburg. Officials: Gerald Huey, Ray McKinley, Wilbur Miller.

HARTFORD CITY: Dunkirk 31–17 Pennville; Redkey 35–15 Bryant; Portland 39–22 Poling; Madison Twp. 36–18 Roll; Hartford City 50–13 Montpelier; Redkey 22–20 Dunkirk; Portland 27–26 Madison Twp; Hartford City 42–27 Redkey; Hartford City 40–25 Portland. Officials: Ora Davis, Mark Williams.

HUNTINGTON: Andrews 28–22 Huntington Twp.; Markle 20–19 Rock Creek Center; Roanoke 27–6 Wayne Twp.; Salamonie Twp. 31–12 Jefferson Twp.; Union Twp. 35–18 Bippus; Lancaster 46–7 Monument City; Huntington 23–17 Clear Creek; Andrews 32–23 Markle;

Roanoke 21–15 Salamonie Twp.; Lancaster Center 19–15 Union Twp.; Huntington 32–7 Andrews; Roanoke 16–11 Lancaster Center; Huntington 15–5 Roanoke. Officials: Mode Cranor, Basil R. Hosier, George Yarnelle.

INDIANAPOLIS: Shortridge 30–23 Ben Davis; Acton 34–24 Castleton; Tech 31–15 Washington; Warren Central 24–11 Broad Ripple; Manual Training 27–23 Decatur Central; Southport 42–18 New Bethel; New Augusta 38–27 Oaklandon; Beech Grove 27–21 Lawrence; Shortridge 33–20 Acton; Tech 34–20 Warren Central; Southport 28–18 Manual;; New Augusta 28–23 Beech Grove; Tech 23–16 Shortridge; Southport 33–11 New Augusta; Tech 30–27 Southport. Officials: Harry Briggs, Blair Gullion, Nate Kaufman.

KENDALLVILLE: Avilla 38–30 LaOtto; Ligonier 45–26 Cromwell; Orange Twp. 34–25 Albion; Wawaka 31–25 Wolf Lake; Avilla 27–25 Kendallville (ot); Ligonier 41–33 Orange Twp.; Wawaka 31–30 Avilla; Ligonier 29–24 Wawaka. Officials: Ward Gilbert, Carl Porter.

KENTLAND: Kentland 37–9 Mt. Ayr; Goodland 83–3 Kniman; Brook 41–6 DeMotte; Morocco 31–14 Fair Oaks; Remington 69–12 Hanging Grove; Kentland 24–18 Rensselaer; Brook 34–30 Goodland (ot); Morocco 29–27 Remington; Kentland 21–17 Brook; Morocco 28–27 Kentland. Officials: Joe Brown, Lloyd B. Hart.

KOKOMO: New London 28–19 West Middleton; Kokomo 20–12 Russiaville; Union Twp. 21–13 Clay Twp.; Howard Twp. 20–12 Ervin Twp.; Jackson Twp. 21–18 Greentown; Kokomo 29–19 New London; Howard Twp. 21–15 Union Twp.; Kokomo 44–18 Jackson Twp.; Kokomo 48–15 Howard Twp. Officials: L. E. Fink, John Gant.

LAFAYETTE: Buck Creek 2–0 Stockwell (forfeit); Clarks Hill 34–14 Monitor; Battle Ground 27–13 Romney; Lafayette 45–20 Wea; West Lafayette 28–18 Klondike; West Point 33–27 Montmorenci; Jackson Twp. 28–15 Dayton; Buck Creek 23–22 Clarks Hill; Battle Ground 30–16 Lafayette; West Lafayette 35–18 West Point; Jackson Twp. 19–18 Buck Creek; West Lafayette 24–23 Battle Ground; West Lafayette 23–19 Jackson Twp. Officials: B.E. Bayh, Reid McLain, Lowell Sparks.

LAPORTE: Hanna 27–17 Kingsbury; Stillwell 23–15 Union Twp.; Union Mills 26–23 Westville; Michigan City 43–16 Clinton Twp.; LaPorte 49–7 Mill Creek; LaCrosse 30–20 Rolling Prairie; Wanatah 42–21 Springfield Twp.; Stillwell 23–22 Hanna; Michigan City 38–14 Union Mills; LaPorte 44–24 LaCrosse; Wanatah 33–14 Stillwell; Michigan City 31–14 LaPorte; Michigan City 55–16 Wanatah. Officials: Allen Klinck, T. R. Smith, Edmund Tully.

LEBANON: Zionsville 36–27 Central; Advance 18–14 Jamestown; Lebanon 56–11 Whitestown; Dover 27–23 Pinnell; Zionsville 26–19 Thorntown; Lebanon 33–26 Advance; Zionsville 15–14 Dover; Lebanon 39–19 Zionsville. Officials: Forrest Ballinger, George Bender.

LINTON: Midland 28–14 Scotland; Solsberry 47–12 Newberry; Linton 32–18 Lyons; Jasonville 19–18 Owensburg; Bloomfield 24–18 Switz City; Midland 28–26 Solsberry; Linton 30–17 Jasonville; Bloomfield 35–19 Midland; Linton 25–24 Bloomfield. Officials: Gerald Powell, Wayne Watson.

LOGANSPORT: Twelve Mile 25–24 New Waverly; Royal Center 31–29 Lucerne; Young America 26–23 Galveston Onward 27–10 Noble Twp. Logansport 72–11 Metea; Washington Twp. 28–25 Walton; Royal Center 31–26 Twelve Mile; Young America 30–29 Onward; Logansport 60–22 Washington Twp.; Young America 21–15 Royal Center; Logansport 44–23 Young America. Officials: Charles Garrett, O. F. Helvie.

MADISON: Lovett 31–14 Paris Crossing; Central 42–25 Saluda; Deputy 43–16 San Jacinto;

Tourney Time

Dupont 28–26 Hanover; Scottsburg 81–8 Marion Twp.; Madison 30–20 North Madison; Austin 34–9 Lexington; Central 29–16 Lovett; Dupont 32–20 Deputy; Madison 28–26 Scottsburg; Central 30–27 Austin; Madison 23–15 Dupont; Madison 33–24 Central. Officials: Richard Miller, Robert L. Todd, Ralph Miller.

MARION: Upland 22–19 Van Buren; Fairmount 24–17 Mathews; Sweetser 20–18 Swayzee; Jonesboro 27–21 Gas City; Marion 40–24 Upland; Fairmount 25–22 Sweetser; Marion 29–16 Jonesboro; Marion 26–18 Fairmount. Officials: Layall Fisher, Daniel Guild.

MILAN: Holton 35–26 Osgood; Sunman 19–16 Versailles; New Marion 46–22 Napoleon; Milan 40–13 Cross Plains; Batesville 31–13 Sunman; New Marion 35–28 Holton; Batesville 32–22 Milan; Batesville 42–30 New Marion. Officials: A. L. Bruce, Charles Brehm.

MISHAWAKA: South Bend Central 31–17 Lakeville; Madison Twp. 33–10 Greene Twp.; Mishawaka 36–19 New Carlisle; Walkerton 34–21 South Bend Wilson; Washington-Clay 36–16 Warren Twp.; South Bend Riley 27–14 North Liberty; Central 35–33 Madison Twp.; Mishawaka 40–12 Walkerton; Riley 41–28 Washington-Clay; Mishawaka 31–22 Central; Riley 27–24 Mishawaka. Officials: Kenneth Barr, George Lambert.

MONON: Liberty Twp. 31–28 Reynolds; Brookston 36–19 Wolcott; Monon 16–13 Chalmers; Monticello 36–10 Round Grove; Burnettsville 20–16 Idaville; Brookston 41–27 Liberty Twp.; Monon 23–19 Monticello; Brookston 41–27 Burnettsville; Brookston 28–24 Monon. Officials: Clarence Barrett, C. Wilbur McCorkle.

MUNCIE: Eaton 31–13 DeSoto; Albany 26–23 Gaston; Yorktown 29–20 Cowan; Muncie 27–19 Daleville; Royerton 27–18 Harrison; Selma 18–17 Burris; Center 26–25 Eaton; Yorktown 28–19 Albany; Muncie 26–16 Royerton; Selma 26–15 Center; Muncie 24–23 Yorktown; Muncie 44–14 Selma. Officials: Glenn Adams, Donald Coar, Lundy Welborn.

NAPPANEE: Baugo Twp. 34–26 Jefferson Twp.; Middlebury 50–27 Millersburg; Elkhart 30–19 Concord Twp.; Goshen 32–15 Bristol; Nappanee 31–24 New Paris; Middlebury 33–29 Baugo Twp.; Elkhart 22–16 Goshen; Nappanee 43–12 Middlebury; Nappanee 32–15 Elkhart. Officials: R. L. Rahbar, George Russell.

NEW ALBANY: Henryville 39–21 Georgetown; Jeffersonville 70–14 Laconia; New Salisbury 36–21 New Amsterdam; New Albany 80–4 New Middletown; Borden 24–15 Mauckport; Corydon 44–18 New Washington; Charlestown 32–14 Lanesville; Silver Creek 45–15 Elizabeth; Jeffersonville 40–17 Henryville; New Albany 59–16 New Salisbury; Corydon 37–20 Borden; Silver Creek 30–22 Charlestown; Jeffersonville 35–18 New Albany; Silver Creek 26–17 Corydon; Jeffersonville 40–25 Silver Creek. Officials: Paul Garrison, Edward DeGroote, Robert Taylor.

NEW CASTLE: New Castle 48–11 Mt. Summit; Cadiz 31–26 Kennard; Straughn 30–23 Spiceland; Middletown 39–31 Sulphur Springs; Knightstown 20–15 Lewisville; Mooreland 24–21 New Lisbon; New Castle 43–20 Cadiz; Middletown 32–21 Straughn; Knightstown 31–19 Mooreland; New Castle 46–7 Middletown; New Castle 24–12 Knightstown. Officials: Fletcher Kerr, Houston Meyer.

OAKLAND CITY: Oakland City 24–15 Fort Branch; Patoka 25–16 Mackey; Francisco 19–17 Haubstadt; Owensville 32–22 Hazleton; Princeton; 30–26 Mt. Olympus; Oakland City 28–25 Patoka; Owensville 20–18 Francisco; Princeton 29–24 Oakland City; Princeton 21–19 Owensville. Officials: James Adams, John Hoffman.

PAOLI: Paoli 22–12 French Lick; Salem 28–24 Hardinsburg; Orleans 18–16 West Baden; Pekin 24–21 Campbellsburg; Paoli 42–18 Monroe Twp.; Salem 12–11 Orleans; Paoli 27–15

Pekin; Paoli 33–15 Orleans. Officials: Borden Purcell, Clyde Waters.

PERU: Jefferson Twp. 25–22 Deedsville; Peru 25–15 Butler Twp.; Gilead 37–32 Converse; Macy 39–31 Amboy; Chili 43–28 Bunker Hill; Clay Twp. 39–18 Jefferson Twp.; Peru 33–17 Gilead; Chili 31–26 Macy; Peru 42–21 Clay Twp.; Peru 50–21 Chili. Officials: Lavon Carey, Winston Robbins.

PETERSBURG: Stendal 45–18 Winslow; Huntingburg 30–27 Holland; Spurgeon 63–12 Birdseye; Jasper 38–16 Ireland; Petersburg 34–22 Otwell; Dubois 28–23 Cuzco; Velpen 28–19 Union; Huntingburg 23–22 Stendal; Jasper 41–18 Spurgeon; Petersburg 40–19 Dubois; Huntingburg 24–16 Velpen; Jasper 38–22 Petersburg; Jasper 23–7 Huntingburg. Officials: Leonard Mayhugh, Harley Jurgens, John Lyskowinski.

PLYMOUTH: Bourbon 38–17 West Twp.; Bremen 36–21 Tyner; Culver 33–18 Argos; Tippecanoe 24–22 Grovertown; Plymouth 41–8 Center Twp.; North Judson 33–9 Hamlet; Knox 58–20 LaPaz; Bourbon 22–13 San Pierre; Bremen 21–11 Culver; Plymouth 27–17 Tippecanoe; North Judson 44–23 Knox; Bremen 18–14 Bourbon; North Judson 21–20 Plymouth; North Judson 38–20 Bremen. Officials: R. G. Campbel, R. P. Chambers, G. M. Kinzel.

RICHMOND: Richmond 35–9 Hagerstown; Economy 19–16 Whitewater; Boston 22–21 Fountain City; Centerville 34–17 Huntsville; Greensfork 36–13 Webster; Milton 37–13 Williamsburg; Richmond 25–20 Cambridge City; Boston 22–15 Economy; Centerville 22–20 Greensfork; Richmond 24–18 Milton; Boston 39–25 Centerville; Richmond 38–23 Boston. Officials: Frederick Shroyer, M. J. Cleary, Raymond Yoos.

RISING SUN: Patriot 19–15 Rising Sun; Bright 21–17 Vevay; Guilford 23–22 Dillsboro; Aurora 33–22 Moores Hill; Lawrenceburg 39–23 Patriot; Guilford 21–19 Bright; Aurora 26–22 Lawrenceburg; Guilford 18–17 Aurora. Officials: Will Smith, Gerald Bottorff.

RUSHVILLE: New Salem 28–17 Milroy; Arlington 26–24 Raleigh; Carthage 27–24 Gings (ot); Rushville 42–14 Morton; Manila 55–18 Glenwood; New Salem 24–21 Mays; Arlington 28–27 Carthage (2ot); Rushville 25–13 Manila; New Salem 38–22 Arlington; Rushville 28–24 New Salem. Officials: Frederick Mackey, George Seidensticker.

SEYMOUR: Tampico 23–7 Scipio; Seymour 39–11 Houston; Vallonia 35–21 Freetown; Clearspring 47–10 Hayden; Medora 26–11 Brownstown; Cortland 27–21 Crothersville; Seymour 43–8 Tampico; Vallonia 21–19 Clearspring; Medora 26–18 Cortland; Seymour 32–6 Vallonia; Seymour 42–6 Medora. Officials: George Bair, Wendell Heath.

SHELBYVILLE: Boggstown 25–19 Clifford; Columbus 39–28 Fairland; Morristown 39–27 Mt. Auburn; Shelbyville 32–28 Waldron; Flat Rock 27–23 Moral Twp.; Hawcreek Twp. 32–26 Boggstown; Columbus 30–16 Morristown; Shelbyville 30–9 Flat Rock; Hawcreek Twp. 21–15 Columbus; Shelbyville 33–18 Hawcreek Twp. Officials: Paul Williams, Guy Woods.

SHERIDAN: Atlanta 18–16 Westfield; Arcadia 18–15 Carmel; Fishers 12–7 Cicero; Sheridan 47–7 Goldsmith; Tipton 26–14 Walnut Grove; Noblesville 33–20 Windfall; Prairie Twp. 22–16 Kempton; Sharpsville 25–23 Atlanta; Arcadia 25–22 Fishers; Tipton 26–12 Sheridan; Noblesville 28–22 Prairies Twp.; Arcadia 19–13 Sharpsville; Tipton 23–22 Noblesville; Tipton 27–24 Arcadia. Officials: A. E. Pitcher, Harry Vandivier, Herbert Vaulk.

SULLIVAN: Sullivan 21–15 Dugger; Pleasantville 27–20 Shelburn; Farmersburg 17–14 Fairbanks; Graysville 39–17 New Lebanon; Carlisle 31–12 Merom; Hymera 25–20 Sullivan; Farmersburg 34–32 Pleasantville; Carlisle 14–13 Graysville; Hymera 17–15 Farmersburg; Carlisle 22–16 Hymera. Officials: Robert Greene, Irvin Springer.

Tourney Time

TELL CITY: Derby 31–30 Leavenworth; Tobinsport 16–14 Rome; Cannelton 63–11 Leopold; Union Twp. 29–24 Troy; Tell City 41–29 Oil Twp.; Marengo 28–11 Milltown; Bristow 46–14 Derby; Cannelton 27–10 Tobinsport; Tell City 45–25 Union Twp.; Bristow 21–13 Marengo; Tell City 33–32 Cannelton; Bristow 24–22 Tell City. Officials: Joe Armstrong, William Pointer, Herbert Robinson.

TERRE HAUTE: Glenn 33–11 Otter Creek; Wiley 32–15 Honey Creek; Garfield 19–16 Gerstmeyer; Pimento 24–23 Riley; West Terre Haute 29–15 Blackhawk; State Training 37–9 Concannon; Fontanet 23–16 Glenn; Wiley 15–11 Garfield; W. Terre Haute 27–23 Pimento; State Training 14–12 Fontanet; Wiley 36–15 West Terre Haute; Wiley 33–15 State Training. Officials: George Graham, George Kerr, Dean Malaska.

VALPARAISO: Valparaiso 33–7 Boone Grove; Chesterton 20–12 Lowell; Wheeler 23–8 Portage; Morgan Twp. 32–19 Hebron; Washington Twp. 22–13 Merrillville; Crown Point 27–17 Liberty Center; Valparaiso 19–14 Chesterton; Wheeler 23–9 Morgan Twp.; Crown Point 19–15 Washington Twp.; Valparaiso 29–24 Wheeler; Valparaiso 26–7 Crown Point. Officials: Forrest Wood, Elmer Posey.

VINCENNES: Bruceville 27–17 Fritchton; Bicknell 38–14 Wheatland; Oaktown 42–16 Monroe City; Freelandville 32–20 Edwardsport; Gibault 21–19 Decker (ot); Vincennes 60–6 Sandborn; Bruceville 41–16 Decker Chapel; Bicknell 34–17 Oaktown; Gibault 33–19 Freelandville; Vincennes 24–18 Bruceville; Bicknell 27–18 Gibault; Vincennes 30–17 Bicknell. Officials: W. V. Slyker, Lloyd Messersmith, H. A. Gottfried.

WABASH: Somerset 26–22 Chester Twp.; Roann 25–18 Chippewa; Lagro 32–21 Lafontaine; Linlawn 33–18 Urbana; North Manchester 30–23 Laketon; Wabash 52–18 Lincolnville; Somerset 25–20 Roann; Lagro 17–16 Linlawn; Wabash 46–10 North Manchester; Somerset 25–16 Lagro; Wabash 37–12 Somerset. Officials: Fernie Trigalet, J. Clayton Hughes.

WARSAW: Etna Green 22–21 Atwood; Mentone 43–15 Silver Lake; Leesburg 27–18 Milford; Pierceton 45–17 Sidney; Claypool 26–15 Syracuse; Warsaw 48–19 Burket; Beaver Dam 29–16 North Webster; Mentone 40–10 Etna Green; Pierceton 26–18 Leesburg; Warsaw 33–17 Claypool; Beaver Dam 12–10 Mentone; Warsaw 34–26 Pierceton; Beaver Dam 40–32 Warsaw. Officials: Hugh Vandivier, P. B. Kriegbaum, Clive Markley.

WASHINGTON: Elnora 30–10 Trinity Springs; Epsom 12–11 Shoals; Loogootee 48–6 Raglesville; Odon 33–22 Glendale; Washington 23–15 Barr Twp.; Plainville 53–15 Burns City; Elnora 41–13 Alfordsville; Loogootee 33–13 Epsom; Washington 30–18 Odon; Plainville 32–13 Elnora; Washington 39–16 Loogootee; Washington 30–16 Plainville. Officials: W. S. Fellmy, Fred Alwood, Raymond Sparks.

WINAMAC: Akron 48–10 Monterey; Fulton 37–18 Francesville; Kewanna 25–12 Grass Creek; Rochester 19–13 Richland Center; Pulaski 32–11 Talma; Medaryville 26–16 Star City; Winamac 36–16 Leiters Ford; Fulton 25–18 Akron; Rochester 31–19 Kewanna; Pulaski 34–9 Medaryville; Fulton 22–19 Winamac; Rochester 22–11 Pulaski. Officials: A. T. Krider, J. Alvin Taylor, LeRoy Shine.

WINCHESTER: Jefferson 29–24 Jackson; McKinley 33–11 Lincoln; Saratoga 26–19 Modoc; Wayne 41–14 Stoney Creek; Lynn 30–29 Farmland; Parker 38–6 Losantville; Union City 28–21 Spartanburg; Winchester 25–17 Ridgeville; McKinley 33–29 Jefferson (2ot); Wayne 27–15 Saratoga; Lynn 25–18 Parker; Union City 26–20 Winchester; Wayne 23–19 McKinley; Union City 30–29 Lynn; Union City 42–14 Lynn. Officials: P. G. Kessler, Palmer Sponsler, Lloyd Miller.

IHSAA Scores | *1930–1939*

1934 REGIONALS

ANDERSON: Indianapolis Tech 19–18 Plainfield; Anderson 21–17 Mt. Comfort; Tech 20–13 Anderson. Officials: B. E. Bayh, Forrest Wood.
AUBURN: Ligonier 23–22 Angola; Beaver Dam 35–30 Columbia City; Beaver Dam 34–33 Ligonier. Officials: Ward Gilbert, Will Smith.
COLUMBUS: North Vernon 30–27 Shelbyville; Franklin 34–19 Madison; North Vernon 29–25 Franklin (ot). Officials: Winston Ashley, George Williams.
EVANSVILLEl: Dale 32–22 Bristow; Princeton 30–26 Reitz; Princeton 21–19 Dale. Officials: Frank Jarrell, Vaughn Russell.
FORT WAYNE: Hartford City 31–17 Ossian; Huntington 30–20 South Side; Hartford city 32–23 Huntington. Officials: H. E. Vandivier, Joel Wilt.
GREENCASTLE: Pine Village 36–21 Clinton; Greencastle 28–25 New Richmond; Greencastle 33–26 Pine Village. Officials: Dillon Geiger, Borden Purcell.
JEFFERSONVILLE: Jeffersonville 22–13 Paoli; Seymour 24–14 Mitchell; Jeffersonville 26–24 Seymour. Officials: C. D. Manhart, Russell Pickett.
LAFAYETTE: Lebanon 35–33 West Lafayette; Frankfort 31–15 Fowler; Lebanon 26–22 Frankfort. Officials: O. F. Helvie, Orville Jones.
LOGANSPORT: Camden 19–17 Peru; Logansport 48–18 Brookston; Logansport 34–9 Camden. Officials: Glenn Adams, Lundy Welborn.
MARION: Tipton 23–21 Kokomo; Wabash 28–23 Marion; Wabash 28–17 Tipton. Officials: J. Clayton Hughes, Stanley Porter.
MARTINSVILLE: Brazil 35–33 Bloomington; Linton 32–25 Wiley (Terre Haute); Brazil 23–9 Linton. Officials: Blair Gullion, Charles Jensen.
MUNCIE: New Castle 14–9 Muncie; Richmond 29–20 Union City; Richmond 18–12 New Castle. Officials: Dale Miller, George Vaulk.
ROCHESTER: Nappanee 27–22 Fulton; North Judson 22–18 South Bend Riley; North Judson 30–29 Nappanee (ot). Officials: George Russell, Fletcher Kerr.
RUSHVILLE: Batesville 32–12 Guilford; Rushville 32–26 Connersville; Batesville 35–34 Rushville. Officials: Houston Meyer, Paul Williams.
VALPARAISO: Hammond 64–14 Morocco; Valparaiso 26–24 Michigan City; Hammond 19–17 Valparaiso (ot). Officials: Carl Burt, Lowell Lenon.
VINCENNES: Vincennes 25–23 Washington (2ot); Jasper 32–17 Carlisle; Jasper 27–26 Vincennes (ot). Officials: Irvin Springer, Nate Kaufman.

1934 FINALS—March 16, 17

INDIANAPOLIS (Butler Fieldhouse): Logansport 31–20 North Judson; Hartford City 31–26 Princeton; Jasper 30–15 North Vernon; Richmond 40–12 Beaver Dam; Indianapolis Tech 24–19 Batesville; Hammond 40–31 Greencastle; Lebanon 37–31 Brazil; Jeffersonville 30–28 Wabash; Logansport 21–12 Hartford City; Jasper 29–27 Richmond; Tech 30–20 Hammond; Jeffersonville 41–20 Lebanon; Logansport 31–28 Jasper; Tech 34–25 Jeffersonville; Logansport 26–19 Tech. Officials: B.E. Bayh, O.F. Helvie, Stanley Porter, Carl Burt, Vaughn Russell.

Tourney Time

1935 SECTIONALS

ANDERSON: Anderson 32–10 Alexandria; Elwood 24–22 Lapel; Summitville 37–21 Frankton; Markleville 34–24 Pendleton. Anderson 41–17 Lapel; Markleville 41–34 Summitville; Anderson 43–22 Markleville. Officials: R.P. Chambers, Clarence Grogan.

ATTICA: Attica 31–16 Hillsboro; Williamsport 36–20 West Lebanon; Pine Village 25–15 Covington; Veedersburg 21–20 Kingman; Attica 54–4 Wallace; Williamsport 21–17 Pine Village; Veedersburg 28–27 Attica; Williamsport 26–21 Veedersburg. Officials: Frank Jarrell, Paul Lovell.

AURORA: Aurora 40–24 Dillsboro; Rising Sun 26–19 Moores Hill; Vevay 27–23 Bright; Lawrenceburg 34–22 Patriot; Aurora 33–19 Guilford; Vevay 32–13 Rising Sun; Aurora 24–23 Lawrenceburg; Aurora 23–18 Vevay. Officials: Thomas Baker, Custer Baker.

BEDFORD: Bedford 47–16 Oolitic; Fayetteville 24–21 Heltonville; Tunnelton 28–18 Shawswick; Williams 32–17 Huron; Mitchell 34–20 Springville; Bedford 36–13 Marshall Twp.; Fayetteville 22–21 Tunnelton; Mitchell 33–19 Williams; Bedford 43–33 Fayetteville; Mitchell 23–21 Bedford. Officials: H. A. Gottfried, Irvin Springer.

BLOOMFIELD: Jasonville 24–22 Scotland; Solsberry 62–11 Newberry; Lyons 46–10 Midland; Bloomfield 23–18 Owensburg; Linton 31–11 Switz City; Solsberry 23–19 Jasonville; Lyons 35–24 Bloomfield; Linton 30–15 Solsberry; Lyons 39–18 Linton. Officials: Herbert Robinson, James Watts

BLUFFTON: Rockcreek 34–12 Chester Center; Lancaster 35–22 Ossian; Berne 34–23 Union; Kirkland 20–15 Monroe; Bluffton 43–11 Jefferson; Hartford Twp. 30–7 Pleasant Mills; Petroleum 21–19 Liberty Center; Rockcreek 52–12 Geneva; Berne 34–10 Lancaster; Bluffton 17–15 Kirkland; Petroleum 25–17 Hartford Twp.; Berne 26–15 Rockcreek; Bluffton 25–8 Petroleum; Berne 30–28 Bluffton. Officials: Alfred Jackson, Leonard B. Moore, Lloyd Miller.

BRAZIL: Spencer 28–4 Gosport; Van Buren 26–15 Cory; Ashboro 32–12 Clay City; Quincy 39–15 Jefferson Twp.; Bowling Green 22–19 Patricksburg; Brazil 32–7 Freedom; Spencer 34–25 Van Buren; Ashboro 31–20 Quincy; Brazil 50–18 Bowling Green; Spencer 27–20 Ashboro; Brazil 36–11 Spencer. Officials: Raymond Meier, Myron Moore.

CANNELTON: Cannelton 26–20 Derby; Leavenworth 33–28 Oil Twp.; Marengo 22–21 Troy; Milltown 62–19 Leopold; Tell City 31–6 Bristow; Cannelton 31–22 Union Twp.; Marengo 21–20 Leavenworth; Tell City 33–15 Milltown; Cannelton 29–16 Marengo; Tell City 22–14 Cannelton. Officials: William E. Pointer, Fred Alwood.

COLUMBIA CITY: Churubusco 33–25 South Whitley; Jefferson Center 21–16 Washington Center; Columbia City 60–14 Wolf Lake; Larwill 36–14 Etna; Churubusco 31–25 Coesse; Columbia City 34–23 Jefferson Center; Churubusco 29–24 Larwill; Columbia City 38–26 Churubusco. Officials: Carl Porter, Paul Bateman.

CONNERSVILLE: Harrison Twp. 54–20 Orange; Brookville 24–18 Liberty; Connersville 49–16 Harrisburg; Brownsville 29–23 Fairview; Laurel 30–28 Bentonville; Springfield Twp. 50–16 Oldenburg; Everton 28–25 Alquina; Whitewater Twp. 34–30 Harrison Twp.; Connersville 40–25 Brookville; Brownsville 40–19 Laurel; Everton 27–24 Springfield Twp.; Connersville 68–13 Whitewater Twp.; Brownsville 34–32 Everton; Connersville 43–30 Brownsville. Officials: Philip Kessler, Palmer Sponsler, Norman Morrison.

CRAWFORDSVILLE: Crawfordsville 27–11 New Ross; New Market 17–15 Darlington; Linden 36–33 Wingate; Ladoga 26–20 Waynetown; Alamo 28–22 New Richmond; Waveland 21–14 Bowers; Crawfordsville 25–22 New Market; Linden 27–19 Ladoga; Waveland 33–29 Alamo;

IHSAA Scores / 1930–1939

Linden 30–25 Crawfordsville; Waveland 20–11 Linden. Officials: Walter Moss, Wayne Watson.

DANVILLE: Danville 21–16 Lizton; Amo 22–18 New Winchester; Plainfield 31–17 Clayton; Brownsburg 36–16 Stilesville; Pittsboro 36–17 North Salem; Danville 24–23 Avon (ot); Plainfield 27–22 Amo; Pittsboro 19–9 Brownsburg; Plainfield 35–23 Danville; Plainfield 26–12 Pittsboro. Officials: Doxie Reeves, Forrest Ballinger.

DELPHI: Monroe Twp. 52–18 Adams Twp.; Delphi 21–10 Cutler; Rock Creek 26–22 Deer Creek; Camden 22–12 Burlington; Flora 52–18 Carrollton; Delphi 21–17 Rock Creek; Camden 23–9 Flora; Camden 22–19 Delphi. Officials: H. E. Vandivier, Elmer Posey.

EVANSVILLE: Griffin 34–18 Cynthiana; New Harmony 23–20 Newburgh; Elberfeld 25–24 Mt. Vernon; Bosse 37–17 Millersburg; Wadesville 21–17 Chandler; Poseyville 17–16 Stewartsville; Central 27–22 Reitz; New Harmony 26–23 Griffin; Bosse 28–15 Elberfeld; Poseyville 24–10 Wadesville; Central 27–16 New Harmony; Bosse 40–7 Poseyville; Bosse 18–16 Central. Officials: Hulett Crecelius, B.E. Bayh, Donald Wilder.

FORT WAYNE: Elmhurst 25–19 Woodburn; Lafayette Central 36–25 Monmouth; New Haven 24–23 Harlan; Hoagland 33–19 Huntertown; Central 44–14 Arcola; Decatur 32–22 Leo; North Side 36–13 Monroeville; South Side 32–23 Elmhurst; Lafayette Central 38–29 New Haven; Central 34–22 Hoagland; North Side 32–24 Decatur; South Side 36–11 Lafayette Central; Central 28–27 North Side; South Side 36–23 Central. Officials: George Williams, Mark Williams, L. E. Fink.

FRANKFORT: Scircleville 25–17 Kirklin; Frankfort 32–17 Forest; Jefferson 24–2 Sugar Creek; Rossville 27–17 Michigantown; Colfax 36–19 Jackson Twp.; Scircleville 21–17 Mulberry; Frankfort 36–20 Jefferson; Rossville 23–17 Colfax; Frankfort 43–16 Scircleville; Frankfort 47–19 Rossville. Officials: John Gant, Houston Meyer.

FRANKLIN: Edinburg 53–18 Van Buren Twp.; Greenwood 38–14 Trafalgar; Masonic Home 44–9 Nashville; Union Twp. 58–6 Jackson Twp.; Clark Twp. 46–18 Nineveh; Franklin 31–13 Whiteland; Center Grove 33–11 Hopewell; Greenwood 26–22 Edinburg; Union Twp. 27–26 Masonic Home; Franklin 31–18 Clark Twp.; Greenwood 22–16 Center Grove; Franklin 25–19 Union Twp.; Franklin 34–13 Greenwood. Officials: Ray McKinley, Guy Woods, Harry Briggs.

GARRETT: Ashley 50–13 Pleasant Lake; Angola 39–26 Concord Twp.; Auburn 42–10 Orland; Butler 28–20 Garrett; Fremont 31–18 Scott Center; Spencerville 27–15 Hamilton; Salem Center 30–16 Metz; Ashley 35–18 Waterloo; Auburn 21–19 Angola; Butler 35–13 Fremont; Spencerville 50–13 Salem Center; Auburn 29–14 Ashley; Butler 39–23 Spencerville; Auburn 22–17 Butler. Officials: A. H. Cornwell, W. E. Thurston, Walter Fisher.

GARY: Froebel 48–17 East Gary Edison; Emerson 74–12 Garfield. Horace Mann 41–22 Hobart; Whiting 37–25 Wallace; Clark 38–9 Tolleston; Griffith 25–23 Calumet Twp.; Hammond 32–23 East Chicago Washington; East Chicago Roosevelt 37–23 Hammond Tech; Emerson 23–20 Froebel; Whiting 27–26 Horace Mann; Griffith 31–23 Clark; Hammond 35–9 Roosevelt; Emerson 35–19 Whiting; Hammond 46–21 Griffith; Hammond 42–23 Emerson. Officials: Forrest Wood, Lundy Welborn, Ward Gilbert.

GOODLAND: Kentland 45–18 Fair Oaks; Brook 31–8 Hanging Grove; Rensselaer 43–21 Wheatfield; Morocco 53–16 Kniman; Remington 27–18 DeMotte; Goodland 31–19 Mt. Ayr; Kentland 50–9 Tefft; Rensselaer 17–12 Brook; Morocco 39–31 Remington; Kentland 27–14 Goodland; Morocco 36–35 Rensselaer; Kentland 46–17 Morocco. Officials: Wayne Cunningham, Will Kinkaid, Louis Donchin.

Tourney Time

GOSHEN: Bristol 26–25 New Paris; Goshen 33–18 Concord; Baugo Twp. 29–25 Millersburg; Middlebury 51–20 Jefferson Twp.; Nappanee 33–24 Elkhart; Wakarusa 31–23 Bristol; Goshen 20–16 Baugo Twp.. Nappanee 38–20 Middlebury; Goshen 26–11 Wakarusa; Nappanee 35–18 Goshen. Officials: Lawrence Gaunt, Walter Cook.

GREENCASTLE: Belle Union 39–6 Putnamville; Bainbridge 24–16 Green Twp.; Greencastle 23–21 Rockville. Russellville 30–23 Marshall; Roachdale 37–31 Cloverdale; Union Twp. 26–24 Reelsville; Fillmore 33–24 Bridgeton; Belle Union 22–19 Bainbridge; Greencastle 18–14 Russellville; Roachdale 34–12 Union Twp.; Belle Union 26–15 Fillmore; Roachdale 23–17 Greencastle; Roachdale 24–19 Belle Union. Officials: Dana Chandler. Robert Hold, Gerald O. Powell.

GREENFIELD: McCordsville 32–14 Mt. Comfort; Wilkinson 37–30 Greenfield; Eden 33–17 Westland; Fortville 39–19 New Palestine; Maxwell 29–11 Charlottesville. Wilkinson 35–18 McCordsville; Fortville 31–19 Eden; Maxwell 35–24 Wilkinson; Fortville 24–21 Maxwell (ot). Officials: Layall Fisher, Lloyd Miller.

GREENSBURG: Letts 31–25 Jackson; Sandusky 24–17 Clarksburg; Westport 29–20 Vernon; New Point 39–16 Zenas; Butlerville 34–15 St. Paul; North Vernon 56–16 Letts; Sandusky 23–22 Westport; New Point 27–24 Butlerville; North Vernon 25–18 Greensburg; New Point 36–15 Sandusky; North Vernon 49–19 New Point. Officials: Russell Pickett, Reid McLain, George Bender.

HARTFORD CITY: Pennville 25–18 Hartford City; Roll 24–16 Poling; Madison Twp. 26––25 Portland; Montpelier 32–30 Redkey; Dunkirk 24–11 Bryant; Pennville 24–19 Roll; Madison Twp. 35–27 Montpelier; Pennville 26–20 Dunkirk; Pennville 23–13 Madison Twp. Officials: Condict Smith, Raymond Trobaugh.

HUNTINGTON: Andrews 25–22 Rock Creek Center; Union Twp. 22–21 Banquo; Clear Creek Twp. 34–26 Bippus; Salamonie Twp. 40–14 Polk Twp.; Lancaster Center 32–19 Markle; Huntington 35–22 Huntington Twp.; Roanoke 30–15 Jefferson Twp.; Andrews 40–23 Union Twp.; Salamonie Twp. 38–20 Clear Creek Twp.; Huntington 34–23 Lancaster Center; Roanoke 30–17 Andrews; Huntington 29–21 Salamonie Twp.; Roanoke 21–20 Huntington. Officials: George Huey, Basil Hosier, George Yarnelle.

INDIANAPOLIS: New Bethel 26–20 Beech Grove; Shortridge 34–14 Broad Ripple; Castleton 24–22 Decatur Central; Manual 30–23 New Augusta; Ben Davis 49–17 Oaklandon; Washington 35–21 Lawrence; Tech 26–18 Warren Central; Southport 20–18 Acton; Shortridge 36–20 New Bethel; Manual 22–16 Castleton; Ben Davis 30–17 Washington; Southport 23–20 Tech; Shortridge 27–16 Manual; Ben Davis 23–20 Southport; Ben Davis 24–22 Shortridge. Officials: Glenn M. Adams, Walter Marks, T. R. Smith.

JASPER: Ireland 28–16 Birdseye; Jasper 54–15 Cuzco; Holland 68–13 Dubois. Velpen 43–12 Union; Stendal 26–14 Spurgeon; Huntingburg 29–26 Petersburg; Otwell 28–22 Winslow; Jasper 31–20 Ireland; Holland 39–23 Velpen; Huntingburg 25–15 Stendal; Jasper 41–16 Otwell; Huntingburg 29–27 Holland; Huntingburg 28–18 Jasper. Officials: John Lyskowinski, Leonard Mayhugh, Walter Ringer.

KENDALLVILLE: Wawaka 26–19 Albion; Ligonier 43–7 Springfield Twp.; Wolcottville 32–17 Scott; Topeka 22–20 Cromwell; LaGrange 32–30 Orange Twp.; Lima 27–23 LaOtto (ot); Kendallville 29–16 Brighton; Avilla 37—19 Shipshewana; Ligonier 29–26 Wawaka; Wolcottville 22–19 Topeka (ot); LaGrange 27–20 Lima; Kendallville 36–24 Avilla; Ligonier 23–13 Wolcottville; LaGrange 36–28 Kendallville; Ligonier 34–19 LaGrange. Officials: Ora M. Davis, Ralph Parker, Louis Briner.

IHSAA Scores | 1930–1939

KOKOMO: Kokomo 30–18 Union Twp.; Clay Twp. 28–20 Jackson Twp.; Russiaville 32–25 West Middleton; Greentown 21–15 Howard Twp.; New London 25–21 Ervin Twp.; Kokomo 35–13 Clay Twp.; Russiaville 17–14 Greentown; Kokomo 37–18 New London; Kokomo 25–20 Russiaville. Officials: Karl Dickerson, Clyde Gentry.

LAFAYETTE: Jackson Twp. 23–22 Stockwell; Klondike 32–21 Romney; Buck Creek 31–8 Dayton; Lafayette 22–20 West Lafayette; Clarks Hill 29–26 West Point; Wea 27–8 Monitor; Battle Ground 25–18 Montmorenci; Klondike 24–17 Jackson Twp.; Lafayette 38–24 Buck Creek; Clarks Hill 38–18 Wea; Battle Ground 26–21 Klondike; Lafayette 34–20 Clarks Hill; Lafayette 32–22 Battle Ground. Officials: Charles G. Garrett, O. F. Helvie, Richard Roberts.

LAPORTE: Union Mills 24–20 Westville; Michigan City 60–15 Stillwell; Springfield Twp. 26–22 Hanna; Rolling Prairie 20–17 Union Twp.; Clinton Twp. 24–14 Millcreek; Wanatah 31–23 LaCrosse; LaPorte 27–15 Kingsbury; Michigan City 44–23 Union Mills; Rolling Prairie 21–12 Springfield Twp.; Clinton Twp. 27–25 Wanatah; Michigan City 32–19 LaPorte; Rolling Prairie 25–22 Clinton Twp.; Michigan City 42–17 Rolling Prairie. Officials: Allen H. Klinck, Lowell D. Sparks, Edmund Tully.

LEBANON: Jamestown 22–18 Zionsville; Lebanon 47–21 Pinnell; Whitestown; 24–21 Dover; Advance 48–21 Central; Thorntown 27–18 Jamestown; Lebanon 56–13 Whitestown; Advance 24–22 Thorntown; Lebanon 26–19 Advance. Officials: Carl Burt, R. G. Campbell.

LOGANSPORT: Galveston 39–20 Lucerne; Metea 25–22 Noble Twp.; Twelve Mile 26–18 Young America; Logansport 58–20 New Waverly; Royal Center 32–22 Onward; Walton 26–24 Washington Twp.; Galveston 20–14 Metea; Logansport 44–19 Twelve Mile; Royal Center 21–18 Walton; Logansport 28–19 Galveston; Logansport 36–13 Royal Center. Officials: Winston Ashley, Dean Malaska.

LYNN: Lynn 30–24 Spartanburg; Parker 21–17 Ridgeville; Wayne 22–20 Lincoln; Farmland 20–17 Stoney Creek; Saratoga 44–18 Modoc; Winchester 37–7 Losantville; Jefferson 23–11 McKinley; Union City 32–15 Jackson; Lynn 16–11 Parker; Farmland 28–17 Wayne; Winchester 51–24 Saratoga; Union City 46–28 Jefferson; Farmland 29–16 Lynn; Union City 18–15 Winchester; Farmland 22–21 Union City. Officials: Blair Gullion, Clive I. Markley, Everett Campbell.

MARION: Marion 33–13 Jefferson Twp.; Sims Twp. 25–21 Sweetser; Fairmount 34–25 Van Buren; Jonesboro 30–22 Gas City; Marion 47–26 Sims Twp.; Fairmount 24–19 Jonesboro; Marion 37–9 Fairmount. Officials: George Russell, Thomas Fields.

MARTINSVILLE: Martinsville 36–11 Smithville; Paragon 30–12 Unionville; Bloomington 47–21 Eminence; Stinesville 19–17 Monrovia; Mooresville 33–21 Ellettsville; Martinsville 26–19 Morgantown; Bloomington 32–20 Paragon; Mooresville 28–25 Stinesville; Martinsville 23–22 Bloomington; Martinsville 28–24 Mooresville. Officials: Vaughn Russell, C. O. Walls.

MILAN: Batesville 18–13 Versailles; New Marion 28–19 Cross Plains; Milan 38–14 Napoleon; Osgood 22–17 Holton; Sunman 27–26 Batesville; Milan 30–28 New Marion; Osgood 27–23 Sunman (ot); Milan 32–21 Osgood. Officials: Will Smith, Robert M. Downey.

MISHAWAKA: Lakeville 31–13 North Liberty; South Bend Riley 45–11 South Bend Wilson; Madison Twp. 48–11 Warren Twp.; New Carlisle 25–22 Greene Twp.; Walkerton 43–21 Washington-Clay; Mishawaka 27–18 South Bend Central; Lakeville 23–18 Riley; New Carlisle 25–24 Madison Twp.; Mishawaka 41–26 Walkerton; New Carlisle 27–22 Lakeville; Mishawaka 32–16 New Carlisle. Officials: A. T. Krider, J. Alvin Taylor.

Tourney Time

MONTICELLO: Brookston 26–16 Wolcott; Reynolds 49–4 Burnettsville; Chalmers 43–21 Liberty Twp.; Monon 34–22 Idaville; Monticello 37–17 Round Grove; Brookston 31–17 Reynolds; Monon 27–21 Chalmers; Monticello 23–18 Brookston; Monticello 24–18 Monon. Officials: Lavon Carey, Glenn Farrell.

MUNCIE: Burris 18–12 Selma; Central 39–14 Albany; Yorktown 30–22 Gaston; Cowan 29–24 Center Twp.; Daleville 26–19 DeSoto; Harrison Twp. 20–18 Eaton (ot); Burris 24–9 Royerton; Central 31–21 Yorktown; Daleville 25–18 Cowan; Burris 28–19 Harrison Twp.; Central 31–12 Daleville; Central 37–14 Burris. Officials: Daniel Guild, Maurice Tudor, Harry Coolman.

NEW ALBANY: Jeffersonville 81–8 Lanesville; New Amsterdam 23–16 New Washington; New Albany 53–22 Borden; Corydon 48–9 Elizabeth; Silver Creek 29–27 New Salisbury; Mauckport 35–14 Laconia; Henryville 43–15 New Middletown; Charlestown 36–21 Georgetown; Jeffersonville 60–14 New Amsterdam; New Albany 28–21 Corydon; Silver Creek 35–17 Mauckport; Henryville 26–15 Charlestown; Jeffersonville 20–17 New Albany; Silver Creek 30–18 Henryville; Jeffersonville 49–15 Silver Creek. Officials: John B. Wilson, Paul Garrison, Ralph J. Black.

NEW CASTLE: Cadiz 26–16 Knightstown; Mt. Summit 21–20 Sulphur Springs; New Castle 34–8 New Lisbon; Kennard 13–12 Spiceland; Middletown 25–8 Straughn; Mooreland 15–12 Lewisville; Cadiz 34–19 Mt. Summit; New Castle 28–11 Kennard; Middletown 32–14 Mooreland; New Castle 38–18 Cadiz; New Castle 44–12 Middletown. Officials: Robert Nipper, Richard Miller.

NEWPORT: Montezuma 29–21 Bloomingdale; Hillsdale 24–17 Newport; Tangier 29–19 Mecca; Clinton 31–25 Cayuga; Rosedale 27–23 Saint Bernice; Dana 31–18 Perrysville; Montezuma 26–22 Hillsdale; Clinton 26–23 Tangier; Dana 26–11 Rosedale; Clinton 33–31 Montezuma; Clinton 22–19 Dana. Officials: Harry Conover, Albert Etter.

NORTH JUDSON: Culver 52–12 West; San Pierre 22–17 Hamlet; Bourbon 23–17 Tippecanoe; Argos 31–24 Center Twp.; Grovertown 16–14 Knox; North Judson 24–9 Tyner; Bremen 35–23 LaPaz; Culver 25–20 Plymouth; Bourbon 32–16 San Pierre; Argos 29–20 Grovertown; North Judson 31–27 Bremen (2ot); Culver 24–15 Bourbon; North Judson 30–21 Argos; North Judson 22–21 Culver. Officials: Clarence F. Barrett, Charles Bennett, George Allesee.

OXFORD: Ambia 43–18 Pine Twp.; Earl Park 32–24 Wadena; Otterbein 19–16 Oxford; Fowler 45–19 Raub; Gilboa 32–16 Boswell; Ambia 29–15 Freeland Park; Earl Park 31–30 Otterbein (ot); Gilboa 24–22 Fowler; Earl Park 27–20 Ambia; Earl Park 21–11 Gilboa. Officials: Orville Jones, Forrest Roe.

PERU: Peru 61–10 Amboy; Bunker Hill 32–13 Jefferson Twp.; Butler Twp. 30–18 Gilead; Deedsville 38–17 Converse; Clay Twp. 59–15 Macy; Peru 46–23 Chili; Bunker Hill 21–18 Butler Twp.; Clay Twp. 40–22 Deedsville; Peru 26–16 Bunker Hill; Peru 30–28 Clay Twp.. Officials: Joe Dienhart, Leon Fadely.

PRINCETON: Princeton 26–22 Haubstadt; Fort Branch 21–19 Owensville; Hazleton 19–18 Patoka; Francisco 23–16 Mackey; Oakland City 32–27 Mt. Olympus; Princeton 25–16 Fort Branch; Francisco 27–23 Hazleton; Princeton 27–18 Oakland City; Princeton 32–19 Francisco. Officials: Clarence Myles, Edward B. DeGroote.

RICHMOND: Richmond 29–23 Greensfork; Boston 35–30 Huntsville; Cambridge City 30–19 Hagerstown; Milton 51–7 Fountain City; Centerville 26–14 Williamsburg; Whitewater 18–8 Webster; Richmond 32–17 Economy; Cambridge City 29–27 Boston; Centerville 33–31 Milton;

Richmond 36–20 Whitewater; Centerville 22–16 Cambridge City; Richmond 50–10 Centerville. Officials: A. E. Pitcher, Leroy Shine, Frederick J. Shroyer.

ROCKPORT: Luce Twp. 34–13 Tennyson; Boonville 48–4 Yankeetown; Selvin 32–15 Folsomville; Lynnville 28–21 Rockport; Chrisney 22–21 Gentryville; Grandview 25–22 Dale; Boonville; 45–14 Luce Twp.; Lynnville 22–20 Selvin; Grandview 32–20 Chrisney; Lynnville 17–16 Boonville; Lynnville 29–17 Grandview. Officials: Joe Armstrong, W. V. Slyker.

RUSHVILLE: Rushville 29–17 New Salem; Gings 29–20 Glenwood; Mays 24–23 Manilla; Arlington 39–21 Raleigh; Milroy 26–23 Carthage; Rushville 30–13 Morton Memorial; Gings 23–21 Mays; Arlington 32–17 Milroy; Rushville 53–16 Gings; Rushville 46–16 Arlington. Officials: Nate Kaufman, Gale Robinson.

SALEM: Monroe Twp. 22–18 Campbellsburg; West Baden 21–14 Pekin; Orleans 19–18 Hardinsburg; Salem 23–17 Paoli; French Lick 23–16 Monroe Twp.; West Baden 32–22 Orleans; Salem 26–22 French Lick (ot); West Baden 20–17 Salem. Officials: Gerald Bottorff, James Adams.

SCOTTSBURG: Lovett 26–24 Saluda; Austin 33–10 Paris Crossing; Central 51–14 San Jacinto; Dupont 34–17 Madison Twp.; North Madison 33–17 Lexington; Scottsburg 36–11 Hanover; Madison 27–19 Deputy; Austin 25–21 Lovett; Central 25–15 Dupont; Scottsburg 21–12 North Madison; Madison 25–19 Austin; Scottsburg 29–12 Central; Madison 19–14 Scottsburg. Officials: George Bair, Robert Taylor, Robert L. Todd.

SEYMOUR: Vallonia 24–19 Tampico; Clearspring 47–17 Freetown; Seymour 42–5 Hayden; Crothersville 50–12 Scipio; Brownstown 39–22 Houston; Medora 44–10 Cortland; Clearspring 32–22 Vallonia; Seymour 15–13 Crothersville; Medora 19–15 Brownstown; Seymour 32–21 Clearspring; Seymour 27–19 Medora. Officials: A. L. Bruce, Wendell Heath.

SHELBYVILLE: Moral 43–21 Clifford; Boggstown 59–29 Mt. Auburn; Hawcreek Twp. 41–21 Fairland; Columbus 33–16 Flat Rock; Morristown 30–27 Waldron; Shelbyville 26–16 Moral; Hawcreek Twp. 25–17 Boggstown; Columbus 30–18 Morristown; Shelbyville 26–16 Hawcreek Twp.; Shelbyville 21–12 Columbus. Officials: Norman Dunlap, Raymond Hobbs.

SULLIVAN: Merom 28–25 Carlisle; Graysville 33–14 Hymera; Sullivan 11–8 Dugger; Fairbanks 14–10 New Lebanon; Shelburn 22–19 Farmersburg; Merom 23–14 Pleasantville; Sullivan 19–13 Graysville; Shelburn 24–14 Fairbanks; Sullivan 26–13 Merom; Sullivan 42–11 Shelburn. Officials: John Hoffman, Elmer Weber.

TERRE HAUTE: West Terre Haute 31–10 Prairie Creek; Wiley 34–16 Riley; Blackhawk 19–18 Gerstmeyer; Honey Creek 44–19 Concannon; Glenn 36–17 Fontanet; Garfield 40–11 Pimento; State Training 30–9 Otter Creek; Wiley 36–7 West Terre Haute; Honey Creek 31–17 Blackhawk; Garfield 18–11 Glenn; Wiley 21–16 State Training; Garfield 32–22 Honey Creek; Wiley 29–27 Garfield. Officials: George Graham, Hal Harris, Lloyd Messersmith.

TIPTON: Tipton 28–19 Walnut Grove; Kempton 20–19 Fisher; Noblesville 23–13 Atlanta; Sharpsville 16–12 Cicero; Prairie Twp. 23–20 Carmel; Sheridan 18–17 Windfall; Arcadia 22–19 Westfield; Tipton 23–17 Kempton. Noblesville 29–13 Sharpsville; Sheridan 15–12 Prairie Twp.; Tipton 34–15 Arcadia; Noblesville 30–16 Sheridan; Tipton 25–19 Noblesville. Officials: Herbert Vaulk, J. L. Mertz, L. R. Lenon.

VALPARAISO: Liberty Center 27–20 Dyer; Wheeler 26–17 Hebron; Portage Twp. 37–12 Merrillville; Morgan Twp. 24–17 Lowell; Valparaiso 50–12 Boone Grove; Crown Point 28–16 Washington Twp.; Chesterton 32–25 Liberty Twp.; Wheeler 40–14 Portage Twp.; Valparaiso 24–

Tourney Time

16 Morgan Twp.; Chesterton 39–25 Crown Point; Valparaiso 24–20 Wheeler; Valparaiso 32–25 Chesterton. Officials: George R. Lambert, Walter N. Geller, Fernie Trigalet.

VINCENNES: Vincennes 39–11 Gibault; Freelandville 22–19 Oaktown; Bicknell 31–18 Wheatland; Decker Chapel 28–14 Edwardsport; Fritchton 27–17 Sandborn; Decker 51–9 Monroe City; Vincennes 49–17 Bruceville; Freelandville 20–18 Bicknell; Decker Chapel 21–20 Fritchton (ot); Vincennes 15–11 Decker. Freelandville 18–17 Decker Chapel; Vincennes 24–20 Freelandville. Officials: Charles A. Jensen, Clyde Castle, George Kerr.

WABASH: Lincolnville 21–17 Chippewa; Wabash 33–19 Lafontaine; Lagro 29–25 Urbana; Linlawn 29–19 Chester Twp.; Somerset 15–10 Laketon; Roann 20–17 North Manchester; Wabash 35–9 Lincolnville; Lagro 22–21 Linlawn; Somerset 37–17 Roann; Wabash 33–20 Lagro; Wabash 18–15 Somerset. Officials: Mode Cranor, Joel D. Wilt.

WARSAW: Pierceton 32–30 Beaver Dam; Milford 39–23 North Webster; Mentone 31–21 Sidney; Atwood 39–33 Syracuse; Etna Green 30–15 Burket; Leesburg 28–22 Claypool; Warsaw 45–15 Silver Lake; Pierceton 27–24 Milford; Mentone 48–14 Atwood; Etna Green 24–21 Leesburg; Warsaw 53–14 Pierceton; Mentone 45–17 Etna Green; Mentone 32–20 Warsaw. Officials: J. Clayton Hughes, Donald Coar, Von Crowe.

WASHINGTON: Barr Twp. 20–18 Washington; Plainville 45–11 Trinity Springs; Burns City 32–15 Glendale; Odon 58–7 Raglesville; Loogootee 36–7 Alfordsville; Shoals 42–20 Epsom; Barr Twp. 21–19 Plainville; Odon 33–19 Burns City; Loogootee 23–10 Shoals; Barr Twp. 35–8 Odon; Barr Twp. 29–19 Loogootee. Officials: W. S. Fellmy, William Coulter.

WINAMAC: Kewanna 25–12 Star City; Pulaski 27–12 Francesville; Grass Creek 21–19 Talma (ot); Leiters Ford 23–21 Medaryville; Winamac 25–13 Akron; Fulton 25–16 Monterey; Rochester 33–13 Richland Center; Pulaski 24–20 Kewanna (ot); Leiters Ford 21–13 Grass Creek; Winamac 25–9 Fulton; Rochester 35–14 Pulaski; Winamac 41–19 Leiters Ford; Rochester 33–22 Winamac. Officials: Ralph Eades, Lawrence Rahbar, G. M. Kinzel.

1935 REGIONALS

ATTICA: Roachdale 22–16 Williamsport; Clinton 19–14 Waveland; Roachdale 36–22 Clinton. Officials: G. L. Russell, Lawrence Rahbar.

AUBURN: Columbia City 39–26 Ligonier; Mentone 27–13 Auburn; Mentone 41–15 Columbia City. Officials: J. Clayton Hughes, O. F. Helvie.

BLOOMINGTON: Brazil 24–21 Martinsville; Lyons 36–19 Wiley; Brazil 24–22 Lyons. Officials: Winston Ashley, John Wilson.

COLUMBUS: Franklin 34–29 North Vernon; Shelbyville 49–17 Madison; Shelbyville 28–24 Franklin. Officials: Irvin Springer, Charles Jensen.

EVANSVILLE: Princeton 24–22 Tell City; Lynnville 20–19 Bosse; Princeton 22–12 Lynnville. Officials: George Bair, Norman Dunlap.

FRANKFORT: Lafayette 38–22 Earl Park. Frankfort 26–24 Lebanon; Frankfort 31–29 Lafayette. Officials: Vaughn Russell, Lundy Welborn.

HUNTINGTON: Berne 18–16 Roanoke; Fort Wayne South Side 38–16 Pennville; Berne 23–17 South Side. Officials: Stanley Porter, Lowell Lenon.

INDIANAPOLIS: Ben Davis 28–24 Plainfield; Anderson 29–15 Fortville; Anderson 28–21 Ben Davis. Officials: B. E. Bayh, Orville Jones.

KOKOMO: Tipton 31–19 Kokomo; Wabash 28–27 Marion (2ot); Tipton 28–20 Wabash. Officials: Houston Meyer, Joel Wilt.
LAPORTE: Hammond 27–13 Kentland; Michigan City 27–18 Valparaiso; Michigan City 27–24 Hammond. Officials: Daniel Guild, Clarence Grogan.
LOGANSPORT: Logansport 24–11 Peru; Monticello 24–22 Camden; Logansport 22–17 Monticello. Officials: Glenn Adams, Charles G. Garrett.
MITCHELL: Seymour 16–14 West Baden. Jeffersonville 37–22 Mitchell; Jeffersonville 48–21 Seymour. Officials: Dale Miller, Nate Kaufman.
MUNCIE: New Castle 43–17 Farmland; Richmond 24–22 Muncie (ot); Richmond 30–19 New Castle. Officials: Carl Burt, Hal Harris.
ROCHESTER: Rochester 45–19 North Judson. Nappanee 26–20 Mishawaka; Nappanee 33–30 Rochester. Officials: Ward Gilbert, Hugh Vandivier.
RUSHVILLE: Connersville 44–18 Milan. Rushville 31–16 Aurora; Rushville 35–25 Connersville. Officials: George Williams, A. E. Pitcher.
WASHINGTON: Barr Twp. 22–17 Vincennes; Sullivan 35–20 Huntingburg; Barr Twp. 29–23 Sullivan. Officials: Thomas Baker, Russell Pickett.

1935 FINALS—March 15, 16

INDIANAPOLIS (Butler Fieldhouse): Rushville 34–32 Princeton; Richmond 34–17 Frankfort; Michigan City 35–24 Mentone; Jeffersonville 41–36 Montgomery; Berne 24–22 Roachdale; Shelbyville 27–21 Logansport; Anderson 31–22 Brazil; Nappanee 37–33 Tipton; Richmond 32–23 Rushville; Jeffersonville 26–23 Michigan City, Shelbyville 28–17 Berne, Anderson 33–23 Nappanee; Jeffersonville 33–28 Richmond; Anderson 30–28 Shelbyville (ot); Anderson 23–17 Jeffersonville. Officials: Carl Burt, Glenn Adams, Stanley Porter, Nate Kaufman, Vaughn Russell.

1936 SECTIONALS

ANDERSON: Anderson 35–17 Summitville; Lapel 26–25 Markleville; Pendleton 31–7 Frankton; Alexandria 25–19 Elwood; Anderson 26–20 Lapel; Pendleton 34–33 Alexandria; Anderson 28–14 Pendleton. Officials: Nate Kaufman, M. E. Somers.
ATTICA: Kingman 32–24 Hillsboro; Attica 21–14 Pine Village; Cayuga 26–24 Covington; Veedersburg 49–21 Wallace; Perrysville 25–13 Williamsport; Kingman 37–24 West Lebanon; Attica 61–14 Cayuga; Veedersburg 22–20 Perrysville; Kingman 27–25 Attica (ot); Kingman 25–16 Veedersburg. Officials: Harry Briggs, Frank Jarrell.
AURORA: Aurora 34–25 Rising Sun; Vevay 30–27 Guilford; Bright 31–29 Lawrenceburg (ot); Moores Hill 41–20 Dillsboro; Aurora 50–7 Patriot; Vevay 32–15 Bright; Aurora 40–21 Moores Hill; Aurora 31–24 Vevay. Officials: F. M. Klayer, Robert L. Todd.
BEDFORD: Tunnelton 18–15 Fayetteville; Bedford 62–5 Huron; Mitchell 46–21 Springville; Shawswick 26–20 Marshall Twp.; Heltonville 27–23 Williams; Oolitic 41–21 Tunnelton; Bedford 26–24 Mitchell; Shawswick 42–21 Heltonville; Bedford 32–18 Oolitic; Bedford 35–20 Shawswick. Officials: Charles A. Jensen, Clyde Castle.
BLOOMINGTON: Smithville 15–9 Unionville; Paragon 22–18 Bloomington; Eminence

Tourney Time

22–21 Monrovia (ot); Ellettsville 22–17 Stinesville; Martinsville 52–12 Mooresville; Smithville 25–18 Morgantown; Paragon 29–23 Eminence; Martinsville 49–11 Ellettsville; Paragon 26–14 Smithville; Martinsville 36–25 Paragon. Officials: Karl Dickerson, Clarence Grogan.

BLUFFTON: Lancaster 31–30 Ossian; Hartford Twp. 53–17 Geneva; Petroleum 41–19 Jefferson; Rockcreek 28–25 Bluffton; Union Center 44–37 Chester; Liberty Center 34–19 Monroe; Berne 38–19 Kirkland; Lancaster 59–23 Pleasant Mills; Petroleum 21–18 Hartford Twp.; Union Center 21–16 Rockcreek; Liberty Center 28–27 Berne; Lancaster 28–18 Petroleum; Union Center 31–19 Liberty Center; Union Center 40–30 Lancaster. Officials: Gerald Huey, Don Jordan, Frederick J. Shroyer.

BOONVILLE: Yankeetown 2–0 Selvin (forfeit); Dale 48–14 Rockport; Lynnville 25–19 Chrisney; Grandview 39–26 Gentryville; Luce Twp. 39–33 Folsomville; Boonville 52–22 Tennyson; Dale 73–14 Yankeetown; Lynnville 40–28 Grandview; Boonville 26–25 Luce Twp.; Lynnville 49–21 Dale; Lynnville 26–22 Boonville. Officials: Joe Armstrong, Walter Ringer.

BRAZIL: Brazil 33–26 Gosport; Van Buren Twp. 36–23 Freedom; Clay City 33–25 Jefferson Twp.; Spencer 42–22 Patricksburg; Bowling Green 33–25 Staunton; Cory 37–18 Quincy; Ashboro 28–23 Brazil; Clay City 26–17 Van Buren Twp.; Spencer 50–24 Bowling Green; Ashboro 33–21 Cory; Spencer 26–20 Clay City; Spencer 44–25 Ashboro. Officials: Robert Hold, Raymond Meier, Fletcher Kerr.

CLINTON: Rosedale 43–12 Mecca; Newport 43–23 Bellmore; Montezuma 25–11 Green Twp.; St. Bernice 27–24 Bridgeton; Dana 34–18 Bloomingdale; Tangier 22–21 Marshall; Clinton 48–15 Hillsdale; Rockville 29–28 Rosedale; Montezuma 20–16 Newport; Dana 40–18 St. Bernice; Tangier 28–26 Clinton; Montezuma 25–23 Rockville; Dana 32–21 Tangier; Dana 24–17 Montezuma. Officials: Myron Moore, William Ellis, George Graham.

COLUMBIA CITY: Coesse 46–25 Etna Twp.; Washington Center 23–15 South Whitley; Churubusco 26–18 Larwill; Columbia City 43–20 Jefferson Center; Coesse 31–30 Wolf Lake; Churubusco 32–17 Washington Center; Columbia City 45–23 Coesse; Columbia City 45–25 Churubusco. Officials: Paul Bateman, Harold McSwane.

CONNERSVILLE: Alquina 47–29 Springfield Twp.; Harrisburg 44–7 Orange; Liberty 29–28 Everton; Brookville 24–22 Laurel; Connersville 40–19 Bentonville; Brownsville 34–21 Harrison Twp.; Fairview 27–18 Whitewater Twp.; Alquina 47–33 Oldenburg; Harrisburg 25–24 Liberty; Connersville 27–14 Brookville; Brownsville 38–35 Fairview; Harrisburg 30–29 Alquina; Connersville 42–30 Brownsville; Connersville 45–18 Harrisburg. Officials: Hal Harris, Palmer Sponsler, Guy Woods.

CRAWFORDSVILLE: Alamo 25–18 Darlington; Wingate 40–15 New Market; Bowers 32–22 Waynetown; Crawfordsville 36–26 Linden; New Richmond 35–22 Waveland; Ladoga 33–20 New Ross; Wingate 48–28 Alamo; Crawfordsville 66–25 Bowers; Ladoga 41–26 New Richmond; Crawfordsville 34–30 Wingate; Crawfordsville 33–28 Ladoga. Officials: Norman Dunlap, Lloyd Messersmith.

CULVER: Knox 50–16 West Twp.; Argos 30–27 North Judson; Bourbon 44–19 Grovertown; Culver 36–24 LaPaz; Hamlet 24–19 Center Twp.; San Pierre 26–19 Bremen; Plymouth 26–19 Tyner; Knox 30–24 Tippecanoe; Bourbon 26–14 Argos; Culver 37–26 Hamlet; Plymouth 60–14 San Pierre; Knox 33–28 Bourbon; Culver 32–31 Plymouth; Culver 35–32 Knox. Officials: Andrew Hatrak, George Russell, Lawrence Rahbar.

DANVILLE: Pittsboro 25–24 Brownsburg; Clayton 34–26 Amo; Plainfield 35–25 New

Winchester; North Salem 32–27 Stilesville; Danville 18–17 Lizton; Avon 32–15 Pittsboro; Plainfield 32–20 Clayton; Danville 24–16 North Salem; Plainfield 32–31 Avon (ot); Plainfield 29–23 Danville. Officials: J. Paul Jones, Cecil Tharp.

DELPHI: Deer Creek 25–23 Cutler; Flora 18–15 Camden; Rockfield 31–12 Adams Twp.; Delphi 50–8 Carrollton; Burlington 33–18 Deer Creek; Flora 21–16 Rockfield; Delphi 31–27 Burlington (ot); Delphi 18–12 Flora. Officials: Glenn Farrell, Elmer Posey.

EAST CHICAGO: Dyer 25–7 East Chicago Garfield; East Chicago Washington 37–13 Lowell; Merrillville 21–17 Calumet Twp.; Hammond Tech 19–18 East Chicago Roosevelt; Hammond High 29–21 Whiting; Crown Point 26–20 Griffith; Clark 46–18 Dyer; Washington 30–13 Merrillville; Hammond High 54–19 Hammond Tech; Clark 30–23 Crown Point; Hammond High 45–14 Washington; Hammond High 25–18 Clark. Officials: Carl Burt, Doxie Reeves, Condict Smith.

ELKHART: Nappanee 35–18 Millersburg; Middlebury 33–28 Wakarusa; Goshen 37–29 Concord Twp.; Baugo Twp. 46–24 Jefferson; Elkhart 46–16 New Paris; Nappanee 29–17 Bristol; Goshen 22–16 Middlebury; Elkhart 36–24 Baugo Twp.; Goshen 21–13 Nappanee; Goshen 21–19 Elkhart (ot). Officials: R. Wayne Cunningham, O. F. Helvie.

EVANSVILLE: Bosse 32–21 Poseyville; Wadesville 26–24 Stewartsville; Cynthiana 25–23 New Harmony; Reitz 29–28 Elberfeld; Newburgh 42–22 Millersburg; Central 50–14 Chandler; Mt. Vernon 40–24 Griffin; Bosse 45–27 Wadesville; Reitz 52–21 Cynthiana; Central 54–22 Newburgh; Bosse 23–17 Mt. Vernon; Central 39–34 Reitz; Central 37–22 Bosse. Officials: Harry Conover; Jr., John Hoffman, Rollie W. Kirchoff.

FORT WAYNE: South Side 27–21 Hoagland; Decatur 23–19 Elmhurst; New Haven 33–20 Monmouth; Monroeville 36–22 Arcola; Central 45–24 Leo; North Side 41–20 Huntertown; Lafayette Central 41–19 Harlan; South Side 30–18 Woodburn; Decatur 37–27 New Haven; Central 45–30 Monroeville. North Side 49–35 Lafayette Central; South Side 36–25 Decatur; Central 42–26 North Side; Central 50–23 South Side. Officials: Richard Roberts, Dana Chandler, Walter Thurston.

FOWLER: Fowler 27–17 Gilboa Twp.; Boswell 26–24 Wadena; Oxford 53–18 Raub; Earl Park 25–8 Ambia; Freeland Park 37–27 Pine Twp.; Otterbein 28–21 Fowler; Oxford 34–31 Boswell; Earl Park 31–17 Freeland Park; Oxford 33–25 Otterbein; Earl Park 31–24 Oxford. Officials: R. G. Campbell, Raymond Trobaugh.

FRANKFORT: Colfax 33–21 Jackson Twp.; Rossville 37–12 Mulberry; Forest 30–15 Sugar Creek; Michigantown 25–16 Kirklin; Frankfort 57–15 Scircleville; Colfax 27–24 Washington Twp.; Rossville 44–26 Forest; Frankfort 38–9 Michigantown; Rossville 39–25 Colfax; Frankfort 40–13 Rossville. Officials: Winston Ashley, Lawrence Gaunt.

FRANKLIN: Clark Twp. 36–18 Trafalgar; Greenwood 20–12 Whiteland; Masonic Home 18–17 Edinburg; Nineveh 37–22 Helmsburg; Union Twp. 48–16 Nashville; Franklin 17–12 Center Grove; Van Buren Twp. 44–28 Clark Twp.; Masonic Home 27–22 Greenwood; Union Twp. 45–31 Nineveh; Franklin 35–15 Van Buren Twp.; Masonic Home 18–12 Union Twp.; Franklin 24–20 Masonic Home. Officials: Raymond Hobbs, Russell Pickett, Ralph E. Parker.

GARRETT: Orland 30–16 Scott Center; Angola 26–12 Pleasant Lake; Concord Twp. 41–17 Fremont; Auburn 47–21 Salem Center; Spencerville 19–17 Butler; Ashley 48–16 Hamilton; Garrett 29–13 Waterloo; Orland 20–19 Metz; Angola 38–33 Concord Twp.; Auburn 27–23 Spencerville; Garrett 40–22 Ashley; Angola 34–14 Orland; Auburn 31–23 Garrett; Auburn 32–30

Tourney Time

Angola. Officials: Clive Markley, H. E. Vandivier, Max Bullock.

GARY: Horace Mann 23–14 Morgan Twp.; Froebel 66–13 Washington Twp.; Wheeler 49–16 Boone Grove. Hobart 49–36 East Gary Edison; Portage Twp. 40–26 Liberty Center (Porter Co.); Wallace 42–20 Chesterton; Valparaiso 52–15 Tolleston; Emerson 45–21 Hebron; Froebel 17–14 Horace Mann; Hobart 37–36 Wheeler; Wallace 45–16 Portage Twp Emerson 35–28 Valparaiso; Froebel 36–29 Hobart; Emerson 33–20 Wallace; Froebel 37–35 Emerson. Officials: George Lambert, Joel Wilt, L. E. Fink.

GREENCASTLE: Russellville 24–20 Putnamville; Roachdale 44–29 Fillmore; Belle Union 27–8 Reelsville; Greencastle 34–29 Cloverdale; Bainbridge 24–21 Russellville; Roachdale 29–24 Belle Union; Greencastle 32–9 Bainbridge; Greencastle 37–16 Roachdale. Officials: Thomas Baker, Houston Meyer.

GREENFIELD: Maxwell 34–33 McCordsville; Eden 27–21 Charlottesville; Wilkinson 43–22 New Palestine; Greenfield 41–18 Westland; Fortville 17–16 Mt. Comfort; Maxwell 41–39 Eden; Greenfield 43–30 Wilkinson; Maxwell 24–23 Fortville; Greenfield 45–28 Maxwell. Officials: Custer Baker, Gale Robinson.

GREENSBURG: St. Paul 37–11 Letts; Greensburg 48–16 Westport; Sandusky 22–21 North Vernon; Jackson 37–26 Clarksburg; Burney 39–15 Butlerville; New Point 42–9 Vernon; St. Paul 47–10 Zenas; Greensburg 30–18 Sandusky; Burney 28–27 Jackson; St. Paul 34–16 New Point; Greensburg 30–13 Burney; Greensburg 54–23 St. Paul. Officials: Don White, George Williams, C. T. Brehm.

HUNTINGBURG: Jasper 31–18 Petersburg. Huntingburg 48–11 Dubois; Winslow 39–23 Birdseye; Otwell 20–19 Ireland; Stendal 36–34 Cuzco; Holland 56–22 Union; Spurgeon 28–24 Velpen; Jasper 17–16 Huntingburg; Winslow 29–16 Otwell; Holland 39–27 Stendal; Jasper 22–19 Spurgeon; Holland 27–23 Winslow; Jasper 36–24 Holland. Officials: Gerald Bottorff, William Coulter, Fred Alwood.

HUNTINGTON: Roanoke 47–25 Andrews; Jefferson Twp. 24–15 Monument City; Huntington Twp. 29–18 Banquo; Huntington 29–17 Lancaster; Warren 34–21 Rockcreek; Bippus 41–27 Markle; Clear Creek 29–17 Union Center; Roanoke 26–16 Jefferson; Huntington 27–23 Huntington Twp.; Bippus 27–24 Warren; Roanoke 26–12 Clear Creek; Huntington 33–24 Bippus; Roanoke 21–18 Huntington. Officials: Leon Fadely, L. B. Moore, Robert H. Simison.

INDIANAPOLIS: Oaklandon 29–18 New Augusta. Broad Ripple 29–24 Lawrence; Shortridge 36–29 Decatur Central; Washington 23–21 Acton; Tech 67–7 Castleton; Southport 25–23 Ben Davis; Warren Central 24–18 Beech Grove; Manual Training 37–22 New Bethel; Broad Ripple 43–21 New Augusta; Shortridge 21–19 Washington; Tech 34–17 Southport; Manual Training 40–30 Warren Central; Shortridge 30–27 Broad Ripple; Tech 23–19 Manual Training; Shortridge 29–18 Tech. Officials: T. R. Smith, Allen H. Klinck, Orville Jones.

KENDALLVILLE: Wawaka 33–22 LaOtto; Cromwell 22–21 Lima; Orange Twp. 28–16 Scott; Springfield Twp. 15–13 Topeka; Brighton 19–13 Avilla; Ligonier 40–31 LaGrange; Kendallville 38–23 Shipshewana; Albion 36–16 Wolcottville; Cromwell 32–29 Wawaka; Orange Twp. 41–14 Springfield Twp.; Ligonier 38–21 Brighton; Kendallville 47–17 Albion; Orange Twp. 22–20 Cromwell; Ligonier 34–19 Kendallville; Ligonier 36–18 Orange Twp. Officials: Louis Briner, Harry Coolman, Von Crowe.

KOKOMO: Clay Twp. 34–29 Jackson Twp.; Howard Twp. 30–29 Greentown; Kokomo 55–14 Ervin Twp.; New London 21–20 West Middleton; Union Twp. 32–25 Russiaville; Howard

Twp. 35–29 Clay Twp.; Kokomo 25–13 New London; Howard Twp. 35–18 Union Twp.; Kokomo 56–23 Howard Twp. Officials: Forrest Ballinger, Edmund Tully.

LAFAYETTE: West Lafayette 31–25 Battle Ground; Jackson 28–16 Stockwell; Buck Creek 28–21 Dayton; Wea 34–16 Romney; Clarks Hill 35–21 Klondike; Lafayette 35–28 West Point; Montmorenci 39–19 Monitor; West Lafayette 32–22 Jackson; Wea 21–20 Buck Creek; Jefferson 61–12 Clarks Hill; West Lafayette 29–21 Montmorenci; Jefferson 45–25 Wea; West Lafayette 31–30 Jefferson. Officials: Jim Puett, G. M. Kinzel, Lowell D. Sparks.

LAPORTE: Wanatah 36–31 Westville; Rolling Prairie 29–28 Hanna; Michigan City 37–17 Mill Creek; LaPorte 37–27 Union Twp.; Union Mills 39–21 Springfield; Kingsbury 26–20 Stillwell; Clinton Twp. 29–23 Lacrosse; Rolling Prairie 44–34 Wanatah; LaPorte 30–23 Michigan City; Union Mills 55–26 Kingsbury; Clinton Twp. 26–25 Rolling Prairie; LaPorte 43–22 Union Mills; LaPorte 59–24 Clinton Twp. Officials: John S. Walker, Charles G. Garrett, G. N. Schumacher.

LEBANON: Lebanon 46–29 Dover; Zionsville 21–17 Advance; Jamestown 20–16 Thorntown; Pinnell 40–20 Whitestown; Lebanon 52–27 Perry Central; Jamestown 30–24 Zionsville; Lebanon 62–28 Pinnell; Lebanon 34–31 Jamestown. Officials: Daniel Guild, M. J. Cleary.

LOGANSPORT: Royal Center 35–16 Metea; Galveston 29–17 Noble Twp.; Logansport 43–21 Onward; Washington Twp. 16–15 Twelve Mile; New Waverly 26–21 Walton; Young America 21–20 Lucerne; Royal Center 37–32 Galveston; Logansport 60–10 Washington Twp.; New Waverly 26–25 Young America. Logansport 38–23 Royal Center; Logansport 82–18 New Waverly. Officials: A. T. Krider, J. Alvin Taylor.

LYONS: Lyons 33–19 Midland. Bloomfield 48–15 Newberry; Switz City 29–16 Scotland; Linton 36–29 Owensburg (2ot); Jasonville 33–25 Solsberry; Bloomfield 31–21 Lyons; Linton 35–23 Switz City; Bloomfield 29–20 Jasonville; Linton 21–15 Bloomfield. Officials: Wendell Heath, Elmer Weber.

MADISON: Scottsburg 26–15 Hanover; Deputy 43–20 Dupont; Austin 35–20 Paris Crossing; Madison 46–14 Lexington; Central 36–21 North Madison; Saluda 30–11 Marion Twp.; Scottsburg 44–25 Deputy; Madison 39–15 Austin; Central 26–12 Saluda; Madison 23–22 Scottsburg; Central 34–31 Madison. Officials: John Lyskowinski, John H. Gant.

MARION: Marion 32–15 Jonesboro; Gas City 28–23 Jefferson Twp.; Fairmount 37–14 Sweetser; Sims Twp. 22–18 Van Buren; Marion 25–21 Gas City; Fairmount 24–12 Sims Twp.; Marion 17–16 Fairmount. Officials: Glenn M. Adams, Ralph C. Eades.

MILAN: Batesville 31–27 Napoleon; Versailles 22–20 Lovett; Sunman 69–2 Cross Plains; New Marion 47–14 San Jacinto; Milan 21–20 Holton; Batesville 26–24 Osgood. Sunman 31–19 Versailles; Milan 42–22 New Marion; Batesville 29–22 Sunman; Milan 23–22 Batesville. Officials: R. N. Taylor, Hermon Phillips.

MISHAWAKA: Madison Twp. 37–23 North Liberty; South Bend Central 40–25 Walkerton; Green Twp. 27–25 Washington-Clay; Warren Twp. 39–34 Wilson; Mishawaka 38–29 Lakeville; South Bend Riley 44–20 South Bend Washington; Madison Twp. 30–20 New Carlisle; Central 48–28 Greene Twp.; Mishawaka 56–13 Warren Twp.; Riley 27–19 Madison Twp.; Mishawaka 29–28 Central; Riley 30–29 Mishawaka. Officials: Donald Coar, Louis Donchin, Millard Easton.

MONON: Wolcott 34–26 Burnettsville; Chalmers 41–34 Idaville; Monon 33–26 Round Grove; Brookston 35–24 Monticello; Reynolds 36–25 Buffalo; Wolcott 25–24 Chalmers; Monon 28–24 Brookston; Wolcott 24–22 Reynolds; Monon 27–18 Wolcott. Officials: Albert Etter, Herbert Vaulk.

Tourney Time

MUNCIE: Center 23–19 DeSoto; Burris 52–27 Eaton; Daleville 33–29 Cowan; Albany 30–23 Royerton; Central 43–22 Yorktown; Gaston 40–16 Harrison Twp.; Center 17–15 Selma; Burris 31–25 Daleville; Central 26–21 Albany; Gaston 27–19 Center; Central 32–27 Burris (ot); Central 46–15 Gaston. Officials: J. H. McClure, Lundy Welborn, Walter Moss.

NEW ALBANY: Corydon 34–16 Franklin Twp.; Silver Creek 43–31 Borden; Charlestown 40–21 Henryville; New Amsterdam 34–30 New Washington; Georgetown 36–27 Laconia; New Middletown 29–9 Elizabeth; New Albany 23–13 Jeffersonville; New Salisbury 37–27 Mauckport; Corydon 43–23 Silver Creek; Charlestown 41–26 New Amsterdam; Georgetown 31–15 New Middletown; New Albany 53–14 New Salisbury; Corydon 31–25 Charlestown; New Albany 48–20 Georgetown. Officials: Hulett Crecelius, Robert Hoffman, Herbert Robinson.

NEW CASTLE: Middletown 32–28 Sulphur Springs; Spiceland 28–24 Mooreland; Lewisville 30–23 New Lisbon; Straughn 29–26 Mt. Summit; Cadiz 25–22 Knightstown; New Castle 46–13 Kennard; Spiceland 30–20 Middletown; Lewisville 37–14 Straughn; New Castle 35–22 Cadiz; Lewisville 21–19 Spiceland; New Castle 26–14 Lewisville. Officials: A. E. Pitcher, Alfred Jackson.

OWENSVILLE: Mt. Olympus 24–21 Patoka; Haubstadt 26–25 Mackey; Hazleton 23–21 Francisco; Owensville 52–14 Oakland City; Princeton 43–27 Fort Branch; Mt. Olympus 51–19 Haubstadt; Owensville 35–16 Hazleton; Princeton 40–21 Mt. Olympus; Princeton 50–39 Owensville. Officials: John B. Wilson, Edward B. DeGroote.

PAOLI: French Lick 23–20 West Baden; Orleans 36–22 Pekin; Hardinsburg 35–13 Little York; Paoli 51–19 Morgan Twp.; Salem 45–18 Monroe Twp.; French Lick 52–14 Campbellsburg; Orleans 42–26 Hardinsburg; Paoli 27–22 Salem; French Lick 34–33 Orleans; Paoli 52–26 French Lick. Officials: Paul Garrison, Leonard Mayhugh.

PERU: Deedsville 25–18 Amboy; Butler Twp. 30–4 Gilead; Macy 20–15 Mexico; Bunker Hill 29–12 Chili; Peru 36–13 Converse; Clay Twp. 48–33 Deedsville; Butler Twp. 28–23 Macy; Peru 34–29 Bunker Hill; Clay Twp. 25–17 Butler Twp.; Peru 44–42 Clay Twp. Officials: Layall Fisher, J. Clayton Hughes.

PORTLAND: Roll 32–19 Gray; Ridgeville 34–17 Bryant; Montpelier 28–21 Poling; Redkey 30–27 Pennville; Hartford City 43–28 Dunkirk; Madison 46–34 Portland; Roll 40–21 Jefferson; Ridgeville 32–26 Montpelier; Hartford City 34–27 Redkey; Madison 27–25 Roll; Ridgeville 25–21 Hartford City; Ridgeville 24–21 Madison. Officials: Lloyd Miller, Leroy Shine, Everett Campbell.

REMINGTON: Morocco 21–13 Fair Oaks; Remington 30–17 Wheatfield; Kentland 37–16 Kniman; Rensselaer 41–12 Kankakee Twp.; Brook 29–22 DeMotte; Goodland 51–16 Mt. Ayr; Remington 36–16 Morocco; Rensselaer 36–21 Kentland; Goodland 24–22 Brook; Rensselaer 26–16 Remington; Rensselaer 26–21 Goodland. Officials: Clarence Barrett, Forrest Wood.

RICHMOND: Hagerstown 33–29 Centerville; Whitewater 25–22 Williamsburg; Milton 29–19 Fountain City; Richmond 37–26 Cambridge City; Boston 26–24 Economy; Greensfork 38–14 Webster; Hagerstown 38–21 Whitewater; Richmond 40–20 Milton; Greensfork 32–18 Boston; Richmond 24–20 Hagerstown; Greensfork 34–20 Richmond. Officials: Reid McLain, M. E. Tudor.

ROCHESTER: Medaryville 26–17 Richland Center; Fulton 12–11 Leiters Ford. Winamac 31–21 Kewanna; Francesville 35–33 Grass Creek; Star City 30–26 Talma; Akron 47–15 Monterey; Rochester 41–21 Pulaski; Medaryville 27–17 Fulton; Winamac 31–21 Francesville; Akron 40–24

Star City; Rochester 30–17 Medaryville; Winamac 26–24 Akron; Winamac 30–26 Rochester. Officials: R. P. Chambers, Lavon Carey, Forrest Roe.

RUSHVILLE: Morton Memorial 32–9 Mays; Arlington 23–21 Gings; Rushville 34–17 Carthage; New Salem 39–27 Manilla; Raleigh 2–0 Milroy (forfeit); Morton Memorial 33–19 Arlington; Rushville 32–20 New Salem; Morton Memorial 25–16 Raleigh; Rushville 43–23 Morton Memorial. Officials: Basil Rosier, Carl Porter.

SEYMOUR: Vallonia 37–19 Cortland; Tampico 29–17 Scipio; Brownstown 32–20 Seymour; Crothersville 33–24 Medora; Freetown 39–32 Hayden; Vallonia 40–12 Houston; Brownstown 40–27 Tampico; Crothersville 28–13 Freetown. Brownstown 40–2 Vallonia; Brownstown 25–24 Crothersville. Officials: Robert M. Downey, George Bender.

SHELBYVILLE: Moral Twp. 35–22 Waldron; Morristown 35–15 Flat Rock; Fairland 30–29 Clifford; Shelbyville 61–6 Mt. Auburn; Hawcreek Twp. 36–30 Boggstown; Columbus 27–24 Moral Twp.; Morristown 40–24 Fairland; Shelbyville 31–11 Hawcreek Twp.; Columbus 45–21 Morristown; Shelbyville 27–21 Columbus. Officials: Walter Fisher, Norman Morrison.

SHERIDAN: Prairie Twp. 24–18 Carmel; Noblesville 27–20 Arcadia; Sharpsville 36–22 Fishers; Kempton 22–18 Goldsmith; Tipton 39–18 Atlanta; Westfield 22–20 Walnut Grove; Sheridan 37–20 Windfall; Cicero 33–32 Prairie Twp. (2ot); Noblesville 42–23 Sharpsville; Tipton 37–31 Kempton; Sheridan 27–14 Westfield; Noblesville 41–16 Cicero; Tipton 33–10 Sheridan; Tipton 44–18 Noblesville. Officials: Cecil Harmon, Dean Malaska, Joe Dienhart.

SULLIVAN: Sullivan 30–13 New Lebanon; Pleasantville 28–24 Fairbanks; Hymera 28–19 Carlisle; Farmersburg 37–18 Shelburn; Merom 21–17 Graysville; Dugger 36–26 Sullivan; Hymera 39–27 Pleasantville; Farmersburg 35–24 Merom; Dugger 32–23 Hymera; Dugger 33–22 Farmersburg. Officials: George Bair, Herbert A. Gottfried.

TELL CITY: Leavenworth 23–19 Marengo; Oil Twp. 52–17 Leopold; Cannelton 34–18 Bristow; Troy 38–18 Derby; Tell City 42–20 Union Twp.; Leavenworth 31–27 Milltown; Cannelton 36–13 Oil Twp.; Troy 31–24 Tell City; Cannelton 25–17 Leavenworth; Cannelton 28–20 Troy. Officials: W. S. Fellmy, C. D. Manhart.

TERRE HAUTE: Blackhawk 20–17 Concannon; Laboratory 36–22 Pimento; Wiley 36–25 Glenn; Riley; 43–19 Prairie Creek; Otter Creek 23–16 West Terre Haute; Fontanet 20–14 Gerstmeyer; Garfield 28–19 Honey Creek; Blackhawk 25–24 Laboratory; Wiley 47–19 Riley; Fontanet 28–19 Otter Creek; Garfield 25–19 Blackhawk; Wiley 35–26 Fontanet; Wiley 35–24 Garfield. Officials: Clyde Gentry, George Kerr, W. V. Slyker.

VINCENNES: Decker 21–14 Bruceville; Sandborn 32–17 Monroe City; Vincennes 54–11 Wheatland; Bicknell 23–10 Fritchton; Edwardsport 24–20 Freelandville; Decker Chapel 18–17 Oaktown; Decker 34–11 Sandborn; Vincennes 49–5 Bicknell; Decker Chapel 24–4 Edwardsport; Vincennes 27–8 Decker; Vincennes 46–23 Decker Chapel. Officials: Irvin Springer, Donald Wilder.

WABASH: Chippewa 24–18 Laketon; Chester Twp. 33–18 Roann; Urbana 28–24 Lincolnville; Wabash 34–6 Lagro; North Manchester 21–10 Somerset; Lafontaine 32–15 Linlawn; Chippewa 30–27 Chester Twp.; Wabash 36–14 Urbana; Lafontaine 25–23 North Manchester; Wabash 42–5 Chippewa; Wabash 35–22 Lafontaine. Officials: L. R. Lenon, J. L. Mertz.

WARSAW: Warsaw 38–20 Beaver Dam; Silver Lake 37–19 Claypool; Mentone 26–21 Atwood; Pierceton 21–17 Burket; Sidney 28–20 Etna Green; Milford 44–17 North Webster; Syracuse 35–18 Leesburg; Warsaw 39–12 Silver Lake; Mentone 39–29 Pierceton; Milford 37–13

Tourney Time

Sidney; Warsaw 22–12 Syracuse; Milford 46–24 Mentone; Warsaw 39–20 Milford. Officials: Charles Bennett, Walter Cook, Thomas Fields.

WASHINGTON: Montgomery 101–19 Raglesville; Washington 62–24 Alfordsville; Shoals 36–23 Epsom; Plainville 36–13 Burns City; Loogootee 40–22 Trinity Spring; Odon 46–15 Elnora; Montgomery 42–14 Glendale; Washington 52–20 Shoals; Plainville 23–15 Loogootee; Montgomery 28–14 Odon; Washington 23–19 Plainville; Washington 30–15 Montgomery. Officials: J. Ralph Black, William E. Pointer, Paul Lovell.

WINCHESTER: Jackson 34–16 Lincoln; Spartanburg 23–21 Wayne Twp. (ot); McKinley 29–20 Green Twp.; Modoc 15–14 Stoney Creek; Union City 38–18 Farmland; Winchester 47–16 Saratoga; Huntsville 41–14 Losantville; Parker 25–21 Lynn; Spartanburg 21–19 Jackson; McKinley 24–23 Modoc; Winchester 31–14 Union City; Parker 37–17 Huntsville; Spartanburg 24–18 McKinley; Winchester 21–16 Parker; Winchester 39–24 Spartanburg. Officials: Philip Kessler, Will F. Smith, Fred White.

1936 REGIONALS

ANDERSON: Anderson 23–21 Indianapolis Shortridge; Plainfield 36–27 Greenfield; Anderson 22–16 Plainfield. Officials: Glenn Adams, J. H. McClure.

AUBURN: Columbia City 48–37 Auburn; Warsaw 27–20 Ligonier; Warsaw 35–27 Columbia City. Officials: L. E. Fink, Lowell Sparks.

EVANSVILLE: Central 30–25 Cannelton; Lynnville 31–28 Princeton; Central 28–24 Lynnville. Officials: C. D. Manhart, Russell Pickett.

FORT WAYNE: Central 41–21 Ridgeville; Union Center 32–15 Roanoke; Central 51–13 Union Center. Officials: Winston Ashley, C. G. Garrett.

GREENCASTLE: Crawfordsville 35–18 Kingman; Greencastle 38–21 Dana; Crawfordsville 29–20 Greencastle. Officials: Stanley Porter, Walter Fisher.

GREENSBURG: Greensburg 39–26 Central (Madison); Shelbyville 21–19 Franklin; Shelbyville 34–23 Greensburg. Officials: Hal Harris, C. O. Walls.

LAFAYETTE: Frankfort 52–12 Lebanon; West Lafayette 29–18 Earl Park; Frankfort 48–12 West Lafayette. Officials: Thomas Baker, Norman Dunlap.

LOGANSPORT: Logansport 37–24 Monon; Delphi 30–26 Peru; Logansport 28–19 Delphi. Officials: Lundy Welborn, Houston Meyer.

MARION: Kokomo 24–21 Tipton; Marion 38–19 Wabash; Kokomo 26–22 Marion. Officials: O. F. Helvie, Donald Coar.

MARTINSVILLE: Martinsville 42–27 Linton; Terre Haute Wiley 34–27 Spencer; Martinsville 46–31 Wiley. Officials: Nate Kaufman, George Williams.

MITCHELL: Paoli 32–31 Bedford (3ot; winner determined by free throws); New Albany 37–21 Brownstown; New Albany 37–34 Paoli. Officials: Irvin Springer, Carl Porter.

MUNCIE: New Castle 39–14 Winchester; Greens Fork 25–22 Muncie; New Castle 33–20 Greens Fork. Officials: Joel Wilt, Daniel Guild.

NAPPANEE: Goshen 37–21 Winamac; South Bend Riley 28–25 Culver; Riley 18–16 Goshen. Officials: George L. Russell, Lawrence Rahbar.

RUSHVILLE: Connersville 30–25 Aurora; Rushville 47–13 Milan; Connersville 43–19 Rushville. Officials: Orville Jones, Allen H. Klinck.

VALPARAISO: Gary Froebel 26–13 Rensselaer; Hammond 35–34 LaPorte (ot); Froebel 21–16 Hammond. Officials: Carl Burt, J. Clayton Hughes.

WASHINGTON: Washington 45–28 Dugger; Vincennes 27–24 Jasper; Washington 28–23 Vincennes. Officials: Paul Garrison, Charles A. Jensen.

1936 SEMI–FINALS

GARY: Logansport 31–27 South Bend Riley; Frankfort 35–29 Gary Froebel; Frankfort 28–27 Logansport. Officials: Joel Wilt, Carl Burt.

INDIANAPOLIS: Crawfordsville 24–17 Shelbyville; Anderson 27–15 Connersville; Anderson 27–12 Crawfordsville. Officials: Glenn Adams, Orville Jones.

MUNCIE: New Castle 18–15 Warsaw; Ft. Wayne Central 36–26 Kokomo; Central 24–18 New Castle. Officials: Winston Ashley, O. F. Helvie.

VINCENNES: Washington 43–30 Martinsville; Evansville Central 27–25 New Albany; Central 37–36 Washington. Officials: Nate Kaufman, Charles Jensen.

1936 FINALS—March 28

INDIANAPOLIS (Butler Fieldhouse): Ft. Wayne Central 36–29 Evansville Central Ft. Wayne; Frankfort 34–18 Anderson; Frankfort 50–24 Central. Officials: Nate Kaufman, Glenn Adams.

1937 SECTIONALS

ANDERSON: Anderson 55–15 Frankton; Elwood 19–15 Summitville; Alexandria 32–31 Lapel; Pendleton 41–19 Markleville; Anderson 14–6 Elwood; Alexandria 18–15 Pendleton; Anderson 21–16 Alexandria. Officials: Nate Kaufman, Allen Klinck.

ANGOLA: Hamilton 2–0 Angola (forfeit); St. Joe 52–15 Freemont; Auburn 41–14 Orland; Garrett 35–24 Ashley; Butler 27–19 Salem Center; Spencerville 49–19 Pleasant Lake; Waterloo 44–29 Metz. St. Joe 47–24 Hamilton; Garrett 31–27 Auburn; Spencerville 27–26 Butler; Waterloo 41–29 St. Joe; Garrett 42–22 Spencerville; Garrett 29–26 Waterloo. Officials: Phil N. Eskew, Harold Johnson, George Nulf.

ATTICA: Covington 47–10 Wallace; Pine Village 24–23 Attica; Hillsboro 55–31 Perrysville; Veedersburg 35–27 Kingman; Williamsport 17–16 West Lebanon; Covington 26–25 Pine Village; Veedersburg 29–27 Hillsboro; Williamsport 26–19 Covington; Williamsport 35–32 Veedersburg (2ot). Officials: Robert Hold, William Lucus.

AURORA: Rising Sun 15–14 Lawrenceburg; Milan 37–20 Guilford; Sunman 51–20 Dillsboro; Aurora 30–16 Moores Hill; Bright 48–13 Cross Plains; Vevay 28–15 Patriot; Milan 27–21 Rising Sun; Aurora 26–24 Sunman (ot); Vevay 37–22 Bright; Aurora 34–23 Milan; Vevay 24–17 Aurora. Officials: Palmer Sponsler, Tom Sutton.

BEDFORD: Mitchell 45–19 Williams; Bedford 36–21 Fayetteville; Heltonville 23–22 Tunnelton; Marshal Twp. 25–22 Oolitic; Shawswick 32–14 Huron; Mitchell 54–12 Springville; Bedford 57–13 Heltonville; Shawswick 26–17 Marshall Twp.; Bedford 39–30 Mitchell; Bedford 38–11 Shawswick. Officials: Hulett Crecelius, John Wilson.

Tourney Time

BLUFFTON: Chester Center 55–15 Pleasant Mills; Berne 35–19 Geneva; Bluffton 29–28 Lancaster; Liberty Center 26–22 Monroe; Rockcreek 36–22 Hartford Twp.; Ossian 25–24 Union; Petroleum 39–18 Jefferson Twp.; Chester Center 39–16 Kirkland; Berne 25–22 Bluffton; Rockcreek 47–32 Liberty Center; Ossian 46–25 Petroleum; Berne 29–28 Chester Center; Ossian 33–24 Rockcreek; Berne 30–20 Ossian. Officials: Al Jackson, Frederick Shroyer, Walter Thurston.

BRAZIL: Gosport 22–13 Clay City; Ashboro 31–25 Patricksburg; Brazil 40–19 Posey Twp.; Quincy 33–23; Freedom; Spencer 30–12 Jefferson Twp.; Van Buren 41–33 Bowling Green; Gosport 24–12 Cory; Brazil 30–12 Ashboro; Spencer 28–13 Quincy; Gosport 28–27 Van Buren; Brazil 22–18 Spencer; Brazil 23–19 Gosport. Officials: Hal Harris, Paul Lovell, J. Raymond Trobaugh.

BROWNSBURG: Plainfield 37–23 Amo; Danville 41–15 Stilesville; North Salem 30–17 Clayton; Brownsburg 34–20 Avon; New Winchester 25–24 Pittsboro; Lizton 42–12 Speedway; Plainfield 44–27 Danville; Brownsburg 21–19 North Salem; New Winchester 38–22 Lizton; Plainfield 25–20 Brownsburg; Plainfield 48–24 New Winchester. Officials: Orville Jones, William Ellis.

CANNELTON: Oil Twp. 18–13 Bristow; Tell City 63–13 Milltown; Cannelton 31–30 Marengo; Troy 30–21 Oil Twp.; Tell City 20–18 Cannelton; Tell City 28–27 Troy. Officials: Joe Armstrong, Harold Schulte.

CLINTON: Dana 32–19 Newport; Montezuma 28–14 Marshall. Cayuga 23–14 Tangier; Bloomingdale 27–20 Green Twp.; Rosedale 22–17 Hillsdale; Clinton 50–14 Union Twp.; St. Bernice 35–34 Bridgeton; Rockville 34–15 Mecca; Dana 24–23 Montezuma; Cayuga 24–13 Bloomingdale; Rosedale 28–26 Clinton; St. Bernice 34–31 Rockville; Dana 31–22 Cayuga; Rosedale 35–31 St. Bernice; Dana 38–24 Rosedale. Officials: George Kerr, Ralph Pearson, Walter Ringer.

CONNERSVILLE: Fairview 23–10 Oldenburg; Springfield Twp. 33–29 Laurel; Bentonville 29–26 Harrison Twp.; Whitewater 30–13 Brownsville; Connersville 40–17 Orange Twp.; Everton 30–28 Harrisburg; Brookville 29–21 Alquina; Liberty 24–18 Fairview; Bentonville 34–23 Springfield Twp.; Connersville 44–16 Whitewater; Everton 33–29 Brookville; Bentonville 22–15 Liberty; Connersville 40–16 Everton; Connersville 31–17 Bentonville. Officials: B. R. Hosier, Russell Pickett, Robert Simison.

CRAWFORDSVILLE: Ladoga 30–21 New Richmond; Waveland 24–12 Darlington. Alamo 40–31 Bowers; Linden 36–26 Waynetown; Crawfordsville 38–14 New Market; New Ross 45–22 Wingate; Ladoga 29–19 Waveland; Linden 42–33 Alamo. Crawfordsville 44–21 New Ross; Linden 40–31 Ladoga; Crawfordsville 54–25 Linden. Officials: Forrest Ballinger, Joe Kelly.

DUNKIRK: Montpelier 35–18 Gray. Roll 33–21 Poling; Redkey 30–29 Dunkirk; Hartford City 47–21 Madison Twp.; Ridgeville 32–22 Pennville; Portland 46–22 Bryant; Montpelier 40–25 Jefferson; Redkey 35–29 Roll; Hartford City 39–31 Ridgeville; Montpelier 28–22 Portland; Hartford City 26–18 Redkey; Hartford City 36–25 Montpelier. Officials: Aaron Belcher, Louis Briner, Donald Dickie.

EAST CHICAGO: Whiting 32–19 Roosevelt; Crown Point 47–20 Gary Miller; Griffith 47–10 Merrillville; Washington 101–14 Garfield; Hammond 26–18 Hammond Tech; Hammond Clark 63–14 Dyer; Lowell 36–26 Calumet Twp.; Whiting 39–22 East Gary Edison; Griffith 38–18 Crown Point; Hammond High 26–24 Washington; Clark 55–25 Lowell; Whiting 32–26 Griffith; Hammond High 36–18 Clark; Hammond High 34–23 Whiting. Officials: L. E. Fink, Forrest M. Wood, Max Bullock.

EVANSVILLE: Elberfeld 44–35 Wadesville; Central 22–20 Mt. Vernon; Bosse 30–21

IHSAA Scores | 1930–1939

Chandler; Newburgh 31–13 Millersburg; Poseyville 33–22 Griffin; Reitz 44–29 Cynthiana; Stewartsville 35–25 New Harmony; Central 49–11 Elberfeld; Bosse 36–18 Newburgh; Reitz 32–18 Poseyville; Central 30–18 Stewartsville; Reitz 36–22 Bosse; Central 29–19 Reitz. Officials: Herbert Edwards, Rollie Kirchoff, Clarence Myles.

FLORA: Flora 19–18 Delphi; Cutler 26–16 Adams Twp.; Carrollton 22–18 Rockfield; Burlington 29–24 Deer Creek. Flora 26–21 Camden; Carrollton 20–18 Cutler (ot); Flora 26–17 Burlington; Flora 24–16 Carrollton. Officials: Glenn Farrell, Myron Moore.

FORT WAYNE: South Side 47–16 Elmhurst; Decatur 40–31 Huntertown; Central 83–11 Woodburn; Harlan 31–15 Arcola. Hoagland 39–21 Lafayette Central; North Side 38–29 New Haven; Monroeville 34–19 Monmouth; South Side 47–23 Leo; Central 47–28 Decatur; Hoagland 34–15 Harlan; North Side 43–33 Monroeville; Central 35–21 South Side; North Side 35–28 Hoagland; Central 37–28 North Side. Officials: Dana Chandler, Joel Wilt, Condict Smith.

FRANKFORT: Frankfort 64–14 Sugar Creek Twp.; Scircleville 41–23 Colfax; Jackson Twp.; 27–19 Washington Twp.; Michigantown 34–17 Kirklin; Mulberry 34–17 Forest; Rossville 21–20 Frankfort; Scircleville 36–25 Jackson Twp.; Michigantown 31–22 Mulberry; Rossville 25–22 Scircleville; Rossville 34–24 Michigantown. Officials: Fletcher Kerr, Reid McLain.

FRANKLIN: Franklin 33–16 Greenwood; Trafalgar 37–13 Nashville; Union Twp. 34–20 Masonic Home; Center Grove 51–20 Helmsburg; Whiteland 43–8 Van Buren Twp.; Nineveh 36–23 Clark Twp.; Franklin 22–21 Edinburg; Union Twp. 48–17 Trafalgar; Center Grove 43–28 Whiteland; Franklin 48–22 Nineveh; Union Twp. 23–15 Center Grove; Franklin 34–27 Union Twp. Officials: Winston Ashley, Lloyd Messersmith, Robert Ball.

GARY: Tolleston 22–16 Portage Twp.; Valparaiso 31–29 Hobart; Wheeler 27–18 Boone Grove; Wallace 34–23 Morgan Twp.; Emerson 54–22 Chesterton; Horace Mann 30–22 Froebel; Hebron 31–21 Washington Twp.; Liberty Center 21–18 Kouts; Valparaiso 23–17 Tolleston; Wallace 32–20 Wheeler; Emerson 37–23 Horace Mann; Liberty Center (Porter Co.) 27–25 Hebron; Wallace 34–29 Valparaiso; Emerson 55–20 Liberty Center; Emerson 36–13 Wallace. Officials: T. R. Smith, Dan Guild, George Vaulk.

GREENCASTLE: Roachdale 28–25 Cloverdale; Russellville 26–24 Bainbridge; Putnamville 20–19 Fillmore (2ot); Greencastle 46–7 Belle Union; Roachdale 18–16 Reelsville; Russellville 27–14 Putnamville; Greencastle 51–18 Roachdale; Greencastle 25–16 Russellville. Officials: Raymond Hobbs, Forrest Roe.

GREENFIELD: Fortville 25–22 Eden; Greenfield 42–30 Westland; Mt. Comfort 36–20 New Palestine; McCordsville 39–29 Wilkinson; Charlottesville 31–25 Maxwell; Fortville 47–33 Greenfield; Mt. Comfort 31–26 McCordsville; Fortville 36–20 Charlottesville; Fortville 34–31 Mt. Comfort. Officials: Frank Jarrell, Houston Meyer.

GREENSBURG: Jackson 35–19 Westport; New Point 26–13 Letts; Osgood 27–11 Sandusky; Greensburg 44–13 St. Paul; Clarksburg 26–17 Napoleon; Batesville 33–12 Burney; Jackson 36–23 New Point; Greensburg 45–18 Osgood; Clarksburg 19–16 Batesville; Greensburg 58–21 Jackson; Greensburg 27–22 Clarksburg. Officials: A. E. Pitcher, Charles Brehm.

HUNTINGTON: Bippus 51–31 Rock Creek; Andrews 37–26 Jefferson; Clear Creek 30–26 Polk Twp.; Union 26–24 Banquo; Roanoke 16–15 Salamonie Twp.; Lancaster 33–15 Markle; Huntington 50–7 Huntington Twp.; Andrews 36–24 Bippus; Clear Creek 28–24 Union; Lancaster 28–26 Roanoke; Andrews 27–24 Huntington; Clear Creek 28–24 Lancaster; Clear Creek 33–15 Andrews. Officials: Everett Campbell, Thomas Fields, Harold McSwane.

Tourney Time

INDIANAPOLIS: Tech 49–15 Warren Central; Broad Ripple 29–28 Manual (ot). Decatur Central 55–24 Lawrence; Washington 31–26 Oaklandon; New Bethel 36–17 Castleton; Ben Davis 28–19 New Augusta. Shortridge 18–13 Southport; Beech Grove 27–22 Acton; Tech 31–11 Broad Ripple; Decatur Central 28–25 Washington; Ben Davis 42–25 New Bethel; Shortridge 36–20 Beech Grove; Tech 27–24 Decatur Central; Ben Davis 26–25 Shortridge (ot); Tech 38–13 Ben Davis. Officials: Harry Conover, Karl Dickerson, Norman Dunlap.

KENDALLVILLE: Avilla 40–15 Wolf Lake; Brighton 14–13 Scott; Topeka 29–15 Shipshewana; Ligonier 40–16 Wawaka; Albion 30–12 Springfield Twp.; Lima 29–12 Rome City; Kendallville 36–20 Wolcottville; LaGrange 34–27 Cromwell; Avilla 36–18 Brighton; Ligonier 28–16 Topeka; Lima 26–17 Albion; Kendallville 26–20 LaGrange; Avilla 27–24 Ligonier; Kendallville 38–17 Lima; Kendallville 28–25 Avilla. Officials: Harry Coolman, James Craw, Von Crow.

KOKOMO: Howard Twp. 22–21 Ervin Twp.; Kokomo 37–19 New London; Jackson Twp. 31–18 Clay Twp.; West Middleton 28–19 Russiaville; Greentown 28–17 Union Twp.; Kokomo 41–28 Howard Twp.; Jackson Twp. 39–24 West Middleton; Kokomo 17–16 Greentown; Kokomo 30–20 Jackson Twp. Officials: R. G. Campbell, Gerald Huey.

LAFAYETTE: Romney 31–24 Montmorenci; Wea 21–20 West Lafayette; West Point 27–9 Stockwell; Klondike 29–24 Battle Ground; Jackson 26–20 Dayton; Monitor 34–28 Buck Creek; Jefferson 52–12 Clarks Hill; Romney 14–11 Wea; Klondike 41–30 West Point; Monitor 37–23 Jackson Twp.; Jefferson 49–33 Romney; Monitor 28–27 Klondike; Jefferson 54–14 Monitor. Officials: Walter Moss, Edmund Tully, G. M. Kinzel.

LAPORTE: LaCrosse 28–14 Springfield Twp.; LaPorte 47–19 Westville; Rolling Prairie 38–21 Clinton Twp.; Hanna 30–19 Wanatah; Kingsbury 32–22 Mill Creek; Michigan City 23–18 Union Twp.; Union Mills 39–13 Stillwell; LaPorte 54–18 LaCrosse. Rolling Prairie 39–14 Hanna; Michigan City 45–12 Kingsbury; LaPorte 44–19 Union Mills; Michigan City 25–21 Rolling Prairie; LaPorte 48–29 Michigan City. Officials: Ralph Eades, Millard Easton, O. F. Helvie.

LEBANON: Lebanon 43–25 Pinnell; Advance 36–16 Whitestown; Thorntown 36–30 Dover; Zionsville 43–23 Central; Jamestown 32–15 Advance; Monon 29–18 Thorntown; Jamestown 27–18 Zionsville; Lebanon 28–25 Jamestown. Officials: J. L. Mertz, Layall Fisher.

LOGANSPORT: Logansport 38–19 Onward; Twelve Mile 35–20 Young America; Galveston 37–21 Metea; Royal Center 30–26 Noble Twp.; Walton 29–28 Washington Twp.; New Waverly 40–22 Lucerne; Logansport 49–27 Twelve Mile; Royal Center 32–23 Galveston; Walton 29–28 New Waverly; Logansport 21–14 Royal Center; Logansport 61–13 Walton. Officials: Charles Bennett, Charles Garrett.

MARION: Jefferson Twp. 41–14 Jonesboro; Gas City 25–18 Sims Twp.; Marion 41–21 Sweetser; Van Buren 26–17 Fairmount; Jefferson Twp. 23–15 Gas City; Marion 28–24 Van Buren; Marion 27–19 Jefferson Twp. Officials: Joe Dienhart, George Yarnelle.

MARTINSVILLE: Monrovia 32–13 Morgantown; Mooresville 42–27 Ellettsville. Martinsville 60–6 Unionville; Paragon 39–19 Eminence; Smithville 20–19 Stinesville; Monrovia 35–27 Bloomington; Martinsville 49–23 Mooresville; Paragon 28–24 Smithville; Martinsville 22–14 Monrovia; Martinsville 40–16 Paragon. Officials: J. Clayton Hughes, Lundy Welborn.

MISHAWAKA: Green Twp. 25–21 Washington-Clay; North Liberty 27–26 New Carlisle; Lakeville 50–24 Wilson; Walkerton 46–39 Washington; Mishawaka 41–35 Riley; Central 43–36 Madison Twp.; North Liberty 27–22 Green Twp.; Lakeville 59–42 Walkerton; Mishawaka 41–39 Central; Lakeville

IHSAA Scores | 1930–1939

45–29 North Liberty; Mishawaka 44–38 Lakeville. Officials: J. Alvin Taylor, A. T. Krider.

MONTICELLO: Buffalo 27–23 Idaville; Brookston 30–21 Round Grove; Monticello 42–13 Burnettsville; Wolcott 40–27 Reynolds; Monon 22–21 Chalmers; Brookston 52–18 Buffalo; Monticello 31–29 Wolcott. Monon 47–28 Brookston; Monon 38–25 Monticello. Officials: K. King Telle, Leon Dulgar.

MOROCCO: Rensselaer 38–16 Tefft; Kentland 29–26 Morocco. DeMotte 17–14 Remington; Brook 36–23 Fair Oaks; Goodland 37–15 Wheatfield; Rensselaer 44–12 Mt. Ayr; Kentland 29–19 DeMotte; Goodland 27–23 Brook; Kentland 23–20 Rensselaer; Goodland 36–4 Kentland. Officials: Albert Etter, Herbert Vaulk.

MUNCIE: Yorktown 28–27 Albany; Gaston 28–18 Daleville; Selma 28–19 Harrison Twp.; Muncie 48–6 Royerton; Eaton 35–33 Center (2ot); DeSoto 31–17 Cowan; Burris 29–28 Yorktown; Gaston 37–23 Selma. Muncie 54–23 Eaton; Burris 33–23 DeSoto. Muncie 45–26 Gaston; Muncie 32–16 Burris. Officials: Thomas Baker, George Williams, L. R. Lenon.

NAPPANEE: Wakarusa 41–27 Millersburg; Nappanee 43–20 Baugo Twp.; Concord Twp.; 47–10 Jefferson Twp.; Goshen 25–17 New Paris; Bristol 32–24 Middlebury; Elkhart 40–37 Wakarusa (ot); Nappanee 56–33 Concord Twp.; Goshen 40–28 Bristol; Elkhart 43–30 Nappanee; Elkhart 30–28 Goshen. Officials: George Lambert, J. H. McClure.

NEW ALBANY: Charlestown 42–1 Elizabeth; New Albany 63–23 New Amsterdam. Henryville 22–21 New Salisbury; Georgetown 33–11 Borden; Mauckport 39–19 New Middletown; Silver Creek 31–8 Laconia; Corydon 35–19 Morgan Twp.; Lanesville 36–22 New Washington; New Albany 50–18 Charlestown; Georgetown 28–15 Henryville; Silver Creek 49–18 Mauckport; Corydon 43–18 Lanesville; New Albany 44–19 Georgetown; Corydon 25–21 Silver Creek; New Albany 47–23 Corydon. Officials: Wendell Heath, Robert Hoffman, Harold Powell.

NEW CASTLE: Knightstown 20–17 Spiceland. Mooreland 23–15 Mt. Summit; Cadiz 53–24 Straughn; New Castle 60–20 New Lisbon; Middletown 39–34 Kennard; Sulphur Springs 22–21 Lewisville. Knightstown 23–22 Mooreland; New Castle 39–27 Cadiz; Middletown 37–29 Sulphur Springs; New Castle 51–18 Knightstown; New Castle 38–19 Middletown. Officials: George Bender, Mark Williams.

NORTH VERNON: Paris Crossing 27–18 San Jacinto. Holton 33–12 Marion Twp.; North Vernon 39–13 New Marion; Versailles 40–13 Vernon; Scipio 34–11 Zenas; Butlerville 31–11 Hayden; Paris Crossing 20–13 Lovett; North Vernon 46–14 Holton; Versailles 49–20 Scipio; Paris Crossing 20–18 Butlerville (ot); North Vernon 49–25 Versailles; North Vernon 53–7 Paris Crossing. Officials: Custer Baker, Gerald Bottorff, Myer Schreiber.

OAKLAND CITY: Owensville 36–9 Mt. Olympus; Fort Branch 31–18 Haubstadt; Mackey 32–19 Francisco; Oakland City 21–18 Princeton; Patoka 35–11 Hazleton; Owensville 20–18 Ft. Branch; Oakland City 20–17 Mackey; Owensville 25–23 Patoka; Owensville 22–14 Oakland City. Officials: Herbert Robinson, Irvin Springer.

OTTERBEIN: Ambia 31–25 Gilboa Twp.; Wadena 24–19 Earl Park; Oxford 27–24 Freeland Park; Pine Twp. 41–15 Raub; Boswell 17–8 Fowler; Otterbein 42–20 Ambia; Wadena 40–27 Oxford; Boswell 34–25 Pine Twp.; Otterbein 42–19 Wadena; Otterbein 25–20 Boswell. Officials: Cyril Prevo, G. W. Strole.

PERU: Clay Twp. 39–14 Converse; Deedsville 42–19 Gilead; Macy 40–20 Chili; Mexico 17–15 Butler; Bunker Hill 37–11 Amboy; Peru 27–24 Clay Twp.; Deedsville 51–21 Macy; Bunker Hill 28–17 Mexico; Peru 30–23 Deedsville; Peru 29–24 Bunker Hill. Officials: Don Jordan, Clive Markley.

Tourney Time

PETERSBURG: Winslow 21–16 Otwell; Jasper 58–5 Union; Stendal 27–21 Ireland; Spurgeon 20–13 Velpen; Holland 26–18 Petersburg; Huntingburg 49–15 Dubois. Cuzco 53–18 Birdseye; Jasper 27–15 Winslow; Spurgeon 30–24 Stendal; Huntingburg 39–21 Holland; Jasper 33–23 Cuzco; Huntingburg 28–14 Spurgeon; Huntingburg 40–34 Jasper. Officials: Leonard Mayhugh, Raymond Meier, Carl Porter.

PLYMOUTH: North Judson 41–30 San Pierre; Hamlet 29–25 Tyner; Grovertown 28–25 LaPaz; Culver 54–13 West High; Plymouth 34–21 Tippecanoe; Bourbon 39–21 Center Twp.; Bremen 19–18 Argos; North Judson 28–25 Knox; Hamlet 31–24 Grovertown; Plymouth 48–33 Culver; Bremen 26–20 Bourbon; North Judson 26–25 Hamlet (ot); Plymouth 28–20 Bremen; Plymouth 37–28 North Judson. Officials: Paul Bateman, Donald Coar, Andrew Hatrak.

RICHMOND: Hagerstown 25–14 Whitewater; Centerville 25–16 Greens Fork; Economy 23–22 Cambridge City; Milton 25–15 Webster; Fountain City 25–16 Williamsburg; Morton 56–18 Boston; Centerville 31–25 Hagerstown; Milton 35–27 Economy; Morton 39–15 Fountain City; Centerville 36–27 Milton; Morton 36–25 Centerville. Officials: Lawrence Gaunt, M. E. Somers.

ROCKPORT: Lynnville 34–19 Selvin; Boonville 55–13 Yankeetown; Rockport 31–25 Tennyson; Luce Twp. 37–22 Folsomville; Dale 34–25 Chrisney; Lynnville 52–21 Gentryville; Boonville 52–18 Rockport; Dale 46–17 Luce Twp.; Lynnville 34–10 Boonville; Dale 32–23 Lynnville. Officials: Edward B. DeGroote, David Royalty.

RUSHVILLE: Morton Memorial 46–22 New Salem; Milroy 38–14 Glenwood; Rushville 28–16 Carthage; Mays 30–11 Gings; Arlington 30–28 Raleigh; Morton Memorial 23–19 Manilla; Rushville 43–15 Milroy; Mays 20–18 Arlington; Rushville 34–16 Morton Memorial; Rushville 33–23. Mays. Officials: Glenn Adams, Gale Robinson.

SALEM: Little York 19–13 Campbellsburg; Hardinsburg 27–11 Monroe Twp.; Paoli 34–17 West Baden; Orleans 36–28 Pekin; French Lick 26–24 Salem; Hardinsburg 41–17 Little York. Paoli 41–12 Orleans; Hardinsburg 21–20 French Lick; Paoli 30–18 Hardinsburg. Officials: John Gant, Charles Henry.

SCOTTSBURG: Austin 17–12 Lexington; Central 25–16 North Madison; Deputy 55–11 Dupont; Madison 42–18 Hanover; Scottsburg 28–12 Saluda; Austin 30–21 Central; Madison 44–33 Deputy; Scottsburg 26–9 Austin; Madison 37–23 Scottsburg. Officials: J. Ralph Black, John Lyskowinski.

SEYMOUR: Freetown 26–19 Medora. Seymour 51–18 Vallonia; Clearspring 23–22 Houston; Tampico 23–16 Cortland; Brownstown 22–18 Crothersville; Seymour 50–19 Freetown; Clearspring 19–18 Tampico; Seymour 31–11 Brownstown; Seymour 57–9 Clearspring. Officials: Clyde Sutton, William Benbow.

SHELBYVILLLE: Shelbyville 31–15 Moral Twp.; Mt. Auburn 29–27 Waldron; Morristown 39–17 Fairland; Clifford 28–12 Flat Rock; Hawcreek Twp. 28–22 Boggstown; Columbus 36–29 Shelbyville; Morristown 67–16 Mt. Auburn; Hawcreek Twp. 27–21 Clifford; Columbus 45–20 Morristown; Columbus 39–20 Hawcreek Twp. Officials: Fred White, Otto Crosley.

SOUTH WHITLEY: Washington Center 36–28 Etna Twp.; Columbia City 55–22 Coesse; Larwill 30–20 South Whitley; Churubusco 28–21 Jefferson Center; Columbia City 46–15 Washington Center; Churubusco 27–23 Larwill; Columbia City 37–20 Churubusco. Officials: Ray Bigler, LeRoy Shine.

SULLIVAN: Farmersburg 35–21 Merom; Dugger 25–20 Pleasantville; Sullivan 41–15 Hymera; Fairbanks 33–15 New Lebanon; Carlisle 17–16 Shelburn; Farmersburg 40–21 Graysville;

Dugger 30–29 Sullivan; Carlisle 22–16 Fairbanks. Dugger 27–16 Farmersburg; Dugger 20–16 Carlisle. Officials: John Hoffman, Gerald Powell.

SWITZ CITY: Jasonville 23–18 Linton; Lyons 23–22 Scotland; Midland 59–16 Newberry; Switz City 37–8 Owensburg; Solsberry 52–19 Worthington; Bloomfield 58–8 Marco; Lyons 23–19 Jasonville; Switz City 23–20 Midland; Bloomfield 18–10 Solsberry; Switz City 32–25 Lyons. Bloomfield 44–27 Switz City. Officials: W. S. Fellmy, Fred Alwood.

TERRE HAUTE: Fontanet 29–22 Garfield; Wiley 35–22 Riley; Glenn 24–22 Gerstmeyer; Pimento 29–26 West Terre Haute; Concannon 27–20 Honey Creek; Otter Creek 28–26 Blackhawk; State Laboratory 36–25 Prairie Creek; Wiley 36–12 Fontanet; Pimento 36–20 Glenn; Concannon 28–23 Otter Creek; Wiley 31–24 State Laboratory; Pimento 30–28 Concannon; Wiley 48–26 Pimento. Officials: Clyde Gentry, Clifford Phillips, Cecil Tharp.

TIPTON: Walnut Grove 21–15 Kempton; Prairie Twp. 20–15 Sharpsville; Noblesville 37–27 Windfall; Sheridan 23–22 Tipton; Atlanta 26–22 Carmel; Cicero 18–17 Arcadia; Westfield 24–16 Fishers; Walnut Grove 35–30 Goldsmith; Noblesville 29–28 Prairie Twp.; Atlanta 27–25 Sheridan; Westfield 20–19 Cicero; Noblesville 32–14 Walnut Grove; Atlanta 23–13 Westfield; Atlanta 30–25 Noblesville. Officials: Lavon Carey, Merl Chambers, Doxie Reeves.

VINCENNES: Bicknell 41–21 Fritchton; Sandborn 26–24 Wheatland; Edwardsport 28–27 Oaktown; Freelandville 30–27 Decker Chapel; Bruceville 30–10 Monroe City; Vincennes 28–17 Decker; Bicknell 30–16 Sandborn; Edwardsport 31–30 Freelandville; Vincennes 30–14 Bruceville; Bicknell 20–19 Edwardsport; Vincennes 51–16 Bicknell. Officials: Harry Briggs, William Pointer.

WABASH: Lincolnville 31–29 Linlawn; LaFontaine 37–26 Chester Twp.; North Manchester 32–30 Roann (ot); Lagro 25–22 Somerset; Wabash 62–22 Chippewa; Laketon 25–21 Urbana; LaFontaine 26–23 Lincolnville; Lagro 27–22 North Manchester; Wabash 49–11 Laketon; LaFontaine 24–23 Lagro (ot); Wabash 40–19 LaFontaine. Officials: R. P. Chambers, Hugh Vandivier.

WARSAW: Claypool 41–22 Etna Green; Silver Lake 26–25 Leesburg; Mentone 26–18 Sidney; Pierceton 32–21 Syracuse; Beaver Dam 41–38 North Webster; Milford 60–23 Burket; Warsaw 65–19 Atwood; Claypool 32–30 Silver Lake; Pierceton 36–26 Mentone; Beaver Dam 53–31 Milford; Warsaw 57–29 Claypool. Beaver Dam 37–32 Pierceton; Warsaw 31–29 Beaver Dam (ot). Officials: Lawrence Rahbar. R. Wayne Cunningham, George L. Russell.

WASHINGTON: Elnora 19–18 Loogootee; Plainville 36–18 Barr Twp.; Shoals 43–26 Burns City; Washington 62–13 Raglesville; Glendale 38–18 Trinity Springs; Odon 32–28 Epsom; Elnora 27–22 Alfordsville; Plainville 32–20 Shoals; Washington 60–15 Glendale; Elnora 21–19 Odon; Washington 27–24 Plainville; Washington 49–20 Elnora. Officials: Clyde Castle, William Coulter, Herbert A. Gottfried.

WINAMAC: Medaryville 23–20 Kewanna; Rochester 42–19 Akron; Francesville 30–25 Talma; Richland Center 25–17 Leiters Ford; Pulaski 35–19 Star City; Winamac 22–19 Fulton; Monterey 26–17 Grass Creek; Rochester 22–15 Medaryville; Francesville 37–28 Richland Center; Winamac 33–20 Pulaski; Rochester 19–14 Monterey; Winamac 28–18 Francesville; Rochester 35–19 Winamac. Officials: G. M. Schumacher, Lowell Sparks, Carl Burt.

WINCHESTER: Wayne 51–15 Losantville; Modoc 41–34 Huntsville; Spartanburg 31–14 Green; Saratoga 30–21 Farmland; McKinley 33–23 Jackson; Parker 18–17 Lynn; Union City 38–19 Lincoln; Winchester 45–24 Stoney Creek; Wayne 35–32 Modoc; Saratoga 25–24 Spartanburg;

Tourney Time

Parker 26–21 McKinley; Union City 26–25 Winchester; Wayne 24–22 Saratoga; Union City 16–14 Parker; Wayne 33–29 Union City. Officials: H. Windmiller, Walter Fisher, John Walker.

1937 REGIONALS

ANDERSON: Plainfield 33–24 Indianapolis Tech; Anderson 25–10 Fortville; Anderson 29–21 Plainfield. Officials: Glenn Adams, Orville Jones.

ATTICA: Greencastle 29–22 Dana; Crawfordsville 25–19 Williamsport; Crawfordsville 28–21 Greencastle. Officials: Hal Harris, Hugh Vandivier.

AUBURN: Garrett 29–25 Kendallville; Warsaw 31–20 Columbia City; Warsaw 41–38 Garrett. Officials: O. F. Helvie, G. L. Russell.

BLOOMINGTON: Martinsville 49–16 Wiley; Brazil 23–21 Bloomfield; Martinsville 27–13 Brazil. Officials: Thomas Baker, Irvin Springer.

COLUMBUS: Greensburg 34–24 Franklin; Columbus 43–38 Madison; Greensburg 32–25 Columbus. Officials: George Williams, C. O. Walls.

EVANSVILLE: Central 33–28 Owensville; Dale 21–17 Tell City; Central 28–21 Dale. Officials: Fred Alwood, Carl Porter.

HUNTINGTON: Ft. Wayne Central 41–22 Hartford City; Clear Creek 28–20 Berne; Central 47–21 Clear Creek. Officials: Daniel Guild, Nate Kaufman.

LAFAYETTE: Rossville 40–35 Lebanon; Lafayette 38–27 Otterbein; Lafayette 45–25 Rossville. Officials: G. M. Kinzel, Charles Garrett.

LOGANSPORT: Monon 33–17 Flora; Logansport 29–21 Peru; Logansport 30–26 Monon. Officials: R. L. Rahbar, L E. Fink.

MARION: Wabash 28–23 Kokomo; Marion 23–13 Atlanta; Wabash 30–24 Marion. Officials: Allen Klinck, T. R. Smith.

MICHIGAN CITY: LaPorte 40–28 Gary Emerson; Hammond 41–21 Goodland; Hammond 29–17 LaPorte. Officials:Carl Burt, J. Clayton Hughes.

MITCHELL: Bedford 27–25 Seymour; New Albany 34–23 Paoli; Bedford 34–16 New Albany. Officials: Norman Dunlap, Russell Pickett.

MUNCIE: New Castle 17–16 Richmond; Muncie 43–17 Wayne; Muncie 31–19 New Castle. Officials: Winston Ashley, Karl Dickerson.

ROCHESTER: Mishawaka 28–23 Elkhart; Rochester 33–14 Plymouth; Rochester 29–26 Mishawaka. Officials: Lowell Sparks, Lundy Welborn.

RUSHVILLE: Rushville 36–28 Vevay; North Vernon 41–23 Connersville; North Vernon 24–22 Rushville. Officials: Stanley Porter, Walter Fisher.

WASHINGTON: Washington 17–14 Vincennes; Huntingburg 33–24 Dugger; Huntingburg 33–21 Washington. Officials: Leonard Mayhugh, Noble Lyons.

1937 SEMI–FINALS

INDIANAPOLIS: North Vernon 38–17 Greensburg; Anderson 23–21 Crawfordsville; Anderson 26–15 North Vernon. Officials: Carl Burt, Irvin Springer.

LOGANSPORT: Rochester 21–19 Lafayette; Hammond 38–27 Logansport; Rochester 33–24 Hammond. Officials: O. F. Helvie, Nate Kaufman.

MUNCIE: Warsaw 31–26 Wabash; Ft. Wayne Central 43–31 Muncie; Central 37–22 Warsaw. Officials: Glenn Adams, Orville Jones.

VINCENNES: Huntingburg 35–30 Evansville Central; Martinsville 38–22 Bedford; Huntingburg 34–21 Martinsville. Officials: Winston Ashley, Thomas Baker.

1937 STATE FINALS—March 27

INDIANAPOLIS (Butler Fieldhouse): Huntingburg 30–28 Ft. Wayne Central; Anderson 28–16 Rochester; Anderson 33–23 Huntingburg. Officials: Nate Kaufman, Carl Burt.

1938 SECTIONALS

AMBIA: Wadena 52–22 Raub; Oxford 32–23 Boswell; Earl Park 48–22 Pine Twp.; Ambia 40–26 Gilboa Twp.; Fowler 31–18 Freeland Park; Otterbein 36–28 Wadena; Oxford 42–34 Earl Park; Ambia 37–26 Fowler; Oxford 29–23 Otterbein; Oxford 48–32 Ambia. Officials: C. E. Baer, Clifford Phillips.

ANDERSON: Lapel 16–14 Pendleton. Elwood 29–21 Alexandria; Summitville 34–21 Frankton; Anderson 22–16 Markleville; Lapel 27–19 Elwood; Anderson 42–18 Summitville; Anderson 37–22 Lapel. Officials: Gale Robinson, J. Clayton Hughes.

ATTICA: Perrysville 28–17 Newtown; Attica 35–30 Covington; Williamsport 33–11 Wallace; Pine Village 27–23 West Lebanon; Veedersburg 41–23 Mellott; Kingman 33–31 Hillsboro; Attica 35–17 Perrysville; Williamsport 37–21 Pine Village; Kingman 37–25 Veedersburg; Williamsport 27–25 Attica; Williamsport 23–8 Kingman. Officials: Dean Malaska, Walter Ringer.

BATESVILLE: Holton 31–27 Batesville; Napoleon 44–26 New Marion; Sunman 52–28 Cross Plains; Milan 33–14 Versailles; Center Twp. 25–23 Holton; Sunman 45–37 Napoleon; Center Twp. 33–29 Milan; Sunman 23–22 Center Twp. Officials: Russell Bratton, A. E. Pitcher.

BEDFORD: Mitchell 41–20 Heltonville; Bedford 32–17 Oolitic; Marshall Twp. 31–25 Springville; Tunnelton 56–14 Huron; Fayetteville 33–20 Shawswick; Bedford 31–24 Mitchell; Marshall Twp. 29–21 Tunnelton; Bedford 43–32 Fayetteville; Bedford 36–16 Marshall Twp. Officials: Glenn Adams, Charles Henry.

BLOOMFIELD: Midland 57–19 Newberry; Bloomfield 45–15 Worthington; Linton 25–20 Switz City; Lyons 25–17 Scotland; Jasonville 32–23 Solsberry; Owensburg 39–19 Marco; Bloomfield 56–28 Midland; Lyons 34–25 Linton; Jasonville 28–19 Owensburg; Bloomfield 30–21 Lyons; Bloomfield 41–38 Jasonville. Officials: Robert Derrington, Clarence Tolbert.

BLOOMINGTON: Bloomington 35–29 Paragon; Ellettsville 39–22 Unionville; Smithville 41–19 Stinesville; Monrovia 56–25 Eminence; Martinsville 43–25 Mooresville; Bloomington 40–29 Morgantown; Ellettsville 38–21 Smithville; Martinsville 34–22 Monrovia; Bloomington 27–21 Ellettsville; Martinsville 29–24 Bloomington. Officials: Carl Porter, Orville Jones.

BLUFFTON: Hartford Twp. 31–24 Jackson; Union 51–13 Jefferson; Rockcreek 50–28 Pleasant Mills; Bluffton 52–22 Chester Center; Petroleum 35–28 Geneva; Kirkland 40–17 Monroe; Ossian 26–21 Berne; Liberty Center 32–30 Lancaster; Union 38–26 Hartford Twp.; Bluffton 22–20 Rockcreek Twp.; Petroleum 33–26 Kirkland; Ossian 55–45 Liberty Center; Bluffton 32–22 Union; Ossian 51–22 Petroleum; Bluffton 26–25 Ossian. Officials: Cecil Young, Harold McSwane, George Lambert.

Tourney Time

BOONVILLE: Dale 35–27 Selvin; Lynnville 35–28 Chrisney; Tennyson 54–17 Yankeetown; Luce Twp. 41–11 Grandview; Boonville 37–22 Rockport; Folsomville 34–16 Gentryville; Dale 44–27 Tennyson; Lynnville 26–13 Luce Twp.; Boonville 39–29 Folsomville. Dale 30–23 Lynnville; Dale 32–30 Boonville (2ot). Officials: John B. Wilson, John Hoffman.

BRAZIL: Bowling Green 38–30 Freedom; Posey Twp. 40–35 Quincy; Brazil 36–23 Clay City; Spencer 43–25 Cory; Patricksburg 35–34 Van Buren Twp.; Ashboro 39–31 Jefferson Twp.; Gosport 49–33 Bowling Green; Posey Twp. 41–40 Brazil; Spencer 58–28 Patricksburg; Ashboro 26–17 Gosport; Spencer 40–30 Posey Twp.; Spencer 28–25 Ashboro. Officials: Joe Dienhart, Robert Hold, Raymond Trobaugh.

COLUMBIA CITY: Washington Center 31–19 South Whitley; Columbia 48–25 Jefferson Center; Churubusco 39–29 Larwill; Coesse 36–13 Etna Twp.; Columbia City 45–30 Washington Center; Churubusco 40–27 Coesse; Columbia 52–28 Churubusco. Officials: G. L. Russell, R. Wayne Cunningham.

CONNERSVILLE: Liberty 59–22 Everton; Brownsville 39–7 Oldenburg; Harrisburg 39–27 Orange; Brookville 37–14 Whitewater; Alquina 60–17 Laurel; Springfield Twp. 51–0 Fairview; Connersville 48–32 Bentonville; Liberty 28–19 Harrison Twp.; Harrisburg 33–15 Brownsville; Brookville 34–23 Alquina; Connersville 38–31 Springfield Twp.; Liberty 33–23 Harrisburg; Brookville 32–22 Connersville; Liberty 22–14 Brookville. Officials: Fred Pierson, Frank Shamel, Myer Schreiber.

CRAWFORDSVILLE: Crawfordsville 31–25 Linden; Darlington 34–19 New Richmond; Wingate 36–21 Bowers; Waynetown 37–35 New Market; Ladoga 27–23 Alamo; New Ross 26–19 Waveland; Crawfordsville 35–24 Darlington; Wingate 41–32 Waynetown; Ladoga 28–26 New Ross; Crawfordsville 50–19 Wingate; Crawfordsville 46–22 Ladoga. Officials: Albert Etter, K. King Telle.

DANVILLE: Plainfield 35–19 Pittsboro; New Winchester 31–24 Clayton; Brownsburg 42–27 North Salem; Amo 31–30 Lizton; Danville 68–40 Stilesville; Plainfield 36–21 Avon; Brownsburg 42–32 New Winchester; Danville 41–31 Amo; Brownsburg 31–17 Plainfield; Brownsburg 41–32 Danville. Officials: Cyril Prevo, Harry Briggs.

DELPHI: Cutler 28–27 Camden; Delphi 31–19 Deer Creek; Flora 24–7 Burlington; Rockfield 46–23 Adams Twp.; Cutler 52–14 Carrollton; Delphi 20–11 Flora; Rockfield 21–20 Cutler; Delphi 20–16 Rockfield. Officials: Ralph King, Forrest Roe.

EVANSVILLE: Stewartsville 24–21 Griffin; Bosse 32–29 Cynthiana; Reitz 54–27 Elberfeld; Mt. Vernon 32–28 Millersburg; Central 73–13 Wadesville; New Harmony 30–23 Newburgh; Poseyville 29–16 Chandler; Bosse 44–27 Stewartsville; Mt. Vernon 26–24 Reitz; Central 63–14 New Harmony; Poseyville 30–27 Bosse; Central 33–16 Mt. Vernon; Central 37–25 Poseyville. Officials: Harry Conover, Fred Alwood, Hulett Crecelius.

FORT WAYNE: South Side 50–24 Huntertown; Decatur 45–30 Monmouth; Harlan 33–32 Lafayette Central; Central 56–23 Woodburn; New Haven 38–24 Monroeville; Hoagland 37–20 Elmhurst; North Side 29–19 Leo; South Side 68–29 Arcola; Decatur 55–25 Harlan; Central 33–19 New Haven; North Side 42–37 Hoagland (ot); South Side 62–37 Decatur; Central 43–30 North Side; South Side 23–15 Central. Officials: Ed Anglemyer, George Yarnelle, Harry Coolman.

FRANKFORT: Michigantown 35–27 Washington Twp.; Forest 19–18 Scircleville; Rossville 37–33 Colfax; Kirklin 39–27 Mulberry; Frankfort 48–15 Sugar Creek; Michigantown 33–25 Jackson Twp.; Rossville 39–36 Forest; Frankfort 53–22 Kirklin; Rossville 42–28 Michigantown;

IHSAA Scores | 1930–1939

Frankfort 44–23 Rossville. Officials. Hugh Bergstrom, Walter Fisher.

FRANKLIN: Whiteland 43–13 Jackson Twp.; Masonic Home 33–22 Van Buren Twp.; Edinburg 25–24 Greenwood; Franklin 34–14 Nashville; Center Grove 39–21 Union Twp.; Nineveh 27–17 Clark Twp.; Whiteland 49–23 Trafalgar; Edinburg 26–20 Masonic Home; Franklin 26–20 Center Grove; Whiteland 34–26 Nineveh; Franklin 27–14 Edinburg; Franklin 22–19 Whiteland. Officials: Norman Dunlap, Ira Willis, George Williams.

GARRETT: Scott Center 20–18 Orland; Metz 34–25 Concord Twp.; Fremont 50–31 Pleasant Lake; Spencerville 31–22 Hamilton; Waterloo 36–33 Auburn; Ashley 26–18 Angola; Butler 30–25 Salem Center; Garrett 83–9 Scott Center; Fremont 40–20 Metz; Waterloo 34–23 Spencerville; Butler 33–28 Ashley; Garrett 50–31 Fremont; Waterloo 43–37 Butler; Garrett 35–33 Waterloo. Officials: James Craw, Walter Thurston, Phil N. Eskew.

GARY: Chesterton 41–14 Liberty Center; Boone Grove 45–14 Washington Twp.; Wheeler 52–34 Morgan Twp.; Horace Mann 31–28 Valparaiso; Froebel 40–16 Kouts; Emerson 59–17 Hebron; Wallace 44–26 Jackson Twp.; Tolleston 41–25 Portage; Chesterton 36–11 Boone Grove; Horace Mann 43–13 Wheeler; Emerson 30–26 Froebel; Wallace 19–18 Tolleston; Horace Mann 22–20 Chesterton; Emerson 37–28 Wallace; Emerson 27–19 Horace Mann. Officials: Max Bullock, Forest M. Wood, L. E. Fink.

GOSHEN: Wakarusa 38–25 Middlebury; Nappanee 52–16 Jefferson Twp.; Goshen 32–26 Bristol; Concord Twp. 32–26 New Paris; Elkhart 50–9 Millersburg; Wakarusa 44–27 Baugo Twp.; Goshen 30–24 Nappanee; Elkhart 42–33 Concord Twp.; Wakarusa 28–26 Goshen; Elkhart 41–37 Wakarusa (ot). Officials: Earl Scott, Dana Chandler.

GREENCASTLE: Putnamville 29–26 Belle Union; Cloverdale 29–25 Roachdale; Greencastle 53–20 Reelsville; Bainbridge 43–25 Russellville; Fillmore 28–17 Putnamville; Greencastle 52–22 Cloverdale; Bainbridge 39–25 Fillmore; Greencastle 43–33 Bainbridge. Officials: G. Elwood Hookey, Fletcher Kerr.

GREENFIELD: Maxwell 26–11 Charlottesville; Wilkinson 33–22 Mt. Comfort; Fortville 32–30 McCordsville (ot); Greenfield 36–29 Eden; New Palestine 41–27 Westland; Wilkinson 38–31 Maxwell; Fortville 45–30 Greenfield; Wilkinson 30–24 New Palestine; Fortville 44–32 Wilkinson. Officials: Thomas Baker, Otto Crosley.

GREENSBURG: Greensburg 38–12 St. Paul; Jackson 49–14 Vernon; Westport 28–24 Butlerville; Burney 18–15 Clarksburg; North Vernon 35–18 Sandusky; Newpoint 35–8 Zenas; Greensburg 26–13 Letts; Jackson 37–22 Westport; North Vernon 30–11 Burney; Greensburg 47–19 New Point; Jackson 28–24 North Vernon; Greensburg 32–15 Jackson. Officials: Mark Williams, Evan Crawley, G. P. Silver.

HAMMOND: East Chicago Washington 36–16 Dyer; East Gary Edison 48–25 Lowell; Griffith 45–16 Miller; Clark 31–24 Whiting; Hobart 39–29 Hammond Tech; Calumet Twp. 37–22 Merrillville; Hammond High 45–23 Crown Point; Roosevelt 34–25 Washington; Griffith 22–18 Edison; Clark 44–35 Hobart; Hammond High 71–21 Calumet Twp.; Roosevelt 40–25 Griffith; Hammond High 22–19 Clark; Hammond High 28–22 Roosevelt. Officials: T. R. Smith, Dan Guild, George Vaulk.

HARTFORD CITY: Hartford City 37–21 Bryant; Pennville 32–30 Redkey; Dunkirk 33–20 Jefferson; Ridgeville 44–29 Poling; Montpelier 31–25 Portland; Madison Twp. 31–27 Roll; Hartford City 77–20 Gray; Dunkirk 24–22 Pennville; Ridgeville 37–36 Montpelier; Hartford City 30–24 Madison; Ridgeville 25–24 Dunkirk; Ridgeville 39–29 Hartford City. Officials: Paul

Tourney Time

Bateman, Lavon Carey, Carl Burt.

HUNTINGTON: Roanoke 41–32 Salamonie Twp.; Lancaster Center 41–32 Rock Creek; Banquo 31–20 Bippus; Monument City 44–23 Jefferson Twp.; Huntington Twp. 28–17 Markle; Andrews 40–23 Clear Creek; Huntington 39–29 Union Twp.; Roanoke 29–24 Lancaster Center; Banquo 25–21 Monument City; Huntington Twp. 30–19 Andrews; Huntington 30–28 Roanoke; Banquo 32–26 Huntington Twp.; Huntington 45–25 Banquo. Officials: Ray Bigler, Donald Coar, Cleo Wysong.

INDIANAPOLIS: Ben Davis 51–34 Oaklandon; Washington 46–34 Warren Central; Tech 39–14 Franklin Twp.; Manual 20–19 Lawrence; Decatur Central 35–22 Broad Ripple; Shortridge 44–19 Castleton; Southport 38–11 Speedway; Beech Grove 27–21 New Augusta; Washington 28–25 Ben Davis; Tech 39–27 Manual; Shortridge 41–35 Decatur Central; Southport 30–27 Beech Grove; Tech 25–23 Washington; Shortridge 24–23 Southport; Shortridge 32–29 Tech. Officials: Raymond Hobbs, Fred White, Allen Klinck.

JASPER: Ireland 24–13 Winslow; Dubois 32–19 Petersburg; Jasper 80–23 Birdseye Otwell 22–21 Spurgeon (ot); Stendal 38–35 Holland; Huntingburg 37–9 Cuzco; Dubois 36–27 Ireland; Jasper 46–25 Otwell; Huntingburg 49–27 Stendal; Jasper 38–31 Dubois; Jasper 30–25 Huntingburg. Officials: John Gant, Irvin Springer.

JEFFERSONVILLE: New Salisbury 24–14 New Middletown; Silver Creek 35–20 Henryville; New Albany 78–11 Lanesville; New Washington 34–20 Elizabeth; Charlestown 43–24 Laconia; Mauckport 25–18 New Amsterdam; Borden 32–30 Georgetown (ot); Jeffersonville 37–20 Corydon; New Salisbury 41–28 Silver Creek; New Albany 69–6 New Washington; Charlestown 50–33 Mauckport; Jeffersonville 76–23 Borden; New Albany 71–6 New Salisbury; Jeffersonville 58–19 Charlestown; New Albany 18–13 Jeffersonville. Officials: Clyde Castle, Fred Steelman, Charles Jensen.

KENDALLVILLE: Ligonier 28–19 Wolcottville. Scott 31–21 Shipshewana; Brighton 32–31 Wolf Lake (ot); Wawaka 39–37 Rome City (ot); Kendallville 41–16 Springfield Twp.; Avilla 27–25 Lima (ot); LaGrange 42–30 Albion; Cromwell 39–21 Topeka; Ligonier 24–19 Scott; Brighton 33–20 Wawaka; Kendallville 47–32 Avilla; Lagrange 43–17 Cromwell; Ligonier 31–23 Brighton; Kendallville 28–26 LaGrange; Kendallville 39–28 Ligonier. Officials: Harrison Berkey, Clive Markley, Thomas Fields, Lores Lehman.

KOKOMO: Jackson Twp. 26–19 Howard Twp.; Kokomo 43–12 West Middleton; Greentown 35–18 Union Twp.; Ervin Twp. 14–12 Russiaville (2ot); New London 34–21 Clay Twp.; Kokomo 54–23 Jackson Twp.; Greentown 44–9 Ervin Twp.; Kokomo 81–23 New London; Kokomo 42–22 Greentown. Officials: Al Jackson, Wm. Kendall.

LAFAYETTE: Montmorenci 38–16 Buck Creek; West Point 31–16 Stockwell; Jefferson 40–19 Monitor; Battle Ground 23–21 Klondike; Dayton 27–14 Clarks Hill; West Lafayette 41–18 Wea; Romney 18–14 Jackson Twp.; West Point 24–19 Montmorenci; Jefferson 72–16 Battle Ground; West Lafayette 29–15 Dayton; West Point 31–25 Romney; Jefferson 32–30 West Lafayette (ot); Jefferson 45–17 West Point. Officials: A. T. Krider, J. Alvin Taylor, Wendell Heath.

LAPORTE: Stillwell 49–19 Wanatah; LaPorte 43–17 Rolling Prairie; Union Twp. 35–33 Westville; Michigan City 20–16 LaCrosse; Clinton Twp. 23–18 Union Mills; Mill Creek 27–25 Springfield Twp.; Kingsbury 19–17 Hanna (ot); LaPorte 57–24 Stillwell; Union Twp. 34–31 Michigan City; Clinton Twp. 33–27 Mill Creek; LaPorte 59–17 Kingsbury; Union Twp. 39–34 Clinton Twp.; LaPorte 58–20 Union Twp. Officials: Lowell Lenon, Lawrence Gaunt, G. W. Strole.

IHSAA Scores | 1930–1939

LAWRENCEBURG: Bright 23–18 Moores Hill; Lawrenceburg 26–13 Patriot; Guilford 24–20 Rising Sun; Vevay 27–24 Dillsboro; Aurora 30–20 Bright; Lawrenceburg 29–20 Guilford; Vevay 33–30 Aurora; Lawrenceburg 37–28 Vevay. Officials: Gerald Bottorff, Hal Harris.

LEBANON: Zionsville 32–24 Central; Pinnell 35–19 Thorntown; Advance 42–17 Whitestown; Lebanon 44–24 Jamestown; Dover 32–29 Zionsville; Pinnell 25–23 Advance; Lebanon 51–18 Dover; Lebanon 37–34 Pinnell. Officials: George Nulf, Karl Dickerson.

LOGANSPORT: Royal Center 52–14 Noble Twp.; Young America 29–24 Washington Twp.; New Waverly 31–28 Walton; Twelve Mile 40–31 Onward; Galveston 29–23 Lucerne; Logansport 57–18 Metea; Royal Center 27–25 Young America; Twelve Mile 32–23 New Waverly; Logansport 20–17 Galveston; Royal Center 48–24 New Waverly; Royal Center 25–21 Logansport. Officials: Doxie Reeves, Condict Smith.

MADISON: Scottsburg 30–16 Dupont; Madison 38–21 Lexington; Deputy 24–16 Saluda; North Madison 43–14 Paris Crossing; Central 66–24 Lovett; Austin 48–12 Marion Twp.; Hanover 46–15 San Jacinto; Madison 32–22 Scottsburg; Deputy 28–18 North Madison; Austin 45–34 Central; Madison 26–23 Hanover (ot); Austin 35–19 Deputy; Madison 24–22 Austin (ot). Officials: Herbert Edwards, Carl Ross, Robert Froman.

MARION: Swayzee 26–25 Sweetser; Jefferson 21–20 Jonesboro; Fairmount 22–20 Gas City (ot); Marion 40–20 Van Buren; Jefferson 23–13 Swayzee; Marion 36–27 Fairmount; Marion 35–18 Jefferson. Officials: Nate Kaufman, M. E. Somers.

MARSHALL: Union Twp. 28–26 St. Bernice; Tangier 29–28 Rosedale (ot); Clinton 50–31 Cayuga; Rockville 29–25 Mecca; Dana 47–19 Marshall; Montezuma 47–27 Bloomingdale; Bridgeton 26–17 Hillsdale; Newport 56–32 Green Twp.; Tangier 37–24 Union Twp.; Clinton 35–33 Rockville; Dana 67–37 Montezuma; Bridgeton; 39–25 Newport; Clinton 40–23 Tangier; Dana 41–26 Bridgeton; Clinton 30–21 Dana. Officials: William L. Ball, D. C. Moffett.

MISHAWAKA: New Carlisle 36–20 Wilson; Washington-Clay 35–28 South Bend Riley; Lakeville 46–36 Madison Twp.; Mishawaka 37–23 Greene Twp.; South Bend Washington 36–34 South Bend Central; North Liberty 51–33 Walkerton; New Carlisle 48–32 Washington-Clay; Mishawaka 35–29 Lakeville; Washington 53–43 North Liberty; Mishawaka 33–25 New Carlisle; Washington 32–26 Mishawaka. Officials: Edmund Tully, Harold Johnson.

MONON: Round Grove 18–15 Buffalo; Monticello 26–19 Brookston; Wolcott 40–28 Chalmers; Monon 34–27 Reynolds; Idaville 30–26 Burnettsville; Monticello 41–18 Round Grove; Monon 46–28 Wolcott; Monticello 37–19 Idaville; Monticello 33–29 Morton. Officials: Wm. Lucus, H. Windmiller.

MOROCCO: Goodland 33–13 Kentland; Wheatfield 34–18 Fair Oaks; Brook 68–16 Hanging Grove; Remington 71–15 Kniman; Rensselaer 27–15 Morocco; Kankakee Twp. 24–21 DeMotte; Goodland 21–20 Mount Ayr; Wheatfield 25–22 Brook; Rensselaer 31–23 Remington; Goodland 25–19 Kankakee Twp.; Rensselaer 33–23 Wheatfield; Rensselaer 45–30 Goodland. Officials: Leon Dulgar, H. D. McNew, Robert Taylor.

MUNCIE: Muncie Central 34–16 Daleville; Burris 43–19 Harrison; Gaston 31–25 Eaton; DeSoto 30–27 Selma; Albany 28–22 Royerton; Center 38–21 Yorktown; Muncie Central 53–23 Cowan; Burris 29–23 Gaston; DeSoto 21–19 Albany; Muncie 31–21 Center; Burris 8–23 DeSoto; Muncie Central 30–27 Burris. Officials: Ray Scott, Cecil Tharp, Winston Ashley.

NEW CASTLE: Mooreland 30–15 Mount Summit; Sulphur Springs 29–27 New Castle;

213

Tourney Time

Straughn 31–24 Spiceland; Lewisville 30–15 New Lisbon; Knightstown 27–26 Kennard. Middletown 53–19 Cadiz; Mooreland 36–33 Sulphur Springs; Lewisville 27–24 Straughn; Middletown 24–21 Knightstown; Mooreland 22–18 Lewisville; Middletown 32–29 Mooreland. Officials: Maurice Tudor, Jacob McClure.

NOBLESVILLE: Kempton 19–16 Atlanta; Arcadia 34–17 Windfall; Carmel 23–11 Westfield; Tipton 37–27 Noblesville; Prairie Twp. 29–19 Cicero; Sharpsville 30–28 Fishers; Sheridan 43–21 Walnut Grove; Kempton 26–20 Goldsmith; Carmel 18–17 Arcadia; Tipton 42–26 Prairie Twp.; Sheridan 35–23 Sharpsville; Carmel 22–15 Kempton; Sheridan 25–19 Tipton; Sheridan 24–18 Carmel. Officials: Gerald Huey, Fred Shroyer, John Walker.

PAOLI: Campbellsburg 23–18 Morgan Twp.; Salem 41–28 French Lick; Orleans 55–29 Pekin; Little York 34–23 Monroe Twp.; Paoli 32–31 Hardinsburg; West Baden 47–35 Campbellsburg; Salem 32–25 Orleans; Paoli 41–23 Little York; Salem 29–27 West Baden (ot); Paoli 34–32 Salem (2ot). Officials: George Bair, Reid Mc-Lain.

PERU: Jefferson Twp. 30–27 Chili; Bunker Hill 37–17 Macy; Gilead 26–20 Amboy; Butler Twp. 31–22 Deedsville; Clay Twp. 30–21 Converse; Peru 51–27 Jefferson Twp.; Bunker Hill 20–13 Gilead; Clay Twp. 20–15 Butler Twp.; Peru 42–20 Bunker Hill; Peru 42–19 Clay Twp. Officials: Layall Fisher, R. P. Chambers.

PIERCETON: North Webster 51–23 Burket; Mentone 35–12 Etna Green; Milford 33–30 Syracuse; Sidney 29–20 Silver Lake; Pierceton 38–23 Leesburg; Atwood 35–23 Claypool; Warsaw 28–22 Beaver Dam; Mentone 19–17 North Webster; Sidney 31–15 Milford; Pierceton 39–30 Atwood; Warsaw 27–19 Mentone; Sidney 13–12 Pierceton; Warsaw 23–19 Sidney. Officials: Walter Cook, Lowell Sparks, Louis Briner.

PLYMOUTH: Culver 45–28 Grovertown; Plymouth 29–11 Tippecanoe; Argos 42–26 LaPaz; Bremen 34–26 Knox; Bourbon 28–20 Center Twp.; San Pierre 23–21 West Twp.; Hamlet 35–27 North Judson; Culver 49–30 Tyner; Argos 34–30 Plymouth; Bremen 22–17 Bourbon; Hamlet 43–22 San Pierre; Culver 47–27 Argos; Bremen 40–36 Hamlet; Culver 36–26 Bremen. Officials: M. E. Easton, Charles Garrett, George Kinzel.

PRINCETON: Francisco 30–26 Patoka; Fort Branch 59–19 Wabash Twp.; Mackey 30–19 Hazleton; Oakland City 42–22 Mount Olympus; Owensville 29–23 Princeton; Francisco 42–30 Haubstadt; Mackey 35–28 Fort Branch; Owensville 39–34 Oakland City; Mackey 23–17 Francisco; Owensville 23–17 Mackey. Officials: David Royalty, William Coulter.

RICHMOND: Cambridge City 34–12 Webster; Greensfork 22–20 Centerville; Milton 34–21 Boston; Richmond 28–16 Williamsburg; Hagerstown 34–18 Whitewater; Fountain City 27–14 Economy; Greensfork 36–23 Cambridge City; Richmond 36–18 Milton; Hagerstown 36–18 Fountain City; Richmond 42–22 Greensfork; Richmond 42–23 Hagerstown. Officials: Lundy Welborn, Aaron Belcher.

RUSHVILLE: Mays 49–19 Gings; Milroy 31–19 Raleigh; Arlington 42–8 Glenwood; Morton Memorial 26–10 Manilla; Carthage 36–17 New Salem; Rushville 47–23 Mays; Milroy 43–36 Arlington; Morton Memorial 39–27 Carthage; Rushville 36–15 Milroy; Rushville 27–19 Morton Memorial. Officials: B. R. Hosier, Clyde Gentry.

SEYMOUR: Seymour 32–17 Brownstown; Houston 30–18 Tampico; Scipio 19–18 Hayden; Clearspring 50–28 Vallonia; Medora 32–14 Cortland; Crothersville 18–16 Freetown; Seymour 42–19 Houston; Clearspring 56–22 Scipio; Medora 19–17 Crothersville; Seymour 33–28 Clearspring; Seymour 31–12 Medora. Officials: J. Ralph Black, Custer Baker.

IHSAA Scores | 1930–1939

SHELBYVILLE: Shelbyville 30–19 Flat Rock; Morristown 39–25 Boggstown; Columbus 50–25 Waldron; Fairland 32–23 Clifford; Moral Twp. 43–23 Mt. Auburn; Shelbyville 27–12 Hawcreek Twp.; Columbus 49–28 Morristown; Fairland 29–22 Moral Twp.; Columbus 37–18 Shelbyville; Columbus 59–37 Fairland. Officials: Everett Campbell, Russell Pickett.

SULLIVAN: Sullivan 56–29 Hymera; Dugger 37–14 Carlisle; Graysville 32–20 New Lebanon; Shelburn 30–22 Merom; Fairbanks 31–21 Pleasantville; Sullivan 27–16 Farmersburg; Dugger 45–23 Graysville; Shelburn 30–29 Fairbanks; Dugger 30–29 Sullivan (3ot); Dugger 34–23 Shelburn. Officials: Rollie Kirchoff, Herbert Robinson.

TELL CITY: Troy 42–22 Bristow; Cannelton 53–27 Union Twp.; Marengo 41–21 Oil Twp.; Tell City 49–8 Milltown; Cannelton 36–30 Troy; Tell City 29–20 Marengo; Tell City 33–28 Cannelton. Officials: W. S. Fellmy, John Lyskowinski.

TERRE HAUTE: West Terre Haute 34–28 Riley; Gerstmeyer 36–19 Prairie Creek; Blackhawk 15–14 Glenn; Otter Creek 37–27 Pimento; Laboratory 34–15 Fontanet; Wiley 33–24 Garfield; Concannon 32–20 Honey Creek. Gerstmeyer 27–19 West Terre Haute; Otter Creek 34–16 Blackhawk; Wiley 30–18 Laboratory; Gerstmeyer 17–16 Concannon; Wiley 37–24 Otter Creek; Wiley 57–31 Gerstmeyer. Officials: Frank Jarrell, Robert Simison, Ralph Pearson

VINCENNES: Bruceville 50–14 Fritchton; Decker 25–16 Monroe City; Freelandville 33–25 Wheatland; Bicknell 20–17 Decker Chapel; Vincennes 57–15 Sandborn; Oaktown 23–20 Edwardsport; Decker 30–26 Bruceville; Freelandville 35–30 Bicknell; Vincennes 42–26 Oaktown; Freelandville 32–26 Decker; Vincennes 51–12 Freelandville. Officials: George Kerr, Robert Hoffman.

WABASH: North Manchester 36–20 LaFontaine; Roann 35–24 Lagro; Laketon 27–25 Chippewa; Linlawn 29–25 Lincolnville; Somerset 27–22 Chester Twp.; Wabash 44–28 Urbana; North Manchester 33–18 Roann; Laketon 34–17 Linlawn; Wabash 32–24 Somerset; North Manchester 39–23 Laketon; Wabash 19–15 North Manchester. Officials: J. L. Mertz, LeRoy Shine.

WASHINGTON: Plainville 54–12 Raglesville; Washington 34–14 Glendale; Barr Twp. 36–17 Trinity Springs; Epsom 42–22 Burns City; Shoals 39–27 Alfordsville; Odon 45–34 Elnora; Plainville 49–25 Loogootee; Washington 33—26 Barr Twp.; Shoals 42–31 Epsom; Plainville 50–19 Odon; Washington 38–23 Shoals; Plainville 28–18 Washington. Officials: Walter Marks, R. F. Meier, William Pointer.

WINAMAC: Star City 32–21 Francesville; Monterey 25–22 Grass Creek; Medaryville 22–14 Talma; Rochester 36–18 Richland Center; Akron 29–14 Leiters Ford; Pulaski 34–21 Fulton; Star City 26–14 Kewanna; Winamac 30–29 Monterey; Rochester 28–18 Medaryville; Pulaski 38–24 Akron; Star City 22–21 Winamac; Rochester 34–19 Pulaski; Rochester 28–19 Star City. Officials: Herbert Vaulk, Don Veller, Freeman Cox.

WINCHESTER: Wayne 26–15 Spartanburg; Stoney Creek 29–14 Losantville; Parker 38–23 Farmland; McKinley 23–19 Union City; Modoc 29–27 Saratoga; Jackson 27–24 Lynn; Winchester 29–17 Huntsville; Lincoln 34–33 Green; Stoney Creek 29–16 Wayne; Parker 44–29 McKinley; Jackson 48–24 Modoc; Winchester 27–25 Lincoln; Parker 30–23 Stoney Creek; Jackson 30–26 Winchester; Parker 41–39 Jackson. Officials: Forrest Ballinger, Donald Dickie, Von Crowe.

Tourney Time

1938 REGIONALS

ANDERSON: Anderson 23–18 Fortville; Shortridge 46–33 Brownsburg; Anderson 25–17 Shortridge. Officials: Karl Dickerson, Lundy Welborn.

CLINTON: Crawfordsville 44–28 Clinton; Greencastle 26–22 Williamsport; Greencastle 32–31 Crawfordsville. Officials: Irvin Springer, Win. Pointer.

EVANSVILLE: Owensville 31–29 Dale; Central 39–20 Tell City; Central 29–15 Owensville. Officials: Frank Jarrell, Russell Pickett.

FORT WAYNE: Ridgeville 33–32 Bluffton (ot); South Side 38–19 Huntington; South Side 54–25 Ridgeville. Officials: Thomas Baker, George Williams.

GREENSBURG: Franklin 28–23 Madison; Columbus 34–22 Greensburg; Columbus 35–24 Franklin. Officials: Gale Robinson, Winston Ashley.

LAFAYETTE: Lafayette 36–25 Lebanon; Frankfort 55–27 Oxford; Frankfort 30–26 Lafayette. Officials: Walter Cook, Lowell Sparks.

LOGANSPORT: Royal Center 23–20 Monticello (ot); Delphi 33–24 Peru; Delphi 24–15 Royal Center. Officials: Carl Burt, J. Clayton Hughes.

MARION: Sheridan 31–28 Kokomo; Marion 31–19 Wabash; Sheridan 25–24 Marion (ot). Officials: Charles Garrett, R. Wayne Cunningham.

MARTINSVILLE: Martinsville 39–20 Spencer; Wiley 34–24 Bloomfield; Martinsville 39–30 Wiley. Officials: Nate Kaufman, Fred Alwood.

MICHIGAN CITY: Emerson 25–23 Rensselaer; Hammond 33–23 LaPorte; Hammond 29–17 Emerson. Officials: Dan Guild, George Vaulk.

MUNCIE: Richmond 38–30 Middletown; Muncie Central 36–8 Parker; Muncie Central 39–26 Richmond. Officials: Orville Jones, T. R. Smith.

NEW ALBANY: New Albany 36–19 Paoli; Bedford 24–21 Seymour; Bedford 34–27 New Albany. Officials: Noble Lyons, Stanley Porter.

ROCHESTER: Washington (South Bend) 28–25 Elkhart; Rochester 28–26 Culver (2ot); Rochester 33–26 Washington. Officials: G. M. Kinzel, Hal Harris.

RUSHVILLE: Liberty 40–35 Lawrenceburg; Rushville 37–16 Sunman; Rushville 25–22 Liberty. Officials: C. O. Walls, Allen Klinck.

WARSAW: Kendallville 36–29 Garrett; Warsaw 25–23 Columbia City; Kendallville 27–26 Warsaw. Officials: G. L. Russell, L. E. Fink.

WASHINGTON: Plainville 34–28 Jasper; Vincennes 25–23 Dugger; Plainville 43–37 Vincennes. Officials: Glen Adams, Clyde Castle.

1938 SEMI—FINALS

INDIANAPOLIS: Greencastle 31–19 Rushville; Columbus 38–36 Anderson; Columbus 45–37 Greencastle. Officials: Carl Burt L. E. Fink.

LAFAYETTE: Frankfort 27–14 Delphi; Hammond 23–19 Rochester; Hammond 32–17 Frankfort; Officials: Irvin Springer, Nate Kaufman.

MUNCIE: Muncie Central 49–33 Kendallville; Ft. Wayne South Side 39–13 Sheridan; South Side 37–33 Muncie Central. Officials: Glenn Adams, Thomas Baker.

VINCENNES: Martinsville 31–23 Plainville; Bedford 31–20 Evansville Central; Bedford 21–20 Martinsville (2ot). Officials: Winston Ashley, Orville Jones.

IHSAA Scores | 1930–1939

1938 FINALS—March 26
INDIANAPOLIS (Butler Fieldhouse): Hammond 39–24 Bedford; Ft. Wayne South Side 40–34 Columbus; South Side (Ft. Wayne) 34–32 Hammond. Officials: Nate Kaufman, Carl Burt.

1939 SECTIONALS
ANDERSON: Markleville 31–26 Pendleton; Alexandria 52–19 Frankton; 34–26 Lapel; Anderson 49–18 Summitville; Markleville 29–23 Alexandria; Anderson 31–28 Elwood; Anderson 30–23 Markleville. Officials: Nate Kaufman, Herbert Edwards.

ANGOLA: Waterloo 45–23 Metz; Auburn 29–17 Butler; Hamilton 22–21 Salem Center; Pleasant Lake 50–16 Scott Center; Orland 34–23 Concord Twp.; Ashley 29–27 Spencerville; Garrett 21–20 Angola; Waterloo 53–28 Fremont; Auburn 38–24 Hamilton; Pleasant Lake 36–31 Orland; Garrett 29–24 Ashley; Auburn 38–29 Waterloo; Garrett 34–12 Pleasant Lake; Auburn 37–29 Garrett. Officials: Don Veller, Claron Veller, Norris Ward.

ATTICA: Wallace 29–20 Mellott; Williamsport 29–11 Perrysville; Covington 35–20 West Lebanon; Hillsboro 32–14 Newtown; Pine Village 39–37 Attica; Kingman 27–21 Veedersburg; Williamsport 22–11 Wallace; Hillsboro 27–23 Covington; Pine Village 32–26 Kingman; Hillsboro 30–28 Williamsport; Pine Village 36–26 Hillsboro. Officials: Doxie Reeves, Forrest Roe.

AURORA: Vevay 30–22 Guilford; Lawrenceburg 37–9 Patriot; Aurora 38–12 Dillsboro; Moores Hill 25–19 Bright; Vevay 28–24 Rising Sun; Aurora 40–33 Lawrenceburg; Vevay 22–19 Moores Hill; Aurora 31–24 Vevay. Officials: Frank Shamel, Fred Pierson.

BATESVILLE: Milan 32–29 New Marion; Holton 37–35 Napoleon (ot); Batesville 43–12 Cross Plains; Sunman 30–20 Versailles; Osgood 37–26 Milan; Batesville 30–18 Holton; Osgood 36–23 Milan; Osgood 29–27 Batesville. Officials: Mike Layden, Myer Schreiber.

BEDFORD: Tunnelton 32–27 Oolitic; Marshall Twp. 40–19 Huron; Mitchell 51–26 Fayetteville; Springville 32–14 Williams; Bedford 43–14 Heltonville; Tunnelton 34–24 Shawswick; Mitchell 35–18 Needmore; Bedford 32–26 Springville; Mitchell 28–25 Tunnelton; Mitchell 32–22 Bedford. Officials: Rollie W. Kirchoff, Walter Marks.

BLOOMFIELD: Jasonville 33–19 Lyons; Linton 29–16 Owensburg; Switz City 28–19 Scotland; Midland 49–28 Newberry; Bloomfield 39–23 Marco; Solsberry 27–22 Worthington; Jasonville 43–22 Linton; Switz City 31–30 Midland; Bloomfield 30–16 Solsberry; Jasonville 32–28 Switz City; Bloomfield 35–33 Jasonville. Officials: Harold Schulte, Carl Porter.

BLUFFTON: Berne 35–33 Pleasant Mills. Ossian 42–16 Rockcreek Center; Petroleum 34–32 Liberty Center; Bluffton 43–16 Jackson Center; Chester Center 26–22 Monroe; Union Center 34–29 Geneva; Lancaster Central 47–17 Jefferson Twp.; Kirkland 24–21 Hartford Twp.. Ossian 35–26 Berne; Bluffton 41–24 Petroleum; Union Center 39–32 Chester Center.; Lancaster Central 35–26 Kirkland; Ossian 31–29 Bluffton; Lancaster Central 31–22 Union Center; Ossian 43–22 Lancaster. Officials: Fred J. Schroyer, James R. Craw, George Yarnelle.

BOONVILLE: Lynnville 44–16 Millersburg; Boonville 27–17 Chandler; Newburgh 26–22 Elberfeld; Selvin 51–33 Yankeetown. Folsomville 27–18 Tennyson; Lynnville 33–24 Boonville; Newburgh 47–33 Selvin; Lynnville 43–27 Folsomville; Lynnville 44–20 Newburgh. Officials: Clarence Tolbert, Clarence Riggs.

BOSWELL: Wadena 22–16 Earl Park; Otterbein 35–30 Freeland Park; Fowler 40–21 Gilboa

217

Tourney Time

Twp.; Boswell 30–24 Ambia. Oxford 46–22 York Twp.; Wadena 36–32 Pine Twp.; Fowler 28–24 Otterbein; Oxford 32–21 Boswell; Fowler 36–29 Wadena; Oxford 37–21 Fowler. Officials: Max Hildreth, G. W. Strole.

CANNELTON: Oil Twp. 29–22 Bristow; Chrisney 28–22 Tell City; Cannelton 25–6 Gentryville; Troy 26–129 Luce Twp.; Rockport 18–14 Grandview; Dale 46–23 Oil Twp.; Cannelton 25–23 Chrisney (ot); Rockport 36–17 Troy; Dale 21–19 Cannelton; Dale 34–18 Rockport. Officials: August Banko, John B. Wilson.

CLINTON: Rockville 33–26 Bridgeton; Clinton 36–20 Cayuga; Bloomingdale 39–16 Green Twp. Marshall 29–28 Hillsdale (ot); Rosedale 36–7 St. Bernice; Montezuma 31–22 Tangier; Dana 53–24 Newport; Mecca 39–30 Bellmore; Clinton 21–19 Rockville; Marshall 28–25 Bloomingdale; Rosedale 32–23 Montezuma; Mecca 38–23 Dana; Clinton 38–15 Marshall; Rosedale 25–22 Mecca; Clinton 35–17 Rosedale. Officials: Robert H. Simison, Jack Cox, George Kerr.

COLUMBIA CITY: Larwill 35–22 Washington Center; Columbia City 48–21 South Whitley; Jefferson Center 34–27 Etna; Churubusco 38–28 Coesse; Columbia City 48–34 Larwill; Churubusco 46–33 Jefferson Center; Columbia City 54–33 Churubusco. Officials: Von Crow, J. Clayton Hughes.

CONNERSVILLE: Everton 32–30 Brownsville; Brookville 62–11 Fairview; Connersville 46–15 Whitewater; Liberty 27–26 Harrison Twp.; Harrisburg 46–24 Bentonville; Alquina 36–27 Springfield Twp.; Orange 36–29 Laurel; Brookville 43–23 Everton; Connersville 45–17 Liberty; Harrisburg 23–18 Alquina; Brookville 46–19 Orange; Connersville 44–35 Harrisburg; Connersville 38–31 Brookville. Officials: Russell Bratton, Leonard Mayhugh, Wendell Heath.

CRAWFORDSVILLE: Alamo 34–21 New Richmond; Wingate 25–20 Ladoga; Crawfordsville 44–15 Linden; Darlington 35–23 Waynetown; Waveland 30–29 Bowers; New Ross 32–29 New Market; Wingate 38–26 Alamo; Darlington 25–21 Crawfordsville; Waveland 23–12 New Ross; Wingate 28–25 Darlington; Waveland 32–23 Wingate. Officials: Hal Harris, Frank Jarrell.

DANVILLE: Brownsburg 38–20 Amo; Danville 25–15 Plainfield; Clayton 20–16 North Salem; Pittsboro 21–17 Stilesville; New Winchester 37–16 Avon; Brownsburg 35–26 Lizton; Clayton 23–20 Danville; New Winchester 34–16 Pittsboro; Clayton 29–27 Brownsburg; New Winchester 35–25 Clayton. Officials: Robert Taylor, Raymond Trobaugh.

EAST CHICAGO: Edison 55–38 Crown Point; Hammond Tech 51–20 Wirt; Lowell 37–35 Calumet Twp. (ot); Washington 42–17 Merrillville; Clark 43–20 Griffith; Whiting 36–21 Hobart; Roosevelt 33–21 Dyer; Hammond 33–25 Edison; Tech 43–26 Lowell; Clark 35–20 Washington; Whiting 38–37 Roosevelt; Hammond 47–32 Tech; Whiting 29–27 Clark; Hammond 31–27 Whiting. Officials: LeRoy Shine, L. E. Fink, George Lambert.

ELKHART: Elkhart 44–33 Middlebury; Bristol 35–24 Jamestown; Wakarusa 31–26 Jefferson; Concord 50–29 Millersburg; Nappanee 37–32 New Paris; Elkhart 38–14 Goshen; Wakarusa 30–26 Bristol; Concord 38–36 Nappanee; Elkhart 26–20 Wakarusa; Elkhart 43–34 Concord. Officials: Donald Coar, Cecil Young.

EVANSVILLE: Griffin 44–14 Wadesville; Central 79–17 Mt. Vernon; Bosse 41–14 Cynthiana; Poseyville 36–28 New Harmony; Reitz 30–10 Stewartsville; Central 30–11 Griffin; Bosse 38–15 Poseyville; Central 27–20 Reitz; Bosse 28–22 Central. Officials: Harry Conover, Jr., Orville Jones.

FLORA: Burlington 23–22 Carrollton; Deer Creek 54–13 Adams Twp.; Cutler 25–16 Rockfield; Delphi 48–28 Camden; Flora 32–22 Burlington; Cutler 33–24 Deer Creek; Delphi

IHSAA Scores | 1930–1939

26–16 Flora; Delphi 32–26 Cutler. Officials: Joe Dienhart, Ray Bigler.

FORT BRANCH: Princeton 38–23 Oakland City; Fort Branch 23–21 Hazelton; Owensville 24–18 Mt. Olympus; Mackey 32–21 Patoka; Francisco 42–12 Haubstadt; Princeton 35–24 Fort Branch; Owensville 40–24 Mackey; Francisco 35–34 Princeton; Owensville 35–19 Francisco. Officials: Clarence Myles, Walter Ringer.

FORT WAYNE: Decatur 42–31 Woodburn; South Side 38–32 Central; Leo 49–28 Lafayette Central. Elmhurst 37–27 Monmouth; Hoagland 27–26 Harlan; New Haven 51–26 Arcola; North Side 35–18 Monroeville; Decatur 35–32 Huntertown (ot); South Side 34–17 Leo; Hoagland 30–28 Elmhurst. North Side 33–24 New Haven; South Side 36–25 Decatur; North Side 35–32 Hoagland; South Side 33–28 North Side. Officials: Lowell D. Sparks, George Williams, Walter A. Cook.

FRANKFORT: Colfax 31–21 Kirklin; Michigantown 35–30 Washington Twp.; Scircleville 23–19 Mulberry; Jackson Twp. 34–31 Forest; Frankfort 65–14 Sugar Creek; Rossville 34–29 Colfax; Michigantown 28–17 Scircleville; Frankfort 42–18 Jackson Twp.; Michigantown 37–35 Rossville; Frankfort 57–25 Michigantown. Officials: Daniel D. Guild, Reid H. McLain.

FRANKLIN: Van Buren Twp. 29–22 Nashville; Trafalgar 39–18 Jackson Twp.; Whiteland 47–23 Clark Twp.; Center Grove 34–18 Nineveh; Masonic Home 30–23 Greenwood; Franklin 35–15 Union Twp.; Trafalgar 46–20 Van Buren Twp.; Center Grove 27–25 Whiteland; Franklin 19–18 Masonic Home; Center Grove 46–32 Trafalgar; Franklin 38–22 Center Grove. Officials: Walter Fisher, Clyde Sutton.

GREENCASTLE: Greencastle 37–19 Fillmore; Bainbridge 22–17 Cloverdale; Russellville 39–21 Putnamville; Belle Union 29–19 Reelsville; Greencastle 36–20 Roachdale; Russellville 32–18 Bainbridge; Greencastle 46–33 Belle Union; Greencastle 42–28 Russellville. Officials: Robert Hold, Karl Dickerson.

GREENFIELD: New Palestine 27–21 McCordsville; Charlottesville 33–26 Eden; Fortville 28–27 Wilkinson; Maxwell 30–22 Mt. Comfort. Greenfield 32–9 Westland; New Palestine 27–26 Charlottesville; Maxwell 20–19 Fortville; Greenfield 34–25 New Palestine; Greenfield 39–18 Maxwell. Officials: Fred White, Stanley Porter.

GREENSBURG: Sandusky 31–21 Vernon; North Vernon 43–14 Clarksburg; Letts 31–21 Westport; Greensburg 27–12 St. Paul; Butlerville 22–18 Newpoint; Burney 43–18 Zenas; Jackson 38–27 Sandusky; North Vernon 58–22 Letts; Greensburg 56–15 Butlerville; Burney 27–14 Jackson; North Vernon 40–29 Greensburg; North Vernon 34–20 Burney. Officials: Russell Pickett, G. Elwood Hookey, B. R. Hosier.

HARTFORD CITY: Hartford City 41–19 Bryant; Portland 29–23 Gray; Dunkirk 29–25 Jefferson. Ridgeville 46–24 Poling; Montpelier 28–19 Roll; Redkey 29–27 Madison Twp.; Hartford City 28–20 Pennville; Portland 30–22 Dunkirk; Ridgeville 29–27 Montpelier; Redkey 36–31 Hartford City; Portland 41–28 Ridgeville; Redkey 35–31 Portland. Officials: H. Windmiller, H. D. McNew, Louis Briner.

HUNTINGBURG: Stendal 48–33 Dubois; Winslow 37–16 Birdseye; Spurgeon 32–29 Holland; Otwell 40–24 Cuzco; Ireland 27–19 Petersburg; Jasper 34–26 Huntingburg; Stendal 44–22 Winslow; Otwell 37–35 Spurgeon; Jasper 44–22 Ireland; Stendal 33–22 Otwell; Stendal 37–35 Jasper. Officials: Fred Alwood, John Lyskowinski.

HUNTINGTON: Salamonie Twp. 26–25 Lancaster Center; Andrews 37–13 Jefferson; Banquo 31–18 Polk Twp.; Union Twp. 47–23 Markle; Rock Creek 32–30 Bippus; Huntington

Tourney Time

31–30 Jackson Twp.; Huntington Twp. 27–17 Clear Creek; Salamonie Twp. 39–21 Andrews; Union 32–25 Banquo; Huntington 40–26 Rock Creek; Warren 39–19 Salamonie Twp.; Union 32–30 Huntington; Union 24–15 Warren. Officials: Aaron Belcher, Mark Williams, Otho Piper.

INDIANAPOLIS: Speedway 28–25 Manual; Southport 34–20 Tech; Warren Central 29–27 Ben Davis; Oaklandon 24–23 Castleton; Beech Grove 24–20 Franklin Twp.; Decatur Central 44–30 New Augusta; Shortridge 36–23 Broad Ripple; Washington 30–26 Lawrence; Southport 47–27 Speedway; Oaklandon 42–39 Warren Central; Decatur Central 31–23 Beech Grove; Shortridge 34–30 Washington; Southport 57–11 Oaklandon. Decatur Central 34–22 Shortridge; Southport 40–28 Decatur Central. Officials: John H. McClure, Clyde Gentry, Lundy Welborn.

JEFFERSONVILLE: New Albany 82–21 Mauckport; Charleston 36–27 Borden; Georgetown 33–21 Laconia; Silver Creek 45–18 Elizabeth; New Washington 33–21 Lanesville; Jeffersonville 47–15 New Amsterdam; Corydon 23–16 New Salisbury; Henryville 35–24 New Middletown; New Al6any 24–13 Charlestown; Silver Creek 27–13 Georgetown; Jeffersonville 38–14 New Washington; Corydon 44–19 Henryville; New Albany 35–24 Silver Creek; Jeffersonville 23–18 Corydon; New Albany 35–32 Jeffersonville. Officials: Robert Derrington, A. E. Pitcher, William E. Pointer.

KENDALLVILLE: Topeka 41–24 Lima; Cromwell 34–29 LaGrange; Wolcottville 29–25 Springfield Twp.; Kendallville 21–19 Scott; Avilla 22–20 Ligonier; Rome City 26–18 Brighton; Albion 21–15 Shipshewana; Wolf Lake 47–24 Wawaka; Topeka 22–18 Cromwell; Kendallville 45–27 Wolcottville; Avilla 39–31 Rome City; Wolf Lake 32–22 Albion; Kendallville 46–24 Topeka; Avilla 32–22 Wolf Lake; Kendallville 40–25 Avilla. Officials: R. Wayne Cunningham, Charles G. Garrett, George L. Russell.

KOKOMO: Greentown 29–17 New London; Russiaville 26–15 Howard Twp.; Jackson Twp. 23–16 Ervin Twp.; Clay Twp. 30–27 Union Twp.; Kokomo 49–28 W. Middleton; Greentown 44–28 Russiaville; Jackson Twp. 31–21 Clay Twp.; Kokomo 33–17 Greentown; Kokomo 45–22 Jackson Twp. Officials: Forrest Ballinger, Otto Crosley.

LAFAYETTE: Lafayette 46–21 Monitor; Montmorenci 22–19 Romney; West Lafayette 83–17 Dayton; Stockwell 37–28 Wea; Battle Ground 24–23 Clarks Hill; Lafayette 48–18 Montmorenci; West Point 36–24 Wea; Klondike 20–18 Buck Creek; West Lafayette 35–28 West Point; Klondike 40–31 Stockwell; Lafayette 34–21 Battle Ground; West Lafayette 39–17 Klondike; Lafayette 33–28 West Lafayette. Officials: Norman Dunlap, Millard Easton, Edmund Tully.

LAPORTE: Kingsbury 33–31 LaCrosse (ot); Union Mills 35–22 Clinton Twp.; Wanatah 32–20 Mill Creek; Michigan City 24–23 Stillwell; Rolling Prairie 33–13 Springfield; LaPorte 49–16 Union Twp.; Westville 24–16 Hanna; Union Mills 33–28 Kingsbury; Michigan City 36–22 Wanatah; LaPorte 35–20 Rolling Prairie; Westville 39–31 Union Mills; LaPorte 45–21 Michigan City; LaPorte 51–21 Westville. Officials: Allen H. Klinck, G. M. Kinzel, Ed Anglemeyer.

LEBANON: Thorntown 32–30 Pinnell; Jamestown 38–19 Whitestown; Zionsville 31–27 Dover; Lebanon 56–15 Advance; Central 30–23 Thorntown; Zionsville 42–31 Jamestown; Lebanon 57–35 Central; Lebanon 54–36 Zionsville. Officials: Layall Fisher, Albert Etter.

LOGANSPORT: Logansport 41–24 Onward; Young America 45–19 Lucerne; Galveston 32–26 Washington Twp.; Walton 40–26 New Waverly; Royal Center 38–23 Twelve Mile; Logansport 46–17 Metea; Young America 27–21 Galveston; Royal Center 38–29 Walton; Logansport 31–20 Young America; Logansport 34–27 Royal Center. Officials: J. Alvin Taylor, A. T. Krider.

MARION: Swayzee 22–16 Van Buren; Gas City 32–16 Fairmount; Sweetser 28–24 Jonesboro;

IHSAA Scores | 1930–1939

Marion 30–23 Jefferson; Swayzee 26–24 Gas City; Marion 52–14 Sweetser; Marion 48–30 Swayzee. Officials: Gerald Huey, Ralph Eades.

MARTINSVILLE: Mooresville 36–35 Morgantown; Stinesville 41–22 Eminence; Monrovia 37–25 Paragon; Martinsville 67–20 Unionville; Bloomington 42–24 Smithville; Mooresville 39–36 Ellettsville; Monrovia 35–29 Stinesville; Bloomington 33–13 Martinsville; Mooresville 37–31 Monrovia; Bloomington 52–48 Mooresville. Officials: T. R. Smith, Stephen Baker.

MISHAWAKA: South Bend Riley 52–27 Washington; Lakeville 44–24 Wilson; Madison Twp. 50–30 Walkerton; Mishawaka 30–24 North Liberty; New Carlisle 40–25 Green Twp.; Central 53–29 Washington-Clay; Riley 46–29 Lakeville; Mishawaka 50–21 Madison Twp.; Central 29–27 New Carlisle; Mishawaka 38–28 Riley; Mishawaka 41–35 Central. Officials: Dana Chandler, George Nulf.

MONTICELLO: Monticello 50–23 Burnettsville; Chalmers 33–20 Reynolds; Monon 32–18 Buffalo; Idaville 21–20 Round Grove (3ot); Brookston 26–24 Wolcott (ot); Monticello 36–32 Chalmers; Monon 28–20 Idaville; Monticello 26–19 Brookston; Monticello 32–25 Monon. Officials: Herbert Vaulk, George Vaulk.

MUNCIE: Eaton 32–12 Daleville; Gaston 49–28 Harrison; DeSoto 35–27 Selma; Royerton 18–17 Center; Burris 32–27 Cowan; Yorktown 39–20 Albany; Muncie 43–24 Eaton; Gaston 31–20 DeSoto; Burris 32–30 Royerton (ot); Muncie 35–26 Yorktown; Burris 43–25 Gaston; Burris 33–31 Muncie. Officials: Raymond Hobbs, Dean Malaska, G. P. Silver.

NEW CASTLE: Middletown 32–27 Straughn; New Castle 48–22 Mt. Summit; Mooreland 25–24 Lewisville; Kennard 30–25 Cadiz; Spiceland 43–15 New Lisbon; Knightstown 30–18 Sulphur Springs. New Castle 28–25 Middletown; Mooreland 35–23 Kennard; Spiceland 30–27 Knightstown; New Castle 34–31 Mooreland; New Castle 45–33 Spiceland. Officials: Gale Robinson, J. L. Mertz.

PERU: Peru 54–8 Butler; Deedsville 25–14 Macy. Bunker Hill 38–21 Gilead; Chili 32–25 Mexico; Clay 48–36 Converse; Peru 40–26 Amboy; Bunker Rill 49–33 Deedsville; Clay 29–14 Chili; Peru 36–25 Bunker Hill; Peru 27–25 Clay (ot). Officials: Ralph King, Leon Dulgar.

PLYMOUTH: LaPaz 33–30 San Pierre; Knox 47–23 West Twp.; Plymouth 39–17 Hamlet; Culver 28–22 Argos; Bremen 25–22 Bourbon; Tyner 36–27 Grovertown; North Judson 46–21 Tippecanoe; LaPaz 36–20 Center Twp.; Knox 31–21 Plymouth; Bremen 26–25 Culver; North Judson 35–30 Tyner; Knox 51–33 LaPaz; Bremen 29–26 North Judson; Knox 36–34 Bremen (ot). Officials: Harold McSwane, C. E. Baer, Hugh Bergstrom.

RENSSELAER: Remington 40–19 DeMotte; Morocco 36–19 Fair Oaks; Kentland 32–31 Mount Ayr; Wheatfield 44–24 Kankakee Twp.; Rensselaer 22–21 Goodland; Brook 29–25 Remington. Morocco 39–21 Kentland; Rensselaer 25–22 Wheatfield; Brook 31–23 Morocco; Rensselaer 34–19 Brook. Officials: Carl Burt, Condict A. Smith.

RICHMOND: Hagerstown 33–20 Economy; Whitewater 20–15 Boston; Milton 35–24 Williamsburg; Richmond 36–9 Webster; Cambridge City 28–20 Fountain City; Centerville 35–16 Greensfork; Hagerstown 31–26 Whitewater; Richmond 38–14 Milton; Centerville 37–12 Cambridge City; Richmond 31–18 Hagerstown; Richmond 36–29 Centerville. Officials: Al Jackson, John S. Walker.

ROCHESTER: Fulton 20–15 Talma; Medaryville 36–31 Star City; Akron 29–27 Rochester (ot); Pulaski 38–30 Leiters Ford; Monterey 39–34 Kewanna; Winamac 30–26 Richland Center; Grass Creek 42–28 Francesville; Medaryville 24–17 Fulton; Akron 28–21 Pulaski; Winamac

Tourney Time

29–27 Monterey (ot); Grass Creek 28–20 Medaryville; Winamac 30–29 Akron; Winamac 44–37 Grass Creek. Officials: Lawrence Gaunt, Harold Johnson, Earl Scott.

RUSHVILLE: Rushville 38–22 Morton Memorial; Mays 32–23 Gings; Raleigh 51–14 Glenwood; Carthage 19–12 Manilla; Arlington 28–27 New Salem; Rushville 24–20 Milroy; Raleigh 28–19 Mays; Arlington 27–20 Carthage; Rushville 35–20 Raleigh; Rushville 39–10 Arlington. Officials: Glenn Adams, Clifford Phillips.

SALEM: West Baden 45–22 Milltown; Marengo 24–17 Orleans; Hardinsburg 33–26 Little York; Salem 39–13 Campbellsburg; French Lick 36–30 Morgan Twp.; Paoli 28–27 Pekin. West Baden 26–21 Marengo; Salem 26–17 Hardinsburg; French Lick 28–19 Paoli; Salem 17–15 West Baden; Salem 37–29 French Lick. Officials: John Gant, William Coulter.

SCOTTSBURG: Deputy 45–18 Paris Crossing. Lexington 60–23 Marion Twp.; Hanover 36–29 North Madison; Madison 22–21 Austin; Scottsburg 18–17 Central; Dupont 37–24 Saluda; San Jacinto 35–15 Lovett; Lexington 29–26 Deputy; Madison 30–21 Hanover; Scottsburg 26–23 Dupont; Lexington 41–17 San Jacinto; Scottsburg 30–29 Madison; Scottsburg 37–23 Lexington. Officials: Gerald Bottorff, Max Thompson, H. Wilbur May.

SEYMOUR: Freetown 47–26 Scipio; Tampico 28–24 Vallonia; Seymour 62–12 Hayden; Medora 35–24 Crothersville; Clearspring 46–26 Cortland; Brownstown 68–16 Houston; Freetown 51–18 Tampico; Seymour 32–28 Medora; Brownstown 35–30 Clearspring; Seymour 50–18 Freetown; Seymour 36–28 Brownstown. Officials: Charles Henry, George Bender.

SHELBYVILLE: Fairland 30–29 Morristown (ot); Waldron 43–24 Mt. Auburn; Columbus 38–30 Shelbyville; Hope 32–30 Moral Twp.; Clifford 62–25 Flat Rock; Fairland 39–28 Boggstown; Waldron 43–32 Columbus; Clifford 30–20 Hope; Waldron 39–29 Fairland; Waldron 33–32 Clifford (ot). Officials: Hulett Crecelius, Thomas Baker.

SHERIDAN: Kempton 2–0 Goldsmith (forfeit); Prairie Twp. 37–21 Walnut Grove; Westfield 21–19 Windfall; Tipton 44–24 Fishers; Noblesville 26–19 Cicero; Atlanta 24–22 Sharpsville; Carmel 26–23 Arcadia; Sheridan 26–16 Kempton; Prairie Twp. 35–22 Westfield; Tipton 46–31 Noblesville; Carmel 31–22 Atlanta; Sheridan 39–21 Prairie Twp.; Tipton 31–25 Carmel; Tipton 33–26 Sheridan. Officials: H. P. Berkey, Everett W. Campbell, William Lucus..

SPENCER: Clay City 19–16 Brazil; Freedom 29–19 Patricksburg; Ashboro 24–16 Jefferson Twp.. Bowling Green 32–21 Cory; Spencer 31–20 Van Buren Twp.; Gosport 37–7 Quincy; Clay City 22–12 Posey Twp.; Ashboro 30–16 Freedom; Spencer 28–26 Bowling Green; Clay City 26–25 Gosport; Spencer 41–25 Ashboro; Spencer 18–17 Clay City. Officials: Herbert Robinson, Raymond Huffman, D. C. Moffett.

SULLIVAN: Hymera 39–38 Pleasantville; Sullivan 47–16 Carlisle; Farmersburg 19–18 Shelburn; Graysville 34–25 Merom; Union (Dugger) 52–27 New Lebanon; Hymera 33–23 Fairbanks; Sullivan 25–24 Farmersburg; Union 32–31 Graysville; Sullivan 47–28 Hymera; Sullivan 31–23. Union. Officials: Evan Crawley, Harry E. Briggs.

TERRE HAUTE: Glenn 30–25 Laboratory; Gerstmeyer 47–18 Riley; Honey Creek 30–29 Wiley; Garfield 31–18 Fontanet; Otter Creek 31–21 Pimento; Concannon 52–17 Prairie Creek; W. Terre Haute 45–21 Blackhawk; Gerstmeyer 41–30 Glenn; Garfield 27–22 Honey Creek. Concannon 19–17 Otter Creek; Gerstmeyer 54–34 W. Terre Haute; Garfield 38–28 Concannon; Garfield 29–22 Gerstmeyer; Officials: Fletcher Kerr, Cecil Tharp, William Kendall.

VALPARAISO: Chesterton 31–15 Wheeler; Tolleston 36–15 Hebron; Horace Mann 55–12 Washington Twp.; Valparaiso 26–21 Emerson; Wallace 45–17 Portage; Morgan Twp. 31–22 Kouts;

Liberty Center 26–19 Jackson Twp.; Froebel 51–12 Boone Grove; Tolleston 25–17 Chesterton; Valparaiso 28–22 Horace Mann; Wallace 35–15 Morgan Twp.; Froebel 54–23 Liberty Center; Valparaiso 29–21 Tolleston; Wallace 23–20 Froebel; Valparaiso 40–34 Wallace. Officials: W. E. Thurston, Forest M. Wood, Winston Ashley.

VINCENNES: Edwardsport 36–24 Monroe City; Vincennes 22–19 Decker; Sandborn 38–18 Oaktown; Decker Chapel 29–13 Fritchton; Wheatland 44–27 Bruceville; Bicknell 37–35 Freelandville; Vincennes 38–19 Edwardsport; Sandborn 30–26 Decker Chapel; Bicknell 33–31 Wheatland (ot); Vincennes 36–28 Sandborn; Vincennes 24–17 Bicknell. Officials: Irvin Springer, Clyde Castle.

WABASH: Laketon 33–31 Linlawn (ot); Chippewa 34–33 Lafontaine; Wabash 37–13 Chester Twp.; North Manchester 44–21 Lincolnville; Somerset 37–20 Lagro; Roann 31–21 Urbana; Laketon 35–23 Chippewa; Wabash 47–14 North Manchester; Roann 39–21 Somerset; Wabash 32–20 Laketon; Wabash 33–31 Roann. Officials: K. King Telle, L. R. Lenon.

WARSAW: Burket 27–22 Etna Green; Beaver Dam 40–35 Silver Lake; Claypool 34–30 Syracuse; Atwood 26–22 Sidney; Mentone 27–25 Warsaw; Pierceton 33–20 Leesburg; Milford 38–33 North Webster; Beaver Dam 36–25 Burket; Atwood 28–25 Claypool; Mentone 30–22 Pierceton; Milford 34–18 Beaver Dam; Mentone 38–15 Atwood; Mentone 34–24 Milford. Officials: Paul Bateman, M. E. Somers, Clive I. Markley.

WASHINGTON: Montgomery 26–20 Elnora; Plainville 59–15 Burns City; Shoals 22–21 Washington; Alfordsville 19–18 Odon; Loogootee 45–24 Epsom; Trinity Springs 28–20 Glendale; Plainville 46–31 Montgomery; Shoals 24–17 Alfordsville; Loogootee 49–13 Glendale; Plainville 24–20 Shoals; Loogootee 24–14 Plainville. Officials: Robert Hoffman, J. Ralph Black.

WINCHESTER: Lynn 30–12 Modoc; Stoney Creek 40–9 Lincoln; Saratoga 29–10 Losantville; Winchester 54–32 Wayne; Union City 29–21 Farmland; Parker 49–22 McKinley; Jackson 37–24 Green; Spartanburg 27–23 Huntsville; Stoney Creek 31–23 Lynn; Winchester 42–28 Saratoga; Parker 32–27 Union City; Jackson 30–27 Spartanburg; Stoney Creek 32–24 Winchester; Parker 34–25 Jackson; Parker 38–32 Stoney Creek. Officials: Harry R. Coolman, Phillip Eskew, Thomas Fields.

1939 REGIONALS

ANDERSON: New Winchester 34–32 Southport. Anderson 42–21 Greenfield; Anderson 40–31 New Winchester. Officials: Gale Robinson, Orville Jones.

AUBURN: Columbia City 31–29 Mentone; Auburn 34–27 Kendallville; Auburn 42–35 Columbia City. Officials: J. Alvin Taylor, A. T. Krider.

BLOOMINGTON: Garfield 30–28 Spencer (ot); Bloomington 39–29 Bloomfield; Garfield 29–24 Bloomington. Officials: William Pointer, George Bender.

EVANSVILLE: Bosse 36–23 Lynnville; Owensville 30–26 Dale; Bosse 28–26 Owensville. Officials: Frank Jarrell, Norman Dunlap.

GARY: LaPorte 27–20 Hammond; Rensselaer 28–27 Valparaiso; LaPorte 40–34 Rensselaer. Officials: T. R. Smith, J. Clayton Hughes.

GREENCASTLE: Greencastle 45–25 Pine Village; Clinton 24–19 Waveland; Greencastle 29–21 Clinton. Officials: Thomas Baker, Fred Alwood.

GREENSBURG: Franklin 43–19 Waldron; North Vernon 31–27 Scottsburg; Franklin 29–27

Tourney Time

North Vernon (ot). Officials: John H. McClure, Lundy Welborn.
   HUNTINGTON: Ossian 35–27 Union Twp.; South Side 29–26 Redkey; Ossian 42–28 South Side. Officials: Glen Adams, Charles G. Garrett.
   LAFAYETTE: Frankfort 44–31 Lafayette; Lebanon 27–26 Oxford; Frankfort 58–25 Lebanon. Officials: Carl Burt, C. O. Walls.
   LOGANSPORT: Logansport 28–25 Peru; Monticello 30–28 Delphi; Logansport 43–34 Monticello. Officials: L. E. Fink, George L. Russell.
   MARION: Kokomo 35–26 Marion; Tipton 40–30 Wabash; Kokomo 56–44 Tipton. Officials: Winston Ashley, Lowell Sparks.
   MUNCIE: New Castle 43–36 Parker; Burris 45–30 Richmond; Burris 35–31 New Castle. Officials: Allen H. Klinck, Carl Dickerson.
   NEW ALBANY: Salem 32–28 Mitchell; Seymour 34–26 New Albany; Salem 25–18 Seymour. Officials: Irvin Springer, Clyde Castle.
   PLYMOUTH: Mishawaka 36–26 Knox; Elkhart 43–20 Winamac; Elkhart 27–22 Mishawaka. Officials: George Williams, Stanley Porter.
   RUSHVILLE: Aurora 46–38 Connersville; Rushville 36–34 Osgood; Aurora 36–24 Rushville. Officials: Nate Kaufman, Hal Harris.
   VINCENNES: Stendal 30–23 Loogootee; Vincennes 37–22 Sullivan; Vincennes 35–24 Stendal. Officials: T. Noble Lyons, Reid H. McLain.
   1939 SEMI–FINALS
   EVANSVILLE: Vincennes 28–18 Salem; Bosse 31–23 Garfield; Bosse 37–22 Vincennes. Officials: Nate Kaufman, T. Noble Lyons.
   HAMMOND: Frankfort 38–31 LaPorte; Elkhart 44–28 Logansport; Frankfort 42–32 Elkhart. Officials: Thomas Baker, Carl Dickerson.
   INDIANAPOLIS: Anderson 32–25 Greencastle; Franklin 27–25 Aurora (ot); Franklin 16–13 Anderson. Officials: Glenn Adams, Carl Burt.
   MUNCIE: Burris 31–26 Auburn; Kokomo 30–29 Ossian; Burris 37–28 Kokomo. Officials: Winston Ashley, L. E. Fink.

1939 FINALS—March 25
   INDIANAPOLIS (Butler Fieldhouse): Frankfort 32–28 Bosse; Franklin 31–25 Burris; Frankfort 36–22 Franklin. Officials: Nate Kaufman, Tom Baker.

1940–1949

1940 SECTIONALS
   ANDERSON: Lapel 37–34 Summitville; Anderson 13–4 Frankton; Pendleton 36–33 Elwood; Alexandria 48–19 Markleville; Lapel 24–23 Anderson; Alexandria 23–16 Pendleton; Lapel 35–34 Alexandria. Officials: Karl Dickerson, Cecil Tharp.

IHSAA Scores | 1940–1949

ATTICA: Williamsport 50–24 West Lebanon; Covington 47–20 Hillsboro; Pine Village 37–25 Perrysville; Kingman 29–10 Mellott; Attica 39–25 Veedersburg; Wallace 40–20 Newtown; Williamsport 32–26 Covington; Kingman 22–19 Pine Village; Attica 48–17 Wallace; Kingman 34–29 Williamsport; Attica 43–32 Kingman. Officials: Reid H. McLain, G. W. Strole.

BATESVILLE: Center Twp. (Osgood) 34–27 Sunman; Napoleon 47–46 Milan; Holton 32–26 Versailles; Batesville 32–19 Cross Plains; Center Twp. 32–21 New Marion; Napoleon 31–28 Holton; Batesville 41–28 Center Twp.; Batesville 63–25 Napoleon. Officials: Otto Crosley, Forrest Ballinger.

BLOOMFIELD: Worthington 25–22 Owensburg; Jasonville 44–30 Marco; Solsberry 24–18 Scotland; Linton 55–15 Newberry; Bloomfield 28–22 Switz City; Midland 50–36 Lyons; Jasonville 41–21 Worthington; Linton 31–29 Solsberry (ot); Bloomfield 46–27 Midland; Jasonville 39–38 Linton; Bloomfield 36–26 Jasonville. Officials: Clarence B. Tolbert, Walter N. Ringer.

BLOOMINGTON: Smithville 42–24 Paragon; Martinsville 55–38 Eminence; Ellettsville 27–25 Morgantown (ot); Monrovia 47–45 Mooresville (ot); Bloomington 48–18 Unionville; Smithville 37–25 Stinesville; Martinsville 53–26 Ellettsville; Bloomington 53–27 Monrovia; Martinsville 35–17 Smithville; Bloomington 31–28 Martinsville. Officials: Herbert H. Edwards, George T. Bender.

BLUFFTON: Liberty Center 32–28 Bluffton; Chester Center 37–34 Rockcreek; Lancaster Central 28–26 Ossian; Union Center 34–21 Petroleum; Liberty Center 49–23 Jackson; Chester Center 26–19 Lancaster Central; Liberty Center 37–33 Union Center; Chester Center 28–27 Liberty Center. Officials: Harold McSwane, Condict A. Smith.

BOONVILLE: Elberfeld 22–14 Newburgh; Boonville 50–13 Selvin; Lynnville 48–13 Yankeetown; Millersburg 26–23 Chandler; Tennyson 33–23 Folsomville; Boonville 35–24 Elberfeld; Lynnville 48–16 Millersburg; Boonville 53–28 Tennyson; Lynnville 32–30 Boonville. Officials: Hulett Crecelius, August Banko.

BUTLER: Auburn 44–13 Butler; Fremont 31–22 Concord Twp.; Spencerville 45–35 Metz; Pleasant Lake 39–32 Salem Center; Churubusco 38–33 Ashley; Waterloo 43–13 Hamilton; Garrett 54–35 Angola; Orland 40–33 Scott Center; Auburn 48–17 Fremont; Spencerville 44–42 Pleasant Lake; Waterloo 49–28 Churubusco; Garrett 55–26 Orland; Auburn 47–28 Spencerville; Garrett 38–27 Waterloo; Garrett 42–36 Auburn. Officials: Walter E. Thurston, Russell H. Arndt, Forest M. Wood.

CLINTON: Newport 26–23 Hillsdale; Bridgeton 39–24 Saint Bernice; Marshall 43–32 Green Twp.; Clinton 34–19 Rosedale; Rockville 44–24 Tangier; Bloomingdale 33–32 Cayuga; Montezuma 32–29 Mecca; Dana 36–30 Bellmore; Bridgeton 47–33 Newport; Clinton 32–22 Marshall; Rockville 36–22 Bloomingdale; Dana 34–32 Montezuma; Clinton 39–37 Bridgeton; Rockville 45–20 Dana; Rockville 43–21 Clinton. Officials: G. Elwood Hookey, Albert Etter, Evan Crawley.

CONNERSVILLE: Kitchel 39–22 Springfield Twp.; Bentonville 29–28 Fairview; Brookville 44–33 Laurel; Whitewater 35–29 Everton; Brownsville 28–19 Alquina; Connersville 51–8 Orange; Harrisburg 30–24 Liberty; Kitchel 34–19 Bentonville; Brookville 43–18 Whitewater; Connersville 51–24 Brownsville; Kitchel 27–21 Harrisburg; Connersville 44–22 Brookville; Connersville 47–33 Kitchel. Officials: Stephen Baker, Aaron Belcher, Herbert P. Dukes.

CRAWFORDSVILLE: Darlington 32–30 Wingate; New Market 44–27 Waveland; New Ross 35–17 Alamo; Waynetown 35–31 New Richmond; Linden 34–33 Ladoga; Crawfordsville

34–25 Bowers; New Market 21–17 Darlington; Waynetown 34–25 New Ross; Crawfordsville 33–15 Linden; New Market 36–31 Waynetown; Crawfordsville 40–32 New Market. Officials: T. R. Smith, H. D. McNew.

DANVILLE: Plainfield 30–19 Amo; Pittsboro 25–22 Brownsburg; North Salem 24–20 Stilesville; Danville 39–22 Avon; Lizton 32–25 New Winchester; Clayton 21–19 Plainfield; Pittsboro 19–14 North Salem; Lizton 34–32 Danville; Pittsboro 24–23 Clayton; Pittsboro 22–19 Lizton. Officials: Robert H. Simison, D. C. Moffett.

DECATUR: Monmouth 29–17 Jefferson Twp.; Berne 26–24 Decatur; Pleasant Mills 39–21 Hartford Twp.; Geneva 39–36 Monroe; Kirkland 41–25 Monmouth; Pleasant Mills 38–24 Berne; Kirkland 39–35 Geneva; Pleasant Mills 39–21 Kirkland. Officials: Vaughn Crow, Donald K. Coar.

DELPHI: Burlington 26–11 Deer Creek; Delphi 30–23 Rockfield; Cutler 38–29 Camden; Flora 30–21 Adams Twp.; Burlington 32–18 Carrollton; Cutler 43–27 Delphi; Burlington 29–28 Flora; Cutler 30–23 Burlington. Officials: Dan Guild, Walter A. Cook.

EVANSVILLE: Reitz 40–21 Bosse; New Harmony 24–20 Stewartsville; Central 38–16 Cynthiana; Wadesville 30–21 Griffin; Mount Vernon 28–27 Poseyville; Reitz 26–23 New Harmony; Central 52–19 Wadesville; Reitz 45–15 Mount Vernon; Central 30–25 Reitz. Officials: Robert J. Hoffman, Harry Conover.

FORT WAYNE: Monroeville 22–20 New Haven; South Side 58–33 Lafayette Center; Leo 49–27 Jefferson Center; Hoagland 35–33 Huntertown; Central 36–22 Arcola; Elmhurst 45–31 Woodburn; North Side 70–27 Coesse; Columbia City 43–32 Harlan; South Side 52–14 Monroeville; Leo 51–26 Hoagland; Central 66–39 Elmhurst; North Side 51–29 Columbia City; South Side 44–28 Leo; North Side 27–24 Central; South Side 32–27 North Side. Officials: J. Alvin Taylor, A. T. Krider, Dana Chandler.

FRANKFORT: Frankfort 41–19 Mulberry; Washington Twp. 25–21 Scircleville; Rossville 28–22 Sugar Creek; Jackson Twp. 38–20 Kirklin; Michigantown 38–29 Forest; Frankfort 40–24 Colfax; Rossville 38–22 Washington Twp.; Michigantown 40–33 Jackson Twp.; Frankfort 36–11 Rossville; Frankfort 36–27 Michigantown. Officials: Phil N. Eskew, Frank Jarrell.

FRANKLIN: Center Grove 35–17 Clark Twp.; Masonic Home 33–26 Nineveh; Jackson Twp. 20–17 Trafalgar; Union Twp. 26–20 Edinburg; Greenwood 40–22 Whiteland; Nashville 38–16 Van Buren Twp.; Franklin 41–25 Center Grove; Masonic Home 37–25 Jackson Twp.; Greenwood 44–36 Union Twp.; Franklin 47–20 Nashville; Greenwood 36–20 Masonic Home; Greenwood 33–29 Franklin. Officials: Ralph M. King, Raymond J. Trobaugh, Allen H. Klinck.

GREENCASTLE: Bainbridge 40–17 Fillmore; Roachdale 56–28 Reelsville; Belle Union 19–17 Cloverdale; Greencastle 49–14 Putnamville; Bainbridge 36–30 Russellville; Roachdale 39–30 Belle Union; Bainbridge 32–29 Greencastle; Bainbridge 33–22 Roachdale. Officials: George L. Kerr, Winston Ashley.

GREENFIELD: Greenfield 38–23 Howe (Indianapolis); New Palestine 31–30 Maxwell; Eden 32–29 Wilkinson; Charlottesville 42–40 Westland. Mount Comfort 28–17 McCordsville; Greenfield 23–21 Fortville; Eden 22–20 New Palestine; Charlottesville 46–27 Mount Comfort. Greenfield 42–10 Eden; Greenfield 37–28 Charlottesville. Officials: Fred Pierson, Fred R. White.

GREENSBURG: Newpoint 26–15 Burney; Clarksburg 31–12 Vernon; Sandusky 62–33 Zenas; Greensburg 34–32 Jackson (ot); Saint Paul 37–14 Butlerville; North Vernon 39–19 Sandcreek; Clarksburg 32–20 Newpoint; Greensburg 37–24 Sandusky; North Vernon 26–23

Saint Paul; Greensburg 31–27 Clarksburg; North Vernon 32–30 Greensburg. Officials: Nate Kaufman, Everett W. Campbell.

HAMMOND: Roosevelt 58–31 Gary Edison; Clark 43–31 Merrillville; Tech 37–21 Dyer; Washington 24–23 Hammond High; Whiting 45–36 Calumet Twp.; Wirt 31–30 Hobart; Griffith 43–17 Crown Point; East Gary Edison 34–23 Lowell; Clark 25–21 Roosevelt; Tech 36–28 Washington; Whiting 63–34 Wirt; East Gary Edison 33–20 Griffith; Tech 31–29 Clark; Whiting 41–34 East Gary Edison; Tech 40–35 Whiting. Officials: Ed Anglemyer, LeRoy Shine, J. Clayton Hughes.

HARTFORD CITY: Pennville 32–28 Ridgeville; Montpelier 45–33 Redkey; Bryant 16–12 Poling; Portland 42–26 Dunkirk; Gray 29–17 Jefferson; Madison Twp. 41–35 Roll; Pennville 29–28 Hartford City; Montpelier 17–15 Bryant; Portland 35–23 Gray; Madison Twp. 28–21 Pennville; Portland 22–20 Montpelier; Portland 33–28 Madison Twp. Officials: James R. Craw, Harry Coolman, Lundy Welborn.

HUNTINGTON: Salamonie Twp. 27–18 Markle; Clear Creek 39–28 Jefferson Twp.; Andrews 27–25 Union Twp.; Rock Creek Center 23–18 Banquo; Lancaster Center 41–23 Polk Twp.; Bippus 47–28 Washington Center; South Whitley 23–19 Huntington Twp.; Huntington 44–33 Jackson Twp.; Salamonie Twp. 31–25 Clear Creek; Andrews 34–19 Rock Creek Center; Lancaster Center 49–30 Bippus; Huntington 57–18 South Whitley; Salamonie Twp. 26–24 Andrews; Huntington 35–26 Lancaster Center; Huntington 39–21 Salamonie Twp. Officials: Herman Byers, Otho L. Piper, Thomas Fields.

INDIANAPOLIS: Southport 46–23 New Augusta; Decatur Central 24–22 Tech; Washington 31–27 Speedway; Warren Central 35–28 Oaklandon; Shortridge 32–22 Broad Ripple; Castleton 27–23 Lawrence; Manual 30–20 Beech Grove; Franklin Twp. 30–23 Ben Davis; Decatur Central 38–22 Southport; Washington 33–24 Warren Central; Shortridge 66–16 Castleton; Manual 34–24 Franklin Twp.; Decatur Central 46–28 Washington; Shortridge 31–22 Manual; Shortridge 30–26 Decatur Central. Officials: B. R. Hosier, Norman Dunlap, Orville Jones.

JEFFERSONVILLE: New Albany 58–14 New Amsterdam; Jeffersonville 51–28 Mauckport; Borden 49–35 Lanesville; Silver Creek 66–19 New Middletown; New Salisbury 33–30 Laconia; Henryville 29–26 Elizabeth; Charlestown 31–22 Georgetown; Corydon 29–19 New Washington; New Albany 21–18 Jeffersonville; Silver Creek 50–26 Borden; Henryville 33–26 New Salisbury; Charlestown 25–23 Corydon; New Albany 41–30 Silver Creek; Charlestown 44–26 Henryville; New Albany 41–21 Charlestown. Officials: Irvin Springer, Charles A. Jensen, Clyde Castle.

KENDALLVILLE: Shipshewana 37–23 Lima; LaGrange 47–31 Wawaka; Brighton 24–14 Albion; Wolf Lake 34–23 Topeka; Kendallville 39–17 Scott Center; Avilla 55–24 Cromwell; Rome City 31–24 Ligonier; Wolcottville 56–20 Springfield Twp.; LaGrange 52–29 Shipshewana; Wolf Lake 41–24 Brighton; Kendallville 34–32 Avilla; Rome City 34–31 Wolcottville; Wolf Lake 19–18 LaGrange; Kendallville 33–21 Rome City; Kendallville 38–18 Wolf Lake. Officials: R. W. Warring, Cecil E. Young, Lawrence Gaunt.

KOKOMO: New London 43–23 West Middleton; Greentown 34–24 Ervin Twp.; Russiaville 26–12 Clay Twp.; Union Twp. 42–26 Jackson Twp.; Kokomo 67–23 Howard Twp.; Greentown 34–21 New London; Union Twp. 32–29 Russiaville; Kokomo 48–32 Greentown; Kokomo 90–12 Union Twp. Officials: Harold S. Johnson, Clay Layman.

LAFAYETTE: Battle Ground 26–24 Klondike; Romney 37–18 Clarks Hill; Wea 31–26 Stockwell; West Lafayette 35–31 Jackson Twp.; Montmorenci 40–25 Monitor; Lafayette 56–24

Tourney Time

Buck Creek; West Point 56–17 Dayton; Battle Ground 31–28 Romney; West Lafayette 19–16 Wea; Lafayette 40–22 Montmorenci; West Point 31–22 Battle Ground; Lafayette 34–28 West Lafayette; Lafayette 44–19 West Point. Officials: Norris D. Ward, Claron Veller, O. Don Edmonds.

LAWRENCEBURG: Patriot 22–21 Vevay; Lawrenceburg 33–23 Rising Sun; Dillsboro 25–22 Moores Hill; Aurora 52–38 Guilford; Patriot 38–23 Bright; Lawrenceburg 39–28 Dillsboro; Patriot 29–20 Aurora; Lawrenceburg 48–17 Patriot. Officials: Paul Cly, Max Thompson.

LEBANON: Dover 35–33 Whitestown; Zionsville 51–17 Advance; Jamestown 26–22 Pinnell; Thorntown 39–33 Central; Lebanon 76–34 Dover; Zionsville 42–29 Jamestown; Lebanon 55–20 Thorntown; Lebanon 38–28 Zionsville. Officials: George W. Yarnell, L. R. Lenon.

LOGANSPORT: New Waverly 36–35 Lucerne; Washington Twp. 41–29 Twelve Mile; Walton 30–20 Metea; Royal Center 39–29 Galveston; Logansport 36–29 Young America; Onward 36–29 New Waverly; Washington Twp. 31–29 Walton; Logansport 48–26 Royal Center; Onward 32–27 Washington Twp.; Logansport 58–22 Onward. Officials: George R. Lambert, K. King Telle.

MARION: Fairmount 27–23 Sweetser; Marion 35–20 Jonesboro; Gas City 26–17 Swayzee; Van Buren 31–25 Jefferson; Marion 34–22 Fairmount; Gas City 39–34 Van Buren; Marion 30–22 Gas City. Officials: Thomas Baker, Robert P. Cline.

MICHIGAN CITY: Union Mills 24–19 Wanatah; LaPorte 47–28 Kingsbury; LaCrosse 36–23 Westville; Michigan City 48–16 Stillwell; Union Twp. 36–28 Mill Creek; Springfield Twp. 35–16 Hanna; Rolling Prairie 58–19 Clinton Twp.; LaPorte 38–27 Union Mills; Michigan City 53–23 LaCrosse; Union Twp. 37–23 Springfield Twp.; LaPorte 40–24 Rolling Prairie; Michigan City 49–17 Union Twp.; LaPorte 36–34 Michigan City. Officials: George W. Nulf, Harrison P. Berkey, Herman E. Schuler.

MISHAWAKA: Lakeville 43–34 North Liberty; South Bend Central 29–13 New Carlisle; Mishawaka 54–31 Madison Twp.; Washington 43–32 Washington-Clay; Greene Twp. 28–26 Wilson; Riley 51–14 Walkerton; Central 49–15 Lakeville; Washington 25–17 Mishawaka; Riley 40–24 Greene Twp.; Central 46–26 Washington; Riley 33–31 Central. Officials: R. W. Cunningham, Charles G. Garrett.

MITCHELL: Williams 33–28 Heltonville; Needmore 21–19 Tunnelton; Bedford 46–22 Fayetteville; Oolitic 55–10 Huron; Springfield 35–32 Shawswick; Mitchell 34–16 Williams; Bedford 47–19 Needmore; Springville 28–27 Oolitic; Mitchell 27–13 Bedford; Mitchell 64–34 Springville. Officials: Robert Derrington, Fred W. Alwood.

MONTICELLO: Monon 40–27 Wolcott; Brookston 46–27 Idaville; Buffalo 35–13 Burnettsville; Round Grove 31–25 Chalmers; Monticello 38–24 Reynolds; Brookston 45–22 Monon; Round Grove 27–20 Buffalo; Brookston 41–38 Monticello; Brookston 44–27 Round Grove. Officials: William R. Kendall, J. L. Mertz.

MUNCIE: Gaston 35–23 Cowan; Burris 34–20 Royerton; Central 50–30 Albany; Daleville 35–29 Yorktown; DeSoto 27–25 Selma; Center 58–20 Eaton; Gaston 30–20 Harrison Twp.; Burris 41–33 Central; Daleville 36–20 DeSoto; Center 27–25 Gaston; Burris 48–20 Daleville; Burris 43–34 Center. Officials: Harold M. Porter, Doxie Reeves, Clyde Gentry.

NAPPANEE: Goshen 34–30 Elkhart; Middlebury 33–26 Millersburg; Concord 38–33 New Paris; Nappanee 30–28 Wakarusa (ot); Jamestown 26–21 Jefferson; Goshen 41–23 Bristol; Concord 41–33 Middlebury; Nappanee 37–23 Jamestown; Concord 41–36 Goshen; Nappanee 27–26 Concord. Officials: Charles E. Baer, Hugh Bergstrom.

NEW CASTLE: Middletown 45–26 Cadiz; Lewisville 31–30 Straughn; Knightstown 37–35

Sulphur Springs; Kennard 34–23 New Lisbon; New Castle 38–25 Spiceland; Mooreland 60–23 Mount Summit; Middletown 28–27 Lewisville; Knightstown 25–19 Kennard; New Castle 47–32 Mooreland; Middletown 30–28 Knightstown; New Castle 39–34 Middletown. Officials: Clifford N. Phillips, Raymond Huffman.

OWENSVILLE: Hazleton 36–28 Mackey; Francisco 22–21 Patoka; Mount Olympus 29–28 Fort Branch; Princeton 44–24 Haubstadt; Oakland City 40–23 Owensville; Francisco 22–19 Hazleton; Princeton 36–28 Mount Olympus; Oakland City 26–24 Francisco; Oakland City 31–30 Princeton. Officials: Fred Wilder, Gerald Aishe.

OXFORD: Freeland Park 51–24 Raub; Wadena 35–19 Earl Park; Boswell 45–27 Gilboa Twp.; Otterbein 37–28 Ambia; Fowler 53–12 Pine Twp.; Freeland Park 35–28 Oxford; Boswell 32–30 Wadena (ot); Fowler 35–33 Otterbein; Freeland Park 36–26 Boswell; Freeland Park 36–23 Fowler. Officials: Clarence Myles, James F. Conover.

PAOLI: Hardinsburg 20–19 Campbellsburg; Orleans 60–38 Little York; Marengo 50–16 English; Morgan Twp. 24–22 French Lick; Paoli 36–28 Pekin; Salem 46–25 Milltown; West Baden 27–22 Hardinsburg; Orleans 31–25 Marengo; Paoli 46–30 Morgan Twp.; Salem 35–22 West Baden; Paoli 28–27 Orleans; Salem 36–19 Paoli. Officials: Clarence Riggs, Carl B. Jerger, J. Ralph Black.

PERU: Clay Twp. 37–29 Peru; Amboy 32–22 Bunker Hill; Mexico 33–31 Deedsville; Converse 55–31 Butler; Macy 25–21 Gilead; Clay Twp. 32–27 Chili; Amboy 45–20 Mexico; Converse 44–34 Macy; Amboy 23–20 Clay Twp.; Amboy 27–25 Converse (ot). Officials: Layall Fisher, Forrest Roe.

PETERSBURG: Petersburg 34–30 Otwell; Ireland 55–39 Jasper; Stendal 43–28 Holland; Winslow 29–28 Dubois (ot); Huntingburg 55–24 Spurgeon; Petersburg 52–24 Cuzco; Ireland 48–29 Stendal; Huntingburg 40–28 Winslow; Petersburg 20–19 Ireland; Huntingburg 36–22 Petersburg. Officials; William M. Coulter, Charles W. Henry.

PIERCETON: Leesburg 37–16 Claypool; Silver Lake 24–19 Atwood; Burket 34–31 Etna Twp.; Beaver Dam 27–25 Pierceton; Sidney 26–24 Larwill; Milford 38–34 Syracuse; Etna Green 22–13 Warsaw; Mentone 25–23 North Webster; Leesburg 38–23 Silver Lake; Beaver Dam 47–22 Burket; Sidney 46–31 Milford; Mentone 35–25 Etna Green; Beaver Dam 48–45 Leesburg; Mentone 35–25 Sidney; Mentone 20–11 Beaver Dam. Officials: Don Veller, Emery L. Druckamiller, Paul Bateman.

PLYMOUTH: North Judson 34–17 Tippecanoe; Bourbon 45–26 West Twp.; LaPaz 44–20 Center Twp.; Plymouth 41–24 Knox; Bremen 32–30 Culver; Hamlet 28–25 Argos; Tyner 28–27 San Pierre; North Judson 54–22 Grovertown; LaPaz 21–18 Bourbon; Plymouth 39–24 Bremen; Hamlet 38–24 Tyner; LaPaz 31–26 North Judson; Plymouth 26–19 Hamlet; Plymouth 39–22 LaPaz. Officials: H. Windmiller, Louis A. Briner, M. E. Somers.

RENSSELAER: Rensselaer 35–14 Mount Ayr; Morocco 37–20 Tefft; Remington 32–20 DeMotte; Kentland 26–23 Wheatfield; Brook 31–20 Fair Oaks; Rensselaer 33–12 Goodland; Remington 26–22 Morocco; Brook 40–24 Kentland; Rensselaer 29–27 Remington; Brook 35–29 Rensselaer. Officials: Max Hildreth, Robert N. Taylor.

RICHMOND: Economy 27–12 Milton; Hagerstown 29–24 Greens Fork; Centerville 37–24 Boston; Lincoln 29–26 Whitewater; Webster 31–24 Fountain City; Richmond 40–22 Williamsburg; Hagerstown 32–17 Economy; Centerville 34–21 Cambridge City; Richmond 50–25 Webster; Hagerstown 41–30 Centerville; Richmond 46–28 Hagerstown. Officials: Clyde

S. Sutton, William N. Reimann.

RUSHVILLE: Morton Memorial 43–32 Arlington; Carthage 37–18 Raleigh; Rushville 61–20 Manilla; Milroy 26–21 Mays; Morton Memorial 43–16 New Salem; Rushville 48–14 Carthage; Morton Memorial 44–29 Milroy; Rushville 50–21 Morton Memorial. Officials: Mark Williams, Russell L. Bratton.

SCOTTSBURG: Dupont 21–18 Paris Crossing (ot); Madison 36–21 Saluda; Central 39–28 Hanover; Scottsburg 32–23 Deputy; North Madison 27–19 Austin; Dupont 33–23 Lexington; Madison 45–26 Central; Scottsburg 38–22 North Madison; Madison 29–26 Dupont; Madison 41–22 Scottsburg. Officials: John Lyskowinski, Myer Schreiber.

SEYMOUR: Seymour 51–23 Scipio; Tampico 25–22 Crothersville; Brownstown 49–22 Clearspring; Medora 24–21 Cortland; Freetown 45–18 Hayden; Seymour 57–18 Vallonia; Brownstown 47–22 Tampico; Medora 30–24 Freetown; Seymour 39–14 Brownstown; Seymour 34–16 Medora. Officials: John Blankenship, A. E. Pitcher.

SHELBYVILLE: Fairland 37–33 Clifford; Columbus 52–22 Boggstown; Hope 22–20 Mount Auburn; Shelbyville 26–16 Flat Rock; Morristown 27–25 Waldron; Moral Twp. 41–26 Fairland; Columbus 41–17 Hope; Shelbyville 22–21 Morristown; Columbus 40–32 Moral Twp.; Columbus 27–24 Shelbyville. Officials: Al Jackson, Leonard Mayhugh.

SPENCER: Cory 33–29 Bowling Green; Van Buren Twp. 28–24 Patricksburg; Gosport 35–27 Jefferson Twp.; Posey Twp. 43–23 Ashboro; Spencer 31–8 Freedom; Clay City 45–21 Quincy; Brazil 39–27 Cory; Gosport 38–28 Van Buren Twp.; Posey Twp. 28–15 Spencer; Clay City 25–20 Brazil; Gosport 22–16 Posey Twp.; Gosport 23–16 Clay City. Officials: Leon Dulgar, Robert Hold, Rollie Kirchoff.

SULLIVAN: Hymera 35–29 Pleasantville; Farmersburg 18–16 New Lebanon; Sullivan 48–20 Merom; Dugger 31–29 Carlisle (ot); Graysville 33–27 Shelburn; Hymera 40–18 Fairbanks; Sullivan 56–20 Farmersburg; Dugger 22–21 Graysville; Hymera 37–34 Sullivan; Dugger 36–24 Hymera. Officials: Arad A. McCutchan, Edmund Tully.

TELL CITY: Gentryville 46–18 Bristow; Cannelton 24–16 Troy; Rockport 29–21 Grandview; Dale 55–18 Oil Twp.; Chrisney 39–23 Luce Twp.; Tell City 50–28 Gentryville; Cannelton 31–13 Rockport; Dale 37–18 Chrisney; Cannelton 24–23 Tell City; Dale 29–22 Cannelton. Officials: John B. Wilson, J. Clinton Dougherty.

TERRE HAUTE: Wiley 40–14 Blackhawk; Fontanet 39–29 Laboratory; Otter Creek 33–22 Honey Creek; Gerstmeyer 30–24 Riley; Prairie Creek 30–28 Glenn; West Terre Haute 45–22 New Goshen; Garfield 27–13 Pimento; Fontanet 44–27 Wiley; Otter Creek 26–25 Gerstmeyer; West Terre Haute 37–36 Prairie Creek; Garfield 33–20 Fontanet; West Terre Haute 26–24 Otter Creek; Garfield 36–31 West Terre Haute. Officials: G. P. Silver, Dean Malaska, Raymond Hobbs.

TIPTON: Westfield 20–17 Carmel; Kempton 39–17 Windfall; Tipton 55–31 Goldsmith; Arcadia 40–17 Fishers; Sheridan 32–14 Noblesville; Atlanta 28–24 Sharpsville; Walnut Grove 30–28 Prairie Twp.; Cicero 28–24 Westfield; Kempton 31–24 Tipton; Sheridan 31–18 Arcadia; Atlanta 19–17 Walnut Grove; Kempton 28–26 Cicero; Sheridan 27–21 Atlanta; Sheridan 27–25 Kempton. Officials: Walter Floyd, Gerald L. Huey, Clive Markley.

VALPARAISO: Tolleston (Gary) 53–15 Chesterton; Froebel (Gary) 58–14 Kouts; Wheeler 34–20 Morgan Twp.; Wallace (Gary) 34–30 Valparaiso; Portage 21–20 Washington Twp.; Liberty 25–13 Jackson Twp.; Horace Mann (Gary) 44–18 Boone Grove; Emerson (Gary) 47–17 Hebron;

Froebel 40–24 Tolleston ; Wallace 54–31 Wheeler; Portage 29–27 Liberty; Horace Mann 20–16 Emerson; Froebel 29–21 Wallace ; Horace Mann 29–13 Portage; Froebel 17–15 Horace Mann. Officials: George R. Vaulk,; J. H. McClure, L. E. Fink.

VINCENNES: Vincennes 55–19 Wheatland; Bruceville 36–35 Decker; Bicknell 46–31 Monroe City; Edwardsport 35–14 Oaktown; Sandborn 30–28 Freelandville; Decker Chapel 43–25 Fritchton; Vincennes 42–16 Bruceville; Edwardsport 38–35 Bicknell; Sandborn 40–26 Decker Chapel; Vincennes 44–28 Edwardsport; Vincennes 54–27 Sandborn. Officials: Harry E. Briggs, Walter E. Marks.

WABASH: Somerset 30–20 Chippewa; Chester 20–18 Linlawn; Wabash 32–17 Lagro; Laketon 42–27 Lincolnville; North Manchester 29–26 Roann; LaFontaine 36–28 Urbana; Somerset 28–19 Chester; Wabash 26–23 Laketon; North Manchester 44–13 LaFontaine; Wabash 40–15 Somerset; North Manchester 22–18 Wabash. Officials: George L. Williams, Daniel McLaughlin.

WASHINGTON: Montgomery 44–14 Glendale; Loogootee 33–30 Epsom; Plainville 58–25 Alfordsville; Elnora 28–21 Trinity Springs; Burns City 20–18 Odon; Washington 41–23 Shoals; Loogootee 27–19 Montgomery; Plainville 57–23 Elnora; Washington 40–14 Burns City; Plainville 30–23 Loogootee; Washington 29–20 Plainville. Officials: William E. Pointer, Carl Porter.

WINAMAC: Winamac 30–17 Leiters Ford; Talma 36–34 Montgomery; Kewanna 33–24 Fulton; Rochester 24–22 Akron; Grass Creek 21–19 Francesville; Medaryville 33–24 Richland Center; Star City 30–16 Pulaski; Winamac 33–17 Talma; Rochester 32–21 Kewanna; Medaryville 21–19 Grass Creek; Star City 35–30 Winamac; Rochester 27–13 Medaryville; Rochester 30–13 Star City. Officials: Hal Harris, Herbert Vaulk, William F. Lucus.

WINCHESTER: Winchester 47–34 Spartanburg; Union City 28–21 Saratoga; Wayne Twp. 35–21 Losantville; Green Twp. 24–21 Jackson Twp.; Farmland 56–31 Lincoln; Lynn 34–32 McKinley; Parker 51–23 Huntsville; Stoney Creek 37–16 Modoc; Union City 34–20 Winchester; Green Twp. 24–19 Wayne Twp.; Farmland 30–26 Lynn; Parker 50–31 Stoney Creek; Union City 31–29 Green Twp.; Parker 26–24 Farmland; Parker 31–29 Union City. Officials: Lores L. Lehman, H. Wilbur May, Donald Dickie.

1940 REGIONALS

AUBURN: Mentone 37–25 Pleasant Mills; Garrett 36–26 Kendallville; Garrett 35–28 Mentone. Officials: J. H. McClure, Walter Cook.

BEDFORD: Mitchell 29–24 Salem; New Albany 29–25 Seymour; Mitchell 37–31 New Albany. Officials: Wm. E. Pointer, Wm. Coulter.

BRAZIL: Gosport 45–27 Bloomfield; Bloomington 24–20 Garfield (Terre Haute); Bloomington 39–20 Gosport. Officials: Karl Dickerson Hal Harris.

CRAWFORDSVILLE: Rockville 41–36 Attica; Crawfordsville 39–23 Bainbridge; Crawfordsville 39–31 Rockville. Officials: L. E. Fink, Forest Wood.

EVANSVILLE: Lynnville 42–16 Oakland City; Dale 26–25 Central; Lynnville 33–21 Dale. Officials: C.O. Walls, Frank Jarrell;

FRANKLIN: North Vernon 38–35 Greenwood; Columbus 40–28 Madison; North Vernon 43–41 Columbus. Officials: Clyde Castle, Irvin Springer.

Tourney Time

FORT WAYNE: South Side 34–26 Portland; Huntington 38–27 Chester Center; South Side 30–24 Huntington. Officials: Winston Ashley, George Williams.
GARY: Froebel 46–29 LaPorte; Hammond Tech 44–41 Brook; Hammond Tech 26–25 Froebel. Officials: Louis Briner, Dana Chandler.
INDIANAPOLIS: Lapel 37–35 Greenwood; Shortridge 43–22 Pittsboro; Lapel 39–36 Shortridge. Officials: Allen H. Klinck, Robert Hoffman.
JASPER: Washington 52–30 Dugger; Vincennes 25–24 Huntingburg; Washington 29–26 Vincennes. Officials: G. P. Silver, Dean Malaska.
LAFAYETTE: Freeland Park 45–44 Lebanon; Lafayette 30–28 Frankfort; Lafayette 40–17 Freeland Park. Officials Orville Jones, Lawrence Gaunt.
MARION: Kokomo 42–17 North Manchester; Marion 42–18 Sheridan; Kokomo 34–32 Marion. Officials: A. T. Krider, J. Alvin Taylor.
MUNCIE: Burris 34–30 Richmond; New Castle 52–27 Parker; New Castle 59–31 Burris. Officials: Thomas Baker, George Vaulk.
PERU: Logansport 40–27 Amboy; Brookston 35–31 Cutler; Logansport 52–47 Brookston. Officials: Lowell D. Sparks, Charles G. Garrett.
PLYMOUTH: South Bend Riley 28–21 Plymouth; Rochester 26–21 Nappanee; Riley 44–32 Rochester. Officials: Philip Eskew, Lundy Welborn.
RUSHVILLE: Rushville 36–30 Batesville; Lawrenceburg 43–30 Connersville; Rushville 53–35 Lawrenceburg. Officials: Nate Kaufman, T. R. Smith

1940 SEMI–FINALS

ANDERSON: Lapel 34–33 Rushville; North Vernon 34–31 Crawfordsville; Lapel 42–25 North Vernon. Officials: L. E. Fink, Orville Jones.
LOGANSPORT: Hammond Tech 33–23 South Bend Riley; Logansport 31–30 Lafayette; Hammond Tech 39–33 Logansport. Officials: Winston Ashley, Karl Dickerson.
MUNCIE: Ft. Wayne South Side 45–34 Garrett; New Castle 40–38 Kokomo; South Side 39–37 New Castle. Officials: Nate Kaufman, Allen H. Klinck.
VINCENNES: Mitchell 47–27 Lynnville; Washington 32–30 Bloomington; Mitchell 20–19 Washington. Officials: Thomas Baker, George Williams.

1940 FINALS—March 30

INDIANAPOLIS (Butler Fieldhouse): Hammond Tech 38–36 Lapel; Mitchell 23–20 Ft. Wayne South Side; Hammond Tech 33–21 Mitchell. Officials: Nate Kaufman, Thomas Baker.

1941 SECTIONALS

ANDERSON: Elwood 37–34 Summitville; Pendleton 46–25 Frankton; Lapel 30–23 Alexandria; Anderson 34–31 Markleville; Pendleton 41–32 Elwood; Anderson 40–22 Lapel; Anderson 30–29 Pendleton. Officials: Karl Dickerson, Frank Luzar.
ATTICA: Attica 38–15 Kingman; Mellott 24–7 Perrysville; Covington 32–15 Newton; Veedersburg 32–25 Williamsport; Hillsboro 48–45 West Lebanon; Pine Village 60–20 Wallace;

IHSAA Scores / 1940–1949

Attica 52–23 Mellott; Veedersburg 36–22 Covington; Pine Village 32–21 Hillsboro; Veedersburg 29–26 Attica; Pine Village 30–15 Veedersburg. Officials: Doxie Reeves, George Vaulk.

AURORA: Dillsboro 36–35 Rising Sun; Vevay 55–27 Moores Hill; Aurora 46–24 Lawrenceburg; Patriot 47–34 Guilford; Dillsboro 49–32 Bright; Aurora 50–39 Vevay; Dillsboro 28–26 Patriot; Aurora 59–27 Dillsboro. Officials: Gene McNutt, Don McBride.

BATESVILLE: Sunman 43–31 New Marion; Versailles 29–19 Holton; Cross Plains 33–31 Center Twp.; Batesville 30–27 Milan; Napoleon 28–26 Sunman; Versailles 26–19 Cross Plains; Batesville 51–19 Napoleon; Batesville 34–31 Versailles. Officials: R. P. Cline, Nate Kaufman.

BEDFORD: Springville 44–27 Williams; Mitchell 54–15 Huron; Fayette 50–36 Shawswick; Heltonville 19–17 Marshall Twp.; Bedford 55–17 Tunnelton; Oolitic 43–27 Springville; Mitchell 55–28 Fayetteville; Bedford 52–18 Heltonville; Mitchell 46–27 Oolitic; Bedford 46–28 Mitchell. Officials: Harry Briggs, Robert Hoffman.

BLOOMFIELD: Bloomfield 35–33 Linton; Switz City 40–18 Scotland; Lyons 35–22 Midland; Marco 27–23 Newberry; Solsberry 45–24 Owensburg; Jasonville 34–14 Worthington; Switz City 24–15 Bloomfield; Lyons 45–25 Marco; Jasonville 28–22 Solsberry; Lyons 19–18 Switz City; Jasonville 36–32 Lyons. Officials: M. E. Frump, Roland Baker.

BLUFFTON: Chester Center 35–19 Jackson Center; Bluffton 37–28 Rockcreek Center; Ossian 34–28 Liberty Center; Petroleum 37–33 Union Center; Chester Center 40–37 Lancaster; Ossian 27–21 Bluffton; Chester Center 37–32 Petroleum; Ossian 39–24 Chester Center. Officials: Ralph King, B. R. Hosier.

BOONVILLE: Millersburg 38–14 Chandler; Selvin 32–29 Elberfeld; Yankeetown 38–32 Tennyson; Lynnville 40–24 Folsomville; Boonville 32–18 Newburgh; Millersburg 40–29 Elberfeld; Lynnville 50–18 Yankeetown; Millersburg 28–26 Boonville; Lynnville 54–24 Millersburg. Officials: Clarence Riggs, Charles Kruzan.

BRAZIL: Gosport 53–25 Patricksburg; Cory 24–14 Jefferson Twp.; Freedom 28–21 Quincy; Ashboro 21–14 Bowling Green; Spencer 39–15 Van Buren Twp.; Brazil 45–8 Posey Twp.; Gosport 33–25 Clay City; Cory 38–24 Freedom; Spencer 45–17 Ashboro; Gosport 32–22 Brazil; Spencer 34–27 Cory; Gosport 37–35 Spencer. Officials: William Ellis, Albert Etter, Herbert Vaulk.

BROWNSTOWN: Brownstown 41–33 Vallonia; Freetown 38–13 Crothersville; Medora 58–19 Hayden; Cortland 53–22 Tampico; Scipio 34–33 Clearspring; Seymour 49–29 Brownstown; Freetown 33–31 Medora; Cortland 33–17 Scipio; Seymour 39–29 Freetown; Seymour 41–21 Cortland. Officials: Kermit Spurgeon, John Lyskowinski.

CANNELTON: Troy 22–20 Rockport; Chrisney 26–14 Grandview; Tell City 46–21 Gentryville; Cannelton 50–15 Bristow; Dale 45–14 Luce Twp.; Troy 24–10 Oil Twp.; Tell City 28–22 Chrisney; Cannelton 32–28 Dale; Tell City 28–15 Troy; Tell City 45–15 Cannelton. Officials: Carl Ross, Gerald Aishe.

CLINTON: Dana 32–21 Bellmore; Montezuma 36–31 Rosedale; Newport 45–26 Marshall; Rockville 26–23 Bridgeton; Saint Bernice 32–24 Bloomingdale; Tangier 40–27 Green Twp.; Clinton 39–30 Mecca; Cayuga 43–27 Hillsdale; Dana 46–23 Montezuma; Rockville 45–35 Newport; Tangier 41–30 Saint Bernice; Cayuga 35–30 Clinton; Dana 37–26 Rockville; Cayuga 29–28 Tangier; Dana 23–22 Cayuga. Officials: Charles Jensen, George Kerr, Clyde Gentry.

CONNERSVILLE: Connersville 47–22 Brownsville; Everton 36–24 Whitewater; Harrisburg 35–27 Orange; Brookville 36–22 Fairview; Liberty 40–22 Springfield Twp.; Alquina 33–28 Laurel; Kitchel 36–22 Bentonville; Connersville 60–37 Everton; Brookville 45–32 Harrisburg;

Tourney Time

Alquina 38–26 Liberty; Connersville 34–25 Kitchel; Brookville 33–21 Alquina; Connersville 41–31 Brookville. Officials: Hal Harris, Al Jackson, Maurice Wooden.

CRAWFORDSVILLE: Crawfordsville 44–26 New Ross; Ladoga 35–14 New Richmond; New Market 33–16 Waveland; Linden 28–25 Wingate; Darlington 34–20 Alamo; Bowers 41–32 Waynetown; Crawfordsville 54–30 Ladoga; New Market 37–29 Linden; Darlington 26–24 Bowers; Crawfordsville 59–24 New Market; Crawfordsville 28–24 Darlington. Officials: George Bender, John Blankenship.

DANVILLE: Plainfield 41–37 Brownsburg; Clayton 30–20 New Winchester; Pittsboro 30–10 Lizton; Avon 29–28 Stilesville; Danville 40–17 North Clayton; Danville 41–40 Avon; Pittsboro 30–17 Amo; Pittsboro 30–28 Salem; Amo 43–41 Plainfield (2ot); Pittsboro 28–26 Danville. Officials: Robert Simison, J. L. Mertz.

DECATUR: Kirkland 38–28 Jefferson Twp.; Monroe 32–23 Hartford Twp.; Decatur 29–26 Berne; Pleasant Mills 37–32 Geneva. Kirkland 34–28 Monmouth; Decatur 45–39 Monroe; Pleasant Mills 36–25 Kirkland; Decatur 34–32 Pleasant Mills. Officials: Harold McSwane, J. Clayton Hughes.

EVANSVILLE: New Harmony 26–18 Cynthiana; Central 82–13 Griffin; Mount Vernon 28–22 Poseyville; Bosse 32–12 Stewartsville; Reitz 28–26 New Harmony; Mount Vernon 25–23 Central (ot); Bosse 38–21 Reitz; Bosse 39–21 Mount Vernon. Officials: Hulett Crecelius, Clarence Myles.

FLORA: Adams Twp. 28–25 Carrollton; Delphi 46–36 Cutler; Camden 32–30 Rockfield; Flora 27–23 Deer Creek; Burlington 48–30 Adams Twp.; Delphi 49–37 Camden; Flora 31–17 Burlington; Delphi 39–38 Flora. Officials: Hardy Songer, Hugh McNew.

FORT WAYNE: New Haven 42–25 Lafayette Central; Central 54–46 South Side; Elmhurst 34–27; Arcola; Coesse 26–25 Harlan; Maumee Twp. 43–31 Leo; North Side 31–22 Huntertown; Hoagland 40–33 Jefferson Center; Columbia City 51–15 Monroeville; Central 49–25 New Haven; Elmhurst 44–31 Coesse North Side 56–25 Maumee Twp.; Columbia City 43–36 Hoagland; Central 39–26 Elmhurst; North Side 52–34 Columbia City; North Side 40–31 Central. Officials: Claron Veller, 0. Don Edmonds, Norris Ward.

FOWLER: Fowler 49–8 Pine Twp.; Otterbein 38–17 Gilboa; Boswell 36–33 Raub; Oxford 34–24 Ambia; Freeland Park 38–25 Wadena; Fowler 39–17 Earl Park; Otterbein 29–26 Boswell; Freeland Park 38–29 Oxford; Fowler 22–21 Otterbein; Freeland Park 47–32 Fowler. Officials: Raymond Trobaugh, L. R. Lenon.

FRANKFORT: Frankfort 29–21 Rossville; Jackson Twp. 40–30 Forest; Scircleville 28–22 Michigantown; Sugar Creek Twp. 24–17 Kirklin; Washington Twp. 40–26 Mulberry; Frankfort 23–21 Colfax; Jackson Twp. 44–27 Scircleville; Sugar Creek Twp. 29–27 Washington Twp.; Jackson Twp. 39–37 Frankfort; Jackson Twp. 39–30 Sugar Creek Twp. Officials: Norman Dunlap, Walter Marks.

FRANKLIN: Nineveh 43–32 Edinburg; Center Grove 41–26 Nashville; Franklin 32–15 Clark; Whiteland 42–21 Van Buren Twp.; Trafalgar 24–23 Masonic Home; Union Twp. 53–23 Helmsburg; Greenwood 45–15 Nineveh; Franklin 39–27 Center Grove; Trafalgar 25–22 Whiteland; Greenwood 39–27 Union Twp.; Franklin 44–33 Trafalgar; Greenwood 28–27 Franklin. Officials Mark Williams: Max Thompson, Leonard Mayhugh.

GARRETT: Orland 34–28 Hamilton; Angola 71–33 Scott Center; Garrett 39–24 Fremont; Churubusco 60–23 Metz; Butler 31–25 Waterloo; Auburn 59–25 Salem Center; Pleasant Lake

IHSAA Scores | 1940–1949

33–31 Spencerville (ot); Concord Twp. 39–38 Ashley (ot); Angola 46–11 Orland; Churubusco 33–26 Garrett; Auburn 40–23 Butler; Pleasant Lake 47–27 Concord Twp.; Angola 34–29 Churubusco; Auburn 39–31 Pleasant Lake; Auburn 40–24 Angola. Officials: Lores Lehman, R. W. Warring, Harold S. Johnson.

GARY: East Chicago Washington 39–19 Wirt; Froebel 39–22 Whiting; East Chicago Roosevelt 47–36 Dyer; Tolleston 39–26 Emerson ; Horace Mann 31–29 Hammond Tech; Gary Edison 33–22 Calumet Twp.; Wallace 57–35 Clark ; Hammond High 42–19 Griffith; Froebel 36–26 Washington; Tolleston 40–39 Roosevelt; Horace Mann 58–14 Gary Edison; Hammond High 54–29 Wallace; Froebel 42–36 Tolleston; Horace Mann 29–22 Hammond High; Froebel 42–33 Horace Mann. Officials: Walter Thurston, Ed Anglemyer, L. E. Fink.

GOSHEN: Concord 34–27 Nappanee; Wakarusa 44–39 Bristol; Elkhart 54–12 Millersburg; New Paris 29–23 Goshen; Middlebury 29–27 Jefferson; Concord 43–29 Baugo Twp.; Elkhart 44–43 Wakarusa; New Paris 23–21 Middlebury; Concord 48–42 Elkhart; New Paris 36–29 Concord. Officials: Otho Piper, George Lambert.

GREENCASTLE: Russellville 37–25 Cloverdale; Roachdale 43–27 Reelsville; Greencastle 64–17 Belle Union; Bainbridge 25–21 Fillmore; Russellville 28–23 Roachdale; Greencastle 55–23 Bainbridge; Greencastle 49–24 Russellville. Officials: James Conover, Harry Conover.

GREENFIELD: Mount Comfort 33–32 Oaklandon; Greenfield 36–30 Mc–Cordsville; Fortville 44–42 Charlottesville; New Palestine 30–26 Westland; Maxwell 53–36 Eden; Mount Comfort 33–25 Wilkinson; Fortville 46–36 Greenfield; Maxwell 30–27 New Palestine; Mount Comfort 24–22 Fortville; Maxwell 35–33 Mount Comfort. Officials: H. Wilbur May, Frank Jarrell.

GREENSBURG: New Point 29–15 Vernon; Greensburg 52–18 Butlerville; North Vernon 41–25 Clarksburg; Sandusky 22–17 Burney; Saint Paul 27–23 Zenas; Jackson 30–18 Sandcreek; Greensburg 35–26 New Point; Sandusky 43–28 North Vernon; Saint Paul 32–27 Jackson; Greensburg 31–28 Sandusky; Saint Paul 33–24 Greensburg. Officials: Harold Porter, William Reimann.

HARTFORD CITY: Bryant 48–23 Hartford City; Portland 33–29 Ridgeville; Pennville 28–25 Montpelier; Madison Twp. 27–19 Jefferson; Poling 34–33 Redkey (ot); Roll 37–21 Gray; Dunkirk 37–35 Bryant (2ot); Portland 28–24 Pennville; Madison Twp. 37–34 Poling; Roll 25–19 Dunkirk; Portland 45–28 Madison Twp.; Portland 37–26 Roll. Officials: Dean Malaska, Walter Floyd, G. P. Silver.

HUNTINGTON: Jackson Twp. 41–32 Lancaster Twp.; Salamonie Twp. 33–14 Jefferson Twp.; Clear Creek 33–19 Huntington Twp.; Union Twp. 23–21 Rock Creek Center; Markle 36–28 Polk Twp.; South Whitley 38–29 Washington; Andrews 36–17 Bippus; Huntington 80–21 Banquo; Jackson Twp. 31–26 Salamonie Twp.; Clear Greek 32–23 Union Twp.; South Whitley 37–34 Markle; Huntington 40–26 Andrews; Jackson Twp. 45–25 Clear Creek; Huntington 44–27 South Whitley; Huntington 45–23 Jackson Twp.. Officials: Clay Layman, John Waller, Don Veller.

INDIANAPOLIS: Manual 36–30 Southport; Decatur Central 31–25 Tech; New Augusta 43–32 Castleton; Shortridge 44–18 Lawrence; Warren Central 38–34 Broad Ripple; Ben Davis 46–25 Beech Grove; Speedway 32–30 Washington; Howe 33–23 Franklin Twp.; Decatur Central 50–25 Manual; Shortridge 33–27 New Augusta; Ben Davis 26–22 Warren Central; Speedway 31–22 Howe; Decatur Central 34–28 Shortridge; Ben Davis 34–23 Speedway; Decatur Central 35–20 Ben Davis. Officials: Raymond Hobbs, Aaron Belcher, Cecil Tharp.

Tourney Time

JASPER: Winslow 27–26 Huntingburg; Jasper 34–21 Petersburg; Spurgeon 31–29 Dubois; Otwell 33–25 Ireland; Holland 60–23 Jefferson Twp.; Cuzco 27–20 Stendal; Winslow 30–29 Jasper; Spurgeon 25–15 Otwell; Holland 35–22 Cuzco; Winslow 24–23 Spurgeon; Winslow 25–19 Holland. Officials: Carl Jerger, Rollie Kirchoff.

JEFFERSONVILLE: New Middletown 32–30 Elizabeth; Jeffersonville 56–21 Henryville; Corydon 68–24 Borden; Lanesville 30–23 New Amsterdam; New Albany 40–22 Charlestown; Mauckport; 39–19 New Salisbury; Silver Creel; 28–18 New Washington; Georgetown 35–15 Laconia; Jeffersonville 64–26 New Middletown; Corydon 60–14 Lanesville; New Albany 53–24 Mauckport; Silver Creek 44–23 Georgetown; Jeffersonville 21–20 Corydon; New Albany 50–32 Silver Creek; Jeffersonville 34–32 New Albany. Officials: Myer Schreiber, Lawrence Young, J. Ralph Black.

KENDALLVILLE: Lagrange 26–24 Wolf Lake (ot); Shipshewana 32–25 Wawaka; Kendallville 46–27 Lima; Rome City 35–25 Springfield Twp.; Ligonier 23–20 Scott; Avilla 39–27 Brighton; Wolcottville 50–27 Topeka Cromwell 36–35 Albion; LaGrange 38–19 Shipshewana; Kendallville 50–24 Rome City; Avilla 30–17 Ligonier; Wolcottville 44–27 Cromwell; LaGrange 33–25 Kendallville; Avilla 23–20 Wolcottville; Avilla 31–17 La–Grange. Officials: Everett Campbell, Donald Dickie, Thomas Fields.

KOKOMO: Greentown 46–25 New London; Howard Twp. 40–14 Clay Twp.; Kokomo 37–23 West Middleton; Jackson Twp. 30–25 Ervin Twp.; Union Twp. 55–31 Russiaville; Greentown 22–18 Howard Twp.; Kokomo 43–21 Jackson Twp.; Union Twp. 36–33 Greentown; Kokomo 42–22 Union Twp.. Officials: Dana Chandler, Gerald Huey;

LAFAYETTE: Lafayette 35–28 Stockwell; Wea 32–26 Dayton; Monitor 23–22 Romney; Klondike 28–22 Montmorenci; Clarks Hill 25–22 Jackson Twp.; West Point 38–28 West Lafayette; Battle Ground 27–19 Buck Creek; Lafayette 51–7 Wea; Klondike 23–19 Monitor; West Point 50–20 Clarks Hills; Lafayette 28–22 Battle Ground; West Point 25–22 Klondike; Lafayette 33–22 West Point. Officials: Orville Jones, Evan Crawley, Charles DeBusk.

LAPORTE: Michigan City 56–45 Clinton Twp.; Wanatah 37–26 Springfield Twp.; Rolling Prairie 44–36 LaCrosse; Hanna 28–26 Union Twp.; Union Mills 30–23 Westville; Mill Creek 24–11 Stillwell; LaPorte 43–20 Kingsbury; Michigan City 46–19 Wanatah; Rolling Prairie 56–27 Hanna; Union Mills 44–18 Mill Creek; Michigan City 39–34 LaPorte; Rolling Prairie 29–26 Union Mills; Rolling Prairie 37–31 Michigan City. Officials: Louis Briner, Paul Bateman, H. Windmiller.

LEBANON: Jamestown 33–30 Dover; Lebanon 59–22 Thorntown; Whitestown 51–41 Advance; Central 47–46 Zionsville; Pinnell 39–37 Jamestown; Lebanon 56–26 Whitestown; Central 37–32 Pinnell; Lebanon 55–25 Central. Officials: Reid McLain, T. R. Smith.

LOGANSPORT: Metea 31–27 New Waverly; Washington Twp. 24–23 Onward; Logansport 40–24 Walton; Lucerne 28–26 Young America; Twelve Mile 32–30 Royal Center; Metea 24–19 Galveston; Logansport 44–34 Washington Twp.; Twelve Mile 22–20 Lucerne (ot); Logansport 58–24 Metea; Logansport 31–30 Twelve Mile. Officials: R. Wayne Cunningham, Charles Garrett.

MADISON: Saluda 40–21 Central; Madison 25–24 Scottsburg; North Madison 26–25 Dupont; Deputy 47–12 Paris Crossing; Lexington 33–15 Hanover; Austin 27–19 Saluda; Madison 40–14 North Madison; Lexington 36–20 Deputy; Madison 40–14 Austin; Madison 35–19 Lexington. Officials: Wendell Ballard, A. E. Pitcher.

MARION: Marion 55–24 Sweetser; Gas City 48–14 Jefferson; Van Buren 31–28 Sims Twp.; Fairmount 38–33 Jonesboro; Marion 47–33 Gas City; Fairmount 26–25 Van Buren; Marion

48–20 Fairmount. Officials: Allen Klinck, Condict Smith.

MARTINSVILLE: Monrovia 28–26 Morgantown; Martinsville 38–30 Mooresville; University 51–39 Smithville; Eminence 30–29 Stinesville; Bloomington 51–43 Ellettsville; Unionville 33–25 Paragon; Martinsville 38–22 Monrovia; Eminence 38–36 University; Bloomington 52–28 Unionville; Martinsville 47–29 Eminence; Bloomington 43–35 Martinsville. Officials: Thomas Baker, Layall Fisher.

MONTICELLO: Monticello 34–26 Monon; Brookston 48–21 Round Grove; Chalmers 28–24 Idaville; Burnettsville 46–28 Wolcott; Buffalo 36–31 Reynolds; Brookston 30–28 Monticello; Chalmers 45–25 Burnettsville; Brookston 50–39 Buffalo; Brookston 27–26 Chalmers (ot). Officials: H. P. Berkey, William Lucus.

MOROCCO: Wheatfield 28–25 Goodland; Rensselaer 36–30 Mount Ayr; Remington 28–25 Brook; DeMotte; 29–27 Tefft; Morocco 36–27 Fair Oaks; Wheatfield 32–27 Kentland; Rensselaer 39–31 Remington; DeMotte 28–24 Morocco; Rensselaer 39–17 Wheatfield; Rensselaer 34–24 DeMotte. Officials: Charles E. Baer, Hugh Bergstrom.

MUNCIE: Center 38–34 Royerton; Gaston 37–22 Daleville; Selma 36–24 Eaton; Harrison Twp. 26–25 Cowan (ot); Muncie Central 33–29 Albany; Burris 59–26 Yorktown; Center 49–28 DeSoto Gaston 35–13 Selma; Muncie Central 50–24 Harrison Twp.; Burris 52–32 Center; Muncie 40–30 Gaston; Burris 32–29 Muncie Central. Officials: Herbert Edwards, C. N. Phillips, and C.O. Walls.

NEW CASTLE: New Castle 42–26 Straughn; Sulphur Springs 35–19 Cadiz; Mt. Summit 28–16 Lewisville; New Lisbon 34–32 Spiceland; Knightstown 37–33 Kennard; Middletown 41–33 Mooreland; New Castle 46–34 Sulphur Springs; New Lisbon 34–28 Mount Summit; Middletown 36–34 Knightstown; New Castle 36–31 New Lisbon; New Castle 43–26 Middletown. Officials: Fred Pierson, Clayton Patterson.

NOBLESVILLE: Walnut Grove 46–35 Cicero; Carmel 29–27 Windfall; Sharpsville 39–20 Prairie Twp.; Fishers 42–29 Westfield; Tipton 35–13 Goldsmith; Sheridan 36–31 Atlanta; Noblesville 58–15 Kempton; Walnut Grove 35–32 Arcadia; Sharpsville 39–37 Carmel; Tipton 35–22 Fishers; Sheridan 34–33 Noblesville; Walnut Grove 33–30 Sharpsville; Tipton 35–27 Sheridan; Tipton 37–29 Walnut Grove. Officials: Daniel McLaughlin, Winston Ashley, Clive Markley.

OAKLAND CITY: Hazleton 22–20 Patoka; Princeton 43–21 Owensville; Mount Olympus 26–25 Haubstadt; Oakland City 29–17 Mackey; Fort Branch 37–16 Francisco; Princeton 29–21 Hazleton; Mount Olympus 27–22 Oakland City; Fort Branch 32–28 Princeton; Fort Branch 26–24 Mount Olympus. Officials: Paul Kelly, Fred Wilder.

PERU: Peru 58–26 Butler; Bunker Hill 44–27 Deedsville; Gilead 32–20 Jefferson Twp.; Clay Twp. 26–20 Chili; Converse 30–23 Amboy; Peru 43–29 Macy; Bunker Hill 51–24 Gilead; Converse 32–27 Clay Twp.; Peru 33–31 Bunker Hill; Peru 37–35 Converse. Officials: A. T. Krider, J. Alvin Taylor.

PLYMOUTH: North Judson 37–29 Argos; Culver 47–19 Tippecanoe; Center 40–38 Bourbon; Bremen 38–15 West Twp.; Plymouth 53–34 LaPaz; San Pierre 27–12 Grovertown; Knox 47–22 Hamlet; North Judson 48–23 Tyner; Culver 40–25 Center; Plymouth 37–32 Bremen; Knox 34–33 San Pierre; Culver 42–29 North Judson; Plymouth 41–30 Knox; Plymouth 44–42 Culver. Officials: E. L. Druckamiller, Donald Coar, James R. Craw.

RICHMOND: Centerville 49–34 Greensfork; Hagerstown 49–20 Whitewater; Fountain City

Tourney Time

39–26 Williamsburg; Boston 27–20 Milton; Economy 52–26 Webster; Richmond 64–22 Lincoln; Hagerstown 38–34 Centerville; Boston 24–21 Fountain City; Richmond 61–32 Economy; Hagerstown 14–6 Boston; Richmond 38–28 Hagerstown. Officials: Fred White, Stephen Baker.

ROCHESTER: Pulaski 34–33 Winamac (ot); Richland Center 32–29 Grass Creek; Francesville 31–10 Monterey; Star City 33–31 Akron; Kewanna 42–34 Fulton; Medaryville 33–22 Talma; Rochester 42–18 Leiters Ford; Pulaski 28–25 Richland Center; Star City 21–17 Francesville; Kewanna 31–29 Medaryville; Rochester 40–22 Pulaski; Kewanna 30–29 Star City; Rochester 42–32 Kewanna. Officials: Max Hildreth, William Kendall, Phil Eskew.

RUSHVILLE: Mays 34–15 New Salem; Rushville 40–21 Morton Memorial; Manilla 32–28 Arlington; Milroy 28–16 Raleigh; Carthage 28–24 Mays; Rushville 55–20 Manilla; Milroy 33–15 Carthage; Rushville 34–25 Milroy. Officials: Forrest Ballinger, Otto Crosley.

SALEM: Morgan Twp. 65–30 Little York; French Lick 38–23 West Baden; English 28–23 Leavenworth; Pekin 36–23 Hardinsburg; Salem 26–22 Milltown; Paoli 56–27 Campbellsburg; Marengo 36–30 Orleans; French Lick 38–28 Morgan Twp.; Pekin 48–20 English; Salem 42–18 Paoli; French Lick 38–25 Marengo; Salem 42–22 Pekin; Salem 29–19 French Lick. Officials: Robert Derrington, Carl Porter, W. N. Ringer.

SHELBYVILLE: Moral Twp. 23–13 Boggstown; Morristown 39–26 Mount Auburn; Waldron 42–27 Fairland; Shelbyville 43–21 Clifford; Columbus 59–26 Flat Rock; Moral Twp. 38–24 Hope; Waldron 32–23 Morristown; Shelbyville 28–25 Columbus; Moran Twp. 37–31 Waldron; Shelbyville 28–21 Moral Twp.. Officials: Clyde Sutton, George Williams.

SOUTH BEND: Mishawaka 38–29 Green Twp.; Washington-Clay 37–19 Walkerton; North Liberty 33–29 New Carlisle; Wilson 29–23 Lakeville; Riley 44–38 Madison Twp.; Washington 27–20 Adams; Central 38–29 Mishawaka; North Liberty 36–29 Washington-Clay; Riley 40–32 Wilson; Central 48–35 Washington; Riley 35–27 North Liberty; Central 45–20 Riley. Officials: M. E. Somers, Lundy Welborn, Lawrence Gaunt.

SULLIVAN: Sullivan 35–31 Fairbanks; Merom 37–24 Pleasantville; New Lebanon 21–15 Farmersburg; Hymera 40–23 Graysville; Dugger 43–38 Carlisle; Shelburn 30–23 Sullivan; Merom 17–15 New Lebanon; Hymera 28–24 Dugger; Shelburn 41–33 Merom; Shelburn 35–25 Hymera. Officials: Robert Hold, Leon Dulgar.

TERRE HAUTE: Gerstmeyer 30–22 Fontanet; Blackhawk 21–20 Prairie Creek; Otter Creek 22–19 Wiley; Garfield 27–23 Riley; Laboratory 34–25 West Terre Haute; Honey Creek 51–12 New Goshen; Pimento 29–14 Glenn; Gerstmeyer 42–22 Concannon; Otter Creek 34–15 Blackhawk; Garfield 25–21 Laboratory; Honey Creek 23–19 Pimento; Gerstmeyer 31–17 Otter Creek; Garfield 26–18 Honey Creek; Gerstmeyer 36–20 Garfield. Officials: Byron Alexander, Fred Alwood, and Clarence Tolbert.

VALPARAISO: Merrillville 29–24 Lowell; Wheeler 30–14 Jackson; Portage 66–2 Washington; Valparaiso 37–17 Liberty Center; Hebron 22–20 Morgan Twp.; Chesterton 20–19 Boone Grove; Hobart 42–32 Kouts; East Gary Edison 40–30 Crown Point; Merrillville 25–22 Wheeler; Valparaiso 33–25 Portage; Hebron 41–27 Chesterton; East Gary Edison 33–17 Hobart; Merrillville 22–21 Valparaiso; East Gary Edison 50–24 Hebron; East Gary Edison 32–24 Merrillville. Officials: Gerald W. Strole, LeRoy Shine, K. King Telle.

VINCENNES: Bruceville 26–25 Decker; Bicknell 36–23 Wheatland; Sandborn 38–33 Fritchton; Freelandville 35–34 Vincennes; Edwardsport 29–22 Decker Chapel; Monroe City 30–25 Oaktown; Bruceville 49–28 Bicknell; Freelandville 46–28 Sandborn; Monroe City 26–21

IHSAA Scores | 1940–1949

Edwardsport; Freelandville 23–17 Bruceville; Freelandville 53–27 Monroe City. Officials: William Coulter, William Pointer.

WABASH: Somerset 42–19 Lagro; Chester Twp. 32–29 North Manchester; Laketon 37–29 Wabash. Urbana 42–28 Chippewa; LaFontaine 29–22 Lincolnville; Roann 36–25 Linlawn; Somerset 32–27 Chester Twp.; Laketon 34–28 Urbana; Roann 33–26 LaFontaine; Somerset 31–27 Laketon; Somerset 38–28 Roann. Officials: Ralph Eades, Forrest Shaw.

WARSAW: Syracuse 45–19 Beaver Dam; Etna Green 39–28 Milford; Atwood 36–22 Burket; Silver Lake 39–31 Claypool; Sidney 34–32 North Webster; Warsaw 36–21 Leesburg; Pierceton 26–19 Mentone; Larwill 38–28 Syracuse; Atwood 37–25 Etna Green; Sidney 41–27 Silver Lake; Pierceton 32–28 Warsaw; Atwood 33–28 Larwill; Pierceton 21–14 Sidney; Pierceton 35–19 Atwood. Officials: Vaughn Crow, Cecil Young, Russell Arndt.

WASHINGTON: Washington 60–14 Odon; Plainville 45–30 Epsom; Shoals 39–23 Elmore Twp.; Trinity Springs 25–23 Glendale; Burns City 15–14 Alfordsville; Loogootee 24–21 Montgomery; Washington 52–35 Plainville; Shoals 65–18 Trinity Springs; Loogootee 43–17 Burns City; Washington 36–28 Shoals; Washington 48–26 Loogootee. Officials: Clyde Castle, Irvin Springer.

WINCHESTER: Lincoln 33–25 Modoc; Winchester 51–30 Green; Spartanburg 29–28 Huntsville; Union City 29–16 Lynn; Saratoga 47–32 Stoney Creek; McKinley 28–25 Farmland; Parker 45–22 Jackson; Wayne 42–18 Losantville; Winchester 47–20 Lincoln; Union City 28–27 Spartanburg; Saratoga 46–28 McKinley; Parker 40–33 Wayne; Winchester 33–24 Union City; Parker 25–23 Saratoga; Parker 33–32 Winchester. Officials: Everett Goshorn, Gerald Alexander, George Chestnut.

1941 REGIONALS

ANDERSON: Anderson 55–26 Maxwell; Decatur Central 42–30 Pittsboro; Anderson 27–21 Decatur Central. Officials: L. E. Fink, J. Clayton Hughes.

ATTICA: Crawfordsville 37–18 Dana; Greencastle 34–26 Pine Village; Crawfordsville 44–38 Greencastle. Officials: Winston Ashley, Philip Eskew.

EVANSVILLE: Fort Branch 22–19 Tell City; Bosse 40–19 Lynnville; Bosse 31–24 Fort Branch. Officials: Frank Jarrell, Orville Jones.

FORT WAYNE: Pierceton 28–26 Avilla; North Side 40–16 Auburn; North Side 30–23 Pierceton. Officials: J. Alvin Taylor, A. T. Krider.

GARY: Rensselaer 29–26 Rolling Prairie; Froebel 32–26 East Gary Edison; Froebel 36–32 Rensselaer. Officials: Allen H. Klinck, Karl Dickerson.

GREENSBURG: Shelbyville 36–28 Greenwood; Madison 30–21 Saint Paul; Madison 30–24 Shelbyville. Officials: Dana Chandler, K. King Telle.

HUNTINGTON: Huntington 41–34 Ossian; Portland 40–36 Decatur; Huntington 52–38 Portland. Officials: C. O. Walls, Paul Bateman.

LAFAYETTE: Freeland Park 35–28 Jackson Twp.; Lafayette 32–20 Lebanon (ot); Lafayette 43–29 Freeland Park. Officials: Charles G. Garrett, R. Wayne Cunningham.

LOGANSPORT: Logansport 38–32 Peru; Brookston 47–29 Delphi; Logansport 45–25 Brookston. Officials: Louis Briner, Hal Harris.

MARION: Tipton 42–35 Marion; Kokomo 44–27 Somerset; Kokomo 29–20 Tipton.

Tourney Time

Officials: G. P. Silver, Dean Malaska.

MUNCIE: New Castle 35–33 Richmond; Burris 50–28 Parker; Burris 39–31 New Castle. Officials: George Bender, Nate Kaufman.

NEW ALBANY: Bedford 26–25 Salem; Jeffersonville 38–33 Seymour; Bedford 49–42 Jeffersonville. Officials: Robert Hoffman, William Pointer.

RUSHVILLE: Rushville 42–41 Connersville; Aurora 47–35 Batesville; Rushville 47–34 Aurora. Officials: T. R. Smith, Fred White.

SOUTH BEND: Central 28–19 Rochester; Plymouth 41–31 New Paris; Central 44–34 Plymouth. Officials: Thomas Baker, George Williams.

TERRE HAUTE: Gerstmeyer 26–25 Jasonville; Bloomington 36–26 Gosport; Bloomington 29–15 Gerstmeyer. Officials: Clyde Castle, Irvin Springer.

WASHINGTON: Washington 52–34 Shelburn; Freelandville 47–45 Winslow; Washington 54–43 Freelandville. Officials: Clyde Gentry, Clyde Sutton.

1941 SEMI-FINALS

HAMMOND: Gary Froebel 43–32 Logansport; South Bend Central 27–21 Lafayette; Froebel 37–36 Central. Officials: Winston Ashley, Nate Kaufman.

INDIANAPOLIS: Rushville 36–29 Anderson; Madison 45–43 Crawfordsville; Madison 39–30 Rushville. Officials: Allen H. Klinck, T. R. Smith.

MUNCIE: Kokomo 41–38 Huntington; Ft. Wayne North Side 46–40 Burris; Kokomo 41–32 North Side. Officials: L. E. Fink, Karl Dickerson;

VINCENNES: Bedford 41–37 Bloomington; Washington 44–27 Bosse;; Washington 44–32 Bedford. Officials: Thomas Baker, George Williams

1941 STATE FINALS—March 22

INDIANAPOLIS (Butler Fieldhouse): Madison 29–27 Froebel; Washington 48–32 Kokomo; Washington 39–33 Madison. Officials: Thomas Baker, L. E. Fink.

1942 SECTIONALS

ANDERSON: Elwood 39–36 Pendleton; Anderson 36–26 Markleville; Summitville 30–26 Alexandria; Lapel 39–30 Frankton; Anderson 39–27 Elwood; Lapel 40–25 Summitville; Anderson 39–35 Lapel. Officials: Orville Jones, C. O. Walls.

ATTICA: Wallace 24–22 Richland Twp.; Hillsboro 34–30 Pine Village; Perrysville 27–21 Kingman; Veedersburg 53–25 West Lebanon; Attica 28–21 Williamsport; Covington 42–12 Wallace; Hillsboro 37–30 Perrysville; Attica 45–30 Veedersburg; Covington 22–21 Hillsboro; Attica 28–22 Covington. Officials: Raymond Hobbs, Reid McLain.

AUBURN: Butler 42–40 Garrett; Metz 43–39 Pleasant Lake; Ashley 52–37 Hamilton; Salem Center 35–12 Scott Center; Waterloo 45–21 Orland; Spencerville 35–34 Angola; Auburn 57–38 Concord Twp.; Fremont 45–27 Churubusco; Butler 39–32 Metz; Ashley 48–26 Salem Center; Waterloo 43–37 Spencerville; Auburn 47–29 Fremont; Butler 45–28 Ashley; Auburn 70–31 Waterloo; Butler 46–44 Auburn. Officials: Walter Moss, Daniel McLaughlin, Russell Arndt.

IHSAA Scores | 1940–1949

BATESVILLE: Napoleon 38–33 Versailles; Cross Plains 26–18 Holton; Milan 33–28 Osgood; Batesville 39–26 Sunman; Napoleon 42–32 New Marion; Cross Plains 25–24 Milan; Napoleon 36–34 Batesville (ot); Cross Plains 33–20 Napoleon. Officials: Layall Fisher, Harold Porter.

BLOOMINGTON: University 31–30 Morgantown; Ellettsville 46–37 Mooresville; Martinsville 32–22 Bloomington; Monrovia 38–34; Unionville; Paragon 41–22 Eminence; Stinesville 47–28 Smithville; Ellettsville 35–34 University; Monrovia 20–18 Martinsville; Stinesville 42–25 Paragon; Monrovia 31–26 Ellettsville; Monrovia 29–23 Stinesville. Officials: George Bender, Clayton Patterson.

BLUFFTON: Union Center 46–37 Petroleum; Lancaster 36–32 Rockcreek; Liberty Center 60–36 Jackson; Chester 45–39 Ossian; Bluffton 48–38 Union Center; Liberty Center 51–30 Lancaster; Chester 49–21 Bluffton; Liberty Center 46–41 Chester. Officials: Ed Anglemeyer, Clayton Hughes.

BOONVILLE: Lynnville 41–27 Newburgh; Selvin 22–14 Chandler; Elberfeld 27–26 Tennyson; Yankeetown 41–27 Millersburg; Boonville 46–27 Folsomville; Lynnville 32–20 Selvin; Yankeetown 37–35 Elberfeld; Boonville 31–23 Lynnville; Boonville 52–22 Yankeetown. Officials: Clarence Tolbert, George Inman.

BRAZIL: Brazil 61–17 Jefferson Twp.; Gosport 45–20 Bowling Green; Spencer 56–24 Quincy; Clay City 45–20 Freedom; Patricksburg 29–25 Ashboro; Cory 27–26 Van Buren Twp.; Brazil 42–31 Staunton; Spencer 31–29 Gosport; Clay City 49–22 Patricksburg; Brazil 40–23 Cory; Spencer 41–36 Clay City; Brazil 45–36 Spencer. Officials: Byron Alexander, Bernard Lampe, James Conover.

CLINTON: Cayuga 29–16 Hillsdale; Marshall 24–23 St. Bernice; Mecca 33–32 Newport; Montezuma 30–26 Bellmore; Rockville 32–22 Greene Twp.; Bridgeton 39–36 Tangier; Bloomingdale 27–25 Dana; Clinton 35–15 Rosedale; Cayuga 41–30 Marshall; Montezuma 48–35 Mecca; Rockville 43–29 Bridgeton; Clinton 35–25 Bloomingdale; Montezuma 21–20 Cayuga; Clinton 33–25 Rockville; Clinton 39–23 Montezuma. Officials: Dean Malaska, Walter Floyd, G. P. Silver.

CONNERSVILLE: Orange 40–25 Laurel; Alquina 38–24 Whitewater; Everton 33–25 Fairview; Connersville 58–15 Bentonville; Liberty 30–28 Brookville; Brownsville 32–23 Springfield Twp.; Kitchel 36–24 Harrisburg; Alquina 31–17 Orange; Connersville 70–15 Everton; Liberty 38–28 Brownsville; Kitchel 31–20 Alquina; Connersville 36–30 Liberty; Kitchel 42–40 Connersville (2ot). Officials: Max Thompson, John Walker, Max Casey.

CRAWFORDSVILLE: Crawfordsville 61–34 Bowers; Wingate 51–32 Waveland; Ladoga 32–22 Waynetown; New Market 36–29 Linden; Darlington 34–19 New Richmond; New Ross 50–27 Alamo; Crawfordsville 55–23 Wingate; New Market 33–29 Ladoga; Darlington 36–35 New Ross; Crawfordsville 46–16 New Market; Crawfordsville 68–26 Darlington. Officials: Frank Jarrell, Frank Luzar.

DECATUR: Jefferson 32–30 Geneva; Hartford 39–19 Monmouth; Decatur 30–29 Kirkland; Berne 41–40 Monroe; Pleasant Mills 44–32 Jefferson; Decatur 42–37 Hartford; Pleasant Mills 30–27 Berne; Pleasant Mills 31–18 Decatur. Officials: Clive Markley, Thomas Fields.

DELPHI: Camden 45–29 Adams; Deer Creek 25–23 Carrollton; Flora 30–25 Burlington; Cutler 42–18 Rockfield; Camden 32–22 Delphi; Flora 28–25 Deer Creek; Cutler 37–27 Camden; Flora 36–30 Cutler. Officials: William Lucus, Karl Dickerson.

EAST CHICAGO: Hobart 44–40 Lowell; East Chicago Roosevelt 35–34 East Gary Edison; East Chicago Washington 48–41 Wheeler; Dyer 33–32 Griffith; Hammond Clark 54–28 Wirt; Whiting 45–26 Crown Point; Hammond Tech 46–32 Merrillville; Hammond 47–33 Hobart;

Tourney Time

Roosevelt 38–35 Washington; Clark 55–28 Dyer; Hammond Tech 36–22 Whiting; Roosevelt 40–32 Hammond; Clark 39–34 Hammond Tech; Roosevelt 54–30 Clark. Officials: Leroy Shine, Norris Ward, Claron Veller.

ELKHART: Nappanee 27–24 Middlebury; Bristol 29–27 Millersburg; Baugo Twp. 41–22 Concord; Goshen 28–27 Elkhart; Wakarusa 38–36 New Paris; Nappanee 35–15 Jefferson; Bristol 27–25 Jamestown; Goshen 41–38 Wakarusa; Nappanee 18–16 Bristol; Goshen 39–19 Nappanee. Officials: Robert Nulf, Harold McSwane.

EVANSVILLE: Central 29–22 Mt. Vernon; New Harmony 29–20 Cynthiana; Poseyville 32–24 Stewartsville; Reitz 37–24 Wadesville; Bosse 32–18 Griffin; Central 44–25 New Harmony; Reitz 36–19 Poseyville; Central 33–20 Bosse; Central 32–21 Reitz. Officials: Robert Hoffman, Rollie Kirchoff.

FORT WAYNE: Lafayette Central 27–26 Arcola; Central 35–28 North Side; Columbia City 52–25 Huntertown; South Side 46–23 Woodburn; New Haven 44–19 Harlan; Elmhurst 22–21 Hoagland; Monroeville 42–25 Coesse; Leo 67–25 Jefferson Center; Central 55–17 Lafayette Central; South Side 35–23 Columbia City; Hoagland 39–31 New Haven; Leo 61–23 Monroeville; Central 44–38 South Side; Leo 52–32 Hoagland; Central 52–24 Leo. Officials Fred White, Lores Lehman, Lawrence Gaunt.

FRANKFORT: Scircleville 38–19 Kirklin; Michigantown 31–27 Washington Twp.; Sugar Creek 25–20 Forest; Colfax 34–22 Mulberry; Frankfort 30–26 Jackson Twp.; Rossville 37–22 Scircleville; Michigantown 35–33 Sugar Creek; Frankfort 37–25 Colfax; Rossville 29–28 Michigantown; Frankfort 25–22 Rossville. Officials: J. L. Mertz, Clyde Gentry.

FRANKLIN: Edinburg 55–21 Van Buren; Whiteland 55–32 Helmsburg; Nineveh 33–20 Nashville; Greenwood 55–29 Trafalgar; Union Twp. 30–28 Center Grove; Franklin 38–20 Clark Twp.; Masonic Home 35–19 Edinburg; Whiteland 29–28 Nineveh; Greenwood 46–23 Union Twp.; Greenwood 30–23 Whiteland; Franklin 37–30 Masonic Home; Franklin 26–23 Greenwood. Officials: Herbert Dukes, Charles DeBusk, Kermit Spurgeon.

GARY: Hebron 27–26 Jackson Center; Emerson 44–25 Chesterton; Gary Edison 49–38 Morgan Twp.; Tolleston 37–33 Valparaiso; Horace Mann 57–40 Portage ; Froebel 70–18 Washington Twp.; Boone Grove 34–28 Liberty Center; Wallace 56–22 Kouts; Emerson 54–26 Hebron; Tolleston 47–30 Gary Edison; Horace Mann 35–31 Froebel; Wallace 58–13 Boone Grove; Emerson 36–32 Tolleston; Horace Mann 31–24 Wallace; Horace Mann 35–20 Emerson. Officials: W. E. Thurston, Forrest Shaw, L. E. Fink.

GREENCASTLE: Russellville 28–26 Roachdale; Cloverdale 35–34 Reelsville; Greencastle 67–32 Belle Union; Fillmore 35–23 Bainbridge; Cloverdale 48–30 Russellville; Greencastle 44–33 Fillmore; Greencastle 45–23 Russellville. Officials: Forrest Ballinger, Otto Crosley.

GREENFIELD: Greenfield 42–28 Charlottesville; Eden 43–21 Westland; Mt. Comfort 29–24 New Palestine; Wilkinson 44–37 McCordsville; Fortville 31–23 Maxwell; Greenfield 38–31 Eden; Mt. Comfort 27–25 Wilkinson; Greenfield 36–33 Fortville (ot); Greenfield 47–27 Mt. Comfort. Officials: Stephen Baker, Gerald Alexander.

GREENSBURG: Sandcreek 34–32 New Point; Greensburg 51–23 Zenas; St. Paul 36–28 Clarksburg; Sandusky 52–38 Vernon; North Vernon 48–31 Burney; Jackson Twp. 44–21 Butlerville; Greensburg 45–20 Sandcreek; Sandusky 39–31 St. Paul; North Vernon 45–27 Jackson; Greensburg 49–37 Sandusky; Greensburg 33–30 North Vernon. Officials: Hal Harris, Samuel Kelley.

HARTFORD CITY: Redkey 35–23 Gray; Portland 35–17 Poling; Pennville 38–29 Dunkirk; Madison 40–22 Jefferson; Montpelier 30–29 Hartford City; Roll 41–20 Bryant; Ridgeville 24–23 Redkey; Pennville 36–27 Portland; Montpelier 50–28 Madison; Ridgeville 20–18 Roll; Pennville 43–29 Montpelier; Pennville 33–28 Ridgeville. Officials: Al Jackson, George Chestnut, B. R. Hosier.

HUNTINGTON: Andrews 47–30 Lancaster; South Whitley 30–9 Banquo; Jefferson Twp. 24–15 Polk Twp.; Jackson Twp. 41–27 Markle; Bippus 26–24 Clear Creek; Rock Creek Center 42–29 Washington Center; Union Twp. 27–23 Salamonie Twp.; Huntington 52–23 Huntington Twp.; Andrews 45–29 South Whitley; Jackson Twp. 57–30 Jefferson Twp.; Rock Creek 47–23 Bippus; Huntington 24–19 Union Twp.; Jackson Twp. 37–35 Andrews; Huntington 57–18 Rock Creek; Huntington 36–35 Jackson Twp. Officials: Lundy Welborn, M.E. Somers, Jacob McClure.

INDIANAPOLIS: Howe 37–30 Southport; Washington 39–35 Speedway; Ben Davis 44–34 Broad Ripple; Decatur Central 41–25 Franklin Twp.; Beech Grove 29–23 Shortridge; Lawrence Central 38–37 Warren Central; Manual 24–22 New Augusta; Tech 33–32 Howe; Washington 32–31 Ben Davis; Decatur Central 34–31 Beech Grove; Lawrence Central 39–33 Manual; Washington 34–30 Tech; Lawrence Central 33–30 Decatur Central; Lawrence Central 31–23 Washington. Officials: Clifford Phillips, T. R. Smith, Cecil Tharp.

JASPER: Huntingburg 54–28 Otwell; Winslow 36–25 Holland; Dubois 38–37 Petersburg; Jasper 44–24 Cuzco; Ireland 39–22 Stendal; Spurgeon 38–26 Birdseye; Winslow 41–32 Huntingburg; Jasper 55–29 Dubois; Spurgeon 36–28 Ireland; Jasper 51–43 Winslow; Jasper 49–38 Spurgeon. Officials: Carl Jerger, Fred Wampler.

JEFFERSONVILLE: Salisbury 35–18 Laconia; Silver Creek 36–28 Henryville; Elizabeth 35–20 Lanesville; New Albany 49–20 New Middleton; Jeffersonville 55–20 Mauckport; Georgetown 24–22 Borden; Corydon 41–31 Charlestown; New Washington 56–22 New Amsterdam; Silver Creek 50–20 New Salisbury; New Albany 52–28 Elizabeth; Jeffersonville 46–23 Georgetown; Corydon 40–34 New Washington; New Albany 30–26 Silver Creek; Jeffersonville 27–23 Corydon; Jeffersonville 46–29 New Albany. Officials: Roland Baker, Hulett Crecelius, Fred Wilder.

KENDALLVILLE: Lima 38–25 Scott; Albion 32–26 Brighton; Cromwell 24–22 Topeka; Ligonier 31–26 Wawaka; Kendallville 39–26 Avilla; LaGrange 36–13 Springfield Twp.; Wolf Lake 34–31 Wolcottville; Shipshewana 37–36 Rome City (ot); Albion 28–17 Lima; Ligonier 17–14 Cromwell; Kendallville 35–25 LaGrange; Wolf Lake 35–24 Shipshewana; Albion 23–20 Ligonier; Wolf Lake 28–13 Kendallville; Wolf Lake 39–23 Albion. Officials: H. Windmiller, R. W. Warring, Louis Briner.

KOKOMO: Kokomo 41–22 Ervin; Clay Twp. 32–29 Russiaville; Greentown 60–20 New London; Jackson Twp. 34–27 West Middleton; Union Twp. 20–17 Howard Twp.; Kokomo 45–20 Clay Twp.; Greentown 40–20 Jackson Twp.; Kokomo 47–15 Union Twp.; Greentown 22–15 Kokomo. Officials: George Vaulk, Herbert Vaulk.

LAFAYETTE: West Lafayette 26–23 Klondike; Romney 34–23 Stockwell; Lafayette 66–12 Wea; Dayton 39–14 Clarks Hill; Montmorenci 34–17 Jackson Twp.; Battle Ground 39–24 West Point; Monitor 31–25 Buck Creek; West Lafayette 29–28 Romney; Lafayette 45–15 Dayton; Battle Ground 38–31 Montmorenci; West Lafayette 30–28 Monitor; Lafayette 61–31 Battle Ground; Lafayette 40–22 West Lafayette. Officials: Allen Klinck, Norman Dunlap, G. W. Strole.

LAWRENCEBURG: Rising Sun 45–40 Bright; Moores Hill 36–32 Patriot; Aurora 34–32

Tourney Time

Lawrenceburg; Dillsboro 32–26 Vevay; Rising Sun 41–37 Guilford; Aurora 43–17 Moores Hill; Dillsboro 41–38 Rising Sun; Aurora 48–28 Dillsboro. Officials: Lawrence Young, Norman Miller.

LEBANON: Whitestown 32–31 Advance; Lebanon 27–25 Thorntown; Jamestown 42–23 Zionsville; Central 48–42 Pinnell; Whitestown 41–19 Dover; Lebanon 44–32 Jamestown; Whitestown 37–24 Central; Lebanon 48–20 Whitestown. Officials: George Merkle, Thomas Baker.

LINTON: Switz City 29–28 Jasonville; Solsberry 40–28 Worthington; Owensburg 31–30 Scotland; Bloomfield 33–30 Midland; Lyons 66–21 Newberry 46–35 Marco; Switz City 35–32 Solsberry; Bloomfield 45–17 Owensburg; Linton 44–29 Lyons; Switz City 26–25 Bloomfield; Linton 37–35 Switz City. Officials: Charles Kruzan, Clarence Myles.

LOGANSPORT: Galveston 34–31 Lucerne; Royal Center 32–19 Metea; Logansport 43–19 Young America; Walton 44–35 Washington Twp.; Onward 33–21 New Waverly; Twelve Mile 36–35 Galveston; Logansport 22–20 Royal Center; Walton 38–33 Onward; Logansport 44–18 Twelve Mile; Logansport 44–20 Walton. Officials: Leonard Mayhugh, Herbert Edwards.

MADISON: Madison 56–16 Saluda; Paris Crossing 27–21 Dupont; Lexington 40–20 Deputy; Austin 32–24 Central; North Madison 37–31 Hanover; Madison 47–20 Scottsburg; Lexington 62–26 Paris Crossing; Austin 28–24 North Madison; Madison 40–23 Lexington; Madison 46–15 Austin. Officials: Ross Dorsett, Don McBride.

MARION: Marion 45–27 Jonesboro; Fairmount 19–14 Gas City; Van Buren 40–31 Jefferson Twp; Swayzee 32–26 Sweetser; Fairmount 42–40 Marion; Swayzee 41–28 Van Buren; Fairmount 31–28 Swayzee. Officials: Ralph King, H. D. McNew.

MICHIGAN CITY: Wanatah 47–21 Hanna; Michigan City 61–34; Rolling Prairie; LaCrosse 34–6 Mill Creek; Clinton Twp. 42–36 Westville; LaPorte 29–17 Union Twp.; Union Mills 53–23 Kingsbury; Springfield Twp. 48–19 Stillwell; Michigan City 45–26 Wanatah; Clinton Twp. 36–28 LaCrosse; LaPorte 42–32 Union Mills; Michigan City 54–27 Springfield Twp.; LaPorte 32–23 Clinton Twp.; Michigan City 36–30 LaPorte. Officials: Wayne Cunningham, Charles Garrett, Max Hildreth.

MITCHELL: Marshall Twp. 38–35 Huron; Mitchell 30–27 Shawswick; Springville 34–26 Williams; Bedford 43–23 Fayettsville; Oolitic 34–23 Tunnelton; Marshall Twp. 40–30 Heltonville; Mitchell 49–23 Springville; Bedford 44–29 Oolitic; Mitchell 39–26 Marshall Twp.; Bedford 25–24 Mitchell. Officials: Irvin Springer, Clyde Castle.

MONTICELLO: Monticello 33–29 Chalmers; Burnettsville 43–35 Idaville; Monon 38–19 Reynolds; Buffalo 29–20 Wolcott; Monticello 37–32 Brookston; Monon 47–37 Burnettsville; Monticello 47–21 Buffalo; Monticello 29–23 Monon. Officials: Ralph Eades, Doxie Reeves.

MOROCCO: Rensselaer 20–12 DeMotte; Remington 38–30 Goodland; Kentland 35–30 Tefft; Morocco 29–19 Fair Oaks; Mt. Ayr 31–30 Wheatfield; Brook 27–26 Rensselaer (ot); Remington 39–26 Kentland; Mt. Ayr 25–17 Morocco; Brook 32–23 Remington; Brook 36–24 Mt. Ayr. Officials: Albert Etter, Robert Hold.

MUNCIE: Royerton 55–41 Albany; DeSoto 40–36 Center; Gaston 48–31 Eaton; Yorktown 37–23 Harrison; Burris 47–29 Central; Selma 43–27 Daleville; Albany 52–21 Cowan; DeSoto 40–36 Gaston; Burris 47–32 Yorktown; Selma 51–36 Albany; Burris 38–24 DeSoto; Burris 49–30 Selma. Officials: Evan Crawley, Phil Eskew, Walter Marks.

NEW CASTLE: Mooreland 23–22 Kennard; Mt. Summit 38–27 New Lisbon; Middletown

42–17 Sulphur Springs; Spiceland 34–24 Knightstown; Straughn 29–27 New Castle; Lewisville 41–31 Cadiz; Mooreland 48–28 Mt. Summit; Middletown 43–36 Spiceland; Straughn 35–15 Lewisville; Mooreland 38–31 Middletown; Straughn 30–26 Mooreland. Officials: A. T. Krider, Myron Weldy.

OTTERBEIN: Ambia 31–30 Raub; Oxford 30–29 Fowler (ot); Otterbein 45–23 Boswell; Freeland Park 33–15 Earl Park; Wadena 49–35 Pine Twp.; Ambia 41–39 Gilboa; Otterbein 36–33 Oxford; Freeland Park 30–24 Wadena; Otterbein 53–26 Ambia; Otterbein 36–32 Freeland Park. Officials: Devon Eaton, King Telle.

PAOLI: Orleans 42–31 Milltown; Morgan Twp. 27–18 Campbellsburg; French Lick 60–34 English; Hardinsburg 59–24 Little York; Salem 40–26 Paoli; Pekin 40–38 West Baden; Marengo 52–31 Leavenworth; Orleans 45–35 Morgan Twp.; French Lick 47–32 Hardinsburg; Salem 34–31 Pekin; Orleans 27–21 Marengo; French Lick 37–29 Salem; French Lick 56–36 Orleans. Officials: Carl Porter, Robert Derrington, R. P. Cline.

PERU: Bunker Hill 28–26 Converse; Peru 52–26 Gilead; Macy 39–27 Butler Twp. Chili 25–17 Jefferson Twp.; Clay Twp. 27–25 Amboy; Bunker Hill 53–19 Deedsville; Peru 37–24 Macy; Clay 21–20 Chili; Peru 47–20 Bunker Hill; Peru 54–26 Clay. Officials: Otho Piper, Raymond Trobaugh.

PLAINFIELD: Clayton 25–21 Lizton; North Salem 30–19 Danville; Stilesville 45–25 New Winchester; Brownsburg 42–27 Plainfield; Avon 48–35 Amo; Pittsboro 20–18 Clayton; North Salem 34–28 Stilesville; Brownsburg 32–27 Avon; Pittsboro 38–27 North Salem; Brownsburg 23–22 Pittsboro. Officials: A. E. Pitcher, John Blankenship.

PLYMOUTH: Grovertown 38–19 LaPaz; Culver 50–36 Plymouth; Tippecanoe 43–18 Hamlet; Bourbon 31–21 Center Twp.; Argos 51–16 Tyner; San Pierre 43–35 North Judson; Bremen 37–29 Knox; Grovertown 34–24 West Twp.; Culver 41–34 Tippecanoe; Bourbon 26–22 Argos; Bremen 37–25 San Pierre; Culver 43–23 Grovertown; Bremen 25–24 Bourbon; Culver 34–23 Bremen. Officials: E. L. Druckamiller, Hugh Bergstrom, C. E. Baer.

PRINCETON: Owensville 25–24 Mackey; Princeton 50–26 Francisco; Fort Branch 30–27 Hazleton; Oakland City 40–30 Mount Olympus; Haubstadt 36–31 Patoka; Owensville 30–29 Princeton; Fort Branch 34–16 Oakland City; Owensville 37–33 Haubstadt; Fort Branch 39–28 Owensville. Officials: Arad McCutchan, Carl Ross.

RICHMOND: Centerville 22–16 Boston; Williamsburg 52–21 Webster; Whitewater 29–21 Greens Fork; Lincoln 24–22 Fountain City; Richmond 34–23 Economy; Hagerstown 30–17 Milton; Centerville 33–15 Williamsburg; Cambridge City 26–18 Whitewater; Richmond 44–27 Hagerstown; Centerville 18–16 Cambridge City; Richmond 36–22 Centerville. Officials: Winston Ashley, Clyde Sutton.

RUSHVILLE: Morton Memorial 39–16 Carthage; Mays 30–28 Milroy; Arlington 39–35 New Salem; Rushville 49–22 Raleigh; Morton Memorial 47–25 Manilla; Arlington 43–33 Mays; Morton Memorial 48–20 Rushville; Arlington 32–31 Morton Memorial. Officials: Wilbur May, Fred Pierson.

SEYMOUR: Brownstown 36–28 Cortland; Seymour 53–16 Freetown; Medora 53–27 Scipio; Crothersville 30–20 Tampico; Vallonia 34–24 Hayden; Brownstown 49–25 Clearspring; Seymour 41–31 Medora; Crothersville 26–22 Vallonia; Seymour 40–33 Brownstown; Seymour 45–11 Crothersville. Officials: John Lyskowinski, William Reimann.

SHELBYVILLE: Hope 36–26 Clifford; Morristown 19–18 Waldron; Shelbyville 65–22 Mt.

Tourney Time

Auburn; Columbus 36–27 Fairland; Flat Rock 46–29 Moral Twp.; Hope 20–18 Boggstown; Shelbyville 19–12 Morristown; Columbus 39–30 Flat Rock; Shelbyville 43–13 Hope; Columbus 39–34 Shelbyville. Officials: Dana Chandler, George Williams.

SHERIDAN: Atlanta 41–32 Sharpsville; Fishers 33–27 Goldsmith; Noblesville 45–19 Prairie Twp.; Kempton 27–26 Carmel; Arcadia 47–35 Cicero; Tipton 42–21; Westfield; Walnut Grove 60–39 Windfall; Sheridan 27–24 Atlanta; Fishers 38–25 Noblesville; Arcadia 47–31 Kempton; Tipton 30–25 Walnut Grove; Fishers 26–22 Sheridan; Tipton 49–22 Arcadia; Tipton 61–21 Fishers. Officials: William Ellis, Jack O'Neal, Aaron Belcher.

SOUTH BEND: Central 30–22 Adams; Riley 55–20 Walkerton; Wilson 32–21 Greene; Madison 52–28 Lakeville; North Liberty 29–27 Washington; Washington-Clay 34–33 Mishawaka; Central 36–21 New Carlisle; Riley 60–37 Wilson; North Liberty 42–36 Madison; Central 37–30 Washington-Clay; North Liberty 22–19 Riley; Central 36–32 North Liberty. Officials: Donald Coar, William Kendall, Paul Bateman.

SULLIVAN: Pleasantville 30–27 Shelburn; Fairbanks 36–26 Merom; Sullivan 51–21 Farmersburg; Dugger 27–25 Graysville; New Lebanon 27–23 Carlisle; Pleasantville 46–28 Hymera; Sullivan 51–32 Fairbanks; Dugger 51–30 New Lebanon; Sullivan 46–35 Pleasantville; Sullivan 42–26 Dugger. Officials: Walter Ringer, William Pointer.

TELL CITY: Tell City 25–24 Dale; Troy 26–20 Grandview; Cannelton 42–17 Gentryville; Rockport 48–16 Luce Twp.; Tell City 43–19 Chrisney; Cannelton 40–25 Troy; Tell City 30–22 Rockport; Tell City 41–21 Cannelton. Officials: Kenneth Ostermeyer, David Royalty.

TERRE HAUTE: Laboratory 52–22 Blackhawk; Honey Creek 37–24 Gerstmeyer; Concannon 57–11 New Goshen; Riley 28–19 Prairie Creek; Pimento 27–25 Garfield; Fontanet 28–22 Glenn; Wiley 44–31 Otter Creek; Laboratory 47–35 West Terre Haute; Honey Creek 30–25 Concannon; Pimento 39–32 Riley; Wiley 52–26 Fontanet; Laboratory 41–36 Honey Creek; Wiley 34–23 Pimento; Wiley 58–45 Laboratory. Officials: Walter Loman, George Kerr, Edward Stuteville.

VINCENNES: Decker 37–20 Sandborn; Fritchton 25–23 Oaktown; Wheatland 44–29 Edwardsport; Vincennes 40–24 Decker Chapel; Bicknell 29–19 Freelandville; Bruceville 29–24 Monroe City; Decker 32–26 Fritchton (ot); Vincennes 44–24 Wheatland; Bicknell 16–15 Bruceville; Decker 26–25 Vincennes; Bicknell 26–21 Decker. Officials: Ralph Black, Harry Briggs.

WABASH: Somerset 37–24 Chippewa; Wabash 24–9 Lagro; Roann 54–26 Urbana; Laketon 32–22 Linlawn; North Manchester 41–21 Chester Twp.; Somerset 30–29 LaFontaine; Wabash 32–26 Roann; North Manchester 24–23 Laketon; Somerset 26–25 Wabash; North Manchester 31–28 Somerset. Officials: Everett Goshorn, Clay Layman.

WARSAW: Etna Green 37–36 Milford; Mentone 33–25 Burket; Sidney 51–39 North Webster; Pierceton 32–14 Claypool; Leesburg 36–28 Larwill; Atwood 32–30 Silver Lake; Warsaw 51–36 Syracuse; Etna Green 46–42 Beaver Dam; Sidney 39–37 Mentone (ot); Pierceton 40–23 Leesburg; Warsaw 56–33 Atwood; Sidney 31–25 Etna Green; Warsaw 38–19 Pierceton; Warsaw 45–32 Sidney. Officials: Donald Dickie, Cecil Young, Vaughn Crow.

WASHINGTON: Shoals 60–25 Trinity Springs; Elmore Twp. 35–27 Alfordsville; Epsom 28–23 Glendale; Barr Twp. 48–33 Odon; Washington 57–23 Loogootee; Shoals 38–33 Plainville; Elnora 37–22 Epsom; Washington 50–30 Barr Twp.; Elnora 21–18 Shoals; Washington 55–17 Elnora. Officials: Clarence Riggs, William Coulter.

WINAMAC: Winamac 44–26 Talma; Kewanna 47–27 Francesville; Richland Center 27–22 Leiters Ford; Grass Creek 45–36 Medaryville; Rochester 41–32 Star City; Fulton 47–18 Monterey;

IHSAA Scores / 1940–1949

Akron 41–34 Pulaski; Winamac 42–25 Kewanna; Richland Center 34–33 Grass Creek; Fulton 23–13 Rochester; Winamac 34–33 Akron (ot); Fulton 44–23 Richland Center; Fulton 31–21 Winamac. Officials: Don Veller, H.P. Berkey, Omer Bixel.

WINCHESTER: Saratoga 35–25 Lynn; Parker 53–52 Lincoln; Winchester 53–22 Green Twp.; Wayne 38–31 Modoc; Farmland 31–18 Huntsville; Union City 43–24 Losantville; McKinley 34–28 Stoney Creek; Spartanburg 46–27 Jackson; Saratoga 27–24 Parker; Winchester 52–25 Wayne; Union City 31–12 Farmland; McKinley 26–24 Spartanburg (2ot); Winchester 40–34 Saratoga; Union City 41–15 McKinley; Winchester 45–34 Union City. Officials: John Hilligoss, George Collyer, Marvin Todd.

1942 REGIONALS

BEDFORD: Bedford 40–23 Seymour; Jeffersonville 35–32 French Lick; Bedford 32–26 Jeffersonville. Officials: King Telle, William Coulter.

EVANSVILLE: Central 44–21 Tell City; Boonville 33–28 Fort Branch; Central 38–36 Boonville (3ot). Officials: Hulett Crecelius, Norman Dunlap.

FORT WAYNE: Central 47–33 Warsaw; Wolf Lake 31–27 Butler; Wolf Lake 39–24 Central. Officials: Thomas Baker, George Williams.

GREENCASTLE: Crawfordsville 39–27 Attica; Greencastle 37–34 Clinton; Crawfordsville 42–29 Greencastle. Officials: Clyde Castle, Irvin Springer.

HAMMOND: Horace Mann 31–26 Michigan City; East Chicago Roosevelt 40–29 Brook; Horace Mann 40–24 Roosevelt. Officials: Cecil Young, Louis Briner.

HUNTINGTON: Huntington 54–40 Liberty Center; Pennville 28–23 Pleasant Mills; Huntington 59–20 Pennville. Officials: L. E. Fink, Walter Thurston.

INDIANAPOLIS: Lawrence Central 39–27 Brownsburg; Anderson 41–29 Greenfield; Lawrence Central 32–29 Anderson. Officials: Karl Dickerson, Philip Eskew.

LAFAYETTE: Lafayette 38–18 Lebanon; Frankfort 42–34 Otterbein; Frankfort 26–24 Lafayette. Officials: George Bender, Lawrence Gaunt.

LOGANSPORT: Flora 28–25 Monticello; Logansport 27–23 Peru; Logansport 42–25 Flora. Officials: R. Wayne Cunningham, Charles G. Garrett.

MARION: Fairmount 33–32 North Manchester; Tipton 29–13 Greentown; Tipton 55–25 Fairmount. Officials: A. T. Krider, Clayton Hughes.

MARTINSVILLE: Terre Haute Wiley 51–25 Monrovia; Linton 55–45 Brazil; Wiley 48–47 Linton. Officials: Dana Chandler, Robert Hoffman.

MUNCIE: Burris 48–36 Winchester; Richmond 65–46 Straughn; Burris 37–28 Richmond. Officials: Frank Jarrell, Paul Bateman.

RUSHVILLE: Kitchel 33–29 Arlington; Aurora 42–29 Cross Plains; Aurora 55–33 Kitchel. Officials: Dean Malaska, G. P. Silver.

SHELBYVILLE: Madison 32–29 Greensburg; Franklin 31–29 Columbus; Madison 40–18 Franklin. Officials: T. R. Smith, Cecil Tharp.

SOUTH BEND: Culver 29–28 Goshen; Central 51–21 Fulton; Central 38–31 Goshen. Officials: Allen Klinck, C. O. Walls.

WASHINGTON: Jasper 36–31 Bicknell; Washington 53–29 Sullivan; Washington 27–24 Jasper. Officials: Winston Ashley, William E. Pointer.

Tourney Time

1942 SEMI-FINALS

ANDERSON: Crawfordsville 30–29 Madison; Lawrence Central 38–36 Aurora; Crawfordsville 42–38 Lawrence Central. Officials: L. E. Fink, Allen Klinck.

HAMMOND: South Bend Central 24–22 Logansport (ot); Frankfort 45–32 Gary Horace Mann; Frankfort 28–24 Central. Officials: T. R. Smith, Karl Dickerson.

MUNCIE: Tipton 45–38 Huntington; Burris 49–21 Wolf Lake; Burris 42–30 Tipton. Officials: Winston Ashley, George Bender.

VINCENNES: Washington 22–20 Evansville Central; Bedford 37–26 Terre Haute Wiley; Washington 37–20 Bedford. Officials: Thomas Baker, George Williams.

1942 FINALS—March 21

INDIANAPOLIS (Butler Fieldhouse): Washington 42–32 Frankfort; Muncie Burris 42–27 Crawfordsville; Washington 24–18 Burris. Officials: Thomas Baker, L.E. Fink.

1943 SECTIONALS

ANDERSON: Alexandria 46–33 Summitville; Anderson 45–33 Elwood; Markleville 45–37 St. Mary's; Lapel 39–37 Pendleton; Alexandria 33–25 Frankton; Markleville 38–36 Anderson; Lapel 37–35 Alexandria; Lapel 35–27 Markleville. Officials: Allen Klinck, H. D. McNew.

ANGOLA: Garrett 45–34 Churubusco; Auburn 54–25 Orland; Angola 51–21 Scott Center; Metz 36–34 Fremont; Waterloo 43–32 Hamilton; Butler 37–35 Spencerville; Ashley 36–27 Pleasant Lake; St. Joe 44–42 Salem Center; Auburn 42–29 Garrett; Angola 62–33 Metz; Waterloo 45–40 Butler; Ashley 33–27 St. Joe; Auburn 46–29 Angola; Waterloo 51–35 Ashley; Auburn 54–22 Waterloo. Officials: Lloyd Bryan, George Merkle, Marvin Todd.

ATTICA: Kingman 34–24 West Lebanon; Hillsboro 49–43 Attica; Veedersburg 47–21 Perrysville; Williamsport 30–21 Covington; Pine Village 54–18 Wallace; Hillsboro 33–30 Kingman; Williamsport 38–27 Veedersburg; Hillsboro 35–32 Pine Village; Hillsboro 33–20 Williamsport. Officials: Doxie Reeves, Cecil Tharp.

AURORA: Lawrenceburg 50–21 Dillsboro; Rising Sun 44–12 Moores Hill; Aurora 27–20 Guilford; Vevay 41–29 Patriot; Lawrenceburg 33–21 Bright; Aurora 24–22 Rising Sun; Lawrenceburg 38–22 Vevay; Aurora 26–24 Lawrenceburg (ot). Officials: Max Thompson, J. T. Haywood.

BATESVILLE: Sunman 47–18 New Marion; Osgood 49–18 Versailles; Holton 34–33 Milan; Batesville 27–18 Cross Plains; Sunman 45–29 Napoleon; Holton 27–23 Osgood (ot); Batesville 32–29 Sunman (ot); Batesville 32–22 Holton. Officials: Paul Cly, Walter Loman.

BEDFORD: Oolitic 51–26 Fayetteville; Marshall Twp. 44–33 Shawswick; Huron 60–31 Tunnelton; Bedford 47–23 Mitchell; Oolitic 64–42 Williams. Marshall Twp. 43–36 Huron; Bedford 28–25 Oolitic; Bedford 54–21 Marshall Twp. Officials: Harry Briggs, Jewell Young.

BLUFFTON: Liberty Center 42–40 Petroleum; Chester Center 41–16 Lancaster Central; Bluffton 26–24 Jackson Center; Union Center 39–34 Ossian; Liberty Center 36–29 Rockcreek Center; Bluff– ton 29–20 Chester Center; Liberty Center 29–26 Union Center; Bluffton 36–33 Liberty Center. Officials: Harold McSwane, Otho Piper.

IHSAA Scores | 1940–1949

BOONVILLE: Yankeetown 41–18 Selvin; Newburgh 33–12 Folsomville; Boonville 59–5 Chandler; Lynnville 31–22 Millersburg; Elberfeld 29–23 Tennyson; Yankeetown 37–21 Newburgh; Boonville 44–32 Lynnville; Yankeetown 36–13 Elberfeld; Boonville 54–26 Yankeetown. Officials: Lawrence Young, Clarence Riggs.

BRAZIL: Spencer 58–29 Patricksburg; Posey Twp. 44–13 Jefferson Twp.; Brazil 43–29 Gosport; Cory 31–24 Ashboro; Van Buren 37–26 Bowling Green; Freedom 21–20 Clay City; Spencer 55–19 Quincy; Brazil 62–20 Posey Twp.; Cory 45–30 Van Buren; Spencer 63–29 Freedom; Brazil 40–24 Cory; Brazil 38–29 Spencer. Officials: Frank Luzar, James Conover, Bernard Lampe.

CANNELTON: Tell City 26–22 Troy; Grandview 41–29 Gentryville; Chrisney 32–31 Rockport; Cannelton 34–20 Dale; Tell City 35–17 Luce Twp.; Chrisney 30–18 Grandview; Tell City 38–28 Cannelton; Tell City 38–17 Chrisney. Officials: Carl Jerger, Robert Rose.

CONNERSVILLE: Brownsville 2–0 Bentonville (forfeit); Connersville 34–31 Springfield Twp.; Everton 29–28 Whitewater; Kitchel 30–17 Brookville; Harrisburg 60–23 Laurel; Orange 40–39 Liberty; Alquina 33–20 Fairview; Connersville 55–31 Brownsville; Kitchel 50–17; Everton; Orange 51–39 Harrisburg; Connersville 36–20 Alquina; Kitchel 44–27 Orange; Kitchel 36–35 Connersville (2ot). Officials: Stephen Baker, Cloyd Julian, Wilbur May.

CLINTON: Rosedale 37–24 St. Bernice; Tangier 52–29 Bellmore; Clinton 41–16 Hillsdale; Montezuma 42–27 Newport; Rockville 30–24 Mecca; Bridgeton 39–23 Dana; Marshall 26–23 Cayuga; Bloomingdale 43–26 Greene Twp.; Tangier 37–23 Rosedale; Clinton 35–31 Montezuma; Rockville 35–33 Bridgeton; Marshall 36–27 Bloomingdale; Clinton 31–20 Tangier; Rockville 52–38 Marshall; Clinton 28–21 Rockville. Officials: W. N. Ringer, George Kerr, Lowell Willis.

CRAWFORDSVILLE: Bowers 27–23 New Market; Alamo 48–30 Wingate; Darlington 37–24 Waveland; Ladoga 34–20 Waynetown; New Ross 43–29 Linden; Crawfordsville 42–20 Bowers; Alamo 43–35 Darlington; Ladoga 30–25 New Ross; Crawfordsville 43–29 Alamo; Crawfordsville 41 29 Ladoga. Officials: T. R. Smith, Norman Dunlap.

DANVILLE: Speedway 39–24 Lizton; Plainfield 33–21 Danville. North Salem 51–23 New Winchester; Amo 25–17 Clayton; Brownsburg 35–23 Stilesville; Pittsboro 41–30 Avon; Plainfield 23–22 Speedway; Amo 29–27 North Salem; Pittsboro 33–26 Brownsburg; Plainfield 32–31 Amo; Plainfield 30–22. Officials: Robert Hold, Donald Cooper.

DECATUR: Berne 34–22 Pleasant Mills. Monroe 41–15 Monmouth; Kirkland 33–19 Jefferson Twp.; Decatur 39–27 Geneva; Hartford Center 41–19 Decatur Catholic; Monroe 33–25 Berne; Decatur 36–19 Kirkland; Monroe 24–22 Hartford Center; Monroe 36–23 Decatur. Officials: Everett Goshorn, Arthur Lloyd.

EAST CHICAGO: Washington 48–24 Hobart; Roosevelt 42–35 Hammond; Clark 56–36 Wheeler; Whiting 41–26 Crown Point; Hammond Tech 34–28 Lowell; Merrillville 51–23 Dyer; Griffith 50–30 Central Catholic; Portage 43–30 Edison; Roosevelt 36–33 Washington (ot); Clark 40–29 Whiting; Hammond Tech 39–30 Merrillville; Portage Twp. 56–29 Griffith; Clark 44–42 Roosevelt; Hammond Tech 42–29 Portage; Clark 33–29 Hammond Tech. Officials: Paul Bateman, Russell Arndt, Cecil Young.

EVANSVILLE: Central 45–22 Washington; Memorial 49–15 Griffin; Reitz 26–24 Poseyville; Lincoln 45–25 Cynthiana; Mt. Vernon 22–21 New Harmony; Wadesville 28–13 Stewartsville; Central 25–24 Bosse; Memorial 29–25 Reitz; Mt. Vernon 55–34 Lincoln; Central 66–10 Wadesville; Memorial 56–37 Mt. Vernon; Central 49–30 Memorial. Officials: Clarence Tolbert, Roy Johnson, Ralph Green.

Tourney Time

FLORA: Flora 32–9 Deer Creek. Cutler 38–24 Adams Twp.; Carrollton 35–18 Rockfield; Delphi 28–24 Camden; Burlington 39–36 Flora; Cutler 34–20 Carrollton; Burlington 30–28 Delphi; Burlington 23–21 Cutler. Officials: Otto Albright, Ross Dean.

FORT BRANCH: Princeton 45–19 Owensville; Ft. Branch 23–10 Francisco; Mt. Olympus 27–22 Patoka; Hazleton 41–29 Haubstadt; Mackey 24–22 Oakland City; Princeton 68–19 Lincoln; Ft. Branch 28–26 Mt. Olympus (ot); Mackey 40–26 Hazleton; Princeton 50–29 Ft. Branch; Princeton 60–34 Mackey. Officials: Irvin Springer, William Coulter.

FORT WAYNE: Monroeville 37–35 Maumee Twp.; South Side 27–15 New Haven; Central 58–36 Elmhurst; North Side 36–15 Lafayette Central; Hoagland 52–27 Coesse; Leo 62–31 Concordia; Central Catholic 45–28 Harlan; Huntertown 46–21 Arcola; South Side 47–21 Monroeville; Central 37–34 North Side; Leo 29–27 Hoagland; Huntertown 35–34 Central Catholic; Central 25–24 South Side; Huntertown 36–32 Leo; Central 62–49 Huntertown. Officials: A. T. Krider, Myron Weldy, R. W. Warring.

FOWLER: Boswell 26–24 Fowler; Freeland Park 32–15 Earl Park; Pine Twp. 39–22 Wadena; Otterbein 29–17 Gilboa; Raub 30–21 Ambia; Oxford 26–14 Boswell; Freeland 35–23 Pine; Raub 26–18 Otterbein; Oxford 25–24 Freeland; Oxford 26–14 Raub. Officials: George Vaulk, Herbert Vaulk.

FRANKFORT: Colfax 52–27 Washington Twp.; Michigantown 30–23 Mulberry; Rossville 38–15 Sugar Creek Twp.; Frankfort 46–16 Jackson; Twp.; Kirklin 20–18 Forest; Colfax 50–32 Scircleville; Michigantown 32–31 Rossville; Frankfort 33–23 Kirklin; Colfax 33–19 Michigantown; Frankfort 29–17 Colfax. Officials: A. E. Pitcher, Layall Fisher.

FRANKLIN: Center Grove 35–33 Edinburg; Whiteland 32–28 Franklin; Greenwood 42–34 Nineveh; Nashville 47–41 Helmsburg; Clark 58–13 Van Buren; Union 47–39 Masonic Home; Center Grove 47–17 Trafalgar; Greenwood 23–22 Whiteland; Clark 33–30 Nashville; Center Grove 32–24 Union; Greenwood 29–27 Clark; Center Grove 23–19 Greenwood. Officials: Aaron Belcher, Harold Porter, Robert Hobbs.

FRENCH LICK: Marengo 52–27 Little York; West Baden 39–20 Milltown; French Lick 48–31 Pekin; Hardinsburg 34–29 Leavenworth (ot); Salem 46–32 English; Campbellsburg 57–55 Orleans; Paoli 53–27 Marengo; French Lick 59–38 West Baden; Salem 55–30 Hardinsburg; Paoli 58–39 Campbellsburg; French Lick 43–34 Salem; French Lick 36–35 Paoli. Officials: John Lyskowinski, Fred Wampler, Loren Harris.

GARY: Emerson 34–30 Wirt; Wallace 74–28 Washington Twp.; Edison 58–39 Liberty Center; Froebel 62–23 Kouts; Horace Mann 47–19 Boone Grove; Tolleston 27–26 Roosevelt; Valparaiso 46–29 Hebron; Chesterton 40–33 Morgan Twp.; Wallace 37–32 Emerson; Froebel 55–39 Edison; Horace Mann 35–26 Tolleston; Valparaiso 70–24 Chesterton; Wallace 45–40 Froebel; Valparaiso 46–33 Horace Mann; Wallace 60–40 Valparaiso. Officials: L. E. Fink, W. E. Thurston, Norris Ward.

GREENCASTLE: Fillmore 47–39 Belle Union; Greencastle 29–28 Roachdale; Bainbridge 41–17 Cloverdale; Russellville 49–8 Reelsville; Greencastle 45–30 Fillmore; Bainbridge 26–25 Russellville; Greencastle 33–32 Bainbridge (ot). Officials :Charles Kruzan, Hardy Songer.

GREENFIELD: Maxwell 48–24 McCordsville; Greenfield 40–20 New Palestine; Wilkinson 30–21 Charlottesville; Eden 36–34 Mt. Comfort; Fortville 31–19 Westland; Greenfield 48–35 Maxwell; Eden 32–15 Wilkinson; Greenfield 29–12 Fortville; Greenfield 52–23 Eden. Officials: George Williams, Thomas Stirling.

GREENSBURG: Greensburg 63–27 Sandcreek; North Vernon 32–23 Jackson; Sandusky 39–23 Zenas; New Point 25–14 Vernon; Burney 33–29 St. Paul; Clarksburg 40–27 Butlerville;

IHSAA Scores | 1940–1949

Greensburg 43–37 North Vernon; New Point 30–26 Sandusky; Burney 31–26 Clarksburg; Greensburg 41–18 New Point; Greensburg 72–21 Burney. Officials: William Newbold, Cleon Reynolds.

HARTFORD CITY: Dunkirk 50–32 Roll; Pennville 57–27 Redkey; Portland 39–25 Ridgeville; Hartford City 36–16 Jefferson; Montpelier 39–26 Madison; Dunkirk 46–26 Poling; Portland 28–22 Pennville; Hartford City 37–22 Montpelier; Dunkirk 39–38 Portland. Dunkirk 43–42 Hartford City. Officials: Clay Layman, E. D. Milhon.

HUNTINGTON: Jefferson Center 44–40 Jefferson Twp.; Andrews 43–29 Lancaster Center; Salamonie Twp. 31–29 Jackson Twp.; Rockcreek Center 19–17 Wayne Twp.; Huntington 30–25 Union. Huntington Catholic 37–32 Bippus; Clear Creek 44–30 Polk Twp.; Huntington Twp. 49–16 Markle; Andrews 44–26 Jefferson Center; Salamonie Twp. 54–19 Rock Creek Center; Huntington 45–20 Huntington Catholic; Clear Creek 28–24 Huntington Twp.; Andrews 27–21 Salamonie Twp.; Huntington 31–23 Clear Creek; Andrews 29–23 Huntington. Officials: Louis Briner, H. Windmiller, Fred White.

INDIANAPOLIS: Lawrence 35–30 Warren; Ben Davis 37–34 Broad Ripple; Shortridge 44–22 Crispus Attucks; Beech Grove 29–28 School for the Deaf; Howe 34–23 Decatur Central; Washington 33–17 Cathedral; Manual 35–18 Sacred Heart; Tech 38–35 Southport; Lawrence 45–35 Ben Davis; Shortridge 39–26 Beech Grove; Howe 28–27 Washington; Tech 49–31 Manual; Lawrence 35–33 Shortridge; Howe 32–31 Tech; Lawrence 42–39 Howe. Officials: C. N. Phillips, Lawrence Gaunt, Phil N. Eskew.

JASPER: Holland 32–27 Petersburg; Jasper 70–21 Ireland; Spurgeon 48–26 Stendal; Huntingburg 26–24 Dubois; Otwell 37–35 Cuzco; Winslow 66–26 Jefferson Twp.; Jasper 43–33 Holland; Huntingburg 39–38 Spurgeon; Winslow 42–26 Otwell; Jasper 47–35 Huntingburg; Jasper 32–28 Winslow. Officials: Frank Jarrell, Evan Crawley.

JEFFERSONVILLE: Elizabeth 40–33 New Amsterdam; Mauckport 41–30 Lanesville; New Albany 65–19 Borden; Jeffersonville 45–26 Corydon; Silver Creek 48–31 North Middletown; New Salisbury 34–24 Palmyra; North Washington 30–20 Georgetown; New Albany 43–21 Mauckport; Jeffersonville 22–21 Silver Creek; New Salisbury 29–25 New Washington; New Albany 63–22 Elizabeth; Jeffersonville 52–32 New Salisbury; Jeffersonville 42–36 New Albany (ot). Officials: Robert Hoffman, Hulett Crecelius, David Royalty.

KENDALLVILLE: Cromwell 20–15 Albion; Wolf Lake 21–13 Brighton; Shipshewana 36–31 LaGrange; Avilla 31–22 Ligonier; Wawaka 41–30 Rome City; Wolcottville 51–29 Howe Military; Kendallville 39–22 Scott; Lima 25–24 Topeka; Cromwell 28–18 Wolf Lake; Avilla 44–41 Shipshewana; Wolcottville 55–28 Wawaka; Kendallville 58–13 Lima; Avilla 31–29 Cromwell; Kendallville 36–26 Wolcottville; Kendallville 37–33 Avilla. Officials: Donald Coar, Donald Dickie, Kenneth Michel.

KOKOMO: West Middleton 35–27 Union Twp.; Greentown 44–19 Ervin Twp.; Jackson Twp. 33–24 Clay Twp.; Russiaville 41–27 New London; Kokomo 43–13 West Middleton; Greentown 25–19 Jackson Twp.; Kokomo 45–28 Russiaville; Kokomo 23–19 Greentown. Officials: John Walker, Frank Kresler.

LAFAYETTE: Battleground 37–21 West Lafayette; Romney 32–23 Shadeland; Jackson Twp. 39–37 Wea; Stockwell 66–21 Montmorenci; Clarks Hill 26–23 West Point; Jefferson 56–27 Buck Creek; Monitor 58–25 Dayton; Battleground 24–23 Klondike; Romney 56–28 Jackson Twp.; Clarks Hill 46–35 Stockwell; Monitor 41–36 Jefferson; Battleground 33–25 Romney; Monitor 30–29

Tourney Time

Clarks Hill; Monitor 41–35 Battleground. Officials: G. P. Silver, Dean Malaska ,Walter Floyd.

LAPORTE: Wanatah 37–28 Springfield; St. Mary's 52–32 Clinton Twp.; Jackson Center 45–30 Kingsbury; Michigan City 79–29 Mill Creek; LaCrosse 37–29 Union Twp.; LaPorte 73–21 Stillwell; Rolling Prairie 49–21 Hanna; Westville 25–23 Union Mills; St. Mary's 32–20 Wanatah; Michigan City 51–36 Jackson Center; LaPorte 31–20 LaCrosse; Rolling Prairie 30–28 Westville; Michigan City 46–29 St. Mary's; LaPorte 45–22 Rolling Prairie; Michigan City 42–37 LaPorte. Officials: R. Wayne Cunningham, Charles McManus, Sam Massette.

LEBANON: Whitestown 41–34 Advance; Lebanon 58–37 Zionsville; Thorntown 34–22 Pinnell; Jamestown 40–30 Central; Pike Twp. 33–20 Dover; Lebanon 57–27 Whitestown; Thorntown 44–19 Jamestown; Lebanon 44–23 Pike Twp.; Lebanon 40–29 Thorntown. Officials: Herbert Edwards, Jim Crowe.

LOGANSPORT: Lucerne 37–35 Galveston; Walton 33–31 Washington Twp.; Logansport 65–35 Young America; Royal Center 37–19 Onward; New Waverly 23–18 Metea; Lucerne 22–18 Twelve Mile; Logansport 46–17 Walton; Royal Center 40–25 New Waverly; Logansport 57–14 Lucerne; Logansport 40–27 Royal Center. Officials: Clyde Gentry, Joe Mullins.

MADISON: Madison 56–25 Deputy; Austin 23–19 Saluda; Hanover 31–18 Dupont; North Madison 31–24 Paris Crossing; Scottsburg 33–24 Central; Madison 56–16 Austin; North Madison 26–23 Hanover; Madison 47–30 Scottsburg; Madison 44–22 North Madison. Officials: Norman Miller, Alvin Heller.

MARION: Sweetser 34–22 Van Buren; Jonesboro 46–32 Gas City; Jefferson Twp. 36–28 Swayzee; Marion 44–16 St. Paul; Sweetser 40–39 Fairmount; Jefferson Twp. 23–22 Jonesboro; Marion 36–21 Sweetser; Marion 43–28 Jefferson Twp. Officials: Forrest Ballinger, Otto Crosley.

MARTINSVILLE: Mooresville 42–36 Monrovia; Martinsville 47–15 Unionville; Bloomington 59–35 Stinesville; University 48–31 Paragon; Ellettsville 54–22 Smithville; Morgantown 36–25 Eminence. Martinsville 46–30 Mooresville; Bloomington 34–31 University; Ellettsville 46–25 Morgantown; Martinsville 29–25 Bloomington; Martinsville 53–41 Ellettsville. Officials: William Reimann, Al Jackson.

MONTICELLO: Monticello 51–25 Burnettsville; Reynolds 41–25 Buffalo; Monon 32–27 Chalmers; Brookston 32–15 Wolcott; Round Grove 28–27 Idaville; Monticello 52–20 Reynolds; Brookston 33–23 Monon; Monticello 26–21 Round Grove; Monticello 29–27 Brookston. Officials: Albert Etter, Robert Etter.

MUNCIE: Burris 59–23 Eaton; Yorktown 53–30 Harrison; Center 38–36 DeSoto; Gaston 38–32 Daleville; Central 39–32 Royerton. Selma 36–30 Cowan; Burris 63–25 Albany; Center 23–13 Yorktown; Central 51–22 Gaston; Burris 45–22 Selma; Center 29–27 Central; Burris 34–22 Center. Officials: Thomas Baker, Raymond Hobbs, Fred Pierson;

NAPPANEE: Goshen 41–29 New Paris; Concord 49–18 Millersburg; Elkhart 45–33 Wakarusa; Nappanee 32–30 Baugo; Middlebury 47–34 Jefferson; Goshen 45–30 Bristol; Elkhart 47–42 Concord; Nappanee 39–34 Middlebury; Elkhart 37–34 Goshen; Elkhart 70–46 Nappanee. Officials: Joe Dienhart, Hubert Whitaker.

NEW CASTLE: Kennard 36–34 Lewisville; Knightstown 30–29 Middletown; Spiceland 49–31 Mt. Summit; Straughn 40–25 Sulphur Springs; Mooreland 41–17 Cadiz; New Castle 50–24 New Lisbon; Knightstown 41–39 Kennard; Spiceland 43–31 Straughn; New Castle 64–24 Mooreland. Spiceland 29–28 Knightstown; New Castle 59–33 Spiceland. Officials: George Bender, John Hilligoss.

IHSAA Scores | 1940–1949

PERU: Jefferson 32–19 Deedsville; Converse 33–12 Chili; Macy 43–26 Butler; Clay 31–21 Amboy; Peru 60–15 Gilead; Jefferson 41–37 Bunker Hill; Converse 59–40 Macy; Peru 50–12 Clay; Converse 34–14 Jefferson; Peru 22–18 Converse. Officials: William Lucas, John Janzaruk.

PLYMOUTH: North Judson 67–30 Tyner; LaPaz 33–24 Tippecanoe; Argos 43–34 West Twp.; San Pierre 47–24 Hamlet; Bourbon 46–44 Plymouth; Culver 52–37 Grovertown; Knox 39–38 Bremen (ot); North Judson 50–18 LaPaz; Argos 38–29 San Pierre. Bourbon 34–33 Culver; Knox 29–28 North Judson. Bourbon 24–23 Argos (ot); Bourbon 46–26 Knox. Officials: G. W. Strole, Tom Ciecka, George Collyer.

RENSSELAER: Kentland 33–26 Mt. Ayr; Remington 33–26 Rensselaer; Tefft 31–24 Fair Oaks; St. Joseph 39–32 DeMotte; Goodland 33–29 Brook; Wheatfield 45–35 Morocco; Remington 43–36 Kentland; Tefft 33–30 St. Joseph; Wheatfield 41–22 Goodland; Remington 58–28 Tefft. Remington 37–34 (ot.) Wheatfield. Officials: Forest M. Shaw, Lester Collins.

RICHMOND: Cambridge City 35–32 Williamsburg; Fountain City 42–25 Webster; Centerville 37–15 Greens Fork; Hagerstown 25–22 Milton; Whitewater 40–18 Boston; Richmond 36–26 Economy; Fountain City 27–26 Cambridge City; Centerville 34–24 Hagerstown; Richmond 40–25 Whitewater; Centerville 33–21 Fountain City; Richmond 33–26 Centerville. Officials: Hal Harris, William Ellis.

ROCHESTER: Akron 35–11 Kewanna; Richland Center 27–23 Francesville; Fulton 53–26 Pulaski; Grass Creek 32–30 Star City; Rochester 58–18 Medaryville; Winamac 17–16 Monterey; Akron 44–32 Richland Center; Fulton 36–33 Grass Creek; Rochester 47–18 Winamac; Akron 36–34 Fulton (ot); Rochester 45–23 Akron. Officials: J. L. Mertz, Harrison Berkey.

RUSHVILLE: Manilla 32–31 Mays; Morton Memorial 31–25 Carthage; Rushville 46–28 Raleigh. New Salem 36–34 Milroy; Arlington 36–28 Manilla; Morton Memorial 36–34 Rushville; New Salem 42–41 Arlington; New Salem 33–30 Morton Memorial. Officials: Ross Dorsett, Don McBride.

SEYMOUR: Hayden 35–32 Tampico; Freetown 22–17 Crothersville; Clearspring 38–24 Cortland; Brownstown 32–30 Medora; Seymour 54–22 Scipio; Freetown 42–31 Hayden; Brownstown 48–35 Clearspring; Seymour 30–18 Freetown; Seymour 36–33 Brownstown (ot). Officials: Jack O'Neal, Roland Baker.

SHELBYVILLE: Mount Auburn 47–36 Moral; Columbus 40–27 Franklin Twp.; Flat Rock 31–26 Clifford; Shelbyville 51–16 Boggstown; Fairland 30–25 Hope; Morristown 38–22 Waldron; Columbus 46–25 Mt. Auburn; Shelbyville 45–23 Flat Rock; Morristown 32–30 Fairland; Shelbyville 39–33 Columbus; Morristown 24–22 Shelbyville. Officials: Karl Dickerson, Max Casey.

SOUTH BEND: New Carlisle 35–24 Greene Twp.; Riley 30–26 Central Catholic; Mishawaka 43–35 Wilson; Central 47–27 Washington; Washington-Clay 49–41 Madison Twp.; Adams 50–28 Walkerton; North Liberty 41–31 Lakeville; Riley 47–39 New Carlisle; Central 31–30 Mishawaka; Washington-Clay 43–42 Adams; Riley 36–25 North Liberty; Central 40–28 Washington-Clay; Central 29–26 Riley. Officials: Ed Anglemyer, Omer Bixel, Devon Eaton.

SULLIVAN: Dugger 60–24 New Lebanon; Hymera 39–21 Pleasantville. Carlisle 27–17 Farmersburg; Sullivan 43–20 Merom. Graysville 33–9 Fairbanks; Dugger 46–36 Shelburn; Carlisle 36–33 Hymera. Sullivan 42–21 Graysville; Dugger 32–31 Carlisle; Sullivan 33–29 Dugger. Officials: Clayton Petterson, Clarence Myles.

TERRE HAUTE: West Terre Haute 47–35 Glenn; Prairie Creek 35–19 Riley; Gerstmeyer 35–20 Pimento; Concannon 43–22 Blackhawk; Laboratory 45–27 Honey Cheek; Otter Creek

36–28 Garfield; Wiley 47–32 Fontanet; West Terre Haute 44–29 Prairie Creek; Gerstmeyer 35–24 Concannon; Laboratory 50–23 Otter Creek; Wiley 60–45 West Terre Haute; Gerstmeyer 26–17 Laboratory; Wiley 44–27 Gerstmeyer. Officials: Edward Stuteville, Charles DeBusk, Carl Porter.

TIPTON: Cicero 28–24 Carmel; Walnut Grove 38–27 Fishers; Sharpsville 30–24 Noblesville; Arcadia 34–27 Windfall; Tipton 41–36 Westfield; Kempton 37–27 Goldsmith; Sheridan 42–35 Atlanta; Cicero 30–27 Prairie; Walnut Grove 36–18 Sharpsville; Tipton 48–39 Arcadia; Sheridan 53–5 Kempton; Walnut Grove 29–27 Cicero; Sheridan 38–37 Tipton; Sheridan 41–30 Walnut Grove. Officials: Raymond Trobaugh, Leland Wright, Gerald Alexander.

VINCENNES: Monroe City 26–25 Bicknell; Freelandville 32–28 Bruceville; Sandborn 38–24 Wheatland; Vincennes 33–25 Fritchton; Oaktown 33–29 Edwardsport. Decker 39–25 Decker Chapel; Monroe City 27–14 Freelandville; Vincennes 36–27 Sandborn; Decker 36–13 Oaktown; Vincennes 32–19 Monroe City; Decker 28–20 Vincennes. Officials: William Pointer, Robert Derrington.

WABASH: North Manchester 41–32 Washington Center; Roann 27–23 Laketon; Chester Twp. 42–29 Somerset; LaFontaine 36–31 Linlawn; South Whitley 55–27 Lincolnville; Wabash 37–22 Chippewa; Urbana 29–19 Largo; North Manchester 27–25 Roann; Chester Twp. 37–28 LaFontaine; Wabash 32–30 South Whitley (2ot); North Manchester 43–20 Urbana; Wabash 33–27 Chester Twp.; Wabash 31–30 North Manchester. Officials: Jacob McClure, Wayne Mosbaugh, Lundy Welborn.

WARSAW: Beaver Dam 28–17 Leesburg; Warsaw 47–25 Larwill; Etna Green 42–25 Syracuse; Columbia City 34–25 North Webster; Milford 53–36 Sidney; Atwood 23–22 Silver Lake; Pierceton 26–19 Mentone; Claypool 52–22 Burket; Warsaw 64–26 Beaver Dam; Etna Green 33–20 Columbia City; Milford 34–29 Atwood; Pierceton 50–22 Claypool; Warsaw 41–35 Etna Green; Pierceton 42–26 Milford; Warsaw 36–32 Pierceton. Officials: J. Clayton Hughes, E. L. Druckamiller, James Koons.

WASHINGTON: Loogootee 33–31 Plainville; Washington 41–23 Alfordsville; Trinity Springs 38–29 Epsom; Elmore Twp. 30–21 Glendale; Washington Catholic 28–27 Shoals; Barr Twp. 38–22 Odon; Washington 29–24 Loogootee; Elnora 34–25 Trinity Springs; Barr Twp. 47–23 Washington Catholic; Washington 47–25 Elnora; Washington 24–17 Barr Twp. Officials: Ted Fehring, H. W. Gross.

WINCHESTER: Winchester 54–32 Lincoln; McKinley 35–32 Spartansburg; Farmland 38–32 Jackson; Stoney Creek 34–32 Parker; Huntsville 23–13 Losantville; Union City 31–23 Modoc; Saratoga 42–29 Wayne; Winchester 38–23 Lynn; Farmland 39–34 McKinley; Stoney Creek 34–24 Huntsville; Saratoga 34–28 Union City; Winchester 45–24 Farmland; Stoney Creek 32–27 Saratoga; Winchester 49–18 Stoney Creek. Officials: Clive Markley, Gerald Powell, Herbert Bramwell.

WORTHINGTON: Switz City 50–16 Solsberry; Worthington 39–18 Newberry; Midland 39–30 Marco; Bloomfield 52–10 Scotland; Linton 56–12 Owensburg; Switz City 37–21 Lyons; Midland 26–21 Worthington; Linton 40–27 Bloomfield; Switz City 33–19 Midland; Linton 53–34 Switz City. Officials: J. Clinton Dougherty, Harold Loge.

1943 REGIONALS

ANDERSON: Lapel 29–24 Plainfield; Greenfield 37–28 Lawrence; Greenfield 38–20 Lapel. Officials: Louis A. Briner, William N. Reimann.

BLOOMINGTON: Brazil 29–27 Linton; Martinsville 42–37 Terre Haute Wiley; Martinsville 37–20 Brazil. Officials: Karl Dickerson, Irvin Springer.

CLINTON: Hillsboro 36–33 Crawfordsville; Clinton 41–37 Greencastle; Clinton 51–40 Hillsboro. Officials: William E. Pointer, William M. Coulter.

EVANSVILLE: Central 43–39 Boonville; Princeton 47–33 Tell City; Central 39–26 Princeton. Officials: W. N. Ringer, Robert Hoffman.

FORT WAYNE: Central 37–27 Auburn; Warsaw 49–46 Kendallville; Central 59–43 Warsaw. Officials: Walter E. Thurston, Norris Ward.

HAMMOND: Gary Wallace 49–34 Clark ; Michigan City 39–34 Remington; Wallace 46–33 Michigan City. Officials: Phil N. Eskew, Lawrence Gaunt.

HUNTINGTON: Monroe 39–38 Bluffton; Andrews 50–42 Dunkirk; Monroe 37–34 Andrews. Officials: Harold McSwane, Cecil E. Young.

LAFAYETTE: Frankfort 38–31 Monitor; Lebanon 37–19 Oxford; Lebanon 48–30 Frankfort. Officials: L.E. Fink, A.T. Krider.

MARION: Marion 40–20 Sheridan; Kokomo 35–21 Wabash; Marion 46–39 Kokomo. Officials: Fred R. White, Jacob H. McClure.

MUNCIE: New Castle 41–37 Burris; Richmond 48–42 Winchester; Richmond 44–26 New Castle. Officials: Frank Jarrell, C. N. Phillips.

NEW ALBANY: Jeffersonville 38–33 French Lick; Bedford 40–29 Seymour; Bedford 36–32 Jeffersonville. Officials: G. P. Silver, Dean Malaska.

PERU: Peru 40–33 Logansport; Monticello 26–24 Burlington; Peru 36–34 Monticello. Officials: George Vaulk, J. Clayton Hughes.

RUSHVILLE: Batesville 30–21 New Salem; Kitchel 43–33 Aurora; Batesville 37–25 Kitchel. Officials: T. R. Smith, Cecil Tharp.

SHELBYVILLE: Greensburg 27–25 Center Grove; Madison 48–27 Morristown; Madison 51–41 Greensburg. Officials: George Bender, Herbert Edwards.

SOUTH BEND: Rochester 39–26 Bourbon; Elkhart 47–43 Central; Rochester 52–41 Elkhart. Officials: Allen Klinck, Paul Bateman.

WASHINGTON: Jasper 33–26 Decker; Washington 25–22 Sullivan; Jasper 33–31 Washington. Officials: Thomas Baker, George Williams.

1943 SEMI–FINALS

HAMMOND: Lebanon 49–34 Rochester; Gary Wallace 37–25 Peru; Lebanon 48–32 Wallace. Officials: Thomas Baker, George Williams.

INDIANAPOLIS: Batesville 26–20 Madison; Greenfield 53–37; Clinton. Batesville 27–20 Greenfield. Officials: L. E. Fink, William Pointer.

MUNCIE: Ft. Wayne Central 46–24 Monroe; Marion 44–35 Richmond; Central 44–23 Marion. Officials: Karl Dickerson, George Bender.

VINCENNES: Jasper 37–34 Martinsville; Bedford 36–25 Evansville Central; Bedford 46–29 Jasper. Officials: Allen Klinck, T.R. Smith.

Tourney Time

1943 FINALS—March 20

INDIANAPOLIS (State Fairgrounds, new Coliseum): Lebanon 36–35 Bedford; Ft. Wayne Central 33–24 Batesville; Ft. Wayne Central 45–40 Lebanon. Officials: Thomas Baker, Allen Klinck.

1944 SECTIONALS

ANDERSON: Anderson 38–20 Pendleton; Alexandria 52–38 Summitville; Frankton 39–38 Markleville; Lapel 61–35 St. Mary's; Anderson 38–25 Elwood; Alexandria 41–29 Frankton; Anderson 58–32 Lapel; Anderson 44–30 Alexandria. Officials: C. N. Phillips, T. R. Smith.

ATTICA: Williamsport 34–6 Wallace; Perrysville 39–28 Richland Twp.; Veedersburg 41–29 Kingman; Covington 48–29 West Lebanon; Hillsboro 34–19 Pine Village; Attica 34–23 Williamsport; Veedersburg 29–26 Perrysville; Hillsboro 33–24 Covington; Veedersburg 34–32 Attica; Hillsboro 37–33 Veedersburg. Officials: Cecil Tharp, Doxie Reeves.

BATESVILLE: Batesville 42–19 Osgood; Sunman 41–27 Cross Plains; Versailles 37–29 Milan; Holton 31–30 Napoleon; Batesville 70–20 New Marion; Sunman 31–30 Versailles; Batesville 25–14 Holton; Batesville 35–18 Sunman. Officials: Paul Cly, W. N. Reimann.

BEDFORD: Mitchell 57–32 Huron; Oolitic 53–26 Fayetteville; Marshall Twp. 34–20 Tunnelton; Bedford 64–21 Heltonville; Mitchell 56–31 Shawswick; Oolitic 32–23 Marshall Twp.; Bedford 50–25 Mitchell; Bedford 34–24 Oolitic. Officials: Frank Jarrell, Evan Crawley.

BLOOMFIELD: Midland 35–24 Newberry; Scotland 38–14 Jasonville; Linton 61–17 Owensburg; Switz City 25–16 Lyons; Worthington 46–18 Solsberry; Marco 26–20 Bloomfield; Midland 30–19 Scotland; Switz City 42–37 Linton; Marco 21–20 Lyons; Switz City 37–19 Midland; Switz City 32–21 Marco. Officials: Hosea Russell, Lowell Willis.

BLOOMINGTON: Mooresville 33–32 Martinsville; Bloomington 40–36 Eminence; Ellettsville 53–30 Monrovia; Stinesville 29–26 Morgantown; University 46–16 Smithville; Paragon 34–25 Unionville; Mooresville 34–29 Bloomington; Stinesville 35–34 Ellettsville; University 33–21 Paragon; Mooresville 42–38 Stinesville; Mooresville 42–39 University (ot). Officials: Irvin Springer, Donald Bright.

BLUFFTON: Chester Center 42–26 Ossian; Rockcreek 34–27 Petroleum; Liberty Center 42–23 Lancaster Central; Bluffton 52–28 Jackson Center; Union Center 43–36 Chester Center; Liberty Center 29–26 Rockcreek; Union Center 30–28 Bluffton; Liberty Center 38–36 Union Center. Officials: Gerald Powell, Fred White.

BOONVILLE: Selvin 26–16 Folsomville; Lynnville 29–28 Newburgh; Boonville 41–27 Yankeetown; Elberfeld 45–19 Chandler; Millersburg 43–20 Selvin; Boonville 48–20 Lynnville; Elberfeld 40–24 Millersburg; Boonville 49–31 Elberfeld. Officials: William Hartley, David Royalty.

BROWNSTOWN: Cortland 33–22 Scipio; Hayden 30–25 Vallonia; Clearspring 32–14 Freetown; Seymour 53–26 Tampico; Medora 29–27 Crothersville; Brownstown 44–31 Cortland; Clearspring 30–18 Hayden; Medora 24–23 Seymour; Brownstown 37–28 Clearspring; Brownstown 41–30 Medora. Officials: Wayne Hammond, Cyril Birge.

BUTLER: Waterloo 44–17 Scott Center; Pleasant Lake 45–25 Hamilton; Auburn 39–27 Salem Center; Churubusco 34–30 Fremont; Butler 39–25 Spencerville; Ashley 40–36 Angola; Garrett 62–26 Orland; Concord Twp. 55–28 Metz; Pleasant Lake 42–32 Waterloo; Auburn.66–22

Churubusco; Butler 47–21 Ashley; Garrett 67–34 Concord Twp.; Auburn 37–28 Pleasant Lake; Garrett 36–32 Butler; Garrett 42–25 Auburn. Officials: R. W. Warring, Myron Weldy, Edwin Anglemyer.

CLINTON: Green Twp. 29–22 Bellmore; Mecca 38–29 Hillsdale; Clinton 50–19 Dana; St. Bernice 40–30 Tangier; Montezuma 32–30 Cayuga; Bridgeton 33–16 Bloomingdale; Rockville 22–19 Rosedale; Marshall 50–18 Newport; Mecca 23–21 Green Twp.; Clinton 29–23 St. Bernice; Bridgeton 25–24 Montezuma; Marshall 38–26 Rockville; Mecca 27–26 Clinton; Bridgeton 38–23 Marshall; Bridgeton 23–15 Mecca. Officials: William Ellis, Dean Malaska, Loren Harris.

CONNERSVILLE: Connersville 45–35 Harrisburg; Fairview 40–27 Whitewater; Springfield Twp. 31–20 Everton; Brookville 37–24 Alquina; Liberty 40–37 Brownsville; Kitchel 50–25 Bentonville; Connersville 50–23 Orange; Springfield Twp. 41–28 Fairview; Liberty 40–23 Brookville; Connersville 44–35 Kitchel; Springfield Twp. 29–27 Liberty; Connersville 38–36 Springfield Twp. Officials: Don C. Dick, Robert O'Neal, Stephen Baker.

CRAWFORDSVILLE: Darlington 37–18 New Market; Alamo 22–18 Ladoga; New Ross 31–27 Linden; Wingate 34–31 Crawfordsville; Waynetown 43–33 Waveland; Darlington 33–26 Alamo; New Ross 45–27 Wingate; Waynetown 31–24 Darlington; Waynetown 27–24 New Ross. Officials: Edward Stuteville, Walter Floyd.

DANVILLE: Plainfield 44–15 Clayton; Charleton 35–16 Brownsburg; Avon 46–39 New Winchester; Pittsboro 34–33 Danville; Lizton 30–26 Stilesville; Amo 32–31 Speedway; North Salem 39–27 Plainfield; Avon 28–26 Charleton; Pittsboro 44–27 Lizton; Amo 33–27 North Salem; Avon 20–19 Pittsboro; Amo 42–39 Avon. Officials Clyde Gentry, Bernard Lampe, Ted Fehring.

DECATUR: Pleasant Mills 63–12 Jefferson; Monmouth 33–20 Monroe; Decatur Catholic 30–22 Kirkland; Berne 55–36 Geneva; Decatur 51–44 Hartford Twp.; Pleasant Mills 25–21 Monmouth; Berne 38–19 Decatur Catholic; Decatur 36–25 Pleasant Mills; Decatur 38–27 Berne. Officials: Clay Layman, E. D. Million.

DELPHI: Delphi 35–22 Flora; Camden 30–20 Cutler; Carrollton 44–17 Rockfield; Burlington 36–19 Adams; Delphi 52–24 Deer Creek; Carrollton 36–35 Camden; Delphi 44–14 Burlington; Delphi 56–27 Carrollton. Officials: Forrest Shaw, Fred Fosler.

EVANSVILLE: Memorial 46–22 Wadesville; Bosse 62–20 B. T. Washington; Reitz 36–17 Central; New Harmony 37–15 Mt. Vernon; Lincoln 44–14 Cynthiana; Poseyville 23–18 Stewartsville; Memorial 33–23 Griffin; Bosse 32–25 Reitz; Lincoln 64–46 New Harmony; Memorial 37–22 Poseyville; Bosse 49–31 Lincoln; Bosse 46–29 Memorial. Officials: Hubert Thomas, Robert Rose, Roy P. Johnson.

FORT WAYNE: North Side 54–27 Hoagland; Huntertown 37–27 Lafayette Central; South Side 37–12 Arcola; Central Catholic 46–16 Harlan; Monroeville 45–25 Coesse; Central 46–32 Concordia; New Haven 49–33 Maumee Twp.; Leo 36–20 Elmhurst; North Side 36–28 Huntertown; South Side 35–28 Central Catholic; Central 59–39 Monroeville; Leo 42–41 New Haven; South Side 39–27 North Side; Central 60–45 Leo; Central 50–39 South Side. Officials: Norris Ward, Phil N. Eskew, Lawrence Gaunt.

FOWLER: Boswell 35–25 Ambia; Otterbein 70–22 Gilboa; Freeland Park 55–35 Pine; Oxford 37–31 Raub; Earl Park 49–23 Wadena; Fowler 30–18 Boswell; Otterbein 44–35 Freeland Park; Oxford 45–35 Earl Park; Fowler 59–26 Otterbein; Fowler 54–34 Oxford. Officials: Omer Bixel, Devon Eaton.

Tourney Time

FRANKFORT: Washington Twp. 57–22 Forest; Colfax 51–35 Kirklin; Rossville 42–28 Jackson Twp.; Frankfort 83–11 Mulberry; Scircleville 39–30 Sugar Creek; Washington Twp. 45–39 Michigantown; Rossville 46–32 Colfax; Frankfort 67–25 Scircleville; Rossville 41–31 Washington Twp.; Frankfort 27–25 Rossville (ot). Officials: Gerald Strole, Herbert Edwards.

FRANKLIN: Whiteland 26–24 Franklin; Edinburg 51–41 Nashville; Nineveh 41–38 Trafalgar; Center Grove 56–18 Van Buren; Clark Twp. 40–33 Union Twp.; Greenwood 81–20 Helmsburg; Whiteland 45–21 Masonic Home; Edinburg 31–22 Nineveh; Center Grove 33–31 Clark Twp.; Whiteland 26–24 Greenwood; Edinburg 34–32 Center Grove; Whiteland 50–25 Edinburg. Officials: A. E. Pitcher, Cleon Reynolds, Thomas Stirling.

GARY: Roosevelt 45–27 Washington Twp.; Gary Edison 36–24 Hebron; Kouts 45–35 Morgan Twp.; Horace Mann 59–27 Liberty Center; Lew Wallace 51–23 Chesterton; Wirt 52–31 Boone Grove; Emerson 54–30 Tolleston; Valparaiso 28–23 Froebel; Roosevelt 34–32 Gary Edison; Horace Mann 41–30 Kouts; Lew Wallace 48–25 Wirt; Emerson 62–37 Valparaiso; Horace Mann 36–29 Roosevelt; Emerson 33–31 Lew Wallace; Emerson 47–38 Horace Mann. Officials: Cecil Young, Lundy Welborn, Paul Bateman.

GOSHEN: Elkhart 45–31 Nappanee; Middlebury 54–36 Wakarusa; Millersburg 26–20 Jefferson; Goshen 47–39 Concord; Baugo 43–32 New Paris; Elkhart 32–26 Bristol; Middlebury 57–31 Millersburg; Goshen 45–36 Baugo; Elkhart 32–26 Bristol; Middlebury 57–31 Millersburg; Goshen 45–36 Baugo; Elkhart 41–30 Middlebury; Elkhart 31–26 Goshen. Officials: Tom Ciecka, Elmer Millbranth.

GREENCASTLE: Cloverdale 45–40 Reelsville; Bainbridge 43–28 Belle Union; Greencastle 37–18 Russellville; Roachdale 48–22 Fillmore; Bainbridge 42–28 Cloverdale; Greencastle 35–33 Roachdale (2ot); Bainbridge 49–40 Greencastle. Officials: Harold Porter, Robert Fink.

GREENFIELD: Wilkinson 27–20 McCordsville; Greenfield 48–42 Charlottesville; Maxwell 37–16 Westland; Mt. Comfort 37–22 New Palestine; Fortville 33–31 Eden; Greenfield 32–25 Wilkinson; Mt. Comfort 40–37 Maxwell (ot); Greenfield 47–32 Fortville; Greenfield 33–30 Mt. Comfort. Officials: Al Jackson, William Newbold.

GREENSBURG: Butlerville 32–22 Zenas; Clarksburg 31–27 Burney; North Vernon 33–16 Vernon; New Point 28–17 Sandcreek; Greensburg 45–37 Jackson; Sandusky 38–25 St. Paul; Clarksburg 45–31 Butlerville; North Vernon 31–23 New Point; Greensburg 59–25 Sandusky; North Vernon 31–28 Clarksburg; Greensburg 39–32 North Vernon. Officials: Fred Pierson, Don McBride.

HAMMOND: East Gary Edison 41–36 Roosevelt; Hammond Tech 37–26 Hobart. Hammond 49–34 Crown Point; Griffith 30–23 Lowell; Catholic Central 52–27 Portage; Washington 44–36 Merrillville. Wheeler 50–32 Dyer. Clark 46–35 Whiting; East Gary Edison 42–31 Hammond Tech; Hammond 30–29 Griffith; Washington 49–37 Catholic Central; Clark 59–17 Wheeler; Hammond 50–43 East Gary Edison; Washington 34–26 Clark; Hammond 32–26 Washington. Officials: L. E. Fink, Harrison Berkey, Walter Thurston.

HARTFORD CITY: Hartford City 55–27 Jefferson; Roll 56–28 Poling; Redkey 35–23 Ridgeville; Portland 38–24 Madison Twp. Pennville 34–33 Dunkirk; Montpelier 59–17 Bryant; Hartford City 34–33 Roll; Redkey 31–26 Portland; Montpelier 40–27 Pennville; Hartford City 43–36 Redkey; Montpelier 32–30 Hartford City. Officials: Arthur Lloyd, Joe Metzger.

HUNTINGTON: Clear Creek 44–21 Andrews; Union Twp. 39–36 Wayne Twp.; Huntington 37–34 Huntington Catholic; Jackson Twp. 28–27 Salamonie Twp.; Huntington Twp. 33–27

Bippus; Jefferson Center 41–34 Rock Creek Center; Polk 64–16 Markle; Jefferson Twp. 34–32 Lancaster Twp.; Union Twp. 28–26 Clear Creek; Jackson Twp. 31–29 Huntington; Huntington Twp. 51–40 Jefferson Center; Polk Twp. 57–25 Jefferson Twp.; Union Twp. 30–28 Jackson Twp.; Huntington Twp. 22–18 Polk Twp.; Huntington Twp. 37–27 Union Twp. Officials: George Collyer, Otho Piper, Marvin Todd.

INDIANAPOLIS: Sacred Heart 42–39 Beech Grove; Cathedral 48–23 School for the Deaf Howe 42–28 Manual; Crispus Attucks 47–34 Washington; Ben Davis 41–39 Lawrence; Tech 35–29 Broad Ripple; Shortridge 36–30 Decatur Central; Southport 35–33 Warren Central; Cathedral 37–35 Sacred Heart; Howe 45–27 Crispus Attucks; Tech 30–29 Ben Davis; Shortridge 35–32 Southport; Howe 45–34 Cathedral; Shortridge 50–33 Tech; Howe 53–48 Shortridge. Officials: Norman Dunlap, Roland Baker, Robert Hoffman.

JASPER: Dubois 49–29 Jefferson Twp.; Jasper 53–47 Huntingburg; Otwell 41–16 Ireland; Holland 41–36 Stendal; Petersburg 36–32 Winslow; Spurgeon 50–22 Cuzco; Jasper 61–37 Dubois; Otwell 31–28 Holland; Spurgeon 37–32 Petersburg; Jasper 70–31 Otwell; Jasper 50–43 Spurgeon. Officials: William Pointer, Robert Derrington.

JEFFERSONVILLE: Silver Creek 27–25 Corydon; Charlestown 39–38 Henryville; Borden 41–39 Mauckport; New Salisbury 27–7 New Middletown; Jeffersonville 37–30 New Albany; Morgan Twp. 53–33 Georgetown; New Washington 50–26 Elizabeth; Lanesville 39–27 New Amsterdam; Silver Creek 45–22 Charlestown; New Salisbury 30–19 Borden; Jeffersonville 53–24 Morgan Twp.; New Washington 48–31 Lanesville; Silver Creek 33–16 New Salisbury; Jeffersonville 59–25 New Washington; Jeffersonville 33–21 Silver Creek. Officials: Theodore Lentz, Irvin Thrasher, Walter Surface.

KENDALLVILLE: Avilla 35–25 LaGrange; Brighton 43–20 Wolcottville; Shipshewana 35–22 Cromwell; Topeka 43–27 Rome City; Albion 42–30 Wawaka; Wolf Lake 40–21 Lima; Ligonier 28–26 Scott; Kendallville 44–28 Howe Military; Avilla 29–27 Brighton (2ot); Shipshewana 47–32 Topeka; Wolf Lake 47–27 Albion; Kendallville 33–24 Ligonier; Shipshewana 35–26 Avilla; Wolf Lake 25–21 Kendallville (ot); Shipshewana 41–28 Wolf Lake. Officials: Russell Arndt, Jim Crowe, H. Windmiller.

KOKOMO: Russiaville 65–34 Clay Twp.; Howard Twp. 40–28 Jackson Twp.; Greentown 49–18 West Middleton; Kokomo 85–24 Union Twp.; Ervin Twp. 36–35 New London; Russiaville 32–26 Howard Twp.; Kokomo 38–22 Greentown; Russiaville 40–32 Ervin Twp.; Kokomo 47–19 Russiaville. Officials: George Vaulk, William Lucus.

LAFAYETTE: Clarks Hill 25–18 Montmorenci; Romney 43–31 Battle Ground; Monitor 42–38 Stockwell; West Point 38–26 Dayton; Jefferson 22–18 West Lafayette; Wea 38–36 Jackson; Klondike 40–38 Shadeland; Buck Creek 24–15 Clarks Hill; Romney 38–30 Monitor; Jefferson 45–24 West Point; Klondike 60–30 Wea; Romney 36–27 Buck Creek; Jefferson 49–24 Klondike; Jefferson 45–23 Romney. Officials: Jack O'Neal, Frank Kressler, George Bender.

LAWRENCEBURG: Aurora 36–22 Lawrenceburg; Patriot 42–24 Moores Hill; Bright 39–28 Rising Sun; Guilford 37–17 Vevay; Aurora 45–35 Dillsboro; Patriot 36–34 Bright; Aurora 46–26 Guilford; Aurora 64–32 Patriot. Officials: Arthur Snoddy, Norman Miller.

LEBANON: Lebanon 45–22 Central; New Augusta 56–40 Advance; Whitestown 27–21 Pinnell; Zionsville 52–23 Jamestown; Thorntown 35–23 Dover; Lebanon 31–27 New Augusta; Whitestown 40–35 Zionsville; Thorntown 30–23 Lebanon; Thorntown 24–19 Whitestown. Officials: Forrest Ballinger, Otto Crosley.

Tourney Time

LOGANSPORT: Young America 31–23 Walton; Metea 33–28 Royal Center; Logansport 48–11 Galveston; Twelve Mile 29–24 Lucerne; Onward 30–20 New Waverly; Washington Twp. 29–28 Young America; Logansport 58–36 Metea; Twelve Mile 45–24 Onward; Logansport; 41–17 Washington Twp.; Logansport 48–19 Twelve Mile. Officials: Orval Martin, Albert Etter.

MADISON: Hanover 24–19 Central; Scottsburg 59–29 Paris Crossing; Austin 30–29 North Madison; Dupont 32–12 Deputy; Madison 32–27 Saluda; Scottsburg 41–22 Hanover; Dupont 26–18 Austin; Scottsburg 24–18 Madison; Scottsburg 30–24 Dupont. Officials: Ray Lackey, John Lyskowinski.

MARION: Swayzee 31–23 Fairmount; Gas City 33–19 Jonesboro; Sweetser 43–24 Van Buren; Marion 32–26 Jefferson Twp.; Swayzee 40–25 St. Paul; Gas City 31–22 Sweetser; Swayzee 28–20 Marion; Gas City 30–26 Swayzee. Officials: Donald Dickie, Ross Dean.

MICHIGAN CITY: LaCrosse 45–31 Jackson Twp.; Union Twp. 43–25 Mill Creek; St. Mary's 27–23 Union Mills; Kingsbury 36–31 Wanatah; Westville 35–31 Hanna; LaPorte 56–14 Clinton Twp.; Rolling Prairie 39–23 Stillwell; Michigan City 40–12 Springfield Twp.; La Crosse 35–29 Union Twp.; St. Mary's 34–21 Kingsbury; LaPorte 88–2 Westville; Michigan City 53–21 Rolling Prairie; St. Mary's 29–24 La Crosse; LaPorte 29–25 Michigan City; LaPorte 59–28 St. Mary's. Officials: Charles Kruzan, Jay L. Mertz, Allen Klinck.

MONTICELLO: Monon 37–21 Burnettsville; Monticello 32–30 Chalmers (ot); Brookston 32–18 Wolcott; Idaville 33–22 Reynolds; Buffalo 20–16 Round Grove; Monticello 45–31 Monon; Brookston 36–2 Idaville; Monticello 34–26 Buffalo; Monticello 34–23 Brookston. Officials: George Merkle, F. O. Sonafrank.

MOROCCO: Mt. Ayr 35–14 Rensselaer; Brook 46–22 St. Joseph; Demotte 30–25 Fair Oaks; Kentland 26–19 Tefft; Goodland 39–2 Wheatfield; Remington 26–21 Morocco; Mt. Ayr 27–23 Brook; Demotte 32–12 Kentland; Goodland 39–25 Remington; Mt. Ayr 18–15 Demotte; Mt. Ayr 38–24 Goodland. Officials: Robert Etter, Herbert Vault.

MUNCIE: Yorktown 39–32 Albany; Daleville 39–24 Harrison Twp. Center 24–18 Selma; Royerton 45–21 Cowan; Burris 55–37 DeSoto; Gaston 31–30 Eaton; Central 44–39 Yorktown; Center 42–28 Daleville; Burris 48–31 Royerton; Central 45–24 Gaston; Burris 34–26 Center; Burris 40–19 Central. Officials: G. P. Silver, John Hilligoss, Karl Dickerson.

NEW CASTLE: New Lisbon 58–32 Sulphur Springs; New Castle 37–24 Knights–town; Spiceland 43–34 Mt. Summit; Straughn 34–25 Kennard; Mooreland 47–25 Cadiz; Lewisville 48–25 Middletown; New Castle 43–26 New Lisbon; Spiceland 36–24 Straughn; Mooreland 39–32 Lewisville; New Castle 61–40 Spiceland; New Castle 64–26 Mooreland. Officials: Ross Dorsett, James Haywood.

NOBLESVILLE: Windfall 28–21 Walnut Grove; Jackson Central 58–8 Kempton; Westfield 34–20 Prairie Twp.; Sharpsville 48–14 Goldsmith; Noblesville 27–26 Fishers; Tipton 40–22 Sheridan; Windfall 34–26 Carmel; Jackson Central 51–35 Westfield; Noblesville 44–31 Sharpsville; Tipton 31–21 Windfall; Noblesville 43–34 Jackson Central; Tipton 45–31 Noblesville. Officials: John Walker, Leland Wright, Aaron Belcher.

OWENSVILLE: Patoka 33–32 Ft. Branch; Oakland City 43–31 Mt. Olympus; Owensville 31–29 Francisco; Mackey 29–26 Hazleton; Princeton 36–17 Haubstadt; Patoka 35–22 Oakland City; Mackey 35–34 Owensville; Princeton 24–20 Patoka; Princeton 43–38 Mackey. Officials: William Coulter, Carl Jerger.

PERU: Clay Twp. 25–15 Chili; Butler Twp. 35–29 Macy; Converse 63–29 Deedsville; Peru

IHSAA Scores | 1940–1949

32–23 Amboy; Bunker Hill 34–29 Gilead; Jefferson Twp. 31–28 Clay Twp.; Converse 49–24 Butler Twp.; Bunker Hill 33–16 Peru; Converse 49–20 Jefferson Twp.; Converse 46–22 Bunker Hill. Officials: Raymond Trobaugh, Hugh McNew.

PLYMOUTH: Plymouth 53–34 Argos; Knox 39–34 Grovertown; LaPaz 59–20 Hamlet; Bremen 42–30 Tippecanoe; Culver 46–44 San Pierre; North Judson 53–34 West Twp.; Bourbon 60–35 Tyner; Plymouth 44–29 Knox; Bremen 53–31 LaPaz; Culver 55–31 North Judson; Plymouth 33–30 Bourbon; Culver 40–25 Bremen; Culver 41–26 Plymouth. Officials: Hugh Bergstrom, Charles McManus, and James Koons.

RICHMOND: Fountain City 28–14 Boston; Richmond 19–17 Hagerstown; Centerville 52–13 Cambridge City; Greens Fork 41–18 Economy; Williamsburg 46–24 Webster; Whitewater 30–27 Milton; Richmond 33–30 Fountain City; Centerville 42–30 Greens Fork; Williamsburg 26–25 Whitewater (ot); Centerville 28–26 Richmond (ot); Centerville 38–36 Williamsburg. Officials: George Williams, Alvin Heller.

RUSHVILLE: Arlington 33–23 Milroy; New Salem 50–29 Raleigh; Carthage 35–30 Manilla; Mays 31–27 Morton Memorial; Arlington 28–25 Rushville; New Salem 35–22 Carthage; Arlington 37–33 Mays (ot); New Salem 39–36 Arlington. Officials: Frank White, Wilbur May.

SALEM: Salem 63–27 Leavenworth; French Lick 64–24 Milltown; Orleans 38–20 English; Paoli 39–31 West Baden; Hardinsburg 47–13 Little York; Pekin 33–23 Campbellsburg; Salem 46–23 Marengo; French Lick 29–25 Orleans; Paoli 79–14 Hardinsburg; Salem 41–20 Pekin; Paoli 28–26 French Lick; Paoli 30–23 Salem. Officials: John Torphy, Roy Dayton, Lawrence Young.

SHELBYVILLE: Moral Twp. 32–18 Boggstown; Franklin Twp. 45–33 Flat Rock; Morristown 36–20 Clifford; Columbus 46–22 Mt. Auburn; Waldron 38–36 Fairland; Shelbyville 40–32 Hope; Moral Twp. 34–27 Franklin Twp.; Columbus 48–40 Morristown; Shelbyville 45–23 Waldron; Columbus 35–19 Moral Twp.; Shelbyville 36–35 Columbus. Officials: Tom Baker, Layall Fisher.

SOUTH BEND: Adams 56–23 Wilson; New Carlisle 33–31 North Liberty; Mishawaka 42–41 Washington (ot); Central 44–31 Lakeville; Madison Twp. 43–27 Walkerton; South Bend Catholic 37–36 Greene Twp.; Riley 57–19 Central Catholic; Adams 52–23 Washington-Clay; Mishawaka 37–32 New Carlisle; Central 50–37 Madison; Riley 63–17 South Bend Catholic; Adams 35–22 Mishawaka; Central 51–37 Riley; Adams 36–30 Central. Officials: LeRoy Shine, R. Wayne Cunningham, Sam Massette.

SPENCER: Freedom 32–30 Patricksburg; Ashboro 45–28 Van Buren Twp.; Brazil 69–29 Staunton; Bowling Green 42–41 Gosport; Clay City 38–34 Cory; Quincy 36–21 Jefferson Twp.; Spencer 27–21 Freedom; Brazil 45–29 Ashboro; Bowling Green 39–37 Clay City; Spencer 39–32 Quincy; Brazil 49–29 Bowling Green. Brazil 29–21 Spencer. Officials: Harry Briggs, Donald Cooper, James Conover.

SULLIVAN: Hymera 21–19 Farmersburg; Carlisle 27–21 New Lebanon; Dugger 46–27 Merom; Shelburn 23–22 Graysville; Fairbanks 40–15 Pleasantville; Sullivan 28–24 Hymera; Dugger 32–30 Carlisle; Shelburn 39–24 Fairbanks; Sullivan 42–24 Dugger; Sullivan 31–24 Shelburn. Officials: Otto Albright, Hulett Crecelius.

TELL CITY: Luce Twp. 40–19 Gentryville; Troy 42–22 Chrisney; Cannelton 42–36 Rockport; Dale 36–29 Tell City; Troy 26–23 Luce Twp.; Dale 34–23 Cannelton; Dale 35–31 Troy. Officials: W.J. McCoskey, Don DeVault.

TERRE HAUTE: State Laboratory 49–35 Gerstmeyer; Riley 24–19 Blackhawk; Otter Creek 42–28 Honey Creek; Fontanet 44–36 Concannon; Garfield 55–28 Glenn; Pimento 31–28 Wiley;

Tourney Time

West Terre Haute 44–23 Prairie Creek; State Laboratory 35–28 Riley; Fontanet 31–28 Otter Creek; Garfield 42–40 Pimento; State Laboratory 36–30 West Terre Haute; Garfield 27–24 Fontanet; State Laboratory 42–31 Garfield. Officials: Hal Harris, Robert Hobbs, Walter Loman.

VINCENNES: Decker Chapel 31–27 Edwardsport; Decker 25–14 Bruceville; Monroe City 43–30 Oaktown; Fritchton 34–26 Wheatland; Vincennes 40–37 Sandborn; Freelandville 37–35 Bicknell; Decker 57–31 Decker Chapel; Monroe City 39–31 Fritchton; Vincennes 46–27 Freelandville; Decker 30–29 Monroe City; Decker 36–30 Vincennes (ot). Officials: Walter Ringer, Clarence Riggs.

WABASH: Chester 27–24 Laketon; Central 39–26 Lincolnville; Somerset 49–38 Washington Center; Linlawn 32–31 Roann; Lafontaine 34–25 Urbana; Wabash 34–30 South Whitley; Lagro 25–18 Chippewa; Chester 32–30 Central; Linlawn 40–38 Somerset; Wabash 56–23 LaFontaine; Chester 42–29 Lagro; Wabash 35–29 Linlawn; Chester 43–28 Wabash. Officials: Donald Coar, Lloyd Bryan, Paul Kelly.

WARSAW: Syracuse 48–18 Leesburg; Pierceton 45–42 Columbus City; Etna Green 43–24 Atwood; Mentone 43–35 Milford; North Webster 30–26 Silver Lake; Larwill 35–30 Beaver Dam; Sidney 48–20 Burket; Warsaw 49–25 Claypool; Pierceton 41–39 Syracuse; Mentone 39–35 Etna Green; Larwill 45–23 North Webster; Warsaw 39–26 Sidney; Pierceton 33–31 Mentone; Warsaw 34–31 Larwill; Warsaw 30–26 Pierceton. Officials: Kenneth Michel, Herbert Brammel, Hardy Songer.

WASHINGTON: Plainville 21–20 Glendale; Shoals 31–22 Alfordsville; Washington 48–35 Barr Twp.; Odon 35–31 Epsom; Washington Catholic 54–43 Elmore Twp.; Loogootee 43–20 Plainville; Washington 34–20 Shoals; Washington Catholic 45–28 Odon; Washington 38–23 Loogootee; Washington 41–33 Washington Catholic. Officials: Clarence Myles, Clayton Patterson.

WINAMAC: Winamac 49–24 Talina; Star City 36–32 Monterey; Akron 42–31 Francesville; Medaryville 31–24 Pulaski; Leiters Ford 39–35 Richland Center; Fulton 44–24 Kewanna; Rochester 29–21 Grass Creek; Star City 26–25 Winamac; Akron 56–26 Medaryville; Fulton 41–19 Leiters Ford; Rochester 40–32 Star City; Akron 49–30 Fulton; Rochester 43–26 Akron. Officials: Harold McSwane, Jacob McClure, Wayne Mosbaugh.

WINCHESTER: Winchester 60–31 Losantville; Stoney Creek 37–22 Spartanburg; Parker 48–12 Huntsville; Lynn 39–27 McKinley; Saratoga 27–18 Lincoln; Union City 40–33 Jackson Twp.; Farmland 41–18 Green Twp.; Modoc 39–38 Wayne; Winchester 27–21 Stoney Creek; Parker 48–46 Lynn; Saratoga 36–35 Union City; Farmland 43–31 Modoc; Parker 36–33 Winchester; Saratoga 30–22 Farmland; Parker 41–37 Saratoga. Officials: Max Casey, Eugene Glaze, John Magnabosco.

1944 REGIONALS

BRAZIL: Brazil 38–33 State High; Mooresville 35–30 Switz City; Mooresville 43–41 Brazil. Officials: Karl Dickerson, Robert Hoffman.

CRAWFORDSVILLE: Bainbridge 40–33 Hillsboro; Waynetown 54–33 Bridgeton; Waynetown 46–45 Bainbridge (2ot). Officials: George Bender, Herbert Edwards.

EVANSVILLE: Boonville 33–24 Princeton; Bosse 38–22 Dale; Bosse 43–35 Boonville. Officials: W. N. Ringer, Norman Dunlap.

FT. WAYNE: Warsaw 36–34 Shipshewana; Central 43–36 Garrett; Central 38–24 Warsaw. Officials: L. E. Fink, Walter Thurston.

HAMMOND: Gary Emerson 36–23 Hammond; LaPorte 47–28 Mt. Ayr; LaPorte 45–29

Emerson. Officials: Paul Bateman, George Vaulk.
   HUNTINGTON: Decatur 44–36 Liberty Center; Montpelier 29–27 Huntington Twp.; Decatur 39–25 Montpelier. Officials: Lawrence Gaunt, Philip Eskew.
   INDIANAPOLIS: Anderson 46–33 Howe; Greenfield 26–22 Amo; Anderson 49–22 Greenfield. Officials: T. R. Smith, Walter Reimann.
   LAFAYETTE: Frankfort 29–27 Fowler; Thorntown 36–31 Lafayette; Frankfort 34–33 Thorntown (2ot). Officials: Frank Jarrel, A. N. Phillips.
   LOGANSPORT: Delphi 41–33 Monticello; Converse 48–29 Logansport; Converse 45–35 Delphi. Officials: Clyde Gentry, Cecil Tharp.
   MARION: Gas City 27–23 Chester Twp.; Kokomo 32–23 Tipton; Kokomo 57–29 Gas City. Officials: Norris Wood ,G.P. Silver
   MUNCIE: Burris 44–31 Parker; New Castle 49–41 Centerville; Burris 31–30 New Castle. Officials: Dean Malaska, Fred White.
   RUSHVILLE: Aurora 24–20 Batesville; New Salem 39–30 Connersville; Aurora 40–34 New Salem. Officials: George Williams, Thomas Baker.
   SEYMOUR: Bedford 43–34 Brownstown; Jeffersonville 48–27 Paoli; Bedford 29–22 Jeffersonville. Officials: Irvin Springer, Roy P. Johnson
   SHELBYVILLE: Scottsburg 39–35 Shelbyville; Whiteland 35–34 Greensburg; Whiteland 28–25 Scottsburg. Officials: Allen Klinck, Evan Crawley.
   SOUTH BEND: Adams 34–24 Rochester; Culver 34–23 Elkhart; Culver 33–31 Adams. Officials: Harold McSwane, Cecil Young.
   WASHINGTON: Washington 30–19 Decker; Jasper 41–33 Sullivan; Washington 41–38 Jasper. Officials: William E. Pointer, William Coulter.

1944 SEMI-FINALS

   ANDERSON: Whiteland 46–37 Waynetown; Anderson 37–18 Aurora; Anderson 40–21 Whiteland. Officials: L. E. Fink, William Pointer.
   HAMMOND: Culver 26–17 Converse; LaPorte 44–34 Frankfort; LaPorte 24–23 Culver. Officials: Karl Dickerson, T. R. Smith.
   MUNCIE: Ft. Wayne Central 41–31 Decatur; Kokomo 39–35 Burris; Kokomo 35–28 Ft. Wayne Central. Officials :C. N. Phillips, Thomas Baker.
   VINCENNES: Washington 20–16 Bedford; Evansville Bosse 46–33 Mooresville; Bosse 40–34 Washington. Officials: Allen Klinck, George Bender.

1944 FINALS—March 18

   INDIANAPOLIS (State Fairgrounds, new Coliseum): Kokomo 30–26 Anderson; Evansville Bosse 41–38 LaPorte; Bosse 39–35 Kokomo. Officials: Allen Klinck, Karl Dickerson.

1945 SECTIONALS

   ANDERSON: Alexandria 42–38 St. Mary's; Summitville 43–33 Frankton; Lapel 35–33 Markleville; Anderson 47–23 Pendleton; Lapel 45–36 Summitville; Anderson 61–29 Elwood;

Tourney Time

Anderson 46–31 Lapel. Officials: A. E. Pitcher, Herbert Edwards.

ATTICA: Williamsport 41–33 Cayuga; Pine Village 30–20 West Lebanon; Veedersburg 28–23 Perrysville; Covington 45–15 Newport; Kingman 47–32 Wallace; Hillsboro 39–31 Attica; Williamsport 27–18 Richland Twp.; Veedersburg 40–27 Pine Village; Covington 53–31 Kingman; Hillsboro 21–18 Williamsport; Covington 39–20 Veedersburg; Covington 27–13 Hillsboro. Officials: Donald Cooper, Norman Morrison, Herbert Vaulk.

AURORA: Vevay 35–19 Bright; Aurora 55–33 Moores Hill; Lawrenceburg 30–26 Rising Sun; Dillsboro 26–21 Guilford; Vevay 31–10 Patriot; Lawrenceburg 35–29 Aurora; Vevay 22–18 Patriot; Lawrenceburg 32–27 Vevay. Officials: Norman Miller, Robert Hodgers.

BATESVILLE: Napoleon 31–20 Holton; Versailles 25–21 Milan; New Marion 25–21 Cross Plains; Center Twp. (Osgood) 33–26 Sunman; Batesville 31–21 Napoleon; Versailles 46–34 New Marion; Batesville 51–35 Center Twp.; Batesville 40–30 Versailles. Officials: Paul Cly, Wayne Hammond.

BLUFFTON: Rockcreek Center 37–36 Ossian; Chester Center 49–36 Liberty Center; Union Center 38–32 Bluffton; Petroleum 55–30 Jackson Center; Rockcreek Center 40–22 Lancaster Central; Chester Center 46–39 Union Center; Petroleum 62–29 Rockcreek Center; Chester Center 43–32 Petroleum. Officials: Kenneth Michel, Donald Coar.

BOONVILLE: Boonville 48–20 Newburgh; Selvin 37–19 Folsomville; Chandler 34–22 Yankeetown; Lynnville 45–17 Millersburg; Elberfeld 59–24 Tennyson; Boonville 81–5 Selvin; Lynnville 33–26 Chandler; Boonville 32–30 Elberfeld (2ot); Boonville 42–27 Lynnville. Officials: Clarence Riggs, David Royalty.

BRAZIL: Posey Twp. 23–15 Van Buren Twp.; Gosport 36–26 Clay City; Brazil 50–18 Freedom; Cory 38–14 Jefferson Twp.; Spencer 42– 35 Ashboro; Bowling Green 44–37 Quincy; Staunton 46–19 Patricksburg; Brazil 64–28 Gosport; Spencer 42–34 Cory; Bowling Green 50–46 Staunton; Spencer 43–42 Brazil; Spencer 56–37 Bowling Green. Officials: Cleon Reynolds, Robert Quillen, James Conover.

CANNELTON: Cannelton 25–21 Chrisney; Rockport 40–22 Troy; Dale 31–30 Luce Twp.; Tell City 40–29 Cannelton; Dale 19–18 Rockport; Tell City 51–29 Dale. Officials Leland Terrell, Carl Jerger.

CONNERSVILLE: Liberty 46–20 Orange; Everton.25–22 Connersville; Fairview 32–25 Whitewater; Springfield Twp. 38–22 Bentonville; Kitchel 31–29 Alquina; Brownsville 24–23 Brookville; Liberty 39–26 Harrisburg; Everton 48–27 Fairview; Kitchel 24–18 Springfield Twp.; Liberty 28–27 Brownsville; Everton 26–25 Kitchel; Liberty 29–26 Everton. Officials: Wilbur May, Norman Freeland, Burl Shook.

CRAWFORDSVILLE: Waynetown 50–47 New Ross; Alamo 39–30 Darlington; Linden 40–31 New Market; Waveland 26–19 Ladoga; Crawfordsville 54–17 Wingate; Waynetown 57–9 Bowers; Alamo 47–29 Linden; Crawfordsville 51–36 Waveland; Waynetown. 53–41 Alamo; Waynetown 29–27 Crawfordsville. Officials: Herbert Schwomeyer, Robert Hobbs.

DANVILLE: Amo 34–29 Charlton; Avon 53–23 New Winchester; North Salem 34–31 Plainfield; Speedway 45–20 Lizton; Brownsburg 41–21 Stilesville; Pittsboro 37–36 Clayton; Danville 49–16 Amo; Avon 20–18 North Salem; Speedway 37–30 Brownsburg; Danville 59–29 Pittsboro; Speedway 33–20 Avon; Danville 25–24 Speedway. Officials: Thomas Stirling, Charles Whitworth, Norman Dunlap.

DECATUR: Kirkland 39–22 Pleasant Mills; Geneva 40–28 Monroe; Decatur Catholic 41–15

IHSAA Scores | 1940–1949

Jefferson; Monmouth 44–27 Hartford Center; Berne 34–18 Decatur; Geneva 30–29 Kirkland; Monmouth 30–29 Decatur Catholic; Berne 51–27 Geneva; Berne 44–34 Monmouth. Officials: Richard Kolp, Donald Dickie.

EVANSVILLE: Lincoln 44–28 Griffin; Wadesville 31–28 Booker T. Washington; Central 30–24 New Harmony; Reitz 29–27 Poseyville; Memorial 74–34 Cynthiana; Bosse 44–20 Mt. Vernon; Wadesville 34–20 Lincoln; Central 40–29 Reitz; Bosse 38–37 Memorial; Central 41–23 Wadesville; Bosse 50–35 Central. Officials: Ted Fehring, Clayton Patterson.

ELKHART: Millersburg 28–25 Jefferson Twp.; Elkhart 43–36 Wakarusa; Goshen 34–29 Bristol; Baugo Twp. 40–34 Middlebury; Nappanee 32–21 New Paris; Concord Twp. 41–25 Millersburg; Elkhart 37–26 Goshen; Baugo Twp. 33–27 Nappanee; Elkhart 42–30 Concord Twp.; Baugo Twp. 41–28 Elkhart. Officials: Elmer Millbranth, Phil Eskew.

FARMLAND: Saratoga 47–23 Green Twp.; Parker 42–22 Modoc; Lynn 33–31 Union City; Wayne Twp. 38–30 Lincoln; Winchester 30–25 Huntsville; Stoney Creek 46–37 Losantville; Jackson 39–37 Farmland; Spartanburg 50–25 McKinley; Parker 41–39 Saratoga; Lynn 50–34 Wayne; Winchester 34–28 Stoney Creek; Jackson 28–26 Spartanburg; Parker 36–33 Lynn; Winchester 45–35 Jackson; Parker 55–38 Winchester. Officials: Leonard Ireland, Herschel Eastman, Max Casey.

FLORA: Camden 37–26 Cutler; Carrollton 54–26 Adams Twp.; Delphi 35–29 Burlington; Flora 53–24 Rockfield; Camden 36–35 Deer Creek; Delphi 39–21 Carrollton; Flora 27–19 Camden; Flora 42–35 Delphi. Officials: William Lucus, George Vaulk.

FORT WAYNE: Central 59–25 Woodburn; New Haven 40–28 Central Catholic; South Side 39–21 Harlan; Leo 32–31 Huntertown; Elmhurst 31–28 Lafayette Central; North Side 38–18 Arcola; Concordia 37–25 Monroeville; Hoagland 45–35 Coesse; Central 53–33 New Haven; South Side 30–26 Leo; North Side 39–33; Elmhurst; Concordia 52–35 Hoagland; South Side 34–31 Central; North Side 40–38 Concordia; North Side 30–28 South Side. Officials: John Walker,, John Magnabosco, L.E. Fink.

FOWLER: Oxford 31–20 Freeland Park; Earl Park 42–21 Raub; Ambia 37–34 Gilboa; Fowler 47–43 Boswell; Otterbein 43–27 Wadena; Oxford 72–13 Pine Twp.; Earl Park 41–40 Ambia; Fowler 46–42 Otterbein; Oxfoxd 43–26 Earl Park; Oxford 28–20 Fowler. Officials: E.S. Stuteville, Frank Kresler.

FRANKFORT: Washington Twp. 31–20 Forest; Jackson Twp. 40–29 Colfax; Michigantown 46–23 Sugar Creek; Rossville 48–20 Mulberry; Frankfort 65–41 Kirklin; Washington Twp. 42–31 Scirlceville; Jackson Twp. 26–23 Michigantown; Frankfort 38–34 Rossville (ot); Washington Twp. 32–31 Jackson Twp. (2ot); Frankfort 48–34 Washington Twp. Officials: Leland Wright, Karl Dickerson.

FRANKLIN: Center Grove 41–17 Union Twp.; Trafalgar 40–34 Van Buren Twp.; Whiteland 27–18 Greenwood; Franklin 23–19 Edinburg; Clark Twp. 65–21 Nashville; Nineveh 49–25 Helmsburg; Trafalgar 26–25 Center Grove; Franklin 20–19 Whiteland; Clark Twp. 31–15 Nineveh; Franklin 47–20 Trafalgar; Franklin 34–31 Clark. Officials: J. T. Haywood, Arthur Snoddy.

GARRETT: Fremont 32–27 Churubusco; Waterloo 47–25 Spencerville; Hamilton 59–11 Scott Center; Auburn 59–19 Metz; Garrett 32–22 Butler; Angola 35–18 Orland; Ashley 51–30 Salem; Pleasant Lake 48–46 Concord Twp.; Waterloo 53–38 Fremont; Auburn 52–20 Hamilton; Angola 41–32 Garrett; Ashley 38–33 Pleasant Lake; Auburn 48–33 Waterloo; Ashley 37–36 Angola; Auburn 57–36 Ashley. Officials: Marvin Todd, Otho Piper. Omer Bixel.

Tourney Time

GARY: Wirt 67–23 Liberty Center; Horace Mann 26–23 Gary Edison; Wallace 65–34 Morgan Twp.; Emerson 50–27 Valparaiso; Tolleston 63–38 Washington Twp.; Roosevelt 29–26 Froebel; Chesterton 25–20 Boone Grove; Kouts 42–17 Hebron; Horace Mann 42–27 William A. Wirt; Emerson 40–39 Wallace; Tolleston 37–36 Roosevelt; Kouts 28–18 Chesterton; Emerson 37–35 Horace Mann; Kouts 40–35 Tolleston; Emerson 60–16 Kouts. Officials: R. W. Warring, Paul Boehm, Walter Thurston.

GREENCASTLE: Roachdale 48–27 Cloverdale; Fillmore 34–13 Clinton Center; Bainbridge 27–20 Reelsville; Greencastle 33–20 Russellville; Roachdale 45–33 Belle Union; Bainbridge 47–27 Fillmore; Roachdale 33–31 Greencastle; Bainbridge 37–33 Roachdale. Officials: Walter Loman, William Ellis.

GREENFIELD: Greenfield 40–18 Mt. Comfort; Eden 40–27 McCordsville; New Palestine 37–36 Charlottesville; Fortville 47–32 Maxwell; Wilkinson 38–28 Westland; Eden 43–28 Greenfield; New Palestine 43–40 Fortville; Eden 61–30 Wilkinson; Eden 58–38 New Palestine. Officials: Al Jackson, Dale Morey.

GREENSBURG: Greensburg 33–18 Sandusky; Clarksburg 38–37 North Vernon; New Point 43–24 Zenas; Jackson 31–30 Vernon; St. Paul 33–32 Burney; Butlerville 44–29 Sandcreek; Greensburg 47–21 Clarksburg; New Point 37–34 Jackson; St. Paul 37–27 Butlerville; Greensburg 36–21 New Point; Greensburg 41–21 St. Paul. Officials: Stephen Baker, Alvin Heller.

HAMMOND: Merrillville 48–38 Crown Point; Hammond High 51–31 Griffith; Hammond Tech 46–23 Wheeler; Portage 36–35 Roosevelt; Washington 59–25 Catholic Central; Hammond Clark 41–35 Whiting; East Gary Edison 57–37 Lowell; Hobart 46–27 Dyer; Hammond High 57–41 Merrillville; Hammond Tech 48–31 Portage; Washington 43–29 Hammond Clark; Edison 58–41 Hobart; Hammond High 35–30 Hammond Tech; Edison 38–37 Washington; Hammond High 57–40 Edison. Officials: Cecil Young, G. W. Strole, Paul Bateman.

HARTFORD CITY: Pennville 29–28 Montpelier; Dunkirk 48–34 Roll; Portland 43–32 Jefferson Twp.; Ridgeville 52–36 Poling; Hartford City 50–22 Madison Twp.; Redkey 44–32 Bryant; Dunkirk 36–23 Pennville; Portland 53–28 Ridgeville; Hartford City 46–28 Redkey; Dunkirk 41–36 Portland; Dunkirk 44–26 Hartford City. Officials: Marvin Dick, Gene McNutt.

HUNTINGTON: Huntington 51–19 Jefferson Center; Polk Twp. 34–30 Lancaster Center; Union Twp. 37–35 Jefferson Twp.; Bippus 38–25 Wayne Twp.; Huntington Twp. 57–18 Rock Greek Center; Salamonie Twp. 29–27 Huntington Catholic; Andrews 55–31 Markle; Clear Creek Twp. 43–35 Jackson Twp.; Huntington 36–30 Polk Twp.; Union Twp. 40–28 Bippus; Huntington Twp. 45–31 Salamonie Twp.; Clear Creek Twp. 45–27 Andrews; Huntington 56–34 Union Twp.; Clear Creek Twp. 42–38 Huntington Twp.; Huntington 29–25 Clear Creek Twp. Officials: F. O. Sonafrank, Lowell Barnett, Aaron Belcher.

INDIANAPOLIS: Crispus Attucks 30–25 Manual; Shortridge 34–26 School for the Deaf; Ben Davis 36–31 Tech; Broad Ripple 44–38 Southport; Howe 38–33 Beech Grove; Decatur Central 31–30 Washington; Warren Central 40–33 Cathedral; Sacred Heart 38–37 Lawrence Central; Crispus Attucks 30–28 Shortridge; Broad Ripple 40–37 Ben Davis; Howe 53–30 Decatur Central; Warren Central 40–33 Sacred Heart; Broad Ripple 51–28 Crispus Attucks; Howe 40–34 Warren Central; Broad Ripple 41–23 Howe. Officials: T. R. Smith, Eugene Glaze, Thomas Baker.

JASPER: Jasper 75–23 Ireland; Spurgeon 28–22 Otwell; Jefferson Twp. 31–21 Cuzco; Huntingburg 42–31 Petersburg; Holland 42–38 Stendal; Winslow 52–24 Dubois; Jasper 43–30 Spurgeon; Huntingburg 64–23 Birdseye; Holland 35–33 Winslow (3ot); Jasper 49–28

Huntingburg; Jasper 61–30 Holland. Officials: William E. Pointer, William Coulter.

JEFFERSONVILLE: Silver Creek 57–31 Georgetown; Lanesville 41–18 New Middletown; Corydon 47–27 New Washington; Jeffersonville 61–8 Laconia; Henryville 36–25 Borden; New Albany 61–14 New Salisbury; Mauckport 40–15 Elizabeth; Charlestown 40–18 New Amsterdam; Silver Creek 45–21 Lanesville; Jeffersonville 58–37 Corydon; New Albany 64–30 Henryville; Charlestown 38–22 Mauckport; Jeffersonville 25–22 Silver Creek; New Albany 65–35 Charlestown; Jeffersonville 31–29 New Albany. Officials: Max Thompson, Francis Myers, Walter Surface.

KENDALLVILLE: Shipshewana 49–30 Howe Military; Cromwell 53–22 Topeka; Kendallville 29–27 Avilla; Wolf Lake 45–22 Scott; Albion 34–16 Ligonier; Wawaka 36–20 Brighton; Wolcottville 39–27 Rome City; LaGrange 28–19 Lima; Cromwell 37–31 Shipshewana; Kendallville 24–23 Wolf Lake; Albion 36–26 Wawaka; LaGrange 29–23 Wolcottville; Cromwell 26–23 Kendallville; LaGrange 45–38 Albion; Cromwell 33–32 LaGrange. Officials: Lundy Welborn, Arthur Lloyd, Louis Briner.

KOKOMO: Russiaville 41–32 Union Twp.; Howard Twp. 50–33 Ervin Twp.; Greentown 48–20 West Middleton; Jackson Twp. 39–21 New London; Kokomo 69–29 Clay Twp.; Howard Twp. 45–31 Russiaville; Greentown 43–21 Jackson Twp.; Kokomo 38–21 Howard Twp.; Kokomo 34–27 Greentown. Officials: C. N. Phillips, Herbert Brammell

LAFAYETTE: West Lafayette 43–19 Monitor; Wea 28–25 Jackson; West Point 39–20 Dayton; Stockwell 34–30 Romney; Montmorenci 38–21 Shadeland; Lafayette 52–33 Buck Creek; Clarks Hill 38–32 Klondike; Battle Ground 40–29 West Lafayette; West Point 40–21 Wea; Stockwell 46–26 Montmorenci; Lafayette 40–11 Clarks Hill; Battle Ground 32–25 West Point; Lafayette 34–24 Stockwell; Lafayette 66–22 Battle Ground. Officials: Sam Massette, G. P. Silver, Hal Harris.

LAPORTE: LaPorte 69–32 Westville; Wanatah 44–34 Kingsbury; Hanna 56–37 LaCrosse; Springfield 28–19 Clinton; Michigan City 94–27 Stillwell; Rolling Prairie 38–35 Union Twp.; Union Mills 26–24 St. Mary's; Jackson Center 39–28 Mill Creek; LaPorte 59–23 Wanatah; Hanna 38–15 Springfield; Michigan City 55–24 Rolling Prairie; Union Mills 45–21 Jackson Center; LaPorte 54–23 Hanna; Michigan City 64–21 Union Mills; Michigan City 44–33 LaPorte. Officials: Charles Kruzan, Charles McManus, Jim Crowe.

LEBANON: Jamestown 30–29 Pinnell; Dover 32–30 Lebanon; Zionsville 28–26 Central; Pike Twp. 26–16 Advance; Thorntown 30–26 Whitestown; Jamestown; 41–29 Dover; Zionsville 45–30 Pike Twp.; Thorntown 32–22 Jamestown; Zionsville 30–29 Thorntown. Officials: Forrest Ballinger, Otto Crosley.

LINTON: Jasonville 26–20 Solsberry; Lyons 51–28 Owensburg; Linton 44–19 Midland; Marco 51–12 Newberry; Scotland 37–20 Switz City; Bloomfield 45–28 Worthington; Lyons 33–25 Jasonville; Linton 49–34 Marco; Bloomfield 36–31 Scotland; Linton 63–39 Lyons; Linton 53–35 Bloomfield. Officials: Lowell Willis, H.W. Gross.

LOGANSPORT: Young America 35–25 Royal Center; Logansport 44–20 Onward; Lucerne 38–36 Galveston; New Waverly 33–31 Twelve Mile; Washington Twp. 41–24 Metea; Young America 27–26 Walton; Logansport 48–24 Lucerne; Washington Twp. 41–19 New Waverly; Logansport 63–38 Young America; Logansport 47–32 Washington Twp. Officials: Jack O'Neal, George Bender.

MADISON: Hanover 30–21 Austin; Central 27–25 North Madison; Scottsburg 50–32 Saluda; Dupont 54–23 Deputy; Madison 47–18 Paris Crossing; Hanover 46–23 Central;

Tourney Time

Scottsburg 29–17 Dupont; Madison 43–24 Hanover; Madison 26–24 Scottsburg. Officials: Ross Dorsett, Howard Wright.

MARION: Gas City 34–24 Swayzee; Sweetser 40–35 Van Buren; St. Paul 37–16 Jefferson Twp.; Fairmount 36–28 Jonesboro; Gas City 39–29 Marion; St. Paul 35–29 Sweetser; Fairmount 28–27 Gas City; Fairmount 40–23 St. Paul. Officials: Layall Fisher, Don Bright.

MARSHALL: Rockville 46–12 Union Twp.; Mecca 33–24 Bloomingdale; Montezuma 36–25 Greene Twp.; Rosedale 26–25 Marshall; Bridgeton 36–33 St. Bernice; Tangier 45–29 Dana; Clinton 42–32 Hillsdale; Mecca 31–25 Rockville; Rosedale 31–23 Montezuma; Tangier 27–24 Bridgeton; Clinton 37–30 Mecca; Tangier 48–25 Rosedale; Clinton 39–31 Tangier. Officials: W.N. Ringer, William J. McCoskey, Loren Harris.

MARTINSVILLE: Ellettsville 45–33 Mooresville; University 47–23 Stinesville; Monrovia 50–45 Smithville; Martinsville 50–25 Eminence; Morgantown 59–19 Paragon; Bloomington 48–13 Unionville; University 53–28 Ellettsville; Martinsville 50–20 Monrovia; Bloomington 59–25 Morgantown; University 52–37 Martinsville; Bloomington 43–30 University. Officials: Cyril Birge, Hulett Crecelius.

MITCHELL: Mitchell 43–22 Tunnelton; Oolitic 44–24 Huron; Fayetteville 40–30 Heltonville; Bedford 56–18 Shawswick; Mitchell 49–32 Marshall Twp.; Fayetteville 49–42 Oolitic; Bedford 55–32 Mitchell; Bedford 74–47 Fayetteville. Officials: Frank Jarrell, Evan Crawley.

MONTICELLO: Monticello 39–19 Buffalo; Brookston 51–36 Burnettsville; Idaville 28–26 Wolcott; Monon 38–23 Chalmers; Round Grove 30–27 Reynolds; Monticello 43–30 Brookston; Monon 52–36 Idaville; Monticello 45–19 Round Grove; Monticello 47–29 Monon. Officials: Albert Etter, Orville Martin.

MUNCIE: Daleville 42–22 Gaston; Yorktown 57–20 Harrison; Central 65–26 Center; Burris 34–27 Albany; Cowan 30–24 DeSoto; Royerton 36–35 Selma; Eaton 34–24 Daleville; Central 38–28 Yorktown; Burris 44–28 Cowan; Royerton 33–31 Eaton; Central 43–25 Burris; Central 43–34 Royerton. Officials: Theodore Lentz, LeRoy Shine, Dean Malaska.

NEW CASTLE: Knightstown 46–44 New Lisbon; New Castle 40–22 Straughn; Mooreland 32–30 Sulphur Springs; Middletown 26–20 Mt. Summit; Spiceland 37–34 Kennard; Lewisville 51–27 Cadiz; New Castle 39–30 Knightstown; Mooreland 31–26 Middletown; Lewisville 32–31 Spiceland; Mooreland 24–21 New Castle; Lewisville 31–29 Mooreland. Officials: Walter Floyd, Frank White.

OAKLAND CITY: Patoka 31–29 Princeton; Mackey 35–28 Hazleton; Oakland City 39–27 Lincoln; Mt. Olympus 33–30 Francisco (ot); Owensville 33–18 Haubstadt; Patoka 38–30 Ft. Branch; Mackey 36–16 Oakland City; Owensville 35–31 Mt. Olympus (ot); Patoka 39–34 Mackey; Owensville 26–25 Patoka. Officials: Don DeVault, Irvin Springer.

PAOLI: Hardinsburg 42–38 Leavenworth; Morgan Twp. 51–20 Milltown; Orleans 50–21 Marengo; Paoli 64–32 Campbellsburg; French Lick 27–21 Salem; West Baden Springs 44–32 Pekin; English 48–22 Little York; Morgan Twp. 34–28 Hardinsburg; Paoli 56–32 Orleans; West Baden Springs 49–31 French Lick; English 26–24 Morgan Twp.; Paoli 30–18 West Baden Springs; Paoli 67–22 English. Officials: Irvin Thrasher, Ivan Sprinkle, John Lyskowinski.

PERU: Gilead 28–24 Converse; Chili 40–29 Deedsville; Clay Twp. 53–23 Butler Twp.; Peru 53–29 Amboy; Bunker Hill 44–25 Mexico; Gilead 24–21 Macy; Clay Twp. 37–35 Chili; Peru 47–27 Bunker Hill; Clay Twp. 38–25 Gilead; Peru 65–28 Clay Twp. Officials: Clay Layman, Raymond Trobaugh.

IHSAA Scores | 1940–1949

PLYMOUTH: Bremen 47–34 Tippecanoe; Plymouth 38–29 San Pierre; Argos 34–29 LaPaz; Bourbon 55–27 Tyner; Grovertown 42–29 Hamlet; Culver 63–27 North Judson; Knox 34–31 West; Plymouth 33–20 Bremen; Bourbon 49–39 Argos; Culver 67–31 Grovertown; Plymouth 60–28 Knox; Culver 43–28 Bourbon; Culver 40–39 Plymouth. Officials: Fred White, Ed Anglemyer; Norris Ward.

RENSSELAER: Remington 54–31 Goodland; Fair Oaks 42–33 Morocco; Rensselaer 37–24 Brook; Wheatfield 41–26 Kankakee Twp.; DeMotte 35–34 St. Joseph; Kentland 35–34 Mt. Ayr; Remington 45–21 Fair Oaks; Rensselaer 44–38 Wheatfield; DeMotte 35–32 Kentland; Remington 47–44 Rensselaer; Remington 51–45 DeMotte. Officials: Wayne Cunningham, Hugh Bergstrom.

RICHMOND: Hagerstown 33–22 Milton; Fountain City 41–21 Webster; Richmond 33–30 Centerville; Whitewater 33–17 Economy; Green's Fork 42–30 Williamsburg; Cambridge City 33–28 Boston; Fountain City 37–31 Hagerstown; Richmond 31–18 Whitewater; Green's Fork 26–24 Cambridge City; Richmond 41–33 Fountain City; Richmond 47–25 Green's Fork. Officials: John Janzaruk, George Williams.

ROCHESTER: Star City 24–23 Fulton; Akron 49–27 Leiters Ford; Francesville 49–25 Kewanna; Rochester 40–39 Winamac; Talma 40–25 Medaryville; Monterey 35–28 Richland Center; Grass Creek 35–26 Pulaski; Star City 35–32 Akron; Rochester 49–36 Francesville; Talma 31–28 Monterey; Grass Creek 24–19 Star City; Rochester 45–33 Talma; Rochester 40–29 Grass Creek. Officials: Jay L. Mertz, Gerald Powell, Don Edmonds.

RUSHVILLE: New Salem 26–24 Milroy; Carthage 28–16 Arlington; Rushville 46–23 Morton Memorial; Raleigh 33–32 Mays; New Salem 41–18 Manilla; Rushville 37–19 Carthage; New Salem 55–32 Raleigh; Rushville 54–36 New Salem. Officials: John Hilligoss, Ray Lackey.

SEYMOUR: Cortland 40–24 Hayden; Clearspring 60–27 Scipio; Brownstown 41–31 Medora; Seymour 34–29 Vallonia; Freetown 25–24 Crothersville; Clearspring 40–30 Cortland; Brownstown 31–30 Seymour; Clearspring 36–30 Freetown; Brownstown 32–21 Clearspring. Officials: W. N. Reimann, Verrollton Shaul.

SHELBYVILLE: Shelbyville 38–34 Clifford; Franklin Twp. 35–21 Flat Rock; Moral Twp. 38–25 Fairland; Hope 27–19 Waldron; Morristown 35–26 Mt. Auburn; Columbus 34–33 Boggstown; Shelbyville 47–39 Franklin Twp.; Hope 48–27 Moral Twp.; Morristown 36–25 Columbus; Hope 24–19 Shelbyville; Hope 29–21 Morristown. Officials Harold Porter and John Gwin.

SHERIDAN: Westfield 29–22 Carmel; Sharpsville 46–34 Windfall; Sheridan 28–26 Noblesville; Tipton 43–19 Jefferson Twp.; Walnut Grove 30–24 Fishers; Jackson Central 62–29 Prairie Twp.; Sharpsville 41–24 Westfield; Tipton 34–26 Sheridan; Jackson Central 44–26 Walnut Grove; Tipton 45–29 Sharpsville; Jackson Central 37–30 Tipton. Officials: Cecil Tharp, Robert Gatewood.

SOUTH BEND: Riley 55–32 Madison Twp.; Central 53–32 Washington-Clay; Mishawaka 43–20 New Carlisle; Washington 47–29 South Bend Catholic; Central Catholic 39–20 Greene; Adams 40–38 Wilson (ot); Lakeville 43–35 North Liberty; Riley 68–45 Walkerton; Central 40–38 Mishawaka; Washington 26–19 Central Catholic; Lakeville 34–29 Adams; Riley 36–28 Central; Washington 44–34 Lakeville; Riley 45–24 Washington. Officials: J.H. McClure, Allen Klinck, Harold McSwane.

SULLIVAN: Hymera 40–25 Pleasantville; Carlisle 37–26 Merom; Farmersburg 34–26 New Lebanon; Sullivan 44–16 Fairbanks; Shelburn 33–32 Graysville; Dugger 17–16 Hymera;

Tourney Time

Farmersburg 36–25 Carlisle; Sullivan 36–24 Shelburn; Farmersburg 43–36 Dugger (ot); Sullivan 45–32 Farmersburg. Officials: Clarence Myles, Hubert Thomas.

TERRE HAUTE: Garfield 40–35 Fontanet; Laboratory 46–19 West Terre Haute; Gerstmeyer 41–32 Concannon; Honey Creek 30–27 Otter Creek; Wiley 50–22 Glenn; Pimento 42–33 Riley; Garfield 36–23 Laboratory; Gerstmeyer 32–29 Honey Creek; Wiley 30–27 Pimento; Gerstmeyer 65–54 Garfield; Gerstmeyer 43–38 Wiley. Officials: Clyde Gentry, Lawrence Young.

VINCENNES: Fritchton 30–21 Decker; Oaktown 46–31 Edwardsport; Vincennes 41–19 Monroe City; Freelandville 33–23 Decker Chapel; Bruceville 35–27 Wheatland; Bicknell 35–24f Sandborn; Oaktown 21–19 Fritchton (ot); Vincennes 30–26 Freelandville; Bicknell 30–29 Bruceville; Vincennes 24–18 Oaktown; Bicknell 37–26 Vincennes. Officials: Roland Baker, Harry Briggs.

WABASH: South Whitley 45–22 Roann; North Manchester 59–19 Somerset; Washington Center 54–40 Urbana; Chester Twp. 46–31 Lagro; Wabash 41–21 Linlawn; Laketon 38–17 Lincolnville; Chippewa 28–26 LaFontaine; North Manchester 44–28 South Whitley; Chester 62–23 Washington Center; Wabash 39–27 Laketon; North Manchester 45–33 Chippewa; Wabash 45–31 Chester Twp.; Wabash 35–27 North Manchester. Officials: Harrison Berkey, Frank Walls, E. D. Milhon.

WARSAW: Etna Green 41–33 Columbia City; North Webster 48–37 Sidney; Milford 57–47 Leesburg; Silver Lake 68–48 Burket; Syracuse 52–32 Larwill; Pierceton 58–26 Mentone; Warsaw 34–28 Beaver Dam; Atwood 37–35 Claypool; North Webster 45–38 Etna Green; Silver Lake 47–29 Milford; Syracuse 52–40 Pierceton; Warsaw 50–35 Atwood; Silver Lake 48–28 North Webster; Syracuse 38–28 Warsaw; Syracuse 43–31 Silver Lake. Officials: Devon Eaton, Forrest Shaw, George Merkle.

WASHINGTON: Washington 27–22 Catholic; Alfordsville 26–18 Odon; Elmore Twp. 42–19 Epsom; Barr Twp. 40–24 Shoals; Loogootee 58–20 Glendale; Washington 38–22 Plainville; Elmore Twp. 52–17 Alfordsville; Loogootee 36–34 Barr Twp.; Washington 34–27 Elmore Twp.; Washington 29–26 Loogootee. Officials: Robert Derrington, W.E. Hartley.

1945 REGIONALS

ANDERSON: Danville 33–32 Anderson; Broad Ripple 50–39 Eden; Broad Ripple 51–28 Danville. Officials: Karl Dickerson, Clyde Gentry.

ATTICA: Waynetown 36–33 Clinton; Covington 49–17 Bainbridge; Covington 32–28 Waynetown. Officials: Dean Malaska, George Vaulk.

BEDFORD: Jeffersonville 48–40 Paoli; Bedford 57–32 Brownstown; Bedford 45–38 Jeffersonville. Officials: William S. Pointer, William Coulter.

EVANSVILLE: Tell City 43–23 Owensville; Bosse 49–37 Boonville; Bosse 77–44 Tell City. Officials: Norman Dunlap, Roland Baker.

FORT WAYNE: Auburn 57–39 Cromwell; Syracuse 37–33 North Side (ot); Auburn 56–32 Syracuse. Officials: Walter Thurston, Norris Ward.

HAMMOND: Michigan City 47–26 Gary Emerson; Hammond 50–38 Remington; Hammond 48–42 Michigan City. Officials: L. E. Fink,. Jim Crowe.

HUNTINGTON: Huntington 50–29 Chester Center; Berne 39–37 Dunkirk; Huntington 51–31 Berne. Officials: Fred White, Harold McSwane.

LAFAYETTE: Oxford 38–33 Zionsville; Frankfort 38–37 Lafayette; Oxford 33–31 Frankfort.

Officials: Allen Klinck, W.N. Ringer.
 LOGANSPORT: Monticello 26–24 Flora (2ot) Logansport 58–34 Peru; Logansport 40–31 Monticello. Officials: Dr. G.P. Silver, Phil Eskew.
 MARION: Wabash 25–23 Fairmount; Kokomo 59–24 Jackson Central; Kokomo 62–36 Wabash. Officials: Thomas Baker, Omer Bixel.
 MUNCIE: Muncie Central 39–25 Richmond; Lewisville 36–25 Parker; Central 41–29 Lewisville. Officials: George Bender, Herbert Edwards.
 RUSHVILLE: Rushville 32–19 Batesville; Lawrenceburg 26–20 Liberty; Rushville 50–35 Lawrenceburg. Officials: John Walker, Aaron Belcher.
 SHELBYVILLE: Franklin 46–36 Madison; Hope 38–27 Greensburg; Hope 41–38 Franklin. Officials: Evan Crawley, Jack O'Neal.
 SOUTH BEND: Riley 37–23 Rochester; Baugo Twp. 40–34 Culver; Riley 50–25 Baugo Twp. Officials: Paul Bateman, Cecil Young.
 TERRE HAUTE: Linton 60–39 Spencer; Gerstmeyer 44–43 Bloomington; Gerstmeyer 50–45 Linton. Officials: T. R. Smith, Cecil Tharp.
 VINCENNES: Jasper 50–30 Bicknell; Sullivan 37–31 Washington; Jasper 65–35 Sullivan. Officials: C.N. Phillips, Frank Jarrell.

1945 SEMI–FINALS

 BLOOMINGTON: Jasper 41–36 Gerstmeyer; Bosse 44–34 Bedford; Bosse 55–32 Jasper. Officials: C. N. Phillips, George Bender.
 INDIANAPOLIS: Broad Ripple 54–36 Hope; Rushville 39–38 Covington; Broad Ripple 54–40 Rushville. Officials Allen Klinck, Phil Eskew.
 LAFAYETTE: South Bend Riley 37–25 Hammond; Logansport 37–22 Oxford; Riley 43–21 Logansport. Officials: Thomas Baker, William E. Pointer.
 MUNCIE: Muncie Central 39–36 Auburn; Huntington 29–28 Kokomo; Huntington 42–37 Central. Officials: T. R. Smith, Walter Thurston.

1945 FINALS—March 17

 INDIANAPOLIS (State Fairgrounds, new Coliseum): Bosse 37–35 Broad Ripple; Riley 39–28 Huntington; Bosse 46–36 Riley; Officials: T. R. Smith, C. N. Phillips

1946 SECTIONALS

 AMBIA: Fowler 51–31 Freeland Park; Oxford 57–33 Raub; Ambia 53–30 Pine Twp.; Otterbein 32–26 Earl Park; Boswell 59–36 Gilboa; Fowler 56–29 Wadena; Oxford 53–20 Ambia; Boswell 36–31 Otterbein; Fowler 33–32 Oxford; Boswell 43–40 Fowler. Officials: Charles McManus, Leland Wright, Charles Marshall.
 ANDERSON: Lapel 47–20 Markleville; Anderson 40–21 Elwood; St. Mary's 47–27 Frankton; Pendleton 42–40 Summitville; Lapel 45–38 Alexandria; Anderson 57–38 St. Mary's; Lapel 36–33 Pendleton; Anderson 50–33 Lapel. Officials: William Reimann, Ray Lackey.
 ATTICA: Perrysville 25–19 Wallace; Pine Village 46–34 Hillsboro; Kingman 35–34

Tourney Time

Williamsport; Covington 42–18 Veedersburg; Attica 36–28 Richland Twp.; Perrysville 23–18 West Lebanon; Pine Village 34–33 Kingman; Attica 29–21 Covington; Pine Village 25–23 Perrysville; Attica 43–16 Pine Village. Officials: Karl Dickerson, William Lucus, Robert Connaroe.

AUBURN: Garrett 56–41 Salem Center; Auburn 56–31 Pleasant Lake; Churubusco 44–42 Orland (ot); Concord Twp. 48–39 Fremont; Ashley 56–37 Metz; Butler 29–28 Waterloo; Spencerville 48–38 Hamilton; Angola 53–19 Scott Center; Auburn 48–26 Garrett; Concord Twp. 45–39 Churubusco; Ashley 62–39 Butler; Angola 61–21 Spencer–ville; Auburn 48–22 Concord Twp.; Ashley 39–38 Angola; Ashley 44–41 Auburn. Officials: Arthur Lloyd, Lloyd Bryan, George Merkle.

BATESVILLE: Versailles 51–26 Cross Plains; Milan 38–31 Batesville; Napoleon 42–24 Osgood; Sunman 49–16 Holton; Versailles 44–29 New Marion; Milan 38–37 Napoleon; Sunman 39–36 Versailles; Milan 30–29 Sunman. Officials: Arthur Snoddy, Robert Quillen.

BEDFORD: Shawswick 37–28 Williams; Fayetteville 47–21 Tunnelton; Bedford 34–23 Mitchell; Oolitic 44–38 Marshall; Heltonville 30–18 Huron; Shawswick 35–32 Fayetteville; Bedford 36–23 Oolitic; Shawswick 51–18 Heltonville; Bedford 56–23 Shawswick. Officials: C.N. Phillips, Francis Myers, William E. Shaefer.

BLOOMINGTON: Bloomington 57–17 Paragon; Smithville 37–36 Mooresville; Morgantown 47–24 Eminence; Martinsville 43–40 Unionville; University 39–27 Monrovia; Bloomington 35–26 Ellettsville; Morgantown 37–35 Smithville; University 42–29 Martinsville; Bloomington 31–29 Morgantown; University 37–30 Bloomington. Officials: Stephen Baker, Walter N. Ringer, William McCoskey.

BLUFFTON: Union Center 33–24 Jackson Center; Lancaster Central 40–29 Bluffton; Chester Center 34–30 Liberty Center; Ossian 37–36 Rockcreek Center; Petroleum 34–30 Union Center; Lancaster Central 39–20 Chester Center; Petroleum 47–35 Ossian; Petroleum 35–29 Lancaster Central. Officials: Joe Metzger, Gerald Powell.

BOONVILLE: Boonville 47–15 Chandler; Newburgh 59–16 Tennyson; Lynnville 69–23 Millersburg; Elberfeld 44–15 Folsomville; Boonville 59–18 Newburgh; Lynnville 48–26 Elberfeld; Boonville 58–50 Lynnville. Officials: Hulett Crecelius, Odilo Berger.

CLINTON: Hillsdale 36–30 Green Twp.; St. Bernice 29–19 Montezuma; Clinton 69–23 Union Twp.; Marshall 31–30 Bloomingdale; Rosedale 26–20 Cayuga; Tangier 37–25 Newport; Rockville 33–32 Bridgeton (ot); Dana 44–27 Mecca; St. Bernice 35–33 Hillsdale (ot); Clinton 41–31 Marshall; Tangier 40–28 Rosedale; Rockville 50–33 Dana; Clinton 41–28 St. Bernice; Rockville 30–27 Tangier; Clinton 35–28 Rockville. Officials: Clyde Gentry, Chester Elson, Clayton Patterson.

CONNERSVILLE: Brownsville 37–21 Brookville; Springfield 36–25 Whitewater; Harrisburg 60–41 Bentonville; Alquina 62–22 Laurel; Liberty 44–32 Kitchel; Orange 40–23 Fairview; Connersville 29–23 Everton; Brownsville 34–33 Springfield; Harrisburg 36–35 Alquina; Orange 30–28 Liberty; Brownsville 34–28 Connersville; Harrisburg 26–16 Orange; Brownsville 42–35 Harrisburg. Officials: John Magnabosco, Richard Kolp, Alvy Havens.

CRAWFORDSVILLE: Waveland 47–38 Waynetown; Linden 37–31 Ladoga; New Ross 52–25 Wingate; Crawfordsville 84–22 New Richmond; Alamo 45–30 New Market; Darlington 69–20 Bowers; Linden 47–45 Waveland; Crawfordsville 72–24 New Ross; Darlington 45–39 Alamo; Crawfordsville 40–28 Linden; Crawfordsville 55–44 Darlington. Officials: Lawrence Leland, Raymond Trobaugh, Harry Briggs.

DANVILLE: North Salem 38–17 Stilesville; Brownsburg 58–27 Lizton; Avon 49–28 Pittsboro;

IHSAA Scores | 1940–1949

Amo 35–28 Plainfield; Danville 35–15 Clayton; Speedway 40–34 New Winchester; Brownsburg 48–20 North Salem; Avon 46–34 Amo; Danville 27–25 Speedway; Brownsburg 48—24 Avon; Danville 49–46 Brownsburg. Officials: Robert Gatewood, George Williams, Otto Albright.

DECATUR: Kirkland 41–26 Jefferson; Monmouth 48–28 Decatur Catholic; Berne 39–26 Hartford; Pleasant Mills 30–24 Geneva; Decatur 47–36 Monroe; Monmouth 47–33 Kirkland; Berne 48–28 Pleasant Mills; Decatur 28–27 Monmouth; Berne 29–28 Decatur. Officials: Lundy Welborn, J. L. Mertz.

DELPHI: Camden 35–29 Rockfield; Flora 57–15 Deer Creek; Carrollton 33–28 Burlington; Delphi 48–19 Adams Twp.; Camden 41–35 Cutler; Flora 53–22 Carrollton; Camden 30–21 Delphi; Flora 36–29 Camden. Officials: Forrest Ballinger, Otto Crosley.

EVANSVILLE: Poseyville 35–28 New Harmony; Central 49–21 Cynthiana; Reitz 52–35 Lincoln; Memorial 46–34 Bosse; Griffin 40–37 Wadesville; Mt. Vernon 30–24 Poseyville; Central 54–36 Reitz; Memorial 68–28 Griffin; Central 41–17 Mt. Vernon; Central 31–28 Memorial. Officials: Cyril Birge, Robert Hoffman, T. M. Dunlevy.

FARMLAND: Union City 41–18 Lincoln; Huntsville 45–40 Wayne; Farmland 33–30 Winchester; McKinley 43–36 Lynn; Parker 35–31 Losantville; Saratoga 42–33 Green; Spartanburg 61–17 Modoc; Jackson 32–29 Stoney Creek; Union City 40–28 Huntsville; Farmland 40–17 McKinley; Parker 39–23 Saratoga; Spartanburg 39–23 Jackson; Farmland 46–33 Union City; Parker 35–23 Spartanburg– Farmland 39–38 Parker (ot). Officials: George Collyer, Layall Fisher, Burl McKenzie.

FORT WAYNE: North Side 38–28 Concordia; Central Catholic 45–36 Harlan; Huntertown 29–27 Elmhurst; South Side 33–19 New Haven; Hoagland 45–24 Lafayette Central; Woodburn 48–27 Arcola; Leo 28–26 Coesse; Central 53–39 Monroeville; North Side 31–28 Central Catholic; South Side 51–24 Huntertown; Woodburn 38–32 Hoagland; Central 53–34 Leo; South Side 36–33 North Side; Central 51–30 Woodburn; Central 51–42 South Side. Officials: Lowell Barnett, John Hilligoss, Phil Eskew.

FRANKFORT: Michigantown 36–25 Washington Twp.; Rossville 64–18 Kirklin; Colfax 31–23 Scircleville; Frankfort 50–15 Mulberry; Jackson Twp. 42–24 Sugar Creek; Michigantown 59–26 Forest; Rossville 40–26 Colfax; Frankfort 41–25 Jackson Twp.; Rossville 32–22 Michigantown; Rossville 43–34 Frankfort. Officials: Thomas Baker, Ted Lentz, Joe Mullins.

FRANKLIN: Whiteland 40–35 Greenwood; Edinburg 44–33 Helmsburg; Nashville 31–28 Trafalgar; Franklin 57–18 Van Buren; Center Grove 32–27 Union; Nineveh 34–29 Clark; Whiteland 58–24 Edinburg: Franklin 70–36 Nashville; Nineveh 28–23 Center Grove; Franklin 32–23 Whiteland; Franklin 52–21 Nineveh. Officials: John Simon, Robert Hobbs, Robert Fink.

GARY: Gary Edison 49–40 Kouts; Froebel 45–42 Emerson (ot); Wirt 63–51 Morgan Twp.; Horace Mann 30–27 Valparaiso; Wallace 50–25 Hebron; Roosevelt 47–24 Liberty Center; Tolleston 47–27 Washington Twp.; Boone Grove 34–27 Chesterton; Edison 30–24 Froebel; Horace Mann 44–28 William A. Wirt; Wallace 40–30 Roosevelt; Tolleston 51–22 Boone Grove; Edison 37–29 Horace Mann; Wallace 53–37 Tolleston; Gary Edison 28–26 Wallace. Officials: L.E. Fink, G.W. Strole, Jim Crowe.

GREENCASTLE: Bainbridge 39–20 Fillmore; Greencastle 33–26 Cloverdale; Russellville 30–29 Roachdale; Reelsville 42–21 Belle Union; Bainbridge 40–14 Clinton Center; Greencastle 26–25 Russellville; Reelsville 39–37 Bainbridge; Reelsville 26–14 Greencastle. Officials: Thomas Stirling, Walter Floyd.

273

Tourney Time

GREENFIELD: Greenfield 38–19 Mt. Comfort; Fortville 51–32 McCordsville; Eden 51–28 New Palestine Maxwell 33–30 Westland; Wilkinson 45–25 Charlottesville; Fortville 35–33 Greenfield; Eden 50–27 Maxwell; Fortville 33–32 Wilkinson; Eden 41–23 Fortville. Officials: Cecil Tharp, Leon Hodson.

GREENSBURG: Greensburg 51–26 Zenas; Butlerville 30–13 Burney; Vernon 32–19 Clarksburg; North Vernon 41–30 Jackson Twp.; Sandcreek 33–32 Sandusky; New Point 41–31 St. Paul; Greensburg 40–30 Butlerville; North Vernon 39–25 Vernon; Sandcreek 29–19 New Point; Greensburg 27–25 North Vernon; Sandcreek 43–40 Greensburg. Officials: Estal Conover, John Townsend, Earl Townsend.

HAMMOND: Catholic Central 44–43 Griffith; Lowell 67–41 Wheeler; Portage 43–33 Hobart; Roosevelt 52–32 Dyer; Hammond Tech 49–38 Clark; Merrillville 51–38 Crown Point; Hammond 60–28 East Gary Edison; East Chicago Washington 61–47 Whiting; Lowell 47–37 Catholic Central; Portage 32–21 Roosevelt; Hammond Tech 56–34 Merrillville; Washington 40–36 Hammond; Lowell 52–45 Portage; Washington 36–32 Hammond Tech; Washington 59–23 Lowell. Officials: Norris Ward, R. W. Warring, Walter Thurston.

HARTFORD CITY: Hartford City 33–32 Montpelier; Redkey 54–33 Bryant; Portland 65–22 Poling; Roll 53–42 Ridgeville; Pennville 38–34 Dunkirk (ot); Madison Twp. 34–26 Jefferson; Hartford City 49–29 Gray; Portland 44–27 Redkey; Pennville 29–28 Roll; Hartford City 38–31 Madison Twp.; Portland 36–27 Pennville; Portland 29–11 Hartford City. Officials: Walter Loman, John Goodwin, Oris DeVol.

HUNTINGTON: Salamonie Twp. 79–17 Wayne; Huntington Twp. 31–30 Roan-oke; Clear Creek 43–34 Rock Creek Center; Jefferson (Huntington Co.) 40–23 Andrews; Lancaster 33–29 Huntington Catholic; Jefferson (Whitley Co.) 41–35 Bippus; Huntington 47–17 Markle; Polk Twp. 50–29 Union Twp.; Salamonie Twp. 28–21 Huntington Twp.; Clear Creek 50–39 Jefferson (Huntington Co.); Lancaster 58–29 Jefferson (Whitley Co.); Huntington 48–30 Polk Twp.; Salamonie Twp. 35–23 Clear Creek; Huntington 37–29 Lancaster; Huntington 49–30 Salamonie Twp. Officials: Devon Phelps, Donald Dickey, John Walker.

INDIANAPOLIS: Washington 54–34 Decatur Central; Sacred Heart 39–34 Crispus Attucks; Howe 32–30 Warren Central; Tech 47–38 Ben Davis; Manual 42–41 Broad Ripple; Beech Grove 34–30 Lawrence; Cathedral 32–25 Southport; Shortridge 57–25 School for the Deaf; Washington 48–46 Sacred Heart; Tech 42–23 Howe; Beech Grove 46–28 Manual; Cathedral 32–21 Shortridge; Tech 42–35 Washington; Cathedral 30–20 Beech Grove; Tech 26–25 Cathedral. Officials: Evan Crawley, Ross Dorsett, Allen Klinck.

JASPER: Stendal 41–28 Dubois; Petersburg 60–19 Jefferson; Winslow 72–24 Cuzco; Jasper 59–30 Holland; Spurgeon 48–27 Ireland; Huntingburg 52–34 Otwell; Petersburg 38–36 Stendal (ot); 54–21 Winslow; Spurgeon 44–31 Huntingburg; Jasper 41–39 Petersburg; Jasper 51–41 Spurgeon. Officials: H. W. Gross, Don DeVault, Loren Harris.

KENDALLVILLE: Wolf Lake 38–27 Ligonier; Albion 40–23 Scott; Kendallville 47–18 LaGrange; Wolcottville 42–33 Howe Military; Cromwell 52–31 Rome City; Avilla 32–23 Lima; Wawaka 60–21 Brighton; Shipshewana 43–27 Topeka; Albion 35–33 Wolf Lake; Kendallville 40–39 Wolcottville; Cromwell 42–39 Avilla; Shipshewana 38–34 Wawaka; Kendallville 44–33 Albion; Cromwell 38–33 Shipshewana; Kendallville 29–25 Cromwell. Officials: Dwight Byerly, Dean Geyer, Walter Bonham.

KOKOMO: Howard Twp. 45–31 Russiaville; Kokomo 41–24 Union Twp.; Greentown 37–

21 Ervin Twp.; Jackson Twp. 56–35 West Middleton; Clay Twp. 38–37 New London; Kokomo 59–16 Howard Twp.; Greentown 29–27 Jackson Twp.; Kokomo 58–15 Clay Twp.; Kokomo 12–6 Greentown. Officials: Herschel Eastman, Orval Martin.

LAFAYETTE: Buck Creek 41–19 Shadeland; Klondike 47–36 Jackson Twp.; Stockwell 31–28 West Point; West Lafayette 35–26 Clarks Hill; Lafayette 58–30 Battle Ground; Wea 33–29 Dayton; Romney 40–36 Montmorenci (ot); Buck Creek 78–40 Monitor; Klondike 56–37 Stockwell; Lafayette 54–27 West Lafayette; Romney 42–29 Wea; Buck Creek 44–34 Klondike (ot); Lafayette 53–26 Romney; Lafayette 59–29 Buck Creek. Officials: William Ellis, Frank Jarrell, Wayne Mosbaugh.

LAWRENCEBURG: Aurora 44–35 Vevay; Moores Hill 33–24 Guilford; Rising Sun 41–23 Patriot; Lawrenceburg 45–30 Dillsboro; Bright 42–40 Aurora; Rising Sun 35–34 Moores Hill; Lawrenceburg 45–22 Bright; Lawrenceburg 57–25 Rising Sun. Officials: Burl Shook, John Gwin.

LEBANON: Thorntown 36–23 Perry Central; Whitestown 41–32 Jamestown; Lebanon 26–23 Dover; Zionsville 46–36 Pike Twp.; Pinnell 40–23 Advance; Whitestown 30–28 Thorntown; Zionsville 31–26 Lebanon; Whitestown 25–24 Pinnell; Whitestown 33–24 Zionsville. Officials: Donald Cooper, Albert Etter.

LOGANSPORT: Onward 43–20 Lucerne; Logansport 60–26 Twelve Mile; Washington Twp. 46–34 Galveston; New Waverly 43–27 Walton; Royal Center 37–20 Young America; Onward 45–34 Metea; Logansport 32–26 Washington Twp.; New Waverly 48–44 Royal Center; Logansport 29–13 Onward; Logansport 49–30 New Waverly. Officials: Doxie Reeves, Clay Layman, Rome Zink.

MADISON: Madison 42–28 Hanover; North Madison 28–23 Central; Scottsburg 39–15 Saluda; Austin 38–30 Dupont; Deputy 38–15 Paris Crossing; Madison 65–22 North Madison; Scottsburg 28–24 Austin; Madison 63–7 Deputy; Madison 36–35 Scottsburg. Officials: Walter N. Surface, Norman Freeland.

MARION: Jefferson Twp. 29–22 Sweetser; St. Paul 34–26 Van Buren; Fairmount 26–23 Jonesboro; Marion 28–17 Swayzee; Gas City 34–21 Jefferson Twp.; St. Paul 24–21 Fairmount; Gas City 37–34 Marion; Gas City 16–8 St. Paul. Officials: John Janzaruk, Max Casey.

MICHIGAN CITY: LaPorte 55–11 Hanna; St. Mary 47–31 Springfield; Westville 44–24 LaCrosse; Rolling Prairie 42–23 Jackson; Union Mills 38–7 Stillwell; Wanatah 35–28 Clinton Twp.; Mill Creek 41–38 Kingsbury; Michigan City 65–31 Union Twp.; LaPorte 44–27 St. Mary; Rolling Prairie 30–24 Westville; Union Mills 29–28 Wanatah; Michigan City 70–17 Mill Creek; LaPorte 49–25; Rolling Prairie; Michigan City 46–24 Union Mills; LaPorte 45–33 Michigan City. Officials: Wayne Cunningham, Charles Garrett, Paul Boehm.

MONTICELLO: Monticello 33–22 Brookston; Chalmers 33–27 Idaville; Reynolds 47–22 Wolcott; Monon 49–35 Round Grove; Buffalo 27–17 Burnettsville; Monticello 41–25 Chalmers; Monon 48–33 Reynolds; Monticello 46–22 Buffalo; Monticello 41–28 Monon. Officials: E. S. Stuteville, Norman Morrison.

MOROCCO: Brook 43–35 Mt. Ayr; Kentland 52–26 Tefft; Morocco 42–23 Goodland; St. Joseph 42–34 Remington; Rensselaer 43–12 Fair Oaks; Wheatfield 36–31 DeMotte; Brook 38–37 Kentland; Morocco 37–35 St. Joseph; Rensselaer 49–24 Wheatfield; Brook 38–34 Morocco; Rensselaer 40–19 Brook. Officials: Fred Vaulk, Elmer Millbranth, E. J. Vennon.

MUNCIE: Royerton 43–28 Eaton; Yorktown 66–21 Harrison; Selma 46–35 Albany; Central 33–19 Cowan: Burris 40–19 Center; DeSoto 40–28 Gaston; Royerton 50–29 Daleville; Yorktown 34–32 Selma; Central 32–24 Burris; Royerton 30–23 DeSoto; Central 46–26 Yorktown; Central

Tourney Time

46–36 Royerton. Officials: Marvin Todd, Wilbur May, Herbert Edwards.

NAPPANEE: Bristol 53–30 Jefferson Twp.; Concord 40–30 Millersburg; Wakarusa 47–32 Baugo Twp.; Middlebury 61–52 New Paris; Elkhart 61–27 Nappanee; Bristol 38–29 Goshen; Wakarusa 45–36 Concord; Elkhart 72–35 Middlebury; Bristol 43–30 Wakarusa; Elkhart 59–37 Bristol. Officials: Cecil Young, Devon Eaton, James L. Koons.

NEW ALBANY: New Washington 27–20 Georgetown; New Salisbury 45–30 Laconia; Charlestown 53–40 Mauckport; New Albany 36–29 Silver Creek; Corydon 48–36 New Middletown; Elizabeth 32–29 New Amsterdam; Jeffersonville 61–19 Borden; Henryville 53–29 Lanesville; New Washington 52–31 New Salisbury; New Albany 62–17 Charlestown; Corydon 59–24 Elizabeth; Jeffersonville 48–35 Henryville; New Albany 44–20 New Washington; Jeffersonville 52–35 Corydon; New Albany 45–42 Jeffersonville. Officials: Wayne Hammond, Howard Wright, Roland Baker.

NEW CASTLE: Lewisville 33–29 Kennard; Mooreland 33–29 Straughn (ot); Knightstown 42–34 Cadiz; Spiceland 51–18 New Lisbon; New Castle 28–11 Mt. Summit; Sulphur Springs 37–26 Middletown; Lewisville 38–34 Mooreland; Knightstown 41–30 Spiceland; New Castle 52–16 Sulphur Springs; Knightstown 40–36 Lewisville; New Castle 68–34 Knightstown. Officials: Maurice Jordan, Jack O'Neal, Leonard Ireland.

PAOLI: Campbellsburg 47–46 Morgan Twp.; French Lick 47–33 West Baden Springs; English 56–30 Little York; Hardinsburg 38–14 Milltown; Pekin 39–33 Marengo; Paoli 38–32 Orleans; Salem 51–25 Campbellsburg; French Lick 50–32 English; Hardinsburg 40–27 Pekin; Salem 34–24 Paoli; French Lick 39–32 Hardinsburg; French Lick 45–42 Salem. Officials: Ivan Sprinkle, Robert Hodgers, Carl Jerger.

PERU: Clay Twp. 44–38 Chili; Macy 33–31 Deedsville; Peru 53–37 Gilead; Converse 55–20 Butler Twp.; Bunker Hill 33–29 Mexico; Clay Twp. 36–20 Macy; Peru 37–21 Converse; Bunker Hill 28–25 Clay Twp.; Peru 20–16 Bunker Hill. Officials: Herbert Vaulk, Forrest Shaw.

PLYMOUTH: Argos 49–24 West Twp.; Bremen 31–17 Bourbon; Culver 57–28 Tyner; Tippecanoe 38–36 San Pierre; Plymouth 71–45 Grovertown; LaPaz 50–32 Hamlet; North Judson 50–34 Knox; Bremen 41–21 Argos; Culver 54–26 Tippecanoe; Plymouth 56–40 LaPaz; Bremen 53–36 North Judson; Culver 50–38 Plymouth; Culver 44–42 Bremen. Officials: Paul Bateman, John Cover, Myron Weldy.

PRINCETON: Mackey 37–30 Mt. Olympus; Hazleton 41–34 Lincoln; Ft. Branch 29–27 Princeton (ot); Patoka 45–30 Francisco; Haubstadt 37–25 Owensville; Mackey 39–29 Oakland City; Ft. Branch 48–27 Hazleton; Patoka 35–24 Haubstadt; Mackey 32–31 Ft. Branch (ot); Mackey 37–31 Patoka. Officials: Robert Derrington, William Hartley, Alfred W. Rose.

RICHMOND: Centerville 54–41 Green's Fork; Fountain City 46–37 Cambridge City; Boston 49–31 Milton; Webster 32–31 Williamsburg; Richmond 59–39 Whitewater; Hagerstown 87–32 Economy; Fountain City 32–28 Centerville; Boston 55–40 Webster; Richmond 46–40 Hagerstown; Fountain City 49–32 Boston; Richmond 53–52 Fountain City. Officials: Arthur Gage, George Bender, J. T. Haywood.

RUSHVILLE: Morton Memorial 34–25 Arlington; Milroy 55–29 Raleigh; New Salem 37–22 Manilla; Rushville 53–39 Mays; Morton Memorial 30–21 Carthage; Milroy 40–27 New Salem; Rushville 59–36 Morton; Milroy 43–40 Rushville. Officials: Herbert Schwomeyer, Don McBride.

SEYMOUR: Freetown 30–21 Medora; Clearspring 32–23 Hayden; Seymour 67–17 Tampico; Vallonia 58–23 Cortland; Brownstown 39–35 Crothersville; Clearspring 50–37 Freetown; Seymour

44–31 Vallonia; Brownstown 41–38 Clearspring; Seymour 41–35 Brownstown. Officials: Harold Porter, Kermit Spurgeon.

SHELBYVILLE: Shelbyville 50–20 Hope; Columbus 54–26 Flat Rock; Morristown 26–17 Fairland; Franklin Twp. 61–18 Clifford; Mt. Auburn 32–31 Boggstown; Moral 52–32 Waldron; Columbus 59–46 Shelbyville; Franklin Twp. 43–41 Morristown; Moral 38–35 Mt. Auburn; Columbus 43–22 Franklin Twp.; Columbus 60–41 Moral. Officials: Eugene Glaze, Dean Malaska, Al Jackson.

SOUTH BEND: Wilson 49–23 South Bend Catholic; New Carlisle 34–33 Washington-Clay; Walkerton 61–32 Greene Twp.; Washington 45–30 Madison Twp.; Mishawaka 54–27 Central Catholic; Adams 40–36 Riley (ot); Central 30–26 Lakeville; Wilson 36–33 North Liberty; New Carlisle 41–31 Walkerton; Washington 46–40 Mishawaka; Central 48–41 Adams; New Carlisle 52–36 Wilson; Central 37–30 Washington; Central 51–47 New Carlisle (ot). Officials: Hugh Bergstrom, Fred White, Sam Massette.

SPENCER: Ashboro 44–11 Coal City; Spencer 44–20 Clay City; Van Buren 20–19 Brazil; Gosport 39–33 Bowling Green; Staunton 56–25 Quincy; Cory 50–19 Freedom; Ashboro 48–34 Patricksburg; Spencer 37–25 Van Buren; Staunton 44–40 Gosport; Cory 23–20 Ashboro; Spencer 47–37 Cory. Officials: Hal Harris, J.C. LaFollette, Clarence Myles.

SULLIVAN: Farmersburg 45–36 Fairbanks; New Lebanon 55–20 Pleasantville; Carlisle 51–28 Merom; Dugger 51–23 Graysville; Sullivan 41–36 Hymera; Shelburn 28–26 Farmersburg; Carlisle 33–32 New Lebanon; Sullivan 46–20 Dugger; Shelburn 31–29 Carlisle; Sullivan 55–29 Shelburn. Officials: Cecil Bosstick, Irvin Thrasher, Edward Campbell.

TELL CITY: Troy 36–30 Selvin; Rockport 46–44 Tell City; Dale 35–27 Luce Twp.; Cannelton 46–21 Chrisney; Rockport 57–27 Troy; Cannelton 45–24 Dale; Cannelton 51–41 Rockport. Officials: David Royalty, Clyde Castle.

TERRE HAUTE: Concannon 42–21 Prairie Creek; Honey Creek 43–31 Wiley; West Terre Haute 31–21 Fontanet; Pimento 39–38 Black Hawk; Garfield 43–23 Riley; Laboratory 41–20 Glenn; Gerstmeyer 36–27 Otter Creek; Honey Creek 48–24 Concannon; Pimento 42–31 West Terre Haute; Laboratory 28–22 Garfield; Honey Creek 39–31 Gerstmeyer; Laboratory 43–28 Pimento; Honey Creek 45–43 Laboratory (ot). Officials: G. P. Silver, Frank White, Fred Fechtman.

TIPTON: Sheridan 34–25 Carmel; Noblesville 38–28 Walnut Grove; Sharpsville 39–32 Jackson Central; Westfield 37–33 Jefferson Twp.; Tipton 45–31 Prairie Twp.; Windfall 34–28 Fishers; Noblesville 31–30 Sheridan; Sharpsville 46–19 Westfield; Tipton 47–32 Windfall; Noblesville 29–22 Sharpsville; Tipton 32–28 Noblesville. Officials: Noble Benbow, Marvin Dick, Herbert Brammell.

VINCENNES: Wheatland 41–23 Fritchton; Freelandville 40–31 Decker; Edwardsport 35–19 Decker Chapel; Vincennes 57–30 Bruceville; Bicknell 59–29 Monroe City; Oaktown 31–28 Sandborn: Freelandville 36–35 Wheatland; Vincennes 35–26 Edwardsport; Bicknell 30–24 Oaktown; Vincennes 40–24 Freelandville; Vincennes 46–33 Bicknell. Officials: William Reed, William E. Pointer, William Coulter.

WABASH: Lagro 42–28 Chippewa; North Manchester 40–27 Washington Center; Chester Twp. 40–30 Laketon; LaFontaine 29–27 Lincolnville (ot); Urbana 50–34 Somerset; Wabash 55–29 South Whitley; Linlawn 33–32 Roann (ot); Lagro 23–20 North Manchester; Chester Twp. 62–45 LaFontaine; Wabash 68–25 Urbana; Lagro 23–21 Linlawn; Wabash 55–34 Chester Twp.;

Tourney Time

Wabash 62–34 Lagro. Officials: J.H. McClure, Aaron Belcher, J.W. Johnson.

WARSAW: Beaver Dam 46–29 Burket; Warsaw 37–33 Columbia City; Etna Green 55–37 Sidney; Syracuse 46–36 North Webster; Milford 53–25 Atwood; Pierceton 41–32 Mentone; Silver Lake 42–40 Claypool; Leesburg 36–15 Larwill; Warsaw 34–23 Beaver Dam; Etna Green 24–20 Syracuse; Milford 36–29 Pierceton; Silver Lake 34–27 Leesburg; Warsaw 29–27 Etna Green; Milford 39–34 Silver Lake; Milford 24–19 Warsaw. Officials: Harold McSwane, Donald Coar, Louis Briner.

WASHINGTON: Washington Catholic 31–29 Shoals; Barr Twp. 58–14 Alfordsville; Epsom 41–26 Odon; Loogootee 32–31 Elmore Twp.; Washington 46–30 Plainville; Washington Catholic 38–18 Glendale; Epsom 45–37 Barr Twp.; Washington 33–32 Loogootee; Washington Catholic 29–16 Epsom; Washington 31–30 Washington Catholic. Officials: Irvin Springer, Robert Hudson, Lawrence Young.

WINAMAC: Talma 28–26 Leiters Ford; Winamac 35–25 Monterey; Fulton 41–34 Richland Center; Akron 32–26 Star City; Kewanna 20–19 Pulaski; Rochester 50–27 Medaryville; Francesville 42–27 Grass Creek; Winamac 44–28 Talma; Fulton 57–37 Akron; Rochester 59–27 Kewanna; Winamac 44–31 Francesville; Fulton 45–34 Rochester; Winamac 43–34 Fulton. Officials: George Vaulk, Charles Kruzan, Otho Piper.

WORTHINGTON: Worthington 40–31 Newberry; Linton 32–20 Midland; Switz City 46–19 Owensburg; Solsberry 39–25 Scotland; Jasonville 35–33 Bloomfield; Marco 45–37 Lyons; Linton 54–23 Worthington; Switz City 41–27 Solsberry; Jasonville 36–21 Marco; Linton 42–16 Switz City; Linton 30–20 Jasonville. Officials: J. D. Nickle, Norman Dunlap, Hubert Thomas.

1946 REGIONALS

ANDERSON: Anderson 51–33 Eden; Indianapolis Tech 34–30 Danville; Anderson 45–39 Tech. Officials: Fred White, George Vaulk.

EVANSVILLE: Central 36–32 Cannelton; Boonville 49–39 Mackey; Central 50–35 Boonville. Officials: C.N. Phillips, Evan Crawley.

FORT WAYNE: Ashley 43–41 Kendallville; Central 35–30 Milford; Central 66–51 Ashley. Officials: Thomas Baker, John Magnabosco.

GREENCASTLE: Crawfordsville 40–23 Clinton; Reelsville 41–40 Attica (ot); Crawfordsville 44–29 Reelsville. Officials: G. P. Silver, Jack O'Neal.

HAMMOND: East Chicago Washington 44–20 Gary Edison; LaPorte 54–40 Rensselaer; Washington 53–46 LaPorte. Officials: Paul Bateman, Cecil Young.

HUNTINGTON: Berne 35–30 Huntington; Portland 41–34 Petroleum; Portland 41–38 Berne. Officials: Cecil Tharp, Herbert Edwards.

JEFFERSONVILLE: Bedford 57–28 French Lick; New Albany 42–30 Seymour; Bedford 33–31 New Albany. Officials: Ray Lackey, William Reimann.

LAFAYETTE: Rossville 43–25 Boswell; Lafayette 68–34 Whitestown; Lafayette 44–38 Rossville. Officials: Jim Crowe, Norris Ward.

LOGANSPORT: Logansport 32–25 Monticello; Flora 32–27 Peru; Flora 56–31 Logansport. Officials: Walter , L. E. Fink.

MARION: Gas City 36–34 Wabash; Kokomo 37–32 Tipton; Gas City 38–28 Kokomo. Officials: George Bender, Marvin Todd.

MARTINSVILLE: Honey Creek 45–32 Spencer; Linton 36–34 University (ot); Linton 27–23 Honey Creek. Officials: William Pointer, William Coulter.

MUNCIE: Central 37–35 New Castle (3ot); Richmond 46–29 Farmland; Richmond 32–31 Central. Officials: Karl Dickerson, Clyde Gentry.

RUSHVILLE: Milroy 40–39 Brownsville; Lawrenceburg 43–26 Milan; Lawrenceburg 55–29 Milroy. Officials: Dean Malaska, Walter Surface.

SHELBYVILLE: Franklin 50–24 Sandcreek; Columbus 53–39 Madison; Franklin 29–21 Columbus. Officials: Walter Ringer, Frank Jarrell.

SOUTH BEND: Culver 38–34 Winamac; Elkhart 37–33 Central; Culver 38–35 Elkhart. Officials: Allen Klinck, Phil Eskew.

VINCENNES: Sullivan 35–24 Washington; Jasper 49–26 Vincennes; Jasper 39–35 Sullivan. Officials: Roland Baker, Robert Derrington.

1946 SEMI-FINALS

BLOOMINGTON: Evansville Central 39–28 Linton; Jasper 47–31 Bedford; Central 41–39 Jasper. Officials: Phil Eskew, G.P. Silver, Walter Thurston.

INDIANAPOLIS: Crawfordsville 36–33 Franklin; Anderson 43–32 Lawrenceburg; Anderson 67–39 Crawfordsville. Officials: Jim Crowe, Paul Bateman, William Pointer.

LAFAYETTE: Culver 35–33 East Chicago Washington; Flora 50–48 Lafayette; Flora 37–35 Culver. Officials: Thomas Baker, Walter N. Ringer, George Bender.

MUNCIE: Ft. Wayne Central 49–43 Richmond (ot); Gas City 37–33 Portland; Central 60–39 Gas City. Officials: Allen Klinck, Dean Malaska, C.N. Phillips.

1946 FINALS—March 16

INDIANAPOLIS (Butler Fieldhouse): Anderson 39–36 Evansville Central; Ft. Wayne Central 61–50 Flora; Anderson 67–53 Ft. Wayne Central. Officials: Walter Thurston, George Bender, C. N. Phillips.

1947 SECTIONALS

ANDERSON: Markleville 43–42 Alexandria; Frankton 49–33 Elwood, Pendleton 43–34 Summitville; St. Mary's 49–45 Lapel; Anderson 44–33 Markleville; Pendleton 42–33 Frankton; Anderson 41–31 St. Mary's; Pendleton 43–39 Anderson. Officials: Ross Dorsett, Frank Luzar.

ATTICA: West Lebanon 38–33 Hillsboro; Covington 32–18 Williamsport; Kingman 45–28 Wallace; Veedersburg 43–33 Richland Twp.; Attica 25–18 Perrysville; West Lebanon 42–40 Pine Village; Covington 27–21 Kingman; Attica 37–28 Veedersburg; Covington 47–24 West Lebanon; Covington 23–21 Attica. Officials: Clayton Patterson, Robert Gatewood, Cecil Bosstick.

AUBURN: Churubusco 40–31 Metz; Orland 49–25 Scott Center; Spencerville 56–32 Pleasant Lake; Auburn 49–37 Concord Twp.; Fremont 48–28 Ashley; Angola 52–22 Salem Center; Garrett 46–26 Waterloo; Butler 51–36 Hamilton; Churubusco 52–48 Orland; Spencerville 36–29 Auburn; Fremont 36–33 Angola; Garrett 40–28 Butler; Spencerville 37–36 Churubusco; Garrett 35–28 Fremont; Spencerville 38–29 Garrett. Officials: Walter Bonham, Otho Piper, Oris DeVol.

Tourney Time

AURORA: Bright 50–44 Rising Sun; Aurora 70–44 Vevay; Lawrenceburg 54–26 Moores Hill; Guilford 44–28 Patriot; Bright 43–37 Dillsboro; Lawrenceburg 58–34 Aurora; Bright 55–32 Guilford; Lawrenceburg 65–30 Bright. Officials: L. Howard Wright, Walter Surface.

BATESVILLE: Napoleon 56–25 Holton; Milan 55–21 New Marion; Osgood 35–28 Versailles; Batesville 33–25 Cross Plains; Napoleon 69–22 Sunman; Osgood 42–30 Milan; Napoleon 44–24 Batesville; Napoleon 37–28 Osgood. Officials: Walter Floyd, Thomas Stirling.

BEDFORD: Oolitic 49–33 Tunnelton; Bedford 58–19 Williams; Fayetteville 60–12 Huron; Shawswick 47–21 Heltonville; Marshall Twp. 35–33 Mitchell; Bedford 27–22 Oolitic; Shawswick 47–43 Fayetteville; Bedford 59–31 Marshall Twp.; Bedford 40–30 Shawswick. Officials: Herb Edwards, Hulett Crecelius.

BLUFFTON: Bluffton 36–34 Lancaster; Ossian 44–30 Liberty Center; Rockcreek Center 34–24 Union Center; Chester Center 50–41 Petroleum; Bluffton 70–27 Jackson Center; Ossian 40–24 Rockcreek Center; Chester Center 42–35 Bluffton; Chester Center 38–36 Ossian. Officials: John Goodwin, James Koons.

BOONVILLE: Newburgh 31–25 Folsomville; Millersburg 45–31 Selvin; Lynnville 72–29 Chandler; Boonville 70–23 Tennyson; Newburgh 50–47 Elberfeld; Lynnville 62–32 Millersburg; Boonville 56–39 Newburgh; Boonville 45–43 Lynnville. Officials: Alfred W. Rose, Carl Jerger.

BOSWELL: Wadena 29–27 Earl Park; Oxford 61–14 Raub; Fowler 42–14 Pine Twp.; Boswell 42–40 Gilboa; Freeland Park 45–44 Ambia; Otterbein 52–26 Wadena; Oxford 43–27 Fowler; Boswell 45–27 Freeland Park; Otterbein 33–31 Oxford; Otterbein 35–31 Boswell. Officials: Noble Benbow, Herbert Brammel, A.M. Franklin.

BRAZIL: Clay City 42–20 Jefferson Twp.; Brazil 61–38 Posey Twp.; Bowling Green 51–19 Quincy; Spencer 41–26 Ashboro; Cory 41–40 Gosport; Van Buren Twp. 35–26 Patricksburg; Clay City 38–31 Freedom; Brazil 68–26 Bowling Green; Cory 28–26 Spencer; Clay City 28–26 Van Buren Twp.; Cory 36–34 Brazil; Cory 38–25 Clay City. Officials: Lowell Willis, William J. McKoskey, W. N. Ringer.

CANNELTON: Tell City 70–18 Oil Twp.; Richland 81–8 Gentryville; Dale 42–31 Troy; Cannelton 51–24 Rockport; Tell City 53–43 Chrisney; Dale 47–37 Richland; Tell City 35–33 Cannelton; Tell City 37–24 Dale. Officials: Lester Cornwell, Irvin Thrasher.

CLINTON: Clinton 51–27 Newport; Dana 37–31 Greene Twp.; Cayuga 43–31 Mecca; Rosedale 44–24 Bloomingdale; Montezuma 47–21 Union Twp.; St. Bernice 32–27 Rockville; Bridgeton 35–30 Hillsdale; Tangier 40–36 Marshall; Clinton 55–30 Dana; Rosedale 50–29 Cayuga; Montezuma 50–40 St. Bernice; Tangier 42–34 Bridgeton; Clinton 35–29 Rosedale; Tangier 56–35 Montezuma; Clinton 34–19 Tangier. Officials: Lawrence Leland, Warren Williams, Robert Hobbs.

CONNERSVILLE: Connersville 72–46 Springfield Twp.; Everton 40–29 Whitewater; Harrisburg 53–35 Alquina; Liberty 60–36 Brookville; Bentonville 34–27 Laurel; Kitchel 38–37 Orange; Brownsville 53–25 Fairview; Everton 27–24 Connersville; Liberty 46–42 Harrisburg; Bentonville 43–38 Kitchel; Everton 44–43 Brownsville; Liberty 65–31 Bentonville; Everton 28–24 Liberty. Officials: Ted Lentz, Lowell Barnett, Herschel Eastman,

CRAWFORDSVILLE: Darlington 49–23 New Ross; New Market 59–18 Bowers; Alamo 56–30 New Richmond; Crawfordsville 91–19 Wingate; Ladoga 50–46 Waveland; Waynetown 35–33 Linden; New Market 41–32 Darlington; Crawfordsville 56–24 Alamo; Ladoga 30–29 Waynetown; Crawfordsville 46–37 New Market; Crawfordsville 38–24 Ladoga. Officials: J. D.

IHSAA Scores / 1940–1949

Nickle, Orval Martin, Hubert Thomas.

DANVILLE: Avon 54–34 North Salem; Brownsburg 44–32 North Winchester; Clayton 38–23 Speedway; Danville 39–25 Plainfield; Lizton 39–37 Amo; Pittsboro 36–34 Stilesville; Avon 39–35 Brownsburg; Clayton 45–31 Danville; Pittsboro 48–30 Lizton; Clayton 45–38 Avon; Clayton 44–32 Pittsboro. Officials: George Danforth, Cecil Tharp, Norman Morrison.

DECATUR: Decatur 46–43 Pleasant Mills; Monroe 42–35 Decatur Catholic; Jefferson 38–37 Geneva; Kirkland 36–34 Monmouth; Berne 39–37 Hartford; Monroe 35–30 Decatur; Kirkland 48–42 Jefferson; Monroe 29–25 Berne; Monroe 38–29 Kirkland. Officials: Burl McKenzie, Charles Bobilya.

EVANSVILLE: Lincoln 52–39 Griffin; Central 42–35 Memorial; Reitz 64–39 Mount Vernon; Wadesville 53–29 Cynthiana; Bosse 65–33 Poseyville; Lincoln 49–36 New Harmony; Central 47–33 Reitz; Bosse 43–32 Wadesville; Central 62–26 Lincoln; Central 52–51 Bosse. Officials: Frank Jarrell, Norman Dunlap, Walter E. Marks.

FARMLAND: Winchester 50–21 Wayne; Stoney Creek 46–30 McKinley; Union City 55–43 Green; Saratoga 35–26 Jackson; Farmland 75–32 Huntsville; Spartanburg 52–26 Lincoln; Parker 42–39 (ot) Losantville; Modoc 43–29 Lynn; Winchester 71–38 Stoney Greek; Union City 41–28 Saratoga; Spartanburg 50–45 Farmland; Parker 67–33 Modoc; Winchester 34–22 Union City; Spartanburg 49–41 Parker; Spartanburg 48–44 (ot) Winchester. Officials: J.W. Johnson. Joe Metzger, Marvin Todd.

FLORA: Flora 41–25 Carrollton; Delphi 31–26 Camden; Adams Twp. 53–30 Deer Creek; Rockfield 45–31 Burlington; Flora 29–27 Butler; Delphi 45–38 Adams Twp.; Flora 49–22 Rockfield; Flora 35–26 Delphi. Officials: Clay Layman, Myrle Rife.

FORT BRANCH: Fort Branch 57–23 Hazleton; Oakland City 71–19 Lincoln; Francisco 51–47 Haubstadt; Mackey 37–25 Patoka; Princeton 56–43 Owensville; Fort Branch 44–16 Mt. Olympus; Oakland City 47–46 Francisco (ot); Princeton 53–30 Mackey; Fort Branch 47–41 Oakland City; Princeton 47–36 Fort Branch. Officials: W. E. Pointer, David Royalty, Loren Harris.

FORT WAYNE: Central Catholic 38–30 Huntertown; New Haven 25–24 Hoagland; Monroeville 46–34 Arcola; Concordia 43–42 North Side; Elmhurst 48–37 Lafayette Central; Maumee Twp. 41–26 Coesse; South Side 53–25 Leo; Central 63–23 Harlan; Central Catholic 45–34 New Haven; Concordia 37–35 Monroeville; Elmhurst 31–30 Maumee Twp.; South Side 54–42 Central; Central Catholic 38–35 Concordia; South Side 33–13 Elmhurst; South Side 27–17 Central Catholic. Officials: R.W. Warring, Raymond Trobaugh, Paul Boehm.

FRANKFORT: Colfax 43–24 Washington Twp.; Frankfort 36–21 Sugar Creek; Jackson Twp. 35–25 Mulberry; Rossville 68–24 Michigantown; Scircleville 39–36 Forest; Colfax 54–25 Kirklin; Frankfort 46–40 Jackson Twp.; Rossville 55–25 Scircleville; Colfax 52–29 Frankfort; Rossville 46–37 Colfax. Officials: Hal Harris, Eugene Glaze, Harold Porter.

FRANKLIN: Center Grove 67–26 Van Buren; Franklin 57–30 Trafalgar; Greenwood 38–28 Helmsburg; Whiteland 39–38 Union; Clark 47–25 Nineveh; Nashville 34–31 Edinburg; Franklin 35–30 Center Grove; Greenwood 29–27 Whiteland; Clark 51–34 Nashville; Franklin 33–24 Greenwood; Franklin 39–29 Clark, Officials: Charles D. Jones, Frank White, John Janzaruk.

GARY–VALPARAISO: (At Gary): Horace Mann 43–29 Gary Edison; Tolleston 46–28 Roosevelt; Froebel 52–21 Wirt; Emerson 63–37 Lew Wallace; Tolleston 48–47 Horace Mann; Emerson 41–34 Froebel; (At Valparaiso): Valparaiso 56–33 Hebron; Kouts 38–21 Liberty Center; Chesterton 34–23 Washington Twp.; Boone Grove 23–21 Morgan Twp.; Valparaiso 37–26 Kouts;

Chesterton 42–23 Boone Grove; Chesterton 34–33 Valparaiso; (At Gary): Emerson 54–37 Tolleston; Emerson 59–29 Chesterton. Officials: Walter E. Thurston, Alvin Vincent, Norris Ward, Frank Kresler.

GOSHEN: New Paris 52–34 Bristol; Jefferson Twp. 34–31 Middlebury; Wakarusa 29–28 Goshen; Concord 36–31 Millersburg; Elkhart 33–21 Nappanee; Baugo 43–36 New Paris; Jefferson Twp. 30–28 Wakarusa; Elkhart 45–23 Concord; Baugo 40–24 Jefferson Twp.; Elkhart 30–28 Baugo. Officials: George Collyer, Victor Griewank, Stanley Dubis.

GREENCASTLE: Bainbridge 57–10 Clinton Center; Greencastle 46–24 Fillmore; Cloverdale 36–27 Reelsville; Roachdale 44–41 Belle Union; Bainbridge 60–35 Russellville; Greencastle 41–29 Cloverdale; Bainbridge 34–28 Roachdale; Greencastle 37–36 Bainbridge. Officials: Earl Townsend, John Townsend.

GREENFIELD: Charlottesville 33–26 New Palestine; Fortville 48–25 McCordsville; Mt. Comfort 43–37 Maxwell; Greenfield 42–34 Eden; Wilkinson 42–31 Charlottesville; Fortville 32–22 Mt. Comfort; Greenfield 37–33 Wilkinson; Fortville 43–21 Greenfield. Officials: Clyde Gentry, J. C. Lafollette.

GREENSBURG: Jackson Twp. 53–14 Zenas; North Vernon 43–19 Vernon; Burney 41–28 New Point; Butlerville 33–25 Sandusky; Clarksburg 67–23 Sandcreek; Greensburg 50–26 St. Paul; North Vernon 54–37 Jackson Twp.; Burney 63–33 Butlerville; Clarksburg 35–33 Greensburg; North Vernon 43–36 Burney; North Vernon 38–24 Clarksburg. Officials: Robert Hodgers, Don Veller, Wilbur May.

HAMMOND–EAST CHICAGO: (At Hammond): Hammond High 45–18 Lowell; Dyer 41–26 Crown Point; Clark 52–36 Griffith; Tech 45–28 Noll; (At East Chicago): Roosevelt 51–29 Portage; Whiting 48–36 Merrillville; Washington 75–30 Wheeler; Hobart 62–40 East Gary Edison; (At Hammond): Hammond High 58–18 Dyer; Clark 62–46 Tech; (At East Chicago): Whiting 49–36 Roosevelt; Washington 58–32 Hobart; (At Hammond): Hammond High 47–42 Clark; (At East Chicago): Washington 49–33 Whiting; (At Hammond): Washington 44–37 Hammond High. Officials: L. E. Fink, Paul Hostetlar, Jim Crowe, Dean Geyer.

HARTFORD CITY: Redkey 48–36 Madison Twp.; Pennville 51–29 Ridgeville; Gray 38–33 Montpelier; Roll 45–26 Poling; Portland 73–13 Bryant; Dunkirk 52–26 Jefferson; Hartford City 34–29 Redkey; Pennville 39–27 Gray; Portland 42–41 Roll; Hartford City 38–36 Dunkirk; Portland 52–33 Pennville; Portland 33–32 Hartford City. Officials: Joe Mullins, Leland Wright, Arthur Lloyd.

HUNTINGTON: Bippus 43–22 Banquo; Huntington 62–40 Huntington Catholic; Roanoke 29–23 Andrews; Huntington Twp. 41–35 Warren; Rock Creek Center 35–26 Markle; Lancaster Twp. 52–47 Jefferson (Huntington Co.); Union Twp. 38–35 Monument City; Jefferson (Whitley Co.) 42–41 Clear Creek; Huntington 68–20 Bippus; Roanoke 40–30 Huntington Twp.; Lancaster Twp. 47–29 Rock Creek Center; Jefferson (Whitley Co.) 38–36 Union Twp.; Huntington 39–22 Roanoke; Lancaster Twp. 40–32 Jefferson (Whitley Co.); Huntington 66–29 Lancaster Twp. Officials: Alvy Havens, Gail Gaddis, Gerald Powell.

INDIANAPOLIS: Warren Central 36–35 Howe; Cathedral 35–34 Tech; Broad Ripple 28–27 Washington; Crispus Attucks 39–38 Decatur Central; Ben Davis 42–40 Sacred Heart; Southport 32–31 Shortridge; Beech Grove 39–31 School for the Deaf; Lawrence 35–26 Manual; Warren Central 50–36 Cathedral; Broad Ripple 50–28 Crispus Attucks; Southport 55–49 Ben Davis; Lawrence 43–32 Beech Grove; Warren Central 48–43 Broad Ripple; Southport 37–33 Lawrence;

IHSAA Scores | 1940–1949

Southport 39–35 Warren Central. Officials: John Walker, John Magnabosco, Phil N. Eskew.

JASPER: Stendal 52–34 Ireland; Spurgeon 45–39 Otwell; Winslow 51–24 Cuzco; Jasper 67–21 Dubois; Huntingburg 58–23 Petersburg; Holland 61–40 Birdseye; Spurgeon 60–31 Stendal; Jasper 45–34 Winslow; Huntingburg 52–36 Holland; Jasper 65–41 Spurgeon; Jasper 36–27 Huntingburg. Officials: Irvin Springer, Robert Hudson, Robert Derrington.

JEFFERSONVILLE: Laconia 41–36 Lanesville; Jeffersonville 73–18 Georgetown; Henryville 52–32 New Middletown; Scribner 35–32 Borden; New Salisbury 31–26 Corydon; Charlestown 48–41 New Amsterdam; New Albany 90–25 Elizabeth; Silver Creek 56–31 Mauckport; Jeffersonville 64–18 Laconia; Henryville 43–34 Scribner; New Salisbury 25–22 Charlestown; Silver Creek 55–42 New Albany; Jeffersonville 57–36 Henryville; Silver Creek 40–29 New Salisbury; Jeffersonville 44–32 Silver Creek. Officials: Ivan Sprinkle, Edward Straith-Miller, Cyril Birge.

KENDALLVILLE: Wawaka 45–27 Wolf Lake; Cromwell 40–22 Albion; Kendallville 58–14 Brighton; Avilla 35–27 Rome City; Howe Military 29–28 Lima; Ligonier 41–39 Topeka; Wolcottville 35–20 LaGrange; Shipshewana 34–32 Scott. Wawaka 43–20 Cromwell; Kendallville 45–31 Avilla; Ligonier 30–24 Howe Military; Wolcottville 41–24 Shipshewana; Kendallville 32–25 Wawaka; Wolcottville 46–33 Ligonier; Kendallville 38–34 Wolcottville. Officials: Rome Zink, Devon Phelps, R. Wayne Cunningham.

KOKOMO: Russiaville 45–26 Clay; Howard Twp. 53–41 West Middleton; Ervin 42–38 New London; Kokomo 52–21 Jackson; Union 38–36 Greentown; Russiaville 42–30 Howard Twp.; Kokomo 60–32 Ervin; Union 51–27 Russiaville; Kokomo 51–34 Union. Officials: Forrest Ballinger, Otto Crosley.

LAFAYETTE: Buck Creek 42–30 West Point; Shadeland 42–40 Jackson Twp.; Romney 39–26 Dayton; West Lafayette 44–34 Stockwell; Wea 36–31 Klondike; Lafayette 79–14 Clarks Hill; Monitor 38–34 Montmorenci; Buck Creek 41–37 Battle Ground (ot); Shadeland 36–32 Romney (ot); West Lafayette 56–39 Wea; Lafayette 71–23 Monitor; Shadeland 48–41 Buck Creek; Lafayette 59–28 West Lafayette; Lafayette 74–33 Shadeland. Officials: William Schaefer, Robert Hoffman, Wayne Hammond.

LAPORTE: Clinton Twp. 34–22 Union Mills; Hanna 48–39 Kingsbury; Mill Creek, 52–25 Wanatah; LaCrosse 39–34 Rolling Prairie; Union Twp. 34–33 Springfield; LaPorte 61–26 Jackson Twp.; Westville 33–20 St. Mary's; Michigan City 64–18 Stillwell; Clinton Twp. 34–32 Hanna; LaCrosse 47–26 Mill Creek; LaPorte 71–17 Union Twp.; Michigan City 50–39 Westville; Clinton Twp. 32–20 LaCrosse; Michigan City 31–29 LaPorte; Michigan City 40–17 Clinton Twp. Officials: E. L. Aldrich, John Cover, Hugh Bergstrom.

LEBANON: Zionsville 43–37 Pinnell; Lebanon 67–26 Pike Twp.; Thorntown 34–26 Whitestown; Perry Central 35–33 Advance; Dover 53–41 Jamestown; Zionsville 35–32 Lebanon; Thorntown 45–28 Perry Central; Zionsville 28–23 Dover; Zionsville 51–44 Thorntown. Officials: Herbert Vaulk, Fred Vaulk.

LINTON: Lyons 39–23 Marco; Bloomfield 75–12 Owensburg; Solsberry 55–39 Newberry; Jasonville 46–26 Switz City; Linton 47–28 Midland; Worthington 32–30 Scotland; Bloomfield 43–32 Lyons; Jasonville 77–34 Solsberry; Linton 56–33 Worthington; Jasonville 54–26 Bloomfield; Linton 68–39 Jasonville. Officials: Clarence Myles, Fred Fechtman, Odilo Berger.

LOGANSPORT: Washington Twp. 45–38 Twelve Mile; Logansport 41–37 Onward; New Waverly 46–32 Walton; Young America 52–35 Lucerne; Metea 47–43 Royal Center; Washington Twp. 35–26 Galveston; Logansport 42–33 New Waverly; Young America 36–14 Metea; Logansport

Tourney Time

35–33 Washington Twp.; Logansport 55–42 Young America. Officials: Leonard Ireland, Charles Marshall, William Ellis.

MADISON: Austin 35–33 Dupont (2ot); Madison 77–32 Saluda; Scottsburg 34–23 New Washington; Hanover 34–24 Paris Crossing; Central 32–26 North Madison; Deputy 40–32 Lexington; Madison 57–30 Austin; Hanover 35–28 Scottsburg; Central 42–34 Deputy; Madison 35–24 Hanover; Madison 56–31 Central. Officials: Leland Terrell, Roland Baker, Robert Fink.

MARION: Marion 33–20 St. Paul; Jefferson Twp. 51–39 Van Buren; Sweetser 59–34 Jonesboro; Gas City 42–32 Fairmount; Marion 15–11 Swayzee; Jefferson Twp. 47–36 Sweetser; Marion 31–28 Gas City; Marion 59–28 Jefferson Twp. Officials: Lores Lehman, J. L. Mertz.

MARTINSVILLE: Ellettsville 47–30 Eminence; University 69–44 Smithville; Stinesville 42–30 Unionville; Bloomington 36–34 Mooresville; Martinsville 35–34 Monrovia; Morgantown 52–25 Paragon; Ellettsville 50–39 University; Bloomington 36–35 Stinesville; Martinsville 48–29 Morgantown; Ellettsville 42–34 Bloomington; Ellettsville 45–36 Martinsville. Officials: E.S. Stuteville, G.P. Silver, Charles Northam.

MONTICELLO: Chalmers 35–26 Buffalo; Idaville 20–18 Burnettsville; Monon 48–25 Reynolds; Brookston 45–32 Monticello; Round Grove 28–20 Wolcott; Chalmers 32–23 Idaville; Monon 28–24 Brookston; Round Grove 38–28 Chalmers; Monon 53–27 Round Grove. Officials: Doxie Reeves, Albert Etter.

MUNCIE: Cowan 45–44 Center; Selma 34–29 Daleville; Harrison 38–30 Gaston; Burris 47–34 Albany; Central 28–26 Yorktown; Royerton 47–39 DeSoto; Eaton 30–28 Cowan; Selma 45–34 Harrison; Burris 46–41 Central; Royerton 51–47 Eaton; Burris 35–21 Selma; Burris 40–33 Royerton. Officials: Fred White, Max Casey, Don McBride.

NEW CASTLE: Middletown 53–34 Kennard; Mooreland 33–32 New Castle; Lewisville 50–19 New Lisbon; Knightstown 24–23 Cadiz; Straughn 54–36 Mt. Summit; Spiceland 47–33 Sulphur Springs; Middletown 48–40 Mooreland; Knightstown 34–24 Lewisville; Spiceland 38–37 Straughn; Knightstown 44–43 Middletown; Spiceland 39–35 Knightstown. Officials: Walter Moss, Dean Malaska, Burl Shook.

NOBLESVILLE: Jackson Central 24–18 Sheridan; Tipton 49–44 Fishers; Prairie Twp. 32–18 Jefferson Twp.; Windfall 42–34 Walnut Grove; Noblesville 43–29 Carmel; Sharpsville 42–30 Westfield; Tipton 49–36 Jackson Central; Windfall 42–40 Prairie Twp.; Noblesville 27–23 Sharpsville; Tipton 53–51 Windfall; Tipton 45–40 Noblesville. Officials: John Simon, James Haywood, John Gwin.

NORTH MANCHESTER: Chippewa 42–34 Linlawn; Chester Twp. 53–35 Washington Center; South Whitley 65–37 Lagro; Lincolnville 38–30 Urbana; Wabash 42–40 Laketon (2ot); North Manchester 43–40 Roann; La Fontaine 44–26 Somerset; Chester Twp. 40–29 Chippewa; South Whitley 50–34 Lincolnville; North Manchester 42–37 Wabash; Chester Twp. 38–18 La Fontaine; North Manchester 53–47 South Whitley; North Manchester 36–34 Chester Twp. (2ot). Officials: Harold McSwane, Donald Dickey, James E. Ridge.

PAOLI: West Baden 26–25 Little York; Morgan Twp. 76–22 Leavenworth; Hardinsburg 44–14 English; French Lick 53–36 Milltown; Salem 54–29 Campbellsburg; Marengo 55–32 Pekin; Paoli 31–27 Orleans; West Baden 41–38 Morgan Twp.; Hardinsburg 45–41 French Lick; Marengo 45–36 Salem; Paoli 42–37 West Baden; Marengo 47–29 Hardinsburg; Marengo 37–26 Paoli. Officials: Clarence Tolbert, Robert Rose, Edgar Braun.

PERU: Converse 39–22 Chili; Peru 75–37 Mexico; Clay Twp. 86–7 Butler Twp.; Bunker Hill

43–28 Macy; Deedsville 35–33 Gilead; Peru 66–31 Converse; Clay Twp. 31–28 Bunker Hill; Peru 76–32 Deedsville; Peru 42–32 Clay Twp. Officials: William Lucus, Leon Hodson, Frank Eakin

PLYMOUTH: Culver 60–28 West Twp.; Argos 48–32 Hamlet; North Judson 53–35 San Pierre; Bremen 52–44 Plymouth; Grovertown 55–50 Knox; Bourbon 55–50 Tyner; LaPaz 37–34 Tippecanoe (ot); Culver 58–28 Argos; Bremen 53–44 North Judson; Culver 48–28 LaPaz; Bremen 54–42 Bourbon; Culver 52–48 Bremen. Officials: Allen Klinck, DeVon Eaton, Wayne Murphy.

RENSSELAER: Goodland 45–42 Fair Oaks; Morocco 50–39 Demotte; Brook 39–30 Wheatfield; Kankakee Twp. 32–23 Remington; St. Joseph 50–32 Mt. Ayr; Rensselaer 56–27 Kentland; Morocco 50–35 Goodland; Kankakee Twp. 42–41 Brook; Rensselaer 39–37 St. Joseph; Morocco 45–25 Kankakee Twp.; Rensselaer 53–50 Morocco. Officials: Harold Carlson, Sam Massette, Edward Herbert.

RICHMOND: Richmond 65–29 Green's Fork; Cambridge City 68–44 Whitewater; Webster 38–35 Williamsburg; Economy 38–36 Milton; Fountain City 52–27 Centerville; Hagerstown 65–24 Boston; Richmond 58–44 Cambridge City; Webster 67–53 Economy; Hagerstown 46–45 Fountain City (ot); Richmond 82–37 Webster; Richmond 52–37 Hagerstown. Officials: Joe Conover, Jack O'Neal, Herbert Schwomeyer.

ROCHESTER: Rochester 53–26 Richland Center; Kewanna 49–42 Talma; Winamac 44–18 Grass Creek; Akron 44–37 Leiters Ford; Pulaski 37–27 Medaryville; Star City 29–26 Francesville; Monterey 50–49 Fulton; Rochester 59–26 Kewanna; Winamac 43–30 Akron; Pulaski 41–36 Star City; Rochester 44–33 Monterey; Winamac 46–28 Pulaski; Winamac 44–36 Rochester. Officials: Charles McManus, E. J. Vennon, Bruce Swinford.

RUSHVILLE: Milroy 39–29 Carthage; New Salem 43–33 Manilla; Arlington 43–34 Morton Memorial; Rushville 53–37 Mays; Milroy 43–40 Raleigh; Arlington 41–37 New Salem; Rushville 45–34 Milroy; Arlington 56–55 Rushville. Officials: Maurice Jordan, John Hilligoss.

SEYMOUR: Freetown 31–29 Cortland; Seymour 58–27 Hayden; Brownstown 38–32 Crothersville; Medora 46–43 Clearspring; Vallonia 50–24 Tampico; Seymour 39–30 Freetown; Brownstown 52–46 Medora; Seymour 59–52 Vallonia; Seymour 49–43 Brownstown. Officials: Ray Lackey, William Reimann.

SHELBYVILLE: Shelbyville 60–20 Mt. Auburn; Waldron 30–25 Flat Rock; Columbus 44–30 Fairland; Clifford 31–29 Hope; Boggstown 39–36 Moral Twp.; Franklin Twp. 64–41 Morristown; Shelbyville 53–24 Waldron; Columbus 75–36 Clifford; Franklin Twp. 55–35 Boggstown; Shelbyville 48–36 Columbus; Shelbyville 56–28 Franklin Twp. Officials: C. N. Phillips, George Bender, Melvin Wilson.

SOUTH BEND: Lakeville 49–37 New Carlisle; Madison Twp. 43–35 Riley; North Liberty 46–24 Greene Twp.; Washington 43–40 Mishawaka; Washington-Clay 54–31 Walkerton; Central 49–34 Adams; Central Catholic 41–35 Woodrow Wilson; South Bend Catholic 46–30 Lakeville; Madison Twp. 68–32 North Liberty; Washington-Clay 47–46 Washington; Central 76–28 Central Catholic; Madison Twp. 60–31 South Bend Catholic; Central 68–54 Washington-Clay; Central 74–53 Madison Twp. Officials: Don Polizotto, Paul Bateman, Cecil Young.

SULLIVAN: Sullivan 29–24 Farmersburg; New Lebanon 51–45 Pleasantville; Carlisle 36–16 Fairbanks; Hymera 30–23 Dugger; Shelburn 54–25 Graysville; Sullivan 41–34 Merom; New Lebanon 29–22 Carlisle; Shelburn 29–28 Hymera; New Lebanon 44–23 Sullivan: Shelburn 32–25 New Lebanon. Officials: Otto Albright, Kenneth Merder, Robert Quillen.

TERRE HAUTE: Honey Creek 52–39 Blackhawk; Riley 44–43 Glenn (2ot); Garfield 66–44

Tourney Time

Laboratory; West Terre Haute 55–35 Prairie Creek; Gerstmeyer 45–37 Otter Creek, Concannon 48–30 Fontanet; Wiley 59–26 Pimento; Honey Creek 48–34 Riley; Garfield 31–22 West Terre Haute; Gerstmeyer 37–33 Concannon; Wiley 37–35 Honey Creek; Garfield 48–28 Gerstmeyer; Garfield 64–35 Wiley. Officials: Evan Crawley, Layall Fisher, Donald Cooper.

VINCENNES: Decker 33–30 Wheatland; Vincennes 44–34 Monroe City; Bruceville 41–23 Freelandville; Edwardsport 30–27 Fritchton; Decker Chapel 48–37 Sandborn; Bicknell 52–30 Oaktown; Vincennes 36–25 Decker; Bruceville 37–24 Edwardsport; Bicknell 43–31 Decker Chapel; Vincennes 37–34 Bruceville; Vincennes 34–17 Bicknell. Officials: Kermit Spurgeon, Clyde Castle, William Hartley.

WARSAW: Warsaw 49–35 Etna Green; North Webster 32–28 Claypool; Leesburg 41–36 Syracuse; Milford 72–40 Larwill; Mentone 45–24 Columbia City; Silver Lake 50–26 Burkett; Pierceton 51–25 Sidney; Beaver Dam 46–33 Atwood; Warsaw 53–22 North Webster; Leesburg 45–39 Milford; Silver Lake 47–29 Mentone; Pierceton 46–38 Beaver Dam; Warsaw 43–31 Leesburg; Silver Lake 59–49 Pierceton; Silver Lake 52–36 Warsaw. Officials: Lloyd Bryan, Myron Weldy, Dwight Byerly.

WASHINGTON: Plainville 30–29 Washington; Barr Twp. 63–34 Glendale; Washington Catholic 52–21 Odon; Loogootee 57–35 Epsom; Shoals 59–24 Alfordsville; Elnora 42–39 Plainville; Washington Catholic 38–36 Barr Twp.; Shoals 42–41 Loogootee; Washington Catholic 57–38 Elnora; Washington Catholic 42–40 Shoals. Officials: William Coulter, Don DeVault, Roy Brann.

1947 REGIONALS

BEDFORD: Bedford 40–33 Jeffersonville; Seymour 54–25 Marengo; Bedford 50–37 Seymour. Officials: C.N. Phillips, Clyde Castle, Evan Crawley.

BLOOMINGTON: Terre Haute Garfield 48–36 Linton; Ellettsville 33–32 Cory; Garfield 48–47 Ellettsville. Officials: Cecil Tharp, Wilbur May, Robert Derrington.

CLINTON: Clinton 31–28 Covington; Crawfordsville 45–27 Greencastle; Clinton 44–37 Crawfordsville. Officials: William Coulter, Walter Floyd, William Pointer.

EVANSVILLE: Princeton 55–45 Tell City; Central 57–44 Boonville; Central 66–33 Princeton. Officials: Roland Baker, Walter Surface, Walter N. Ringer.

FORT WAYNE: Ft. Wayne South Side 49–26 Spencerville; Silver Lake 35–34 Kendallville; South Side 54–26 Silver Lake. Officials: Walter Thurston, Devon Eaton, Jim Crowe.

GREENSBURG: Shelbyville 44–38 Madison; North Vernon 37–34 Franklin; Shelbyville 55–23 North Vernon. Officials: Robert Hoffman, Norman Dunlap, Cyril Birge.

HAMMOND: Gary Emerson 47–43 Rensselaer; East Chicago Washington 43–28 Michigan City; Washington 51–42 Emerson. Officials: Allen Klinck, Raymond Trobaugh, Phil Eskew.

HUNTINGTON: Huntington 58–32 Chester Center; Portland 36–33 Monroe; Huntington 55–53 Portland. Officials: Dean Malaska, Maurice Jordan, George Bender.

INDIANAPOLIS: Southport 45–41 Fortville; Pendleton 55–44 Clayton; Pendleton 51–46 Southport. Officials: L. E. Fink, Don McBride, Norris Ward.

LAFAYETTE: Lafayette 57–42 Zionsville; Rossville 48–36 Otterbein; Rossville 51–50 Lafayette. Officials: Marvin Todd, Arthur Lloyd, Fred White.

LOGANSPORT: Logansport 47–45 Monon; Peru 48–46 Flora; Logansport 58–37 Peru. Officials: Clyde Gentry, Charles McManus, Hugh Bergstrom.

MARION: Kokomo 45–39 Tipton; Marion 50–44 N. Manchester; Marion 39–37 Kokomo. Officials: Herbert Edwards, John Hilligoss, G. P. Silver.

MUNCIE: Spartanburg 36–29 Spiceland; Burris 44–39 Richmond; Burris 51–40 Spartanburg. Officials: Frank Jarrell, Cecil Young, Paul Bateman.

RUSHVILLE: Lawrenceburg 47–30 Everton; Napoleon 48–47 Arlington; Lawrenceburg 59–35 Napoleon. Officials: Jay Mertz, George Collyer, Jack O'Neal.

SOUTH BEND: Elkhart 34–32 Winamac; Central 48–39 Culver; Central 33–30 Elkhart. Officials: John Magnabosco, Sam Massette, John Walker.

VINCENNES: Shelburn 42–36 Washington Catholic; Vincennes 46–39 Jasper; Shelburn 40–34 Vincennes. Officials: Ross Dorsett, Ray Lackey, William Reimann.

1947 SEMI–FINALS

BLOOMINGTON: Terre Haute Garfield 64–47 Shelburn; Evansville Central 42–38 Bedford; Garfield 43–38 Central. Officials: Paul Bateman, Jim Crowe, George Bender.

INDIANAPOLIS: Shelbyville 48–39 Clinton; Lawrenceburg 45–41 Pendleton; Shelbyville 44–37 Lawrenceburg. Officials: Allen Klinck, Roland Baker, Marvin Todd.

LAFAYETTE: South Bend Central 44–41 Rossville; East Chicago Washington 59–32 Logansport; Washington 43–38 Central. Officials: Dean Malaska, G. P. Silver, C. N. Phillips.

MUNCIE: Marion 39–32 Ft. Wayne South Side; Muncie Burris 71–62 Huntington (ot); Marion 40–32 Burris. Officials: William Pointer, Ray Lackey, Walter Thurston.

1947 FINALS—March 22

INDIANAPOLIS (Butler Fieldhouse): Terre Haute Garfield 59–50 Marion; Shelbyville 54–46 East Chicago Washington; Shelbyville 68–58 Garfield. Officials: George Bender, Dean Malaska, Walter Thurston.

1948 SECTIONALS

ANDERSON: Lapel 46–43 Elwood; Anderson 54–38 Summitville; Pendleton 41–40 Alexandria (ot); St. Mary's 48–36 Frankton; Markleville 42–36 Lapel (ot); Anderson 42–40 Pendleton (ot); Markleville 51–35 St. Mary's; Anderson 54–47 Markleville. Officials: Don McBride, John Hilligoss.

ATTICA: Attica 52–15 Kingman; Hillsboro 47–32 Williamsport; Veedersburg 47–42 Pine Village; Richland Twp. 42–21 Wallace; Covington 35–25 West Lebanon; Attica 46–35 Perrysville; Veedersburg 42–36 Hillsboro; Covington 51–34 Richland Twp.; Attica 59–38 Veedersburg; Attica 36–29 Covington. Officials: Herbert Brammell, Noble Benbow, Roderick Witt.

AUBURN–GARRETT: (At Auburn): Garrett 55–38 Salem Center; Angola 49–26 Hamilton; Orland 35–18 Concord Twp.; Churubusco 50–27 Scott Center; (At Garrett): Spencerville 45–43 Auburn; Waterloo 68–29 Pleasant Lake; Butler 38–33 Metz; Fremont 47–34 Ashley; (At Auburn): Garrett 36–34 Angola; Churubusco 50–49 Orland; (At Garrett): Waterloo 38–32 Spencerville; Fremont 45–33 Butler; (At Auburn): Garrett 27–22 Churubusco; Fremont 37–32 Waterloo; Garrett 60–26 Fremont. Officials: Donald Dickie, Don Lieberum, Marvin Todd, Robert Dornte.

Tourney Time

BATESVILLE: Batesville 49–30 Cross Plains; Osgood 39–31 Sunman; Holton 47–41 Versailles (ot); Napoleon 45–44 Milan; Batesville 53–39 New Marion; Holton 53–30 Osgood; Napoleon 35–18 Batesville; Napoleon 37–32 Holton. Officials: Charles D. Jones, L. Howard Wright.

BEDFORD: Marshall Twp. 33–32 Shawswick; Fayetteville 52–29 Huron; Bedford 41–33 Mitchell; Oolitic 55–43 Williams; Tunnelton 43–26 Heltonville; Marshall Twp. 52–40 Fayetteville; Bedford 44–39 Oolitic; Marshall Twp. 51–47 Tunnelton; Bedford 48–21 Marshall Twp. Officials: William Pointer, Ivan Sprinkle.

BLOOMINGTON: University 35–34 Stinesville; Morgantown 56–24 Eminence; Ellettsville 57–26 Paragon; Bloomington 44–29 Monrovia; Mooresville 63–27 Unionville; Martinsville 50–22 Smithville; University 43–32 Morgantown; Bloomington 51–35 Ellettsville; Martinsville 37–34 Mooresville; Bloomington 50–29 University; Bloomington 34–32 Martinsville. Officials: S.T. Proffitt, Cyril Birge, Norman Dunlap.

BLUFFTON: Petroleum 40–37 Liberty Center; Lancaster Central 37–35 Ossian; Chester Center 48–38 Bluffton; Jackson Center 32–24 Union Center; Petroleum 56–32 Rockcreek Center; Chester Center 20–19 Lancaster Central; Petroleum 31–29 Jackson Center; Chester Center 30–25 Petroleum. Officials: Forrest L. Ballinger, Otto Crosley.

BOONVILLE: Lynnville 66–60 Millersburg; Chandler 58–42 Tennyson; Newburgh 46–24 Folsomville; Elberfeld 62–43 Selvin; Boonville 43–38 Lynnville; Newburgh 38–35 Chandler; Boonville 66–47 Elberfeld; Boonville 49–39 Newburgh. Officials: Edgar Braun, Lee Albin.

BRAZIL: Gosport 48–39 Staunton; Brazil 49–31 Spencer; Freedom 48–42 Patricksburg; Clay City 48–31 Ashboro; Cory 44–34 Coal City; Van Buren 72–43 Quincy; Gosport 85–39 Bowling Green; Brazil 56–34 Freedom; Cory 47–33 Clay City; Van Buren 54–34 Gosport; Brazil 53–39 Cory; Brazil 47–32 Van Buren. Officials: Loren Harris, J. D. Nickle, Edward Stuteville.

BROOK (St. Joseph's College): Rensselaer 74–40 Kentland; Goodland 54–51 Remington; Kankakee Twp. 46–40 Wheatfield; Demotte 39–27 Fair Oaks; Mt. Ayr 33–32 Morocco; Brook 40–37 Rensselaer; Kankakee Twp. 58–50 Goodland; Mt. Ayr 37–32 Demotte; Brook 57–33 Kankakee Twp.; Brook 50–40 Mt. Ayr. Officials: John Cover, Bruce Swinford, Doxie Reeves.

CLINTON: Mecca 51–26 Bridgeton; Rosedale 66–36 Cayuga; Marshall 67–25 Bellmore W. Twp.; Clinton 52–43 Green Twp.; Hillsdale 38–33 Bloomingdale; Tangier 48–36 Newport; Dana 46–43 Rockville; Montezuma 44–34 St. Bernice; Mecca 34–28 Rosedale; Marshall 49–42 Clinton; Tangier 38–24 Hillsdale; Dana 56–40 Montezuma; Mecca 41–27 Marshall; Dana 47–30 Tangier; Dana 49–40 Mecca. Officials: Lowell Willis, Clarence Myles, Kenneth Merder.

CONNERSVILLE: Springfield Twp. 40–23 Laurel; Alquina 62–35 Orange; Liberty 40–36 Harrisburg; Whitewater 48–28 Bentonville; Connersville 49–42 Brookville; Brownsville 38–31 Fairview; Springfield Twp. 40–29 Kitchel; Liberty 39–37 Alquina; Connersville 71–35 Whitewater; Springfield Twp. 35–30 Brownsville; Connersville 45–43 Liberty; Connersville 38–32 Springfield Twp. Officials: Edward Straith–Miller, Robert Quillen, Chester C. Elson.

CRAWFORDSVILLE: Crawfordsville 37–25 New Market; Linden 46–42 Darlington; Ladoga 61–25 Wingate; Alamo 70–34 Bowers; New Ross 50–41 New Richmond; Waynetown 40–32 Waveland; Crawfordsville 58–36 Linden; Ladoga 53–42 Alamo; Waynetown 48–44 New Ross; Crawfordsville 51–41 Ladoga; Crawfordsville 57–39 Waynetown. Officials: Warren Williams, Allen Klinck, Leland Wright.

DANVILLE: Clayton 45–22 Pittsboro; Danville 48–29 Brownsburg; North Salem 32–26 New

Winchester; Charlton 35–34 Stilesville; Avon 46–35 Plainfield; Speedway 39–37 Amo; Clayton 34–25 Lizton; Danville 47–31 North Salem; Avon 45–41 Charlton; Speedway 45–32 Clayton; Avon 43–35 Danville; Speedway 41–26 Avon. Officials: Otto Albright, William McCoskey, Charles Marshall.

DECATUR: Hartford 32–25 Geneva; Decatur 44–43 Monmouth; Kirkland 33–32 Berne; Decatur Catholic 42–29 Pleasant Mills; Monroe 44–36 Jefferson; Hartford 40–36 Decatur; Decatur Catholic 29–26 Kirkland; Hartford 41–35 Monroe; Hartford 42–29 Decatur Catholic. Officials: Clay Layman, Gene Winks.

DELPHI: Burlington 58–23 Rockfield; Camden 30–25 Carrollton; Delphi 49–34 Cutler; Flora 57–27 Adams Twp.; Deer Creek 29–27 Burlington; Delphi 48–46 Camden (2ot); Flora 69–27 Deer Creek; Delphi 39–31 Flora. Officials: Frank Kresler Jr., Norman Morrison.

ELKHART: Elkhart 46–24 Jefferson Twp.; New Paris 37–29 Middlebury; Bristol 37–23 Millersburg; Elkhart 51–50 New Paris; Goshen 34–32 Baugo Twp.; Concord 46–25 Nappanee; Wakarusa 39–34 Goshen; Elkhart 45–25 Bristol; Wakarusa 41–37 Concord; Elkhart 39–34 Wakarusa. Officials: Hugh Bergstrom, E.L. Aldrich, Don Polizotto, Harold Carlson.

EVANSVILLE: Memorial 78–36 Cynthiana; Central 50–27 Wadesville; Griffin 52–43 New Harmony; Lincoln 56–52 Poseyville; Bosse 71–33 Mount Vernon; Reitz 55–44 Memorial; Central 59–45 Griffin; Bosse 44–37 Lincoln; Central 47–42 Reitz; Central 56–46 Bosse. Officials: Roland Baker, Clarence Tolbert, Leland Terrell.

FARMLAND: Lynn 45–38 Wayne; Lincoln 36–32 Huntsville; Saratoga 52–37 Modoc; Spartanburg 39–31 McKinley; Losantville 31–25 Jackson; Parker 56–34 Stoney Creek; Winchester 53–40 Union City; Farmland 46–31 Green Twp.; Lynn 56–35 Lincoln; Spartanburg 46–45 Saratoga; Parker 55–30 Losantville; Winchester 70–61 Farmland; Spartanburg 39–30 Lynn; Parker 55–48 Winchester; Parker 45–31 Spartanburg. Officials: Eugene Glaze, Charles Northam, John Gwin.

FORT WAYNE: (At North Side): Arcola 53–39 Coesse; Central 49–25 Huntertown; Harlan 41–33 Elmhurst; Concordia 37–34 South Side; Central 79–45 Arcola; Concordia 54–51 Harlan; (At South Side): North Side 38–26 New Haven; Leo 35–33 Hoagland; Monroeville 50–45 Central Catholic; Woodburn 54–32 Lafayette Central; North Side 45–37 Leo; Monroeville 50–35 Woodburn; (At North Side): Central 52–36 Concordia; Monroeville 44–33 North Side; Monroeville 38–32 Central. Officials: George Bender, Lores Lehman, Jim Crowe, Jay Mertz.

FRANKFORT: Washington Twp. 37–35 Kirklin; Forest 38–33 Jackson Twp.; Scircleville 39–33 Mulberry; Frankfort 41–29 Michigantown; Rossville 75–58 Colfax; Washington Twp. 48–37 Sugar Creek; Forest 43–32 Scircleville; Rossville 46–44 Frankfort (ot); Forest 41–39 Washington Twp.; Rossville 67–31 Forest. Officials: Herschel Eastman, Robert Hobbs, Lowell Barnett.

FRANKLIN: Greenwood 41–39 Center Grove; Edinburg 55–32 Nineveh; Van Buren 54–47 Clark; Union 41–22 Nashville; Trafalgar 31–30 Whiteland; Franklin 50–30 Helmsburg; Greenwood 55–36 Edinburg; Union 57–36 Van Buren; Franklin 39–24 Trafalgar; Greenwood 33–28 Union; Franklin 34–33 Greenwood. Officials: Roy Gardner, Yank Terry, Joe Conover.

GARY–VALPARAISO: (At Gary): Emerson 47–35 Lew Wallace; Horace Mann 40–38 Froebel; Wirt 59–43 Tolleston; Roosevelt 39–32 Gary Edison; (At Valparaiso): Valparaiso 43–37 Chestertown; Liberty Center 42–31 Boone Grove; Kouts 47–34 Hebron; Morgan Twp. 45–41 Washington Twp.; (At Gary): Emerson 48–40 Horace Mann; Gary Wirt 55–52 Gary Roosevelt; (At Valparaiso): Valparaiso 30–25 Liberty Center; Kouts 66–38 Morgan Twp.; (At Gary): Emerson

Tourney Time

58–40 Gary Wirt; Kouts 33–29 Valparaiso; Emerson 55–34 Kouts. Officials: Paul Boehm, R.W. Warring, Victor Griewank, Devon Phelps.

GREENCASTLE: Roachdale 45–28 Cloverdale; Greencastle 56–26 Reelsville; Belle Union 41–39 Russellville; Bainbridge 37–28 Fillmore; Greencastle 54–33 Roachdale; Bainbridge 48–37 Belle Union; Greencastle 48–31 Bainbridge. Officials: G.P. Silver, Robert Gatewood.

GREENFIELD: Mt. Comfort 37–35 Wilkinson; Fortville 42–29 Eden; Franklin Twp. 67–35 Maxwell; Greenfield 66–29 McCordsville; New Palestine 61–44 Charlottesville; Fortville 40–37 Mt. Comfort; Greenfield 41–37 Franklin Twp.; Fortville 47–28 New Palestine; Greenfield 47–35 Fortville. Officials: Cecil Tharp, William McNamara.

GREENSBURG: Sandusky 43–35 St. Paul; Greensburg 41–24 Sandcreek; Burney 77–35 Butlerville; North Vernon 39–11 New Point; Clarksburg 34–29 Vernon; Jackson 59–22 Zenas; Greensburg 43–36 Sandusky; North Vernon 40–27 Burney; Clarksburg 43–28 Jackson; Greensburg 39–26 North Vernon; Greensburg 44–27 Clarksburg. Officials: Robert Fink, Arthur M. Gross, John Simon.

HAMMOND–EAST CHICAGO: (At Hammond): Lowell 41–36 Noll; Hammond High 48–43 Griffith; Hammond Tech 55–35 Crown Point; Hammond Clark 61–24 Dyer; Hammond High 39–35 Lowell; Tech 56–52 Clark; (At East Chicago): East Chicago Roosevelt 53–48 Portage; East Chicago Washington 48–35 Merrillville; Whiting 58–42 Hobart; East Gary Edison 33–24 Wheeler; Washington 48–46 Roosevelt; Whiting 62–32 East Gary Edison; (At Hammond): Hammond High 37–23 Tech; Washington 39–35 Whiting; Hammond High 36–34 Washington. Officials: Paul Bateman, Alvin Vincent, Cecil Young, Myron Weldy.

HARTFORD CITY: Ridgeville 75–31 Poling; Gray 41–30 Bryant; Jefferson (Randolph Co.) 39–37 Montpelier; Redkey 60–20 Madison Twp.; Roll 31–29 Hartford City; Dunkirk 49–44 Pennville; Portland 61–25 Ridgeville; Jefferson 51–18 Gray; Redkey 46–34 Roll; Portland 52–42 Dunkirk; Jefferson 37–25 Redkey; Portland 59–34 Jefferson. Officials: Walter Moss, Phillip Kammerer, Raymond Trobaugh.

HUNTINGTON: Union Twp. 50–37 Rock Creek Center; Clear Creek 29–27 Bippus; Huntington Twp. 48–15 Wayne Twp.: Huntington 54–37 Jackson Twp.; Jefferson (Columbia City) 55–47 Jefferson (Warren); Andrews 53–34 Markle; Huntington Catholic 39–33 Lancaster Center; Salamonie Twp. 48–43 Polk Twp.; Clear Creek 35–29 Union Twp.; Huntington 51–34 Huntington Twp.; Jefferson (Columbia City) 47–41 Andrews; Huntington Catholic 54–53 Salamonie Twp.; Huntington 60–21 Clear Creek; Huntington Catholic 57–34 Jefferson (Columbia City); Huntington 43–27 Huntington Catholic. Officials: Otho Piper, James Ridge, Walter Bonham.

INDIANAPOLIS: Tech 58–21 School for the Deaf; Crispus Attacks 66–37 Beech Grove; Cathedral 34–30 Southport; Lawrence Central 52–32 Sacred Heart; Decatur Central 35–27 Manual; Howe 54–41 Ben Davis; Warren Central 49–44 Shortridge; Washington 39–37 Broad Ripple; Crispus Attacks 46 45 Tech; Lawrence Central 45–44 Cathedral; Decatur Central 45–40 Howe; Washington 57–48 Warren Central; Lawrence Central 43–42 Crispus Attacks; Washington 47–39 Decatur Central; Washington 62–43 Lawrence Central. Officials: W.N. Reimann, H. F. McNaught, Ray Lackey.

JASPER: Winslow 45–36 Petersburg; Spurgeon 39–29 Dubois; Otwell 53–40 Birdseye; Huntingburg 59–55 Holland; Jasper 44–34 Ireland; Stendal 50–25 Cuzco; Spurgeon 54–48 Winslow; Huntingburg 66–41 Otwell; Jasper 49–33 Stendal; Spurgeon 62–58 Huntingburg;

Jasper 51–49 Spurgeon. Officials: August Banko, William Coulter, Kermit Spurgeon.

JEFFERSONVILLE: Jeffersonville 107–23 New Middletown, Laconia 45–24 Mauckport; Scribner 38–33 Borden; Henryville 58–26 New Amsterdam; New Albany 62–16 Georgetown; Corydon 50–36 Charlestown; Silver Creek 69–29 Elizabeth; Lanesville 63–35 Taylor; Jeffersonville 73–39 Laconia; Henryville 43–41 Scribner; New Albany 57–28 Corydon; Silver Creek 68–41 Lanesville; Jeffersonville 53–41 Henryville; New Albany 51–40 Silver Creek; New Albany 53–31 Jeffersonville. Officials: Robert Grannan, Paul Neal, Robert Hoffman.

KENDALLVILLE–ALBION: (At Kendallville): Ligonier 44–32 Howe Military; Avilla 31–27 Rome City; Albion 55–43 Wolf Lake; Brighton 37–34 Lima; Avilla 36–35 Ligonier; Albion 53–25 Brighton; (At Albion): Kendallville 54–30 Wolcottville; Shipshewana 47–33 Scott; Wawaka 49–32 LaGrange; Cromwell 32–28 Topeka; Shipshewana 43–38 Kendallville; Wawaka 56–23 Cromwell; (At Kendallville): Albion 46–26 Avilla; Wawaka 44–26 Shipshewana; Wawaka 41–38 Albion. Officials: George Collyer, Lloyd Bryan, Joe Metzger, Dwight Byerly.

KOKOMO: Ervin Twp. 48–47 Union Twp.; Kokomo 59–13 New London; Greentown 61–25 Russiaville; Howard Twp. 57–42 W. Middleton; Clay Twp. 41–36 Jackson Twp.; Kokomo 69–24 Ervin Twp.; Greentown 43–26 Howard Twp.; Kokomo 51–21 Clay Twp.; Kokomo 19–17 Greentown. Officials: Hal Harris, Frank White.

LAFAYETTE: Clarks Hill 41–28 Monitor; Buck Creek 54–34 Wea; Lafayette 67–38 Battle Ground; Dayton 42–40 Montmorenci; West Point 34–25 Jackson Twp.; Shadeland 42–39 Stockwell; Klondike 61–38 Romney; West Lafayette 50–41 Clarks Hill; Lafayette 54–16 Buck Creek; Dayton 36–30 West Point; Klondike 57–51 Shadeland; Lafayette 51–38 West Lafayette; Klondike 47–37 Dayton; Lafayette 78–37 Klondike. Officials: Myrle Rife, Frank Jarrell, Herbert Schwomeyer.

LAWRENCEBURG: Lawrenceburg 49–34 Guilford; Aurora 49–37 Moores Hill; Dillsboro 49–40 Bright; Patriot 44–42 Vevay; Lawrenceburg 59–36 Rising Sun; Aurora 53–41 Dillsboro; Lawrenceburg 66–27 Patriot; Lawrenceburg 46–26 Aurora. Officials: James Sanders, Maurice Jordan.

LEBANON: Thorntown 59–35 Pike Twp.; Zionsville 39–25 Pinnell; Perry Central 50–46 Dover; Whitestown 45–27 Jamestown; Lebanon 52–33 Advance; Thorntown 41–30 Zionsville; Perry Central 33–32 Whitestown; Lebanon 44–41 Thorntown; Lebanon 50–30 Perry Central. Officials: Joe Mullins, Albert Etter.

LINTON: Scotland 57–50 Switz City; Bloomfield 51–37 Lyons; Linton 79–23 Owensburg; Solsberry 46–19 Midland; Jasonville 62–28 Marco; Worthington 37–36 Scotland; Linton 40–34 Bloomfield; Solsberry 45–41 Jasonville; Linton 50–39 Worthington; Solsberry 61–56 Linton. Officials: Cecil Bosstick, William Schaefer, Gilbert Smith.

LOGANSPORT: Logansport 57–39 Metea; Onward 44–32 Galveston Washington Twp. 47–34 Twelve Mile; Walton 56–39 New Waverly; Young America 41–31 Lucerne; Logansport 46–28 Royal Center; Washington Twp. 53–43 Onward; Walton 37–30 Young America; Logansport 32–21 Washington Twp.; Logansport 48–33 Walton. Officials: Lawrence Leland, Clayton Patterson, Art Cosgrove.

MADISON: Central 40–25 New Washington; Dupont 50–38 Deputy; Scottsburg 43–39 Austin; Saluda 53–35 North Madison; Lexington 50–46 Paris Crossing; Madison 74–37 Hanover; Central 42–34 Dupont; Scottsburg 33–32 Saluda (ot); Madison 81–21 Lexington; Scottsburg 48–38 Central; Madison 67–44 Scottsburg. Officials: Robert Cherry, Harold Porter, Wayne Hammond.

Tourney Time

MARION: Gas City 54–39 Jonesboro; Fairmount 43–28 St. Paul; Marion 52–29 Van Buren; Sweetser 45–33 Swayzee; Gas City 28–27 Jefferson Twp.; Marion 40–24 Fairmount; Gas City 34–22 Sweetser; Marion 45–38 Gas City. Officials: William Ellis, Charles Bobilya.

MICHIGAN CITY: Westville 60–43 Hanna; Stillwell 45–38 Clinton Twp.; Union Mills 43–41 La Crosse; LaPorte 75–22 Jackson Twp.; Michigan City 58–32 St. Mary's; Kingsbury 50–30 Union Twp.; Wanatah 43–38 Mill Creek; Rolling Prairie 34–32 Springfield Twp.; Westville 59–41 Stillwell; LaPorte 63–29 Union Mills; Michigan City 55–34 Kingsbury; Rolling Prairie 64–35 Wanatah; LaPorte 57–37 Westville; Michigan City 57–38 Rolling Prairie; Michigan City 58–54 LaPorte. Officials: Stanley Dubis, Dean Geyer, L.E. Fink.

MONTICELLO: Monticello 40–14 Wolcott; Burnettsville 36–24 Round Grove; Monon 45–34 Reynolds; Brookston 55–40 Idaville; Buffalo 53–40 Chalmers; Monticello 39–31 Burnettsville; Brookston 50–37 Monon; Monticello 48–27 Buffalo; Brookston 38–27 Monticello. Officials: Fred Fechtman, Donald Cooper.

MUNCIE: Albany 64–27 Harrison; Royerton 70–29 Gaston; Central 53–35 Cowan; Daleville 32–25 Selma; Center 35–32 Eaton; Burris 52–40 DeSoto; Albany 36–35 Yorktown; Central 47–37 Royerton; Center 43–25 Daleville; Burris 59–41 Albany; Central 61–40 Center; Central 54–32 Burris. Officials: Wilbur May, Burl Shook, J.W. Johnson.

NEW CASTLE: Cadiz 46–44 Lewisville (ot); Spiceland 34–30 Sulphur Springs; Middletown 47–28 Mt. Summit; Knightstown 45–35 Kennard; Straughn 55–52 Mooreland (ot); New Castle 59–19 New Lisbon; Spiceland 37–35 Cadiz; Middletown 49–46 Knightstown; New Castle 36–32 Straughn; Middletown 48–34 Spiceland; New Castle 40–38 Middletown (ot). Officials: Wray Holbrook, C.N. Phillips, James Haywood.

OWENSVILLE–OAKLAND CITY: (At Owensville): Mackey 56–24 Lincoln; Francisco 30–26 Mt. Olympus; Princeton 59–42 Owensville; Mackey 47–33 Francisco; (At Oakland City): Patoka 29–28 Haubstadt; Oakland City 47–21 Hazleton; Patoka 53–38 Ft. Branch; (At Owensville): Princeton 57–52 Mackey; Patoka 41–15 Oakland City; Princeton 67–39 Patoka. Officials: William Hartley, Robert Rose, Robert Hudson, Don DeVault.

OXFORD: Freeland Park 42–34 Ambia; Wadena 33–24 Gilboa; Fowler 32–27 Otterbein; Boswell 50–30 Raub; Oxford 46–10 Pine Twp.; Freeland Park 38–26 Earl Park; Wadena 38–32 Fowler; Oxford 30–25 Boswell; Freeland Park 31–29 Wadena; Freeland Park 41–26 Oxford. Officials: Herbert Vaulk, Fred Vaulk, Meredyth Delph.

PAOLI: Morgan Twp. 45–36 Hardinsburg; Mt. St. Francis 55–53 New Salisbury; English 31–26 Depauw; Pekin 38–32 Campbellsburg; West Baden 53–32 Milltown; French Lick 59–48 Marengo; Paoli 46–30 Orleans; Morgan Twp. 52–45 Salem; Mt. St. Francis 64–40 English; West Baden 43–32 Pekin; French Lick 33–28 Paoli; Mt. St. Francis 48–43 Morgan Twp.; French Lick 49–43 West Baden; Mt. St. Francis 43–42 French Lick. Officials: Herschel Bales, Hugh Thrasher, Hulett Crecelius.

PERU: Peru 42–31 Converse; Bunker Hill 36–18 Chili; Clay Twp. 62–17 Butler Twp.; Gilead 42–34 Jefferson Twp. (Mexico); Deedsville 25–23 Macy; Peru 49–21 Bunker Hill; Gilead 39–33 Clay Twp.; Peru 53–13 Deedsville; Peru 62–33 Gilead. Officials: John Walker, Ward Mosbaugh.

PLYMOUTH: North Judson 40–36 Argos; Tyner 39–37 Bourbon; Knox 51–28 San Pierre; Hamlet 71–35 West High; LaPaz 57–38 Tippecanoe; Bremen 45–39 Grovertown; Culver 49–39 Plymouth; North Judson 51–44 Tyner; Knox 53–39 Hamlet; LaPaz 62–42 Bremen; Culver 51–43 North Judson; LaPaz 58–56 Knox; Culver 70–52 LaPaz. Officials: Charles McManus, Arthur

IHSAA Scores | 1940–1949

Lloyd, E.J. Vennon.

RICHMOND: Cambridge City 46–33 Greensfork; Hagerstown 58–38 Milton; Williamsburg 53–47 Webster; Boston 39–32 Economy; Richmond 53–44 Fountain City; Whitewater 47–41 Centerville; Hagerstown 52–43 Cambridge City; Williamsburg 46–37 Boston; Richmond 77–41 Whitewater; Hagerstown 37–26 Williamsburg; Richmond 36–33 Hagerstown. Officials: Alvin Heller, Evan Crawley, G. Ross Dorsett.

RUSHVILLE: Carthage 35–27 Manilla; Arlington 45–28 Milroy; Mays 55–35 Raleigh; Morton Memorial 50–46 New Salem; Rushville 32–23 Carthage; Arlington 44–38 Mays; Rushville 43–33 Morton Memorial; Rushville 35–28 Arlington. Officials: Frank Luzar, Tom Stirling.

SEYMOUR: Vallonia 58–26 Cortland; Clearspring 44–42 Brownstown; Medora 28–24 Crothersville; Freetown 40–29 Tampico; Seymour 48–14 Hayden; Vallonia 44–29 Clearspring; Freetown 45–30 Medora; Seymour 41–37 Vallonia; Seymour 52–32 Freetown. Officials: Herbert Edwards, James Patterson.

SHELBYVILLE: Shelbyville 34–29 Boggstown; Columbus 65–38 Moral Twp.; Flat Rock 44–37 Clifford; Mt. Auburn 53–39 Hope; Morristown 52–43 Waldron; Shelbyville 42–39 Fairland; Columbus 45–25 Flat Rock; Morristown 49–40 Mt. Auburn; Columbus 61–44 Shelbyville; Columbus 68–38 Morristown. Officials: Clyde Gentry, J.C. LaFollette, Jack O'Neal.

SHERIDAN: Fishers 52–32 Carmel; Windfall 58–39 Walnut Grove; Tipton 44–43 Jackson Central; Prairie Twp. 45–43 Westfield; Sharpsville 53–40 Jefferson Twp.; Sheridan 52–50 Noblesville (ot); Fishers 40–39 Windfall; Prairie Twp. 55–47 Tipton; Sharpsville 48–43 Sheridan; Prairie Twp. 44–33 Fishers; Sharpsville 34–27 Prairie Twp. Officials: Wilbur Schumacker, Orval Martin, Cloyd Julian.

SOUTH BEND: New Carlisle 44–40 Madison Twp.; North Liberty 53–40 South Bend Catholic; Central 38–36 Mishawaka; Riley 41–39 New Carlisle; Central 41–28 North Liberty; Central Catholic 47–42 Green Twp.; Lakeville 34–29 Walkerton; Adams 46–34 Wilson; Washington 43–35 Washington-Clay; Lakeville 43–34 Central Catholic; Adams 51–44 Washington; Central 54–47 Riley; Adams 55–30 Lakeville; Central 57–39 Adams. Officials: Sam Massette, Edward Herbert, Devon Eaton, M. E. Somers.

SULLIVAN: New Lebanon 41–23 Fairbanks; Sullivan 39–34 Carlisle; Dugger 28–25 Pleasantville; Merom 47–45 Farmersburg (ot); Shelburn 58–30 Graysville; New Lebanon 33–19 Hymera; Dugger 48–34 Sullivan; Shelburn 51–32 Merom; New Lebanon 30–23 Dugger; Shelburn 34–31 New Lebanon (ot). Officials: Roy Brann, Hubert Thomas, A.M. Franklin.

TELL CITY: Tell City 52–40 Luce Twp.; Troy 36–35 Chrisney; Cannelton 61–37 Leavenworth; Rockport 52–43 Oil Twp.; Tell City 56–48 Dale; Cannelton 41–38 Troy; Tell City 37–27 Rockport; Cannelton 37–35 Tell City. Officials: Wilfred Susott, Robert Derrington.

TERRE HAUTE: Glenn 44–41 Honey Creek; Wiley 106–26 Fayette; Pimento 48–32 Blackhawk; Fontanet 36–32 Concannon; Garfield 55–40 Riley; Otter Creek 37–31 Laboratory; Gerstmeyer 34–28 West Terre Haute, Prairie Creek 49–47 Glenn; Wiley 63–43 Pimento; Garfield 57–36 Fontanet; Gerstmeyer 41–38 Otter Creek; Wiley 57–33 Prairie Creek; Garfield 44–35 Gerstmeyer; Wiley 45–44 Garfield. Officials: Paul Dazey, Dean Malaska, Odilo Berger.

VINCENNES: Monroe City 41–37 Bicknell; Decker 45–28 Fritchton; Bruceville 56–37 Freelandville; Vincennes 49–26 Decker Chapel; Edwardsport 47–42 Wheatland; Sandborn 36–34 Oaktown; Decker 39–38 Monroe City; Vincennes 30–27 Bruceville; Edwardsport 37–33 Sandborn; Vincennes 46–29 Decker; Vincennes 56–35 Edwardsport. Officials: Lloyd Whipple,

Tourney Time

Clyde Castle, Irvin Thrasher.

WABASH: Roann 39–38 North Manchester; Wabash 61–38 Lincolnville; LaFontaine 45–37 Lagro; Linlawn 51–40 Roann; Wabash 49–30 LaFontaine; South Whitley 57–40 Somerset; Urbana 38–35 Washington Center; Chester 50–39 Chippewa; South Whitley 47–43 Laketon; Chester 58–40 Urbana; Wabash 59–50 Linlawn; Chester 52–34 South Whitley; Chester 51–39 Wabash. Officials: John Magnabosco, Burl McKenzie, Leon Hodson, George Danforth.

WARSAW: Columbia City 63–29 Atwood; Leesburg 40–32 Pierceton. Beaver Dam 34–27 Claypool; Etna Green 35–33 Warsaw; Leesburg 50–48 Columbia City; Beaver Dam 44–38 Etna Green; Mentone 48–31 Burkett; North Webster 35–28 Silver Lake; Milford 48–26 Syracuse; Sidney 41–31 Larwill; Mentone 36–34 North Webster; Milford 74–34 Sidney; Beaver Dam 45–38 Leesburg; Milford 66–41 Mentone; Milford 58–38 Beaver Dam. Officials: Walter Thurston, James Koons, Norris Ward, Robert Hughes.

WASHINGTON: Shoals 27–23 Odon; Barr Twp. 54–21 Epsom; Loogootee 51–33 Elmore Twp.; Plainville 58–23 Alfordsville; Washington 31–29 Washington Catholic; Barr Twp. 39–26 Shoals; Loogootee 45–31 Plainville; Barr Twp. 38–25 Washington; Loogootee 36–35 Barr Twp. Officials: Alfred Rose, David Royalty.

WINAMAC: Star City 36–31 Leiters Ford; Richland Center 41–21 Kewanna; Rochester 50–31 Francesville; Akron 63–39 Fulton; Winamac 56–16 Medaryville; Talma 31–30 Grass Creek; Monterey 47–34 Pulaski; Richland Center 23–22 Star City; Akron 42–36 Rochester; Winamac 61–38 Talma, Richland Center 32–30 Monterey; Akron 51–36 Winamac; Richland Center 38–34 Akron. Officials: Paul Hostetler, John Janzaruk, Gerald Powell.

1948 REGIONALS

CRAWFORDSVILLE: Attica 45–40 Greencastle; Crawfordsville 51–34 Dana; Crawfordsville 52–49 Attica. Officials: Hugh Bergstrom, Sam Massette, Norman Dunlap.

EVANSVILLE: Central 47–35 Boonville; Princeton 49–36 Cannelton; Central 64–47 Princeton. Officials: W. N. Reimann, Herbert Edwards, Ray Lackey.

FORT WAYNE: Monroeville 51–46 Milford; Garrett 65–50 Wawaka; Monroeville 37–25 Garrett. Officials: Wilbur May, Charles McManus, Allen Klinck.

HAMMOND: Hammond 51–47 Gary Emerson; Michigan City 63–51 Brook; Hammond 48–40 Michigan City. Officials: Jim Crowe, Devon Eaton, Walter Thurston.

HUNTINGTON: Portland 53–26 Chester Center; Hartford Center 51–32 Huntington; Portland 51–38 Hartford Center. Officials: Clyde Gentry, John Magnabosco, John Walker.

INDIANAPOLIS: Anderson 39–38 Greenfield; Indianapolis Washington 60–44 Speedway; Anderson 45–41 Washington. Officials: Cecil Young, Maurice Jordan, Cyril Birge.

JEFFERSONVILLE: New Albany 58–44 Bedford; Seymour 35–18 St. Francis; New Albany 39–29 Seymour. Officials: Dean Malaska, Eugene Glaze, William Coulter.

LAFAYETTE: Lafayette 45–37 Lebanon; Rossville 63–35 Freeland Park; Lafayette 58–46 Rossville. Officials: Don McBride, John Hilligoss, George Bender.

LOGANSPORT: Logansport 38–35 Brookston; Peru 45–44 Delphi; Peru 44–43 Logansport. Officials: Arthur Lloyd, George Collyer, Cecil Tharp.

MARION: Marion 53–29 Sharpsville; Chester Twp. 48–46 Kokomo; Chester Twp. 76–54 Marion. Officials: Paul Boehm, Ross Dorsett, Paul Bateman.

MARTINSVILLE: Bloomington 44–42 Terre Haute Wiley; Solsberry 51–49 Brazil; Bloomington 60–35 Solsberry. Officials: Robert Hoffman, Clarence Tolbert, Clyde Castle.

MUNCIE: Parker 45–39 New Castle; Muncie Central 48–36 Richmond; Central 54–39 Parker. Officials: Norris Ward, L. E. Fink, Jack O'Neal.

RUSHVILLE: Connersville 31–29 Rushville; Lawrenceburg 41–29 Napoleon; Lawrenceburg 46–36 Connersville. Officials: Lores Lehman, Walter Bonham, Roland Baker.

SHELBYVILLE: Columbus 43–39 Franklin; Madison 65–38 Greensburg; Madison 55–40 Columbus. Officials: William E. Pointer, Robert Derrington, Evan Crawley.

SOUTH BEND: Elkhart 41–36 Culver; Central 65–45 Richland Center; Central 40–38 Elkhart. Officials: Marvin Todd, J. W. Johnson, Jay L. Mertz.

VINCENNES: Jasper 48–22 Shelburn; Vincennes 51–48 Loogootee; Jasper 48–43 Vincennes. Officials: C.N. Phillips, Frank Jarrell, G.P. Silver.

1948 SEMI–FINALS

BLOOMINGTON: Evansville Central 61–49 Bloomington; Jasper 53–50 New Albany; Central 54–40 Jasper. Officials: Marvin Todd, Jack O'Neal, Jim Crowe, George Bender.

INDIANAPOLIS: Anderson 39–38 Madison; Lawrenceburg 43–39 Crawfordsville; Anderson 44–43 Lawrenceburg. Officials: C. N. Phillips, Walter Thurston, William E. Pointer, Clyde Castle.

LAFAYETTE: Peru 45–44 South Bend Central; Lafayette 44–39 Hammond; Lafayette 60–53 Peru. Officials: Paul Bateman, Roland Baker, Ray Lackey, W.N. Reimann.

MUNCIE: Portland 65–54 Chester Twp.; Muncie Central 49–38 Monroeville; Central 56–47 Portland. Officials: Dean Malaska, Allen Klinck, G.P. Silver, Robert Hoffman.

1948 FINALS—March 20

INDIANAPOLIS (Butler Fieldhouse): Evansville Central 48–40 Muncie Central; Lafayette 60–48 Anderson; and Lafayette 54–42 Evansville Central . Officials: Dean Malaska, G.P. Silver, Jim Crowe, Paul Bateman.

1949 SECTIONALS

ANDERSON: Summitville 49–40 Alexandria; Pendleton 42–36 Frankton; Markleville 48–42 St. Mary's; Lapel 45–43 Anderson; Summitville 54–43 Pendleton; Markleville 63–57 Lapel; Summitville 68–43 Markleville. Officials: J. C. LaFollette, Norman Morrison.

ATTICA: Richland Twp. 33–32 Covington; Attica 65–45 Hillsboro; Pine Village 43–38 West Lebanon; Veedersburg 40–26 Wallace; Perrysville 45–36 Kingman; Richland Twp. 37–36 Williamsport; Attica 58–36 Pine Village; Perrysville 41–30 Veedersburg; Attica 50–47 Richland Twp.; Attica 57–30 Perrysville. Officials: Roy Brann, M. N. Delph, Harry Frick.

AUBURN–GARRETT: (At Auburn): Churubusco 45–17 Hamilton; Auburn 52–43 Butler; Spencerville 38–26 Orland; Garrett 52–50 Ashley; Auburn 62–39 Churubusco; Garrett 42–39 Spencerville; (At Garrett): Angola 57–47 Metz; Fremont 62–29 Scott Center; Salem Center 43–38 Pleasant Lake; Waterloo 49–48 Concord Twp.; Angola 56–37 Fremont; Salem Center 53–39

Tourney Time

Waterloo; (At Auburn): Auburn 57–33 Garrett; Angola 52–39 Salem Center; Auburn 71–47 Angola. Officials: Robert Dornte, Lloyd Bryan, Everett Havens, Burl McKenzie, Gerald Strickler, Gerald Reinke.

AURORA: Dillsboro 51–39 Rising Sun; Guilford 45–42 Aurora; Bright 49–34 Moores Hill; Patriot 35–33 Vevay; Lawrenceburg 66–37 Dillsboro; Guilford 53–30 Bright; Lawrenceburg 61–30 Patriot; Lawrenceburg 66–34 Guilford. Officials: James Patterson, Wray Holbrook.

BATESVILLE: Batesville 44–39 Holton; Milan 36–34 Versailles Osgood 34–25 Cross Plains; New Marion 44–42 Napoleon; Batesville 55–32 Sunman; Milan 33–24 Osgood; Batesville 25–23 New Marion; Batesville 50–40 Milan. Officials: Leon Hodson, George Danforth

BEDFORD: Huron 34–23 Fayetteville; Bedford 48–29 Shawswick; Marshall Twp. 41–39 Mitchell (ot); Tunnelton 39–38 Williams, Oolitic 45–22 Heltonville; Bedford 54–23 Huron; Tunnelton 43–37 Marshall Twp.; Bedford 37–36 Oolitic; Bedford 45–30 Tunnelton. Officials: Robert Hoffman, Warren Dee Williams.

BLUFFTON: Lancaster Central 38–34 Union Center; Bluffton 46–45 Liberty Center; Rockcreek Center 37–31 Ossian; Petroleum 41–40 Jackson Center; Lancaster Central 63–40 Chester Center; Bluffton 40–32 Rockcreek; Lancaster Central 42–34 Petroleum; Lancaster Central 40–25 Bluffton. Officials: Jay Mertz, Oscar Samuels

BOONVILLE: Tennyson 36–13 Millersburg; Newburgh 43–31 Elberfeld; Boonville 37–34 Chandler; Lynnville 62–14 Selvin; Tennyson 45–26 Folsomville; Boonville 45–43 Newburgh; Lynnville 29–28 Tennyson; Lynnville 43–41 Boonville. Officials: Robert Rose, William Coulter.

BRAZIL: Quincy 36–33 Staunton; Ashboro 44–27 Bowling Green; Patricksburg 30–20 Cory; Brazil 39–19 Van Buren; Spencer 41–28 Clay City; Gosport 59–32 Coal City; Quincy 47–27 Freedom; Patricksburg 30–26 Ashboro; Brazil 55–40 Spencer; Gosport 48–27 Quincy; Brazil 33–30 Patricksburg; Brazil 40–35 Gosport. Officials: Roland Baker, Robert Fink, Roderick Witt.

CANNELTON: Dale 76–30 Leavenworth; Cannelton 61–36 Oil Twp.; Rockport 51–39 Chrisney; Tell City 70–29 Troy; Dale 40–34 Luce Twp.; Cannelton 76–37 Rockport; Dale 51–41 Tell City; Dale 43–33 Cannelton. Officials: Donald DeVault, William Dixon.

CLINTON: Tangier 44–39 Bridgeton; St. Bernice 45–32 Union Twp.; Mecca 41–37 Montezuma; Bloomingdale 63–35 Cayuga; Rosedale 41–37 Newport; Rockville 47–30 Hillsdale; Clinton 45–34 Marshall; Dana 57–39 Greene Twp.; Tangier 57–28 St. Bernice; Bloomingdale 59–37 Mecca; Rockville 41–36 Rosedale; Clinton 45–28 Dana; Bloomingdale 22–14 Tangier; Clinton 40–27 Rockville; Clinton 35–29 Bloomingdale. Officials: Charles Marshall, Foster Nichols, Evan Crawley, Robert Quillen.

CONNERSVILLE: Whitewater 43–34 Alquina; Bentonville 50–34 Fairview; Brookville 49–31 Springfield Twp.; Liberty 43–34 Harrisburg; Connersville 59–24 Kitchel; Orange 43–18 Laurel; Brownsville 62–39 Whitewater; Brookville 44–35 Bentonville; Connersville 48–32 Liberty; Brownsville 43–41 Orange; Connersville 45–26 Brookville; Connersville 33–23 Brownsville. Officials: C.O. Walls, James Sanders, John Simon.

CRAWFORDSVILLE: Ladoga 46–28 New Ross; New Market 47–40 New Richmond; Crawfordsville 46–29 Waynetown; Waveland 32–26 Linden; Bowers 40–32 Darlington; Alamo 46–40 Wingate; New Market 46–45 Ladoga; Waveland 40–37 Crawfordsville; Bowers 52–42 Alamo; Waveland 42–41 New Market (ot); Waveland 66–48 Bowers. Officials: William Schaefer, Allen Klinck, Gil Smith.

DANVILLE: Speedway 48–36 Danville; North Salem 47–33 Pittsboro; Avon 37–35 New

Winchester; Amo 55–30 Lizton; Charlton 46–33 Stilesville; Plainfield 52–51 Clayton; Speedway 43–33 Brownsburg; Avon 44–36 North Salem; Amo 54–49 Charlton; Speedway 56–31 Plainfield; Amo 40–39 Avon; Amo 51–44 Speedway. Officials: A. M. Franklin, Herbert Brammell, Ray Lackey.

DECATUR: Decatur Catholic 41–22 Pleasant Mills; Kirkland Twp. 44–42 Geneva; Monroe 57–34 Monmouth; Berne 41–37 Jefferson Twp.; Decatur 44–36 Hartford Twp.; Kirkland Twp. 41–34 Decatur Catholic; Monroe 50–31 Berne; Decatur 49–38 Kirkland Twp.; Decatur 56–37 Monroe. Officials: George Collyer, Roscoe Hall.

DEMOTTE (St. Joseph's College): DeMotte 44–20 Tefft; Brook 43–20 Fair Oaks; Remington 52–43 Morocco; Wheatfield 34–25 Kentland; Goodland 39–29 Mt. Ayr; Rensselaer 51–23 DeMotte; Remington 35–24 Brook; Wheatfield 46–23 Goodland; Rensselaer 34–18 Remington; Rensselaer 49–26 Wheatfield. Officials: Herbert Vaulk, Fred Vaulk, Noble Benbow.

ELWOOD: Greentown 54–40 Northwestern; Jackson Twp. 49–40 Russiaville; Kokomo 48–37 Elwood; Western 58–39 Union Twp.; Jackson Twp. 52–40 Greentown; Kokomo 47–38 Western; Kokomo 42–41 Jackson Twp. Officials: Charles Northam, Arthur Gross.

EVANSVILLE: Memorial 68–41 Cynthiana; Bosse 68–32 Poseyville; Lincoln 38–36 Reitz; Griffin 37–33 Wadesville; Mt. Vernon 44–33 New Harmony; Central 51–48 Memorial; Bosse 55–52 Lincoln; Griffin 63–51 Mt Vernon; Central 43–38 Bosse; Central 64–44 Griffin. Officials: G. P. Silver, Kenneth Merder, Clayton Nichols.

FARMLAND: Winchester 47–42 Green; Saratoga 62–47 Union City; Lynn 44–34 Losantville; Spartanburg 59–37 Stoney Creek; Jackson 53–48 Wayne; Farmland 57–22 Lincoln; Parker 36–32 McKinley; Huntsville 55–40 Modoc; Winchester 41–28 Saratoga; Spartanburg 34–33 Lynn; Jackson 43–39 Farmland; Parker 51–40 Huntsville; Winchester 48–38 Spartanburg; Parker 40–30 Jackson; Winchester 47–31 Parker. Officials: Roy Gardner, Robert Hughes, Clay Layman, Francis Richards.

FLORA: Delphi 82–26 Adams Twp.; Cutler 48–36 Burlington; Camden 44–30 Carrollton; Deer Creek 39–20 Rockfield; Flora 45–40 Delphi; Camden 31–24 Cutler; Flora 43–32 Deer Creek; Camden 47–41 Flora. Officials: Otto Albright, Charles DeBusk.

FORT BRANCH: Princeton 60–32 Mt. Olympus; Francisco 39–34 Mackey; Owensville 55–49 Princeton; Fort Branch 66–22 Hazelton; Oakland City 75–29 Patoka; Fort Branch 58–52 Haubstadt; Fort Branch 60–57 Oakland City; Francisco 33–31 Owensville; Fort Branch 44–39 Francisco. Officials: Wilford Susott, Alfred Rose, David Royalty, Lloyd Whipple.

FORT WAYNE: Harlan 41–35 Leo; Coesse 41–39 Maumee Twp. (Woodburn); South Side 42–27 Lafayette Central; North Side 71–29 Arcola; Coesse 40–38 Harlan; North Side 46–36 South Side; Monroeville 43–31 Elmhurst; New Haven 40–39 Concordia; Central 46–33 Central Catholic; Hoagland 37–29 Huntertown; Monroeville 37–31 Haven; Central 54–37 Hoagland; North Side 46–30 Coesse; 49–42 Monroeville; Central 51–49 North Side. Officials: Don Polizotto, Edward Herbert, Harold Nelson, Hugh Bergstrom, Harold Carlson, Frank Sanders.

FRANKFORT: Washington Twp.46–26 Forest; Colfax 26–24 Kirklin; Frankfort 49–41 Sugar Creek; Rossville 62–38 Scircleville; Mulberry 43–36 Jackson Twp.; Michigantown 46–24 Washington Twp.; Frankfort 28–10 Colfax; Rossville 39–31 Mulberry; Frankfort 34–23 Michigantown; Frankfort 52–39 Rossville. Officials: Melvin Wilson, Paul Dazey, Ralph Renegar.

FRANKLIN: Union 68–21 Van Buren; Franklin 66–43 Nineveh; Center Grove 48–42 Edinburg; Whiteland 56–32 Clark; Helms 54–46 Trafalgar; Greenwood 56–44 Nashville; Union

Tourney Time

46–37 Franklin; Whiteland 36–33 Center Grove; Helmsburg 42–39 Greenwood; Whiteland 52–32 Union; Helmsburg 38–29 Whiteland. Officials: Robert Cherry, Kermit Spurgeon, John Magnabosco.

GARY–VALPARAISO: (At Gary): William A. Wirt 36–32 Emerson; Horace Mann 39–36 Tolleston; Gary Edison 46–44 Roosevelt; Froebel 52–34 Lew Wallace; Horace Mann 48–44 William A. Wirt; Froebel 52–50 Gary Edison; (At Valparaiso): Valparaiso 58–32 Liberty Center; Morgan Twp. 53–41 Boone Grove; Chesterton 42–38 Hebron; Kouts 39–35 Washington Twp.; Valparaiso 50–39 Morgan Twp.; Chesterton 52–40 Kouts; (At Gary): Horace Mann 42–41 Froebel; Valparaiso 52–37 Chesterton; Horace Mann 43–34 Valparaiso. Officials: Paul Bateman, Don Lieberum, Paul Hostetler, Ed Kurtz.

GREENCASTLE: Roachdale 37–26 Reelsville; Belle Union 44–35 Bainbridge; Greencastle 52–41 Russellville; Fillmore 46–30 Cloverdale; Roachdale 48–41 Belle Union; Fillmore 32–24 Greencastle; Fillmore 28–26 Roachdale. Officials: Otto Crosley, Forrest Ballinger.

GREENFIELD: McCordsville 32–22 Maxwell; Greenfield 40–35 New Palestine; Franklin Twp. 40–20 Mt. Comfort; Charlottesville 39–27 Wilkinson; Fortville 54–34 Eden; Greenfield 68–45 McCordsville; Franklin Twp. 38–24 Charlottesville; Fortville 45–39 Greenfield; Fortville 53–32 Franklin Twp.. Officials: Thomas Stirling, Harold Porter.

GREENSBURG: Burney 61–34 Vernon; North Vernon 47–42 Jackson Twp.; Clarksburg 40–30 New Point; Greensburg 56–40 St. Paul; Sandusky 51–41 Sandcreek Twp.; Burney 48–36 North Vernon; Greensburg 58–36 Clarksburg; Burney 44–28 Sandusky; Greensburg 68–40 Burney. Officials: Jack O'Neal, John Gwin.

HAMMOND: Clark 42–39 Tech; Noll 47–43 Crown Point; Griffith 56–51 Dyer; Hammond High 53–48 Lowell; East Gary Edison 48–40 East Chicago Washington; Portage 42–38 Merrillville; East Chicago Roosevelt 49–18 Wheeler; Whiting 49–35 Hobart; Clark 81–43 Noll; Hammond High 47–44 Griffith; Portage 38–34 East Gary Edison; East Chicago Roosevelt 46–40 Whiting; Hammond High 44–40 Clark; East Chicago Roosevelt 45–34 Portage; Hammond High 44–37 East Chicago Roosevelt. Officials: Marvin Todd, Art Cosgrove, Walter Bonham, Frank Kresler.

HARTFORD CITY: Jefferson (Randolph Co.) 56–48 Dunkirk; Ridgeville 67–38 Gov. I.P. Gray; Roll 42–38 Bryant; Montpelier 39–38 Redkey; Hartford City 71–24 Madison Twp.; Pennville 51–18 Poling; Jefferson 41–27 Portland; Roll 45–37 Ridgeville; Hartford City 50–30 Montpelier; Jefferson 42–28 Pennville; Roll 33–29 Hartford City; Jefferson 51–36 Roll. Officials: Wilbur May, James Ridge, Ward Mosbaugh.

HUNTINGTON: Huntington Catholic 63–33 Salamonie Twp.; Jackson Twp. 44–23 Rock Creek; Jefferson Center 48–44 Clear Creek; Polk Twp. 42–41 Huntington Twp.; Andrews 55–46 Lancaster Center; Union Twp. 40–28 Bippus; Huntington 79–24 Wayne Twp.; Jefferson Twp. 60–22 Markle; Huntington Catholic 43–41 Jackson Twp.; Jefferson Center 45–43 Polk Twp.; Union Twp. 41–39 Andrews; Huntington 55–29 Jefferson Twp.; Huntington Catholic 54–38 Jefferson Center; Huntington 41–20 Union Twp.; Huntington Catholic 41–39 Huntington. Officials: Walter Moss, Gerald Alexander, Leland Wright, James Koons.

INDIANAPOLIS: Cathedral 28–26 Sacred Heart; Lawrence Central 41–38 Warren Central; Broad Ripple 52–47 Howe; Southport 47–46 Beech Grove; Tech 42–40 Washington; Shortridge 42–32 Manual; School for the Deaf 35–32 Decatur Central; Crispus Attucks 40–29 Ben Davis; Lawrence Central 50–49 Cathedral; Southport 43–39 Broad Ripple; Tech 38–28 Shortridge; Crispus Attucks 44–31 School for the Deaf; Southport 39–36 Lawrence Central; Tech 45–37

Crispus Attucks; Tech 49–48 Southport. Officials: Don McBride, Burl Shook, John Hilligoss, Maurice Jordan.

JASPER: Huntingburg 47–28 Otwell; Jasper 56–26 Dubois; Holland 59–35 Birdseye; Petersburg 50–35 Ireland; Winslow 76–23 Stendal; Huntingburg 40–39 Spurgeon; Jasper 36–28 Holland; Winslow 48–38 Petersburg; Jasper 44–35 Huntingburg; Jasper 48–39 Winslow. Officials: Clyde Castle, Robert Derrington, Eugene Perkins.

JEFFERSONVILLE: Corydon 45–29 Henryville; Borden 51–36 New Middleton; New Albany 64–22 Elizabeth; Scribner 69–36 New Amsterdam; Jeffersonville 66–21 Lanesville; Mauckport 68–39 Laconia; Charlestown 61–19 Taylor; Silver Creek 59–32 Georgetown; Corydon 47–26 Borden; New Albany 49–26 Scribner; Jeffersonville 72–44 Mauckport; Silver Creek 48–38 Charlestown; New Albany 43–30 Corydon; Jeffersonville 58–47 Silver Creek; Jeffersonville 41–32 New Albany. Officials: Irvin Thrasher, Leland Terrell, Ed Straith-Miller, Howard Wright.

KENDALLVILLE–ALBION: (At Albion): Topeka 52–26 Springfield Twp.; Wolcottville 34–32 Lima; Howe Military 59–47 Wawaka; Wolf Lake 31–29 LaGrange (ot); Topeka 40–36 Wolcottville; Howe Military 50–36 Wolf Lake; (At Kendallville): Kendallville 47–29 Shipshewana; Avilla 42–32 Scott; Ligonier 40–33 Rome City; Albion 40–39 Brighton; Kendallville 43–40 Albion 41–39 Ligonier; (At Kendallville): Howe Military 36–23 Topeka; Kendallville 47–41 Albion; Howe Military 39–38 Kendallville (ot). Officials: J. W. Johnson, Myron Weldy, Ray E. Aldrich, M. E. Somers, William Harmon.

LAFAYETTE: Battle Ground 42–35 West Point; West Lafayette 62–33 Wea; Klondike 55–38 Buck Creek; Shadeland 57–56 Twp.; Stockwell 56–41 Monitor; Jefferson 76–34 Montmorenci; 43–42 Romney; Battle Ground 63–26 Clarks Hill; West Lafayette 61–42 Klondike; Shadeland 50–43 Stockwell; Jefferson 47–38 Dayton; West Lafayette 47–41 Battle Ground; Jefferson 75–34 Shadeland; Jefferson 50–35 West Lafayette. Officials: Donald Cooper, Herschel Eastman, Cecil Bosstick, S.T. Proffitt.

LAPORTE: Mill Creek 35–30 Rolling Prairie; Stillwell 56–27 Springfield Twp.; Hanna 49–33 Wanatah; Clinton Twp. 56–31 Jackson Twp.; St. Mary's 48–38 La Crosse; Michigan City 45–25 Union La Porte 57–25 Union Mills; Westville 32–22 Kingsbury; Mill Creek 40–39 Stillwell; Clinton 52–43 Hanna; Michigan City 31–25 St. Mary's; La Porte 49–34 Westville; Mill Creek 37–34 Clinton; LaPorte 38–30 Michigan City; LaPorte 51–31 Mill Creek. Officials: Charles McManus, Maurice De Schryver, Sam Massette, William Ellis.

LEBANON: Thorntown 37–33 Dover; Lebanon 36–28 Jackson Twp.; Whitestown 40–38 Pike Twp.; Zionsville 63–30 Perry Central; Thorntown 42–32 Pinnell; Lebanon 42–37 Whitestown; Zionsville 48–35 Thorntown; Zionsville 41–40 Lebanon. Officials: W.N. Reimann, Cloyd Julian.

LINTON: Linton 38–37 Marco; Solsberry 53–42 Scotland; Jasonville 40–22 Lyons; Bloomfield 51–40 Midland; Worthington 58–42 Switz City; Linton 33–29 Solsberry; Bloomfield 58–41 Jasonville; Worthington 39–34 Linton; Worthington 47–45 Bloomfield (ot). Officials: Layall Fisher, Loren Mitchell.

LOGANSPORT: Galveston 62–40 Onward; Logansport 64–36 Young America; Lucerne 53–39 New Waverly; Twelve Mile 62–32 Metea; Washington Twp. 48–35 Royal Center; Galveston 30–26 Walton; Logansport 62–43 Lucerne; Washington Twp. 43–39 Twelve Mile; Galveston 29–28 Logansport; Washington Twp. 38–29 Galveston. Officials: Dean Geyer, Edward Stuteville, Byron Alexander.

Tourney Time

MADISON: New Washington 43–32 North Madison; Saluda 45–42 Deputy; Central 43–33 Paris Crossing; Austin 53–28 Dupont; Madison 63–27 Lexington; Scottsburg 64–30 Hanover; New Washington 53–23 Saluda; Austin 56–47 Central; Madison 64–30 Scottsburg; New Washington 27–26 Austin; Madison 88–40 New Washington. Officials: Morris Stevens, Alvin Heller, Herschel Bales.

MARION: Fairmount 42–39 Van Buren; Mississinewa 57–34 Sweetser; Swayzee 50–49 Jefferson Twp. (ot); Marion 66–43 St. Paul; Fairmount 39–37 Mississinewa; Marion 58–54 Swayzee; Marion 40–34 Fairmount. Officials: Harold McSwane, Walter Stebing.

MARTINSVILLE: University 79–62 Unionville; Martinsville 64–32 Paragon; Stinesville 58–39 Eminence; Bloomington 67–42 Ellettsville; Monrovia 47–45 Smithville; Mooresville 51–49 Morgantown; Martinsville 41–30 University; Bloomington 74–56 Stinesville; Mooresville 47–44 Monrovia; Bloomington 37–34 Martinsville; Bloomington 53–43 Mooresville. Officials: Odilo Berger, Loren Harris, Frank White.

MONTICELLO: Brookston 51–33 Monon; Monticello 65–35 Burnettsville; Wolcott 43–32 Idaville; Chalmers 40–33 Buffalo; Brookston 50–35 Reynolds; Monticello 49–46 Wolcott. Brookston 50–25 Chalmers; Brookston 42–30 Monticello. Officials: Joe Mullins, Raymond Trobaugh.

MUNCIE: Selma 46–37 Yorktown; Eaton 39–31 Harrison; Burris 54–49 Center; Cowan 42–39 Daleville; DeSoto 54–50 Gaston; Central 67–39 Royerton; Albany 52–50 Selma; Burris 47–34 Eaton; Cowan 49–28 DeSoto; Central (Muncie) 54–17 Albany; Burris (Muncie) 41–37 Cowan; Central (Muncie) 46–37 Burris. Officials: Lores Lehman, James Haywood, Cecil Tharp.

NAPPANEE: Wakarusa 44–31 Cromwell; New Paris 33–17 Elkhart; Nappanee 47–41 Bristol; New Paris 30–17 Wakarusa; Goshen 34–31 Middlebury; Concord 48–35 Jefferson; Millersburg 38–33 Baugo Twp.; Concord 33–27 Goshen; New Paris 43–30 Nappanee; Concord 58–24 Millersburg; Concord 42–25 New Paris. Officials: Gene Winks, Victor Griewank, John Janzaruk.

NEW CASTLE: Straughn 32–31 Middletown; Mt. Summit 35–27 Kennard; New Lisbon 46–41 Lewisville; Straughn 47–38 Mt. Summit; New Castle 59–29 Knightstown; Sulphur Springs 56–43 Mooreland; Cadiz 39–38 Spiceland; New Castle 73–41 Sulphur Springs; Straughn 53–34 New Lisbon; New Castle 40–16 Cadiz; New Castle 61–34 Straughn. Officials: Myrle Rife, Ross Dorsett, William McNamara.

OTTERBEIN: Ambia 41–28 Boswell; Otterbein 46–34 Wadena; Fowler 49–39 Freeland Park; Earl Park 48–35 Pine Twp.; Gilboa 41–31 Raub; Oxford 39–33 Ambia; Fowler 31–28 Otterbein; Gilboa 36–34 Earl Park; Fowler 43–30 Oxford; Fowler 53–33 Gilboa. Officials: Clayton Patterson, Clarence Myles, Robert Gregory.

PAOLI: Paoli 59–29 English; West Baden 53–40 Salem; Orleans 33–31 Mt. St. Frances; Campbellsburg 43–42 Pekin; Morgan Twp. 61–26 Hardinsburg; French Lick 69–29 Depauw; New Salisbury 45–43 Milltown; Paoli 48–40 Marengo; West Baden 41–40 Orleans; Morgan Twp. 57–35 Campbellsburg; French Lick 60–47 New Salisbury; Paoli 52–40 West Baden; Morgan Twp. 59–26 French Lick; Paoli 59–41 Morgan Twp. Officials: Ivan Sprinkle, Chris Moritz, Edgar Braun, Robert Grannan.

PERU: Mexico 46–37 Chili; Clay Twp. 63–20 Butler Twp.; Bunker Hill 54–40 Converse; Gilead 52–46 Deedsville; Peru 56–34 Macy; Clay Twp. 43–35 Mexico; Bunker Hill 42–37 Gilead; Peru 54–30 Clay Twp.; Peru 40–32 Bunker Hill. Officials: Norris Ward, Albert Etter.

PLYMOUTH: LaPaz 55–46 Grovertown; Culver 65–41 Tyner; Tippecanoe 55–48 Bremen; LaPaz 78–39 West Twp.; Culver 67–35 Tippecanoe; Hamlet 52–36 Argos; North Judson 66–20

San Pierre; Plymouth 53–50 Bourbon; Hamlet 37–34 Knox; North Judson 56–27 Plymouth; LaPaz 66–49 Culver; North Judson 45–38 Hamlet; North Judson 53–51 LaPaz. Officials: DeVon Eaton, Charles Meade, Bruce Swinford.

RICHMOND: Centerville 49–37 Cambridge City; Webster 51–37 Boston; Richmond 55–40 Hagerstown; Whitewater 49–39 Williamsburg; Fountain City 60–21 Milton; Greens Fork 53–35 Economy; Centerville 46–36 Webster; Richmond 73–35 Whitewater; Fountain City 28–25 Greens Fork; Richmond 42–40 Centerville; Fountain City 40–34 Richmond. Officials: Eugene Sparks, Robert Hobbs, John Walker.

ROCHESTER: Richland Center 49–30 Fulton; Akron 70–25 Rochester 40–37 Monterey; Grass Creek 59–34 Francesville; Medaryville 40–39 Talma; Leiters Ford 43–42 Star City; Winamac 55–45 Kewanna; Richland Center 44–38 Akron; Rochester 41–36 Grass Creek; Leiters Ford 48–35 Medaryville; Winamac 47–45 Richland Center; Rochester 45–32 Leiters Ford; Rochester 40–36 Winamac. Officials: John Cover, Phillip Kammerer, Verlin Jackson.

RUSHVILLE: Carthage 59–50 Milroy; Arlington 41–39 Morton Memorial; New Salem 74–40 Manilla; Rushville 53–39 Mays; Carthage 59–24 Raleigh; New Salem 41–40 Arlington; Rushville 42–33 Carthage; Rushville 54–50 New Salem. Officials: Eugene Glaze, Lowell Barnett.

SEYMOUR: Brownstown 39–38 Cortland; Medora 55–43 Crothersville; Seymour 65–28 Hayden; Freetown 54–43 Clearspring; Vallonia 53–41 Tampico; Medora 48–46 Brownstown (2ot); Freetown 30–25 Seymour; Medora 42–38 Vallonia; Medora 48–38 Freetown. Officials: Herbert Schwomeyer, Wilbur Schumacher.

SHELBYVILLE: Shelbyville 57–18 Boggstown; Moral Twp. 59–44 Mt. Auburn; Morristown 52–38 Hope; Fairland 61–34 Clifford; Columbus 53–27 Flat Rock; Shelbyville 23–16 Waldron; Morristown 58–48 Moral Twp.; Fairland 45–41 Columbus; Morristown 34–23 Shelbyville; Fairland 59–40 Morristown. Officials: C. N. Phillips, Joe Conover, Charles Jones.

SOUTH BEND: Greene Twp. 59–55 Walkerton; Wilson 53–38 South Bend Catholic, Central 42–41 Mishawaka; Washington 37–33 Greene Twp.; Central 58–34 Wilson; North Liberty 36–34 Central Catholic; Riley 46–41 Madison Twp.; Washington-Clay 36–22 Adams; New Carlisle 38–36 Lakeville; North Liberty 44–42 Riley; Washington-Clay 61–46 New Carlisle; Central 36–27 Washington; Washington-Clay 54–39 North Liberty; Central 45–27 Washington-Clay. Officials: Stanley Dubis, John Tatum, Arthur Lloyd, Richard Duffield.

SULLIVAN: New Lebanon 27–23 Hymera; Shelburn 53–35 Merom; Sullivan 60–42 Fairbanks; Dugger 52–17 Carlisle; Graysville 44–32 Farmersburg; New Lebanon 35–29 Pleasantville; Shelburn 37–30 Sullivan; Dugger 49–45 Graysville; Shelburn 46–36 New Lebanon; Shelburn 35–31 Dugger. Officials: Yank Terry, Ray Manaugh, Frank Smith.

TERRE HAUTE: Glenn 54–23 Fayette; Gerstmeyer 65–41 West Terre Haute; Wiley 40–39 Prairie Creek; Garfield 45–40 Fontanet; Laboratory 57–53 Honey Creek; Riley 43–37 Concannon; Blackhawk 37–35 Pimento; Glenn 43–30 Otter Creek; Gerstmeyer 42–31 Wiley; Laboratory 49–41 Garfield; Riley 63–46 Blackhawk; Glenn 47–46 Gerstmeyer; Laboratory 57–42 Riley; Laboratory 56–53 Glenn. Officials: Lowell Willis, J. B. Williams, Clarence Tolbert, Wayne Hammond.

TIPTON: Tipton 55–33 Walnut Grove; Sheridan 53–31 Windfall; Sharpsville 26–22 Prairie; Sheridan 41–40 Tipton; Carmel 44–35 Jefferson Twp.; Westfield 45–40 Jackson Central; Fishers 31–30 Noblesville; Westfield 44–42 Carmel; Sheridan 27–25 Sharpsville; Westfield 44–24 Fishers; Sheridan 45–32 Westfield. Officials: Herbert Edwards, Raymond King, Lawrence Leland, Melvin Newlin.

Tourney Time

VINCENNES: Bruceville 52–43 Decker; Fritchton 56–29 Freelandville; Monroe City 54–38 Wheatland; Oaktown 35–13 Decker Chapel; Bicknell 56–35 Edwardsport; Vincennes 49–33 Sandborn; Fritchton 35–31 Bruceville; Monroe City 66–31 Oaktown; Vincennes 61–51 Bicknell; Monroe City 55–44 Fritchton; Monroe City 49–48 Vincennes. Officials: Robert W. Babbs, Robert Hudson, Cyril Birge.

WABASH (Honeywell gymnasium): Chester Twp. 70–27 Somerset; Wabash 15–4 Laketon; Roann 50–36 Chippewa; Chester 47–24 South Whitley; Wabash 52–44 Roann; (Wabash High School gymnasium): North Manchester 54–46 Washington Center; Lafontaine 32–28 Linlawn; Lagro 32–30 Lincolnville; North Manchester 49–35 Urbana; Lafontaine 55–46 Lagro; (Honeywell): Wabash 53–35 Chester; LaFontaine 54–50 North Manchester; Wabash 62–32 LaFontaine. Officials: Devon Phelps, Don Engle, Alvin Vincent, Robert Windsor.

WARSAW: Etna Green 40–27 Claypool; Beaver Dam 51–45 Larwill; Sidney 32–29 Burkett (2ot); Syracuse 44–41 Atwood; Leesburg 47–39 Silver Lake; North Webster 51–49 Milford (ot); Pierceton 48–41 Mentone; Warsaw 43–41 Columbia City; Beaver Dam 40–38 Etna Green; Syracuse 53–27 Sidney; North Webster 43–40 Leesburg; Warsaw 50–46 Pierceton; Syracuse 63–62 Beaver Dam (ot); Warsaw 65–48 North Webster; Syracuse 57–53 Warsaw. Officials: Dwight Byerly, Charles Bobilya, H. F. Naught, Leonard Lupold.

WASHINGTON: Odon 42–32 Epsom; Barr Twp. 52–42 Shoals; Washington 52–30 Plainville; Washington Catholic 45–28 Elnora; Loogootee 78–26 Alfordsville; Barr Twp. 77–39 Odon; Washington Catholic 42–36 Washington; Loogootee 33–28 Barr Twp.; Loogootee 51–37 Washington Catholic. Officials: August Banko, Hugh Thrasher.

1949 REGIONALS

ATTICA: Fillmore 35–27 Waveland; Attica 43–42 Clinton (ot); Attica 62–32 Fillmore. Officials: Devon Eaton, George Collyer, Arthur Lloyd.

BEDFORD: Bedford 48–41 Jeffersonville; Paoli 59–40 Medora; Bedford 28–24 Paoli. Officials: Jack O'Neal, Clyde Castle, Robert Hobbs.

BLOOMINGTON: Bloomington 61–39 Worthington; Terre Haute Laboratory 63–59 Brazil; Bloomington 43–39 Laboratory. Officials: Cyril Birge, Robert Derrington, William Coulter.

EVANSVILLE: Central 42–34 Lynnville; Dale 59–35 Ft. Branch; Central 45–38 Dale. Officials: Clarence Tolbert, Lowell Willis, Evan Crawley.

FORT WAYNE: Auburn 45–20 Howe Military; Central 59–46 Syracuse; Auburn 51–47 Central. Officials: Don McBride, John Hilligoss, Eugene Glaze.

GREENSBURG: Fairland 52–46 Greensburg; Madison 59–30 Helmsburg; Madison 56–37 Fairland. Officials: Roland Baker, Raymond Trobaugh, Lores Lehman.

HAMMOND: LaPorte 65–45 Gary Horace Mann; Hammond High 58–46 Rensselaer; Hammond 55–41 LaPorte. Officials: Harold McSwane, J. W. Johnson, Jay Mertz.

HUNTINGTON: Lancaster Central 53–41 Decatur; Jefferson (Randolph Co.) 41–35 Huntington Catholic; Jefferson Twp. 36–34 Lancaster Central. Officials: Herbert Edwards, James Haywood, Sam Massette.

INDIANAPOLIS: Fortville 69–53 Amo; Summitville 49–42 Tech; Summitville 61–41 Fortville. Officials: Wilbur May, Norris Ward, Marvin Todd.

LAFAYETTE: Zionsville 59–49 Fowler; Frankfort 52–36 Lafayette; Frankfort 40–38

Zionsville. Officials: John Walker, Victor Griewank, Robert Hoffman.

LOGANSPORT: Camden 34–30 Washington Twp. (Cass Co.); Brookston 49–47 Peru; Brookston 54–41 Camden. Officials: Maurice Jordan, Thomas Stirling, John Magnabosco.

MARION: Wabash 50–33 Sheridan; Kokomo 57–36 Marion; Kokomo 55–53 Wabash. Officials: C. N. Phillips, Stanley Dubis, Don Polizotto.

MUNCIE: New Castle 54–44 Winchester; Central 43–22 Fountain City; New Castle 30–28 Central. Officials: William Reimann, Walter Bonham, Ray Lackey.

RUSHVILLE: Connersville 43–41 Rushville (2ot); Lawrenceburg 45–29 Batesville; Lawrenceburg 51–34 Connersville. Officials: G.P. Silver, Lawrence Leland, Herbert Schwomeyer.

SOUTH BEND: Central 46–40 Concord Twp.; Rochester 44–35 North Judson; Central 52–26 Rochester. Officials: Charles McManus, Hugh Bergstrom, Paul Bateman.

VINCENNES: Monroe City 35–34 Loogootee; Jasper 61–52 Shelburn; Jasper 57–55 Monroe City. Officials: Allen Klinck, Irvin Thrasher, Cecil Tharp.

1949 SEMI-FINALS

BLOOMINGTON: Jasper 41–33 Bedford; Bloomington 62–46 Evansville Central ; Jasper 50–49 Bloomington. Officials: Marvin Todd, Don McBride, Ray Lackey, William Reimann.

INDIANAPOLIS: Lawrenceburg 61–49 Attica; Madison 53–38 Summitville; Madison 47–40 Lawrenceburg. Officials: Allen Klinck, Lores Lehman, Paul Bateman, Robert Hoffman.

LAFAYETTE: Frankfort 47–35 Hammond High; South Bend Central 66–35 Brookston; Central 59–55 Frankfort. Officials: C.N. Phillips, Clyde Castle, Jack O'Neal, Eugene Glaze.

MUNCIE: Auburn 54–43 Kokomo; New Castle 49–43 Jefferson (Randolph County); Auburn 45–43 New Castle. Officials: Roland Baker, Cyril Birge, G. P. Silver, Charles McManus.

1949 FINALS—March 19

INDIANAPOLIS (Butler Fieldhouse): Madison 53–40 South Bend Central; Jasper 53–48 Auburn; Jasper 62–21 Madison. Officials: Roland Baker, Jack O'Neal, C. N. Phillips, Marvin Todd.

1950–1959

1950 SECTIONALS

ANDERSON: Lapel 58–48 Pendleton; Anderson 67–35 Summitville; Markleville 43–35 Frankton; St. Mary's 53–38 Alexandria; Anderson 46–43 Lapel; Markleville 44–38 St. Mary's; Anderson 59–43 Markleville. Officials: Allen Klinck, John Walker.

ATTICA: Covington 42–35 Hillsboro; Perrysville 57–27 Pine Village; West Lebanon 57–49 Kingman; Richland Twp. 56–26 Wallace; Attica 53–32 Veedersburg; Covington 44–25 Williamsport; Perrysville 53–32 West Lebanon; Richland Twp. 37–34 Attica; Covington 26–25

Tourney Time

Perrysville; Richland Twp. 32–31 Covington. Officials: Ed Kurtz, Clarence Myles, Gil Smith.

BATESVIILLE: Versailles 47–40 Sunman; Osgood 64–47 New Marion; Holton 24–23 Napoleon; Milan 43–39 Cross Plains; Batesville 57–30 Versailles; Osgood 41–21 Holton; Batesville 51–50 Milan; Batesville 39–35 Osgood. Officials: Forest Ballinger, Otto Crosley.

BEDFORD: Mitchell 62–36 Fayettsville; Marshall Twp. 46–42 Oolitic; Shawswick 54–33 Tunnelton; Campbellsburg 56–28 Heltonville; Bedford 55–36 Orleans; Williams 57–41 Huron; Mitchell 42–33 Marshall Twp.; Campbellsburg 48–43 Shawswick; Bedford 51–35 Williams; Mitchell 57–36 Campbellsburg; Mitchell 36–31 Bedford. Officials: Odilo Berger, Cyril Birge, Wilbur Schumacher.

BLOOMINGTON: Mooresville 78–44 Eminence; Smithville 44–43 Monrovia; Morgantown 46–27 Paragon; Ellettsville 55–35 Martinsville; Stinesville 47–41 University; Bloomington 77–53 Unionville; Smithville 58–57 Mooresville; Ellettsville 53–38 Morgantown; Bloomington 68–30 Stinesville; Ellettsville 73–64 Smithville; Ellettsville 61–47 Bloomington. Officials: Robert Hoffman, Otto Hurrle, Ivan Sprinkle.

BLUFFTON: Ossian 37–33 Chester Center; Lancaster Central 24–17 Jackson Twp.; Bluffton 48–30 Ossian; Rockcreek 76–34 Liberty Center Petroleum 39–37 Union Center; Rockcreek Center 59–57 Petroleum (ot); Lancaster Central 47–46 Rockcreek Center. Officials: Walter Bonham, Joe Mullins.

BOONVILLE: Newburgh 57–53 Elberfeld; Tennyson 57–43 Selvin; Lynnville 47–30 Folsomville; Chandler 48–47 Boonville (ot); Newburgh 64–38 Millersburg; Lynnville 51–39 Tennyson; Chandler 55–40 Newburgh; Chandler 57–44 Lynnville. Officials: August Banko, Lester Cornwell.

BRAZIL: Van Buren 56–24 Quincy; Gosport 47–38 Ashboro; Posey Twp. 53–40 Cory; Brazil 46–34 Clay City; Jefferson Twp. 41–36 Bowling Green; Patricksburg 61–32 Freedom; Van Buren 43–32 Spencer; Gosport 53–40 Posey Twp.; Brazil 69–32 Jefferson Twp.; Patricksburg 46–40 Van Buren; Brazil 49–44 Gosport; Brazil 60–49 Patricksburg. Officials: Kenneth Merder, Bruce Swinford, Bill Wood.

CLINTON: Bloomingdale 44–43 St. Bernice; Tangier 45–35 Green Twp.; Mecca 44–43 Newport; Rockville 46–40 Marshall; Rosedale 46–23 Union Twp.; Montezuma 34–31 Bridgeton; Clinton 33–24 Hillsdale; Cayuga 51–43 Dana; Bloomingdale 39–30 Tangier; Rockville 43–34 Mecca; Rosedale 66–39 Montezuma; Clinton 67–40 Cayuga; Rockville 51–40 Bloomingdale; Clinton 56–38 Rosedale; Clinton 48–37 Rockville. Officials: Byron Alexander, Paul Dazey, Robert Gregory, J. C. LaFollette.

CONNERSVILLE: Fairview 37–33 Springfield Twp.; Harrisburg 50–46 Liberty; Whitewater 38–36 Laurel; Brookville 50–39 Bentonville; Alquina 36–34 Brownsville; Connersville 67–32 Kitchel; Fairview 48–32 Harrisburg; Brookville 67–28 Whitewater; Alquina 34–31 Connersville; Brookville 41–39 Fairview; Brookville 55–38 Alquina. Officials: Roy Gardner, Alvin Heller, Chris Moritz.

CRAWFORDSVILLE: Darlington 36–21 Linden; Crawfordsville 45–17 Waynetown; Ladoga 50–33 Alamo; Crawfordsville 37–20 Darlington; New Richmond 41–31 Wingate; New Market 59–41 Bowers; Waveland 46–39 New Ross; New Market 63–36 New Richmond; Crawfordsville 56–35 Ladoga; New Market 54–44 Waveland; New Market 51–43 Crawfordsville. Officials: Noble Benbow, Herbert Brammell, S.T. Proffitt.

DANVILLE: Danville 51–38 Amo; Avon 58–39 Pittsboro; Lizton 45–40 Brownsburg;

Plainfield 43–36 Clayton; Charlton 50–28 Stilesville; Speedway 37–18 North Salem; New Winchester 44–35 Danville; Avon 55–28 Lizton; Charlton 44–40 Plainfield; Speedway 45–30 New Winchester; Avon 32–29 Charlton; Speedway 45–27 Avon. Officials: Cecil Bosstick, J. D. Nickle, William Reimann.

DECATUR: Decatur Catholic 39–37 Berne; Hartford Center 53–40 Jefferson Twp.; Decatur 51–44 Adams Central; Geneva 37–34 Monmouth; Central 73–43 Pleasant Mills; Decatur 53–48 Hartford Center; Decatur Catholic 61–53 Geneva; Decatur 58–46 Decatur Catholic. Officials: Phil Kammerer, Norris Ward.

DELPHI: Camden 45–22 Burlington; Flora 58–50 Buck Creek (ot); Deer Creek 42–39 Carrollton; Cutler 43–39 Delphi; Flora 51–48 Camden; Cutler 44–42 Deer Creek; Flora 58–29 Cutler. Officials: Fred Vaulk, Herbert Vaulk.

EVANSVILLE: Reitz 69–30 New Harmony; Cynthiana 52–51 Mount Vernon; Lincoln 56–24 Griffin; Mater Dei 52–34 Poseyville; Bosse 50–41 Wadesville; Central 33–27 Memorial; Reitz 65–33 Cynthiana; Lincoln 51–40 Mater Dei; Bosse 57–46 Central; Lincoln 47–39 Reitz; Bosse 56–44 Lincoln. Officials: Eugene Perkins, Clarence Tolbert, Robert Rose.

FARMLAND: Union City 73–28 Losantville; Parker 50–44 Spartanburg; Farmland 50–44 Saratoga; Lynn 43–40 Winchester; Jackson Twp. 57–33 Modoc; Green Twp. 58–31 Huntsville; Wayne Twp. 37–25 McKinley; Stoney Creek 33–29 Lincoln; Parker 45–37 Union City; Lynn 41–36 Farmland; Jackson Twp. 42–35 Green Twp.; Stoney Creek 42–34 Wayne Twp.; Lynn 48–37 Parker; Stoney Creek 46–37 Jackson Twp.; Lynn 53–41 Stoney Creek. Officials: Wilbur May, Morris Stevens, Gerald Strickler, Meredyth Delph.

FORT BRANCH–PRINCETON: (At Fort Branch): Oakland City 54–28 Hazleton; Haubstadt 41–38 Fort Branch; Oakland City 56–44 Patoka; (At Princeton): Mackey 60–32 Mount Olympus; Princeton 61–48 Francisco; Owensville 52–34 Mackey; (At Fort Branch): Oakland City 51–41 Haubstadt; Princeton 63–50 Owensville; Princeton 72–50 Oakland City. Officials: Edmund Cissna, William Coulter, Loren Harris, James Parker.

FORT WAYNE: (At North Side): Harlan 59–50 Lafayette Central; New Haven 41–38 Central Catholic; Concordia 52–49 Arcola; North Side 71–52 Elmhurst; Harlan 45–43 New Haven; North Side 57–47 Concordia; (At South Side): Central 58–33 Coesse; Leo 52–51 Huntertown; Hoagland 47–45 Monroeville (ot); South Side 62–27 Maumee Twp.; Central 66–48 Leo; South Side 46–36 Hoagland; (At North Side): North Side 55–43 Harlan; Central 36–34 South Side; North Side 52–39 Central. Officials: Stanley Dubis, Oscar Samuels, William Yohler, Sam Massette, John Tatum, Victor Mettle.

FOWLER: Ambia 61–14 Pine Twp.; Oxford 47–39 Boswell; Earl Park 49–32 Gilboa Twp.; Otterbein 46–34 Fowler; Freeland Park 61–30 Raub; Ambia 52–31 Wadena; Earl Park 28–26 Oxford; Freeland Park 49–37 Otterbein; Earl Park 37–32 Ambia; Freeland Park 41–26 Earl Park. Officials: Donald Cooper, Melvin Newlin, Foster Nichols.

FRANKFORT: Michigantown 57–47 Scircleville; Colfax 39–22 Washington Twp.; Frankfort 46–39 Jackson Twp.; Rossville 49–40 Mulberry; Forest 48–24 Kirklin; Michigantown 41–39 Sugar Creek Frankfort 58–25 Colfax; Forest 37–36 Rossville; Frankfort 33–32 Michigantown; Frankfort 48–44 Forest. Officials: Raymond King, Lawrence Leland, Warren Williams.

FRANKLIN: Center Grove 56–55 Clark Twp.; Nineveh 49–36 Van Buren Twp.; Whiteland 26–19 Helmsburg; Greenwood 41–40 Bargersville; Nashville 48–40 Trafalgar; Edinburg 42–37 Franklin; Center Grove 41–32 Nineveh; Whiteland 50–39 Greenwood; Edinburg 58–33 Nashville;

Tourney Time

Whiteland 46–41 Center Grove; Whiteland 44–38 Edinburg. Officials: Gerald Alexander, Ward Mosbaugh, Clayton Patterson.

GARRETT–AUBURN: (At Garrett): Angola 42–39 Butler; Fremont 52–44 Orland; Garrett 48–27 Waterloo; Auburn 76–41 Metz; Angola 56–54 Fremont; Auburn 54–44 Garrett; (At Auburn): Churubusco 68–23 Scott; Spencerville 49–37 Hamilton; Ashley 38–35 Salem Center; Pleasant Lake 37–28 Concord Twp.; Spencerville 52–50 Churubusco (ot); Ashley 51–46 Pleasant Lake; (At Garrett): Auburn 54–39 Angola; Ashley 51–46 Spencerville; Auburn 53–45 Ashley. Officials: George Collyer, Gerald Imel, Kermit Leininger, Merle Shively, Marvin Todd, Myron Weldy.

GARY–VALPARAISO: (At Gary): Gary Edison 47–10 Tolleston; Froebel 42–40 Wallace Horace Mann 56–53 William A. Wirt; Emerson 41–38 Roosevelt; Froebel 56–29 Edison; Emerson 38–31 Horace Mann; (At Valparaiso): Hebron 43–40 Chesterton; Kouts 43–24 Boone Grove; Valparaiso 47–15 Liberty Center; Morgan Twp. 52–34 Washington Twp.; (At Gary): Froebel 52–37 Emerson; Valparaiso 44–42 Kouts; Froebel 58–37 Valparaiso. Officials: Charles Bobilya, William Ellis, Don Lieberum, Gene Winks.

GOSHEN: Goshen 67–42 Millersburg; Middlebury 50–44 Baugo Twp.; Elkhart 38–27 Concord Twp.; Middlebury 60–47 Goshen; Jefferson Twp. 40–38 New Paris; Nappanee 47–36 Bristol; Wakarusa 65–54 Cromwell; Jefferson Twp. 29–28 Nappanee; Elkhart 50–44 Middlebury; Wakarusa 36–32 Jefferson Twp.; Elkhart 51–34 Wakarusa. Officials: John Cover, Robert Hughes, Arthur Lloyd.

GREENCASTLE: Russellville 37–25 Cloverdale; Greencastle 61–43 Fillmore; Belle Union 39–33 Reelsville; Roachdale 46–38 Bainbridge; Greencastle 45–40 Russellville; Belle Union 43–33 Roachdale; Greencastle 59–39 Belle Union. Officials: David Albright, Harold Porter.

GREENFIELD: Greenfield 51–45 Eden; Charlottesville 36–30 New Palestine; Fortville 31–29 Wilkinson; Franklin Twp. 50–42 Maxwell; McCordsville 41–27 Mount Comfort; Charlottesville 55–47 Greenfield; Franklin Twp. 40–27 Fortville; McCordsville 39–33 Charlottesville; Franklin Twp. 58–48 McCordsville. Officials: Robert Cherry, Don McBride.

GREENSBURG: St. Paul 57–42 North Vernon; Jackson Twp. 52–48 Burney; Greensburg 73–49 Sandusky; New Point 45–31 Vernon; Sandcreek 59–50 Clarksburg; Jackson Twp. 49–45 St. Paul; Greensburg 53–41 New Point; Jackson Twp. 47–44 Sandcreek; Greensburg 64–48 Jackson Twp. Officials: Herbert Schwomeyer, John Williams.

HAMMOND–EAST CHICAGO: (At Hammond): Griffith 62–49 Bishop Noll; Clark 57–54 Hammond Tech (ot); Hammond 60–38 Lowell; Crown Point 47–41 Dyer; Griffith 57–50 Clark; Hammond 54–34 Crown Point; Washington 60–47 Merrillville; (At East Chicago): Roosevelt 69–44 Whiting; East Gary 75–37 Wheeler; Hobart 53–50 Portage; Roosevelt 60–57 Washington; Hobart 67–62 East Gary Edison; (At Hammond): Hammond 55–43 Griffith; East Chicago Roosevelt 58–52 Hobart; Hammond 40–37 East Chicago Roosevelt (ot). Officials: Devon Eaton, Dean Geyer, Victor Griewank, Paul Hostetler.

HARTFORD CITY: Montpelier 50–43 Roll; Dunkirk 39–35 Madison Twp.; Portland 64–52 Hartford City; Jefferson 42–29 Ridgeville; Gray 45–39 Pennville; Redkey 58–45 Bryan; Montpelier 69–34 Poling; Portland 34–33 Dunkirk; Jefferson 45–32 Gray; Montpelier 41–38 Redkey; Portland 45–36 Jefferson; Portland 43–40 Montpelier (ot). Officials: Richard Duffield, Charles Jones, Burl McKenzie.

HUNTINGTON: Huntington Twp. 48–38 Wayne Twp.; Jefferson Twp. 51–23 Markle; Union

IHSAA Scores | 1950–1959

Twp. 56–35 Clear Creek; Polk Twp. 51–24 Rockcreek Center; Jackson Twp. 33–25 Salamonie Twp.; Huntington 48–41 Huntington Catholic; Bippus 63–52 Jefferson Center; Lancaster Twp. 34–32 Andrews; Huntington Twp. 38–34 Jefferson Twp.; Union Twp. 45–30 Polk Twp.; Huntington 41–37 Jackson Twp.; Lancaster Twp. 46–45 Bippus; Union Twp. 39–23 Huntington Twp.; Huntington 57–46 Lancaster Twp.; Huntington 40–29 Union Twp. Officials: Don Engle, Clay Layman, Frank Sanders, Raymond Trobaugh.

INDIANAPOLIS: Howe 45–43 Lawrence Central; Shortridge 52–38 Sacred Heart; Washington 67–49 Beech Grove; Tech 56–36 Warren Central; Broad Ripple 59–47 Decatur Central; Ben Davis 36–35 Crispus Attucks; Cathedral 50–36 School for the Deaf; Southport 43–42 Manual; Howe 48–41 Shortridge; Tech 48–30 Washington; Broad Ripple 55–43 Ben Davis; Cathedral 54–48 Southport; Tech 51–34 Howe; Broad Ripple 48–41 Cathedral; Tech 38–36 Broad Ripple. Officials: Lowell Barnett, Evan Crawley, Herschel Eastman, Lowell Willis.

JASPER: Ireland 53–29 Birdseye, Huntingburg 62–40 Dubois; Spurgeon 42–40 Stendal; Holland 57–43 Otwell; Jasper 62–32 Petersburg; Winslow 72–26 Ireland; Huntingburg 69–37 Spurgeon; Jasper 55–51 Holland; Winslow 45–38 Huntingburg; Winslow 64–46 Jasper. Officials: Roland Baker, Frank Smith, Leland Terrell.

KENDALLVILLE–ALBION: (At Kendallville): Kendallville 64–24 LaGrange; Lima 41–38 Rome City; Wawaka 49–33 Scott; Shipshewana 32–31 Ligonier; Kendallville 59–26 Lima; Wawaka 45–34 Shipshewana; (At Albion): Wolf Lake 45–40 Topeka; Brighton 58–45 Springfield Twp.; Avilla 43–34 Wolcottville; Albion 45–39 Howe Military; Brighton 60–53 Wolf Lake; Avilla 50–44 Albion; (At Kendallville): Brighton 52–40 Avilla (ot); Kendallville 64–31 Wawaka; Kendallville 54–48 Brighton. Officials: Lloyd Bryan, Everett Cass, Robert Dornte, Roscoe Hall, Everett Havens, Loris Jacobs.

KOKOMO: Greentown 69–38 Galveston; Union 51–50 Western; Elwood 58–24 Jackson Twp.; Kokomo 55–54 Northwestern; Greentown 46–38 Union Twp.; Kokomo 44–39 Elwood; Greentown 48–47 Kokomo. Officials: Harold McSwane, Robert Windsor.

LAFAYETTE: Klondike 50–46 Wea; Clarks Hill 39–24 Stockwell; Battle Ground 43–36 Dayton; West Lafayette 53–44 Romney; Point 47–46 Montmorenci; Monitor 43–39 Jackson Twp.; Lafayette 68–34 Shadeland; Klondike 40–38 Clarks Hill; West Lafayette 45–40 Battle Ground; Monitor 49–48 West Point; Lafayette 50–37 Klondike; West Lafayette 43–40 Monitor; Lafayette 41–35 West Lafayette. Officials: Art Cosgrove, Norman Morrison Ed Straith-Miller.

LEBANON: Lebanon 58–28 Pinnell; Jackson Twp. 52–44 Dover. Zionsville 68–50 Pike Twp.; Thorntown 54–53 Perry Central; Whitestown 52–43 Lebanon; Zionsville 45–42 Jackson Twp.; Whitestown 57–44 Thorntown; Zionsville 38–34 Whitestown. Officials: Kenneth Smartz ,Thomas Stirling.

LINTON: Bloomfield 42–38 Switz City (ot); Linton 35–28 Scotland; Marco 57–32 Worthington; Solsberry 40–34 Lyons; Jasonville 31–22 Midland; Bloomfield 35–31 Linton; Marco 37–36 Solsberry; Bloomfield 50–49 Jasonville; Marco 46–31 Bloomfield. Officials: Robert Babbs, A.M. Franklin.

LOGANSPORT: Logansport 90–26 New Waverly; Washington Twp. 36–34 Lucerne; Onward 44–42 Royal Center; Young America 43–40 Walton; Twelve Mile 54–39 Metea; Logansport 53–38 Washington Twp.; Young America 43–30 Onward; Logansport 53–44 Twelve Mile; Logansport 54–50 Young America. Officials: Verlin Jackson, John Magnabosco.

MADISON: Madison 84–36 Deputy; Scottsburg 60–43 Austin; New Washington 47–31

307

Tourney Time

North Madison; Lexington 73–28 Paris Crossing; Central 34–29 Hanover; Saluda 41–38 Dupont; Madison 63–33 Scottsburg; Lexington 50–38 New Washington; Central 41–33 Saluda; Madison 103–39 Lexington; Madison 95–28 Central. Officials: Robert Fink, Robert Quillen, James Sanders.

MARION: Sweetser 48–39 Van Buren; Marion 46–36 Fairmount; Swayzee 54–41 Jefferson Twp.; Mississinewa 46–27 St. Paul; Marion 66–36 Sweetser; Swayzee 45–42 Mississinewa; Marion 63–43 Swayzee. Officials: Charles Northam, James Ridge.

MICHIGAN CITY: St. Mary's 43–32 Hanna; Michigan City 59–30 Clinton Twp.; Mill Creek 46–37 Jackson Twp.; Westville 47–35 Springfield Twp.; LaCrosse 50–31 Union Twp.; Wanatah 29–27 Kingsbury; Stillwell 52–51 LaPorte; Union Mills 60–39 Rolling Prairie; Michigan City 56–50 St. Mary's; Westville 51–32 Mill Creek; Wanatah 47–46 LaCrosse; Union Mills 52–49 Stillwell; Michigan City 40–38 Westville; Union Mills 61–31 Wanatah; Union Mills 54–44 Michigan City. Officials: Harry Frick, Eddie Herbert, Frank Kresler, Don Polizotto.

MONTICELLO: Brookston 39–34 Monticello; Chalmers 54–41 Reynolds; Monon 55–46 Idaville; Burnettsville 38–35 Buffalo; Brookston 43–40 Wolcott; Chalmers 52–44 Monon; Brookston 56–43 Burnettsville; Brookston 46–34 Chalmers. Officials: Leon Hodson, Edward Stuteville.

MUNCIE: Yorktown 60–40 Eaton; Burris 50–45 Albany; Harrison Twp. 56–46 DeSoto; Royerton 56–40 Gaston; Cowan 40–36 Daleville; Central 59–29 Center; Yorktown 36–28 Selma; Harrison Twp. 45–44 Burris; Royerton 68–38 Cowan; Central 73–59 Yorktown; Royerton 55–38 Harrison Twp.; Central 56–37 Royerton. Officials: Herbert Edwards, Robert Hobbs, James Patterson.

NEW ALBANY: Mauckport 50–20 New Middletown; Charlestown 60–40 Borden; Silver Creek 50–32 Elizabeth; New Salisbury 43–35 Henryville; Georgetown 57–27 Laconia; Lanesville 69–29 New Amsterdam; Corydon 48–32 Taylor; New Albany 57–31 Scribner; Charlestown 55–47 Mauckport (ot); Silver Creek 48–35 New Salisbury; Georgetown 58–47 Lanesville; New Albany 63–42 Corydon; Silver Creek 54–48 Charlestown; New Albany 61–23 Georgetown; New Albany 42–32 Silver Creek. Officials: Edgar Braun, Clayton Nichols, Yank Terry, Hugh Thrasher.

NEW CASTLE: Middletown 61–45 Mooreland; Knightstown 57–30 Cadiz; Straughn 40–38 Kennard; Middletown 48–36 Knightstown; Spiceland 39–37 Sulphur Springs; New Castle 71–18 New Lisbon; Mount Summit 59–27 Lewisville, New Castle 80–23 Spiceland; Middletown 47–32 Straughn; New Castle 52–31 Mount Summit; New Castle 61–40 Middletown. Officials: Cloyd Julian, Lores Lehman, Ted Sims.

PAOLI: French Lick 45–42 West Baden (ot); English 53–42 Hardinsburg; Paoli 67–35 Pekin; Salem 82–30 Morgan Twp.; Mount St. Francis 53–48 Marengo; Milltown 46–16 DePauw; English 43–38 French Lick; Paoli 56–44 Salem; Mount St. Francis 52–34 Milltown; Paoli 62–43 English; Paoli 64–40 Mount St. Francis. Officials: Ray Manaugh, Eugene Sparks, Kermit Spurgeon.

PERU: Macy 43–40 Clay Twp.; Gilead 60–38 Chili; Peru 69–58 Jefferson Twp.; Bunker Hill 66–36 Butler Twp.; Converse 51–39 Deedsville; Gilead 52–33 Macy; Peru 70–49 Bunker Hill; Converse 44–41 Gilead; Converse 46–40 Peru. Officials: Eugene Glaze, Francis Richards.

PLYMOUTH: Bourbon 57–51 LaPaz; Bremen 57–55 Knox; Grovertown 59–34 San Pierre; Bourbon 58–27 West Twp.; Grovertown 64–50 Bremen; Plymouth 63–51 Argos; North Judson 56–48 Tippecanoe; Hamlet 44–40 Tyner; Culver 50–27 Plymouth; North Judson 59–49 Hamlet; Bourbon 50–43 Grovertown; North Judson 58–41 Culver, Bourbon 62–61 North Judson.

IHSAA Scores | 1950–1959

Officials: Leonard Lupold, Charles McManus, H. F. McNaught.

RENSSELAER: Rensselaer 65–28 Goodland; Wheatfield 41–20 Mount Ayr; Brook 44–31 DeMotte; Remington 37–32 Kentland; Kankakee 35–34 Fair Oaks; Rensselaer 57–41 Morocco; Wheatfield 40–36 Brook; Remington 38–30 Kankakee; Wheatfield 45–40 Rensselaer; Wheatfield 59–39 Remington. Officials: Harold Carlson, Albert Etter, Jack Small.

RICHMOND: Webster 42–25 Greensfork; Fountain City 68–31 Williamsburg; Richmond 72–31 Economy; Milton 32–25 Boston; Hagerstown 44–38 Cambridge City; Whitewater 52–45 Centerville; Fountain City 29–27 Webster; Richmond 53–18 Milton; Hagerstown 44–40 Whitewater; Richmond 52–11 Fountain City; Richmond 59–41 Hagerstown. Officials: Wayne Hammond, James Haywood, Wray Holbrook.

RUSHVILLE: Rushville 73–24 Orange; Manilla 51–44 Raleigh; Carthage 44–42 Mays; New Salem 42–30 Arlington; Morton Memorial 50–36 Milroy; Rushville 46–29 Manilla; Carthage 40–38 New Salem; Rushville 58–36 Morton Memorial; Rushville 66–45 Carthage. Officials: Paul Neal, Melvin Wilson.

SEYMOUR: Medora 58–50 Hayden; Seymour 76–29 Clearspring; Brownstown 29–25 Tampico; Crothersville 46–45 Freetown; Vallonia 43–27 Cortland; Seymour 40–33 Medora; Brownstown 53–43 Crothersville; Vallonia 46–36 Seymour; Vallonia 65–27 Brownstown. Officials: Joe Conover, John Simon.

SHELBYVILLE: Shelbyville 45–37 Clifford; Columbus 54–37 Waldron; Boggstown 47–44 Hope; Morristown 44–32 Moral Twp.; Mount Auburn 33–25 Flat Rock; Fairland 40–35 Shelbyville; Columbus 53–42 Boggstown; Mount Auburn 62–55 Morristown; Fairland 62–55 Columbus; Fairland 60–41 Mount Auburn. Officials: John Hilligoss, Maurice Jordan, Howard Plough.

SHERIDAN–NOBLESVILLE: (At Sheridan): Carmel 58–41 Sharpsville; Noblesville 37–32 Prairie Twp.; Sheridan 59–50 Jackson Central; Carmel 72–42 Noblesville; (At Noblesville): Tipton 63–42 Windfall; Walnut Grove 43–40 Westfield; Jefferson Twp. 49–39 Fishers; Tipton 57–28 Walnut Grove; (At Sheridan): Sheridan 48–36 Carmel; Tipton 49–41 Jefferson Twp.; Sheridan 51–39 Tipton. Officials: Charles DeBusk, Jack O'Neal, Ralph Renegar, Frank White.

SOUTH BEND: Central 80–44 Greene Twp.; Wilson 40–33 North Liberty; Walkerton 50–38 Madison Twp.; Central 69–46 Riley; Walkerton 60–49 Wilson; Central Catholic 47–20 Catholic; Washington-Clay 56–43 Lakeville; Mishawaka 49–42 Washington; Adams 51–37 New Carlisle; Washington-Clay 50–36 Central Catholic; Adams 41–39 Mishawaka; Central 66–41 Walkerton; Washington-Clay 55–45 Adams; Central 52–24 Washington-Clay, Officials: E. L. Aldrich, Hugh Bergstrom, J.W. Johnson, Toy Jones, Harold Nelson.

SULLIVAN: Farmersburg 53–45 Shelburn; Graysville 49–41 Merom; Dugger 51–40 Pleasantville; Sullivan 41–36 Carlisle; Hymera 61–33 New Lebanon; Farmersburg 56–32 Fairbanks; Graysville 41–35 Dugger; Sullivan 51–40 Hymera; Farmersburg 47–43 Graysville; Sullivan 53–34 Farmersburg. Officials: Robert Grannan, Alfred Rose, Wilfred Susott.

TELL CITY: Chrisney 59–36 Leavenworth; Tell City 51–32 Cannelton; Rockport 34–27 Troy; Dale 67–28 Bristow; Oil Twp. 55–54 Luce Twp.; Tell City 65–33 Chrisney; Dale 29–26 Rockport; Tell City 79–52 Oil Twp.; Tell City 72–33 Dale. Officials: Kenneth Huber, Lloyd Whipple.

TERRE HAUTE: Wiley 54–22 Fayette; Otter Creek 52–38 Honey Creek; Fontanet 51–42 Concannon; Glenn 45–33 Laboratory; Pimento 53–44 West Terre Haute; Gerstmeyer 68–19

Tourney Time

Blackhawk; Riley 64–32 Prairie –Creek; Wiley 50–39 Garfield; Fontanet 60–41 Otter Creek; Glenn 72–44 Pimento; Gerstmeyer 61–42 Riley; Fontanet 42–41 Wiley; Gerstmeyer 45–41 Glenn; Gerstmeyer 44–42 Fontanet (ot). Officials: George Danforth, Walter Moss, C.O. Walls, Roderick Witt.

VEVAY: Patriot 47–40 Bright; Aurora 50–37 Vevay; Moores Hill 51–37 Guilford; Lawrenceburg 60–24 Dillsboro; Rising Sun 57–26 Patriot; Aurora 67–39 Moores Hill; Lawrenceburg 56–37 Rising Sun; Lawrenceburg 49–40 Aurora. Officials: John Gwin, Burl Shook.

VINCENNES: Decker Chapel 41–36 Oaktown; Monroe City 45–39 Wheatland; Bicknell 51–25 Edwardsport; Freelandville 51–48 Decker (ot); Vincennes 41–30 Central Catholic; Fritchton 60–37 Sandborn; Bruceville 46–37 Decker Chapel; Monroe City 57–42 Bicknell; Vincennes 56–46 Freelandville; Fritchton 52–38 Bruceville; Vincennes 63–57 Monroe City; Vincennes 70–36 Fritchton. Officials: Roy Brann, Robert Derrington, Don DeVault.

WABASH: Roann 43–38 Urbana; South Whitley 47–36 Chester Twp.; Laketon 36–21 Lagro; Roann 40–28 LaFontaine; South Whitley 42–30 Laketon; Wabash 48–45 North Manchester; Washington Center 52–41 Somerset; Linlawn 53–35 Chippewa; Wabash 72–35 Washington Center; Roann 41–28 South Whitley; Wabash 64–32 Linlawn; Wabash 41–40 Roann. Officials: Paul Bateman, Dwight Byerly, Charles Marshall.

WARSAW: Columbia City 60–53 Milford; Pierceton 61–46 Silver Lake; Warsaw 63–42 Burket; North Webster 82–48 Sidney; Mentone 59–44 Larwill; Syracuse 52–49 Atwood; Leesburg 64–44 Claypool; Etna Green 66–43 Beaver Dam; Columbia City 52–37 Pierceton; Warsaw 44–41 North Webster; Syracuse 58–54 Mentone; Leesburg 56–49 Etna Green; Columbia City 61–52 Warsaw; Syracuse 56–42 Leesburg; Columbia City 59–52 Syracuse. Officials: Arthur Gross, Ray Nemeth, Myrle Rife, Walter Stebing.

WASHINGTON: Loogootee 70–41 Barr Twp.; Elmore Twp. 49–39 Plainville; Washington 70–22 Alfordsville; Washington Catholic 64–27 Epsom; Odon 49–37 Shoals; Loogootee 65–52 Elmore Twp.; Catholic 34–28 Washington; Loogootee 59–38 Odon; Loogootee 63–52 Catholic. Officials: William Dixon, Irvin Thrasher.

WINAMAC: Monterey 40–30 Leiters Ford; Fulton 53–36 Francesville; Richland Center 49–38 Winamac; Grass Creek 36–33 Akron; Kewanna 49–25 Pulaski; Medaryville 31–22 Rochester; Star City 51–44 Talma; Fulton 68–43 Monterey; Richland Center 51–36 Grass Creek; Medaryville 54–41 Kewanna; Star City 46–37 Fulton; Richland Center 49–34 Medaryville; Richland Center 43–23 Star City. Officials: John Janzaruk, Charles Meade, Gerald Reinke.

1950 REGIONALS

BEDFORD: Vallonia 33–30 Mitchell; New Albany 51–33 Paoli; New Albany 53–32 Vallonia. Officials: Robert Derrington, Clarence Tolbert, Lloyd Whipple.

EVANSVILLE: Tell City 61–45 Princeton; Bosse 69–51 Chandler; Bosse 52–46 Tell City. Officials: Cyril Birge, S.T. Proffitt, Irvin Thrasher.

FORT WAYNE: North Side 62–61 Decatur; Auburn 46–39 Kendallville; Auburn 57–39 North Side. Officials: Herschel Eastman, Devon Eaton, Victor Griewank.

GREENCASTLE: Greencastle 54–45 New Market; Clinton 60–54 Richland Twp.; Clinton 57–50 Greencastle. Officials: James Haywood, John Hilligoss, Ed Straith-Miller.

HAMMOND: Hammond 73–40 Union Mills; Gary Froebel 46–27 Wheatfield; Hammond

45–42 Froebel . Officials: Paul Bateman, Allen Klinck, Arthur Lloyd.

INDIANAPOLIS: Anderson 55–39 Speedway; Tech 59–29 Franklin Twp.;Tech 56–50 Anderson. Officials: Walter Bonham, J.W. Johnson, Harold McSwane.

KOKOMO: Wabash 35–30 Converse; Sheridan 45–42 Greentown; Sheridan 39–34 Wabash. Officials: Hugh Bergstrom, Evan Crawley, Ed Stuteville.

LAFAYETTE: Frankfort 50–33 Zionsville; Lafayette 72–42 Freeland Park; Lafayette 46–36 Frankfort. Officials: Lowell Barnett, Jack O'Neal, Lowell Willis.

LOGANSPORT: Logansport 39–33 Brookston; Richland Center 58–55 Flora (ot); Richland Center 45–35 Logansport. Officials: Stanley Dubis, Herbert Edwards, Wayne Hammond.

MARION: Marion 53–45 Portland; Lancaster Central 61–35 Huntington; Marion 53–37 Lancaster Central. Officials: E.L. Aldrich, Charles McManus, Thomas Stirling.

MARTINSVILLE: Terre Haute Gerstmeyer 41–35 Brazil; Ellettsville 68–37 Marco; Ellettsville 68–45 Gerstmeyer. Officials: Joe Conover, William Reimann, Raymond Trobaugh.

MUNCIE: New Castle 56–35 Lynn; Muncie Central 41–39 Richmond; New Castle 45–37 Central. Officials: Robert Hoffman, Lawrence Leland, Charles McManus.

RUSHVILLE: Rushville 55–45 Lawrenceburg; Batesville 51–39 Brookville; Rushville 47–28 Batesville. Officials: Charles Bobilya, Maurice Jordan, Marvin Todd.

SHELBYVILLE: Fairland 39–32 Whiteland; Madison 53–42 Greensburg; Madison 65–48 Fairland. Officials: Wilbur May, Kenneth Merder, Don McBride.

SOUTH BEND: Bourbon 56–40 Elkhart; South Bend Central 73–56 Columbia City; Central 69–38 Bourbon. Officials: George Collyer, Lores Lehman, Don Polizotto.

VINCENNES: Vincennes 54–33 Sullivan; Winslow 68–52 Loogootee; Winslow 74–63 Vincennes. Officials: Eugene Glaze, Robert Hobbs, Herbert Schwomeyer.

1950 SEMI–FINALS

BLOOMINGTON: New Albany 56–43 Ellettsville; Winslow 75–55 Bosse ; New Albany 52–36 Winslow. Officials: Paul Bateman, Eugene Glaze, John Hilligoss, Lores Lehman.

INDIANAPOLIS: Madison 55–46 Tech; Rushville 67–60 Clinton; Madison 64–49 Rushville. Officials: Cyril Birge, Victor Griewank, Robert Hoffman, Charles McManus.

LAFAYETTE: South Bend Central 43–34 Richland Center; Lafayette 50–46 Hammond; Lafayette 55–53 Central. Officials: Roland Baker, Walter Bonham, Don McBride, Marvin Todd.

MUNCIE: Sheridan 54–45 New Castle; Marion 57–51 Auburn; Marion 61–45 Sheridan. Officials: Evan Crawley, Allen Klinck, Jack O'Neal, William Reimann.

1950 FINALS—March 18

INDIANAPOLIS (Butler Fieldhouse): Madison 50–49 Marion; Lafayette 41–39 New Albany; Madison 67–44 Lafayette. Officials: Roland Baker, Jack O'Neal, William Reimann, Marvin Todd.

1951 SECTIONALS

AMBIA: Otterbin 49–37 Earl Park; Freeland Park 40–32 Oxford; Ambia 44–27 Pine Twp.;

Tourney Time

Gilboa 57–18 Wadena; Fowler 56–40 Boswell, Otterbein 44–40 Freeland Park; Ambia 46–35 Gilboa; Otterbein 42–34 Fowler; Otterbein 59–32 Ambia. Officials: Otto Albright, Melvin Newlin.

ANDERSON: Anderson 62–41 Pendleton; Markleville 41–40 Alexandria ; Lapel 56–55 St. Mary's; Summitville 42–40 Frankton; Anderson 48–40 Markleville; Lapel 55–40 Summitville; Anderson 86–42 Lapel. Officials: Jack O' Neal, Cloyd Julian.

ATTICA: Attica 48–38 Hillsboro, Veedersburg 59–57 Kingman; Richland Twp. 39–22 West Lebanon; Covington 60–40 Wallace; Pine Village 37–34 Williamsport; Attica 53–27 Perrysville; Richland Twp. 71–38 Veedersburg; Covington 50–45 Pine Village; Richland Twp. 61–49 Attica; Covington 47–43 Richland Twp. Officials: Evan Crawley, Leonard Benedetto, Herbert Vaulk.

AUBURN–GARRETT: (At Auburn): Garrett 66–47 Metz; Spencerville 57–48 Scott Center; Butler 55–54 Salem Center; Concord Twp. 56–48 Waterloo; Spencerville 41–39 Garrett; Butler 68–50 Concord Twp.; (At Garrett): Orland 70–55 Pleasant Lake; Churubusco 39–36 Hamilton; Auburn 94–50 Ashley; Fremont 57–55 Angola; Orland 58–55 Churubusco; Auburn 58–50 Fremont; (At Auburn): Spencerville 42–40 Butler; Auburn 83–38 Orland; Auburn 61–43 Spencerville. Officials: Robert Dornte, Lloyd Bryan, Don McCoy, Paul Hostetler, Richard Duffield, Phil Bail.

BEDFORD: Oolitic 64–30 Heltonville; Marshall Twp. 49–46 Mitchell; Orleans 54–43 Campbellsubrg; Bedford 86–30 Huron; Shawswick 59–42 Fayetteville; Tunnelton 35–32 Williams; Oolitic 60–35 Marshall Twp.; Bedford 44–36 Orleans; Shawswick 66–41 Tunnelton; Bedford 66–57 Oolitic; Bedford 83–53 Shawswick. Officials: Gil Smith, Ken Merder, Roy Brann.

BLUFFTON: Jackson Twp. 50–48 Petroleum; Rockcreek Center 39–37 Bluffton; Jackson Twp. 41–29 Liberty Center; Lancaster Central 49–45 Chester Center; Ossian 42–26 Union Center; Rockcreek Center 41–33 Jackson Twp.; Lancaster Central 48–43 Ossian; Lancaster Central 46–41 Rockcreek Center. Officials: James Ridge, Wesley Oler.

BOONVILLE: Millersburg 45–41 Folsomville; Boonville 50–30 Newburgh; Tennyson 44–32 Selvin; Chandler 45–41 Lynnville; Elberfeld 52–43 Millersburg; Boonville 47–28 Elberfeld; Chandler 33–28 Tennyson; Boonville 51–36 Chandler. Officials: Hugh Thrasher, Ivan Sprinkle.

BRAZIL: Gosport 62–34 Quincy; Ashboro 38–37 Spencer; Coal City 41–40 Bowling Green; Patricksburg 54–30 Cory; Van Buren 49–43 Clay City; Staunton 42–41 Brazil; Gosport 60–26 Freedom; Ashboro 62–28 Coal City; Patricksburg 58–42 Van Buren; Staunton 41–38 Gosport; Ashboro 41–40 Patricksburg; Staunton 46–45 Ashboro. Officials: Harold Porter, Oran Hollandbeck, Loren Harris.

CONNERSVILLE: Bentonville 49–46 Springfield Twp.; Brownsville 58–36 Fairview; Connersville 93–40 Whitewater; Brownsville 50–35 Bentonville; Alquina 68–26 Laurel; Brookville 63–39 Kitchel; Liberty 42–38 Harrisburg; Brookville 50–34 Alquina; Connersville 44–43 Brownsville; Brookville 63–50 Liberty; Connersville 48–41 Brookville. Officials: George Danforth, Don McBride, Gerald Alexander.

CRAWFORDSVILLE: New Market 57–33 Waynetown; Linden 58–47 Alamo; Waveland 36–24 New Richmond; New Market 63–47 Linden; Darlington; 64–41 Wingate; Ladoga 66–38 Bowers; Crawfordsville 70–35 New Ross; Darlington 53–48 Ladoga; Waveland 32–30 New Market; Crawfordsville 50–37 Darlington; Waveland 46–44 Crawfordsville. Officials: Harry Frick, Otto Hurrle, Meredyth Delph.

DANVILLE: New Winchester 46–44 Amo; Danville 60–55 Speedway; Stilesville 60–49

Pittsboro; Plainfield 51–46 Clayton; Charlton 58–25 Lizton; Brownsburg 44–40 Avon; North Salem 60–44 New Winchester; Danville 60–50 Stilesville; Plainfield 53–34 Charton; Brownsburg 60–45 North Salem; Danville 59–51 Plainfield; Brownsburg 58–56 Danville (2ot). Officials: Leon Hodson, Jack Small, Clarence Myles.

DECATUR: Jefferson 58–55 Pleasant Mills; Berne 45–33 Adams Central; Decatur 67–47 Decatur Catholic; Hartford Center 51–44 Geneva; Jefferson 57–50 Monmouth; Decatur 63–40 Berne; Hartford Center 68–56 Jefferson; Decatur 69–40 Hartford Center. Officials: William Ellis, Merle Shivley.

DELPHI: Deer Creek 43–42 Cutler; Delphi 61–41 Buck Creek; Flora 61–50 Camden; Burlington 53–39 Carrollton; Delphi 59–33 Deer Creek; Flora 86–46 Burlington; Delphi 60–58 Flora. Officials: Arthur Gross, Ward Mosbaugh.

ELKHART: Nappanee 52–43 Middlebury; Goshen 84–59 Millersburg; Elkhart 68–46 Wakarusa; Nappanee 85–65 Goshen; Bristol 55–52 Scott; Jefferson 56–50 Concord; Baugo 62–41 New Paris; Jefferson 68–58 Bristol; Elkhart 70–43 Nappanee; Baugo 72–40 Jefferson; Elkhart 70–63 Baugo. Officials: Don Yohe, Harold Nelson, John Tatum.

EVANSVILLE: Bosse 46–30 Griffin; Mater Dei 63–39 Wadesville; Memorial 52–34 Lincoln; Poseyville 39–38 Cynthiana; Central 64–49 New Harmony; Reitz 72–56 Mt. Vernon; Bosse 52–37 Mater Dei; Memorial 51–43 Poseyville; Retiz 66–52 Central; Bosse 45–31 Memorial; Reitz 78–39 Bosse. Officials: Edgar Braun, Cyril Birge, Frank Smith.

FARMLAND: Saratoga 63–53 Losantville; Jackson 59–55 Huntsville (ot); Parker 63–40 Green; Farmland 75–51 Modoc; Union City 52–50 Spartanburg; Winchester 47–42 Stoney Creek; Lynn 38–36 Wayne; McKinley 48–36 Saratoga; Parker 57–35 Jackson; Farmland 48–46 Union City; Winchester 57–42 Lynn; Parker 53–36 McKinley; Winchester 39–36 Farmland; Winchester 58–55 Parker. Officials: James Haywood, Bill Garrett, Oscar Samuels, Myrle Rife.

FORT WAYNE: (At North Side): Elmhurst 38–25 Coesse; Hoagland 49–41 Central Catholic; Central 47–45 Monroeville; North Side 40–31 New Haven; Elmhurst 54–49 Hoagland; Central 53–49 North Side; (At South Side): South Side 85–32 Lafayette Central; Concordia 66–40 Maumee Twp.; Huntertown 53–45 Arcola; Leo 62–52 Harlan; South Side 54–53 Concordia; Huntertown 50–49 Leo; (At North Side): Central 64–42 Elmhurst; Huntertown 47–37 South Side; Central 57–50 Huntertown. Officials: Don Polizotto, Wayne Hammond, James Davidson, Charles McManus, Toy Jones, Clarence Timmons.

FRANKFORT: Kirklin 42–23 Scircleville; Frankfort 67–10 Jefferson; Rossville 58–42 Jackson; Mulberry 62–47 Sugar Creek; Colfax 45–43 Michigantown; Frankfort 62–33 Kirklin; Rossville 41–37 Mulberry; Frankfort 25–23 Colfax; Rossville 44–41 Frankfort. Officials: Joe Mullins, Raymond Trobaugh.

FRANKLIN: Edinburg 75–34 Van Buren; Whiteland 33–26 Nineveh; Center Grove 52–47 Nashville; Helmsburg 48–47 Trafalgar; Clark 60–44 Greenwood; Franklin 57–42 Union; Edinburg 52–26 Whiteland; Center Grove 52–45 Helmsburg; Clark 53–48 Franklin; Edinburg 55–54 Center Grove; Edinburg 57–55 Clark. Officials: Howard Plough, Wilbur May, Roderick Witt.

GARY–VALPARAISO: (At Gary): Wirt 43–36 Tolleston; Froebel 72–28 Horace Mann; Roosevelt 47–46 Lew Wallace; Emerson 65–51 Gary Edison; Froebel 72–39 W.A. Wirt; Roosevelt 55–30 Emerson; (At Valparaiso): Valparaiso 54–37 Chesterton; Calumet Twp. 50–46 Boone Grove (ot); Kouts 66–34 Morgan Twp.; Hebron 65–33 Liberty Twp.; Valparaiso 65–34 Calumet

Tourney Time

Twp.; Kouts 48–39 Hebron; (At Gary): Froebel 44–42 Roosevelt; Valparaiso 67–32 Kouts; Froebel 68–48 Valparaiso. Officials: Marvin Todd, Paul Bateman, Devon Eaton, Gerald Reinke.

GREENCASTLE: Roachdale 67–52 Bainbridge; Fillmore 48–47 Greencastle; Russellville 41–35 Reelsville; Belle Union 53–35 Cloverdale; Fillmore 45–41 Roachdale; Belle Union 46–44 Russellville; Fillmore 47–41 Belle Union. Officials: Frank White, Robert Quillen.

GREENFIELD: Wilkinson 58–34 Maxwell; Franklin Twp. 73–47 Eden; McCordsville 31–30 Fortville; Charlottesville 45–43 Greenfield; New Palestine 58–50 Mt. Comfort; Franklin Twp. 60–47 Wilkinson; McCordsville 50–36 Charlottesville; Franklin Twp. 68–39 New Palestine; Franklin Twp. 41–39 McCordsville. Officials: Lawrence Leland, Robert Windsor.

GREENSBURG: Greensburg 77–53 Sandusky; North Vernon 62–50 Sandcreek; Burney 48–46 New Point; Jackson 47–41 St. Paul; Clarksburg 48–37 Vernon; Greensburg 72–46 North Vernon; Jackson 39–31 Burney; Greensburg 59–41 Clarksburg; Jackson 59–58 Greensburg. Officials: Clayton Nichols, Kenneth Smartz.

HAMMOND–EAST CHICAGO: (At Hammond): Clark 64–34 Dyer; Crown Point 55–47 Tech; Bishop Noll 58–57 Hammond; Griffith 59–23 Lowell; Clark 65–32 Crown Point; Bishop Noll 48–42 Griffith; (At East Chicago): Washington 72–47 Portage Twp.; Hobart 35–27 Whiting; Roosevelt 66–44 Wheeler; Merrillville 64–57 East Gary Edison; Washington 79–53 Hobart; Roosevelt 60–51 Merrillville; (At Hammond): Clark 53–43 Bishop Noll; Roosevelt 59–54 Washington; Roosevelt 56–45 Clark. Officials: Victor Griewank, Edward Stuteville, H.F. McNaught, Charles Meade.

HARTFORD CITY: Hartford City 57–43 Redkey; Gray 59–50 Bryant; Dunkirk 50–40 Portland; Montpelier 69–41 Poling, Ridgeville 54–42 Pennville; Roll 42–38 Jefferson (Randolph County); Hartford City 77–39 Madison Twp.; Gray 54–49 Dunkirk; Montpelier 46–45 Ridgeville; Roll 49–47 Hartford City; Montpelier 44–43 Gray; Roll 40–38 Montpelier. Officials: Ralph Renegar, Loris Jacobs, Burl Shook.

HUNTINGTON: Salamonie Twp. 52–46 Clear Creek; Jefferson Twp. (Warren) 54–29 Markle; Polk Twp. 48–42 Jefferson Twp. (Columbia City); Jackson Twp. 49–42 Andrews; Huntington 66–33 Huntington Twp.; Lancaster Twp. 49–41 Huntington Catholic; Union Twp. 39–32 Bippus; Rockcreek Center 51–41 Wayne Twp.; Salamonie Twp. 51–45 Jefferson Twp. (Warren); Jackson 41–39 Polk Twp.; Lancaster Twp. 59–57 Huntington; Union Twp. 55–35 Rockcreek Center; Jackson Twp. 42–38 Salamonie Twp.; Union Twp. 53–34 Lancaster Twp.; Union Twp. 42–37 Jackson Twp.. Officials: Charles Bobilya, Kermit Leininger, Dwight Byerly, Maurice Criswell.

INDIANAPOLIS: Manual 54–45 Lawrence Central; Howe 18–6 Beech Grove; Shortridge 62–42 School for the Deaf; Southport 71–52 Washington; Ben Davis 48–40 Decatur Central; Crispus Attucks 58–43 Sacred Heart; Broad Ripple 51–49 Tech; Cathedral 59–55 Warren Central; Howe 37–35 Manual Southport 44–42 Shortridge; Crispus Attucks 84–54 Ben Davis; Cathedral 49–47 Broad Ripple; Howe 52–42 Southport; Crispus Attucks 71–37 Cathedral; Crispus Attucks 71–43 Howe. Officials: Lores Lehman, Gerald Strickler, Irvin Thrasher, Leland Terell.

JASPER: Dubois 57–48 Stendal; Petersburg 79–37 Birdseye; Holland 56–35 Spurgeon; Jasper 49–29 Ireland; Huntingburg 49–37 Otwell; Winslow 67–54 Dubois; Petersburg 55–42 Holland; Jasper 40–37 Huntingburg; Winslow 61–48 Petersburg; Winslow 49–42 Jasper. Officials: Robert Derrington, Lowell Willis, William Dixon.

JEFFERSONVILLE–NEW ALBANY: (At Jeffersonville): Silver Creek 43–33 Borden; Henryville 62–53 Laconia; New Washington 40–38 Taylor; Jeffersonville 62–25 Charlestown;

Silver Creek 55–33 Henryville; Jeffersonville 66–48 New Washington; (At New Albany): Scribner 42–32 New Salisbury; New Middletown 45–39 Georgetown; New Albany 72–35 Lanesville; Corydon 37–31 Elizabeth; New Middletown 45–38 Scribner; New Albany 82–35 Corydon; (At Jeffersonville): Jeffersonville 32–30 Silver Creek; New Albany 53–34 New Middletown; New Albany 51–38 Jeffersonville. Officials: Joe Conover, Eugene Perkins, Eugene Bell, Roland Baker, James Sanders, Kenneth Smock.

KENDALLVILLE: Wawaka 53–41 Topeka; Brighton 59–52 Springfield Twp.; Wolcottville 56–48 Wolf Lake; Kendallville 60–44 Rome City; Albion 41–39 Howe Military; Avilla 48–41 Cromwell; Lima 56–54 LaGrange (2ot); Ligonier 52–44 Shipshewana; Wawaka 51–44 Brighton; Kendallville 30–26 Wolcottville; Albion 49–41 Avilla; Ligonier 60–36 Lima; Kendallville 54–43 Wawaka; Ligonier 41–32 Albion; Kendallville 55–48 Ligonier. Officials: Don Lieberum, Robert Hughes, Burl McKenzie, Gerald Imel.

KOKOMO: Kokomo 55–35 Eastern; Elwood 50–42 Clay Twp; Western 47–32 Galveston; Northwestern 47–27 Forest; Kokomo 48–46 Elwood (ot); Northwestern 66–48 Western; Kokomo 47–36 Northwestern. Officials: Walter Bonham, Charles Northam.

LAFAYETTE: West Point 51–48 Shadeland; Lafayette 56–30 Montmorenci; Jackson Twp. 62–43 Clarks Hill; Wea 51–49 Stockwell (ot); Monitor 52–31 Battle Ground; Klondike 43–42 West Lafayette; Romney 57–34 Dayton; Lafayette 52–28 West Point; Jackson Twp. 53–36 Wea; Klondike 59–56 Monitor; Lafayette 66–26 Romney; Jackson Twp. 61–41 Klondike; Lafayette 81–38 Jackson Twp. Officials: Eugene Glaze, Warren Williams, Ed Kurtz.

LAPORTE: Michigan City 63–16 Wanatah; Jackson Twp. 42–37, Stillwell; St. Mary's 56–35 LaCrosse; LaPorte 51–28 Union Mills; Hanna 57–34 Kingsburg; Rolling Prairie 62–39 Clinton Twp.; Washington Twp. 40–39 Union Twp. Westville 37–35 Mill Creek; Michigan City 49–26 Jackson Twp.; LaPorte 54–36 St. Mary's; Rolling Prairie 39–37 Hanna; Westville 44–36 Washington Twp.; Michigan City 43–41 LaPorte; Rolling Prairie 46–33 Westville; Rolling Prairie 43–38 Michigan City. Officials: Hugh Bergstrom, Vic Mettler, Sam Massette, Andrew White.

LAWRENCEBURG: Moores Hill 46–22 Guilford; Lawrenceburg 53–43 Bright; Aurora 48–39 Rising Sun; Patriot 36–33 Vevay; Dillsboro 39–36 Moores Hill; Aurora 32–30 Lawrenceburg; Patriot 36–33 Dillsboro; Aurora 51–19 Patriot. Officials: Robert Cherry, Morris Stevens.

LEBANON: Thorntown 58–19 Pinnell; Lebanon 56–32 Jackson Twp.; Pike Twp. 50–40 Dover; Perry Central 57–55 Whitestown; Thorntown 56–48 Zionsville; Lebanon 47–35 Pike Twp.; Thorntown 51–35 Perry Central; Lebanon 61–39 Thorntown. Officials: Forrest Ballinger, Otto Crosley.

LINTON: Jasonville 60–49 Lyons; Marco 60–46 Scotland; Linton 63–40 Bloom-field; Switz City 41–33 Worthington; Solsberry 50–46 Midland; Jasonville 48–25 Marco; Linton 54–51 Switz City; Solsberry 50–49 Jasonville (ot); Linton 78–46 Solsberry. Officials: Cy Proffitt, Paul Grimes.

LOGANSPORT: Walton 61–24 Young America; Royal Center 54–26 Metea; Logansport 66–45 Washington Twp.; Lucerne 57–40 Twelve Mile; Walton 64–19 New Waverly; Logansport 77–39 Royal Center; Lucerne 59–49 Walton; Logansport 63–48 Lucerne. Officials: John Janzaruk, Paul Dazey.

MADISON: Madison 76–51 North Madison; Scottsburg 37–35 Central; Saluda 51–49 Austin (ot); Lexington 63–41 Deputy; Hanover 88–33 Paris Crossing; Madison 65–46 Dupont; Saluda 52–32 Scottsburfg; Lexington 57–44 Hanover; Madison 65–45 Saluda; Madison 72–51 Lexington. Officials: Odilo Berger, Alvin Heller, Kermit Spurgeon.

MARION: Mississinewa 55–42 Jefferson Twp.; Marion 45–31 Saint Paul; Van Buren 61–55 Sweetser; Fairmount 41–39 Swayzee; Marion 62–29 Mississinewa; Fairmount 69–50 Van Buren; Marion 48–46 Fairmount (ot). Officials: George Collyer, John Williams

MARTINSVILLE: Mooresville 51–46 Paragon; Bloomington 59–39 Martinsville; Eminence 35–34 Monrovia; Smithville 65–55 University; Ellettsville 30–17 Morgantown; Stinesville 53–48 Unionville; Bloomington 45–41 Mooresville; Smithville 74–37 Eminence; Ellettsville 69–42 Stinesville; Bloomington 51–49 Smithville; Bloomington 64–48 Ellettsville. Officials: William Reimann, Clarence Tolbert, Robert Rose.

MONTICELLO: Monticello 48–33 Reynolds; Chalmers 49–30 Idaville; Wolcott 43–35 Round Grove; Monon 50–37 Burnettsville; Brookston 50–23 Buffalo; Monticello 53–37 Chalmers; Monon 67–36 Wolcott; Brookston 41–38 Monticello; Brookston 37–33 Monon. Officials: Noble Benbow, Herbert Brammell.

MUNCIE: Yorktown 60–46 Daleville; Harrison Twp. 45–35 Center; Burris 42–21 Cowan; Central 44–21 Selma; Gaston 47–38 DeSoto; Eaton 55–26 Albany; Royerton 44–31 Yorktown; Burris 63–37 Harrison; Central 67–34 Gaston; Eaton 48–46 Royerton; Central 55–38 Burris; Central 77–42 Eaton. Officials: Frank Luzar, Robert Greogry, John Hilligoss.

NEW CASTLE: Middletown 59–36 Kennard; Straughn 68–45 Sulphur Springs; Mooreland 56–40 Lewisville; Middletown 67–57 Straughn; Mt. Summit 71–46 Cadiz; New Castle 86–19 New Lisbon; Spiceland 40–38 Knightstown; New Castle 62–39 Mt. Summit; Middletown 67–39 Mooreland; New Castle 67–37 Spiceland; Middletown 57–47 New Castle. Officials: John Simon, John Gwin, Maurice Miles.

OWENSVILLE: Owensville 37–26 Mt. Olympus; Oakland City 42–38 Mackey; Ft. Branch 65–35 Hazelton; Haubstadt 52–50 Francisco; Princeton 51–20 Patoka; Oakland City 50–45 Owensville; Ft. Branch 68–51 Haubstadt; Princeton 65–30 Oakland City; Princeton 50–41 Ft. Branch. Officials: Robert Grannan, Willard Ketner.

PAOLI: Peking 49–46 Milltown; French Lick 65–63 Hardinsburg; Marengo 48–43 Salem; West Baden Springs 46–43 Morgan Twp.; English 56–48 Paoli; Mt. St. Francis 71–44 Leavenworth; French Lick 47–37 Pekin; Marengo 60–33 West Baden Springs; Mt. St. Francis 65–62 English; Marengo 44–39 French Lick; Mt. St. Francis 62–50 Marengo. Officials: Gerald Clapp, Chris Moritz, Edmund Cissna.

PERU: Peru 78–34 Butler Twp.; Macy 52–34 Deedsville; Converse 55–30 Gilead; Bunker Hill 37–36 Chili; Peru 71–44 Jefferson Twp.; Macy 48–37 Converse; Peru 45–21 Bunker Hill; Peru 77–36 Macy. Officials: Harold McSwane, Roscoe Hall.

PLYMOUTH: Hamlet 51–45 Bourbon; Tyner 52–50 Culver; Argos 55–50 Plymouth; Hamlet 49–47 North Judson; Argos 57–37 Tyner; Tippecanoe 47–43 San Pierre; LaPaz 64–39 Bremen; Knox 62–49 Grovertown; Tippecanoe 43–36 West Twp.; LaPaz 58–55 Knox; Hamlet 41–33 Argos; LaPaz 33–28 Tippecanoe; LaPaz 48–47 Hamlet. Officials: Stanley Dubis, Verlin Jackson, Gerald Vowell.

RENSSELAER: DeMotte 41–39 Kankakee Twp.; Mt. Ayr 52–41 Fair Oaks; Kentland 50–39 Brook; Rensselaer 51–35 Wheatfield; Morocco 42–35 Remington; DeMotte 43–28 Goodland; Kentland 48–31 Mt. Ayr; Rensselaer 42–27 Morocco; Kentland 54–49 DeMotte; Rensselaer 69–43 Kentland. Officials: E.L. Aldrich, Bruce Swinford, David Albright.

RICHMOND: Fountain City 56–25 Williamsburg; Economy 47–31 Boston; Centerville 28–26 Greens Fork; Richmond 52–23 Milton; Cambridge City 45–38 Webster; Hagerstown

IHSAA Scores | 1950–1959

44–20 Whitewater; Fountain City 38–21 Economy; Centerville 36–33 Richmond; Cambridge City 37–30 Hagerstown; Fountain City 34–27 Centerville; Cambridge City 43–42 Fountain City. Officials: Everett Campbell, Melvin Wilson, James Patterson.

ROCHESTER: Richland Center 55–36 Star City; Grass Creek 60–38 Pulaski; Rochester 48–35 Kewanna; Winamac 65–42 Leiters Ford; Fulton 40–34 Francesville; Akron 23–17 Monterey; Medaryville 99–45 Talma; Richland Center 52–43 Grass Creek; Winamac 48–42 Rochester; Fulton 43–34 Akron; Richland Center 60–51 Medaryville; Winamac 68–51 Fulton; Winamac 57–51 Richland Center. Officials: Arthur Lloyd, Gene Winks, Francis Richards.

ROCKPORT: Tell City 55–38 Dale; Cannelton 55–47 Luce Twp.; Oil Twp. 48–45 Bristow; Chrisney 44–33 Rockport; Tell City 57–36 Troy; Cannelton 56–52 Oil Twp.; Tell City 51–29 Chrisney; Tell City 63–36 Cannelton. Officials: Gus Banko, James Parker.

ROCKVILLE: Montezuma 45–43 Rockville; Rosedale 49–37 Dana; Hillsdale 43–42 Bloomingdale; St. Bernice 39–33 Bellmore; Clinton 64–34 Greene Twp.; Tangier 61–36 Bridgeton; Mecca 44–40 Marshall; Cayuga 56–33 Newport; Montezuma 35–31 Rosedale; St. Bernice 44–41 Hillsdale; Clinton 55–47 Tangier; Cayuga 72–59 Mecca; Montezuma 54–47 St. Bernice; Cayuga 44–36 Clinton; Cayuga 39–38 Montezuma. Officials: Albert Etter, Melbourne Pope, Charles Marshall, Bill Wood.

RUSHVILLE: Rushville 66–39 Arlington; Carthage 78–47 Mays; New Salem 47–25 Raleigh; Morton Memorial 65–35 Manilla; Orange 68–41 Milroy; Rushville 59–31 Carthage; Morton Memorial 58–42 New Salem; Rushville 64–44 Orange; Rushville71–29 Morton Memorial. Officials: Herbert Schwomeyer, William Schumacher.

SEYMOUR: Seymour 72–37 Tampico; Cortland 53–47 Brownstown; Vallonia 51–44 Freetown; Medora 80–41 Hayden; Crothersville 52–40 Clearspring; Seymour 48–37 Cortland; Medora 52–43 Vallonia; Seymour 71–51 Crothersville; Seymour 51–40 Medora. Officials: Roy Gardner, Paul Neal.

SHELBYVILLE: Hope 43–35 Mt. Auburn; Shelbyville 53–32 Boggstown; Columbus 63–31 Morristown; Waldron 67–35 Flat Rock; Fairland 63–54 Clifford; Moral Twp. 45–36 Hope; Columbus 61–59 Shelbyville; Waldron 56–49 Fairland; Columbus 59–50 Moral Twp.; Columbus 55–51 Waldron. Officials: Herschell Eastman, Lowell Barnett, William Yohler.

SOUTH BEND: Mishawaka 71–53 Lakeville; Washington 58–44 Adams; Washington-Clay 65–44 New Carlisle; Mishawaka 71–70 Washington (ot); Walkerton 64–44 Catholic; Riley 67–44 North Liberty; Madison Twp. 77–48 Greene Twp.; Central 53–35 Central Catholic; Walkerton 45–40 Riley; Madison Twp. 72–56 Central; Washington-Clay 58–55 Mishawaka; Madison Twp. 59–52 Walkerton; Washington-Clay 76–49 Madison Twp. Officials: Dean Geyer, Frank Sanders, John Cover.

SULLIVAN: Farmersburg 48–27 Gill Twp.; Sullivan 49–34 Dugger; Fairbanks 39–36 Graysville; Carlisle 45–30 Hymera; Pleasantville 50–38 Shelburn; Farmersburg 52–51 Sullivan; Carlisle 31–30 Fairbanks; Farmersburg 44–43 Pleasantville (2ot); Carlisle 45–36 Farmersburg. Officials: Cecil Bosstick, LeRoy Heminger.

TERRE HAUTE: Glenn 29–25 Laboratory; Gerstmeyer 41–32 Concannon; West Terre Haute 45–27 Fontanet; Honey Creek 52–44 Otter Creek; Riley 70–33 Blackhawk; Wiley 40–29 New Goshen; Pimento 48–42 Prairie Creek; Glenn 32–16 Garfield; Gerstmeyer 43–37 West Terre Haute; Honey Creek 51–44 Riley; Wiley 66–28 Pimento; Glenn 40–31 Gerstmeyer; Honey Creek 47–45 Wiley (2ot); Glenn 48–31 Honey Creek. Officials: Robert Hoffman, Clarence Brown,

Clayton Patterson, Robert Babbs.

TIPTON: Jefferson Twp. 42–36 Fisher; Tipton 44–32 Carmel; Jackson Central 57–51 Westfield; Tipton 42–40 Jefferson; Sheridan 52–30 Walnut Grove; Windfall 57–56 Sharpsville; Noblesville 47–29 Prairie Twp.; Sheridan 63–61 Windfall; Jackson Central 51–43 Tipton; Sheridan 54–40 Noblesville; Sheridan 57–44 Jackson Central. Officials: John Magnabosco, Ted Sims, J.C. LaFollette, Charles D. Jones.

VERSAILLES: Batesville 50–35 Milan, Osgood 46–41 New Mexico; Holton 48–39 Versailles; Napoleon 51–33 Cross Plains; Batesville 53–25 Sunman; Holton 38–36 Osgood; Batesville 31–27 Napoleon; Batesville 32–30 Holton. Officials: Wray Holbrook, Robert Fink.

VINCENNES: Vincennes 64–39 Bruceville; Monroe City 63–40 Decker Chapel; Central Catholic 50–36 Fritchton; Decker 42–35 Wheatland; Bicknell 66–44 Oaktown; Sandborn 49–44 Freelandville; Vincennes 71–40 Edwardsport; Monroe City 49–46 Central Catholic; Decker 46–37 Bicknell; Vincennes 71–32 Sandborn; Decker 50–41 Monroe City; Vincennes 27–26 Decker. Officials: Robert Hobbs, Vesper Moore, Lloyd Whipple.

WABASH: White's Institute 45–41 Somerset; Wabash 73–45 Laketon; Urbana 48–47 Washington Center; Wabash 51–31 White's Institute; South Whitley 65–34 Linlawn; North Manchester 70–39 LaFontaine; Chester Twp. 51–41 Chippewa; Roan 61–54 Largo; South Whitley 63–62 North Manchester; Roann 59–46 Chester; Wabash 60–34 Urbana; South Whitley 53–48 Roann; Wabash 62–43 South Whitley. Officials: Walter E. Stebing, Leonard Lupold, John Burger.

WARSAW: Atwood 58–38 Claypool; Mentone 64–44 Sidney; Etna Green 49–42 Leesburg; Columbia City 71–58 Larwill; Silver Lake 69–51 Burket; Syracuse 58–53 Beaver Dam; Warsaw 61–50 North Webster; Milford 37–32 Pierceton; Atwood 41–39 Mentone; Etna Green 63–40 Columbia City; Syracuse 73–54 Silver Lake; Warsaw 67–52 Milford; Etna Green 50–44 Atwood; Warsaw 57–47 Syracuse; Warsaw 64–53 Etna Green. Officials: Clay Layman; Everett Cass, Myron Weldy, William Brainerd.

WASHINGTON: Washington Catholic 51–47 Washingtohn; Plainville 76–49 Elmore Twp.; Barr Twp. 54–41 Odon; Loogootee 83–16 Epsom; Alfordsville 40–37 Shoals; Washington Catholic 61–58 Plainville; Loogootee 63–61 Barr Twp.(2ot); Washington Catholic 63–33 Alfordsville; Loogootee 58–47 Washington Catholic. Officials: Ed Straith-Miller, Eugene Sparks.

1951 REGIONALS

BLOOMINGTON: Glenn 42–25 Linton; Bloomington 50–24 Posey Twp.; Glenn 52–43 Bloomington. Officials: Robert Hobbs, John Gwin, Wilbur May, Roy Gardner.

CLINTON: Covington 33–32 Fillmore; Waveland 62–51 Cayuga; Covington 50–49 Waveland. Officials: Robert Derrington, Robert Gregory, Lowell Willis, Kenneth Merder.

EVANSVILLE: Princeton 49–38 Tell City, Reitz 64–36 Boonville; Retiz 56–50 Princeton. Officials: Roland Baker, Leland Terrell, Clarence Tolbert, Robert Rose.

FORT WAYNE: Auburn 50–45 Central; Decatur 78–65 Kendallville; Auburn 76–61 Decatur. Officials: Stanley Dubis, Joe Mullins, Don McBride, Charles Northam.

GREENSBURG: Edinburg 42–41 Madison; Columbus 71–66 Jackson Twp.; Edinburg 51–50 Columbus. Officials: John Hilligoss, Leon Hodson, Herbert Schwomeyer, James Sanders.

HAMMOND: Roosevelt 64–47 Rolling Prairie; Froebel 76–56 Rensselaer; Froebel 63–46 Roosevelt. Officials: Walter Bonham, Robert Dornte, Lores Lehman, Gerald Strickler.

IHSAA Scores | 1950–1959

INDIANAPOLIS: Anderson 82–43 Brownsburg; Attucks 60–36 Franklin Twp.; Attucks 81–80 Anderson. Officials: Charles McManus, Lloyd Whipple, Don Polizotto, H.F. McNaught.
KOKOMO: Kokomo 45–43 Sheridan; Peru 61–47 Wabash; Kokomo 71–37 Peru. Officials: Paul Bateman, Cloyd Julian, George Collyer, Paul Hostetler.
LAFAYETTE: Lebanon 56–54 Otterbein (ot); Lafayette 46–34 Rossville; Lafayette 54–30 Lebanon. Officials: Hugh Bergstrom, E.L. Aldrich, Marvin Todd, Herschell Eastman.
LOGANSPORT: Brookston 43–41 Logansport; Winamac 71–69 Delphi, Brookston 40–38 Winamac. Officials: Victor Griewank, James Patterson, E.S. Stuteville, Lowell Barnett.
MARION: Marion 58–33 Union Twp.; Lancaster Central 46–43 Roll; Marion 86–54 Lancaster Central. Officials: Irvin Thrasher, J.C. Lafollette, James Haywood, Joe Conover.
MUNCIE: Middletown 67–48 Winchester; Muncie Central 70–26 Cambridge City; Muncie Central 57–44 Middletown. Officials: Devon Eaton, Charles Meade, William Reimann, Ed Straith-Miller.
NEW ALBANY: Bedford 52–50 Seymour; New Albany 75–49 Mt. St. Francis; New Albany 65–51 Bedford. Officials: Cyril Burge, Wayne Hammond, Robert Hoffman, Alvin Heller.
RUSHVILLE: Batesville 68–65 Connersville (ot); Rushville 57–49 Aurora; Batesville 65–54 Rushville. Officials: Harold McSwane, Don Lieberum, Jack O'Neal, Eugene Perkins.
SOUTH BEND: Washington-Clay 70–57 LaPaz; Elkhart 68–43 Warsaw; Elkhart 50–39 Washington-Clay. Officials: Arthur Lloyd, Charles Bobilya, Eugene Glaze, Oscar Samuels.
VINCENNES: Winslow 58–44 Vincennes; Loogootee 44–33 Carlisle; Winslow 57–55 Loogootee. Officials: Evan Crawley, S.T. Proffitt, Lawrence Leland, Warren (Dee) Williams.

1951 SEMI-FINALS

BLOOMINGTON: New Albany 55–53 Winslow, Reitz 56–46 Glenn; Reitz 65–51 New Albany. Officials: Charles McManus, Don Polizotto, Lores Lehman, Marvin Todd.
INDIANAPOLIS: Batesville 45–37 Edinburg; Chrispus Attucks 71–31 Covington; Crispus Attucks 62–42 Batesville. Officials: Walter Bonham; Paul Bateman, Don McBride, Robert Hoffman.
KOKOMO: Muncie Central 60–44 Kokomo; Auburn 57–41 Marion; Muncie Central 53–39 Auburn. Officials: Victor Griewank, Jack O'Neal, Eugene Glaze, Evan Crawley.
LAFAYETTE: Elkhart 43–26 Brookston; Lafayette Jefferson 50–49 Gary Froebel; Jefferson 55–50 Elkhart. Officials: John Hilligoss, Roland Baker, Cyril Birge, William Reimann.

1951 FINALS—March 17

INDIANAPOLIS (Butler Fieldhouse): Evansville Reitz 66–59 Crispus Attucks; Muncie Central 51–41 Lafayette Jefferson; Muncie Central 60–58 Evansville Reitz. Officials: Charles McManus, Walter Bonham, Robert Hoffman, Cyril Birge, William Reimann, Don McBride.

1952 SECTIONALS

ANDERSON: Frankton 63–57 Markleville; Elwood 68–28 Lapel; Alexandria 66–45 St. Mary's; Anderson 44–33 Pendleton; Frankton 58–50 Summitville; Elwood 46–43 Alexandria;

Tourney Time

Anderson 59–51 Frankton; Anderson 44–38 Elwood. Officials: Wilbur May, Maurice Jordan.

AURORA: Aurora 55–23 Patriot; Guilford 49–46 Dillsboro; Lawrenceburg 47–31 Bright; Rising Sun 58–30 Vevay; Aurora 77–19 Moores Hill; Lawrenceburg 40–31 Guilford; Aurora 50–38 Rising Sun; Aurora 50–29 Lawrenceburg. Officials: Leroy Heminger, Paul Grimes.

BEDFORD: Mitchell 53–34 Heltonville; Huron 60–50 Tunnelton; Fayetteville 58–39 Williams; Shawswick 58–35 Campbellsburg; Oolitic 61–57 Bedford; Orleans 76–54 Marshal Twp.; Mitchell 67–47 Huron; Shawswick 82–44 Fayetteville; Orleans 56–55 Oolitic; Shawswick 53–47 Mitchell; Shawswick 84–68 Orleans. Officials: Kermit Spurgeon, Evan Crawley, Paul Neal.

BLOOMINGTON: Paragon 61–32 Eminence; Monrovia 53–40 Morgantown; Bloomington 53–45 Mooresville; Ellettsville 50–31 Smithville; University 42–35 Stinesville; Martinsville 52–43 Unionville; Monrovia 51–49 Paragon; Ellettsville 69–55 Bloomington; Martinsville 49–27 University; Ellettsville 36–23 Monrovia; Ellettsville 37–35 Martinsville. Officials: Clayton Patterson, James Patterson, Wray Holbrook.

BLUFFTON: Bluffton 63–44 Union Center; Lancaster 39–34 Liberty Center; Bluffton 50–37 Rockcreek; Ossian 64–57 Chester Center; Jackson 53–43 Petroleum; Bluffton 61–31 Lancaster; Ossian 49–48 Jackson; Bluffton 57–48 Ossian. Officials: William Yohler, Lowell Barnett.

BOSWELL: Ambia 55–35 Boswell; Earl Park 57–42 Gilboa; Freeland Park 53–33 Otterbein; Fowler 71–13 Pine Twp.; Oxford 66–27 Wadena; Earl Park 69–39 Ambia; Fowler 43–39 Freeland Park; Earl Park 57–33 Oxford; Earl Park 31–29 Fowler. Officials: Charles Marshall, J. D. Nickle.

BRAZIL: Gosport 64–36 Patricksburg; Ashboro 62–33 Staunton; Van Buren 51–19 Cory; Brazil 69–29 Bowling Green; Spencer 47–42 Freedom; Coal City 58–28 Coalmont; Clay City 62–36 Quincy; Ashboro 60–53 Gosport; Brazil 73–44 Van Buren; Spencer 65–47 Jefferson Twp.; Clay City 34–23 Ashboro; Brazil 67–34 Spencer; Brazil 49–46 Clay City. Officials: E. S. Stuteville, Ken Merder, Clarence Myles.

CLINTON: Bridgeton 51–42 Cayuga; Clinton 68–44 Greene Twp.; Hillsdale 49–48 Rockville; Rosedale 52–36 Montezuma; St. Bernice 54–51 Marshall; Dana 27–23 Tangier; Bloomingdale 50–41 Mecca; Newport 53–42 Bellmore; Clinton 43–40 Bridgeton; Rosedale 44–35 Hillsdale; Dana 73–49 St. Bernice; Bloomingdale 58–39 Newport; Rosedale 49–37 Clinton; Dana 71–58 Bloomingdale; Rosedale 42–30 Dana. Officials: Cloyd Julian, Charles Hopkins, Lawrence Benedetto, Clarence Brown.

CONNERSVILLE: Brownsville 49–47 Harrisburg; Brookville 45–26 Bentonville; Connersville 75–35 Harrison Twp.; Brownsville 37–36 Brookville; Liberty 49–40 Fairview; Alquina 69–38 Laurel; Springfield Twp. 70–49 Whitewater; Alquina 59–43 Liberty; Connersville 44–35 Brownsville; Springfield Twp. 50–41 Alquina; Connersville 57–31 Springfield Twp. Officials: Frank Carnes, Charles Northam, James Davidson.

COVINGTON: Hillsboro 49–35 Wallace; Covington 72–65 Attica; Pine Village 58–56 West Lebanon; Williamsport 75–48 Veedersburg; Richland Twp. 58–42 Perrysville; Hillsboro 47–45 Kingman; Covington 55–53 Pine Village; Richland Twp. 52–49 Williamsport; Covington 51–49 Hillsboro; Richland Twp. 56–54 Covington (ot). Officials: Harold Porter, Kenneth Smartz, Cecil Bosstick.

CRAWFORDSVILLE: Crawfordsville 58–37, Alamo; Linden 51–36 Ladoga; Waveland 67–44 New Richmond; Crawfordsville 70–55 Linden; Waynetown 66–44 New Ross; Darlington 53–35 Bowers; New Market 49–35 Wingate; Waynetown 56–47 Darlington; Waveland 59–58 Crawfordsville (ot); New Market 71–58 Waynetown; Waveland 65–45 New Market. Officials:

IHSAA Scores | 1950–1959

James Boswell, Joe Mullins, Ward Mosbaugh.

DANVILLE: Avon 71–36 Charlton, Brownsburg 60–40 Lizton; North Salem 43–35 Danville; Amo 45–27 Pittsboro; New Winchester 46–34 Clayton; Speedway 55–48 Stilesville; Plainfield 45–44 Avon; Brownsburg 56–41 North Salem; New Winchester 53–49 Amo; Speedway 41–39 Plainfield; Brownsburg 51–39 New Winchester; Speedway 53–50 Brownsburg. Officials: Melvin Newlin, David Albright, John Simon.

DECATUR: Hartford Center 50–48 Berne; Geneva 60–58 Monmouth; Decatur 55–50 Hartford Center; Pleasant Mills 60–57 Decatur Catholic; Adams Central 60–48 Jefferson; Decatur 61–53 Geneva; Pleasant Mills 73–52 Adams Central; Decatur 49–46 Pleasant Mills. Officials: Verlin Jackson Charles Bobilya.

EVANSVILLE: Reitz 45–44 Griffin; New Harmony 69–60 Wadesville; Central 66–50 Bosse; Lincoln 51–31 Cynthiana; Mt. Vernon 57–45 Mater Dei; Poseyville 57–48 Memorial; New Harmony 61–54 Reitz; Central 65–39 Lincoln; Mt. Vernon 65–56 Poseyville; Central 57–34 New Harmony; Central 65–52 Mt. Vernon. Officials: Vesper Moore, Wayne Hammond, Robert Rose.

FORT WAYNE: (At North Side): Harlan 48–41 Maumee Twp.; Leo 47–43 South Side; Huntertown 41–38 Elmhurst; North Side 60–38 New Haven; Leo 53–32 Harlan; North Side 70–44 Huntertown. (At South Side): Hoagland 65–39 Lafayette Central; Monroeville 45–26 Coesse; Central Catholic 61–35 Arcola; Central 64–41 Concordia; Hoagland 63–42 Monroeville; Central 64–38 Central Catholic; (At North Side): Central 45–25 Hoagland; North Side 47–35 Leo; Central 62–56 North Side. Officials: Dean Geyer, Frank Sanders, Dale Miller, E.L. Aldrich, Andrew White, Gene Davis.

FRANKFORT: Frankfort 46–36 Colfax; Mulberry 55–54 Rossville; Scircleville 36–34 Jackson Twp.; Forest 48–46 Michigantown; Kirklin 54–32 Washington Twp.; Frankfort 59–43 Sugar Creek; Mulberry 53–40 Scircleville; Kirklin 55–44 Forest; Frankfort 38–37 Mulberry; Frankfort 41–39 Kirklin. Officials: Robert Hobbs, Melbourne Pope, Clarence Timmons.

FRANKLIN: Clark 46–39 Nashville; Greenwood 73–35 Nineveh; Union 50–42 Edinburg; Whiteland 47–35 Helmsburg; Center Grove 58–40 Van Buren; Trafalgar 44–42 Franklin; Clark 69–56 Greenwood; Union 34–33 Whiteland; Trafalgar 46–39 Center Grove; Union 49–46 Clark; Union 57–42 Trafalgar. Officials: Fred Marlow, Eugene Glaze, Charles Jones.

GARRETT–AUBURN: (At Garrett): Fremont 50–36 Spencerville; Auburn 59–33 Concord Twp.; Butler 48–45 Orland; Angola 54–44 Ashley; Churubusco 53–38 Pleasant Lake; Scott Center 62–38 Metz; (At Auburn): Waterloo 46–33 Hamilton; Garrett 52–32 Salem Center; Auburn 59–37 Fremont; Butler 53–50 Angola; Scott Center 67–45 Churubusco; Waterloo 36–34 Garrett; (At Garrett): Auburn 48–17 Butler; Scott Center 59–55 Waterloo; Auburn 72–53 Scott Center. Officials: George Collier, Kermit Leininger, Edward Burke, Burl McKenzie, Everett Cass, Lawrence Gradeless.

GARY: Roosevelt 79–49 Calumet Twp.; Emerson 46–42 Hobart; Tolleston 40–39 East Gary Edison; Horace Mann 44–36 William A. Wirt; Roosevelt 48–36 Emerson; Gary Edison 79–29 Portage Twp.; Tolleston 72–42 Horace Mann; Froebel 36–35 Lew Wallace; Roosevelt 40–36 Gary Edison; Tolleston 30–29 Froebel; Tolleston 37–35 Roosevelt. Officials: Myron Weldy, Victor Griewank, John Janzaruk.

GREENCASTLE: Greencastle 65–40 Reelsville; Fillmore 36–31 Cloverdale; Roachdale 76–50 Russellville; Bainbridge 45–27 Belle Union; Greencastle 41–32 Fillmore; Roachdale 61–37

Tourney Time

Bainbridge; Greencastle 67–36 Roachdale. Officials: Noble Benbow, Herbert Brammel.

GREENFIELD: Greenfield 57–52 Franklin Twp.; Fortville 47–37 Eden; Wilkinson 64–25 Mt. Comfort; Charlottesville 70–56 McCordsville; Maxwell 45–42 New Palestine; Greenfield 38–34 Fortville; Wilkinson 65–56 Charlottesville; Greenfield 58–39 Maxwell; Greenfield 77–55 Wilkinson. Officials: Richard Tiernan, H. Burl Shook.

GREENSBURG: Burney 49–43 St. Paul; Vernon 51–50 Jackson; Greensburg 67–35 New Point; North Vernon 61–45 Sandusky; Clarksburg 62–55 Sandcreek; Burney 67–66 Vernon; North Vernon 48–42 Greensburg; Burney 52–38 Clarksburg; North Vernon 63–52 Burney. Officials: Leon Hodson, George Danforth.

HAMMOND: Roosevelt 49–39 Dyer; Tech 57–50 Crown Point (ot); Hammond 57–55 Washington; Roosevelt 59–50 Tech; Merrillville 51–38 Griffith; Clark 53–51 Whiting; Bishop Noll 59–44 Lowell; Clark 54–48 Merrillville; Hammond 51–45 Roosevelt; Clark 37–30 Bishop Noll; Hammond 51–41 Clark. Officials: John Tatum, Walter Bonham, Dan Lieberum.

HARTFORD CITY: Pennville 46–41 Ridgeville; Bryant 42–40 Roll; Redkey 78–45 Poling; Gray 64–36 Madison– Portland 47–32 Montpelier; Hartford City 50–47 Dunkirk; Bryant 49–38 Pennville; Redkey 64–51 Gray; Portland 57–56 Hartford City; Redkey 57–49 Bryant; Redkey 45–42 Portland. Officials: Wayne Crispen. Raymond Trobaugh, Francis Richards.

HUNTINGBURG: Ireland 41–37 French Lick; Otwell 49–46 Holland; West Baden 40–35 Stendal; Spurgeon 62–61 Winslow; Huntingburg 45–43 Dubois; Jasper 80–31 Birdseye; Ireland 58–56 Otwell, Spurgeon 48–39 West Baden; Jasper 62–45 Huntingburg; Spurgeon 54–39 Ireland; Jasper 52–47 Spurgeon. Officials: Edgar Braun, Lloyd Whipple, Eugene Perkins.

HUNTINGTON: Roanoke 69–60 Jefferson Twp. (Huntington); Catholic 51–42 Rock Creek; Andrews 47–34 Salamonie Twp.; Bippus 63–52 Huntington Twp.; Union Twp. 55–43 Polk Twp.; Jefferson Twp. (Whitley) 55–36 Wayne Twp.; Huntington 77–37 Lancaster Twp.; Clear Creek 50–39 Markle; Roanoke 40–38 Catholic; Bippus 51–50 Andrews; Jefferson Twp. (Whitely) 52–44 Union Twp.; Huntington 74–42 Clear Creek; Roanoke 57–51 Bippus; Huntington 33–18 Jefferson Twp. (Whitley); Huntington 60–41 Roanoke. Officials: Arthur Gross, William Brainerd, Leonard Lupold, Everett Campbell.

INDIANAPOLIS: Manual 49–47 Warren Central; Broad Ripple 49–48 Washington; Ben Davis 58–44 Lawrence Central; Decatur Central 39–37 Sacred Heart; Tech 63–27 Beech Grove; Crispus Attucks 55–49 Cathedral; Howe 66–32 School for the Deaf; Southport 74–50 Shortridge; Decatur Central 43–41 Ben Davis; Tech 63–60 Crispus Attucks; Howe 56–54 Southport; Decatur Central 50–35 Broad Ripple; Tech 46–44 Howe; Tech 39–37 Decatur Central. Officials: Marvin Todd, Eugene Sparks, Robert Dornte, James Sanders.

JEFFERSONVILLE: Milltown 48–40 Pekin, Silver Creek 43–34 Hardinsburg; Taylor 45–44 Henryville (ot); Jeffersonville 51–49 Salem; Leavenworth 35–29 New Washington; Marengo 30–26 Borden; Charlestown 49–35 Milltown; Silver Creek 47–33 Taylor; Jeffersonville 85–29 Leavenworth; Charlestown 41–40 Marengo; Jeffersonville 49–47 Silver Creek (ot); Jeffersonville 67–41 Charlestown. Officials: Odilo Berger, Chris Moritz, Cyril Birge.

KENDALLVILLE: Springfield Twp. 42–40 Brighton; Rome City 54–49 Cromwell; Kendallville 45–38 Wolcottville; Howe Military 58–45 Topeka; Wolf Lake 45–43 Avilla; LaGrange 68–42 Lima; Ligonier 60–49 Wawaka; Albion 64–62 Shipshewana; Rome City 53–44 Springfield Twp.; Kendallville 57–45 Howe Military; Wolf Lake 50–48 LaGrange; Albion 76–40 Ligonier; Kendallville 60–47 Rome City; Albion 64–39 Wolf Lake; Kendallville 52–46 Albion. Officials:

IHSAA Scores / 1950–1959

Paul Hostetler, Dwight Byerly, Merle Shively, Bill Garrett.

KOKOMO: Delphi 51–38 Northwestern; Kokomo 82–37 Eastern; Camden 57–32 Burlington; Flora 58–27 Cutler; Deer Creek 47–43 Carrollton; Delphi 62–42 Western; Kokomo 26–15 Camden; Flora 70–14 Deer Creek; Kokomo 61–52 Delphi; Kokomo 36–28 Flora. Officials: Herschel Eastman, Arthur Lloyd, James Ridge.

LAFAYETTE: Klondike 66–31 Dayton; Montmorenci 19–7 Clarks Hill; Lafayette 53–34 Jackson Twp.; West Lafayette 50–41 Romney; Stockwell 60–48 West Point; Battle Ground 45–41 Shadeland; Monitor 53–42 Wea; Klondike 62–33 Buck Creek; Lafayette 55–41 Montmorenci; West Lafayette 60–47 Stockwell; Monitor 56–41 Battle Ground; Lafayette 53–30 Klondike; Monitor 40–32 West Lafayette; Lafayette 60–41 Monitor. Officials: Otto Hurrle, Roderick Witt, Toy Jones, Gerald Alexander.

LEBANON: Thorntown 39–35 Jackson Twp.; Zionsville 74–57 Pike Twp.; Perry Central 61–39 Whitestown; Lebanon 65–28 Pinnell; Thorntown 49–31 Dover; Zionsville 51–44 Perry Central; Lebanon 43–41 Thorntown; Lebanon 66–49 Zionsville. Officials: Robert Crouch, Frank White.

LINTON: Bloomfield 73–28 Scotland; Linton 76–29 Worthington; Solsberry 36–28 Marco; Jasonville 62–54 Lyons; Midland 42–32 Switz City; Linton 52–50 Bloomfield; Jasonville 45–26 Solsberry; Linton 55–33 Midland; Jasonville 56–55 Linton. Officials: Gilbert Smith, Oran Hollandbeck.

LOGANSPORT: Royal Center 56–52 Metea; Washington Twp. 54–27 Young America; Walton 40–35 Lucerne; Logansport 35–29 Galveston; Twelve Mile 39–30 New, Waverly; Royal Center 38–34 Washington Twp.; Logansport 44–27 Walton; Royal Center 58–29 Twelve Mile; Logansport 37–35 Royal Center. Officials: J.C. LaFollette, Robert Sosbe.

LYNNVILLE: Elberfeld 37–17 Tennyson; Boonville 47–41 Newburgh; Millersburg 62–28 Selvin; Lynnville 65–14 Folsomville; Elberfeld 36–28 Chandler; Boonville 58–32 Millersburg; Lynnville 42–18 Elberfeld; Boonville 46–38 Lynnville. Officials: Robert Grannan, James Parker.

MADISON: Dupont 50–44 Deputy; Hanover 61–58 Central; Austin 53–41 Paris Crossing; North Madison 52–37 Saluda; Madison 76–34 Lexington; Scottsburg 59–50 Dupont; Hanover 64–26 Austin; Madison 52–40 North Madison; Hanover 52–41 Scottsburg; Madison 46–43 Hanover. Officials: Roy Gardner, Gerald Clapp, George Temple.

MARION: Fairmount 41–40 Mississinewa; Jefferson 53–46 Sweetser; Van Buren 61–22 St. Paul; Marion 58–34 Swayzee; Fairmount 51–37 Jefferson; Marion 68–33 Van Buren; Marion 51–44 Fairmount. Officials: Lores Lehman, Jack Small.

MICHIGAN CITY: Westville 58–28 St. Mary's; LaPorte 59–28 Kingsbury; Michigan City 70–24 Stillwell; Mill Creek 56–26 Hanna; Union Mills 60–47 Union Twp.; Rolling Prairie 43–37 Clinton Twp.; LaPorte 79–39 Westville; Michigan City 54–46 Mill Creek; Rolling Prairie 61–40 Union Mills; Michigan City 57–44 LaPorte; Michigan City 77–34 Rolling Prairie. Officials: Harold Nelson, Devon Eaton, William Ellis.

MONTICELLO: Burnettsville 51–45 Reynolds; Monticello 56–29 Buffalo; Chalmers 45–40 Idaville; Monon 49–33 Round Grove; Brookston 67–36 Wolcott; Monticello 85–60 Burnettsville; Monon 45–41 Chalmers; Monticello 47–41 Brookston; Monon 34–33 Monticello. Officials: Meredyth Delph and Paul Dazey.

MUNCIE: Central 83–31 Harrison Twp.; Selma 48–41 Cowan; Gaston 39–38 Yorktown; Albany 43–38 DeSoto; Burris 59–36 Eaton; Center 44–21 Daleville; Central 61–36 Royerton;

323

Tourney Time

Gaston 45–43 Selma; Burris 79–43 Albany; Central 49–24 Center; Burris 48–36 Gaston; Central 71–56 Burris. Officials: Gerald Strickler, Leland Terrell, Charles Meade.

NAPPANEE: Nappanee 46–42 Middlebury; Concord Twp. 77–57 Scott; Jefferson 51–40 Bristol; Nappanee 57–50 Concord Twp. (ot) Elkhart 59–39 Millersburg; Goshen 59–45 Baugo Twp.; Wakarusa 54–48 New Paris; Elkhart 63–38 Goshen; Nappanee 63–44 Jefferson, Elkhart 69–43 Wakarusa; Elkhart 47–45 Nappanee (ot). Officials: Richard Duffield, Sam Massette, Walter Stebing.

NEW ALBANY: Georgetown 56–44 New Salisbury; Morgan Twp. 58–56 New Middletown; New Albany 68–47 English; Corydon 44–43 Elizabeth; Paoli 56–51 Lanesville; Laconia 44–40 Mt. St. Francis; Morgan Twp. 68–33 Georgetown; New Albany 90–31 Corydon; Paoli 59–40 Laconia; New Albany 47–31 Morgan Twp.; New Albany 82–47 Paoli. Officials: William Yaggi, Robert Hoffman, Hugh Thrasher.

NEW CASTLE: New Castle 67–50 Straughn; Knightstown 44–28 New Lisbon; Spiceland 44–40 Kennard; New Castle 67–49 Knightstown; Mooreland 59–30 Sulphur Springs; Middletown 66–36 Cadiz; Mt. Summit 51–34 Lewisville; Middletown 78–41 Mooreland; New Castle 72–53 Spiceland; Middletown 40–38 Mt. Summit (3ot); New Castle 63–51 Middletown. Officials: James Lentz, Lawrence Leland, James Haywood.

NOBLESVILLE: Jackson Central 47–29 Prairie Twp. Westfield 63–45 Sharpsville; Tipton 60–49 Carmel; Jackson Central 64–54 Westfield; Windfall 58–49 Fishers; Sheridan 44–29 Noblesville; Walnut Grove 46–41 Jefferson Twp.; Sheridan 42–38 Windfall; Tipton 49–47 Jackson Central; Sheridan 46–27 Walnut Grove; Sheridan 69–32 Tipton. Officials: Robert Gregory, Homer Owens, Clayton Nichols, Robert Windsor.

OWENSVILLE: Fort Branch 56–45 Oakland City; Patoka 44–39 Hazleton; Mackey 44–38 Francisco; Princeton 57–27 Mt. Olympus; Haubstadt 44–37 Owensville; Ft. Branch 62–36 Patoka; Princeton 58–46 Mackey; Ft. Branch 49–40 Haubstadt; Princeton 64–52 Ft. Branch. Officials: William Dixon, Lowell Willis.

PERU: Bunker Hill 72–45 Butler Twp.; Peru 71–33 Chili; Mexico 59–43 Gilead; Macy 45–44 Clay Twp.; Deedsville 50–46 Converse; Peru 61–48 Bunker Hill; Macy 49–41 Mexico; Peru 58–45 Deedsville; Peru 63–36 Macy. Officials: Bruce Swinford, Norris Ward.

PLYMOUTH: Knox 74–53 Hamlet; LaPaz 46–41 San Pierre; North Judson 55–38 Argos; Knox 65–41 Bremen; North Judson 91–62 LaPaz; Plymouth 62–49 Tippecanoe; Bourbon 53–46 Tyner; Grovertown 51–49 West; Plymouth 32–22 Culver; Bourbon 48–43 Grovertown; Knox 54–50 North Judson; Plymouth 57–35 Bourbon; Knox 62–60 Plymouth. Officials: Eddie Herbert, John Burger, Arthur Hiduke.

RENSSELAER: Kentland 59–30 Brook; DeMotte 45–43 Fair Oaks; Rensselaer 55–40 Kankakee; Wheatfield 43–38 Mt. Ayr; Morocco 45–42 Goodland; Kentland 64–51 Remington; Rensselaer 51–45 DeMotte; Morocco 46–26 Wheatfield; Kentland 51–43 Rensselaer; Kentland 58–55 Morocco (ot). Officials: Herbert Vaulk, John Cover, Gerald Vowell.

RICHMOND: Milton 49–21 Webster; Fountain City 49–36 Greens Fork; Richmond 80–15 Whitewater; Centerville 66–29 Boston; Hagerstown 47–45 Cambridge City; Economy 53–42 Williamsburg; Fountain City 36–34 Milton; Richmond 45–43 Centerville; Hagerstown 35–34 Economy; Richmond 56–42 Fountain City; Richmond 51–41 Hagerstown. Officials: Oscar Samuels, Herbert Schwomeyer, Joe Conover.

RUSHVILLE: Morton Memorial 53–36 Milroy; Rushville 74–31 Arlington; New Salem 62–

IHSAA Scores | 1950–1959

24 Manilla; Carthage 77–32 Mays; Raleigh 37–35 Orange; Rushville 62–44 Morton Memorial; New Salem 40–39 Carthage; Rushville 50–48 Raleigh; New Salem 39–29 Rushville. Officials: John Hilligoss, Wesley Oler.

SEYMOUR: Crothersville 43–38 Cortland; Vallonia 57–38 Freetown; Brownstown 69–25 Hayden; Seymour 49–36 Clearspring; Medora 67–21 Tampico; Vallonia 39–29 Crothersville; Seymour 51–48 Brownstown; Medora 51–41 Vallonia; Seymour 68–49 Medora. Officials: Ed Straith-Miller, Robert Cherry.

SHELBYVILLE: Shelbyville 50–27 Hope; Morristown 39–27 Fairland; Moral Twp. 64–62 Flat Rock; Columbus 84–20 Boggstown; Waldron 74–43 Clifford, Shelbyville 63–22 Mt. Auburn; Moral Twp. 63–42 Morristown, Columbus 53–46 Waldron; Shelbyville 48–38 Moral Twp.; Shelbyville 52–40 Columbus. Officials: Dee Williams, John Gwin, Morris Stevens.

SOUTH BEND: Greene 58–46 Central Catholic; New Carlisle 72–63 Catholic; Mishawaka 54–48 Madison Twp.; New Carlisle 70–64 Greene; Central 68–46 Walkerton; Riley 60–33 North Liberty; Adams 62–52 Washington; Washington-Clay 61–39 Lakeville, Riley 47–40 Central; Adams 66–52 Washington-Clay; Mishawaka 58–51 New Carlisle; Riley 60–51 Adams; Riley 53–42 Mishawaka. Officials: Stan Dubis, Don Polizotto, Don Yohe.

SULLIVAN: Carlisle 56–34 Gill Twp.; Farmersburg 52–44 Dugger; Sullivan 74–57 Shelburn; Graysville 63–38 Fairbanks; Hymera 61–53 Pleasantville; Carlisle 58–40 Farmersburg; Sullivan 51–33 Grayville; Carlisle 45–40 Hymera; Carlisle 30–26 Sullivan. Officials: Robert Babbs, Clyde Boyer.

TELL CITY: Dale 46–44 Tell City, Chrisney 58–44 Oil Twp.; Rockport 50–37 Bristow; Cannelton 85–58 Richland; Troy 45–43 Dale; Chrisney 42–39 Rockport; Cannelton 52–32 Troy; Cannelton 48–43 Chrisney. Officials: Kenneth Blankenbaker, Yank Terry.

TERRE HAUTE: Wiley 66–26 Blackhawk; Otter Creek 50–48 Concannon; Garfield 52–51 Riley; Laboratory 59–56 Fayette; Gerstmeyer 89–36 Fontanet; Pimento 65–41 Prairie Creek; Glenn 53–44 West Terre Haute; Wiley 50–40 Honey Creek; Garfield 67–50 Otter Creek; Gerstmeyer 72–55 Laboratory; Glenn 44–36 Pimento; Garfield 47–41 Wiley; Glenn 50–44 Gerstmeyer; Garfield 56–45 Glenn. Officials: Irvin Thrasher, Frank Smith, Frank Luzar, John Williams.

VALPARAISO: Hebron 64–34 Kouts; Chesterton 68–41 Boone Grove; Valparaiso 60–24 Jackson Twp.; Chesterton 63–52 Hebron; Wheeler 43–41 Wanatah; Morgan Twp. 56–53 Liberty Twp.; LaCrosse 69–43 Washington Twp.; Wheeler 51–42 Morgan Twp.; Valparaiso 50–48 Chesterton; LaCrosse 49–48 Wheeler; Valparaiso 69–38 LaCrosse. Officials: Ed Kurtz, Paul Bateman, Gene Winks.

VERSAILLES: Batesville 48–33 Milan; Osgood 51–22 Sunman; Napoleon 41–39 Holton; Versailles 58–19 New Marion; Batesville 64–42 Cross Plains; Osgood 61–37 Napoleon; Batesville 55–37 Versailles; Batesville 54–37 Osgood. Officials: Maurice Miles, Howard Plough.

VINCENNES: Decker 50–43 Central Catholic; Bicknell 48–43 Sandborn; Bruceville 55–48 Edwardsport; Monroe City 50–48 Freelandville; Vincennes 56–34 Fritchton; Decker Chapel 55–41 Wheatland; Decker 65–41 Oaktown; Bruceville 60–37 Bicknell; Vincennes 42–37 Monroe City; Decker 61–47 Decker Chapel; Vincennes 65–39 Bruceville; Vincennes 51–43 Decker. Officials: Roy Brann, Ivan Sprinkle, Roland Baker.

WABASH: Washington Center 50–31 Laketon; Chester Twp. 61–38 Linlawn; White's 48–42 LaFontaine–, Chester Twp. 46–42 Washington Center; Roann 60–53 Somerset; North Manchester 61–34 Lagro; South Whitley 71–31 Chippewa; Wabash 54–27 Urbana; Roann 50–33 North

Tourney Time

Manchester; Wabash 49–48 South Whitley; Chester Twp. 36–33 White's; Wabash 47–35 Roann; Wabash 60–43 Chester Twp. Officials: Lloyd Bryan, Gerald Imel, Maurice Criswell.

WARSAW: Burket 57–42 Claypool; Atwood 82–42 Beaver Dam; Etna Green 46–35 Leesburg; Warsaw 70–49 Sidney; Columbia City 51–46 Milford; Syracuse 69–41 Mentone; Pierceton 41–36 North Webster; Silver Lake 76–45 Larwill; Atwood 58–54 Burket; Warsaw 59–57 Etna Green; Columbia City 76–49 Syracuse; Pierceton 65–54 Silver Lake; Warsaw 66–51 Atwood; Columbia City 49–47 Pierceton; Warsaw 68–62 Columbia City. Officials: Loris Jacobs, Ray Nemeth, Roscoe Hall, William Findling.

WASHINGTON: St. Johns 57–48 Alfordsville; Washington 82–37 Shoals; Plainville 64–43 Petersburg; Catholic 65–46 Elmore Twp.; Barr Twp. 72–42 Odon; Loogootee 63–36 Epsom; Washington 75–35 St. Johns; Catholic 62–41 Plainville; Barr Twp. 60–43 Loogootee; Washington 64–33 Catholic; Barr Twp. 58–52 Washington. Officials: John Park, S.T. Proffitt, Willard Ketner.

WINAMAC: Grass Creek 52–44 Francesville; Rochester 38–27 Leiters Ford; Fulton 69–33 Talma; Richland Center 43–40 Akron; Kewanna 44–35 Star City; Medaryville 60–43 Monterey; Winamac 37–34 Pulaski; Rochester 50–46 Grass Creek; Fulton 60–58 Richland Center; Medaryville 54–48 Kewanna; Winamac 47–44 Rochester; Medaryville 68–61 Fulton; Winamac 50–44 Medaryville. Officials: Donald Dick, William Etter, Walter McFatridge.

WINCHESTER: Parker 47–35 Union City; Stoney Creek 70–39 Spartanburg; Green Twp. 43–39 Lynn; Jefferson 52–31 Losantville; Winchester 55–30 Huntsville; Modoc 52–33 McKinley; Farmland 41–40 Wayne Twp.; Jackson Twp. 57–43 Saratoga; Parker 48–42 Stoney Creek; Jefferson 42–34 Green Twp.; Winchester 36–31 Modoc; Farmland 42–37 Jackson Twp.; Jefferson 42–40 Parker; Winchester 43–35 Farmland; Winchester 43–42 Jefferson. Officials: Don McBride, Phil Bail, Jerry Steiner, Donald McCoy.

1952 REGIONALS

CRAWFORDSVILLE: Richland Twp. 49–42 Rosedale; Greencastle 39–38 Waveland; Greencastle 47–44 Richland Twp. Officials: Lowell Barnett, Paul Hostetler, Herschel Eastman, William Ellis.

EVANSVILLE: Central 59–53 Boonville; Princeton 65–47 Cannelton; Central 66–50 Princeton. Officials: Evan Crawley, Kermit Spurgeon, Irvin Thrasher and Ken Merder.

FORT WAYNE: Auburn 49–46 Central; Decatur 63–56 Kendallville; Auburn 84–52 Decatur. Officials: Don Polizotto, John Gwin, Maurice Jordan, Frank White.

HAMMOND: Hammond 56–49 Michigan City; Valparaiso 47–45 Tolleston; Hammond 59–49 Valparaiso. Officials: Marvin Todd, Robert Dornte, Wayne Hammond, Charles Meade.

INDIANAPOLIS: Greenfield 61–49 Speedway; Tech 47–46 Anderson; Tech 70–46 Greenfield. Officials: Joe Conover, Joe Mullins, Roland Baker, E. S. Stuteville.

JEFFERSONVILLE: New Albany 43–41 Seymour (2ot); Jeffersonville 53–46 Shawswick; New Albany 61–48 Jeffersonville. Officials: Herb Schwomeyer, Roy Gardner, Lawrence Leland, James Patterson.

KOKOMO: Sheridan 47–31 Wabash; Kokomo 69–49 Peru; Kokomo 37–30 Sheridan. Officials: James Haywood, John Burger, Wilbur May, Warren Williams.

LAFAYETTE: Lafayette 52–45 Frankfort; Earl Park 56–53 Lebanon; Lafayette 50–45 Earl

Park. Officials: Stan Dubis, Gerald Strickler, Charles Northam, Devon Eaton.

LOGANSPORT: Logansport 63–46 Monon; Kentland 64–41 Winamac; Logansport 64–51 Kentland. Officials: George Collyer, E. L. Aldrich, Ed Straith-Miller, Eddie Herbert.

MARION: Redkey 49–36 Huntington; Marion 59–48 Bluffton; Marion 55–54 Redkey. Officials: Don McBride, Dean Geyer, Arthur Lloyd, Charles Bobilya.

MARTINSVILLE: Ellettsville 52–50 Brazil (2ot); Garfield 46–41 Jasonville; Garfield 57–38 Ellettsville. Officials: Lowell Willis, Cloyd Julian, John Hilligoss, Robert Gregory.

MUNCIE: Richmond 57–46 Winchester; Central 72–49 New Castle; Central 50–39 Richmond. Officials: Walter Bonham, Eugene Sparks, Lores Lehman, James Sanders.

RUSHVILLE: Batesville 46–31 New Salem; Aurora 54–43 Connersville; Batesville 63–44 Aurora. Officials: Robert Hoffman, Leon Hodson, Lloyd Whipple, Robert Rose.

SHELBYVILLE: Shelbyville 52–32 Madison; Union Twp. 49–48 North Vernon; Shelbyville 67–25 Union Twp. Officials: Cyril Birge, Eugene Perkins, S. T. Proffitt, J.C. Lafollette.

SOUTH BEND: Knox 67–65 Warsaw (ot); Elkhart 53–45 Riley; Elkhart 62–48 Knox. Officials: Paul Bateman, Don Lieberum, Victor Griewank, John Janzaruk.

VINCENNES: Jasper 60–59 Barr Twp.; Vincennes 60–48 Carlisle; Vincennes 54–47 Jasper. Officials: Eugene Glaze, Oscar Samuels, Robert Hobbs, Leland Terrell.

1952 SEMI-FINALS

BLOOMINGTON: Evansville Central 56–54 Terre Haute Garfield (4ot); New Albany 56–49 Vincennes; New Albany 52–50 Evansville Central. Officials: Walter Bonham, Lawrence Leland, Marvin Todd, Paul Bateman.

INDIANAPOLIS: Shelbyville 46–34 Batesville; Tech 66–52 Greencastle; Tech 60–33 Shelbyville. Officials: Lores Lehman, Lowell Barnett, Don McBride, John Hilligoss.

LAFAYETTE: Logansport 45–43 Hammond; Lafayette 39–37 Elkhart; Lafayette 54–37 Logansport. Officials: Robert Hoffman, Cyril Birge, Eugene Glaze, Herb Schwomeyer.

MUNCIE: Muncie Central 64–39 Auburn; Kokomo 62–58 Marion; Muncie Central 62–60 Kokomo. Officials: Roland Baker, Victor Griewank, Don Polizotto, Stan Dubis.

1952 FINALS—March 22

INDIANAPOLIS (Butler Fieldhouse): Indianapolis Tech 56–49 Lafayette Jefferson; Muncie Central 68–67 New Albany; Central 68–49 Tech. Officials: Cyril Birge, John Hilligoss, Don McBride, Don Polizotto, Robert Hoffman, Walter Bonham.

1953 SECTIONALS

ANDERSON: Frankton 59–49 Pendleton; Alexandria 42–36 St. Mary's; Elwood 56–46 Lapel; Anderson 46–43 Summitville (ot); Frankton 57–55 Markleville; Alexandria 50–33 Elwood; Anderson 64–62 Frankton; Alexandria 64–54 Anderson. Officials: Marvin Todd, Frank Sanders.

ATTICA: Williamsport 51–36 West Lebanon; Kingman 49–41 Wallace; Attica 73–41 Hillsboro; Covington 68–59 Pine Village; Perrysville 51–35 Veedersburg; Williamsport 48–40 Richland Twp.; Attica 61–42 Kingman; Covington 56–48 Perrysville; Attica 63–45 Williamsport;

Tourney Time

Attica 57–53 Covington. Officials: Clarence Brown, David Albright, Robert Brees.

AUBURN–GARRETT: (At Auburn): Auburn 72–41 Hamilton; Orland 57–52 Churubusco; Angola 55–48 Garrett; Metz 56–54 Pleasant Lake; Auburn 62–40 Orland; Angola 81–50 Metz; (At Garrett): Salem Center 65–41 Ashley; Fremont 67–59 Scott Center; Concord Twp. 71–48 Spencerville; Butler 63–42 Waterloo; Fremont 58–56 Salem Center; Butler 87–51 Concord Twp.; (At Auburn): Auburn 65–45 Angola; Butler 62–59 Fremont; Auburn 69–56 Butler; Officials: John Burger, Leonard Lupold, Ed Trexler, John Janzaruk, Loris Jacobs, Richard Swartz.

BEDFORD: Shawswick 40–37 Marshall Twp.; Campbellsburg 55–52 Fayetteville; Orleans 69–42 Williams; Huron 51–46 Heltonville; Bedford 62–52 Tunnelton; Mitchell 62–51 Oolitic; Shawswick 56–45 Campbellsburg; Orleans 52–44 Huron; Mitchell 46–44 Bedford (ot); Orleans 54–53 Shawswick; Orleans 57–53 Mitchell. Officials: William Yaggi, Robert Rose, Hugh Thrasher.

BLUFFTON: Lancaster Central 55–34 Rockcreek; Chester Center 81–46 Petroleum; Lancaster Central 54–36 Liberty Center; Ossian 64–60 Union Center; Bluffton 65–51 Jackson Center; Lancaster Central 62–49 Chester Center; Ossian 57–55 Bluffton; Ossian 74–56 Lancaster Central. Officials: Frank Carnes, Gene Davis.

BRAZIL: Van Buren Twp. 58–52 Clay City; Staunton 50–47 Cory (ot); Spencer 56–39 Bowling Green; Brazil 74–27 Quincy; Freedom 53–44 Gosport; Ashboro 83–41 Coalmont; Patricksburg 50–44 Coal City; Van Buren Twp. 61–49 Staunton; Brazil 57–51 Spencer; Freedom 67–45 Ashboro; Van Buren Twp. 58–51 Patricksburg; Brazil 69–47 Freedom; Brazil 51–35 Van Buren Twp. Officials: Melvin Newlin, Gil Smith, Robert Davidson.

CONNERSVILLE: Harrisburg 61–41 Harrison Twp.; Liberty 61–46 Fairview; Alquina 58–55 Bentonville; Liberty 60–58 Harrisburg; Springfield Twp. 58–36 Brownsville; Brookville 66–39 Whitewater; Connersville 65–39 Laurel; Springfield Twp. 53–52 Brookville; Alquina 43–42 Liberty; Connersville 50–40 Springfield Twp.; Connersville 52–41 Alquina. Officials: John Evans, Don McBride, William Yohler.

CRAWFORDSVILLE: Wingate 51–44 Alamo; Ladoga 52–41 Waynetown; Craw–fordsville 64–36 Bowers; Ladoga 81–43 Wingate; Linden 52–49 Darlington; New Market 62–39 New Richmond; Waveland 38–34 New Ross; New Market 58–38 Linden; Crawfordsville 46–43 Ladoga; Waveland 59–57 New Market (ot); Waveland 65–60 Crawfordsville. Officials: E. C. Boyer, E.S. Stuteville, Vesper Moore.

DALE: Dale 57–47 Rockport; Chrisney 71–43 Richland; Tell City 60–47 Cannelton; Troy 45–35 Oil Twp.; Ferdinand 55–43 Bristow; Chrisney 49–45 Dale; Tell City 63–53 Troy; Chrisney 66–44 Ferdinand; Tell City 56–44 Chrisney. Officials: Kermit Spurgeon, G.W. Clapp.

DANVILLE: Amo 58–35 Clayton; Charlton 67–58 Brownsburg; Avon 69–53 Speedway; Danville 63–62 North Salem; Plainfield 51–50 Stilesville; New Winchester 48–46 Lizton; Amo 79–49 Pittsboro; Charlton 60–58 Avon; Danville 70–62 Plainfield; Amo 60–45 New Winchester; Charlton 57–50 Danville; Amo 73–51 Charlton. Officials: James Ridge, John Park, Wilbur May.

DECATUR: Monmouth 50–42 Adams Central; Berne 59–47 Jefferson; Monmouth 65–52 Decatur Catholic; Pleasant Mills 79–49 Geneva; Hartford Center 49–38 Decatur; Monmouth 55–39 Berne; Pleasant Mills 62–32 Hartford Center; Monmouth 55–52 Pleasant Mills. Officials: Richard Tiernan, Burl Shook.

EVANSVILLE: Mater Dei 58–56 Wadesville; Reitz 65–58 New Harmony; Central 79–36 Memorial; Mt. Vernon 56–55 Bosse; Cynthiana 67–54 Griffin; Lincoln 68–26 Poseyville; Reitz

96–62 Mater Dei; Central 86–61 Mt. Vernon; Lincoln 54–35 Cynthiana; Central 74–61 Reitz; Central 59–40 Lincoln. Officials: Robert Babbs, James Sanders, Eugene Sparks.

FORT WAYNE: Arcola 75–56 Coesse; Elmhurst 57–53 Hoagland; North Side 73–63 Central Catholic; Harlan 67–44 Woodburn; Leo 51–48 Huntertown; Central 58–52 South Side; Concordia 74–54 New Haven; Monroeville 61–56 Lafayette Central; Elmhurst 49–43 Arcola; North Side 34–30 Harlan; Central 59–44 Leo; Concordia 66–56 Monroeville; North Side 56–55 Elmhurst; Central 64–44 Concordia; Central 53–49 North Side. Officials: Lores Lehman, Homer Owens, Stan Dubis, Harold Carlson.

FRANKFORT: Michigantown 66–55 Sugar Creek; Kirklin 74–46 Washington Twp.; Jackson Twp.50–44 Scircleville; Colfax 60–48 Mulberry; Frankfort 66–50 Forest; Rossville 60–39 Michigantown; Kirklin 66–53 Jackson Twp.; Frankfort 57–42 Colfax; Kirklin 39–37 Rossville: Frankfort 58–43 Kirklin. Officials: Eugene Glaze, James Lentz, Robert Windsor.

FRANKLIN: Franklin 64–49 Union Twp.; Edinburgh 68–51 Helmsburg; Greenwood 51–45 Center Grove; Nineveh 61–44 Van Buren Twp.; Clark Twp. 65–49 Whiteland; Nashville 51–44 Trafalgar; Franklin 63–52 Edinburgh; Greenwood 69–46 Nineveh; Clark Twp. 57–51 Nashville; Greenwood 56–50 Franklin; Clark Twp. 70–50 Greenwood. Officials: Kenneth Blankenbaker, Oscar Samuels, Morris Stevens.

GARY: Tolleston 48–46 Merrillville; Wallace 43–42 Calumet Twp.; Gary Edison 65–50 Hobart; Wallace 47–45 Tolleston; Emerson 73–52 East Gary Edison; Horace Mann 59–47 Wirt; Roosevelt 44–42 Froebel; Horace Mann 55–50 Emerson; Wallace 64–48 Gary Edison; Horace Mann 61–49 Roosevelt; Wallace 52–37 Horace Mann. Officials: Maurice Criswell, H. F. McNaught, Charles Meade.

GOSHEN: Nappanee 57–48 Middlebury; Baugo Twp. 53–30 Millersburg; Jefferson 56–50 Concord; Nappanee 52–49 Baugo Twp.; Elkhart 56–36 Bristol; Goshen 55–40 Scott; Wakarusa 92–54 New Paris; Elkhart 52–30 Goshen; Jefferson 62–48 Nappanee; Elkhart 52–47 Wakarusa; Elkhart 68–51 Jefferson. Officials: Arthur Gross, Don Polizotto, Toy Jones.

GREENCASTLE: Reelsville 88–50 Cloverdale; Roachdale 65–55 Belle Union; Fillmore 58–45 Russellville; Greencastle 58–46 Bainbridge; Reelsville 76–63 Roachdale; Greencastle 46–42 Fillmore; Greencastle 60–57 Reelsville. Officials: Ken Merder, Leonard Benedetto.

GREENFIELD: Eden 63–48 Maxwell; Fortville 53–47 Wilkinson; Charlottesville 62–34 McCordsville; New Palestine 58–57 Mt. Comfort; Franklin Twp. 52–47 Greenfield; Fortville 42–38 Eden; Charlottesville 46–42 New Palestine; Fortville 46–40 Franklin Twp.; Charlottesville 48–45 Fortville. Officials: Herbert Brammel, Noble Benbow.

GREENSBURG: Greensburg 67–43 Burney; St. Paul 38–15 Jackson Twp.; New Point 63–58 Sandcreek; Sandusky 43–40 Vernon; North Vernon 47–35 Clarksburg; Greensburg 49–36 St. Paul; Sandusky 48–43 New Point; Greensburg 61–50 North Vernon; Greensburg 74—44 Sandusky. Officials: John Hilligoss, John Simon.

HAMMOND: Hammond High 50–37 Morton; Bishop Noll 54–29 Lowell; East Chicago Washington 65–49 Tech; Hammond High 61–57 Washington; Clark 66–55 Whiting; East Chicago Roosevelt 68–51 Dyer; Crown Point 32–25 Griffith; Roosevelt 65–60 Clark; Hammond High 58–52 Washington; Roosevelt 74–66 Crown Point; Hammond High 53–51 Roosevelt. Officials: Gene Winks, Victor Griewank, Norris Ward.

HARTFORD CITY: Pennville 54–43 Madison; Montpelier, 74–67 Poling; Roll 59–57 Bryant; Portland 68–67 Redkey; Hartford City 57–50 Dunkirk; Gray 63–42 Pennville; Montpelier

Tourney Time

55–52 Roll; Hartford City 57–43 Portland; Gray 69–60 Montpelier; Hartford City 92–53 Gray. Officials: Merle Shively, Gerald Imel, Ward Mosbaugh.

HUNTINGBURG: Dubois 57–44 Ireland; Holland 59–48 Spurgeon; French Lick 66–44 Winslow; Otwell 49–43 Stendal; West Baden 70–50 Birdseye; Huntingburg 59–49 Jasper; Holland 49–44 Dubois: French Lick 70–55 Otwell; Huntingburg 55–34 West Baden; Holland 40–39 French Lick; Holland 49–46 Huntingburg. Officials: Paul Grimes, Leroy Heminger, William Dixon.

HUNTINGTON: Andrews 48–41 Huntington Twp.: Huntington 68–59 Salamonie Twp.; Clear Creek Twp. 72–49 Union Twp.; Huntington Catholic 64–58 Bippus; Jefferson Twp. (Warren) 59–37 Wayne Twp.; Lancaster Twp. 65–49 Markel; Polk Twp. 57–43 Jefferson Twp. (Columbia City); Roanoke 73–57 Rockcreek; Huntington 80–42 Andrews; Clear Creek Twp. 61–60 Huntington Catholic; Lancaster Twp. 69–46 Jefferson Twp. (Warren); Polk Twp. 58–52 Roanoke; Huntington 44–25 Clear Creek Twp.; Polk Twp. 63–58 Lancaster Twp.; Huntington 38–37 Polk Twp. Officials: Charles Northam, Lawrence Gradeless. Wesley Oler, Clayton Smith.

INDIANAPOLIS: Crispus Attucks 42–22 Decatur Central; Ben Davis 54–43 Tech; Broad Ripple 48–42 Shortridge; Howe 77–44 Beech Grove; Southport 90–46 School for the Deaf; Warren Central 55–39 Lawrence Central; Sacred Heart 46–43 Cathedral; Washington 38—32 Manual; Crispus Attucks 87–52 Ben Davis; Howe 71–59 Broad Ripple; Southport 72–46 Warren Central; Washington 65–63 Sacred Heart; Crispus Attucks 59–48 Howe; Southport 71–70 Washington; Crispus Attucks 106–64 Southport. Officials: Roland Baker, Frank Smith, Lowell Barnett, James Davidson.

JEFFERSONVILLE: Borden 43–38 New Washington; Silver Creel, 58–35 Leavenworth; Pekin 67–58 Henryville; Marengo 71–48 Milltown; Jeffersonville 75–35 Charlestown; Salem 81–42 Hardinsburg; Silver Creek 71–50 Borden; Marengo 50–42 Pekin; Jeffersonville 72–39 Salem; Silver Creek 57–39 Marengo; Jeffersonville 39–35 Silver Creek. Officials: Dwain Laird, Irvin Thrasher, Roy Gardner.

KENDALLVILLE: Shipshewana 51–47 Albion; LaGrange 57–56 Howe Military; Kendallville 36–22 Wawaka; Ligonier 71–39 Springfield Twp.; Avilla 59–44 Lima; Cromwell 41–35 Topeka; Wolf Lake 52–38 Brighton, Rome City 58–50 Wolcottville; LaGrange 57–49 Shipshewana; Kendallville 35–19 Ligonier; Avilla 68–46 Cromwell; Wolf Lake 48–45 Rome City; Kendallville 69–55 LaGrange; Avilla 62–58 Wolf Lake; Kendallville 76–69 Avilla. Officials: George Collyer, Phil Bail, Charles Bobilya, Kermit Leininger.

KOKOMO: Western 55–54 Camden; Delphi 85–46 Deer Creek; Burlington 57–25 Carrollton; Kokomo 52–47 Northwestern; Flora 95–58 Cutler. Eastern 60–54 Western; Delphi 69–42 Burlington; Kokomo 73–69 Flora; Delphi 52–32 Eastern; Kokomo 80–44 Delphi. Officials: Dee Williams, James Boswell, Bruce Swinford.

LAFAYETTE: West Point 54–40 Dayton; Buck Creek 58–56 Jackson Twp.; Montmorenci 70–46 Romney; Klondike 47–39 Wea; Lafayette 57–38 Monitor; Clarks Hill 47–43 Shadeland; West Lafayette 71–46 Battle Ground; Stockwell 62–52 West Point; Montmorenci 81–50 Buck Creek; Lafayette 63–45 Klondike; West Lafayette 69–38 Clarks Hill; Stockwell 56–54 Montmorenci; Lafayette 57–46 West Lafayette; Lafayette 55–42 Stockwell. Officials: Frank Luzar, Wayne Crispen, John Williams, Walter McFatridge.

LEBANON: Whitestown 46–33 Pinnell; Thorntown 62–60 Pike Twp.; Zionsville 68–22 Dover; Lebanon 62–43 Perry Central; Jackson Twp. 66–45 Whitestown; Zionsville 44–39

Thorntown; Lebanon 67–51 Jackson Twp.; Zionsville 67–53 Lebanon. Officials: Roy Brann, Bill Wood.

LINTON: Worthington 52–51 Scotland; Bloomfield 67–41 Midland; Linton 84–41 Jasonville; Marco 45–38 Lyons; Solsberry 62–53 Switz City; Bloomfield 59–36 Worthington; Linton 61–46 Marco; Solsberry 71–38 Bloomfield; Solsberry 56–49 Linton. Officials: Leland Terrell, J. Firman Grimes.

LOGANSPORT: Young America 66–56 Walton; Logansport 78–53 Twelve Mile; Royal Center 75–47 Lucerne; Galveston 73–17 New Waverly; Washington Twp. 56–46 Metea; Logansport 62–42 Young America; Royal Center 44–43 Galveston; Logansport 64–51 Washington Twp.; Logansport 61–51 Royal Center. Officials: Leon Hodson, George Danforth.

LYNNVILLE: Chandler 58–28 Tennyson; Elberfeld 81–37 Folsomville; Lynnville 83–33 Selvin; Boonville 83–22 Millersburg; Chandler 52–42 Newburgh; Lynnville 60–42 Elberfeld; Boonville 72–43 Chandler; Boonville 48–46 Lynnville. Officials: Norman Risley, Lowell Willis.

MADISON: Central 57–55 Hanover; Madison 59–35 Paris Crossing; North Madison 60–58 Dupont; Scottsburg 81–51 Deputy; Lexington 59–52 Saluda; Central 52–48 Austin; Madison 77–61 North Madison; Scottsburg 59–55 Lexington; Madison 80–58 Central; Scottsburg 62–45 Madison. Officials: Robert Cherry, Chris Moritz, Vern Doles.

MARION: Fairmount 53–41 St. Paul's; Van Buren 55–52 Sweetser; Marion 59–58 Jefferson Twp.; Mississinewa 66–33 Swayzee, Fairmount 49–47 Van Buren (ot); Mississinewa 61–34 Marion; Mississinewa 69–49 Fairmount. Officials: Paul Bateman, Francis Richards.

MARTINSVILLE: Morgantown 42–39 Martinsville; Mooresville 68–40 Paragon; Eminence 57–51 Smithville; University 64–62 Monrovia; Bloomington 87–39 Unionville; Stinesville 50–47 Ellettsville; Morgantown 58–48 Mooresville; University 49–38 Eminence; Bloomington 46–40 Stinesville; Morgantown 35–28 University; Bloomington 66–47 Morgantown. Officials: John Masariu, J.C. LaFollette, S.T. Proffitt.

MICHIGAN CITY: Union Mills 68–54 Union Twp.; LaPorte 83–50 Hanna; Rolling Prairie 73–53 Kingsbury; Stillwell 64–48 Clinton Twp.; Mill Creek 61–49 Westville; Michigan City 94–52 LaCrosse; St. Mary's 69–50 Wanatah; Union Mills 45–44 LaPorte; Rolling Prairie 69–51 Stillwell; Michigan City 59–44 Mill Creek; St. Mary's 46–45 Union Mills; Michigan City 60–44 Rolling Prairie; Michigan City 69–44 St. Mary's. Officials: Arthur Lloyd, John Cover, Richard Duffield.

MONTICELLO: Burnettsville 35–33 Chalmers; Idaville 55–52 Buffalo; Wolcott 58–46 Brookston; Reynolds 62–54 Monon; Monticello 48–40 Burnettsville; Wolcott 32–26 Idaville; Monticello 50–48 Reynolds; Wolcott 73–61 Monticello. Officials: Joe Mullins, Raymond Trobaugh.

MUNCIE: Gaston 58–38 DeSoto; Center 74–45 Selma; Muncie Central 94–30 Albany; Yorktown 61–49 Harrison; Cowan 61–56 Eaton; Burris 72–42 Daleville; Gaston 40–38 Royerton; Muncie Central 58—36 Center; Yorktown 56–47 Cowan; Burris 49–42 Gaston; Muncie Central 65–31 Yorktown; Muncie Central 66–47 Muncie Burris. Officials: Don McCoy, Don Lieberum, Walter Bonham.

NEW ALBANY: Paoli 47–44 Laconia; Corydon 48–21 Morgan Twp.; New Albany 78–38 New Salisbury; New Middleton 63–42 Lanesville; English 64–56 Elizabeth; Georgetown 82–40 Mt. St. Francis; Corydon 55–53 Paoli; New Albany 76–62 New Middleton; Georgetown 51–49 English; New Albany 67–41 Corydon; New Albany 83–58 Georgetown. Officials: Robert Laird,

Tourney Time

James Patterson, Fred Marlow.

NEW CASTLE: New Lisbon 57–34 Sulphur Springs; Mt. Summit 46–35 Lewisville; Middletown 57–44 Spiceland; Mt. Summit 38–33 New Lisbon; Cadiz 66–65 Mooreland; Knightstown 72–59 Straughn; New Castle 90–47 Kennard; Knightstown 96–36 Cadiz; Middletown 57–54 Mt. Summit; New Castle 57–54 Knightstown; New Castle 65–51 Middletown. Officials: M. N. Delph, Cloyd Julian, Howard Plough.

OWENSVILLE: Mackey 54–44 Mt. Olympus; Hazleton 67–62 Francisco; Oakland City 73–55 Patoka; Princeton 47–45 Ft. Branch; Owensville 46–45 Haubstadt; Mackey 52–40 Hazleton; Oakland City 63–51 Princeton; Owensville 52–42 Mackey; Owensville 47–42 Oakland City. Officials: Malvern Redman, Ivan Sprinkle.

OXFORD: Earl Park 43–40 Gilboa; Ambia 49–45 Wadena; Fowler 61–41 Otterbein; Boswell 46–44 Freeland Park; Pine Twp. 42–40 Oxford; Ambia 44–33 Earl Park; Fowler 51–48 Boswell; Pine Twp. 48–35 Ambia; Fowler 38–31 Pine Twp. Officials: Paul Dazey, Ed Kurtz.

PERU: Clay Twp. 74–47 Deedsville; Peru 92–52 Converse; Chili 47–30 Gilead; Bunker Hill 73–38 Mexico; Butler Twp. 55–53 Macy; Peru 51–48 Clay Twp.; Bunker Hill 71–47 Chili; Peru 94–45 Butler Twp.; Peru 84–55 Bunker Hill. Officials: Myron Weldy, Ray Nemeth.

PLYMOUTH: North Judson 72–44 Hamlet; West Twp. 64–44 Tippecanoe; San Pierre 61–48 Bremen; Knox 79–62 North Judson; West Twp. 42–40 San Pierre; Culver 52–47 Argos; Tyner 52–48 LaPaz; Plymouth 54–47 Grovertown; Culver 55–47 Bourbon; Plymouth 53–47 Tyner; Knox 37–20 West Twp.; Culver 54–36 Plymouth; Knox 66–50 Culver. Officials: Don Yohe, E. L. Aldrich, Walter Stebing.

RENSSELAER: DeMotte 59–51 Wheatfield; Kentland 66–37 Remington; Mt. Ayr 49–47 Kankakee Twp.; Brook 58–49 Morocco; Fair Oaks 54–50 Goodland; DeMotte 44–42 Rensselaer; Kentland 48–41 Mt. Ayr; Brook 59–51 Fair Oaks; DeMotte 62–55 Kentland; Brook 61–46 DeMotte. Officials: Sam Massette, Charles Marshall, Andrew Hiduke.

RICHMOND: Economy 43–39 Webster; Milton 60–38 Williamsburg; Richmond 54–36 Boston; Hagerstown 72–52 Whitewater; Centerville 45–32 Fountain City; Cambridge City 59–45 Greensfork; Milton 52–42 Economy; Richmond 74–53 Hagerstown; Centerville 59–44 Cambridge City; Richmond 49–40 Milton; Richmond 65–52 Centerville. Officials: Charles Timmons, Gerald Strickler, Clayton Nichols.

ROCHESTER: Kewanna 65–48 Francesville; Rochester 69–42 Grass Creek; Fulton 71–58 Monterey; Richland Center 81–26 Talma; Winamac 80–45 Pulaski; Aubbeenaubbee Twp 48–44 Star City; Akron 56–51 Medaryville; Rochester 57–47 Kewanna; Richland Center 77–68 Fulton; Winamac 62–46 Aubbeenaubbee Twp.; Rochester 45–40 Akron; Richland Center 68–67 Winamac; Richland Center 74–73 Rochester. Officials: Dean Geyer, Roscoe Hall, Everett Havens.

ROCKVILLE: St. Bernice 47–46 Tangier; Bridgeton 69–36 Greene Twp.; Cayuga 54–50 Marshall; Rockville 59–52 Rosedale; Montezuma 40–37 Bloomingdale; Clinton 49–37 Newport; Hillsdale 42–35 Bellmore; Dana 50–44 Mecca; St. Bernice 41–35 Bridgeton; Rockville 61–48 Cayuga; Montezuma 51–41 Clinton; Dana 37–35 Hillsdale; Rockville 14–11 St. Bernice; Montezuma 31–30 Dana; Montezuma 67–52 Rockville. Officials: Robert Gregory, Oran Hollandbeck, Roderick Witt, Byron Arnold.

RUSHVILLE: Raleigh 53–52 Rushville; Morton Memorial 74–37 Mays; Carthage 72–70 Arlington (ot); New Salem 67–35 Manilla; Milroy 71–39 Orange; Morton Memoria l85–51 Raleigh; Carthage 51–44 New Salem; Morton Memorial 55–38 Milroy; Morton Memorial 58–53

IHSAA Scores | 1950–1959

Carthage. Officials: Jerry Steiner, Don Dick.

SEYMOUR: Vallonia 59–44 Freetown; Seymour 76–53 Medora; Crothersville 61–45 Cortland; Hayden 56–41 Tampico; Brownstown 67–33 Clearspring; Seymour 64–48 Vallonia; Hayden 51–50 Crothersville; Brownstown 59–58 Seymour; Brownstown 70–52 Hayden. Officials: Herb Schwomeyer, Arthur Thompson.

SHELBYVILLE: Morristown 57–55 Hope; Columbus 68–55 Flat Rock; Shelbyville 58–43 Fairland; Boggstown 55–53 Clifford; Moral Twp. 66–44 Mt. Auburn; Morristown 68–60 Waldron; Shelbyville 55–49 Columbus; Boggstown 70–67 Moral Twp.; Shelbyville 76–31 Morristown; Shelbyville 56–48 Boggstown. Officials: Evan Crawley, Everett Campbell, Melbourne Pope.

SHERIDAN: Westfield 63–54 Windfall; Sharpsville 46–38 Prairie; Carmel 81–52 Noblesville; Sharpsville 48–45 Westfield; Sheridan 59–39 Walnut Grove; Jackson Central 83–64 Jefferson Twp.; Tipton 94–71 Fishers; Sheridan 89–53 Jackson Central; Carmel 61–52 Sharpsville; Sheridan 70–57 Tipton; Sheridan 58–56 Carmel. Officials: Cecil Bosstick, Lawrence Leland, Jack Small.

SOUTH BEND: Central 54–50 Riley; Washington-Clay 58–48 North Liberty; Mishawaka 84–37 Catholic; Central 73–46 Lakeville; Washington-Clay 62–59 Mishawaka; Madison Twp. 72–64 Greene Twp.; Walkerton 58–56 New Carlisle; Washington 53–52 Adams; Madison Twp. 62–60 Walkerton; Central 91–69 Washington-Clay; Madison Twp. 56–53 Washington; Central 83–68 Madison Twp. Officials: Harold Nelson, John Tatum, Edward Herbert.

SULLIVAN: Fairbanks 62–60 Hymera; Gill Twp. 50–38 Graysville; Farmersburg 64–56 Shelburn; Dugger 89–63 Pleasantville; Sullivan 43–33 Carlisle; Fairbanks 56–50 Gill Twp.; Dugger 60–57 Farmersburg; Sullivan 63–36 Fairbanks; Sullivan 80–59 Dugger. Officials: Odilo Berger, Willard Ketner.

TERRE HAUTE: Riley 67–55 Blackhawk; Laboratory 89–39 Fontanet; Garfield 51–32 Otter Creek; Concannon 75–43 Prairie Creek; Glenn 62–38 Pimento; Gerstmeyer 40–29 Fayette; Wiley 46–43 Honey Creek; Riley 62–43 West Terre Haute; Laboratory 49–44 Garfield; Concannon 65–52 Glenn; Gerstmeyer 55–35 Wiley; Laboratory 64–44 Riley; Gerstmeyer 50–45 Concannon; Gerstmeyer 62–50 Laboratory. Officials: Ed Straith-Miller, Kenneth Smartz, Otto Hurrle, Bob Crouch.

VALPARAISO: Boone Grove 55–44 Washington; Morgan Twp. 65–41 Kouts; Portage Twp. 60–59 Valparaiso; Hebron 75–49 Liberty Center; Chesterton 71–29 Jackson Twp.; Wheeler 59–58 Boone Grove; Portage Twp. 69–45 Morgan Twp.; Hebron 51–45 Chesterton; Wheeler 46–41 Portage Twp.; Hebron 51–42 Wheeler. Officials: Wayne Hammond, William Brainerd, William Ellis.

VERSAILLES: Holton 61–22 Cross Plains; Batesville 51–50 Sunman; Napoleon 60–36 New Marion; Milan 51–23 Osgood; Holton 43–39 Versailles; Batesville 57–32 Napoleon; Milan 27–15 Holton; Milan 42–27 Batesville. Officials: Harold Porter, John Gwin.

VEVAY: Lawrenceburg 60–42 Guilford; Bright 52–24 Patriot; Vevay 64–36 Moores Hill; Aurora 65–58 Rising Sun; Lawrenceburg 69–37 Dillsboro; Vevay 68–51 Bright; Aurora 42–33 Lawrenceburg; Aurora 40–36 Vevay. Officials: James Haywood, Wray Holbrook.

VINCENNES: Decker 51–37 Decker Chapel; Wheatland 57–51 Oaktown; Monroe City 71–69 Bruceville; Freelandville 43–42 Bicknell; Central Catholic 75–48 Fritchton; Sandborn 59–55 Vincennes; Wheatland 61–60 Decker; Monroe City 70–55 Freelandville; Sandborn 73–63 Central Catholic; Monroe City 44–33 Wheatland; Monroe City 75–44 Sandborn. Officials: Charles Fouty, Cyril Birge, Paul Neal.

Tourney Time

WABASH: Noble Twp. 64–52 Lagro; Chester Twp. 51–35 Urbana; Wabash 55–53 South Whitley; LaFontaine 67–47 Noble Twp.; Wabash 80–63 Chester Twp.; North Manchester 66–55 White's; Laketon 64–54 Roann; Somerset 79–74 Washington Center; North Manchester 75–48 Laketon; Wabash 48–42 LaFontaine; North Manchester 94–68 Somerset; Wabash 58–45 North Manchester. Officials: Edward Burke, Bill Larkin, Paul Hostetler.

WARSAW: Syracuse 54–48 Etna Green; Sidney 75–53 Atwood; Leesburg 47–40 Pierceton; Larwill 58–50 Claypool; Mentone 58–56 Beaver Dam; Silver Lake 71–47 Burkett; Warsaw 77–42 Columbia City; North Webster 61–54 Milford; Sidney 60–51 Syracuse; Leesburg 63–60 Larwill; Silver Lake 49–44 Mentone; North Webster 65–38 Warsaw; Sidney 59–48 Leesburg; North Webster 56–52 Silver Lake; North Webster 53–34 Sidney. Officials: Lloyd Bryan, Gerald Vowell, Dwight Byerly, Bill Garrett.

WASHINGTON: Washington 80–50 Odon; St. John's 54–50 Loogootee; Alfordsville 72–29 Epsom; Petersburg 80–33 Plainville; Washington Catholic 91–40 Shoals; Barr Twp. 77–46 Elnora; Washington 61–41 St. John's; Petersburg 75–59 Alfordsville; Washington Catholic 58–56 Barr Twp.; Washington 70–49 Petersburg; Washington 73–49 Washington Catholic. Officials: J. D. Nickle, Lloyd Whipple, Joseph Hunter.

WINCHESTER: Parker 47–43 Spartanburg; Ridgeville 57–38 McKinley; Saratoga 41–40 Jefferson; Union 70–58 Stoney Creek; Winchester 40–33 Jackson; Union City 43–42 Lynn; Farmland 47–41 Green; Parker 61–54 Wayne; Ridgeville 54–32 Saratoga; Union 55–45 Winchester; Union City 61–36 Farmland; Parker 51–35 Ridgeville; Union 50–45 Union City; Parker 54–33 Union. Officials: Robert Dornte, Everett Cass, Burl McKenzie, William Findling.

1953 REGIONALS

BEDFORD: Brownstown 67–64 Orleans; Jeffersonville 64–53 New Albany; Jeffersonville 77–60 Brownstown. Officials: Evan Crawley, Ken Merder, Cloyd Julian, Lowell Willis.

BLOOMINGTON: Brazil 54–46 Solsberry; Gerstmeyer 57–48 Bloomington; Gerstmeyer 51–43 Brazil. Officials: Cyril Birge, Leroy Heminger, Lloyd Whipple, William Dixon.

COVINGTON: Montezuma 81–66 Waveland; Attica 59–49 Greencastle; Attica 63–48 Montezuma. Officials: Charles Meade, Maurice Criswell, Herb Schwomeyer, Leon Hodson.

EVANSVILLE: Tell City 56–54 Boonville; Central 80–37 Owensville; Central 82–54 Tell City. Officials: S.T. Proffitt, Frank Smith, Ed Straith-Miller, Paul Neal.

FORT WAYNE: Monmouth 75–60 Kendallville; Central 60–31 Auburn; Central 75–46 Monmouth. Officials: Victor Griewank, E.L. Aldrich, Eugene Glaze, Frank Sanders.

HAMMOND: Lew Wallace 67–49 Hebron; Hammond 55–46 Michigan City; Lew Wallace 58–54 Hammond. Officials: Gerald Strickler, Burl McKenzie, Walter Bonham, Dean Geyer.

INDIANAPOLIS: Amo 59–52 Charlottesville; Crispus Attucks 62–57 Alexandria; Crispus Attucks 72–46 Amo. Officials: Leland Terrell, James Haywood, John Hilligoss, Wilbur May.

KOKOMO: Kokomo 75–59 Peru; Sheridan 49–42 Wabash; Kokomo 47–45 Sheridan. Officials: Lores Lehman, Stan Dubis, Paul Grimes, J.C. LaFollette.

LAFAYETTE: Zionsville 74–46 Fowler; Frankfort 58–56 Lafayette (2ot); Zionsville 61–56 Frankfort. Officials: Don Lieberum, Robert Rose, Don Polizotto, John Janzaurk.

LOGANSPORT: Brook 61–58 Wolcott; Logansport 72–48 Richland Center; Logansport 51–37 Brook. Officials: Paul Bateman, Charles Bobilya, Don McBride, John Burger.

MARION: Hartford City 63–55 Ossian; Mississinewa 57–49 Huntington; Hartford City 67–64 Mississinewa (ot). Officials: Roland Baker, Roy Gardner, Paul Hostetler, Robert Gregory.
MUNCIE: Richmond 57–51 New Castle; Muncie Central 78–50 Parker; Richmond 54–52 Muncie Central (2ot). Officials: Lawrence Leland, James Patterson, Dee Williams, Joe Mullins.
RUSHVILLE: Milan 53–51 Morton Memorial (2ot); Connersville 51–40 Aurora; Milan 24–22 Connersville. Officials: Eugene Sparks, Oscar Samuels, James Sanders, Kermit Spurgeon.
SHELBYVILLE: Shelbyville 37–33 Scottsburg; Greensburg 70–66 Clark Twp.; Shelbyville 68–43 Greensburg. Officials: Lowell Barnett, James Davidson, Charles Northam, John Gwin.
SOUTH BEND: North Webster 69–55 Knox; Central 67–53 Elkhart; Central 68–49 North Webster. Officials: Robert Dornte, Arthur Lloyd, Marvin Todd, George Collyer.
VINCENNES: Washington 75–57 Monroe City; Holland 61–60 Sullivan; Washington 67–56 Holland. Officials: Wayne Hammond, Edward S. Stuteville, Irvin Thrasher, Roy Brann.

1953 SEMI-FINALS
FORT WAYNE: Hartford City 71–53 Kokomo; Richmond 46–41 Central; Richmond 62–44 Hartford City. Officials: Lawrence Leland, Charles Meade, Don Polizotto, Wayne Hammond, Herbert Schwomeyer, Irvin Thrasher.
INDIANAPOLIS: Shelbyville 46–44 Crispus Attucks; Milan 49–48 Attica (ot); Milan 43–21 Shelbyville. Officials: Lores Lehman, Stan Dubis, Don McBride, S.T. Proffitt, Cyril Birge, Lloyd Whipple.
LAFAYETTE: South Bend Central 72–69 Logansport (ot); Gary Wallace 65–56 Zionsville; South Bend Central 61–54 Gary Wallace. Officials: Roland Baker, Roy Gardner, John Hilligoss, Charles Northam, Eugene Glaze, Dee Williams.
BLOOMINGTON: Gerstmeyer 67–51 Jeffersonville; Evansville Central 56–45 Washington; Gerstmeyer 78–71 Central. Officials: Walter Bonham, Victor Griewank, Paul Bateman, Lowell Barnett, Marvin Todd, Robert Dornte.

1953 FINALS—March 21
INDIANAPOLIS (Butler Fieldhouse): South Bend Central 56–37 Milan; Terre Haute Gerstmeyer 48–40 Richmond; Central 42–41 Gerstmeyer. Officials: John Hilligoss, Victor Griewank, Lores Lehman, Eugene Glaze, Don Polizotto, Lawrence Leland.

1954 SECTIONALS
ANDERSON: Alexandria 60–45 St. Mary's; Lapel 55–46 Markleville; Anderson 55–52 Elwood; Summitville 62–61 Frankton (ot); Alexandria 46–40 Pendleton; Anderson 51–35 Lapel; Alexandria 58–27 Summitville; Alexandria 65–51 Anderson. Officials: Homer Owens, John Hilligoss.
BEDFORD: Bedford 75–58 Williams; Orleans 66–53 Fayetteville; Paoli 60–58 Shawswick; Oolitic 74–55 Mitchell; Marshall Twp. 57–42 Huron; Heltonville 73–69 Tunnelton; Bedford 59–54 Orleans; Oolitic 63–54 Paoli; Heltonville 46–34 Marshall Twp.; Oolitic 56–53 Bedford (ot); Oolitic 86–48 Heltonville. Officials: Vern Doles, Lowell Willis, Odilo Berger.

Tourney Time

BLOOMINGTON: Martinsville 58–55 Morgantown; Stinesville 66–53 Unionville; Smithville 49–34 University; Eminence 50–41 Monrovia; Ellettsville 72–47 Paragon; Mooresville 57–52 Bloomington; Martinsville 77–57 Stinesville; Smithville 63–51 Eminence; Ellettsville 77–42 Mooresville; Martinsville 54–52 Smithville; Martinsville 64–59 Ellettsville. Officials: John Thomas, Ed Straith-Miller, Ivan Sprinkle.

BRAZIL: Spencer 36–34 Coal City; Cory 51–42 Patricksburg; Brazil 73–61 Staunton; Clay City 76–74 Van Buren (ot); Freedom 61–42 Coalmont; Gosport 50–44 Bowling Green; Spencer 55–38 Ashboro; Brazil 44–39 Cory; Clay City 45–44 Freedom (ot); Gosport 59–56 Spencer; Brazil 59–37 Clay City; Brazil 59–50 Gosport. Officials: Leonard Benedetto, Henry Pearcy, John Simon.

CLINTON: St. Bernice 83–49 Bellmore; Mecca 58–56 Tangier; Clinton 54–51 Cayuga; Rosedale 71–44 Greene Twp.; Montezuma 73–60 Bloomingdale; Rockville 63–47 Dana; Hillsdale 64–55 Bridgeton; Newport 68–61 Marshall; Mecca 50–39 St. Bernice; Clinton 45–40 Rosedale; Montezuma 58–49 Rockville; Newport 58–37 Hillsdale; Mecca 52–43 Clinton; Montezuma 56–54 Newport; Montezuma 67–57 Mecca. Officials: Charles Marshall, James Murphy, Bruce Swinford, Leo Ponto,

CONNERSVILLE: Alquina 86–42 Fairview; Brookville 65–49 Brownsville; Connersville 69–40 Springfield; Brookville 51–38 Alquina; Harrisburg 54–36 Harrison Twp.; Liberty 83–56 Whitewater; Harrisburg 72–53 Laurel; Connersville 53–44 Brookville; Harrisburg 42–30 Liberty; Connersville 67–46 Harrisburg. Officials: Charles Timmons, Everett Campbell, Earnest Baldwin.

COVINGTON: Perrysville 58–55 Hillsboro; Williamsport 82–40 Wallace; Covington 49–45 Kingman; Attica 50–40 Veedersburg; Pine Village 61–51 West Lebanon; Richland Twp. 66–56 Perrysville; Covington 61–47 Williamsport; Attica 42–39 Pine Village; Richland Twp. 63–47 Covington; Attica 70–62 Richland Twp. Officials: Roy Brann, Everett Boyer, Ed Kurtz.

CRAWFORDSVILLE: New Ross 60–45 Coal Creek Central; Linden 42–38–Waveland; Darlington 59–50 Bowers; New Ross 57–43 Linden; Ladoga 66–47 Waynetown; Crawfordsville 60–41 New Market; Ladoga 53–34 Alamo; New Ross 53–41 Darlington; Crawfordsville 59–49 Ladoga; New Ross 59–54 Crawfordsville. Officials: Irvin Thrasher, John Park, Willard Ketner.

DALE: Tell City 47–40 Chrisney; Troy 62–24 Bristow; Luce Twp. 72–44 Oil Twp.; Rockport 17–11 St. Ferdinand; Dale 39–31 Cannelton; Tell City 50–40 Troy; Rockport 50–34 Luce Twp.; Dale 55–44 Tell City; Rockport 47–45 Dale. Officials: Malvern Redman, Harold Gourley.

DANVILLE: New Winchester 59–48 Plainfield; Danville 62–59 Stilesville; Lizton 60–58 Speedway; North Salem 55–48 Avon; Clayton 69–32 Pittsboro; Amo 54–49 Charlton; Brownsburg 36–32 New Winchester; Danville 44–43 Lizton; Clayton 58–56 North Salem; Brownsburg 47–42 Amo; Danville 53–48 Clayton; Danville 48–43 Browns–burg. Officials: Fred Marlow, John Evans, William Findling.

DECATUR: Decatur 66–50 Hartford Center; Monmouth 73–67 Decatur Catholic; Decatur 59–49 Geneva; Pleasant Mills 56–52 Berne; Adams Central 68–55 Jefferson; Monmouth 57–47 Decatur; Pleasant Mills 62–54 Adams Central; Monmouth 63–58 Pleasant Mills. Officials: Frank Carnes, Gene Davis.

EVANSVILLE: Central 70–55 Griffin; Poseyville 58–53 Cynthiana; Lincoln 55–40 Mt. Vernon; Reitz 82–46 Wadesville; New Harmony 58–54 Memorial; Bosse 70–60 Mater Dei; Central 66–34 Poseyville; Lincoln 34–32 Reitz; Bosse 51–49 New Harmony; Central 46–45 Lincoln; Central 70–60 Bosse. Officials: Norman Risley, S.T. Proffitt, Cyril Birge.

IHSAA Scores | 1950–1959

FORT WAYNE: North Side 49–35 Leo; Central Catholic 72–41 Woodburn; South Side 34–32 Harlan; Elmhurst 49–26 Lafayette Central; Concordia 61–53 New Haven; Arcola 59–52 Coesse; Central 70–40 Hoagland; Huntertown 72–53 Monroeville; North Side 80–57 Central Catholic; South Side 65–52 Elmhurst; Concordia 71–53 Arcola; Central 69–42 Huntertown; North Side 50–48 South Side; Concordia 53–48 Central; North Side 59–56 Concordia (ot). Officials: Lowell Barnett. Wesley Oler, John Janzaruk, Harold Nelson.

FRANKFORT: Kirklin 67–38 Mulberry; Michigantown 78–40 Washington Twp.; Colfax 58–32 Sugar Creek; Rossville 77–66 Forest; Scircleville 47–46 Jackson Twp.; Frankfort 58–50 Kirklin; Michigantown 55–49 Colfax (ot); Rossville 57–53 Scircleville, Frankfort 70–61 Michigantown; Frankfort 62–44 Rossville. Officials: Oscar Samuels, John Tatum, Melvin Newlin.

FRANKLIN: Whiteland 45–31 Nineveh; Greenwood 47–37 Center Grove; Franklin 54–34 Nashville; Trafalgar 62–56 Union; Edinburg 49–47 Clark; Helmsburg 59–49 Van Buren; Whiteland 50–36 Greenwood; Franklin 65–41 Trafalgar; Edinburg 49–45 Helmsburg; Franklin 59–28 Whiteland; Franklin 47–36 Edinburg. Officials: G.W. Clapp, M. N. Delph, Don Dick.

GARRETT–AUBURN: (At Garrett): Auburn 66–37 Pleasant Lake; Waterloo 63–47 Metz; Concord–Spencer 60–52 Ashley; Butler 69–50 Scott Center; Auburn 49–45 Waterloo; Butler 70–67 Concord Spencer (ot); (At Auburn): Garrett 57–49 Salem Center; Hamilton 52–50 Orland; Churubusco 74–57 Angola; Garrett 57–51 Fremont; Churubusco 68–62 Hamilton; (At Garrett): Auburn 69–49 Butler; Garrett 56–55 Churubusco; Auburn 42–41 Garrett. Officials: Raymond Trobaugh, Walter McFatridge, Charles Garber, Gerald Imel, Bill Garrett, Eldo Fewell.

GARY: Froebel 58–39 Wallace; Roosevelt 56–34 Horace Mann; Merrillville 70–53 Emerson; Tolleston 50–36 Gary Edison; Roosevelt 52–47 Froebel; Tolleston 51–47 Merrillville; East Gary Edison 50–46 Wirt; Hobart 47–43 Calumet Twp.; Roosevelt 52–44 Tolleston; Hobart 57–55 East Gary Edison; Roosevelt 72–52 Hobart. Officials: Gene Winks, Victor Griewank, Dean Geyer.

GREENCASTLE: Fillmore 64–45 Russellville; Greencastle 59–32 Belle Union; Cloverdale 69–65 Bainbridge; Reelsville 53–51 Roachdale; Fillmore 57–51 Greencastle; Cloverdale 51–49 Reelsville; Fillmore 69–57 Cloverdale. Officials: Paul Dazey, Bill Wood.

GREENFIELD: Fortville 72–52 Franklin Twp.; Wilkinson 54–44 Charlottesville; Eden 72–41 McCordsville; Greenfield 53–43 Maxwell; Mt. Comfort 56–29 New Palestine; Fortville 48–46 Wilkinson; Greenfield 50–48 Eden; Fortville 57–41 Mt. Comfort; Fortville 51–49 Greenfield. Officials: John Gwin, Joe Garoffolo.

GREENSBURG: Greensburg 81–41 Sandcreek; Sandusky 63–62 New Point; St. Paul 49–28 Jackson Twp.; Burney 49–46 North Vernon; Vernon 65–51 Clarksburg; Greensburg 63–37 Sandusky; Burney 55–52 St. Paul; Greensburg 58–45 Vernon; Greensburg 77–49 Burney. Officials: Leroy Heminger, Kenneth Blankenbaker.

HAMMOND: Morton 63–49 Dyer; 62–50 Tech; Clark 84–79 Crown Point; Morton 59–55 Noll; Hammond High 65–54 Whiting; Griffith 65–45 Lowell; East Chicago Washington 74–57 East ChicagoRoosevelt; Hammond High 47–45 Griffith; Clark 64–62 Morton; Hammond High 64–47 Washington; Hammond High 73–62 Clark. Officials: Maurice Criswell, H.F. McNaught, Charles Meade.

HARTFORD CITY: Montpelier 52–21 Gray; Bryant 78–50 Pennville; Portland 72–51 Poling; Hartford City 69–33 Roll; Dunkirk 71–33 Madison; Montpelier 51–44 Redkey; Portland 64–53 Bryant; Hartford City 60–49 Dunkirk; Portland 56–45 Montpelier; Hartford City 66–57 Portland. Officials: Morris Stevens, Toy Jones, Roy Kilby.

Tourney Time

HUNTINGBURG: Winslow 86–42 Birdseye; Dubois 50–39 Ireland; Huntingburg 52–46 Holland; Jasper 49–44 Stendal; Otwell 60–54 Spurgeon; French Lick 36–33 West Baden; Winslow 59–46 Dubois; Huntingburg 57–47 Jasper; French Lick 50–31 Otwell; Winslow 56–48 Huntingburg; Winslow 67–53 French Lick. Officials: J. Firman Grimes, Roland Baker, Kermit Spurgeon.

HUNTINGTON: Bippus 63–35 Wayne Twp.; Huntington Twp. 59–48 Roanoke; Salamonie Twp. 57–50 Jefferson Twp. (Warren); Huntington 60–50 Andrews; Clear Creek 68–36 Union Twp; Jefferson Center (Columbia City) 40–37 Markle; Lancaster Twp. 62–47 Rock Creek; Huntington Catholic 91–44 Bippus; Huntington Twp. 46–45 Salamonie Twp; Huntington 58–42 Clear Creek; Lancaster Twp. 75–63 Jefferson Center (Columbia City); Huntington Twp. 44–43 Huntington Catholic; Huntington 55–45 Lancaster Twp.; Huntington 68–46 Huntington Twp. Officials: Paul Hostetler, Gene Butts, Roscoe Hall, Walter Stebing.

INDIANAPOLIS: Lawrence Central 39–38 Southport; Crispus Attucks 86–54 Ben Davis; Broad Ripple 81–44 School for the Deaf; Sacred Heart 67–50 Beech Grove; Warren Central 49–47 Manual; Shortridge 63–54 Howe; Tech 63–28 Decatur Central; Washington 55–50 Cathedral; Crispus Attucks 64–32 Lawrence Central; Broad Ripple 55–54 Sacred Heart; Warren Central 58–51 Shortridge; Tech 61–56 Washington; Crispus Attucks 70–52 Broad Ripple; Tech 60–45 Warren Central; Crispus Attucks 53–46 Tech. Officials: Joe Mullins, Jack Small, Roy Gardner, Don Lieberum.

JEFFERSONVILLE: New Washington 73–45 Hardinsburg; Silver Creek 37–29 Salem; Jeffersonville 90–48 Charlestown; Borden 61–41 Pekin; Henryville 63–61 Providence; Campbellsburg 48–45 New Washington; Jeffersonville 54–45 Silver Creek; Henryville 52–50 Borden (ot); Jeffersonville 81–43 Campbellsburg; Jeffersonville 77–45 Henryville. Officials: James Patterson, Wray Holbrook, Robert Cherry.

KENDALLVILLE: Shipshewana 46–42 Cromwell; Brighton 57–43 Springfield Twp.; Avilla 79–75 Wawaka; Wolcottville 69–39 Topeka; Kendallville 73–41 Rome City; Howe Military 48–46 Wolf Lake; Ligonier 66–49 Lima; LaGrange 60–57 Albion; Shipshewana 51–44 Brighton; Avilla 71–43 Wolcottville; Howe Military 61–59 Kendallville: LaGrange 73–71 Ligonier (ot.); Avilla 61–45 Shipshewana; LaGrange 60–36 Howe Military; LaGrange 60–49 Avilla. Officials: Everett Havens, Lloyd Bryan, Ray Nemeth, Thomas Demark.

KOKOMO: Camden 56–42 Cutler; Flora 87–29 Deer Creek; Eastern 112–21 Carrollton; Kokomo 51–50 Northwestern; Delphi 59–44 Burlington; Western 62–57 Camden; Flora 60–58 Eastern; Kokomo 83–41 Delphi; Flora 53–50 Western (ot); Kokomo 69–64 Flora (ot). Officials: Robert Dornte, Arthur Lloyd, Lawrence Gradeless.

LAFAYETTE: Shadeland 70–43 Romney; Klondike 51–47 West Lafayette; Stockwell 55–47 Battle Ground; Buck Creek 75–72 Clarks Hill; Lafayette 99–35 Wea; Dayton 48–42 Monitor; West Point 71–35 Jackson Twp; Shadeland 61–56 Montmorenci; Klondike 45–43 Stockwell (2ot); Lafayette 96–54 Buck Creek; Dayton 43–40 West Point; Klondike 44–42 Shadeland; Lafayette 60–39 Dayton; Lafayette 69–39 Klondike. Officials: Lawrence Leland, Robert Spay; Paul Grimes, Robert Sosbe.

LAWRENCEBURG: Lawrenceburg 51–33 Patriot; Aurora 57–40 Guilford; Vevay 53–40 Bright; Rising Sun 61–45 Moores Hill; Lawrenceburg 54–29 Dillsboro; Aurora 47–37 Vevay; Lawrenceburg 46–41 Rising Sun; Aurora 46–39 Lawrenceburg. Officials: Robert Laird, Dwain Laird.

LEBANON: Lebanon 58–48 Dover; Zionsville 78–57 Whitestown; Pike Twp. 53–52 Perry Central; Jackson Twp. 47–46 Thorntown; Lebanon 53–39 Pinnell; Pike Twp. 50–49 Zionsville (2ot.); Lebanon 59–45 Jackson Twp.; Lebanon 55–42 Pike Twp. Officials: Clayton Smith, William Yohler.

LINTON: Bloomfield 63–37 Marco; Midland 55–47 Jasonville; Linton 67–52 Lyons; Solsberry 79–22 Scotland; Switz City 83–72 Worthington; Bloomfield 72–54 Midland; Linton 63–55 Solsberry; Switz City 65–56 Bloomfield; Linton 63–57 Switz City. Officials: Thomas Hoffman, Charles Fouty.

LOGANSPORT: Lucerne 64–42 New Waverly; Logansport 83–30 Tipton Twp.; Galveston 50–45 Young America; Washington Twp. 73–48 Twelve Mile; Metea 51–50 Royal Center; Logansport 64–25 Lucerne, Washington Twp. 49–43 Galveston; Logansport 67–30 Metea; Logansport 88–48 Washington Twp. Officials: Gerald Strickler, Leonard Lupold.

LYNNVILLE: Selvin 54–39 Tennyson; Newburgh 70–28 Folsomville; Lynnville 44–37 Elberfeld; Chandler 55–36 Millersburg; Boonville 53–34 Selvin; Lynnville 63–49 Newburgh; Boonville 40–38 Chandler (ot); Lynnville 46–45 Boonville (ot). Officials: Robert Davidson, Vesper Moore.

MADISON: Central 35–34 Austin; Madison 88–59 Lexington; Scottsburg 98–59 Dupont; Hanover 54–50 Deputy; Paris Crossing 63–42 Saluda; Madison 55–45 Central; Scottsburg 64–53 Hanover; Madison 94–84 Paris Crossing; Scottsburg 50–48 Madison. Officials: Eugene Sparks, James Sanders.

MARION: Swayzee 64–43 Sweetser; Mississinewa 67–28 Van Buren; Marion 72–44 Jefferson Twp.; Fairmount 81–43 St. Paul; Mississinewa 50–29 Swayzee; Marion 61–46 Fairmount; Mississinewa 55–47 Marion. Officials: Don McBride, James Ridge.

MICHIGAN CITY: Westville 68–53 Stillwell; Clinton Twp. 48–38 Kingsbury; Union Twp. 60–50 LaCrosse; Rolling Prairie 68–63 LaPorte; St. Mary 62–33 Wanatah; Union Mills 50–39 Mill Creek; Michigan City 70–30 Hanna; Westville 49–38 Clinton Twp.; Union Twp. 52–47 Rolling Prairie; Union Mills 67–56 St. Mary; Michigan City 77–34 Westville; Union Mills 62–54 Union Twp.; Michigan City 71–49 Union Mills. Officials: Frank Sanders, Merle Shively, Sam Massette.

MUNCIE: Daleville 64–53 Harrison Twp.; Gaston 64–63 Albany; Yorktown 67–61 Royerton; Center 64–57 Eaton; Burris 68–47 Selma; Central 89–38 Cowan; Daleville 66–61 DeSoto; Yorktown 60–42 Gaston; Burris 61–44 Center; Central 94–32 Daleville; Burris 61–43 Yorktown; Central 63–54 Burris. Officials: Wayne Crispen, Clarence Brown, Dee Williams, R. Wayne Smith.

NAPPANEE: Baugo Twp. 52–39 Scott; Bristol 56–50 Wakarusa; Goshen 62–58 New Paris; Baugo Twp. 60–55 Bristol; Nappanee 75–66 Jefferson Twp.; Elkhart 63–53 Middlebury; Millersburg 73–70 Concord Twp.; Elkhart 48–47 Nappanee; Goshen 61–56 Baugo Twp.; Elkhart 78–35 Millersburg; Elkhart 79–51 Goshen. Officials: John Sebastian, Stan Dubis, E.L. Aldrich.

NEW ALBANY: English 61–38 Leavenworth; Lanesville 57–48 Morgan Twp.; Laconia 61–37 Georgetown; Milltown 52–40 New Middleton; Elizabeth 65–58 Marengo; Corydon 59–39 Mt. St. Francis; New Albany 75–43 New Salisbury; Lanesville 55–54 English; Laconia 59–45 Milltown; Corydon 61–46 Elizabeth; New Albany 100–66 Lanesville; Laconia 54–49 Corydon; New Albany 87–56 Laconia. Officials: Frank Smith, Oran Hollandbeck, Noel Genth.

NEW CASTLE: Straughn 60–50 Knightstown (ot); New Castle 86–64 Sulphur Springs;

Tourney Time

Mooreland 76–64 Cadiz; Straughn 49–47 New Castle; Lewisville 50–41 Mt. Summit; Middletown 80–54 New Lisbon; Spiceland 67–47 Kennard; Middletown 75–41 Lewisville; Straughn 52–49 Mooreland; Middletown 73–48 Spiceland; Middletown 55–42 Straughn. Officials: Byron Arnold, Wayne Hammond, Robert Crouch.

OSSIAN: Ossian 59–53 Jackson; Bluffton 60–50 Union Center; Chester Center 60–58 Lancaster Central; Rockcreek 58–53 Liberty Center; Ossian 52–44 Petroleum; Bluffton 45–37 Chester Center; Ossian 60–54 Rockcreek (ot); Bluffton 40–33 Ossian. Officials: Burl Shook, Leon Hodson.

OTTERBEIN: Gilboa 61–41 Wadena; Ambia 48–33 Freeland Park; Fowler 55–38 Boswell; Pine Twp. 54–44 Earl Park; Otterbein 59–57 Oxford; Ambia 47–45 Gilboa; Fowler 42–35 Pine Twp.; Otterbein 46–38 Ambia; Fowler 69–39 Otterbein. Officials: Roderick Witt, David Albright.

OWENSVILLE: Ft. Branch 52–46 Owensville; Francisco 56–44 Hazleton; Oakland City 71–46 Mackey; Princeton 69–45 Haubstadt; Patoka 50–36 Mt. Olympus; Ft. Branch 47–43 Francisco; Princeton 52–44 Oakland City; Ft. Branch 57–45 Patoka; Ft. Branch 66–50 Princeton. Officials: Kenneth Merder, Tyrus Rice.

PERU: Bunker Hill 60–33 Gilead; Converse 50–37 Chili; Peru 68–40 Clay. Twp.; Mexico 82–71 Macy; Deedsville 41–38 Butler Twp.; Converse-Jackson 34–32 Bunker Hill; Peru 75–40 Mexico; Converse-Jackson 56–33 Deedsville; Peru 41–37 Converse-Jackson. Officials: Marvin Todd, Everett Cass.

PLYMOUTH: San Pierre 53–41 Culver; Argos 29–21 Knox; Grovertown 58–55 West Twp.; LaPaz 59–56 San Pierre; Argos 79–46 Grovertown; North Judson 77–57 Tyner; Hamlet 58–51 Tippecanoe; Plymouth 54–52 Bourbon; North Judson 54–46 Bremen; Plymouth 56–47 Hamlet; LaPaz 46–43 Argos; North Judson 56–35 Plymouth; LaPaz 48–47 North Judson (ot). Officials: Paul Bateman, Richard Duffield, Burl McKenzie.

RENSSELAER: DeMotte 57–42 Wheatfield; Goodland 42–41 Fair Oaks; Morocco 43–37 Mt. Ayr; Brook 52–51 Rensselaer: Kentland 77–37 Remington; DeMotte 60–32 Kankakee Twp.; Goodland 46–39 Morocco; Kentland 61–53 Brook; DeMotte 60–49 Goodland; Kentland 57–45 DeMotte. Officials: E.S. Stuteville, Harley Collins, Anthony Lazar.

RICHMOND: Richmond 81–46 Whitewater; Cambridge City 64–44 Webster; Milton 41–31 Centerville; Hagerstown 48–45 Williamsburg; Fountain City 51–33 Boston; Economy 38–37 Greens Fork; Richmond 70–37 Cambridge City; Milton 60–48 Hagerstown; Fountain City 52–31 Economy; Milton 41–34 Richmond; Milton 55–43 Fountain City. Officials: Arthur Thompson, Eugene Glaze, Gil Smith.

RUSHVILLE: Orange 46–40 Arlington; New Salem 69–45 Manilla; Rushville 49–27 Milroy; Mays 50–46 Raleigh; Carthage 52–48 Morton Memorial; New Salem 48–37 Orange; Rushville 67–51 Mays; Carthage 45–42 New Salem; Rushville 54–53 Carthage. Officials: Noble Benbow, Herbert Brammell.

SEYMOUR: Freetown 59–43 Tampico; Medora 56–55 Crothersville (ot); Seymour 56–43 Vallonia; Clearspring 58–40 Cortland; Brownstown 79–58 Hayden; Medora 83–43 Freetown; Seymour 78–60 Clearspring; Medora 64–52 Brownstown; Seymour 100–68 Medora. Officials: Robert Rose, James Lentz.

SHELBYVILLE: Waldron 67–45 Mt. Auburn; Moral Twp. 69–39 Flat Rock; Columbus 65–56 Boggstown; Hope 82–57 Clifford; Morristown 57–51 Fairland; Waldron 57–41 Shelbyville; Columbus 51–48 Moral Twp.; Morristown 57–48 Hope; Columbus 54–52 Waldron; Columbus

52–44 Morristown. Officials: Herbert Schwomeyer, John Holmes, Kenneth Smartz.

SHERIDAN: Noblesville 51–44 Sharpsville; Fishers 49–44 Carmel; Westfield 68–54 Jackson Central; Fishers 83–63 Noblesville; Sheridan 69–55 Windfall; Jefferson Twp. 70–60 Prairie Twp.; Tipton 42–34 Walnut Grove; Sheridan 70–49 Jefferson Twp.; Fishers 58–56 Westfield; Sheridan 42–29 Tipton; Sheridan 52–46 Fishers. Officials: Charles Northam, Wilbur May, Glenn Lantz.

SOUTH BEND: Central 67–50 Washington-Clay; North Liberty 38–36 Walkerton (2ot); Adams 72–62 New Carlisle; Central 51–46 Riley; Adams 68–47 North Liberty; Madison Twp. 68–61 Lakeville; Mishawaka 80–51 Greene Twp.; St. Joseph 60–48 Washington; Mishawaka 81–55 Madison Twp.; Central 68–53 Adams; Mishawaka 59–49 St. Joseph; Central 75–60 Mishawaka. Officials: Don McCoy, Robert Kramer, Don Polizotto.

SULLIVAN: Sullivan 57–47 Graysville; Hymera 64–54 Shelburn; Farmersburg 67–53 Gill Twp.; Dugger 43–39 Carlisle; Pleasantville 52–43 Fairbanks; Sullivan 64–39 Hymera; Farmersburg 62–59 Dugger; Sullivan 51–40 Pleasantville; Farmersburg 57–55 Sullivan (ot). Officials: Leland Terrell, Lester Cornwell.

TERRE HAUTE: Schulte 63–53 Fontanet; Garfield 81–58 Riley; Gerstmeyer 69–45 Pimento; Glenn 77–63 Blackhawk; Otter Creek 69–32 Prairie Creek; Laboratory 57–50 West Terre Haute; Wiley 58–48 Concannon; Honey Creek 50–36 Fayette; Garfield 64–46 Schulte; Gerstmeyer 102–66 Glenn; Laboratory 62–43 Otter Creek; Honey Creek 61–56 Wiley; Gerstmeyer 44–42 Garfield; Honey Creek 72–61 Laboratory; Gerstmeyer 86–52 Honey Creek. Officials: Clayton Nichols, Melbourne Pope, Paul Neal, James Boswell, Winfield Jacobs.

VALPARAISO: Wheeler 47–44 Chesterton; Liberty Twp. 61–46 Jackson Twp.; Boone Grove 77–60 Morgan Twp.; Hebron 50–33 Kouts; Valparaiso 47–40 Portage Twp.; Wheeler 51–38 Washington Twp.; Boone Grove 72–65 Liberty Twp.; Hebron 59–37 Valparaiso; Boone Grove 61–55 Wheeler; Hebron 62–45 Boone Grove. Officials: Norris Ward, Robert Brees, Bill Larkin.

VERSAILLES: Sunman 51–45 Holton; Versailles 59–30 New Marion; Batesville 62–57 Napoleon; Milan 83–36 Cross Plains; Osgood 50–38 Sunman; Versailles 43–38 Batesville; Milan 44–32 Osgood; Milan 57–43 Versailles. Officials: John Williams, Cloyd Julian.

VINCENNES: Freelandville 72–48 Oaktown; Monroe City 60–50; Sandborn 63–48 Bruceville; Vincennes 80–51 Bicknell; Central Catholic 69–49 Decker Chapel; Fritchton 64–52 Decker; Freelandville 68–56 Monroe City; Vincennes 57–35 Sandborn; Central Catholic 56–49 Fritchton; Vincennes 78–46 Freelandville; Vincennes 63–58 Central Catholic. Officials: Joseph Hunter, Lloyd Whipple, Hugh Thrasher.

WABASH: North Manchester 71–37 Lagro; Somerset 44–42 Roann; Wabash 73–53 Noble Twp.; South Whitley 60–55 North Manchester; Wabash 70–35 Somerset; Urbana 53–45 Washington Center; LaFontaine 41–37 White's; Chester Twp. 73–55 Laketon; LaFontaine 48–34 Urbana; Wabash 75–71 South Whitley; LaFontaine 49–40 Chester Twp.; Wabash 52–50 LaFontaine. Officials: Loris Jacobs, Richard Swartz, Lores Lehman.

WARSAW: Columbia City 52–50 Silver Lake; Warsaw 67–56 North Webster; Atwood 60–55 Claypool; Milford 67–51 Syracuse; Sidney 62–55 Etna Green; Mentone 88–68 Larwill; Pierceton 55–54 Beaver Dam; Leesburg 61–54 Burket; Warsaw 74–63 Columbia City; Milford 60–47 Atwood; Mentone 67–58 Sidney; Pierceton 50–47 Leesburg; Warsaw 59–51 Milford; Mentone 78–68 Pierceton; Mentone 72–55 Warsaw. Officials: George Collyer, Phil Bail, John Burger, Myron Weldy.

WASHINGTON: Washington Catholic 78–46 Plainville; Alfordsville 52–35 Shoals; Loogootee

Tourney Time

65–47 Elmore Twp.; Washington 61–42 Petersburg; Loogootee St. John's 63–47 Odon; Barr Twp. 72–26 Epsom; Alfordsville 56–55 Washington Catholic; Washington 73–54 Loogootee; Barr Twp. 69–49 Loogootee St. John's; Washington 72–38 Alfordsville; Washington 52–49 Barr Twp, Officials: William Yaggi, William Dixon, Wilfred Susott.

WINAMAC: Kewanna 52–48 Winamac (ot); Talma 57–56 Fulton; Richland Center 71–52 Star City; Grass Creek 44–43 Pulaski; Rochester 74–60 Akron; Medaryville 87–78 Monterey; Francesville 63–53 Aubbeenaubbee Twp.; Kewanna 70–24 Talma; Richland Center 57–52 Grass Creek; Rochester 62–53 Medaryville; Kewanna 52–43 Francesville; Richland Center 57–56 Rochester; Kewanna 39–37 Richland Center. Officials: John Cover, Edward Burke, Andrew Hiduke.

WINCHESTER: Ridgeville 69–53 Jefferson; Union City 55–48 Spartanburg; Winchester 68–39 Saratoga; Union 67–48 Green Twp.; Parker 58–51 Farmland; Lynn 51–45 Wayne Twp.; McKinley 67–51 Stoney Creek; Ridgeville 53–43 Jackson; Union City 71–51 Winchester; Union 53–45 Parker (ot); Lynn 43–41 McKinley; Union City 81–38 Ridgeville; Lynn 48–45 Union; Union City 40–38 Lynn. Officials: James Haywood, John DeMoss, Howard Plough, Karl Bly.

WOLCOTT: Monon 44–40 Burnettsville; Idaville 52–44 Buffalo; Wolcott 71–51 Monticello; Brookston 51–49 Reynolds; Monon 61–51 Chalmers; Wolcott 65–57 Idaville; Brookston 70–57 Monon; Wolcott 55–49 Brookston. Officials: Ward Mosbaugh, Robert Windsor.

1954 REGIONALS

EVANSVILLE: Rockport 66–35 Lynnville; Central 67–64 Ft. Branch (ot); Central 70–57 Rockport. Officials: Leland Terrell, Leroy Heminger, Roland Baker, Paul Grimes.

FORT WAYNE: North Side 68–54 Monmouth; Auburn 60–53 LaGrange; North Side 65–56 Auburn. Officials: John Hilligoss, Wilbur May, Charles Meade, James Haywood.

GREENCASTLE: Montezuma 55–52 Fillmore; New Ross 51–46 Attica; Montezuma 70–61 New Ross. Officials: Eugene Sparks, Morris Stevens, James Sanders, Wray Holbrook.

HAMMOND: Hammond High 59–53 Gary Roosevelt; Michigan City 58–56 Hebron; Hammond High 67–49 Michigan City. Officials: Robert Dornte, Jack Small, Don Lieberum, E.S. Stuteville.

HUNTINGBURG: Winslow 59–51 Vincennes; Washington 68–63 Farmersburg; Winslow 61–51 Washington. Officials: Herbert Schwomeyer, Frank Smith, Dee Williams, Kenneth Smartz.

INDIANAPOLIS: Alexandria 70–57 Danville; Crispus Attucks 54–44 Fortville; Crispus Attucks 64–48 Alexandria. Officials: Marvin Todd, Frank Sanders, Charles Northam, James Patterson.

JEFFERSONVILLE: Seymour 71–65 Oolitic; Jeffersonville 65–46 New Albany; Jeffersonville 58–50 Seymour. Officials: Lloyd Whipple, William Dixon, Cyril Birge, Ivan Sprinkle.

KOKOMO: Kokomo 60–43 Peru; Sheridan 64–52 Wabash; Kokomo 45–44 Sheridan. Officials: Gerald Strickler, Roy Gardner, Dean Geyer, John Janzaruk.

LAFAYETTE: Fowler 52–50 Frankfort; Lafayette 55–52 Lebanon; Lafayette 71–43 Fowler. Officials: Victor Griewank, Roy Brann, Lowell Willis, George Collyer.

LOGANSPORT: Logansport 87–47 Wolcott; Kentland 60–49 Kewanna; Logansport 72–47 Kentland. Officials: Wayne Hammond, Arthur Lloyd, Cloyd Julian, Oscar Samuels.

MARION: Mississinewa 64–49 Hartford City; Bluffton 38–27 Huntington; Mississinewa

54–36 Bluffton. Officials: Ed Straith-Miller, John Gwin, Paul Bateman, John Burger.

MARTINSVILLE: Terre Haute Gerstmeyer 67–49 Brazil; Martinsville 67–59 Linton; Gerstmeyer 71–62 Martinsville. Officials: Lawrence Leland, Leon Hodson, Don McBride, Robert Rose.

MUNCIE: Muncie Central 61–38 Union City; Middletown 61–41 Milton; Muncie Central 57–52 Middletown. Officials: Stan Dubis, Burl McKenzie, Don Polizotto, E. L. Aldrich.

RUSHVILLE: Milan 58–34 Rushville; Aurora 67–51 Connersville; Milan 46–38 Aurora. Officials: Lowell Barnett, Clayton Nichols, Irvin Thrasher, Ken Merder.

SHELBYVILLE: Columbus 72–67 Greensburg; Scottsburg 55–53 Franklin; Columbus 63–50 Scottsburg. Officials: S.T. Proffitt, John Williams, Eugene Glaze, Kermit Spurgeon.

SOUTH BEND: Elkhart 68–47 Mentone; South Bend Central 88–51 LaPaz; Elkhart 70–61 Central. Officials: Lores Lehman, Maurice Criswell, Joe Mullins, H.F. McNaught.

1954 SEMI—FINALS

BLOOMINGTON: Terre Haute Gerstmeyer 49–46 Jeffersonville; Evansville Central 58–47 Winslow; Terre Haute Gerstmeyer 55–44 Evansville Central. Officials: Eugene Glaze, Lowell Barnett, Lores Lehman, Joe Mullins, Charles Meade, Roy Gardner,

FORT WAYNE: Muncie Central 62–48 North Side; Mississinewa 66–55 Kokomo; Muncie Central 63–48 Mississinewa. Officials: Roland Baker, Don McBride, Stan Dubis, Eugene Sparks, Lawrence Leland, Herb Schwomeyer.

INDIANAPOLIS: Milan 44–34 Montezuma; Crispus Attucks 68–67 Columbus; Milan 65–52 Crispus Attucks. Officials: S.T. Proffitt, Lloyd Whipple, Victor Griewank, Robert Dornte, Don Polizotto, Cyril Birge.

LAFAYETTE: Elkhart 47–43 Lafayette Jefferson; Hammond 58–46 Logansport; Elkhart 63–53 Hammond. Officials: Dee Williams, Wayne Hammond, John Hilligoss, Ed Straith-Miller, Marvin Todd, Charles Northam.

1954 FINALS—March 20

INDIANAPOLIS (Butler Fieldhouse): Muncie Central 59–50 Elkhart; Milan 60–48 Terre Haute Gerstmeyer; Milan 32–30 Muncie Central. Officials: S.T. Proffitt, Charles Meade, Lawrence Leland, Stan Dubis, Marvin Todd, Cyril Birge.

1955 SECTIONALS

ADAMS CENTRAL: Berne 47–43 Hartford Center; Monmouth 62–57 Decatur; Decatur Catholic 56–43 Berne; Adams Central 57–48 Pleasant Mills; Geneva 63–36 Jefferson; Monmouth 50–49 Decatur Catholic; Geneva 43–41 Adams Central (2ot); Monmouth 56–53 Geneva (ot). Officials: William Yohler, Earnest Baldwin.

ANDERSON: Alexandria 45–33 Pendleton; Anderson 85–48 Frankton; Lapel 68–37 St. Mary's; Markleville 61–44 Summitville; Alexandria 41–34 Elwood; Anderson 58–42 Lapel; Markleville 59–45 Alexandria; Anderson 67–45 Markleville. Officials: Dee Williams, Wesley Oler, Richard Tiernan.

Tourney Time

ATTICA: Veedersburg 69–61 Kingman; Richland Twp. 80–51 Wallace; Covington 39–35 Perrysville (ot); Attica 39–36 Williamsport; West Lebanon 42–41 Pine Village; Hillsboro 64–62 Veedersburg; Richland Twp. 56–45 Covington; Attica 64–42 West Lebanon; Hillsboro 46–45 Richland Twp.; Attica 54–48 Hillsboro. Officials: Raymond Trobaugh, Eldo Fewell, Walter Frye.

AUBURN–GARRETT: (At Auburn): Metz 47–46 Ashley; Angola 63–41 Waterloo; Garrett 58–46 Scott Center; Fremont 62–49 Churubusco; Angola 66–52 Metz; Garrett 41–36 Fremont; (At Garrett): Butler 52–38 Orland; Auburn 67–50 Pleasant Lake; Salem Center 62–60 Hamilton; Butler 56–41 Riverdale; Auburn 76–61 Salem Center; (At Auburn): Angola.56–55 Garrett; Auburn 56–52 Butler; Auburn 65–57 Angola. Officials: Phil Bail, Glen Dunn, Paul Hostetler, James Murray.

AURORA: Aurora 56–36 Dillsboro; Lawrenceburg 49–32 Patriot; Vevay 63–52 Rising Sun; Bright 35–32 Guilford; Aurora 74–41 Moores Hill; Vevay 48–41 Lawrenceburg; Aurora 74–41 Bright; Vevay 44–42 Aurora. Officials: Robert Cherry, Wray Holbrook, Gilbert Beagle.

BEDFORD: Paoli 60–46 Tunnelton; Huron 49–45 Heltonville; Bedford 46–42 Mitchell; Orleans 68–52 Fayetteville; Shawswick 68–61 Needmore; Oolitic 52–50 Williams; Paoli 66–38 Huron; Bedford 67–56 Orleans; Oolitic 55–47 Shawswick; Paoli 56–41 Bedford; Paoli 50–48 Oolitic (ot). Officials: Henry Pearcy, Cyril Birge, Tyrus Rice.

BLUFFTON: Rockcreek 55–53 Ossian; Petroleum 69–44 Jackson Twp.; Chester Center 64–58 Lancaster Central; Bluffton 71–47 Liberty Center; Union Center 58–44 Rockcreek; Chester Center 47–44 Petroleum; Bluffton 65–52 Union Center; Bluffton 46–35 Chester Center. Officials: Roscoe Hall, Walter Stebing, William May.

BRAZIL: Brazil 43–40 Spencer; Patricksburg 51–46 Gosport; Coalmont 68–57 Coal City; Staunton 58–41 Bowling Green; Freedom 57–50 Ashboro; Clay City 60–47 Cory; Brazil 58–44 Van Buren; Patricksburg 56–51 Coalmont; Staunton 54–31 Freedom; Brazil 56–40 Clay City; Patricksburg 46–44 Staunton; Brazil 57–33 Patricksburg. Officials: Melbourne Pope, Clarence Brown, Charles Marshall.

COLUMBUS: Clifford 53–47 Hope; Flat Rock 35–34 Boggstown; Mt. Auburn 52–40 Fairland; Shelbyville 53–38 Moral Twp.; Columbus 65–35 Waldron; Clifford 51–49 Flat Rock; Shelbyville 72–41 Mt. Auburn; Columbus 52–46 Clifford; Columbus 47–44 Shelby-ville. Officials: Cloyd Julian, Bill Wood.

CONNERSVILLE: Harrisburg 75–38 Brownsville; Brookville 56–48 Laurel; Alquina 59–37 Fairview; Brookville 66–47 Harrisburg; Springfield Twp. 42–26 Harrison Twp.; Liberty 49–44 Whitewater; Connersville 68–33 Orange; Liberty 49–14 Springfield Twp.; Alquina 57–41 Brookville; Connersville 57–42 Liberty; Connersville 83–44 Alquina. Officials: Leonard Benedetto, Homer Owens, Ward Mosbaugh.

CRAWFORDSVILLE: Linden 67–44 Coal Greek Central; New Market 54–38 Alamo; Waveland 80–53 Waynetown; Linden 54–40 New Market; New Ross 59–40 Darlington; Crawfordsville 79–50 Ladoga; New Ross 73–61 Bowers; Linden 50–43 Waveland; Crawfordsville 74–39 New Ross; Crawfordsville 56–37 Linden. Officials: Gilbert Smith, Glen Lantz, Joseph Thomas.

DANVILLE: Danville 61–58 New Winchester; Clayton 63–52 Brownsburg; Amo 61–42 Pittsboro; Charlton 60–56 Avon; Plainfield 68–44 Stilesville; Speedway 69–59 Lizton; Danville 57–43 North Salem; Amo 53–40 Clayton; Plainfield 71–48 Charlton; Speedway 64–62 Danville; Plainfield 65–40 Amo; Speedway 73–59 Plainfield. Officials: James Murphy, Leo Ponto, Bruce Swinford.

IHSAA Scores / 1950–1959

ELKHART: Goshen 76–61 Jefferson; Wakarusa 54–42 Scott; New Paris 71–49 Baugo Twp.; Millersburg 68–67 Concord; Nappanee 48–47 Elkhart; Middlebury 56–34 Bristol; Wakarusa 63–56 Goshen; Millersburg 46–41 New Paris; Nappanee 53–45 Middlebury; Wakarusa 61–59 Millersburg; Nappanee 56–39 Wakarusa. Officials: Don McCoy, Joe Mullins, Robert Dornte.

EVANSVILLE: New Harmony 57–44 Mt. Vernon; Cynthiana. 47–41 Wadesville; Reitz 52–49 Bosse; Lincoln 51–41 Memorial; Central 67–49 Mater Dei; Griffin 59–56 Poseyville; New Harmony 62–36 Cynthiana; Reitz 61–51 Lincoln; Central 85–35 Griffin; Reitz 50–45 New Harmony; Reitz 60–53 Central. Officials: Winfield Jacobs, Frank Smith, Vesper Moore.

FORT WAYNE: Hoagland 54–52 Coesse; Huntertown 48–47 Lafayette Central (ot); South Side 69–56 Leo; Woodburn 51–47 Elmhurst; Monroeville 72–62 New Haven; Concordia 78–36 Arcola; North Side 57–48 Central Catholic; Central 36–21 Harlan; Hoagland 44–43 Huntertown (ot); South Side 64–41 Woodburn; Concordia 65–52 Monroeville; North Side 58–56 Central; South Side 84–36 Hoagland; North Side 85–65 Concordia; North Side 63–52 South Side. Officials: Eugene Glaze, Charles Timmons, Charles Northam, Lawrence Gradeless.

FOWLER: Oxford 57–50 Ambia; Wadena 38–20 Earl Park; Fowler 34–23 Gilboa; Otterbein 61–46 Boswell; Freeland Park 42–29 Pine Twp.; Oxford 67–27 Raub; Fowler 58–31 Wadena; Otterbein 56–46 Freeland Park; Fowler 57–39 Oxford; Fowler 37–27 Otterbein. Officials: Melvin Newlin, John Park, Ira Ray Williams.

FRANKFORT: Kirklin 39–37 Jackson Twp.; Colfax 63–48 Mulberry; Frankfort 75–41 Sugar Creek; Michigantown 46–40 Forrest; Scircleville 62–44 Washington Twp.; Rossville 55–46 Kirklin; Frankfort 46–38 Colfax; Michigantown 42–40 Scircleville; Frankfort 76–58 Rossville; Frankfort 62–41 Michigantown. Officials: James Davidson, Paul Dazey, M.N. Delph.

GARY: Lew Wallace 72–47 Hobart; Gary Edison 58–51 Horace Mann; Tolleston 84–45 East Gary Edison; Froebel 69–56 Emerson; Merrillville 78–42 Calumet Twp.; Roosevelt 64–54 William A. Wirt, Lew Wallace 68–66 Gary Edison; Froebel 67–64 Tolleston; Roosevelt 62–54 Merrillville; Froebel 67–58 Lew Wallace; Roosevelt 89–61 Froebel. Officials: Edward Burke, Charles Meade, Maurice Criswell.

GREENCASTLE: Russellville 79–33 Belle Union; Greencastle 56–42 Bainbridge; Cloverdale 79–57 Reelsville; Fillmore 70–41 Roachdale; Greencastle 66–58 Russellville; Fillmore 67–61 Cloverdale; Fillmore 69–58 Greencastle. Officials: John Williams, Jerry Steiner.

GREENFIELD: Eden 57–53 McCordsville (ot); Greenfield 58–44 Mt. Comfort; Maxwell 47–43 New Palestine; Wilkinson 49–27 Charlottesville; Fortville 65–56 Franklin Twp.; Eden 79–53 Greenfield; Wilkinson 63–45 Maxwell; Fortville 50–46 Eden; Wilkinson 55–53 Fortville. Officials: Frank Carnes, Gene Davis.

GREENSBURG: Burney 55–49 New Point; Vernon 47–41 Saint Paul; Sandcreek 49–42 Jackson Twp.; Greensburg 88–49 Clarksburg; Sandusky 55–44 North Vernon; Burney 68–56 Vernon; Greensburg 50–44 Sandcreek; Sandusky 53–37 Burney; Greensburg 49–46 Sandusky. Officials: Herb Schwomeyer, John J. Holmes.

GREENWOOD: Union Twp. 59–57 Nashville; Center Grove 48–41 Whiteland; Clark Twp. 39–33 Nineveh; Edinburg 49–43 Helmsburg; Franklin 63–45 Trafalgar; Greenwood 68–37 Van Buren; Center Grove 56–42 Union Twp.; Edinburg 67–39 Clark Twp.; Franklin 53–40 Greenwood; Center Grove 58–51 Edinburg; Franklin 61–55 Center Grove. Officials: Fred Marlow, John Gwin, Howard Plough.

HAMMOND: East Chicago Washington 64–58 East Chicago Roosevelt; Crown Point 62–37

Tourney Time

Lowell; Clark 49–43 Morton; Washington 59–58 Crown Point; Noll 94–44 Tech; Hammond High 79–44 Griffith; Whiting 76–54 Dyer; Hammond High 73–65 Noll; Washington 66–54 Clark; Hammond High 61–50 Whiting; Hammond High 59–50 Washington. Officials: Walt McFatridge, H.F. McNaught, Paul Bateman.

HARTFORD CITY: Montpelier 58–39 Madison Twp.; Hartford City 91–35 Gray; Dunkirk 67–48 Redkey; Portland 63–62 Roll; Bryant 66–55 Pennville; Montpelier 63–50 Poling; Hartford City 72–37 Dunkirk; Bryant 73–64 Portland; Hartford City 49–37 Montpelier; Hartford City 67–57 Bryant. Officials: Wilbur May, Arthur Lloyd, Glen Wisler.

HUNTINGBURG: Holland 59–52 Jasper; Winslow 68–44 Dubois; French Lick 59–34 Birdseye; Otwell 56–35 Spurgeon; West Baden 51–22 Stendal; Huntingburg 52–35 Ireland; Holland 48–45 Winslow; Otwell 51–41 French Lick; Huntingburg 62–36 West Baden; Holland 56–27 Otwell; Huntingburg 55–50 Holland. Officials: Robert Davidson, Lloyd Whipple, Joseph Hunter.

HUNTINGTON: Huntington Twp. 58–56 Huntington; Andrews 57–53 Salamonie Twp.; Rock Creek 73–71 Jefferson Twp. (Columbia City); Union Twp. 46–38 Huntington Catholic; Clear Creek 82–35 Wayne Twp.; Bippus 60–29 Markle; Roanoke 55–51 Lancaster Twp.; Huntington Twp. 63–48 Jefferson Twp. (Warren); Andrews 58–53 Rock Creek; Union Twp. 67–57 Clear Creek; Roanoke 72–56 Bippus; Huntington Twp. 58–57 Andrews; Roanoke 54–49 Union Twp.; Huntington Twp. 44–38 Roanoke. Officials: Gerald Strickler, Thomas Demark, Norris Ward, Ray Nemeth.

INDIANAPOLIS: Manual 53–52 Warren Central; Crispus Attucks 79–51 Washington; Cathedral 72–33 Lawrence Central; Broad Ripple 51–44 Sacred Heart; Ben Davis 34–27 Beech Grove; Shortridge 72–45 Decatur Central; Tech 72–48 School for the Deaf; Howe 54–53 Southport; Crispus Attucks 87–36 Manual; Broad Ripple 61–52 Cathedral; Shortridge 60–52 Ben Davis; Tech 68–59 Howe; Crispus Attucks 33–19 Broad Ripple; Shortridge 45–39 Tech; Crispus Attucks 73–59 Shortridge. Officials: Marvin Todd, William Findling, Roland Baker, J. Firman Grimes.

JEFFERSONVILLE: Charlestown 80–54 Henryville; New Washington 53–39 Borden; Providence 52–50 Jeffersonville; Silver Creek 52–38 Salem; Campbellsburg 49–42 Hardinsburg; Charlestown 74–40 Pekin; Providence 56–36 New Washington; Silver Creek 68–47 Campbellsburg; Providence 56–51 Charlestown; Silver Creek 35–28 Providence. Officials: Leland Terrell, Leroy Heminger, William Yaggi.

KENDALLVILLE: Rome City 48–33 Topeka; Kendallville 52–46 Wolcottville; Ligonier 72–57 Brighton; Avilla 83–39 Springfield Twp.; Wawaka 76–49 Albion; LaGrange 70–59 Shipshewana; Lima 39–37 Wolf Lake; Howe Military 56–44 Cromwell; Kendallville 40–33 Rome City; Avilla 62–59 Ligonier; Wawaka 77–58 LaGrange; Howe Military 37–33 Lima; Avilla 57–51 Kendallville; Wawaka 69–53 Howe Military; Avilla 69–66 Wawaka. Officials: John Burger, Joseph Bella, John Janzaruk, Richard Swartz.

KOKOMO: Western 37–29 Camden; Northwestern 56–37 Delphi; Burlington 79–44 Deer Creek; Flora 48–44 Eastern, Kokomo 93–21 Carrolton; Western 41–40 Cutler; Northwestern 59–34 Burlington; Kokomo 65–45 Flora; Northwestern 58–49 Western; Northwestern 64–62 Kokomo. Officials: Lowell Barnett, Don Lieberum, Merle Shively.

LAFAYETTE: Dayton 54–52 Wea; Jackson Twp. 62–56 West Point; Buck Creek 50–49 Montmorenci; Shadeland 66–44 Romney; Monitor 62–57 Clarks Hill; Klondike 81–38 Stockwell; West Lafayette 53–50 Battle Ground; Lafayette 80–27 Dayton; Buck Creek 65–57 Jackson Twp.; Shadeland 44–29 Monitor; Klondike 43–40 West Lafayette; Lafayette 61–22 Buck

Creek; Klondike 53–42 Shadeland; Lafayette 65–43 Klondike. Officials: Clayton Nichols, Willard Ketner, Robert Crouch, Charles Garber.

LINTON: Switz City 77–28 Scotland; Solsberry 50–42 Lyons; Linton 55–49 Jasonville; Bloomfield 64–33 Worthington; Marco 49–41 Midland; Switz City 62–38 Solsberry; Bloomfield 77–59 Linton; Switz City 67–28 Marco; Switz City 80–61 Bloomfield. Officials: Noel Genth, Norman Shields.

LOGANSPORT: Royal Center 76–39 Young America; Metea 54–48 Lucerne; Washington Twp. 57–54 Tipton Twp.; Twelve Mile 47–40 New Waverly; Galveston 56–47 Logansport; Royal Center 63–46 Metea; Twelve Mile 40–36 Washington Twp.; Royal Center 57–45 Galveston; Royal Center 68–47 Twelve Mile. Officials: Lawrence Leland, Roy Kilby.

LYNNVILLE: Tennyson 62–15 Folsomville; Selvin 55–38 Millersburg; Newburgh 49–35 Elberfeld; Chandler 39–28 Lynnville; Boonville 66–46 Tennyson; Newburgh 44–41 Selvin; Boonville 57–55 Chandler; Newburgh 52–51 Boonville. Officials: Thomas Hoffman, Kenneth Blankenbaker, James Schwenk.

MADISON: Shawe Memorial 56–24 Lexington; Scottsburg 98–38 Hanover; Austin 77–58 Dupont; Madison 56–43 Deputy; Paris Crossing 88–56 Central; Shawe Memorial 60–35 Saluda; Scottsburg 52–35 Austin; Madison 61–37 Paris Crossing; Scottsburg 83–42 Shawe Memorial; Scottsburg 17–16 Madison. Officials: Paul Grimes, John Evans, James Beyer.

MARION: Swayzee 49–40 Jefferson Twp.; Fairmount 59–57 Bennett; Mississinewa 38–32 Sweetser; Marion 72–60 Van Buren; Fairmount 43–37 Swayzee; Marion 43–35 Mississinewa; Fairmount 64–62 Marion (2ot). Officials: John Hilligoss, Everett Cass.

MARTINSVILLE: Eminence 46–42 Monrovia; University (Bloomington) 62–55 Smithville; Unionville 51–44 Stinesville; Mooresville 77–74 Martinsville; Bloomington 67–57 Ellettsville; Morgantown 97–53 Paragon; University (Bloomington) 48–44 Eminence; Unionville 64–59 Mooresville; Bloomington 62–53 Morgantown; Unionville 58–30 University (Bloomington); Bloomington 47–43 Unionville. Officials: Lester Cornwell, Eugene Sparks, Lowell Willis.

MICHIGAN CITY: Union Twp. 64–48 Union Mills; Clinton Twp. 60–38 LaCrosse; Michigan City 66–44 Rolling Prairie; Wanatah 42–36 Stilwell; Mill Creek 62–43 Westville; St. Mary's 49–32 Kingsbury; LaPorte 69–26 Hanna; Union Twp. 71–62 Clinton Twp.; Michigan City 78–34 Wanatah; St. Mary's 59–55 Mill Creek; LaPorte 81–56 Union Twp.; Michigan City 75–44 St. Mary's; Michigan City 46–42 LaPorte. Officials: Robert Kramer, Andrew Hiduke, Ernest Sohl.

MONTICELLO: Brookston 37–31 Buffalo; Chalmers 38–32 Idaville; Monticello 48–31 Burnettsville; Wolcott 63–61 Monon; Brookston 67–42 Reynolds; Monticello 48–32 Chalmers; Wolcott 59–54 Brookston; Monticello 72–48 Wolcott. Officials: David Albright, Robert Spay, James Morrison.

MUNCIE: Selma 67–54 Harrison; Muncie Central 84–42 Muncie Burris; Daleville 61–45 Center; Gaston 58–49 DeSoto; Royerton 38–37 Cowan; Yorktown 62–47 Albany; Eaton 57–46 Selma; Muncie Central 84–35 Daleville; Gaston 57–54 Royerton; Yorktown 75–62 Eaton; Muncie Central 76–38 Gaston; Muncie Central 71–59 Yorktown. Officials: Frank Sanders, Richard Duffield, Don McBride.

NEW ALBANY: Elizabeth 76–51 Central (Corydon); English 55–52 Lanesville; Milltown 53–25 Mt. St. Francis; Morgan Twp. 53–34 Leavenworth; Laconia 43–26 Marengo; New Albany 115–52 Georgetown; New Salisbury 54–50 Elizabeth; English 63–47 Milltown; Morgan Twp. 59–52 Laconia; New Albany 68–49 New Salisbury; Morgan Twp. 66–48 English; New Albany 87–54 Morgan Twp. Officials: Odilo Berger, Vern Dales, Irvin Thrasher.

Tourney Time

NEW CASTLE: New Castle 48–34 Mooreland; Middletown 58–49 Straughn; Knightstown 54–51 Sulphur Springs; New Castle 44–43 Middletown; Spiceland 65–61 New Lisbon; Lewisville 53–49 Kennard; Cadiz 62–58 Mt. Summit; Lewisville 76–51 Spiceland; New Castle 64–54 Knightstown; Lewisville 44–42 Cadiz (2ot); New Castle 51–38 Lewisville. Officials: Karl Bly, James Patterson, John Thomas.

PERU: Converse 42–34 Gilead; Bunker Hill 66–50 Deedsville; Peru 66–44 Mexico; Chili 50–47 Clay Twp.; Butler Twp. 62–51 Macy; Converse 46–45 Bunker Hill; Peru 72–37 Chili; Converse 55–30 Butler Twp.; Peru 60–47 Converse. Officials: Noble Benbow, Herbert Brammell.

PLYMOUTH: Argos 35–34 Grovertown; Bremen 42–30 West Twp.; San Pierre 43–42 Plymouth; Bourbon 44–41 Argos; Bremen 65–50 San Pierre; Culver 55–33 Hamlet; North Judson 49–35 Knox; Tyner 63–61 Tippecanoe; LaPaz 70–53 Culver; North Judson 78–50 Tyner; Bourbon 46–42 Bremen; LaPaz 45–35 North Judson; LaPaz 54–52 Bourbon. Officials: Lores Lehman, Sam Massette, Loris Jacobs.

PRINCETON: Oakland City 42–41 Mt. Olympus (ot); Hazleton 79–52 Mackey; Princeton 39–38 Ft. Branch (ot); Francisco 56–50 Haubstadt (ot); Patoka 49–47 Owensville (ot); Oakland City 62–41 Hazleton; Princeton 62–50 Francisco; Patoka 67–51 Oakland City; Patoka 60–50 Princeton. Officials: Fred Hodge, Wilfred Susott.

RENSSELAER: Morocco 67–47 DeMotte; Brook 54–45 Kankakee Twp.; Rensselaer 67–55 Remington; Fair Oaks 57–47 Mt. Ayr; Goodland 81–46 Wheatfield; Kentland 44–42 Morocco; Brook 53–33 Rensselaer; Goodland 64–53 Fair Oaks; Brook 44–36 Kentland; Goodland 66–58 Brook. Officials: Victor Griewank, Gene Winks, R. Wayne Smith.

RICHMOND: Williamsburg 50–37 Economy; Fountain City 47–37 Whitewater; Cambridge City 55–50 Boston (ot); Centerville 50–43 Webster; Greens Fork 48–36 Milton; Richmond 55–48 Hagerstown; Williamsburg 49–36 Fountain City; Centerville 47–30 Cambridge City; Richmond 70–37 Greens Fork; Williamsburg 47–23 Centerville; Richmond 58–40 Williamsburg. Officials: Don Dick, Roy Gardner, Everett Campbell.

ROCHESTER: Rochester 72–54 Medaryville; Star City 72–56 Aubbeenaubbee Twp.; Francesville 55–38 Kewanna; Rochester 54–44 Richland Center; Francesville 66–57 Star City; Winamac 81–57 Monterey; Akron 85–54 Talma; Fulton 68–61 Grass Creek; Winamac 64–52 Pulaski; Akron 95–72 Fulton; Francesville 61–45 Rochester; Akron 64–51 Winamac; Francesville 58–42 Akron. Officials: Harley Collins, Robert Brees, Gary Nelson.

ROCKVILLE: Rosedale 77–41 Bellmore; Greene Twp. 63–56 St. Bernice; Rockville 57–55 Marshall; Clinton 70–40 Bridgeton; Hillsdale 55–51 Cayuga; Newport 50–48 Mecca (ot); Bloomingdale 39–34 Tangier; Montezuma 52–44 Dana; Rosedale 67–44 Greene Twp.; Clinton 62–56 Rockville; Hillsdale 45–38 Newport; Bloomingdale 51–41 Montezuma; Clinton 61–49 Rosedale; Bloomingdale 46–38 Hillsdale; Clinton 51–45 Bloomingdale. Officials: Otto Hurrle, Roderick Witt, James Boswell, Joseph Garoffolo.

RUSHVILLE: Rushville 49–37 Milroy; Carthage 56–54 Mays; New Salem 59–50 Manilla; Morton Memorial 75–64 Arlington; Morristown 93–49 Raleigh; Rushville 57–49 Carthage; Morton Memorial 59–58 New Salem; Rushville 34–25 Morristown; Rushville 79–59 Morton Memorial. Officials: James Sanders, James Ridge.

SEYMOUR: Crothersville 61–54 Clearsprings; Medora 89–57 Hayden; Brownstown 68–39 Vallonia; Seymour 99–44 Tampico; Cortland 54–45 Freetown; Medora 60–58 Crothersville; Seymour 73–57 Brownstown; Cortland 55–43 Medora; Seymour 90–63 Cortland. Officials:

Dwain Laird, Robert Laird.

SHERIDAN: Sheridan 67–59 Walnut Grove; Windfall 38–35 Jefferson Twp.; Fishers 68–61 Prairie; Sheridan 63–52 Windfall; Westfield 70–55 Carmel; Jackson Central 81–41 Sharpsville; Tipton 60–55 Noblesville; Jackson Central 55–44 Westfield; Sheridan 58–54 Fishers; Tipton 60–55 Jackson Central; Sheridan 67–49 Tipton. Officials: Robert Windsor, Ed Straith-Miller, Wayne Crispen.

SOUTH BEND: New Carlisle 79–60 Madison Twp.; Mishawaka 66–61 Central; Adams 51–46 St. Joseph's; Washington-Clay 51–46 New Carlisle; Mishawaka 61–52 Adams; Riley 51–42 Lakeville; Washington 35–31 Green Twp.; Walkerton 72–42 North Liberty; Riley 71–51 Washington; Mishawaka 70–55 Washington Clay; Riley 68–47 Walkerton; Mishawaka 70–53 Riley. Officials: John Sebastian, Gene Butts, Stan Dubis.

SULLIVAN: Farmersburg 56–53 Hymera; Gill Twp. 59–53 Sullivan; Dugger 68–58 Shelburn; Graysville 75–63 Fairbanks; Carlisle 58–42 Pleasantville; Gill Twp. 62–55 Farmersburg; Dugger 75–52 Graysville; Gill Twp. 56–50 Carlisle; Gill Twp. 77–53 Dugger. Officials: Robert Rose, Norman Risley.

TELL CITY: Rockport 59–31 Oil Twp.; Tell City 65–50 Cannelton; St. Ferdinand 52–29 Troy; Richland (Luce Twp.) 55–38 Chrisney; Dale 70–39 Bristow; Tell City 38–36 Rockport; St. Ferdinand 52–49 Richland (Luce Twp.); Tell City 57–45 Dale (2ot); Tell City 28–20 St. Ferdinand. Officials: G.W. Clapp, Charles Fouty.

TERRE HAUTE: Glenn 81–34 Fontanet; Concannon 57–50 Otter Creek; Honey Creek 37–32 Prairie Creek; Riley 63–60 Laboratory; Wiley 45–40 Pimento; Schulte 51–34 Fayette; Garfield 58–48 West Terre Haute; Gerstmeyer 94–48 Blackhawk; Concannon 60–48 Glenn; Riley 73–54 Honey Creek; Wiley 45–41 Schulte; Garfield 56–49 Gerstmeyer; Concannon 58–56 Riley; Garfield 67–61 Wiley; Garfield 65–51 Concannon. Officials: Jack Small, Robert Sosbe, Arthur Thompson, Byron Arnold.

THORNTOWN: Thorntown 64–57 Lebanon; Perry Central 60–40 Dover; Zionsville 70–29 Whitestown; Pike Twp. 64–55 Pinnell; Thorntown 59–35 Jackson Twp.; Zionsville 59–43 Perry Central; Thorntown 50–36 Pike Twp.; Zionsville 66–54 Thorntown. Officials: Leon Hodson, James Lentz, Ronald Bland.

VALPARAISO: Portage Twp. 73–37 Jackson Twp.; Chesterton 78–44 Morgan Twp.; Liberty Twp. 71–55 Wheeler; Hebron 69–61 Boone Grove; Kouts 56–43 Washington Twp.; Portage Twp. 62–60 Valparaiso; Chesterton 64–46 Liberty Twp.; Kouts 55–51 Hebron; Chesterton 47–44 Portage Twp.; Chesterton 47–21 Kouts. Officials: Dean Geyer, Myron Weldy, John Fee.

VERSAILLES: Napoleon 44–38 Sunman; Versailles 63–49 New Marion; Cross Plains 43–40 Osgood; Milan 50–36 Batesville; Holton 50–39 Napoleon; Versailles 66–39 Gross Plains; Milan 47–39 Holton; Milan 37–35 Versailles (2ot); Officials: James Haywood, Kermit Spurgeon, Wendell Baker.

VINCENNES: Wheatland 66–51 Bicknell; Central Catholic 62–35 Decker; Sandborn 64–55 Bruceville; Vincennes 87–62 Fritchton; Monroe City 68–58 Decker Chapel; Freelandville 87–46 Oaktown; Central Catholic 64–45 Wheatland; Vincennes 58–38 Sandborn; Freelandville 79–56 Monroe City; Vincennes 48–46 Central Catholic; Vincennes 57–51 Freelandville. Officials: Harold Gourley, S. T. Proffitt, William Dixon.

WABASH: South Whitley 52–42 Noble Twp.; Urbana 60–52 Laketon; LaFontaine 57–49 Chester Twp.; South Whitley 53–35 Roann; LaFontaine 33–32 Urbana; Wabash 83–47 Lagro;

Tourney Time

Somerset 60–41 White's; North Manchester 59–40 Washington Center; Wabash 47–30 Somerset; South Whitley 51–43 LaFontaine; Wabash 71–38 North Manchester; Wabash 63–48 South Whitley. Officials: Leonard Lupold, Gerald Imel, Burl McKenzie.

WARSAW: Milford 34–32 Mentone; Pierceton 69–44 Leesburg; Atwood 53–47 Sidney; Etna Green 66–60 Silver Lake; Columbia City 53–38 North Webster; Burket 51–44 Beaver Dam; Syracuse 62–36 Larwill; Warsaw 70–52 Claypool; Pierceton 59–41 Milford; Etna Green 54–40 Atwood; Columbia City 61–40 Burket; Warsaw 63–45 Syracuse; Etna Green 58–54 Pierceton; Warsaw 61–51 Columbia City; Warsaw 87–54 Etna Green. Officials: Darl March, Anthony Lazar, Bill Larkin, John Cover.

WASHINGTON: Loogootee St. John's 55–51 Epsom; Petersburg 56–52 Elmore Twp.; Loogootee High 52–46 Odon; Washington Catholic 54–51 Plainville; Washington High 48–41 Barr Twp.; Shoals 68–49 Alfordsville; St John's 58–53 Petersburg; Loogootee High 71–54 Washington Catholic; Washington High 93–55 Shoals; St. John's 67–60 Loogootee High; Washington High 81–38 St. John's. Officials: Roger Emmert, Robert Sweet, Malvern Redman.

WINCHESTER: Union City 71–62 Stoney Creek; Farmland 51–19 Green Twp.; Ridgeville 51–50 Wayne Twp.; Spartanburg 56–47 McKinley; Saratoga 51–49 Lynn; Union 49–45 Parker; Jackson Twp. 55–40 Jefferson; Union City 49–46 Winchester; Farmland 70–50 Ridgeville; Spartanburg 55–41 Saratoga; Union 50–37 Jackson Twp.; Farmland 56–50 Union City; Union 63–44 Spartanburg; Farmland 62–51 Union. Officials: Oscar Samuels, Johannes Dienelt, Bill Garrett, Everett Havens.

1955 REGIONALS

BLOOMINGTON: Switz City 55–41 Terre Haute Garfield;; Brazil 51–43 Bloomington; Switz City 66–58 Brazil. Officials: Cyril Birge, Kermit Spurgeon, Lloyd Whipple, John Gwin.

COLUMBUS: Greensburg 59–54 Franklin; Columbus 58–51 Scottsburg; Columbus 33–32 Greensburg. Officials: Lawrence Leland, William Dixon, Robert Rose, Joseph Hunter.

COVINGTON: Fillmore 61–53 Clinton; Crawfordsville 46–29 Attica; Crawfordsville 58–42 Fillmore. Officials: Lowell Barnett, Oscar Samuels, Lowell Willis, Gene Winks.

ELKHART: Warsaw 65–53 LaPaz; Mishawaka 52–49 Nappanee (ot); Mishawaka 63–52 Warsaw. Officials: Marvin Todd, Everett Campbell; Eugene Glaze, Andrew Hiduke.

EVANSVILLE: Reitz 56–42 Tell City; Newburgh 70–58 Patoka; Reitz 57–52 Newburgh. Officials: Dee Williams, Clayton Nichols, Cloyd Julian, John Williams.

FORT WAYNE: North Side 80–46 Avilla; Auburn 82–67 Monmouth; North Side 66–56 Auburn. Officials: Stan Dubis, Maurice Criswell, Ed Straith-Miller, Dean Geyer.

HAMMOND: Gary Roosevelt 66–57 Hammond High; Michigan City 55–51 Chesterton; Gary Roosevelt 58–51 Michigan City. Officials: Joe Mullins, Frank Sanders, Lores Lehman, William Findling.

HUNTINGBURG: Washington 65–63 Gill Twp.; Vincennes 54–45 Huntingburg; Vincennes 62–60 Washington (ot). Officials: Leland Terrell, Wray Holbrook, Roland Baker, James Patterson.

INDIANAPOLIS: Anderson 46–43 Speedway; Crispus Attucks 95–42 Wilkinson; Crispus Attucks 76–51 Anderson. Officials: Eugene Sparks, Burl McKenzie, James Sanders, Frank Smith.

JEFFERSONVILLE: Paoli 70–60 Seymour; New Albany 77–66 Silver Creek; New Albany 86–60 Paoli. Officials: James Haywood, Robert Cherry, Roy Gardner, Paul Grimes.

KOKOMO: Northwestern 60–43 Peru; Sheridan 54–52 Wabash; Sheridan 57–53 Northwestern. Officials: John Hilligoss, Wilbur May, Robert Dornte, Roscoe Hall.

LAFAYETTE: Lafayette 48–47 Frankfort; Zionsville 39–37 Fowler; Lafayette 63–41 Zionsville. Officials: Paul Bateman, John Janzaruk, Irvin Thrasher, John Burger.

LOGANSPORT: Francesville 65–54 Goodland; Monticello 73–60 Royal Center; Monticello 53–48 Francesville. Officials: Don McBride, Everett Cass, Don Lieberum, Leon Hodson.

MARION: Bluffton 49–48 Fairmount; Hartford City 56–47 Huntington Twp.; Hartford City 51–46 Bluffton. Officials: Charles Northam, Wesley Oler, Victor Griewank, David Albright.

MUNCIE: Richmond 70–57 New Castle; Muncie Central 73–44 Farmland; Muncie Central 67–56 Richmond. Officials: Charles Meade, H. F. McNaught, Herb Schwomeyer, Jack Small.

RUSHVILLE: Milan 42–40 Connersville; Rushville 57–41 Vevay; Rushville 53–42 Milan. Officials: Gerald Strickler, S.T. Proffitt, Arthur Lloyd, Leroy Heminger.

1955 SEMI–FINALS

BLOOMINGTON: New Albany 84–41 Switz City; Vincennes 53–52 Reitz ; New Albany 86–58 Vincennes. Officials: Don McBride, Lowell Barnett, Charles Meade, Maurice Criswell, Marvin Todd, Eugene Glaze.

ELKHART: Mishawaka 51–43 Hartford City; Ft. Wayne North Side 63–56 Sheridan; North Side 54–48 Mishawaka. Officials: Stan Dubis, Ed Straith-Miller, Herb Schwomeyer, H.F. McNaught, Lawrence Leland, Dee Williams.

INDIANAPOLIS: Crispus Attucks 80–62 Columbus; Muncie Central 65–48 Rushville; Crispus Attucks 71–70 Muncie Central. Officials: Roy Gardner, Charles Northam, Robert Dornte, Joe Mullins, Cyril Birge, John Hilligoss.

LAFAYETTE: Gary Roosevelt 71–52 Crawfordsville; Lafayette Jefferson 59–47 Monticello; Gary Roosevelt 59–46 Jefferson. Officials: S.T. Proffitt, Eugene Sparks, Lores Lehman, Gerald Strickler, Roland Baker, Lloyd Whipple.

1955 FINALS—March 19

INDIANAPOLIS (Butler Fieldhouse): Crispus Attucks 79–67 New Albany; Gary Roosevelt 68–66 Ft. Wayne North Side; Crispus Attucks 97–74 Gary Roosevelt. Officials: Roy Gardner, Stan Dubis, Herb Schwomeyer, Lowell Barnett, S. T. Proffitt, Charles Meade.

1956 SECTIONALS

ADAMS CENTRAL: Monmouth 45–41 Hartford; Pleasant Mills 67–57 Geneva; Monmouth 78–61 Adams Central; Decatur Catholic 87–62 Jefferson; Decatur 65–63 Berne-French; Monmouth 70–64 Pleasant Mills; Decatur 63–61 Decatur Catholic (2ot); Monmouth 72–71 Decatur. Officials: Merle Shively, Lewis Goshert.

ANDERSON: Frankton 64–50 St. Mary's; Pendleton 52–50 Lapel; Elwood 86–50 Summitville; Alexandria 68–48 Highland; Anderson 80–65 Markleville; Frankton 60–47 Pendleton; Elwood 54–46 Alexandria; Anderson 67–58 Frankton; Anderson 62–54 Elwood. Officials: Marvin Todd, Don McCoy.

Tourney Time

BEDFORD: Shawswick 84–63 Huron; Paoli 65–47 Heltonville: Mitchell 97–41 Tunnelton; Marshall Twp. 52–43 Williams; Fayetteville 57–54 Oolitic; Bedford 78–72 Orleans; Shawswick 82–67 Paoli; Mitchell 86–62 Marshall Twp.; Bedford 69–39 Fayetteville; Mitchell 51–30 Shawswick; Mitchell 74–59 Bedford. Officials: Ivan Risley, S. T. Proffitt, Norman Risley.

BLOOMINGTON: Unionville 61–57 Monrovia; Mooresville 79–60 Paragon; Morgantown 75–63 Ellettsville; Martinsville 72–60 Stilesville; Smithville 76–53 Eminence; Bloomington 63–39 University; Mooresville 79–73 Unionville; Morgantown 71–68 Martinsville; Bloomington 88–53 Smithville; Morgantown 98–76 Mooresville; Morgantown 75–67 Bloomington. Officials: Robert Laird, Cyril Birge, Dwain Laird.

BLUFFTON: Jackson Twp. 50–47 Petroleum; Bluffton 38–35 Liberty Center; Union Center 76–58 Chester Center; Lancaster Central 71–51 Ossian; Rockcreek Center 59–50 Jackson Twp.; Bluffton 77–71 Union Center; Lancaster Central 43–40 Rockcreek Center; Bluffton 70–61 Lancaster Central. Officials: Leon Hodson, Everett Havens, Marion Acton.

BRAZIL: Freedom 70–55 Coal City; Brazil 39–21 Bowling Green; Patricksburg 66–63 Gosport; Staunton 65–50 Clay City; Spencer 76–62 Van Buren; Cory 44–41 Ashboro; Freedom 61–40 Coalmont; Brazil 67–37 Patricksburg; Staunton 77–62 Spencer; Freedom 39–38 Cory; Brazil 53–46 Staunton; Brazil 61–46 Freedom. Officials: Paul Dazey, Ira Ray Williams, Lowell Willis.

CENTER GROVE: Union 48–39 Edinburg; Center Grove 72–56 Nineveh; Greenwood 55–51 Franklin; Decatur Central 70–60 Whiteland; Southport 72–52 Clark; Helmsburg 54–41 Trafalgar; Center Grove 60–59 Union; Greenwood 59–48 Decatur Central; Southport 76–42 Helmsburg; Greenwood 47–41 Center Grove; Southport 86–37 Greenwood. Officials: Earnest Baldwin, Roy Gardner, William Yohler.

CHURUBUSCO–GARRETT (At Churubusco): Auburn 48–44 Angola; Hamilton 58–32 Pleasant Lake; Garrett 77–48 Churubusco; Auburn 43–39 Waterloo; Garrett 71–70 Hamilton; Garrett 54–53 Auburn; (At Garrett): Fremont 78–35 Metz; Butler 69–60 Orland; Ashley 61–48 Riverdale; Fremont 58–31 Salem Center; Butler 64–58 Ashley; (At Churubusco): Garrett 54–53 Auburn; Fremont 76–66 Butler; Fremont 67–52 Garrett. Officials: Ray Nemeth, Thomas Demark, Don McBride, Richard Dermody.

CLINTON: Tangier 53–46 Marshall; Dana 67–47 Bloomingdale; Mecca 49–45 Rockville; Hillsdale 63–54 St. Bernice; Newport 62–51 Bridgeton; Union Twp. 69–53 Greene Twp.; Rosedale 64–57 Cayuga; Clinton 78–50 Montezuma; Dana 67–45 Tangier; Mecca 62–42 Hillsdale; Union Twp. 48–40 Newport; Clinton 57–51 Rosedale; Mecca 44–43 Dana; Clinton 76–48 Bellmore; Clinton 74–55 Mecca. Officials: Robert Sosbe, Noble Benbow, Leo Ponto, Jack Small.

COLUMBUS: Hope 41–39 Nashville; Shelbyville 67–42 Flatrock; 53–46 Moral Twp.; Columbus 72–59 Mt. Auburn; Boggstown 67–39 Van Buren; Waldron 51–46 Fairland; Shelbyville 58–34 Hope; Columbus 55–47 Clifford; Waldron 53–48 Boggstown; Columbus 52–50 Shelbyville; Columbus 58–37 Waldron. Officials: Ralph F. Box, Roland Baker, Robert Babbs.

CONNERSVILLE: Laurel 71–41 Brownsville; Brookville 54–53 Whitewater; Alquina 52–51 Harrisburg; Brookville 43–39 Laurel (ot); Connersville 77–40 Fairview; Harrison Twp. 56–48 Springfield Twp.; Liberty 61–44 Orange; Connersville 68–40 Kitchel; Alquina 59–48 Brookville; Connersville 59–48 Liberty; Connersville 88–54 Alquina. Officials: James Beyer, Robert Crouch, Byron Arnold.

COVINGTON: Hillsboro 51–49 Williamsport; Attica 57–47 Veedersburg; West Lebanon 49–30 Wallace; Pine Village 59–56 Kingman; Covington 53–52 Richland Twp.; Perrysville 45–44

Hillsboro; West Lebanon 43–40 Attica; Covington 48–46 Pine Village; Perrysville 39–37 West Lebanon; Covington 47–40 Perrysville. Officials: Roderick Witt, Joe Garoffolo, Melvin Newlin.

CRAWFORDSVILLE: Alamo 48–35 Linden; Darlington 67–57 Coal Creek Central; New Ross 45–41 Crawfordsville; Darlington 58–53 Alamo; Ladoga 64–45 New Market; Waveland 47–45 Waynetown; New Ross 52–46 Darlington; Ladoga 51–43 Waveland; New Ross 38–23 Ladoga. Officials: Ott Hurrle, Arthur Thompson.

DANVILLE: Lizton 56–50 Charlton; Danville 59–52 Amo; Speedway 62–55 Avon; Pittsboro 84–67 Clayton; Brownsburg 87–48 New Winchester; Stilesville 71–62 Plainfield; North Salem 69–59 Lizton; Danville 49–45 Speedway; Brownsburg 49–44 Pittsboro; Stilesville 66–62 North Salem; Danville 51–44 Brownsburg. Danville 59–58 Stilesville. Officials: Joe Thomas, W. L. Ketner, John Park.

ELKHART: Millersburg 61–54 Bristol; Nappanee 53–50 Wakarusa; Middlebury 49–36 New Paris; Concord Twp. 58–53 Jefferson Twp.; Baugo Twp. 54–52 Goshen; Elkhart 63–50 Newbury Van Buren Twp.; Millersburg 59–42 Topeka; Middlebury 42–39 Nappanee; Baugo Twp. 53–52 Concord Twp.; Elkhart 55–27 Millersburg; Middlebury 47–41 Baugo Twp.; Elkhart 37–35 Middlebury. Officials: Robert Kramer, Andrew Hiduke, Richard Duffield.

EVANSVILLE: Central 68–42 Cynthiana; Mt. Vernon 47–44 Poseyville; Memorial 74–53 Bosse; Lincoln 63–48 New Harmony; Wadesville 67–59 Griffin; Reitz 59–57 Mater Dei; Central 75–50 Mt. Vernon; Lincoln 55–54 Memorial; Reitz 58–45 Wadesville; Lincoln 59–49 Central; Lincoln 58–53 Reitz. Officials: Robert Davidson, Robert Rose, Charles Fouty.

FORT WAYNE: New Haven 64–52 Woodburn; Central Catholic 88–70 Concordia; South Side 53–42 Hoagland; North Side 51–45 Central; Coesse 57–44 Arcola; Elmhurst 69–50 Huntertown; Lafayette Central 69–60 Monroeville; Harlan 66–53 Leo; Central Catholic 94–70 New Haven; South Side 66–51 North Side; Elmhurst 59–42 Coesse; Harlan 51–49 Lafayette Central; South Side 69–65 Central Catholic (ot); Elmhurst 50–46 Harlan; South Side 54–41 Elmhurst. Officials: Frank Sanders, Gene Butts, Oscar Samuels, Wayne Crispen.

FOWLER: Ambia 35–23 Earl Park; Oxford 68–50 Pine Twp.; Fowler 41–36 Wadena; Otterbein 62–45 Gilboa Twp.; Boswell 79–68 Freeland Park; Ambia 67–60 Oxford; Fowler 60–53 Otterbein; Ambia 38–36 Boswell; Ambia 56–52 Fowler. Officials: Glenn Lantz, Robert Spay.

FRANKFORT: Colfax 53–50 Frankfort; Rossville 71–66 Michigantown; Mulberry 73–65 Scircleville; Sugar Creek 66–46 Washington Twp.; Jackson Twp. 47–43 Forest; Kirklin 55–51 Colfax; Mulberry 58–51 Rossville; Jackson Twp. 32–31 Sugar Creek; Mulberry 46–36 Kirklin; Jackson Twp. 42–37 Mulberry (ot). Officials: Gene Winks, Bill Wood, Robert Brees.

GARY: East Gary Edison 82–71 Hobart; Calumet Twp. 48–42 Horace Mann; Roosevelt 46–37 Wirt; Lew Wallace 62–51 Merrillville; Froebel 54–42 Tolleston; Gary Edison 82–52 Emerson; East Gary Edison 79–68 Calumet Twp.; Roosevelt 89–50 Lew Wallace; Froebel 47–45 Gary Edison; Roosevelt 85–54 East Gary Edison; Froebel 62–56 Roosevelt. Officials: Victor Griewank, Walt McFatridge, H. F. McNaught.

GREENCASTLE: Cloverdale 62–60 Fillmore (2ot); Russellville 61–46 Bainbridge; Greencastle 82–48 Reelsville; Roachdale 48–33 Belle Union; Russellville 70–61 Cloverdale; Greencastle 56–42 Roachdale; Greencastle 90–48 Russellville. Officials: Cloyd Julian, John J. Holmes.

GREENFIELD: Fortville.62–51 McCordsville; Charlottesville 59–56 Franklin Twp.; Greenfield 62–60 Wilkinson; New Palestine 68–51 Mount Comfort; Hancock Central 67–57 Fortville; Charlottesville 59–57 Greenfield; Hancock Central 58–51 New Palestine; Hancock

Tourney Time

Central 68–57 Charlottesville. Officials: James Ridge, James Lentz, John Priest.

GREENSBURG: Jackson Twp. 69–52 North Vernon; Sandusky 57–53 Clarksburg; Sandcreek, 43–40 New Point; Greensburg 44–42 Burney; St. Paul 63–50 Vernon; Jackson Twp. 68–46 Sandusky; Greensburg 76–50 Sandcreek, St. Paul 48–41 Jackson Twp.; St. Paul 44–42 Greensburg. Officials: Richard Tiernan, Karl Bly.

HAMMOND: Morton 86–76 Crown Point; Hammond High 68–58 Noll; Clark 78–62 Dyer; Hammond High 77–66 Morton; East Chicago Washington 78–60 Whiting; East Chicago Roosevelt 66–54 Lowell; Griffith 83–75 Tech (ot); East Chicago Washington 91–70 East Chicago Roosevelt; Hammond High 72–46 Clark; East Chicago Washington 86–53 Griffith; Hammond High 82–61 East Chicago Washington. Officials: Joseph Bella, Charles Meade, Lawrence Gradeless.

HARTFORD CITY: Roll 67–65 Portland; Poling 72–69 Madison; Bryant 62–48 Gray; Dunkirk 57–44 Pennville; Hartford City 82–70 Montpelier; Roll 82–60 Redkey; Poling 75–69 Bryant; Hartford City 47–14 Dunkirk; Roll 64–40 Poling; Hartford City 53–31 Roll. Officials: John Gwin, William May, James Murray.

HUNTINGBURG: Stendal 45–39 Birdseye; Winslow 67–65 Holland; Otwell 46–40 Spurgeon; West Baden 53–40 Ireland; Huntingburg 58–54 French Lick; Jasper 72–35 Dubois; Winslow 69–47 Stendal; West Baden 40–31 Otwell; Jasper 62–50 Huntingburg; Winslow 57–48 West Baden; Jasper 73–68 Winslow (ot). Officials: Ronald Bland, Eugene Sparks, Vesper Moore.

HUNTINGTON: Union Twp. 73–52 Lancaster Twp.; Clear Creek 80–63 Markle; Salamonie Twp. 75–71 Rockcreek Center; Huntington Catholic 83–55 Jefferson Two. (Warren); Huntington 89–63 Huntington Twp.; Andrews 72–65 Jefferson Center (Columbia City); Roanoke 52–49 Bippus; Clear Creek 67–63 Union Twp.; Huntington Catholic 79–52 Salamonie Twp.; Huntington 90–48 Andrews; Clear Creek 59–53 Roanoke; Huntington 72–57 Huntington Catholic; Clear Creek 78–76 Huntington. Officials: Everett Cass, Johannes Dienelt, Charles Garber.

INDIANAPOLIS: Shortridge 49–47 Tech; Ben Davis 71–61 Warren Central; Broad Ripple 50–44 Scecina Memorial; Lawrence 58–46 Sacred Heart; Howe 81–55 Wood; Attucks 91–30 Beech Grove; Cathedral 81–50 School for the Deaf; Manual 49–48 Washington (ot); Shortridge 53–43 Ben Davis; Broad Ripple 54–52 Lawrence (ot); Attucks 72–58 Howe; Cathedral 57–51 Manual; Shortridge 50–42 Broad Ripple; Attucks 57–49 Cathedral; Attucks 53–48 Shortridge. Officials: John Hilligoss, Wesley Oler, Charles Northam, Homer Owens.

JEFFERSONVILLE: Henryville 57–54 Salem; Silver Creek 49–47 New Washington; Providence 87–44 Hardinsburg; Jeffersonville 91–67 Campbellsburg; Charlestown 69–47 Borden; Henryville 53–42 Pekin; Providence 71–51 Silver Creek Charlestown 59–58 Jeffersonville; Providence 72–49 Henryville; Providence 71–56 Charlestown. Officials: Paul Grimes, Vern Doles, Noel Genth.

KENDALLVILLE: Brighton 84–72 LaGrange; Rome City 54–51 Wolcottville; Avilla 70–34 Wolf Lake; Wawaka 87–42 Springfield Twp.; Lima 55–49 Kendallville; Albion 67–49 Cromwell; Ligonier 72–48 Howe Military; Brighton 69–58 Rome City; Avilla 68–48 Wawaka; Albion 57–49 Lima; Brighton 69–67 Ligonier (ot); Avilla 55–50 Albion; Avilla 59–42 Brighton. Officials: Gerald Imel, Edward Burke, Bill Garrett.

KNOX: Winamac 90–44 San Pierre; Aubbeenaubbee 72–54 Pulaski; Francesville 55–54 Monterey (2ot); Grovertown 74–47 Star City; Knox 55–41 Hamlet; North Judson 70–48 Medaryville; Winamac 75–32 Aubbeenaubbee; Grovertown 61–49 Francesville; Knox 41–38

North Judson; Winamac 24–19 Grovertown; Winamac 41–29 Knox. Officials: Myron Weldy, Roy Kilby, Burl McKenzie.

KOKOMO: Eastern 67–37 Deer Creek; Western 72–63 Northwestern; Delphi 76–54 Camden; Flora 79–53 Cutler; Kokomo 101–28 Burlington; Eastern 63–52 Western, Delphi 67–45 Flora; Eastern 70–64 Kokomo; Eastern 49–48 Delphi. Officials: Dee Williams, Charles Timmons.

LAFAYETTE: West Point 56–51 Jackson Twp.; Klondike 75–43 Romney; Jefferson 83–35 Lauramie Twp.; West Lafayette 84–39 Buck Creek; Wea 63–62 Shadeland; Dayton 67–44 Montmorenci; Monitor 81–52 Battle Ground; Klondike 46–31 West Point; Jefferson 50–37 West Lafayette; Dayton 53–51 Wea; Monitor 53–46 Klondike; Jefferson 57–36 Dayton; Jefferson 54–35 Monitor. Officials: Joe Mullins, Ward Mosbaugh, Robert Windsor.

LEBANON: Dover 81–60 Perry Central; Pike 50–41 Wells; Zionsville 58–48 Lebanon; Pinnell 68–59 Thorntown; Dover 80–68 Whitestown; Zionsville 63–51 Pike; Pinnell 63–59 Dover; Zionsville 73–38 Pinnell. Officials: Don Dick, Henry Pearcy, Merle Hill.

LOGANSPORT: Kewanna 75–49 Tipton Twp.; Logansport 81–37 Twelve Mile; Grass Creek, 83–63 Galveston; Royal Center 98–39 New Waverly; Washington Twp. 69–40 Young America; Lucerne 62–40 Metea; Logansport 64–41 Kewanna; Grass Creek 57–56 Royal Center; Washington Twp. 58–42 Lucerne; Logansport 82–57 Grass Creek; Logansport 75–49 Washington Twp. Officials: Gary Nelson, Norris Ward, John Burger.

LYNNVILLE: Lynnville 46–44 Chandler; Tennyson 66–48 Millersburg; Boonville 61–28 Folsomville; Selvin 57–47 Elberfeld; Newburgh 59–44 Lynnville; Boonville 64–37 Tennyson; Newburgh 51–30 Selvin; Boonville 80–52 Newburgh. Officials: Harold Gourley, David Schellhase, Donald Boyer.

MADISON: Shawe Memorial 79–22 Dupont; Scottsburg 72–45 Lexington; Paris Crossing 53–48 Deputy; Madison 85–45 Hanover; Austin 63–45 Central; Shawe Memorial 74–45 Saluda; Scottsburg 78–58 Paris Crossing, Madison 80–68 Austin; Scottsburg 59–53 Shawe Memorial; Scottsburg 46–44 Madison. Officials: Ed Straith-Miller, Wendell Baker, Gilbert Beagle.

MARION: Jefferson Twp. 50–40 Sweetser; Mississinewa 71–29 Van Buren; Marion 71–44 Fairmount; Swayzee 82–45 Bennett; Mississinewa 75–48 Jefferson Twp.; Marion 76–51 Swayzee; Marion 57–56 Mississinewa. Officials: Robert Dornte, John Janzaruk.

MICHIGAN CITY: LaCrosse 46–43 Kingsbury; Mill Creek 52–34 Stillwell; Michigan City 111–43 St. Mary's; Hanna 84–43 Clinton Twp.; Union Twp. 73–66 Wanatah; LaPorte 74–40 Union Mills; Rolling Prairie 67–53 Westville; Mill Creek 30–28 LaCrosse; Michigan City 85–62 Hanna; LaPorte 84–53 Union Twp.; Mill Creek 66–63 Rolling Prairie; Michigan City 71–64 LaPorte; Michigan City 77–63 Mill Creek. Officials: Maurice Criswell, Richard Swartz, John Fee.

MONTICELLO: Monticello 66–44 Burnettsville; Buffalo 60–41 Idaville; Monon 62–53 Wolcott; Brookston 55–41 Reynolds; Monticello 89–32 Chalmers; Buffalo 61–60 Monon; Monticello 56–49 Brookston; Monticello 71–57 Buffalo. Officials: Dean Geyer, R. Wayne Smith, Jimmy Dimitroff.

MUNCIE: Royerton 65–51 Albany; Burris 56–49 Cowan; Eaton 67–44 Selma; Harrison Twp. 68–49 Desoto; Gaston 63–55 Daleville; Yorktown 56–45 Center; Muncie Central 71–62 Royerton; Eaton 64–61 Burris; Harrison Twp. 57–44 Gaston; Muncie Central 82–45 Yorktown; Eaton 68–35 Harrison Twp.; Muncie Central 75–52 Eaton. Officials: James Haywood, Robert Cherry, James Boswell, Carter L. Caton.

Tourney Time

NEW ALBANY: Laconia 61–32 Leavenworth; New Albany 82–53 Lanesville; North Central 48–47 Morgan Twp.; Corydon 52–39 Milltown; Marengo 52–51 Mt. St. Francis; Georgetown 63–57 English; Elizabeth 44–43 Laconia; New Albany 82–55 North Central; Marengo 59–56 Corydon; Elizabeth 67–60 Georgetown; New Albany 106–64 Marengo; New Albany 57–52 Elizabeth. Officials: Thomas Hoffman James Schwenk, Fred Marlow.

NEW CASTLE: Mooreland 68–64 Mt. Summit; Cadiz 61–50 Straughn; Middletown 79–42 Sulphur Springs; Cadiz 45–41 Mooreland; Knightstown 57–35 New Lisbon; New Castle 55–53 Lewisville (2ot); Spiceland 59–50 Kennard; Knightstown 73–58 New Castle; Middletown 62–51 Cadiz; Knightstown 53–51 Spiceland; Middletown 56–37 Knightstown. Officials: Norman Shields, Clayton Nichols, Winfield Jacobs.

NOBLESVILLE: Sheridan 53–36 Fishers; Jefferson Twp. (Kempton) 64–55 Noblesville; Westfield 47–41 Carmel; Walnut Grove 52–42 Prairie Twp.; Windfall 51–39 Sharpsville; Jackson Central 44–43 Tipton; Jefferson Twp. 48–43 Sheridan; Walnut Grove 73–45 Westfield; Jackson Central 46–45 Windfall; Jefferson Twp. (Kempton) 55–53 Walnut Grove; Jefferson Twp. (Kempton) 43–42 Jackson Central. Officials: Lowell Barnett, James Murphy, Howard Plough.

PERU: Fulton 56–48 Clay Twp.; Gilead 63–36 Butler Twp.; Akron 58–55 Bunker Hill; Converse 61–39 Mexico; Chili 62–54 Deedsville (ot); Peru 91–36 Macy; Fulton 64–53 Gilead; Akron 58–52 Converse; Peru 58–50 Chili; Akron 73–51 Fulton; Akron 64–56 Peru. Officials: Phil Bail, Herb Schwomeyer, Roscoe Hall.

PLYMOUTH: Bourbon 58–35 Tyner; LaPaz 52–43 Plymouth; Argos 68–51 Bremen; LaPaz 78–69 Bourbon; Rochester 80–59 West Twp.; Tippecanoe 76–49 Talma; Richland Center 76–60 Culver; Tippecanoe 56–55 Rochester; LaPaz 62–55 Argos; Richland Center 62–56 Tippecanoe; LaPaz 71–54 Richland Center. Officials: Anthony Lazar, Stanley Dubis, Leonard Lupold.

PRINCETON: Mt. Olympus 45–42 Hazelton; Fort Branch 60–37 Haubstadt; Francisco 41–36 Patoka; Owensville 80–55 Oakland City; Princeton 67–47 Mackey; Fort Branch 83–61 Mt. Olympus; Owensville 57–42 Francisco; Princeton 50–34 Fort Branch; Princeton 70–43 Owensville. Officials: J. Firman Grimes, Robert Sweet.

RENSSELAER: Morocco 61–37 Mt. Ayr; Goodland 64–47 Remington; DeMotte 75–54 Tefft; Rensselaer 63–46 Fair Oaks; Wheatfield 65–59 Brook; Morocco 69–61 Kentland; DeMotte 63–61 Goodland (ot); Rensselaer 43–41 Wheatfield (ot); Morocco 56–50 DeMotte; Morocco 65–58 Rensselaer. Officials: John Cover, Sam Massette, Glen Wisler.

RICHMOND: Williamsburg 49–46 Fountain City; Hagerstown 62–36 Whitewater; Milton 46–35 Webster; Richmond 70–29 Boston; Cambridge City 47–46 Economy; Centerville 73–35 Greens Fork; Hagerstown 59–57 Williamsburg; Richmond 62–41 Milton; Centerville 50–49 Cambridge City; Richmond 73–57 Hagerstown; Richmond 54–44 Centerville. Officials: John Evans, William Findling, M.N. Delph.

RUSHVILLE: Arlington 78–65 Manilla; Milroy 73–61 Morton Memorial; Morristown 94–68 New Salem; Rushville 71–57 Mays; Arlington 66–55 Carthage; Morristown 67–58 Milroy; Rushville 54–45 Arlington; Rushville 88–78 Morristown. Officials: Eugene Glaze, Gene Davis, Carl Bruns.

SEYMOUR: Vallonia 59–54 Crothersville; Seymour 78–51 Cortland; Medora 67–48 Tampico; Freetown 60–55 Brownstown; Hayden 58–57 Clearspring; Seymour 70–50 Vallonia; Medora 74–63 Freetown; Seymour 86–52 Hayden; Seymour 92–38 Medora. Officials: Jerry Steiner, John Williams.

IHSAA Scores | 1950–1959

SOUTH BEND: Walkerton 64–48 Greene Twp.; Lakeville 87–76 New Carlisle; Adams 80–40 Madison Twp.; Central 62–30 Walkerton; Lakeville 65–62 Adams; Washington 63–40 North Liberty; St. Joseph's 55–50 Washington Clay; Mishawaka 76–65 Riley; Washington 69–48 St. Joseph's; Central 80–59 Lakeville; Washington 80–74 Mishawaka; Central 66–64 Washington. Officials: Harley Collins, Bill Larkin, Don Lieberum.

SULLIVAN: Carlisle 64–46 Pleasantville; Shelburn 77–55 Graysville; Hymera 69–48 Farmersburg; Gill Twp. 55–49 Fairbanks; Sullivan 56–36 Dugger; Carlisle 65–42 Shelburn; Hymera 63–41 Gill Twp.; Sullivan 46–45 Carlisle; Hymera 60–43 Sullivan. Officials: Walter Frye, Wilfred Susott.

SWITZ CITY: Solsberry 59–40 Worthington; Switz City 62–42 Jasonville; Bloomfield 78–63 Marco; Midland 78–52 Lyons; Linton 45–44 Solsberry; Switz City 81–64 Bloomfield; Midland 58–49 Linton; Switz City 68–52 Midland. Officials: Leroy Heminger, Leonard Benedetto, James Parker.

SYRACUSE: Mentone 58–44 Beaver Dam; North Webster 53–39 Sidney; Leesburg 64–44 Claypool; Syracuse 53–52 Silver Lake; Warsaw 61–42 Larwill; Pierceton 63–49 Columbia City; Etna Green 52–49 Atwood; Mentone 76–64 Milford; Leesburg 51–47 North Webster; Warsaw 75–57 Syracuse; Pierceton 75–46 Etna Green; Mentone 57–43 Leesburg; Warsaw 61–55 Pierceton; Warsaw 47–45 Mentone. Officials: Lores Lehman, Harold Braden, Gerald Strickler, Donald Hollman.

TELL CITY: St. Ferdinand 50–46 Oil Twp.; Bristow 46–35 Richland Twp.; Dale 78–40 Tell City; Rockport 45–24 Chrisney; Cannelton 54–45 Troy; Ferdinand 62–53 Bristow; Dale 56–39 Rockport; Cannelton 52–48 St. Ferdinand (ot); Dale 58–49 Cannelton. Officials: Malvern Redman, Fred Hodge.

TERRE HAUTE: Garfield 54–49 Riley; Honey Creek 61–58 Schulte; Gerstmeyer 50–47 State; Glenn 71–61 Fontanet; New Goshen 40–33 Otter Creek; Wiley 65–56 West Terre Haute; Prairie Creek 58–34 Pimento; Concannon 93–53 Blackhawk; Garfield 67–51 Honey Creek; Gerstmeyer 59–54 Glenn; Wiley 58–40 New Goshen; Concannon 62–37 Prairie Creek; Gerstmeyer 64–62 Garfield; Wiley 55–34 Concannon; Gerstmeyer 59–53 Wiley. Officials: Joe Hunter, Clarence Brown, Melbourne Pope, Gilbert Smith, William McDonald.

VALPARAISO: Wheeler 59–58 Morgan Twp.; Liberty Twp. 86–32 Jackson Twp.; Portage 49–48 Valparaiso; Boone Grove 52–42 Washington Twp.; Hebron 67–50 Kouts; Chesterton 74–55 Wheeler; Portage 93–63 Liberty Twp.; Boone Grove 58–51 Hebron; Portage 60–51 Chesterton; Portage 52–46 Boone Grove. Officials: Ernest Sohl, Victor Wukovits, George Sobek.

VERSAILLES: Sunman 41–38 New Marion; Cross Plains 44–42 Napoleon; Versailles 42–37 Osgood; Milan 50–46 Batesville; Holton 63–55 Sunman; Versailles 76–49 Cross Plains; Milan 37–15 Holton; Milan 53–36 Versailles. Officials: Leland Terrell, Kenneth Blankenbaker, Edwin Miller.

VEVAY: Vevay 78–45 Moores Hill; Dillsboro 56–52 Guilford; Lawrenceburg 65–52 Patriot; Rising Sun 72–53 Bright; Vevay 61–59 Aurora; Lawrenceburg 55–49 Dillsboro; Vevay 40–39 Rising Sun (2ot); Vevay 46–44. Lawrenceburg. Officials: James Patterson, John Thomas, Grayson Mahin.

VINCENNES: Vincennes 74–48 Wheatland; Bruceville 39–34 Fritchton; Central Catholic 59–48 Monroe City; Decker 48–32 Decker Chapel; Freelandville 44–42 Sandborn; Bicknell 59–54 Oaktown; Vincennes 68–64 Bruceville; Central Catholic 72–60 Decker; Bicknell 61–56 Freelandville; Vincennes 69–61 Central Catholic; Vincennes 96–58 Bicknell. Officials: Roger

Tourney Time

Emmert, Lloyd Whipple, Lester Cornwell.

WABASH: LaFontaine 44–37 White's; North Manchester 56–46 Urbana; Wabash 61–54 Somerset, North Manchester 59–53 LaFontaine; South Whitley 59–40 Roann; Noble Twp. 56–54 Chester Twp.; Lagro 82–41 Laketon; South Whitley 76–59 Noble Twp.; Wabash 68–61 North Manchester; South Whitley 61–44 Lagro; Wabash 65–64 South Whitley. Officials: Darl March, Paul Bateman, Walter Stebing.

WASHINGTON: Barr Twp. 62–30 Epsom; Plainville 71–66 Petersburg; St. John's Loogootee 67–47 Washington Catholic; Loogootee High 61–52 Alfordsville; Washington 78–45 Odon; Shoals 73–46 Elmore Twp.; Plainville 65–51 Barr Twp.; Loogootee 48–45 St. John's; Washington 59–58 Shoals; Plainville 63–58 Loogootee; Plainville 65–55 Washington. Officials: Tyrus Rice, James Sanders, Frank Smith.

WINCHESTER: Union Twp. 82–53 Stoney Creek; Winchester 40–36 Parker; Lynn 68–57 Spartanburg; McKinley 41–34 Ridgeville; Green 47–38 Wayne; Union City 64–54 Farmland; Ward Twp. 46–39 Jackson; Winchester 49–44 Union Twp.; Lynn 59–57 McKinley; Union City 70–36 Green; Winchester 31–26 Ward Twp.; Lynn 64–51 Union City; Winchester 42–40 Lynn. Officials: Everett Campbell, Frank Carnes, James Davidson.

1956 REGIONALS

COLUMBUS: Scottsburg 68–54 St. Paul; Southport 71–49 Columbus; Scottsburg 72–60 Southport. Officials: Lloyd Whipple, Malvern Redman, Cyril Birge, John Gwin.

ELKHART: Elkhart 71–55 LaPaz; South Bend Central 51–48 Warsaw; Elkhart 59–53 South Bend Central. Officials: Charles Northam, Homer Owens, Oscar Samuels, William Findling.

EVANSVILLE: Boonville 57–56 Evansville Lincoln; Princeton 58–56 Dale; Princeton 52–50 Boonville. Officials: Eugene Sparks, S. T. Proffitt, James Sanders, Joseph Hunter.

FORT WAYNE: Monmouth 80–58 Fremont; Fort Wayne South Side 64–54 Avilla; Fort Wayne South Side 66–59 Monmouth. Officials: Lowell Barnett, Harley Collins, H. F. McNaught, Wesley Oler.

GREENCASTLE: Clinton 58–48 Greencastle; New Ross 58–52 Covington; New Ross 63–50 Clinton. Officials: Leland Terrell, Robert Cherry, Frank Smith, Fred Marlow.

HAMMOND: Hammond High 66–65 Michigan City; Gary Froebel 76–75 Portage Twp.; Gary Froebel 74–70 Hammond High. Officials: Robert Dornte, Paul Bateman, Marvin Todd, Don McCoy.

HUNTINGBURG: Hymera 63–59 Plainville; Jasper 62–60 Vincennes; Jasper 86–60 Hymera. Officials: Ed Straith-Miller, Leroy Heminger, Cloyd Julian, Paul Grimes.

INDIANAPOLIS: Crispus Attucks 61–48 Anderson; Hancock Central 64–45 Danville; Crispus Attucks 99–43 Hancock Central. Officials: Charles Meade, Everett Campbell, Don Lieberum, Everett Cass.

JEFFERSONVILLE: Seymour 93–60 Providence; New Albany 93–60 Mitchell; New Albany 64–62 Seymour. Officials: Robert Rose, James Boswell, Lowell Willis, Clayton Nichols.

KOKOMO: Wabash 69–64 Akron; Eastern 58–52 Jefferson Twp.; Wabash 59–52 Eastern. Officials: Gerald Strickler, Burl McKenzie, Don McBride, Gene Winks.

LAFAYETTE: Jackson Twp. 71–38 Ambia; Lafayette Jefferson 68–58 Zionsville; Jefferson 55–36 Jackson Twp. Officials: James Haywood, Dean Geyer, James Patterson, Lores Lehman.

IHSAA Scores | 1950–1959

LOGANSPORT: Logansport 78–45 Morocco; Monticello 56–47 Winamac; Logansport 60–54 Monticello. Officials: Dee Williams, Victor Griewank, Herbert Schwomeyer, John Janzaruk.

MARION: Clear Creek 76–71 Bluffton (ot); Marion 68–63 Hartford City; Marion 86–53 Clear Creek. Officials: John Hilligoss, Roscoe Hall, Stan Dubis, Andrew Hiduke.

MARTINSVILLE: Morgantown 85–67 Brazil; Gerstmeyer 91–70 Switz City; Gerstmeyer 83–67 Morgantown. Officials: Roy Gardner, Jack Small, Eugene Glaze, Charlie Timmons.

MUNCIE: Muncie Central 62–59 Richmond; Middletown 42–37 Winchester; Muncie Central 65–59 Middletown. Officials: Maurice Criswell, Jerry Steiner, Frank Sanders, Lawrence Gradeless.

RUSHVILLE: Connersville 64–49 Rushville; Milan 64–57 Vevay; Connersville 58–55 Milan. Officials: Roland Baker, Winfield Jacobs, Joe Mullins, John Williams.

1956 SEMI-FINALS

BLOOMINGTON: Terre Haute Gerstmeyer 55–52 Jasper; Princeton 59–39 New Albany; Gerstmeyer Terre Haute 69–58 Princeton. Officials: Lowell Barnett, Don Lieberum, Don McBride, Ed Straith-Miller, Stan Dubis, Joe Mullins.

FORT WAYNE: Fort Wayne South Side 69–58 Wabash; Elkhart 72–69 Marion; Elkhart 70–64 Fort Wayne South Side. Officials: John Hilligoss, Herb Schwomeyer, Eugene Sparks, Jim Patterson, Charles Meade, Maurice Criswell.

INDIANAPOLIS: Scottsburg 66–59 Muncie Central; Crispus Attucks 67–49 Connersville; Crispus Attucks 67–42 Scottsburg. Officials: Roy Gardner, H.F. McNaught, Marvin Todd, Robert Dornte, Roland Baker, Lloyd Whipple.

LAFAYETTE: Lafayette Jefferson 56–51 Logansport; Gary Froebel 56–41 New Ross; Lafayette Jefferson 71–58 Gary Froebel. Officials: Robert Rose, Dee Williams, S.T. Proffitt, Gerald Strickler, Cyril Birge, Charles Northam..

1956 FINALS—March 17

INDIANAPOLIS (Butler Fieldhouse): Jefferson (Lafayette) 54–52 Elkhart; Crispus Attucks (Indianapolis) 68–59 Gerstmeyer (Terre Haute); Crispus Attucks (Indianapolis) 79–57 Jefferson (Lafayette). Officials: Herb Schwomeyer, Dee Williams, Lowell Barnett, Robert Dornte, Roy Gardner, Charles Northam.

1957 SECTIONALS

ADAMS CENTRAL: Decatur 47–28 Monmouth; Berne 61–58 Pleasant Mills; Adams Central 48–47 Geneva; Hartford Center 74–46 Decatur Catholic; Berne 44–42 Decatur (2ot); Hartford Center 61–46 Adams Central; Hartford Center 60–49 Berne. Officials: John Hilligoss, Richard Tiernan.

ANDERSON: Elwood 65–60 Madison Heights; Anderson 60–41 Alexandria; Highland 53–34 Pendleton; Elwood 67–53 Anderson; Frankton 73–54 Markleville; Summitville 47–34 Lapel; Frankton 66–62 St. Mary's; Elwood 69–54 Highland; Frankton 57–53 Summitville; Elwood 57–50 Frankton. Officials: Gerald Strickler, Ed Straith-Miller, Thomas Dean.

Tourney Time

ATTICA: Hillsboro 81–57 Wallace; Attica 51–49 Covington; Veedersburg 68–48 Pine Village; Richland Twp. 71–64 Williamsport; West Lebanon 70–40 Perrysville; Hillsboro 62–40 Kingman; Veedersburg 70–67 Attica; Richland Twp. 60–53 West Lebanon; Veedersburg 71–52 Hillsboro; Richland Twp. 75–73 Veedersburg. Officials: Joe Thomas, Charles Fouty, DeVere Hoffman.

BEDFORD: Paoli 52–41 Orleans; Bedford 62–42 Oolitic; Shawswick 59–37 Mitchell; Marshall Twp. 43–41 Huron (ot); Tunnelton 58—55 Fayetteville; Williams 60–58 Heltonville; Bedford 57–45 Paoli; Marshall Twp. 57–43 Shawswick; Williams 64–51 Tunnelton; Bedford 51–47 Marshall Twp.; Bedford 53–42 Williams. Officials: Leonard Benedetto, Lowell Willis, Robert Davidson.

BLUFFTON: Bluffton 78–63 Jackson; Liberty Center 61–57 Chester Center; Ossian 68–42 Petroleum; Rockcreek 85–48 Union; Bluffton 66–52 Lancaster Central; Liberty Center 52–49 Ossian; Bluffton 70–57 Rockcreek; Bluffton 62–42 Liberty Center. Officials: Charles Northam, James Ridge, David Habegger.

CENTER GROVE: Decatur Central 61–32 Center Grove; Greenwood 75–62 Helmsburg; Nineveh 47–33 Clark; Edinburg 45–38 Whiteland; Southport 75–49 Franklin; Trafalgar 51–50 Union; Decatur Central 46–42 Greenwood; Nineveh 44–38 Edinburg; Southport 72–47 Trafalgar; Nineveh 46–44 Decatur Central (2ot); Southport 56–31 Nineveh. Officials: Vern Doles, Eugene Sparks, Wesley Oler.

CHURUBUSCO–AUBURN: (At Churubusco): Auburn 56–53 Orland; Churubusco 82–27 Flint; Fremont 52–32 Riverdale; Butler 83–48 Hamilton; Churubusco 38–30 Auburn; Fremont 70–53 Butler; (At Auburn): Angola 75–46 Salem Center; Ashley 45–35 Waterloo; Garrett 57–43 Pleasant Lake; Angola 64–36 Metz; Garrett 63–44 Ashley; (At Churubusco): Fremont 48–33 Churubusco; Garrett 49–41 Angola; Garrett 53–41 Fremont. Officials: Victor Wukovits, Edgar Powers, John Burger, Lewis Goshert.

CLAY CITY: Brazil 60–38 Cory; Freedom 55–28 Ashboro; Van Buren 65–47 Bowling Green; Staunton 56–45 Coal City; Gosport 56–52 Coalmont; Spencer 48–40 Patricksburg; Brazil 58–39 Clay City; Freedom 57–47 Van Buren; Staunton 61–42 Gosport; Spencer 41–32 Brazil; Staunton 63–45 Freedom; Staunton 27–24 Spencer. Officials: Henry Pearcy, James Parker, LeRoy Heminger, Cloyd Thompson.

COLUMBUS: Moral Twp. 67–44 Boggstown; Waldron 66–38 Fairland; Clifford 48–42 Van Buren; Columbus 82–57 Mt. Auburn; Shelbyville 82–54 Flatrock; Hope 53–49 Nashville; Moral Twp. 56–51 Waldron; Columbus 75–26 Clifford; Shelbyville 67–46 Hope; Columbus 59–53 Moral Twp.; Columbus 48–46 Shelbyville. Officials: Edwin Miller, Frank Smith, Don Shiflet.

CONNERSVILLE: Alquina 51–34 Orange: Connersville 72–34 Springfield; Whitewater 68–47 Brownsville; Connersville 61–58 Alquina; Laurel 50–47 Liberty; Brookville 91–26 Fairview; Harrisburg 65–51 Harrison Twp.; Laurel 51–46 Brookville; Connersville 75–46 Whitewater; Harrisburg 62–50 Laurel; Connersville 66–53 Harrisburg. Officials: Don McBride, John Evans, Gilbert Beagle.

CRAWFORDSVILLE: Crawfordsville 64–62 Waveland; Ladoga 63–55 Coal Creek Central; Darlington 54–52 New Ross; Crawfordsville 64–51 Ladoga; New Market 61–46 Waynetown; Alamo 58–32 Linden; Crawfordsville 53–47 Darlington; New Market 55–48 Alamo; Crawfordsville 86–41 New Market. Officials: Paul Grimes, Roderick Witt.

DANVILLE: Amo 60–58 New Winchester; North Salem 57–55 Pittsboro; Charlton 51–46 Avon; Danville 45–34 Lizton; Brownsburg 62–58 Speedway; Clayton 72–58 Stilesville; Plainfield 70–59 Amo; North Salem 64–60 Charlton; Brownsburg 53–46 Danville; Clayton 67–62 Plainfield;

IHSAA Scores | 1950–1959

North Salem 72–55 Brownsburg; North Salem 81–47 Clayton. Officials: Melvin Newlin, Grayson Mahin, Ward Mosbaugh.

DILLSBORO: Aurora 82–47 Dillsboro; Moores Hill 46–40 Guilford (ot); Rising Sun 65–55 Vevay; Bright 66–61 Patriot; Aurora 79–65 Lawrenceburg; Rising Sun 43–38 Moores Hill; Aurora 72–52 Bright; Aurora 67–56 Rising Sun. Officials: Karl Bly, Howard Plough, Cloyd Thompson.

EAST CHICAGO: Hammond Noll 87–79 Washington; Clark 59–44 Morton; Tech 57–55 Whiting; Noll 69–41 Clark; Hammond High 50–34 Dyer; Lowell 59–55 Griffith; Roosevelt 73–48 Crown Point; Hammond High 74–51 Lowell; Noll 51–36 Tech; Hammond High 47–46 Roosevelt; Noll 78–40 Hammond High. Officials: John Fee, H. F. McNaught, William Findling.

ELKHART: Jefferson 38–35 Bristol; New Paris 59–53 Topeka; Goshen 64–48 Concord; Nappanee 62–56 Baugo Twp.; Elkhart 70–45 Shipshewana-Scott; Millersburg 61–60 Middlebury; Wakarusa 58–51 Jefferson; New Paris 44–40 Goshen; Elkhart 43–38 Nappanee; Wakarusa 56–49 Millersburg; Elkhart 41–39 New Paris; Elkhart 70–32 Wakarusa. Officials: Phil Bail, Harold Braden, Victor Griewank.

EVANSVILLE: Cynthiana 56–34 New Harmony; Bosse 74–51 Wadesville; Mater Dei 71–44 Poseyville; Central 57–39 North; Lincoln 34–8 Mt. Vernon; Memorial 48–47 Reitz; Griffin 49–41 Cynthiana: Bosse 57–41 Mater Dei; Lincoln 52–39 Central; Memorial 48–43 Griffin; Lincoln 69–51 Bosse; Lincoln 70–40 Memorial. Officials: J. Firman Grimes, Vesper Moore, S. T. Proffitt.

FORT WAYNE: Concordia 63–39 Huntertown; Central 77–58 Leo; Harlan 63–53 Monroeville; South Side 34–16 North Side; New Haven 74–62 Hoagland; Woodburn 65–60 Coesse; Elmhurst 82–75 Lafayette Central; Central Catholic 43–38 Arcola; Central 64–56 Concordia; South Side 65–34 Harlan; New Haven 67–58 Woodburn; Central Catholic 78–44 Elmhurst; South Side 56–45 Central; Central Catholic 59–41 New Haven; South Side 44–40 Central Catholic. Officials: Dean Geyer, Richard Swartz, Thomas Demark, Ray Nemeth.

FOWLER: Ambia 50–38 Wadena; Otterbein 45–42 Boswell; Oxford 85–40 Earl Park; Pine Twp. 57–28 Freeland Park; Gilboa 42–39 Fowler; Otterbein 47–44 Ambia; Oxford 67–56 Pine Twp.; Otterbein 65–34 Gilboa; Otterbein 56–51 Oxford. Officials: Paul Dazey, Joe Garoffolo.

FRANKFORT: Mulberry 44–37 Michigantown; Frankfort 65–37; Sugar Creek; Forest 66–60 Washington Twp.; Colfax 61–45 Kirklin; Scircleville 60–47 Jackson Twp.; Rossville 59–37 Mulberry; Forest 53–50 Frankfort (ot); Colfax 63–45 Scircleville; Rossville 59–47 Forest; Colfax 62–55 Rossville. Officials: Jerry Steiner, Darl March, Darrell Snodgrass.

GARY: Froebel 61–45 Emerson; Calumet Twp. 66–42 Wirt; Roosevelt 101–57 East Gary Edison; Horace Mann 67–48 Merrillville; Gary Edison 59–36 Tolleston; Hobart 56–49 Lew Wallace; Froebel 57–44 Calumet Twp.; Roosevelt 61–58 Horace Mann; Gary Edison 81–54 Hobart; Roosevelt 73–69 Froebel; Roosevelt 58–57 Gary Edison. Officials: Burl McKenzie, Don Lieberum, Lawrence Gradeless.

GREENCASTLE: Greencastle 84–59 Russellville; Bainbridge 60–48 Cloverdale; Roachdale 46–42 Belle Union; Reelsville 73–49 Fillmore; Greencastle 70–46 Bainbridge; Roachdale 79–53 Reelsville; Greencastle 47–41 Roachdale. Officials: Dee Williams, John Park.

GREENFIELD: Charlottesville 69–66 Hancock Central; New Palestine 88–71 Mt. Comfort; Franklin Twp. 78–65 Wilkinson; Fortville 69–55 McCordsville; Charlottesville 62–60 Greenfield; New Palestine 78–60 Franklin Twp.; Charlottesville 69–61 Fortville; New Palestine 67–64 Charlottesville. Officials: James Haywood, Earnest Baldwin, Wray Holbrook.

Tourney Time

GREENSBURG: New Point 56–51 St. Paul; Greensburg 65–55 North Vernon; Vernon 72–71 Burney; Jackson 62–47 Sandcreek; Clarksburg 60–45 Sandusky; New Point 50–40 Greensburg; Jackson 70–56 Vernon; New Point 50–41 Clarksburg; Jackson 73–41 New Point. Officials: James Lentz, Gene Davis.

HARTFORD CITY: Montpelier 62–60 Pennville; Redkey 82–56 Poling; Portland 83–81 Madison Twp.; Roll 74–43 Gray; Hartford City 87–68 Dunkirk; Bryant 76–75 Montpelier (ot); Portland 74–59 Redkey; Hartford City 85–69 Roll; Portland 70–50 Bryant; Hartford City 69–53 Portland. Officials: Joe Mullins, Walter McFatridge, Richard Duffield.

HUNTINGBURG: Winslow 70–53 Huntingburg; Birdseye 59–56 Stendal; West Baden 49–48 Holland; Dubois 73–53 French Lick; Jasper 58–44 Ireland; Spurgeon 58–54 Otwell; Winslow 86–40 Birdseye; West Baden 57–50 Dubois; Jasper 85–33 Spurgeon; West Baden 57–54 Winslow; Jasper 77–63 West Baden. Officials: Don Boyer, Robert Rose, Malvern Redman.

HUNTINGTON: Roanoke 61–27 Bippus; Huntington 75–60 Clear Creek; Union 64–54 Andrews; Jefferson (Warren) 77–44 Jefferson (Whitley Co.); Lancaster 54–42 Rock Creek; Warren 67–62 Huntington Twp.; Roanoke 41–40 Huntington Catholic; Huntington 65–53 Union; Jefferson (Warren) 71–51 Lancaster; Warren 50–47 Roanoke; Huntington 52–26 Jefferson (Warren); Huntington 75–42 Warren. Officials: Charles Timmons, Meredyth N. Delph, John Janzaruk.

INDIANAPOLIS: Lawrence Central 59–53 Sacred Heart; Beech Grove 62–42 Washington; Wood 66–64 Cathedral; Crispus Attucks 56—34 Scecina; Tech 69–50 Broad Ripple; Shortridge 70–56 School for the Deaf; Ben Davis 50–45 Manual; Warren Central 64–58 Howe; Beech Grove 56–55 Lawrence Central; Crispus Attucks 61–55 Wood; Tech 66–51 Shortridge; Ben Davis 58–57 Warren Central; Crispus Attucks 69–29 Beech Grove; Tech 72–52 Ben Davis; Crispus Attucks 50–44 Tech. Officials: James Patterson, Everett Campbell, James Davidson, Frank Carnes.

JEFFERSONVILLE: Charlestown 53–38 New Washington, Henryville 40–39 Campbellsburg; Silver Creek 51–45 Hardinsburg; Jeffersonville 63–52 Salem; Providence 77–56 Clarksville; Pekin 64–49 Borden; Charlestown 37–30 Henryville; Jeffersonville 49–35 Silver Creek; Providence 67–47 Pekin; Jeffersonville 50–49 Charlestown; Providence 67–54 Jeffersonville. Officials: James Schwenk, Roland Baker, Leland Terrell.

KENDALLVILLE: Avilla 87–70 Lima; Brighton 63–56 Howe Military; Wolcottville 56–53 Wolf Lake; Ligonier 61–58 Rome City; Albion 65–43 Springfield Twp.; Wawaka 64–59 Cromwell; Kendallville 38–36 LaGrange; Brighton 66–62 Avilla; Wolcottville 65–62 Ligonier; Albion 66–57 Wawaka; Kendallville 58–54 Brighton; Albion 53–52 Wolcottville; Kendallville 50–45 Albion. Officials: Gene Winks, Wayne Smith, Merle Shively.

KNOX: Monterey 79–77 Francesville (2ot); Grovertown 77–58 Medaryville; North Judson 75–53 Star City; Aubbeenaubbee 73–39 Pulaski; Knox 45–37 Hamlet; Winamac 80–31 San Pierre; Grovertown 77–58 Medaryville; North Judson 75–53 Star City; Aubbeenaubbee 73–65 Monterey; North Judson 76–53 Aubbeenaubbee; Winamac 57–45 Knox; North Judson 65–61 Grovertown; North Judson 46–42 Winamac. Officials: Charles Garber, Stan Dubis, Glen Wisler.

KOKOMO: Camden 67–54 Eastern; Cutler 68–41 Burlington; Delphi 71–57 Deer Creek; Kokomo 45–42 Western; Northwestern 64–57 Flora; Camden 80–38 Cutler; Delphi 65–55 Kokomo; Northwestern 47–43 Camden; Delphi 43–40 Northwestern. Officials: Marvin Todd, John Williams.

LAFAYETTE: West Lafayette 68–41 Montmorenci; Klondike 67–27 Lauramie Twp.; Dayton 63–49 Southwestern; Lafayette 90–36 Buck Creek; Monitor 67–50 Battle Ground; West Lafayette

IHSAA Scores | 1950–1959

50–47 Klondike; Lafayette 75–38 Dayton; West Lafayette 49–42 Monitor; Lafayette 59–40 West Lafayette. Officials: Cloyd Julian, John Holmes.

LOGANSPORT: Logansport 60–59 Royal Center; Galveston 60–59 Tipton Twp.; Washington Twp. 50–29 Twelve Mile; Metea 65–41 Young, America; Grass Creek 67–65 Kewanna (ot); Lucerne 57–44 New Waverly; Logansport 74–50 Galveston; Washington Twp. 96–47 Metea; Grass Creek 75–52 Lucerne; Logansport 64–62 Washington Twp.; Logansport 67–59 Grass Creek. Officials: Everett Cass, Oscar Samuels, Gerald Imel.

LYNNVILLE: Lynnville 49–38 Millersburg; Chandler 69–67 Boonville; Newburgh 66–58 Selvin; Elberfeld 51–43 Tennyson; Lynnville 77–58 Chandler; Newburgh 45–44 Elberfeld; Lynnville 35–34 Newburgh. Officials: Ivan Risley, Norman Risley.

MARION: Mississinewa 59–32 Fairmount; Bennett 53–45 Jefferson Twp.; Marion 74–53 Van Buren; Sweetser 51–45 Swayzee; Mississinewa 57–35 Bennett; Marion 61–54 Sweetser; Marion 68–62 Mississinewa. Officials: Frank Sanders, Roy Kilby.

MARTINSVILLE: Eminence 52–41 Unionville; Mooresville 51–39 Ellettsville; Smithville 39–36 University; Bloomington 49–47 Morgantown; Martinsville 80–36 Monrovia; Stinesville 52–43 Eminence; Mooresville 52–51 Smithville; Martinsville 43–39 Bloomington (ot); Mooresville 48–36 Stinesville; Martinsville 60–56 Mooresville. Officials: James Sanders, Noel Genth, Robert Sweet.

MICHIGAN CITY: LaPorte 86–33 Stillwell; Union Twp. 70–69 Wanatah (ot); Mill Creek 79–59 Hanna; Westville 68–61 St. Mary's; Michigan City 75–50 LaCrosse; Rolling Prairie 78–36 Clinton Twp.; Union Mills 77–57 Kingsbury; LaPorte 57–42 Union Twp.; Mill Creek 50–46 Westville; Michigan City 87–66 Rolling Prairie; LaPorte 70–55 Union Mills; Michigan City 81–54 Mill Creek; Michigan City 63–55 LaPorte. Officials: Paul Bateman, Gary Nelson, Carter Caton.

MONTICELLO: Monon 61–44 Brookston; Burnettsville 80–51 Chalmers; Monticello 71–43 Idaville; Wolcott 69–35 Buffalo; Monon 75–48 Reynolds; Monticello 57–56 Burnettsville; Monon 71–67 Wolcott; Monticello 73–67 Monon. Officials: Robert Sosbe, Robert Brees, George Davenport.

MUNCIE: Harrison 56–37 Yorktown; Gaston 71–44 Daleville; Muncie Central 77–42 Albany; Eaton 72–60 Cowan; Royerton 56–51 Center; Selma 50–43 Burris; Harrison 64–52 DeSoto; Muncie Central 69–47 Gaston; Eaton 62–61 Royerton; Harrison 57–38 Selma; Muncie Central 71–59 Eaton; Muncie Central 68–44 Harrison. Officials: Clayton Nichols, Johannes Dienelt, Robert Dornte.

NEW ALBANY: Corydon 68–51 Leavenworth; English 56–39 Morgan Twp.; Marengo 33–26 Georgetown; Elizabeth 62–32 Mt. St. Francis; Laconia 58–39 Milltown; North Central 63–44 Lanesville; Corydon 51–45 New Albany; Laconia 58–55 Elizabeth; Corydon 32–30 North Central; Marengo 49–43 Laconia; Marengo 64–60 Corydon. Officials: Ralph Box, Joseph Hunter, Norman Shields.

NEW CASTLE: Kennard 56–35 New Lisbon; Knightstown 69–53 Lewisville 64–37 Mt. Summit; Kennard 73–60 Knightstown; New Castle 65–29 Spiceland; Middletown 56–41 Cadiz; Sulphur Springs 59–57 Mooreland; New Castle 69–54 Middletown; Lewisville 49–48 Kennard; New Castle 90–54 Sulphur Springs; New Castle 70–64 Lewisville (ot). Officials: Floyd Reed, James Boswell, Arthur Thompson.

NOBLESVILLE: Sheridan 69–49 Walnut Grove; Windfall 61–26 Prairie Twp.; Carmel 71–58 Fishers; Sharpsville 43–34 Westfield; Jackson Central 45–44 Tipton; Noblesville 59–34

Tourney Time

Jefferson Twp.; Windfall 64–55 Sheridan; Carmel 69–40 Sharpsville; Noblesville 67–55 Jackson Central; Windfall 79–53 Carmel; Noblesville 58–54 Windfall. Officials: Ira Williams, Jack Small, Gene Butts.

PERU: Deedsville 72–43 Gilead; Akron 89–35 Butler Twp.; Peru 54–36 Converse; Bunker Hill 20–19 Clay Twp.; Chili 64–50 Mexico; Fulton 60–59 Macy (2ot); Deedsville 75–64 Akron; Peru 44–43 Bunker Hill; Fulton 53–52 Chili; Peru 55–50 Deedsville; Peru 65–45 Fulton. Officials: James Murray, Norris Ward, Myron Weldy.

PLYMOUTH: Talma 53–40 Tyner; Bourbon 66–58 Culver; Plymouth 68–51 Tippecanoe; Bourbon 67–54 Talma; Rochester 81–50 LaPaz; Argos 87–49 West Twp.; Bremen 71–69 Richland Center (ot); Argos 80–72 Rochester; Plymouth 67–46 Bourbon; Argos 43–28 Bremen; Plymouth 63–60 Argos. Officials: Andrew Hiduke, Ernest Sohl, John Sebastian.

PRINCETON: Oakland City 47–43 Mt. Olympus; Ft. Branch 53–51 Francisco; Owensville 85–24 Hazelton; Mackey 42–39 Haubstadt; Princeton 80–55 Patoka; Ft. Branch 65–55 Oakland City; Owensville 61–58 Mackey; Princeton 51–47 Ft. Branch; Princeton 60–48 Owensville. Officials: Ken Merder, Thomas Hoffman.

RENSSELAER: Wheatfield 69–45 Fair Oaks; DeMotte 70–60 Morocco; Brook 70–65 Remington; Goodland 66–49 Mt. Ayr; Rensselaer 66–59 Kentland; Wheatfield 59–51 Tefft; Brook 70–64 DeMotte; Rensselaer 61–59 Goodland (ot); Wheatfield 67–64 Brook; Rensselaer 73–48 Wheatfield. Officials: Anthony Lazar, Nick Reff, Leo Ponto.

RICHMOND: Richmond 70–63 Cambridge City; Williamsburg 76–49 Economy; Hagerstown 47–45 Boston (ot); Whitewater 73–50 Milton; Centerville 57–48 Greens Fork; Fountain City 63–48 Webster; Richmond 58–55 Williamsburg; Hagerstown 53–50 Whitewater; Centerville 55–51 Fountain City (ot); Richmond 62–41 Hagerstown; Richmond 65–53 Centerville. Officials: John Priest, Robert Cherry, Fred Marlow.

ROCKVILLE: Montezuma 80–57 Hillsdale; Newport 58–54 Mecca; Tangier 35–34 Cayuga; Bloomingdale 52–50 St. Bernice; Rockville 47–44 Rosedale; Dana 60–36 Marshall; Clinton 65–45 Bridgeton; Montezuma 77–45 Bellmore; Tangier 62–49 Newport; Rockville 73–34 Bloomingdale; Clinton 64–60 Dana; Tangier 72–60 Montezuma; Rockville 54–50 Clinton; Tangier 42–36 Rockville. Officials: Melbourne Pope, Merle Hill, Gilbert Smith, Wendell Baker.

RUSHVILLE: Arlington 67–52 Manilla; Morristown 77–56 Mays; Carthage 55–52 New Salem; Morton Memorial 65–63 Milroy; Arlington 67–51 Rushville; Morristown 66–64 Carthage (ot); Morton Memorial 66–61 Arlington (ot); Morristown 67–55 Morton Memorial. Officials: Homer Owens, William May, Morris Davis.

SCOTTSBURG: Lexington 64–45 Saluda; Shawe 64–35 Dupont; Scottsburg 90–43 Central; Austin 47–43 Deputy; Hanover 52–32 Paris Crossing; Madison 78–53 Lexington; Scottsburg 76–58 Shawe Memorial; Austin 49–45 Hanover; Madison 62–48 Scottsburg; Madison 68–58 Austin. Officials: Robert Laird, Kenneth Blankenbaker, Dwain Laird.

SEYMOUR: Clearspring 60–43 Tampico; Brownstown 59–54 Medora; Seymour 77–69 Crothersville; Vallonia 51–50 Freetown; Cortland 39–37 Hayden; Brownstown 47–44 Clearspring; Seymour 85–50 Vallonia; Cortland 50–44 Brownstown; Seymour 67–49 Cortland, Officials: Roy Gardner, Carl Bruns.

SOUTH BEND: Lakeville 89–52 Madison Twp.; Riley 59–42 New Carlisle; Washington-Clay 57–50 Greene Twp.; Lakeville 73–62 Washington; Riley 65–48 Washington-Clay; Central 52–32 Adams; Mishawaka 86–52 St. Joseph; Walkerton 50–38 North Liberty; Central 77–72

IHSAA Scores | 1950–1959

Mishawaka; Lakeville 65–48 Riley; Central 44–26 Walkerton; Central 56–48 Lakeville. Officials: Wayne Crispen, Glen Lantz, Maurice Criswell.

SULLIVAN: Hymera 60–43 Fairbanks; Sullivan 63–46 Farmersburg; Dugger 61–40 Graysville; Carlisle 74–45 Pleasantville; Shelburn 54–49 Gill Twp.; Sullivan 57–36 Hymera; Dugger 61–59 Carlisle; Sullivan 64–54 Shelburn; Sullivan 71–48 Dugger. Officials: Harold Gourley, Donald Hubbard.

SWITZ CITY: Bloomfield 65–44 Midland; Solsberry 56–47 Lyons; Linton 37–29 Worthington; Switz City 66–44 Marco; Bloomfield 57–55 Jasonville (ot); Solsberry 54–45 Linton; Bloomfield 64–42 Switz City; Solsberry 53–34 Bloomfield. Officials: William McDonald, Walter Frye, Wallace Reeve.

SYRACUSE: Warsaw 55–48 Atwood; Etna Green 43–38 Leesburg; Syracuse 58–50 Beaver Dam; Columbia City 72–37 Larwill; Silver Lake 62–49 Claypool; Mentone 46–44 Milford (3ot); Pierceton 64–42 Sidney; North Webster 46–45 Warsaw; Etna Green 75–50 Syracuse; Silver Lake 52–43 Columbia City; Pierceton 55–42 Mentone; Etna Green 55–45 North Webster; Pierceton 56–46 Silver Lake; Pierceton 63–60 Etna Green. Officials: Harley Collins, William Hile, Joseph Bella, Marion Acton.

TELL CITY: Dale 70–37 Cannelton; St. Ferdinand 52–47 Troy; Tell City 56–53 Oil Twp.; Luce Twp. 56–48 Chrisney; Rockport 53–49 Bristow; Dale 43–42 St. Ferdinand; Tell City 56–42 Luce Twp.; Dale 50–26 Rockport; Dale 40–38 Tell City (3ot). Officials: Lester Cornwell, Roger Emmert.

TERRE HAUTE: Honey Creek 42–36 Prairie Creek; Garfield 84–54 Fontanet; Otter Creek 48–34 Riley; Wiley 64–49 Glenn; Gerstmeyer 64–51 West Terre Haute; Pimento 60–48 Blackhawk; Schulte 60–55 Concannon; Laboratory 63–54 New Goshen; Garfield 60–39 Honey Creek; Wiley 72–54 Otter Creek; Gerstmeyer 82–50 Pimento; Schulte 64–54 Laboratory; Garfield 43–38 Wiley; Gerstmeyer 62–42 Schulte; Gerstmeyer 73–65 Garfield. Officials: Cyril Birge, Jimmy Dimitroff, Winfield Jacobs, Noble Benbow.

VALPARAISO: Kouts 65–55 Liberty Twp.; Hebron 78–76 Morgan Twp.; Portage 68–31 Wheeler; Valparaiso 86–76 Chesterton; Boone Grove 79–46 Jackson Twp.; Kouts 58–42 Washington Twp.; Hebron 62–57 Portage; Valparaiso 54–51 Boone Grove; Kouts 66–55 Hebron; Valparaiso 61–57 Kouts. Officials: Robert Kramer, Bill Larkin, Ed Burke.

VERSAILLES: Cross Plains 43–35 Napoleon; Batesville 51–36 Osgood; Milan 50–31 New Marion; Sunman 40–37 Holton; Versailles 62–30 Cross Plains; Batesville 55–44 Milan; Versailles 72–49 Sunman; Versailles 61–43 Batesville. Officials: John Thomas, James Beyer, Oscar Melson.

VINCENNES: Monroe City 69–49 Decker Chapel; Decker 60–54 Bicknell; Vincennes 73–53 Oaktown; Bruceville 55–42 Freelandville; Wheatland 51–50 Fritchton; Sandborn 71–42 Central Catholic; Monroe City 74–57 Edwardsport; Vincennes 80–61 Decker; Wheatland 66–64 Bruceville; Sandborn 60–51 Monroe City; Vincennes 55–54 Wheatland; Sandborn 65–59 Vincennes. Officials: W. L. Ketner, Tyrus Rice, Robert Babbs, Wray Holbrook.

WABASH: Somerset 65–61 Chester; LaFontaine 46–41 Roann; Noble Twp. 65–56 Laketon; LaFontaine 64–49 Somerset; Wabash 67–63 South Whitley; Lagro 68–32 White's; Urbana 64–50 North Manchester; Wabash 35–26 Lagro; LaFontaine 62–52 Noble Twp.; Wabash 41–37 Urbana; Wabash 63–58 LaFontaine. Officials: Robert Spay, Robert Windsor, William Yohler.

WASHINGTON: Plainville 59–46 Washington Catholic; Loogootee St. Johns 88–49 Elmore Twp.; Petersburg 78–49 Shoals; Loogootee 66–42 Alfordsville; Washington 54–39 Barr

Tourney Time

Twp.; Odon 66–37 Epsom; Loogootee St. Johns 54–53 Plainville; Petersburg 77–59 Loogootee; Washington 54–44 Odon; Petersburg 62–56 Loogootee St. Johns; Washington 65–46 Petersburg. Officials: Fred Hodge, Lloyd Whipple, Dave Schellhase.

WINCHESTER: Union City 59–51 Spartanburg; Winchester 54–53 Farmland; Lynn 71–57 Green Twp.; Ridgeville 55–46 Ward Twp.; Parker 88–59 Jackson Twp.; Union Twp. 35–26 Stoney Creek; McKinley 69–39 Wayne Twp.; Winchester 62–49 Union City; Ridgeville 67–54 Lynn; Parker 63–59 Union Twp.; Winchester 51–37 McKinley; Ridgeville 64–52 Parker; Winchester 69–41 Ridgeville. Officials: Don McCoy, Don Hollman, Roscoe Hall.

ZIONSVILLE: Lebanon 64–54 Pinnell; North Central 54–51 Wells; Pike Twp. 67–56 Whitestown; Zionsville 71–67 Dover; Thorntown 61–39 Perry Central; North Central 51–49 Lebanon; Zionsville 68–49 Pike Twp.; Thorntown 46–39 North Central; Thorntown 55–44 Zionsville. Officials: Lowell Barnett, Charles Posey.

1957 REGIONALS

BLOOMINGTON: Solsberry 54–52 Staunton; Gerstmeyer 66–55 Martinsville; Gerstmeyer 84–52 Solsberry. Officials: Lowell Barnett, Fred Marlow, Oscar Samuels, Robert Cherry.

COLUMBUS: Columbus 81–68 Jackson Twp.; Southport 68–65 Madison; Southport 47–46 Columbus. Officials: Dee Williams, James Boswell, Charles Northam, Homer Owens.

COVINGTON: Crawfordsville 56–46 Richland Twp.; Greencastle 65–44 Tangier; Greencastle 66–57 Crawfordsville. Officials: Roland Baker, Gene Winks, Leland Terrell, William Findling.

EAST CHICAGO: Gary Roosevelt 76–61 Valparaiso; Michigan City 50–47 Hammond Noll; Gary Roosevelt 89–65 Michigan City. Officials: Joe Mullins, Thomas Demark, Maurice Criswell, Jack Small.

ELKHART: South Bend Central 66–55 Elkhart; Pierceton 51–49 Plymouth; South Bend Central 89–42 Pierceton. Officials: H. F. McNaught, Don McCoy, Gerald Strickler, Burl McKenzie.

EVANSVILLE: Lincoln 55–53 Princeton; Dale 67–45 Lynnville; Lincoln 63–57 Dale. Officials: Robert Rose, Lowell Willis, Winfield Jacobs, Robert Davidson.

FORT WAYNE: Fort Wayne South Side 56–40 Hartford Center; Garrett 63–45 Kendallville; South Side 63–36 Garrett. Officials: Cloyd Julian, James Haywood, John Williams, James Davidson.

HUNTINGBURG: Jasper 59–51 Washington; Sandborn 39–32 Sullivan; Jasper 47–37 Sandborn. Officials: Eugene Sparks, Joe Hunter, James Sanders, S.T. Proffitt.

INDIANAPOLIS: Elwood 80–68 New Palestine; Attucks 80–49 North Salem; Attucks 78–68 Elwood. Officials: John Hilligoss, Charles Timmons, Don McBride, Wayne Crispen.

JEFFERSONVILLE: Seymour 64–55 Providence; Marengo 65–48 Bedford; Seymour 66–60 Marengo. Officials: Lloyd Whipple, Malvern Redman, Cyril Birge, Leroy Heminger.

KOKOMO: Delphi 72–52 Peru; Noblesville 69–59 Wabash; Noblesville 59–47 Delphi. Officials: Frank Sanders, Wesley Oler, Paul Grimes, Victor Griewank.

LAFAYETTE: Lafayette 59–52 Otterbein; Colfax 45–34 Thorntown; Lafayette 62–47 Colfax. Officials: Stan Dubis, Harley Collins, Ed Straith-Miller, Everett Cass.

LOGANSPORT: North Judson 55–43 Rensselaer; Monticello 78–72 Logansport; Monticello 71–59 North Judson. Officials: Robert Dornte, Roscoe Hall, Dean Geyer, Lawrence Gradeless.

MARION: Marion 77–43 Huntington; Hartford City 65–48 Bluffton; Marion 72–58

Hartford City. Officials: Roy Gardner, Clayton Nichols, James Patterson, John Janzaruk.

MUNCIE: New Castle 62–53 Richmond; Muncie Central 85–45 Winchester; Muncie Central 69–61 New Castle. Officials: Marvin Todd, Walt McFatridge, Don Lieberum, Gerald Imel.

RUSHVILLE: Connersville 54–45 Morristown; Aurora 65–63 Versailles; Connersville 66–65 Aurora. Officials: Frank Smith, Everett Campbell, Jerry Steiner, Robert Sosbe.

1957 SEMI-STATES

EVANSVILLE: Jasper 69–67 Lincoln (2ot); Gerstmeyer 82–54 Seymour; Gerstmeyer 75–66 Jasper. Officials: Dee Williams, Jerry Steiner, Robert Rose, Frank Smith, Roy Gardner, James Patterson.

FORT WAYNE: South Bend Central 74–50 Fort Wayne South Side; Noblesville 57–55 Marion; South Bend Central 75–62 Noblesville. Officials: Stan Dubis, Joe Mullins, H. F. McNaught, S. T. Proffitt, Lowell Barnett, Charles Northam.

INDIANAPOLIS: Southport 71–54 Muncie; Attucks 63–39 Connersville; Attucks 60–50 Southport. Officials: Cyril Birge, Lloyd Whipple, Robert Dornte, Frank Sanders, Roland Baker, Maurice Criswell.

LAFAYETTE: Lafayette Jefferson 68–56 Monticello; Gary Roosevelt 62–45 Greencastle; Lafayette Jefferson 50–48 Gary Roosevelt. Officials: Don Lieberum, Eugene Sparks, Marvin Todd, Gerald Strickler, John Hilligoss, Don McBride.

1957 FINALS—March 23

INDIANAPOLIS (Butler Fieldhouse): South Bend Central 54–36 Lafayette Jefferson; Indianapolis Crispus Attucks 85–71 Terre Haute Gerstmeyer; South Bend Central 67–55 Indianapolis Crispus Attucks. Officials: Dee Williams, Gerald Strickler, H. F. McNaught, Joe Mullins, Charles Northam, Lloyd Whipple.

1958 SECTIONALS

ADAMS CENTRAL: Decatur Catholic 73–30 Pleasant Mills; Hartford Center 48–47 Adams Central; Geneva 45–35 Monmouth; Berne 47–44 Decatur; Hartford Center 71–69 Decatur Catholic (2ot); Berne 49–47 Geneva (ot); Berne 44–42 Hartford Center. Officials: Paul Bateman, Roy Kilby.

ANDERSON: Highland 52–44 Frankton; Madison Heights 78–58 St. Mary's; Elwood 79–59 Markleville; Madison Heights 78–66 Highland; Anderson 64–59 Summitville; Lapel 56–53 Alexandria; Anderson 58–57 Pendleton; Elwood 55–52 Madison Heights; Anderson 62–50 Lapel; Anderson 67–57 Elwood. Officials: James W. Boswell, Arthur Thompson, Fred Marlow.

AVILLA: Wawaka 55–48 Ligonier; Lima 79–32 Springfield Twp.; Kendallville 58–43 Rome City; Wolf Lake 69–43 Wolcottville; Avilla 46–45 LaGrange; Albion 54–50 Cromwell; Howe Military 65–43 Brighton; Wawaka 64–46 Lima; Wolf Lake 58–52 Kendallville; Albion 77–64 Avilla; Howe Military 47–37 Wawaka; Wolf Lake 69–66 Albion; Howe Military 63–57 Wolf Lake. Officials: Norris Ward, Carter L. Caton, Myron Weldy, Edgar C. Powers.

BEDFORD: Williams 59–42 Tunnelton; Mitchell 49–47 Shawswick (ot); Orleans 48–43 Paoli;

Tourney Time

Huron 60–46 Heltonville; Bedford 57–51 Fayetteville; Marshall Twp. 38–36 Oolitic; Mitchell 63–52 Williams; Orleans 47–26 Huron; Bedford 52–34 Marshall Twp.; Mitchell 59–49 Orleans; Bedford 38–36 Mitchell (ot). Officials: Kenneth Blankenbaker, Carl Bruns, Noel Genth.

BLOOMINGTON: Ellettsville 55–46 University; Morgantown 79–37 Eminence; Bloomington 66–37 Unionville; Martinsville 65–51 Stinesville; Mooresville 68–60 Smithville; Ellettsville 55–41 Monrovia; Bloomington 70–41 Morgantown; Martinsville 65–61 Mooresville; Bloomington 50–46 Ellettsville; Bloomington 79–67 Martinsville. Officials: Robert C. Rose, Donald R. Boyer, Robert B. Sweet.

BLUFFTON: Bluffton 8l–74 Lancaster Central; Union 63–47 Liberty, Center; Jackson 50–43 Chester Center; Ossian 64–37 Petroleum; Bluffton 65–52 Rockcreek; Jackson 40–38 Union; Bluffton 56–46 Ossian; Bluffton 64–50 Jackson. Officials: Bob Butterbaugh, Robert Spay, Gerald Imel.

BROOKVILLE: Harrisburg 50–45 Springfield; Alquina 57–49 Laurel; Liberty 48–36 Harrison Twp.; Alquina 54–51 Harrisburg; Brookville 75–28 Whitewater; Brownsville 49–25 Fairview; Connersville 64–41 Orange; Brookville 88–37 Brownsville; Liberty 34–32 Alquina; Brookville 42–36 Connersville; Brookville 44–30 Liberty. Officials: Dwain Laird, Cloyd T. Thompson, Wendell Baker.

BROWNSBURG: Stilesville 53–44 Lizton; Speedway 48–37 Charlton; Amo 62–46 Pittsboro; Brownsburg 57–41 North Winchester; North Salem 61–57 Clayton (ot); Plainfield 56–55 Avon (ot) Stilesville 70–62 Danville; Amo 55–43 Speedway; Brownsburg 53–52 North Salem; Plainfield 75–52 Stilesville; Amo 49–47 Brownsburg (2ot); Amo 59–57 Plainfield. Officials: William May, John Sheets, Robert Cherry.

CENTER GROVE: Whiteland 38–30 Union; Decatur Central 66–45 Center Grove; Trafalgar 60–55 Edinburg; Southport 42–40 Greenwood; Franklin 36–33 Nineveh; Helmsburg 39–37 Clark (2ot); Decatur Central 44–37 Whiteland; Trafalgar 57–52 Southport; Helmsburg 41–40 Franklin; Decatur Central 41–29 Trafalgar; Decatur Central 55–46 Helmsburg. Officials: Don McBride, William McDonald, Charles Fouty.

CHURUBUSCO–GARRETT (At Churubusco): Riverdale 81–46 Orland; Garrett 51–31 Churubusco; Fremont 81–58 Bellefountain; Riverdale 61–52 Salem Center; Fremont 44–42 Garrett; (At Garrett): Waterloo 72–45 Pleasant Lake; Butler 94–29 Flint; Ashley 52–45 Auburn; Angola 64–60 Waterloo; Butler 98–71 Ashley; (At Churubusco): Fremont 58–41 Riverdale, Butler 51–40 Angola; Fremont 67–53 Butler. Officials: Charles Timmons, James Murray, Dean B. Geyer, Donald E. Orlosky.

CLINTON: St. Bernice 66–61 Bellmore; Rosedale 73–53 Hillsdale: Clinton 55–53 Cayuga; Tangier 48–43 Bridgeton; Montezuma 64–46 Dana; Bloomingdale 60–46 Marshall; Rockville 61–55 Mecca; Newport 63–61 St. Bernice (2ot); Rosedale 58–55 Clinton; Montezuma 70–54 Tangier; Rockville 48–38 Bloomingdale; Rosedale 54–48 Newport; Rockville 59–54 Montezuma; Rockville 56–52 Rosedale. Officials: Jimmy Dimitroff, James Ruby, John Masariu, Carl Petercheff.

COLUMBUS: Columbus 55–40 Fairland; Waldron 64–40 Van Buren: Flat Rock 68–50 Hauser; Shelbyville 87–45 Mt. Auburn; Moral Twp. 63–56 Nashville; Columbus 72–55 Boggstown; Waldron 47–45 Flat Rock; Shelbyville 66–26 Moral Twp.; Waldron 65–61 Columbus; Shelbyville 40–33 Waldron. Officials: Clayton Nichols, L.C. Thorne, John J. Holmes.

COVINGTON: Covington 40–34 Veedersburg; Pine Village 63–54 Hillsboro; Attica 61–36

Kingman; Richland Twp. 78–58 Wallace; West Lebanon 58–55 Perrysville; Covington 49–46 Williamsport; Attica 53–35 Pine Village; Richland Twp. 52–50 West Lebanon (ot); Attica 50–48 Covington (2ot); Attica 63–50 Richland Twp. Officials: Merle Hill, Leo R. Ponto, George J. Neff.

CRAWFORDSVILLE: Crawfordsville 57–46 New Market; Alamo 73–52 Ladoga; Linden 68–57 Waynetown; Crawfordsville 64–62 Alamo; Darlington 68–57 New Ross; Waveland 72–67 Coal Creek Central; Crawfordsville 78–49 Linden; Waveland 70–45 Darlington; Crawfordsville 59–43 Waveland. Officials: Howard Cosand, Devere Hoffman, Dee Williams.

DILLSBORO: Lawrenceburg 64–41 Bright; Dillsboro 73–40 Patriot; Vevay 49–44 Moores Hill; Aurora 49–36 Guilford; Rising Sun 52–47 Lawrenceburg; Vevay 67–60 Dillsboro; Rising Sun 64–62 Aurora; Vevay 57–47 Rising Sun. Rising Sun. Officials: James F. Davis, Vern E. Doles and John Evans.

EAST CHICAGO: Roosevelt 69–39 Dyer; Whiting 54–49 Hammond Tech; Crown Point 54–52 Hammond High; Roosevelt 80–52 Whiting; Morton 58–50 Clark; Washington 63–46 Griffith; Noll 64–38 Lowell; Washington 78–54 Morton; Roosevelt 64–59 Crown Point; Washington 65–48 Bishop Noll; Washington 62–56 Roosevelt. Officials: Burl McKenzie, Don Lieberum, Maurice Criswell.

ELKHART: Millersburg 60–44 Bristol, Elkhart 92–40 Wakarusa; Mishawaka 79–46 Nappanee; Middlebury 53–46 Jefferson; New Paris 62–40 Topeka; Goshen 56–52 Concord; Shipshewana Scott 64–48 Baugo Twp.; Elkhart 64–41 Millersburg; Mishawaka 58–49 Middlebury; New Paris 76–50 Goshen; Elkhart 65–40 Shipshewana Scott; Mishawaka 68–59 New Paris; Elkhart 52–43 Mishawaka. Officials: Harley G. Collins, Johannes P. Dienelt, Stan Dubis, Donald W. Hollman.

EVANSVILLE: Mater Dei 51–47 Memorial; Mt. Vernon 62–44 New Harmony; Griffin 55–35 Poseyville; Lincoln 42–37 Bosse; Cynthiana 51–40 Wadesville; Central 50–45 North; Mater Dei 45–43 Reitz; Mt. Vernon 57–54 Griffin; Lincoln 79–32 Cynthiana; Central 51–48 Mater Dei (ot); Mt. Vernon 66–58 Lincoln; Central 58–57 Mt. Vernon. Officials: James W. Sanders, Ralph F. Box, Eugene Sparks.

FORT WAYNE: Lafayette Central 57–52 Elmhurst; Central 67–59 Central Catholic; New Haven 62–60 Harlan; South Side 68–40 Leo; North Side 61–25 Coesse; Huntertown 54–46 Monroeville; Concordia 91–75 Hoagland; Woodburn 49–41 Arcola; Central 63–44 Lafayette Central; South Side 67–53 New Haven; Huntertown 51–49 North Side; Concordia 73–54 Woodburn; South Side 60–56 Central (ot); Concordia 49–45 Huntertown; South Side 55–34 Concordia. Officials: John Hilligoss, Wesley Oler, Lawrence Gradeless, Victor J. Wukovits.

FOWLER: Wadena 44–31 Gilboa: Earl Park 52–46 Pine; Freeland Park 61–57 Oxford; Ambia 74–42 Raub; Otterbein 58–38 Fowler; Boswelll 51–35 Wadena; Freeland Park 57–54 Earl Park; Otterbein 52–32 Ambia; Boswell 49–43 Freeland Park; Otterbein 46–32 Boswell Officials: Noble Benbow, Morris Davis, John Park.

FRANKFORT: Sugar Creek 35–28 Jackson Twp.; Rossville 55–36 Scircleville; Kirklin 67–55 Mulberry; Michigantown 52–46 Colfax; Frankfort 73–61 Forest; Sugar Creek 41–40 Washington Twp.; Rossville 53–49 Kirklin; Frankfort 62–37 Michigantown; Rossville 42–30 Sugar Creek; Rossville 51–46 Frankfort. Officials: Paul Grimes, William Yohler, Gerald Strole, Jr.

GARY: Calumet Twp. 72–48 Lew Wallace; Horace Mann 61–50 Hobart; Gary Edison 64–59 Wirt; Roosevelt 72–38 Tolleston; Merrillville 81–70 East Gary Edison; Froebel 70–55 Emerson; Calumet Twp. 66–50 Horace Mann; Roosevelt 87–39 Gary Edison; Froebel 72–60

Tourney Time

Merrillville; Roosevelt 76–65 Calumet Twp.; Froebel 77–70 Roosevelt. Officials: Joseph J. Bella, H.F. McNaught, William R. Findling.

GREENCASTLE: Belle Union 47–46 Roachdale; Bainbridge 67–49 Fillmore; Greencastle 61–53 Cloverdale; Reelsville 79–60 Russellville; Bainbridge 49–34 Belle Union; Greencastle 61–56 Reelsville; Bainbridge 55–42 Greencastle. Officials: Leland Terrell, Walter Swift.

GREENFIELD: Franklin Twp. 74–42 Wilkinson; Charlottesville 56–53 Greenfield; Fortville 53–32 McCordsville; Mt. Comfort 67–66 Palestine; Hancock Central 61–51 Franklin Twp.; Charlottesville 56–54 Fortville (ot); Hancock Central 50–48 Mt. Comfort; Charlottesville 65–40 Hancock Central. Officials: Charles Posey, Mel Pope, Joe Garoffolo.

GREENSBURG: Clarksburg 68–61 Sandcreek; Greensburg 40–38 New Point; North Vernon 50–47 St. Paul; Jackson Twp. 59–57 Sandusky; Vernon 62–54 Burney; Clarksburg 54–52 Greensburg; North Vernon 48–42 Jackson Twp.; Clarksburg 63–49 Vernon; North Vernon 65–51 Clarksburg. Officials: John M. Priest, Eugene Lillie, M.N. Delph.

HARTFORD CITY: Portland 60–50 Hartford City; Bryant 68–59 Redkey; Madison 60–54 Poling; Montpelier 53–34 Gray; Roll 59–56 Pennville; Dunkirk 70–60 Portland; Bryant 74–61 Madison; Montpelier 79–47 Roll; Bryant 56–55 Dunkirk; Bryant 66–50 Montpelier. Officials: Robert Dornte, Roscoe Hall, James Ridge.

HUNTINGBURG: Jasper 61–54 Winslow; Huntingburg 74–38 Otwell; Spurgeon 60–50 St. Ferdinand; Holland 76–46 Stendal; Ireland 62–36 Birdseye; Springs Valley 63–59 Dubois; Huntingburg 67–53 Jasper; Holland 71–69 Spurgeon; Springs Valley 67–48 Ireland; Huntingburg 46–45 Holland; Springs Valley 66–41 Huntingburg. Officials: Harold Shiflet, Jr., Winfield Jacobs, Don Shiflet.

HUNTINGTON: Jefferson Twp. 74–53 Union; Clear Creek 54–52 Huntington Catholic; Andrews 88–59 Bippus; Huntington Twp. 70–51 Rock Creek; Lancaster Twp. 65–48 Jefferson Center; Huntington 49–47 Salamonie Twp.; Roanoke 67–62 Jefferson Twp.; Clear Creek, 59–46 Andrews; Huntington Twp. 67–48 Lancaster Twp.; Huntington 55–47 Roanoke; Huntington Twp. 66–56 Clear Creek; Huntington Twp. 47–38 Huntington. Officials: Ed Burke, Lauren Griffith, Oscar T. Samuels.

INDIANAPOLIS: Broad Ripple 62–57 Warren Central; Manual 61–54 Washington; School for the Deaf 58–49 Sacred Heart; Ben Davis 60–50 Shortridge; Scecina 79–55 Cathedral; Howe 85–60 Beech Grove; Tech 75–54 Wood; Crispus Attucks 56–35 Lawrence Central; Broad Ripple 71–61 Manual; Ben Davis 63–44 School for the Deaf; Scecina 71–63 Howe; Crispus Attucks 61–50 Tech; Ben Davis 52–51 Broad Ripple (2ot); Crispus Attucks 70–68 Scecina (2ot); Crispus Attucks 71–48 Ben Davis. Officials: Joe Mullins, Marion Acton, Walt McFatridge, Thomas E. Dean.

JEFFERSONVILLE: Providence 61–43 Henryville; New Washington 88–48 Campbellsburg; Clarksville 68–41 Hardinsburg; Salem 63–51 Borden; Charlestown 50–42 Silver Creek; Jeffersonville 91–56 Pekin; Providence 60–53 New Washington; Salem 53–42 Clarksville; Jeffersonville 81–68 Charlestown; Salem 66–64 Providence; Jeffersonville 91–55 Salem. Officials: Julian Piercefield, Cyril Birge, Tyrus R. Rice.

KENTLAND: Wheatfield 70–47 Fair Oaks; Goodland 68–32 Tefft; Rensselaer 52–51 Morocco; Remington 60–50 Mt. Ayr; Brook 66–43 Kentland; DeMotte 57–53 Wheatfield; Rensselaer 62–47 Goodland; Brook 66–52 Remington; Rensselaer 60–56 DeMotte; Rensselaer 49–47 Brook (2ot). Officials: Ira Ray Williams, John C. Sebastian, John H Arnold.

KNOX: Francesville 54–46 Star City; Grovertown 66–50 Pulaski; Knox 68–48 San Pierre;

Winamac 51–34 Hamlet; Medaryville 74–71 Aubbeenaubbee Twp. (2ot); North Judson 83–37 Monterey; Grovertown 43–40 Francesville; Winamac 75–64 Knox; North Judson 56–42 Medaryville; Grovertown 44–42 Winamac (ot); North Judson 47–37 Grovertown. Officials: Lewis B. Goshert, Jack T. Small, Richard Duffield.

KOKOMO: Kokomo 86–33 Burlington; Camden 52–49 Northwestern; Western 75–73 Deer Creek; Delphi 73–59 Cutler; Flora 72–62 Eastern; Kokomo 105–45 Camden; Delphi 58–46 Western; Kokomo 96–61 Flora; Kokomo 91–53 Delphi. Officials: Everett W. Campbell, Robert D. Sosbe, James E. Patterson.

LAFAYETTE: Southwestern 60–53 Montmorenci; Lafayette Jefferson 84–31 Monitor; Klondike 41–36 Dayton; Buck Creek 55–39 Battle Ground; West Lafayette 67–29 Central Catholic; Southwestern 70–56 Lauramie; Lafayette Jefferson 51–38 Klondike; West Lafayette 83–54 Buck Creek; Lafayette Jefferson 56–34 Southwestern; Lafayette Jefferson 50–46 West Lafayette. Officials: S.T. Proffitt, John B. Williams, Glen Wisler.

LOGANSPORT: Logansport 79–33 Metea; Galveston 57–47 Kewanna; Tipton Twp. 47–44 Washington Twp.; Lucerne 57–41 Twelve Mile; Young America 50–42 Grass Creek; Royal Center 80–30 New Waverly; Logansport 85–49 Galveston; Tipton Twp. 71–53 Lucerne; Royal Center 61–43 Young America; Logansport 69–48 Tipton Twp.; Royal Center 59–51 Logansport. Officials: William Goshert, Victor Griewank, Richard Swartz.

LYNNVILLE: Tennyson 54–47 Selvin; Newburgh 65–54 Chandler; Elberfeld 63–41 Lynnville; Boonville 55–45 Millersburg; Newburgh 68–48 Tennyson; Elberfeld 52–41 Boonville; Newburgh 64–54 Elberfeld. Officials: Lowell K. Willis, Earle R. Wolfe.

MARION: Marion 76–46 Bennett; Sweetser 80–63 Van Buren; Swayzee 72–60 Jefferson Twp.; Mississinewa 59–49 Fairmount; Marion 56–31 Sweetser, Swayzee 49–48 Mississinewa (ot); Marion 74–56 Swayzee. Officials: Jerry Steiner, Harold Braden.

MICHIGAN CITY: Michigan City 95–43 Union Twp.; Mill Creek 63–35 Wanatah; LaPorte 81–50 LaCrosse; Rolling Prairie 69–36 Kingsbury; Union Mills 63–32 Westville; St. Mary's 62–38 Stillwell; Hanna 61–29 Clinton; Michigan City 91–39 Mill Creek; LaPorte 66–62 Rolling Prairie; St. Mary's 71–58 Union Mills; Michigan City 73–26 Hanna; LaPorte 69–36 St. Mary's; Michigan City 63–46 LaPorte. Officials: Robert Kramer, Nick Reff, Ernest Sohl, Anthony Lazar, Jr.

MONTICELLO: Idaville 79–56 Burnettsville; Monticello 95–43 Chalmers; Monon 69–31 Buffalo; Wolcott 81–61 Brookston; Idaville 72–60 Reynolds; Monticello 69–49 Monon; Wolcott 27–24 Idaville; Monticello 99–57 Wolcott, Officials: William E. Farrar, Gilbert Smith, Merle Shively.

MUNCIE: Harrison Twp 62–43 Gaston; Daleville 55–50 Selma; Muncie Central 90–55 Eaton; Yorktown 74–56 Cowan; Royerton 82–48 DeSoto; Burris 51–34 Albany; Harrison Twp. 89–44 Center; Muncie Central 64–32 Daleville; Royerton 83–46 Yorktown; Harrison Twp. 70–48 Burris; Muncie Central 61–51 Royerton; Muncie Central 71–49 Harrison Twp. Officials: Wayne Crispen, Robert Laird, Roy W. Gardner.

NEW ALBANY: Corydon 62–46 Milltown; English 57–46 Morgan Twp.; Lanesville 64–45 Elizabeth; Leavenworth 60–49 Marengo; New Albany 71–64 Georgetown; Laconia 61–55 North Central; Corydon 59–55 English; Leavenworth 73–47 Lanesville; New Albany 84–50 Laconia ; Cordon 64–58 Leavenworth; New Albany 83–72 Corydon. Officials: Russell Owens, John M. Thomas, James J. Beyer.

NEW CASTLE: New Castle 76–71 Lewisville; Knightstown 72–51 Spiceland; Mooreland 68–

57 Straughn; Knightstown 60–55 New Castle; Mt. Summit 59–53 Sulphur Springs; Middletown 70–43 Cadiz; Knightstown 59–53 Mooreland; Middletown 54–52 Mt. Summit; Knightstown 54–45 Middletown. Officials: Karl Bly, Howard Plough, Charles Northam.

NOBLESVILLE: Jackson Central 50–41 Carmel; Noblesville 66–31 Sharpsville; Sheridan 45–41 Tipton; Noblesville 48–46 Jackson Central; Prairie Twp. 49–47 Jefferson Twp.; Walnut Grove 54–45 Fishers; Windfall 74–52 Westfield; Walnut Grove 59–45 Prairie Twp.; Noblesville 65–44 Sheridan; Windfall 46–43 Walnut Grove; Noblesville 69–66 Windfall (ot). Officials: James Carey, James Davidson, Gene Davis.

PERU: Converse 46–45 Bunker Hill; Clay Twp. 57–48 Gilead; Peru 91–32 Butler Twp.; Fulton 50–49 Deedsville, Akron 55–47 Chili; Converse 88–31 Mexico; Peru 54–49 Clay Twp. (ot); Akron 55–46 Fulton; Peru 48–46 Converse; Peru 60–56 Akron (ot). Officials: Marvin Todd, Gary Nelson, David Habegger.

PLYMOUTH: West Twp. 59–57 Richland Center; Argos 60–38 Talma; Tyner 61–56 Bourbon; Argos 66–65 West Twp. (ot); Culver 47–41 Bremen; Plymouth 72–60 Rochester; LaPaz 79–70 Tippecanoe; Plymouth 73–56 Culver; Tyner 47–43 Argos; LaPaz 48–46 Plymouth; LaPaz 59–42 Tyner. Officials: William R. Hile, Bill Larkin, Darl March.

PRINCETON: Ft Branch 65–49 Patoka; Haubstadt 69–20 Hazleton; Francisco 52–44 Oakland City; Mackey 64–54 Mt. Olympus; Princeton 66–50 Owensville; Ft. Branch 68–41 Haubstadt; Mackey 60–58 Francisco (2ot); Princeton 56–49 Ft. Branch; Princeton 46–42 Mackey. Officials: Ivan I. Risley, Wallace R. Reeve, Norman L. Risley.

RICHMOND: Economy 43–39 Greensfork; Williamsburg 62–47 Boston; Fountain City 69–58 Centerville; Richmond 71–42 Whitewater; Hagerstown 65–49 Cambridge City; Milton 56–54 Webster; Williamsburg 62–53 Economy; Richmond 66–52 Fountain City; Hagerstown 64–53 Milton; Richmond 80–42 Williamsburg; Richmond 49–48 Hagerstown. Officials: Don E. Hurst, James Haywood, Gilbert A. Beagle.

RUSHVILLE: Arlington 82–67 Morristown; Milroy 59–50 Mays; Rushville 63–49 Carthage; New Salem 78–47 Manilla; Arlington 67–35 Morton Memorial; Rushville 60–46 Milroy; Arlington 64–48 New Salem; Rushville 51–46 Arlington. Officials: James E. Lentz, LeRoy F. Heminger, Richard J. Tierman.

SCOTTSBURG: Madison Shawe 45–42 Scottsburg Madison 62–44 Deputy, Saluda 82–63 Dupont; Hanover 72–57 Lexington; Austin 67–52 Madison Central; Madison Shawe 59–47 Paris Crossing; Madison 80–52 Saluda; Austin 56–44 Hanover; Madison 58–44 Madison Shawe; Madison 67–58 Austin. Officials: Roland Baker, Wray Holbrook, Harold Mason.

SEYMOUR: Crothersville 63–45 Tampico; Freetown 76–50 Clearspring; Brownstown 64–49 Hayden; Seymour 64–50 Cortland: Medora 52–40 Vallonia; Freetown 71–58 Crothersville; Seymour 60–54 Brownstown; Freetown 66–58 Medora; Seymour 74–58 Freetown. Officials: Norman Shields, Don C. Stimson, Frank Smith.

SOUTH BEND: St. Joseph's 58–53 Washington-Clay; Riley 70–48 Lakeville; Greene Twp. 55–38 North Liberty; St. Joseph's 48–36 Riley; Washington 69–55 Madison Twp.; Central 56–36 Walkerton; Adams 87–43 New Carlisle; Washington 67–64 Central; St. Joseph's 85–51 Greene Twp.; Adams 60–50 Washington; Adams 62–58 St. Joseph's. Officials: John F. Fee, Frank Sanders, Jr., Gene Butts.

SPENCER: Staunton 68–47 Freedom; Clay City 55–37 Cory; Van Buren 51–34 Coal City; Brazil 82–59 Gosport; Bowling Green 43–23 Ashboro; Coalmont 56–39 Patricksburg; Staunton

IHSAA Scores | 1950–1959

69–60 Spencer; Van Buren 52–33 Clay City; Brazil 60–59 Bowling Green; Staunton 61–46 Coalmont; Van Buren 67–65 Brazil (ot); Staunton 72–49 Van Buren. Officials: Edwin L. Miller, Raymond Robison, Edward Straith–Miller.

SULLIVAN: Dugger 63–34 Blackhawk; North Central 52–43 Hymera; Graysville 59–56 Carlisle; Pleasantville 65–64 Pimento; Prairie Creek 67–55 Sullivan; Dugger 58–55 North Central; Graysville 77–49 Pleasantville; Dugger 50–45 Prairie Creek; Dugger 57–48 Graysville. Officials: Melvin L. Newlin, Fred Hodge, James W. Schwenk.

SWITZ CITY: Linton 70–53 Switz City; Midland 69–50 Marco; Bloomfield 71–61 Lyons; Worthington 66–54 Jasonville; Linton 65–41 Solsberry; Midland 74–69 Bloomfield; Linton 67–53 Worthington; Linton 70–63 Midland. Officials: W.L. Ketner, Lester R. Cornwell, Leonard F. Benedetto.

SYRACUSE: Milford 79–58 Larwill; Leesburg 39–38 Atwood; North Webster 62–42 Pierceton; Etna Green 65–49 Beaver Dam; Syracuse 71–57 Columbia City; Silver Lake 44–42 Mentone (2ot); Claypool 58–54 Sidney; Warsaw 63–49 Milford; North Webster 104–51 Leesburg; Etna Green 69–56 Syracuse; Claypool 63–41 Silver Lake; North Webster 52–49 Warsaw; Etna Green 49–32 Claypool; Etna Green 59–53 North Webster. Officials: Don McCoy, Robert Cowan, Charles Garber, Jr., John A. Zehring.

TELL CITY: Rockport 59–39 Luce Twp.; Cannelton 84–43 Bristow: Dale 54–37 Tell City; Chrisney 67–43 Troy; Rockport 62–43 Oil Twp.; Dale 67–36 Cannelton; Chrisney 43–41 Rockport; Dale 66–38 Chrisney. Officials: Howard E. Risley, Dave Schellhase, Donald L. Hubbard.

TERRE HAUTE: Garfield 78–59 Fontanet; Glenn 71–60 Schulte; Otter Creek 68–66 West Terre Haute; Honey Creek 67–48 Laboratory; New Goshen 66–51 Riley; Gerstmeyer 70–67 Concannon; Garfield 63–43 Wiley; Otter Creek 56–48 Glenn; Honey Creek 70–55 New Goshen: Gerstmeyer 63–58 Garfield; Otter Creek, 79–58 Honey Creek; Gerstmeyer 81–55 Otter Creek. Officials: Robert R. Davidson, Roger J. Emmert, Lloyd G. Whipple.

VALPARAISO: Kouts 70–60 Portage; Hebron 64–34 Wheeler; Morgan 63–46 Washington Twp.; Hebron 67–46 Kouts; Chesterton 58–53 Boone, Grove; Valparaiso 71–32 Jackson Twp; Chesterton 79–30 Liberty; Hebron 61–52 Morgan Twp.; Valparaiso 77–63 Chesterton; Valparaiso 60–55 Hebron. Officials: Thomas Demark, Ray L. Nemeth, Robert Brees.

VERSAILLES: Holton 48–46 Batesville; Cross Plains 60–58 New Marion; Versailles 55–46 Napoleon; Milan 44–42 Osgood (ot); Holton 53–45 Sunman; Versailles 52–41 Cross Plains; Holton 44–43 Milan; Versailles 65–44 Holton. Officials: Charles E. Stumpf, Joseph F. Hunter, Grayson J. Mahin.

VINCENNES: Vincennes 69–36 Bicknell; Sandborn 75–55 Oaktown; Central Catholic 62–37 Edwardsport; Decker 55–43 Decker Chapel; Bruceville 78–48 Fritchton; Wheatland 55–48 Freelandville; Vincennes 75–60 Monroe City; Central Catholic 47–46 Sandborn; Decker 55–39 Bruceville; Vincennes 70–55 Wheatland; Decker 55–47 Central Catholic; Vincennes 74–52 Decker. Officials: Thomas A. Hoffman, Donald Ray Call, Malvern G. Redman.

WABASH: Wabash 61–55 Manchester; Laketon 62–45 Somerset; Noble Twp. 87–54 White's; Wabash 58–49 Laketon; LaFontaine 52–48 Lagro; Urbana 67–55 South Whitley; LaFontaine 68–43 Roann; Wabash 62–59 Noble Twp.; LaFontaine 49–39 Urbana; Wabash 73–66 LaFontaine. Officials: Homer Owens, Jr., Glen Lantz, Ward Mosbaugh.

WASHINGTON: St. John's 62–46 Epsom; Odon 50–45 Barr Twp.; Washington Catholic 66–52 Alfordsville; Loogootee 86–67 Petersburg; Washington 81–70 Plainville; Shoals 77–64

Tourney Time

Elnora; Odon 72–54 St. John's; Loogootee 57–54 Washington Catholic; Washington 66–55 Shoals; Odon 66–59 Loogootee; Washington 71–58 Odon. Officials: Lloyd D. Grimes, J. Firman Grimes, Vesper Moore.

WINCHESTER: Spartanburg 61–44 Lynn; Winchester 69–57 Union City; Farmland 74–70 Jackson; Ridgeville 49–48 White River; Parker 75–46 Stoney Creek; Ward 58–42 Green; Spartanburg 58–51 Union; Winchester 49–34 Farmland; Parker 77–49 Ridgeville; Ward 63–42 Spartanburg; Parker 76–66 Winchester; Parker 47–42 Ward. Officials: Floyd A. Reed, Robert C. Showalter, Gerald Strickler.

ZIONSVILLE: Zionsville 68–42 Pinnell; North Central 73–52 Wells; Thorntown 59–40 Perry Central; Pike Twp. 68–47 Whitestown; Lebanon 50–28 Dover; Zionsville 55–50 North Central; Thorntown 67–42 Pike Twp.; Zionsville 49–48 Lebanon; Zionsville 70–62 Thorntown. Officials: Earnest V. Baldwin, Walter Frye, Jr., Frank H. Carnes.

1958 REGIONALS

COLUMBUS: Decatur Central 60–43 North Vernon; Madison 44–40 Shelbyville; Madison 63–58 Decatur Central. Officials: Leland Terrell, Frank Carnes, Lowell Willis, Robert Davidson.

EAST CHICAGO: Valparaiso 67–52 Froebel; East Chicago Washington 71–69 Michigan City; Washington 80–69 Valparaiso. Officials: Frank Sanders, William Larkin, Marvin Todd, Don McCoy.

ELKHART: South Bend Adams 52–48 Etna Green; Elkhart 58–47 LaPaz; Elkhart 58–57 South Bend Adams. Officials: Joe Mullins, Walt McFatridge, Maurice Criswell, Everett Campbell.

EVANSVILLE: Dale 72–53 Newburgh; Princeton 57–46 Evansville Central; Princeton 55–53 Dale. Officials: Frank Smith, Joseph Hunter, Roland Baker, Winfield Jacobs.

FORT WAYNE: Berne 37–33 Howe Military; Ft. Wayne South Side 61–48 Fremont; South Side 68–51 Berne. Officials: Jack Small, Harley Collins, H. F. McNaught, Thomas Demark.

GREENCASTLE: Crawfordsville 70–38 Rockville; Attica 56–52 Bainbridge; Crawfordsville 85–41 Attica. Officials: Lloyd Whipple, Dwain Laird, Leroy Heminger, James Haywood.

HUNTINGBURG: Vincennes 65–49 Washington; Springs Valley 63–54 Dugger; Springs Valley 62–59 Vincennes (ot). Officials: James Boswell, John Williams, Clayton Nichols, S.T. Proffitt.

INDIANAPOLIS: Crispus Attucks 67–60 Charlottesville; Anderson 65–54 Amo; Anderson 51–50 Crispus Attucks. Officials: Don McBride, Robert Sosbe, John Hilligoss, Robert Spay.

JEFFERSONVILLE: Seymour 65–59 New Albany; Jeffersonville 77–63 Bedford; Jeffersonville 85–67 Seymour. Officials: Robert Rose, Norman Risley, Paul Grimes, Robert Cherry.

KOKOMO: Kokomo 64–54 Noblesville; Wabash 92–52 Peru; Kokomo 73–58 Wabash. Officials: Dee Williams, Lawrence Gradeless, Roy Gardner, Charles Timmons.

LAFAYETTE: Rossville 57–52 Zionsville; Lafayette Jefferson 46–33 Otterbein; Lafayette Jefferson 50–48 Rossville. Officials: Dean Geyer, Robert Dornte, Oscar Samuels, Roscoe Hall.

LOGANSPORT: North Judson 38–30 Rensselaer; Monticello 62–58 Royal Center; North Judson 61–44 Monticello. Officials: Stan Dubis, Gerald Imel, Gerald Strickler, James Davidson.

MARION: Bluffton 57–46 Bryant; Marion 62–52 Huntington Twp.; Bluffton 58–44 Marion. Officials: James Sanders, Edward Straith-Miller, Eugene Sparks, Victor Griewank.

MARTINSVILLE: Terre Haute Gerstmeyer 98–61 Linton; Bloomington 55–53 Staunton;

Gerstmeyer 66–50 Bloomington. Officials: Cyril Birge, Malvern Redman, Charles Northam, Homer Owens.

MUNCIE: Muncie Central 63–41 Parker; Richmond 67–53 Knightstown; Muncie Central 70–60 Richmond. Officials: James E. Patterson. Fred M. Marlow, Jerry Steiner, Burl R. McKenzie.

RUSHVILLE: Rushville 55–48 Brookville; Vevay 71–56 Versailles: Rushville 48–43 Vevay. Officials: Don Lieberum, William Findling, Wesley Oler, Wayne Crispen.

1958 SEMI–STATES

EVANSVILLE: Princeton 71–67 Jeffersonville; Springs Valley 66–55 Terre Haute Gerstmeyer; Springs Valley 71–54 Princeton. Officials: Dee Williams, James Boswell, James Patterson, Paul Grimes, Roy Gardner, Jerry Steiner.

FORT WAYNE: Ft. Wayne South Side 71–49 Bluffton; Elkhart 59–57 Kokomo; Ft. Wayne South Side 76–44 Elkhart. Officials: Maurice Criswell, Charles Northam, H. F. McNaught, S.T. Proffitt, Roland Baker, Eugene Sparks.

INDIANAPOLIS: Muncie Central 55–53 Rushville (ot); Anderson 68–48 Madison; Muncie Central 53–52 Anderson. Officials: Lloyd Whipple, Gerald Strickler, Cyril Birge, Frank Sanders, Marvin Todd, Stan Dubis.

LAFAYETTE: Crawfordsville 61–51 Lafayette Jefferson; East Chicago Washington 56–55 North Judson; Crawfordsville 70–59 East Chicago Washington. Officials: Joe Mullins, Don Lieberum, Robert Rose, Frank Smith, John Hilligoss, Don McBride.

1958 FINALS—March 22

INDIANAPOLIS (Butler Fieldhouse): Ft. Wayne South Side 55–42 Springs Valley; Crawfordsville 53–45 Muncie Central; South Side 63–34 Crawfordsville. Officials: Joe Mullins, Lloyd Whipple, Gerald Strickler, Maurice Criswell, H. F. McNaught, James Patterson.

1959 SECTIONALS

ADAMS CENTRAL: Hartford Center 56–37 Berne; Geneva 47–36 Pleasant Mills; Decatur 61–44 Adams Central; Decatur Catholic 65–38 Monmouth; Hartford Center 66–43 Geneva; Decatur 72–61 Decatur Catholic; Decatur 50–34 Hartford Center. Officials: Charles Northam, Robert C. Showalter.

ATTICA: Attica 62–52 Covington; Kingman 57–54 West Lebanon; Veedersburg 72–51 Wallace; Perrysville 50–48 Pine Village; Hillsboro 59–45 Richland Twp.; Attica 83–49 Williamsport; Veedersburg 62–54 Kingman; Hillsboro 51–36 Perrysville; Attica 49–48 Veedersburg; Attica 88–51 Hillsboro. Officials: Walter Frye, Jr., William B. McDonald, James Ruby.

BEDFORD: Williams 56–54 Orleans; Shawswick 65–60 Bedford; Paoli 84–62 Fayetteville; Mitchell 65–52 Marshall Twp.; Heltonville 60–55 Huron, Oolitic 53–47 Tunnelton; Shawswick 73–57 Williams: Mitchell 80–76 Paoli; Oolitic 54–50 Heltonville; Shawswick 73–60 Mitchell; Shawswick 43–33 Oolitic. Officials: Carl P. Petercheff, J. Firman Grimes, Harold Mason.

BLUFFTON: Ossian 53–34 Union Center; Bluffton 71–57 Petroleum; Lancaster Central

Tourney Time

63–57 Jackson; Rockcreek 51–50 Liberty Center; Ossian 50–29 Chester Center; Bluffton 60–53 Lancaster, Central; Ossian 55–54 Rockcreek (2ot); Ossian 46–44 Bluffton (ot). Officials: William Goshert, Wayne Crispen, M.N. Delph.

BOONVILLE: Boonville 58–44 Millersburg; Newburgh 48–22 Selvin; Lynnville 47–39 Elberfeld; Tennyson 28–16 Chandler; Newburgh 47–45 Boonville; Tennyson 36–31 Lynnville; Newburgh 43–40 Tennyson. Officials: Norman L. Risley, Ivan Risley.

BROWNSBURG: North Salem 61–55 Danville; Clayton 68–49 Lizton; Brownsburg 80–40 Pittsboro; Avon 56–55 Chariton; Stilesville 63–50 Plainfield; Amo 65–64 New Winchester; North Salem 62–41 Clayton; Brownsburg 58–37 Avon; Amo 65–64 Stilesville; Brownsburg 55–45 North Salem; Brownsburg 62–44 Amo. Officials: Walter Swift, Merle Hill, Leo R. Ponto.

CARMEL: Prairie Twp. 61–60 Sharpsville; Noblesville 61–40 Jefferson; Windfall 61–60 Tipton; Sheridan 71–32 Jackson Central; Fishers 65–54 Walnut Grove; Carmel 74–47 Westfield; Noblesville 61–54 Prairie Twp.; Sheridan 49–39 Windfall; Carmel 44–42 Fishers (3ot); Noblesville 51–41 Sheridan; Noblesville 45–33 Carmel. Officials: James Beyer, Dwain Laird, Charles Garber, Jr.

CHURUBUSCO–AUBURN: (At Auburn): Waterloo 52–49 Riverdale (ot); Angola 51–40 Auburn; Butler 60–57 Garrett; Angola 47–42 Waterloo; (At Churubusco): Ashley 59–56 Orland; Churubusco 58–38 Fremont; Bellefountain 63–44 Salem Center; Ashley 53–43 Churubusco; (At Churubusco): Bellefountain 46–45 Ashley; Angola 81–68 Butler; Angola 62–50 Bellefountain. Officials: Gerald Strickler, Floyd A. Reed, Johannes P. Dienelt, Robert G. Cowan.

COLUMBIA CITY: Warsaw 68–52 Etna Green; Pierceton 66–51 Atwood; Larwill 66–56 Sidney; Claypool 72–54 Milford; Mentone 82–48 North Webster; Syracuse 57–54 South Whitley; Columbia City 66–36 Leesburg; Warsaw 71–59 Pierceton; Larwill 63–43 Claypool; Mentone 57–48 Syracuse; Columbia City 68–57 Warsaw; Mentone 51–43 Larwill; Columbia City 64–49 Mentone. Officials: Ray Nemeth, Richard Gebhart, Edgar Powers, Richard Morrison.

COLUMBUS: Southwestern 51–47 Hauser; Shelbyville 47–43 Triton; Nashville 68–56 Helmsburg; Waldron 53–41 Columbus; Shelbyville 70–56 Southwestern; Nashville 72–69 Waldron; Nashville 62–59 Shelbyville. Officials: Lloyd Whipple, Joseph Hunter.

CONNERSVILLE: Brookville 71–33 Harrison Twp., Liberty 70–66 Laurel; Springfield Twp. 40–38 Whitewater (2ot); Fayette Central 45–41 Brownsville; Connersville 59–34 Alquina; Brookville 64–44 Liberty; Springfield Twp. 40–37 Fayette Central; Brookville 59–57 Connersville (2ot); Brookville 52–45 Springfield Twp.. Officials: Charles Timmons, William Yohler, Don C. Stimson.

CRAWFORDSVILLE: Crawfordsville 59–42 Waynetown; New Ross 40–21 Coal Creek Central; Ladoga 64–54 Waveland; Crawfordsville 51–45 New Ross; Alamo 54–48 Linden; Darlington 49–45 New Market; Crawfordsville 57–46 Ladoga; Alamo 53–48 Darlington; Crawfordsville 63–48 Alamo. Officials: Robert Laird, Donald Call, Jimmy Dimitroff.

DILLSBORO: Vevay 93–47 Moores Hill; Aurora 68–62 Rising Sun; Lawrenceburg 52–50 Guilford; Bright 64–44 Patriot; Vevay 70–47 Dillsboro; Aurora 56–49 Lawrenceburg; Vevay 79–40 Bright; Aurora 57–54 Vevay. Officials: Charles E. Stumpf, Lowell Smith, Raymond M. Robison, James Haywood.

EAST CHICAGO: Hammond Morton 79–61 Tech; Bishop Noll 75–39 Dyer; East Chicago Washington 74–46 Highland; Griffith 65–59 Morton; East Chicago Washington 71–44 Noll; Whiting 53–45 East Chicago Roosevelt; Grown Point 66–46 Clark; Hammond High 72–49

Lowell; Crown Point 74–54 Whiting; Washington 98–67 Griffith; Crown Point 54–52 Hammond High (ot); Washington 77–51 Crown Point. Officials: Victor J. Wukovits, William E. Hemphill, H. F. McNaught.

ELKHART: Shipshewana-Scott 69–42 Millersburg; Elkhart 58–46 Nappanee; Concord 78–45 Goshen; Wakarusa 59–36 Topeka; Penn 49–44 Bristol; Jefferson 44–43 New Paris; Middlebury 48–33 Baugh Twp.; Elkhart 60–49 Shipshewana-Scott; Concord 69–37 Wakarusa; Jefferson 52–46 Penn; Elkhart 62–50 Middlebury; Concord 49–43 Jefferson; Elkhart 58–56 Concord. Officials: Bill Larkin, Ernest Sohl. Richard Duffield, Roy Kilby.

EVANSVILLE: Mt. Vernon 83–71 Poseyville; Bosse 55–54 Central; North 74–46 Wadesville; Lincoln 91–40 Griffin; Reitz 69–34 Cynthiana; Mater Dei 80–44 New Harmony; Memorial 81–73 Mt. Vernon; Bosse 73–50 North; Lincoln 72–63 Reitz; Mater Dei 79–56 Memorial; Bosse 72–58 Lincoln; Bosse 58–51 Mater Dei. Officials: Charles A. Fouty, Howard E. Risley, Robert C. Rose.

FORT WAYNE: Arcola 52–50 Elmhurst (ot); Huntertown 66–61 North Side; South Side 63–33 Monroeville; Concordia 54–51 Harlan; Leo 58–30 Hoagland; New Haven 81–57 Woodburn; Central 78–75 Central Catholic; Huntertown 84–53 Arcola; South Side 79–44 Concordia; Leo 64–60 New Haven; Central 52–37 Huntertown; South Side 79–56 Leo; South Side 73–61 Central. Officials: Thomas Dean, Marion Acton, William R. Findling, Gene Butts.

FOWLER: Fowler 75–40 Gilboa; Boswell 54–47 Freeland Park; Ambia 64–30 Raub; Pine Twp. 34–31 Earl Park; Fowler 62–37 Wadena; Ambia 57–40 Boswell; Otterbein 70–53 Pine Twp.; Fowler 54–46 Otterbein. Officials: Darl March, William Hile, John Howard Arnold.

FRANKFORT: Frankfort 68–50 Jackson Twp.; Rossville 56–23 Mulberry; Kirklin 68–40 Scircleville; Forest 65–59 Michigantown; Colfax 61–26 Sugar Creek; Frankfort 62–47 Washington Twp.; Rossville 75–36 Kirklin; Forest 63–50 Colfax; Rossville 59–57 Frankfort; Rossville 64–54 Forest. Officials: James W. Davidson, Gene P. Davis, Earnest V. Baldwin.

GARY: Horace Mann 97–38 River Forest; Lew Wallace 56–50 Gary Edison; Roosevelt 93–48 Merrillville; Calumet 67–63 Tolleston; Emerson 73–56 Hobart; Froebel 73–44 East Gary Edison; Wirt 79–66 Horace Mann; Roosevelt 71–60 Lew Wallace; Emerson 62–60 Calumet; Froebel 82–56 Wirt; Roosevelt 85–44 Emerson; Roosevelt 72–63 Froebel. Officials: Ed Burke, Carter L. Caton, Myron Weldy.

GREENCASTLE: Bainbridge 76–51 Cloverdale; Belle Union 57–49 Fillmore; Reelsville 49–34 Russellville; Roachdale 74–66 Greencastle; Bainbridge 67–52 Belle Union; Reelsville 60–57 Roachdale; Bainbridge 69–53 Reelsville. Officials: LeRoy Heminger, Norman Shields.

GREENSBURG: Greensburg 75–56 Jackson; St. Paul 52–34 Clarksburg; Sandcreek 49–45 Sandusky; Vernon 51–40 New Point; North Vernon 64–56 Burney; St. Paul 47–45 Greensburg; Sandcreek 68–44 Vernon: North Vernon 76–52 St. Paul; North Vernon 63–55 Sandcreek. Officials: Karl Bly, Glen L. Bonsett, John B. Williams.

HARTFORD CITY: Dunkirk 67–52 Redkey; Montpelier 69–41 Madison Twp.; Bryant 81–42 Gray; Hartford City 49–48 Pennville; Portland 59–50 Poling; Dunkirk 101–55 Roll; Bryant 55–50 Montpelier; Hartford City 89–63 Portland; Dunkirk 71–53 Bryant; Dunkirk 88–69 Hartford City. Officials: Don Lieberum, Thomas A. Hoffman, Grayson J. Mahin.

HUNTINGBURG: Springs Valley 58–33 Otwell; Holland 71–38 Birdseye; Winslow 58–48 St. Ferdinand; Dubois 60–59 Spurgeon; Jasper. 87–60 Stendal; Huntingburg 73–46 Ireland; Springs Valley 67–61 Holland; Winslow 60–53 Dubois; Huntingburg 68–58 Jasper; Springs Valley 54–47 Winslow; Huntingburg 41–39 Springs Valley. Officials: Donald L. Hubbard, Robert

Tourney Time

R. Davidson, Roger J. Emmert.

HUNTINGTON: Clear Creek 55–54 Salamonie Twp.; Lancaster Twp. 66–65 Lafayette Central; Huntington Catholic 53–51 Rock Creek; Union Twp. 75–64 Roanoke; Huntington Twp. 63–40 Jefferson; Andrews 55–54 Huntington; Clear Creek 53–48 Lancaster Twp.; Huntington Catholic 77–63 Union; Andrews 59–58 Huntington Twp.; Huntington Catholic 58–47 Clear Creek; Huntington Catholic 46–43 Andrews. Officials: Howard Cosand, Dean B. Geyer, Richard M. Swartz.

INDIANAPOLIS: Lawrence Central 60–56 North Central; Crispus Attucks 79–65 Broad Ripple; Ben Davis 67–65 Warren Central; Scecina 72–48 Pike Twp.; Tech 83–58 Speedway; Washington 60–50 Cathedral; Shortridge 81–54 School for the Deaf; Crispus Attucks 89–44 Lawrence Central; Ben Davis 86–63 Scecina; Tech 64–59 Washington; Crispus Attucks 63–62 Shortridge; Tech 68–64 Ben Davis; Crispus Attucks 78–68 Tech. Officials: Maurice Criswell, John F. Fee, Robert H. Spay, Glen Wisler.

JEFFERSONVILLE: Charlestown 55–44 Clarksville; New Washington 66–57 Henryville; Providence 56–54 Silver Creek; New Albany 97–46 Borden; Jeffersonville 56–49 Georgetown; New Washington 53–51 Charlestown; New Albany 71–60 Providence; Jeffersonville 86–49 New Washington; New Albany 68–66 Jeffersonville. Officials: Vern E. Doles, Noel Genth, Paul Grimes.

KENDALLVILLE: LaGrange 55–53 Ligonier (3ot); Lima 46–41 Springfield Twp.; Cromwell 53–51 Wawaka; Albion 33–32 Avilla; Kendallville 73–50 Rome City; Howe Military 58–50 Wolf Lake; Brighton 45–33 Wolcottville; LaGrange 75–41 Lima; Albion 48–40 Cromwell; Howe Military 37–35; Kendallville; Brighton 47–43 LaGrange; Howe Military 46–38 Albion; Brighton 46–40 Howe Military. Officials: Robert J. Dornte, Harold Braden, Burl McKenzie, James Murray.

KENTLAND: Goodland 66–40 Tefft; Rensselaer 57–45 Morocco; Kentland 51–50 Remington; Wheatfield 60–39 Fair Oaks; Mt. Ayr 62–61 Brook (ot); DeMotte 75–55 Goodland; Rensselaer 65–42 Kentland; Wheatfield 67–51 Mt. Ayr; Rensselaer 60–40 DeMotte; Rensselaer 59–45 Wheatfield. Officials: Victor Griewank, Morris Davis, Richard Robinson.

KNOX: Winamac 59–58 Walkerton (ot); Grovertown 53–43 Hamlet; Medaryville 54–52 Aubbeenaubbee; North Judson 64–47 Knox; San Pierre 54–36 Pulaski; Monterey 54–41 Star City; Grovertown 59–46 Winamac; North Judson 40–25 Medaryville; San Pierre 56–48 Monterey; North Judson 59–48 Grovertown; North Judson 67–43 San Pierre. Officials: Gary G. Nelson, Robert Kramer, Robert C. Brees.

KOKOMO: Kokomo 51–43 Eastern; Western 58–54 Camden; Northwestern 63–58 Delphi; Flora 74–65 Burlington; Kokomo 81–41 Western; Northwestern 89–68 Flora; Kokomo 78–52 Northwestern. Officials: Jerry Steiner, John Holmes.

LAFAYETTE: Montmorenci 64–61 Southwestern; Jefferson 59–51 East Tipp; Klondike 55–41 Lauramie; Dayton 80–46 Battleground; West Lafayette 62–30 Central Catholic; Jefferson 67–50 Montmorenci; Klondike 49–47 Dayton; Jefferson 55–42 West Lafayette; Jefferson 68–46 Klondike. Officials: Mel Pope, Gilbert Smith, Walt McFatridge.

LOGANSPORT: Young America 64–63 Tipton Twp.; Twelve Mile 55–49 Galveston; Metea 73–69 Royal Center; Washington Twp. 58–51 Lucerne; Logansport 53–44 Kewanna; Grass Creek 60–53 New Waverly; Twelve Mile 64–51 Young America; Washington Twp. 57–53 Metea; Logansport 90–53 Grass Creek; Washington Twp. 72–45 Twelve Mile; Logansport 69–49 Washington Twp. Officials: William E. Farrar, Frank Sanders, Jr., Louis B. Goshert.

MADISON HEIGHTS: Madison Heights 64–54 Highland; Summitville 60–52 Frankton;

IHSAA Scores | 1950-1959

Anderson 59–41 Lapel; Madison Heights 92–72, Summitville; St. Mary's 57–39 Wilkinson; Alexandria 60–50 Markleville; Pendleton 52–50 Elwood (ot); Alexandria 65–40 St. Mary's; Anderson 50–25 Madison Heights; Alexandria 44–40 Pendleton; Alexandria 47–38 Anderson. Officials: Don Hurst, John Hilligoss, Clayton Nichols.

MARION: Jefferson Twp. 64–58 Van Buren; Fairmount 64–58 Swayzee; Marion 86–40 Bennett; Mississinewa 68–51 Sweetser; Fairmount 62–42 Jefferson Twp.; Marion 69–58 Mississinewa; Marion 49–40 Fairmount. Officials: Wesley Oler, Homer Owens, Jr.

MARTINSVILLE: Eminence 51–44 Unionville; Ellettsville 52–50 Bloomington University (2ot); Morgantown 56–53 Monrovia; Bloomington 62–51 Smithville; Martinsville 70–41 Stinesville; Mooresville 61–54 Eminence; Ellettsville 56–52 Morgantown; Martinsville 72–52 Bloomington; Ellettsville 53–50 Mooresville; Martinsville 69–53 Ellettsville. Officials: Eugene Sparks, Lowell K. Willis, James F. Davis.

MICHIGAN CITY: Michigan City 99–31 Hanna; LaCrosse 55–45 Westville; Union Twp. 42–39 Wanatah; Mill Creek 70–46 Stillwell; Rolling, Prairie 56–42 Kingsbury; St. Mary's 66–60 Union Mills; LaPorte 73–32 Clinton Twp.; Michigan City 91–40 LaCrosse; Mill Creek 42–28 Union Twp.; St. Mary's 63–39 Rolling Prairie; Michigan City 83–64 LaPorte; Mill Creek 56–48 St. Mary's; Michigan City 72–40 Mill Creek. Officials: Stan Dubis, John Sebastian, Merle Shively, Wayne Smith.

MISHAWAKA: South Bend Adams 60–50 Mishawaka; Riley 61–48 Washington-Clay; Central 81–47 Madison Twp.; Adams 75–61 Riley; Washington 76–60 New Carlisle; Lakeville 69–55 North Liberty; St. Joseph 67–57 Greene Twp.; Washington 72–67 Lakeville; Central 54–45 Adams; Washington 80–74 St. Joseph; Central 63–56 Washington. Officials: DeVere Hoffman, Harley Collins, Glenn Lantz.

MONON: Brookston 59–48 Burnettsville; Monon 58–49 Reynolds; Wolcott 55–49 Francesville (ot); Chalmers 60–42 Buffalo; Idaville 58–56 Monticello; Monon 64–62 Brookston (ot); Wolcott 62–53 Chalmers; Monon 50–46 Idaville; Wolcott 71–59 Monon. Officials: Nick Reff, Joe Garoffolo, Anthony Lazar.

MUNCIE: Burris 67–65 Eaton; Selma 56–55 Center; Royerton 64–57 Albany; DeSoto 61–52 Daleville; Yorktown 63–51 Gaston; Central 77–30 Cowan; Burris 71–54 Harrison; Royerton 72–54 Selma; DeSoto 64–57 Yorktown; Central 73–57 Burris; DeSoto 61–56 Royerton; Central 99–51 DeSoto. Officials: Joe Mullins, Robert B. Sosbe, Marvin Todd.

NEW CASTLE: Mooreland 55–49 Mt. Summit; New Castle 89–45 Sulphur Springs; Middletown 62–58 Spiceland; New Castle 63–33 Mooreland; Knightstown 57–45 Straughn; Lewisville 63–50 Cadiz; New Castle 79–61 Middletown; Knightstown 67–53 Lewisville; New Castle 71–54 Knightstown. Officials: Everett Campbell, Gilbert Beagle, James Patterson.

PERU: Akron 63–45 Gilead; Fulton 49–46 Beaver Dam (ot); Peru 65–50 Mexico; Clay Twp. 86–50 Deedsville; Converse 57–42 Bunker Hill; Akron 51–50 Chili; Peru 53–39 Fulton; Converse 53–50 Clay Twp.; Peru 75–59 Akron; Converse 81–55 Peru. Officials: Maurice Davis, Don Hollman, Don McCoy.

PLYMOUTH: LaPaz 63–50 Bourbon; Rochester 63–36 Talma; Plymouth 56–50 Richland Center; Rochester 72–63 LaPaz; West Twp. 60–44 Tippecanoe; Argos 52–47 Bremen; Culver 70–68 Tyner; Argos 65–46 West Twp.; Plymouth 47–42 Rochester; Argos 64–55 Culver; Plymouth 44–36 Argos. Officials: Lauren Griffith, Jack Small, John Sheets.

PRINCETON: Francisco 59–47 Mt. Olympus; Oakland City 84–54 Mackey; Owensville

Tourney Time

65–42 Hazelton; Patoka 61–57 Haubstadt; Ft. Branch 71–70 Princeton; Oakland City 75–59 Francisco; Owensville 35–33 Patoka; Ft. Branch 69–60 Oakland City; Ft. Branch 84–58 Owensville. Officials: James Schwenk, Earle R. Wolfe, Donald R. Boyer.

RICHMOND: Richmond 71–53 Fountain City; Greensfork 63–54 Williamsburg; Cambridge City 64–54 Centerville; Economy 61–55 Whitewater; Hagerstown 71–58 Milton; Boston 51–49 Webster; Richmond 47–43 Greensfork; Cambridge City 63–58 Economy; Hagerstown 45–43 Boston; Richmond 41–33 Cambridge City; Hagerstown 51–45 Richmond. Officials: Charles Posey, Roy W. Gardner, David R. Habegger.

ROCKVILLE: Rockville 45–29 Mecca; Turkey Run 48–43 Dana; Rosedale 66–41 Newport; Clinton 46–33 Cayuga; Bridgeton 33–31 Hillsdale; Montezuma 47–45 St. Bernice; Rockville 86–47 Bellmore; Rosedale 43–41 Turkey Run; Clinton 60–31 Bridgeton; Rockville 63–54 Montezuma; Clinton 69–58 Rosedale; Rockville 45–43 Clinton. Officials: George Neff, James Eads, Frank Smith.

RUSHVILLE: Carthage 69–39 Milroy; Manilla 80–51 Mays; Rushville 80–56 Morristown; New Salem 77–55 Morton Memorial; Arlington 70–68 Charlottesville (ot); Manilla 73–71 Carthage; Rushville 70–56 New Salem; Arlington 60–57 Manilla; Rushville 77–68 Arlington. Officials: James E. Ridge, John M. Priest, Don McBride.

SALEM: Corydon 62–52 English-Sterling; Pekin 87–64 Marengo. Morgan Twp. 53–39 South Central; Milltown 66–34 Hardinsburg; Salem 61–48 Campbellsburg; North Central 78–45 Lanesville; Corydon 73–45 Pekin; Morgan Twp. 60–30 Milltown; Salem 68–54 North Central; Morgan Twp. 51–46 Corydon; Salem 50–41 Morgan Twp. Officials: Russell Owens, Cyril Birge, Julian G. Piercefield.

SCOTTSBURG: Hanover 72–66 Saluda; Madison Central 82–53 Paris Crossing; Scottsburg 69–41 Dupont; Deputy 71–41 Lexington; Madison 71–56 Madison Shawe; Austin 69–56 Hanover; Madison Central 44–42 Scottsburg; Madison 92–40 Deputy; Austin 63–51 Madison Central; Madison 73–49 Austin. Officials: Ed Straith-Miller, Wendell Baker, Edwin T. Miller.

SEYMOUR: Cortland 65–53 Crothersville; Medora 72–51 Tampico; Seymour 75–51 Freetown; Clearspring 67–63 Brownstown; Hayden 56–52 Vallonia; Cortland 62–59 Medora; Seymour 72–54 Clearspring: Cortland 50–48 Hayden (ot); Seymour 67–47 Cortland. Officials: Winfield H. Jacobs, John M. Thomas, Dee Williams.

SOUTHPORT: Fortville 69–64 Mt. Comfort (ot); New Palestine 59–55 Decatur Central; Sacred Heart 72–46 Greenfield; Southport 52–29 Hancock Central; Howe 68–58 Franklin Twp.; Wood 67–29 McCordsville; Manual 72–33 Beech Grove; Fortville 57–53 New Palestine; Southport 52–39 Sacred Heart; Howe 76–59 Wood; Manual 65–45 Fortville; Southport 65–43 Howe; Southport 43–41 Manual (ot). Officials: Oscar T. Samuels, Frank Carnes, James W. Sanders, Fred M. Marlow.

SPENCER: Brazil 55–27 Coal City; Patricksburg 56–43 Clay City; Van Buren 83–43 Cory; Spencer 54–51 Freedom; Coalmont 72–68 Gosport; Staunton 43–26 Ashboro; Brazil 72–64 Bowling Green; Van Buren 61–44 Patricksburg; Spencer 68–47 Coalmont; Brazil 60–49 Staunton; Van Buren 64–50 Spencer; Brazil 56–54 Van Buren. Officials: Robert B. Sweet, Wallace Reeve, Leland Terrell.

SULLIVAN: Prairie Creek 68–42 Pimento; Graysville 68–48 Blackhawk; Dugger 46–42 Pleasantville; Sullivan 83–63 North Central; Carlisle 50–45 Hymera; Prairie Creek 54–46 Graysville; Sullivan 55–52 Dugger; Prairie Creek 50–45 Carlisle; Sullivan 42–41 Prairie Creek.

Officials: Don Shifiet, Harold Shifiet, Jr., Henry E. Pearcy.

SWITZ CITY: Bloomfield 69–52 Solsberry; Switz City 67–48 Jasonville; Linton 70–53 Midland; Worthington 54–47 L & M; Bloomfield 75–41 Switz City; Worthington 74–56 Linton; Bloomfield 38–33 Worthington. Officials: S. T. Proffitt, William Bitzegaio.

TELL CITY: Cannelton 45–42 Chrisney; Bristow 46–34 Troy; Tell City 64–13 Luce Twp.; Rockport 40–35 Oil Twp.; Dale 60–46 Leavenworth; Cannelton 46–34 Bristow; Tell City 42–35 Rockport; Dale 52–42 Cannelton; Tell City 55–44 Dale. Officials: Lester R. Cornwell, Charles M. Sallee, Kenneth H. Blankenbaker.

TERRE HAUTE: Gerstmeyer 87–45 Honey Creek; Wiley 59–50 Fontanet; Otter Creek 55–52 Garfield; Concannon 77–49 New Goshen; State 69–62 Glenn; Schulte 83–43 West Terre Haute; Gerstmeyer 65–33 Riley; Wiley 61–48 Otter Creek; Concannon 62–61 State; Gerstmeyer 76–61 Schulte; Wiley 63–52 Concannon; Gerstmeyer 68–53 Wiley. Officials: John F. Masariu, Charlie Lentz, James W. Boswell.

VALPARAISO: Boone Grove 63–54 Washington; Portage 82–65 Hebron; Valparaiso 93–34 Morgan; Kouts 48–44 Wheeler; Chesterton 69–62 Jackson; Boone Grove 86–44 Liberty Twp.; Valparaiso 97–60 Portage; Chesterton 66–65 Kouts; Valparaiso 87–58 Boone Grove; Valparaiso 109–74 Chesterton. Officials: Lawrence Gradeless, Darrell L. Snodgrass, Gerald W. Strole, Jr.

VERSAILLES: Versailles 69–61 Cross Plains; Osgood 85–44 Holton; Sunman 54–39 Napoleon; New Marion 58–55 Milan; Versailles 81–60 Batesville; Sunman 46–37 Osgood; Versailles 68–55 New Marion; Versailles 75–54 Sunman. Officials: L. C. Thorne, Arthur Thompson, Wray Holbrook.

VINCENNES: Vincennes 80–50 Decker Chapel; Bicknell 75–59 Wheatland; Bruceville 51–49 Oaktown; Monroe City 67–47 Fritchton; Decker 70–59 Edwardsport; Central Catholic 61–48 Freelandville; Vincennes 60–45 Sandborn; Bicknell 55–47 Bruceville; Monroe City 56–43 Decker; Vincennes 75–45 Central Catholic; Monroe City 61–56 Bicknell; Vincennes 68–52 Monroe City. Officials: Fred Hodge, Ralph F. Box, Roland C. Baker.

WABASH: Urbana 51–38 Somerset; Wabash 57–29 Lagro; Roann 65–60 Silver Lake (ot); Wabash 63–32 Urbana; Noble Twp. 65–59 Laketon; Lafontaine 51–34 White's; Noble Twp. 69–53 Manchester; Wabash 61–55 Roann; Noble Twp. 53–42 Lafontaine; Wabash 74–55 Noble Twp. Officials: Gerald Imel, James Carey, Eugene Lillie.

WASHINGTON: Shoals 67–50 Petersburg; St. John's 78–52 Epsom; Odon 60–42 Elnora; Washington Catholic 62–46 Plainville; Washington 65–51 Loogootee; Barr Twp. 48–41 Alfordsville; Shoals 64–47 St. John's; Odon 58–34 Washington Catholic; Washington 44–43 Barr Twp.; Odon 52–38 Shoals; Odon 59–56 Washington. Officials: W. L. Ketner, Malvern G. Redman, Harold E. Gourley.

WHITELAND: Union 58–48 Greenwood; Edinburg 51–39 Clark; Whiteland 60–29 Nineveh; Franklin 29–20 Center Grove; Trafalgar 52–51 Union; Edinburg 48–41 Whiteland; Franklin 42–25 Trafalgar; Edinburg 39–37 Franklin (2ot). Officials: Richard C. Foster, Jr., Robert J. Cherry, Noble Benbow.

WINCHESTER: Farmland 49–42 Ridgeville; Parker 25–24 Union City-Wayne; Spartanburg 51–38 Ward-Jackson; Lynn 62–46 Union Twp.; Winchester 73–52 White River; Parker 24–23 Farmland; Spartanburg 61–40 Lynn; Parker 67–51 Winchester; Parker 28–15 Spartanburg. Officials: Richard Tiernan, William May, Howard Plough.

ZIONSVILLE: Lebanon 73–40 Whitestown; Zionsville 64–37 Perry Central; Pinnell 51–44

Tourney Time

Wells; Thorntown 57–43 Dover; Zionsville 42–36 Lebanon; Thorntown 57–56 Pinnell; Zionsville 47–46 Thorntown (ot). Officials: Ira Ray Williams, John J. Hinga.

1959 REGIONALS

BLOOMINGTON: Bloomfield 68–58 Gerstmeyer; Brazil 57–54 Martinsville; Brazil 67–58 Bloomfield. Officials: William Findling, Wayne Crispen, Robert Rose, Robert Sosbe.

COLUMBUS: Nashville 68–56 North Vernon; Madison 60–44 Edinburg; Madison 93–62 Nashville. Officials: Roland Baker, J. Firman Grimes, Cyril Birge, Norman Risley.

CONNERSVILLE: Rushville 84–66 Aurora; Versailles 39–35 Brookville; Rushville 76–68 Versailles. Officials: Eugene Sparks, James Sanders, Winfield Jacobs, Frank Carnes.

COVINGTON: Bainbridge 62–49 Rockville; Crawfordsville 55–46 Attica; Bainbridge 62–50 Crawfordsville. Officials: Homer Owens, John Fee, Wesley Oler, Lowell Willis.

EAST CHICAGO: East Chicago Washington 67–52 Gary Roosevelt; Michigan City 94–74 Valparaiso; Washington 92–76 Michigan City. Officials: Maurice Criswell, Walt McFatridge, Jack Small, Robert Spay.

ELKHART: Columbia City 72–58 Elkhart; South Bend Central 62–50 Plymouth; South Bend Central 63–46 Columbia City. Officials: Gerald Strickler, Gerald Imel, Oscar Samuels, Thomas Dean.

EVANSVILLE: Evansville Bosse 73–31 Newburgh; Tell City 55–53 Ft. Branch; Tell City 61–55 Bosse. Officials: Paul Grimes, Leroy Heminger, Robert Laird, James Patterson.

FORT WAYNE: Angola 56–33 Brighton; Ft. Wayne South Side 59–51 Decatur; South Side 82–58 Angola. Officials: Joe Mullins, Charlie Timmons, Dean Geyer, Bill Larkin.

HUNTINGBURG: Odon 63–61 Vincennes; Huntingburg 71–54 Sullivan; Odon 60–58 Huntingburg. Officials: Jerry Steiner, John Williams, Dee Williams, Vern Doles.

INDIANAPOLIS: Southport 58–35 Brownsburg; Indianapolis Attucks 60–53 Alexandria; Attucks 75–47 Southport. Officials: Charles Northam, Charles Fouty, Marvin Todd, Don McCoy.

JEFFERSONVILLE: New Albany 65–57 Seymour; Shawswick 69–57 Salem; New Albany 65–59 Shawswick. Officials: Lloyd Whipple, Robert Davidson, Malvern Redman, Roger Emmert.

KOKOMO: Noblesville 58–49 Converse; Kokomo 89–52 Wabash; Kokomo 81–62 Noblesville. Officials: Stan Dubis, Everett Campbell, Don McBride, Leland Terrell.

LAFAYETTE: Rossville 61–56 Zionsville; Lafayette Jefferson 59–53 Fowler; Jefferson 47–45 Rossville. Officials: Don Lieberum, Burl McKenzie, John Hilligoss, Harley Collins.

LOGANSPORT: Wolcott 62–56 Rensselaer; Logansport 53–47 North Judson; Logansport 81–46 Wolcott. Officials: Frank Smith, Ed Straith-Miller, Clayton Nichols, Arthur Thompson.

MARION: Marion 70–36 Huntington Catholic; Dunkirk 59–44 Ossian; Marion 73–52 Dunkirk. Officials: Frank Sanders, Jr., Fred Marlow, H. F. McNaught, Joseph Hunter.

MUNCIE: Parker 52–41 Hagerstown; Muncie Central 80–61 New Castle; Muncie Central 57–46 Parker. Officials: Roy Gardner, Robert Cherry, James Boswell, Lawrence Gradeless.

1959 SEMI-STATES

FORT WAYNE: Kokomo 92–90 Fort Wayne South Side; Marion 61–60 South Bend Central; Kokomo 66–55 Marion. Officials: Roy Gardner, Frank Smith, Stan Dubis, Paul Grimes, Dee

Williams, James Boswell.

EVANSVILLE: New Albany 57–55 Tell City; Odon 78–65 Brazil; New Albany 70–68 Odon (2ot). Officials: Don McBride, John Hilligoss, Wesley Oler, Maurice Criswell, Joe Mullins, Charles Northam.

INDIANAPOLIS: Indianapolis Attucks 82–80 Madison; Muncie Central 77–72 Rushville; Attucks 64–62 Muncie Central. Officials: H.F. McNaught, Gerald Strickler, Lloyd Whipple, Frank Sanders, Roland Baker, Don Lieberum.

LAFAYETTE: Lafayette Jefferson 56–52 East Chicago Washington; Logansport 76–62 Bainbridge; Logansport 61–56 Lafayette Jefferson. Officials: James Patterson, Robert Rose, Jerry Stainer, Eugene Sparks, Marvin Todd, Cyril Birge.

1959 FINALS—March 29

INDIANAPOLIS (Butler Fieldhouse): Indianapolis Attucks 76–50 Logansport; Kokomo 58–56 New Albany (ot); Attucks 92–54 Kokomo. Officials: James Patterson, Frank Sanders, Maurice Criswell, Robert Rose, Dee Williams, Roy Gardner.

1960–1969

1960 SECTIONALS

ADAMS CENTRAL: Hartford Center 55–53 Decatur Catholic; Adams Central 62–47 Geneva; Decatur 72–48 Pleasant Mills; Berne 82–54 Monmouth, Adams Central 47–34 Hartford Center; Berne 44–43 Decatur (2ot); Berne 64–62 Adams Central. Officials: Gene Butts, William Farrar.

BEDFORD: Paoli 91–68 Marshall Twp.; Shawswick 75–56 Williams; Mitchell 71–57 Fayetteville; Bedford 83–56 Heltonville; Oolitic 70–52 Tunnelton; Orleans 68–50 Huron; Paoli 85–56 Shawswick; Mitchell 63–57 Bedford; Orleans 65–64 Oolitic (2ot); Mitchell 71–69 Paoli (2ot); Mitchell 51–46 Orleans. Officials: Wallace R. Reeve, Robert C. Rose, Glen L. Bonsett.

BLUFFTON: Ossian 65–60 Union Center; Chester Center 65–48 Liberty Center; Petroleum 58–56 Rockcreek Center; Bluffton 77–47 Jackson Twp.; Ossian 75–55 Lancaster Central; Chester Center 64–56 Petroleum (2ot); Bluffton 79–68 Ossian; Bluffton 84–40 Chester Center. Officials: Dale Van Houten, Joe Mullins, Glen Wisler.

BOONVILLE: Castle 63–41 Lynnville; Elberfeld 80–52 Selvin; Boonville 71–49 Millersburg; Tennyson 54–52 Luce Twp. (2ot); Castle 42–52 Elberfeld; Boonville 58–39 Tennyson; Boonville 44–39 Castle. Officials: Lowell Willis, Robert Sweet.

BROWNSBURG: Brownsburg 65–53 New Winchester; Avon 53–49 Pittsboro; Danville 70–38 Charlton; Plainfield 70–39 Clayton; North Salem 61–54 Amo; Stilesville 69–66 Lizton (2ot); Brownsburg 72–58 Avon; Plainfield 68–54 Danville; North Salem 75–43 Stilesville; Plainfield 63–45 Brownsburg; North Salem 79–63 Plainfield. Officials: Harry W. Green, Charles A. Fouty, John J. Hinga.

Tourney Time

CARMEL: Tipton 58–50 Westfield; Noblesville 65–53 Carmel; Jackson Central 63–42 Fishers; Walnut Grove 43–34 Windfall; Sheridan 48–47 Sharpsville; Noblesville 74–53 Tipton; Jackson Central 50–48 Walnut Grove; Sheridan 28–23 Noblesville; Sheridan 45–31 Jackson Central. Officials: Richard D. Robinson, Jim Ladd, James E. Ridge.

CENTER GROVE: Center Grove 67–47 Greenwood; Franklin 76–56 Clark; Edinburg 61–57 Trafalgar; Union 53–31 Nineveh; Center Grove 36–34 Whiteland; Franklin 52–44 Edinburg; Center Grove 64–48 Union; Center Grove 49–46 Franklin. Officials: Charles Stumpf, Frank Smith, Gilbert Beagle.

CHURUBUSCO–GARRETT (At Churubusco): Churubusco 68–55 Auburn; Angola 51–39 Ashley; Garrett 48–43 Riverdale; Angola 66–53 Churubusco; (At Garrett): Orland 69–42 Salem Center; Hamilton 62–50 Fremont; Waterloo 62–56 Butler; Orland 72–55 Hamilton; (At Churubusco): Garrett 46–41 Angola; Waterloo 69–49 Orland; Waterloo 39–34 Garrett. Officials: David R. Habegger, Don A. Yager, Lewis B. Goshert, William Goshert.

CLAY CITY: Patricksburg 42–41 Staunton; Cory 57–48 Clay City; Freedom 61–48 Gosport; Bowling Green 57–48 Coal City; Brazil 58–30 Van Buren; Coalmont 52–50 Spencer; Patricksburg 71–56 Cory; Freedom 65–55 Bowling Green; Brazil 75–39 Coalmont; Freedom 47–41 Patricksburg; Brazil 69–47 Freedom. Officials: Earle R. Wolfe, Mel Pope, Donald R. Boyer.

CLINTON: Rosedale 70–50 Mecca; Montezuma 72–58 Dana; Clinton 66–36 St. Bernice; Rockville 62–36 Cayuga; Bridgeton 63–38 Hillsdale; Turkey Run 75–59 Newport; Montezuma 58–56 Rosedale (2ot); Rockville 67–55 Clinton; Turkey Run 50–43 Bridgeton; Rockville 65–49 Montezuma; Rockville 59–41 Turkey Run. Officials: Allen Voorhis, Noble Benbow, Richard Foster, Jr.

CLINTON CENTRAL: Prairie 40–27 Mulberry; Clinton Central 72–36 Jefferson Twp.; Rossville 52–45 Jackson Twp.; Frankfort 85–52 Colfax; Prairie 55–39 Washington Twp.; Clinton Central 71–63 Rossville; Frankfort 85–60 Prairie; Clinton Central 79–71 Frankfort. Officials: Walter R. Swift, Ira Ray Williams, Charlie Timmons

COLUMBIA CITY: Pierceton 77–67 Milford; Columbia City 73–50 Claypool; Larwill 71–42 Sidney; North Webster 65–47 Leesburg; Mentone 61–58 Syracuse (ot); Warsaw 55–53 Atwood; South Whitley 70–62 Etna Green; Columbia City 74–60 Pierceton; North Webster 68–54 Larwill: Mentone 64–57 Warsaw; Columbia City 73–54 South Whitley; North Webster 57–43 Mentone; Columbia City 86–60 North Webster. Officials: Earnest V. Baldwin, James B. Carey, Frank Carnes, Eugene Lillie.

COLUMBUS:: Shelbyville 54–41 Triton; Columbus 96–50 Nashville; Southwestern 52–51 Helmsburg; Waldron 68–39 Hauser; Columbus 74–43 Shelbyville; Waldron 63–42 Southwestern; Waldron 47–45 Columbus. Officials: Roy W. Gardner, John M. Priest.

CONNERSVILLE: Liberty 47–45 Laurel; Alquina 77–38 Brownsville; Brookville 66–28 Springfield Twp.; Fayette Central 55–34 Harrison Twp.; Connersville 67–36 Whitewater; Alquina 53–47 Liberty; Fayette Central 54–52 Brookville; Connersville 60–38 Alquina; Connersville 72–45 Fayette Central. Officials: Charles Lentz, Neal D. Jay, Paul Grimes.

CRAWFORDSVILLE:: Darlington 46–45 Waveland; Crawfordsville 66–54 Coal Creek Central; New Market 67–55 Ladoga; Crawfordsville 66–45 Darlington; New Ross 61–45 Alamo; Linden 74–57 Waynetown; Crawfordsville 46–33 New Market; New Ross 62–52 Linden; Crawfordsville 53–42 New Ross. Officials: James S. Eads, Danny P. Jacobs, Ralph F. Box.

EAST CHICAGO:: Highland 83–47 Dyer; Hammond Noll 88–52 Lowell; Hammond High

IHSAA Scores | 1960–1969

57–53 Whiting; Highland 68–57 Clark; Hammond High 70–66 Noll; East Chicago Washington 54–50 Hammond Tech; Griffith 60–56 Hammond Morton; East Chicago Roosevelt 71–46 Crown Point; Washington 57–42 Griffith; Highland 82–60 Hammond High; Washington 60–48 Roosevelt; Washington 83–66 Highland. Officials: Carter L. Caton, Joseph J. Bella, Lawrence Gradeless.

ELKHART: Middlebury 65–61 Penn; New Paris 82–71 Shipshewana; Scott; Baugo Twp. 60–42 Jefferson Twp.; Goshen 80–57 Nappanee; Elkhart 57–44 Wakarusa; Bristol 59–55 Millersburg; Concord 93–38 Topeka; Middlebury 65–47 New Paris; Goshen 56–41 Baugo Twp.; Elkhart 65–43 Bristol; Concord 63–57 Middlebury; Elkhart 66–63 Goshen; Elkhart 61–55 Concord. Officials: Don McCoy, Ned Brenizer, Johannes P. Dienelt, Robert C. Cowan.

EVANSVILLE: Mt. Vernon 82–67 North Posey; Central 64–62 Bosse; Lincoln 77–74 Memorial; Mater Dei 76–52 New Harmony; Reitz 73–55 Rex Mundi; North 74–64 Mt. Vernon: Lincoln 65–49 Central; Reitz 83–67 Mater Dei; Lincoln 61–42 North: Lincoln 60–53 Reitz. Officials: Leland Terrell, Robert R. Davidson, Norman Shields.

FORT WAYNE: Ft. Wayne North Side 77–60 Woodland; Harlan 84–80 Arcola (2ot); Huntertown 59–54 Hoagland; Central Catholic 61–39 New Haven; Central 81–64 South Side; Ft. Wayne Concordia 95–66 Monroeville; Leo 70–65 Elmhurst (2ot); Harlan 76–60 North Side; Huntertown 60–59 Central Catholic; Central 93–75 Concordia; Leo 45–43 Harlan; Central 72–45 Huntertown; Central 38–34 Leo. Officials: Wayne Crispen, Bill Hile, Robert H. Spay, John H. Arnold.

FOWLER: Otterbein 49–32 Ambia; Fowler 75–30 Wadena; Oxford 64–57 Pine Twp.; Freeland Park 81–64 Gilboa; Earl Park 64–46 Raub; Otterbein 50–45 Boswell; Fowler 40–37 Oxford; Freeland Park 59–50 Earl Park; Fowler 47–41 Otterbein: Fowler 41–39 Freeland Park. Officials: George Neff, Howard Cosand, Harry D. Inskeep.

GARY: Wirt 61–60 Lew Wallace; Froebel 86–59 Calumet Twp.; Hobart 63–52 Emerson; Gary Edison 65–64 East Gary Edison; Roosevelt 81–51 Tolleston; Merrillville 58–48 River Forest; Horace Mann 57–48 William A. Wirt; Froebel 71–64 Hobart; Roosevelt 95–42 Edison; Horace Mann 61–59 Merrillville; Roosevelt 76–65 Froebel; Roosevelt 85–57 Horace Mann. Officials: Thomas Dean, Richard M. Swartz, Dean B. Geyer.

GREENCASTLE: Bainbridge 60–44 Roachdale; Greencastle 80–54 Fillmore; Belle Union 50–42 Russellville; Cloverdale 50–49 Reelsville; Greencastle 60–57 Bainbridge; Cloverdale 73–55 Belle Union; Greencastle 65–60 Cloverdale. Officials: John F. Masariu, Carl Petercheff.

GREENSBURG: Greensburg 66–63 Sandcreek (2ot); North Vernon 75–36 Sandusky; St. Paul 59–45 Burney; Clarksburg 46–36 New Point; Vernon 45–44 Jackson; Greensburg 78–68 North Vernon; St. Paul 39–38 Clarksburg; Greensburg 75–55 Vernon; Greensburg 56–53 St. Paul. Officials: James Davis, Howard Plough, Gerl Furr.

HUNTINGBURG: Springs Valley 88–60 Birdseye; Huntingburg 59–49 Dubois; Jasper 69–59 Ireland; Ferdinand 61–55 Otwell; Holland 56–48 Stendal; Winslow 51–48 Spurgeon; Huntingburg 55–45 Springs Valley; Jasper 61–54 St. Ferdinand; Winslow 61–44 Holland; Jasper 65–59 Huntingburg; Jasper 84–38 Winslow. Officials: Kenneth Blankenbaker, Malvern Redman, Joseph Hunter.

HUNTINGTON: Huntington 74–33 Jefferson Twp.; Andrews 63–39 Roanoke; Huntington Catholic 65–59 Clear Creek; Lancaster Twp. 72–70 Lafayette Central; Huntington Twp. 79–55 Rock Creek; Salamonie Twp. 71–50 Union Twp.; Huntington 64–57 Andrews; Lancaster Twp.

Tourney Time

74–73 Huntington Catholic; Huntington Twp. 65–57 Salamonie Twp.; Huntington 62–55 Lancaster Twp.; Huntington 71–57 Huntington Twp. Officials: Floyd A. Reed, Everett W. Campbell, William H. Yohler.

INDIANAPOLIS: Cathedral 65–60 Scecina; Tech 44–29 Speedway; Shortridge 69–56 Crispus Attucks; North Central 50–32 School for the Deaf; Warren Central 60–55 Pike Twp.; Ben Davis 58–44 Lawrence Central; Broad Ripple 67–53 Washington; Tech 64–55 Cathedral; Shortridge 60–53 North Central; Ben Davis 66–59 Warren Central; Tech 67–58 Broad Ripple; Shortridge 53–45 Ben Davis, Tech 55–44 Shortridge. Officials: John Hilligoss, William May, Homer Owens, Jr., Robert C. Showalter.

JEFFERSONVILLE: Silver Creek 49–48 Borden; New Washington 81–68 Georgetown; Providence 58–47 Henryville; Jeffersonville 74–68 Charlestown; New Albany 65–54 Clarksville; Silver Creek 84–61 New Washington; Providence 65–61 Jeffersonville (2ot); New Albany 68–58 Silver Creek; New Albany 70–53 Providence. Officials: James Schwenk, Raymond M. Robison, Cyril Birge.

KENDALLVILLE: Ligonier 67–55 Springfield Twp.; Kendallville 71–46 Avilla; Rome City 44–39 LaGrange; Cromwell 58–46 Wawaka; Brighton,57–53 Wolcottville; Albion 82–30 Wolf Lake; Howe Military 57–54 Lima; Kendallville 55–44 Ligonier; Cromwell 36–35 Rome City; Albion 50–39 Brighton; Kendallville 57–35 Howe Military; Albion 65–50 Cromwell; Albion 62–44 Kendallville. Officials: Victor Wukovits, Wayne Smith, Ray L. Nemeth, Edgar C. Powers.

KENTLAND: Fair Oaks, 52–39 Tefft; Kentland 46–44 Brook: Rensselaer 51–49 Morocco; DeMotte 72–43 Mt. Ayr; Goodland 60–51 Wheatfield; Remington 57–38 Fair Oaks; Kentland 41–36 Rensselaer; Goodland 54–53 DeMotte (2ot); Kentland 46–40 Remington; Goodland 61–38 Kentland. Officials: Leo Ponto, Darl March, Richard Pattengale.

KNOX: Knox 56–47 San Pierre; North Judson 48–45 Walkerton; Grovertown 41–31 Star City; Medaryville 64–46 Aubbennaubbee Twp.; Monterey 60–42 Hamlet: Knox 60–52 Winamac; North Judson 77–32 Grovertown; Monterey 52–47 Medaryville; Knox 45–43 North Judson; Knox 78–47 Monterey. Officials: W. Merle Hill, Anthony Lazar, Ronald E. Jones.

KOKOMO: Northwestern 59–57 Flora; Eastern 69–51 Western; Kokomo 94–35 Camden; Delphi 83–37 Burlington; Northwestern 60–57 Eastern; Kokomo 72–67 Delphi; Kokomo 96–66 Northwestern. Officials: Wesley N. Oler, John F. Fee.

LAFAYETTE: East Tipp 68–56 Lauramie Twp.; Klondike 72–67 Dayton; Battle Ground 56–51 Montmorenci; Lafayette Jefferson 72–52 Southwestern; West Lafayette 73–48 Central Catholic; Klondike 63–43 East Tipp; Lafayette Jefferson 60–42 Battle Ground; West Lafayette 61–53 Klondike; Lafayette Jefferson 54–44 West Lafayette. Officials: Charles Garber, Jr., Eugene E. Marks, William R. Findling.

LOGANSPORT: Twelve Mile 73–34 Young America; Royal Center 48–46 Grass Creek; Washington Twp. 50–44 Kewanna; Metea 97–43 Galveston; Logansport 83–25 Lucerne; Twelve Mile 65–47 Tipton Twp.; Royal Center 52–40 Washington Twp.; Logansport 78–59 Metea; Twelve Mile 69–43 Royal Center; Logansport 56–54 Twelve Mile. Officials: Jack T. Small, Darrell Snodgrass, James Benecke, Sr.

MADISON HEIGHTS: Summitville 62–58 St. Mary's; Alexandria 61–46 Frankton; Anderson 66–40 Markleville; Alexandria 63–37 Summitville; Madison Heights 76–62 Lapel; Elwood 38–36 Highland; Madison Heights 71–65 Pendleton; Alexandria 20–18 Anderson; Elwood 72–54 Madison Heights; Elwood 54–43 Alexandria. Officials: Don McBride, Jimmy Dimitroff, Richard Tiernan.

IHSAA Scores | 1960–1969

MARION: Oak Hill 53–52 Marion; Mississinewa 69–43 Bennett; Fairmount 59–58 Van Buren; Swayzee 68–58 Jefferson Twp.; Oak Hill 45–40 Mississinewa; Swayzee 72–61 Fairmount; Oak Hill 54–48 Swayzee. Officials: Frank Sanders, Jr., Roy Kilby.

MARTINSVILLE: Eminence 60–58 Martinsville (3ot); Smithville 73–64 Unionville; Ellettsville 63–53 Stinesville; University 67–47 Morgantown; Bloomington 86–48 Mooresville; Eminence 75–54 Monrovia; Ellettsville 57–49 Smithville; Bloomington 85–62 University; Ellettsville 72–48 Eminence; Bloomington 82–51 Ellettsville, Officials: Oscar T. Samuels, Wray D. Holbrook, Grayson J. Mahin.

MICHIGAN CITY: Hanna 60–44 Kingsbury; Stillwell 75–67 Rolling Prairie; Clinton Twp. 59–47 Wanatah; Union Twp. 61–42 St. Mary's; Michigan City 94–36 LaCrosse; Union Mills 59–51 Westville; LaPorte 91–41 Mill Creek; Hanna 54–45 Stillwell; Union Twp. 56–50 Clinton Twp.; Michigan City 89–39 Union Mills; LaPorte 82–30 Hanna; Michigan City 71–43 Union Twp.; Michigan City 76–64 LaPorte. Officials: Maurice Criswell, Richard Morrison, Burl McKenzie, Gary Nelson.

MILAN: Versailles 73–55 Batesville; Sunman 72–65 Milan; Napoleon 64–59 Cross Plains; New Marion 76–71 Osgood; Versailles 94–65 Holton; Napoleon 46–40 Sunman; Versailles 72–68 New Marion; Versailles 74–51 Napoleon. Officials: Jack Mercer, Jerry Steiner, John Holmes.

MISHAWAKA: North Liberty 59–49 Madison; Washington 73–40 New Carlisle; South Bend Central 59–51 Riley; Washington 68–49 North Liberty; Adams 82–52 Lakeville; Mishawaka 39–37 Washington-Clay; St. Joseph 43–29 Greene Twp.; Adams 55–34 Mishawaka; Central 63–52 Washington; St. Joseph 53–51 Adams; St. Joseph 58–52 Central. Officials: James Buckley, Stanley Dubis, Bill Larkin.

MONON: Monticello 67–57 Reynolds; Wolcott 68–45 Chalmers; Brookston 43–27 Monon; Idaville 61–41 Buffalo; Francesville 57–48 Burnettsville; Monticello 49–41 Wolcott; Brookston 64–52 Idaville; Monticello 74–50 Francesville; Brookston 71–54 Monticello. Officials: Morris Davis, Jerry Jones, Richard Gebhart.

MUNCIE: Gaston 55–49 Yorktown; Eaton 68–54 Harrison Twp.; Selma 60–36 Center; Burris 48–37 Albany; Royerton 57–55 DeSoto; Central 90–49 Daleville; Cowan 60–52 Gaston; Selma 64–60 Eaton; Royerton 63–61 Burris; Central 65–26 Cowan; Royerton 55–44 Selma; Central 97–68 Royerton. Officials: Arthur Thompson, Edwin L. Miller, Dee Williams.

NEW CASTLE: Mooreland 69–57 Cadiz; New Castle 94–59 Lewisville; Spiceland 56–53 Straughn; Middletown 61–58 Sulphur Springs; Knightstown 94–66 Wilkinson; Mooreland 73–64 Mt. Summit; New Castle 88–82 Spiceland; Middletown 65–62 Knightstown; New Castle 71–59 Mooreland; Middletown 81–74 New Castle. Officials: John B. Williams, Dwain Laird, Harold E. Mason.

PERU: Peru 86–47 Mexico; Deedsville 67–54 Akron; Clay Twp. 68–40 Chili; Fulton 55–53 Gilead; Bunker Hill 77–58 Beaver Dam; Peru 65–49 Deedsville; Clay Twp. 69–61 Fulton; Bunker Hill 44–43 Peru; Bunker Hill 64–54 Clay. Officials: Robert Dornte, John Sheets, Don Lieberum.

PLYMOUTH: Talma 48–45 Argos; Richland Center 71–44 West Twp.; Rochester 63–51 Bourbon; Richland Center 87–58 Talma; Tippecanoe 96–66 Tyner; Bremen 82–62 LaPaz; Plymouth 64–48 Culver; Tippecanoe 68–58 Bremen; Rochester 62–56 Richland Center; Plymouth 41–38 Tippecanoe; Plymouth 43–41 Rochester. Officials: Nick Reff, John Sebastian, James Tansey.

Tourney Time

PORTLAND: Montpelier 44–43 Roll; Pennville 68–64 Portland; Hartford City 62–59 Dunkirk; Poling 63–28 Gray; Madison Twp. 51–35 Bryant; Montpelier 61–52 Redkey; Pennville 76–75 Hartford City (2ot); Poling 58–42 Madison Twp.; Montpelier 68–48 Pennville; Montpelier 75–58 Poling. Officials: Fred Marlow, Maurice Davis, Robert Henne.

PRINCETON: Hazleton 53–49 Mt. Olympus; Owensville 58–45 Mackey; Ft. Branch 61–58 Haubstadt; Princeton 62–46 Patoka; Francisco 76–67 Oakland City; Owensville 63–48 Hazleton; Ft. Branch 68–67 Princeton (2ot); Owensville 60–56 Francisco; Ft. Branch 64–32 Owensville. Officials: Howard Risley, Donald Lynch, William Bitzegaio.

RICHMOND: Richmond 63–38 Greens Fork; Williamsburg 60–59 Hagerstown; Milton 51–31 Boston; Centerville 76–66 Economy; Cambridge City 71–53 Whitewater; Fountain City 74–46 Webster; Richmond 74–58 Williamsburg; Milton 65–55 Centerville; Cambridge City 79–71 Fountain City; Richmond 50–46 Milton; Richmond 77–59 Cambridge City. Officials: Darrel McFall, James Boswell, John Thomas.

RISING SUN: Aurora 49–36 Rising Sun; Lawrenceburg 75–56 Dillsboro; Moores Hill 60–32 Patriot; North Dearborn 50–33 Vevay; Lawrenceburg 64–56 Aurora; Moores Hill 82–80 North Dearborn (2ot); Lawrenceburg 83–52 Moores Hill. Officials: James E. Patterson, Robert Wells.

RUSHVILLE: Arlington 52–48 Charlottesville; Morton Memorial 51–48 Carthage; Morristown 66–44 Mays; Manilla 71–38 Milroy; Rushville 88–41 New Salem; Morton Memorial 57–42 Arlington; Morristown 82–49 Manilla; Rushville 69–50 Morton Memorial; Rushville 86–57 Morristown. Officials: Don Stimson, Alan Smith, Marion Acton.

SALEM: North Central 51–40 Hardinsburg; Morgan Twp. 58–49 Salem; English 34–29 Milltown; South Central 49–43 Lanesville; Corydon 74–47 Marengo; Pekin 60–57 Campbellsburg; Morgan Twp. 42–31 North Central; English 65–53 South Central; Corydon 44–33 Pekin; Morgan Twp. 42–28 English; Corydon 48–45 Morgan Twp. Officials: Ivan Risley, Norman Risley, James Beyer.

SCOTTSBURG: Madison Central 82–63 Paris Crossing; Madison 86–43 Austin; Madison Shawe 67–64 Deputy; Scottsburg 54–43 Dupont; Hanover 75–70 Saluda; Madison Central 50–38 Lexington; Madison 96–46 Madison Shawe; Scottsburg 55–42 Hanover; Madison 81–42 Madison Central; Madison 76–51 Scottsburg. Officials: Winfield Jacobs, Don Shiflet, Harold Shiflet, Jr., Richard Sweet.

SEYMOUR: Hayden 48–42 Vallonia; Brownstown 64–50 Tampico; Cortland 52–39 Freetown; Medora 69–52 Clearspring; Seymour 73–41 Crothersville; Brownstown 56–42 Hayden; Medora 50–47 Cortland; Seymour 61–53 Brownstown; Seymour 83–71 Medora. Officials: Don Hurst, John Bush, Robert Cherry.

SOUTHPORT: Decatur Central 46–45 Sacred Heart; Vernon Twp. 83–56 Mt. Comfort; Beech Grove 54–53 Indianapolis Howe; Franklin Twp. 87–55 Hancock Central; Indianapolis Manual 62–44 Greenfield; Southport 62–59 Indianapolis Wood; New Palestine 58–53 Decatur Central; Vernon Twp. 69–54 Beech Grove; Indianapolis Manual 58–53 Franklin Twp.; Southport 64–59 New Palestine; Indianapolis Manual 62–48 Vernon Twp.; Indianapolis Manual 71–61 Southport. Officials: Vern Doles, L. C. Thorne, Roland Baker

SULLIVAN: Blackhawk 50–43 Prairie Creek; North Central 79–40 Graysville; Sullivan 60–35 Pimento; Hymera 52–37 Dugger; Carlisle 62–44 Pleasantville; North Central 57–50 Blackhawk; Sullivan 47–38 Hymera; Carlisle 41–36 North Central; Carlisle 40–37 Sullivan. Officials: William McDonald, Donald Call, Walter Frye, Jr.

SWITZ CITY: Worthington 57–48 Midland: L & M 60–58 Solsberry; Switz City 44–40 Linton; Bloomfield 92–51 Jasonville; Worthington 54–30 L & M; Bloomfield 29–15 Switz City; Bloomfield 47–30 Worthington. Officials: Noel Genth, Russell Owens.

TELL CITY: Dale 54–40 Leavenworth; Tell City 51–49 Oil Twp.; Rockport 56–40 Bristow; Cannelton 62–48 Chrisney; Tell City 52–50 Dale; Rockport 59–51 Cannelton; Tell City 51–36 Rockport. Officials: Roger Emmert, Lowell Smith.

TERRE HAUTE: Riley 61–48 New Goshen; Garfield 60–38 Concannon; Gerstmeyer 83–41 West Terre Haute; Fontanet 51–49 Otter Creek; Wiley 57–51 Glenn; Laboratory 42–33 Schulte; Riley 64–48 Honey Creek; Garfield 76–66 Gerstmeyer; Wiley 68–61 Fontanet; Riley 47–42 Laboratory; Garfield 57–56 Wiley; Garfield 71–63 Riley. Officials: Robert Laird, James Ruby, Wendell Baker.

VALPARAISO: Washington Twp. 57–49 Morgan Twp.; Portage Twp. 95–52 Liberty Twp.; Chesterton 72–45 Hebron; Boone Grove 45–43 Jackson Twp. (2ot); Valparaiso 78–62 Kouts; Wheeler 72–64 Washington Twp.; Portage Twp. 72–63 Chesterton; Valparaiso 80–63 Boone Grove; Portage Twp. 74–57 Wheeler; Valparaiso 80–66 Portage Twp. Officials: Robert Kramer, Ernest W. Sohl, John Ward.

VINCENNES: Bruceville 66–64 Fritchton; Sandborn 50–35 Oaktown, Vincennes 93–38 Edwardsport; Central Catholic 51–45 Wheatland, Decker 58–49 Freelandville; Decker Chapel 66–55 Bicknell; Monroe City 74–64 Bruceville; Vincennes 70–40 Sandborn; Decker 54–47 Central Catholic; Decker Chapel 69–68 Monroe City; Vincennes 74–50 Decker; Vincennes 85–60 Decker Chapel. Officials: Harold Gourley, Charles Sallee, J. Firman Grimes.

WABASH: Noble 60–37 Lagro; Somerset 64–53 Roann; LaFontaine 69–63 Urbana (2ot); Noble 73–44 Somerset; Manchester 67–49 White's; Wabash 54–53 Laketon; Manchester 65–46 Silver Lake; Noble 69–53 LaFontaine; Manchester 60–53 Wabash; Manchester 62–53 Noble. Officials: Harold Braden, DeVere Hoffman, Glen Dunn

WASHINGTON: Washington Catholic 56–52 St. John's; Elnora 66–63 Shoals, Odon 101–81 Barr Twp.; Plainville 49–48 Loogootee; Washington 65–34 Petersburg; Alfordsville 64–46 Epsom, Elnora 67–56 Washington Catholic; Odon 65–38 Plainville; Washington 82–27 Alfordsville: Odon 81–64 Elnora; Washington 57–42 Odon. Officials: Donald Hubbard, Lloyd Whipple, Lester Cornwell.

WILLIAMSPORT: Richland Twp. 55–36 Kingman; Perrysville 69–63 Attica, Covington 83–52 Seeger; Veedersburg 63–44 Wallace; Williamsport 89–59 Hillsboro, Pine Village 58–53 Richland Twp.; Covington 79–62 Perrysville, Williamsport 71–63 Veedersburg; Covington 79–48 Pine Village; Covington 62–53 Williamsport. Officials: Joe Garoffolo, Robert Brees, William Malloy.

WINCHESTER: Union City-Wayne 81–38 Ridgeville; Parker 55–45 Farmland; Spartanburg 67–55 Union Twp.; Winchester Driver 50–43 Lynn; Union City Wayne 67–58 Ward-Jackson; Parker 80–50 Spartanburg; Driver 52–51 Union City Wayne; Parker 70–41 Driver. Officials: Lauren Griffith, Marvin Todd, Thomas Hoffman.

ZIONSVILLE: Zionsville 53–50 Lebanon; Thorntown 69–38 Wells; Pinnell 65–54 Dover; Perry Central 62–59 Whitestown; Thorntown 56–43 Zionsville; Pinnell 48–34 Perry Central; Thorntown 58–46 Pinnell. Officials: Walt McFatridge, Max Andress.

Tourney Time

1960 REGIONALS
COLUMBUS: Madison 71–58 Center Grove: Greensburg 51–50 Waldron; Madison 81–54 Greensburg. Officials: Joe Mullins, Walt McFatridge, Malvern Redman, Roger Emmert.

CONNERSVILLE: Rushville 82–59 Connersville; Versailles 72–71 Lawrenceburg; Rushville 99–70 Versailles. Officials: James Boswell, John Williams, Homer Owens, Jr., Arthur Thompson.

EAST CHICAGO: Gary Roosevelt 75–74 Michigan City; East Chicago Washington 79–60 Valparaiso; East Chicago Washington 60–58 Gary Roosevelt. Officials: Wesley Oler, John Fee, Bill Larkin, Wayne Crispen.

ELKHART: South Bend St. Joseph 62–50 Columbia City; Elkhart 69–41 Plymouth; Elkhart 60–53 St. Joseph. Officials: Jack Small, Floyd Reed, William R. Findling, David Habegger.

EVANSVILLE: Tell City 68–38 Fort Branch; Evansville Lincoln 70–56 Boonville; Tell City 56–46 Lincoln. Officials: Winfield Jacobs, Kenneth Blankenbaker, Robert Rose, Donald Boyer.

FORT WAYNE: Ft. Wayne Central 84–57 Waterloo; Albion 61–59 Berne; Central 87–72 Albion. Officials: Everett Campbell, Frank Carnes, Oscar Samuels, Glen Wisler.

GREENCASTLE: Covington 66–64 Greencastle; Rockville 59–48 Crawfordsville; Covington 87–51 Rockville. Officials: Roland Baker, Robert Davidson, Joseph Hunter, Norman Risley.

HUNTINGBURG: Washington 64–62 Jasper; Carlisle 50–41 Vincennes; Carlisle 35–33 Washington. Officials: Frank Smith, Wendell Baker, Paul Grimes, Robert Cherry.

INDIANAPOLIS: Manual 71–51 North Salem; Tech 62–43 Elwood; Tech 46–45 Manual. Officials: Maurice Criswell, J. Firman Grimes, Marvin Todd, Leland Terrell.

JEFFERSONVILLE: Seymour 77–57 Corydon; New Albany 59–57 Mitchell; New Albany 73–67 Seymour. Officials: James Patterson, John Thomas, Roy Gardnerd Vern Doles.

KOKOMO: Kokomo 82–35 Bunker Hill; Sheridan 37–36 Manchester; Kokomo 46–35 Sheridan. Officials: Jerry Steiner, Roy Kilby, John Hilligoss, Fred Marlow.

LAFAYETTE: Lafayette Jefferson 58–47 Thorntown; Clinton Central 83–53 Fowler; Lafayette 57–50 Clinton Central. Officials Stanley Dubis, Thomas Dean, Lawrence Gradeless, Charles Fouty.

LOGANSPORT: Logansport 69–59 Knox; Brookston 70–42 Goodland: Logansport 69–52 Brookston. Officials: Dee Williams, Dwain Laird, Don Lieberum, Charlie Timmons.

MARION: Oak Hill 54–49 Montpelier; Bluffton 60–50 Huntington; Bluffton 66–63 Oak Hill. Officials: Don McBride, Robert Laird, Dean Geyer, John Sheets.

MARTINSVILLE: Bloomington 62–53 Brazil; Terre Haute Garfield 66–48 Bloomfield; Bloomington 57–50 Garfield. Officials: Lloyd Whipple, Lowell Willis, Cyril Birge, James Schwenk.

NEW CASTLE: Muncie Central 64–36 Parker; Middletown 75–71 Richmond; Muncie Central 112–65 Middletown. Officials: Frank Sanders, Jr., Ira Ray Williams, Don McCoy, Robert Spay.

1960 SEMI—STATES
EVANSVILLE: Tell City 26–24 Carlisle; Bloomington 70–52 New Albany; Bloomington 76–42 Tell City. Officials: Roy Gardner, James Patterson, Jerry Steiner, Paul Grimes, Dee Williams, James Boswell.

IHSAA Scores | 1960–1969

FORT WAYNE: Ft. Wayne Central 68–56 Elkhart; Bluffton 89–85 Kokomo (2ot); Central 93–67 Bluffton. Officials: John Hilligoss, Wesley Oler, Maurice Criswell, Jack Small, Cyril Birge, Robert Rose.
INDIANAPOLIS: Madison 74–60 Rushville; Muncie Central 48–44 Tech; Muncie Central 72–64 Madison. Officials: Lloyd Whipple, Don McCoy, Joe Mullins, Bill Larkin, Stanley Dubis, Frank Smith.
LAFAYETTE: East Chicago Washington 66–59 Logansport; Covington 60–51 Lafayette Jefferson; Washington 77–51 Covington. Officials: Roland Baker, Everett Campbell, Don McBride, Don Lieberum, Marvin Todd, Frank Sanders.

1960 FINALS—March 19

INDIANAPOLIS (Butler Fieldhouse): Muncie Central 102–66 Bloomington; East Chicago Washington 62–61 Fort Wayne Central; East Chicago Washington 75–59 Muncie Central. Officials: Don Lieberum, Robert Rose, Frank Smith, Jerry Steiner, Frank Sanders, James Boswell.

1961 SECTIONALS

ADAMS CENTRAL: Decatur 75–52 Pleasant Mills; Adams Central 72–52 Geneva; Hartford Center 64–61 Monmouth; Berne-French 79–53 Decatur Catholic; Decatur 76–70 Adams Central; Berne-French 56–39 Hartford Center; Berne-French 51–46 Decatur. Officials: Wesley Oler, Richard Gebhart, Harold Ashbrook.
ATTICA: Richland Twp. 68–53 Williamsport; Attica 92–40 Wallace; Veedersburg 58–56 Kingman; Perrysville 48–47 Hillsboro; Covington 77–52 Seeger; Richland 64–52 Pine Village; Attica 68–38 Veedersburg; Perrysville 70–66 Covington; Attica 39–23 Richland; Attica 80–63 Perrysville. Officials: Jack Mercer, George Neff, John Ward.
BEDFORD: Tunnelton 65–49 Huron; Shawswick 77–41 Williams; Mitchell 92–76 Orleans; Bedford 60–48 Oolitic; Paoli 78–57 Heltonville; Marshall Twp. 46–31 Fayetteville; Tunnelton 63–54 Shawswick; Bedford 73–62 Mitchell; Paoli 65–53 Marshall Twp.; Bedford 77–60 Tunnelton; Bedford 74–65 Paoli. Officials: Richard Sweet, Lloyd Whipple, Robert Sweet.
BLUFFTON: Hoagland 65–53 Chester Center; Liberty Center 46–44 Union Center (ot); Ossian 67–50 Lancaster Central; Bluffton 73–47 Rockcreek Center; Petroleum 55–53 Jackson Twp. (ot); Hoagland 66–60 Liberty Center; Bluffton 71–61 Ossian; Petroleum 58–57 Hoagland; Bluffton 43–30 Petroleum. Officials: William May, Robert Henne, Don McBride.
BOONVILLE: Castle 74–44 Lynnville; Tennyson 53–51 Elberfeld; Luce Twp. 58–45 Selvin; Boonville 76–70 Millersburg; Castle 63–40 Tennyson; Boonville 68–31 Luce Twp.; Castle 62–61 Boonville. Officials: Charles Sallee, Donald Lynch, William Bateman.
BROWNSBURG: Amo 40–35 Charlton; North Salem 42–33 Pittsboro; Avon 59–37 Stilesville; Clayton 60–58 Brownsburg; Danville 72–58 Lizton; Plainfield 72–49 New Winchester; North Salem 70–65 Amo; Clayton 48–36 Avon; Plainfield 71–53 Danville; Clayton 59–56 North Salem; Plainfield 58–52 Clayton. Officials: Charles Stumpf, John Thomas, John Priest.
CARMEL: Sheridan 60–52 Jackson Central; Noblesville 71–59 Fishers; Tipton 57–49 Walnut Grove; Westfield 43–36 Windfall; Carmel 64–58 Sharpsville; Noblesville 66–64 Sheridan (2ot); Westfield 58–50 Tipton; Noblesville 61–59 Carmel; Noblesville 79–62 Westfield. Officials: John

Tourney Time

Fee, Richard Foster, Winfield Jacobs.

CHESTERTON: Chesterton 60–55 Kouts; Jackson Twp. 52–51 Liberty Twp. (ot); Morgan Twp. 76–50 Wheeler; Portage Twp. 73–39 Washington Twp.; Valparaiso 80–61 Hebron; Chesterton 55–43 Boone Grove; Jackson Twp. 61–56 Morgan Twp.; Valparaiso 68–57 Portage Twp.; Chesterton 93–43 Jackson Twp.; Valparaiso 52–44 Chesterton. Officials: Robert Brees, Gary Nelson, John Gassensmith.

CHURUBUSCO–HAMILTON: (At Churubusco): Fremont 74–57 Waterloo; Auburn 60–54 Orland; Garrett 70–51 Hamilton; Fremont 76–64 Auburn; (At Hamilton): Angola 76–60 Riverdale; Churubusco 63–43 Salem Center; Butler 64–61 Ashley; Angola 62–60 Churubusco (ot); (At Churubusco): Garrett 62–57 Fremont; Angola 63–47 Butler; Garrett 62–43 Angola. Officials: Carter Caton, Glen Dunn, Edgar Powers, Robert Reed.

CLINTON CENTRAL: Frankfort 68–67 Rossville; Clinton Central 63–31 Colfax; Prairie 54–34 Jefferson (Frankfort); Jackson Twp. 57–43 Jefferson Twp. (Kempton); Frankfort 68–30 Mulberry; Clinton Central 47–42 Prairie; Frankfort 73–58 Jackson Twp.; Frankfort 55–54 Clinton Central. Officials: Robert Wells, James Beyer, Wendell Baker.

COLUMBIA CITY: Mentone 65–41 Larwill; Milford 85–60 Pierceton; Columbia City 82–35 Sidney; Warsaw 63–45 Etna Green; North Webster 94–54 Leesburg; Atwood 51–50 Syracuse; Claypool 40–38 South Whitley; Milford 39–36 Mentone (ot); Columbia City 46–43 Warsaw; North Webster 75–49 Atwood; Milford 68–50 Claypool; Columbia City 66–46 North Webster; Columbia City 71–63 Milford. Officials: Oscar Samuels, Richard Freeman, David Habegger and Don Yager.

COLUMBUS: Hauser 52–47 Waldron; Nashville 69–56 Triton; Columbus 80–52 Helmsburg; Shelbyville 52–33 Southwestern; Nash 49–46 Hauser; Columbus 77–64 Shelbyville; Columbus 61–57 Nashville. Officials: Kenneth Blankenbaker, Mel Pope, Francis Terrell.

CONNERSVILLE: Liberty 80–30 Brownsville; Springfield Twp. 65–50 Alquina; Connersville 72–46 Fayette–Central; Brookville 83–35 Laurel; Whitewater Twp. 47–33 Harrison Twp.; Liberty 66–53 Springfield Twp.; Connersville 65–58 Brookville; Liberty 66–56 Whitewater Twp.; Connersville 62–43 Liberty. Officials: Wray Holbrook, John Holmes, Vern Doles.

CRAWFORDSVILLE: Ladoga 55–46 Waveland; Alamo 46–31 Waynetown; Crawfordsville 45–44 New Market; Ladoga 34–31 Alamo; Darlington 43–36 Coal Creek Central; New Ross 45–43 Linden; Crawfordsville 59–37 Ladoga; New Ross 52–50 Darlington (2ot); New Ross 51–44 Crawfordsville. Officials: John Sheets, Harry Inskeep, James Boswell.

EAST CHICAGO: Hammond Tech 64–40 Dyer; Hammond High 65–50 Noll; East Chicago Roosevelt 56–44 Highland; Griffith 63–59 Tech; Hammond High 79–70 East Chicago Roosevelt; Crown Point 57–44 Lowell; Clark 27–26 Morton; East Chicago Washington 58–45 Whiting; Clark 57–53 Crown Point; Griffith 48–47 Hammond High; East Chicago Washington 59–57 Clark; East Chicago Washington 70–42 Griffith. Officials: Dean Geyer, Donald Edwards, Zeke Williams, Eugene Marks.

ELKHART: Penn 61–58 Millersburg; Baugo Twp. 75–67 New Paris; Shipshewana-Scott 75–58 Jefferson Twp.; Elkhart 73–49 Middlebury; Nappanee 53–43 Wakarusa; Concord 83–29 Topeka; Goshen 79–36 Bristol; Penn 59–43 Baugo Twp.; Elkhart 67–51 Shipshewana-Scott; Concord 86–50 Nappanee; Goshen 77–57 Penn; Elkhart 63–60 Concord; Elkhart 78–44 Goshen. Officials: Stanley Dubis, Anthony Lazar, Glen Wisler, John Arnold.

EVANSVILLE: Central 67–61 North; New Harmony 52–47 North Posey; Mater Dei 64–

48 Memorial; Bosse 66–59 Reitz; Rex Mundi 73–70 Mt. Vernon; Central 71–63 Lincoln; Mater Dei 82–54 New Harmony; Bosse 68–61 Rex Mundi; Central 23–8 Mater Dei; Bosse 55–53 Central. Officials: J. Firman Grimes, Glen Bonsett, William Malloy.

FORT WAYNE: South 79–29 Monroeville; New Haven 69–61 Arcola; Leo 74–65 Bishop Luers; North 62–55 Central Catholic; Concordia 80–60 Harlan; Central 66–42 Elmhurst; Huntertown 56–52 Woodland; South 70–44 New Haven; Leo 66–48 North; Central 74–70 Concordia; South 56–38 Huntertown; Central 58–46 Leo; South 52–46 Central. Officials: Joe Mullins, James Carey, Charles Garber, William Yohler.

FOWLER: Boswell 47–28 Raub; Pine Twp. 61–31 Wadena; Fowler 42–39 Otterbein; Oxford 57–50 Freeland Park; Ambia 68–38 Earl Park; Boswell 63–40 Pine Twp.; Fowler 52–39 Oxford; Ambia 61–45 Boswell; Ambia 72–70 Fowler. Officials: Joe Garoffolo, Eldon Horney, Morris Davis.

GARY: Horace Mann 64–57 Gary Edison; Tolleston 52–49 Emerson; Lew Wallace 78–76 Hobart (2ot); Calumet 62–59 Merrillville; Roosevelt 107–33 River Forest; William A. Wirt 59–51 East Gary Edison Froebel 69–56 Horace Mann; Lew Wallace 55–49 Tolleston; Roosevelt 85–55 Calumet; Froebel 69–49 William A. Wirt; Roosevelt 75–56 Lew Wallace; Roosevelt 66–58 Froebel. Officials: Lawrence Gradeless, Joseph Bella, Burl McKenzie and James Tansey.

GREENCASTLE: Reelsville 72–56 Fillmore; Cloverdale 62–45 Russellville; Bainbridge 62–59 Belle Union; Greencastle 71–62 Roachdale; Cloverdale 75–71 Reelsville; Greencastle 78–39 Bainbridge; Greencastle 75–64 Cloverdale. Officials: Edwin Miller, W. Merle Hill, Richard Pattengale.

GREENSBURG: Greensburg 60–52 Clarksburg; Vernon 56–55 New Point; Jackson Twp. 56–54 Sandcreek; North Vernon 84–57 Burney; St. Paul 75–35 Sandusky; Greensburg 83–47 Vernon; North Vernon 62–59 Jackson Twp.; Greensburg 46–45 St. Paul; North Vernon 75–73 Greensburg. Officials: Earnest Baldwin, Jack Goen, James Ridge.

HUNTINGBURG: Huntingburg 80–55 St. Ferdinand: Ireland 63–47 Otwell; Jasper 97–60 Springs Valley; Holland 81–42 Birdseye; Winslow 42–32 Stendal; Dubois 59–42 Spurgeon; Huntingburg 67–59 Ireland; Jasper 64–52 Holland; Winslow 54–52 Dubois; Jasper 68–57 Huntingburg; Jasper 85–58 Winslow. Officials: Raymond Robison, Harold Gourley, Howard Risley.

HUNTINGTON: Rock Creek 63–61 Andrews; Huntington Twp. 57–41 Lafayette Central; Huntington Catholic 59–46 Jefferson Twp.; Huntington 60–35 Clear Creek; Roanoke 80–61 Union Twp.; Salamonie Twp. 53–52 Lancaster Twp.; Huntington Twp. 87–62 Rock Creek; Huntington 69–41 Huntington Catholic; Roanoke 38–36 Salamonie Twp.; Huntington 78–63 Huntington Twp.; Huntington 57–56 Roanoke. Officials: Gary Muncy, Charlie Timmons, Neal Jay.

INDIANAPOLIS: Ben Davis 76–33 School for the Deaf; Tech 58–57 Shortridge; Scecina 70–68 Pike; Cathedral 77–59 Warren Central; Washington 65–50 Broad Ripple; North Central 50–46 Speedway; Crispus Attucks 71–45 Lawrence; Tech 76–56 Ben Davis; Cathedral 45–36 Scecina; Washington 69–64 North Central (ot); Crispus Attucks 74–50 Tech; Cathedral 61–40 Washington; Crispus Attucks 68–61 Cathedral. Officials: Frank Carnes, Robert Showalter, Wayne Crispen, Bill Hile.

JEFFERSONVILLE: New Albany 68–46 Clarksville; Silver Creek 46–43 Jeffersonville; Henryville 45–43 Charlestown; Providence 72–66 Georgetown; New Washington 50–47 Borden;

Tourney Time

Silver Creek 58–49 New Al;bany; Providence 59–50 Henryville; Silver Creek 70–32 New Washington; Silver Creek 50–39 Providence. Officials: L. C. Thorne, Ralph Box, Roland Baker.

KENDALLVILLE: Cromwell 68–45 Springfield Twp.; Ligonier 65–50 Brighton; Wawaka 64–56 Lima (ot); LaGrange 56–47 Howe Military; Avilla 71–56 Wolf Lake; Rome City 63–53 Albion; Kendallville 83–45 Wolcottville; Ligonier 69–40 Cromwell; Wawaka 53–49 LaGrange (ot); Avilla 59–44 Rome City; Kendallville 55–44 Ligonier; Avilla 79–46 Wawaka; Kendallville 63–46 Avilla. Officials: Gene Butts, Kent Adams, Lewis Goshert, William Goshert.

KENTLAND: Goodland 63–56 Tefft; Wheatfield 58–56 Brook; Fair Oaks 70–56 Remington; DeMotte 63–54 Mt. Ayr; Rensselaer 44–43 Kentland; Morocco 47–45 Goodland; Wheatfield 95–55 Fair Oaks; Rensselaer 58–46 DeMotte; Wheatfield 73–63 Morocco; Rensselaer 82–71 Wheatfield. Officials: Noble Benbow, Howard Cosand, Jonnie Webber.

KOKOMO: Eastern 65–50 Camden; Kokomo 70–38 Delphi; Western 51–46 Burlington; Flora 64–49 Northwestern; Kokomo 76–41 Eastern; Flora 62–61 Western (ot); Kokomo 95–52 Flora. Officials: Frank Sanders, Roy Kilby, Ned Brenizer.

LAFAYETTE: Southwestern 83–63 Dayton; Battle Ground 64–50 Lauramie Twp.; West Lafayette 80–68 Montmorenci; Lafayette Jefferson 69–40 Central Catholic; Klondike 63–59 East Tipp; Battle Ground 69–62 Southwestern; Lafayette Jefferson 59–47 West Lafayette; Battle Ground 56–41 Klondike; Lafayette Jefferson 98–43 Battle Ground. Officials. Darl March, John Zehring, Bill Larkin.

LOGANSPORT: Washington Twp. 41–38 Royal Center; Metea 59–57 Galveston; Twelve Mile 64–39 Lucerne; Tipton Twp. 54–51 Grass Creek; Logansport 91–47 Kewanna; Washington Twp. 69–43 Young America; Twelve Mile 50–48 Metea; Logansport 79–54 Tipton Twp.; Twelve Mile 68–46 Washington Twp.; Logansport 56–38 Twelve Mile. Officials: Marvin Todd, Walter Swift, Leo Ponto.

MADISON: Madison 96–36 Lexington; Scottsburg 59–58 Southwestern; Austin 62–47 Deputy; Paris Crossing 57–51 Dupont; Madison 73–67 Shawe Memorial; Austin 61–45 Scottsburg; Madison 86–44 Paris Crossing; Madison 89–61 Austin. Officials: Clifford Runnebohm, Paul Grimes, Darrell McFall.

MADISON HEIGHTS: Elwood 35–33 Highland (ot); Anderson 53–46 Lapel; Madison Heights 68–67 Frankton; Elwood 48–44 Anderson; Markleville 56–39 Pendleton; Alexandria 44–38 Summitville; St. Mary's 67–59 Markleville; Elwood 80–76 Madison Heights; Alexandria 62–38 St. Mary's; Alexandria 62–40 Elwood. Officials: Gerald Strickler, Thomas Dean, Allen Voorhis.

MANCHESTER: Urbana 92–53 Roann; Noble 79–51 Silver Lake; Somerset 77–37 Lagro; Laketon 66–62 Manchester; LaFontaine 77–61 White's; Wabash 92–77 Urbana; Noble 72–42 Somerset; LaFontaine 84–79 Laketon; Wabash 77–68 Noble; Wabash 74–73 LaFontaine. Officials: Maurice Criswell, Lauren Griffith, Robert Wendt.

MARION: Oak Hill 72–42 Van Buren; Mississinewa 79–46 Bennett; Swayzee 60–47 Fairmount; Marion 54–49 Jefferson Twp.; Oak Hill 76–60 Mississinewa; Marion 51–46 Swayzee; Oak Hill 69–52 Marion. Officials: Arthur Thompson, Robert Dornte, Maurice Davis.

MARTINSVILLE: University 49–46 Mooresville; Martinsville 70–60 Unionville; Ellettsville 66–51 Monrovia; Bloomington 65–38 Stinesville; Eminence 71–43 Smithville; University 71–62 Morgantown; Ellettsville 59–57 Martinsville; Bloomington 62–49 Eminence; Ellettsville 68–57 University; Ellettsville 68–57 Bloomington. Officials: Donald Boyer, Gilbert Beagle, John Bush.

IHSAA Scores | *1960–1969*

MICHIGAN CITY: Westville 67–45 Hanna; LaCrosse 74–58 Union Mills; LaPorte 64–38 Stillwell; Michigan City 91–44 Kingsbury; Mill Creek 49–46 Rolling Prairie; St. Mary's 71–46 Wanatah; Union Twp. 68–50 Clinton Twp.; LaCrosse 63–61 Westville; Michigan City 68–56 LaPorte; St. Mary's 43–42 Mill Creek; Union Twp. 89–54 LaCrosse; Michigan City 99–49 St. Mary's; Michigan City 78–42 Union Twp. Officials: Ernest Sohl, Ralph E. Cox, Thomas Hoffman, Ronald Jones.

MILAN: Holton 60–50 Versailles; Sunman 58–57 Batesville; New Marion 55–53 Milan (2ot); Jac-Cen-Del 65–61 Cross Plains; Sunman 61–38 Holton; New Marion 60–56 Jac-Cen-Del; New Marion 54–51 Sunman. Officials: Gerl Furr, Max Andress, Jack Cummings.

MISHAWAKA: New Carlisle 39–32 Green Twp.; North Liberty 69–53 Madison Twp.; Mishawaka 50–41 South Bend St. Joseph; North Liberty 60–55 New Carlisle; South Bend Washington 69–62 Riley; Adams 59–39 Washington-Clay; Central 66–41 Lakeville; Washington 58–57 Adams; Mishawaka 66–59 North Liberty; Central 68–65 Washington; Central 73–56 Mishawaka. Officials: Walter Oliver, Robert Kramer, Jack Small.

MONON: Brookston 49–44 Monon; Francesville 79–65 Idaville; Reynolds 56–45 Monticello; Burnettsville 59–40 Chalmers; Wolcott 69–46 Buffalo; Brookston 61–54 Francesville; Reynolds 61–53 Burnettsville; Brookston 57–51 Wolcott; Brookston 63–55 Reynolds. Officials: John Sebastian, George Avery, Robert Spay.

MUNCIE: Royerton 39–31 Eaton; Daleville 65–59 Cowan (ot); DeSoto 66–56 Yorktown; Central 96–28 Center; Harrison Twp. 55–48 Selma; Burris 57–52 Gaston; Royerton 43–39 Albany (ot); DeSoto 63–62 Daleville; Central 62–33 Harrison Twp.; Burris 80–74 Royerton; Central 84–40 DeSoto; Central 80–37 Muncie Burris. Officials: James Patterson, James Ruby, Fred Marlow, Don Hollman.

NEW CASTLE: Wilkinson 61–59 Sulphur Springs; Lewisville 72–70 Middletown; Mt. Summit 60–47 Cadiz; New Castle 81–46 Straughn; Mooreland 54–49 Spiceland; Knightstown 67–55 Wilkinson; Lewisville 81–61 Mt. Summit; New Castle 79–67 Mooreland; Lewisville 76–60 Knightstown; Lewisville 56–49 New Castle. Officials: Homer Owens, Robert Cherry, Charles Lentz.

PERU: Peru 99–40 Deedsville; Gilead 92–65 Beaver 60–57 Chili; Clay Twp. 68–63 Bunker Hill; Mexico 65–56 Fulton; Peru 64–35 Gilead; Akron 53–51 Clay Twp.; Peru 69–36 Mexico; Peru 108–50 Akron. Officials: Floyd Reed, William Farrar, Jimmy Dimitroff.

PLYMOUTH: Tippecanoe 43–42 Talma; Bremen 45–44 Plymouth; Bourbon 59–57 Richland Center (ot); Bremen 73–56 Tippecanoe; Argos 61–53 West Twp.; Rochester 66–57 LaPaz; Culver 88–76 Tyson; Rochester 65–34 Argos; Bremen 70–53 Bourbon; Rochester 77–69 Culver; Bremen 71–68 Rochester. Officials: William Ryan, Johannes Dienelt, Richard Swartz.

PORTLAND: Portland 65–57 Pennville; Dunkirk 79–44 Poling; Hartford City 65–51 Montpelier; Redkey 59–58 Madison Twp.; Bryant 69–56 Roll; Portland 77–40 Gray; Dunkirk 60–59 Hartford City; Redkey 43–41 Bryant; Dunkirk 84–66 Portland; Dunkirk 70–56 Redkey. Officials: Don Lieberum, Harold Braden, Dale Van Houten.

PRINCETON: Ft. Branch 65–47 Mt. Olympus; Princeton 61–48 Francisco; Patoka 60–48 Hazelton; Haubstadt 60–54 Owensville; Oakland City 57–56 Mackey (ot); Ft. Branch 64–62 Princeton; Haubstadt 58–57 Patoka; Ft. Branch 92–58 Oakland City; Haubstadt 14–12 Ft. Branch (3ot). Officials: Lester Cornwell, Kenneth Payne, Lowell Smith.

RICHMOND: Centerville 91–39 Webster; Whitewater 103–25 Economy; Richmond 82–38

Tourney Time

Boston; Fountain City 71–60 Milton; Hagerstown 86–43 Greens Fork; Cambridge City 57–47 Williamsburg; Centerville 74–67 Whitewater; Richmond 66–62 Fountain City; Cambridge City 57–47 Hagerstown; Centerville 56–53 Richmond; Cambridge City 60–56 Centerville. Officials: James Benecke, Dwain Laird, Gerald Imel.

RISING SUN: Rising Sun 72–55 Aurora; Vevay 99–25 Patriot; Dillsboro 77–52 North Dearborn; Lawrenceburg 84–57 Moores Hill; Rising Sun 67–56 Vevay; Dillsboro 55–51 Lawrenceburg; Dillsboro 69–64 Rising Sun. Officials: Richard Tiernan, Jim Ladd, Don Snedeker.

ROCKVILLE: Mecca 34–33 Hillsdale; Clinton 92–49 Cayuga; Rosedale 66–31 St. Bernice; Montezuma 54–46 Newport; Rockville 53–52 Turkey Run; Dana 68–38 Mecca; Clinton 63–60 Rosedale; Montezuma 47–44 Rockville; Clinton 77–71 Dana; Clinton 68–62 Montezuma (ot). Officials: Jerry Steiner, Darrell Snodgrass, Donald Call.

RUSHVILLE: Rushville 73–57 Morton Memorial; Morristown 84–60 Arlington; New Salem 56–52 Milroy; Manilla 57–40 Carthage; Charlottesville 57–55 Mays; Morristown 67–62 Rushville; New Salem 57–53 Manilla; Morristown 72–67 Charlottesville; Morristown 76–56 New Salem. Officials: John Williams, Royce McCullough, Russell Owens.

SALEM: Pekin 64–59 Lanesville; South Central 66–52 Hardinsburg; Corydon 60–58 Milltown; Campbellsburg 81–43 Marengo; Salem 64–48 North Central; English 40–39 Morgan Twp.; Pekin 78–45 South Central; Corydon 79–74 Campbellsburg; Salem 65–51 English; Corydon 74–73 Pekin (ot); Corydon 78–68 Salem. Officials: Alan Smith, James Schwenk, Wallace Reeve.

SEYMOUR: Brownstown 58–47 Crothersville; Seymour 53–35. Cortland; Clearspring 66–51 Freetown; Tampico 82–62 Medora; Vallonia 60–58 Brownstown; Seymour 63–56 Clearspring; Vallonia 80–64 Tampico; Seymour 73–52 Vallonia. Officials: Marvin Cave, John Masariu, Grayson Mahin.

SOUTHPORT: Hancock Central 74–56 Indianapolis Howe; Indianapolis Manual 64–44 New Palestine; Greenfield 56–50 Indianapolis Sacred Heart; Franklin Central 79–46 Mt. Comfort; Beech Grove 70–52 Decatur Central; Southport 39–37 Indianapolis Wood; Vernon Twp. 67–54 Hancock Central; Indianapolis Manual 76–49 Greenfield; Franklin Central 68–43 Beech Grove; Vernon Twp. 54–42 Southport; Indianapolis Manual 61–35 Franklin Central; Indianapolis Manual 58–41 Vernon Twp. Officials: John Hilligoss, Don Hurst, Everett Campbell, Marion Acton.

SPENCER: Spencer 70–52 Gosport; Cory 51–46 Coal City; Coalmont 56–51 Patricksburg; Staunton 73–71 Bowling Green; Brazil 69–59 Van Buren; Clay City 64–46 Freedom; Spencer 66–41 Cory; Coalmont 69–63 Staunton; Brazil 82–46 Clay City; Spencer 48–43 Coalmont; Brazil 63–44 Spencer. Officials: Harold Mason, Lowell Willis, Julian Piercefield.

SULLIVAN: Sullivan 42–21 Pimento; North Central 54–44 Blackhawk; Carlisle 49–46 Pleasantville; Prairie Creek 58–35 Hymera; Graysville 52–42 Dugger; North Central 61–59 Sullivan; Carlisle 46–29 Prairie Creek; North Central 67–44 Graysville; North Central 51–48 Carlisle. Officials: Danny Jacobs, Ben Olsson, Leland Terrell.

SWITZ CITY: Worthington 49–40 Solsberry; Midland 56–54 Switz City; Linton 79–42 Jasonville; Bloomfield 66–38 L & M; Worthington 62–48 Midland; Bloomfield 53–49 Linton; Bloomfield 71–55 Worthington. Officials: Cyril Birge, Donald Hubbard, Earle Wolfe.

TELL CITY: Tell City 73–36 Oil Twp.; Dale 59–45 Leavenworth; Cannelton 48–46 Rockport; Chrisney 47–40 Bristow; Tell City 76–40 Dale; Cannelton 68–48 Chrisney; Tell City 58–47 Cannelton. Officials: Norman Risley, Ivan Risley, James DeGroote,

TERRE HAUTE: Otter Creek 45–44 Honey Creek; Glenn 75–47 West Vigo; Laboratory 73–48 Riley; Gerstmeyer 69–65 Wiley; Garfield 65–55 Fontanet; Schulte 66–46 New Goshen; Glenn 78–61 Otter Creek; Gerstmeyer 54–44 Laboratory; Garfield 64–55 Schulte; Gerstmeyer 46–42 Glenn; Gerstmeyer 87–71 Garfield. Officials: James Eads, Robert Rose, Carl Petercheff.

VINCENNES: Wheatland 54–53 Bicknell; Edwardsport 51–43 Sandborn; Monroe City 79–55 Bruceville; Vincennes 88–54 Central Catholic; Freelandville 65–41 Oaktown; Decker Chapel 62–56 Decker; Wheatland 43–41 Fritchton; Monroe City 52–49 Edwardsport; Vincennes 62–46 Freelandville; Decker Chapel 38–37 Wheatland; Monroe City 93–78 Vincennes; Monroe City 60–49 Decker Chapel. Officials: Roger Emmert, William Bitzegaio, Norman Shields, Wayne Myers.

WASHINGTON: Odon 76–68 St. John's; Washington 71–63 Petersburg; Washington Catholic 56–38 Epsom; Plainville 70–41 Elnora; Loogootee 52–14 Alfordsville; Shoals 62–61 Barr Twp.; Washington 81–56 Odon; Washington Catholic 66–59 Plainville; Loogootee 57–40 Shoals; Washington 62–58 Washington Catholic; Loogootee 72–46 Washington. Officials: Lloyd Baugh, Donald Shiflet, Robert Davidson.

WHITELAND: Trafalgar 57–54 Center Grove (ot). Greenwood 57–46 Franklin; Clark Twp. 43–40 Union Twp.; Edinburg 66–41 Nineveh; Whiteland 49–42 Trafalgar; Greenwood 56–53 Clark Twp; Edinburg 66–64 Whiteland; Greenwood 54–35 Edinburg. Officials: James Davis, Frank Smith, Howard Plough.

WINAMAC: Monterey 77–46 Walkerton; Knox 70–40 Aubbeenaubbee Twp.; Hamlet 60–40 Grovertown; North Judson 42–30 Star City; Winamac 52–44 Medaryville; Monterey 62–34 San Pierre; Knox 72–47 Hamlet; North Judson 43–35 Winamac; Monterey 67–57 Knox; Monterey 51–46 North Judson. Officials: Victor Wukovits, Ray Nemeth, Harry Green.

WINCHESTER: Driver 72–65 Lynn; Parker 53–45 Union; Union City-Wayne 81–51 Spartanburg; Ward-Jackson 68–65 Ridgeville; Farmland 55–53 Driver; Parker 65–62 Union City-Wayne; Ward-Jackson 60–58 Farmland; Ward-Jackson 66–65 Parker. Officials: Robert Cowan, Robert Laird, William Findling.

ZIONSVILLE: Thorntown 62–53 Zionsville; Pinnell 66–24 Perry Central; Whitestown 55–42 Dover; Lebanon 68–47 Wells; Thorntown 40–31 Pinnell; Lebanon 85–40 Whitestown; Lebanon 62–58 Thorntown. Officials: Charles Fouty, Eugene Lillie, Bob Fisher.

1961 REGIONALS

BLOOMINGTON: Brazil 75–64 Terre Haute Gerstmeyer; Bloomfield 63–56 Ellettsville; Bloomfield 51–48 Brazil. Officials: Robert Spay, Arthur Thompson, John Fee, Norman Risley.

COLUMBUS: Madison 72–58 North Vernon; Columbus 76–41 Greenwood; Columbus 63–59 Madison. Officials: Robert Rose, Lowell Willis, Lloyd Whipple, James Schwenk.

CONNERSVILLE: Connersville 90–65 Dillsboro; New Marion 66–54 Morristown; Connersville 66–59 New Marion. Officials: Don Lieberum, David Habegger, Paul Grimes, Floyd Reed.

COVINGTON: New Ross 57–47 Attica; Greencastle 74–52 Clinton; New Ross 64–45 Greencastle. Officials: Wesley Oler, Wendell Baker, Maurice Criswell, Leland Terrell.

EAST CHICAGO: Michigan City 52–50 Valparaiso; Gary Roosevelt 66–60 East Chicago Washington; Gary Roosevelt 77–68 Michigan City. Officials: Jack Small, John Sheets, Frank Sanders, Roy Kilby.

Tourney Time

ELKHART: Elkhart 80–37 Bremen; Columbia City 67–65 South Bend Central; Elkhart 54–52 Columbia City. Officials: Wayne Crispen, Frank Carnes, Everett Campbell, Charlie Timmons.
EVANSVILLE: Tell City 47–37 Haubstadt; Evansville Bosse 68–54 Castle; Tell City 56–53 Bosse. Officials: Roland Baker, Donald Shiflet, Frank Smith, Charles Fouty.
FORT WAYNE: Berne 68–58 Garrett; Ft. Wayne South Side 62–54 Kendallville; Berne 56–42 South Side. Officials: Lawrence Gradeless, Victor Wukovits, Thomas Dean, Dean Geyer.
HUNTINGBURG: Jasper 50–46 Loogootee; Monroe City 53–51 North Central; Jasper 76–75 Monroe City. Officials: James Patterson. Kenneth Blankenbaker, Jerry Steiner, J.F. Grimes.
INDIANAPOLIS: Crispus Attucks 53–43 Alexandria; Manual 66–54 Plainfield; Manual 55–44 Crispus Attucks. Officials: Joe Mullins, Glen Wisler, Winfield Jacobs, Robert Cherry.
JEFFERSONVILLE: Corydon 59–56 Seymour; Silver Creek 65–60 Bedford; Corydon 75–62 Silver Creek. Officials: Cyril Birge, Roger Emmert, Robert Davidson, Donald Boyer.
KOKOMO: Kokomo 95–64 Peru; Noblesville 77–62 Wabash; Kokomo 92–59 Noblesville. Officials: James Boswell, John Thomas, John Williams, Zeke Williams.
LAFAYETTE: Lebanon 91–47 Ambia; Frankfort 67–62 Lafayette Jefferson (ot); Lebanon 87–71 Frankfort. Officials: Homer Owens, Robert Laird, Gerald Strickler, William Findling.
LOGANSPORT: Monterey 68–58 Brookston; Logansport 76–62 Rensselaer; Logansport 72–56 Monterey. Officials: Don McBride, Oscar Samuels, Stanley Dubis, Robert Kramer.
MARION: Huntington 69–56 Dunkirk; Bluffton 71–69 Oak Hill; Huntington 70–59 Bluffton. Officials: John Hilligoss, James Beyer, Fred Marlow, Dwain Laird.
NEW CASTLE: Muncie Central 56–33 Cambridge City; Lewisville 47–33 Ward-Jackson; Muncie Central 50–41 Lewisville. Officials: Bill Larkin, Jimmy Dimitroff, Marvin Todd, Vern Doles.

1961 SEMI–STATES

EVANSVILLE: Tell City 62–53 Bloomfield; Jasper 86–65 Corydon; Tell City 64–60 Jasper. Officials: Jerry Steiner, Wayne Crispen, Joe Mullins, Wesley Oler, James Boswell, Robert Rose.
FORT WAYNE: Berne 66–52 Elkhart; Kokomo 85–55 Huntington; Kokomo 75–63 Berne. Officials: Jack Small, Paul Grimes, Homer Owens, Winfield Jacobs, Stanley Dubis, Bill Larkin.
INDIANAPOLIS: Manual 61–49 Connersville; Muncie Central 77–66 Columbus; Manual 62–59 Muncie Central. Officials: Frank Sanders, Lloyd Whipple, Cyril Birge, Maurice Criswell, Marvin Todd, John Hilligoss.
LAFAYETTE: Logansport 83–51 New Ross; Lebanon 62–61 Gary Roosevelt; Logansport 84–65 Lebanon. Officials: Don Lieberum, Lawrence Gradeless, Don McBride, Roland Baker, James Patterson, Everett Campbell.

1961 FINALS—March 18

INDIANAPOLIS (Butler Fieldhouse): Indianapolis Manual 70–55 Tell City; Kokomo 87–66 Logansport; Kokomo 68–66 Manual (ot). Officials: Jack Small. Paul Grimes, James Boswell, Jerry Steiner, Don Lieberum, Frank Smith.

IHSAA Scores | 1960–1969

1962 SECTIONALS

ADAMS CENTRAL: Decatur Catholic 66–57 Adams Central; Decatur 84–57 Geneva; Monmouth 65–52 Hartford Center; Berne-French 71–54 Pleasant Mills; Decatur 67–63 Decatur Catholic; Berne-French 81–62 Monmouth; Berne-French 75–59 Decatur. Officials: Roy Kilby, Eugene Lillie, Melvin Fuller.

ANDERSON: Alexandria 58–50 Frankton; Highland 61–51 Lapel; St. Mary's 42–41 Madison Heights; Anderson 88–47 Summitville; Pendleton 65–54 Elwood; Markleville 56–55 Alexandria; Highland 56–48 St. Mary's; Anderson 57–56 Pendleton (ot); Markleville 79–57 Highland; Anderson 87–81 Markleville. Officials: Frank Sanders, Howard Risley, Edwin Miller, Charles Northam.

ANGOLA: Auburn 72–53 Orland; Angola 72–63 Churubusco; Ashley 57–54 Waterloo; Angola 57–56 Auburn; Butler 67–48 Riverdale; Fremont 58–41 Salem Center; Garrett 51–32 Hamilton; Butler 67–65 Fremont; Butler 56–54 Garrett; Angola 70–43 Ashley; Angola 63–57 Butler. Officials: Lawrence Gradeless, Richard Morrison, Joseph Bella, Richard Gebhart.

BEDFORD: Marshall Twp. 56–55 Paoli (ot); Bedford 67–46 Mitchell; Tunnelton 103–80 Orleans; Huron 79–46 Fayetteville; Oolitic 88–65 Williams; Shawswick 86–45 Heltonville; Bedford 53–51 Marshall Twp.; Tunnelton 74–60 Huron; Shawswick 58–56 Oolitic; Bedford 73–62 Tunnelton; Bedford 81–68 Shawswick. Officials: Roger Emmert, Darrell McFall, Herod Toon, James DeGroote.

BLUFFTON: Hoagland 70–58 Lancaster Central; Liberty Center 68–61 Union Center; Rock Creek 65–52 Jackson Twp.; Bluffton 72–60 Chester Center; Ossian 49–31 Petroleum; Liberty Center 74–67 Hoagland; Bluffton 76–62 Rock Creek; Ossian 62–57 Liberty Center (2ot); Bluffton 68–58 Ossian. Officials: Robert Cowan, Harold Ashbrook, Lauren Griffith.

BOONVILLE: Millersburg 73–53 Elberfeld; Boonville 90–55 Lynnville; Tennyson 52–42 Selvin; Castle 77–43 Luce Twp.; Boonville 105–64 Millersburg; Castle 63–27 Tennyson; Castle 84–51 Boonville. Officials: Norman Shields, Earle Wolfe, William Fields.

BROWNSBURG: Stilesville 62–53 Amo; Danville 55–54 Avon; Clayton 64–46 North Salem; Charlton 51–44 Lizton; Plainfield 52–48 New Winchester; Pittsboro 61–53 Brownsburg; Danville 76–52 Stilesville; Clayton 73–55 Charlton; Plainfield 85–65 Pittsboro; Danville 40–37 Clayton; Plainfield 51–49 Danville. Officials: James Beyer, John Mikels, Eldon Horney, John Ward.

CARMEL: Tipton 62–51 Sheridan; Jackson Central 59–54 Fishers; Noblesville 79–61 Walnut Grove; Carmel 68–40 Westfield; Tipton 86–71 Jackson Central; Noblesville 61–52 Carmel; Noblesville 79–73 Tipton. Officials: John Hilligoss, Gene Butts, Don Snedeker.

CHESTERTON: Hebron 61–37 Liberty Twp.; Chesterton 71–43 Boone Grove; Valparaiso 68–33 Washington Twp.; Portage 76–57 Morgan Twp.; Kouts 70–50 Wheeler; Hebron 60–59 Jackson Twp.; Valparaiso 62–61 Chesterton; Portage 58–45 Kouts; Valparaiso 77–56 Hebron; Valparaiso 68–57 Portage. Officials: Jack Small, George Avery, Donald Edwards, Zeke Williams.

CLAY CITY: Spencer 80–57 Patricksburg; Brazil 59–58 Gosport. Clay City 74–70 Coal City; Bowling Green 58–56 (ot); Freedom 57–56 Van Buren; Spencer 55–50 Brazil; Bowling Green 67–48 Clay City; Spencer 65–52 Freedom; Spencer 82–51 Bowling Green. Officials: Lester Cornwell, Robert Davidson, William Bateman.

CLINTON: Clinton 56–40 Turkey Run; Cayuga 58–55 Montezuma; Rockville 96–35 Mecca; Rosedale 63–43 Newport; Clinton 67–51 Cayuga; Rockville 66–37 Rosedale; Rockville 61–54 Clinton. Officials: Walter Swift, Joseph Garoffolo, George Neff.

399

Tourney Time

CLINTON CENTRAL: Rossville 94–64 Lauramie Twp.; Clinton Prairie 88–46 Dayton; Jefferson Twp. 57–40 Prairie Twp.; Frankfort 75–69 Clinton Central; Rossville 80–77 Clinton Prairie; Frankfort 72–40 Jefferson Twp.; Rossville 83–57 Frankfort. Officials: Lewis Goshert, Charles Sallee, Gary Muncy.

COLUMBIA CITY: South Whitley 53–50 Etna Green; North Webster 79–42 Sidney; Warsaw 64–52 Pierceton; Syracuse 83–64 Milford; Claypool 61–50 Atwood; Columbia City 76–58 Larwill; Mentone 83–50 Leesburg; South Whitley 64–42 North Webster; Warsaw 68–63 Syracuse; Columbia City 62–55 Claypool; Mentone 56–39 South Whitley; Warsaw 61–51 Columbia City; Mentone 65–61 Warsaw. Officials: Earnest Baldwin, Harold Braden, William Ryan, Neal Jay.

COLUMBUS: Shelbyville 57–55 Hauser; Waldron 67–46 Southwestern; Columbus 84–56 Ninevah; Brown County 65–55 Triton; Shelbyville 61–59 Waldron (ot); Brown County 66–63 Columbus; Shelbyville 86–70 Brown County. Officials: James Boswell, John Holmes, James Davis.

CONNERSVILLE: Liberty 68–43 Fayette Central; Whitewater Twp.69–50 Milton; Alquina 56–43 Laurel; Connersville 65–51 Brookville; Liberty 71–58 Whitewater Twp.; Connersville 65–44 Alquina; Connersville 90–54 Liberty. Officials: Don McBride, Allen Voorhis, Maurice Gardner.

COVINGTON: Seeger 70–63 Williamsport; Pine Village 63–44 Wallace; Attica 75–39 Kingman; Perrysville 70–55 Veedersburg; Hillsboro 53–48 Richland Twp.; Seegar 47–45 Covington; Attica 91–63 Pine Village; Perrysville 62–46 Hillsboro; Attica 69–41 Seegar; Attica 86–64 Perrysville. Officials: Mel Pope, Donald Lynch, Jerry Baker, Lowell Willis.

CRAWFORDSVILLE: Ladoga 60–37 Coal Creek Central; Waynetown 51–49 New Market; Crawfordsville 54–43 Waveland; Ladoga 64–52 Waynetown; New Ross 94–56 Alamo; Darlington 56–46 Linden; Ladoga 52–46 Crawfordsville; New Ross 79–52 Darlington: New Ross 60–46 Ladoga. Officials: Dwain Laird, Francis Terrell, John Fee.

EAST CHICAGO: Hammond Noll 69–42 Dyer; Hammond Clark 64–43 Highland; Lowell 68–65 Tech; East Chicago Washington 90–67 Noll; Clark 65–59 Lowell; Hammond High 83–59 Crown Point; Whiting 67–45 Griffith; Morton 81–50 East Chicago Roosevelt; Whiting 57–46 Hammond High; East Chicago Washington 68–51 Clark; Morton 65–60 Whiting; East Chicago Washington 91–65 Morton. Officials: Ray Nemeth, James Tansey, John Gassensmith, Richard Swartz.

ELKHART: Penn 62–48 Wakarusa; Concord 70–56 Bristol; Goshen 92–37 Topeka; New Paris 68–35 Shipshewana-Scott; Middlebury 60–59 Nappanee; Baugo Twp. 75–50 Millersburg; Elkhart 91–34 Jefferson; Penn 69–59 Concord; Goshen 70–52 New Paris; Baugo Twp. 87–70 Middlebury; Elkhart 84–47 Penn; Goshen 64–54 Baugo Twp.; Elkhart 80–62 Goshen. Officials: Robert Spay, Robert Reed, Eugene Marks, Robert Kramer.

EVANSVILLE: Central 85–57 Mt. Vernon; Bosse 92–56 North Posey; Reitz 68–67 Lincoln; Mater Dei 69–51 New Harmony; North 61–46 Memorial; Rex Mundi 79–49 Central; Bosse 68–57 Reitz; North 82–54 Mater Dei; Bosse 57–54 Rex Mundi; Bosse 88–71 North. Officials: Robert Rose, L.C. Thorne, Richard Sweet, Don Shiflet.

FORT WAYNE: Central 73–50 Concordia; Central Catholic 61–49 Woodlan; New Haven 69–55 Leo; Elmhurst 51–42 South Side; Monroeville 67–60 Harlan; North Side 44–27 Huntertown; Bishop Luers 45–43 Arcola; Central 70–59 Central Catholic; Elmhurst 72–59 New Haven; North

IHSAA Scores | 1960–1969

Side 69–37 Monroeville; Central 81–64 Bishop Luers; Elmhurst 49–46 North Side; Central 71–57 Elmhurst. Officials: Dean Geyer, Marvin Cave, William Goshert, Charlie Timmons.

FRANKLIN: Union Twp. 55–49 Clark Twp.; Franklin 63–47 Whiteland; Center Grove 68–47 Edinburg; Greenwood 77–62 Trafalgar; Franklin 41–28 Union Twp.; Greenwood 64–48 Center Grove; Franklin 56–47 Greenwood. Officials: Richard Foster, Danny Jacobs, Robert Wells.

GARY: Tolleston 74–34 River Forest; Calumet 67–60 Hobart; Lew Wallace 72–60 Emerson; Roosevelt 78–55 Wirt; Horace Mann 63–61 Merrillville; Froebel 91–43 Gary Edison; East Gary Edison 67–46 Andrean; Tolleston 81–48 Calumet; Roosevelt 57–55 Lew Wallace; Froebel 77–46 Horace Mann; Tolleston 61–58 East Gary Edison; Froebel 89–60 Roosevelt; Froebel 67–53 Tolleston. Officials: Maurice Criswell, John Sheets, Ronald Hosinski, Edgar Powers.

GREENCASTLE: Cloverdale 52–50 Reelsville; Greencastle 54–44 Fillmore; Bainbridge 86–71 Roachdale; Belle Union 64–53 Russellville; Greencastle 57–36 Cloverdale; Bainbridge 77–57 Belle Union; Bainbridge 94–72 Greencastle. Officials: Jimmy Dimitroff, Darrell Snodgrass, Ben Olsson.

GREENSBURG: Sandusky 66–52 Vernon; St. Paul 64–33 Clarksburg; Burney 75–45 New Point; Jackson Twp. 72–61 North Vernon; Greensburg 59–52 Sandcreek; St. Paul 67–60 Sandusky; Jackson Twp. 79–48 Burney; Greensburg 43–37 St. Paul; Greensburg 64–47 Jackson Twp. Officials: James Ruby, Jack Longnecker, Richard Tiernan.

HUNTINGBURG: Dubois 81–48 Spurgeon; Jasper 91–38 Birdseye; St. Ferdinand 49–45 Holland (ot); Huntingburg 63–48 Otwell; Ireland 85–47 Stendal; Springs Valley 91–50 Winslow; Jasper 75–62 Dubois; St. Ferdinand 60–53 Huntingburg; Ireland 75–59 Springs Valley; Jasper 75–62 St. Ferdinand; Jasper 59–51 Ireland. Officials: Charles Fouty, William Bitzegaio, Kenneth Payne, Lowell Smith.

HUNTINGTON: Roanoke 74–49 Clear Creek; Andrews 74–55 Huntington Twp.; Huntington 75–58 Lancaster Twp.; Union Twp. 53–46 Lafayette Central; Huntington Catholic 63–50 Jefferson Twp.; Salamonie Twp. 63–40 Rock Creek; Roanoke 72–71 Andrews; Huntington 75–46 Union Twp.; Huntington Catholic 56–45 Salamonie Twp.; Huntington 71–47 Roanoke; Huntington 62–58 Huntington Catholic. Officials: Jerry Steiner, Art Thompson, Jonnie Webber, Kent Adams.

INDIANAPOLIS: Crispus Attucks 96–57 Scecina; Broad Ripple 80–53 Warren Central; Speedway 58–49 Pike; Tech 80–52 Ben Davis; Cathedral 88–52 Arlington; Lawrence Central 66–58 School for the Deaf; Shortridge 70–43 North Central; Crispus Attucks 67–60 Broad Ripple; Speedway 54–53 Tech; Cathedral 73–56 Lawrence Central; Crispus Attucks 62–50 Shortridge; Speedway 64–49 Cathedral; Crispus Attucks 54–53 Speedway. Officials: Wesley Oler, William May, Don Hurst, Marion Acton.

JEFFERSONVILLE: Providence 66–41 New Washington; Charlestown 38–19 Borden; Clarksville 58–55 Henryville; Jeffersonville 62–61 New Albany (ot); Georgetown 58–57 Silver Creek; Charlestown 51–48 Providence; Clarksville 68–62 Jeffersonville; Charlestown 84–63 Georgetown; Charlestown 67–54 Clarksville. Officials: Lloyd Whipple, Royce McCullough, Gilbert Beagle.

KENDALLVILLE: Ligonier 78–29 Howe Military; Springfield Twp. 55–35 Wolcottville; Avilla 99–42 Wolf Lake; Kendallville 84–42 Wawaka; Rome City 66–58 Cromwell; Albion 78–62 LaGrange; Lima 60–58 Brighton; Ligonier 82–62 Springfield Twp.; Kendallville 78–60 Avilla; Albion 58–44 Rome City; Ligonier 71–51 Lima, Albion 58–42 Kendallville; Ligonier 63–51

401

Tourney Time

Albion. Officials: Wayne Crispen, James Benecke, Don Yager, Don Lieberum, Donald Lozier.

KENTLAND: Fowler 66–64 Otterbein (2ot); Oxford 57–47 Freeland Park, Boswell 56–45 Ambia; Kentland 64–43 Goodland; Fowler 54–42 Oxford; Kentland 44–43 Boswell; Fowler 66–63 Kentland. Officials: Charles Garber, John Arnold, Eugene Carrabine.

KNOX: Hamlet 54–52 Aubbeenaubbee Twp.; Grovertown 62–45 Monterey; Walkerton 63–50 Star City; Knox 69–66 Winamac (ot); North Judson 56–54 Medaryville; San Pierre 59–47 Hamlet; Walkerton 55–45 Grovertown, Knox 59–56 North Judson; Walkerton 52–40 San Pierre: Knox 58–39 Walkerton. Officials: Thomas Dean, Norris Boomershine, Walter Oliver, Ernie Sohl.

KOKOMO: Delphi 62–57 Camden; Western 62–58 Eastern; Kokomo 74–31 Windfall; Sharpsville 86–63 Carroll; Northwestern 72–61 Delphi; Kokomo 76–53 Western; Sharpsville 66–62 Northwestern; Kokomo 87–45 Sharpsville. Officials: Harry Green, Frank Carnes, John Thomas.

LAFAYETTE: Central Catholic 65–54 Battle Ground; West Lafayette 54–47 Southwestern; Klondike 62–57 East Tipp; Lafayette Jefferson 105–44 Montmorenci; West Lafayette 62–57 Central Catholic (ot); Lafayette Jefferson 100–37 Klondike; Lafayette Jefferson 71–47 West Lafayette. Officials: Joe Mullins, Robert Wendt, George Dunleavy.

LOGANSPORT: South Caston 51–43 Tipton Twp.; Lucerne 42–36 Washington Twp.; Logansport 69–41 Kewanna; Galveston 61–47 Young America; Royal Center 48–45 South Caston; Logansport 61–53 Lucerne; Royal Center 53–44 Galveston; Logansport 58–45 Royal Center. Officials: Dale Van Houten, David Habegger, Harry Inskeep.

MADISON: Madison 83–35 Dupont; Scottsburg 59–54 Southwestern; Deputy 69–44 Lexington; Shawe Memorial 81–66 Austin; Madison 71–43 Scottsburg; Shawe Memorial 63–52 Deputy; Madison 75–39 Shawe Memorial. Officials: Winfield Jacobs, Wendell Baker, Louis Schmalfeldt.

MANCHESTER: Manchester 81–73 Silver Lake; Laketon 69–56 Roann; White's 61–58 LaFontaine; Wabash 82–51 Urbana; Noble 81–55 Lagro; Manchester 65–56 Laketon, Wabash 65–60 White's; Noble 70–67 Manchester; Noble 85–78 Wabash. Officials: Victor Wukovits, Maurice Davis, Everett Campbell.

MARION: Bennett 56–51 Swayzee; Oak Hill 70–53 Mississinewa; Van Buren 60–44 Fairmount; Marion 80–55 Jefferson Twp.; Oak Hill 70–51 Bennett; Marion 74–64 Van Buren; Oak Hill 80–77 Marion. Officials: Bill Larkin, Robert Showalter, Gil Baumgartner.

MARTINSVILLE: Bloomington University 76–60 Mooresville; Unionville 79–57 Smithville; Ellettsville 62–52 Martinsville; Bloomington High 76–59 Monrovia; Eminence 83–44 Morgantown; Bloomington University 85–62 Stinesville; Ellettsville 81–55 Unionville; Eminence 67–51 Bloomington High; Ellettsville 68–53 Bloomington University; Eminence 61–58 Ellettsville. Officials: James Patterson, Clifford Runnebohm, Jack Gardner, Robert Sweet, Charles Daum.

MICHIGAN CITY: Michigan City 65–60 LaPorte; Wanatah 68–47 Mill Creek; Clinton Twp. 60–46 LaCrosse; Rolling Prairie 71–57 St. Mary's; Stillwell 70–50 Union Mills; Hanna 74–65 Union Twp.; Westville 69–39 Kingsbury; Michigan City 95–59 Wanatah; Clinton Twp. 69–64 Rolling Prairie; Hanna 63–62 Stillwell; Michigan City 71–53 Westville; Clinton Twp. 68–64 Hanna; Michigan City 83–45 Clinton Twp, Officials: Stanley Dubis, Don Hollman, Robert Crane, Glen Wisler.

MILAN: Holton 69–63 Batesville; Sunman 64–54 Milan; Jac-Cen-Del 75–65 Cross Plains; New Marion 50–48 Versailles; Holton 59–54 Sunman; New Marion 59–57 Jac-Cen-Del (2ot); Holton 62–49 New Marion. Officials: Fred Marlow, Charles Stumpf, Marvin Heaton.

MONON: Burnettsville 49–47 Monticello; Wolcott 61–31 Buffalo; Reynolds 57–43 Francesville; Monon 59–41 Idaville; Brookston 66–36 Chalmers; Burnettsville 41–37 Wolcott; Monon 54–45 Reynolds; Brookston 62–52 Burnettsville; Brookston 77–60 Monon. Officials: Richard Pattengale, John Zehring, Thomas Hoffman.

MUNCIE: Eaton 61–50 Daleville; Albany 56–52 DeSoto; Muncie Central 74–58 Yorktown; Royerton 49–44 Muncie Burris; Harrison Twp. 65–44 Selma; Center 74–54 Cowan; Gaston 66–41 Eaton; Muncie Central 65–49 Albany; Royerton 78–47 Harrison Twp.; Gaston 55–45 Center; Muncie Central 60–55 Royerton; Muncie Central 83–69 Gaston. Officials: John Williams, Julian Piercefield, Jack Mercer, Charlie Lentz.

NEW CASTLE: Cadiz 68–53 Mt. Summit; Knightstown 78–36 Lewisville; Straughn 71–62 Mooreland; Middletown 67–37 Wilkinson; Spiceland 48–46 New Castle; Sulphur Springs 69–65 Cadiz (ot); Knightstown 79–50 Straughn; Middletown 46–38 Spiceland; Knightstown 54–49 Sulphur Springs; Middletown 49–38 Knightstown. Officials: Gerald Strickler, Robert Fisher, Francis Fiddler, Robert Laird.

PERU: Peru 71–58 North Miami; Bunker Hill 54–51 Akron; North Caston 39–34 Beaver Dam; Clay Twp. 69–58 Somerset; Peru 58–55 Bunker Hill; Clay Twp. 59–56 North Caston; Clay Twp. 62–51 Peru. Officials: Darl March, William Yohler, Wayne Targgart.

PLYMOUTH: Talma 57–44 Argos; Tippecanoe 66–47 West Twp.; Bremen 65–58 LaPaz; Tippecanoe 55–44 Talma; Rochester 59–50 Richland Center; Plymouth 70–52 Tyner; Bourbon 73–63 Culver; Plymouth 56–51 Rochester; Bremen 46–36 Tippecanoe; Bourbon 59–45 Plymouth; Bourbon 56–55 Bremen. Officials: Don McCoy, Richard Freeman, Gerald Sweet, Ned Brenizer.

PORTLAND: Pennville 78–60 Montpelier; Dunkirk 102–39 Roll; Hartford City 66–33 Madison Twp.; Redkey 64–51 Gray; Portland 87–57 Bryant; Pennville 76–53 Poling; Hartford City 54–53 Dunkirk (ot); Portland 72–49 Redkey; Pennville 69–53 Hartford City; Pennville 58–57 Portland (ot). Officials: John Priest, Jim Ladd, Max Hensler, James Ridge.

PRINCETON: Owensville 72–56 Hazleton; Mackey 84–57 Patoka; Ft. Branch 59–47 Haubstadt; Princeton 63–58 Oakland City; Mt. Olympus 58–52 Francisco; Owensville 50–48 Mackey (ot); Ft. Branch 61–51 Princeton; Mt. Olympus 82–61 Owensville; Ft. Branch 71–51 Mt. Olympus. Officials: Wayne Myers, John Mayhugh, William Malloy.

RENSSELAER: Remington 41–27 Brook; Rensselaer 70–40 Tefft; Wheatfield 72–70 DeMotte; Mt. Ayr 69–66 Morocco; Remington 61–40 Fair Oaks; Rensselaer 73–70 Wheatfield; Remington 59–57 Mt. Ayr; Rensselaer 43–42 Remington. Officials: Anthony Lazar, Lloyd Chambers, William Farrar.

RICHMOND: Hagerstown 93–69 Williamsburg; Webster 66–35 Economy; Whitewater 58–57 Greens Fork; Richmond 101–57 Fountain City; Centerville 63–45 Cambridge City; Hagerstown 87–43 Boston; Webster 72–53 Whitewater; Richmond 64–49 Centerville; Hagerstown 77–34 Webster; Richmond 83–68 Hagerstown. Officials: Floyd Reed, Carl Petercheff, John Bush, James Carey.

RISING SUN: Aurora 82–38 Vevay; North Dearborn 63–36 Patriot; Lawrenceburg 68–62 Moores Hill (ot); Rising Sun 64–56 Dillsboro; North Dearborn 62–52 Aurora; Lawrenceburg 65–61 Rising Sun; North Dearborn 64–56 Lawrenceburg. Officials: Robert Cherry, Howard Plough, William Williamson.

Tourney Time

RUSHVILLE: Carthage 58–57 Manilla; Milroy 53–51 Mays; Rushville 63–50 Charlottesville; Arlington 58–47 Morton Memorial; Morristown 86–68 New Salem; Carthage 59–57 Milroy; Arlington 60–54 Rushville; Morristown 59–53 Carthage; Morristown 59–51 Arlington. Officials: Jack Goen, James Eads, Vern Doles.

SALEM: Campbellsburg 61–46 Salem; Morgan Twp. 66–39 Lanesville; Marengo 32–29 Milltown; North Central 44–43 South Central; Pekin 57–51 English; Corydon 85–56 Hardinsburg; Morgan Twp. 51–41 Campbellsburg; North Central 46–22 Marengo; Corydon 63–41 Pekin; Morgan Twp. 46–44 North Central; Morgan Twp. 54–51 Corydon. Officials: Cyril Birge, Lloyd Baugh, Norman Chestnut, Max Andress.

SEYMOUR: Vallonia 58–53 Freetown; Seymour 70–39 Cortland; Crothersville 50–47 Medora; Tampico 68–54 Brownstown; Clearspring 74–53 Vallonia; Seymour 72–45 Crothersville; Clearspring 65–44 Tampico; Seymour 84–54 Clearspring. Officials: Howard Morgan, Norman Risley, Ivan Risley.

SOUTH BEND: New Carlisle 49–47 Lakeville; Adams 67–38 Greene Twp.; Washington 62–61 Riley (ot); Adams 63–47 New Carlisle; Mishawaka 63–52 Washington-Clay; North Liberty 61–58 Madison Twp.; Central 58–47 St. Joseph's; Mishawaka 75–56 North Liberty; Adams 53–51 Washington; Central 63–51 Mishawaka; Central 54–53 Adams. Officials: William Hile, Ronald Jones, Ralph Cox, John Sebastian.

SOUTHPORT: Indianapolis Washington 67–43 Decatur Central; Sacred Heart 52–51 Hancock Central; Southport 91–57 Vernon Twp.; New Palestine 70–63 Beech Grove; Franklin Central 65–57 Wood; Howe 94–47 Mt. Comfort; Manual 64–57 Greenfield (ot); Washington 82–56 Sacred Heart; Southport 77–58 New Palestine; Franklin Central 68–46 Howe; Washington 69–53 Manual; Southport 67–59 Franklin Central; Southport 67–59 Washington. Officials: Homer Owens, Donald Call, Russell Owens, J. Firman Grimes.

SULLIVAN: Hymera 43–35 Pleasantville; Carlisle 62–35 Oaktown; North Central 76–50 Coalmont; Sullivan 57–34 Dugger; Carlisle 78–63 Hymera; Sullivan 63–54 North Central; Carlisle 60–46 Sullivan. Officials: Donald Hubbard, Ralph Box, Raymond Vescovi.

SWITZ CITY: Midland 62–59 Switz City, Bloomfield 60–53 L & M; Linton 61–52 Jasonville; Worthington 64–53 Eastern (Greene Co.); Bloomfield 59–48 Midland; Linton 58–45 Worthington; Bloomfield 44–42 Linton. Officials: James Schwenk, Morris Davis, Paul Meyer.

TELL CITY: Tell City 90–41 Chrisney; Cannelton 83–44 Bristow; Oil Twp. 55–47 Dale; Rockport 64–44 Leavenworth; Tell City 69–44 Cannelton; Rockport 53–44 Oil Twp.; Tell City 80–49 Rockport. Officials: Roland Baker, Wallace Reeve, Charles Adams.

TERRE HAUTE: Garfield 66–52 West Vigo; Honey Creek 49–39 Wiley; Gerstmeyer 53–42 Laboratory; Staunton 73–71 Schulte (ot); Garfield 53–48 Honey Creek; Gerstmeyer 77–58 Staunton; Garfield 53–42 Gerstmeyer. Officials: Donald Boyer, Harold Gourley, John Manka.

VINCENNES: Bruceville 57–42 Decker; Freelandville 53–49 Monroe City; Fritchton 55–54 Sandborn; Decker Chapel 70–62 Edwardsport; Vincennes 77–56 Bicknell; Central Catholic 60–59 Wheatland; Freelandville 48–46 Bruceville; Fritchton 56–46 Decker Chapel; Vincennes 69–57 Central Catholic; Freelandville 55–51 Fritchton; Vincennes 64–46 Freelandville. Officials: Kenneth Blankenbaker, Edward Trexler, Jack Cummings and Ray Robison.

WASHINGTON: Petersburg 70–60 Odon; Shoals 88–55 Plainville; Washington High 71–56 Washington Catholic; Barr Twp. 85–47 Elnora; Loogootee High 72–52 Alfordsville; Loogootee St. John's 50–47 Epsom; Shoals 58–56 Petersburg (ot); Washington 69–53 Montgomery; Loogootee

High 71–45 Loogootee St. John's; Washington 54–36 Shoals; Loogootee 62–54 Washington. Officials: Paul Grimes, Harold Mason, James Lear, Glen Bonsett.
WINCHESTER: Ward-Jackson 70–48 Spartanburg; Lynn 61–51 Ridgeville; Union City-Wayne 54–49 Farmland; Union 72–63 Parker; Driver 58–47 Ward-Jackson; Union City-Wayne 67–62 Lynn; Driver 61–58 Union; Union City-Wayne 86–50 Driver. Officials: Fred Kehoe, Gerald Imel, Johannes Dienelt.
ZIONSVILLE: Zionsville 93–63 Dover; Whitestown 69–61 Thorntown, Pinnell 74–47 Wells; Lebanon 83–50 Perry Central; Whitestown 53–49 Zionsville; Pinnell 69–66 Lebanon; Pinnell 61–50 Whitestown. Officials: William Findling, Leo Ponto, Gordon McCain.

1962 REGIONALS

COLUMBUS: Greensburg 57–47 Shelbyville; Madison 67–47 Franklin; Madison 77–60 Greensburg. Officials: William Malloy, Don Hubbard, Kenneth Blankenbaker, Roger Emmert, Joe Mullins, Bill Hile.
CONNERSVILLE: Connersville 58–57 Morristown; Holton 52–50 North Dearborn; Connersville 73–54 Holton. Officials: John Sheets, Glen Bonsett, Wendell Baker, Earnest Baldwin, Paul Grimes, Don Shiflet.
EAST CHICAGO: East Chicago Washington 84–72 Michigan City; Gary Froebel 77–72 Valparaiso; East Chicago Washington 68–66 Gary Froebel. Officials: Dean Geyer, Joe Bella, Victor Wukovits, Charles Garber, Lawrence Gradeless, Gene Butts.
ELKHART: Elkhart 81–45 Bourbon; South Bend Central 58–57 Mentone; Elkhart 66–62 South Bend Central. Officials: Robert Cowan, John Arnold, Maurice Criswell, Anthony Lazar, Gerald Strickler, Marion Acton.
EVANSVILLE: Evansville Bosse 76–61 Fort Branch; Castle 67–64 Tell City; Bosse 84–53 Castle. Officials: Dwain Laird, Gilbert Beagle, Robert Laird, Lowell Smith, James Patterson, Vern Doles.
FORT WAYNE: Angola 57–56 Berne-French; Ft. Wayne Central 92–56 Ligonier; Ft. Wayne Central 59–45 Angola. Officials: Homer Owens, William May, John Hilligoss, Howard Risley, Wesley Oler, Robert Showalter.
GREENCASTLE: Attica 74–61 New Ross; Rockville 80–64 Bainbridge; Attica 71–63 Rockville. Officials: Robert Cherry, Donald Boyer, Lloyd Whipple, Earle Wolfe, Wayne Crispen, Robert Davidson.
HUNTINGBURG: Jasper 48–45 Carlisle; Vincennes 55–53 Loogootee; Jasper 63–56 Vincennes. Officials: J. Firman Grimes, Norman Shields, Arthur Thompson, Jimmy Dimitroff, James Boswell, John Thomas.
INDIANAPOLIS: Anderson 68–66 Indianapolis Crispus Attucks; Southport 70–57 Plainfield; Anderson 59–57 Southport. Officials: Robert Spay, Thomas Dean, Jack Small, Don Hollman, Cyril Birge, John Fee.
JEFFERSONVILLE: Bedford 49–47 Charlestown; Seymour 88–63 Morgan Twp.; Seymour 59–49 Bedford. Officials: James Schwenk, Marvin Cave, Robert Rose, Harold Gourley, Jerry Steiner, James Beyer.
KOKOMO: Kokomo 109–73 Noble; Noblesville 69–51 Clay; Kokomo 83–69 Noblesville. Officials: Fred Marlow, Edgar Powers. Don Hurst, Walter Swift, Stanley Dubis, David Habegger.

Tourney Time

LAFAYETTE: Rossville 78–76 Fowler; Lafayette Jefferson 84–69 Pinnell; Lafayette Jefferson 95–81 Rossville. Officials: Norman Risley, Ernest Sohl, Roland Baker, Floyd Reed, Bill Larkin, Robert Kramer.

LOGANSPORT: Logansport 64–50 Brookston; Knox 67–53 Rensselaer; Knox 47–43 Logansport. Officials: Ray Nemeth, Richard Swartz, Roy Kilby, Morris Davis, Everett Campbell, Gerald Imel.

MARION: Oak Hill 72–60 Bluffton; Huntington 61–39 Pennville; Huntington 69–58 Oak Hill. Officials: Don McCoy, Harry Inskeep, Frank Sanders, Darl March, Charles Fouty, Glen Wisler.

MARTINSVILLE: Eminence 61–48 Terre Haute Garfield; Bloomfield 55–47 Spencer; Eminence 65–47 Bloomfield. Officials: Frank Carnes, Richard Pattengale, William Findling, James Ruby, Don McBride, Zeke Williams.

NEW CASTLE: Middletown 71–60 Union City-Wayne; Muncie Central 83–63 Richmond; Muncie Central 60–58 Middletown (2ot), Officials: John Williams, Raymond Robison, Don Lieberum, Richard Foster, Winfield Jacobs, Lewis Goshert.

1962 SEMI–STATES

EVANSVILLE: Seymour 78–63 Eminence; Evansville Bosse 70–68 Jasper; Evansville Bosse 77–57 Seymour. Officials: Robert Spay, John Fee, Wesley Oler, Fred Marlow, Everett Campbell, Homer Owens.

FORT WAYNE: Elkhart 61–58 Fort Wayne Central; Kokomo 67–53 Huntington: Kokomo 73–70 Elkhart. Officials: Winfield Jacobs, Kenneth Blankenbaker, Robert Rose, Dwain Laird, Bill Larkin, James Boswell.

INDIANAPOLIS: Madison 73–64 Connersville; Anderson 71–60 Muncie Central; Madison 91–81 Anderson. Officials: Jack Small, Robert Davidson, Stanley Dubis, David Habegger, Wayne Crispen, Lawrence Gradeless.

LAFAYETTE: East Chicago Washington 66–47 Attica; Lafayette Jefferson 66–41 Knox; East Chicago Washington 67–66 Lafayette Jefferson. Officials: Paul Grimes, Roger Emmert, Don Lieberum, Charles Fouty, Jerry Steiner, Frank Sanders.

1962 FINALS—March 17

INDIANAPOLIS (Butler Fieldhouse): Evansville Bosse 79–75 Madison; East Chicago Washington 74–73 Kokomo; Bosse 84–81 Washington. Officials: Wayne Crispen, Bill Larkin, Everett Campbell, Winfield Jacobs, Jerry Steiner, Paul Grimes.

1963 SECTIONALS

ADAMS CENTRAL: Berne 66–41 Geneva; Decatur Catholic 39–37 Pleasant Mills; Adams Central 67–61 Decatur; Monmouth 82–58 Hartford Center; Berne 53–37 Decatur Catholic; Monmouth 70–59 Adams Central; Berne 63–61 Monmouth. Officials: Richard Swartz, Wayne Targgart, James Davis.

ANDERSON: St. Mary's 57–52 Markleville; Summitville 52–51 Elwood; Alexandria 58–52 Madison Heights; Anderson 60–47 Highland; Pendleton 70–57 Frankton; St. Mary's 71–51

IHSAA Scores | 1960–1969

Lapel; Alexandria 59–41 Summitville; Anderson 70–60 Pendleton; Alexandria 56–44 St. Mary's; Alexandria 36–33 Anderson. Officials: Don McCoy, Jim Ladd, Marvin Heaton, Glen Wisler.

ANGOLA–CHURUBUSCO: (At Angola): Auburn 50–41 Fremont; Churubusco 72–61 Waterloo; Garrett 62–30 Salem Center; Auburn 90–77 Churubusco; (At Churubusco): Ashley 71–57 Butler; Angola 62–26 Riverdale; Orland 58–55 Hamilton; Angola 51–50 Ashley; (At Angola): Garrett 51–44 Auburn; Angola 86–70 Orland; Angola 62–47 Garrett. Officials: Edgar Powers, James Tansey, Richard Freeman, Ray Nemeth.

BEDFORD: Mitchell 44–38 Shawswick; Orleans 61–48 Fayetteville; Paoli 75–48 Oolitic, Tunnelton 66–38 Heltonville; Bedford 44–38 Huron; Marshall Twp. 71–50 Williams; Mitchell 45–42 Orleans; Tunnelton 73–67 Paoli (ot); Bedford 54–41 Marshall Twp.; Mitchell 48–45 Tunnelton; Bedford 65–32 Mitchell. Officials: Harold E. Gourley, Robert Wells, Raymond Vescovi, William Malloy.

BLUFFTON: Lancaster Central 59–23 Chester Center: Jackson Center 62–38 Petroleum; Liberty Center 56–54 Rockcreek; Bluffton 62–47 Hoagland; Ossian 60–55 Lancaster Central; Liberty Center 55–34 Jackson Center; Bluffton 61–55 Ossian; Bluffton 66–53 Liberty Center. Officials: Bill Hile, Max Hensler, Charlie Stumpf.

BOONVILLE: Boonville 73–31 Stendal; Elberfeld 70–58 Millersburg; Castle 68–45 Spurgeon; Luce Twp. 46–44 Lynnville; Boonville 88–58 Elberfeld; Castle 65–55 Luce Twp.; Boonville 69–52 Castle. Officials: Ralph Box, Paul Meyer, James Lear.

BROWNSBURG: North Salem 68–44 Lizton; Plainfield 65–59 Clayton; Danville 79–55 Stilesville; Brownsburg 56–36 New Winchester; Charlton 59–49 Amo; Avon 72–59 Pittsboro; Plainfield 68–49 North Salem; Danville 73–52 Brownsburg; Avon 55–52 Chariton; Danville 58–48 Plainfield; Danville 49–44 Avon. Officials: Earnest Baldwin, Jerry Baker, Joe Smelcer, Robert Showalter.

CARMEL: Noblesville 34–24 Carmel; Sheridan 55–54 Jackson Central; Tipton 79–50 Walnut Grove; Fishers 53–44 Westfield; Noblesville 58–43 Sheridan; Tipton 71–52 Fishers; Noblesville 51–42 Tipton. Officials: William May, Loyd Chambers, Walter Swift.

CHESTERTON: Morgan Twp. 63–44, Wheeler; Valparaiso 89–30 Liberty Twp.; Hebron 90–50 Jackson Twp.; Portage 70–47 Washington Twp.; Boone Grove 55–54 Kouts; Chesterton 75–41 Morgan Twp.; Valparaiso 86–60 Hebron; Portage 56–55 Boone Grove; Valparaiso 72–67 Chesterton; Valparaiso 72–49 Portage. Officials: Wayne Crispen, Richard Brainerd, Ronald Hosinski, Gene Butts.

CLINTON CENTRAL: Rossville 72–44 Jefferson Twp.; Clinton Prairie 71–67 Clinton Central (ot); Dayton 74–58 Prairie Twp.; Frankfort 59–36 Lauramie Twp.; Clinton Prairie 85–69 Rossville; Frankfort 89–54 Dayton; Frankfort 89–66 Clinton Prairie. Officials: Gerald Imel, Donald Lozier, Gilbert Beagle.

COLUMBUS: Shelbyville 74–52 Hauser; Southwestern 59–52 Brown County; Columbus 75–54 Waldron; Triton 69–46 Nineveh; Shelbyville 66–61 Southwestern; Columbus 83–55 Triton; Columbus 80–55 Shelbyville. Officials: John Hilligoss, Francis Fiddler, Norman Risley.

CONNERSVILLE: Laurel 38–36 Fayette Central; Connersville 63–43 Liberty; Brookville 62–38 Whitewater Twp.; Milton 55–45 Alquina; Connersville 68–45 Laurel; Brookville 44–38 Milton; Connersville 59–58 Brookville. Officials: J. F. Grimes, Carl Schnebelt, Charles Lentz.

CRAWFORDSVILLE: Darlington 47–44 Waynetown; Crawfordsville 58–48 New Market; New Ross 52–37 Linden; Crawfordsville 65–44 Darlington; Waveland 45–39 Ladoga; Coal Creek

Tourney Time

Central 64–55 Alamo; Crawfordsville 57–46 New Ross; Waveland 51–46 Coal Creek Central; Crawfordsville 60–48 Waveland. Officials: John Arnold, Donald Lynch, Max Andress.

EAST CHICAGO: Highland 55–45 Hammond Gavit; Hammond Clark 61–57 Crown Point; Tech 64–61 Lowell (ot); Highland 55–53 Dyer; Clark 69–40 Tech; East Chicago Roosevelt 58–50 Whiting; Hammond High 71–61 Griffith; East Chicago Washington 83–72 Morton; Noll 67–52 Roosevelt; Washington 64–62 Hammond High; Highland 66–54 Clark; Washington 64–53 Noll; Washington 61–43 Highland. Officials: Bill Larkin, George Avery, Robert Wendt, Darl March.

ELKHART: Topeka 77–44 Jefferson; Elkhart 69–25 Wakarusa; Middlebury 70–57 Millersburg; Goshen 61–40 Baugo Twp.; New Paris 79–40 Shipshewana Scott; Penn 80–52 Bristol; Nappanee 79–70 Concord; Elkhart 65–38 Topeka; Goshen 69–43 Middlebury; Penn 68–61 New Paris; Nappanee 60–57 Elkhart; Goshen 74–64 Penn; Goshen 74–68 Nappanee. Officials: Thomas Hoffman, Harold Ashbrook, Robert Crane, Ron Jones.

EVANSVILLE: North 61–60 Memorial; Reitz 77–55 Mater Dei; North Posey 62–57 Harrison; Rex Mundi 88–42 New Harmony; Bosse 93–53 Mt. Vernon; Central 74–54 North; Reitz 62–45 North Posey; Bosse 78–62 Rex Mundi; Central 57–47 Reitz; Bosse 77–53 Central. Officials: Dwain Laird, Wallace Reeve, Kenneth Payne, Robert Laird.

FORT WAYNE: Central 74–37 Monroeville; New Haven 51–49 South Side; Concordia 67–57 Arcola; Leo 68–64 Woodlan (ot); Central Catholic 69–59 Elmhurst; Harlan 55–54 Huntertown; North Side 83–63 Bishop Luers; Central 72–55 New Haven; Concordia 68–54 Leo; Central Catholic 77–68 Harlan; North Side 58–46 Central; Concordia 68–61 Central Catholic; Concordia 55–51 North Side. Officials: James Boswell, Jonnie Webber, John Gassensmith, Darrel McFall.

GARY: Horace Mann 73–72 Hobart; Tolleston 73–41 Andrean; Merrillville 74–63 Wirt; Roosevelt 87–63 Froebel; Gary Edison 77–64 River Forest; Lew Wallace 63–60 Emerson; Calumet 83–61 East Gary Edison; Tolleston 64–48 Horace Mann; Roosevelt 87–48 Merrillville; Lew Wallace 66–59 Gary Edison; Tolleston 80–54 Calumet; Roosevelt 91–48 Lew Wallace; Roosevelt 67–50 Tolleston. Officials: Jack Small. John Mikels, Gordon McCain, Zeke Williams.

GREENCASTLE: Belle Union 73–60 Reelsville Roachdale 65–60 Cloverdale; Bainbridge 70–54 Russellville; Greencastle 47–46 Fillmore; Roachdale 86–79 Belle Union; Greencastle 70–59 Bainbridge; Greencastle 78–68 Roachdale. Officials: John Thomas, Billy Walker, James Beyer.

GREENSBURG: Jackson Twp. 70–61 Sandusky; Burney 68–52 North Vernon; Sandcreek 50–48 New Point; Saint Paul 60–47 Clarksburg; Greensburg 76–45 Vernon; Jackson Twp. 78–56 Burney; Saint Paul 47–40 Sandcreek; Greensburg 66–58 Jackson Twp.; Greensburg 58–35 Saint Paul. Officials: Norman Shields, Ray Ward, Donald Call.

HARTFORD CITY: Bryant 60–57 Hartford City; Dunkirk 84–48 Poling; Montpelier 46–44 Pennville; Redkey 75–48 Gray; Madison Twp. 63–62 Portland; Bryant 66–63 Dunkirk; Redkey 87–71 Montpelier; Bryant 71–55 Madison Twp.; Bryant 69–62 Redkey. Officials: James Benecke, Boynton Robson, Richard Vendrely.

HUNTINGBURG: Dubois 48–46 Holland; Huntingburg 57–55 Otwell; Jasper 73–43 Birdseye; Springs Valley 78–67 St. Ferdinand; Ireland 62–46 Winslow, Huntingburg 48–47 Dubois (ot); Springs Valley 72–59 Jasper; Ireland 71–55 Huntingburg; Ireland 20–19 Springs Valley. Officials: Robert Rose, Robert Hertzberger, Robert Sweet.

HUNTINGTON: Andrews 51–50 Lancaster Twp.; Union Twp. 64–51 Rockcreek; Jefferson

Twp. 65–47 Lafayette Central; Salamonie Twp. 34–31 Roanoke; Huntington 73–16 Clear Creek; Huntington Catholic 68–46 Huntington Twp.; Union Twp. 51–49 Andrews; Jefferson Twp. 44–43 Salamonie Twp.; Huntington 54–21 Huntington Catholic; Union Twp. 69–42 Jefferson Twp.; Huntington 90–36 Union Twp. Officials: Wesley Oler, John Ward, Allen Voorhis, Joseph Bella.

INDIANAPOLIS: Scecina 56–46 Arlington; Ben Davis 57–49 Lawrence; Cathedral 70–55 Pike; Broad Ripple 70–49 Warren Central; North Central 95–35 School for the Deaf; Tech 62–38 Speedway; Shortridge 52–34 Scecina; Cathedral 78–58 Ben Davis; Broad Ripple 68–55 North Central; Tech 70–60 Shortridge; Broad Ripple 61–50 Cathedral; Broad Ripple 67–56 Tech. Officials: Homer Owens, Eugene Lillie, Ned Brenizer, Floyd Reed.

JEFFERSONVILLE: Henryville 71–50 New Washington; Silver Creek 52–51 Charlestown; Jeffersonville 70–32 Borden; New Albany 44–43 Georgetown; Clarksville 52–51 Providence; Silver Creek 72–71 Henryville; Jeffersonville 65–44 New Albany; Clarksville 58–56 Silver Creek (2ot); Jeffersonville 59–47 Clarksville. Officials: Fred Marlow, William Bateman, John Bush.

KENDALLVILLE: Albion 47–45 Kendallville; LaGrange 56–48 Wolf Lake; Wawaka 57–45 Wolcottville; Cromwell 70–41 Springfield Twp.; Brighton 55–52 Avilla (ot); Lima 71–70 Ligonier; Albion 73–44 LaGrange; Wawaka 64–50 Cromwell; Brighton 72–69 Lima; Albion 56–52 Wawaka; Albion 65–61 Brighton (ot). Officials: William Findling, Jack Goen, Fred Kehoe, Robert Fisher.

KENTLAND: Fowler 90–47 Ambia; Kentland 48–47 Goodland, Oxford 67–55 Boswell; Otterbein 90–62 Freeland Park; Fowler 65–47 Kentland; Otterbein 70–58 Oxford; Fowler 53–51 Otterbein. Officials: Jim Ruby, Herod Toon, Ralph Cox.

KOKOMO: Kokomo 65–47 Delphi; Western 59–55 Sharpsville; Northwestern 74–63 Camden; Windfall 64–52 Carroll; Kokomo 84–53 Eastern; Western 45–42 Northwestern; Kokomo 87–62 Windfall; Kokomo 66–53 Western. Officials: David Habegger, Robert Reed, Howard Risley.

LAFAYETTE: West Lafayette 51–44 Klondike; Southwestern 52–40 Battleground; Lafayette Jefferson 77–56 Central Catholic; East Tipp 60–55 Montmorenci; West Lafayette 44–40 Southwestern; Lafayette Jefferson 62–43 East Tipp; Lafayette Jefferson 80–46 West Lafayette. Officials: James Patterson, Dale VanHouten, Don Hollman.

LOGANSPORT: Royal Center 78–49 Lucerne; Kewanna 68–48 Young America; Galveston 70–58 Tipton Twp.; Logansport 72–51 Washington Twp.; Royal Center 49–47 Kewanna; Logansport 58–48 Galveston; Royal Center 60–50 Logansport. Officials: Stanley Dubis, Sam Reed, Julian Piercefield.

MADISON: Madison 68–42 Lexington; Scottsburg 72–57 Austin; Deputy 78–54 Dupont; Shawe Memorial 66–60 Southwestern; Madison 76–74 Scottsburg; Shawe Memorial 60–59 Deputy; Madison 80–58 Shawe Memorial. Officials: Robert Cherry, Morris Cohen, Marvin Cave.

MANCHESTER: South Whitley 57–55 Silver Lake; Southwood 66–58 Sidney; Northfield 62–50 Manchester; Wabash 66–32 White's; South Whitley 58–54 Southwood; Northfield 57–49 Wabash; South Whitley 61–54 Northfield. Officials: John Holmes, Jack Longnecker, Maurice Davis.

MARION: Mississinewa 89–67 Fairmount; Swayzee 64–61 Oak Hill; Bennett 77–59 Van Buren; Marion 63–48 Jefferson Twp.; Swayzee 61–59 Mississinewa; Marion 88–65 Bennett; Marion 65–57 Swayzee. Officials: Roy Kilby, Jack Gardner, Wendell Baker.

MARTINSVILLE: Eminence 74–65 Smithville; Morgantown 55–41 Unionville; Martinsville

Tourney Time

61–52 Mooresville; Stinesville 77–63 University; Ellettsville 58–47 Monrovia; Bloomington 62–58 Eminence; Martinsville 70–25 Morgantown; Stinesville 64–59 Ellettsville; Martinsville 49–39 Bloomington; Martinsville 92–29 Stinesville. Officials: James Schwenk, Don Snedeker, Leo Kelly, Harry Green.

MICHIGAN CITY: LaPorte 74–46 Rolling Prairie; Westville 62–60 LaCrosse; South Central 72–53 Mill Creek; St. Mary's 89–62 Kingsbury; Michigan City 98–49 Stillwell; Union Twp. 85–52 Wanatah; LaPorte 84–59 Westville; St. Mary's 71–52 South Central; Michigan City 89–57 Union Twp.; LaPorte 83–57 St. Mary's; Michigan City 66–62 LaPorte. Officials: Robert Spay, William Farrar, Norris Boomershine, Anthony Lazar.

MILAN: Jac-Cen-Del 58–55 Versailles; Milan 40–37 Holton; Batesville 66–48 Sunman; New Marion 63–44 Cross Plains; Milan 54–48 Jac-Cen-Del; Batesville 54–53 New Marion; Batesville 74–70 Milan (2ot). Officials: Harold Mason, Charles Tabereaux, Ben Olsson.

MONON: Monon 69–65 Burnettsville; Chalmers 41–34 Wolcott; Monticello 75–45 Buffalo; Reynolds 44–43 Francesville; Brookston 61–48 Idaville; Morton 71–46. Chalmers; Monticello 68–58 Reynolds; Monon 61–52 Brookston; Monticello 83–72 Monon. Officials: Lewis Goshert, James Cox, William Goshert.

MUNCIE: Gaston 40–37 Cowan; Selma 77–58 Harrison Twp.; Daleville 60–52 Center; Muncie Central 73–46 Yorktown; Muncie Southside 77–51 Eaton; Muncie Burris 61–55 Royerton; Albany 53–38 DeSoto; Selma 67–49 Gaston; Central 89–48 Daleville; Southside 70–41 Burris; Albany 53–45 Selma; Central 77–53 Southside; Central 79–41 Albany. Officials: John Fee, Carl Petercheff, R. Gerald Sweet, Glen Bonsett.

NEW CASTLE: Knightstown 72–56 Straughn; Mooreland 67–56 Greenfield; Mt. Summit 76–51 Cadiz; Hancock Central 70–69 Lewisville; Wilkinson 61–55 Spiceland; Sulphur Springs 78–74 Vernon Twp.; New Castle 62–54 Middletown; Knightstown 78–57 Mooreland; Hancock Central 73–69 Mt. Summit; Wilkinson 71–61 Sulphur Springs; New Castle 84–62 Knightstown; Wilkinson 56–47 Hancock Central; New Castle 105–73 Wilkinson. Officials: Arthur Thompson, Jack Mercer, Francis Terrell, Charles Sallee.

PERU: North Miami 51–46 South Caston; Peru 86–75 North Caston; Rochester 54–39 Bunker Hill; Clay 69–52 Akron; Peru 68–49 North Miami; Clay 67–66 Rochester; Peru 73–53 Clay. Officials: Richard Pattengale, James Burt, Morris Davis.

PLYMOUTH: Tippecanoe 63–55 LaPaz (ot); Bourbon 73–40 Tyner; Plymouth 58–40 Argos; Bourbon 76–50 Tippecanoe; Richland Center 54–52 Talma; Bremen 62–50 West Twp.; Culver 60–51 Richland Center (ot); Plymouth 77–61 Bourbon; Culver 46–38 Bremen; Plymouth 55–53 Culver. Officials: Ernie Sohl, Richard A. Lederman, David Schwartz, Don Lieberum.

PRINCETON: Princeton 54–48 Patoka; Francisco 75–49 Hazleton; Owensville 69–51 Mackey; Oakland City 64–53 Haubstadt; Ft. Branch 79–28 Mt. Olympus; Princeton 93–35 Francisco; Owensville 50–49 Oakland City (ot); Ft. Branch 46–45 Princeton (ot); Ft. Branch 59–36 Owensville. Officials: Don Shiflet, Noble Rector, L.C. Thorne.

RENSSELAER: Mt. Ayr 69–39 Tefft; Wheatfield 64–40 Fair Oak; Rensselaer 64–61 Remington; DeMotte 73–54 Brook; Mt. Ayr 57–47 Morocco; Rensselaer 51–48 Wheatfield; DeMotte 55–51 Mt. Ayr; Rensselaer 55–47 DeMotte. Officials: Victor Wukovits, Kent Adams, Charles Garber.

RICHMOND: Centerville 58–45 Fountain City; Hagerstown 92–35 Boston; Richmond 91–74 Williamsburg; Cambridge City 70–64 Whitewater; Hagerstown 67–44 Centerville;

Richmond 90–62 Cambridge City; Richmond 86–42 Hagerstown. Officials: Paul Grimes, Gary Muncy, Lauren Griffith.

RISING SUN: Rising Sun 96–36 Patriot; Aurora 68–63 Lawrenceburg; North Dearborn 70–47 Vevay; Moores Hill 63–36 Dillsboro; Rising Sun 84–74 Aurora; North Dearborn 66–50 Moores Hill; Dearborn 77–60 Rising Sun. Officials: Raymond Robison, Louis Schmalfeldt, Clifford Runnebohm.

ROCKVILLE: Cayuga 68–55 Montezuma; Rockville 73–47 Clinton; Turkey Run 56–51 Mecca; Newport 60–51 Rosedale; Rockville 65–42 Cayuga; Newport 46–45 Turkey Run (ot); Rockville 83–49 Newport. Officials: Maurice Criswell, Norman Chestnut, Jack Cummings.

RUSHVILLE: Charlottesville 45–43 Mays; Rushville 53–46 Manilla; Carthage 83–74 Milroy; New Salem 37–36 Arlington; Morristown 91–44 Morton Memorial; Rushville 66–44 Charlottesville; New Salem 74–60 Carthage; Morristown 69–52 Rushville; Morristown 76–73 New Salem. Officials: John Sheets, Russell Rogers, Richard Foster.

SALEM: Morgan Twp. 61–48 Lanesville; South Central 76–61 Marengo; Corydon 66–41 North Central; Salem 80–39 Hardinsburg; Pekin 65–62 Campbellsburg; Morgan Twp. 60–47 Milltown; Corydon 64–57 South Central; Salem 85–62 Pekin; Morgan Twp. 42–37 Corydon; Salem 38–36 Morgan Twp. Officials: Winfield Jacobs, Gene Wilm, William Gray, Royce McCullough.

SEYMOUR: Clearspring 56–54 Cortland; Seymour 73–49 Freetown; Brownstown 71–70 Medora; Tampico 57–47 Crothersville; Seymour 81–60 Clearspring; Brownstown 71–46 Tampico; Seymour 43–41 Brownstown. Officials: Richard Sweet, William Pittman, James Eads.

SOUTH BEND: Riley 57–50 Adams; Washington-Clay 64–58 Greene Twp.; Central 74–39 Madison Twp.; Riley 76–51 Washington-Clay; Washington 42–33 St. Joseph's; Lakeville 63–57 North Liberty; Mishawaka 63–55 New Carlisle; Washington 67–57 Lakeville; Central 65–59 Riley; Mishawaka 64–61 Washington; Central 78–58 Mishawaka. Officials: Marion Acton, Eugene Marks, George Dunleavy, Robert Kramer.

SOUTHPORT: Wood 87–45 New Palestine; Manual 58–56 Howe; Southport 81–68 Decatur Central; Sacred Heart 81–63 Mt. Comfort; Washington 82–69 Beech Grove; Wood 63–39 Franklin Central; Southport 80–68 Manual; Washington 80–78 Sacred Heart; Southport 64–55 Wood; Southport 72–70 Washington. Officials: Charles Fouty, James Carey, Neal Jay, Thomas Dean.

SPENCER: Brazil 72–58 Patricksburg; Van Buren 72–52 Gosport; Cory 55–46 Clay City; Freedom 49–31 Bowling Green; Spencer 81–50 Coal City; Brazil 71–60 Van Buren; Freedom 72–69 Cory (ot); Spencer 79–69 Brazil; Freedom 56–55 Spencer. Officials: Donald Hubbard, Jack Chestnut, Charles Daum.

SULLIVAN: Sullivan 62–56 Hymera; North Central 73–43 Oaktown; Pleasantville 58–51 Coalmont; Carlisle 64–58 Dugger; Sullivan 63–62 North Central; Carlisle 73–50 Pleasantville; Sullivan 42–38 Carlisle. Officials: Roland Baker, Ed Scott, Lloyd Baugh.

SWITZ CITY: Switz City 55–45 Worthington; L & M 57–54 Linton; Midland 55–47 Eastern; Bloomfield 72–30 Jasonville; L & M 56–41 Switz City; Bloomfield 59–41 L & M. Officials: Vern Doles, Marvin Vail, Charles Adams.

TELL CITY: Dale 78–52 Leavenworth; Tell City 77–42 English; Cannelton 42–39 Perry Central; Chrisney 66–50 Rockport; Tell City 49–25 Dale; Chrisney 47–46 Cannelton (ot); Tell City 68–43 Chrisney. Officials: Earle Wolfe, Charles Bertram, Howard Morgan.

Tourney Time

TERRE HAUTE: Gerstmeyer 63–45 Honey Creek; Staunton 60–54 Laboratory; West Vigo 63–53 Schulte; Garfield 51–49 Wiley; Gerstmeyer 58–56 Staunton; Garfield 57–54 West Vigo (ot) Garfield 76–62 Gerstmeyer. Officials: Robert Davidson, Maurice Gardner, Russell Owens.

VINCENNES: Vincennes 89–33 Wheatland; Bruceville 77–64 Central Catholic; Bicknell 67–46 Freelandville; Monroe City 79–61 Decker; Vigo 51–40 Fritchton; Vincennes 70–38 Bruceville; Monroe City 59–54 Bicknell; Vincennes 58–57 Vigo; Vincennes 71–53 Monroe City. Officials: Lowell Smith, Frank Bradshaw, Danny Jacobs.

WARSAW: Leesburg 63–48 Claypool; Pierceton 75–53 Milford; Warsaw 85–49 North Webster; Larwill 79–68 Syracuse; Columbia City 77–69 Etna Green; Mentone 69–47 Leesburg; Warsaw 60–54 Pierceton; Columbia City 65–58 Larwill; Mentone 64–45 Warsaw; Columbia City 78–69 Mentone. Officials: Larry Gradeless, Donald Edwards, Eugene Linn, Jimmy Dimitroff.

WASHINGTON: Washington Catholic 39–25 Elnora; Loogootee High 84–56 Petersburg; Shoals 51–50 Odon; Alfordsville 58–56 Epsom; Washington High 71–64 Plainville; Loogootee St. John's 53–46 Barr Twp.; Loogootee High 92–61 Washington Catholic; Alfordsville 73–68 Shoals; Washington 51–47 Loogootee St. John's; Loogootee High 72–41 Alfordsville; Washington High 58–51 Loogootee High. Officials: Roger Emmert, William Williamson, Walter Vanover, James DeGroote.

WHITELAND: Edinburg 47–45 Whiteland (ot); Union Twp. 63–62 Franklin; Greenwood 59–55 Trafalgar; Center Grove 59–43 Clark Twp.; Union Twp. 53–44 Edinburg; Greenwood 75–71; Center Grove (ot); Greenwood 64–49 Union Twp. Officials: Ken Blankenbaker, William Fields, Wayne Myers.

WILLIAMSPORT: Perrysville 85–36 Hillsboro; Seeger 69–53 Veedersburg; Kingman 67–53 Wallace; Williamsport 58–53 Covington; Richland Twp. 76–52 Pine Village; Perrysville 68–51 Attica; Seeger 65–54 Kingman; Williamsport 73–62 Richland Twp.; Seeger 74–59 Perrysville; Williamsport 59–57 Seeger. Officials: Jerry Steiner, John Manka, Bobby Goble, Donald Boyer.

WINAMAC: San Pierre 72–41 Star City; Knox 66–53 Walkerton; Winamac 66–64 Grovertown; Hamlet 46–41 Monterey; Aubbeenaubbee Twp. 47–46 North Judson; San Pierre 64–35 Medaryville; Knox 52–44 Winamac; Aubbeenaubbee Twp. 56–49 Hamlet; Knox 54–38 San Pierre; Knox 62–59 Aubbeenaubbee Twp. (ot). Officials: Joe Mullins, Gil Baumgartner, Donald Koester, Harry Inskeep.

WINCHESTER: Farmland 76–67 Ridgeville; Parker 85–79 Driver; Union 85–68 Spartanburg; Union City-Wayne 65–58 Lynn; Parker 43–35 Farmland; Union 65–63 Union City-Wayne; Parker 73–67 Union. Officials: John Williams, Frank Hoagburg, Don Yager.

ZIONSVILLE: Zionsville 78–47 Perry Central; Thorntown 87–46 Whitestown; Wells 40–29 Pinnell; Lebanon 46–36 Dover; Zionsville 60–37 Thorntown; Wells 58–56 Lebanon; Wells 47–46 Zionsville. Officials: Everett Campbell, Melvin Fuller, Don Hurst.

1963 REGIONALS

COLUMBUS: Madison 67–55 Greensburg; Columbus 77 –63 Greenwood; Columbus 69–49 Madison. Officials: Donald Boyer, Eugene Lillie, Zeke Williams, John Sheets, Jerry Steiner, Marion Acton.

CONNERSVILLE: Connersville 81–53 Batesville; Morristown 69–53 North Dearborn; Connersville 75–61 Morristown. Officials: Wayne Crispen, Howard Risley, John Williams, Danny

IHSAA Scores | 1960–1969

Jacobs, Thomas Dean, Gerald Imel.

COVINGTON: Crawfordsville 64–53 Rockville; Greencastle 62–53 Williamsport; Greencastle 51–48 Crawfordsville. Officials: Charles Garber, Ron Jones, Don Lieberum, Harry Inskeep, Bill Larkin, Lowell Smith.

EAST CHICAGO: East Chicago Washington 63–43 Valparaiso; Michigan City 88–83 Gary Roosevelt; Washington 81–67 Michigan City. Officials: Floyd Reed, Richard Pattengale, Lewis Goshert, William Goshert, Robert Spay Don Hollman.

ELKHART: Goshen 99–67 Plymouth; South Bend Central 77–41 Columbia City; South Bend Central 53–51 Goshen. Officials: John Fee, Earnest Baldwin, Wendell Baker, Darrell McFall, Stanley Dubis, Robert Showalter.

EVANSVILLE: Tell City 82–51 Boonville; Bosse 65–51 Ft. Branch; Bosse 60–41 Tell City. Officials: John Thomas, Don Hurst, Robert Cherry, Norman Shields, Max Andress, James Beyer.

FORT WAYNE: Berne 74–65 Concordia; Angola 62–49 Albion; Berne 54–52 Angola (ot). Officials: William Findling, Gilbert Beagle, J. F. Grimes, Richard Foster, Arthur Thompson, Thomas Hoffman.

HUNTINGBURG: Ireland 75–63 Sullivan; Washington 55–49 Vincennes; Ireland 39–37 Washington. Officials: Morris Davis, Russel Owens, Fred Marlow, Jim Ruby, Glen Wisler, Marvin Cave.

INDIANAPOLIS: Broad Ripple 85–60 Danville; Southport 57–51 Alexandria; Broad Ripple 71–61 Southport. Officials: Robert Rose, Bill Hile, Roger Emmert, Roy Kilby, Wesley Oler, James Schwenk.

JEFFERSONVILLE: Seymour 76–65 Salem; Jeffersonville 66–55 Bedford, Seymour 54–48 Jeffersonville. Officials: Earle Wolfe, Donald Hubbard, James Boswell, John Holmes, Charles Fouty, William Malloy.

KOKOMO: Noblesville 62–58 Peru; Kokomo 84–54 South Whitley; Noblesville 69–68 Kokomo. Officials: Vern Doles, Ray Nemeth, Robert Davidson, Lauren Griffith, Dwain Laird, Robert Laird.

LAFAYETTE: Wells 67–64 Frankfort; Lafayette Jefferson 92—82 Fowler, Jefferson 77–52 Wells. Officials: William May, Ned Brenizer, Dave Habegger, Arthur Lazar, Don McCoy, Victor Wukovits.

LOGANSPORT: Monticello 61–49 Knox; Royal Center 72–60 Rensselaer; Royal Center 66–51 Monticello. Officials: Homer Owens, Walter Swift, Joseph Bella, Donald Call, Winfield Jacobs, Ernie Sohl.

MARION: Huntington 60–28 Bryant; Marion 85–65 Bluffton; Huntington 69–61 Marion (3ot). Officials: Paul Grimes, Edgar Powers, Richard Swartz, Richard Sweet, Jimmy Dimitroff, Glenn Bonsett.

NEW CASTLE: New Castle 80–55 Parker; Muncie Central 64–56 Richmond; Muncie Central 69–58 New Castle. Officials: John Arnold, Harry Green, Ken Blankenbaker, Don Shiflet, Larry Gradeless, Gene Butts.

TERRE HAUTE: Bloomfield 59–51 Martinsville; Garfield 71–40 Freedom; Garfield 67–45 Bloomfield. Officials: Raymond Robison, Wallace Reeve, Jack Small, Robert Kramer, Everett Campbell, Harold Gourley.

Tourney Time

1963 SEMI–STATES

EVANSVILLE: Bosse 61–36 Ireland; Terre Haute Garfield 52–51 Seymour; Garfield 60–55 Bosse. Officials; Wayne Crispen, Jack Small, Jerry Steiner, Floyd Reed, Authur Thompson, David Habegger.

FORT WAYNE: South Bend Central 76–42 Berne; Huntington 79–68 Noblesville; South Bend Central 74–53 Huntington. Officials: Paul Grimes, John Williams, Winfield Jacobs, Fred Marlow, Wesley Oler, Charles Fouty.

INDIANAPOLIS: Broad Ripple 55–51 Connersville; Muncie Central 79–70 Columbus; Muncie Central 76–67 Broad Ripple. Officials: John Fee, Ken Blankenbaker, Robert Spay, Homer Owens, Bill Larkin, Robert Davidson.

LAFAYETTE: Lafayette 73–68 East Chicago Washington; Royal Center 67–46 Greencastle; Lafayette 81–66 Royal Center. Officials: Everett Campbell, Dwain Laird, Roger Emmert, Robert Cherry, Larry Gradeless, Roy Kilby.

1963 FINALS—March 23

INDIANAPOLIS (Butler Fieldhouse): Muncie Central 73–71 Lafayette Jefferson; South Bend Central 72–45 Terre Haute Garfield; Muncie Central 65–61 South Bend Central; Officials: Wayne Crispen, Wesley Oler, Bill Larkin, Jack Small, Everett Campbell, Winfield Jacobs.

1964 SECTIONALS

ADAMS CENTRAL: Decatur 46–44 Geneva; Berne 71–58 Monroeville; Adams Central 59–57 Hoagland; Monmouth 72–68 Decatur Catholic; Berne 49–46 Decatur; Adams Central 61–58 Monmouth; Adams Central 78–60 Berne. Officials: Charles Garber, Jonnie Webber, Lewis Goshert.

ANDERSON: Madison Heights 70–62 Pendleton; Anderson 98–50 Frankton; Lapel 70–62 Summitville; Elwood 81–46 Markleville; Alexandria 53–51 Highland; Madison Heights 75–61 St. Mary's; Anderson 76–49 Lapel; Elwood 49–43 Alexandria; Anderson 71–64 Madison Heights; Anderson 68–52 Elwood. Officials: Homer Owens, Harold Ashbrook, Morris Cohen, William May.

ANGOLA: Ashley 87–38 Springfield Twp.; LaGrange 52–47 Fremont; Hamilton 64–46 Lima; Brighton 56–51 Orland; Wolcottville 54–49 Salem Center; Ashley 53–35 Angola; LaGrange 48–44 Hamilton; Brighton 64–47 Wolcottville; Ashley 72–55 LaGrange; Ashley 51–42 Brighton. Officials: William Goshert, Norris Boomershine, Melvin Fuller, John Gassensmith.

BEDFORD: Paoli 72–54 Mitchell; Tunnelton 57–55 Heltonville; Oolitic 45–42 Shawswick; Marshall Twp. 66–59 Orleans; Bedford 61–53 Fayetteville; Paoli 78–51 Tunnelton; Marshall Twp. 59–50 Oolitic; Paoli 70–56 Bedford; Marshall Twp. 84–80 Paoli. Officials: Donald Hubbard, Carl Schnebelt, James Eads.

BLUFFTON: Rockcreek 69–58 Jackson Center; Liberty Center 64–45 Chester Center; Lancaster Central 54–50 Ossian; Bluffton 81–75 Petroleum; Liberty Center 57–52 Rockcreek; Lancaster Central 69–51 Bluffton; Liberty Center 66–61 Lancaster Central. Officials: Harry Inskeep, Wayne Targgart, Francis Terrell.

BOONVILLE: Boonville 69–24 Elberfeld; Millersburg 69–59 Spurgeon; Lynnville 54–51 Stendal; Castle 70–49 Luce Twp.; Boonville 60–40 Millersburg; Castle 67–53 Lynnville; Boonville 57–54 Castle. Officials: Bob Davidson, Norman Chestnut, Jack Cummings.

BROWNSBURG: Stilesville 80–72 Amo; Brownsburg 63–51 North Salem; Danville 85–50 Lizton; Pittsboro 72–54 Avon; Clayton 84–50 Charlton; Stilesville 72–70 Plainfield; Danville 72–54 Brownsburg; Clayton 65–63 Pittsboro (ot); Danville 73–64 Stilesville; Danville 62–53 Clayton. Officials: Fred Marlow, Don Lynch, Max Hensler, Max Andress

CARMEL: Carmel 85–58 Fishers; Sheridan 70–54 Jackson Central; Noblesville 95–53 Walnut Grove; Tipton 104–71 Westfield; Sheridan 61–48 Carmel; Noblesville 75–72 Tipton (ot); Noblesville 77–74 Sheridan. Officials: Bob Showalter, Wayne Myers, Richard Sweet.

CHESTERTON: Boone Grove 52–45 Wheeler; Kouts 57–32 Washington Twp.; Valparaiso 95–50 Portage; Morgan Twp. 69–66 Jackson Twp.; Chesterton 67–39 Liberty Twp.; Boone Grove 55–39 Kouts; Valparaiso 90–56 Morgan Twp.; Chesterton 77–41 Boone Grove; Valparaiso 91–72 Chesterton. Officials: Don McCoy, Robert Wendt, Walter Swift.

CLINTON: Turkey Run 67–62 Cayuga; Rockville 74–57 Clinton; Rosedale 78–43 Kingman; Montezuma 73–44 Newport; Turkey Run 71–68 Rockville (4ot); Montezuma 57–47 Rosedale; Turkey Run 60–57 Montezuma. Officials: Norman Risley, Louis Schmalfeldt, William Bateman.

COLUMBUS: Brown County 69–65 Southwestern; Triton 79–67 Nineveh; Columbus 84–40 Shelbyville; Waldron 54–49 Hauser; Triton 55–54 Brown County, Columbus 109–69 Waldron; Columbus 105–74 Triton. Officials: Wayne Crispen, John Manka, Kenneth Payne.

CONNERSVILLE: Whitewater 56–54 Laurel; Liberty 78–51 Fayette Central; Brookville 66–45 Straughn; Alquina 64–57 Connersville; Liberty 66–61 Whitewater; Brookville 42–33 Alquina, Brookville 53–44 Liberty. Officials: Glen Bonsett, Boynton Robson, Ben Olsson.

COVINGTON: Williamsport 94–87 Richland Twp.; Pine Village 66–58 Hillsboro; Perrysville 70–46 Wallace; Covington 86–68 Seeger; Attica 72–56 Veedersburg; Williamsport 61–52 Pine Village; Covington 69–62 Perrysville; Williamsport 69–67 Attica; Williamsport 46–45 Covington. Officials: John Williams, Francis Fiddler, Allen Voorhis.

CRAWFORDSVILLE: Ladoga 67–49 Linden; Crawfordsville 68–34 Darlington; New Market 45–44 Waynetown; Crawfordsville 98–66 Ladoga; Waveland 72–56 New Ross; Alamo 42–41 Coal Creek Central; Crawfordsville 58–45 New Market; Waveland 69–56 Alamo; Crawfordsville 69–51 Waveland. Officials: Charles Fouty, Billy Maroney, William Malloy.

EAST CHICAGO: East Chicago Washington 63–57 Gary Edison; Merrillville 89–44 Gary Andrean; Lowell 69–63 Hobart; Washington 60–48 Merrillville; Crown Point 64–58 Whiting; East Chicago Roosevelt 87–60 Hammond Clark; Washington 88–59 Lowell; Crown Point 66–60 Roosevelt; Washington 64–62 Crown Point. Officials: Wesley Oler, Ronald Hosinski, Joseph Bella, Roger DeYoung.

ELKHART: Baugo Twp. 65–49 Middlebury; Wakarusa 61–48 Millersburg; Elkhart 69–49 Goshen; Concord 62–53 Topeka; Penn 95–63 Bristol; Nappanee 81–55 Shipshewana-Scott; New Paris 77–41 Jefferson; Baugo Twp. 58–56 Wakarusa; Elkhart 71–49 Concord; Penn 68–58 Nappanee; New Paris 62–43 Baugo Twp.; Elkhart 67–46 Penn; Elkhart 67–43 New Paris. Officials: Floyd Reed, Eugene Carrabine, Eugene Linn, Ralph Cox.

EVANSVILLE: Rex Mundi 27–25 Mt. Vernon; Bosse 63–45 Harrison; North 61–49 New Harmony; Memorial 86–62 North Posey; Mater Dei 47–42 Central; Rex Mundi 75–59 Reitz; North 70–51 Bosse; Memorial 40–39 Mater Dei; Rex Mundi 68–56 North; Rex Mundi 87–53

Tourney Time

Memorial. Officials: Ken Blankenbaker, Ralph Box, Lloyd Baugh, Raymond Robison.

FORT WAYNE: Central Catholic 81–65 Woodlan; Harlan 75–63 Arcola; North Side 63–35 South Side; Concordia 69–54 Bishop Luers; New Haven 79–68 Leo; Central 73–66 Huntertown; Central Catholic 77–58 Elmhurst; North Side 69–59 Harlan; Concordia 84–73 New Haven; Central 79–63 Central Catholic; North Side 72–68 Concordia; Central 50–47 North Side. Officials: Wendell Baker, Jack Goen, Fred Kehoe, Eugene Marks.

FRANKFORT: Rossville 80–58 Jefferson Twp.; Frankfort 68–65 Dayton; Lauramie Twp. 65–54 Delphi; Clinton Prairie 61–54 Clinton Central; Rossville 68–60 Frankfort; Clinton Prairie 60–57 Lauramie Twp.; Clinton Prairie 67–60 Rossville. Officials: James Beyer, Ed Scott, Robert Reed.

FRANKLIN: New Palestine 62–58 Trafalgar; Whiteland 74–59 Edinburg; Franklin 75–73 Greenwood; Center Grove 67–58 Clark; Whiteland 61–54 New Palestine; Franklin 67–65 Center Grove; Franklin 69–60 Whiteland. Officials: James Schwenk, Russell Rogers, Harry Green.

GARY: Emerson 46–41 Wirt; River Forest 62–49 East Gary Edison; Froebel 85–67 Lew Wallace; Roosevelt 109–48 Horace Mann; Emerson 68–57 River Forest; Froebel 95–89 Roosevelt; Froebel 82–49 Gary Emerson. Officials: Ray Nemeth, Richard Brainerd, Vic Wukovits.

GREENCASTLE: Greencastle 66–60 Cloverdale; Fillmore 78–63 Reelsville; Belle Union 71–64 Russellville; Bainbridge 60–53 Rosedale; Greencastle 81–77 Fillmore; Bainbridge 64–23 Belle Union; Greencastle 64–52 Bainbridge. Officials: Glen Wisler, William Pittman, Charlie Lentz.

GREENSBURG: Sandcreek 71–63 Vernon; Clarksburg 59–55 St. Paul; Burney 84–77 Jackson Twp.; North Vernon 67–62 Greensburg; New Point 74–64 Sandcreek; Clarksburg 64–56 Burney; North Vernon 62–61 New Point; Clarksburg 74–72 North Vernon. Officials: Arthur Thompson, Don Shields, Robert Fisher.

HAMMOND: Hammond Noll 76–71 Dyer Central; Gary Tolleston 72–55 Highland; Hammond High 78–64 Griffith; Tolleston 77–73 Noll; Calumet 79–63 Gavit; Tech 57–46 Morton; Tolleston 80–59 Hammond High; Calumet 91–54 Tech; Tolleston 76–69 Calumet. Officials: Lawrence Gradeless, Bobby Goble, Marion Acton.

HUNTINGBURG: Springs Valley 71–54 Otwell; Huntingburg 85–64 Holland; St. Ferdinand 61–49 Jasper; Dubois 68–48 Ireland; Winslow 57–54 Birdseye; Springs Valley 67–62 Huntingburg; St. Ferdinand 53–42 Dubois; Springs Valley 66–56 Winslow; Springs Valley 77–74 St. Ferdinand (2ot). Officials: Robert Laird, Jack Chestnut, Carl Petercheff.

HUNTINGTON: Rock Creek 78–58 Andrews; Roanoke 71–43 Jefferson; Lancaster 59–46 Huntington Catholic; Huntington 69–43 Clear Creek; Union 60–56 Warren; Rock Creek 68–54 Huntington Twp.; Roanoke 78–57 Lancaster; Huntington 72–46 Union; Roanoke 53–47 Rock Creek; Huntington 69–30 Roanoke. Officials: J. F. Grimes, Ray Ward, Kenneth Barnes, Darrell McFall.

INDIANAPOLIS: Warren Central 65–57 Ben Davis; North Central 62–61 Arlington; Cathedral 91–70 Lawrence Central; Tech 86–51 Scecina; Broad Ripple 71–38 Chatard; Shortridge 79–28 Indiana School for Deaf; Crispus Attucks 59–34 Northwest; Warren Central 73–66 North Central; Tech 81–66 Cathedral; Broad Ripple 56–49 Shortridge; Crispus Attucks 71–56 Warren Central; l Tech 72–63 Broad Ripple; Tech 81–77 Crispus Attucks. Officials: Roy Kilby, Lauren Griffith, Gary Muncy, Don Hollman.

JEFFERSONVILLE: Providence 58–52 New Albany; Silver Creek 79–77 Clarksville; Jeffersonville 58–48 Henryville; Charlestown 76–42 Borden; Providence 78–69 Georgetown

(2ot); Silver Creek 53–51 Jeffersonville (ot) ; Providence 80–62 Charlestown; Silver Creek 69–58 Providence. Officials: James Patterson, Charles Daum, Norman Shields.

KENDALLVILLE: Avilla 60–46 Wawaka; Eastside 79–52 Wolf Lake; Garrett 77–54 Churubusco; Waterloo 50–31 Cromwell; Kendallville 72–60 Ligonier; Auburn 73–59 Albion; Eastside 64–34 Avilla; Garrett 79–59 Waterloo; Auburn 61–52 Kendallville; Garrett 57–45 Eastside; Garrett 65–54 Auburn. Officials: John Arnold, Neal Jay, Gordon McCain, James Carey.

KENTLAND: Goodland 63–55 Otterbein; Kentland 79–63 Ambia; Oxford 73–60 Brook; Fowler 69–46 Boswell; Kentland 71–63 Goodland; Fowler 46–44 Oxford; Fowler 61–52 Kentland. Officials: Richard Gebhart, Donald Koester, George Dunleavy.

KNOX: Aubbeenaubbee Twp. 64–50 Monterey; Oregon-Davis 48–47 San Pierre; North Judson 79–44 Walkerton; Winamac 61–47 Star City; Aubbeenaubbee Twp. 72–55 Knox; North Judson 70–53 Oregon-Davis; Winamac 62–47 Aubbeenaubbee Twp.; North Judson 51–46 Winamac. Officials: Gerald Imel, Lloyd Chambers, James Benecke.

KOKOMO: Kokomo 61–50 Western; Maconaquah 71–46 Camden; Windfall 66–60 Eastern; Northwestern 82–70 Carroll; Kokomo 81–44 Sharpsville–Prairie; Maconaquah 77–57 Windfall; Kokomo 83–53 Northwestern; Kokomo 66–48 Maconaquah. Officials: Don Lieberum, Richard Freeman, James Tansey.

LAFAYETTE: Battleground 72–46 Montmorenci; West Lafayette 78–52 East Tipp; Jefferson 89–60 Central Catholic; Southwestern 78–59 Klondike; West Lafayette 60–28 Battleground; Jefferson 95–60 Southwestern; Jefferson 64–59 West Lafayette. Officials: Anthony Lazar, James Cox, Howard Risley,

LOGANSPORT: North Caston 59–52 Logansport; North Miami 43–41 South Caston; Pioneer 62–47 Peru; Cass 92–43 Kewanna; North Caston 50–46 North Miami; Pioneer 59–45 Cass; Pioneer 62–55 North Caston. Officials: Thomas Hoffman, Gil Baumgartner, George Avery.

MADISON: Scottsburg 85–61 Deputy; Shawe Memorial 69–54 Dupont; Madison 71–67 Southwestern; New Washington 72–61 Lexington; Shawe Memorial 76–64 Scottsburg; Madison 87–52 New Washington; Madison 64–63 Shawe Memorial. Officials: John Thomas, Bill Gray, Danny Jacobs.

MANCHESTER: Sidney 85–56 Akron; Southwood 84–54 White's; South Whitley 81–67 Wabash; Manchester 79–54 Northfield; Sidney 69–62 Silver Lake; South Whitley 89–71 Southwood; Manchester 101–82 Sidney; Manchester 71–62 South Whitley. Officials: Earnest Baldwin, Samuel Reed, John Ward.

MARION: Mississinewa 50–43 Bennett; Swayzee 66–59 Marion; Oak Hill 55–39 Van Buren; Jefferson 71–58 Fairmount; Swayzee 48–46 Mississinewa; Oak Hill 59–50 Jefferson; Swayzee 38–37 Oak Hill (3ot). Officials: Marvin Cave, Don Lozier, Kent Adams.

MARTINSVILLE: Stinesville 54–51 Smithville; Martinsville 87–61 Bloomington; Monrovia 62–57 Morgantown; Ellettsville 72–43 Unionville; Eminence 54–52 Mooresville; University 74–61 Stinesville; Martinsville 71–50 Monrovia; Eminence 71–57 Ellettsville; Martinsville 54–47 University; Martinsville 72–63 Eminence. Officials: Robert Spay, Howard Morgan, Marvin Vail, Lowell Smith.

MICHIGAN CITY: LaPorte 96–49 Kingsbury; LaCrosse 86–80 Westville; St. Mary's 83–75 Wanatah; Rolling Prairie 63–60 Union Twp.; South Central 64–57 Stillwell; Michigan City 98–58 Mill Creek; LaPorte 97–59 LaCrosse; St. Mary's 68–46 Rolling Prairie; Michigan City 67–44 South Central; LaPorte 91–69 St. Mary's; Michigan City 76–74 LaPorte. Officials: Zeke Williams,

Tourney Time

Dale VanHouten, Joe Smelcer, Bill Hile.

MILAN: Cross Plains 65–58 New Marion; Batesville 62–56 Milan; Jac-Cen-Del 74–71 Versailles; Holton 74–73 Sunman (ot); Batesville 82–57 Cross Plains; Holton 81–76 Jac-Cen-Del; Holton 78–60 Batesville. Officials: Eugene Lillie, Jack Longnecker, William Fields.

MONON: Wolcott 64–57 Chalmers; Twin Lakes 77–58 Medaryville; Remington 66–43 Brookston; North White 79–62 Francesville; Wolcott 66–64 Twin Lakes; North White 57–54 Remington; North White 69–57 Wolcott. Officials: Robert Kramer, Robert Crane, Ernie Sohl.

MUNCIE: Eaton 55–48 Cowan; Gaston 53–50 Yorktown; Selma 55–52 Muncie Burris; Muncie Southside 66–35 Harrison Twp.; Daleville 81–44 DeSoto; Royerton 63–41 Albany; Eaton 51–49 Gaston; Muncie Southside 64–61 Selma; Royerton 73–59 Daleville; Muncie Southside 74–39 Eaton; Muncie Southside 83–68 Royerton. Officials: Gene Butts, Clifford Runnebohm, Richard Lederman, Don Hurst.

NEW CASTLE: Mt. Summit 79–60 Wilkinson; Knightstown 53–44 Mooreland; New Castle 91–36 Middletown; Greenfield 65–61 Mt. Vernon; Spiceland 58–50 Cadiz; Hancock Central 60–44 Sulphur Springs; Mt. Summit 56–55 Knightstown; New Castle 82–60 Greenfield; Hancock Central 45–44 Spiceland; New Castle 75–60 Mt. Summit; New Castle 89–47 Hancock Central. Officials: David Habegger, Don Yager, Frank Hoagburg, Don Shiflet.

PLYMOUTH: Triton 69–62 Bremen; Argos 54–50 West Twp.; Culver 70–51 Tyner; Argos 64–49 Triton; LaPaz 54–50 Plymouth; Rochester 48–36 Richland Center; Culver 80–64 Argos; LaPaz 56–53 Rochester; Culver 65–54 LaPaz. Officials: Bill Larkin, Richard Vendrely, Jim Ruby.

PORTLAND: Hartford City 62–38 Gray; Montpelier 60–34 Dunkirk; Portland 69–48 Pennville; Bryant 59–58 Redkey; Montpelier 67–65 Hartford City; Portland 60–48 Bryant; Portland 65–57 Montpelier. Officials: John Holmes, James Burt, Don Snedeker.

PRINCETON: Owensville 61–52 Oakland City (ot); Haubstadt 60–51 Mt. Olympus; Mackey 54–51 White River; Princeton 80–34 Francisco; Fort Branch 71–53 Owensville; Mackey 65–56 Haubstadt; Princeton 62–54 Fort Branch; Princeton 38–32 Mackey. Officials: Robert Sweet, Rudy Tabereaux, Jerry Baker.

RENSSELAER: DeMotte 65–43 Fair Oaks; Morocco 51–32 Tefft; Rensselaer 69–57 Mt. Ayr; Wheatfield 67–64 Hebron; Rensselaer 65–52 Wheatfield; DeMotte 74–53 Morocco; DeMotte 62–58 Rensselaer. Officials: Edgar Powers, Don Edwards, Jack Gardner.

RICHMOND: Centerville 60–59 Whitewater-Fountain City; Richmond 78–40 Spartanburg; Lewisville 62–56 Williamsburg-Webster; Hagerstown 52–50 Cambridge City; Richmond 50–45 Centerville; Hagerstown 67–51 Lewisville; Richmond 54–44 Hagerstown. Officials: Robert J. Cherry, David Schwartz, Harold Mason.

RISING SUN: Aurora 68–63 Vevay; Dillsboro 64–47 Rising Sun; Lawrenceburg 80-44 Patriot; North Dearborn 92–54 Moores Hill; Dillsboro 60–58 Aurora; North Dearborn 70–55 Lawrenceburg; North Dearborn 56–46 Dillsboro. Officials: James Davis, Wayne VanSickle, Marvin Heaton.

RUSHVILLE: Charlottesville 58–57 Manilla; New Salem 77–60 Arlington; Rushville 66–60 Morristown; Milroy 80–67 Mays; Carthage 60–47 Morton Memorial; New Salem 86–71 Charlottesville Rushville 75–60 Milroy; New Salem 77–69 Carthage; Rushville 72–54 New Salem. Officials: Everett Campbell, Robert Manor, Charles Sallee.

SALEM: Corydon 67–52 Pekin; Morgan Twp. 45–35 North Central; Milltown 61–51 Marengo; Salem 56–51 West Washington; South Central 68–67 Lanesville; Corydon 65–51

Morgan Twp.; Milltown 48–45 Salem; Corydon 90–50 South Central; Corydon 53–51 Milltown. Officials: Dwain Laird, Walter Vanover, John Bush.

SEYMOUR: Brownstown 69–65 Crothersville; Medora 83–78 Cortland; Seymour 77–57 Freetown; Austin 76–74 Clearspring; Brownstown 85–69 Medora; Seymour 80–64 Austin; Seymour 79–70 Brownstown. Officials: Robert Rose, Ray Vescovi, Wallace Reeve.

SOUTH BEND: St. Joseph's 71–54 Riley; Mishawaka 60–58 Washington (ot); Madison 81–74 North Liberty; Mishawaka 70–62 St. Joseph's; Adams 85–58 Clay; Central 96–74 New Carlisle; Lakeville 64–55 Greene; Central 67–49 Adams; Mishawaka 80–76 Madison (ot); Central 97–58 Lakeville; Central 64–61 Mishawaka. Officials: Tom Dean, John Mikels, R. Gerald Sweet, Ned Brenizer.

SOUTHPORT: Howe 71–66 Southport (ot); Wood 76–57 Decatur Central; Washington 67–54 Manual; Beech Grove 59–51 Franklin Central; Howe 83–66 Sacred Heart; Washington 84–55 Wood; Howe 59–56 Beech Grove; Howe 75–64 Washington. Officials: John Fee, Jim Ladd, John Sheets.

SULLIVAN: Pleasantville 69–55 Hymera; North Central 85–50 Dugger; Shakamak 89–64 Coal City; Carlisle 50–44 Sullivan; North Central 59–57 Pleasantville; Shakamak 77–56 Carlisle; Shakamak 75–73 North Central. Officials: Harold Gourley, Charles Adams, Richard Pattengale.

SWITZ CITY: Worthington 63–60 Elnora; Eastern 69–59 Linton; Bloomfield 71–57 L&M; Switz City 98–61 Freedom; Eastern 65–45 Worthington; Bloomfield 66–48 Switz City; Bloomfield 77–44 Eastern. Officials: Jack Small, William Williamson, Gene Wilm.

TELL CITY: Tell City 69–47 Leavenworth; Dale 79–52 English; Chrisney 66–40 Rockport; Perry Central 52–47 Cannelton; Tell City 68–50 Dale; Perry Central 59–48 Chrisney; Tell City 55–40 Perry Central. Officials: Donald Call, Paul Meyer, L. C. Thorne.

TERRE HAUTE: Schulte 69–66 Staunton (2ot); Honey Creek 42–31 Gerstmeyer; Wiley 55–52 Laboratory; Garfield 63–54 West Vigo; Schulte 45–42 Honey Creek; Garfield 40–38 Wiley (ot); Garfield 55–54 Schulte (4ot). Officials: Roger Emmert, Frank Bradshaw, James DeGroote.

VAN BUREN: Gosport 65–62 Bowling Green; Brazil 65–42 Patricksburg; Spencer 93–84 Cory; Van Buren 78–63 Clay City; Brazil 78–68 Gosport; Spencer 74–57 Van Buren; Spencer 73–71 Brazil. Officials: Earle Wolfe, Billy Lee Walker, Herod Toon.

VINCENNES: Petersburg 69–62 Central Catholic; Fritchton 69–62 Wheatland; North Knox 95–56 Decker; Vincennes 76–59 Monroe City; Petersburg 62–60 Fritchton; North Knox 89–72 Vincennes; North Knox 86–68 Petersburg. Officials: Winfield. Jacobs, Richard Crays, Noble Rector.

WARSAW: Larwill 75–65 Leesburg; Columbia City 96–59 North Webster; Warsaw 96–61 Syracuse; Mentone 70–62 Claypool; Milford 74–72 Pierceton; Columbia City 86–65 Larwill; Warsaw 97–74 Mentone; Columbia City 104–78 Milford; Columbia City 80–74 Warsaw. Officials: Stan Dubis, David Parry, Ron Jones.

WASHINGTON: Washington 65–64 Plainville; Loogootee 80–48 Alfordsville; Loogootee St. John 62–60 Barr Twp. (ot); Shoals 77–59 Washington Catholic; Washington 70–51 Odon; Loogootee 60–50 Loogootee St. John; Shoals 75–67 Washington; Loogootee 71–64 Shoals. Officials: Jimmy Dimitroff, Charles Bertram, Jack Mercer.

WINCHESTER: Monroe Central 71–53 Ridgeville; Center 72–70 Lynn (ot); Driver 114–72 Madison Twp.; Union City 63–59 Union; Center 62–60 Monroe Central; Driver 91–67 Union City; Driver 87–56 Center. Officials: Richard Foster, Maurice Gardner, Robert Wells.

ZIONSVILLE: Lebanon 81–54 Pinnell; Granville-Wells 64–58 Speedway; Zionsville 74–60

Tourney Time

Pike; Thorntown 62–59 Dover; Lebanon 69–59 Wells; Zionsville 69–59 Thorntown; Lebanon 54–51 Zionsville. Officials: Vern Doles, Melvin Botkin, Charles Stumpf.

1964 REGIONALS

COLUMBUS: Columbus 83–41 Madison; Franklin 69–67 Clarksburg; Columbus 117–70 Franklin. Officials: Bob Showalter, Earle Wolfe, Earnest Baldwin, Lauren Griffith, Jack Small, Howard Risley.

CONNERSVILLE: Brookville 73–54 Holton; Rushville 57–41 North Dearborn; Rushville 78–60 Brookville. Officials: Kenneth Blankenbaker, J. F. Grimes, Winfield Jacobs, Harold Mason, William Goshert, Harry Inskeep.

EAST CHICAGO: Michigan City 106–87 Gary Froebel; Gary Tolleston 84–62 East Chicago Washington; Gary Tolleston 93–83 Michigan City. Officials: Gerald Imel, Richard Foster, Thomas Dean, John Arnold, Wayne Crispen, Harry Green.

ELKHART: Elkhart 71–39 Culver; South Bend Central 85–68 Columbia City; Elkhart 73–65 South Bend Central. Officials: Richard Pattengale, John Holmes, Robert Spay, Robert Fisher, Homer Owens, Bill Hile.

EVANSVILLE: Rex Mundi 69–66 Tell City; Princeton 56–54 Boonville; Rex Mundi 85–61 Princeton. Officials: Walter Swift, Danny Jacobs, Fred Marlow, Darrell McFall, Glen Wisler, Marvin Cave.

FORT WAYNE: Ashley 62–57 Adams Central; Garrett 76–72 Central, Ft. Wayne; Garrett 62–59 Ashley. Officials: John Sheets, Ralph Cox, Dwain Laird, Edgar Powers, Robert Krammer, Ernie Sohl.

GREENCASTLE: Greencastle 82–79 Turkey Run; Crawfordsville 63–62 Williamsport; Greencastle 114–84 Crawfordsville. Officials: Everett Campbell, Harold Gourley, Floyd Reed, James Davis, Roger Emmert, Donald Hubbard.

HUNTINGBURG: Springs Valley 72–64 North Knox; Loogootee 49–46 Bloomfield; Springs Valley 84–69 Loogootee. Officials: Don Hurst, Francis Terrell, James Beyer, Charles Stumph, John Williams, William Malloy.

INDIANAPOLIS: Indianapolis Howe 75–49 Danville; Anderson 75–65 Tech; Howe 68–64 Anderson. Officials: Eugene Butts, Richard Sweet, Don McCoy, Thomas Huffman, Bill Larkin, Zeke Williams.

JEFFERSONVILLE: Seymour 67–65 Corydon; Marshall Twp. 75–69 Silver Creek; Seymour 87–68 Marshall Twp. Officials: Jimmy Dimitroff, Howard Morgan, Robert Laird, Donald Call, Arthur Thompson, Jim Ruby

KOKOMO: Lebanon 67–63 Manchester; Kokomo 68–66 Noblesville; Kokomo 71–51 Lebanon. Officials: Max Andress, Kenneth Payne, Don Shiflet, Wallace Reeve, Larry Gradeless, Norman Shields.

LAFAYETTE: Lafayette 73–61 Clinton Prairie; North White 63–60 Fowler; Lafayette 89–75 North White. Officials: Marion Acton, Ronald Jones, Lewis B. Goshert, George Avery, Robert Rose, Raymond Robison.

LOGANSPORT: Pioneer 63–60 DeMotte; Valparaiso 77–68 North Judson; Valparaiso 64–62 Pioneer. Officials: David Habegger, Robert Reed, Robert Cherry, Vic Wukovits, Charles Fouty, Anthony Lazar.

MARION: Swayzee 65–61 Liberty Center (9ot- all-time Indiana record); Huntington 68–54 Portland; Huntington 58–33 Swayzee. Officials: John Thomas, William May, Vern Doles, Eugene Marks, Wendell Baker, Joseph Bella.

NEW CASTLE: Richmond 79–69 Winchester; Muncie South 62–59 New Castle; Muncie South 80–79 Richmond. Officials: Roy Kilby, Lowell Smith, Glen Bonsett, Don Hollman, John Fee, Ned Brenizer.

TERRE HAUTE: Martinsville 69–60 Spencer; Garfield 90–88 Shakamak; Martinsville 50–44 Garfield. Officials: James W. Schwenk, Richard C. Gebhart, Robert Davidson, Charles Garber, Jr., Wesley Oler, Eugene R. Lillie.

1964 SEMI-STATES

EVANSVILLE: Seymour 86–71 Springs Valley; Rex Mundi 78–53 Martinsville; Rex Mundi 76–53 Seymour. Officials: Robert Spay, Robert Cherry, Wayne Crispen, Wendell Baker, Winfield Jacobs, Jack Small.

FORT WAYNE: Huntington 76–61 Kokomo; Elkhart 80–70 Garrett; Huntington 64–58 Elkhart, Officials: Everett Campbell, Roger Emmert, Robert Davidson, Glen Wisler, Charles Fouty, Arthur Thompson.

INDIANAPOLIS: Columbus 81–56 Howe; Rushville 82–72 Muncie Southside; Columbus 79–62 Rushville. Officials: John Fee, David Habegger, Wesley Oler, Gerald Imel, Roy Kilby, Floyd Reed.

LAFAYETTE: Valparaiso 80–77 Greencastle, Lafayette 95–64 Gary Tolleston; Lafayette 73–67 Valparaiso. Officials: Homer Owens, John Williams, Bill Larkin, Thomas Dean, Ken Blankenbaker, Larry Gradeless.

1964 FINALS—March 21

INDIANAPOLIS (Butler Fieldhouse): Huntington 71–67 Columbus; Lafayette Jefferson 74–61 Evansville Rex Mundi; Lafayette Jefferson 58–55 Huntington. Officials: Everett Campbell, Larry Gradeless, Wesley Oler, Charles Fouty, Winfield Jacobs, Robert Spay.

1965 SECTIONALS

ADAMS CENTRAL: Decatur 58–48 Monroeville; Monmouth 63–53 Hoagland; Berne 67–66 Decatur Catholic; Adams Central 71–65 Woodlan; Decatur 80–63 Monmouth; Adams Central 80–63 Monmouth; Adams Central 70–67 Decatur. Officials: Bob Showalter, Jim Carey, Don Snedeker.

ANDERSON: Anderson 78–66 Elwood; Alexandria 82–67 Summitville; St. Mary's 64–60 Daleville; Madison Heights 63–56 Pendleton; Markleville 66–62 Frankton (ot); Lapel 70–60 Highland; Anderson 68–58 Alexandria; Madison Heights 81–58 St. Mary's; Markleville 61–56 Lapel (ot); Anderson 73–61 Madison Heights; Anderson 72–46 Markleville. Officials: Winfield Jacobs, Donald Edwards, Jerry Larrison, Don Hurst.

ANGOLA: Ashley 59–57 Shipshewana-Scott; Lakeland 98–43 Fremont; Topeka 77–54 Prairie Heights; Hamilton 63–45 Angola; Lakeland 86–56 Ashley; Topeka 66–60 Hamilton; Lakeland

Tourney Time

83–44 Topeka. Officials: David Habegger, Frank Hoagburg, Don Yager.

BEDFORD: Paoli 50–47 Tunnelton; Marshall Twp. 80–66 Bedford; Orleans 53–52 Fayetteville; Shawswick 67–53 Heltonville; Oolitic 65–59 Mitchell; Marshall Twp. 78–61 Paoli; Orleans 58–55 Shawswick; Marshall Twp. 44–43 Oolitic; Orleans 54–48 Marshall Twp. Officials: James Ruby, Noble Rector, William Phillips, Clifford Runnebohm.

BLUFFTON: Ossian 86–38 Liberty Center; Bluffton 55–51 Lancaster Central; Salamonie Twp. 52–51 Chester Center (ot); Petroleum 52–50 Jackson Center; Ossian 61–35 Bluffton; Salamonie Twp. 65–43 Petroleum; Ossian 69–30 Salamonie Twp.. Officials: James Davis, Duane Conrad, Jim Ladd.

BOONVILLE: Boonville 95–66 Luce Twp.; Lynnville 78–45 Stendal: Elberfeld 82–51 Millersburg; Castle 95–36 Spurgeon; Boonville 80–56 Lynnville; Castle 85–58 Elberfeld; Boonville 83–63 Castle. Officials: Howard Morgan, Richard Crays, Rudy Tabereaux.

BRAZIL: Spencer 104–34 Bowling Green; Brazil 92–62 Patricksburg; Van Buren 82–45 Clay City; Cory 60–56 Gosport; Spencer 84–70 Brazil; Van Buren 92–32 Cory; Spencer 65–62 Van Buren. Officials: Roger Emmert, Marvin Vail, Wallace Reeve.

BROWNSBURG: Avon 69–47 Charlton; Cascade 92–62 Plainfield; North Salem 51–49 Brownsburg; Danville 67–55 Pittsboro, Cascade 71–38 Avon; Danville 95–56 North Salem; Cascade 72–56 Danville. Officials: Robert Fisher, Harold Gray, Jack Goen.

CARMEL: Westfield 78–61 Walnut Grove; Noblesville. 78–64 Jackson Central; Tipton 84–66 Carmel; Sheridan 68–65 Fishers; Noblesville 74–51 Westfield; Tipton 94–58 Sheridan; Tipton 70–58 Noblesville. Officials: Charles Fouty, Raymond Mitrione, William Malloy.

CAYUGA: North Vermillion 82–60 Rockville; Turkey Run 107–57 Kingman; Clinton 61–50 Alamo; Montezuma 65–48 Rosedale; North Vermillion 60–50 Turkey Run; Montezuma 69–47 Clinton; North Vermillion 80–58 Montezuma. Officials: Earle Wolfe, Robert Wendt, Carl Petercheff.

CHESTERTON: Chesterton 55–46 Boone Grove; Portage 77–74 Jackson Twp.; Valparaiso 77–63 Wheeler; Kouts 59–41 Washington Twp.; Morgan Twp. 59–52 Liberty Twp.; Portage 57–54 Chesterton; Valparaiso 89–64 Kouts; Portage 79–56 Morgan Twp.; Valparaiso 97–79 Portage. Officials: Edgar Powers, Jr., Gary Muncy, Arthur Largent, Richard Pattengale.

COLUMBUS: Columbus 94–44 Waldron; Brown County 91–73 Southwestern; Triton Central 75–53 Hauser; Shelbyville 64–46 Nineveh; Columbus 87–69 Brown County; Shelbyville 63–61 Triton (ot); Columbus 87–59 Shelbyville. Officials: Lauren Griffith, Herod Toon, Allen Voorhis.

CONNERSVILLE: Brookville 95–51 Laurel; Liberty 66–62 Connersville; Straughn 77–62 Alquina; Whitewater 72–54 Fayette Central; Brookville 69–42 Liberty; Whitewater 82–76 Straughn; Brookville 78–46 Whitewater. Officials: Ray Robison, Robert Kirk, Marvin Cave.

COVINGTON: Richland Twp. 63–61 Covington; Williamsport 75–73 Pine Village; Seeger 58–47 Veedersburg; Attica 89–43 Hillsboro: Williamsport 65–51 Richland Twp.; Attica 69–52 Seeger; Williamsport 54–50 Attica. Officials: John Arnold, Ray Ward, Warren Keyser.

CRAWFORDSVILLE: Crawfordsville 75–60 Waveland; Waynetown 63–60 Ladoga; Darlington 47–45 Coal Creek Central; New Ross 67–58 New Market; Crawfordsville 66–50 Waynetown, New Ross 72–52 Darlington; Crawfordsville 72–68 New Ross. Officials: Richard Sweet, Bobby Goble, Kenneth Payne.

EAST CHICAGO: Gary Tolleston 73–49 Gary Edison; Calumet 61–55 East Chicago

Roosevelt; Hammond Noll 73–55 Andrean; Tolleston 62–58 Calumet; East Chicago Washington 93–46 Hobart; Merrillville 71–67 Crown Point; Tolleston 72–63 Noll; Washington 100–69 Merrillville; Washington 71–57 Tolleston. Officials: Robert Spay, Norris Boomershine, Richard Brainerd, Lewis Goshert.

ELKHART: New Paris 65–63 Millersburg; Elkhart 72–57 Goshen; Middlebury 51–50 Wakarusa; Concord 101–64 Jefferson; Penn 89–42 Jimtown; Nappanee 98–36 Bristol; Elkhart 84–47 New Paris; Middlebury 74–68 Concord; Penn 67–61 Nappanee; Elkhart 77–62 Middlebury; Penn 64–62 Elkhart. Officials: Charles Garber, Joe Smelcer, Roger DeYoung, Richard Gebhart.

EVANSVILLE: North 72–43 New Harmony; Bosse 50–48 Mt. Vernon; Central 50–45 Reitz; Memorial 90–73 Mater Dei; Harrison 78–67 Rex Mundi; Bosse 66–60 North; Central 56–51 Memorial; Bosse 62–59 Harrison; Central 70–58 Bosse. Officials: James Patterson, Wayne Myers, Morris Cohen, John Thomas.

FORT WAYNE: North Side 78–55 Central Catholic; Central 64–52 Harlan; Concordia 92–62 Arcola; Elmhurst 80–51 Leo; South Side 65–63 Huntertown (ot); New Haven 73–65 Bishop Luers; North Side 58–42 Central; Elmhurst 69–58 Concordia; New Haven 68–56 8outh Side; North Side 79–47 Elmhurst; North Side 78–52 New Haven. Officials: Lawrence Gradeless, Harold Ashbrook, Eugene Linn, Charles Sallee.

FRANKFORT: Clinton Prairie 60–54 Linden; Delphi 59–53 Lauramie Twp.; Clinton Central 73–42 Dayton; Frankfort 80–66 Rossville; Clinton Prairie 50–44 Delphi; Frankfort 60–59 Clinton Central; Frankfort 81–61 Clinton Prairie. Officials: Don Hollman, Larry Pinkerton, Ronald Hosinski.

GARY: Froebel 95–54 East Gary Edison; Lew Wallace 69–66 River Forest; Emerson 59–52 Wirt; Roosevelt 78–39 Mann; Froebel 89–62 Lew Wallace; Roosevelt 112–45 Emerson; Roosevelt 66–64 Froebel. Officials: John Fee, Russell Freeland, William Goshert.

GREENCASTLE: Greencastle 98–67 Russellville; Cloverdale 95–81 Bainbridge; Fillmore 77–71 Belle Union; Reelsville 76–61 Roachdale; Cloverdale 74–62 Greencastle; Fillmore 73–69 Reelsville; Cloverdale 78–66 Fillmore. Officials: Fred Marlow, William Gray, William Bateman.

GREENSBURG: Burney 60–42 New Point; Greensburg 53–31 Saint Paul; North Vernon 72–52 Clarksburg; Jackson Twp. 63–53 Sandcreek; Greensburg 73–51 Burney; North Vernon 58–36 Jackson Twp.; North Vernon 60–51 Greensburg. Officials: Ken Blankenbaker, Melvin Botkin, James P. Carey.

HAMMOND: Hammond High 69–42 Lowell; Griffith 63–52 Morton; Clark 71–57 Gavit; Hammond High 54–51 Griffith; Tech 76–68 Whiting; Highland 58–47 Dyer Central; Hammond High 69–62 Clark; Tech 53–47 Highland; Hammond High 84–73 Tech. Officials: Jack Small, John Mikels, Lloyd Chambers, John Sheets.

HUNTINGBURG: Birdseye 83–78 Holland (3ot); Huntingburg 62–51 Jasper; Ireland 79–57 Otwell; Springs Valley 68–60 Dubois; St. Ferdinand 54–52 Winslow: Huntingburg 74–54 Birdseye; Springs Valley 61–60 Ireland; Huntingburg 77–68 St. Ferdinand; Springs Valley 72–65 Huntingburg. Officials: Jimmy Dimitroff, John Manka, Russell Rogers, Max Andress.

HUNTINGTON: Huntington Twp. 45–43 Jefferson; Clear Creek 75–67 Roanoke; Union 50–38 Rock Creek; Andrews 62–61 Lancaster; Huntington High 71–41 Huntington Catholic; Huntington Twp. 63–57 Clear Creek; Union 71–54 Andrews; Huntington High 62–42 Huntington Twp.; Huntington High 44–41 Union. Officials: John Williams, Fred Kehoe, Byron Weaver, Harry Inskeep.

Tourney Time

INDIANAPOLIS: Crispus Attucks 57–42 Scecina; Ben Davis 77–75 Shortridge; Tech 58–50 Broad Ripple; Cathedral 65–55 Warren Central; North Central 55–50 Lawrence Central; Arlington 94–52 Chatard; Northwest 72–56 School for the Deaf; Ben Davis 69–59 Crispus Attucks; Cathedral 58–56 Tech; North Central 79–68 Arlington; Ben Davis 77–62 Northwest; Cathedral 72–71 North Central; Ben Davis 66–57 Cathedral. Officials: Wayne Crispen, Gene Marks, Marvin Heaton, Thomas Dean.

JEFFERSONVILLE: Providence 67–66 Georgetown; Silver Creek 83–61 Borden; New Albany 100–60 Clarksville; Jeffersonville 131–78 Henryville; Providence 65–58 Silver Creek; New Albany 67–65 Jeffersonville; Providence 77–65 New Albany. Officials: Robert Cherry, Walter Vanover, Donald Hubbard.

KENDALLVILLE: Auburn 67–65 Albion; Wolf Lake 66–58 Cromwell; Kendallville 75–71 Avilla; Waterloo 63–62 Churubusco; Eastside 83–48 Wawaka; Garrett 57–26 Ligonier; Auburn 60–48 Wolf Lake; Waterloo 87–52 Kendallville; Garrett 70–52 Eastside; Waterloo 47–40 Auburn; Garrett 47–38 Waterloo. Officials: Earnest Baldwin, Billy Maroney, Audley Cragun, Samuel Reed.

KENTLAND: Fowler 61–49 Oxford; Brook 71–55 Boswell; Kentland 65–59 Ambia; Mt. Ayr 76–41 Morocco; Fowler 70–48 Brook; Kentland 69–56 Mt. Ayr; Kentland 67–60 Fowler. Officials: Anthony Lazar, Donald Reinholt, Robert Sweet.

KOKOMO: Kokomo 58–49 Eastern; Northwestern 72–71 Windfall; Sharpsville 69–66 Carroll; Maconaquah 54–44 Western; Kokomo 83–47 Northwestern; Maconaquah 74–50 Sharpsville; Kokomo 67–51 Maconaquah. Officials: Homer Owens, Wayne VanSickle, Gene Butts.

LAFAYETTE: Jefferson 75–55 West Lafayette; Central Catholic 75–44 East Tipp; Southwestern 78–50 Klondike; Battle Ground 60–42 Montmorenci; Jefferson 64–52 Central Catholic; Battle Ground 67–60 Southwestern; Jefferson 89–52 Battle Ground. Officials: Floyd Reed, Boynton Robson, Francis Terrell.

LAWRENCEBURG: Moores Hill 41–35 Patriot; Dillsboro 72–55 North Dearborn; Aurora 62–55 Rising Sun; Vevay 74–64 Lawrenceburg; Dillsboro 63–46 Moores Hill; Aurora 77–62 Vevay; Aurora 68–55 Dillsboro. Officials: John Holmes, Roger McGriff, Jack Mercer.

LOGANSPORT: Pioneer 70–35 Camden; Caston 63–62 Kewanna (ot); Logansport 57–50 Peru; Cass 75–71 North Miami; Caston 50–49 Pioneer (ot); Logansport 62–61 Cass; Logansport 60–52 Caston. Officials: Gerald Imel, Paul Leamon, Charlie Stumpf.

MADISON: New Washington 84–63 Dupont; Shawe Memorial 93–47 Lexington; Madison 78–60 Charlestown; Southwestern 86–60 Deputy; Shawe Memorial 82–72 New Washington; Madison 63–57 Southwestern; Madison 64–48 Shawe Memorial. Officials: Glen Wisler, Lloyd Baugh, Harold Mason.

MANCHESTER: Manchester 76–64 Northfield; Southwood 75–51 White's; Wabash 93–62 South Whitley; Silver Lake 85–65 Akron; Manchester 81–63 Southwood; Silver Lake 65–63 Wabash; Manchester 63–56 Silver Lake. Officials: Joseph Bella, Robert Manor, Neal Jay.

MARION: Fairmount 66–65 Oak Hill; Swayzee 55–54 Jefferson; Mississinewa 68–65 Van Buren; Marion 86–54 Bennett; Fairmount 55–50 Swayzee; Marion 78–58 Mississinewa; Marion 71–55 Fairmount. Officials: Zeke Williams, Richard Vendrely, Walter Swift.

MARTINSVILLE: Mooresville 65–54 Monrovia; University 72–59 Unionville; Bloomington 99–68 Smithville; Martinsville 90–63 Morgantown; Edgewood 68–43 Eminence; University 56–54 Mooresville; Bloomington 69–64 Martinsville; University 60–57 Edgewood; Bloomington

77–65 University. Officials: Richard Foster, Max Hensler. David Avery, Raymond Vescovi.

MICHIGAN CITY: New Carlisle 66–63 South Central; St. Mary's 78–61 Rolling Prairie; Wanatah 79–75 LaCrosse; Westville 75–72 Union Twp.; Michigan City 56–48 LaPorte; New Carlisle 116–67 St. Mary's; Westville 78–72 Wanatah; Michigan City 95–59 New Carlisle; Michigan City 95–48 Westville. Officials: Robert Kramer, Gordon McCain, Don Lozier, Ernie Sohl.

MILAN: Sunman 61–60 Milan; Batesville 80–68 Versailles; Jac-Cen-Del 63–48 Cross Plains; Holton 67–54 New Marion; Sunman 70–66 Batesville; Jac-Cen-Del 82–65 Holton; Jac-Cen-Del 69–57 Sunman. Officials: William May, Kenneth Barnes, Donald Call.

MONON: Medaryville 78–57 Tefft; Brookston 51–44 Twin Lakes; Wheatfield 60–54 Chalmers; North White 70–53 Francesville; Brookston 69–60 Medaryville; Wheatfield 62–59 North White; Wheatfield 47–42 Brookston. Officials: Robert Reed, David Schwartz, John Gassensmith.

MUNCIE: Burris 90–47 Eaton; Southside 76–38 Harrison; Royerton 69–57 Cowan; Central 80–59 Yorktown; Gaston 85–78 Selma; Albany 70–64 DeSoto; Southside 79–68 Burris (ot); Central 79–73 Royerton; Gaston 85–62 Albany; Southside 79–68 Central; Southside 67–57 Gaston. Officials: Dwain Laird, Richard Freeman, William Pittman, Robert Laird.

NEW CASTLE: Mt. Vernon 69–53 Cadiz; Greenfield 63–56 Middletown; New Castle 100–48 Sulphur Springs; Blue River 66–44 Hancock Central; Knightstown 76–59 Spiceland; Mt. Vernon 66–61 Greenfield; New Castle 63–58 Blue River; Mt. Vernon 77–64 Knightstown; New Castle 81–61 Mt. Vernon. Officials: Roy Kilby, Jack Gardner, Richard Lederman, Marion Acton.

PLYMOUTH: Plymouth 93–69 LaPaz; Triton 89–57 West; Argos 65–63 Walkerton (ot); Bremen 92–62 Tyner; Triton 77–59 Plymouth; Bremen 65–36 Argos; Triton 68–67 Bremen. Officials: Ron Jones, James Cox, Ralph Cox.

PORTLAND: Montpelier 75–50 Gray; Pennville 67–61 Bryant; Geneva 71–59 Dunkirk; Portland 77–58 Hartford City; Montpelier 79–57 Pennville; Portland 65–36 Geneva; Montpelier 63–59 Portland (ot). Officials: Howard Risley, William VanSickle, John Bush.

PRINCETON: Princeton 93–45 Francisco; Ft. Branch 68–60 Haubstadt; Oakland City 74–64 Owensville; North Posey 51–41 Mackey; Mt. Olympus 76–46 White River; Princeton 61–48 Ft. Branch; Oakland City 60–57 North Posey; Princeton 83–60 Mt. Olympus; Princeton 91–65 Oakland City. Officials: Norman Shields, Jack Cummings, Norman Chestnut, Ben Olsson.

RICHMOND: Randolph Southern 72–67 Centerville; Webster-Williamsburg 73–39 Whitewater-Fountain City; Hagerstown 56–53 Lewisville; Richmond 58–56 Cambridge City; Webster-Williamsburg 45–43 Randolph Southern; Hagerstown 71–58 Richmond; Hagerstown 57–51 Webster-Williamsburg. Officials: Glen Bonsett, Francis Fiddler, Robert Wells.

RUSHVILLE: Mays 70–69 Morristown; Carthage 86–60 Morton Memorial; Milroy 74–72 Manilla; Rushville 85–72 Eastern Hancock; New Salem 88–70 Arlington; Carthage 66–62 Mays; Rushville 73–60 Milroy; New Salem 72–56 Carthage; Rushville 72–59 New Salem. Officials: Don Shiflet, Louis Schmalfeldt, Billy Lee Walker, William Fields.

SALEM: Corydon 64–58 Marengo; North Central 62–57 Eastern; Milltown 58–41 South Central; Salem 65–62 West Washington: Morgan Twp. 74–40 Lanesville; Corydon 72–45 North Central; Milltown 54–52 Salem; Morgan Twp. 54–43 Corydon; Morgan Twp. 68—48 Milltown. Officials: Harold Gourley, Frank Bradshaw, Bruce Knecht, James DeGroote.

SEYMOUR: Cortland 65–64 Medora; Crothersville 68–66 Clearspring: Scottsburg 82–73

Tourney Time

Austin; Seymour 89–58 Brownstown; Crothersville 84–69 Cortland; Seymour 81–80 Scottsburg; Seymour 96–68 Crothersville. Officials: Robert Davidson, Gene Wilm, Charles Adams.

SOUTH BEND: Central 67–55 Mishawaka; St. Joseph 72–60 Riley; Adams 63–55 Clay (ot); Central 74–70 St. Joseph; Washington 73–46 North Liberty; Lakeville 86–53 Greene Twp.; Central 61–49 Adams; Washington 63–49 Lakeville; Washington 63–62 Central. Officials: Stanley Dubis, Wayne Targgart, James Burt, Thomas Hoffman.

SOUTHPORT: Indianapolis Wood 90–72 Decatur Central; Southport 80–62 Franklin Central; Indianapolis Howe 77–59 Sacred Heart; Washington 90–43 Chartrand; Manual 69–61 Beech Grove; Wood 85–62 Southport; Washington 80–66 Howe; Manual 75–70 Wood (ot); Washington 67–61 Manual. Officials: Everett Campbell, Eugene Lillie, Gil Baumgartner, Bill Hile.

SULLIVAN: Sullivan 73–40 Dugger; North Central 72–63 Shakamak; Pleasantville 63–57 Carlisle; Hymera 68–62 Coal City; Sullivan 60–59 North Central; Pleasantville 69–61 Hymera; Sullivan 70–57 Pleasantville. Officials: Darrel McFall, Robert Rohleder, Charles Bertram.

SWITZ CITY: Worthington 62–55 Linton Stockton; Bloomfield 48–34 Odon; Eastern 60–54 Elnora; L & M 56–41 Central; Bloomfield 47–36 Worthington; L & M 52–50 Eastern; Bloomfield 51–39 L & M. Officials: Arthur Thompson, Charles Daum, Russell Owens.

TELL CITY: Perry Central 58–42 English; Chrisney 64–53 Rockport; Tell City 63–55 Leavenworth; Dale 65–51 Cannelton; Chrisney 65–57 Perry Central; Dale 52–45 Tell City; Chrisney 73–59 Dale. Officials: Vern Doles, Jack Chestnut, Maurice Gardner.

TERRE HAUTE: Laboratory 58–57 West Vigo (ot); Gerstmeyer 71–64 Honey Creek; Wiley 53–51 Staunton; Schulte 59–58 Garfield; Laboratory 62–60 Gerstmeyer; Schulte 37–34 Wiley (ot); Laboratory 58–52 Schulte. Officials: James Schwenk, David Loewenstein, Charlie Lentz.

VINCENNES: Petersburg 83–66 Monroe City; Vincennes 71–63 Wheatland; North Knox 74–66 Central Catholic; Decker 65–60 Fritchton; Vincennes 92–65 Petersburg; North Knox 109–67 Decker; Vincennes 63–46 North Knox. Officials: James Beyer, Donald Shields, William Williamson.

WARSAW: North Webster 78–57 Larwill; Warsaw 73–29 Syracuse; Pierceton 85–63 Milford; Columbia City 74–54 Mentone; Claypool 87–85 Leesburg; Warsaw 79–46 North Webster; Pierceton 74–68 Columbia City; Warsaw 80–72 Claypool; Warsaw 62–47 Pierceton. Officials: Harry Green, Donald Koester, Clair Robison, George Avery.

WASHINGTON: Washington 55–43 Washington Catholic; Plainville 77–51 Alfordsville; Loogootee 78–59 Shoals; Loogootee St. John's 61–53 Montgomery; Washington 83–43 Plainville; Loogootee 56–52 Loogootee St. John's; Washington 59–48 Loogootee. Officials: Wendell Baker, Carl Schnebelt, James Eads.

WHITELAND: Whiteland 80–64 Clark Twp.; Greenwood 79–64 Edinburg; Franklin 71–43 Trafalgar; Center Grove 79–38 New Palestine; Greenwood 80–71 Whiteland; Franklin 73–61 Center Grove; Greenwood 72–66 Franklin. Officials: Lowell Smith, John Tucker, L.C. Thorne.

WINAMAC: Aubbeenaubbee 53–49 Star City; Winamac 66–61 North Judson; Richland Center 68–65 Monterey; Knox 81–51 Oregon-Davis; Rochester 68–63 Culver: Winamac 103–43 Aubbeenaubbee; Knox 39–29 Richland Center; Winamac 60–39 Rochester; Winamac 79–55 Knox. Officials: Ray Nemeth, George Dunleavy, Martin Burdette, James Tansey.

WINCHESTER: Driver (Winchester) 104–69 Redkey; Madison Twp. 83–55 Ridgeville; Union (Modoc) 63–62 Center; Monroe Central 68–64 Union City (ot); Driver 100–66 Madison Twp.; Monroe Central 79–59 Union (Modoc); Monroe Central 74–64 Driver. Officials: J. Firman

Grimes. Gary Janeway, Dale Van Houten.

WOLCOTT: DeMotte 37–32 Fair Oaks; Remington 40–39 Wolcott; Otterbein 91–75 Rensselaer; Hebron 90–45 Goodland; DeMotte 68–53 Remington; Otterbein 74–67 Hebron; Otterbein 70–68 DeMotte. Officials: James Benecke, Melvin Fuller, Jonnie Webber.

ZIONSVILLE: Wells 69–65 Zionsville; Thorntown 92–51 Lizton; Speedway 63–54 Lebanon; Pike 84–54 Brebeuf; Wells 61–54 Thorntown; Speedway 73–59 Pike; Speedway 52–47 Wells. Officials: Danny Jacobs, Jerry Baker, John Ward.

1965 REGIONALS

COLUMBUS: Columbus 105–79 North Vernon; Madison 106–86 Greenwood; Columbus 78–75 Madison. Officials: Harold Gourley, James DeGroote, James Schwenk, Howard Morgan, Homer Owens, William May.

CONNERSVILLE: Brookville 91–63 Jac-Cen-Del; Aurora 71–70 Rushville (ot); Brookville 76–61 Aurora. Officials: Don Hollman, David Habegger, Charles Fouty, Harry Green, John Arnold, William Malloy.

COVINGTON: Cloverdale 81–60 Crawfordsville; North Vermillion 87–83 Williamsport; Cloverdale 84–70 North Vermillion. Officials: Earnest Baldwin, Robert Fisher, Robert Spay, Richard Gebhart, Robert Davison, Anthony Lazar.

EAST CHICAGO: Gary Roosevelt 79–64 Hammond High; East Chicago Washington 86–68 Valparaiso; Gary Roosevelt 84–70 East Chicago Washington. Officials: Bill Hile, Gene Marks, Zeke Williams, Walter Swift, Roy Kilby, Richard Pattengale.

ELKHART: Penn 87–81 Warsaw; South Bend Washington 65–55 Michigan City; South Bend Washington 95–66 Penn. Officials: Jimmy Dimitroff, Charles Sallee, John Sheets, Richard Foster, Everett Campbell, Eugene Lillie.

EVANSVILLE: Chrisney 68–62 Central; Princeton 82–53 Boonville; Princeton 66–46 Chrisney. Officials: Raymond Robison, Kenneth Payne, Donald Call, Richard Sweet, Glen Bonsett, Lauren Griffith.

FORT WAYNE: North Side 70–59 Lakeland; Garrett 59–43 Adams Central; North Side 59–55 Garrett. Officials: Charles Garber, Joseph Bella, Wendall Baker, James Ruby, Jack Small, Harold Mason.

HUNTINGBURG: Washington 77–58 Springs Valley; Bloomfield 59–56 Vincennes; Bloomfield 56–51 Washington. Officials: Darrel McFall, John Holmes, Ken Blankenbaker, Jack Mercer, Dwain Laird, Robert Laird.

INDIANAPOLIS: Washington 81–66 Ben Davis; Anderson 58–49 Cascade; Washington 75–71 Anderson. Officials: Winfield Jacobs, Danny Jacobs, Edgar Powers, Robert Reed, John Fee, Marion Acton.

JEFFERSONVILLE: Providence 56–43 Orleans; Seymour 78–62 Morgan Twp.; Seymour 76–69 Providence. Officials: Roger Emmert, James Davis, Howard Risley, Wallace Reeve, Glen Wisler, Charlie Stumpf.

KOKOMO: Kokomo 62–60 Speedway; Manchester 69–64 Tipton; Kokomo 98–57 Manchester. Officials: Floyd Reed, Ron Jones, Ernie Sohl, Ralph Cox, Robert Kramer, Thomas Hoffman.

LAFAYETTE: Lafayette Jeff 70–60 Frankfort; Kentland 58–52 Otterbein; Lafayette 73–44

Tourney Time

Kentland. Officials: Gene Butts, Don Snedeker, Lawrence Gradeless, Harry Inskeep, Robert Cherry, Robert Showalter.

LOGANSPORT: Winamac 61–51 Logansport; Triton 72–70 Wheatfield; Triton 67–64 Winamac. Officials: John Thomas, James Benecke, Don Shiflet, Francis Terrell, John Williams, Marvin Cave

MARION: Ossian 80–73 Montpelier; Marion 66–60 Huntington; Marion 83–64 Ossian. Officials: Fred Marlow, Norman Shields, Arthur Thompson, George Avery, J. Firman Grimes, Don Hurst.

NEW CASTLE: Muncie Southside 80–64 Monroe Central; New Castle 72–47 Hagerstown; Muncie Southside 67–65 New Castle. Officials: James Beyer, Max Andress, Gerald Imel, William Goshert, Wayne Crispen, Lewis Goshert.

TERRE HAUTE: Spencer 88–75 Terre Haute Laboratory; Bloomington 62–59 Sullivan; Bloomington 60–54 Spencer. Officials: Vern Doles, Donald Hubbard, Lowell Smith, John Ward, Thomas Dean, Earle Wolfe.

1965 SEMI–STATES

EVANSVILLE: Princeton 55–45 Bloomfield; Seymour 57–54 Bloomington; Princeton 57–50 Seymour. Officials: Charles Fouty, Arthur Thompson, Homer Owens, Glen Wisler, Jimmy Dimitroff, John Williams.

FORT WAYNE: Fort Wayne North Side 78–74 Kokomo; South Bend Washington 70–66 Marion; Fort Wayne North Side 58–55 South Bend Washington. Officials: Everett Campbell, John Thomas, John Fee, Robert Kramer, Winfield Jacobs, Ken Blankenbaker.

INDIANAPOLIS: Washington 79–63 Brookville; Muncie Southside 78–70 Columbus; Washington 69–52 Muncie Southside. Officials: Robert Davidson, James Schwenk, Floyd Reed, Thomas Dean, Lawrence Gradeless, Zeke Williams.

LAFAYETTE: Gary Roosevelt 72–61 Lafayette Jeff; Triton 70–67 Cloverdale; Gary Roosevelt 103–61 Triton. Officials: Dave Habegger, Gerald Imel, Roger Emmert, Roy Kilby, Robert Spay, Wendell Baker.

1965 FINALS—March 20

INDIANAPOLIS (Butler Fieldhouse): Indianapolis Washington 88–76 Princeton; Fort Wayne North Side 74–65 Gary Roosevelt; Indianapolis Washington 64–57 North Side. Officials: Robert Spay, Homer Owens, Lawrence Gradeless, Art Thompson, Charles Fouty, Roger Emmert.

1966 SECTIONALS

ANDERSON: Elwood 60–48 Pendleton; Markleville 69–68 Alexandria; Madison Heights 80–58 St. Mary's; Highland 57–44 Frankton; Anderson 91–56 Daleville; Markleville 81–79 Elwood (ot); Madison Heights 91–53 Highland; Anderson 91–67 Markleville; Anderson 83–70 Madison Heights. Officials: Jack Small, Allen Voorhis, Gary Muncy, Bill Hile.

ANGOLA: Topeka 60–58 Angola; Fremont 58–53 Prairie Heights; Waterloo 70–56 Shipshewana-Scott; Ashley 54–49 Lakeland; Eastside 53–51 Hamilton (ot); Fremont 71–53

Topeka; Waterloo 67–57 Ashley; Eastside 45–38 Fremont; Eastside 45–31 Waterloo. Officials: Gene Butts, Melvin Botkin, Arthur Largent, Don Lozier.

BEDFORD: Bedford 56–55 Marshall Twp.; Paoli 59–55 Fayetteville; Shawswick 56–46 Orleans; Oolitic 90–60 Tunnelton; Mitchell 82–59 Heltonville; Bedford 68–57 Paoli; Shawswick 66–60 Oolitic; Bedford 68–61 Mitchell; Bedford 63–56 Shawswick. Officials: Earle Wolfe, Roger McGriff, Louis Schmalfeldt, Marvin Cave.

BLOOMINGTON: Unionville 80–67 Morgantown; Eminence 64–63 University; Martinsville 59–44 Smithville; Bloomington 81–74 Edgewood; Unionville 94–69 Eminence; Bloomington 80–65 Martinsville; Unionville 69–68 Bloomington. Officials: James Schwenk, James R. Carey, Donald Hubbard.

BLUFFTON: Decatur 72–60 Liberty Center; Lancaster Central 74–61 Bluffton; Petroleum 58–56 Monmouth; Ossian 101–43 Chester Center; Decatur Catholic 88–61 Jackson Center; Lancaster Central 60–58 Decatur; Ossian 69–55 Petroleum; Decatur Catholic 64–57 Lancaster Central; Decatur Catholic 70–62 Ossian. Officials: John Williams, Billy Walker, Ray Mitrione, John Bush.

BOONVILLE: Castle 80–72 Haubstadt; South Spencer 79–53 Tecumseh; Stendal 59–57 Mackey; Boonville 71–45 Spurgeon; Castle 58–56 South Spencer; Boonville 81–57 Stendal; Boonville 88–73 Castle. Officials: William Malloy, Fred Myers, John Tucker.

BRAZIL: Reelsville 59–57 Spencer; Cloverdale 99–60 Patricksburg; Van Buren 83–69 Staunton; Brazil 94–55 Gosport; Cloverdale 68–48 Reelsville; Van Buren 79–75 Brazil; Cloverdale 71–51 Van Buren. Officials: Jim Ruby, Clair Robison, Howard Morgan.

BROWNSBURG: Pittsboro 69–49 Monrovia; Plainfield 57–49 Avon; Danville 62–61 Brownsburg; Mooresville 83–39 Charlton; Plainfield 61–52 Pittsboro; Mooresville 68–61 Danville; Mooresville 63–55 Plainfield. Officials: Danny Jacobs, Jim Ladd, Richard Crays.

CARMEL: Noblesville 55–51 Westfield; Lapel 75–72 Hamilton Heights; Tipton 57–48 Fishers; Carmel 67–62 Sheridan; Noblesville 76–63 Lapel; Carmel 81–63 Tipton; Carmel 58–56 Noblesville. Officials: Robert Reed, Earnest Baldwin, Wayne Van Sickle.

CHESTERTON: Portage 66–42 Washington Twp.; Wheeler 70–66 Jackson Twp.; Valparaiso 87–52 Morgan Twp.; Chesterton 61–39 Liberty Twp.; Portage 84–69 Wheeler; Valparaiso 87–67 Chesterton; Valparaiso 81–72 Portage. Officials: Ray Nemeth, Richard Brainerd, Richard Freeman.

COLUMBUS: Ninevah 55–53 Brown County; Columbus 105–48 Hauser; Shelbyville 66–53 Southwestern; Waldron 63–62 Edinburg; Columbus 93–48 Ninevah; Shelbyville 78–32 Waldron; Columbus 73–64 Shelbyville. Officials: Robert Davidson, James Cox, Charles Garber.

CONNERSVILLE: Laurel 73–70 Fayette Central; Connersville 90–59 Union; Straughn 80–73 Alquina; Brookville 54–49 Liberty; Connersville 78–57 Laurel; Brookville 68–47 Straughn; Brookville 62–41 Connersville. Officials: Howard Risley, McKee Munk, Jack Cummings.

COVINGTON: Pine Village 61–56 Seeger; Turkey Run 56–49 Covington; Attica 83–61 Fountain Central; North Vermillion 83–55 Williamsport; Turkey Run 72–69 Pine Village; Attica 74–48 North Vermillion; Turkey Run 60–59 Attica. Officials: Francis Terrell, Rudy Tabereaux, Jim Eads.

CRAWFORDSVILLE: Coal Creek Central 91–79 Crawfordsville; Ladoga 51–48 Waynetown; New Market 70–44 Alamo; New Ross 76–60 Waveland; Coal Creek Central 73–60 Ladoga; New Ross 72–63 New Market; Coal Creek Central 80–71 New Ross. Officials: Eugene Lillie, Ben

Tourney Time

Olsson, Robert Fisher.

CROWN POINT: Griffith 65–51 Boone Grove; Merrillville 63–57 Hebron; Crown Point 76–46 Dyer; Lowell 78–50 Kouts; Merrillville 44–41 Griffith; Crown Point 65–49 Lowell; Crown Point 68–52 Merrillville. Officials: Edgar Powers, Max Hensler, John Gassensmith.

EAST CHICAGO: Calumet 72–45 Gary Andrean; East Chicago Washington 45–39 Hammond Noll; East Chicago Roosevelt 72–63 Hobart; Tolleston 70–57 Gary Edison; Washington 51–38 Calumet; East Chicago Roosevelt 65–62 Tolleston; Washington 80–69 East Chicago Roosevelt. Officials: Roy Kilby, Harold Gray, Joe Smelcer.

ELKHART: Goshen 86–52 Bristol; Nappanee 67–58 Wakarusa; Concord 63–48 Middlebury; Elkhart 64–51 Penn; New Paris 61–52 Millersburg; Jefferson 70–68 Jimtown; Goshen 62–54 Nappanee; Elkhart 68–49 Concord; Jefferson 56–50 New Paris; Elkhart 66–63 Goshen (ot); Elkhart 77–56 Jefferson. Officials: Ernie Sohl, Frank Hoagburg, Gary Janeway, George Avery.

EVANSVILLE: Memorial 59–51 Central; Rex Mundi 79–40 Mater Dei; Harrison 71–56 North; Reitz 60–57 Bosse; Memorial 71–62 Rex Mundi; Harrison 42–34 Reitz; Memorial 63–61 Harrison. Officials: Charles Fouty, Noble J. Rector, Robert B. Sweet.

FORT WAYNE (#1): Snider 82–65 Hoagland; South Side 54–49 Woodlan; Huntertown 68–53 Dwenger; Monroeville 62–52 Luers; South Side 52–36 Snider; Monroeville 53–51 Huntertown; South Side 54–37 Monroeville. Officials: Bob Showalter, Ray Ward, John Arnold.

FORT WAYNE (#2): Central 80–59 Central Catholic; New Haven 74–68 Arcola; North Side 74–54 Concordia; Elmhurst 78–71 Leo; New Haven 65–63 Central (ot) North Side 52–47 Elmhurst; North Side 64–45 New Haven. Officials: Arthur Thompson, Samuel Reed, Charlie Lentz.

FRANKFORT: Frankfort 64–60 East Tipp; Rossville 61–59 Wainwright (ot); Delphi 62–54 Linden; Clinton Central 71–48 Clinton Prairie; Rossville 56–54 Frankfort (2ot); Clinton Central 80–59 Delphi; Clinton Central 61–46 Rossville. Officials: Thomas Hoffman, Bill Gray, Charles Stumpf.

FRANKLIN: Franklin 60–59 Triton Central; Morristown 71–53 Center Grove; Whiteland 83–62 Trafalgar; Greenwood 92–60 New Palestine; Franklin 60–59 Morristown; Greenwood 77–68 Whiteland; Greenwood 71–67 Franklin. Officials: Winfield Jacobs, Jerry A. Baker, William Bateman.

GARY: Horace Mann 51–42 Wirt; Lew Wallace 91–83 East Gary Edison; Roosevelt 85–35 Emerson; Froebel 97–56 River Forest; Horace Mann 64–54 Lew Wallace; Roosevelt 96–87 Froebel; Roosevelt 81–65 Horace Mann. Officials: Robert H. Spay, Duane F. Conrad, Norris Boomershine.

GREENCASTLE: Fillmore 55–51 Cascade; Rockville 72–53 North Salem; Russellville 70–52 Roachdale; Bainbridge 83–71 Greencastle; Fillmore 89–52 Rockville; Bainbridge 97–66 Russellville; Bainbridge 89–75 Fillmore. Officials: Robert Cherry, Norman Chestnut, Wallace Reeve.

GREENSBURG: Greensburg 89–46 St. Paul; Clarksburg 46–43 Sandcreek; New Point 62–53 Burney; Milroy 84–71 Jackson; Greensburg 61–36 Clarksburg; Milroy 84–61 New Point; Greensburg 87–62 Milroy. Officials: Homer Owens, Herod Toon, Robert Manor.

HAMMOND: Morton 71–61 Highland; Tech 80–69 Gavit; Whiting 80–65 Munster; Hammond High 72–50 Clark; Morton 64–63 Tech; Hammond High 64–54 Whiting; Hammond High 75–60 Morton. Officials: Zeke Williams, Billy Maroney, Walter Swift.

HUNTINGBURG: Jasper 95–29 Birdseye; Ireland 63–58 Winslow; Springs Valley 54–50

Holland; Dubois 78–72 Huntingburg; Jasper 62–39 Ireland; Springs Valley 66–61 Dubois; Springs Valley 59–57 Jasper (2ot) Officials: Dwain Laird, Donald Shields, Wayne Myers.

HUNTINGTON: Huntington 66–43 Huntington Twp.; Huntington Catholic 77–62 Rock Creek; Clear Creek 65–32 Andrews; Lancaster 55–44 Salamonie Twp; Roanoke 74–59 Union; Huntington 52–47 Huntington Catholic; Clear Creek 59–54 Lancaster; Huntington 73–27 Roanoke; Huntington 58–47 Clear Creek. Officials: Robert Laird, Bobby Goble, Don Reinholt, Ron Hosinski.

INDIANAPOLIS (Hinkle Fieldhouse): Washington 90–60 Broad Ripple; Tech 83–54 North Central; Ben Davis 66–63 Arlington; Cathedral 74–65 Crispus Attucks; Tech 83–74 Washington; Cathedral 66–53 Ben Davis; Tech 69–58 Cathedral. Officials: Gerald Imel, Harold Ashbrook, Kenneth Payne.

INDIANAPOLIS (Coliseum): Wood 79–46 Chatard; Howe 72–42 Warren Central; Northwest 71–65 Scecina; Lawrence Central 51–50 Shortridge; Howe 66–59 Wood; Northwest 65–63 Lawrence Central; Howe 61–51 Northwest. Officials: Everett Campbell, David Avery, Richard Foster.

JEFFERSONVILLE: New Albany 85–18 Lanesville; Silver Creek 60–58 Clarksville; Jeffersonville 100–61 Georgetown; Providence 71–44 Borden; New Albany 68–66 Silver Creek; Jeffersonville 64–62 Providence; New Albany 55–50 Jeffersonville. Officials: John Thomas, David Loewenstein, Harold Mason.

KENDALLVILLE: Wolf Lake 74–73 Avilla; Ligonier 57–51 Auburn (ot); Garrett 89–36 Cromwell; Albion 66–43 Wawaka; Churubusco 72–71 Kendallville; Wolf Lake 83–67 Ligonier; Garrett 44–23 Albion; Wolf Lake 65–60 Churubusco; Garrett 83–50 Wolf Lake. Officials: Gene Marks, Kenneth Barnes, Larry Pinkerton, Eugene Linn.

KENTLAND: Oxford 95–58 Ambia; Remington 63–46 Goodland; Mt. Ayr 54–52 Boswell; Brook 66–46 Kentland; Fowler 61–36 Morocco; Oxford 43–42 Remington; Brook 37–31 Mt. Ayr; Fowler 52–37 Oxford: Fowler 44–38 Brook. Officials: Thomas Dean, Melvin Fuller, William Van Sickle, Robert Wendt.

KNOX: Knox 79–62 North Judson; Culver 68–64 Monterey; Winamac 66–50 Walkerton; Aubbeenaubbee Twp. 88–60 LaCrosse; Rochester 54–38 Oregon Davis; Knox 64–58 Culver; Winamac 89–43 Aubbeenaubbee Twp.; Knox 50–49 Rochester; Knox 72–60 Winamac. Officials: Stan Dubis, James Burt, Wayne Targgart, Anthony Lazar.

KOKOMO: Sharpsville–Prairie 75–66 Eastern; Maconaquah 47–40 Western; Kokomo 90–53 Carroll; Northwestern 65–40 Windfall; Sharpsville-Prairie 63–51 Maconaquah; Kokomo 74–45 Northwestern; Kokomo 123–70 Sharpsville-Prairie. Officials: Robert Kramer, Don Yager, Joseph Bella.

LAFAYETTE: Otterbein 62–55 Montmorenci; Central Catholic 65–59 Battle Ground; Jefferson 96–46 Klondike; West Lafayette 79–58 Southwestern; Otterbein 75–58 Central Catholic; Jefferson 69–54 West Lafayette; Jefferson 79–54 Otterbein. Officials: Don Shiflet, Eugene Carrabine, Donald Call.

LAVILLE: Bremen 81–37 Tyner; North Liberty 77–55 Argos; Plymouth 65–61 Triton; LaVille 65–54 South Bend Jackson; Bremen 55–45 North Liberty; Plymouth 59–48 LaVille; Bremen 46–44 Plymouth. Officials: Ralph Cox, Roger DeYoung, Dale Van Houten.

LAWRENCEBURG: Aurora 87–58 North Dearborn; Rising Sun 50–46 Patriot; Dillsboro 70–65 Whitewater; Lawrenceburg 63–44 Moores Hill; Aurora 68–51 Rising Sun; Lawrenceburg 55–51

Tourney Time

Dillsboro; Aurora 55–53 Lawrenceburg. Officials: William May, Robert Wells, Byron Weaver.

LOGANSPORT: Logansport 86–52 Kewanna; Pioneer 68–65 Cass; Caston 59–50 Star City; Peru 50–48 North Miami; Logansport 12–10 Pioneer; Peru 51–47 Caston; Logansport 29–19 Peru. Officials: Floyd Reed, Donald Koester, John Holmes.

MADISON: Madison 81–60 Vevay; Charlestown 58–56 Shawe Memorial; Southwestern 82–57 Henryville; Deputy 62–60 New Washington, Madison 56–54 Charlestown (ot); Southwestern 99–77 Deputy; Madison 93–77 Southwestern. Officials: Fred Marlow, William Pittman, Don Snedeker.

MANCHESTER: Northfield 76–14 South Whitley; Wabash 61–57 Silver Lake (ot); Akron 75–70 White's; Manchester 62–52 Southwood; Northfield 69–60 Wabash; Manchester 87–54 Akron; Manchester 66–55 Northfield. Officials: Glen Wisler, Jack Gardner, Richard Pattengale.

MARION: Oak Hill 62–50 Fairmount; Marion Bennett 69–64 Mississinewa; Marion 73–65 Summitville; Montpelier 85–57 Eastbrook; Oak Hill 68–66 Marion Bennett; Marion 65–53 Montpelier; Marion 72–59 Oak Hill. Officials: J. Firman Grimes, William Williamson, Donald Edwards.

MICHIGAN CITY: Michigan City 97–50 St. Mary's; LaPorte 92–54 Westville; New Carlisle 80–71 Wanatah; South Central 93–89 Rolling Prairie; Michigan City 72–51 LaPorte; South Central 63–58 New Carlisle; Michigan City 88–49 South Central. Officials: John Fee, John Mikels, Richard Gebhart.

MILAN: Versailles 88–80 Milan; Sunman 106–42 New Marion; Jac-Cen-Del 127–35 Cross Plains; Batesville 96–74 Holton; Sunman 93–77 Versailles; Jac-Cen-Del 87–73 Batesville; Sunman 88–73 Jac-Cen-Del. Officials: Jack Mercer, Jerry Larrison, Francis Fiddler.

NORTH WHITE: DeMotte 73–64 Wolcott; North White 67–63 Francesville; Rensselaer 75–70 Medaryville; Frontier 72–61 Twin Lakes; DeMotte 87–66 Wheatfield; Rensselaer 69–61 North White; Frontier 74–71 DeMotte; Frontier 78–60 Rensselaer. Officials: Lawrence Gradeless, George Dunleavy, David Schwartz, Charles Sallee.

MUNCIE: Muncie Southside 91–61 Muncie Burris; Gaston 77–70 Cowan; Muncie Central 67–50 Royerton; Albany 80–46 Harrison Twp., Yorktown 63–53 Selma; DeSoto 72–67 Eaton; Muncie Southside 55–32 Gaston; Muncie Central 71–53 Albany; Yorktown 85–65 DeSoto; Muncie Southside 53–51 Muncie Central; Muncie Southside 83–64 Yorktown. Officials: Raymond Robison, Gordon McCain, Paul Leamon, Darrel McFall.

NEW CASTLE: Middletown 89–56 Sulphur Springs; Mt. Vernon 59–57 Knightstown; Greenfield 76–56 Blue River; New Castle 93–57 Hancock Central; Spiceland 67–50 Cadiz; Mt. Vernon 71–51 Middletown; New Castle 79–70 Greenfield; Mt. Vernon 67–56 Spiceland; Mt. Vernon 66–65 New Castle. Officials: Don Hollman, Carl Petercheff, John Manka, Ned Brenizer.

PORTLAND: Adams Central 58–47 Dunkirk; Bryant 66–38 Pennville; Geneva 77–45 Berne; Portland 58–46 Hartford City; Adams Central 56–54 Bryant (ot); Geneva 72–69 Portland (ot); Adams Central 70–51 Geneva. Officials: Harry Green, Morris Cohen, Maurice Gardner.

PRINCETON: Mt. Vernon 68–58 Ft. Branch; North Posey 85–57 New Harmony; Princeton 67–59 Owensville; Oakland City 69–30 Francisco; North Posey 66–43 Mt. Vernon; Oakland City 70–59 Princeton; North Posey 50–43 Oakland City. Officials: Richard Sweet, Robert Kirk, William Fields.

RICHMOND: Webster-Williamsburg 68–66 Hagerstown; Richmond 87–34 Whitewater-Fountain City; Cambridge City 57–55 Randolph Southern (ot); Lewisville 71–55 Centerville; Richmond 73–41 Webster-Williamsburg; Cambridge City 56–53 Lewisville; Richmond 74–61

IHSAA Scores | 1960-1969

Cambridge City. Officials: Wendell Baker, Richard Lederman, William Goshert.

RUSHVILLE: Carthage 62–47 Mays; Morton Memorial 57–55 Arlington; Rushville 60–47 Eastern Hancock; Manilla 79–69 New Salem; Carthage 56–44 Morton Memorial; Rushville 72–43 Manilla; Rushville 55–41 Carthage. Officials: Ken Blankenbaker, Martin Burdette, Jonnie Webber.

SALEM: Marengo 80–50 Eastern; Corydon 68–46 South Central; Morgan Twp. 76–66 Salem; North Central 69–46 Milltown; West Washington 60–52 Marengo; Corydon 56–48 Morgan Twp.; North Central 65–48 West Washington; North Central 59–52 Corydon. Officials: James Beyer, Boynton Robson, Clifford Spears, James Davis.

SEYMOUR: Brownstown 74–58 Medora; Seymour 94–65 Clearspring; Austin 67–62 Scottsburg; North Vernon 94–40 Crothersville; Seymour 77–60 Brownstown; North Vernon 79–61 Austin; North Vernon 76–70 Seymour. Officials: Jimmy Dimitroff, William Phillips, Harry Inskeep.

SOUTH BEND: Central 88–67 St. Joseph; Riley 65–62 Adams: Clay 53–50 Mishawaka; Washington 80–42 LaSalle; Central 69–57 Riley; Washington 64–56 Clay; Central 97–83 Washington. Officials: Wayne Crispen, Russell Freeland, James P. Carey.

SOUTHPORT: Chatard 81–45 School for the Deaf; Southport 72–64 Franklin Central; Decatur Central 88–51 Sacred Heart; Beech Grove 67–49 Manual; Southport 75–50 Chartrand; Beech Grove 84–67 Decatur Central, Beech Grove 68–67 Southport. Officials: Glen Bonsett, Carl Schnebelt, John Ward.

SULLIVAN: Shakamak 105–53 Dugger; Sullivan 65–45 Cory; North Central 54–43 Hymera; Carlisle 68–67 Clay City; Shakamak 78–61 Sullivan; North Central 69–63 Carlisle; Shakamak 60–52 North Central. Officials: Robert Emmert, Frank Bradshaw, Charles Daum.

SWITZ CITY: Switz City Central 30–29 Eastern; L & M 61–51 Worthington; Linton-Stockton 65–52 Odon; Bloomfield 56–46 Elnora; Switz City Central 60–47 L & M; Linton-Stockton 59–49 Bloomfield; Linton-Stockton 63–54 Switz City Central. Officials: Harold Gourley, James DeGroote, Walter S. Vanover.

TELL CITY: Dale 76–59 Leavenworth; English 63–56 Ferdinand; Chrisney 56–52 Cannelton; Tell City 66–40 Perry Central; Dale 50–40 English; Tell City 70–52 Chrisney; Tell City 80–70 Dale. Officials: Lowell Smith, Warren Keyser, Russell Rogers.

TERRE HAUTE: Gerstmeyer 76–70 Honey Creek; Garfield 92–64 Schulte; West Vigo 71–60 Montezuma; Laboratory 50–42 Clinton; Wiley 68–64 Rosedale; Garfield 66–55 Gerstmeyer; Laboratory 52–39 West Vigo; Garfield 53–46 Wiley; Garfield 57–39 Laboratory. Officials: James Patterson, Raymond Vescovi, Charles Bertram, L. C. Thorne.

VINCENNES: Wheatland 47–46 Fritchton; Central Catholic 74–53 Decker; Vincennes 69–63 Monroe City; North Knox 65–50 Petersburg; Central Catholic 61–46 Wheatland; Vincennes 74–63 North Knox; Vincennes 52–44 Central Catholic. Officials: Vern Doles, Jack Chestnut, Russell Owens.

WARSAW: Pierceton 64–57 North Webster; Milford 79–55 Larwill; Mentone 72–61 Claypool; Warsaw 105–61 Leesburg: Columbia City 68–39 Syracuse; Pierceton 77–68 Milford; Warsaw 58–40 Mentone, Columbia City 66–56 Pierceton; Warsaw 46–44 Columbia City. Officials: David Habegger, Jack Goen, Richard Venderly, Neal Jay

WASHINGTON: Loogootee 65–39 Otwell; Loogootee St. John's 71–60 Shoals; Washington Catholic 53–44 Plainville; Washington 60–46 Barr–Reeve; Loogootee 71–49 Loogootee St.

Tourney Time

John's; Washington 67–65 Washington Catholic; Washington 53–46 Loogootee (ot) Officials: Max Andress, Gene Wilm, Clifford Runnebohm.

WINCHESTER: Union City 71–55 Center; Union 67–59 Ridgeville; Monroe Central 88–71 Madison; Redkey 75–70 Driver; Union City 71–58 Union; Redkey 81–73 Monroe Central; Union City 77–44 Redkey. Officials: Don Hurst, Bruce Knecht, James Benecke.

ZIONSVILLE: Speedway 62–52 Darlington; Brebeuf 61–59 Zionsville; Lebanon 72–58 Thorntown; Pike 82–64 Wells; Speedway 68–48 Brebeuf; Lebanon 77–54 Pike; Lebanon 63–61 Speedway. Officials: Marion Acton, Marvin Heaton, Gilbert Baumgartner.

1966 REGIONALS

ANDERSON: Adams Central 53–51 Carmel; Anderson 91–62 Marion; Anderson 87–63 Adams Central. Officials: Gene Butts, John Gassensmith, Robert Kramer, Robert Reed, John Fee, Gene Marks.

COLUMBUS: Columbus 81–72 Madison; Greensburg 88–79 Greenwood; Greensburg 74–62 Columbus. Officials: Bill Hile, Richard Gebhart, John Arnold, Wallace Reeve, David Habegger, John Ward.

CONNERSVILLE: Brookville 69–42 Sunman; Aurora 97–73 Rushville; Aurora 62–54 Brookville. Officials: J. Firman Grimes, Lowell Smith, Wayne Crispen, Gil Baumgartner, Francis Terrell, James Benecke.

COVINGTON: Coal Creek Central 82–75 Turkey Run; Bainbridge 90–70 Fowler; Bainbridge 85–74 Coal Creek. Officials: Marvin Cave, Howard Morgan, James Schwenk, Joseph Bella, Jimmy Dimitroff, Earle Wolfe.

EAST CHICAGO: Hammond High 67–53 Crown Point; East Chicago Washington 73–62 Gary Roosevelt; East Chicago Washington 71–52 Hammond High. Officials: Eugene Lillie, Robert Fisher, Floyd Reed, Marion Acton, Charles Fouty, William Malloy.

ELKHART: South Bend Central 78–77 Warsaw; Michigan City 74–43 Elkhart; Michigan City 79–72 South Bend Central. Officials: Charles Garber, George Dunleavy, Art Thompson, Jack Mercer, Zeke Williams, Darrel McFall.

EVANSVILLE: Memorial 92–67 North Posey; Boonville 84–75 Tell City; Memorial 78–62 Boonville. Officials: Robert H. Laird, Harold E. Mason, James L. Ruby, James J. Beyer, Dwain Laird, Harold Ashbrook.

FORT WAYNE: Fort Wayne South 53–35 Eastside; Garrett 62–61 Fort Wayne North; Fort Wayne South 45–40 Garrett. Officials: William May, George Avery, Robert Spay, Tom Hoffman, Lawrence Gradeless, Harry Inskeep.

HUNTINGBURG: Springs Valley 69–44 Linton; Vincennes 46–39 Washington; Vincennes 66–56 Springs Valley. Officials: Wendall Baker, Robert Wells, Glen Bonsett, Donald Call, John Williams, Walter Swift.

INDIANAPOLIS: Tech 78–60 Mooresville; Beech Grove 51–50 Indianapolis Howe; Indianapolis Tech 72–63 Beech Grove. Officials: Don Hollman, Ned Brenizer, Roy Kilby, William Goshert, Winfield Jacobs, Raymond Robison.

JEFFERSONVILLE: North Vernon 71–67 Bedford; North Central (Ramsey) 71–68 New Albany; North Vernon 84–62 North Central. Officials: Robert Davidson, Donald Hubbard, Harold Gourley, James DeGroote, Homer Owens, Don Snedeker.

KOKOMO: Kokomo 76–48 Manchester; Huntington 81–50 Decatur Catholic; Kokomo 69–51 Huntington. Officials: Edgar Powers, Richard Freeman, Don Hurst, Kenneth Payne, Robert Cherry, Danny Jacobs.

LAFAYETTE: Lebanon 72–57 Frontier; Lafayette Jefferson 82–41 Clinton Central; Lebanon 82–70 Lafayette. Officials: Gerald Imel, Ray L. Nemeth, Ernest Sohl, Ralph Cox, John Thomas, Charles Stumpf.

LOGANSPORT: Valparaiso 73–52 Knox; Logansport 69–41 Bremen; Logansport 82–78 Valparaiso. Officials: Glen Wisler, James Davis, Fred Marlow, Don Shiflet, Everett Campbell, Vern Doles.

NEW CASTLE: Richmond 69–62 Muncie Southside; Mt. Vernon 69–63 Union City; Richmond 68–54 Mt. Vernon. Officials: Ken Blankenbaker, Richard Sweet, Richard Foster, Wayne Myers, Tom Dean, John Holmes.

TERRE HAUTE: Shakamak 62–53 Garfield; Cloverdale 70–62 Unionville; Cloverdale 82–65 Shakamak. Officials: Howard Risley, John Bush, Roger Emmert, Harry Green, Robert Showalter, Charles Sallee.

1966 SEMI—STATES

EVANSVILLE: Cloverdale 76–57 Vincennes; North Vernon 80–63 Memorial; Cloverdale 73–66 North Vernon. Officials: Roy Kilby, Art Thompson, Wendell Baker, Homer Owens, Jimmy Dimitroff, John B. Williams.

FORT WAYNE: Anderson 69–68 Fort Wayne South Side; Michigan City 74–66 Kokomo; Michigan City 90–81 Anderson. Officials: Roger Emmert, Glen Wisler, Robert Davidson, Robert Kramer, Charles Fouty, John Thomas.

INDIANAPOLIS: Greensburg 74–70 Richmond; Tech 81–64 Aurora; Tech 79–75 Greensburg. Officials: John Fee, Gerald Imel, Robert Spay, Ernie Sohl, Larry Gradeless, Zeke Williams.

LAFAYETTE: Lebanon 65–64 Logansport; East Chicago Washington 78–74 Bainbridge; Washington 59–58 Lebanon. Officials: Kenneth Blankenbaker, Robert Laird, David Habegger, James Schwenk, Tom Dean, Floyd Reed.

1966 FINALS—March 19

INDIANAPOLIS (Hinkle Fieldhouse): Michigan City Elston 81–64 East Chicago Washington; Indianapolis Tech 58–51 Cloverdale; Michigan City Elston 63–52 Tech. Officials: Art Thompson, David Habeggar, Roger Emmert, Kenneth Blankenbaker, Homer Owens, John Fee.

1967 SECTIONALS

ANDERSON: Pendleton 63–60 Daleville; Madison Heights 74–59 Anderson; Alexandria 80–76 Markleville; Highland 75–59 Frankton; Madison Heights 89–80 Pendleton; Alexandria 63–62 Highland; Madison Heights 93–75 Alexandria. Officials: Don Hollman, Bill Gray, John Hilligoss, Charles Stumpf.

BEDFORD: Tunnelton 50–49 Heltonville; Bedford 60–48 Mitchell; Shawswick 72–64

Tourney Time

Fayetteville; Oolitic 74–42 Marshall Twp.; Bedford 61–54 Tunnelton; Oolitic 76–57 Shawswick, Oolitic 55–49 Bedford. Officials: Glen Wisler, Byron Weaver, William Laird, Fred Marlow.

BLUFFTON: Ossian 75–54 Lancaster Central; Southern Wells 67–66 Decatur; Monmouth 59–48 Adams Central; Bluffton 72–39 Decatur Catholic; Ossian 91–73 Southern Wells; Bluffton 50–48; Monmouth; Bluffton 56–46 Ossian. Officials: Firman Grimes, Wayne Van Sickle, Charles Thompson, Don Hurst.

BOONVILLE: Boonville 69–65 Castle; South Spencer 67–59 Haubstadt; Chrisney 63–43 Mackey; Tecumseh 62–56 Winslow; Boonville 75–69 South Spencer; Chrisney 74–51 Tecumseh; Boonville 58–57 Chrisney. Officials: Wayne Myers, Jerry Baker, Ray Norris, Robert Sweet.

BRAZIL: Brazil 66–50 Van Buren; Spencer 77–73 Gosport (2ot); Staunton 53–45 Reelsville; Brazil 63–58 Cloverdale; Spencer 56–46 Staunton; Brazil 70–61 Spencer. Officials: Vern Doles, Roger McGriff, Robert Rohleder, Harry Green.

BROWNSBURG: Danville 73–65 Monrovia; Plainfield 61–55 Pittsboro; Mooresville 67–58 Avon; Brownsburg 68–37 Charlton; Plainfield 54–53 Danville; Brownsburg 54–53 Mooresville; Plainfield 60–59 Brownsburg. Officials: James Davis, Melvin Botkin, Robert Cherry, Ward Weisel.

CARMEL: Westfield 68–66 Noblesville; Sheridan 74–64 Lapel; Hamilton Heights 111–49 Hamilton Southeastern; Carmel 53–51 Tipton; Sheridan 62–42 Westfield; Carmel 73–70 Hamilton Heights; Carmel 77–50 Sheridan. Officials: James Benecke, James Cox, Donald Schmidt, James Burt.

CHESTERTON: Chesterton 77–57 Liberty Twp.; Morgan Twp. 65–45 Washington Twp.; Jackson Twp. 75–49 Wheeler; Valparaiso 75–60 Portage; Chesterton 92–64 Morgan Twp.; Valparaiso 72–58 Jackson Twp.; Valparaiso 55–47 Chesterton. Officials: Gerald Imel, David Avery, Merl Heckaman, Jack Gardner.

COLUMBIA CITY: Pierceton 60–59 South Whitley (ot) Wolf Lake 63–34 Larwill; Columbia City 65–51 Manchester; Pierceton 78–50 Churubusco; Wolf Lake 59–58 Columbia City; Wolf Lake 76–53 Pierceton. Officials: Thomas Hoffman, Larry Pinkerton, Robert Gilmore, Melvin Fuller.

COLUMBUS: Brown County 85–54 Nineveh; Southwestern 68–63 Edinburg; Waldron 57–53 Hauser; Shelbyville 64–52 Columbus; Brown County 63–61 Southwestern; Shelbyville 68–41 Waldron; Shelbyville 103–69 Brown County. Officials: Everett Campbell, Herod Toon, Robert Wolfe, Robert Showalter.

CONNERSVILLE: Laurel 55–47 Lewisville; Liberty 61–40 Straughn; Brookville 87–39 Union (College Corner); Connersville 92–56 Laurel; Liberty 46–41 Brookville; Liberty 73–65 Connersville. Officials: David Habegger, Myron Moriarity, Bill Strafford, Russell Rogers.

CRAWFORDSVILLE: Waveland 76–71 Waynetown; Ladoga 63–61 Alamo; New Market 78–72 Coal Creek Central; New Ross 78–75 Crawfordsville; Waveland 81–76 Ladoga (ot); New Market 81–63 New Ross; New Market 57–50 Waveland. Officials: James Beyer, Clair Robison, Gene Williams, Raymond Robison.

CROWN POINT: Merrillville 70–58 Boone Grove; Lake Central 88–69 Hebron; Crown Point 72–61 Lowell; Griffith 60–46 Hanover Central; Merrillville 73–59 Lake Central; Griffith 80–64 Crown Point; Griffith 64–47 Merrillville. Officials: Walter Swift, John Mikels, John Lozier, John Ward.

EAST CHICAGO: East Chicago Washington 73–55 Hobart; East Chicago Roosevelt 78–66

IHSAA Scores / 1960–1969

Gary Andrean; Tolleston 66–52 Calumet; Gary Edison 74–67 Hammond Noll; East Chicago Roosevelt 65–63 Washington; Tolleston 82–76 Gary Edison; Tolleston 78–77 East Chicago Roosevelt. Officials: Larry Gradeless, Bobby Goble, Paul Stemm, Robert Reed.

EAST NOBLE: Garrett 59–45 Auburn; Wawaka 67–49 Waterloo; Albion 65–61 Eastside; East Noble 85–53 Cromwell; Garrett 72–64 Wawaka; East Noble 77–57 Albion; East Noble 79–77 Garrett. Officials: Don Edwards, Robert Manor, Patrick King, Richard Brainard.

ELKHART: Elkhart 65–52 Concord; Wakarusa 64–41 Jefferson; Penn 71–60 Millersburg; Nappanee 90–59 Jimtown; Goshen 78–55 Middlebury; Elkhart 81–57 Wakarusa; Nappanee 64–59 Penn; Goshen 56–50 Elkhart; Nappanee 51–43 Goshen. Officials: George Dunleavy, Max Hensler, Arthur Morris, Anthony Lazar.

EVANSVILLE: North 58–54 Reitz; Central 78–66 Memorial; Bosse 70–61 Rex Mundi; Harrison 47–22 Mater Del; North 66–47 Central; Bosse 63–60 Harrison; North 59–44 Bosse. Officials: Arthur Thompson, William Fields, Paul Garriott, Charles Sallee.

FORT WAYNE (#1): New Haven 56–45 Bishop Dwenger; North Side 67–63 Hoagland; South Side 66–65 Central (ot); Central Catholic 101–75 Huntertown; North Side 56–54 New Haven; South Side 78–58 Central Catholic; South Side 39–36 North Side. Officials: Jimmy Dimitroff, Russell Freeland, Donald Leever, Allen Voorhis.

FORT WAYNE (#2): Woodlan 56–47 Arcola; Snider 61–48 Bishop Luers; Concordia 74–55 Monroeville; Elmhurst 75–58 Leo: Snider 78–59 Woodlan; Concordia 36–34 Elmhurst; Snider 56–49 Concordia. Officials: George Avery, John Manka, Troy Ingram, James P. Carey.

FOUNTAIN CENTRAL: Seeger 66–56 Williamsport; North Vermillion 75–71 Pine Village; Attica 63–58 Turkey Run; Covington 73–61 Fountain Central; Seeger 65–55 North Vermillion; Covington 65–63 Attica; Seeger 61–55 Covington. Officials: Robert Laird, Richard Crays, Joseph Dickey, Jack Mercer.

FRANKFORT: Frankfort 60–49 Linden; Clinton Prairie 46–45 Wainwright; Rossville 64–54 East Tipp; Delphi 60–55 Clinton Central; Frankfort 66–50 Clinton Prairie; Delphi 58–56 Rossville; (2ot); Delphi 60–53 Frankfort. Officials: Richard Freeman, Samuel Reed, Kenneth Sussman, Francis Fiddler.

GARY: Gary Roosevelt: 98–64 Emerson; Froebel 78–49 East Gary Edison; Wirt 56–45 River Forest; Horace Mann 76–59 Lew Wallace; Roosevelt 76–68 Froebel; Horace Mann 53–47 Wirt; Roosevelt 69–43 Horace Mann. Officials: Tom Dean, Billy Maroney, George Grygiel, Don Lozier.

GREENCASTLE: Greencastle 90–59 Roachdale; Russellville 50–45 Cascade; North Salem 62–60 Fillmore; Bainbridge 107–67 Rockville; Greencastle 87–51 Russellville; Bainbridge 111–47 North Salem; Bainbridge 94–85 Greencastle. Officials: James Schwenk, Jerry Larrison, Phillip Hardwick, Earle Wolfe.

GREENSBURG: Sandcreek 65–52 Milroy; Jackson 61–50 Clarksburg; St. Paul 68–38 New Point; Greensburg 97–43 Burney; Sandcreek 58–42 Jackson; Greensburg 70–48 St. Paul; Greensburg 51–41 Sandcreek. Officials: Neal Jay, Robert Kirk, Walter Overton, Jack Cummings.

HAMMOND: Hammond Gavit 87–64 Clark; Tech 78–50 Whiting; Munster 72–59 Highland; Morton 65–62 Hammond High; Tech 98–84 Gavit; Munster 76–62 Morton; Tech 88–68 Munster. Officials: Bill Hile, Harold Gray, Jon Gallipo, John Arnold.

HUNTINGBURG: Huntingburg 55–46 Orleans; Holland 89–33 Ireland; Springs Valley 61–53 Dubois; Jasper 67–59 Paoli; Holland 73–62 Huntingburg; Jasper 59–39 Springs Valley; Holland

Tourney Time

62–52 Jasper. Officials: Glen Bonsett, Noble Rector, Michael Hennegan, Carl Schnebelt.

HUNTINGTON: Southwood 71–58 White's; Wabash 73–57 Huntington; Northfield 91–63 Huntington Catholic; Eastbrook 73–68 Southwood; Wabash 68–67 Northfield; Wabash 68–54 Eastbrook. Officials: Richard Foster, James R. Carey, Jerry Struble, Gordon McCain.

INDIANAPOLIS (Hinkle Fieldhouse): Indianapolis Washington 75–66 North Central; Crispus Attucks 64–37 Ritter; Ben Davis 74–54 Arlington; Tech 68–58 Broad Ripple; Washington 70–66 Crispus Attucks; Tech 62–58 Ben Davis; Tech 66–63 Washington. Officials: Winfield Jacobs, Joe Smelcer, Richard Lederman, Robert Fisher.

INDIANAPOLIS (Coliseum): Warren Central 66–41 Chatard; Shortridge 92–61 Howe; Lawrence Central 97–63 Northwest; Scecina 66–63 School for Deaf; Shortridge 63–60 Warren Central (3ot); Lawrence Central 86–63 Scecina; Shortridge 59–53 Lawrence Central. Officials: Homer Owens, Eugene Linn, Fred Myers, William Malloy.

JEFFERSONVILLE: Clarksville 79–56 South Central; New Albany 79–46 Lanesville; Georgetown 85–57 Borden; Jeffersonville 51–43 Providence; New Albany 61–53 Clarksville; Jeffersonville 83–56 Georgetown; New Albany 54–47 Jeffersonville. Officials: James DeGroote, Keith Combs, Jack Williams, Raymond Vescovi.

KNOX: Knox 54–51 North Judson; Monterey 65–58 LaCrosse; Glenn 78–69 Kouts; Oregon-Davis 66–58 Culver; Winamac 74–69 Aubbeenaubbee Twp.; Knox 55–54 Monterey; Oregon-Davis 59–55 Glenn; Winamac 83–46 Knox; Oregon-Davis 60–58 Winamac. Officials: Zeke Williams, Jonnie Webber, James Wehsollek, Eugene Carrabine.

KOKOMO: Carroll 85–60 Windfall; Kokomo 72–40 Eastern; Sharpsville Prairie 70–57 Western; Maconaquah 54–46 Northwestern; Kokomo 59–56 Carroll; Maconaquah 70–53 Sharpsville Prairie; Kokomo 62–41 Maconaquah. Officials: Ned Brenizer, Gary Janeway, Gene Gibson, Norris Boomershine.

LAFAYETTE: Lafayette Jefferson 72–52 Benton Central; Central Catholic 77–60 Frontier; West Lafayette 71–52 Klondike; Battle Ground 66–52 Southwestern; Lafayette Jefferson 81–61 Central Catholic; West Lafayette 65–59 Battle Ground (ot); Lafayette Jefferson 68–48 West Lafayette. Officials: Ernie Sohl, Don Koester, Richard Cook, Marion Acton.

LAKELAND: Angola 66–54 Prairie Heights; Hamilton 74–59 Ligonier; Westview 75–71 Ashley; Lakeland 83–40 Fremont; Hamilton 70–63 Angola; Westview 59–55 Lakeland; Hamilton 69–56 Westview. Officials: Edgar Powers, Don Reinholt, Al Lindahl, Ronald Hosinski.

LAVILLE: Plymouth 56–38 Argos; Bremen 64–40 Mishawaka Marian; North Liberty 53–36 South Bend Jackson; Triton 73–65 LaVille; Plymouth 65–61 Bremen (ot); Triton 59–58 North Liberty; Plymouth 56–46 Triton. Officials: Stan Dubis, Richard Vendrely, Gene Keenan, Gary Muncy.

LAWRENCEBURG: Dillsboro 67–66 North Dearborn; Lawrenceburg 68–52 Whitewater; Aurora 67–34 Patriot; Vevay 88–81 Rising Sun; Lawrenceburg 63–45 Dillsboro; Vevay 62–58 Aurora; Lawrenceburg 59–45 Vevay. Officials: Don Snedeker, Billy Lee Walker, Don Smith, Jim Ladd.

LOGANSPORT: Caston 64–55 Kewanna; Lewis Cass 60–37 Star City; Logansport 72–37 North Miami; Peru 65–54 Pioneer; Lewis Cass 52–42 Caston; Logansport 81–48 Peru; Logansport 69–45 Lewis Cass. Officials: Wendell Baker, Roger DeYoung, Robert Marcinek, Wayne Targgart.

MADISON: Silver Creek 65–64 Southwestern; Charlestown 69–67 Deputy (ot); New Washington 72–43 Henryville; Madison 96–65 Shame Memorial; Silver Creek 58–52 Charlestown;

IHSAA Scores / 1960–1969

Madison 80–50 New Washington; Madison 77–75 Silver Creek. Officials: Don Shiflet, Maurice Gardner, Alan Henshaw, James Ruby.

MARION: Marion 72–46 Fairmount; Elwood 70–42 Oak Hill; Marion Bennett 73–68 Summitville; Marion 80–55 Mississinewa; Elwood 73–56 Marion Bennett; Marion 65–62 Elwood (ot). Officials: John Holmes, Arthur Largent, James Frey, Robert Wells.

MARTINSVILLE: University 65–63 Unionville (ot); Eminence 82–63 Edgewood; Martinsville 78–69 Morgantown; Bloomington 90–54 Smithville; University 70–54 Eminence; Bloomington 65–49 Martinsville; Bloomington 81–51 University. Officials: Wallace Reeve, Bruce Knecht, Thomas Moorman, Richard Pattengale.

MICHIGAN CITY: St. Mary's 81–58 Rolling Prairie; South Central 75–53 Wanatah; Michigan City 89–33 Westville; LaPorte 67–52 New Carlisle; South Central 72–70 St. Mary's; Michigan City 75–43 LaPorte; Michigan City 74–50 South Central. Officials: Roy Kilby, Marty Burdette, Eric Harmon, Gene Butts.

MILAN: Sunman 61–49 Moores Hill; Jac-Cen-Del 73–66 Batesville; Holton 54–50 South Ripley; Sunman 56–52 Milan; Jac-Cen-Del 82–67 Holton; Jac-Cen-Del 70–60 Sunman. Officials: Jack Goen, McKee Munk, Dan Landis, Morris Cohen.

MUNCIE: Albany 68–64 Cowan; Royerton 72–46 Eaton; Burris 63–49 Yorktown; Central 81–52 DeSoto; Muncie Southside 71–60 Wes-Del; Royerton 79–65 Albany; Muncie Central 78–61 Burris; Muncie Southside 66–61 Royerton; Muncie Southside 75–69 Muncie Central. Officials: Gene Marks, Jack Chestnut, Richard Hale, Lewis Goshert.

NEW CASTLE: Sulphur Springs 95–88 Blue River (2ot); Knightstown 66–43 Spiceland; Greenfield 66–50 Cadiz; New Castle 91–55 Middletown; Mt. Vernon 73–58 Hancock Central; Knightstown 86–61 Sulphur Springs; New Castle 62–59 Greenfield; Knightstown 66–53 Mt. Vernon; New Castle 65–52 Knightstown. Officials: Ken Blankenbaker, Paul Leamon, Dick Venable, Gil Baumgartner.

NORTH WHITE: North White 64–51 Medaryville; DeMotte 73–52 Francesville; Wolcott 83–66 Rensselaer; Wheatfield 51–50 Twin Lakes; North White 55–53 DeMotte; Wheatfield 81–69 Wolcott; Wheatfield 53–50 North White. Officials: Richard Sweet, Ed Scott, Peter Kokinda, Dale Van Houten.

PORTLAND: Bryant 68–43 Pennville; South Adams 70–52 Hartford City; Portland 72–59 Dunkirk; Montpelier 73–66 Bryant; South Adams 91–65 Portland; Montpelier 58–51 South Adams. Officials: John Fee, Clifford Spears, Robert Bowman, Harold Ashbrook.

PRINCETON: Oakland City 59–55 Mt. Vernon; North Posey 88–45 Francisco; Owensville 54–46 Princeton; Ft. Branch 71–52 New Harmony; Oakland City 57–43 North Posey; Ft. Branch 73–69 Owensville; Oakland City 67–65 Ft. Branch. Officials: Kenneth Payne, Warren Keyser, Stewart Vickers, William Williamson.

RICHMOND: Richmond 61–36 Whitewater-Fountain City; Cambridge City 66–56 Hagerstown; Centerville 85–65 Randolph-Southern; Richmond 55–34 Webster-Williamsburg; Cambridge City 79–66 Centerville; Richmond 52–48 Cambridge City. Officials: Wayne Crispen, Don Yager, Delmer Knecht, Howard Risley.

RUSHVILLE: Morristown 59–57 Eastern Hancock; Carthage 76–62 New Salem; Rushville 87–53 Morton Memorial; Manilla 62–51 Arlington; Morristown 92–71 Carthage; Rushville 97–51 Manilla; Morristown 91–84 Rushville. Officials: John Williams, Ben Olsson, Louis Zabona, Eugene Lillie.

Tourney Time

SALEM: Corydon 56–52 Milltown (ot); Marengo 83–68 Salem; Morgan Twp. 65–61 North Central; West Washington 66–53 Eastern; Corydon 59–46 Marengo; West Washington 80–63 Morgan Twp.; Corydon 53–37 West Washington. Officials: John Thomas, Walter Vanover, Ronald Ham, Charles Daum.

SEYMOUR: Brownstown 79–57 Clearspring; Crothersville 63–52 Austin; Scottsburg 54–51 North Vernon; Seymour 93–61 Medora; Crothersville 59–55 Brownstown; Seymour 76–71 Scottsburg; Seymour 75–56 Crothersville. Officials: Donald Hubbard, Louis Schmalfeldt, David Lowenstein, Marvin Cave.

SOUTH BEND: Adams 42–38 Washington; Central 86–50 Clay; Riley 53–49 LaSalle; Mishawaka 56–44 St. Joseph; Adams 69–66 Central; Riley 68–66 Mishawaka; Adams 70–58 Riley. Officials: Don Alvarez, Charles Garber, Frank Hoagburg, Floyd Reed.

SOUTH NEWTON: Remington 65–55 Oxford; Fowler 71–49 Morocco; Ambia 57–54 Boswell; South Newton 86–56 Mt. Ayr; Fowler 64–51 Remington; South Newton 73–62 Ambia; Fowler 61–56 South Newton (ot). Officials: Robert Kramer, John Tucker, Thomas Manning, Ray Nemeth.

SOUTHPORT: Southport 90–40 Cathedral; Indianapolis Wood 81–59 Chartrand; Decatur Central 66–41 Kennedy; Beech Grove 63–49 Manual; Southport 61–58 Wood; Decatur Central 62–55 Beech Grove; Southport 50–49 Decatur Central. Officials: Lowell Smith, Norman Chestnut, Lynn Barlow, Danny Jacobs.

SULLIVAN: North Central 93–36 Patricksburg; Shakamak 74–69 Clay City; Dugger 80–72 Cory; North Central 62–52 Sullivan; Dugger 83–80 Shakamak; North Central 84–72 Dugger. Officials: Donald Call, Randall Holland, Frank Hobson, Lloyd Chambers.

SWITZ CITY: Linton-Stockton 63–57 Eastern (ot); Odon 65–61 Worthington-Jefferson; Switz City Central 50–49 L & M; Elnora 53–46 Bloomfield; Linton-Stockton 66–55 Odon; Switz City Central 58–57 Elnora; Linton-Stockton 75–44 Switz City Central. Officials: Roger Emmert, Charles Bertram, Robert Roney, Clifford Runnebohm.

TELL CITY: Tell City 57–38 Dale; Perry Central 65–32 Birdseye; Leavenworth 70–36 English; Saint Ferdinand 66–65 Cannelton (ot); Perry Central 42–34 Tell City; Leavenworth 54–47 Saint Ferdinand; Leavenworth 32–30 Perry Central. Officials: Robert Davidson, Lloyd Baugh, Leroy Schultheis, Rudy Tabereaux.

TERRE HAUTE: Garfield 72–49 Montezuma; Schulte 65–58 Rosedale; Honey Creek 81–74 West Vigo; Wiley 71–63 Clinton; Gerstmeyer 81–46 Laboratory; Garfield 74–67 Schulte; Honey Creek 70–68 Wiley; Garfield 72–53 Gerstmeyer; Garfield 90–79 Honey Creek. Officials: Dwain Laird, William Bateman, William Phillips, Harry Inskeep.

VINCENNES: Central Catholic 78–51 Fritchton; Monroe City 60–47 Decker; Wheatland 71–57 Petersburg; Vincennes 87–69 North Knox; Monroe City 63–61 Central Catholic; Vincennes 91–74 Wheatland; Vincennes 85–65 Monroe City. Officials: Harold Mason, Boynton Robson, Dallas Richards, James Eads.

WARSAW: Syracuse 74–52 North Webster; Mentone 59–46 Milford; Warsaw 71–62 Akron; Rochester 66–63 New Paris; Syracuse 89–86 Mentone; Warsaw 86–60 Rochester; Warsaw 91–50 Syracuse. Officials: Darrell McFall, David Parry, Jerry Scott, Ray Ward.

WASHINGTON: Washington Catholic 68–50 Otwell; Washington 71–63 Plainville; Barr-Reeve 57–48 Loogootee St. John's; Loogootee 82–54 Shoals; Washington 74–51 Washington Catholic; Barr-Reeves 53–49 Loogootee; Washington 75–54 Barr-Reeves. Officials: Harold Gourley, George Oberle, Floyd Riggs, Frank Bradshaw.

IHSAA Scores | 1960–1969

WHITELAND: Whiteland 92–68 Greenwood; New Palestine 89–58 Trafalgar; Center Grove 53–50 Franklin Central; Franklin 77–62 Triton Central; Whiteland 87–67 New Palestine; Center Grove 58–54 Franklin; Whiteland 71–53 Center Grove. Officials: William May, Don Shields, William Van Sickle, Marvin Heaton.
WINCHESTER: Monroe Central 57–53 Redkey; Selma 58–54 Center; Winchester 71–65 Madison Twp.; Union City 68–58 Union; Selma 75–69 Monroe Central; Union City 91–86 Winchester; Selma 56–54 Union City. Officials: Max Andress, David Schwartz, Ronald Beard, John Bush.
ZIONSVILLE: Pike 75–51 Wells; Thorntown 65–59 Darlington; Speedway 61–60 Lebanon; Zionsville 65–60 Brebeuf; Pike 35–28 Thorntown; Speedway 52–48 Zionsville (ot); Speedway 56–54 Pike. Officials: Richard Gebhart, Raymond Mitrione, George Taylor, John Gassensmith.

1967 REGIONALS

ANDERSON: Marion 90–69 Carmel; Madison Heights 73–65 Montpelier; Marion 80–77 Madison Heights. Officials: Ernie Sohl, George Avery, Marion Acton, Max Andress, Winfield Jacobs, Ned Brenizer.
BLOOMINGTON: Terre Haute Garfield 64–53 Brazil; Bloomington 66–54 Seymour; Garfield 76–64 Bloomington. Officials: Raymond Vescovi, Don Snedeker, Bill Hile, Robert Fisher, Robert Showalter, Harold Gourley.
COLUMBUS: Greensburg 69–68 Shelbyville; Madison 76–63 Whiteland; Greensburg 61–60 Madison. Officials: Donald Hubbard, Wallace Reeve, John Williams, Earle Wolfe, Roger Emmert, James DeGroote.
CONNERSVILLE: Jac-Cen-Del 50–49 Lawrenceburg; Liberty 74–64 Morristown; Liberty 64–52 Jac-Cen-Del. Officials: Lowell Smith, John Ward, Roy Kilby, Donald Call, Jimmy Dimitroff, Harold Ashbrook.
EAST CHICAGO: Gary Tolleston 80–72 Hammond Tech; Gary Roosevelt 89–67 Griffith; Gary Roosevelt 85–72 Tolleston. Officials: Edgar Powers, Gene Butts, David Habegger, Gordon McCain, Wendell Baker, Harold Mason.
ELKHART: Michigan City 60–59 South Bend Adams; Warsaw 79–60 Nappanee; Michigan City 83–72 Warsaw. Officials: Wayne Crispen, John Arnold, Robert Kramer, Harry Green, Homer Owens, Marvin Cave.
EVANSVILLE: North 71–60 Oakland City; Boonville 58–39 Leavenworth; North 83–54 Boonville. Officials: James Ruby, Wayne Myers, Ken Blankenbaker, Kenneth Payne, William Malloy, Darrel McFall.
FORT WAYNE: South Side 68–39 Hamilton; Snider 79–61 East Noble; South Side 56–32 Snider. Officials: John Fee, Don Hurst, Robert Laird, Eugene Lillie, Jack Mercer, Howard Risley.
FRANKFORT: Bainbridge 79–42 New Market; Speedway 62–50 Delphi; Bainbridge 79–71 Speedway. Officials: Don Shiflet, William Fields, Don Hollman, James Davis, Larry Gradeless, Robert Reed.
HUNTINGBURG: New Albany 60–59 Holland; Corydon 56–51 Oolitic; New Albany 74–62 Corydon. Officials: Glen Wisler, Maurice Gardner, Harry Inskeep, Danny Jacobs, James Beyer, Richard Sweet.
INDIANAPOLIS: Shortridge 78–55 Southport; Tech 68–41 Plainfield; Shortridge 56–47 Tech. Officials: James Schwenk, Richard Gebhart, Robert Davidson, Gil Baumgartner, Everett

Tourney Time

Campbell, Gene Marks.
KOKOMO: Kokomo 76–60 Wabash; Bluffton 65–61 Wolf Lake; Kokomo 56–44 Bluffton. Officials: Bill May, George Dunleavy, Gerald Imel, Robert Wells, John Thomas, John Gassensmith.
LAFAYETTE: Wheatfield 35–33 Seeger; Lafayette Jefferson 73–59 Fowler; Lafayette Jefferson 81–48 Wheatfield. Officials: Charles Garber, Norris Boomershine, Fred Marlow, John Holmes, Tom Dean, Tom Hoffman.
LOGANSPORT: Plymouth 79–50 Oregon-Davis; Logansport 99–57 Valparaiso; Logansport 65–61 Plymouth. Officials: Firman Grimes, Marvin Heaton, Dwain Laird, John Bush, Floyd Reed, Richard Freeman.
NEW CASTLE: New Castle 71–55 Selma; Richmond 52–48 Muncie Southside; New Castle 76–72 Richmond. Officials: Vern Doles, Gary Muncy, Raymond Robison, James Benecke, Zeke Williams, Walter Swift.
WASHINGTON: Washington 90–72 Linton; Vincennes 85–65 North Central (Farmersburg); Washington 56–54 Vincennes. Officials: Glen Bonsett, Charlie Stumpf, Richard Foster, Allen Voorhis, Art Thompson, Charles Sallee.

1967 SEMI-STATES

EVANSVILLE: Evansville North 66–58 New Albany; Terre Haute Garfield 68–63 Washington; Evansville North 59–58 Terre Haute Garfield. Officials: Gerald Imel, Robert Laird, David Habegger, Wendell Baker, John Fee, Ernie Sohl.
FORT WAYNE: Fort Wayne South 47–43 Michigan City Elston; Marion 78–64 Kokomo; South 68–51 Marion. Officials: Glen Wisler, Zeke Williams, Ken Blankenbaker, Lowell Smith, Art Thompson, Dwain Laird.
INDIANAPOLIS: Indianapolis Shortridge 73–53 Greensburg; New Castle 88–61 Liberty; New Castle 51–49 Indianapolis Shortridge. Officials: Roy Kilby, Robert Showalter, Floyd Reed, Edgar Powers, Tom Dean, Robert Kramer.
LAFAYETTE: Bainbridge 71–67 Logansport; Lafayette Jefferson 65–59 Gary Roosevelt; Lafayette Jefferson 75–72 Bainbridge. Officials: John Williams, Jimmy Dimitroff, Roger Emmert, James Schwenk, Homer Owens, John Thomas.

1967 FINALS—March 18

INDIANAPOLIS (Hinkle Fieldhouse): Evansville North 66–56 New Castle; Lafayette Jefferson 79–70 Fort Wayne South Side; Evansville North 60–58 Lafayette Jefferson. Officials: Glen Wisler, Kenneth Blankenbaker, John Fee, John Williams, David Habegger, Roy Kilby.

1968 SECTIONALS

ANDERSON: Markleville 85–73 Daleville; Madison Heights 72–63 Frankton; Alexandria 75–58 Pendleton; Highland 75–72 Anderson (ot); Madison Heights 64–60 Markleville; Highland 77–73 Alexandria (2ot); Madison Heights 67–52 Highland. Officials: Roy Kilby, Ray Mitrione, Troy Ingram, Marvin Cave.

BEDFORD: Shawswick 65–62 Tunnelton; Fayetteville 62–61 Heltonville; Oolitic 69–40 Mitchell; Bedford 51–36 Marshall Twp.; Fayetteville 76–53 Shawswick; Oolitic 69–44 Bedford; Oolitic 66–45 Fayetteville. Officials: Roger Emmert, David Avery, Randall Holland, Jim DeGroote.

BLUFFTON: Bluffton 71–42 Southern Wells; South Adams 78–69 Eastbrook; Bellmont 70–65 Adams Central (ot); Bluffton 66–48 Norwell; Bellmont 69–62 South Adams; Bluffton 65–57 Bellmont. Officials: John Holmes, Merl Heckaman, Kenneth Miller, Richard Vendrely.

BOONVILLE: Tecumseh 59–57 Haubstadt; South Spencer 60–48 Chrisney; Winslow 59–54 Castle; Dale 68–50 Boonville; Tecumseh 82–58 South Spencer; Dale 60–58 Winslow; Dale 77–69 Tecumseh. Officials: Richard Sweet, Leroy Schultheis, Darrell Eaton, Ben Olsson.

BRAZIL: Staunton 58–53 Van Buren; Rockville 65–45 Reelsville; Brazil 49–48 Rosedale; Staunton 55–51 Montezuma; Brazil 46–45 Rockville; Brazil 55–50 Staunton. Officials: Fred Marlow, Bruce Knecht, Robert Roney, William Bateman.

BROWNSBURG: Brownsburg 90–40 Charlton; Mooresville 67–52 Monrovia; Danville 60–58 Pittsboro; Avon 71–58 Plainfield; Brownsburg 68–58 Mooresville; Avon 74–62 Danville; Brownsburg 92–68 Avon. Officials: Don Hurst, J. Thomas Moorman, Paul Wernke, Lloyd Baugh.

CARMEL: Tipton 69–40 Sheridan; Carmel 94–50 Westfield; Noblesville 71–53 Hamilton Southeast; Hamilton Heights 58–52 Lapel; Carmel 58–54 Tipton; Noblesville 74–71 Hamilton Heights (ot); Carmel 76–66 Noblesville. Officials: Gene Butts, Paul Leamon, Robert Gilmore, Gil Baumgartner.

CHESTERTON: Valparaiso 71–50 Liberty Twp.; Portage 84–65 Jackson Twp.; Chesterton 82–48 Wheeler; Morgan Twp. 78–60 Washington Twp.; Valparaiso 80–53 Portage; Chesterton 85–50 Morgan Twp.; Chesterton 64–60 Valparaiso. Officials: Richard Foster, Lloyd Chambers, Jon Gallipo, John E. Ward.

CLAY CITY: Spencer 79–36 Patricksburg; North Central 73–52 Shakamak; Cloverdale 73–56 Clay City; Spencer 66–50 Gosport; Cloverdale 73–61 North Central; Cloverdale 71–64 Spencer. Officials: Robert Laird, Clifford Runnebohm, Frank Hobson, Max Andress.

COLUMBIA CITY: South Whitley 48–45 Wolf Lake; Manchester 50–46 Pierceton; Columbia City 54–50 Larwill; South Whitley 69–65 Churubusco; Manchester 50–44 Columbia City; Manchester 62–52 South Whitley. Officials: John Gassensmith, Arthur Largent, John Hilligoss, Jack Goen.

COLUMBUS: Greensburg 68–49 Jackson Twp; Brown County 66–56 Hauser; Columbus 82–43 Sandcreek; Edinburg 82–57 Burney; Brown County 59–55 Greensburg; Columbus 86–58 Edinburg; Columbus 102–74 Brown County. Officials: Homer Owens Jr., Jim Ladd, Michael Hennegan, Don Snedeker.

CONNERSVILLE: Connersville 79–55 Lewisville; College Corner 61–51 Liberty; Whitewater 81–78 Straughn; Brookville 61–31 Laurel; Connersville 78–56 College Corner; Whitewater 62–61 Brookville; Connersville 105–80 Whitewater. Officials: James Ruby, Richard Hale, Donald Ford, Robert Wells.

CRAWFORDSVILLE: Crawfordsville 102–49 New Market; Linden 72–64 Ladoga; Coal Creek Central 67–61 New Ross; Waveland 62–53 Waynetown; Crawfordsville 86–61 Linden; Waveland 71–68 Coal Creek Central; Crawfordsville 93–55 Waveland. Officials: Charles Garber, Morris Cohen, Bill Laird, Gene Marks.

Tourney Time

CROWN POINT: Lowell 62–58 Hanover Central; Merrillville 89–75 Hebron; Griffith 87–76 Boone Grove; Crown Point 85–57 Lake Central; Lowell 68–56 Merrillville; Crown Point 75–72 Griffith; Lowell 82–68 Crown Point. Officials: Robert Reed, Billy Maroney, Louis Zabona, Joe Smelcer.

DEKALB: Hamilton 52–51 Fremont; Garrett 60–41 Eastside; DeKalb 85–31 Angola; Hamilton 70–58 Prairie Heights; DeKalb 53–46 Garrett; DeKalb 68–47 Hamilton. Officials: Harold Ashbrook, James R. Carey, Donald Leever, Don Edwards.

EAST CHICAGO: East Chicago Roosevelt 79–57 Gary Andrean; East Chicago Washington 65–59 Hobart; Hammond Noll 89–56 Calumet; Tolleston 72–69 Gary Edison; Washington 74–63 East Chicago Roosevelt; Tolleston 70–62 Noll; Washington 72–60 Tolleston. Officials: Marion Acton, John Mikels, Jerry Struble, Gordon McCain.

EAST NOBLE: West Noble 58–56 Fairfield; Lakeland 65–62 Middlebury; Westview 71–70 East Noble (3ot); West Noble 79–73 Albion; Lakeland 60–57 Westview; Lakeland 76–72 West Noble. Officials: Tom Dean, Ward Weisel, William DeRome, Jonnie Joe Webber.

ELKHART: Jimtown 54–50 Wakarusa; Elkhart 56–53 Goshen (ot); Penn 59–43 Concord; Nappanee 79–47 Jefferson; Elkhart 53–39 Jimtown; Penn 60–56 Nappanee; Penn 67–65 Elkhart (ot). Officials: David Habegger, Russ Freeland, Peter Kokinda, Charles Sallee.

EVANSVILLE: Rex Mundi 67–57 Harrison; North 80–60 Bosse; Reitz 65–54 Central; Memorial 77–69 Mater Dei; North 58–46 Rex Mundi; Reitz 74–51 Memorial; Reitz 69–40 North. Officials: Winfield Jacobs, George Oberle, Robert Kirk, Danny Jacobs.

FORT WAYNE (#1): Monroeville 65–45 Bishop Luers; Bishop Dwenger 66–58 Arcola; New Haven 75–72 Huntertown; Central Catholic 70–58 Elmhurst; Bishop Dwenger 65–56 Monroeville; Central Catholic 74–65 New Haven; Central Catholic 61–49 Bishop Dwenger. Officials: Everett Campbell, Louis Schmalfeldt, Patrick King, James Beyer.

FORT WAYNE (#2): Snider 61–54 North Side; Central 67–43 Woodlan; South Side 67–45 Hoagland; Concordia 63–54 Leo; Central 71–68 Snider; Concordia 78–62 South Side; Central 62–54 Concordia. Officials: Wayne Crispen, Roger DeYoung, Lynn Barlow, Richard Gebbart.

FOUNTAIN CENTRAL: Attica 82–63 Turkey Run; Seeger 72–61 Pine Village; Fountain Central 67–64 Covington; North Vermillion 78–47 Williamsport; Attica 74–63 Seeger; Fountain Central 85–69 North Vermillion; Attica 81–67 Fountain Central. Officials: Dwain Laird, William Phillips, William Strafford, Darrel McFall.

FRANKFORT: Delphi 59–54 Clinton Prairie; Wainwright 79–74 East Tipp; Frankfort 62–58 Carroll; Clinton Central 64–40 Rossville; Wainwright 68–56 Delphi; Frankfort 66–64 Clinton Central; Wainwright 65–62 Frankfort. Officials: Art Thompson, Charles Bertram, Walter Overton, Eugene Lillie.

FRANKLIN: Center Grove 91–60 New Palestine; Whiteland 67–58 Indian Creek; Franklin 61–56 Greenwood; Decatur Central 71–61 Franklin Central; Center Grove 60–56 Whiteland; Franklin 68–66 Decatur Central; Franklin 69–61 Center Grove. Officials: James Schwenk, David Loewenstein, Robert L. Rohleder, William Fields.

GARY: Horace Mann 59–49 River Forest; Gary Roosevelt 97–42 East Gary Edison; Froebel 90–66 Wirt; Emerson 75–56 Wallace; Roosevelt 75–50 Horace Mann; Froebel 67–61 Emerson; Roosevelt 86–78 Froebel. Officials: Edgar Powers, David Parry, Eric Harmon, Ronald Hosinski.

GREENCASTLE: Greencastle 78–75 Bainbridge; Fillmore 82–71 Russellville; North Salem 69–56 Roachdale; Greencastle 73–63 Cascade; North Salem 78–71 Fillmore; Greencastle 93–59

IHSAA Scores | 1960–1969

North Salem. Officials: Jack Chestnut, Ray Ward, Dan Landis, William Williamson.

HAMMOND: Hammond Tech 73–58 Clark; Highland 52–46 Morton; Munster 80–55 Gavit; Hammond High 73–70 Whiting; Tech 78–61 Highland; Munster 83–67 Hammond High; Tech 62–59 Munster. Officials: Norris Boomershine, Don Reinholt, Gene Williams, Rich Freeman.

HUNTINGBURG: St. Ferdinand 71–66 Springs Valley; Ireland 73–45 Birdseye; Holland 67–56 Jasper; Huntingburg 71–68 Dubois; St. Ferdinand 59–44 Ireland; Holland 79–50 Huntingburg; Holland 57–53 St. Ferdinand. Officials: William Malloy, Jerry Baker, Keith Combs, Raymond Wescovi.

HUNTINGTON: Northfield 56–49 Huntington; Huntington Catholic 64–51 White's; Wabash 76–54 Southwood; Northfield 59–41 Huntington Catholic; Northfield 64–60 Wabash. Officials: Harry Green, Harold Gray, Delmar Knecht, James Eads.

INDIANAPOLIS (Hinkle Fieldhouse): Tech 55–40 Arlington; North Central 73–64 Ben Davis; Washington 79–45 Broad Ripple; Crispus Attucks 66–52 Ritter; Tech 63–58 North Central; Washington 68–60 Crispus Attucks; Washington 70–65 Tech. Officials: Zeke Williams, Richard Brainerd, Richard Cook, Bill Hile.

INDIANAPOLIS (Coliseum): Chatard 83–53 Indiana School for the Deaf; Lawrence Central 62–54 Howe; Scecina 73–56 Northwest; Shortridge 47–45 Marshall; Chatard 68–61 Lawrence Central; Shortridge 79–50 Scecina; Shortridge 82–43 Chatard. Officials: Don Hollman, Wayne Van Sickle, Martin Burdette, Gary Muncy.

JEFFERSONVILLE: Clarksville 59–51 Providence; Jeffersonville 79–48 Lanesville; South Central 70–60 Floyd Central; New Albany 73–58 Borden; Jeffersonville 63–60 Clarksville; New Albany 95–72 South Central; Jeffersonville 63–57 New Albany. Officials: Wendell Baker, William Pitman, Frank Corsaro, Francis Fiddler.

KNOX: Winamac, 63–38 Oregon-Davis; Monterey 72–68 Aubbeenaubbee Twp; Knox 64–63 LaCrosse; North Judson 58–44 Culver; Winamac 76–45 Monterey; Knox 62–45 North Judson; Knox 58–56 Winamac. Officials: Robert Kramer, Donald Schmidt, Gerry Scheub, Howard Risley.

KOKOMO: Eastern 54–51 Windfall; Maconaquah 88–52 Taylor; Kokomo 81–48 Western; Sharpsville 78–69 Northwestern; Maconaquah 55–50 Eastern; Kokomo 85–52 Sharpsville; Kokomo 72–57 Maconaquah. Officials: Bob Showalter, Bill Gray, Sidney Ellis, Charlie Stumpf.

LAFAYETTE: Lafayette Jefferson 93–39 Klondike; Southwestern 74–39 Battle Ground; West Lafayette 80–75 Central Catholic (2ot); Jefferson 82–45 Benton Central; West Lafayette 66–51 Southwestern; Lafayette Jefferson 56–55 West Lafayette. Officials: George Avery, Gary Janeway, Myron Moriarity, Eugene Linn.

LAVILLE: Bremen 77–55 Glenn; LaVille 73–61 North Liberty; South Bend Jackson 63–62 Argos; Plymouth 83–72 Mishawaka Marian; LaVille 62–57 Bremen; Plymouth 69–65 South Bend Jackson; LaVille 69–68 Plymouth. Officials: Ernie Sohl, David Schwartz, Dan Alvarez, George Dunleavy.

LAWRENCEBURG: Aurora 96–50 Patriot; Vevay 76–62 Rising Sun; Lawrenceburg 95–61 Dillsboro; North Dearborn 66–59 Aurora; Vevay 79–65 Lawrenceburg; North Dearborn 76–41 Vevay. Officials: Harry Inskeep, Robert Wolfe, Bill Wing, Boynton Robson.

LOGANSPORT: Lewis Cass 91–44 Star City; North Miami 68–61 Caston; Pioneer 69–65 Peru; Logansport 70–43 Kewanna; North Miami 66–61 Lewis Cass; Logansport 84–49 Pioneer; North Miami 61–55 Logansport. Officials: Firman Grimes, Jack Gardner, Arthur Morris, Walter Swift.

Tourney Time

MADISON: Madison 91–56 Deputy, Charlestown 82–62 New Washington; Southwestern 79–56 Henryville; Silver Creek 57–56 Madison Shawe; Madison 78–70 Charlestown; Silver Creek 75–59 Southwestern; Silver Creek 69–57 Madison. Officials: James Davis, Roger McGriff, Ken Sussman, John Bush.

MARION: Mississinewa 75–49 Marion Bennett; Summitville 72–63 Elwood; Marion 72–43 Fairmount; Mississinewa 68–50 Oak Hill; Marion 63–59 Summitville; Marion 70–48 Mississinewa. Officials: Harold Mason, Bobby Goble, Robert Bowman, John Manka.

MARTINSVILLE: Martinsville 82–73 Eminence; Bloomington 84–46 Unionville; Edgewood 77–50 Smithville; Martinsville 77–63 University; Bloomington 67–59 Edgewood; Bloomington 69–61 Martinsville. Officials: Maurice Gardner, Ed Scott, Merle Vickers, Robert Sweet.

MICHIGAN CITY: Michigan City 92–40 Rolling Prairie; LaPorte 74–56 Wanatah; St. Mary's 78–63 Westville; South Central 74–47 New Carlisle; Michigan City 90–52 LaPorte; South Central 77–57 St. Mary's; Michigan City 96–49 South Central. Officials: John Arnold, Richard Lederman, John Lozier, Ned Brenizer.

MILAN: Jac-Cen-Del 77–40 Sunman; South Ripley 81–71 Batesville; Milan 74–56 Moores Hill; Jac-Cen-Del 75–62 Holton; South Ripley 59–57 Milan; Jac-Cen-Del 67–66 South Ripley. Officials: John Williams, Melvin Botkin, Dick Venable, Neal Jay.

MUNCIE: Delta 76–71 Southside, Cowan 65–40 Yorktown; Burris 71–69 Wes-Del (ot); Central 82–61 Albany; Delta 59–47 Cowan; Central 78–66 Burris; Central 55–52 Delta. Officials: Gerald Imel, Frank Hoagburg, Paul Garriott, Vern Doles.

NEW CASTLE: Greenfield 69–64 Shenandoah; Hancock Central 77–56 Spiceland; New Castle 82–68 Mt. Vernon; Knightstown 69–62 Blue River; Greenfield 86–63 Hancock Central; New Castle 53–48 Knightstown; New Castle 90–65 Greenfield. Officials: Floyd A. Reed, James G. Burt, Joseph Louis Dickey, Raymond M. Robison.

NORTH NEWTON: Remington 67–45 Ambia; South Newton 71–64 Oxford; Fowler 63–50 North Newton (2ot), Rensselaer 80–53 Boswell; South Newton 57–53 Remington; Fowler 67–50 Rensselaer; South Newton 56–54 Fowler. Officials: Stanley Dubis, Gene Kennan, Rex Mays, Eugene Carrabine.

NORTH WHITE: Wolcott 70–57 DeMotte; North White 93–62 Kouts; Wheatfield 56–45 West Central; Frontier 70–68 Twin Lakes; Wolcott 75–61 North White; Frontier 60–50 Wheatfield; Frontier 73–60 Wolcott. Officials: Tom Hoffman, Larry Pinkerton, Robert Marcinek, Allen Voorhis.

PAOLI: Morgan Twp. 79–65 North Central; Paoli 63–55 Orleans; West Washington 72–69 Eastern (ot); Corydon 65–50 Salem; Paoli 68–53 Morgan Twp.; Corydon 72–46 West Washington; Paoli 47–41 Corydon. Officials: Earle Wolfe, Jack Williams, David Mounts, Richard Crays.

PORTLAND: Montpelier 64–60 Hartford City; Portland 89–66 Pennville; Bryant 68–51 Dunkirk; Portland 71–69 Montpelier; Portland 58–51 Bryant. Officials: Dale Van Houten, Gene Gibson, Charles Bromelmeier, Wayne Targgart.

PRINCETON: Ft. Branch 66–64 Princeton; Wood Memorial 59–49 Owensville; North Posey 73 –51 Francisco; Mt. Vernon 93–60 New Harmony; Wood Memorial 68–45 Ft. Branch; Mt. Vernon 55–47 North Posey; Mt. Vernon 44–42 Wood Memorial. Officials: Wayne Myers, Don Smith, John Britton, Don Shields.

RICHMOND: Richmond 85–46 Cambridge City; Northeastern 76–63 Hagerstown; Centerville 90–51 Randolph Southern; Richmond 65–52 Northeastern; Richmond 96–60

Centerville. Officials: John Thomas, Al Lindahl, Thomas Neuman, James Benecke.

RUSHVILLE: Eastern Hancock 73–55 New Salem; Rushville 75–47 Arlington; Milroy 79–70 Carthage; Eastern Hancock 72–44 Morton Memorial; Rushville 58–55 Milroy; Eastern Hancock 72–62 Rushville. Officials: Donald Call, Clifford Spears, James Wehsollek, Jim Cox.

SEYMOUR: Seymour 69–58 North Vernon; Austin 67–60 Crothersville; Scottsburg 82–50 Medora; Brownstown 88–32 Clearspring; Seymour 83–67 Austin; Scottsburg 86–81 Brownstown; Scottsburg 83–73 Seymour. Officials: Jack Mercer, Phillip Hardwick, Bill Wullner, Noble Rector.

SHELBYVILLE: Waldron 67–52 Morristown; Triton Central 76–59 North De-catur; Shelbyville 85–47 Southwestern; Waldron 69–56 Manilla (ot); Shelbyville 92–65 Triton Central; Shelbyville 96–44 Waldron. Officials: Ken Blankenbaker, Samuel Reed, Dallas Richards, Jimmy Dimitroff.

SOUTH BEND: Clay 69–49 Mishawaka; Washington 71–69 Central; St. Joseph 40–38 Riley; LaSalle 70–47 Adams; Washington 61–51 Clay; St. Joseph 69–68 LaSalle; St. Joseph 54–48 Washington. Officials: John Fee, William Van Sickle, Thomas Manning, Donald Koester.

SOUTHPORT: Wood 98–77 Chartrand; Southport 45–44 Warren Central (ot); Cathedral 64–39 Kennedy; Beech Grove 63–43 Manual; Southport 54–52 Wood; Cathedral 60–53 Beech Grove; Southport 64–63 Cathedral. Officials: Bill May, George Taylor, Russell Rogers, Marvin Heaton.

SWITZ CITY: Odon 58–50 Worthington; Eastern 62–48 Linton; L&M 56–55 Bloomfield (ot); Elnora 68–67 Switz City; Odon 66–57 Eastern; L&M 87–72 Elnora; L&M 65–55 Odon. Officials: Donald L. Hubbard, Ronald Ham, Charles David Roy, Richard V. Pattengale.

TELL CITY: Cannelton 88–61 English; Milltown 63–43 Marengo; Tell City 57–47 Perry Central; Cannelton 69–68 Leavenworth; Tell City 36–33 Milltown; Tell City 55–45 Cannelton. Officials: Wallace Reeve, McKee Munk, Richard Schleicher, Carl Schnebelt.

TERRE HAUTE: Clinton 64–47 West Vigo; Gerstmeyer 82–61 Laboratory; Schulte 54–47 Garfield; Wiley 66–57 Honey Creek; Clinton 75–65 Gerstmeyer; Wiley 55–41 Schulte; Clinton 57–51 Wiley. Officials: Harold Gourley, Jerry Larrison, Floyd Riggs, Charles Daum.

VINCENNES: Petersburg 83–55 Dugger; Central Catholic 61–48 Sullivan; South Knox 57–46 North Knox; Vincennes 85–46 Petersburg; South Knox 72–67 Central Catholic; Vincennes 67–61 South Knox. Officials: Kenneth Payne, Warren Keyser, Raymond Norris, John Tucker.

WARSAW: Akron 86–73 Rochester; Warsaw 66–42 Triton; Milford 64–59 North Webster; Mentone 87–67 Syracuse; Akron 76–70 Warsaw; Mentone 85–55 Milford; Akron 78–77 Mentone. Officials: James Carey, Ronald Beard, Donald Roudebush, Byron Weaver.

WASHINGTON: Washington 74–62 Washington Catholic; Plainville 60–59 Barr-Reeves; Loogootee St. John's 84–81 Otwell (ot); Loogootee 52–35 Shoals; Washington 65–40 Plainville; Loogootee St. John's 62–51 Loogootee; Washington 57–36 Loogootee St. John's. Officials: Lowell Smith, Rudy Tabereaux, W. Blake Ress, Glen Bonsett.

WINCHESTER: Monroe Central 71–55 Union; Winchester 89–58 Redkey; Wapahani 77–72 Union City; Monroe Central 81–62 Winchester; Monroe Central 79–76 Wapahani. Officials: Glen Wisler, James Frey, Tom Knox, Max Hensler.

ZIONSVILLE: Zionsville 74–69 Darlington; Thorntown 66–57 Speedway; Lebanon 70–68 Brebeuf (ot); Pike 88–62 Wells; Thorntown 66–57 Zionsville; Lebanon 70–69 Pike (ot); Lebanon 80–73 Thorntown. Officials: Don Shiflet, Fred Myers, Jerry Scott, Robert Fisher.

Tourney Time

1968 REGIONALS

ANDERSON: Madison Heights 76–64 Portland; Marion 68–67 Carmel; Marion 52–51 Madison Heights (ot). Officials. Donald Call, Ronald Hosinski, Bill Hile, Richard Freeman, Zeke Williams, Raymond Robison.

BLOOMINGTON: Bloomington 54–52 Clinton (ot); Scottsburg 69–63 Brazil; Bloomington 62–61 Scottsburg. Officials: Earle Wolfe, James P. Carey, Donald Hubbard, Charles Daum, James Davis, Roger Emmert.

COLUMBUS: Columbus 87–80 Franklin; Shelbyville 94–70 Silver Creek; Columbus 83–80 Shelbyville. Officials: Richard Foster, Jack Gardner, Harold Gourley, Raymond Vescovi, Darrell McFall, Richard Sweet.

CONNERSVILLE: Eastern Hancock 64–63 Connersville; Jac-Cen-Del 73–64 North Dearborn; Jac-Cen-Del 61–53 Eastern Hancock. Officials: James Schwenk, Wayne Myers, John Holmes, Gary Muncy, Don Shiflet, Harry Green.

EAST CHICAGO: Gary Roosevelt 98–74 Lowell; East Chicago Washington 64–62 Hammond Tech; Gary Roosevelt 74–68 East Chicago Washington. Officials: Charles Garber Jr., Robert Reed, Robert Laird, James Benecke, John Williams, Harold Ashbrook.

ELKHART: Michigan City 66–63 South Bend St. Joseph; Akron 67–64 Penn; Michigan City 94–77 Akron. Officials: Floyd Reed, John Ward, Firman Grimes, James Ruby, Tom Hoffman, Walter Swift.

EVANSVILLE: Dale 52–40 Mt. Vernon; Reitz 62–41 Tell City; Reitz 65–53 Dale. Officials: Howard Risley, Vern Doles, Marvin Cave, William Fields, Maurice Gardner, Jack Mercer.

FORT WAYNE: Fort Wayne Central Catholic 58–52 Fort Wayne Central; Lakeland 61–53 DeKalb; Central Catholic 72–50 Lakeland. Officials: John Thomas, Charlie Stumpf, John Arnold, Don Snedeker, Arthur Thompson, Gene Marks.

FRANKFORT: Greencastle 81–80 Crawfordsville; Wainwright 78–71 Lebanon; Greencastle 88–66 Wainwright. Officials: Gene Butts, John Gassensmith, Ernie Sohl, George Dunleavy, Robert Kramer, Don Hurst.

HUNTINGBURG: Holland 61–59 Oolitic; Jeffersonville 79–52 Paoli; Jeffersonville 72–70 Holland. Officials: Jimmy Dimitroff, Kenneth Payne, Max Andress, John Bush, Bob Showalter, Charles Sallee.

INDIANAPOLIS: Shortridge 78–54 Brownsburg; Washington 64–53 Southport; Shortridge 72–60 Washington. Officials: William Malloy, Eugene Linn, John Fee, Gordon McCain, Homer Owens, Jim DeGroote.

KOKOMO: Kokomo 71–64 Bluffton; Manchester 80–68 Northfield; Kokomo 70–55 Manchester. Officials: Glen Wisler, Allen Voorhis, Harry Inskeep, Marvin Heaton, Glen Bonsett, Gil Baumgartner.

LAFAYETTE: Attica 52–50 Frontier; Lafayette Jefferson 69–48 South Newton; Attica 69–59 Lafayette Jefferson. Officials: Edgar Powers, Wallace Reeve, Bill May, Donald Koester, Ken Blankenbaker, Lowell Smith.

LOGANSPORT: North Miami 61–41 Knox; Chesterton 88–68 LaVille; North Miami 72–65 Chesterton. Officials: George Avery, Norris Boomershine, Don Hollman, Gerald Imel, Eugene Lillie, Robert Wells.

NEW CASTLE: Richmond 67–58 Monroe Central; Muncie Central 72–62 New Castle; Richmond 67–64 Muncie Central. Officials: Roy Kilby, Jack Chestnut, David Habegger, Richard

Gebhart, Marion Acton, Ned Brenizer.
WASHINGTON: Vincennes 88–63 L&M; Cloverdale 80–57 Washington; Vincennes 87–57 Cloverdale. Officials: James Beyer, Max Hensler, Wendell Baker, Francis Fiddler, Dwain Laird, Danny Jacobs.

1968 SEMI–STATES

EVANSVILLE: Vincennes 77–69 Jeffersonville; Reitz 89–69 Bloomington; Vincennes 71–70 Reitz. Officials: Jimmy Dimitroff, Bill Hile, Roy Kilby, William Malloy, John Williams, Zeke Williams.
FORT WAYNE: Michigan City Elston 90–79 Kokomo; Marion 62–51 Central Catholic; Marion 72–67 Michigan City Elston. Officials: Wendell Baker, Raymond Robison, Robert Kramer, Ernie Sohl, James Schwenk, Robert Laird.
INDIANAPOLIS: Richmond 68–49 Jac-Cen-Del; Shortridge 88–77 Columbus; Shortridge 81–58 Richmond. Officials: Gerald Imel, Don Shiflet, David Habegger, Marion Acton, Ken Blankenbaker, Lowell Smith.
LAFAYETTE: North Miami 73–66 Greencastle; Gary Roosevelt 82–69 Attica; Gary Roosevelt 91–30 North Miami. Officials: Dwain Laird, Bob Showalter, Glen Wisler, Harold Gourley, Floyd Reed, John Thomas.

1968 FINALS—March 16

INDIANAPOLIS (Hinkle Fieldhouse): Gary Roosevelt 65–48 Vincennes; Indianapolis Shortridge 58–56 Marion; Gary Roosevelt 68–60 Indianapolis Shortridge. Officials: John Williams, Floyd Reed, Glen Wisler, James Schwenk, Roy Kilby, Robert Kramer.

1969 SECTIONALS

ANDERSON: Daleville 78–65 Pendleton; Madison Heights 80–68 Markleville; Anderson 95–49 Highland; Frankton 62–61 Alexandria; Madison Heights 92–62 Daleville; Anderson 91–64 Frankton; Anderson 81–62 Madison Heights. Officials: Charles Garber, Jr., Russell Freeland, Phillip Hardwick, Wayne Van Sickle.
BATESVILLE: Batesville 63–60 Milan (ot); Holton 78–64 South Ripley; Jac-Cen-Del 32–26 Sunman; Batesville 82–47 Moores Hill; Jac-Cen-Del 88–51 Holton; Jac-Cen-Del 66–51 Batesville. Officials: Howard Risley, John Manka, George Emery, Jim Ladd.
BEDFORD: Needmore 61–60 Oolitic; Tunnelton 69–41 Heltonville; Fayetteville 65–63 Shawswick; Bedford 61–56 Mitchell; Needmore 63–62 Tunnelton; Bedford 81–65 Fayetteville; Bedford 64–44 Needmore. Officials: Harold Gourley, Keith Combs, Melvin Redman, Raymond Vescovi.
BLUFFTON: Southern Wells 78–76 Adams Central; Eastbrook 87–72 South Adams; Bluffton 62–46 Norwell; Bellmont 68–52 Southern Wells; Bluffton 92–68 Eastbrook; Bluffton 65–60 Bellmont. Officials: Dwain Laird, Patrick King, Gene Williams, James Beyer.
BOONVILLE: Chrisney 79–69 Boonville; Winslow 78–62 South Spencer; Tecumseh 67–56 Dale; Chrisney 75–58 Castle; Winslow 73–56 Tecumseh; Chrisney 88–69 Winslow. Officials:

Tourney Time

Russell Rogers, Don Smith, Jr., John Britton, Robert Kirk.

BRAZIL: Montezuma 76–60 Reelsville; Van Buren 72–59 Rockville; Rosedale 62–61 Staunton; Brazil 56–37 Montezuma; Van Buren 59–54 Rosedale; Brazil 69–51 Van Buren. Officials: John Bush, Lynn Barlow, Paul Wernke, Rudy Tabereaux.

BROWNSBURG: Mooresville 73–64 Pittsboro; Monrovia 93–50 Charlton; Danville 68–61 Brownsburg; Plainfield 80–66 Avon; Mooresville 79–73 Monrovia; Plainfield 71–62 Danville; Plainfield 89–82 Mooresville. Officials: Bill Hile, Richard Sweet, Joe Gallipo, Blake Ress.

CARMEL: Carmel 85–78 Hamilton Southeastern; Tipton 77–45 Sheridan; Noblesville 70–56 Westfield; Lapel 77–69 Hamilton Heights; Carmel 66–56 Tipton (ot); Lapel 76–66 Noblesville; Carmel 84–72 Lapel. Officials: Ronald Hosinski, John Tucker, Louis Zabona, Bob Goble.

CHESTERTON: Jackson Twp. 63–41 Wheeler; Chesterton 67–49 Morgan Twp.; Valparaiso 79–44 Liberty Twp.; Portage 107–52 Washington Twp.; Chesterton 89–63 Jackson Twp.; Valparaiso 84–68 Portage; Valparaiso 73–49 Chesterton. Officials: Roy Kilby, William Van Sickle, Jerry Scott, Gordon McCain.

CLAY CITY: Cloverdale 79–57 North Central; Spencer 94–66 Shakamak; Gosport 35–31 Patricksburg; Cloverdale 62–54 Clay City; Spencer 80–44 Gosport; Cloverdale 82–65 Spencer. Officials: Wallace Reeve, Warren Keyser, Walter Overton, William Williamson.

COLUMBIA CITY: Larwill 63–49 Churubusco; Manchester 66–54 South Whitley; Columbia City 56–52 Pierceton; Larwill 65–53 Manchester; Larwill 75–73 Columbia City. Officials: Harry W. Green, James Richard Carey, Eric Harmon, Robert Manor.

COLUMBUS: Columbus 71–40 South Decatur; Hauser 75–49 Edinburg; Brown County 74–58 Greensburg; Columbus 70–58 Hauser; Columbus 107–89 Brown County. Officials: James F. Davis, Clifford Spears, Dallas Richards, Herod Toon, Jr.

CONNERSVILLE: Brookville 76–50 Liberty; Whitewater 74–70 Laurel; Connersville 57–56 Union; Brookville 72–65 Whitewater; Connersville 83–56 Brookville. Officials: John Holmes, Melvin Botkin, Al Lindahl, Morris Cohen.

CRAWFORDSVILLE: Crawfordsville 72–57 Waynetown; Ladoga 91–49 New Ross; Waveland 56–52 Linden; Coal Creek Central 82–40 New Market; Crawfordsville 54–50 Ladoga (ot); Coal Creek Central 70–63 Waveland; Crawfordsville 72–63 Coal Creek Central. Officials: Winfield Jacobs, Stewart Vickers, Larry Holdcraft, Norman Chestnut.

CROWN POINT: Hebron 68–57 Merrillville; Crown Point 74–43 Griffith; Hanover Central 66–63 Boone Grove; Hebron 70–63 Lake Centra; Crown Point 91–61 Hanover Central; Crown Point 77–64 Hebron. Officials: John Arnold, Harold Gray, George Grygiel, Richard Freeman.

DEKALB: Garrett 90–60 Hamilton; DeKalb 72–49 Prairie Heights (LaGrange); Fremont 60–49 Angola; Garrett 89–57 Eastside; DeKalb 86–36 Fremont; DeKalb 72–63 Garrett. Officials: Robert Reed, George Taylor, Donald Roudebush, Richard Brainerd.

EAST CHICAGO: Hammond Noll 84–75 Calumet; East Chicago Washington 104–92 Hobart; East Chicago Roosevelt 77–61 East Gary Edison; Andrean 67–64 River Forest; Washington 77–76 Noll; Roosevelt 63–59 Andrean; Roosevelt 75–62 Washington. Officials: Zeke Williams, Billy Maroney, John Lozier, John Gassensmith.

EAST NOBLE: West Noble 84–72 Central Noble; Fairfield 67–57 East Noble; Lakeland 46–45 Middlebury; West Noble 59–53 Westview; Fairfield 76–56 Lakeland; Fairfield 68–65 West Noble. Officials: Harold Ashbrook, Eugene Keenan, Ronald Beard, Jack Goen.

ELKHART: Jefferson Twp. 58–53 Wakarusa; Goshen 49–46 Nappanee; Penn 61–44 Concord;

Elkhart 75–43 Jimtown; Goshen 85–66 Jefferson Twp.; Elkhart 70–64 Penn; Goshen 75–64 Elkhart. Officials: Tom Hoffman, Richard Hale, Thomas Neuman, Don Koester.

EVANSVILLE: Rex Mundi 58–47 North; Bosse 69–66 Memorial; Mater Dei 54–49 Harrison; Reitz 56–52 Central; Rex Mundi 80–66 Bosse; Reitz 70–66 Mater Dei; Rex Mundi 72–67 Reitz. Officials: Don Shiflet, Don Shields, McKee Monk, Jack Chestnut.

FORT WAYNE (#1): Snider 53–42 South Side; Central Catholic 55–53 Heritage; Elmhurst 86–65 Woodlan (Woodburn); Central 69–62 Snider; Central Catholic 51–50 Elmhurst; Central Catholic 56–52 Central. Officials: Marion Acton, Neal Jay, Ward Weisel, Eugene Lillie.

FORT WAYNE (# 2): New Haven 69–61 Bishop Luers; Concordia 63–58 Bishop Dwenger; North Side 63–50 Leo; New Haven 79–72 Carroll (Huntertown); North Side 71–57 Concordia; North Side 69–58 New Haven. Officials: Gene Marks, Boynton Robson, Byron Weaver, Don Snedeker.

FOUNTAIN CENTRAL: Attica 61–45 Seeger; Covington 73–72 Williamsport; Turkey Run 84–59 Pine Village; North Vermillion 37–33 Fountain Central; Attica 71–61 Covington; North Vermillion 98–67 Turkey Run; North Vermillion 51–48 Attica. Officials: Wendell Baker, Louis Schmalfeldt, Dick Venable, Larry Inskeep.

FRANKFORT: Rossville 60–49 Delphi; Frankfort 90–61 Clinton Prairie; Sharpsville 67–57 Wainwright; Clinton Central 77–65 Carroll; Rossville 100–92 Frankfort; Sharpsville 61–59 Clinton Central; Rossville 103–88 Sharpsville. Officials: Ernie Sohl, Robert Marcinek, Thomas Meeks, Roger DeYoung.

GARY: Tolleston 93–66 West Side; Gary Roosevelt 73–52 Emerson; Froebel 94–59 Wirt; Mann 76–64 Wallace; Tolleston 77–66 Roosevelt; Froebel 53–45 Mann; Tolleston 73–68 Froebel. Officials: Richard Gebhart, Arthur Largent, Merl Heckaman, Walter Swift.

GREENCASTLE: Russellville 58–46 Roachdale; Cascade (Clayton) 66–64 Bainbridge; Greencastle 80–46 Fillmore; Russellville 58–53 North Salem; Greencastle 76–59 Cascade; Greencastle 80–44 Russellville. Officials: Donald Hubbard, Bruce Knecht, J. Thomas Moorman, Jonnie Joe Webber.

HAMMOND: Tech 74–63 Clark; Munster 66–63 Hammond High; Whiting 76–59 Morton; Gavit 76–69 Highland; Munster 70–68 Tech; Gavit 81–69 Whiting; Munster 92–82 Gavit. Officials: Edgar Powers, David Parry, Richard Cook, Joe Smelcer.

HUNTINGBURG: Dubois 45–36 Birdseye; Springs Valley 80–71 Jasper; Holland 88–66 Ferdinand; Huntingburg 76–74 Ireland; Springs Valley 46–29 Dubois; Holland 70–61 Huntingburg; Springs Valley 54–34 Holland. Officials: Danny Jacobs, Fred Myers, Leroy Schultheis, Kenneth Payne.

HUNTINGTON: White's 48–38 Huntington Catholic; Huntington 62–48 Wabash; Northfield 83–65 Southwood Huntington 76–36 White's (Wabash); Huntington 71–55 Northfield. Officials: Fred Marlow, Wayne Targgart, Robert Frey, John Ward.

INDIANAPOLIS (Hinkle Fieldhouse): Broad Ripple 71–63 Arlington; Washington 73–42 Tech; Crispus Attucks 86–41 Ritter; North Central 71–61 Ben Davis; Washington 105–57 Broad Ripple; Crispus Attucks 79–63 North Central; Washington 90–64 Crispus Attucks. Officials: David Habegger, Noble Rector, Marty Burdette, Bill May.

INDIANAPOLIS (Coliseum): Howe 75–42 School for the Deaf; Northwest 87–72 Scecina; Shortridge 83–41 Lawrence; Chatard 75–66 Marshall; Howe 80–62 Northwest; Shortridge 77–74 Chatard; Shortridge 72–70 Howe. Officials: Wayne Crispen, Carl Schnebelt, Troy Ingram, Lowell Smith.

Tourney Time

JEFFERSONVILLE: Jeffersonville 98–45 Borden; Providence 75–58 Floyd Central (New Albany); Lanesville 78–44 South Central; New Albany 98–66 Clarksville; Jeffersonville 61–59 Providence; New Albany 95–42 Lanesville; New Albany 95–77 Jeffersonville. Officials: James Schwenk, Jerry Larrison, Paul Garriott, Don Call.

KNOX: Culver 78–68 LaCrosse; Winamac 64–59 North Judson (ot); Knox 68–56 Oregon-Davis; Culver 65–60 Winamac; Knox 54–51 Culver. Officials: Richard Pattengale, Peter Kokinda, Charles Bromelmeier, David Schwartz.

KOKOMO: Northwestern 74–73 Eastern; Kokomo High 61–60 Western; Maconaquah 71–52 Windfall; Kokomo Haworth 64–61 Taylor; Kokomo 71–56 Northwestern; Maconaquah 60–57 Haworth; Kokomo 69–64 Maconaquah. Officials: Floyd Reed, Dale Van Houten, Robert Gilmore, Robert Laird.

LAFAYETTE: Lafayette Jefferson 79–68 West Lafayette; East Tipp 73–65 Battle Ground; Central Catholic 62–46 Southwestern; Lafayette Jefferson 54–43 Klondike; East Tipp 60–57 Central Catholic; Lafayette Jefferson 84–56 East Tipp. Officials: Firman Grimes, Arthur Morris, Bill Wing, Gene Butts.

LAVILLE: South Bend Jackson 56–49 Argos (ot); Bremen 78–46 North Liberty; Mishawaka Marian 56–52 Glenn; Plymouth 68–55 LaVille; South Bend Jackson 54–50 Bremen; Mishawaka Marian 66–61 Plymouth; Marian 64–51 Jackson. Officials: James Benecke Jr., Gene Gibson, Rex Mays, Gil Baumgartner.

LAWRENCEBURG: North Dearborn 80–77 Rising Sun (ot); Aurora 70–67 Lawrenceburg; Switzerland County 50–47 Dillsboro; Aurora 76–67 North Dearborn; Aurora 63–57 Switzerland County. Officials: Glen Wisler, Joseph Dickey, Gary Coers, James Eads.

LEBANON: Speedway 68–54 Granville Wells; Brebeuf (Indianapolis) 56–55 Thorntown; Zionsville 74–68 Lebanon; Darlington 83–64 Indianapolis Pike; Speedway 55–48 Brebeuf; Darlington 81–69 Zionsville; Darlington 56–54 Speedway. Officials: Everett Campbell, Jerry Baker, Raymond Norris, Wayne Myers.

LOGANSPORT: Logansport 91–50 Kewanna; Lewis Cass 85–55 Pioneer; Caston 67–64 Peru; Logansport 64–51 North Miami; Lewis Cass 86–60 Caston; Logansport 55–48 Lewis Cass. Officials: Stan Dubis, Gary Janeway, Thomas Manning Jr., James Ruby.

MADISON: Silver Creek 72–70 Shawe Memorial; Madison 77–76 Charlestown; Southwestern 85–69 Henryville; Silver Creek 81–67 New Washington; Madison 75–65 Southwestern; Silver Creek 82–58 Madison. Officials: Jack Mercer, William Phillips, Sidney Ellis, Francis Fiddler.

MARION: Fairmount 65–61 Summitville; Marion 53–25 Mississinewa; Oak Hill 70–57 Marion Bennett; Elwood 81–60 Fairmount; Marion 63–48 Oak Hill; Marion 64–43 Elwood. Officials: Bob Showalter, Robert Wolfe, Tom Knox, Bill Gray.

MARTINSVILLE: Eminence 74–56 Bloomington University; Martinsville 80–63 Unionville; Bloomington 94–69 Edgewood; Eminence 65–64 Smithville; Martinsville 69–68 Bloomington; Martinsville 73–54 Eminence. Officials: Marvin Heaton, Ray Mitrione, Frank Hobson, William Bateman.

MICHIGAN CITY: Marquette 78–72 South Central; Michigan City Elston 96–60 Westville; LaPorte 81–69 New Prairie; Marquette 86–72 Wanatah; Elston 62–59 LaPorte; Elston 78–65 Marquette. Officials: Gerald Imel, Jerry Struble, Gerry Schueb, Gary Muncy.

MUNCIE: Yorktown 69–62 Wes-Del; Muncie Burris 61–52 Albany; Muncie Southside 89–64 Delta; Cowan 60–56 Muncie Central; Yorktown 60–52 Burris; Southside 64–55 Cowan; Southside

41–37 Yorktown. Officials: Don Hollman, Dave Avery, Larry Hollman, Norris Boomershine.

NEW CASTLE: Greenfield 74–64 Blue River (Mt. Summit); Mt. Vernon 80–69 Shenandoah; Hancock Central 82–65 Tri; New Castle 76–51 Knightstown; Greenfield 82–81 Mt. Vernon (ot); Hancock Central 66–55 New Castle; Greenfield 100–56 Hancock Central. Officials: Allen Voorhis, Jim Cox, William Laird, Max Hensler.

NORTH NEWTON: Remington 58–41 South Newton; Benton Central 69–45 North Newton; Rensselaer 76–72 Lowell; Benton Central 75–68 Remington; Rensselaer 52–50 Benton Central. Officials: George Avery, Kenneth Miller, Ron Bella, Lloyd Chambers.

NORTH WHITE: Frontier 84–57 Kouts; Twin Lakes 67–59 Wolcott; North White 62–42 DeMotte; Wheatfield 57–48 West Central; Frontier 85–78 Twin Lakes; Wheatfield 52–49 North White; Frontier 81–58 Wheatfield. Officials: Robert Kramer, Dan Alverez, Dan Landis, Harold Mason.

PAOLI: Corydon 45–36 Morgan Twp.; Eastern (Pekin) 64–49 Orleans; North Central 60–45 Salem; Paoli 51–40 West Washington; Corydon 67–61 Eastern; Paoli 50–36 North Central; Paoli 39–38 Corydon. Officials: Roger Emmert, Ronald Ham, Frank Corsaro, Marvin Cave.

PORTLAND: Montpelier 74–50 Dunkirk; Pennville 71–63 Hartford City; Portland 55–52 Bryant; Montpelier 86–69 Pennville; Portland 69–67 Montpelier. Officials: Robert Wells, Delmar Knecht, Paul Hackleman, Richard Lederman.

PRINCETON: Wood Memorial 64–44 Haubstadt; Mt. Vernon 83–61 New Harmony; Princeton 58–48 Ft. Branch; Owensville 63–50 North Posey; Wood Memorial 79–57 Mt. Vernon; Princeton 64–55 Owensville; Princeton 50–48 Wood Memorial. Officials: Richard Crays, Ed Scott, Richard Schleicher, David Loewenstein.

RICHMOND: Centerville 67–57 Cambridge City; Richmond 90–63 Randolph Southern; Northeastern 66–61 Hagerstown; Richmond 90–46 Centerville; Richmond 86–46 Northeastern. Officials: Darrell McFall, James Burt, James Frey, Richard Vendrely.

RUSHVILLE: Rushville 92–66 Morristown; Eastern Hancock 68–51 Morton Memorial; North Decatur 84–47 Carthage; Rushville 87–58 Eastern Hancock; Rushville 72–65 North Decatur. Officials: Eugene Linn, Ken Sussman, William De Rome, William Pittman.

SEYMOUR: Brownstown Central 89–63 Medora; Seymour 94–38 Clearspring; Austin 61–39 Crothersville; Scottsburg 72–66 Jennings County; Seymour 85–62 Brownstown Central; Scottsburg 93–64 Austin; Scottsburg 103–89 Seymour. Officials: Jim DeGroote, Floyd Riggs, Richard Burrows, Robert Fisher.

SHELBYVILLE: Southwestern 71–53 Triton Central; Shelbyville 93–61 New Palestine; Franklin Central 80–61 Waldron; Shelbyville 75–66 Southwestern; Shelbyville 90–74 Franklin Central. Officials: Jack Gardner, John Hilligoss, Donald Ford, Ben Olsson.

SOUTH BEND: St. Joseph 67–46 Washington; Adams 65–62 Mishawaka; Central 69–63 Riley; La Salle 77–48 Clay; St. Joseph 58–47 Adams; Central 83–68 LaSalle; St. Joseph 64–58 Central. Officials: Arthur Thompson, Paul Leamon, Donald Schmidt, Charles Sallee.

SOUTHPORT: Cathedral 78–68 Chartrand; Southport 77–71 Manual; Warren Central 74–44 Kennedy; Wood 74–62 Beech Grove, Cathedral 69–61 Southport; Warren Central 68–46 Wood; Warren Central 61–49 Cathedral. Officials: Homer Owen, Jr., Sam Reed, James Wehsollek, James P. Carey.

SWITZ CITY: Linton 64–58 Central (Switz City); Bloomfield 68–44 Eastern (Greene Co.); L&M 53–52 Worthington; Bloomfield 60–56 Linton; L&M 55–48 Bloomfield. Officials: Vern

Tourney Time

Doles, David Mounts, Donald Ricketts, Billy Lee Walker.

TELL CITY: Perry Central 106–64 Leavenworth; Tell City 62–54 Milltown; Cannelton 65–47 English–Sterling; Perry Central 52–48 Marengo; Tell City 69–57 Cannelton; Tell City 41–39 Perry Central. Officials: Earl Wolfe, Robert Roney, Darrell Eaton, Charles Bertram.

TERRE HAUTE: Honey Creek 79–54 West Vigo; Gerstmeyer 79–55 Laboratory; Garfield 80–61 Schulte; Wiley 75–52 Clinton; Gerstmeyer 79–69 Honey Creek; Wiley 67–51 Garfield; Wiley 59–51 Gerstmeyer (2ot). Officials: Jimmy Dimitroff; Jack Cummings, William Strafford, William Fields.

VINCENNES: Vincennes 64–48 South Knox; North Knox 83–45 Dugger; Central Catholic 69–48 Petersburg; Lincoln 97–51 Sullivan; North Knox 83–59 Central Catholic; Lincoln 57–49 North Knox. Officials: Don Hurst, George Oberle, Charles Roush, Lauren Griffith.

WARSAW: Warsaw 66–46 Mentone; Rochester 62–50 Wawasee; Triton 63–62 Akron; Warsaw 66–55 Rochester; Warsaw 51–49 Triton. Officials: George Dunleavy, Donald Leever, Edward Ulshafer, Jr., Eugene Carrabine.

WASHINGTON: Barr–Reeve 82–47 Shoals; Otwell 82–66 Washington; North Daviess 60–58 Washington Catholic; Loogootee St. John's 42–37 Loogootee;

Otwell 54–39 Barr–Reeve; North Daviess 83–79 St. John's; Otwell 80–77 North Daviess. Officials: Raymond Robison, Jack A. Williams, Charles Roy, Charles Daum.

WHITELAND: Franklin 68–60 Whiteland; Decatur Central 90–61 Center Grove; Indian Creek 67–53 Greenwood; Franklin 71–50 Decatur Central; Franklin 62–46 Indian Creek. Officials: Glen Bonsett, Michael Hennegan, Bill Wullner, Robert Sweet.

WINCHESTER: Union City 70–60 Union; Winchester 55–54 Wapahani; Monroe Central 74–57 Redkey; Union City 77–65 Winchester; Union City 58–44 Monroe Central. Officials: Frank Hoagburg, Robert Bowman, Charles Thompson, Roger McGriff.

1969 REGIONALS

ANDERSON: Marion 78–65 Anderson; Carmel 77–60 Portland; Marion 58–48 Carmel. Officials: Gerald Imel, James Benecke, John Arnold, Norman Chestnut, Lowell Smith, Gil Baumgartner.

BLOOMINGTON: Scottsburg 92–62 Martinsville; Brazil 67–66 Terre Haute Wiley (ot); Scottsburg 77–65 Brazil. Officials: James Schwenk, Wallace Reeve, Harold Gourley, Raymond Vescovi, Bill May, Jack Mercer.

COLUMBUS: Silver Creek 70–67 Franklin; Shelbyville 79–76 Columbus; Silver Creek 79–68 Shelbyville. Officials: Harold Ashbrook, Marvin Heaton, Donald Hubbard, Charles Daum, Kenneth Payne, Gordon McCain.

CONNERSVILLE: Connersville 78–44 Aurora; Jac-Cen-Del 77–69 Rushville; Jac-Cen-Del 63–57 Connersville. Officials: Darrel McFall, Ben Olsson, Raymond Robison, Richard Crays, Floyd Reed, Max Hensler.

EAST CHICAGO: East Chicago Roosevelt 81–61 Crown Point; Gary Tolleston 68–64 Munster; Gary Tolleston 72–53 Roosevelt. Officials. Harry Green, Jack Gardner, Don Hollman, Norris Boomershine, Roy Kilby, John Ward.

ELKHART: Warsaw 73–60 Larwill; Goshen 77–70 Mishawaka Marian; Goshen 58–54 (ot) Warsaw. Officials: Harold Mason, Richard Vendrely, Robert Wells, Roger DeYoung, David

Habegger, Allen Voorhis.

EVANSVILLE: Rex Mundi 62–56 Tell City; Chrisney 61–49 Princeton; Rex Mundi 81–55 Chrisney. Officials: Glen Bonsett, Jerry Baker, Harry Inskeep, Francis Fiddler, Dwain Laird, John Bush.

FORT WAYNE: Central Catholic 68–59 Fairfield; North Side 49–47 DeKalb; North Side 73–54 Central Catholic. Officials: James Davis, Richard Freeman, Marvin Cave, Bob Goble, Richard Gebhart, Robert Fisher.

FRANKFORT: Rossville 72–64 Greencastle; Crawfordsville 70–66 Darlington; Rossville 75–71 Crawfordsville. Officials: Tom Hoffman, Eugene Carrabine, George Avery, Don Koester, Wendell Baker, Charles Sallee.

HUNTINGBURG: Springs Valley 68–67 New Albany; Bedford 50–47 Paoli; Bedford 68–58 Springs Valley. Officials: Don Hurst, Bill Grey, Zeke Williams, Howard Risley, Firman Grimes, Don Snedecker.

INDIANAPOLIS: Indianapolis Washington 46–38 Shortridge; Warren Central 73–52 Plainfield; Washington 87–41 Warren Central. Officials: Marion Acton, Danny Jacobs, Don Shiflet, Gary Muncy, Bob Showalter, Earl Wolfe.

KOKOMO: Huntington 55–50 Bluffton; Kokomo 82–80 Logansport; Huntington 71–63 Kokomo; Officials: John Holmes, Wayne Van Sickle, Robert Kramer, Ronald Hosinski, Gene Marks, John Gassensmith.

LAFAYETTE: Lafayette Jefferson 80–63 Rensselaer; North Vermillion 86–68 Frontier; North Vermillion 72–71 Lafayette Jefferson. Officials: James Beyer, Richard Sweet, Vern Doles, Jack Chestnut, Robert Laird, Wayne Myers.

NEW CASTLE: Greenfield 67–64 Muncie Southside; Richmond 73–66 Union City; Richmond 62–45 Greenfield. Officials: Gene Butts, Richard Lederman, Charles Garber Jr., William Fields, Bill Hile, Robert Reed.

SOUTH BEND: Michigan City 73–64 Valparaiso; St. Joseph's 72–45 Knox; St. Joseph's 70–68 Michigan City. Officials: James P. Carey, Joe Smelcer, Ernie Sohl, George Dunleavy, Eugene Lillie, Eugene Linn.

WASHINGTON: L&M 68–65 Cloverdale; Vincennes 87–70 Otwell; Vincennes 89–57 L&M. Officials: Jimmy Dimitroff, Morris Cohen, Don Call, Walter Swift, Glen Wisler, James Ruby.

1969 SEMI—STATES

EVANSVILLE: Rex Mundi 65–55 Bedford; Vincennes 75–71 Scottsburg; Vincennes 74–50 Rex Mundi. Officials: Floyd Reed, Bill May, Bob Showalter, Danny Jacobs, Robert Kramer, Ernie Sohl.

FORT WAYNE: North Side 63–55 Goshen; Marion 55–52 Huntington; Marion 67–54 North Side. Officials: Zeke Williams, Harold Gourley, Wendell Baker, Don Shiflet, Jimmy Dimitroff, Robert Laird.

INDIANAPOLIS: Jac-Cen-Del 59–50 Richmond; Indianapolis Washington 85–64 Silver Creek; Indianapolis Washington 96–65 Jac-Cen-Del. Officials: Lowell Smith, Raymond Robison, Glen Wisler, Bill Hile, Roy Kilby, Gene Marks.

LAFAYETTE: Rossville 90–74 North Vermillion; Gary Tolleston 81–75 South Bend St. Joseph; Gary Tolleston 96–79 Rossville; Officials: James Schwenk, Richard Gebhart, Gerald Imel, Darrell McFall, Dwain Laird, Marion Acton.

Tourney Time

1969 FINALS—March 22

INDIANAPOLIS (Hinkle Fieldhouse): Indianapolis Washington 61–60 Marion; Gary Tolleston 77–66 Vincennes; Indianapolis Washington 79–76 Gary Tolleston. Officials: Wendell Baker, Robert Kramer, James Schwenk, Ernie Sohl, Floyd Reed, Zeke Williams.

1970–1979

1970 SECTIONALS

ANDERSON: Madison Heights 78–62 Lapel; Highland 72–63 Alexandria; Dale–ville 76–68 Frankton; Anderson 101–57 Pendleton Heights; Madison Heights 81–55 Highland; Anderson 108–57 Daleville; Madison Heights 75–60 Anderson. Officials: George Avery, Noble Rector, Al Lindahl, Jack Gardner.

BATESVILLE: Batesville 75–58 Sunman; Jac-Cen-Del 66–53 Milan; South Ripley 91–53 Moores Hill; Batesville 60–58 Jac-Cen-Del; South Ripley 69–66 Batesville (2ot). Officials: John Holmes, Joe Dickey, Herb Pruett, Ben Olsson.

BEDFORD: Shawswick 67–66 Tunnelton; Mitchell 69–56 Needmore; Oolitic 56–55 Fayetteville; Bedford 107–43 Heltonville; Mitchell 69–61 Shawswick; Bedford 73–61 Oolitic; Mitchell 71–61 Bedford. Officials: Donald Hubbard, Ronald Ham, Donald Ricketts, Richard Sweet.

BEN DAVIS: Ben Davis 55–54 Lawrence Central; Northwest 67–65 Chatard; Howe 72–33 School for the Deaf; Ben Davis 84–76 Scecina; Nothwest 79–56 Howe; Northwest 76–64 Ben Davis. Officials: Homer Owens, Ed Scott, George Oberle, James P. Carey.

BENTON CENTRAL: Benton Central 60–53 Remington; Rensselaer 61–49 North Newton; South Newton 70–62 Lowell; Benton Central 58–53 Rensselaer; South Newton 71–67 Benton Central. Officials: Officials: Robert Laird, Merle Vickers, Donald Ford, Don Hurst.

BLACKFORD: Portland 78–52 Bryant; Dunkirk 69–57 Pennville; Blackford 76–48 Eastbrook; Portland 62–51 Dunkirk; Blackford 66–49 Portland. Officials: Robert Wells, Thomas Neuman, Bill Graham, Richard Vendrely.

BLUFFTON: Norwell 77–46 Southern Wells; Bluffton 76–59 South Adams; Bellmont 59–55 Adams Central; Bluffton 64–53 Norwell; Bluffton 67–56 Bellmont. Officials: Don Snedeker, Bruce Knecht, Delmar Knecht, Wayne Targgart.

BOONVILLE: Chrisney 76–70 Tecumseh; Dale 78–60 Boonville; South Spencer 80–61 Castle; Tell City 69–54 Cannelton; Dale 56–43 Chrisney; Tell City 73–69 South Spencer; Tell City 94–45 Dale. Officials: Lowell Smith, Richard Schleicher, George Emery, Earle Wolfe.

BRAZIL: Staunton 92–72 Rosedale; Van Buren 68–66 Rockville; Brazil 68–46 Montezuma; Van Buren 64–52 Staunton; Brazil 59–52 Van Buren. Officials: Jack Cummings, Walter Overton, John Koker, John Manka.

BROWNSBURG: Danville 77–53 Monrovia; Plainfield 65–60 Brownsburg; Mooresville 66–64 Avon; Pittsboro 97–65 Charlton; Plainfield 63–61 Danville; Pittsboro 61–46 Mooresville; Plainfield 77–51 Pittsboro. Officials: Kenneth Payne, Don Roudebush, Norman Chestnut,

IHSAA Scores | 1970–1979

Raymond Norris.

CARMEL: Hamilton Southeastern 88–43 Westfield; Carmel 79–59 Noblesville; Hamilton Heights 77–70 Sheridan; Tipton 56–49 Hamilton Southeastern; Carmel 104–82 Hamilton Heights; Carmel 81–74 Tipton. Officials: Danny Jacobs, James Frey, Blake Ress, Richard Lederman.

CASS: Logansport 67–66 Pioneer; Caston 89–76 Kewanna; Peru 59–56 Noth Miami; Cass 60–57 Logansport; Peru 81–54 Caston; Peru 81–62 Cass. Officials: Robert Kramer, Peter Kokinda, Nick Sweigart, Eugene Carrabine.

CHESTERTON: Valparaiso 74–34 Wheeler; Morgan Twp. 87–69 Kouts; Portage 94–66 Washington Twp.; Valparaiso 62–55 Chesterton; Portage 84–83 Morgan Twp.; Valparaiso 82–76 Portage. Officials: John Gassensmith, Rex Mays, Herbert Resler, Bob Goble.

CLAY CITY: Shakamak 96–60 Patricksburg; Clay City 74–64 North Central; Spencer 82–42 Gosport; Clay City 85–76 Shakamak; Spencer 57–55 Clay City. Officials: Vern Doles, Leroy Schultheis, David Mounts, Russell Rogers.

COLUMBIA CITY: Pierceton 80–65 Manchester; South Whitley 84–67 Churubusco; Northfield 77–67 Columbia City; South Whitley 56–52 Pierceton; Northfield 87–67 South Whitley. Officials: George Dunleavy, Patrick King, Ronald Flotow, Richard Brainerd.

COLUMBUS: South Decatur 56–55 Edinburg; Brown County 79–65 Greensburg; Columbus 75–62 Hauser; Brown County 71–63 South Decatur; Columbus 91–69 Brown County. Officials: Wallace Reeve, J. Thomas Moorman, Bill Wullner, Robert Kirk.

CONNERSVILLE: Liberty 67–64 Laurel; Union (College Corner) 55–54 Brookville; Connersville 101–45 Whitewater; Liberty 72–69 Union; Connersville 96–60 Liberty. Officials: Glenn Bonsett, Don Smith, Sr., Tom Meeks, David Schwartz.

CRAWFORDSVILLE: New Ross 75–74 Waveland (2ot); Waynetown 75–59 New Market; Ladoga 65–60 Coal Creek Central; Crawfordsville 64–61 Linden; Waynetown 75–59 New Ross; Crawfordsville 63–61 Ladoga; Waynetown 74–69 Crawfordsville. Officials: William Bateman, George Taylor, Charles Roy, James Cox.

CROWN POINT: Hebron 58–43 Hanover Central; Griffith 79–70 Merrillville; Lake Central 98–79 Boone Grove; Crown Point 78–59 Hebron; Lake Central 64–53 Griffith; Lake Central 50–48 Crown Point. Officials: Zeke Williams, Jerry Scott, Gordon Vanator, Lloyd Chambers.

DEKALB: Hamilton 53–51 Angola; DeKalb 84–63 Eastside; Prairie Heights 70–66 Garrett; Hamilton 63–41 Fremont; DeKalb 81–75 Prairie Heights (ot); DeKalb 81–50 Hamilton. Officials: Richard Gebhart, Harold Gray, William DeRome, Max Hensler.

EAST CHICAGO: Calumet 72–58 Hammond Noll; East Chicago Washington 83–47 Hobart; East Gary Edison 71–65 River Forest; East Chicago Roosevelt 68–46 Calumet; Washington 89–67 Edison; Roosevelt 58–55 Washington. Officials: John Ward, David Parry, Richard Cook, Arthur Largent.

EAST NOBLE: Fairfield 64–52 East Noble; Central Noble 53–50 West Noble; Lakeland 71–47 Westview; Fairfield 64–59 Central Noble; Lakeland 57–56 Fairfield. Officials: Neal Jay, Ward Weisel, Richard Hall, James Eads.

ELKHART: Elkhart 92–61 Concord; Penn 58–50 NorthWood; Northridge 74–69 Goshen; Elkhart 84–65 Jimtown; Penn 75–67 Northridge; Elkhart 74–58 Penn. Officials: Roy Kilby, Don Leever, Kenneth Miller, Gil Baumgartner.

EVANSVILLE: Memorial 82–52 Mater Dei; Central 87–57 Rex Mundi; Harrison 59–57

Tourney Time

Reitz; North 83–58 Bosse; Memorial 82–77 Central; North 91–67 Harrison; Memorial 85–80 North. Officials: Jimmy Dimitroff, William Pittman, Clifford Spears, Jack Mercer.

FT. WAYNE (#1): Central Catholic 60–58 Carroll; Woodlan 85–75 Elmhurst; North Side 66–56 Snider; Central Catholic 76–62 New Haven; North Side 77–67 Woodlan; North Side 66–57 Central Catholic. Officials: Richard Freeman, Paul Garriott, Gene Williams, Marvin Heaton.

FT. WAYNE (#2): Luers 71–60 Heritage; Concordia 70–59 South Side; Leo 67–65 Dwenger; Central 67–54 Luers; Concordia 72–67 Leo; Central 83–51 Concordia. Officials: Firman Grimes, Billy Maroney, Robert Wolfe, Ronald Hosinski.

FOUNTAIN CENTRAL: Fountain Central 82–61 Turkey Run; Attica 69–42 Pine Village; Covington 81–67 Williamsport; North Vermillion 81–64 Seeger; Fountain Central 62–54 Attica; Covington 78–70 North Vermillion; Covington 81–61 Fountain Central. Officials: Ernie Sohl, William Van Sickle, John Hilligoss, Harold Mason.

FRANKFORT: Frankfort 79–76 Clinton Central; Sharpsville-Prairie 67–53 Wainwright; Delphi 92–73 Clinton Prairie; Rossville 77–45 Carroll (Carroll Co.); Sharpsville-Prairie 74–70 Frankfort; Rossville 86–81 Delphi; Rossville 95–54 Sharpsville-Prairie. Officials: Everett Campbell, Louis Zabona, Robert Frey, Eugene Linn.

FRANKLIN: Whiteland 51–46 Center Grove; Franklin 73–65 Indian Creek; Greenwood 67–52 Decatur Central; Whiteland 69–62 Franklin; Greenwood 70–43 Whiteland. Officials: Wayne Van Sickle, Melvin Botkin, Paul Cox, Sam Reed.

GARY: West 70–66 Horace Mann; Wallace 79–59 Emerson; Wirt 62–54 Andrean; Gary Roosevelt 85–73 West Side; Wallace 61–57 Wirt; Roosevelt 77–55 Wallace. Officials: James Ruby, John Lozier, Ron Bella, Joe Smelcer.

GREENCASTLE: North Putnam 84–74 Greencastle; South Putnam 66–55 Cascade; Cloverdale 64–38 North Salem; North Putnam 75–62 South Putnam; North Putnam 72–50 Cloverdale. Officials: John Bush, Jon Gallipo, Bill Wing, James R. Carey.

HAMMOND: Clark 73–41 Whiting; Gavit 61–59 Hammond High; Munster 53–49 Morton; Tech 65–54 Highland; Clark 90–60 Gavit; Munster 59–54 Tech; Clark 78–65 Munster. Officials: Richard Pattengale, Eric Harmon, George Grygiel, Gordon McCain.

HUNTINGBURG: Perry Central 52–46 Ireland; Huntingburg 74–63 Ferdinand; Holland 75–51 Birdseye; Jasper 66–51 Dubois; Huntingburg 64–53 Perry Central; Holland 52–47 Jasper; Huntingburg 55–53 Holland. Officials: Charles Sallee, Lauren Griffith, Jack Williams, Jim DeGroote.

HUNTINGTON: White's 76–54 Southwood; Huntington North 75–65 Wabash; White's 82–62 Huntington Catholic; North 80–56 White's. Officials: Norris Boomershine, Robert Gilmore, Max Rink, Robert Reed.

INDIANAPOLIS: Washington 72–70 Ritter; Crispus Attucks 93–56 Arlington; Shortridge 68–51 Broad Ripple; Tech 90–82 North Central; Attucks 73–69 Washington; Tech 75–69 Shortridge; Crispus Attucks 64–60 Tech. Officials: Marion Acton, Frank Hoagburg, William Laird, Russell Freeland.

JEFFERSONVILLE: New Albany 127–53 Lanesville; Clarksville Providence 112–50 South Central; Jeffersonville 95–74 Floyd Central; New Albany 102–75 Clarksville; Jeffersonville 83–66 Providence; Jeffersonville 84–80 New Albany. Officials: James Beyer, Phil Hardwick, Sidney Ellis, Bill Gray.

KNOX: Knox 58–56 LaCrosse; North Judson 82–56 Culver; Winamac 59–54 Oregon-Davis;

North Judson 83–68 Knox; Winamac 56–49 North Judson. Officials: James Benecke, Sr., Ed Ulshafer, Richard Hale, Billy Walker.
  KOKOMO: Haworth 92–56 Windfall; Maconaquah 83–57 Eastern; Kokomo 96–78 Northwestern; Western 83–78 Taylor (ot); Haworth 65–55 Maconaquah; Kokomo 78–64 Western; Haworth 73–58 Kokomo. Officials: Darrell McFall, Roger McGriff, Robert Marcinek, Don Koester.
  LAFAYETTE: West Lafayette 78–58 Klondike; Southwestern 91–82 Central Catholic; Lafayette Jefferson 99–39 Battle Ground; West Lafayette 74–54 East Tipp; Jefferson 68–43 Southwestern; Jefferson 57–56 West Lafayette. Officials: Gerald Imel, Richard Burrows, Dan Alvarez, Roger DeYoung.
  LaVILLE: Mishawaka Marian 81–56 LaVille; Plymouth 65–47 Bremen; South Bend Jackson 63–55 Argos; Glenn 57–52 North Liberty; Plymouth 68–65 Marian; Glenn 78–68 Jackson; Plymouth 84–43 Glenn. Officials: Wayne Crispen, Thomas Manning, Jr., Ralph Thiery, Jr., Tom Hoffman.
  LAWRENCEBURG: Lawrenceburg 95–37 Dillsboro; North Dearborn 75–64 Rising Sun; Auroro 67–49 Switzerland County; Lawrenceburg 79–57 North Dearborn; Lawrenceburg 59–38 Aurora. Officials: Wendell Baker, Ray Mitrione, James Rider, Carl Schnebelt.
  LEBANON: Speedway 71–66 Thorntown; Brebeuf 67–66 Zionsville, Lebanon 78–59 Pike; Darlington 90–47 Granville Wells; Brebeuf 66–58 Speedway; Lebanon 84–70 Darlington; Lebanon 71–68 Brebeuf. Officials: Don Hollman, Ron Beard, Charles Roush, Paul Leamon.
  MADISON: Southwestern 74–52 New Washington; Silver Creek (Sellersburg) 70–38 Henryville; Madison Shawe 86–84 Charestown (ot); Madison 70–68 Southwestern (ot); Silver Creek 91–62 Shawe; Silver Creek 76–61 Madison. Officials: Bill May, Robert Beeson, Robert Klein, Troy Ingram.
  MARION: Elwood 78–69 Mississinewa; Oak Hill 78–66 Madison-Grant; Marion 85–39 Bennett; Oak Hill 88–82 Elwood; Marion 84–65 Oak Hill. Officials: Howard Risley, Gary Coers, Donald Schmidt, James Burt.
  MARTINSVILLE: University 75–68 Eminence; Bloomington 103–81 Smithville; Unionville 60–58 Edgewood; Bloomington University 59–57 Martinsville; Bloomington 70–44 Unionville; Bloomington 82–51 University. Officials: Bob Showalter, Dave Loewenstein, Thomas Lawrence, Jonnie Webber.
  MICHIGAN CITY: Westville 74–73 Michigan City Marquette; Michigan City 93–48 New Prairie; LaPorte 64–53 South Central; Michigan City 94–44 Westville; Michigan City 96–72 LaPorte. Officials: Harold Ashbrook, Stan Dubis, Merl Heckaman, Larry Holdcraft.
  MUNCIE: Yorktown 74–68 Cowan; Central 79–62 Southside; Wes-Del 91–74 Delta; Burris 62–50 Albany; Central 52–49 Yorktown; Wes-Del 77–50 Burris; Central 71–65 Wes-Del. Officials: Bill Hile, Jerry Larrison, Reginald Cheatham, Charles Garber, Jr.
  NEW CASTLE: Mt. Vernon 68–55 Blue River; New Castle 106–82 Tri; Shenandoah 65–53 Greenfield; Knightstown 59–52 Mt. Vernon; Shenandoah 70–58 New Castle; Shenandoah 54–47 Knightstown. Officials: Don Shiflet, Gene Gibson, Larry Hollman, Dave Avery.
  NORTH WHITE: Wolcott 70–69 Frontier; North White 62–52 Twin Lakes; DeMotte 69–43 Wheatfield; Wolcott 68–53 West Central; DeMotte 57–48 North White; DeMotte 91–71 Wolcott. Officials: Gene Butts, Arthur Morris, Gerry Scheub, Gary Janeway.
  PAOLI: Milltown 77–38 English; Paoli 87–62 Marengo; Springs Valley 54–45 Orleans;

Tourney Time

Milltown 63–47 Leavenworth; Paoli 61–48 Springs Valley; Milltown 61–58 Paoli. Officials: Harold Gourley, Paul Wernke, Richie Moore, Raymond Vescovi.

PRINCETON: Princeton 68–50 Ft. Branch; Owensville 80–70 New Harmony; Wood Memorial 72–42 North Posey; Haubstadt 67–66 Mt. Vernon; Princeton 57–53 Owensville; Wood 78–53 Haubstadt; Wood 65–60 Princeton. Officials: Jack Chestnut, Frank Hobson, Darrell Eaton, Jerry Baker.

RICHMOND: Cambridge City 78–76 Centerville; Richmond 101–53 Hagerstown; Randolph Southern 77–64 Northeastern; Richmond 86–49 Cambridge City; Richmond 103–56 Randolph Southern. Officials: Eugene Lillie, Bill Strafford, Thomas Von Deylen, Dale Van Houten.

RUSHVILLE: Rushville 93–69 Morristown; Carthage 64–48 Eastern Hancock; North Decatur 71–58 Morton Memorial; Rushville 91–67 Carthage; North Decatur 73–60 Rushville. Officials: Rudy Tabereaux, Don Shields, Ronald Kitts, Herod Toon.

SALEM: West Washington 56–55 Borden; North Harrison 76–55 Eastern (Pekin); Corydon 77–59 Salem; North Harrison 65–63 Corydon. Officials: Don Call, Dick Venable, William Hite, Charles Bertram.

SEYMOUR: Scottsburg 95–58 Medora; Austin 90–59 Crothersville; Jennings County 68–66 Brownstown Central; Seymour 80–79 Scottsburg; Jennings County 100–89 Austin; Seymour 84–83 Jennings County. Officials: John Williams, Ken Sussman, Frank Corsaro, Byron Weaver.

SHELBYVILLE: Shelbyville 73–66 Franklin Central; Triton Central 91–66 New Palestine; Southwestern 62–60 Waldron; Shelbyville 78–63 Triton Central; Shelbyville 87–60 Southwestern. Officials: Wayne Myers, McKee Munk, Fred Myers, Jerry Schalburg.

SOUTH BEND: Central 76–67 Clay; St. Joseph's 53–52 Riley; Adams 73–70 Mishawaka; LaSalle 83–55 Washington; St. Joseph's 69–68 Central; LaSalle 76–73 Adams (ot); LaSalle 59–57 St. Joseph's. Officials: Opal Courtney, Francis Fiddler, Danny Landis, Gene Marks.

SOUTHPORT: Indianapolis Manual 68–58 Beech Grove; Roncalli 75–71 Wood; Southport 65–58 Warren Central; Cathedral 87–76 Marshall; Manual 82–59 Roncalli; Southport 87–83 Cathedral; Southport 61–53 Manual. Officials: Gary Muncy, John Tucker, Tom Knox, Marty Burdette.

SWITZ CITY: Worthington 76–53 Eastern; Switz City 58–34 Linton; Bloomfield 82–63 L & M; Worthington 67–65 Switz City (2ot); Bloomfield 103–89 Worthington. Officials: Walter Swift, Floyd Riggs, Paul Hackleman, Boynton Robson.

TERRE HAUTE: Garfield 80–57 Schults; Honey Creek 68–54 West Vigo; Gerstmeyer 40–35 Clinton; Wiley 67–57 Laboratory; Garfield 91–70 Honey Creek; Wiley 56–34 Gerstmeyer; Wiley 78–58 Garfield. Officials: Allen Voorhis, Warren Keyser, Keith Combs, Louis Schmalfeldt.

VINCENNES: South Knox 87–57 Sullivan; Vincennes 94–44 Petersburg; North Knox 91–65 Vincennes Central Catholic; South Knox 87–46 Dugger; Vincennes 65–55 North Knox; South Knox 73–65 Vincennes. Officials: Raymond Robison, John Britton, Melvin Redman, William Fields.

WARSAW: Rochester 60–39 Triton; Wawasee 97–60 Mentone; Warsaw 80–64 Akron; Rochester 80–57 Wawasee; Warsaw 65–58 Rochester. Officials: Floyd Reed, James Wehsollek, Robert Boyle, Harry Green.

WASHINGTON: Loogootee 69–56 Washington Catholic; Washington 56–48 Otwell; Winslow 48–46 Barr-Reeve (ot); Shoals 82–79 North Daviess; Loogootee 66–33 Washington; Winslow 78–71 Shoals; Loogootee 64–55 Winslow. Officials: Arthur Thompson, Dallas Richards,

Glen Clemmons, Harry Inskeep.

WINCHESTER: Union 79–70 Winchester; Wapahani 63–60 Union City; Redkey 77–69 Monroe Central (ot); Union 79–61 Wapahani; Union 102–81 Redkey. Officials: Dwain Laird, Charles Bromelmeier, William Altman, Morris Cohen.

1970 REGIONALS

ANDERSON: Carmel 80–76 Madison Heights; Blackford 80–70 Marion; Carmel 76–67 Blackford. Officials: Wallace Reeve, Norris Boomershine, Glen Bonsett, George Dunleavy, Tom Hoffman, Eugene Carrabine.

BLOOMINGTON: Bloomington 75–73 Terre Haute Wiley (ot); Seymour 74–51 Brazil; Seymour 90–64 Bloomington. Officials: Eugene Lillie, Bob Goble, Harold Ashbrook, Marvin Heaton, Jimmy Dimitroff, Eugene Linn.

COLUMBUS: Shelbyville 84–70 Silver Creek; Columbus 72–71 Greenwood; Columbus 79–73 Shelbyville. Officials: Danny Jacobs, Paul Leamon, Don Hollman, James Benecke, Marion Acton, James P. Carey.

CONNERSVILLE: South Ripley 82–78 North Decatur; Lawrenceburg 81–66 Connersville; South Ripley 74–65 Lawrenceburg. Officials: Richard Gebhart, Frank Hoagburg, Gene Butts, Richard Lederman, Gerald Imel, Richard Vendrely.

ELKHART: Elkhart 87–76 Northfield; Plymouth 71–51 Warsaw; Plymouth 47–45 Elkhart. Officials: Howard Risley, Marty Burdette, Bill May, Max Hensler, Zeke Williams, Don Koester.

EVANSVILLE: Oakland City Wood 57–48 Tell City; Evansville Memorial 73–68 South Knox; Memorial 90–66 Wood. Officials: Wendell Baker, Allen Voorhis, Don Hurst, Morris Cohen, Walter Swift, John Bush.

FORT WAYNE: Fort Wayne North Side 54–52 DeKalb; Fort Wayne Central 55–47 Lakeland; North Side 65–58 Central. Officials: Vern Doles, Wayne Van Sickle, Charles Sallee, Gordon McCain, Raymond Robison, Robert Reed.

GARY: Hammond Clark 61–52 Lake Central; East Chicago Roosevelt 72–64 Gary Roosevelt; East Chicago Roosevelt 72–38 Clark. Officials: Harry Inskeep, Francis Fiddler, Dwain Laird, Gary Muncy, Floyd Reed, Gil Baumgartner.

GREENCASTLE: Lebanon 91–83 North Putnam; Rossville 93–55 Waynetown; Rossville 81–77 Lebanon. Officials: Donald Hubbard, Jack Cummings, James Beyer, Raymond Vescovi, Harold Gourley, Jim DeGroote.

HUNTINGBURG: North Harrison 88–73 Huntingburg; Milltown 72–69 Jeffersonville; Milltown 70–66 North Harrison. Officials: Wayne Myers, Rudy Tabereaux, John Holmes, Robert Wells, James Ruby, Jack Chestnut.

INDIANAPOLIS: Plainfield 72–59 Indianapolis Northwest; Crispus Attucks 87–76 Southport; Crispus Attucks 76–65 Plainfield. Officials: Charles Garber, Jr., Roger DeYoung, George Avery, Joe Smelcer, Roy Kilby, John Gassensmith.

KOKOMO: Kokomo Haworth 91–82 Huntington; Bluffton 64–53 Peru; Haworth 74–58 Bluffton. Officials: Earle Wolfe, Don Snedeker, Ernie Sohl, Jerry Baker, Don Shiflet, Kenneth Payne.

LAFAYETTE: DeMotte 71–50 Covington; Lafayette Jefferson 93–54 South Newton; Jefferson 102–63 DeMotte. Don Call, Ben Olsson, Bob Showalter, William Fields, Robert Kramer, Richard Freeman.

Tourney Time

NEW CASTLE: Shenandoah 76–69 Union; Muncie Central 69–56 Richmond; Muncie Central 82–67 Shenandoah. Officials: Richard Sweet, Ronald Hosinski, Gene Marks, Billy Maroney, Lowell Smith, Norman Chestnut.

SOUTH BEND: Michigan City 78–72 South Bend LaSalle; Valparaiso 95–68 Winamac; Michigan City 95–67 Valparaiso. Officials: Harry Green, Russell Freeland, Bill Hile, John Ward, Darrell McFall, Jack Mercer.

WASHINGTON: Loogootee 62–55 Mitchell; Bloomfield 64–63 Spencer; Loogootee 55–45 Bloomfield. Officials: Harold Mason, Dave Avery, Firman Grimes, Bill Gray, Robert Laird, Jack Gardner.

1970 SEMI–STATES

EVANSVILLE: Loogootee 77–71 Evansville Memorial; Seymour 68–60 Milltown; Loogootee 80–78 Seymour. Officials: Zeke Williams, Bob Showalter, Bill Hile, Richard Gebhart, Floyd Reed, Dwain Laird.

FORT WAYNE: Carmel 61–59 Fort Wayne North Side; Plymouth 71–64 Kokomo Haworth (ot); Carmel 53–52 Plymouth. Officials: Ernie Sohl, George Avery, Harold Gourley, Gene Marks, Jimmy Dimitroff, Robert Laird.

INDIANAPOLIS: Crispus Attucks 89–67 South Ripley; Muncie Central 73–56 Columbus; Muncie Central 86–81 Crispus Attucks. Officials: Don Shiflet, Don Hubbard, Gerald Imel, Bill May, Robert Kramer, Danny Jacobs.

LAFAYETTE: Michigan City 87–80 Rossville; East Chicago Roosevelt 56–54 Lafayette Jefferson; East Chicago Roosevelt 82–78 Michigan City. Officials: Wendell Baker, Ray Robison, Marion Acton, Charles Sallee, Lowell Smith, Darrell McFall.

1970 FINALS—March 21

INDIANAPOLIS (Hinkle Fieldhouse): Carmel 71–62 Loogootee; East Chicago Roosevelt 90–75 Muncie Central; East Chicago Roosevelt 76–62 Carmel. Officials: Ernie Sohl, Bill Hile, Zeke Williams, Harold Gourley, Wendell Baker, Bob Showalter.

1971 SECTIONALS

ANDERSON: Pendleton Heights 106–52 Daleville; Anderson 77–63 Frankton; Alexandria 86–63 Lapel; Madison Heights 52–50 Highland; Anderson 70–69 Pendleton Heights; Madison Heights 56–50 Alexandria; Madison Heights 58–40 Anderson. Officials: Don Snedeker, James Frey, Tom Knox, Richard Vendrely.

BATESVILLE: Sunman 61–59 Milan; Batesville 49–16 South Ripley; Jac-Cen-Del 65–59 Moores Hill; Batesville 86–60 Sunman; Batesville 83–57 Jac-Cen-Del. Officials: Zeke Williams, William DeRome, Larry Freyburger, James Carey.

BEDFORD: Shawswick 83–59 Heltonville; Bedford 64–58 Mitchell; Oolitic 66–63 Needmore (ot); Tunnelton 69–49 Fayetteville; Bedford 86–64 Shawswick; Tunnelton 66–57 Oolitic; Bedford 54–52 Tunnelton (ot). Officials: James Beyer, Richie Moore, Floyd Riggs, Billy Walker.

BELLMONT: Southern Wells 60–58 Bluffton; Bellmont 71–66 Norwell; South Adams 50–

46 Adams Central; Bellmont 57–56 Southern Wells; Bellmont 61–59 South Adams. Officials: Marvin Heaton, Troy Ingram, Joe Edmonds, Harold Gray.

BEN DAVIS: Ben Davis 85–46 Scecina; Northwest 70–65 Howe; Chatard 59–52 Lawrence Central; Speedway 90–50 School for the Deaf; Northwest 90–74 Ben Davis; Speedway 53–49 Chatard; Northwest 64–60 Speedway. Officials: John Ward, Jerry Scott, Paul Wernke, James Cox.

BENTON CENTRAL: Rensselaer 76–47 North Newton; Remington 70–56 Lowell; Benton Central 62–60 South Newton; Remington 54–44 Rensselaer; Benton Central 58–57 Remington (ot). Officials: Kenneth Payne, Ronald Beard, Jack Graham, Jerry Baker.

BLACKFORD: Pennville 66–63 Albany; Dunkirk 53–51 Portland; Blackford 76–52 Bryant; Dunkirk 73–61 Pennville; Blackford 97–61 Dunkirk. Officials: John Bush, Thomas Moorman, Rudy Stegelmann, Wayne Targgart.

BLOOMINGTON: Eminence 72–60 Smithville; Bloomington 85–67 Edgewood; Bloomington University 68–58 Unionville; Martinsville 111–68 Eminence; Bloomington 79–58 University; Bloomington 75–62 Martinsville. Officials: Jack Mercer, Keith Combs, George Emery, Don Shields.

BOONVILLE: Tell City 64–48 Castle; South Spencer 70–63 Cannelton; Boonville 79–66 Chrisney; Dale 88–73 Tecumseh; Tell City 63–56 South Spencer; Dale 78–68 Boonville; Tell City 56–51 Dale. Officials: William Fields, Frank Hobson, James Rider, Richard Crays.

BRAZIL: Van Buren 64–52 Montezuma; Brazil 74–41 Rosedale; Rockville 54–53 Staunton; Brazil 64–59 Van Buren; Brazil 74–62 Rockville. Officials: Harold Mason, Jon Gallipo, Sidney Ellis, Morris Cohen.

BROWNSBURG: Plainfield 87–69 Monrovia; Mooresville 65–62 Avon; Brownsburg 77–67 Danville; Plainfield 60–38 Pittsboro; Brownsburg 71–59 Mooresville; Brownsburg 76–59 Plainfield. Officials: Bill Graham, Richard Gebhart, Leroy Schultheis, Max Hensler.

CALUMET: Calumet 77–73 Hebron; Crown Point 91–53 Hanover Central; Lake Central 88–79 Boone Grove; Griffith 76–49 Merrillville; Crown Point 64–49 Calumet; Griffith 71–68 Lake Central; Crown Point 75–59 Griffith. Officials: Marion Acton, Gene Williams, Kevin Weinberg, Arthur Largent.

CARMEL: Sheridan 58–57 Noblesville; Carmel 86–79 Hamilton Heights; Hamilton Southeastern 58–57 Westfield (ot); Carmel; 73–49 Sheridan; Carmel 72–65 Hamilton Southeastern. Officials: Don Hollman, Al Lindahl, Robert Beeson, Gary Janeway.

CASS: Peru 49–42 Cass; North Miami 92–81 Caston; Logansport 94–85 Kewanna; Pioneer 78–77 Peru; Logansport 92–80 North Miami; Logansport 76–73 Pioneer. Officials: Ernie Sohl, Robert Gilmore, Ed Ulshafer, George Dunleavy.

CHESTERTON: Wheeler 70–49 Washington Twp.; Chesterton 95–50 Kouts; Portage 82–81 Valparaiso; Morgan Twp. 78–39 Wheeler; Portage 58–57 Chesterton; Portage 76–53 Morgan Twp. Officials: Gene Butts, Robert Wolfe, Max Rink, Harold Ashbrook.

CLAY CITY: Owen Valley 60–52 Clay City; Sullivan 80–54 North Central; Dugger 58–54 Shakamak; Owen Valley 78–76 Sullivan (3ot);Owen Valley 72–57 Dugger. Officials: Earle Wolfe, John Hilligoss, Thomas Lawrence, Richard Pattengale.

COLUMBIA CITY: Pierceton 79–59 Churubusco; Columbia 74–62 South Whitley; North Manchester 79–62 Homestead; Pierceton 67–57 Columbia City; North Manchester 70–68 Pierceton. Officials: Darrell McFall, Rex Mays, Norman Hathcoat, John Manka.

COLUMBUS: South Decatur 68–48 Edinburg; Greensburg 68–58 Hauser; Columbus 78–70 Brown County; South Decatur 64–63 Greensburg; Columbus 65–59 South Decatur. Officials: Walter Swift, Darrell Eaton, Herb Pruett, Byron Weaver.

CONNERSVILLE: Connersville 71–65 Brookville; Liberty 96–55 Whitewater Twp.; Union (College Corner) 71–64 Laurel; Connersville 79–58 Liberty; Connersville 98–70 Union. Officials: Vern Doles, Walter Overton, Thomas VonDeylen, Charles Garber, Jr.

CRAWFORDSVILLE: Darlington 69–60 Waynetown; Waveland 73–59 Coal Creek Central; Linden 60–52 New Market; Crawfordsville 77–59 Ladoga; Waveland 82–77 Darlington; Crawfordsville 68–64 Linden; Crawfordsville 80–70 Waveland. Officials: Jimmy Dimitroff, Ward Weisel, Richard Hall, Jack Goen.

DeKALB: Hamilton 67–47 Fremont; Garrett 93–53 Prairie Heights; DeKalb 91–74 Angola; Eastside 84–68 Hamilton; Garrett 80–64 DeKalb; Garrett 80–67 Eastside. Officials: Harry Inskeep, Ron Bella, Larry Jones, Boynton Robson.

EASTBROOK (At Marion Memorial Coliseum)**:** White's 64–63 Eastbrook; Huntington 67–65 Northfield; Huntington Catholic 86–70 Southwood; White's 79–66 Wabash; Huntington 87–61 Huntington Catholic; Huntington 67–63 White's. Officials: Bob Showalter, Blake Ress, Ron McKibben, William Pittman.

EAST CHICAGO: Washington 71–39 East Gary Edison; East Chicago Roosevelt 67–55 River Forest; Hobart 77–66 Hammond Noll; Washington 73–48 Roosevelt; Washington 87–56 Hobart. Officials: Gary Muncy, Richard Hale, William Sorukas, Frank Hoagburg.

EAST NOBLE: Fairfield 65–64 Central Noble; East Noble 28–26 West Noble (ot); Westview 70–65 Lakeland; Fairfield 73–66 East Noble; Fairfield 63–39 Westview. Officials: James Ruby, Donald Leever, Robert Boyle, James R. Carey.

ELKHART: Northridge 78–73 Concord (ot); Penn 73–54 Goshen; Elkhart 88–75 Jimtown; Northwood 68–63 Northridge; Elkhart 68–60 Penn; Elkhart 64–51 Northwood. Officials: Robert Kramer, Dan Alvarez, Opal Courtney, Paul Leamon.

EVANSVILLE CENTRAL: Memorial 60–58 North; Rex Mundi 82–57 Harrison; Central 71–56 Bosse; Reitz 55–54 Mater Dei; Rex Mundi 67–62 Memorial; Reitz 71–58 Central; Reitz 77–71 Rex Mundi. Officials: Wendell Baker, Raymond Norris, Paul Hackelman, Wayne Myers.

FORT WAYNE (#1): Leo 66–65 Snider; Elmhurst 64–61 Central Catholic; Central 76–58 Dwenger; Leo 78–64 Luers; Elmhurst 75–74 Central (ot); Elmhurst 67–63 Leo. Officials: Dwain Laird, Richard Cook, Paul Cox, Bill Gray.

FORT WAYNE (#2): Concordia 56–54 Woodlan; South Side 57–38 Heritage; North Side 66–60 Carroll; Concordia 48–46 New Haven; North Side 60–48 South Side; North Side 47–42 Concordia (ot). Officials: John Gassensmith, George Grygiel, Herbert Resler, Norris Boomershine.

FOUNTAIN CENTRAL: Pine Village 65–63 Seeger; Covington 82–68 Fountain Central; Williamsport 82–61 Attica; Turkey Run 83–67 North Vermillion; Covington 81–68 Pine Village; Williamsport 65–64 Turkey Run; Covington 90–65 Williamsport. Officials: Richard Sweet, Donald Roudebush, Herod Toon, Jr., Francis Fiddler.

FRANKFORT: Tri Central 75–65 Clinton Central; Tipton 63–60 Delphi; Rossville 70–42 Clinton Prairie; Frankfort 69–63 Carroll; Tri Central 53–50 Tipton; Rossville 91–75 Frankfort; Rossville 115–88 Tri Central. Officials: Gene Marks, Thomas Manning, Jr., Charles Roush, Ronald Hosinski.

GARY: Wallace 66–65 Gary Roosevelt; Mann 62–60 Andrean; West Side 72–48 Wirt; Emerson 69–64 Wallace (2ot); West Side 54–47 Mann; West Side 77–62 Emerson. Officials: Robert Reed, Joseph Dickey, Thomas Neuman, Bob Goble.

GREENCASTLE: North Salem 75–68 Cascade; Greencastle 81–46 South Putnam; North Putnam 48–46 Cloverdale; Greencastle 51–50 North Salem; North Putnam 45–43 Greencastle. Officials: Bill May, Delmar Knecht, Gary Koers, Robert Wells.

HAMMOND: Clark 53–50 Gavit; Munster 69–61 Whiting; Highland 62–57 Hammond High; Morton 64–60 Tech; Clark 71–62 Munster; Highland 70–56 Morton; Clark 87–78 Morton. Officials: George Avery, Ron Flotow, John Losier, Lloyd Chambers.

HUNTINGBURG: Jasper 71–45 Holland; Perry Central 61–60 Huntingburg (2ot); Dubois 66–46 Birdseye; Jasper 77–53 Ferdinand; Dubois 86–65 Perry Central; Jasper 86–65 Dubois. Officials: Raymond Robison, Richard Schleicher, James Roberts, Robert Kirk.

INDIANAPOLIS: Washington 57–51 Shortridge; Crispus 69–46 Ritter; Tech 48–45 Arlington; North Central 66–46 Broad Ripple; Washington 65–61 Attucks; Tech 72–66 North Central; Tech 60–58 Washington. Officials: Richard Freeman, George Oberle, Bill Wullner, Dave Avery.

JEFFERSONVILLE: Clarksville Providence 78–75 Clarksville; Floyd Central 84–80 New Albany; Jeffersonville 97–64 South Central; Providence 88–40 Lanesville; Floyd Central 92–91 Jeffersonville; Floyd Central 83–82 Providence. Officials: Don Shiflet, Clifford Spears, Tom Meeks, Don Hubbard.

KNOX: Winamac 66–56 Culver; Knox 85–61 LaCrosse; North Judson 56–41 Oregon–Davis; Knox 79–63 Winamac; Knox 62–60 North Judson (ot). Officials: Gerald Imel, Donald Ford, Ralph Thiery, Jr., Richard Lederman.

KOKOMO: Taylor 64–56 Northwestern; Kokomo Haworth 111–58 Maconaquah; Kokomo 81–57 Eastern; Western 58–52 Taylor; Kokomo 75–66 Haworth; Kokomo 72–50 Western. Officials: Jack Chestnut, Ray Mitrione, Merl Heckaman, Roger DeYoung.

LAFAYETTE: Harrison 40–36 Wainwright; Southwestern 72–64 West Lafayette; Lafayette Jefferson 68–62 Central Catholic; Southwestern 89–70 Harrison; Jefferson 78–77 Southwestern (ot). Officials: Thomas Hoffman, Peter Kokinda, Robert Justak, Sam Reed.

LaVILLE: LaVille 69–46 North Liberty; Glenn 77–66 Argos; South Bend Jackson 56–49 Bremen; Plymouth 65–51 LaVille; Jackson 72–65 Glenn; Plymouth 99–66 Jackson. Officials: Don Koester, Arthur Morris, Gerry Scheub, Billy Maroney.

LAWRENCEBURG: Lawrenceburg 86–58 Dillsboro; Rising Sun 70–52 Switzerland County; North Dearborn 71–68 Aurora; Lawrenceburg 91–70 Rising Sun; Lawrenceburg 75–55 North Dearborn. Officials: Donald Call, Danny Landis, Glen Clemons, Wayne Van Sickle.

LEBANON: Pike 104–59 Granville Wells; Zionsville 93–84 Thorntown; Lebanon 78–66 Brebeuf; Pike 67–50 New Ross; Lebanon 74–57 Zionsville; Lebanon 51–50 Pike. Officials: James Benecke, Sr., Fred Myers, Larry Hollman, Gilbert Baumgartner.

MADISON: Southwestern 72–46 New Washington; Madison Shawe 73–68 Charlestown; Madison 73–68 Silver Creek (ot); Southwestern 61–34 Henryville; Madison 92–63 Shawe; Madison 57–53 Southwestern. Officials: Charles Sallee, Bill Laird, Frank Corsaro, David Loewenstein.

MARION: Oak Hill 69–54 Marion Bennett; Madison-Grant 83–75 Mississinewa; Marion 71–54 Elwood; Oak Hill 76–63 Madison-Grant; Oak Hill 75–71 Marion. Officials: Art

Thompson, Bruce Knecht, Ken Sussman, Allen Voorhis.

MICHIGAN CITY: LaPorte 83–54 Marquette; New Prairie 80–73 Westville; Michigan City 111–39 South Central; LaPorte 80–62 New Prairie; Michigan 101–94 LaPorte. Officials: Jack Gardner, Kenneth Miller, Herbert Hicks, Joe Smelcer.

MUNCIE: Burris 70–48 Wes–Del; Central 63–52 Southside; Yorktown 70–59 Cowan; Northside 94–61 Delta; Central 62–48 Burris; Yorktown 84–69 Northside; Central 55–45 Yorktown. Officials: Russell Freeland, Louis Zabona, Richard Burrows, John Tucker.

NEW CASTLE: New Castle 89–70 Knightstown; Mount Vernon 69–68 Tri; Greenfield 85–49 Blue River; New Castle 64–60 Shenandoah; Greenfield 72–65 Mount Vernon; New Castle 62–59 Greenfield. Officials: Bill Hile, Eric Harmon, Robert Klein, William Van Sickle.

NORTH WHITE: North White 53–52 Frontier; Kankakee Valley 72–48 West Central; Twin Lakes 66–62 Wolcott; Kankakee Valley 59–41 North White; Kankakee Valley 66–54 Twin Lakes. Officials: Don Hurst, Stewart Vickers, Robert Frey, Richard Brainerd.

PAOLI: Leavenworth 72–68 English; Milltown 55–43 Orleans; Paoli 69–54 Marengo; Springs Valley 71–69 Leavenworth (ot); Milltown 52–45 Paoli; Springs Valley 52–51 Milltown. Officials: Robert Laird, Dick Venable, Charles Thompson, Ben Olsson.

PRINCETON: Owensville 67–66 New Harmony; Wood Memorial 75–60 Mt. Vernon; Princeton 80–47 Haubstadt; Ft. Branch 57–43 North Posey; Wood Memorial 39–33 Owensville; Princeton 62–52 Ft. Branch; Princeton 63–50 Wood Memorial. Officials: Lowell Smith, McKee Munk, William Hite, Noble Rector.

RICHMOND: Randolph Southern 61–43 Centerville; Cambridge City 58–55 Northeastern; Richmond 79–43 Hagerstown; Randolph Southern 66–60 Cambridge City; Richmond 74–60 Randolph Southern. Officials: Roy Kilby, Jerry Larrison, Reginald Cheatham, Dale VanHouten.

RUSHVILLE: Eastern Hancock 69–54 North Decatur; Carthage 69–60 Morton Memorial; Rushville 98–56 Morristown; Eastern Hancock 75–51 Carthage; Rushville 110–77 Eastern Hancock. Officials: Jack Cummings, Bill Strafford, James Helms, Carl Schnebelt.

SALEM: Salem 95–65 West Washington; North Harrison 89–74 Borden; Corydon 66–60 Eastern; Salem 86–79 North Harrison; Salem 68–66 Corydon. Officials: Wallace Reeve, David Mounts, John Koker, Louis Schmalfeldt.

SEYMOUR: Jennings County 60–53 Scottsburg; Austin 57–49 Crothersville; Seymour 117–41 Medora; Jennings County 71–58 Brownstown Central; Seymour 105–65 Austin; Seymour 85–74 Jennings County. Officials: Harold Gourley, Paul Garriott, Melvin Redman, James DeGroote.

SHELBYVILLE: Franklin Central 64–56 New Palestine; Waldron 62–47 Triton Central; Shelbyville 69–49 Southwestern; Franklin Central 57–44 Waldron; Franklin Central 54–53 Shelbyville. Officials: Glen Bonsett, Jim Wehsollek, Harold Gibbs, David Schwartz.

SWITZ CITY CENTRAL: Eastern 65–49 L & M; Linton 62–56 Switz City Central; Worthington 45–44 Bloomfield (ot); Linton 70–62 Eastern. Officials: Firman Grimes, Phil Hardwick, John Britton, Warren Keyser.

SOUTH BEND: LaSalle 81–76 Riley; Mishawaka 103–73 Clay; Washington 61–59 Marian; Adams 66–63 St. Joseph's; LaSalle 79–75 Mishawaka; Adams 86–67 Washington; Adams 70–57 LaSalle. Officials: Stanley Dubis, Bob Marcinek, Nick Sweigart, Eugene Carrabine.

SOUTHPORT: Warren Central 84–62 Marshall; Cathedral 81–47 Southport; Manual 75–62 Beech Grove; Wood 89–67 Roncalli; Cathedral 58–57 Warren Central; Manual 82–76 Wood; Cathedral 75–48 Manual. Officials: Gordon McCain, Dallas Richards, Jerry Schalburg, Mel Botkin.

TERRE HAUTE: Gerstmeyer 74–57 Garfield; Schulte 64–61 Laboratory; Wiley 49–47 Clinton; West Vigo 67–65 Honey Creek; Gerstmeyer 66–44 Schulte; Wiley 86–58 West Vigo; Gerstmeyer 62–60 Wiley. Officials: Norman Chestnut, Jack Williams, Donald Ricketts, Marty Burdette.

TRITON: Warsaw 68–46 Mentone; Triton 71–61 Wawasee; Rochester 87–58 Akron; Warsaw 87–79 Triton; Rochester 72–62 Warsaw. Officials: Howard Risley, Ron Kitts, Don Schmidt, Eugene Linn.

VINCENNES: Rivet 92–71 Winslow; South Knox 84–80 North Knox (ot); Vincennes 102–40 Petersburg; South Knox 80–79 Rivet; Vincennes 72–61 South Knox. Officials: Rudy Tabereaux, Ed Scott, Don Smith, Sr., Charles Bertram.

WASHINGTON: Loogootee 54–47 Washington; Barr-Reeve 72–60 Shoals; North Daviess 63–38 Otwell; Loogootee 58–47 Washington Catholic; Barr-Reeve 67–57 North Daviess; Loogootee 59–52 Barr-Reeve. Officials: Raymond Vescovi, Ronald Ham, Larry Collins, Roger McGriff.

WHITELAND: Greenwood 81–60 Whiteland; Franklin 86–50 Indian Creek; Decatur Central 59–58 Center Grove; Franklin 72–51 Greenwood; Franklin 68–65 Decatur Central. Officials: Homer Owens, George Taylor, John Lyskowinski, Russell Rogers.

WINCHESTER: Monroe Central 72–48 Wapahani; Winchester 52–46 Union City; Union 74–69 Redkey; Winchester 67–57 Monroe Central; Winchester 71–60 Union. Officials: John Holmes, Gene Gibson, John Fleischman, James Burt.

1971 REGIONALS

ANDERSON: Carmel 76–64 Blackford; Madison Heights 61–55 Kokomo; Madison Heights 61–55 Carmel. Officials: John Gassensmith, Frank Hoagburg, Donald Hubbard, Don Koester, Walter Swift, Bob Goble.

COLUMBUS: Franklin 52–48 Franklin Central; Bloomington 70–69 Columbus; Bloomington 73–71 Franklin. Officials: Don Snedeker, Harold Gray, Gerald Imel, Gilbert Baumgartner, Gene Marks, Ron Hosinski.

CONNERSVILLE: Batesville 65–56 Connersville; Rushville 51–49 Lawrenceburg; Batesville 83–65 Rushville. Officials: Harold Mason, Morris Cohen, Robert Reed, Rudy Tabereaux, Harold Gourley, James DeGroote.

ELKHART: Rochester 82–71 Plymouth; Elkhart 83–62 Manchester, Elkhart 77–69 Rochester. Officials: John Holmes, Eugene Carrabine, Richard Gebhart, Bill Gray, Harry Inskeep, Gary Muncy.

EVANSVILLE: Reitz 56–51 Vincennes; Tell City 73–48 Princeton; Tell City 74–54 Reitz. Officials: Robert Laird, Jack Chestnut; Firman Grimes, Jack Cummings, Bob Showalter, Robert Wells.

FORT WAYNE: Elmhurst 64–50 North Side; Garrett 76–75 Fairfield; Garrett 71–60 Elmhurst. Officials: Don Shiflet, Marvin Heaton, Jimmy Dimitroff, Arthur Largent, Ernie Sohl, David Avery.

FRANKFORT: Crawfordsville 80–77 North Putnam; Rossville 88–68 Lebanon; Rossville 87–68 Crawfordsville. Officials: Gene Butts, Ben Olsson, Donald Call, Norman Chestnut, James Beyer, Wayne Myers.

GARY: East Chicago Washington 62–51 Hammond Clark; Gary West Side 94–59 Crown Point; Washington 94–89 West Side. Officials: Richard Freeman, Jack Gardner, Howard Risley,

Tourney Time

Eugene Linn, Zeke Williams, Joe Smelcer.

HUNTINGBURG: Salem 58–53 Springs Valley; Jasper 103–42 Linton; Salem 76–73 Jasper. Officials: Darrell McFall, Jerry Baker, Jack Mercer, Max Hensler, Bill May, Francis Fiddler.

INDIANAPOLIS: Cathedral 65–61 Northwest; Tech 82–50 Brownsburg; Tech 83–66 Cathedral. Officials: George Dunleavy, Richard Lederman, James Benecke, Marty Burdette, Robert Kramer, Ray Vescovi.

LAFAYETTE: Jefferson 73–62 Kankakee Valley; Covington 78–70 Benton Central; Jefferson 71–69 Covington. Officials: Raymond Robison, Melvin Botkin, Marion Acton, James Cox, Earle Wolfe, James P. Carey.

MARION: Oak Hill 70–63 Bellmont; Logansport 75–73 Huntington; Oak Hill 73–72 Logansport. Officials ; Thomas Hoffman, William Fields, Vern Doles, Norris Boomershine, Charles Sallee, Russell Freeland.

NEW CASTLE: Richmond 81–75 Muncie Central (ot); New Castle 89–64 Winchester; New Castle 84–79 Richmond (ot). Officials: Don Hollman, Kenneth Payne, Glen Bonsett, Paul Leamon, George Avery, Gordon McCain.

SEYMOUR: Floyd Central 75–59 Bedford; Seymour 89–72 Madison; Floyd Central 93–86 Seymour. Officials: Don Hurst, Richard Crays, John Ward, Richard Vendrely, Bill Hile, Richard Sweet.

SOUTH BEND: Portage 78–77 Adams (ot); Michigan City 82–69 Knox; Michigan City 85–62 Portage. Officials: Jim Ruby, Byron Weaver, Dwain Laird, Roger DeYoung, Wendell Baker, Allen Voorhis.

WASHINGTON: Loogootee 58–52 Owen Valley; Gerstmeyer 42–36 Brazil; Loogootee 51–50 Gerstmeyer. Officials: Lowell Smith, Don Shields, Harold Ashbrook, Wayne Van Sickle, John Bush, Billy Maroney.

1971 SEMI–STATES

EVANSVILLE: Floyd Central 77–68 Salem; Loogootee 51–48 Tell City; Floyd Central 83–74 Loogootee. Officials: Jimmy Dimitroff, Harry Inskeep, Gerald Imel, Don Snedeker, Marion Acton, George Avery.

FORT WAYNE: Elkhart 74–63 Oak Hill; Madison Heights 75–59 Garrett; Elkhart 82–70 Madison Heights. Officials: Darrell McFall, John Ward, Bill Hile, Raymond Robison, Lowell Smith, Charles Sallee.

INDIANAPOLIS: Bloomington 73–53 Indianapolis Tech, New Castle 68–63 Batesville, New Castle 77–65 Bloomington. Officials: Ernie Sohl, Robert Reed, Don Shiflet, Richard Gebhart, Zeke Williams, Gene Marks.

LAFAYETTE: Rossville 94–77 Lafayette Jefferson; East Chicago Washington 93–79 Michigan City; Washington 79–67 Rossville. Officials: Harold Gourley, Bill May, Bob Showalter, Don Hollman, Wendell Baker, Robert Laird.

1971 FINALS—March 20

Last finals at Hinkle Fieldhouse: Elkhart 65–60 New Castle (3ot); East Chicago Washington 102–88 Floyd Central; Washington 70–60 Elkhart. Officials: Bob Showalter, Marion Acton, Bill Hile, Gerald Imel, Harold Gourley, Jimmy Dimitroff.

IHSAA Scores / 1970–1979

1972 SECTIONALS

ANDERSON: Alexandria 58–57 Anderson; Frankton 73–51 Daleville; Pendleton Heights 68–66 Highland; Madison Heights 63–52 Lapel; Alexandria 63–48 Frankton; Madison Heights 84–59 Pendleton Heights; Madison Heights 45–41 Alexandria. Officials: Gene Butts, Blake Ress, Robert Frey, James Burt.

BATESVILLE: Jac-Cen-Del 62–56 South Ripley; Sunman 81–71 Milan; Batesville 86–50 Moores Hill; Jac-Cen-Del 71–56 Sunman; Jac-Cen-Del 70–60 Batesville. Officials: Melvin Botkin, Robert Gilmore, Steve Vannatter, William Van Sickle.

BEDFORD: Tunnelton 54–52 Shawswick; Bedford 100–56 Fayetteville; Mitchell 58–55 Heltonville; Oolitic 60–51 Needmore; Bedford 67–49 Tunnelton; Mitchell 72–60 Oolitic; Bedford 82–47 Mitchell. Officials: Harry Inskeep, David Mounts, James Dunlap, Jerry Larrison.

BEN DAVIS: Speedway 83–78 Northwest (ot); Ben Davis 71–66 Washington; Scecina 68–57 Ritter; Cathedral 97–32 School for the Deaf; Speedway 75–67 Ben Davis; Cathedral 110–71 Scecina; Cathedral 71–63 Speedway. Officials: Norman Chestnut, Bill Wullner, Ron Kitts, Bill Gray.

BENTON CENTRAL: Benton Central 77–66 North White; Tri County 59–58 South Newton; Frontier 61–57 Twin Lakes; Benton Central 77–74 Tri County; Benton Central 72–67 Frontier. Officials: Stan Dubis, William DeRome, Richard Hall (replaced by Phil Barth), Dan Alvarez.

BLACKFORD: Redkey 73–57 Bryant; Dunkirk 89–85 Albany; Blackford 68–53 Pennville; Portland 86–73 Eastbrook; Redkey 95–85 Dunkirk; Blackford 65–53 Portland; Blackford 80–58 Redkey. Officials: Jack Mercer, Andy Phillips, Robert Keys, Jon Gallipo.

BLUFFTON: South Adams 98–80 Bellmont; Bluffton 83–65 Southern Wells; Norwell 62–60 Adams Central; Bluffton 71–69 South Adams (ot); Norwell 63–46 Bluffton. Officials: John Gassensmith, Joseph Dickey, Tom Lawrence (replaced by Gayle Forrest on game 3), Troy Ingram.

BOONVILLE: Tell City 70–59 Tecumseh; Dale 90–58 Cannelton; Boonville 64–56 Chrisney; South Spencer 76–61 Castle; Tell City 77–63 Dale; South Spencer 70–54 Boonville; Tell City 72–70 South Spencer. Officials: Don Shields, Glen Clemmons, Jack Johnson, Dallas Richards.

BRAZIL: Rockville 65–56 Montezuma; Staunton 65–52 Van Buren; Brazil 76–57 Rosedale; Rockville 69–67 Staunton; Rockville 85–80 Brazil. Officials: Earle Wolfe, Frank Hobson, Gary Stiles, Warren Keyser.

BROWNSBURG: Danville 77–72 Mooresville; Brownsburg 91–71 Monrovia; Plainfield 49–39 Pittsboro; Danville 81–80 Avon; Brownsburg 62–60 Plainfield (ot); Brownsburg 85–69 Danville. Officials: Jack Goen, James Wehsollek, Paul Cox, Noble Rector.

CALUMET: Lake Central 83–80 Merrillville; Crown Point 69–63 Griffith; Calumet 59–53 Hanover Central; Hebron 70–64 Boone Grove; Lake Central 61–51 Crown Point; Calumet 71–70 Hebron; Calumet 54–51 Lake Central. Officials: Joe Smelcer, Richard Cook, Max Rink, Dave Avery.

CARMEL: Westfield 62–51 Sheridan; Carmel 60–35 Hamilton Heights; Noblesville 74–65 Hamilton Southeastern; Carmel 65–42 Westfield; Carmel 35–28 Noblesville. Officials: Marion Acton, J. Thomas Moorman, James Helms, Ben Olsson.

CASS: Pioneer 63–48 Caston; Peru 72–70 Kewanna; Logansport 61–56 North Miami; Pioneer 79–63 Cass; Peru 69–45 Logansport; Peru 64–61 Pioneer. Officials: Tom Hoffman, Robert Wolfe,

469

Tourney Time

Frank Walker, Wayne Targgart.

CHESTERTON: Portage 66–60 Chesterton; Valparaiso 82–73 Morgan Twp.; Washington Twp. 69–66 Wheeler; Portage 61–49 Valparaiso; Portage 79–39 Washington Twp. Officials: Richard Freeman, Kenneth Miller, Larry Jones, Billy Maroney.

CLAY CITY: Clay City 58–56 Sullivan (2ot); Owen Valley 71–63 Shakamak; North Central 94–66 Union (Dugger); Clay City 67–55 Owen Valley; Clay City 73–60 North Central. Officials: Raymond Vescovi, Ronald Hamm, Temme Patterson, Charles Bertram.

COLUMBIA CITY: Manchester 62–57 Churubusco; White's 63–61 Northfield (ot); Columbia City 68–52 Whitko; White's 46–41 Manchester; Columbia City 60–59 White's. Officials: Allen Voorhis, Frank Corsaro, Steve Cherry, Robert Marcinek.

COLUMBUS: Brown County 68–64 Hauser; Columbus 78–56 Southwestern; Brown County 60–54 Edinburg; Brown County 69–63 Columbus. Officials: Don Hubbard, J. E. Hennegan, Randall Westfall, Ed Scott.

CONNERSVILLE: Connersville 82–65 Union (College Corner); Brookville 84–61 Liberty; Laurel 64–50 Whitewater; Connersville 93–61 Brookville; Connersville 97–40 Laurel. Officials: Raymond Robison, Leroy Schultheis, John Lyskowinski, Rudy Tabereaux.

DeKALB: Hamilton 85–76 Prairie Heights; Garrett 82–77 Angola; Eastside 54–52 Fremont; DeKalb 72–49 Hamilton; Garrett 59–44 Eastside; Garrett 65–60 DeKalb. Officials: Darrell McFall, Donald Roudebush, Donnie Cranfield, John Manka.

EAST CHICAGO: Hobart 72–55 Hammond Noll; Roosevelt 71–51 Washington; East Gary Edison 69–67 River Forest; Hobart 68–66 Roosevelt (4ot); Hobart 64–58 Edison. Officials: Norris Boomershine, Merle Heckaman, Rudy Stegelmann, Richard Brainerd.

EAST NOBLE: West Noble 67–49 Lakeland; East Noble 63–48 Central Noble; Westview 71–64 Fairfield; East Noble 57–55 West Noble; East Noble 75–72 Westview. Officials: Charles Garber, Ronald Flotow, Larry Freyburgher, John Lozier.

ELKHART: Penn 78–53 Northwood; Elkhart 75–50 Goshen; Northridge 70–68 Concord; Penn 68–55 Jimtown; Elkhart 75–64 Northridge; Penn 58–57 Elkhart. Officials: Ernie Sohl, George Oberle, Larry Hollman, Eugene Carrabine.

EVANSVILLE: Harrison 69–54 Mater Dei; Central 103–85 Memorial; Reitz 77–62 North; Bosse 84–72 Rex Mundi; Central 76–71 Harrison; Reitz 74–72 Bosse; Reitz 100–95 Central. Officials: Kenneth Payne, Richard Schleicher, Jerry Schalburg, Fred Myers.

FORT WAYNE (#1): Carroll 67–56 South Side; Leo 83–70 Homestead; North Side 64–54 Northrop; Heritage 76–59 Concordia; Leo 58–57 Carroll; North Side 59–57 Heritage; North Side 85–73 Leo. Officials: Robert Reed, Clifford Spears, Opal Courtney, Louis Schmalfeldt.

FORT WAYNE (#2): New Haven 73–60 Central Catholic; Wayne 64–56 Woodlan; Snider 76–65 Elmhurst; Dwenger 47–46 Luers; New Haven 65–61 Wayne; Snider 63–55 Dwenger; Snider 62–61 New Haven. Officials: Gordon McCain, George Taylor, Norman Hathcoat, James Cox.

FOUNTAIN CENTRAL: Pine Village 83–67 Fountain Central. Seeger 75–55 Covington; North Vermillion 87–77 Attica; Williamsport 74–65 Turkey Run; Pine Village 76–72 Seeger; North Vermillion 72–71 Williamsport; Pine Village 76–68 North Vermillion. Officials: Donald Koester, Tom Manning, William Hite, Bob Goble.

FRANKFORT: Frankfort 64–55 Clinton Central; Rossville 68–58 Carroll; Clinton Prairie 77–68 Tipton; Frankfort 85–64 Tri Central; Rossville 74–69 Clinton Prairie; Frankfort 67–63

Rossville. Officials: Homer Owens, Peter Kokinda, Donald O'Conner, John Tucker.

FRANKLIN: Franklin 89–56 Greenwood; Center Grove 90–64 Indian Creek; Whiteland 69–68 Decatur Central; Center Grove 72–71 Franklin; Center Grove 59–46 Whiteland. Officials: Jerry Baker, McKee Munk, Gary Eaglin, Russell Rogers.

GARY: Andrean 79–40 Wirt; Gary Roosevelt 81–43 Mann; West Side 60–44 Wallace; Andrean 87–60 Emerson; West Side 49–48 Roosevelt (ot); West Side 88–60 Andrean. Officials: John Ward, Louis Zabona, William Sorukas, Lloyd Chambers.

GREENCASTLE: South Putnam 60–48 Greencastle; Cloverdale 68–61 North Putnam; North Salem 78–62 Cascade; Cloverdale 72–65 South Putnam; Cloverdale 59–55 North Salem. Officials: Gene Marks, Don Smith, Thomas Whitehead, Richard Pattengale.

GREENSBURG: Rushville 62–37 North Decatur; South Decatur 63–57 Waldron; Rushville 68–46 Greensburg; Rushville 52–41 South Decatur. Officials: John Holmes, George Emery, James Roberts, Paul Garriott.

HAMMOND: Morton 55–48 Whiting; Gavit 66–62 Munster; Highland 66–64 Tech; Clark 44–42 Hammond High; Morton 74–70 Gavit; Clark 60–41 Highland; Clark 74–60 Morton. Officials: Zeke Williams (replaced by Rich Bowie), Arthur Largent, Kevin Weinberg, Rex Mays.

HUNTINGBURG: Perry Central 73–52 Dubois; Jasper 84–54 Holland; Forest Park 74–66 Huntingburg; Jasper 81–59 Perry Central; Jasper 61–53 Forest Park. Officials: Wendell Baker, Sidney Ellis, Ronald McKibban, Morris Cohen.

HUNTINGTON: Huntington Catholic 71–58 Southwood; Huntington North 67–60 Wabash; Huntington North 49–46 Huntington Catholic. Officials: Bill May, Joe Edmonds, Richard Clark, Ronald Hosinski.

INDIANAPOLIS: Chatard 49–43 Marshall; Arlington 67–66 Shortridge; Broad Ripple 60–53 Lawrence Central; Tech 60–56 North Central; Arlington 61–58 Chatard; Tech 60–59 Broad Ripple; Tech 70–62 Arlington. Officials: James P. Carey, Tom Know, Thomas Vondeylen, Wayne Van Sickle.

JEFFERSONVILLE: Floyd Central 81–71 Providence; Jeffersonville 94–53 Clarksville; New Albany 72–70 Floyd Central; Jeffersonville 88–62 New Albany. Officials: Don Snedeker, Danny Landis, Robert Beeson, Boynton Robson.

KANKAKEE VALLEY: Rensselaer 86–51 Kankakee Valley; West Central 60–55 North Newton; Lowell 66–62 Kouts; Rensselaer 75–54 West Central; Lowell 47–42 Rensselaer. Officials: Roy Kilby, Al Lindahl, John Fleischman, Max Hensler.

KNOX: Knox 70–67 Winamac (ot); Culver 103–62 Oregon-Davis; North Judson 93–70 LaCrosse; Knox 77–72 Culver; Knox 62–58 North Judson. Officials: Harold Ashbrook, Tom Meeks, Dick Modricker, Richard Vendrely.

KOKOMO: Western 63–46 Maconaquah; Taylor 65–57 Eastern; Haworth 76–57 Northwestern; Kokomo 87–59 Western; Haworth 67–46 Taylor; Haworth 69–68 Kokomo. Officials: George Avery, Bruce Knecht, Robert Klein, James Benecke, Jr.

LAFAYETTE: Central Catholic 86–75 Harrison; Jefferson 74–49 West Lafayette; Delphi 90–89 Central Catholic; Jefferson 88–63 Delphi. Officials: James Ruby, Nick Sweigart, John Wray, David Schwartz.

LAVILLE: Bremen 63–56 North Liberty; South Bend Jackson 75–53 Argos; Plymouth 91–76 Glenn; Bremen 51–49 LaVille; Jackson 59–58 Plymouth; Jackson 61–60 Bremen. Officials: Charles Sallee, Donald Schmidt, John Koker, Marty Burdette.

LAWRENCEBURG: Lawrenceburg 79–56 Rising Sun; North Dearborn 60–49 Switzerland County; Dillsboro 62–58 Aurora (ot); Lawrenceburg 87–58 North Dearborn; Lawrenceburg 80–55 Dillsboro. Officials: Jack Cummings, Ward Weisel, Harold Gibbs, James R. Carey.

LEBANON: Brebeuf 59–46 Lebanon; Zionsville 93–70 Wells; Pike 75–74 Thorntown; Zionsville 81–77 Brebeuf (ot); Pike 70–65 Zionsville. Officials: Glen Bonsett, Ray Mitrione, Wayne Jessup, Dale Van Houten.

MADISON: Southwestern 73–63 Charlestown; Silver Creek 65–59 New Washington; Madison 97–63 Madison Shawe; Southwestern 62–54 Henryville; Madison 59–50 Silver Creek; Madison 72–62 Southwestern. Officials: Jimmy Dimitroff, Bill Graham, David Willoughby, Byron Weaver.

MARION: Marion 48–46 Mississinewa; Oak Hill 82–57 Marion Bennett; Madison-Grant 58–41 Elwood; Marion 59–55 Oak Hill; Marion 78–74 Madison-Grant (ot). Officials: John Bush, William Laird, Herb Resler, Jerry Scott.

MARTINSVILLE: Bloomington University 64–62 Bloomington; Edgewood 83–57 Unionville; Smithville 86–72 Eminence; University 86–81 Martinsville; Edgewood 98–75 Smithville; University 81–62 Edgewood. Officials: Lowell Smith, Floyd Riggs, Donald Ricketts, Eugene Linn.

MICHIGAN CITY: Michigan City Marquette 73–47 Westville; Michigan City Elston 97–45 Michigan City Rogers; LaPorte 94–69 New Prairie; South Central 58–53 Marquette; Elston 100–77 LaPorte; Elston 124–43 South Central. Officials: Don Hollman, Gene Gibson, Robert Boyle, Harold Gray.

MUNCIE: Muncie Central 87–54 Muncie Burris; Wes-Del 78–63 Muncie Southside; Yorktown 64–48 Delta; Muncie Northside 67–59 Cowan; Central 78–61 Wes-Del; Yorktown 79–61 Northside; Yorktown 70–65 Central. Officials: Art Thompson, Eric Harmon, George Grygiel; Jack Gardner.

NEW CASTLE: New Castle 44–32 Knightstown; Tri 92–48 Morton Memorial; Mount Vernon 67–39 Blue River; Eastern Hancock 65–61 Shenandoah; New Castle 62–35 Tri; Mount Vernon 69–47 Eastern Hancock; New Castle 64–55 Mount Vernon. Officials: Gary Muncy, Richard Hale, Roger Pflughaupt, Paul Leamon.

NORTH MONTGOMERY: Crawfordsville 82–61 Southmont; North Montgomery 90–67 Southwestern; Crawfordsville 56–38 Wainwright; Crawfordsville 68–56 North Montgomery. Officials: Robert Laird, Darrell Eaton, Jack Graham, Roger McGriff.

PAOLI: Orleans 87–40 Marengo; Paoli 69–57 Leavenworth; Springs Valley 58–57 West Washington; Milltown 64–48 English; Orleans 62–61 Paoli; Milltown 70–59 Springs Valley; Orleans 64–53 Milltown. Officials: Richard Crays, Melvin Redman, Larry Collins, Robert Kirk.

PRINCETON: Oakland City Wood Memorial 78–46 North Posey; Mount Vernon 84–74 Princeton; Fort Branch 60–59 New Harmony (ot); Haubstadt 67–57 Owensville; Mount Vernon 74–59 Wood Memorial; Fort Branch 72–55 Haubstadt; Mount Vernon 72–64 Fort Branch. Officials: Don Shiflet, Charles Roush, Bruce Mayfield, Ray Norris.

RICHMOND: Richmond 81–41 Northeastern; Hagerstown 59–56 Centerville; Richmond 68–44 Cambridge City; Richmond 66–47 Hagerstown. Officials: Richard Lederman, John Hilligoss, James O'Neal, Carl Schnebelt.

SALEM: Salem 64–63 South Central; Corydon 65–51 North Harrison; Lanesville 75–59 Borden; Eastern 83–60 Salem; Lanesville 57–55 Corydon; Eastern 67–58 Lanesville. Officials:

Harold Gourley, Richie Moore, Ralph Scales, Jack Williams.

SEYMOUR: Seymour 100–66 Austin; Brownstown Central 84–58 Medora; Jennings County 98–57 Crothersville; Seymour 85–71 Scottsburg; Jennings County 90–88 Brownstown Central; Jennings County 91–90 Seymour. Officials: Wallace Reeve, Bill Strafford, Herb Pruett, William Pittman.

SHELBYVILLE: Franklin Central 70–47 Greenfield Central; Triton Central 69–60 New Palestine; Shelbyville 65–64 Morristown (ot); Franklin Central 58–54 Triton Central; Shelbyville 55–49 Franklin Central. Officials: William Fields, James Rider, Don Pope, Ronald Beard.

SOUTH BEND: LaSalle 77–75 Riley (2ot); Adams 92–70 Mishawaka; St. Joseph's 62–54 Washington; Mishawaka Marian 94–75 Clay; Adams 71–70 LaSalle; St. Joseph's 85–51 Marian; St. Joseph's 72–59 Adams. Officials: Robert Kramer, Thomas Neuman, Herbert Hicks, Gil Baumgartner.

SOUTHPORT: Wood 76–61 Roncalli; Attucks 67–60 Southport; Manual 79–70 Warren Central; Howe 70–57 Beech Grove; Attucks 63–48 Wood; Manual 67–58 Howe; Attucks 63–62 Manual. Officials: Frank Hoagburg, Paul Wernke, Gary Coers, Dave Lowenstein.

SWITZ CITY: Bloomfield 71–57 Switz City; L & M 73–71 Worthington; Eastern 59–53 Linton; Bloomfield 96–63 L & M; Bloomfield 58–56 Eastern. Officials: Don Hurst, Delmar Knecht, G. A. Ward, Wayne Myers.

TERRE HAUTE: Laboratory 56–53 Clinton; Terre Haute North 64–53 Terre Haute South; West Vigo 65–62 Schulte; North 76–45 Laboratory; North 75–53 West. Officials: Harold Mason, Phil Hardwick, Reginald Cheatham, Francis Fiddler.

VINCENNES: Vincennes 71–48 Winslow; South Knox 67–60 Petersburg; Rivet 66–54 North Knox; Lincoln 75–40 South Knox; Lincoln 56–45 Rivet. Officials: Howard Risley, Richard Burrows, Leslie Wright, Walter Overton.

WARSAW: Wawasee 84–73 Triton; Warsaw 46–41 Mentone; Rochester 77–59 Akron; Warsaw 78–64 Wawasee; Rochester 60–58 Warsaw. Officials: Roger DeYoung, Gerry Scheub, Robert Justak, Billy Walker.

WASHINGTON: Catholic 68–58 Shoals; Loogootee 100–51 Otwell; Barr-Reeve 61–53 North Daviess; Washington 71–56 Catholic; Loogootee 85–61 Barr-Reeve; Loogootee 62–57 Washington. Officials: Donald Call, Paul Hackleman, Larry Maxwell, Keith Combs.

WINCHESTER: Randolph Southern 101–77 Union; Wapahani 67–61 Monroe Central; Union City 61–58 Winchester; Randolph Southern 96–76 Wapahani; Union City 69–66 Randolph Southern. Officials: Harold Back, Donald Ford, Gary Janeway, Robert Wells.

1972 REGIONALS

ANDERSON: Madison Heights 69–62 Carmel; Blackford 56–54 Kokomo Haworth; Madison Heights 68–64 Blackford. Officials: William Fields, Warren Keyser, Wayne Myers, Roger DeYoung, Richard Freeman, Morris Cohen.

COLUMBUS: Shelbyville 72–65 Bloomington University; Center Grove 74–64 Brown County; Center Grove 69–52 Shelbyville. Officials: James Benecke, Jack Williams, Gene Linn, John Lozier, Norris Boomershine, Billy Maroney.

CONNERSVILLE: Jac-Cen-Del 66–64 Lawrenceburg; Connersville 74–52 Rushsville; Connersville 69–46 Jac-Cen-Del. Officials: Glen Clemons, Donald Shields, Mike Crouch, McKee

Munk, Eugene Linn, Jim Cox.

ELKHART: Penn 76–59 South Bend Jackson; Rochester 82–72 Columbia City; Penn 69–67 Rochester (ot). Officials: Ray Robison, Frank Hoagburg, John Bush, Ward Weisel, Wendell Baker, Bob Goble.

EVANSVILLE: Tell City 73–71 Mt. Vernon; Vincennes 78–55 Evansville Reitz; Vincennes 74–57 Tell City. Officials: Harold Mason, Roger McGriff, John Holmes, Byron Weaver, Donald Call, Bill Gray.

FORT WAYNE: Garrett 84–78 Fort Wayne Snider; East Noble 78–69 Fort Wayne North Side; Garrett 63–49 East Noble. Officials: Harry Inskeep, Troy Ingram, Jim Ruby, Ronald Beard, Tom Hoffman, Donald Koester.

FRANKFORT: Indianapolis Pike 62–59 Cloverdale; Crawfordsville 84–72 Frankfort; Pike 76–64 Crawfordsville. Officials: Lowell Smith, Robert Marcinek, Earle Wolfe, Jack Cummings, Don Hollman, Richard Lederman.

GARY: Hobart 62–53 Calumet; Gary West Side 57–49 Hammond Clark; West Side 73–55 Hobart. Officials: Darrell McFall, Ronald Hosinski, Gene Butts, Paul Leamon, Charles Sallee, Marty Burdette.

INDIANAPOLIS: Attucks 65–61 Tech; Cathedral 99–55 Brownsburg; Cathedral 82–71 Attucks. Officials: Harold Gourley, David Avery, Glen Bonsett, Don Shields, Robert Reed, Richard Vendrely.

LAFAYETTE: Benton Central 71–69 Pine Village; Lafayette Jefferson 85–56 Lowell; Jefferson 79–67 Benton Central. Officials: Bill May, Gary Janeway, Donald Hubbard, Rudy Tabereaux, George Avery, Richard Crays.

MARION: Marion 58–57 Norwell; Huntington North 69–54 Peru; Marion 56–54 Huntington North. Officials: Jimmy Dimitroff, Dan Alvarez, Don Hurst, Robert Kirk, Don Shiflet, Norman Chestnut.

NEW CASTLE: Yorktown 71–59 New Castle; Richmond 100–45 Union City; Richmond 70–51 Yorktown. Officials: Gil Baumgartner, Joe Smelcer, Francis Fiddler, John Gassensmith, Arthur Largent.

SEYMOUR: Madison 91–87 Jennings Co.; Jeffersonville 87–59 Eastern (Pekin); Jeffersonville 78–62 Madison. Officials: Jack Mercer, Wayne Van Sickle, Kenneth Payne, Lloyd Chambers, Gordon McCain, Max Hensler.

SOUTH BEND: Michigan City 91–56 Knox; Portage 60–53 South Bend St. Joseph;s; Michigan City 82–58 Portage. Officials: Gary Muncy, Jon Gallipo, Robert Laird, Jack Gardner, Robert Wells, James P. Carey.

TERRE HAUTE: Bloomfield 61–55 Clay City; Terre Haute North 110–68 Rockville; Terre Haute North 84–52 Bloomfield. Officials: Gene Marks, Dave Loewenstein, Raymond Vescovi, Keith Combs, Ernie Sohl, Eugene Carrabine.

WASHINGTON: Loogootee 70–63 Bedford; Jasper 77–71 Orleans; Jasper 59–58 Loogootee. Officials: Allen Voorhis, Melvin Botkin, Don Snedeker, Jerry Scott, John Ward, Harold Gray.

1972 SEMI—STATES

EVANSVILLE: Jeffersonville 64–46 Jasper; Terre Haute North 58–51 Vincennes; Jeffersonville 62–60 Terre Haute North. Officials: Gene Marks, John Bush, Marion Acton, Jack Mercer, Lowell

Smith, John Ward.

FORT WAYNE: Mishawaka Penn 74–67 Marion; Anderson Madison Heights 83–71 Garrett; Madison Heights 57–48 Penn. Officials: Officials: Darrell McFall, Raymond Vescovi, Jimmy Dimitroff, Charles Sallee, Harold Gourley, Robert Reed.

INDIANAPOLIS: Center Grove 62–61 Richmond; Connersville 76–68 Indianapolis Cathedral; Connersville 72–54 Center Grove. Officials: Ray Robison, Don Hollman, Bill May, John Gassensmith, George Avery, Gordon McCain.

LAFAYETTE: Michigan City Elston 78–64 Lafayette Jefferson; Gary West Side 70–52 Indianapolis Pike; West Side 84–83 Elston (ot). Officials: Robert Laird, Kenneth Payne, Harry Inskeep, Gary Muncy, Don Shiflet, Don Snedeker.

1972 FINALS—March 18

BLOOMINGTON (Indiana University): Gary West Side 75–67 Anderson Madison Heights; Connersville 76–69 Jeffersonville (ot). Connersville 80–63 West Side. Officials: Darrell McFall, Bill May, Jimmy Dimitroff, Gene Marks, Marion Acton, Lowell Smith.

1973 SECTIONALS

ANDERSON: Madison Heights 77–48 Frankton; Anderson 91–52 Lapel; Daleville 71–59 Highland; Alexandria 59–55 Pendleton Heights; Anderson 113–56 Madison Heights; Alexandria 50–42 Daleville; Anderson 57–38 Alexandria. Officials: Robert Reed, Louis Zabona, Robert Keys, Roger DeYoung.

BATESVILLE: Milan 63–57 South Ripley; Batesville 106–44 Moores Hill; Jac-Cen-Del 76–42 Sunman; Milan 57–51 Batesville; Milan 48–46 Jac-Cen-Del. Officials: Don Shields, John Hilligoss, Don Pope, Bill Strafford.

BEDFORD: Bedford 64–39 Fayetteville; Mitchell 63–39 Oolitic; Heltonville 73–65 Tunnelton; Shawswick 20–16 Needmore; Bedford 51–42 Mitchell; Shawswick 62–58 Heltonville; Bedford 70–58 Shawswick. Officials: Harold Mason, Stewart Vickers, Temme Patterson, Jack Williams.

BELLMONT: Bluffton 62–55 Bellmont; South Adams 80–77 Southern Wells; Norwell 60–51 Adams Central; South Adams 71–61 Bluffton; Norwell 75–58 South Adams. Officials: Boynton Robson, Rudy Stegelmann, Gayle Forrest, James R. Carey.

BEN DAVIS: Northwest 86–61 Ben Davis; Cathedral 89–51 School for the Deaf; Speedway 64–61 Scecina; Washington 79–45 Ritter; Cathedral 60–54 Northwest; Speedway 56–55 Washington (2ot); Speedway 63–61 Cathedral. Officials: Gordon McCain, James Rider, Larry Freyburgher, Dallas Richards.

BENTON CENTRAL: Benton Central 69–63 South Newton; Frontier 75–60 Tri County; North White 67–65 Twin Lakes; Frontier 82–76 Benton Central (2ot); Frontier 68–58 North White. Officials: Paul Garriott, William Phillips, Bob Richardson, Clifford Spears.

BLACKFORD: Blackford 81–65 Dunkirk; Portland 70–45 Bryant; Eastbrook 80–53 Redkey; Albany 64–62 Pennville; Portland 77–63 Blackford; Eastbrook 64–56 Albany; Portland 76–60 Eastbrook. Officials: Harry Inskeep, Ronald McKibban, Milton Cooper, Byron Weaver.

BOONVILLE: Tell City 85–72 South Spencer; Castle 61–60 Boonville; Heritage Hills 71–47

Tourney Time

Tecumseh; Tell City 59–34 Cannelton; Heritage Hills 64–58 Castle; Tell City 93–59 Heritage Hills. Officials: Don Hurst, Harold Gibbs, Delmus Aubrey, Ed Scott.

BRAZIL: Brazil 88–55 Staunton; Rockville 81–57 Rosedale; Montezuma 56–48 Van Buren; Brazil 74–55 Rockville; Brazil 46–39 Montezuma (ot). Officials: Wallace Reeve, Frank Corsaro, John Ramey, Roger McGriff.

BROWNSBURG: Pittsboro 73–71 Monrovia (ot); Danville 75–66 Mooresville; Avon 97–71 Brownsburg; Plainfield 34–28 Pittsboro; Avon 77–68 Danville; Plainfield 53–48 Avon. Officials: Bill May, Jerry Schalburg, Harold Back, Jerry Scott.

CALUMET: Hanover Central 67–58 Calumet; Crown Point 69–61 Merrillville; Griffith 57–35 Lake Central; Crown Point 64–56 Hanover Central; Griffith 45–42 Crown Point. Officials: John Gassensmith, Rex Mays, Frank Walker, Richard Brainerd.

CARMEL: Hamilton Heights 69–68 Sheridan (ot); Carmel 67–35 Noblesville; Westfield 73–72 Hamilton Southeastern; Carmel 65–48 Hamilton Heights; Carmel 59–55 Westfield (2ot). Officials: Harold Ashbrook, Charles Roush, Gary Eaglin, Robert Kirk.

CASS: Peru 67–62 Caston; Cass 84–72 Kewanna; North Miami 65–62 Pioneer; Peru 66–63 Logansport; North Miami 86–79 Cass; Peru 76–66 North Miami. Officials: Gil Baumgartner, Joseph Dickey, Leslie Wright, Robert Marcinek.

CLAY CITY: Clay City 101–61 Sullivan; Owen Valley 76–73 Union (Dugger); Shakamak 63–58 North Central; Clay City 62–48 Owen Valley; Clay City 61–59 Shakamak. Officials: Don Hubbard, Richard Schleicher, Dennis Cave, Lloyd Chambers.

COLUMBIA CITY: Whitko 90–70 Churubusco; North Manchester 60–56 Northfield; Columbia City 63–60 Whitko; Columbia City 87–59 North Manchester. Officials: Ronald Beard, Herb Pruett, Robert Carr, Robert Gilmore.

COLUMBUS: Southwestern 63–61 Brown County; Columbus East 42–35 Columbus North; Edinburg 65–58 Hauser; Southwestern 55–53 Columbus East; Edinburg 67–38 Southwestern. Officials: Norman Chestnut, Paul Hackleman, Tom Whitehead, John Manka.

CONNERSVILLE: Connersville 65–64 Union County (ot); Laurel 84–59 Whitewater Twp.; Connersville 40–26 Brookville; Connersville 74–44 Laurel. Officials: Richard Lederman, Robert Boyle, Barry Gerig, Warren Keyser.

DEKALB: Garrett 52–47 Eastside; DeKalb 70–42 Angola; Fremont 78–58 Hamilton; Prairie Heights 58–49 Garrett; Fremont 53–50 DeKalb; Fremont 68–56 Prairie Heights. Officials: Marty Burdette, Richard Hall, Jack Tiede, Troy Ingram.

EAST CHICAGO: Hobart 48–47 Washington; Hammond Noll 41–27 Roosevelt; East Gary Edison 90–75 River Forest; Noll 25–17 Hobart; Noll 33–28 Edison. Officials: Bob Goble, Kenneth Miller, Larry Jones, Harold Gray.

EAST NOBLE: East Noble 66–46 Lakeland; Westview 74–57 Central Noble; Fairfield 65–61 West Noble (ot); Westview 73–72 East Noble; Westview 55–43 Fairfield. Officials: Mel Botkin, Jack Graham, Michael Morlan, James Wehsollek.

ELKHART: Concord 89–83 Jimtown; Northridge 79–58 Northwood; Elkhart Memorial 63–54 Goshen; Penn 60–41 Elkhart Central; Concord 75–52 Northridge; Penn 55–51 Memorial; Penn 57–47 Concord. Officials: Gene Marks, George Taylor, John Fleischman, Gene Gibson.

EVANSVILLE: Central 81–76 Harrison; Mater Dei 58–54 Memorial; Bosse 63–53 North; Reitz 71–50 Central; Bosse 49–44 Mater Dei; Bosse 61–45 Reitz. Officials: Art Thompson, Sidney Ellis, Phil Barth, Phil Hardwick.

IHSAA Scores / 1970–1979

FLOYD CENTRAL: Floyd Central 95–50 South Central; North Harrison 79–68 Corydon; Salem 85–80 Borden; Eastern (Pekin) 69–57 Lanesville; Floyd Cental 79–64 North Harrison; Eastern 70–52 Salem; Floyd Central 98–54 Eastern. Officials: Wendell Baker, Larry Collins, James Dunlap, Ronald Ham.

FORT WAYNE (#1): Leo 57–51 Carroll; Woodlan 73–56 Bishop Luers; Northrop 75–49 Dwenger; Homestead 72–67 Wayne; Woodlan 66–64 Leo (ot); Northrop 75–46 Homestead; Northrop 65–44 Woodlan. Officials: Richard Gebhart, Robert Beeson, Kevin Weinberg, John Lozier.

FORT WAYNE (#2): Snider 100–82 Elmhurst; North Side 80–72 South Side; Concordia 66–65 New Haven; Snider 85–61 Heritage; North Side 68–45 Concordia; North Side 82–71 Snider. Officials: James Ruby, Donald Ford, Robert Klein, Dave Avery.

FOUNTAIN CENTRAL: Covington 67–59 North Vermillion; Seeger 58–44 Pine Village; Fpountain Central 60–49 Attica; Turkey Run 66–64 Williamsport; Covington 54–49 Seeger; Fountain Central 61–49 Turkey Run; Fountain Central 64–60 Covington. Officials: Eugene Carrabine, Darrell Eaton, John Wray, Dan Alvarez.

FRANKFORT: Carroll 71–66 Clinton Prairie; Rossville 80–73 Clinton Central; Frankfort 75–63 Tipton; Carroll 65–59 Tri Central; Frankfort 75–68 Rossville; Frankfort 80–77 Carroll (ot). Officials: George Avery, Jerry Scheub, Carl Pitts, Wayne Myers.

GARY: Gary Roosevelt 70–68 Emerson; Mann 61–58 Andrean; Wallace 91–57 Wirt; Roosevelt 67–61 Mann; Wallace 61–56 Roosevelt. Officials: Jack Gardner, Herb Resler, James Reinebold, John Tucker.

GREENCASTLE: Greencastle 55–53 Cascade; Cloverdale 74–57 South Putnam; North Putnam 80–55 North Salem; Cloverdale 44–43 Greencastle; Cloverdale 64–60 North Putnam (ot). Officials: William Fields, Frank Hobson, Randall Westfall, Rudy Tabereaux.

GREENSBURG: North Decatur 67–58 Waldron; Rushville 87–63 Greensburg; North Decatur 56–50 South Decatur; Rushville 71–68 North Decatur. Officials: Homer Owens, Paul Cox, James Fairchild, Ben Olsson.

HAMMOND: Hammond High 80–75 Tech; Gavit 61–57 Highland; Clark 67–51 Morton; Munster 60–58 Whiting; Hammond High 82–62 Gavit; Clark 41–22 Munster; Hammond High 70–62 Clark. Officials: Marion Acton, Max Rink., William Sorukas, Jon Gallipo.

HUNTINGTON: Huntington 103–59 Southwood; Wabash 88–87 White's (3ot); Huntington 98–53 Huntington Catholic; Huntington 81–60 Wabash. Officials: Robert Wells, Ronald Flotow, Keith Yoder, Ray Mitrione.

INDIANAPOLIS: Shortridge 84–58 Broad Ripple; Chatard 63–61 Marshall; Arlington 57–53 Tech (ot); North Central 64–61 Lawrence Central; Chatard 62–59 Shortridge; North Central 68–62 Arlington; North Central 70–64 Chatard. Officials: Don Hollman. George Grygiel, Joe Edmonds, Eugene Linn.

JEFFERSONVILLE: Clarksville 68–66 Providence; New Albany 71–63 Jeffersonville; New Albany 86–58 Clarksville. Officials: Earle Wolfe, William Hite, Gary Stiles, Danny Jacobs.

KANKAKEE VALLEY: Hebron 62–53 Kankakee Valley; Rensselaer 61–52 West Central; Kouts 72–65 Lowell; Hebron 97–71 North Newton; Rensselaer 60–56 Kouts; Hebron 60–54 Rensselaer. Officials: Richard Vendrely, Merl Heckaman, Donald O'Connor, Dale Van Houten.

KNOX: Knox 77–41 LaCrosse; Winamac 74–51 Culver; North Judson 55–40 Oregon-Davis; Knox 71–48 Winamac; Knox 60–58 North Judson. Officials: Charles Garber, Larry Hollman, Jerry Pieper, Eric Harmon.

Tourney Time

KOKOMO: Haworth 75–57 Northwestern; Kokomo 70–44 Maconaquah; Taylor 72–55 Eastern; Haworth 82–45 Western; Kokomo 69–41 Taylor; Kokomo 82–61 Haworth. Officials: Norris Boomershine, Thomas Neuman, Roger Pflughaupt, Wayne Targgart.

LAFAYETTE: Central Catholic 70–56 Harrison; Jefferson 67–53 Delphi; Catholic 50–49 West Lafayette (ot); Catholic 57–56 Jefferson. Officials: Stan Dubis, Al Lindahl, Opal Courtney, Ray Norris.

LaVILLE: Plymouth 92–42 Bremen; South Bend Jackson 72–47 North Liberty; Glenn 45–39 LaVille; Plymouth 82–64 Argos; Glenn 84–68 Jackson; Plymouth 65–54 Glenn. Officials: Jack Mercer, Nick Sweigart, Don Cranfield, Jerry Larrison.

LAWRENCEBURG: Dillsboro 52–51 Aurora; Lawrenceburg 85–61 North Dearborn; Rising Sun 69–39 Switzerland County; Lawrenceburg 72–48 Dillsboro; Lawrenceburg 77–55 Rising Sun. Officials: Raymond Robison, William Laird, Steve Vannatter, Billy Walker.

LEBANON: Indianapolis 63–50 Wells; Brebeuf 61–55 Zionsville; Lebanon 79–55 Thorntown; Brebeuf 73–53 Pike; Lebanon 59–56 Brebeuf. Officials: Don Shiflet, Delmar Knecht, Robert Justak, Tom Manning.

MADISON: Charlestown 86–61 Henryville; Southwestern 76–64 Madison; Silver Creek 67–59 Madison Shawe; Charlestown 60–59 New Washington; Southwestern 59–46 Silver Creek; Southwestern 69–52 Charlestown. Officials: Darrell McFall, Tom Meeks, George Dixon, Louis Schmalfeldt.

MARION: Madison-Grant 70–60 Marion; Elwood 66–63 Mississinewa; Oak Hill 82–67 Marion Bennett; Madison-Grant 73–68 Elwood; Madison-Grant 73–62 Oak Hill. Officials: Richard Freeman, William Graham, Herbert Hicks, Ron Hosinski.

MARTINSVILLE: Martinsville 69–61 Bloomington North; Bloomington South 93–65 Edgewood; Martinsville 80–65 Eminence; South 76–70 Martinsville. Officials: Jerry Baker, George Emery, Bruce Mayfield, McKee Munk.

MICHIGAN CITY: Elston 57–54 New Prairie; LaPorte 86–53 Westville; Rogers 79–62 South Central; Elston 67–55 Marquette; LaPorte 48–41 Rogers; Elston 50–44 LaPorte. Officials: John Ward, Richard Hale, Thomas VonDeylen, Gary Janeway.

MUNCIE: Delta 61–46 Burris; Southside 67–36 Cowan; Yorktown 59–52 Central; Northside 94–53 Wes–Del; Southside 46–39 Delta; Yorktown 44–42 Northside; Yorktown 50–40 Southside. Officials: Joe Smelcer, Blake Ress, Wayne Jessup, Richard Cook.

NEW CASTLE: Eastern Hancock 83–41 Morton Memorial; New Castle 80–50 Mount Vernon; Shenandoah 70–53 Blue River; Knightstown 47–44 Tri; New Castle 73–31 Eastern Hancock; Shenandoah 63–55 Knightstown; New Castle 85–63 Shenandoah. Officials: Charles Sallee, Bill Wullner, Larry Maxwell, James Benecke.

NORTH MONTGOMERY: Crawfordsville 62–53 Wainwright; Southmont 62–58 Southwestern; Crawfordsville 63–50 North Montgomery; Crawfordsville 63–49 Southmont. Officials: Jack Cummings, Norman Hathcoat, Arthur Morris, William Van Sickle.

PAOLI: Paoli 96–59 English; Leavenworth 65–63 West Washington; Springs Valley 78–47 Milltown; Orleans 99–74 Maremgo; Paoli 73–55 Leavenworth; Orleans 81–65 Springs Valley; Orleans 70–44 Paoli. Officials: Morris Cohen, Richard Burrows, G. A. Ward, Floyd Riggs.

PRINCETON: Wood Memorial 60–45 Haubstadt; Mt. Vernon 78–49 Owensville; Ft. Branch 64–43 New Harmony; Princeton 58–50 North Posey; Mt. Vernon 50–43 Wood Memorial; Princeton 55–53 Ft. Branch; Princeton 54–51 Mt. Vernon. Officials: Jimmy Dimitroff, John

Lyskowinski, Jack Johnson, Leroy Schultheis.

RICHMOND: Richmond 65–38 Centerville; Cambridge City 67–40 Hagerstown; Richmond 81–59 Northeastern; Richmond 67–43 Cambridge City. Officials: Frank Hoagburg, Ed Ulshafer, Gary Muncy, Donald Schmidt.

SEYMOUR: Seymour 91–72 Scottsburg; Jennings County 80–55 Medora; Austin 75–61 Crothersville; Seymour 78–47 Brownstown Central; Jennings County 93–80 Austin; Seymour 91–89 Jennings County. Officials: Ray Vescovi, Don Ricketts, David Willoughby, Keith Combs.

SHELBYVILLE: Shelbyville 52–39 Franklin Central; Morristown 68–60 Triton Central (ot); Greenfield Central 88–67 New Palestine; Shelbyville 56–52 Morristown; Greenfield Central 50–35 Shelbyville. Officials: Lowell Smith, James Roberts, Richard Clark, Ward Weisel.

SOUTH BEND: Adams 86–34 Mishawaka Marian; Washington 83–72 Clay; Riley 73–63 Mishawaka; St. Joseph's 59–56 LaSalle; Adams 87–68 Washington; St. Joseph's 63–61 Riley; Adams 75–67 St. Joseph's. Officials: Thomas Hoffman, Robert Wolfe, Reginald Cheatham, James Cox.

SOUTHPORT: Southport 64–40 Roncalli; Howe 75–55 Wood; Crispus Attucks 77–56 Manual; Warren Central 60–35 Beech Grove; Southport 83–46 Howe; Attucks 55–52 Warren Central; Attucks 87–78 Southport (ot). Officials: Wayne Van Sickle, Don Smith, Ron Kitts, Paul Leamon.

SOUTHRIDGE: Jasper 61–55 Winslow; Forest Park 81–40 Perry Central; Southridge 52–50 Dubois; Jasper 69–64 Forest Park; Jasper 47–46 Southridge. Officials: Robert Laird, Gary Coers, James O'Neal, Bruce Knecht.

SWITZ CITY: Eastern 79–56 Linton; Bloomfield 63–53 L & M; Switz City Central 76–70 Worthington; Eastern 67–61 Bloomfield (ot); Central 55–51 Eastern. Officials: Bill Gray, Richie Moore, Kenneth Cave, Walter Overton.

TERRE HAUTE: South 90–50 Schulte; West Vigo 63–49 Clinton; North 78–30 Laboratory; South 81–61 West Vigo; South 81–65 North. Officials: Howard Risley, Dave Mounts, Mike Bohan, Dave Lowenstein.

TRITON: Warsaw 66–41 Wawasee; Triton 75–58 Mentone; Rochester 69–59 Akron; Warsaw 73–60 Triton; Warsaw 65–56 Rochester. Officials: Don Koester, William DeRome, Richard Bowie, Peter Kokinda.

VALPARAISO: Wheeler 57–55 Morgan Twp.; Chesterton 68–64 Boone Grove; Portage 68–46 Washington Twp.; Valparaiso 64–60 Wheeler; Portage 67–50 Chesterton; Portage 61–60 Valparaiso. Officials: Gene Butts, Robert Frey, Dick Modricker, Billy Maroney.

VINCENNES: Vincennes Rivet 59–51 North Knox; South Knox 73–63 Petersburg; Vincennes 58–48 Rivet; Vincennes 59–49 South Knox. Officials: Richard Crays, Glen Clemons, Robert Maxey, Fred Myers.

WASHINGTON: Loogootee 84–58 Shoals; Washington 62–45 Washington Catholic; North Daviess 60–51 Otwell; Loogootee 61–57 Barr-Reeve; Washington 68–60 North Daviess; Loogootee 69–56 Washington. Officials: John Bush, Melvin Redman, Armond Motz, Charles Bertram.

WHITELAND: Franklin 55–45 Greenwood; Whiteland 83–62 Indian Creek; Center Grove 63–37 Decatur Central; Franklin 79–66 Whiteland; Franklin 65–60 Center Grove. Officials: Don Snedeker, Donald Roudebush, Ralph Scales, Max Hensler.

WINCHESTER: Union City 70–58 Monroe Central; Winchester 94–86 Randolph Southern;

Tourney Time

Wapahani 73–62 Union; Union City 49–48 Winchester; Union City 56–47 Wapahani. Officials: Allen Voorhis, Danny Landis, James Helms, William Pittman.

1973 REGIONALS

ANDERSON: Anderson 87–59 Portland; Carmel 54–41 Kokomo; Anderson 60–50 Carmel. Officials: Norman Chestnut, Dave Lowenstein, Raymond Vescovi, Don Shields, Marion Acton, Don Shields.

COLUMBUS: Franklin 75–46 Greenfield Central; Bloomington South 69–65 Edinburg; Franklin 70–40 Bloomington South. Officials: Marty Burdette, Keith Combs, Joe Smelcer, Jerry Scott, Robert Reed, Troy Ingram.

CONNERSVILLE: Lawrenceburg 47–45 Connersville; Milan 60–59 Rushville; Milan 48–41 Lawrenceburg. Officials: James Ruby, Donald Schmidt, Lowell Smith, Dallas Richards, Gil Baumgartner, Paul Leamon.

ELKHART: Plymouth 88–57 Columbia City; Warsaw 57–54 Penn; Plymouth 53–52 Warsaw (ot). Officials: Robert Wells, Phil Hardwick, Charles Sallee, Byron Weaver, Don Hollman, Richard Crays.

EVANSVILLE: Princeton 47–42 Vincennes; Tell City 69–66 Evansville Bosse (ot); Tell City 75–56 Princeton. Officials: Jack Gardner, Eric Harmon, Jack Mercer, Jerry Larrison, Don Snedeker, Robert Kirk.

FORT WAYNE: Westview 82–71 Fort Wayne North Side; Fort Wayne Northrop 101–43 Fremont; Northrop 64–63 Westview. Officials: John Gassensmith, Bruce Knecht, Howard Risley, Robert Marcinek, George Avery, Morris Cohen.

FRANKFORT: Lebanon 55–40 Cloverdale; Crawfordsville 94–74 Frankfort; Lebanon 69–50 Crawfordsville. Officials: Norris Boomershine, Gene Gibson, Robert Laird, Ronald Hosinski, James Benecke, Rudy Tabereaux.

GARY: Hammond Noll 52–37 Gary Wallace; Hammond High 87–62 Griffith; Noll 55–51 Hammond High. Officials: Max Hensler, John Lozier Allen Voorhis, James Wehsollek, Richard Gebhart, Richard Lederman.

INDIANAPOLIS: Speedway 59–44 Plainfield; Attucks 75–62 North Central; Speedway 56–54 Attucks. Officials: Bob Goble, Dan Alvarez, Gene Butts, Richard Cook, John Ward, Eugene Carrabine.

LAFAYETTE: Frontier 70–58 Hebron; Lafayette Central Catholic 92–68 Fountain Central; Central Catholic 74–55 Frontier. Officials: Don Hurst, Don Shiflet, Tom Hoffman, Leroy Schultheis, Warren Keyser, Jack Cummings.

MARION: Norwell 78–74 Madison-Grant; Huntington 86–79 Peru; Norwell 61–56 Huntington. Officials: Donald Koester, Thomas Manning, Harold Mason, Fred Myers, John Bush, Jerry Baker.

NEW CASTLE: Richmond 52–41 Union City; New Castle 73–37 Yorktown; Richmond 59–52 New Castle. Officials: Wayne Myers, Wayne Targgart, Richard Freeman, David Avery, Gary Muncy, Roger DeYoung.

SEYMOUR: Seymour 65–64 Southwestern; New Albany 69–66 Floyd Central; New Albany 90–72 Seymour. Officials: Bill May, Billy Maroney, Earle Wolfe, Ward Weisel, Eugene Linn, James Cox.

SOUTH BEND: Michigan City Elston 62–56 Portage; South Bend Adams 83–63 Knox;

Adams 90–70 Michigan City. Officials: Wayne Van Sickle, Melvin Botkin, Raymond Robison, Frank Hoagburg, Jimmy Dimitroff, Bill Gray.

TERRE HAUTE: Terre Haute 76–56 Brazil; Clay City 64–50 Switz City; South 60–58 Clay City. Officials: Harold Ashbrook, Charles Bertram, Darrell McFall, Jack Williams, William Fields, Harold Gray.

WASHINGTON: Bedford 53–41 Loogootee; Jasper 68–55 Orleans; Jasper 62–58 Bedford. Officials: Gene Marks, Roger McGriff, Gordon McCain, Ronald Beard, Harry Inskeep, Jon Gallipo.

1973 SEMI–STATES

EVANSVILLE: Tell City 90–71 Terre Haute South; New Albany 72–61 Jasper; New Albany 63–62 Tell City. Officials: Lowell Smith, Gordon McCain, John Ward, Gene Butts, Jimmy Dimitroff, Harry Inskeep.

FORT WAYNE: Fort Wayne Northrop 71–42 Norwell, Anderson 96–84 Plymouth; Anderson 92–69 Northrop. Officials: Bill May, Robert Laird, Don Snedeker, Jack Mercer, Don Shiflet, John Bush.

INDIANAPOLIS: Richmond 48–43 Milan; Franklin 56–45 Speedway; Franklin 67–53 Richmond. Officials: Richard Gebhart, Gary Muncu, Gene Marks, Tom Hoffman, Marion Acton, Robert Reed.

LAFAYETTE: South Bend Adams 57–49 Hammond Noll; Central Catholic 76–64 Lebanon; Adams 87–80 Central Catholic. Officials: Don Hollman, Earle Wolfe, Darrell McFall, Charles Sallee, George Avery, Ray Vescovi.

1973 FINALS—March 17

BLOOMINGTON (Indiana University): New Albany 77–76 Franklin (ot); South Bend Adams 99–95 Anderson; New Albany 84–79 Adams. Officials: Darrell McFall, Charles Sallee, Bill May, Robert Laird, Lowell Smith, Gene Marks.

1974 SECTIONALS

ANDERSON: Madison Heights 64–49 Alexandria; Anderson 73–57 Highland; Pendleton Heights 65–41 Frankton; Lapel 94–59 Daleville; Anderson 73–71 Madison Heights; Lapel 75–64 Pendleton Heights; Anderson 81–58 Lapel. Officials: Marion Acton, Bob Goble, Danny Jacobs, Winfield Jacobs.

BATESVILLE: Milan 58–55 East Central; Batesville 54–45 Jac-Cen-Del; Milan 54–52 South Ripley; Batesville 54–45 Milan. Officials: Bruce Knecht, Jim Roberts, Kenneth Cave, Don Pope.

BEDFORD: Mitchell 66–53 Fayetteville; Bedford 78–41 Needmore; Tunnelton 86–62 Heltonville; Shawswick 72–61 Oolitic; Bedford 69–37 Mitchell; Tunnelton 54–39 Shawswick; Bedford 58–37 Tunnelton. Officials: Robert Laird, Ronald Ham, Dwain Laird, Delmus Aubrey.

BEN DAVIS: Ritter 75–59 School for the Deaf; Ben Davis 69–67 Speedway; Cathedral 68–67 Northwest; Washington 78–70 Scecina; Ben Davis 73–52 Ritter; Cathedral 74–71 Washington; Ben Davis 77–73 Cathedral. Officials: Mel Botkin, Herb Pruett, Gary Muncy, Gary Janeway.

Tourney Time

BENTON CENTRAL: Benton Central 80–78 Twin Lakes; North White 77–65 South Newton; Tri County 68–64 Frontier; North White 74–72 Benton Central; North White 52–45 Tri County. Officials: Ed Scott, Don Cranfield, Dan Landis, Wayne Targgart.

BLACKFORD: Eastbrook 78–76 Pennville (ot); Bryant 80–72 Portland; Albany 66–59 Redkey; Blackford 65–57 Dunkirk; Bryant 67–65 Eastbrook; Blackford 73–50 Albany; Blackford 73–52 Bryant. Officials: Don Snedeker, Don Thompson, Brandon Bryant, Ronald Flotow.

BLUFFTON: South Adams 60–59 Norwell; Bellmont 76–56 Adams Central; Southern Wells 81–78 Bluffton (2ot); Bellmont 82–66 South Adams; Bellmont 68–61 Southern Wells. Officials: Dan Alvarez, Larry Hollman, Dan Yagodnik, Don Roudebush.

BOONVILLE: Castle 78–52 Boonville; Cannelton 69–53 Tecumseh; Tell City 68–63 Heritage Hills; South Spencer 79–73 Castle; Tell City 50–40 Cannelton; Tell City 59–58 South Spencer. Officials: Leroy Schultheis, Richie Moore, Noel Baker, Steve Cherry.

BRAZIL: Van Buren 72–64 Staunton; Montezuma 55–46 Rosedale; Brazil 81–54 Rockville; Van Buren 66–54 Montezuma; Brazil 82–65 Van Buren. Officials: Ray Vescovi, Richard Hall, Pete Deakyne, Louis Schmalfeldt.

BROWNSBURG: Pittsboro 78–47 Monrovia; Mooresville 70–69 Brownsburg (2ot); Avon 76–40 Danville; Pittsboro 50–39 Plainfield; Avon 67–56 Mooresville; Pittsboro 70–69 Avon (2ot); Officials: Wayne Van Sickle, Richard Schleicher, Gary Eaglin, Delmar Knecht.

CALUMET: Crown Point 74–49 Hanover Central; Lake Central 55–53 Griffith; Munster 65–55 Highland; Calumet 62–60 Merrillville (ot); Lake Central 61–57 Crown Point (ot); Calumet 55–45 Munster; Calumet 67–55 Lake Central. Officials: Charles Sallee, Norris Boomershine, Tom Simler, Jon Gallipo.

CARMEL: Sheridan 75–51 Westfield; Hamilton Heights 63–62 Noblesville (ot); Carmel 70–65 Hamilton Southeastern; Hamilton Heights 47–45 Sheridan; Carmel 51–49 Hamilton Heights. Officials: Gene Butts, Rudy Tabereaux, Jerry Petro, Bill Laird.

COLUMBIA CITY: Northfield 67–61 Columbia City; Churubusco 66–65 North Manchester; Whitko 79–64 Northfield; Whitko 76–67 Churubusco. Officials: Officials: Don Koester, Mike Morlan, George Grygiel, Gayle Forrest.

COLUMBUS: North 44–37 East; Hauser 67–65 Brown County; Southwestern 59–52 Edinburgh; North 84–65 Hauser; North 72–58 Southwestern. Officials: Wendell Baker, Tom Pitts, Ralph Scales, Bill Wullner.

CONNERSVILLE: Connersville 97–50 Whitewater; Brookville 91–60 Laurel; Connersville 60–58 Union County; Connersville 63–50 Brookville. Officials: Richard Gebhart, Larry Freyburgher, William Van Sickle, Charles Roush.

DeKalb: DeKalb 101–47 Prairie Heights; Garrett 72–69 Eastside; Angola 75–72 Fremont; DeKalb 83–47 Hamilton; Angola 67–66 Garrett; DeKalb 71–50 Angola. Officials: Richard Vendrely, Tom Knox, Barry Gerig, Max Rink.

EAST CHICAGO: Roosevelt 79–56 River Forest; Washington 54–36 Hobart; Whiting 52–41 East Gary Edison; Washington 47–45 Roosevelt; Washington 60–49 Whiting. Officials: Joe Smelcer, Tom Meeks, George Dixon, Gene Gibson.

EAST NOBLE: West Noble 58–54 Central Noble; East Noble 75–50 Fairfield; Lakeland 69–57 Westview; East 54–50 West; East 73–62 Lakeland. Officials: George Avery, Tom VonDeylen, Robert Gilmore, Paul Leamon.

ELKHART: Elkhart Memorial 66–49 Northwood; Penn 71–55 Goshen; Northridge 64–55

Elkhart Central; Concord 86–62 Jimtown; Memorial 57–56 Penn; Northridge 71–47 Concord; Memorial 56–44 Northridge. Officials: Don Hollman, Gary Scheub, William DeRome, Jerry Scott.

EVANSVILLE: Memorial 61–60 Harrison; Mater Dei 54–46 North; Central 74–70 Reitz; Bosse 74–62 Memorial; Mater Dei 69–68 Central (ot); Bosse 58–50 Mater Dei. Officials: Norman Chestnut, Robert Kirk, Mason Meeks, Mel Redman.

FLOYD CENTRAL: North Harrison 54–53 Floyd Central; Eastern 83–65 Borden; Lanesville 69–62 Corydon; South Central 68–64 Salem (ot); Eastern (Pekin) 69–68 North Harrison; South Central 67–57 Lanesville; South Central 77–64 Eastern. Officials: Jimmy Dimitroff, John Ramey, Jerry Newsom, Wayne Jessup.

FORT WAYNE (#1): Concordia 70–65 Wayne; South Side 66–38 Heritage; North Side 51–39 Leo; Elmhurst 62–53 New Haven; South Side 81–79 Concordia; North Side 72–55 Elmhurst; South Side 69–68 North Side. Officials: Jack Mercer, Phillip Barth, Richard Boer, Peter Kokinda.

FORT WAYNE (#2): Woodlan 64–56 Homestead; Northrop 70–44 Harding; Carroll 56–44 Dwenger; Snider 62–46 Luers; Northrop 75–56 Woodlan; Carroll 61–58 Snider; Northrop 57–47 Carroll. Officials: Richard Cook, Mike Devault, Herbert Hicks, Phillip Hardwick.

FOUNTAIN CENTRAL: Attica 83–69 Turkey Run; Fountain Central 55–46 North Vermillion; Covington 79–70 Seeger; Fountain Central 72–69 Attica; Covington 76–70 Fountain Central. Officials: Earle Wolfe, Larry Maxwell, Kevin Weinberg, Nick Sweigart.

FRANKFORT: Frankfort 58–49 Tri Central; Carroll 84–81 Rossville (ot); Tipton 53–46 Clinton Prairie; Frankfort 56–53 Clinton Central; Carroll 77–74 Tipton (ot); Frankfort 72–70 Carroll. Officials: Tom Hoffman, Paul Cox, Mike Bohan, Lou Zabona.

FRANKLIN: Whiteland 79–73 Decatur Central; Center Grove 72–57 Indian Creek; Franklin 79–40 Greenwood; Center Grove 72–59 Whiteland; Franklin 59–54 Center Grove. Officials: Jerry Larrison, George Emery, Gary Stiles, McKee Munk.

GARY: Gary Roosevelt 52–50 Wallace; Emerson 81–59 Mann; West Side 58–57 Wirt; Roosevelt 66–46 Andrean; West Side 47–41 Emerson; West Side 59–45 Roosevelt. Officials: Gene Marks, Milt Cooper, Ken Miller, Reginald Cheatham.

GREENCASTLE: Cascade 48–47 Cloverdale; Greencastle 61–58 North Salem; South Putnam 78–73 North Putnam (2ot); Greencastle 71–59 Cascade; South Putnam 75–61 Greencastle. Officials: John Lozier, Bill Graham, Allen Youmans, Morris Cohen

GREENSBURG: Rushville 83–70 Waldron; Greensburg 71–66 North Decatur; Rushville 119–61 South Decatur; Rushville 82–72 Greensburg. Officials: Max Hensler, James O'Neal, Jerry Pieper, Glen Clemons.

HAMMOND: Hammond High 63–62 Clark; Morton 66–60 Tech; Noll 56–44 Gavit; Hammond High 75–55 Morton; Hammond High 68–67 Noll. Officials: Jim Cox, Billy Maroney, William Sorukas, Robert Reed.

HUNTINGTON: Southwood 66–64 Wabash; Huntington 78–39 Huntington Catholic; Southwood 78–77 White's; Huntington 77–67 Southwood. Officials: Harold Ashbrook, Merl Heckaman, Carl March, Jack Graham.

INDIANAPOLIS: Shortridge 84–57 Broad Ripple; North Central 83–56 Chatard; Tech 74–66 Lawrence Central; Arlington 83–67 Marshall; Shortridge 65–63 North Central; Arlington 85–82 Tech; Arlington 76–63 Shortridge. Officials: Jack Gardner, Ron Hosinski, Gary Coers, David Lowenstein.

Tourney Time

JEFFERSONVILLE: Clarksville Providence 83–53 Clarksville; Jeffersonville 65–54 New Albany; Jeffersonville 49–45 Providence. Officials: Troy Ingram, Terry Stewart, Ken Gorrell, Jack Cummings.

KANKAKEE VALLEY: Lowell 57–48 West Central; Kankakee Valley 83–58 Kouts; Rensselaer 60–59 North Newton; Hebron 72–45 Lowell; Kankakee Valley 68–67 Rensselaer; Hebron 52–42 Kankakee Valley. Officials: Eugene Carrabine, James Reinebold, Ron Kitts, John Wray.

KNOX: North Judson 64–54 Knox; Culver 70–51 LaCrosse; Oregon-Davis 64–61 Winamac (ot); North Judson 73–43 Culver; North Judson 82–71 Oregon-Davis. Officials: Homer Owens, Frank Hoagburg, Jerry Karstens, Herb Resler.

KOKOMO: Kokomo Haworth 63–57 Eastern; Western 60–44 Taylor; Kokomo 74–55 Northwestern; Haworth 78–66 Maconaquah; Kokomo 65–51 Western; Kokomo 59–56 Haworth. Officials: Tom Manning, Joe Edmonds, Paul Danko, Stan Dubis.

LAFAYETTE: West Lafayette 59–50 Delphi; Harrison 63–61 Central Catholic; Lafayette Jefferson 65–44 West Lafayette; Jefferson 74–53 Harrison. Officials: Don Hurst, Bud Wetzel, Keith Yoder, Bob Marcinek.

La VILLE: Plymouth 66–64 Argos; South Bend Jackson 62–43 North Liberty; La Ville 61–34 Bremen; Plymouth 64–56 Glenn; La Ville 65–53 Jackson; Plymouth 71–65 La Ville. Officials: Eric Harmon, Art Morris, Richard Bowie, Opal Courtney.

LAWRENCEBURG: Dillsboro 61–32 Moores Hill; Aurora 64–60 Switzerland Co.; Lawrenceburg 61–54 Rising Sun; Aurora 64–54 Dillsboro; Lawrenceburg 66–63 Aurora. Officials: William Hite, Roger McGriff, Robert Klein, Allen Voorhis.

LEBANON: Thorntown 80–59 Zionsville; Pike 82–50 Wells; Lebanon 76–42 Brebeuf; Pike 71–63 Thorntown; Lebanon 83–59 Pike. Officials: Don Schmidt, Robert Boyle, Rudy Stegelmann, Larry Jones.

LOGANSPORT: Logansport 57–55 Peru, Pioneer 80–43 Kewanna; North Miami 59–57 Cass (ot); Logansport 80–60 Caston; Pioneer 55–52 North Miami; Logansport 81–56 Pioneer. Officials: Ray Mitrione, John Fleischman, Paul Hackleman, Jerry Schalburg.

MADISON: Southwestern 93–58 Henryville; Charlestown 64–53 Madison; New Washington 96–95 Madison Shawe; Southwestern 73–60 Silver Creek; New Washington 87–80 Charlestown; Southwestern 70–62 New Washington. Officials: John Bush, Darrell Eaton, Armand Motz, Don Smith.

MARION: Mississinewa 61–60 Oak Hill; Madison-Grant 67–57 Marion Bennett; Marion 88–70 Elwood; Madison-Grant 60–47 Mississinewa; Marion 90–73 Madison-Grant. Officials: David Avery, Jack Tiede, Cliff Spears, Robert Beeson.

MARTINSVILLE: Owen Valley 63–43 Eminence; Martinsville 81–56 Edgewood; Bloomington North 68–48 Bloomington South; Martinsville 73–56 Owen Valley; Martinsville 61–60 Bloomington North. Officials: Darrell McFall, Jack Johnson, G. A. Ward, Richard Burrows.

MICHIGAN CITY ROGERS: Marquette 85–77 Westville; Rogers 73–55 South Central; LaPorte 80–52 New Prairie; Elston 96–39 Marquette; LaPorte 68–64 Rogers; Elston 65–57 LaPorte. Officials: Gordon McCain, James Benecke, Sr., Donald O'Connor, Gil Baumgartner.

MUNCIE: Wes-Del 67–54 Burris; Delta 50–37 Cowan; Northside 84–65 Southside; Central 54–42 Yorktown; Delta 73–59 Wes-Del; Northside 90–72 Central; Northside 90–60 Delta. Officials: John Ward, James Rider, Rex Mays, Roger DeYoung.

IHSAA Scores | 1970–1979

NEW CASTLE: New Castle 68–52 Tri; Shenandoah 92–58 Morton Memorial; Eastern Hancock 56–55 Mount Vernon; Blue River 67–64 Knightstown; New Castle 74–66 Shenandoah; Eastern Hancock 82–64 Blue River; Eastern Hancock 63–62 New Castle. Officials: Byron Weaver, Blake Ress, Joe Dickey, Harold Gray.

NORTH MONTGOMERY: North Montgomery 85–58 Southwestern; Wainwright 71–66 Southmont; North Montgomery 81–79 Crawfordsville; North Montgomery 98–81 Wainwright. Officials: James Wehsollek, Dale Van Houten, James Fairchild, Dick Modricker.

PAOLI: Springs Valley 81–60 Paoli; Leavenworth 78–68 West Washington; Marengo 67–61 English; Milltown 72–53 Orleans; Springs Valley 88–62 Leavenworth; Milltown 64–44 Marengo; Springs Valley 63–46 Milltown. Officials: John Manka, Temme Patterson, Ron McKibben, Charles Bertram.

PRINCETON: Mount Vernon 34–32 Owensville; Princeton 67–53 North Posey; Oakland City Wood 59–46 Haubstadt; Fort Branch 66–55 New Harmony; Princeton 71–60 Mount Vernon; Wood 48–45 Fort Branch; Princeton 57–55 Wood. Officials: Harry Inskeep, Bill Gray, Floyd Riggs, Dallas Richards.

RICHMOND: Richmond 105–28 Northeastern; Hagerstown 70–44 Cambridge City; Richmond 52–34 Centerville; Richmond 66–33 Hagerstown. Officials: George Taylor, Ronald Beard, Roger Pflughaupt, Warren Keyser.

SEYMOUR: Seymour 69–63 Scottsburg; Austin 81–48 Medora; Jennings County 74–51 Crothersville; Seymour 65–61 Brownstown Central; Jennings County 79–60 Austin; Seymour 69–58 Jennings County. Officials: Bill May, Tom Whitehead, Richard Crays, Jack Williams.

SHELBYVILLE: Shelbyville 46–40 New Palestine; Greenfield 80–57 Roncalli; Franklin Central 76–64 Morristown; Shelbyville 53–43 Triton Central; Franklin Central 68–65 Greenfield; Shelbyville 40–38 Franklin Central. Officials: Don Shields, Robert Carr, Steve Vannatter, Sid Ellis.

SOUTH BEND: Adams 80–61 LaSalle; Washington 83–57 Riley; Clay 81–61 Mishawaka Marian; Mishawaka 61–40 St. Joseph's; Adams 58–56 Washington; Mishawaka 71–57 Clay; Adams 61–57 Mishawaka. Officials: Marty Burdette, Richard Clark, George Dyer, Ward Weisel.

SOUTHPORT: Southport 89–65 Warren Central; Beech Grove 72–63 Crispus Attucks; Howe 63–60 Perry Meridian (ot); Manual 68–60 Wood; Beech Grove 83–81 Southport (3ot); Manual 78–55 Howe; Manual 64–63 Beech Grove. Officials: Lowell Smith, Raymond Norris, Bruce Mayfield, Richard Freeman.

SOUTHRIDGE: Jasper 80–54 Winslow; Southridge 63–60 Forest Park; Perry Central 53–49 Dubois; Jasper 81–64 Southridge; Jasper 73–49 Perry Central. Officials: Keith Combs, Fred Myers, Frank Hobson, David Mounts.

SULLIVAN: Clay City 83–58 Union (Dugger); Sullivan 88–51 North Central; Clay City 59–58 Shakamak; Clay City 74–44 Sullivan. Officials: William Fields, William Pittman, Harold Gibbs, Jim Ruby.

SWITZ CITY: Linton 65–61 L & M; Bloomfield 73–63 Eastern (Greene Co.); Switz City Central 69–57 Worthington; Linton-Stockton 70–68 Bloomfield; Linton-Stickton 84–82 Switz City Central (2ot). Officials: Don Shiflet, John Lyskowinski, Don Hubbard, Randy Westfall.

TERRE HAUTE: North 83–76 South; Clinton 63–57 Laboratory; West Vigo 65–59 Schulte; North 86–69 Clinton; North 105–71 West Vigo. Officials: Eugene Linn, Walt Overton, Larry Collins, John Hilligoss.

VALPARAISO: Valparaiso 48–42 Portage; Morgan Twp. 69–60 Washington Twp.; Chesterton

Tourney Time

44–39 Boone Grove; Valparaiso 80–44 Wheeler; Chesterton 73–53 Morgan Twp.; Valparaiso 64–59 Chesterton. Officials: Bob Justak, John Tucker, Jim Carey, John Gassensmith.

VINCENNES: Vincennes Rivet 44–38 South Knox; Vincennes 44–40 Petersburg; North Knox 65–59 Rivet; Vincennes 54–43 North Knox. Officials: Wayne Myers, Dennis Cave, David Willoughby, Don Ricketts.

WARSAW: Akron 61–52 Triton; Warsaw 77–53 Mentone; Rochester 75–74 Wawasee; Akron 55–53 Warsaw; Akron 91–89 Rochester (ot). Officials: Richard Lederman, Al Lindahl, Les Wright, Norman Hathcoat.

WASHINGTON: Washington 61–51 Barr–Reeve; Shoals 58–53 North Daviess; Loogootee 57–36 Otwell; Washington 59–56 Washington Catholic; Loogootee 72–37 Shoals; Loogootee 35–34 Washington. Officials: Robert Wolfe, James Helms, Paul Garriott, Harold Back.

WINCHESTER: Randolph Southern 87–66 Union City; Winchester 74–53 Wapahani; Union (Modoc) 72–66 Monroe Central; Winchester 88–83 Randolph Southern; Winchester 68–42 Union. Officials: Dick Hale, Bob Richardson, Tom Neuman, Richard Brainerd.

1974 REGIONALS

ANDERSON: Kokomo 67–63 Carmel; Anderson 68–47 Blackford; Anderson 78–66 Kokomo. Officials: Eugene Carrabine, Gerry Scheub, Darrell McFall, Nick Sweigart, Wayne Van Sickle, Jerry Scott.

COLUMBUS: Martinsville 66–62 Columbus North (ot); Franklin 78–41 Shelbyville; Franklin 69–66 Martinsville. Officials: Harry Inskeep, James Wehsollek, Don Roudebush, Phil Hardwick, Byron Weaver, Ray Vescovi.

CONNERSVILLE: Rushville 62–58 Lawrenceburg; Connersville 73–52 Batesville; Connersville 54–47 Rushville. Officials: Jim Rider, Dave Lowenstein, Don Smith, David Avery, Jimmy Dimitroff, Richard Gebhart.

ELKHART: Elkhart Memorial 82–60 Akron; Plymouth 77–68 Whitko; Memorial 61–56 Plymouth. Officials: John Manka, James Benecke, Norman Hathcoat, Max Hensler, Joe Smelcer, Eugene Linn.

EVANSVILLE: Evansville Bosse 59–51 Tell City; Princeton 63–51 Vincennes; Bosse 71–62 Princeton. Officials: Leroy Schultheis, Bruce Knecht, Dan Jacobs, Winfield Jacobs, Lowell Smith, Jack Gardner.

FORT WAYNE: DeKalb 67–60 East Noble (ot); Northrop 67–51 South Side; Northrop 63–44 DeKalb. Officials: George Taylor, Morris Cohen, Homer Owens, Tom Manning, Marion Acton, Roger DeYoung.

FRANKFORT: Lebanon 74–62 South Putnam; Frankfort 82–77 North Montgomery; Lebanon 68–54 Frankfort. Officials: Harold Gray, George Dixon, Ward Weisel, William Hite, Robert Laird, Richard Freeman.

GARY: Gary West Side 66–61 East Chicago Washington; Hammond High 86–66 Calumet; West Side 75–73 Hammond. Officials: Tom Meeks, Richard Cook, Robert Reed, Roger McGriff, John Ward, George Avery.

INDIANAPOLIS: Arlington 74–43 Pittsboro; Ben Davis 57–53 Manual; Arlington 70–65 Ben Davis. Officials: Robert Justak, Gil Baumgartner, Stan Dubis, Robert Marcinek, John Gallipo, Gordon McCain.

LAFAYETTE: Jefferson 72–50 Covington; Hebron 64–61 North White; Jefferson 81–50 Hebron. Officials: Richard Vendrely, Don Schmidt, Sid Ellis, Gene Butts, Don Hollman, Norman Chestnut.

MARION: Marion 69–65 Huntington North; Logansport 89–74 Bellmont; Logansport 85–67 Marion. Officials: Max Rink, Don Shields, Ron Hosinski, Ron Flotow, Bill May, Gene Marks.

NEW CASTLE: Richmond 71–63 Winchester; Muncie North 78–63 Eastern Hancock; Richmond 73–70 North (ot). Officials: Ed Scott, Jack Mercer, Don Koester, Dan Alvarez, Don Snedeker, Marty Burdette.

SEYMOUR: Seymour 102–62 South Central; Jeffersonville 68–56 Southwestern (Hanover); Jeffersonville 73–63 Seymour. Officials: Steve Cherry, Jack Cummings, Melvin Botkin, Melvin Redman, Keith Combs, Jerry Larrison.

SOUTH BEND: South Bend Adams 75–56 Michigan City Elston; Valparaiso 55–54 North Judson; Valparaiso 71–63 Adams. Officials: James Cox, Ray Mitrione, Tom Hoffman, Eugene Gibson, Don Hurst, Troy Ingram.

TERRE HAUTE: Clay City 71–45 Linton–Stockton; Terre Haute North 89–52 Brazil; Clay City 64–59 North, Officials: Wayne Jessup, Dallas Richards, William Laird, Gary Muncy, Earle Wolfe, Don Shiflet.

WASHINGTON: Springs Valley 60–58 Jasper; Bedford 49–43 Loogootee; Bedford 58–55 Springs Valley. Officials: Wendell Baker, Lou Schmalfeldt; John Bush, Allen Voorhis, Charles Sallee, John Lozier.

1974 SEMI—STATES

EVANSVILLE: Bosse 56–54 Bedford; Jeffersonville 52–46 Clay City; Jeffersonville 63–51 Bosse. Officials: Robert Laird, Troy Ingram, Wayne Van Sickle, John Bush, Darrell McFall, Charles Sallee.

FORT WAYNE: Anderson 66–56 Elkhart Memorial; Fort Wayne Northrop 55–53 Logansport; Fort Wayne Northrop 67–53 Anderson. Officials: Byron Weaver, Gene Butts, Lowell Smith, Richard Freeman, John Ward, Don Shiflet.

INDIANAPOLIS: Franklin 68–62 Indianapolis Arlington; Richmond 65–54 Connersville; Franklin 60–59 Richmond. Officials: Marion Acton, Joe Smelcer, John Gallipo, Gordon McCain, Gene Marks, Gary Muncy.

LAFAYETTE: Lafayette Jefferson 67–62 Gary West Side; Valparaiso 68–63 Lebanon; Lafayette 72–62 Valparaiso. Officials: Marty Burdette, George Avery, Richard Gebhart, Norman Chestnut, Bill May, Jimmy Dimitroff.

1974 FINALS—March 23

BLOOMINGTON (Indiana University): Jeffersonville 63–52 Franklin; Fort Wayne Northrop 63–49 Lafayette Jefferson; Northrop 59–56 Jeffersonville. Officials: Bill May (his last game), Gary Muncy, Jimmy Dimitroff, Don Shiflet, Marion Acton, John Ward.

Tourney Time

1975 SECTIONALS

ANDERSON: Alexandria 65–64 Pendleton Heights; Lapel 61–48 Frankton; Madison Heights 100–45 Daleville; Anderson 60–35 Highland; Alexandria 64–52 Lapel; Madison Heights 70–69 Anderson; Madison Heights 68–54 Alexandria. Officials: Marty Burdette, Robert Beeson, Larry Maxwell, James Benecke, Sr.

BEDFORD–NORTH LAWRENCE: Bedford–North Lawrence 75–59 Eastern (Greene Co.); Mitchell 47–46 Orleans; Bedford-North Lawrence 45–42 Mitchell. Officials: John Bush, Paul Hackleman, Ron McKibban, Don Roudebush.

BEN DAVIS: Speedway 74–52 Scecina; Ben Davis 76–65 Cathedral; Washington 59–37 School for the Deaf; Northwest 96–60 Ritter; Ben Davis 72–65 Speedway; Washington 64–58 Northwest; Washington 69–54 Ben Davis. Officials: Tom Knox, Jerry Baker, Ken Miller, Jerry Karstens.

BENTON CENTRAL: Tri–County 79–66 South Newton; Frontier 31–27 North White (ot); Benton Central 60–51 Twin Lakes; Tri–County 65–58 Frontier; Tri–County 72–56 Benton Central. Officials: Dave Avery, Richard Hall, Vic Gilla, James Wehsollek.

BLACKFORD: Bryant 56–38 Redkey; Eastbrook 86–63 Pennville; Blackford 67–62 Portland; Dunkirk 63–57 Bryant (ot); Blackford 72–67 Eastbrook; Blackford 90–55 Dunkirk. Officials: Richard Gebhart, Tom Simler, Gary Foltz, Harold Ashbrook.

BOONVILLE: Tell City 42–26 Cannelton; Heritage Hills 61–56 Castle; Boonville 76–64 Tecumseh; Tell City 68–63 South Spencer (3ot); Boonville 75–57 Heritage Hills; Tell City 67–42 Boonville. Officials: Jerry Larrison, Bob Richardson, Tad Heminger, Wayne Jessup.

BRAZIL: Brazil 68–43 Rosedale; Staunton 57–48 Rockville; Van Buren 62–46 Montezuma; Staunton 68–61 Brazil; Staunton 60–59 Van Buren. Officials: Officials: Robert Laird, G. A. Ward, Al Youmans, Harry Inskeep.

BROWNSBURG: Pittsboro 47–46 Danville; Plainfield 100–45 Monrovia; Avon 69–51 Brownsburg; Pittsboro 73–59 Mooresville; Avon 45–43 Plainfield; Pittsboro 72–56 Avon. Officials: Homer Owens, McKee Munk, William Hite, Jack Cummings.

CALUMET: Lake Central 59–57 Crown Point; Griffith 74–53 Munster; Merrillville 78–75 Highland; Lake Central 51–48 Calumet; Merrillville 70–62 Griffith; Merrillville 29–22 Lake Central. Officials: John Lozier, Pete Deakyne, Charles Weinkauf, Robert Wolfe.

CARMEL: Carmel 63–47 Noblesville; Hamilton Heights 78–62 Westfield; Sheridan 43–36 Hamilton Southeastern; Hamilton Heights 87–59 Carmel; Hamilton Heights 62–56 Sheridan. Officials: Don Shiflet, George Grygiel, Ken Keller, Don Koester.

COLUMBIA CITY: Manchester 55–47 Churubusco; Columbia City 74–56 Whit–ko; Manchester 79–59 Northfield; Columbia City 80–56 Manchester. Officials: Richard Freeman, Richard Bowie, Frank DeSantis, Tom Hoffman.

COLUMBUS: Brown County 67–60 Southwestern; Columbus North 59–40 Columbus East; Hauser 70–47 Edinburg; North 72–66 Brown County; North 84–50 Hauser. Officials: Gordon McCain, Richard Burrows, Richard Schleicher, Don Shields.

CONNERSVILLE: Laurel 112–71 Cambridge City; Union County 47–46 Connersville; Brookville 88–61 Laurel; Brookville 60–59 Union County. Officials: Dave Lowenstein, Dale Van Houten, Jim Roberts, Norman Hathcoat.

DEKALB: DeKalb 86–58 Hamilton; Eastside 61–54 Prairie Heights; Garrett 54–47 Fremont; Leo 59–58 Angola; DeKalb 60–54 Eastside (ot); Leo 76–65 Garrett; Leo 61–47 DeKalb. Officials:

John Gassensmith, Jerry Pieper, Mike DeVault, Kevin Weinberg.

EAST CENTRAL: Milan 84–66 South Ripley; East Central 86–47 Jac-Cen-Del; Batesville 69–55 Milan; East Central 74–64 Batesville. Officials: Phil Barth, Allen Voorhis, Tom Dull, Tom Meeks.

EAST CHICAGO: Washington 55–43 East Gary Edison; Roosevelt 79–75 River Forest; Hobart 62–46 Whiting; Washington 75–48 Roosevelt; Washington 78–39 Hobart. Officials: Jack Mercer, Tom Neuman, Jon Custer, Phil Hardwick.

EAST NOBLE: West Noble 95–54 Howe Military; Westview 87–47 Bethany Christian; Central Noble 80–63 Fairfield; East Noble 59–52 Lakeland; Westview 71–65 West Noble; East Noble 95–65 Central Noble; East Noble 73–52 Westview. Officials: Ron Hosinski, Ron Kitts, Gayle Forrest, Delmar Knecht.

ELKHART: Northridge 40–33 Jimtown; Elkhart Memorial 70–55 Northwood; Goshen 85–72 Concord; Penn 66–49 Elkhart Central; Northridge 65–62 Memorial; Goshen 60–44 Penn; Northridge 62–56 Goshen. Officials: Tom Manning, Dick Hale, Steve Beres, Reginald Cheatham.

EVANSVILLE: Bosse 71–61 Reitz; Central 65–42 Harrison; Memorial 50–44 North; Bosse 53–39 Mater Dei; Central 44–39 Memorial (ot); Bosse 64–59 Central. Officials: Lowell Smith, Jack Johnson, Don Nester, Milton Cooper.

FLOYD CENTRAL: North Harrison 73–58 Borden; Floyd Central 101–74 Eastern (Pekin); Corydon 71–64 South Central; North Harrison 66–59 Lanesville; Floyd Central 93–69 Corydon; Floyd Central 75–63 North Harrison. Officials: Bruce Knecht, Dwain Laird, Dennie Oxley, Ken Gorrell.

FORT WAYNE (#1): New Haven 77–69 Northrop; North Side 75–51 Woodlan; Carroll 79–59 Concordia; Snider 69–60 New Haven; North Side 91–68 Carroll; North Side 61–58 Snider. Officials: Marion Acton, Mason Meeks, Gren Lefebvre, Eugene Carrabine.

FORT WAYNE (#2): Harding 64–59 Luers; South Side 67–55 Wayne; Homestead 68–67 Elmhurst (ot); Harding 60–48 Dwenger; South Side 53–52 Homestead; South Side 63–58 Harding. Officials: Troy Ingram, Larry Freyburgher, Michael Crouch, Paul Cox.

FOUNTAIN CENTRAL: Seeger 70–59 Covington; Attica 88–68 North Vermillion; Turkey Run 79–58 Fountain Central; Attica 71–69 Seeger; Turkey Run 79–67 Attica. Officials: George Avery, Herbert Hicks, Al Lindahl, Richard Lederman.

FRANKFORT: Rossville 72–50 Tipton; Tri Central 73–71 Clinton Central; Frankfort 91–67 Carroll (Carroll Co.); Rossville 87–66 Clinton Prairie; Frankfort 93–75 Tri Central; Rossville 72–67 Frankfort. Officials: Joe Smelcer, Mark Baltz, Robert DeBroka, George Taylor.

GARY: Mann 70–53 Wirt; West Side 67–54 Gary Roosevelt; Emerson 67–60 Andrean; Wallace 53–42 Mann; Emerson 78–62 West Side; Emerson 93–54 Wallace. Officials: Gil Baumgartner, Brandon Bryant, John Fleischman, Donald Schmidt.

GREENCASTLE: North Putnam 71–50 South Putnam; Cloverdale 65–45 North Salem; Greencastle 67–40 Cascade; North Putnam 79–48 Cloverdale; North Putnam 74–60 Greencastle. Officials: Byron Weaver, Charles Roush, Carl Redman, Robert Kirk.

GREENSBURG: Rushville 89–53 South Decatur; Greensburg 61–60 Waldron; Rushville 91–60 North Decatur; Rushville 69–58 Greensburg. Officials: William Fields, Don Cranfield, Charles Hadley, Richard Clark.

GREENWOOD: Indian Creek 66–61 Decatur Central; Whiteland 75–71 Greenwood; Center Grove 59–49 Franklin; Whiteland 66–65 Indian Creek (ot); Center Grove 60–56 Whiteland.

Tourney Time

Officials: Bill Wullner, James Fairchild, William Johnston, Ray Norris.

HAMMOND: Tech 67–60 Gavit; Morton 61–55 Noll (ot); Hammond High 60–36 Clark; Tech 63–59 Morton; Hammond High 79–74 Tech. Officials: Darrell McFall, Joe Edmonds, Jesse Lynch, James Reinebold.

HUNTINGTON: Huntington North 82–33 White's; Wabash 64–62 Huntington Catholic; North 78–48 Southwood; North 59–55 Wabash. Officials: Norris Boomershine, Dan O'Connor, Bill Graham, Larry Jones.

INDIANAPOLIS: Lawrence Central 74–53 Marshall; Tech 51–49 Broad Ripple; North Central 72–62 Shortridge; Arlington 62–46 Chatard; Tech 50–47 Lawrence Central; North Central 70–62 Arlington; North Central 60–57 Tech. Officials: Roger DeYoung, Opal Courtney, Ralph Scales, Jon Gallipo.

JEFFERSONVILLE: Clarksville 67–65 Jeffersonville; New Albany 56–46 Providence; New Albany 60–50 Clarksville. Officials: Wayne Van Sickle, Herb Pruett, Steve White, Ray Mitrione.

KANKAKEE VALLEY: Rensselaer 60–53 North Newton; Hanover Central 70–51 Kouts; Hebron 70–60 Lowell; Kankakee Valley 64–55 West Central; Rensselaer 59–52 Hanover Central; Kankakee Valley 79–65 Hebron; Kankakee Valley 72–62 Rensselaer. Officials: Jimmy Dimitroff, Richard Brainerd, Robert Keys, Bob Marcinek.

KOKOMO: Maconaquah 55–51 Eastern; Haworth 61–56 Taylor; Kokomo 76–53 Western; Northwestern 63–39 Maconaquah; Kokomo 93–62 Haworth; Kokomo 68–56 Northwestern. Officials: Richard Cook, George Dixon, Tom Herbert, Gerry Scheub.

LAFAYETTE: West Lafayette 59–50 Harrison; Lafayette Jefferson 89–56 Central Catholic; West Lafayette 59–37 Delphi; Jefferson 57–46 West Lafayette. Officials: Norman Chestnut, Richie Moore, Larry Hollman, Paul Leamon.

LAVILLE: South Bend Jackson 54–50 Bremen; Argos 58–55 La Ville; Glenn 77–61 North Liberty; Plymouth 44–42 Jackson (2ot); Glenn 81–75 Argos (2ot); Plymouth 55–52 Glenn. Officials: John Ward, Richard Modricker, William Van Sickle, Dan Alvarez.

LAWRENCEBURG: Aurora 66–55 Lawrenceburg; Rising Sun 89–63 Dillsboro; Switzerland County 62–56 Moores Hill; Aurora 63–61 Rising Sun; Switzerland County 50–47 Aurora (ot). Officials: Morris Cohen, John Wray Jr., John Ramey, Lou Schmalfeldt.

LEBANON: Pike 64–45 Brebeuf; Zionsville 78–67 Western Boone; Lebanon 97–48 Pike; Lebanon 91–54 Zionsville.Officials: Bill Laird, Tom Pitts, Harold Back, Robert Gilmore.

LOGANSPORT: Logansport 70–60 Caston; Pioneer 53–39 Cass; Peru 76–37 Kewanna; Logansport 78–63 North Miami; Peru 59–58 Pioneer; Peru 63–56 Logansport. Officials: Robert Justak, John Tucker, Jerry Newsom, Jerry Petro.

MADISON: Madison 58–54 Silver Creek; New Washington 66–64 Southwestern; Charlestown 73–57 Henryville; Madison 87–64 Madison Shawe; Charlestown 55–44 New Washington; Charlestown 70–56 Madison. Officials: Raymond Vescovi, Bill Pittman, Kenneth Cave, Mel Redman.

MARION: Marion 72–50 Mississinewa; Oak Hill 56–55 Madison-Grant; Elwood 64–48 Marion Bennett; Marion 48–46 Oak Hill; Marion 76–57 Elwood. Officials: Gene Gibson, Ronald Flotow, Roger Pflughaupt, Richard Vendrely.

MARTINSVILLE: Bloomington North 70–55 Bloomington South; Edgewood 60–55 Owen Valley; Martinsville 87–53 Eminence; Bloomington North 61–60 Edgewood; Martinsville 72–62 Bloomington North. Officials: Dallas Richards, Glen Clemons, John Lyskowinski, Wayne Myers.

IHSAA Scores / 1970–1979

MICHIGAN CITY: Elston 61–57 Rogers; Westville 62–59 Marquette; South Central 71–59 New Prairie; Elston 25–18 LaPorte (ot); South Central 60–56 Westville; Elston 70–45 South Central. Officials: Max Hensler, Bill DeRome, Ward Weisel, Frank Hoagburg.

MUNCIE: Yorktown 95–71 Cowan; Delta 67–64 Muncie Southside; Wes-Del 66–47 Muncie Burris; Muncie Northside 61–39 Muncie Central; Delta 43–40 Yorktown; Northside 88–73 Wes-Del; Northside 65–41 Delta. Officials: Gene Butts, Gary Coers, Terry Stewart, Don Snedeker.

NEW CASTLE: Knightstown 68–50 Blue River; Mount Vernon 59–40 Morton Memorial; Tri 64–47 Shenandoah; New Castle 68–47 Eastern Hancock; Mount Vernon 52–40 Knightstown; Tri 62–61 New Castle; Mount Vernon 68–56 Tri. Officials: Don Hollman, Robert Boyle, Gary Janeway, Max Rink.

NORTH JUDSON: Winamac 70–51 Oregon-Davis; Culver Military 86–43 Divine Heart Seminary; North Judson 73–36 LaCrosse; Culver 63–58 Knox; Culver 53–52 Winamac; North Judson 81–31 Culver; North Judson 79–52 Culver Military. Officials: Jack Gardner, Paul Danko, Les Wright, Jerry Scott.

NORTH MONTGOMERY: Crawfordsville 66–56 Southmont; North Montgomery 78–43 Southwestern; Crawfordsville 65–64 Wainwright; North Montgomery 75–73 Crawfordsville. Officials: Eric Harmon, Robert Klein, David Willoughby, Stan Dubis.

PAOLI: West Washington 91–86 Marengo; Springs Valley 81–68 Salem; English 74–69 Leavenworth; Milltown 60–43 Paoli; Springs Valley 65–48 West Washington; Milltown 66–58 English; Springs Valley 66–57 Milltown. Officials: Keith Combs, Bruce Mayfield, Darrell Eaton, Paul Garriott.

PRINCETON: Gibson Southern 54–52 Princeton; North Posey 76–64 Mt. Vernon; Oakland City Wood 63–38 New Harmony; Gibson Southern 75–67 North Posey; Gibson Southern 57–52 Wood. Officials: Don Hurst, Sid Ellis, Delmus Aubrey, Cliff Spears.

RICHMOND: Richmond 84–64 Randolph Southern; Hagerstown 47–42 Northeastern; Richmond 52–43 Centerville; Richmond 74–34 Hagerstown. Officials: Mel Botkin, Rex Mays, Judson Raver, Wayne Targgart.

SEYMOUR: Seymour 73–46 Scottsburg; Austin 92–47 Medora; Jennings County 67–64 Brownstown Central; Seymour 77–45 Crothersville; Jennings County 72–55 Austin; Seymour 74–60 Jennings County. Officials: Ron Beard, James Helms, Temme Patterson, Frank Hobson.

SHELBYVILLE: Greenfield Central 59–54 Triton Central; Franklin Central 61–46 Roncalli; New Palestine 72–67 Shelbyville; Franklin Central 70–51 Greenfield Central; Franklin Central 80–47 New Palestine. Officials: Ed Scott, Bud Wetzel, Dave Atwell, Gary Eaglin.

SOUTH ADAMS: Norwell 70–62 Bluffton; South Adams 76–62 Heritage; Southern Wells 75–63 Bellmont; Norwell 80–59 Adams Central; Southern Wells 68–65 South Adams; Norwell 61–60 Southern Wells. Officials: Billy Maroney, William Sorukas, Keith Yoder, Jack Graham.

SOUTH BEND: Adams 77–45 Clay; Washington 39–36 LaSalle; St. Joseph's 58–53 Riley; Mishawaka 76–40 Mishawaka Marian; Adams 66–62 Washington; Mishawaka 54–52 St. Joseph's; Mishawaka 75–63 Adams. Officials: Harold Gray, Richard Boer, John Elliott, Nick Sweigart.

SOUTHPORT: Wood 67–61 Manual; Howe 69–58 Crispus Attucks; Beech Grove 75–73 Warren Central (ot); Perry Meridian 68–59 Southport; Wood 66–55 Howe; Perry Meridian 70–69 Beech Grove; Wood 72–70 Perry Meridian. Officials: Gene Linn, Robert Carr, George Dyer, Jim Cox.

SOUTHRIDGE: Forest Park 68–51 Dubois; Jasper 71–50 Perry Central; Forest Park 81–72

Southridge; Jasper 75–74 Forest Park (3ot). Officials: John Hilligoss, Larry Collins, Russ Ferrill, Don Ricketts.

SULLIVAN: Union (Dugger) 48–47 Shakamak; Clay City 62–61 North Central; Sullivan 85–50 Union; Clay City 58–55 Sullivan (ot). Officials: Jack Williams, Dennis Cave, Floyd Riggs, Ronald Ham.

SWITZ CITY CENTRAL: Bloomfield 48–34 Worthington; Linton 82–44 L & M; Bloomfield 74–60 Central; Linton 48–30 Bloomfield. Officials: Mike Bohan, Noel Baker, Dan Landis, Charles Bertram.

TERRE HAUTE: South 65–64 Schulte; West Vigo 92–67 Terre Haute State; North 70–43 Clinton; West Vigo 70–67 South; North 90–57 West Vigo. Officials: Winfield Jacobs, Randy Westfall, James Dunlap, Danny Jacobs.

TRITON: Rochester 63–30 Wawasee Prep; Warsaw 67–61 Wawasee; Tippecanoe Valley 67–65 Triton (2ot); Rochester 64–54 Warsaw; Rochester 66–53 Tippecanoe Valley. Officials: Wendell Baker, Dan Yagodnik, Art Morris, Bill Gray.

VALPARAISO: Portage 71–64 Morgan Twp.; Chesterton 87–62 Washington Twp.; Boone Grove 72–50 Wheeler; Valparaiso 64–56 Portage; Chesterton 72–68 Boone Grove; Valparaiso 57–40 Chesterton. Officials: Gene Marks, Barry Gerig, Dale Blosser, Merl Heckaman.

VINCENNES: North Knox 66–55 Vincennes Rivet; Vincennes 42–32 South Knox; Vincennes 43–20 North Knox. Officials: John Manka, Tom Whitehead, Armand Motz, Jr., Paul Grimes.

WASHINGTON: Washington 70–54 North Daviess; Loogootee 62–44 Barr-Reeve; Pike Central 76–59 Washington Catholic; Washington 62–57 Shoals; Loogootee 79–55 Pike Central; Loogootee 45–39 Washington. Officials: Officials: Jim Rider, Ric Baldwin, Jimmie Westerfield, Steve Cherry.

WINCHESTER: Union City 77–59 Union; Monroe Central 62–58 Wapahani (ot); Winchester 66–45 Union City; Winchester 77–47 Monroe Central. Officials: Robert Reed, Lou Zabona, Mark Masariu, Carl March.

1975 REGIONALS

ANDERSON: Madison Heights 71–69 Kokomo; Blackford 84–74 Hamilton Heights; Madison Heights 82–68 Blackford. Officials: James Reinebold, Max Rink, Winfield Jacobs, Carl March, Jerry Larrison, Don Hurst.

COLUMBUS: Columbus North 61–55 Martinsville; Center Grove 66–51 Franklin Central; Columbus North 55–48 Center Grove. Officials: Ron Beard, Jerry Karstens, Dan Alvarez, Gil Baumgartner, Gordon McCain, George Avery.

CONNERSVILLE: East Central 79–55 Switzerland County; Rushville 92–75 Brookville; Rushville 65–60 East Central. Officials: Bob Laird, Norris Boomershine, Jack Gardner, Don Shields, Wendell Baker, Darrell McFall.

ELKHART: Plymouth 71–68 Northridge (3ot); Columbia City 57–55 Rochester; Columbia City 71–62 Plymouth. Officials: Ron Beard, Jerry Karstens, Dan Alvarez, Gil Baumgartner, Gordon McCain, George Avery.

EVANSVILLE: Gibson Southern 47–34 Vincennes; Tell City 77–65 Bosse; Gibson Southern 64–51 Tell City. Officials: Jim Rider, Ken Gorrell, Tom Meeks, Jerry Petro, Phil Hardwick, John Lozier.

FORT WAYNE: North Side 68–39 Leo; East Noble 65–51 South Side; North Side 56–36 East Noble. Officials: Gerry Scheub, Reginald Cheatham, Richard Freeman, Kenneth Miller, Marty Burdette, Jack Mercer.

FRANKFORT: Rossville 55–48 North Montgomery; Lebanon 74–49 North Putnam; Lebanon 57–45 Rossville. Officials: Mel Redman, Milton Cooper, Donald Shiflet, Ronald Ham, Gene Marks, Roger DeYoung.

GARY: Emerson 78–68 Merrillville; Hammond High 76–72 East Chicago Washington; Emerson 72–71 Hammond. Officials: Steve Cherry, Eric Harmon, Jon Gallipo, Billy Maroney, Jimmy Dimitroff, Troy Ingram.

INDIANAPOLIS: Washington 75–74 Wood; North Central 86–59 Pittsboro; Washington 60–55 North Central. Officials: Don Schmidt, Frank Hoagburg, Don Snedeker, Bill Wullner, Marion Acton, Lowell Smith.

LAFAYETTE: Turkey Run 92–75 Kankakee Valley; Lafayette Jefferson 76–42 Tri County; Lafayette 104–59 Turkey Run. Officials: Bill Laird, William Fields, Richard Cook, Dallas Richards, Keith Combs, John Bush.

MARION: Marion 66–44 Norwell; Huntington 65–64 Peru; Marion 73–54 Huntington. Officials: Robert Reed, Tom Knox, Eugene Carrabine, Nick Sweigart, Joe Smelcer, Don Koester.

NEW CASTLE: Muncie North 73–62 Winchester; Richmond 65–54 Mount Vernon; Muncie North 68–62 Richmond. Officials: Stan Dubis, Opal Courtney, Bruce Knecht, Richard Boer, Danny Jacobs, James Benecke, Sr.

SEYMOUR: Floyd Central 70–58 Charlestown; Seymour 66–58 New Albany; Seymour 88–76 Floyd Central. Officials: Max Hensler, Robert Beeson, Harold Gray, Harold Ashbrook, Dave Avery, Richard Gebhart.

SOUTH BEND: Mishawaka 64–52 North Judson; Michigan City Elston 66–55 Valparaiso; Elston 71–67 Mishawaka (2ot). Officials: Merl Heckaman, Jim Wehsollek, Don Hollman, Art Morris, Homer Owens, Gene Butts.

TERRE HAUTE: Terre Haute North 87–66 Staunton; Clay City 55–51 Linton-Stockton; North 58–49 Clay City. Officials: Jerry Scott, Jack Williams, Raymond Vescovi, Cliff Spears, Eugene Linn, Morris Cohen.

WASHINGTON: Jasper 65–57 Bedford-North Lawrence; Loogootee 60–46 Springs Valley; Loogootee 56–48 Jasper. Officials: Gene Gibson, Ralph Scales, Ray Mitrione, Delmar Knecht, Wayne Van Sickle, Byron Weaver.

1975 SEMI—STATES

INDIANAPOLIS: Columbus North 52–48 Indianapolis Washington (ot); Rushville 68–60 Muncie North; North 62–43 Rushville. Officials: Don Hurst, Gene Butts, Richard Gebhart, Don Shiflet, Gene Marks, Joe Smelcer.

EVANSVILLE: Loogootee 58–53 Terre Haute North; Seymour 64–56 Gibson Southern; Loogootee 62–47 Seymour. Officials: Jon Gallipo, Dave Avery, Eugene Linn, Byron Weaver, John Ward, Marty Burdette.

FORT WAYNE: North Side 72–68 Madison Heights; Marion 72–49 Columbia City; Marion 82–61 North Side. Officials: Roger DeYoung, Gordon McCain, Don Koester, Darrell McFall, Jimmy Dimitroff, George Avery.

Tourney Time

LAFAYETTE: Lebanon 59–56 Michigan City Elston; Lafayette Jefferson 61–59 Gary Emerson; Lebanon 59–50 Jefferson. Officials: Keith Combs, Troy Ingram, Danny Jacobs, Wayne Van Sickle, Marion Acton, Lowell Smith.

1975 FINALS—March 22
INDIANAPOLIS (Market Square Arena): Marion 73–65 Lebanon; Loogootee 50–27 Columbus North; Marion 58–46 Loogootee. Officials: Jimmy Dimitroff, Wayne Van Sickle, Marion Acton, Marty Burdette, Gene Marks, Joe Smelcer.

1976 SECTIONALS
ANDERSON: Lapel 58–55 Frankton; Madison Heights 69–54 Daleville; Highland 46–40 Alexandria; Anderson 78–76 Pendleton Heights (2ot); Madison Heights 64–43 Lapel; Highland 58–55 Anderson; Highland 72–44 Madison Heights. Officials: Darrell McFall, Paul Leamon, Robert Boyle, Frank Hoagburg.

BATESVILLE: Milan 69–48 Moores Hill; Batesville 45–44 Jac-Cen-Del; Milan 70–68 South Ripley; Batesville 69–58 Milan. Officials: James Rider, Richard Clark, Bud Wetzel, Ralph Scales.

BEDFORD–NORTH LAWRENCE: Orleans 82–55 Medora; Bedford-North Lawrence 66–55 Mitchell; Bedford-North Lawrence 58–49 Orleans. Officials: Norman Chestnut, Carl Redman, Jack Behme, Donald Rickett.

BEN DAVIS: Washington 69–67 Speedway; Scecina 60–57 Ben Davis; Northwest 73–60 Decatur Central; Pike 106–77 Cathedral; Washington 63–61 Scecina; Northwest 73–66 Pike; Northwest 73–61 Washington. Officials: Wayne Van Sickle, Raymond Norris, Mark Reyher, Steve Cherry.

BENTON CENTRAL: Frontier 85–59 South Newton; Benton Central 88–45 Twin Lakes; Tri County 38–30 North White; Frontier 54–49 Benton Central; Frontier 51–46 Tri County. Officials: Harold Gray, Dick Modricker, Craig Martin, Gene Gibson.

BLACKFORD: Blackford 67–59 Wes-Del; Delta 63–52 Eastbrook; Blackford 66–64 Delta. Officials: Bruce Knecht, Al Lindahl, Thomas Von Deylen, Delmar Knecht.

BOONVILLE: Boonville 52–45 Castle; Tell City 66–58 Heritage Hills; Tecumseh 71–59 Cannelton; Boonville 68–67 South Soencer; Tell City 50–48 Tecumseh; Boonville 57–46 Tell City. Officials: Wayne Myers, Temme Patterson, Randy Westfall, John Tucker.

BRAZIL: Rosedale 78–69 Van Buren; Brazil 78–66 Staunton; Montezuma 58–55 Rockville; Brazil 82–51 Rosedale; Brazil 84–46 Montezuma. Officials: Don Shiflet, Jack Johnson, John Evans, William Fields.

BROWNSBURG: Brownsburg 76–62 Avon; Mooresville 96–62 Danville; Plainfield 84–57 Monrovia; Mooresville 68–61 Brownsburg; Plainfield 60–59 Mooresville. Officials: Ed Scott, Wayne Jessup, Thomas Newlin, Jerry Baker.

CALUMET: Munster 64–51 Merrillville; Griffith 68–62 Calumet; Highland 72–47 Lake Central; Munster 69–67 Crown Point; Highland 57–54 Griffith; Munster 64–59 Highland. Officials: Robert Reed, Larry Jones, Michael DeVault, James Reinebold.

CARMEL: Sheridan 50–37 Hamilton Southeastern; Carmel 59–53 Westfield; Noblesville 70–48 Hamilton Heights; Carmel 66–40 Sheridan; Carmel 44–42 Noblesville. Officials: Eugene

IHSAA Scores | 1970–1979

Linn, Gren Lefebvre, Dale Van Houten, Billy Maroney.

COLUMBIA CITY: Whitko 73–59 Columbia City; Manchester 74–65 Central Noble; Whitko 63–44 Churubusco; Whitko 60–57 Manchester. Officials: James Cox, George Dyer, William Van Sickle, Stan Dubis.

COLUMBUS: Brown County 62–57 Southwestern; Hauser 75–49 Edinburg; Columbus East 77–66 Columbus North; Brown County 77–63 Hauser; Brown County 101–97 East. Officials: Don Snedeker, Bill Graham, Dennie Oxley, George Taylor.

CONNERSVILLE: Connersville 67–58 Cambridge City; Union County 89–77 Laurel; Brookville 84–38 Morton Memorial; Union County 54–48 Connersville; Union County 62–60 Brookville. OfficialsL Jerry Petro, Allen Youmans, Herb Pruett, Bob Carr.

DEKALB: DeKalb 67–45 Prairie Heights; Garrett 68–54 Fremont; Hamilton 49–41 Eastside; Leo 64–47 Angola; DeKalb 59–57 Garrett; Leo 74–55 Hamilton; Leo 55–54 DeKalb (ot). Officials: Gene Butts, Tom Neuman, Thomas Dull, James Benecke.

EAST CENTRAL: Aurora 58–57 Switzerland County; Rising Sun 108–70 Lawrenceburg; Dillsboro 68–61 East Central; Aurora 78–64 Rising Sun; Aurora 83–67 Dillsboro. Officials: Jerry Larrison, Glen Clemons, Rudy Williams, John Manka.

EAST CHICAGO: East Gary Edison 61–48 River Forest; Washington 89–54 Whiting; Roosevelt 42–36 Hammond Noll; Washington 61–41 East Gary Edison; Washington 59–48 Roosevelt. Officials: Richard Cook, William Sorukas, Frank Desantis, John Gassensmith.

EAST NOBLE: Bethany Christian 74–49 Howe Military; East Noble 73–57 West Noble; Westview 78–53 Lakeland; Fairfield 66–60 Bethany Christian (ot); Westview 86–76 East Noble; Westview 78–71 Fairfield. Officials: Rex Mays, Judson Raver, Dale Blosser, Roger Pflughaupt.

ELKHART: Goshen 46–38 Northwood; Penn 45–40 Jimtown; Concord 58–56 Elkhart Memorial; Elkhart Central 76–44 Northridge; Penn 51–50 Goshen; Central 74–57 Concord; Central 65–51 Penn. Officials: Don Schmidt, Paul Danko, David Zurcher, Bob Marcinek.

EVANSVILLE: North 67–53 Harrison; Memorial 54–51 Central; Mater Dei 61–52 Reitz; Bosse 77–64 North; Memorial 66–63 Mater Dei; Bosse 72–64 Memorial. Officials: Winfield Jacobs, George Dixon, William Johnston, Danny Jacobs.

FLOYD CENTRAL: Floyd Central 75–61 Corydon; Borden 56–53 Eastern (Pekin); North Harrison 56–47 South Central; Floyd Central 69–61 Lanesville; North Harrison 83–52 Borden; North Harrison 74–60 Floyd Central. Officials: Reginald Cheatham, Victor Gilla, Leland Thompson, Noel Baker.

FORT WAYNE (#1): Snider 70–59 Woodlan; New Haven 47–45 Luers; Wayne 71–62 Elmhurst; Northrop 76–68 Snider; Wayne 72–66 New Haven (ot); Wayne 71–69 Northrop (ot). Officials: Jon Gallipo, Richard Bowie, Keith Yoder, John Lozier.

FORT WAYNE (#2): Concordia 67–65 South Side (2ot); North Side 52–39 Heritage; Harding 84–72 Carroll; Concordia 57–50 Dwenger; North Side 81–79 Harding (ot); North Side 56–47 Concordia. Officials: James Wehsollek, Donald O'Conner, John Wray, Jr., Milton Cooper.

FOUNTAIN CENTRAL: Fountain Central 88–58 North Vermillion; Seeger 63–59 Covington; Attica 85–66 Turkey Run; Fountain Central 77–63 Seeger; Attica 81–69 Fountain Central. Officials: Jack Gardner, Mark Masariu, Thomas Simler, Ken Gorrell.

FRANKFORT: Tri Central 53–51 Rossville; Frankfort 53–38 Tipton; Clinton Prairie 73–62 Clinton Central; Carroll 69–49 Tri Central; Frankfort 71–66 Clinton Prairie; Frankfort 63–58 Carroll. Officials: Jerry Scott, Wayne Targgart, Richard Brainerd, Nick Sweigart.

Tourney Time

GARY: Mann 64–62 Gary Roosevelt; West Side 55–40 Wirt; Emerson 65–46 Andrean; Mann 79–61 Wallace; West Side 53–47 Emerson; West Side 62–56 Mann. Officials: Jimmy Dimitroff, William Pittman, Jesse Lynch, Phil Hardwick.

GREENCASTLE: North Putnam 72–61 Cascade; Tri West 71–65 South Putnam; Greencastle 73–57 Cloverdale; North Putnam 67–58 Tri-West; North Putnam 68–62 Greencastle. Officials: Gordon McCain, Kenneth Cave, James Miller, Dennis Cave.

GREENSBURG: Waldron 47–36 North Decatur; Rushville 59–54 Greensburg; South Decatur 51–46 Waldron; Rushville 87–51 South Decatur. Officials: Dave Lowenstein, Darrell Eaton, Rick Owens, McKee Munk.

HAMMOND: Tech 65–49 Gavit; Morton 63–54 Hammond High; Tech 73–71 Clark; Morton 60–53 Tech. Officials: Gene Marks, Ken Keller, Dale Cramer, Harold Ashbrook.

HUNTINGTON: Southwood 58–55 Wabash; Homestead 48–46 White's; Huntington 82–33 Northfield; Huntington Catholic 81–79 Southwood; Huntington 61–37 Homestead; Huntington 69–48 Catholic. Officials: Don Koester, Jerry Karstens, Kevin Weinberg, Tom Manning, Jr.

INDIANAPOLIS: Chatard 57–56 Arlington; North Central 71–65 Shortridge; Lawrence Central 74–66 Tech; Broad Ripple 84–66 Marshall; Chatard 80–78 North Central (ot); Lawrence Central 74–60 Broad Ripple; Lawrence Central 80–58 Chatard. Officials: Troy Ingram, Robert Kirk, Gary Eaglin, Eric Harmon.

JAY COUNTY: Winchester 84–51 Randolph Southern; Union City 65–55 Wapahani; Jay County 69–66 Monroe Central; Union City 56–55 Winchester; Jay County 58–50 Union City. Officials: Merl Heckaman, Pete Deakyne, Jerry Christie, Larry Hollman.

JEFFERSONVILLE: Jeffersonville 63–38 Clarksville; New Albany 70–67 Providence; Jeffersonville 73–57 New Albany. Officials: Keith Combs, Larry Collins, Richard Lederman, Ronald Ham.

KANKAKEE VALLEY: Hebron 62–51 Rensselaer; North Newton 64–55 West Central; Lowell 78–69 Hanover Central; Kankakee Valley 79–68 Kouts; Hebron 76–47 North Newton; Lowell 65–60 Kankakee Valley; Hebron 82–67 Lowell. Officials: Ron Beard, Robert DeBroka, Benjamin Hirt, Leslie Wright.

KOKOMO: Western 61–49 Northwestern; Kokomo 63–53 Haworth; Maconaquah 73–70 Eastern; Taylor 59–57 Western; Kokomo 74–53 Maconaquah; Kokomo 78–64 Taylor. Officials: Gil Baumgartner, Dick Hale, Dave Atwell, Jack Mercer.

LAFAYETTE: Central Catholic 60–57 Harrison; Lafayette Jefferson 47–28 West Lafayette; Catholic 63–40 Delphi; Jefferson 72–57 Catholic. Officials: Richard Boer, Terry Stewart, William Gebhart, Gerry Scheub.

La VILLE: Argos 81–48 North Liberty; Plymouth 52–46 Bremen; Glenn 64–53 La Ville; Plymouth 63–56 Argos; Plymouth 68–48 Glenn. Officials: George Avery, Steve Beres, Ronald Beres, Max Hensler.

LEBANON: Lebanon 107–38 School for the Deaf; Brebeuf 73–59 Ritter; Western Boone 66–65 Zionsville (ot); Lebanon 61–46 Brebeuf; Lebanon 74–47 Western Boone. Officials: Opal Courtney, Dan Yagodnik, John Lyskowinski, James Fairchild.

LOGANSPORT: Pioneer 57–54 Caston (2ot); Logansport 66–43 Cass; Peru 59–56 North Miami; Pioneer 81–48 Kewanna; Logansport 47–41 Peru; Logansport 60–44 Pioneer. Officials: Marty Burdette, Michael Crouch, John Elliott, Mel Botkin.

MADISON: Southwestern 66–53 Henryville; Charlestown 83–57 Madison Shawe; Silver

IHSAA Scores | 1970–1979

Creek 74–66 New Washington; Madison 68–43 Southwestern; Charlestown 52–43 Silver Creek; Charlestown 50–45 Madison. Officials: Morris Cohen, Russell Ferrill, Jerome Davis, Bill Gray.

MARION: Madison-Grant 75–68 Elwood; Marion Bennett 66–63 Mississinewa; Marion 86–51 Oak Hill; Bennett 75–71 Madison-Grant; Marion 77–60 Bennett. Officials: Byron Weaver, Larry Freyburgher, Michael Winger, William DeRome.

MARTINSVILLE: Bloomington South 53–44 Edgewood; Martinsville 71–47 Eminence; Bloomington North 67–65 Owen Valley; South 61–52 Martinsville; North 56–52 South. Officials: Robert Wolfe, James Helms, Don Cranfield, Richard Hall.

MICHIGAN CITY: South Central 79–55 Westville; Elston 51–40 Marquette; Rogers 62–58 New Prairie; LaPorte 61–51 South Central; Rogers 67–65 Elston; LaPorte 53–46 Rogers. Officials: Roger DeYoung, Lauren Griffith, Gary Foltz, Tom Knox.

MUNCIE: Yorktown 57–51 Northside; Southside 53–42 Central; Cowan 64–61 Burris; Southside 50–48 Yorktown; Cowan 56–54 Southside (ot). Officials: Homer Owens, Don Thompson, Mark Baltz, Paul Hackleman.

NEW CASTLE: Knightstown 50–36 Mt. Vernon; Tri 67–56 Union; Eastern Hancock 70–49 Shenandoah; New Castle 83–63 Blue River; Tri 64–54 Knightstown; Eastern Hancock 70–68 New Castle; Tri 63–51 Eastern Hancock. Officials: Ray Mitrione, John Fleischman, Bob Richardson, Norris Boomershine.

NORTH JUDSON: LaCrosse 79–67 Culver; Culver Military 74–45 Divine Heart; North Judson 47–46 Knox; Winamac 44–33 Oregon-Davis; LaCrosse 68–64 Culver Military; North Judson 53–51 Winamac; North Judson 54–38 LaCrosse. Officials: Eugene Carrabine, Ronald Flotow, Tom Herbert, George Grygiel.

NORTH MONTGOMERY: Crawfordsville 63–61 North Montgomery; McCutcheon 64–55 Southmont; Crawfordsville 66–57 McCutcheon. Officials: Louis Schmalfeldt, Gary Coers, Armand Motz, Noble Rector.

PAOLI: Paoli 61–56 West Washington; Milltown 67–52 Leavenworth; Salem 78–61 English; Springs Valley 86–74 Marengo; Milltown 61–54 Paoli; Springs Valley 77–69 Salem; Milltown 72–63 Springs Valley. Officials: Mike Bohan, Richie Moore, Robert Klein, John Hilligoss.

PRINCETON: North Posey 62–46 Oakland City Wood; Princeton 66–47 Gibson Southern; New Harmony 69–67 Mr. Vernon (2ot); Princeton 75–58 North Posey; Princeton 75–51 New Harmony. Officials: Phillip Barth, Larry Maxwell, Tad Heminger, Norman Hathcoat.

RICHMOND: Centerville 57–55 Hagerstown; Richmond 83–48 Northeastern; Richmond 75–48 Centerville. Officials: Don Hurst, Charles Hadley, Ric Baldwin, Richard Schleicher.

SEYMOUR: Seymour 89–74 Scottsburg; Jennings County 70–48 Crothersville; Austin 81–66 Brownstown Central; Jennings County 72–69 Seymour; Jennings County 88–68 Austin. Officials: Clifford Spears, Delmus Aubrey, James Roberts, Mason Meeks.

SHELBYVILLE: Greenfield Central 58–53 Morristown; Shelbyville 60–46 New Palestine; Triton Central 57–55 Roncalli; Franklin Central 62–40 Greenfield Central; Shelbyville 77–63 Triton Central; Franklin Central 74–71 Shelbyville. Officials: Bill Wullner, Paul Garriott, Gayle Forrest, Wendell Baker.

SOUTH ADAMS: Bluffton 76–74 Southern Wells; Bellmont 73–72 South Adams; Norwell 86–65 Adams Central; Bluffton 67–66 Bellmont; Bluffton 77–58 Norwell. Officials: Richard Freeman, Jerry Pieper, Jerry Cook, Ron Hosinski.

SOUTH BEND: St. Joseph's 57–45 Adams; Riley 49–44 Clay; Mishawaka 75–55 Mishawaka

Tourney Time

Marian; Washington 54–52 LaSalle; St. Joseph's 61–52 Riley; Washington 81–46 Mishawaka; St. Joseph's 59–52 Washington. Officials: Marion Acton, Charles Weinkauf, Brandon Bryant, Dan Alvarez.

SOUTHPORT: Wood 64–46 Warren Central; Perry Meridian 73–52 Beech Grove; Attucks 76–65 Southport; Manual 64–57 Howe; Perry Meridian 69–68 Wood; Manual 79–71 Attucks (3ot); Perry Meridian 67–63 Manual. Officials: Robert Beeson, Frank Hobson, Richard Eynon, Jerry Newsom.

SOUTHRIDGE: Forest Park 58–42 Jasper; Southridge 72–55 Dubois; Forest Park 60–56 Perry Central; Southridge 57–45 Forest Park. Officials: Harry Inskeep, Jimmie Westerfield, Don Criswell, James Dunlap.

SULLIVAN: Sullivan 90–52 Union (Dugger); Clay City 81–75 North Central; Sullivan 76–66 Shakamak; Clay City 64–63 Sullivan (ot). Officials: Jack Graham, Charles Roush, G. A. Ward, Tom Whitehead.

SWITZ CITY: Eastern (Greene Co.) 73–62 Switz City Central; Linton 72–65 L & M; Worthington 54–52 Bloomfield; Linton 64–55 Eastern; Linton 72–56 Worthington. Officials: Jack Williams, David Willoughby, Jon Custer, Paul Grimes.

TERRE HAUTE: South 65–50 Schulte; Clinton 67–60 North; West Vigo 57–55 Laboratory (ot); South 71–60 Clinton; South 49–48 West Vigo (ot). Officials: Melvin Redman, Max Cameron, Ronald Ramsey, Dallas Richards.

TRITON: Tippecanoe Valley 98–82 Triton; Warsaw 61–52 Rochester; Tippecanoe Valley 105–90 Wawasee; Warsaw 65–61 Tippecanoe Valley. Officials: Robert Justak, Herbert Hicks, Stephen White, Robert Laird.

VALPARAISO: Valparaiso 79–68 Morgan Twp.; Boone Grove 67–58 Washington Twp.; Hobart 67–59 Portage; Chesterton 70–36 Wheeler; Valparaiso 66–62 Boone Grove; Hobart 65–63 Chesterton; Valparaiso 84–66 Hobart. Officials: Joe Smelcer, Art Morris, Joe Edmonds, Ken Miller.

VINCENNES: South Knox 62–55 Vincennes Rivet; Vincennes 50–29 North Knox; South Knox 43–40 Vincennes. Officials: Raymond Vescovi, Don Nester, Mike Cummings, Jack Cummings.

WASHINGTON: Washington 72–53 Pike Central; Loogootee 69–48 Barr-Reeve; Shoals 61–52 North Daviess; Washington 28–24 Washington Catholic; Loogootee 55–47 Shoals; Washington 46–44 Loogootee (ot). Officials: Donald Shields, John Ramey, Dwain Laird, Bill Laird.

WHITELAND: Greenwood 68–53 Indian Creek; Franklin 79–55 Whiteland; Center Grove 68–54 Greenwood; Center Grove 70–69 Franklin (2ot). Officials: Carl March, Bruce Mayfield, Gary Cheeseman, Robert Gilmore.

1976 REGIONALS

ANDERSON: Blackford 66–64 Kokomo; Highland 59–51 Carmel (ot); Highland 54–50 Blackford. Officials: Rex Mays, Robert Laird, Jimmy Dimitrpff, McKee Munk, BobMarcinek, Gene Marks.

COLUMBUS: Franklin Central 61–55 Bloomington North (ot); Brown County 68–66 Center Grove; Brown County 72–70 Franklin Central (2ot). Officials: Raymond Norris, Ronald Ham, Melvin Redman, Norman Hathcoat, Danny Jacobs, Marion Acton.

IHSAA Scores | 1970–1979

CONNERSVILLE: Rushville 86–77 Union County; Aurora 50–49 Batesville; Rushville 86–45 Aurora. Officials: Ken Miller, Don Shiflet, Melvin Botkin, Gene Gibson, Jon Gallipo, Eugene Linn.

ELKHART: Warsaw 58–50 Whiyko; Elkhart Central 64–52 Plymouth; Warsaw 57–55 Elkhart Central. Officials: Officials: John Fleischman, Richard Boer, Roger Pflughaupt, Richard Freeman, Roger DeYoung, Troy Ingram.

EVANSVILLE: Boonville 74–60 Evansville Bosse; Princeton 60–48 South Knox; Boonville 64–57 Princeton. Officials: William Fields, Milton Cooper, Pete Deakyne, Darrell McFall, Jerry Scott, Robert Wolfe.

FORT WAYNE: Fort Wayne Wayne 63–59 Westview; Fort Wayne North Side 61–47 Leo; North Side 65–62 Wayne. Officials: John Hilligoss, Eugene Carrabine, Gary Coers, Robert Reed, Richard Cook, Eric Harmon.

FRANKFORT: Lebanon 56–47 North Putnam; Crawfordsville 63–60 Frankfort; Lebanon 58–54 Crawfordsville. Officials: Carl March, Billy Maroney, Robert Boyle, Frank Hoagburg, Gil Baumgartner, George Avery.

GARY: West Side 75–55 Hammond Morton; East Chicago Washington 79–63 Munster; Washington 79–58 West Side. Officials: Michael Bohan, Harold Gray, Tom Knox, James Cox, Jack Gardner, Joe Smelcer.

INDIANAPOLIS: Perry Meridian 71–58 Plainfield; Northwest 76–65 Lawrence Central; Perry Meridian 74–67 Northwest. Officials: James Rider, Donald Shields, Donald Ricketts, Raymond Vescovi, Winfield Jacobs, Keith Combs.

LAFAYETTE: Lafayette Jefferson 69–48 Attica; Hebron 62–57 Frontier; Jefferson 75–63 Hebron. Officials: Robert Klein, Dan Alvarez, Larry Hollman, Morris Cohen, Byron Weaver, Opal Courtney.

MARION: Marion 74–70 Huntington North; Logansport 76–68 Bluffton; Marion 76–59 Logansport. Officials: Mason Meeks, Dave Lowenstein, John Ramey, Bill Wullner, Don Snedeker, Gene Butts.

NEW CASTLE: Jay County 71–66 Tri; Richmond 73–51 Cowan; Richmond 56–42 Jay County. Officials: Ron Hosinski, Max Hensler, John Lozier, Donald Schmidt, James Wehsollek, Don Koester.

SEYMOUR: Charlestown 57–52 North Harrison; Jeffersonville 77–54 Jennings County; Jeffersonville 72–54 Charlestown. Officials: Richie Moore, Ray Mitrione, Don Hurst, Wendell Baker, Norman Chestnut, Homer Owens.

SOUTH BEND: St. Joseph's 70–60 LaPorte; Valparaiso 78–39 North Judson; Valparaiso 60–52 St. Joseph's. Officials: Jerry Petro, George Taylor, Richard Hall, Steve Cherry, Gordon McCain, Marty Burdette.

TERRE HAUTE: Terre Haute South 51–49 Brazil; Clay City 67–46 Linton; South 78–70 Clay City. Officials: Dick Modricker, Phil Hardwick, Dennis Cave, Kirk Roberts, Jerry Larrison, Wayne Van Sickle.

WASHINGTON: Bedford-North Lawrence 62–60 Southridge; Washington 50–49 Milltown (ot); Bedford-North Lawrence 53–46 Washington. Officials: James Fairchild, Clifford Spears, Joe Edmonds, Jack Williams, Jack Mercer, Ronald Beard.

Tourney Time

1976 SEMI-STATES

EVANSVILLE: Jeffersonville 70–52 Boonville; Terre Haute South 60–53 Bedford North Lawrence; Jeffersonville 60–38 Terre Haute South. Officials: Danny Jacobs, Don Snedeker, Jimmy Dimitroff, Bill Wullner, Gordon McCain, Homer Owens.

FORT WAYNE: Marion 59–57 Anderson; Fort Wayne North Side 57–49 Warsaw; Marion 69–66 North Side (ot). Officials: Opal Courtney, Wayne Van Sickle, Eric Harmon, Joe Smelcer, Troy Ingram, Eugene Linn.

INDIANAPOLIS: Rushville 81–78 Richmond; Perry Meridian 75–64 Brown County; Rushville 92–85 Perry Meridian. Officials: Keith Combs, Jack Gardner, Roger DeYoung, Don Koester, Gene Butts, Marty Burdette.

LAFAYETTE: Lebanon 40–37 Lafayette Jefferson; East Chicago Washington 54–52 Valparaiso; Washington 58–43 Lebanon. Officials: James Wehsollek, Darrell McFall, Marion Acton Donald Shields, George Avery, Gene Marks.

1976 FINALS—March 27

INDIANAPOLIS (Market Square Arena): Rushville 68–59 East Chicago Washington; Marion 49–47 Jeffersonville; Marion 82–76 Rushville. Officials: Homer Owens, Eugene Linn, Darrell McFall, Gene Butts, Gene Marks, Troy Ingram.

1977 SECTIONALS

ANDERSON: Madison Heights 58–56 Lapel; Highland 71–51 Pendleton Heights; Alexandria 62–54 Daleville; Anderson 100–52 Frankton; Madison Heights 56–48 Highland; Anderson 64–58 Alexandria; Anderson 55–52 Madison Heights. Officials: Jack Mercer, Judson Raver, George Grygiel, Jim Cox.

BATESVILLE: Milan 75–74 South Ripley (ot); Batesville 68–56 Moores Hill; Jac-Cen-Del 82–66 Milan; Jac-Cen-Del 67–46 Batesville. Officials: Jerry Petro, Richard Hall, Delmus Aubrey, Mark Masariu.

BEDFORD–NORTH LAWRENCE: Bedford–North Lawrence 56–53 Bloomington South (ot); Mitchell 57–46 Orleans; Bloomfield 80–48 Medora; Bedford-North Lawrence 55–48 Mitchell; Bedford–North Lawrence 67–53 Bloomfield. Officials: Darrell McFall, D. J. Frazer, David Lee, William Graham.

BEN DAVIS: Speedway 75–59 Shortridge; Washington 62–45 Northwest; Pike 73–70 Brebeuf (ot); Ben Davis 80–59 Ritter; Washington 57–54 Speedway; Pike 77–66 Ben Davis; Washington 59–56 Pike. Officials: David Lowenstein, Larry Freyburgher, Tom Crouch, William Fields.

BENTON CENTRAL: Benton Central 44–32 Twin Lakes; South Newton 70–57 North White; Frontier 67–59 Tri–County; Benton Central 72–62 South Newton; Benton Central 53–51 Frontier (4ot). Officials: Morris Cohen, Herb Hicks, Jim Anderson, Steve Beres.

BLACKFORD: Blackford 79–65 Eastbrook; Wes-Del 58–57 Delta; Wes-Del 72–58 Blackford. Officials: Officials: Richard Clark, Bud Wetzel, Leslie Wright, John Manka.

BOONVILLE: Heritage Hills 47–41 Tell City; Castle 84–47 Cannelton; Boonville 94–65 Tecumseh; Heritage Hills 58–55 South Spencer; Boonville 57–50 Castle; Boonville 56–53

IHSAA Scores | 1970–1979

Heritage Hills. Officials: Jerry Scott, Dave Atwell, James Roberts, Jesse Lynch.
  BROWNSBURG: Avon 58–43 Danville; Brownsburg 80–61 Cascade; Mooresville 71–54 Plainfield; Brownsburg 60–56 Avon; Mooresville 50–48 Brownsburg. Officials: Richie Moore, Ric Baldwin, Armand Motz, Ronald Ham.
  CALUMET: Merrillville 57–56 Highland; Munster 69–58 Griffith; Lake Central 63–61 East Gary Edison; Calumet 72–64 Crown Point; Munster 56–48 Merrillville; Calumet 65–51 Lake Central; Munster 76–58 Calumet. Officials: Richard Modricker, George Dixon, Jay Smith, Ken Miller.
  CARMEL: Hamilton Heights 65–57 Sheridan; Carmel 88–56 Westfield; Noblesville 78–50 Hamilton Southeastern; Carmel 77–64 Hamilton Heights; Carmel 59–40 Noblesville. Officials: Marty Burdette, Mike Winger, Keith Yoder, Robert Justak.
  COLUMBIA CITY: Columbia City 91–69 Churubusco; Central Noble 75–54 Manchester; Columbia City 68–50 Whitko; Central Noble 78–70 Columbia City. Officials: Don Thompson, Dale Cramer, Robert Rueth, John Hilligoss.
  COLUMBUS: Columbus East 89–52 Southwestern; Hauser 76–71 Edinburgh; Columbus North 86–62 Brown County; East 54–43 Hauser; East 55–52 North. Officials: Robert Beeson, Vic Gilla, Larry Sintz, Joe Edmonds.
  CONNERSVILLE: Union County 61–51 Laurel; Brookville 64–51 Cambridge City; Connersville 67–39 Morton Memorial; Union County 42–41 Brookville; Union County 56–55 Connersville. Officials: Robert Wolfe, James Fairchild, Gary Woodling, Gene Gibson.
  DeKalb: Eastside 59–56 Hamilton; Prairie Heights 94–84 Fremont; Leo 69–67 Garrett; DeKalb 77–72 Angola; Eastside 67–57 Prairie Heights; DeKalb 66–60 Leo; DeKalb 79–58 Eastside. Officials: George Taylor, Robert DeBroka, Jerome Fawley, Robert Boyle.
  EAST CENTRAL: Aurora 78–62 Dillsboro; Rising Sun 71–67 East Central; Switzerland County 56–54 Lawrenceburg; Aurora 79–70 Rising Sun; Aurora 60–57 Switzerland County. Officials: Norman Hathcoat, Allen Youmans, John Ramey, Bruce Mayfield.
  EAST CHICAGO: Washington 50–48 Hammond Noll; Roosevelt 68–57 Whiting; Washington 51–44 Roosevelt. Officials: Eric Harmon, Ken Keller, Lauren Griffith, John Lozier.
  EAST NOBLE: Fairfield 87–83 Westview; East Noble 69–41 Bethany Christian; West Noble 96–50 Howe Military; Lakeland 65–48 Fairfield; East Noble 63–55 West Noble; Lakeland 78–73 East Noble. Officials: Bruce Knecht, Dan Yagodnik, Steve Skiles, Delmar Knecht.
  ELKHART: Central 68–51 Jimtown; Goshen 92–58 NorthWood; Concord 49–43 Memorial; Penn 56–51 Northridge; Goshen 52–51 Central; Concord 65–44 Penn; Concord 54–49 Goshen. Officials: Don Koester, Larry Jones, Ron Waisnora, Jerry Karstens.
  EVANSVILLE: Memorial 55–48 Harrison; Mater Dei 62–60 Reitz; Central 95–83 North; Bosse 64–52 Memorial; Central 77–72 Mater Dei; Central 89–71 Bosse. Officials: Ken Gorrell, Jack Cummings, Charles Weinkauf, Ray Norris.
  FLOYD CENTRAL: Lanesville 55–45 Borden; North Harrison 68–47 Corydon; Floyd Central 81–49 South Central; Lanesville 63–53 North Harrison; Floyd Central 88–54 Lanesville. Officials: Bill Gray, John Evans, Richard Hughes, Dannis Cave.
  FORT WAYNE (#1): North Side 67–58 Luers; South Side 79–48 Heritage; Harding 72–66 Woodlan; Snider 69–67 North Side; South Side 57–50 Harding; South Side 61–57 Snider. Officials: Opal Courtney, Robert Gilmore, Gene Johnson, Ron Beard.
  FORT WAYNE (#2): Carroll 66–65 New Haven; Wayne 69–51 Elmhurst; Concordia 58–56

Tourney Time

Northrop; Dwenger 52–50 Carroll; Wayne 87–61 Concordia; Wayne 75–59 Dwenger. Officials: Gene Marks, Tad Heminger, Rudy Williams, Frank Desantis.

FOUNTAIN CENTRAL: North Vermillion 66–65 Seeger (ot); Attica 79–69 Turkey Run; Covington 71–65 Fountain Central; Attica 66–54 North Vermillion; Covington 86–66 Attica. Officials: Jimmy Dimitroff, David Willoughby, Roger Fisher, Craig Martin.

FRANKFORT: Frankfort 72–49 Rossville; Tipton 64–63 Tri-Central; Clinton Prairie 65–57 Clinton Central; Frankfort 77–62 Tipton; Frankfort 92–71 Clinton Prairie. Officials: Paul Hardwick, Tom Herbert, Ward Weisel, Merl Heckaman.

FRANKLIN: Center Grove 86–84 Greenwood; Franklin 45–33 Indian Creek; Whiteland 57–52 Center Grove; Franklin 58–57 Whiteland. Officials: Don Snedeker, Thomas Newlin, David Watt, Gary Eaglin.

FRANKLIN CENTRAL: Franklin Central 31–30 Roncalli (ot); Marshall 63–48 Warren Central; Scecina 64–56 Beech Grove; Marshall 52–48 Franklin Central; Marshall 72–65 Scecina. Officials: Wayne Van Sickle, McKee Munk, Michael Crouch, Steve Cherry.

GARY: Gary Roosevelt 63–54 Emerson; Wirt 64–62 Wallace; Mann 66–58 West Side; Roosevelt 66–60 Wirt; Mann 83–61 Roosevelt. Officials: Mike Bohan, Bob Richardson, Leland Thompson, Harold Gray.

GREENCASTLE: North Putnam 70–66 Van Buren; South Putnam 58–56 Greencastle (ot); Cloverdale 63–45 Rockville; South Putnam 56–50 North Putnam; South Putnam 54–51 Cloverdale. Officials: Ed Scott, Charles Bertram, Larry Collins, Jimmie Westerfield.

GREENSBURG: Greensburg 62–56 North Decatur; South Decatur 86–73 Waldron; Greensburg 66–51 Rushville; Greensburg 103–64 South Decatur. Officials: Brandon Bryant, Jon Custer, Steve Welmer, Don Shiflet.

HAMMOND: Clark 58–52 Morton; Hammond High 56–49 Gavit; Andrean 67–49 Tech; Hammond High 71–64 Clark; Andrean 70–66 Hammond High. Officials: Carl March, Richard Hale, Gaylord Fritz, Paul Leamon.

HUNTINGTON: Wabash 66–57 Homestead; Northfield 61–54 White's; Huntington North 91–55 Southwood; Wabash 85–75 Huntington Catholic; North 72–51 Northfield; North 60–51 Wabash. Officials: Troy Ingram, Don Nester, Herb Pruett, Pete Deakyne, Rich Clark. .

INDIANAPOLIS: Arlington 57–50 North Central; Tech 59–53 Broad Ripple; Lawrence North 65–57 Cathedral; Lawrence Central 64–54 Chatard; Arlington 70–69 Tech; Lawrence Central 60–50 Lawrence North; Lawrence Central 54–51 Arlington. Officials: Richard Cook, James Reinebold, James Helms, Bill Wullner.

JAY COUNTY: Union City 80–58 Wapahani; Jay County 51–47 Winchester; Monroe Central 88–87 Randolph Southern; Jay County 62–58 Union City; Jay County 59–57 Monroe Central. Officials: Gene Butts, Tom VonDeylen, James Miller, Ron Hosinski.

JEFFERSONVILLE: Clarksville 75–68 Providence; Jeffersonville 65–40 New Albany. Jeffersonville 68–58 Clarksville. Officials: Don Ricketts, Jerry Newsom, Gary Leistner, Mel Botkin.

KANKAKEE VALLEY: Kankakee Valley 75–62 Kouts; North Newton 75–58 Hanover Central; Lowell 81–57 West Central; Hebron 70–58 Rensselaer; Kankakee Valley 64–41 North Newton; Hebron 63–62 Lowell; Kankakee Valley 53–45 Hebron. Officials: Tom Simler, John Elliott, Dale Blosser, Harold Ashbrook.

KOKOMO: Haworth 91–65 Taylor; Kokomo 87–52 Northwestern; Eastern 48–44 Western

IHSAA Scores | 1970–1979

(ot); Kokomo 61–50 Haworth; Kokomo 51–36 Eastern. Officials: Tom Knox, Mark Baltz, Jerry Pieper, Richard Brainerd.

LAFAYETTE: Carroll 67–42 Harrison; West Lafayette 66–54 Delphi; Jefferson 64–56 Catholic; West Lafayette 65–49 Carroll; Jefferson 37–34 West Lafayette. Officials: John Fleischman, Paul Garriott, Don Criswell, David Zurcher.

LEBANON: Zionsville 64–51 Western Boone; Lebanon 40–38 Tri–-West; Lebanon 51–47 Zionsville. Officials: Louis Schmalfeldt, Jerry Christie, Bill DeRome, Paul Grimes.

LOGANSPORT: Maconaquah 87–60 Caston; Logansport 74–37 North Miami; Pioneer 80–50 Kewanna; Peru 46–43 Cass; Logansport 51–40 Maconaquah; Peru 70–66 Pioneer; Logansport 49–43 Peru. Officials: Richard Boer, Mark Reyher, Kevin Weinberg, Frank Hoagburg.

MADISON: Silver Creek 63–46 Charlestown; Southwestern 64–44 New Washington; Madison 72–64 Henryville; Silver Creek 74–62 Madison Shawe; Southwestern 59–48 Madison; Southwestern 47–45 Silver Creek. Officials: Jerry Larrison, Jack Behme, Jerry Cook, Robert Reed.

MARION: Marion 76–52 Madison–Grant; Oak Hill 65–58 Elwood; Mississinewa 58–57 Marion Bennett; Marion 94–62 Oak Hill; Marion 87–43 Mississinewa. Officials: George Avery, Tom Neuman, Jerry Cook, Robert Reed.

MARTINSVILLE: Martinsville 63–53 Edgewood; Eminence 80–64 Owen Valley; Bloomington North 69–60 Monrovia; Martinsville 74–59 Eminence; Martinsville 68–63 Bloomington North (3ot). Officials: Robert Carr, Dennis Oxley, Mike Cummings, Frank Hobson.

MICHIGAN CITY: Chesterton 95–66 New Prairie; Rogers 73–61 Westville; Elston 73–58 Marquette; Chesterton 66–49 LaPorte; Rogers 55–52 Elston; Rogers 69–55 Chesterton. Officials: Jim Wehsollek, Richard Lederman, Reginald Cheatham, Steve White.

MUNCIE: Central 72–59 Burris; Yorktown 62–61 Northside; Southside 59–52 Cowan; Central 75–57 Yorktown; Central 55–54 Southside. Officials: Donald Schmidt, Noel Baker, Don Resler, Gren Lefebvre.

NEW CASTLE: Eastern Hancock 66–58 Blue River; Tri 62–45 Mt. Vernon; New Castle 70–56 Shenandoah; Knightstown 72–58 Union (Modoc); Tri 53–48 Eastern Hancock; Knightstown 65–61 New Castle; Tri 52–51 Knightstown. Officials: Gene Linn, Roger Pflughaupt, Vic Combs, Jim Benecke.

NORTH JUDSON: Winamac 62–60 Culver Military; South Central; 82–72 Oregon-Davis; North Judson 90–65 Culver Military; LaCrosse 80–51 Knox; South Central 58–56 Winamac; LaCrosse 74–62 North Judson; LaCrosse 67–62 South Central. Officials: Nick Sweigart, Don O'Connor, John Gassessmith, Tom Manning.

NORTH MONTGOMERY: McCutcheon 84–81 Southmont; North Montgomery 63–55 Crawfordsville (ot); North Montgomery 52–50 McCutcheon. Officials: Wendell Baker, Benjamin Hirt, David Long, Dwain Laird.

PAOLI: Springs Valley 59–44 Paoli; Salem 67–49 West Washington; Crawford County 45–26 Eastern (Pekin); Salem 62–47 Springs Valley; Crawford County 57–55 Salem. Officials: John Shields, John Tucker, William Johnston, Jack Graham.

PLYMOUTH: LaVille 80–26 Divine Heart; North Liberty 78–73 Glenn; Plymouth 65–58 Bremen; LaVille 58–37 Argos; Plymouth 84–65 North Liberty; Plymouth 53–40 LaVille. Officials: Clifford Spears, Dale VanHouten, Richard Bowie, Rex Mays.

PRINCETON: New Harmony 48–45 Gibson Southern; North Posey 45–43 Oakland City; Princeton 51–47 Mt. Vernon; New Harmony 69–62 North Posey; Princeton 74–42 New

Tourney Time

Harmony. Officials: Terry Stewart, Paul Hackleman, William Pittman, Richard Eynon.

RICHMOND: Richmond 73–33 Northeastern; Hagerstown 49–48 Centerville; Richmond 72–49 Hagerstown. Officials: Gil Baumgartner, Al Lindahl, Tom Dull, Larry Hollman.

SEYMOUR: Jennings County 87–50 Crothersville; Scottsburg 53–50 Austin; Seymour 78–63 Brownstown Central; Scottsburg 64–56 Jennings County; Seymour 65–63 Scottsburg (ot). Officials: Mel Redman, Jerome Davis, Ric Kingston, Ray Mitrione.

SHELBYVILLE: Shelbyville 81–68 Morristown; Greenfield Central 52–47 New Palestine; Shelbyville 81–64 Triton Central; Greenfield Central 57–51 Shelbyville (ot). Officials: Winfield Jacobs, George Dyer, G. R. Honchell, Gary Cheeseman.

SOUTH ADAMS: South Adams 55–53 Southern Wells; Bluffton 54–53 Norwell; Adams Central 57–54 Bellmont; B;luffton 71–56 South Adams; Bluffton 64–62 Adams Central. Officials: Gary Foltz, Wayne Targgart, Jon Davenport, Mike De Vault.

SOUTH BEND: Adams 92–76 Riley; Mishawaka 69–61 Washington; Clay 62–59 Mishawaka Marian; LaSalle 65–44 St. Joseph's; Adams 74–61 Mishawaka; LaSalle 75–55 Clay; LaSalle 77–71 Adams. Officials: Roger DeYoung, Rick Owens, Phil Sullivan, Phil Barth.

SOUTHPORT: Howe 50–37 Decatur Central; Perry Meridian 80–69 Manual; Wood 95–51 School for the Deaf; Southport 79–54 Attucks; Perry Meridian 58–57 Howe; Southport 56–55 Wood; Southport 62–54 Perry Meridian. Officials: Danny Jacobs, Jim Rider, Glen Clemons, Robert Kirk.

SOUTHRIDGE: Jasper 51–50 Perry Central; Northeast Dubois 58–45 Forest Park; Jasper 63–60 Southridge; Northeast Dubois 60–55 Jasper (ot). Officials: Jack Gardner, Mason Meeks, Ralph Scales, Jack Williams.

SWITZ CITY: Shakamak 82–56 Switz City Central; Bloomfield 49–46 L & M; Worthington 67–62 Linton; Bloomfield 66–62 Shakamak; Worthington 65–62 Bloomfield. Officials: James Dunlap, Temme Patterson, Robert Klein, Carl Redman.

TERRE HAUTE NORTH: Brazil 65–48 Montezuma; Laboratory 86–46 Clinton; North 68–57 Rosedale; Staunton 75–56 Schulte; Brazil 76–67 Laboratory (ot); Staunton 69–60 North; Staunton 59–53 Brazil. Officials: Keith Combs, John Lyskowinski, Ron Carter, Darrel Eaton.

TERRE HAUTE SOUTH: South 64–54 Union (Dugger); North Central 78–55 Sullivan; West Vigo 61–59 Clay City (ot); South 84–60 North Central; South 58–42 West Vigo. Officials: David Avery, Larry Maxwell, Kenneth Cave, Norman Chestnut.

TRITON: Tippecanoe Valley 78–76 Triton (ot); Wawasee 75–66 Rochester; Warsaw 86–74 Tippecanoe Valley; Wawasee 70–66 Warsaw (ot). Officials: Byron Weaver, Harry Inskeep, Charles Hadley, Ron Flotow.

VALPARAISO: Morgan Twp. 62–58 Washington Twp.; Hobart 58–38 Wheeler; Valparaiso 64–48 River Forest; Boone Grove 80–66 Portage; Hobart 61–52 Morgan Twp.; Boone Grove 64–61 Valparaiso; Hobart 54–53 Boone Grove. Officials: Richard Freeman, William Sorukas, William Gebhart, BobMarcinek.

VINCENNES: South Knox 66–52 Vincennes Rivet; Vincennes 59–49 North Knox; South Knox 50–47 Vincennes. Officials: Don Hurst, Robert Laird, Charles Roush, William Laird.

WASHINGTON: Shoals 65–61 Pike Central; Loogootee 54–26 Washington Catholic; Washington 72–48 North Daviess; Shoals 66–59 Barr-Reeve; Washington 28–26 Loogootee; Washington 70–51 Shoals. Officials: Richard Schleicher, Russell Ferrill, Don Dockery, Max Cameron.

1977 REGIONALS

ANDERSON: Carmel 75–51 Wes-Del; Kokomo 53–45 Anderson; Carmel 57–50 Kokomo. Officials: Phil Barth, Robert Kirk, Keith Combs, Jerry Karstens, Troy Ingram, Richard Cook.

COLUMBUS: Columbus East 58–56 Martinsville (ot); Franklin 78–67 Greenfield Central; Columbus East 51–50 Franklin. Officials: Robert Carr, Don Hurst, Mark Masariu, Dave Lowenstein, Eugene Linn, Jack Mercer.

CONNERSVILLE: Union County 66–51 Jac-Cen-Del; Aurora 49–47 Greensburg; Aurora 64–60 Union County. Officials: Don Thompson, Robert Klein, Larry Maxwell, Don Ricketts, Marty Burdette, Gil Baumgartner.

ELKHART: Central Noble 79–64 Concord; Plymouth 75–69 Wawasee; Plymouth 79–64 Central Noble. Officials: Eric Harmon, Judson Raver, Gren LeFebvre, Pete Deakyne, Phillip Hardwick, Byron Weaver.

EVANSVILLE: Boonville 64–53 Princeton; Evansville Central 73–66 South Knox; Central 72–58 Boonville. Officials: Norman Hathcoat, Louis Schmalfeldt, Jesse Lynch, Wendell Baker; Don Shields, Darrell McFall.

FORT WAYNE: South Side 60–57 Wayne; Lakeland 69–61 DeKalb; South Side 61–53 Lakeland. Officials: Robert Reed, Don O'Connor, Richard Boer, Nick Sweigart, Jerry Petro, BobMarcinek.

FRANKFORT: Mooresville 58–48 North Montgomery; Frankfort 40–29 Lebanon; Mooresville 59–56 Frankfort. Officials: Merl Heckaman, George Grygiel, Don Shiflet, Danny Jacobs, Don Koester, Winfield Jacobs.

GARY: Andrean 76–66 Munster; East Chicago Washington 58–50 Gary Mann; Washington 74–53 Andrean. Officials: James Reinebold, Ray Norris, George Dixon, Mason Meeks, Dave Avery, Gene Marks.

INDIANAPOLIS: Lawrence Central 75–54 Marshall; Southport 69–67 Washington; Lawrence Central 77–62 Southport. Officials: Ray Mitrione, Gary Foltz, Harold Gray, Jim Benecke, Opal Courtney, Tom Knox.

LAFAYETTE: Covington 57–55 Kankakee Valley; Lafayette Jefferson 68–55 Benton Central; Jefferson 61–58 Covington. Officials: John Ramey, Robert Gilmore, Ken Miller, Richard Brainerd, George Avery, Gene Butts.

MARION: Huntington North 84–60 Bluffton; Marion 84–73 Logansport; Marion 71–68 North. Officials: John Fleischman, Mike Devault, Robert Wolfe, Ken Gorrell, Don Schmidt, Richard Freeman.

NEW CASTLE: Richmond 57–48 Muncie Central; Tri 46–45 Jay County; Richmond 58–48 Tri. Officials: Jerry Larrison, Gary Eaglin, Harold Ashbrook, Mel Botkin, James Wehsollek, Cliff Spears.

SEYMOUR: Jeffersonville 68–51 Seymour; Floyd Central 68–66 Southwestern (ot); Jeffersonville 83–67 Floyd Central. Officials: Jim Cox, Carl Redman, Mel Redman, Terry Stewart, Wayne Van Sickle, Jack Williams.

SOUTH BEND: LaSalle 60–49 LaCrosse; Michigan City Rogers 64–50 Hobart; LaSalle 59–42 Rogers. Officials: Richard Hale, Dale Van Houten, Jack Gardner, Tom Simler, John Lozier, Bill Wullner.

TERRE HAUTE: South 74–54 Worthington; South Putnam 63–59 Staunton; South 48–42 South Putnam. Officials: Ron Ham, Jim Rider, Carl March, George Dyer, Jerry Scott, Roger DeYoung.

Tourney Time

WASHINGTON: Northeast Dubois 42–37 Crawford County; Washington 66–63 Bedford-North Lawrence (ot); Northeast Dubois 64–61 Washington. Officials: Morris Cohen, Bruce Mayfield, Robert Beeson, Mike Bohan, Jimmy Dimitroff, Don Snedeker.

1977 SEMI-STATES

EVANSVILLE: Terre Haute South 50–46 Jeffersonville; Northeast Dubois 66–64 Evansville Central; South 71–57 Northeast Dubois. Officials: Jerry Scott, Byron Weaver, Jack Mercer, George Avery, Eric Harmon, Eugene Linn.

FORT WAYNE: South Side 63–56 Marion; Carmel 58–54 Plymouth; Carmel 47–43 South Side. Officials: Jerry Petro, Winfield Jacobs, Bob Marcinek, Richard Cook, Don Snedeker, Roger DeYoung.

INDIANAPOLIS: Aurora 68–66 Lawrence Central (ot); Columbus 51–41 Richmond; East 61–57 Aurora. Officials: Donald Schmidt, James Wehsollek, Don Koester, Opal Courtney, Gene Marks, Gene Butts.

LAFAYETTE: East Chicago Washington 62–61 Lafayette Jefferson; South Bend LaSalle 51–35 Mooresville; Washington 63–54 LaSalle. Officials: Wayne Van Sickle, Tom Knox, Darrell McFall, Bill Wullner, Troy Ingram, Marty Burdette.

1977 FINALS—March 27

INDIANAPOLIS (Market Square Arena): East Chicago Washington 66–45 Terre Haute South; Carmel 71–60 Columbus East; Carmel 53–52 Washington. Officials: Troy Ingram, Bill Wullner, Gene Butts, Roger DeYoung, Eugene Linn, Eric Harmon.

1978 SECTIONALS

ANDERSON: Lapel 55–37 Daleville; Anderson 63–50 Madison Heights; Alexandria 69–39 Frankton; Highland 42–37 Pendleton Heights; Anderson 61–53 Lapel; Alexandria 73–56 Highland; Anderson 67–66 Alexandria. Officials: Jerry Petro, Craig Martin, Steve Welmer, Kenneth Gorrell.

BATESVILLE: Jac-Cen-Del 82–55 Moores Hill; South Ripley 70–61 Milan; Batesville 58–52 Jac-Cen-Del; South Ripley 64–56 Batesville. Officials: James Wehsollek, Jerome Davis, Gary Woodling, Robert Carr.

BEDFORD–NORTH LAWRENCE: Bedford–North Lawrence 81–54 Eastern (Greene Co.); Bloomington South 66–44 Orleans; Mitchell 97–64 Medora; Bloomington South 61–59 Bedford–North Lawrence; Bloomington South 53–50 Mitchell. Officials: Jerry Larrison, Allen Youmans, Max Cameron, Bruce Knecht, Charles Weinkauf.

BEN DAVIS: Northwest 68–62 Brebeuf; Washington 48–47 Shortridge; Pike 57–54 Ritter; Ben Davis 75–57 Speedway; Northwest 62–61 Washington; Ben Davis 81–57 Pike; Ben Davis 60–46 Northwest. Officials: Marty Burdette, Judson Raver, John Tucker, Ron Beard.

BENTON CENTRAL: Benton Central 48–41 Twin Lakes; South Newton 55–41 North White; Tri County 60–56 Frontier; Benton Central 72–66 South Newton; Benton Central 62–46

Tri–County. Officials: Richard Boer, Dave Atwell, Thomas Newlin, David Zurcher.

BLACKFORD: Blackford 97–65 Delta; Wes-Del 57–53 Eastbrook; Blackford 58–47 Wes-Del. Officials: Robert Reed, James Helms, Paul Leamon, Michael DeVault.

BOONVILLE: Boonville 42–35 Tell City; Heritage Hills 70–59 South Spencer; Tecumseh 65–51 Cannelton; Boonville 68–48 Castle; Tecumseh 50–48 Heritage Hills; Boonville 68–56 Tecumseh. Officials: Robert Klein, William Pittman, William Johnston, Paul Hackleman.

BROWNSBURG: Plainfield 76–42 Cascade; Brownsburg 101–69 Danville; Avon 54–53 Mooresville; Plainfield 78–75 Brownsburg; Avon 48–46 Plainfield. Officials: Raymond Norris, Steve White, John Ramey, Robert Gilmore.

CALUMET: Highland 53–38 East Gary Edison; Lake Central 47–45 Munster; Calumet 76–61 Crown Point; Merrillville 77–52 Griffith; Highland 69–61 Lake Central; Merrillville 61–60 Calumet; Merrillville 70–60 Highland. Officials: Darrell McFall, Bob Richardson, David Willoughby, Mike Bohan.

CARMEL: Carmel 72–51 Hamilton Southeastern; Westfield 58–55 Noblesville; Sheridan 48–37 Hamilton Heights; Carmel 74–54 Westfield; Carmel 64–40 Sheridan. Officials: Jerry Scott, James Fairchild, G. R. Honchell, Joe Edmonds.

COLUMBIA CITY: Columbia City 68–50 Central Noble; Whitko 73–72 Manchester (ot); Columbia City 71–59 Churubusco; Columbia 45–43 Whitko. Officials: Harold Gray, Jerome Fawley, William Champion, James Reinebold.

COLUMBUS: East 74–48 Brown County; North 84–69 Southwestern; Hauser 73–65 Edinburg; East 47–43 North; East 44–39 Hauser. Officials: Jesse Lynch, Lanny Rossman, Robert Kirk, James Roberts.

CONNERSVILLE: Union County 55–54 Laurel; Brookville 66–43 Cambridge City; Connersville 71–37 Morton Memorial; Brookville 72–52 Union County; Connersville 49–48 Brookville (ot). Officials: Jerry Newsom, Russell Ferrill, Delmus Aubrey, Louis Schmalfeldt.

DEKALB: Garrett 59–40 East Side; Angola 61–51 Prairie Heights; Fremont 64–60 DeKalb; Hamilton 55–53 Leo; Angola 74–48 Garrett; Hamilton 56–49 Fremont; Angola 57–52 Hamilton. Officials: William Sorukas, John Elliott, Kenneth Dickman, Dale Blosser.

EAST CENTRAL: Aurora 61–57 Lawrenceburg; East Central 86–61 Switzerland County; Rising Sun 67–63 Dillsboro; Aurora 81–50 East Central; Aurora 53–51 Rising Sun. Officials: Don Shields, Don Nester, Paul Beatty, Richard Eynon, Marty Burdette.

EAST CHICAGO: Roosevelt 77–48 Washington; Hammond Noll 82–59 Whiting; Noll 51–49 Roosevelt. Officials: Troy Ingram, Kevin Weinberg, Jacob Burton, Richard Bowie.

EAST NOBLE: East Noble 70–67 West Noble; Fairfield 80–42 Howe Military; Lakeland 68–46 Westview; East Noble 66–62 Bethany Christian; Lakeland 73–55 Fairfield; Lakeland 83–54 East Noble. Officials: Ken Miller, Phil Sullivan, Tom Jerles, Frank DeSantis.

ELKHART: NorthWood 57–55 Penn; Elkhart Memorial 67–56 Jimtown; Northridge 69–65 Goshen; Elkhart Central 84–58 Concord; Memorial 79–78 NorthWood; Central 66–57 Northridge; Central 55–52 Memorial. Officials: Clifford Spears, Rick Owens, Scott Healy, Mark Masariu.

EVANSVILLE: Mater Dei 76–67 Reitz; Memorial 45–44 Bosse; Central 61–47 Harrison; North 68–62 Mater Dei; Memorial 50–48 Central; North 73–60 Memorial. Officials: Don Shiflet, Darrell Eaton, William Shobe, Dave Lowenstein.

FLOYD CENTRAL: North Harrison 63–57 Corydon; Floyd Central 86–51 Borden; South

Tourney Time

Central 58–56 Lanesville; Floyd Central 82–49 North Harrison; Floyd Central 71–50 South Central. Officials: Phil Hardwick, Tad Heminger, David Petty, Jack Cummings.

FORT WAYNE (#1): North Side 64–51 Elmhurst; Carroll 74–65 Wayne; Luers 63–60 Concordia; North Side 66–46 Snider; Carroll 55–47 Luers; North Side 89–66 Carroll. Officials: Wayne Van Sickle, Steve Cherry, Daniel Moore, Bill Gray.

FORT WAYNE (#2): Dwenger 65–43 Heritage; South Side 52–43 Woodlan; Northrop 77–45 New Haven; Harding 46–42 Dwenger; South Side 65–58 Northrop; South Side 42–29 Harding. Officials: Tom Manning, Jon Davenport, Warren Benko, Roger DeYoung.

FOUNTAIN CENTRAL: North Vermillion 49–47 Fountain Central (2ot); Covington 74–49 Attica; Seeger 71–58 Turkey Run; Covington 77–69 North Vermillion; Seeger 76–73 Covington. Officials: Leslie Wright, Rushus Williams, Ronald Moore, Paul Garriott.

FRANKFORT: Rossville 47–44 Clinton Central; Frankfort 61–54 Tri-Central; Clinton Prairie 71–66 Tipton; Frankfort 89–55 Rossville; Frankfort 66–64 Clinton Prairie. Officials: Byron Weaver, Larry Maxwell, William DeRome, Richard Freeman.

FRANKLIN CENTRAL: Franklin Central 60–54 Warren Central; Scecina 59–55 Marshall; Beech Grove 56–48 Roncalli; Scecina 60–54 Franklin Central; Scecina 63–51 Beech Grove. Officials: Opal Courtney, Mike Winger, Mark Baltz, Donald Schmidt.

GARY: Wirt 63–54 West Side; Emerson 88–50 Wallace; Gary Roosevelt 92–70 Mann; Emerson 44–41 Wirt; Roosevelt 52–50 Emerson (ot). Officials: Dave Avery, Jay Smith, Dick Modricker, Mark Beck.

GREENCASTLE: Greencastle 63–46 Rockville; Van Buren 70–59 South Putnam; Cloverdale 52–42 North Putnam; Van Buren 75–63 Greencastle; Van Buren 52–36 Cloverdale. Officials: Don Snedeker, Frank Hobson, Dennie Oxley, John Lyskowinski.

GREENSBURG: Greensburg 66–40 North Decatur; Waldron 63–57 South Decatur; Rushville 64–56 Greensburg; Rushville 64–48 Waldron. Officials: Officials: Pete Deakyne, Gary Cheeseman, Don Hittle, Bruce Mayfield.

GREENWOOD: Center Grove 64–62 Whiteland; Indian Creek 68–66 Greenwood; Franklin 65–63 Center Grove; Indian Creek 55–53 Franklin (ot). Officials: Norman Hathcoat, Jack Graham, Ralph Scales, Bud Wetzel, Steve Cherry.

HAMMOND: Andrean 68–51 Clark; Morton 69–67 Hammond High; Gavit 56–44 Tech; Morton 50–48 Andrean; Gavit 64–62 Morton. Officials: Jerry Karstens, Keith Yoder, Ronald Carter, Ronald Flotow.

HUNTINGTON: Southwood 49–47 Huntington Catholic; White's 61–59 Homestead; Huntington North 75–57 Wabash; Northfield 70–68 Southwood; North 86–59 White's; North 81–56 Northfield. Officials: Ken Sussman, Tom Simler, Robert Debroka, Gary Foltz.

INDIANAPOLIS: North Central 60–50 Lawrence Central; Tech 91–75 Broad Ripple; Lawrence North 85–60 Chatard; Cathedral 59–46 Arlington; Tech 68–61 North Central; Cathedral 35–31 Lawrence North; Tech 62–59 Cathedral. Officials: Tom Knox, Robert Boyle, Frank Hoagburg, Gil Baumgartner.

JAY COUNTY: Jay County 59–44 Wapahani; Randolph Southern 60–59 Union City; Monroe Central 70–68 Winchester; Jay County 65–62 Randolph Southern; Jay County 55–35 Monroe Central. Officials: Gene Gibson, Dale Cramer, Tony Primavera, Roger Pflughaupt.

JEFFERSONVILLE: Clarksville 76–65 New Albany; Providence 51–50 Jeffersonville; Clarksville 94–66 Providence. Officials: Winfield Jacobs, Kenneth Cave, Larry Sintz, Dennis Cave.

IHSAA Scores | 1970–1979

KANKAKEE VALLEY: North Newton 65–61 Hanover Central; Lowell 42–40 Kankakee Valley; Hebron 69–66 Kouts; West Central 83–73 Rensselaer; North Newton 48–44 Lowell; Hebron 69–67 West Central; North Newton 52–50 Hebron. Officials: Larry Jones, Dale VanHouten, Ken Keller, Herbert Hicks.

KOKOMO: Kokomo 80–35 Taylor; Eastern 83–54 Northwestern; Haworth 63–60 Western; Kokomo 67–52 Eastern; Kokomo 68–48 Haworth. Officials: Richard Lederman, Benjamin Hirt, Tom Crouch, Delmar Knecht.

LAFAYETTE: Delphi 70–60 Central Catholic; Jefferson 69–51 Carroll; West Lafayette 64–56 Harrison; Delphi 65–58 Jefferson; Delphi 49–36 West Lafayette. Officials: Danny Jacobs, Mark Reyher, Gene Johnson, Charles Hadley.

LEBANON: Zionsville 49–45 Western Boone; Lebanon 57–36 Tri-West; Lebanon 53–51 Zionsville (ot). Officials: Gene Butts, Don Criswell, Charles Roush, Carl March.

LOGANSPORT: Peru 55–50 Logansport; Maconaquah 76–51 Pioneer; North Miami 55–54 Caston; Cass 84–42 Kewanna; Peru 71–54 Maconaquah; Cass 76–60 North Miami; Cass 90–71 Peru. Officials: Richard Cook, Ronald Waisnora, Steve Beres, Robert Marcinek.

MADISON: Silver Creek 81–60 Madison Shawe; Madison 57–51 Southwestern; New Washington 58–46 Henryville; Silver Creek 58–45 Charlestown; Madison 60–56 New Washington; Silver Creek 48–44 Madison. Officials: Wendell Baker, Jimmie Westerfield, David Lee, Temme Patterson.

MARION: Mississinewa 46–42 Oak Hill; Madison-Grant 73–42 Marion Bennett; Marion 75–46 Elwood; Mississinewa 27–25 Madison-Grant; Marion 77–48 Mississinewa. Officials: Gene Marks, Merl Heckaman, Larry Hollman, Richard Brainerd.

MARTINSVILLE: Bloomington North 68–42 Edgewood; Martinsville 80–69 Monrovia; Eminence 93–72 Owen Valley; North 71–60 Martinsville; Eminence 76–64 North. Officials: Robert Beeson, Roger Fisher, Tom Rohr, Gren Lefebvre.

MICHIGAN CITY: Westville 48–47 Rogers; LaPorte 58–46 Chesterton; Elston 70–69 New Prairie; Marquette 44–38 Westville; Elston 67–57 LaPorte; Elston 75–49 Marquette. Officials: Jim Cox, Mike Crouch, Dave Long, George Dyer.

MUNCIE: North 64–37 Cowan; Central 49–41 Yorktown (3ot); Burris 65–56 South; Central 50–47 North; Central 75–32 Burris. Officials: Gary Eaglin, Thomas VonDeylen, Steve Skiles, John Fleischman.

NEW CASTLE: Tri 78–49 Blue River; New Castle 89–47 Mt. Vernon; Knightstown 56–53 Shenandoah; Union 44–38 Eastern Hancock; New Castle 58–52 Tri; Union 44–38 Knightstown; New Castle 77–56 Union. Officials: Rex Mays, Bill Graham, Edward Koors, Terry Stewart.

NORTH JUDSON: Culver 60–51 Culver Military; North Judson 64–55 Knox; Winamac 66–62 Oregon–Davis; South Central 88–57 LaCrosse; North Judson 48–45 Culver; South Central 38–35 Winamac; North Judson 73–57 South Central. Officials: Don Koester, Leland Thompson, Jim Anderson, Dan Yagodnik.

NORTH MONTGOMERY: Southmont 63–57 North Montgomery; Crawfordsville 56–54 McCutcheon; Crawfordsville 63–57 Southmont. Officials: John Hilligoss, David Watt, Ronald Grimes, William Fields.

PAOLI: Paoli 59–57 Eastern (Pekin); Springs Valley 77–6 4 Crawford County; Salem 63–56 West Washington; Paoli 65–57 Springs Valley; Paoli 62–57 Salem. Officials: Norman Chestnut, Larry Collins, Donald Dockery, James Dunlap.

Tourney Time

PLYMOUTH: La Ville 47–45 Glenn; Bremen 68–65 Plymouth; Argos 82–59 North Liberty; Bremen 52–51 La Ville (ot); Argos 46–39 Bremen. Officials: Nick Sweigart, Larry Freyburgher, Herb Pruett, Reginald Cheatham.

PRINCETON: Princeton 83–51 New Harmony; Oakland City 56–47 North Posey; Mt. Vernon 60–58 Gibson Southern; Princeton 52–47 Oakland City; Mt. Vernon 52–48 Princeton. Officials: Robert Wolfe, Don Thompson, Michael Wallpe, Ronald Ham.

RICHMOND: Richmond 92–34 Centerville; Hagerstown 69–68 Northeastern; Richmond 90–50 Hagerstown. Officials: James Benecke, Jerry Pieper, Jerry Christie, Noel Baker.

SEYMOUR: Seymour 72–60 Jennings County; Scottsburg 80–61 Brownstown Central; Austin 74–41 Crothersville; Scottsburg 72–67 Seymour; Scottsburg 47–42 Austin. Officials: Brandon Bryant, Gary Leistner, Richard Hughes, Mel Botkin.

SHELBYVILLE: Shelbyville 91–52 Morristown; Greenfield Central 56–47 Triton Central; Shelbyville 79–60 New Palestine; Shelbyville 64–56 Greenfield Central. Officials: Eugene Linn, Richard Schleicher, William Gebhart, Chuck Weinkauf.

SOUTH ADAMS: Norwell 72–61 South Adams; Southern Wells 63–56 Adams Central; Bellmont 80–75 Bluffton; Norwell 82–64 Southern Wells; Norwell 66–65 Bellmont. Officials: Ray Mitrione, Ric Baldwin, Gaylord Fritz, John Gassessmith, Bruce Knecht.

SOUTH BEND: Riley 64–53 Mishawaka Marian; Clay 66–63 Adams; LaSalle 56–54 Mishawaka (ot); Washington 83–58 St. Joseph's; Clay 65–60 Riley; LaSalle 76–69 Washington; LaSalle 45–44 Clay. Officials: Jimmy Dimitroff, Wayne Targgart, Ronald Ramsey, George Taylor.

SOUTHPORT: Wood 98–93 Southport (2ot); Attucks 64–51 Decatur Central; Perry Meridian 60–58 Manual; Howe 95–56 School for the Deaf; Wood 74–71 Attucks; Perry Meridian 52–48 Howe; Wood 80–58 Perry Meridian. Officials: Bill Wullner, Thomas Neuman, James Miller, Rich Clark.

SOUTHRIDGE: Northeast Dubois 59–53 Forest Park; Jasper 62–49 Southridge; Perry Central 63–55 Northeast Dubois; Perry Central 56–55 Jasper. Officials: Morris Cohen, Glen Clemons, James Saunders, James Rider.

SWITZ CITY: Worthington 66–64 L & M; Shakamak 78–60 Linton; Bloomfield 81–38 Switz City Central; Shakamak 66–65 Worthington; Bloomfield 56–42 Shakamak. Officials: Keith Combs, Rick Kingston, Jim Fish, D. J. Frazer.

TERRE HAUTE NORTH: North 67–57 Laboratory; Staunton 52–35 Rosedale; Brazil 74–60 South Vermillion; North 80–47 Montezuma; Staunton 53–52 Brazil; North 66–44 Staunton. Officials: Jack Williams, Carl Redman, Jack Behme, Mason Meeks.

TERRE HAUTE SOUTH: Sullivan 47–36 Clay City; South 84–52 Union (Dugger); West Vigo 71–59 North Central; South 56–45 Sullivan; South 65–49 West Vigo. Officials: Melvin Redman, Charles Bertram, Victor Gilla, Norman Hathcoat.

TRITON: Wawasee 55–52 Warsaw; Tippecanoe Valley 89–58 Triton; Rochester 50–48 Wawasee; Rochester 53–48 Tippecanoe Valley. Officials: Ward Weisel, Ron Resler, Dave Vendrely, Thomas Dull.

VALPARAISO: Morgan Twp. 66–39 Wheeler; Hobart 62–45 Washington Twp.; Valparaiso 82–74 River Forest; Portage 60–46 Boone Grove; Morgan Twp. 65–55 Hobart; Valparaiso 51–39 Portage; Valparaiso 62–41 Morgan Twp. Officials: John Lozier, George Grygiel, Robert Wasson, Donald O'Connor, Tim Fogarty.

VINCENNES: South Knox 59–53 North Knox; Vincennes 47–36 Vincennes Rivet; Vincennes

49–41 South Knox. Officials: Jack Mercer, Richie Moore, Charles Siebe, Ed Scott.

WASHINGTON: Loogootee 49–44 Barr–Reeve; Washington 79–46 North Daviess; Washington Catholic 63–61 Shoals; Loogootee 53–49 Pike Central (2ot); Washington 74–39 Catholic; Washington 56–33 Loogootee. Officials: Don Hurst, Don Smith, John Evans, McKee Munk.

1978 REGIONALS

ANDERSON: Blackford 62–59 Carmel; Anderson 66–64 Kokomo (ot); Anderson 76–62 Blackford. Officials: Don Shiflet, Dave Atwell, Kenneth Miller, Gary Foltz, Roger DeYoung, Gene Linn.

COLUMBUS: Shelbyville 50–47 Indian Creek; Columbus East 76–61 Eminence; East 50–47 Shelbyville (ot). Officials: Gary Cheeseman, Rich Clark, Harold Gray, Jack Graham, Keith Combs, Don Snedeker.

CONNERSVILLE: Connersville 69–56 Aurora; Rushville 61–54 South Ripley; Connersville 71–59 Rushville. Officials: James Reinebold, Michael Winger, Phillip Hardwick, Ronald Beard, Byron Weaver, Winfield Jacobs.

ELKHART: Argos 49–43 Rochester; Elkhart Central 80–61 Columbia City; Central 80–67 Argos. Officials: Brandon Bryant, Mark Masariu, Richard Modricker, Don Hurst, Nick Sweigart, Chuck Weinkauf.

EVANSVILLE: Evansville North 76–56 Mt. Vernon; Boonville 64–47 Vincennes; Boonville 72–65 North. Officials: Officials: Steve Cherry, Thomas Simler, George Taylor, Robert Beeson, John Lozier, Norman Chestnut.

FORT WAYNE: Lakeland 56–48 Angola; North Side 61–50 South Side; North Side 47–44 Lakeland. Officials: Rick Owens, Richard Brainerd, Jim Cox, Jesse Lynch, James Wehsollek, Don Koester.

FRANKFORT: Crawfordsville 50–48 Avon; Frankfort 65–58 Lebanon; Frankfort 74–58 Crawfordsville. Officials: Jerry Scott, William Fields, Jerry Karstens, Dale Blosser, David Lowenstein, Wayne Van Sickle.

GARY: Hammond Noll 73–71 Gary Roosevelt (ot); Merrillville 62–57 Hammond Gavit; Merrillville 48–47 Noll. Officials: Robert Reed, Donald O'Connor, Marty Burdette, Jack Mercer, Pete Deakyne, Jerry Larrison.

INDIANAPOLIS: Ben Davis 73–67 Wood; Tech 59–55 Scecina; Tech 62–61 Ben Davis. Officials: Jack Williams, Melvin Redman, Richard Freeman, Jack Cummings, Danny Jacobs, Gene Marks.

LAFAYETTE: Seeger 64–59 North Newton; Benton Central 50–49 Delphi; Benton Central 75–62 Seeger. Officials: Darrell Eaton, Wendell Baker, Joe Edmonds, William Graham, Jerry Petro, Richard Boer.

MARION: Cass 79–66 Huntington; Marion 63–61 Norwell (ot); Marion 58–55 Cass (ot). Officials: Thomas Manning, Gren Lefebvre, Robert Gilmore, Steve White, Richard Cook, Opal Courtney.

NEW CASTLE: Muncie Central 57–41 Jay County; Richmond 55–52 New Castle; Central 53–52 Richmond (2ot). Officials: Frank DeSantis, Robert Boyle, Larry Jones, Frank Hoagburg, Tom Knox, Jimmy Dimitroff.

Tourney Time

SEYMOUR: Clarksville 97–86 Silver Creek; Scottsburg 81–62 Floyd Central; Scottsburg 95–77 Clarksville. Officials: John Tucker, Morris Cohen, Ronald Ham, Donald Ricketts, Robert Wolfe, Troy Ingram.

SOUTH BEND: Valparaiso 72–59 Michigan City Elston, South Bend LaSalle 79–55 North Judson; LaSalle 53–52 Valparaiso. Officials: David Avery, John Fleischman, Clifford Spears, Mason Meeks, Gil Baumgartner, Donald Schmidt.

TERRE HAUTE: Bloomfield 49–47 Terrhe Haute North; Terre Haute South 79–77 Van Buren (2ot); South 54–41 Bloomfield. Officials: David Zurcher, Bruce Knecht, Robert Marcinek, Carl Redman, Mike Bohan, Donald Shields.

WASHINGTON: Washington 53–46 Bloomington South; Paoli 66–58 Perry Central; Washington 82–44 Paoli. Officials: Gary Eaglin, Norman Hathcoat, Raymond Norris, James Dunlap, Kenneth Gorrell, Bill Wullner.

1978 SEMI-STATES

EVANSVILLE: Terre Haute South 75–50 Boonville; Washington 81–65 Scottsburg; South 55–53 Washington. Officials: Wayne Van Sickle, Harold Gray, Jerry Petro, Kenneth Gorrell, James Wehsollek, Troy Ingram.

INDIANAPOLIS: Muncie Central 84–64 Connersville; Indianapolis Tech 61–59 Columbus East; Central 70–66 Tech. Officials: Roger DeYoung, Donald Shields, Eugene Linn, John Lozier, Marty Burdette, Gene Marks.

LAFAYETTE: Merrillville 58–50 South Bend LaSalle; Frankfort 70–64 Benton Central; Merrillville 80–68 Frankfort. Officials: Mike Bohan, Donald Schmidt, Tom Knox, Jerry Larrison, Bill Wullner, Jimmy Dimitroff.

SOUTH BEND: Elkhart Central 65–54 Fort Wayne North; Anderson 84–77 Marion (2ot); Central 76–74 Anderson. Officials: Don Snedeker, Byron Weaver, Richard Freeman, Jesse Lynch, Don Koester, Richard Cook.

1978 FINALS—April 15

Tournaments were delayed because of power shortages due to strikes in the coal industry.

INDIANAPOLIS (Market Square Arena): Muncie Central 89–85 Elkhart Central; Terre Haute South 54–53 Merrillville (ot); Central 65–64 South (ot). Officials: Don Koester, Gene Marks, James Wehsollek, Jimmy Dimitroff, Marty Burdette, Richard Cook.

1979 SECTIONALS

ANDERSON: Lapel 66–50 Frankton; Madison Heights 72–70 Alexandria; Highland 74–43 Daleville; Anderson 83–57 Pendleton Heights; Madison Heights 66–54 Lapel; Anderson 76–60 Highland; Anderson 74–67 Madison Heights. Officials: Wayne Van Sickle, Rich Clark, Lanny Rossman, Roger McGriff.

BEDFORD-NORTH LAWRENCE: Bedford-North Lawrence 66–39 Orleans; Bloomington South 44–36 Mitchell; Eastern (Greene Co.) 77–47 Medora; Bedford-North Lawrence 58–57 Bloomington South; Bedford-North Lawrence 72–49 Eastern. Officials: Kenneth Gorrell, Charles

IHSAA Scores | 1970–1979

Bertram, Tom Rohr, Steve Welmer.

BEN DAVIS: Ben Davis 83–64 Ritter; Northwest 59–56 Brebeuf; Pike 60–52 Shortridge; Washington 73–52 Speedway; Ben Davis 77–55 Northwest; Washington 64–57 Pike; Washington 63–46 Ben Davis. Officials: Keith Combs, Richard Hall, Mark Beck, James Dunlap.

BENTON CENTRAL: Twin Lakes 52–51 North White; Benton Central 50–21 South Newton; Tri County 66–61 Frontier; Benton Central 67–59 Twin Lakes; Benton Central 84–42 Tri County. Officials: Winfield Jacobs, Richard Bowie, Ronald Moore, William Sorukas.

BLACKFORD: Delta 67–62 Blackford; Eastbrook 59–56 Wes-Del; Eastbrook 63–53 Delta. Officials: Gary Foltz, Wayne Targgart, Richard Beck, Richard Lederman.

BOONVILLE: South Spencer 60–34 Boonville; Castle 47–46 Heritage Hills; Tecumseh 63–57 Cannelton; South Spencer 42–28 Tell City; Castle 69–68 Tecumseh; South Spencer 42–34 Castle. Officials: Danny Jacobs, Ronald Grimes, Al Christoules, William Fields.

BROWNSBURG: Mooresville 80–58 Plainfield; Brownsburg 50–49 Cascade; Danville 61–60 Avon; Mooresville 67–62 Brownsburg; Mooresville 68–65 Danville. Officials: Don Hurst, Tom Jerles, Doug Bauman, Bill Graham.

CALUMET: Calumet 61–46 Highland; Merrillville 66–39 East Gary Edison; Lake Central 58–48 Griffith; Crown Point 66–54 Munster; Merrillville 59–56 Calumet; Lake Central 71–62 Crown Point; Lake Central 42–34 Merrillville. Officials: Jerry Scott, Jerome Fawley, Benjamin Hirt, Ron Hosinski.

CARMEL: Sheridan 56–48 Westfield; Hamilton Heights 78–56 Hamilton Southeastern; Carmel 66–58 Noblesville; Hamilton Heights 84–58 Sheridan; Carmel 83–51 Hamilton Heights. Officials: Roger DeYoung, John Tucker, Tom Crouch, Dick Modricker.

COLUMBIA CITY: Churubusco 64–62 Manchester (ot); Columbia City 71–69 Central Noble (ot); Whitko 68–55 Churubusco; Whitko 74–50 Columbia City. Officials: Clifford Spears, Jon Davenport, Fred Mohri, Robert Reed.

COLUMBUS: North 84–62 Southwestern; East 57–42 Edinburgh; Brown County 67–61 Hauser; East 52–41 North; East 69–51 Brown County. Officials: Jack Williams, Larry Collins, Thomas Dull, Rudy Williams.

CONNERSVILLE: Brookville 62–53 Connersville; Union County 61–41 Laurel; Cambridge City 88–51 Morton Memorial; Union County 65–39 Brookville; Union County 62–61 Cambridge City. Officials: Terry Stewart, William Gebhart, Jim Saunders, Richard Eynon.

DeKALB: Leo 61–56 Garrett; DeKalb 62–34 Eastside; Hamilton 78–53 Fremont; Angola 59–31 Prairie Heights; DeKalb 70–57 Leo; Angola 54–53 Hamilton; DeKalb 58–54 Angola. Officials: Dave Avery, Ron Kitts, Jay Smith, Pete Deakyne.

EAST CENTRAL: Batesville 60–50 South Ripley; Milan 61–58 East Central; Batesville 90–58 JacCen-Del; Batesville 57–56 Milan. Officials: Wendell Baker, Jim Fish, David Petty, Rick Owens.

EAST CHICAGO: Hammond Noll 62–57 Washington; Roosevelt 57–40 Whiting; Noll 60–58 Roosevelt. Officials: Jesse Lynch, Robert DeBroka, Louis Harmening, Ron Flotow.

EAST NOBLE: Fairfield 67–58 Lakeland; Westview 84–52 West Noble; Bethany Christian 57–45 Howe Military; East Noble 66–47 Fairfield; Westview 101–60 Bethany Christian; Westview 82–71 East Noble. Officials: Don O'Connor, James Miller, Bob Storm, Gene Gibson.

ELKHART: Memorial 100–72 Jimtown; Penn 68–52 Northridge; Concord 58–55 NorthWood; Central 68–57 Goshen; Penn 70–69 Memorial; Central 65–47 Concord; Central

Tourney Time

62–61 Penn. Officials: Norman Hathcoat, Bob Carr, Phil Sullivan, Bill Gray.

EVANSVILLE: Mater Dei 69–57 Harrison; North 58–56 Memorial; Bosse 54–49 Reitz; Central 75–58 Mater Dei; North 64–61 Bosse; North 70–67 Central. Officials: Jimmy Dimitroff, Joseph Gilliland, Ron Ramsey, Louis Schmalfeldt.

FLOYD CENTRAL: North Harrison 50–48 South Central (ot); Floyd Central 79–55 Lanesville; Borden 69–49 Corydon; Floyd Central 62–54 North Harrison; Floyd Central 56–48 Borden. Officials: Robert Beeson, David Watt, William Shobe, David Willoughby.

FORT WAYNE (#1): Concordia 73–67 Heritage; North Side 70–49 Luers; South Side 74–46 New Haven; Concordia 58–46 Wayne; South Side 63–53 North Side; South Side 66–59 Concordia. Officials: Gene Marks, Gary Cheeseman, David Long, Brandon Bryant.

FORT WAYNE (#2): Dwenger 67–61 Northrop; Harding 71–60 Snider; Elmhurst 64–46 Carroll; Dwenger 93–45 Woodlan; Harding 84–77 Elmhurst; Harding 72–62 Dwenger. Officials: Jerry Larrison, Kenneth Dickman, Tony Primavera, Chuck Weinjauf.

FOUNTAIN CENTRAL: North Vermillion 69–56 Covington; Fountain Central 66–64 Seeger; Turkey Run 58–56 Attica; Fountain Central 70–58 North Vermillion; Fountain Central 57–56 Turkey Run. Officials: James Wehsollek, Steve Beres, Scott Healy, Charles Hadley.

FRANKFORT: Frankfort 89–64 Clinton Prairie; Tipton 64–61 Tri Central; Clinton Central 54–52 Rossville; Tipton 56–55 Frankfort; Clinton Central 76–74 Tipton. Officials: Eugene Linn, David Vendrely, Bill Kaylor, Thomas Neuman.

FRANKLIN CENTRAL: Roncalli 46–39 Warren Central; Beech Grove 60–57 Scecina (ot); Franklin Centra; 62–50 Marshall; Beech Grove 50–46 Roncalli; Franklin Central 59–55 Beech Grove. Officials: Norman Chestnut, Don Smith, Sr., James Roberts, Don Shiflet.

GARY: Wirt 69–52 Wallace; Emerson 78–75 West Side; Gary Roosevelt 62–55 Mann; Emerson 75–63 Wirt; Roosevelt 58–57 Emerson. Officials: John Lozier, Jerry Cook, Charles Redinger, Michael DeVault.

GREENCASTLE: Van Buren 80–56 Cloverdale; North Putnam 55–52 Rockville; Greencastle 68–49 South Putnam; Van Buren 65–47 North Putnam; Van Buren 65–50 Greencastle. Officials: Temme Patterson, Don Criswell, Jerry Christie, Ronald Ham.

GREENSBURG: Rushville 66–58 Waldron; South Decatur 80–60 North Decatur; Rushville 60–52 Greensburg; Rushville 65–61 South Decatur. Officials: Morris Cohen, Mike Crouch, Rex Nichols, Herb Pruett.

HAMMOND: Andrean 82–57 Gavit; Morton 71–53 Tech; Hammond High 68–45 Clark; Morton 78–57 Andrean; Hammond High 76–72 Morton. Officials: Frank DeSantis, Jacob Burton, Tim Fogarty, Gren Lefebvre.

HUNTINGTON: Northfield 52–49 Wabash; Homestead 60–52 Huntington Catholic; Huntington North 74–50 White's; Southwood 47–46 Northfield; North 66–54 Homesyead; North 64–59 Southwood. Officials: Richard Cook, Ken Keller, John Gassensmith, Dale Blosser.

INDIANAPOLIS: Broad Ripple 63–62 Cathedral; Tech 77–65 Chatard; Arlington 58–49 Lawrence North; North Central 74–64 Lawrence Central; Broad Ripple 62–53 Tech; North Central 65–50 Arlington; North Central 96–75 Broad Ripple. Officials: Harold Gray, Dave Atwell, Harry Northington, Carl March.

JAY COUNTY: Winchester 66–52 Wapahani; Jay County 59–58 Union City; Randolph Southern 47–46 Monroe Central; Jay County 54–51 Winchester; Jay County 66–62 Randolph Southern. Officials: Tom Knox, Dale VanHouten, Gaylord Fritz, Jim Benecke.

IHSAA Scores | 1970–1979

JEFFERSONVILLE: Clarksville 82–72 Jeffersonville; New Albany 81–74 Providence; Clarksville 79–77 New Albany (ot). Officials: Troy Ingram, Dan Moore, Ed Roush, Paul Garriott.

KANKAKEE VALLEY: West Central 67–62 Kouts; Lowell 55–53 Hebron; Rensselaer Central 71–37 Hanover Central; Kankakee Valley 50–41 North Newton; Lowell 64–61 West Central; Kankakee Valley 47–43 Rensselaer Central; Kankakee Valley 65–46 Lowell. Officials: Rex Mays, Bill Champion, Mike Waisnora, Kevin Weinberg.

KOKOMO: Kokomo 49–40 Northwestern; Western 63–60 Haworth; Eastern 79–72 Taylor; Kokomo 84–61 Western; Kokomo 63–62 Eastern. Officials: Robert Marcinek, David Nichols, Steven Bollier, Daniel Yagodnik.

LAFAYETTE: Carroll 79–57 Central Catholic; West Lafayette 56–47 Delphi; Harrison 69–54 Jefferson; West Lafayette 55–49 Carroll; West Lafayette 47–39 Harrison. Officials: Nick Sweigart, Warren Benko, John Gross, Jr., Herbert Hicks.

LEBANON: Western Boone 59–49 Zionsville; Lebanon 57–55 Tri West; Lebanon 49–35 Western Boone. Officials: Larry Jones, Craig Martin, William Johnston, Mark Reyher.

LOGANSPORT: Peru 88–64 Caston; Cass 59–50 North Miami; Logansport 60–41 Pioneer; Maconaquah 72–57 Kewanna; Peru 49–41 Cass; Logansport 78–66 Maconaquah; Logansport 41–40 Peru (ot). Officials: Jack Mercer, Ron Carter, Lloyd Ahlbrand, Tom Manning.

MADISON: Southwestern 65–59 Madison; Charlestown 67–48 New Washington; Silver Creek 99–73 Madison Shawe; Southwestern 57–45 Henryville; Silver Creek 77–70 Charlestown; Silver Creek 55–47 Southwestern. Officials: Bob Wolfe, Robert Klein, Richard Hughes, Robert Kirk.

MARION: Elwood 73–62 Oak Hill; Marion 72–54 Madison-Grant; Mississinewa 83–49 Marion Bennett; Marion 75–42 Elwood; Marion 87–71 Mississinewa. Officials: Judson Raver, Tom Simler, Keith Yoder, John Fleischman.

MARTINSVILLE: Bloomington 78–53 Eminence; Edgewood 65–52 Monrovia; Owen Valley 72–57 Martinsville; North 71–57 Edgewood; North 67–59 Owen Valley. Officials: Donald Shields, Jack Cummings, Delmus Aubrey, Delmar Knecht.

MICHIGAN CITY: Rogers 70–61 LaPorte; River Forest 85–63 Westville; Elston 82–56 New Prairie; Rogers 72–54 Marquette; Elston 82–67 River Forest; Rogers 91–69 Elston. Officials: George Taylor, Larry Hollman, Paul Leamon, Robert Boyle.

MUNCIE: Central 87–34 Cowan; Southside 65–49 Burris; Northside 56–45 Yorktown; Central 63–38 Southside; Central 61–48 Northside. Officials: Richard Freeman, Edward Koors, G. R, Honchell, Roger Pflughaupt.

NEW CASTLE: Union 60–50 Eastern Hancock; Shenandoah 56–44 Knightstown; New Castle 84–44 Mount Vernon; Tri 50–43 Blue River; Shenandoah 79–46 Union; New Castle 66–38 Tri; New Castle 59–46 Shenandoah. Officials: Frank Hoagburg, David Lee, Robert Wasson, Gary Eaglin.

NORTH JUDSON: North Judson 84–82 Culver Military (2ot); Oregon-Davis 77–62 LaCrosse; South Central 66–45 Knox; Winamac 61–41 Culver Community; Oregon-Davis 68–56 North Judson; South Central 53–49 Winamac; Oregon-Davis 54–48 South Central. Officials: Richard Boer, Ron Waisnora, Al Youmans, James Reinebold, Sr.

NORTH MONTGOMERY: Crawfordsville 62–46 Southmont; North Montgomery 67–58 McCutcheon; Crawfordsville 55–54 North Montgomery. Officials: Melvin Redman, Skip Frazer,

515

Tourney Time

Ivan Burkle, Carl Redman.

PAOLI: Crawford County 84–58 Eastern (Pekin); Springs Valley 74–59 West Washington; Paoli 61–59 Salem (ot); Springs Valley 59–56 Crawford County; Springs Valley 66–60 Paoli. Officials: Ken Sussman, Jack Behme, BobRichardson, Jimmie Westerfield.

PLYMOUTH: Plymouth 58–53 North Liberty; Argos 65–42 Bremen; LaVille 57–48 Glenn; Argos 96–79 Plymouth; Argos 69–59 LaVille. Officials: Jerry Karstens, Don Resler, James Anderson, Dave Zurcher.

PRINCETON: Princeton 78–52 Oakland City; Gibson Southern 87–50 New Harmony; Mt. Vernon 79–63 North Posey; Princeton 85–72 Gibson Southern; Princeton 67–58 Mt. Vernon. Officials: Mason Meeks, Glen Clemons, Gary Woodling, Jack Graham.

RICHMOND: Northeastern 69–67 Centerville; Richmond 97–52 Hagerstown; Richmond 90–43 Northeastern. Officials: Don Snedeker, Paul Cox, Lonnie Eaglin, John Lyskowinski.

SEYMOUR: Scottsburg 56–30 Austin; Jennings County 60–58 Seymour; Brownstown Central 73–66 Crothersville; Scottsburg 68–64 Jennings County; Scottsburg 103–62 Brownstown Central. Officials: Bill Wullner, Donald Nester, Kenneth Cave, Jim Cox.

SHELBYVILLE: Shelbyville 79–53 Greenfield Central; New Palestine 58–46 Morristown; Shelbyville 73–40 Triton Central; Shelbyville 54–46 New Palestine. Officials: Mark Masariu, Leland Thompson, Mike Wallpe, McKee Munk.

SOUTH ADAMS: Bellmont 86–73 Southern Wells; Bluffton 69–54 Norwell; South Adams 80–60 Adams Central; Bellmont 76–73 Bluffton; Bellmont 68–60 South Adams. Officials: Stephen White, Donald Hittle, Paul Beatty, Mark Baltz.

SOUTH BEND: Adams 64–52 St. Joseph's; Riley 71–55 Mishawaka; LaSalle 59–56 Clay; Washington 66–48 Mishawaka Marian; Adams 67–56 Riley; Washington 56–52 LaSalle (ot); Adams 89–65 Washington. Officials: Mike Bohan, Reginald Cheatham, John Evans, Gil Baumgartner.

SOUTH DEARBORN: Switzerland County 59–34 Rising Sun; Lawrenceburg 63–54 South Dearborn; Lawrenceburg 59–55 Switzerland County. Officials: Ward Weisel, William DeRome, Larry Sintz, Larry Freyburgher.

SOUTHPORT: Attucks 61–48 Southport; Decatur Central 55–49 Perry Meridian; Howe 99–32 School for the Deaf; Manual 74–66 Attucks; Howe 66–64 Decatur Central (ot); Howe 88–68 Manual. Officials: Ronald Beard, James Helms, Steven Skiles, Steve Cherry.

SOUTHRIDGE: Northeast Dubois 46–45 Perry Central; Southridge 56–40 Forest Park; Northeast Dubois 64–58 Jasper; Southridge 46–44 Northeast Dubois. Officials: Jerry Newsom, Bruce Mayfield; Richard Alexander, Larry Maxwell.

SWITZ CITY: Bloomfield 50–40 Linton; Switz City 70–68 Worthington; Shakamak 64–52 L & M; Bloomfield 63–50 Switz City; Bloomfield 54–44 Shakamak. Officials: Byron Weaver, Dennis Thomas, Charles Siebe, William Pittman.

TERRE HAUTE NORTH: North 73–43 Montezuma; Brazil 77–57 South Vermillion; Rosedale 68–51 Staunton; North 57–49 Brazil; North 94–73 Rosedale. Officials: Don Ricketts, Tad Heminger, Roger Fisher, Bruce Knecht.

TERRE HAUTE SOUTH: South 66–57 Sullivan; North Central 86–60 West Vigo; Union (Dugger) 79–66 Clay City; South 88–63 North Central; South 89–55 Union. Officials: Richie Moore, Paul Hackleman, Paul Crawford, Darrell Eaton.

TRITON: Tippecanoe Valley 74–37 Triton; Warsaw 70–68 Rochester; Tippecanoe Valley

63–60 Wawasee; Tippecanoe Valley 58–48 Warsaw. Officials: James Fairchild, Joe Edmonds, Jerry Davis, Robert Gilmore.

VALPARAISO: Valparaiso 60–57 Chesterton (ot); Portage 83–48 Wheeler; Morgan Twp. 68–55 Washington Twp.; Boone Grove 66–53 Hobart; Valparaiso 65–60 Portage; Boone Grove 67–54 Morgan Twp.; Valparaiso 59–57 Boone Grove. Officials: Don Schmidt, Mike Winger, Dale Cramer, Merl Heckaman.

VINCENNES: South Knox 51–41 Vincennes Rivet; Vincennes 64–58 North Knox; Vincennes 41–30 South Knox. Officials: Ray Norris, Max Cameron, Donald Dockery, Richard Schleicher.

WASHINGTON: Washington 86–27 Shoals; Loogootee 78–45 North Daviess; Pike Central 54–47 Barr–Reeve; Washington 95–56 Washington Catholic; Loogootee 55–37 Pike Central; Washington 52–49 Loogootee. Officials: Jerry Petro, Thomas Newlin, Gary Myers, Ed Scott.

WHITELAND: Whiteland 63–57 Greenwood; Center Grove 48–46 Indian Creek; Whiteland 77–59 Franklin; Center Grove 52–45 Whiteland. Officials: Dave Lowenstein, Gary Leistner, Frank Hobson, Ray Mitrione.

1979 REGIONALS

ANDERSON: Anderson 89–62 Eastbrook; Carmel 73–56 Kokomo; Anderson 58–56 Carmel. Officials: Danny Jacobs, Tom Manning, Don Ricketts, Jack Williams, Richard Cook, Gene Marks.

COLUMBUS: Shelbyville 77–64 Bloomington North; Columbus 53–36 Center Grove; Shelbyville 42–40 Columbus East. Officials: Ken Sussman, Terry Stewart, James Dunlap, Robert Kirk, Wayne Van Sickle, Norman Hathcoat.

CONNERSVILLE: Lawrenceburg 72–57 Batesville; Rushville 60–50 Union County; Rushville 68–59 Lawrenceburg. Officials: Gary Foltz, Pete Deakyne, Norman Chestnut, Jack Mercer, Chuck Weinkauf, George Taylor.

ELKHART: Elkhart Central 71–60 Tippecanoe Valley; Argos 70–54 Whitko; Argos 84–68 Central. Officials: Steve Skiles, Larry Jones, Ed Scott, Wendell Baker, Harold Gray, John Lozier.

EVANSVILLE: South Spencer 51–48 Evansville North; Princeton 61–53 Vincennes; South Spencer 53–52 Princeton. Officials: Ray Norris, Jack Cummings, Gary Eaglin, Robert Klein, Clifford Spears, Dave Avery.

FORT WAYNE: Harding 65–63 South Side; DeKalb 68–60 Westview; Harding 70–49 DeKalb. Officials: Steve Cherry, Roger McGriff, Kevin Weinberg, Richard Hall, Eugene Linn, Ronald Beard.

FRANKFORT: Crawfordsville 58–53 Lebanon; Mooresville 76–53 Clinton Central; Crawfordsville 66–62 Mooresville. Officials: Robert Boyle, John Fleischman, Richard Boer, Richie Moore, Winfield Jacobs, Tom Knox.

GARY: Hammond High 92–60 Hammond Noll; Gary Roosevelt 61–52 Lake Central; Gary. Roosevelt 72–68 Hammond High. Officials: Thomas Neuman, Rudy Williams, Mike Bohan, Frank Hoagburg, Gil Baumgartner, Donald Schmidt.

INDIANAPOLIS: Howe 76–75 Washington (ot); North Central 83–76 Franklin Central; North Central 69–59 Howe. Officials: Jay Smith, Robert Reed, McKee Munk, Ronald Ham, Frank DeSantis, Roger DeYoung.

LAFAYETTE: West Lafayette 59–46 Kankakee Valley; Fountain Central 58–57 Benton

Tourney Time

Central; West Lafayette 53–43 Fountain Central. Officials: Carl Redman, Don O'Connor, Morris Cohen, Ron Hosinski, Jim Cox, Melvin Redman.
  MARION: Huntington North 76–70 Bellmont; Marion 35–33 Logansport; Marion 84–72 Huntington. Officials: Don Smith, Jim Benecke, Nick Sweigart, Don Snedeker, Richard Freeman, Jerry Petro.
  NEW CASTLE: Jay County 52–51 New Castle; Muncie Central 56–54 Richmond; Central 93–70 Jay County. Officials: Dave Lowenstein, Donald Shields, Jerry Newsom, Jerry Karstens, Kenneth Gorrell, Bill Wullner.
  SEYMOUR: Scottsburg 73–68 Floyd Central; Clarksville 73–71 Silver Creek; Scottsburg 70–68 Clarksville. Officials: William Gebhart, Judson Raver, Rex Mays, Richard Lederman, Rich Clark, Keith Combs.
  SOUTH BEND: Valparaiso 82–54 Oregon-Davis; Michigan City Rogers 58–56 South Bend Adams (ot); Rogers 68–63 Valparaiso. Officials: Jerry Scott, Phillip Sullivan, Robert Beeson, Dick Modricker, Byron Weaver, Troy Ingram.
  TERRE HAUTE: Terre Haute South 66–49 Terre Haute North; Van Buren 89–65 Bloomfield; South 69–60 Van Buren. Officials: Carl March, Gren Lefebvre, Brandon Bryant, Steve Welmer, Jerry Lasrrison, Jimmy Dimitroff.
  WASHINGTON: Washington 62–44 Bedford-North Lawrence; Southridge 66–48 Springs Valley; Washington 70–51 Southridge. Officials: Steven White, Mark Masariu, John Tucker, Bill Gray, James Wehsollek, Jesse Lynch.

1979 SEMI–STATES

EVANSVILLE: Terre Haute South 60–56 South Spencer; Washington 53–52 Scottsburg; South 58–51 Washington. Officials: Byron Weaver, Tom Knox, Jerry Larrison, Don Snedeker, Bill Wullner, Eugene Linn.
  FORT WAYNE: Marion 70–64 Michigan City Rogers; Argos 66–64 Harding; Argos 84–83 Marion. Officials: Troy Ingram, Melvin Redman, Danny Jacobs, Mike Bohan, Jimmy Dimitroff, Wayne Van Sickle.
  INDIANAPOLIS: Muncie Central 70–59 Rushville; North Central 80–61 Shelbyville; Muncie Central 47–46 North Central. Officials: Richard Freeman, James Wehsollek, Ronald Beard, John Lozier, Kenneth Gorrell, Roger DeYoung.
  LAFAYETTE: Anderson 53–49 West Lafayette; Crawfordsville 60–52 Gary Roosevelt; Anderson 87–55 Crawfordsville. Officials: Frank Hoagburg, Gene Marks, Raymond Norris, Jesse Lynch, Richard Cook, Jerry Petro.

1979 FINALS—March 24

INDIANAPOLIS (Market Square Arena): Anderson 74–64 Argos; Muncie Central 60–55 Terre Haute South (ot); Muncie Central 64–60 Anderson. Officials: Kenneth Gorrell, Wayne Van Sickle, John Lozier, Eugene Linn, Jerry Petro, Roger DeYoung.

IHSAA Scores | 1980–1989

1980–1989

1980 SECTIONALS

ANDERSON: Highland 54–40 Alexandria-Monroe; Madison Heights 66–44 Pendleton Heights; Anderson 99–56 Daleville; Lapel 53–50 Frankton; Highland 69–65 Madison Heights (3ot); Anderson 79–56 Lapel; Highland 76–75 Anderson. Officials: Donald Schmidt, Roger Pflughaupt, Edward Koors, John Fleischman.

BEDFORD–NORTH LAWRENCE: Bedford-North Lawrence 57–49 Medora; Mitchell 50–36 Orleans; Bloomington South 53–31 Eastern (Greene Co.); Bedford-North Lawrence 46–37 Mitchell; Bedford-North Lawrence 41–39 Bloomington South. Officials: Dave Loewenstein, Kenneth Cave, Louis Harmening, Carl Redman.

BEN DAVIS: Northwest 79–77 Shortridge; Ben Davis 59–46 Speedway; Washington 68–66 Pike; Brebeuf 66–65 Ritter; Ben Davis 55–51 Northwest; Washington 74–70 Brebeuf; Washington 71–53 Ben Davis. Officials: Don O'Connor, Harry Northington, Jerry Christie, Jack Graham.

BENTON CENTRAL: Twin Lakes 56–55 Frontier; Tri–County 71–53 South Newton; Benton Central 59–34 North White; Twin Lakes 59–53 Tri–County; Twin Lakes 59–58 Benton Central. Officials: Gene Marks, Dale Cramer, Douglas Coddington, Don Criswell.

BLACKFORD: Blackford 56–54 Wes-Del; Delta 58–57 Wapahani; Blackford 72–42 Eastbrook; Delta 60–53 Blackford. Officials: Clifford Spears, Terry Stewart, Dale VanHouten, Herb Pruett.

BOONVILLE: Tell City 48–40 Boonville; Heritage Hills 65–36 Castle; Cannelton 59–57 Tecumseh; South Spencer 46–42 Tell City; Heritage Hills 86–57 Cannelton; Heritage Hills 52–47 South Spencer. Officials: Norman Chestnut, Frank Hobson, Max Cameron, Darrel Eaton.

BROWNSBURG: Mooresville 58–52 Danville; Brownsburg 59–44 Cascade; Plainfield 66–39 Avon; Brownsburg 56–53 Mooresville; Plainfield 54–52 Brownsburg. Officials: Dick Modricker, Craig Martin, Tad Heminger, Carl March.

CALUMET: Highland 43–41 Merrillville; Calumet 56–44 Munster; Lake Central 69–43 Griffith; Crown Point 66–61 Lake Station Edison; Highland 65–53 Calumet; Lake Central 50–43 Crown Point; Lake Central 60–48 Highland. Officials: Gren Lefebvre, William Champion, Tom Rohr, Ron Carter.

CARMEL: Hamilton Heights 69–60 Hamilton Southeastern; Noblesville 57–39 Sheridan; Carmel 72–51 Westfield; Noblesville 81–56 Hamilton Heights; Carmel 59–46 Noblesville. Officials: Frank DeSantis, James Bennecke, John Sorg, Mark Baltz.

CLAY CITY: Sullivan 59–42 Staunton; North Central 45–41 Clay City; Brazil 68–49 Union (Dugger); Sullivan 84–76 North Central (6ot); Brazil 68–54 Sullivan. Officials: Bruce Knecht, Charles Siebe, Phillip Tincher, Jack Cummings.

COLUMBIA CITY: Whitko 67–39 Churubusco; Columbia City 54–50 Central Noble; Manchester 75–67 Whitko; Manchester 66–64 Columbia City. Officials: Gary Cheeseman, Jim Fairchild, Dan Neupauer, Robert Gilmore.

Tourney Time

COLUMBUS NORTH: Columbus North 58–43 Edinburgh; Hauser 58–57 Brown County; Columbus East 58–45 Columbus North; Columbus East 50–32 Hauser. Officials: Mike Bohan, Timothy Fogarty, Robert Dietrick, Tony Primavera.

CONNERSVILLE: Cambridge City 60–41 Brookville; Union County 54–46 Centerville; Connersville 99–32 Laurel, Union County 56–44 Cambridge City; Connersville 49–45 Union County. Officials: Steve Cherry, Mason Meeks, John Stumpf, Norman Hathcoat.

DEKALB: Leo 80–38 Prairie Heights; Angola 78–57 Hamilton; DeKalb 72–52 Fremont; Eastside 57–44 (2ot) Garrett; Leo 71–52 Angola; DeKalb 52–42 Eastside, DeKalb 60–46 Leo. Officials: Frank Hoagburg, Gaylord Fritz, Charles Redinger, Steven Skiles.

EAST CENTRAL: Milan 75–64 South Ripley; East Central 50–49 Batesville; Milan 79—56 Jac-Cen-Del; Milan 59–52 East Central (2ot). Officials: James Wehsollek, Ron Ramsey, Thomas Dull, Charles Hadley.

EAST CHICAGO: Hammond Noll 60–53 Whiting; East Chicago Roosevelt 52–50 East Chicago Washington; Noll 54–44 Roosevelt. Officials: Dave Avery, Michael DeVault, Jon Davenport, Richard Brainerd.

EAST NOBLE: East Noble 62–49 Westview; Lakeland 57–52 West Noble; Bethany Christian 51–43 Howe Military (2ot); Fairfield 93–78 East Noble; Lakeland 60–57 Bethany Christian; Lakeland 47–45 Fairfield. Officials: Ward Weisel, Larry Freyburgher, William DeRome, Jerome Fawley.

ELKHART: Elkhart Central 76–46 Penn; Elkhart Memorial 76–71 North Wood; Concord 59–52 Jimtown; Northridge 59–45 Goshen; Memorial 72–60 Central; Concord 62–53 Northridge; Memorial 80–66 Concord. Officials: Tom Knox, Daniel Yagodnik, Robert Boyle, Richard Calloway.

EVANSVILLE: Bosse 83–35 Evansville Day School; North 44–34 Central; Memorial 72–39 Reitz; Mater Dei 69–65 Harrison; North 67–58 Bosse; Memorial 52–49 Mater Dei; North 44–43 Memorial. Officials: Donald Shields, Glen Clemons, Delmus Aubrey, McKee Munk.

FLOYD CENTRAL: Corydon 63–58 South Central (Elizabeth); Floyd Central 90–75 Borden; Lanesville 65–56 North Harrison, Floyd Central 85–52 Corydon; Floyd Central 62–51 Lanesville. Officials: Bill Wullner, G.R. Honchell, Ed Roush, Roger McGriff.

FORT WAYNE (#1): Northrop 58–31 Luers; Harding 61–52 Elmhurst; Dwenger 90–55 Woodlan; Northrop 58–31 Snider; Harding 79–77 Dwenger, Northrop 53–39 Harding. Officials: Richard Freeman, Jay C. Smith, Fred Mohri, William Sorukas.

FORT WAYNE (#2): South Side 59–44 Wayne; Concordia 45–43 New Haven (ot); Heritage 64–54 Carroll; South Side 59–44 North Side; Concordia 64–54 Heritage (ot); South Side 69–52 Concordia. Officials: Richard Cook, Ronald Flotow, Joe Edmonds, Rich Clark.

FOUNTAIN CENTRAL: Attica 61–54 Fountain Central; Turkey Run 66–48 North Vermillion; Covington 70–66 Seeger; Attica 74–63 Turkey Run; Attica 81–78 Covington (2ot). Officials: Jim Cox, David Long, Mike Crouch, Ed Scott.

FRANKFORT: Clinton Central 77–53 Clinton Prairie, Tipton 57–44 Tri Central, Frankfort 54–52 Rossville; Clinton Central 56–54 Tipton (ot); Clinton Central 66–63 Frankfort. Officials: Roger DeYoung, Larry Hollman, Thomas May, Bob Marcinek.

FRANKLIN: Center Grove 91–86 Franklin; Indian Creek 71–70 Greenwood; Center Grove 96–94 Whiteland (ot); Indian Creek 61–58 Center Grove. Officials: Winfield Jacobs, Tom Crouch, Gary Seitzinger, Danny Jacobs.

FRANKLIN CENTRAL: Franklin Central 66–58 Warren Central; Marshall 56–38 Roncalli; Scecina 54–48 Beech Grove; Franklin Central 59–52 Marshall; Franklin Central 63–51 Scecina. Officials: Stephen White, David Vendrely, Bill Kaylor, Phil Sullivan.

GARY: West Side 67–66 Emerson (ot); Wirt 51–49 Mann; Wallace 69–64 Gary Roosevelt; West Side 51–48 Wirt; Wallace 64–61 West Side (ot). Officials: Ronald Hosinski, Robert Storm, Anthony Zappia, Kevin Weinberg.

GREENCASTLE: Greencastle 59–44 South Putnam; North Putnam 57–43 Cloverdale; Van Buren 65–40 Rockville; Greencastle 79–75 North Putnam; Van Buren 66–60 Greencastle. Officials: Don Shiflet, Joe Gilliland, Larry Nixon, John Evans.

GREENFIELD–CENTRAL: New Palestine 37–34 Mt. Vernon (Fortville); Greenfield-Central 51–37 Eastern Hancock; New Palestine 61–54 Greenfield-Central. Officials: Gene Gibson, James Helms, Robert Wasson, Michael Winger.

GREENSBURG: Greensburg 81–60 North Decatur; South Decatur 48–42 Morton Memorial; Greensburg 36–17 Rushville; Greensburg 47–33 South Decatur. Officials: Jesse Lynch, David Willoughby, Paul Hackleman, Jack Mercer.

HAMMOND: Tech 60–49 Gavit; Hammond High 56–46 Clark; Andrean 71–56 Morton; Hammond High 58–44 Tech; Andrean 71–61 Hammond High. Officials: Mark Masariu, Ken Dickman, Ivan Burkle, Rex Mays.

HUNTINGTON: Homestead 89–40 White's; Southwood 67–52 Huntington Catholic; Huntington North 70–43 Wabash; Homestead 72–42 Northfield; Southwood 61–59 Huntington North; Homestead 57–55 Southwood. Officials: Tom Jerles, Reginald Cheatham, Donald Hittle, Daniel Moore.

INDIANAPOLIS: Broad Ripple 76–69 Chatard; North Central 67–64 Tech (ot); Cathedral 77–71 Lawrence North; Lawrence Central 71–64 Arlington; Broad Ripple 75–60 North Central; Cathedral 68–64 Lawrence Central; Broad Ripple 62–55 Cathedral. Officials: Ronald Beard, Rudy Williams, Paul Cox, Bob Carr.

JAY COUNTY: Jay County 72–49 Union City; Winchester 49–39 Monroe Central; Randolph Southern 83–70 Union (Modoc); Winchester 47–45 Jay County; Winchester 64–53 Randolph Southern. Officials: Troy Ingram, Ken Keller, Robert Stanley, Louis Schmalfeldt.

KANKAKEE VALLEY: Kouts 57–52 Hanover Central; Kankakee Valley 74–52 Rensselaer Central; Lowell 86–51 Washington Twp.; Hebron 72–50 North Newton; Kankakee Valley 64–26 Kouts; Lowell 59–57 Hebron (ot); Kankakee Valley 68–40 Lowell. Officials: Byron Weaver, J. David Lee, George Marlow, Chuck Weinkauf.

KOKOMO: Haworth 59–49 Northwestern; Eastern 80–53 Western; Kokomo 55–42 Taylor; Eastern 68–50 Haworth; Kokomo 45–43 Eastern. Officials: Eugene Linn, Mike Waisnora, Robert Gootee, Nick Sweigart.

LAFAYETTE: Jefferson 80–67 Carroll (Flora); West Lafayette 58–35 Central Catholic; Harrison 55–54 Delphi (ot); Jefferson 51–49 West Lafayette; Jefferson 55–52 Harrison (2ot). Officials: Jerry Petro, Richard Hughes, Bob Harvey, Larry Maxwell.

LEBANON: Western Boone 59–52 Lebanon; Zionsville 69–55 Tri-West Hendricks; Zionsville 62–54 Western Boone. Officials: Richard Boer, Steve Beres, James Anderson, Warren Benko.

LOGANSPORT: Pioneer 55–53 Caston (ot); Cass 90–41 Kewanna; Peru 68–51 Maconaquah; Logansport 58–54 North Miami; Cass 45–40 Pioneer; Logansport 61–48 Peru; Logansport 41–38 Cass. Officials: Bob Wolfe, Dave Zurcher, John Goss, Robert Klein.

Tourney Time

MADISON: Madison Shawe 69–49 Madison; Southwestern (Hanover) 56–54 New Washington; Henryville 50–48 Charlestown (ot); Silver Creek 70–43 Madison Shawe; Henryville 61–54 Southwestern; Silver Creek 65–32 Henryville. Officials: Ken Gorrell, Jim Miller, Paul Crawford, James Deakyne.

MARION: Oak Hill 68–58 Madison Grant; Marion 68–48 Elwood; Mississinewa 51–41 Bennett; Marion 74–56 Oak Hill; Marion 72–38 Mississinewa. Officials: Brandon Bryant, Dale Blosser, Tony Watt, Rick Owens.

MARTINSVILLE: Edgewood 95–66 Owen Valley; Martinsville 86–58 Eminence; Bloomington North 35–33 Monrovia; Edgewood 95–74 Martinsville; Bloomington North 40–36 Edgewood. Officials: Jerry Larrison, Paul Garriott, Larry Gilpin, William Pittman.

MICHIGAN CITY: Rogers 46–26 New Prairie; Elston 74–50 Westville; Marquette 67–50 LaPorte; Rogers 74–71 Elston; Rogers 72–52 Marquette. Officials: Jerry Scott, Tom Simler, Anthony York, Harold Gray.

MUNCIE: Burris 51–41 Southside; Northside 47–40 Yorktown; Central 83–43 Cowan; Northside 46–39 Burris; Central 60–53 Northside. Officials: Jerry Newsom, David Nichols, William Holzer, Richard Eynon.

NEW ALBANY: New Albany 74–66 Providence; Jeffersonville 90–46 Clarksville; New Albany 57–54 Jeffersonville. Officials: Melvin Redman, Charles Bertram, William Nimnicht, James Dunlap. Tournament side was changed from Jeffersonville.

NEW CASTLE: New Castle 63–54 Blue River; Knightstown 71–51 Hagerstown; Tri 74–62 Northeastern; Richmond 63–59 Shenandoah (4ot); New Castle 76–68 Knightstown; Richmond 68–52 Tri; Richmond 40–39 New Castle. Officials: Jimmy Dimitroff, Lanny Rossman, Jerome Vincent, Darrell McFall.

NORTH JUDSON: South Central (Union Mills) 47–38 North Judson; Oregon-Davis 54–24 LaCrosse; Culver Community 61–50 Knox; Winamac 52–45 West Central. Oregon-Davis 56–53 South Central (Union Mills); Winamac 29–27 Culver Community; Oregon-Davis 76–53 Winamac. Officials: Jerry Karstens, Keith Yoder, David Berman, Judson Raver.

NORTH MONTGOMERY: North Montgomery 46–36 Southmont; McCutcheon 51–40 Crawfordsville; North Montgomery 42–38 McCutcheon. Officials: Steve Welmer, Michael Wallpe, Roger Holder, Raymond Norris.

PAOLI: Eastern (Pekin) 75–67 Springs Valley (ot); Crawford County 42–25 Paoli; West Washington 52–50 Salem; Crawford County 93–76 Eastern (Pekin); Crawford County 69–48 West Washington. Officials: Richie Moore, Gary Woodling, Gary Myers, Thomas Newlin.

PLYMOUTH: Plymouth 68–59 Bremen; Argos 70–47 Culver Military; LaVille 66–52 North Liberty; Plymouth 73–60 Glenn; Argos 60–53 LaVille; Argos 67–56 Plymouth. Officials: Ron Waisnora, Rex Nichols, Richard Beck, Herbert Hicks.

PRINCETON: New Harmony 81–63 Oakland City; Mt. Vernon 62–51 Gibson Southern (ot); Princeton 60–50 North Posey; Mt. Vernon 100–50 New Harmony; Princeton 55–46 Mt. Vernon. Officials: John Lyskowinski, James Roberts, Richard Schleicher, Bruce Mayfield.

SEYMOUR: Scottsburg 63–55 Brownstown Central; Crothersville 53–47 Austin; Jennings County 77–52 Seymour; Crothersville 69–56 Scottsburg; Jennings County 74–69 Crothersville. Officials: Don Snedeker, Bill Graham, Larry Sintz, Robert Beeson.

SHELBYVILLE: Shelbyville 66–38 Triton Central; Southwestern 63–61 Morristown; Shelbyville 69–45 Waldron, Shelbyville 53–37 Southwestern. Officials: Wayne VanSickle, William

Shobe, James Keifer, Robert Kirk.

SOUTH ADAMS: South Adams 76–66 Southern Wells; Norwell 69–47 Adams Central; Bellmont 60–51 Bluffton; Norwell 71–58 South Adams; Norwell 69–64 Bellmont. Officials: Mel Botkin, Don Resler, Steven Bollier, Richard Hall.

SOUTH BEND: Riley 66–61 Adams; LaSalle 69–47 St. Joseph's; Clay 62–54 Washington; Mishawaka 73–43 Mishawaka Marion; LaSalle 81–74 Riley; Clay 78—64 Mishawaka; LaSalle 52–50 Clay. Officials: John Lozier, Thomas Neuman, Paul Leamon, Larry Jones, Martin Parmeter.

SOUTH DEARBORN: South Dearborn 63–59 Switzerland County; Lawrenceburg 73–56 Rising Sun; South Dearborn 59–55 Lawrenceburg. Officials: Don Smith, Russell Ferrill, William Amerson, William Fields.

SOUTHPORT: Perry Meridian 93–31 Indiana School for Deaf; Manual 60–52 Southport; Howe 77–45 Park–Tudor; Attucks 62–49 Decatur Central; Manual 63–54 Perry Meridian (ot); Howe 74–70 Attucks; Manual 56–52 Howe. Officials: Gary Eaglin, David Petty, Lonnie Eaglin, George Taylor.

SOUTHRIDGE: Southridge 52–50 Jasper; Northeast Dubois 43–36 Forest Park; Southridge 80–48 Perry Central; Southridge 55–45 Northeast Dubois. Officials: Ronald Ham, Donald Dockery, Larry Collins, Temme Patterson.

SWITZ CITY CENTRAL: Bloomfield 62–40 Linton-Stockton; Shakamak 73–50 Switz City Central; Worthington 59–49 L & M; Bloomfield 55–53 Shakamak; Bloomfield 57–36 Worthington. Officials: Jim Westerfield, Gary Leistner, Bill Johnston, Jack Behme.

TERRE HAUTE: Terre Haute North 85–46 Montezuma; Terre Haute South 76–66 Rosedale; West Vigo 60–58 South Vermillion; South 64–62 North (ot); South 76–41 West Vigo. Officials: Morris Cohen, Don Nester, Jim Fish, Leland Thompson.

TRITON: Tippecanoe Valley 44–39 Wawasee; Rochester 74–68 Triton (2ot); Warsaw 81–60 Tippecanoe Valley; Warsaw 82–62 Rochester. Officials: Gary Foltz, Douglas Bauman, Lloyd Ahlbrand, Wayne Targgart.

VALPARAISO: Hobart 48–47 Boone Grove; Chesterton 57–45 River Forest; Portage 89–67 Morgan Twp.; Valparaiso 86–62 Wheeler, Hobart 66–59 Chesterton; Valparaiso 36–28 Portage; Valparaiso 81–56 Hobart. Officials: Robert Reed, Jim Reinebold, Robert DeBroka, Jerry Cook.

VINCENNES: North Knox 60–59 Vincennes Rivet; Vincennes 51–50 South Knox; Vincennes 44–33 North Knox. Officials: Dave Atwell, Al Christoules, John Tucker, D.J. Frazer.

WASHINGTON: Barr–Reeve 65–56 Shoals; Washington Catholic 64–53 Pike Central; Loogootee 54–39 Washington; Barr–Reeve 73–71 North Daviess (2ot); Washington Catholic 52–34 Loogootee; Barr–Reeve 64–31 Washington Catholic. Officials: Keith Combs, Ronald Grimes, Dennis Thomas, Mark Reyher.

1980 REGIONALS

ANDERSON: Carmel 47–43 Highland; Delta 55–54 Kokomo; Carmel 54–48 Delta. Officials: Donald O'Connor, Steve Welmer, Richard Brainerd, Jerry Cook, Byron Weaver, John Lozier.

COLUMBUS: Shelbyville 50–45 Columbus East; Bloomington North 69–58 Indian Creek; Shelbyville 41–37 Bloomington North. Officials: Phillip Sullivan Jimmie Westerfield; Dave Loewenstein, Donald Dockery, Mel Redman, Keith Combs.

CONNERSVILLE: South Dearborn 70–46 Milan; Connersville 101–68 Greensburg; Connersville 60–46 South Dearborn. Officials: Don Schmidt, Jim Cox, Robert Boyle, David Vendrely, Frank Hoagburg, Eugene Linn.

ELKHART: Warsaw 80–70 Elkhart Memorial; Argos 80–72 Manchester; Warsaw 52–51 Argos. Officials: Robert Klein, Robert Kirk, Jesse Lynch, John Evans, Michael Bohan, Darrell McFall.

EVANSVILLE: Evansville North 58–57 Vincennes; Princeton 52–50 Heritage Hills; Evansville North 66–64 Princeton (3ot). Officials: Terry Stewart, David Petty, Winfield Jacobs, Leland Thompson, Brandon Bryant, Jimmy Dimitroff.

FORT WAYNE: DeKalb 41–32 Lakeland; Fort Wayne South Side 73–63 Northrop; Fort Wayne South Side 53–52 DeKalb. Officials: Mike DeVault, Jerome Karstens, Richard Boer, Warren Benko, Nick Sweigart, Roger DeYoung.

FRANKFORT: Clinton Central 53–43 Plainfield; North Montgomery 40–37 Zionsville (ot); Clinton Central 46–44 North Montgomery (ot). Officials: Don Shiflet, Raymond Norris, Jerry Newton, Richard Eynon, Danny Jacobs, Richard Cook.

GARY: Andrean 61–59 Hammond Noll; Wallace 53–47 Lake Central; Andrean 64–48 Wallace. Officials: Mark Masariu, Robert Carr, Norman Hathcoat, Tom Jerles, Ronald Beard, James Wehsollek.

INDIANAPOLIS: Manual 68–53 Franklin Central; Broad Ripple 58–50 Washington; Broad Ripple 70–57 Manual. Officials: David Avery, David Atwell, Ronald Carter, Robert Beeson, Richard Freeman, Don Snedeker.

LAFAYETTE: Jefferson 60–49 Kankakee Valley; Attica 59–56 Twin Lakes; Jefferson 70–69 Attica. Officials: William Sorukas, Jerome Fawley, Rushus Williams, Bruce Knecht, Frank DeSantis, Robert Marcinek.

MARION: Marion 55–38 Homestead; Norwell 58–48 Logansport; Marion 71–53 Norwell. Officials: Steve Cherry, Daniel Moore, Rich Clark, Rick Owens, Wayne VanSickle, Troy Ingram.

MICHIGAN CITY ROGERS: South Bend LaSalle 76–65 Oregon-Davis; Valparaiso 64–56 Michigan City Rogers; Valparaiso 64–60 South Bend LaSalle. Officials: Roger Pflughaupt, Thomas Neuman, Gene Gibson, George Taylor, Judson Raver, Tom Knox.

NEW CASTLE: Richmond 59–51 Winchester, Muncie Central 63–45 New Palestine; Muncie Central 47–45 Richmond (2ot). Officials: Ron Hosinski, Carl March, Gary Eaglin, Don Smith, Jerry Petro, Gene Marks.

SEYMOUR: Floyd Central 66–65 Jennings County; New Albany 57–43 Silver Creek; New Albany 97–85 Floyd Central. Officials: Morris Cohen, Gary Foltz, James Dunlap, John Behme, Roger McGriff, Jerry Larrison.

TERRE HAUTE SOUTH: Terre Haute South 62–45 Bloomfield; Brazil 62–58 Van Buren; Terre Haute South 64–39 Brazil. Officials: Melvin Botkin, James Deakyne, McKee Munk, John Lyskowinski, Donald Shields, Bill Wullner.

WASHINGTON: Bedford-North Lawrence 56–43 Southridge; Crawford County 54–44 Barr-Reeve; Crawford County 44–40 Bedford-North Lawrence. Officials: Larry Jones, Richard Modricker, Robert Wolfe, Craig Martin, Harold Gray, Kenneth Gorrell.

IHSAA Scores | 1980–1989

1980 SEMI–STATES
EVANSVILLE: New Albany 72–59 Terre Haute South; Crawford County 60–56 Evansville North; New Albany 60–59 Crawford County. Officials: Michael Bohan, Ronald Beard, Brandon Bryant, Byron Weaver, Troy Ingram, Darrel McFall.

FORT WAYNE: Marion 62–57 Warsaw; Fort Wayne South Side 66–64 Valparaiso (3ot); Marion 68–58 South Side. Officials: Don O'Connor, Gene Marks, Jerry Petro, James Wehsollek, Jimmy Dimitroff, Kenneth Gorrell.

INDIANAPOLIS: Broad Ripple 73–65 Connersville; Shelbyville 47–45 Muncie Central; Broad Ripple 64–45 Shelbyville. Officials: Richard Freeman, Nick Sweigart, Frank DeSantis, Roger DeYoung, John Lozier, Richard Cook.

LAFAYETTE: Andrean 60–54 Carmel; Jefferson 62–58 Clinton Central; Andrean 74–62 Jefferson. Officials: Don Snedeker, Keith Combs, Dave Loewenstein, Danny Jacobs, Eugene Linn, Bill Wullner.

1980 FINALS—March 29
INDIANAPOLIS (Market Square Arena): New Albany 69–68 Andrean; Broad Ripple 71–69 Marion; Broad Ripple 73–66 New Albany. Officials: Byron Weaver, John Lozier, Richard Cook, Danny Jacobs, Troy Ingram, Don Snedeker.

1981 SECTIONALS
ANDERSON: Alexandria 65–46 Lapel; Madison Heights 93–51 Daleville; Highland 56–38 Pendleton Heights; Anderson 59–57 Frankton; Madison Heights 74–62 Alexandria; Anderson 107–103 Highland (2ot); Anderson 67–64 Madison Heights. Officials: Troy Ingram, Jim Keifer, Jerry Vincent, Daniel Moore.

BEDFORD–NORTH LAWRENCE: Bedford–North Lawrence 60–27 Orleans; Mitchell 62–40 Eastern (Greene Co.); Bloomington South 64–46 Medora; Bedford–North Lawrence 44–37 Mitchell; Bedford-North Lawrence 38–28 Bloomington South. Officials: Leland D. Thompson, Jim Fish, Bob Harvey, Mark Baltz, Jack Taylor.

BEN DAVIS: Pike 75–63 Shortridge; Brebeuf 78–50 Speedway; Washington 61–56 Northwest; Ben Davis 76–66 Ritter; Pike 51–48 Brebeuf; Ben Davis 40–39 Washington; Pike 41–40 Ben Davis. Officials: Donald J. Schmidt, Timothy R. Fogarty, Ed Koors, Frank Hoagburg.

BENTON CENTRAL: Twin Lakes 64–58 Benton Central; Tri-County 63–54 South Newton; Frontier 88–79 North White; Twin Lakes 62–49 Tri-County; Frontier 52–50 Twin Lakes. Officials: Ray Norris, Ed Scott, Albert Christoules, Mark Reyher.

BLACKFORD: Delta 54–51 Eastbrook; Wapahani 71–59 Wes–Del; Blackford 69–66 Delta; Blackford 52–44 Wapahani. Officials: Tom Knox, Don Resler, Larry Hollman, Judson Raver.

BOONVILLE: Boonville 46–45 Castle; South Spencer 39–37 Heritage Hills; Tell City 74–55 Cannelton; Tecumseh 56–51 Boonville; South Spencer 44–42 Tell City; South Spencer 54–43 Tecumseh. Officials: Larry Maxwell, Robert Kirk, Bob Gentry, Jack Cummings.

BROWNSBURG: Cascade 61–45 Danville; Mooresville 43–41 Avon; Brownsburg 51–50 Plainfield (2ot); Mooresville 68–63 Cascade; Brownsburg 57–44 Mooresville. Officials: George

Taylor, James Fairchild, Lou Harmening, Mel Botkin.

CALUMET: Lake Central 58–57 Munster; Merrillville 71–60 Crown Point; Lake Station Edison 48–45 Calumet; Highland 51–45 Griffith; Merrillville 54–50 Lake Central (2ot); Highland 65–55 Edison; Highland 48–45 Merrillville. Officials: Carl March, Kenneth Dickman, Steve Brown, Harry Northington.

CARMEL: Carmel 63–48 Hamilton Southeastern; Hamilton Heights 74–57 Westfield; Noblesville 65–33 Sheridan; Hamilton Heights 75–56 Carmel; Noblesville 93–62 Hamilton Heights. Officials: Bob Marcinek, John Goss, Jr., James Helms, David Zurcher.

COLUMBIA CITY: Manchester 62–59 Churubusco; Whitko 58–40 Columbia City; Manchester 56–40 Central Noble; Whitko 52–51 Manchester. Officials: Jerry Cook, David Willoughby; Charles Redinger, Jack Graham.

COLUMBUS: Brown County 72–71 Edinburgh (ot); Hauser 38–25 Columbus East; Columbus North 84–50 Brown County; Columbus North 39–35 Hauser. Officials: Bob Carr, Gary Cheesman, Herb Pruett, Paul Cox.

CONNERSVILLE: Union County 41–37 Brookville; Laurel 73–70 Cambridge City; Connersville 62–50 Centerville; Union County 64–54 Laurel; Connersville 53–52 Union County. Officials: Kenneth Gorrell, Glen Clemons, Michael McCarty, John Lyskowinski.

DEKALB: Fremont 46–42 Hamilton; Angola 74–63 Eastside; Garrett 61–53 Leo; DeKalb 95–63 Prairie Heights; Angola 58–50 Fremont; DeKalb 54–52 Garrett; DeKalb 70–55 Angola. Officials: Ron Beard, Joe Edmonds, Samuel Lower, Mark Masariu.

EAST CENTRAL: South Ripley 54–46 Batesville; Milan 65–54 East Central; South Ripley 59–53 Jac-Cen-Del; South Ripley 65–32 Milan. Officials: Tom Neuman, Gaylord Fritz, Bob Wasson, Roger Pflughaupt.

EAST CHICAGO: Whiting 62–50 Hammond Noll; East Chicago Roosevelt 64–47 East Chicago Washington; Whiting 51–50 Roosevelt (ot). Officials: Ron Carter, Bill Champion, Ivan Burkle, Thomas Simler.

EAST NOBLE: Fairfield 82–56 Bethany Christian; East Noble 74–63 Westview; Lakeland 55–29 Howe Military; Fairfield 79–52 West Noble; Lakeland 53–46 East Noble; Lakeland 62–53 Fairfield. Officials: Dave Avery, James Reinebold, Sr., Tim Smith, Robert Reed.

ELKHART: Northridge 63–59 Jimtown; Elkhart Memorial 70–67 Northwood; Penn 57–55 Goshen; Elkhart Central 76–67 Concord; Memorial 65–63 Northridge; Central 58–51 Penn; Memorial 82–81 Central. Officials: Richard Cook, Ron Ramsey, Ronald Flotow, David Primavera.

EVANSVILLE: Mater Dei 62–60 Bosse, Central 63–57 Memorial; North 72–60 Reitz; Harrison 90–48 Day School; Central 49–48 Mater Dei; North 77–70 Harrison; Central 53–51 North (ot). Officials: Jerry Newson, William Fields, Kenneth Cave, Richard Eynon.

FLOYD CENTRAL: South Central 58–52 Borden; Corydon Central 61–53 Lanesville; Floyd Central 71–64 North Harrison; Corydon Central 66–47 South Central; Floyd Central 87–35 Corydon Central. Officials: James Deakyne, Frank Hobson, Max Clouse, Charles Hadley.

FORT WAYNE (#1): South Side 53–39 Snider; Elmhurst 69–54 Luers; Wayne 77–64 North Side; South Side 39–35 Carroll; Wayne 61–54 Elmhurst; Wayne 36–34 South Side. Officials: Jerry Petro, Terry Stewart, Richard Hughes, Dave Atwell.

FORT WAYNE (#2): Harding 65–41 Heritage; Concordia 67–66 Dwenge (5ot); Northrop 65–61 New Haven; Harding 71–50 Woodlan; Concordia 69–54 Northrop; Concordia 52–48

IHSAA Scores | 1980–1989

Harding. Officials: Mike Bohan, Jerome Fawley, Robert DeBroka, David Petty.

FOUNTAIN CENTRAL: Seeger 53–36 Attica; Fountain Central 70–66 Turk Covington 69–55 North Vermillion; Fountain Central 54–49 Seeger; Fountain 68–56 Covington. Officials: Melvin Redman, Larry Collins, Tom Newlin, Carl Redman.

FRANKFORT: Clinton Central; 68–51 Frankfort; Tri-Central 29–28 Tipton; Rossville 55–47 Clinton Prairie; Tri-Central 71–70 Clinton Central; Rossville 62–44 Tri-Central. Officials: Jerry Karstens, Steve Beres, Robert Gootee, Herbert Hicks.

FRANKLIN CENTRAL: Franklin Central 56–53 Warren Central; Roncalli 58–55 Scecina; Marshall 46–41 Beech Grove; Roncalli 32–30 Franklin Central; Marshall 57–53 Roncalli. Officials: Gary Eaglin, Robert Gilmore, Lonnie Eaglin, Rudy Williams.

GARY: Gary Roosevelt 77–73 Mann; Wallace 61–58 Wirt; West Side 51–48 Emerson (ot); Roosevelt 104–63 Wallace; Roosevelt 60–50 West Side. Officials: Frank DeSantis, Dale Cramer, Ross Radtke, Jr., Donald O'Connor.

GREENCASTLE: Cloverdale 64–45 South Putnam; Rockville 67–61 North Putnam (ot); Van Buren 55–52 Greencastle; Cloverdale 64–54 Rockville; Cloverdale 78–51 Van Buren. Officials: Dave Loewenstein, Phillip Tincher, Stephen Fisher, Gary Leistner.

GREENFIELD CENTRAL: Mt. Vernon (Fortville) 57–56 Greenfield-Central; Eastern Hancock 48–47 New Palestine; Eastern Hancock 72–66 Mt. Vernon (2ot). Officials: Larry Freyburgher, William DeRome, Tom Crouch, Ward Weisel.

GREENSBURG: North Decatur 49–34 Morton Memorial; Rushville 62–57 South Decatur; Greensburg 87–54 North Decatur; Greensburg 82–60 Rushville. Officials: James Roberts, Gary Woodling, Fred Hamilton, Steve Welmer.

GREENWOOD: Whiteland 64–48 Center Grove; Indian Creek 71–70 Greenwood; Franklin 51–46 Whiteland, Indian Creek 59–55 Franklin. Officials: Rick Owens, Larry Sintz, Dan Henkle, Don Smith, Sr.

HAMMOND: Morton 69–56 Gavit; Tech 55–50 Clark; Andrean 59–47 Hammond High; Morton 53–48 Tech; Andrean 71–68 Morton. Officials: Bob Wolfe, Paul E. Garriott, Clarence Crain, John D. Tucker.

HUNTINGTON: Homestead 47–45 Huntington North; Northfield 69–54 Huntington Catholic; Wabash 53–51 White's; Homestead 82–43 Southwood; Northfield 64–44 Wabash; Homestead 54–42 Northfield. Officials: Richard Freeman, Jon Davenport, Anthony Zappia, Michael DeVault.

INDIANAPOLIS: Cathedral 83–57 Lawrence Central; Tech 68–62 Arlington; Chatard 71–70 Broad Ripple; Lawrence North 53–52 North Central (2ot); Cathedral 67–54 Tech; Chatard 70–67 Lawrence North; Chatard 68–66 Cathedral. Officials: Eugene Linn, Mike Crouch, Anthany York, Jim Cox.

JAY COUNTY: Jay County 49–35 Monroe Central; Winchester 49–47 Union City; Randolph Southern 61–47 Union (Modoc); Jay County 48–35 Winchester; Jay County 37–35 Randolph Southern (ot). Officials: Rex Mays, Keith Yoder, Robert Clark, Jerry Christie.

JEFFERSONVILLE: New Albany 23–13 Clarksville; Jeffersonville 58–44 Providence; New Albany 51–50 Jeffersonville. Officials: Norman Hathcoat, Robert Stanley, William Holzer, Steve Cherry.

KANKAKEE VALLEY: Kankakee Valley 61–28 Hanover Central; Rensselaer 51–40 North Newton; Boone Grove 82–48 Lowell; Hebron 64–62 Kouts; Kankakee Valley 72 48 Rensselaer;

Boone Grove 50–47 Hebron; Kankakee Valley 74–50 Boone Grove. Officials: Nick Sweigart, August Mohri, Robert Graczyk, Jay Smith.

KOKOMO: Kokomo 55–47 Eastern (Greentown); Haworth 66–54 Taylor; Northwestern 55–43 Western; Kokomo 50–44 Haworth; Northwestern 51–47 Kokomo. Officials: William Sorukas, Robert Storm, Kevin Weinberg, Ron Hosinski.

LAFAYETTE: Central Catholic 63–46 Delphi; Harrison 55–41 West Lafayette; Jefferson 75–62 Carroll (Flora); Harrison 65–58 Central Catholic; Harrison 43–41 Jefferson. Officials: Opal Courtney, Paul Danko, Lloyd Ahlbrand, Mike Waisnora.

LEBANON: Western Boone 61–54 Tri–West; Zionsville 40–37 Lebanon (ot); Western Boone 26–24 Zionsville. Officials: Winfield Jacobs, Larry Nixon, Gary Byrer, Tom Rohr.

LOGANSPORT: Cass 73–64 Peru; Caston 81–64 Maconaquah; North Miami 96–48 Kewanna; Pioneer 53–50 Logansport; Cass 83–69 Caston; Pioneer 62–37 North Miami; Cass 41–39 Pioneer (ot). Officials: Roger DeYoung, James Anderson, Michael Benda, Daniel Yagodnik.

MADISON: Charlestown 59–44 Silver Creek; Madison-Shawe 59–56 New Washington; Madison 44–42 Henryville (ot); Charlestown 49–47 Southwestern; Madison 71–55 Madison-Shawe; Charlestown 55–53 Madison. Officials: Roger McGriff, Louis Schmalfeldt, David Nichols, Mason Meeks.

MARION: Marion 73–43 Elwood; Bennett 67–58 Madison-Grant; Oak Hill 73–58 Mississinewa; Marion 71–37 Bennett; Marion 88–65 Oak Hill. Officials: Wayne VanSickle, Paul Beatty, Jim Pitcher, Don Snedeker.

MARTINSVILLE: Edgewood 64–48 Owen Valley; Martinsville 73–44 Monrovia; Bloomington North 85–66 Eminence; Martinsville 41–39 Edgewood; Bloomington North 42–40 Martinsville (ot). Officials: Norman Chestnut, Darrell Eaton, Richard Schleicher, Bruce Mayfield.

MICHIGAN CITY: Rogers 82–47 New Prairie; Westville 63–48 LaPorte; Elston 52–50 Marquette; Rogers 73–47 Westville; Rogers 61–60 Elston. Officials: Clifford Spears, David Berman, Len Glazier, Rex Nichols.

MUNCIE: Northside 54–50 Central; Burris 64–48 Cowan; Southside 47–45 Yorktown; Northside 17–15 Burris; Southside 45–43 Northside. Officials: Bill Wullner, Paul Crawford, Lanny Rossman, Darrell McFall.

NEW CASTLE: Shenandoah 67–50 Hagerstown; Northeastern 67–62 Tri; Richmond 60–48 Blue River; New Castle 53–48 Knightstown; Shenandoah 62–43 Northeastern; Richmond 47–45 New Castle; Shenandoah 40–39 Richmond. Officials: John Lozier, Steven Skiles, Dick Beck, Larry Jones.

NORTH JUDSON: West Central 43–39 Culver; South Central 55–53 Winamac; Knox 70–66 LaCrosse; Oregon–Davis 72–57 North Judson; South Central 63–59 West Central; Oregon–Davis 92–69 Knox; Oregon–Davis 78–75 South Central (ot). Officials: Dale Blosser, Thomas May, David Vendrely, Mike Winger.

NORTH MONTGOMERY: McCutcheon 49–42 North Montgomery; Southmont 75–62 Crawfordsville; McCutcheon 70–56 Southmont. Officials: Tom Jerles, Douglas Bauman, Charles Siebe, William Shobe.

PAOLI: Salem 62–45 Paoli; Crawford County 50–42 Spring Valley; West Washington 63–53 Eastern (Pekin) (ot); Crawford County 47–40 Salem; Crawford County 88–46 West Washington. Officials: Robert Beeson, G.R. Honchell; Thomas Creech, Bill Graham.

PLYMOUTH: LaVille 64–63 Plymouth, Glenn 71–54 North Liberty; Argos 80–61 Culver Military; LaVille 60–47 Bremen; Argos 72–55 Glenn; Argos 47–41 LaVille. Officials: Gary Foltz, Gene Gibson, Wayne Targgart, Jim Benecke.

PRINCETON: Mt. Vernon 67–57 North Posey; Gibson Southern 81–58 Oakland City Wood; Princeton 60–54 New Harmony; Mt. Vernon 68–59 Gibson Southern; Mt. Vernon 73–64 Princeton. Officials: Ron Grimes, Robert Dietrick, Gary Seitzinger, Donel Criswell.

SEYMOUR: Scottsburg 60–59 Seymour; Brownstown Central 57–46 Austin; Crothersville 40–36 Jennings County; Brownsburg Central 42–39 Scottsburg (ot); Brownstown Central 45–40 Crothersville. Officials: James Dunlap, Jack Behme, Charles Bertram, Keith Combs.

SHELBYVILLE: Shelbyville 66–43 Morristown; Triton Central 82–62 Waldron; Shelbyville 74–28 Southwestern; Shelbyville 35–34 Triton Central (ot). Officials: Rich Clark, Max Cameron, Gary Myers, Don Hittle.

SOUTH ADAMS: Adams Central 50–47 Bluffton; Southern Wells 57–51 South Adams (ot); Norwell 67–41 Bellmont; Southern Wells 67–51 Adams Central; Norwell 58–46 Southern Wells. Officials: James Wehsollek, David Long, William Kachel, Phil Sullivan.

SOUTH BEND: Adams 49–48 St. Joseph's; LaSalle 86–71 Mishawaka; Riley 76–39 Mishawaka Marian; Washington 58–55 Clay (ot); Adams 58–56 LaSalle (ot); Riley 69–67 Washington; Riley 67–54 Adams. Officials: Gene Marks, Richard Calloway, Ralph Cummins, Warren Benko.

SOUTH DEARBORN: Lawrenceburg 63–55 South Dearborn; Switzerland County 81–73 Rising Sun; Lawrenceburg 63–53 Switzerland County. Officials: Steve White, David Watt, Gene Marsh, Jim Miller.

SOUTHPORT: Park Tudor 58–47 Deaf Scgool; Howe 65–58 Manual; Southport 52–50 Perry Meridian; Attucks 40–38 Decatur Central; Howe 73–28 Park Tudor; Southport 47–43 Attucks; Howe 87–65 Southport. Officials: Donald Shields, William Amerson, Gary Hawn, McKee Munk.

SOUTHRIDGE: Jasper 79–43 Perry Central; Southridge 77–64 Forest Park; Jasper 65–61 Northeast Dubois; Jasper 69–68 Southridge. Officials: Richie Moore, Michael Wallpe, William Nimnicht, Robert Klein.

SOUTH VERMILLION: Brazil 57–45 Clay City; Montezuma 60–58 Staunton; South Vermillion 72–38 Rosedale; Brazil 44–43 Montezuma; Brazil 59–37 South Vermillion. Officials: Temme Patterson, William Pittman, Dennis Thomas, Jack Mercer.

SWITZ CITY CENTRAL: Switz City Central 60–58 Linton-Stockton (ot); Shakamak 66–54 Worthington; Bloomfield 42–38 L & M (ot); Switz City Central 41–35 Shakamak; Bloomfield 50–37 Switz City Central. Officials: Don Nester, Paul Hackleman, Denis Ward, Ed Roush.

TERRE HAUTE: Union (Dugger) 69–62 West Vigo; North Central (Farmersburg) 69–50 Sullivan; Terre Haute South 55–47 Terre Haute North; Union 65–57 North Central; Terre Haute South 94–54 Union. Officials: Brandon Bryant, J. David Lee, John Adams, Joe Gilliland.

TRITON: Triton 57–54 Tippecanoe Valley; Warsaw 56–54 Rochester; Triton 69–62 Wawasee; Warsaw 67–57 Triton. Officials: Ron Waisnora, John Sorg, Dale VanHouten, Robert Boyle.

VALPARAISO: River Forest 59–53 Chesterton; Portage 98–67 Washington Twp.; Valparaiso 81–51 Morgan Twp.; Wheeler 63–62 Hobart; Portage 45–44 River Forest; Valparaiso 96–66 Wheeler; Valparaiso 72–61 Portage. Officials: Harold Gray, Craig Martin, Dave Emery, Dick Modricker.

VINCENNES: Vincennes 89–44 North Knox; South Knox 54–47 Vincennes Rivet; Vincennes

Tourney Time

90–53 South Knox. Officials: John Evans, Roger Holder, Robert Davis, Chuck Weinkauf.

WASHINGTON: Loogootee 38–26 Barr-Reeve; Washington 62–42 North Daviess; Pike Central 52–43 Shoals; Loogootee 41–28 Washington Catholic; Washington 62–45 Pike Central; Loogootee 44–33 Washington. Officials: Jerry Larrison, John Stumpf, Douglas Coddington, Jesse Lynch.

1981 REGIONALS

ANDERSON: Anderson 59–53 Noblesville; Northwestern 70–55 Blackford; Anderson 85–67 Northwestern. Officials: David Avery, Craig Martin, Dick Modricker, Larry Jones, Harold Gray, John Lozier.

COLUMBUS: Shelbyville 60–58 Indian Creek (ot); Columbus North 56–45 Bloomington North; Columbus North 52–42 Shelbyville. Officials: Robert Kirk, Dave Loewenstein, Steve Cherry, Norman Hathcoat, Ronald Beard, James Wehsollek.

CONNERSVILLE: Lawrenceburg 55–53 Connersville; South Ripley 76–74 Greensburg; South Ripley 63–62 Lawrenceburg. Officials: Glen Clemons, Donald Shields, Mike Crouch, McKee Munk, Eugene Linn, Jim Cox.

ELKHART: Whitko 63–60 Argos; Warsaw 80–75 Elkhart Memorial; Warsaw 58–55 Whitko. Officials: Larry Maxwell, Jack Mercer, Mark Baltz, Brandon Bryant, Mike Bohan, Darrell McFall.

EVANSVILLE: Vincennes 57–50 Evansville Central; Mt. Vernon 53–51 South Spencer; Vincennes 62–53 Mt. Vernon. Officials: Gary Eaglin, Don Smith, Robert Beeson, Bill Graham, Don Snedeker, Bill Wullner.

FORT WAYNE: Fort Wayne Concordia 67–54 Lakeland; Fort Wayne Wayne 64–51 DeKalb; Fort Wayne Wayne 62–36 Fort Wayne Concordia. Officials: Dale Blosser, Mike DeVault, Dale Cramer, Jerry Karstens, Jerry Cook, Dick Freeman.

FRANKFORT: Western Boone 60–53 Rossville; Brownsburg 51–43 McCutcheon; Brownsburg 44–40 Western Boone. Officials: Keith Combs, Richie Moore, Mark Reyher, Raymond L. Norris, James Dunlap, Melvin Redman.

GARY: Andrean 92–84 Gary Roosevelt (ot); Whiting 61–45 Highland; Andrean 79–71 Whiting. Officials: Roger McGriff, Steve Welmer, David Petty, Richard Eynon, Jerry Newson, Kenneth Gorrell.

INDIANAPOLIS: Chatard 66–65 Pike; Howe 46–40 Marshall; Howe 69–51 Chatard. Officials: Daniel Moore, Tom Jerles, Rick Owens, Rich Clark, Wayne VanSickle, Troy Ingram.

LAFAYETTE: Harrison 51–41 Fountain Central; Kankakee Valley 78–59 Frontier; Kankakee Valley 54–47 Harrison. Officials: George Taylor, Jerry Petro, Bob Carr, Ronald Grimes, Winfield Jacobs, Jack Cummings.

MARION: Homestead 73–62 Norwell; Marion 76–54 Cass; Marion 78–62 Homestead. Officials: Gene Marks, Jerome Fawley, Ron Hosinski, William Sorukas, Donald O'Connor, Frank DeSantis.

MICHIGAN CITY: Michigan City Rogers 65–52 Oregon-Davis; Valparaiso 64–61 South Bend Riley; Valparaiso 81–68 Rogers. Officials: Dave Atwell, Tom Simler, Mark Masariu, Harry Northington, Carl March, Ron Carter.

NEW CASTLE: Shenandoah 71–52 Eastern Hancock, Jay County 54–47 Muncie Southside;

Shenandoah 52–46 Jay County. Officials: Bob Marcinek, Warren Benko, Nick Sweigart, Ron Waisnora, Roger DeYoung, Richard Cook.

SEYMOUR: Floyd Central 66–55 New Albany; Charlestown 60–53 Brownstown Central; Floyd Central 86–81 Charlestown. Officials: Leland Thompson, David Primavera, Terry Stewart, Clifford Spears, Chuck Weinkauf, Jerry Larrison.

TERRE HAUTE: Cloverdale 54–51 Bloomfield, Brazil 66–64 Terre Haute South; Brazil 58—56 Cloverdale. Officials: Robert Klein, Mason Meeks, Ron Ramsey, Louis Schmalfeldt, Bob Wolfe, Jesse Lynch.

WASHINGTON: Crawford County 47–44 Bedford-North Lawrence; Loogootee 53–46 Jasper; Loogootee 61–53 Crawford County. Officials: Judson Raver, Tom Knox, Don Resler, Thomas Neuman, Donald Schmidt, Frank Hoagburg.

1981 SEMI–STATES

EVANSVILLE CENTRAL: Floyd Central 50–47 Loogootee; Vincennes 55–44 Brazil; Vincennes 65–53 Floyd Central. Officials: Frank DeSantis, Norman Hathcoat, Richard Freeman, James Wehsollek, Ron Beard, Don Snedeker.

FORT WAYNE: Warsaw 45–42 Fort Wayne Wayne; Marion 74–68 Valparaiso; Warsaw 64–60 Marion. Officials: Bill Wullner, Steve Welmer, Jerry Petro, Darrell McFall, Nick Sweigert, Ken Gorrell.

INDIANAPOLIS: Shenandoah 74–52 South Ripley; Indianapolis Howe 60–36 Columbus North; Shenandoah 57–49 Indianapolis Howe. Officials: Gene Marks, Bob Marcinek, John Lozier, Melvin Redman, Roger DeYoung, Troy Ingram.

LAFAYETTE: Anderson 74–66 Kankakee Valley; Andrean 67–66 Brownsburg (ot); Anderson 84–80 Andrean. Officials: Tom Knox, James Dunlap, Winfield Jacobs, Eugene Linn, Wayne Van Sickle, Richard Cook.

1981 FINALS—March 21

INDIANAPOLIS (Market Square Arena): Anderson 71–62 Warsaw; Vincennes 72–53 Shenandoah; Vincennes 54–52 Anderson. Officials: Troy Ingram, Richard Freeman, Kenneth Gorrell, Ronald Beard, Roger DeYoung, Nick Sweigart.

1982 SECTIONALS

ANDERSON: Frankton 50–40 Lapel; Madison Heights 64–55 Alexandria; Highland 115–75 Daleville; Anderson 79–61 Pendleton Heights; Madison Heights 44–40 Frankton; Highland 72–71 Anderson (ot); Madison Heights 67–66 Highland. Officials: John Lozier, Bill Champion, Jeffrey Shelhart, Larry Jones.

BEDFORD-NORTH LAWRENCE: Bedford-North Lawrence 42–40 Mitchell; Bloomington North 57–49 Orleans; Bedford-North Lawrence 56–45 Medora; Bedford-North Lawrence 32–30 Bloomington South (ot). Officials: Jimmy Dimitroff, Len Glazier, Max Cameron, Louis Schmalfeldt.

BEN DAVIS: Pike 66–53 Brebeuf, Northwest 75–42 Ritter; Washington 61–59 Ben Davis; Pike 66–peedway; Washington 67–46 Northwest; Washington 72–68 Pike. Officials: Bob Marcinek, John Goss, Robert Graczyk, David Zurcher.

Tourney Time

BENTON CENTRAL: Tri–County 69–51 Twin Lakes; South Newton 67–53 North White; Benton Central 66–62 Frontier; South Newton 65–56 Tri–County; Benton Central 81–74 (ot) South Newton (ot). Officials: Jerome Karstens, Robert Gootee, John Kunkel, James Anderson.

BLACKFORD: Blackford 45–37 Eastbrook; Wes–Del 46–45 Delta; Wapahani 51–48 Blackford; Wes–Del 39–37 Wapahani. Officials: Gary Foltz, Tim Smith, Fred Mohri, Jay Smith.

BOONVILLE: Heritage Hills 37–31 Boonville; South Spencer 62–44 Tell City; Tecumseh 65–55 Cannelton; Heritage Hills 44–43 Castle; Tecumseh 49–47 South Spencer (ot); Heritage Hills 30–27 Tecumseh. Officials: McKee Munk, Gary Woodling, Glen Clemons, Bruce Mayfield.

BROWNSBURG: Plainfield 54–50 Avon; Cascade 53–50 Danville; Brownsburg 60–48 Mooresville; Plainfield 63–56 Cascade; Plainfield 56–54 Brownsburg (2ot). Officials: Rick Owens, Tom Crouch, Gene Marsh, Joe Edmonds,

CALUMET: Merrillville 75–54 Lake Station Edison; Lake Central 43–39 Munster; Crown Point 45–44 Highland; Calumet 72–61 Griffith; Merrillville 54–51 Lake Central; Crown Point 60–59 Calumet; Merrillville 86–68 Crown Point. Officials: Richard Cook, Kevin Weinberg, John Sorg, Bob Storm.

CARMEL: Carmel 60–59 Hamilton Heights (2ot); Sheridan 74–72 Westfield (ot); Noblesville 101–52 Hamilton Southeastern; Sheridan 57–55 Carmel; Noblesville 68–58 Sheridan. Officials: Stephen White, Paul Crawford, David Hurst, Jim Miller.

COLUMBIA CITY: Manchester 67–57 Whitko; Columbia City 52–38 Central Noble; Manchester 71–56 Churubusco; Manchester 56–34 Columbia City. Officials: George Taylor, Michael Wallpe, Douglas Bauman, David Petty.

COLUMBUS: Columbus North 56–48 Brown County; Columbus East 60–45 Hauser; Columbus North 66–51 Edinburgh; North 57–55 East. Officials: Morris Cohen, Donel Criswell, John Tucker, Larry Maxwell.

CONNERSVILLE: Union County 54–45 Laurel; Cambridge City 38–36 Brookville; Connersville 49–18 Centerville; Union County 47–38 Cambridge City; Connersville 55–32 Union County. Officials: Frank Hoagburg, Edward Koors, Gaylord Fritz, Dave Vendrely.

EAST CENTRAL: Jac–Den–Del 59–50 Batesville; East Central 30–16 Milan; South Ripley 46–39 Jac-Cen-Del; South Ripley 60–46 East Central. Officials: Dave Atwell, Gary Myers, Louis Harmening, Thomas Newlin.

DEKALB: Angola 70–55 Fremont; Hamilton 36–35 Garrett; Prairie Heights 56–51 Eastside (2ot); DeKalb 67–57 Leo; Angola 60–21 Hamilton; DeKalb 76–54 Prairie Heights; Angola 58–56 DeKalb. Officials: Richard Freeman, Jon Davenport, Anthony Zappia, Michael DeVault.

EAST CHICAGO: East Chicago Roosevelt 72–55 Whiting; Hammond Noll 75–63 East Chicago Washington; Roosevelt 62–55 Noll. Officials: Jack Mercer, Jim Fish, Douglas Coddington, John Evans.

EAST NOBLE: Fairfield 58–50 West Noble; Lakeland 91–55 Howe Military; East Noble 88–48 Bethany Christian; Westview, 52–48 Fairfield; Lakeland 73–61 East Noble; Lakeland 75–54 Westview. Officials: Mark Masariu, Ron Kitts, Dick Beck, David Long.

ELKHART: Northwood 75–27 Jimtown; Elkhart Memorial 78–67 Goshen; Northridge 70–69 Concord (ot); Elkhart Central 68–64 Penn; Memorial 65–62 Northwood; Central 68–65 Northridge; Memorial 76–63 Central. Officials: Opal Courtney, Paul Danko, David Raabe, Steven Skiles.

EVANSVILLE: Bosse 82–59 Mater Dei; Memorial 54–44 Central; Harrison 106–35

Evansville Christian; North 65–51 Reitz; Bosse 73–47 Memorial; Harrison 67–59 North; Bosse 60–27 Harrison. Officials: Jesse Lynch, John Stumpf, Frank Bodwell, Jerry Larrison.

FLOYD CENTRAL: Corydon 56–38 Borden; Lanesville 77–48 Graceland Christian; Floyd Central 67–42 North Harrison; Corydon 67–49 South Central; Floyd Central 69–40 Lanesville; Corydon 69–61 Floyd Central. Officials: Carl March, Phillip Tincher, Jim Reid, Jack Cummings.

FORT WAYNE (#1): Harding 49–42 Heritage; New Haven 80–69 Elmhurst; Northrop 56–45 Dwenger; Harding 60–44 Woodlan; Northrop 49–35 New Haven; Harding 46–44 Northrop (ot). Officials: Norman Hathcoat, Phil Sullivan, James Fairchild, Rich Clark.

FORT WAYNE (#2): Snider 44–42 Wayne; North Side 75–51 Luers; South Side 58–54 Concordia; Snider 68–47 Carroll; South Side 49–41 North Side; Snider 55–48 South Side. Officials: Bob Carr, Paul Cox, Steven Smith, Herb Pruett.

FOUNTAIN CENTRAL: Seeger 57–51 Turkey Run; North Vermillion 64–56 Attica; Fountain Central 79–52 Covington; North Vermillion 82–63 Seeger; Fountain Central 65–51 North Vermillion. Officials: Don Nester, Clarence Crain, Paul Hackleman, Lanny Rossman.

FRANKFORT: Clinton Prairie 63–55 Tri-Central; Frankfort 68–66 Rossville; Tipton 49–45 Clinton Central; Clinton Prairie 66–58 Frankfort; Clinton Prairie 46–44 Tipton. Officials: Jerry Newsom, Richard Hughes, Ronald James, Richard Eynon.

FRANKLIN CENTRAL: Warren Central 45–38 Franklin Central; Marshall 55–47 Scecina; Roncalli 80–44 Indianapolis Lutheran; Warren Central 53–40 Beech Grove; Marshall 40–36 Roncalli; Warren Central 50–49 Marshall. Officials: Eugene Linn, Mike Crouch, Fred Hamilton, Jim Cox.

GARY: Wirt 54–52 Mann; Gary Roosevelt 73–70 Wallace; Wirt 56–52 West Side; Roosevelt 60–48 Wirt. Officials: Harry Northington, Steven Brown, David Emery, Jerry Christie.

GREENCASTLE: Cloverdale 87–53 Rockville; Van Buren 81–79 North Putnam; Greencastle 66–48 South Putnam; Cloverdale 61–42 Van Buren; Cloverdale 61–43 Greencastle. Officials: Raymond Norris, Tom Rohr, Al Christoules, Mark Reyher.

GREENFIELD CENTRAL: Greenfield Central 64–47 Eastern Hancock; Mt. Vernon (Fortville) 45–42 New Palestine (2ot); Greenfield Central 65–55 Mt. Vernon. Officials: Robert Beeson, Tom Creech, Lonnie Eaglin, Bill Graham.

GREENSBURG: Rushville 84–43 Morton Memorial; Greensburg 58–57 North Decatur; Rushville 65–62 South Decatur; Greensburg 63–58 Rushville. Officials: Mason Meeks, Charles Hadley, William Shobe, Mark Baltz.

HAMMOND: Morton 55–44 Andrean; Hammond High 51–43 Clark; Tech 64–63 Gavit; Hammond High 73–54 Morton; Hammond High 80–63 Tech. Officials: Jerry Cook, Dale Blosser, Robert Reed, William Sorukas.

HUNTINGTON: Homestead 74–50 Wabash; Southwood 69–35 White's; Huntington North 88–45 Northfield; Homestead 83–39 Huntington Catholic; Huntington North 51–41 Southwood; Huntington North 46–45 Homestead. Officials: Don O'Connor, Charles Redinger, Daniel Pfeifer, James Reinebold.

INDIANAPOLIS: Tech 57–56 North Central; Arlington 75–72 Chatard; Broad Ripple 70–66 Lawrence North; Cathedral 22–19 Lawrence Central; Arlington 55–51 Tech; Cathedral 62–55 Broad Ripple; Cathedral 62–60 Arlington. Officials: Wayne Van Sickle, Donald Hittle, Jim Pitcher, Don Snedeker.

Tourney Time

JAY COUNTY: Monroe Central 63–57 Winchester; Randolph Southern 50–39 Union (Modoc); Jay County 43–23 Union City; Randolph Southern 55–49 Monroe Central; Jay County 34–33 Randolph Southern. Officials: Steve Cherry, Robert Dietrick, Larry Gilpin, Jack Graham.

JEFFERSONVILLE: Jeffersonville 73–46 Providence; New Albany 89–48 Clarksville; Jeffersonville 58–56 New Albany. Officials: Keith Combs, Jack Behme, Charles Bertram, James Dunlap.

KANKAKEE VALLEY: Kankakee Valley 58–50 Boone Grove; Rensselaer 61–44 North Newton; Lowell 48–47 Hebron; Kouts 79–45 Hanover Central; Kankakee Valley 48–39 Rensselaer; Lowell 79–63 Kouts; Kankakee Valley 59–38 Lowell. Officials: Jerome Fawley, William Kachek, Ryan Estes, Dale Cramer.

KOKOMO: Northwestern 58–46 Eastern (Greentown); Kokomo 51–50 Haworth (ot); Western 74–69 Taylor; Northwestern 69–52 Kokomo; Northwestern 47–45 Western. Officials: Gene Marks, Richard Calloway, Ralph Cummins, Warren Benko.

LAFAYETTE: Jefferson 62–59 Harrison; Carroll (Flora) 72–57 Central Catholic; Delphi 79–45 West Lafayette; Jefferson 110–63 Carroll; Jefferson 64–52 Delphi. Officials: Roger DeYoung, Michael Benda, John Sebben, Daniel Yagodnik.

LEBANON: Tri–West Hendricks 57–55 Lebanon; Western Boone 41–33 Zionsville; Western Boone 55–49 Tri–West Hendricks (2ot). Officials: Roger Pflughaupt, Bob Wasson, Stephen Bird, Gene Gibson.

LOGANSPORT: North Miami 70–62 Pioneer; Logansport 79–62 Caston; Peru 80–64 Cass; Maconaquah 61–49 North Miami (ot); Peru 69–67 Logansport; Peru 78–70 Maconaquah. Officials: Nick Sweigart, Thomas May, David Pruett, Mike Waisnora.

MADISON: Silver Creek 70–40 Southwestern; Charlestown 72–56 New Washington; Henryville 50–45 Madison Shawe; Silver Creek 39–37 Madison; Henryville 59–57 Charlestown; Silver Creek 67–46 Henryville. Officials: Joe Gilliland, Roger Holder, Bob Gentry, David Lee.

MARION: Oak Hill 57–50 Bennett; Elwood 44–37 Mississinewa; Marion 92–50 Madison Grant; Oak Hill 63–59 Elwood; Marion 52–46 Oak Hill. Officials: Troy Ingram, Tony Watt, Jim Keifer, Dan Moore.

MARTINSVILLE: Owen Valley 64–59 Monrovia; Martinsville 55–50 Eminence; Bloomington North 54–51 Edgewood; Martinsville 55–53 Owen Valley; Bloomington North 54–51 Martinsville. Officials: Temme Patterson, Dennis Thomas, Frank Hobson, Richie Moore.

MICHIGAN CITY: New Prairie 79–73 Westville; Elston 75–64 Marquette; LaPorte 64–62 Rogers (ot); Elston 75–64 New Prairie; Elston 66–53 LaPorte. Officials: Frank DeSantis, Russ Radtke, James Kowalski, Ron Hosinski.

MUNCIE: Burris 37–35 Yorktown; Central 60–52 Cowan; Southside 55–38 Northside; Central 33–29 Burris; Central 48–46 Southside. Officials: Donald Schmidt, Michael Winger, Mathew Turner, Thomas Neuman.

NEW CASTLE: Knightstown 48–45 Blue River; Richmond 63–58 Northeastern; New Castle 73–52 Hagerstown; Shenandoah 64–57 Tri; Richmond 51–36 Knightstown; Shenandoah 66–65 New Castle; Shenandoah 44–42 Richmond. Officials: Tom Knox, Judson Raver, Larry Hollman, Don Resler.

NORTH JUDSON: South Central 54–41 Winamac; North Judson 68–59 Oregon-Davis; Knox 69–53 LaCrosse; Culver Community 51–42 West Central; South Central 58–56 North Judson (ot); Knox 63–59 Culver Community; South Central 50–37 Knox. Officials: James

Wehsollek, Robert Gilmore, Lloyd Ahlbrand, Gary Cheesman.

NORTH MONTGOMERY: North Montgomery 47–44 Southmont; McCutcheon 65–50 Crawfordsville; McCutcheon 61–49 North Montgomery. Officials: Harold Gray, Kenneth Dickman, Mark Hay, Rex Mays.

PAOLI: Paoli 71–54 Eastern (Pekin); Salem 59–56 Springs Valley; Crawford County 54–43 West Washington; Salem 52–46 Paoli; Crawford County 53–52 Salem. Officials: Mel Redman, Robert Davis, William Nimnicht, Carl Redman.

PLYMOUTH: Argos 92–18 Culver Military; LaVille 57–46 Glenn, Plymouth 72–37 Bremen; Argos 40–36 LaVille; Plymouth 55–47 Argos. Officials: Ron Carter, Larry Nixon, Jack Taylor, Timothy Fogarty.

PRINCETON: Mt. Vernon 56–39 New Harmony; Gibson Southern 49–47 Princeton, North Posey 49–43 Oakland City; Mt. Vernon 51–43 Gibson Southern; Mt, Vernon 57–55 North Posey (ot). Officials: Darrel McFall, David Nichols, David Willoughby, Robert Klein.

SEYMOUR: Crothersville 45–42 Brownstown Central; Scottsburg 66–61 Austin; Seymour 64–62 Jennings County; Crothersville 63–55 Scottsburg; Seymour 57–48 Crothersville. Officials: Ken Gorrell, Charles Siebe, Dennis Maude, Jerry Petro, Rick Alexander.

SHELBYVILLE: Waldron 67–66 Southwestern (ot); Shelbyville 68–51 Morristown; Triton Central 50–49 Waldron; Shelbyville 73–55 Triton Central. Officials: Ron Grimes, Gary Leistner, Daniel Henkle, Don Smith, Sr.

SOUTH ADAMS: Bellmont 55–45 South Adams; Southern Wells 51–46 Bluffton; Norwell 42–28 Adams Central; Southern Wells 59–54 Bellmont; Southern Wells 62–43 Norwell. Officials: Ron Beard, Sam Lower, Phil Vidito, Dick Modricker.

SOUTH BEND: Mishawaka 58–41 Mishawaka Marian; LaSalle 53–38 St. Joseph's; Riley 63–54 Clay; Washington 56–47 Adams; LaSalle 80–44 Mishawaka; Washington 64–51 Riley; LaSalle 69–66 Washington (ot). Officials: Chuck Weinkauf, Terry Stewart, John Adams, Jerome Vincent.

SOUTH DEARBORN: Lawrenceburg 61–39 South Dearborn; Switzerland County 62–57 Rising Sun; Lawrenceburg 51–47 Switzerland County. Officials: Mike Bohan, Kenneth Cave, Denis Ward, William Pittman.

SOUTHPORT: Howe 40–37 Decatur Central; Perry Meridian 63–47 Attucks; Manual 53–35 Park Tudor; Southport 65–43 School for the Deaf; Howe 72–58 Perry Meridian; Southport 59–58 Manual; Howe 69–59 Southport. Officials: Dave Loewenstein, Darrell Eaton, Stephen Fisher, Norman Chestnut.

SOUTHRIDGE: Forest Park 32–21 Northeast Dubois; Southridge 66–53 Jasper; Forest Park 61–58 Perry Central; Southridge 48–44 Forest Park. Officials: Clifford Spear, Bob Harvey, Max Clouse, Rex Nichols.

SOUTH VERMILLION: Sullivan 57–49 South Vermillion; North Central (Farmersburg) 59–50 Rosedale; Montezuma 50–39 Union (Dugger); Sullivan 59–58 North Central (Farmersburg); Montezuma 58–49 Sullivan (ot). Officials: Leland Thompson, William Holzer, David Berman, James Deakyne.

SWITZ CITY CENTRAL: Bloomfield 44–40 Eastern (Greene Co.); Worthington 62–61 Switz City Central (2ot); L & M 51–37 Shakamak; Linton-Stockton 75–62 Bloomfield; L & M 61–48 Worthington; Linton–Stockton 63–62 L & M (2ot). Officials: Don Shields, William Amerson, Gary Hawn, James Roberts.

TERRE HAUTE: Brazil 90–70 West Vigo; Terre Haute North 61–43 Staunton Terre Haute

Tourney Time

South 81–43 Clay City; Terre Haute North 63–61 Brazil; Terre Haute, South 66–59 Terre Haute North. Officials: Dave Avery, Ivan Burkle, Patrick Parks, Craig Martin.

TRITON: Rochester 74–57 Tippecanoe Valley; Warsaw 35–30 Triton; Wawasee 57–54 Rochester; Wawasee 49–45 Warsaw. Officials: Rudy Williams, Larry Sintz, Robert Stanley, Tom Jerles.

VALPARAISO: Morgan Twp. 68–55 Hobart; Portage 71–57 Wheeler; Valparaiso 72–71 Chesterton (ot); River Forest 76–55 Washington Twp.; Portage 84–66 Morgan Twp.; Valparaiso 70–65 River Forest; Valparaiso 88–65 Portage. Officials: Bob Wolfe, Tony Primavera, Ron Ramsey, Brandon Bryant. .

VINCENNES: Vincennes 57–36 North Knox; South Knox 71–64 (ot) Vincennes Rivet; Vincennes 62–31 South Knox. Officials: Winfield Jacobs, Gary Byrer, Jerry Judd, Robert Kirk.

WASHINGTON: Washington Catholic 72–51 North Daviess; Loogootee 39–37 PikeCentral; Washington 51–49 Barr–Reeve; Washington Catholic 52–47 Shoals; Loogootee 48–41 Washington; Loogootee 52–43 Washington Catholic. Officials: Steve Welmer, Ed Roush, Michael McCarty, Roger McGriff.

WHITELAND: Whiteland 55–54 Center Grove; Indian Creek 70–64 Greenwood, Whiteland 53–52 Franklin; Indian Creek 41–39 Whiteland. Officials: Bill Wullner, John Lyskowinski, G.R. Honchell, Gary Eaglin.

1982 REGIONALS

ANDERSON: Noblesville 54–53 Northwestern; Madison Heights 68–43 Wes-Del; Madison Heights 53–49 Noblesville. Officials: Mike Waisnora, Nick Sweigart, Warren Benko, Robert Marcinek, Richard Cook, Roger DeYoung.

COLUMBUS: Indian Creek 52–43 Shelbyville; Bloomington North 69–55 Columbus North; Bloomington North 71–66 Indian Creek. Officials: David Zurcher, Daniel Yagodnik, Dale Cramer, Jerome Karstens, Opal Courtney, Richard Freeman.

CONNERSVILLE: Connersville 61–46 Greensburg; Lawrenceburg 69–63 South Ripley (3ot); Connersville 55–46 Lawrenceburg. Officials: Mark Reyher, Raymond Norris, Temme Patterson, James Dunlap, Melvin Redman, Keith Combs.

ELKHART: Plymouth 72–55 Manchester; Elkhart Memorial 85–76 Wawasee; Plymouth 77–74 Elkhart Memorial. Officials: Daniel Moore, Rick Owens, Tony Watt, Stephen White, Wayne Van Sickle, Troy Ingram.

EVANSVILLE: Heritage Hills 65–39 Mt. Vernon; Bosse 53–32 Vincennes; Bosse 78–50 Heritage Hills. Officials: John Lyskowinski, Bruce Mayfield, Michael Crouch, Timothy Fogarty, Jim Cox, Eugene Linn.

FORT WAYNE: Harding 52–50 Angola; Snider 78–45 Lakeland; Harding 64–62 Snider. Officials: Winfield Jacobs, Robert Beeson, Don Smith, Gary Eaglin, Don Snedeker, Bill Wullner.

FRANKFORT: Western Boone 39–35 McCutcheon (2ot); Clinton Prairie 53–52 Plainfield; Western Boone 27–24 Clinton Prairie. Officials: Clifford Spears, Leland Thompson, Terry Stewart, James Deakyne, Chuck Weinkauf, Jerry Larrison.

GARY: Gary Roosevelt 63–62 Hammond; East Chicago Roosevelt 85–74 Merrillville; Gary Roosevelt 76–71 East Chicago Roosevelt. Officials: Herb Pruett, George Taylor, Steve Cherry, Norman Hathcoat, James Wehsollek, Ronald Beard.

INDIANAPOLIS: Cathedral 66–63 Howe; Washington 60–46 Warren Central; Cathedral

61–60 Washington. Officials: Richard Eynon, Jerry Newsom, Roger McGriff, Steve Weimer, Jerry Petro, Kenneth Gorrell.

LAFAYETTE: Kankakee Valley 61–60 Fountain Central; Lafayette Jefferson 74–60 Benton Central; Lafayette Jefferson 67–65 Kankakee Valley (ot); Officials: Jack Mercer, Joseph Gilliland, Brandon Bryant, Michael Bohan, Jimmy Dimitroff, Darrel McFall.

MARION: Huntington North 72–61 Peru; Marion 60–50 Southern Wells; Marion 74–59 Huntington North. Officials: Ronald Grimes, Norm Chestnut, Jack Cummings, Robert Kirk, David Lowenstein, Carl March.

MICHIGAN CITY: South Bend LaSalle 64–63 Valparaiso; Michigan City Elston 70–64 South Central; LaSalle 89–73 Elston. Officials: Mason Meeks, Morris Cohen, Lanny Rossman, David Petty, Robert Wolfe, Jesse Lynch.

NEW CASTLE: Muncie Central 64–50 Greenfield–Central; Jay County 52–51 Shenandoah; Muncie Central 48–46 Jay County (2ot). Officials: Harold Gray, William Champion, David Avery, Richard Modricker, Larry Jones, John Lozier.

SEYMOUR: Jeffersonville 53–47 Seymour; Silver Creek 73–51 Corydon; Jeffersonville 67–44 Saver Creek. Officials: Jerome Fawley, Ronald Hosinski, Dale Blosser, Jerry Cook, Don O'Connor, Frank DeSantis.

TERRE HAUTE: Cloverdale 86–72 Montezuma; Terre Haute South 93–59 Linton; South 60–59 Cloverdale. Officials: Don Resler, Gary Cheesman, Paul Cox, Robert Carr, Tom Knox, Donald Schmidt.

WASHINGTON: Crawford County 43–38 Southridge; Bedford-North Lawrence 44–38 Loogootee; Bedford-North Lawrence 34–33 Crawford County. Officials: Jerry Christie, David Atwell, Mark Masariu, Harry Northington, Ronald Carter, Gene Marks.

1982 SEMI–STATE

EVANSVILLE: Terre Haute South 52–51 Jeffersonville; Evansville Bosse 37–35 Bedford-North Lawrence; Bosse 64–63 South. Officials: Darrel McFall, Michael Bohan, Don Snedeker, Bill Wullner, Wayne Van Sickle, Troy Ingram.

FORT WAYNE: South Bend LaSalle 75–66 Harding; Plymouth 56–55 Marion (ot); Plymouth 77–71 South Bend LaSalle. Officials: Jerry Petro, Jerry Cook, Ron Beard, James Wehsollek, Gene Marks, John Lozier.

INDIANAPOLIS: Indianapolis Cathedral 71–62 Connersville; Muncie Central 69–64 Bloomington North; Indianapolis Cathedral 67–55 Muncie Central. Officials: Nick Sweigart, Bob Marcinek, Richard Cook, Jim Cox, Eugene Linn, Roger DeYoung.

LAFAYETTE: Madison Heights 70–66 Lafayette Jefferson; Gary Roosevelt 38–36 Western Boone; Roosevelt 62–60 Madison Heights. Officials: Jesse Lynch, Jerry Larrison, Don O'Connor, Frank DeSantis, Steve Welmer, Ken Gorrell.

1982 FINALS—March 27

INDIANAPOLIS (Market Square Arena): Plymouth 62–59 Indianapolis Cathedral; Gary Roosevelt 58–57 Evansville Bosse; Plymouth 75–74 Roosevelt (2ot). Officials: Roger DeYoung, Bob Marcinek, Eugene Linn, Frank DeSantis, Wayne Van Sickle, Steve Welmer.

Tourney Time

1983 SECTIONALS

ANDERSON: Highland 82–72 Daleville: Frankton 57–55 Madison Heights; Anderson 66–50 Alexandria; Pendleton Heights 71–43 Lapel; Highland 69–66 Frankton; Anderson 81–56 Pendleton Heights; Anderson 74–73 Highland. Officials: Ronald Carter, Larry Nixon, Jack Taylor, Tim Fogarty.

BEDFORD NORTH LAWRENCE: Bedford–North Lawrence 39–38 Bloomington South; Mitchell 56–49 Orleans; Bedford-North Lawrence 74–39 Medora; Bedford-North Lawrence 59–51 Mitchell. Officials: Mel Redman, Robert Davis, Richard Kay, William Nimnicht.

BEN DAVIS: Washington 97–40 Ritter; Brebeuf 71–65 Pike; Northwest 67–59 Speedway: Washington 68–64 Ben Davis (ot); Brebeuf 74–73 Northwest; Brebeuf 80–74 Washington. Officials: Jim Cox, Fred Hamilton, David Raabe, Mike Crouch.

BENTON CENTRAL: Twin Lakes 56–44 Tri-County; North White 62–46 Frontier; Benton Central 79–70 South Newton; Twin Lakes 61–53 North White; Benton Central 58–47 Twin Lakes. Officials: Roger DeYoung, John Goss, Michael Benda, Dan Yagodnik.

BLACKFORD: Wapahani 54–47 Eastbrook; Blackford 76–51 Wes-Del; Wapahani 58–54 Delta; Wapahani 46–37 Blackford. Officials: Roger Pflughaupt, Bob Wasson, Steve Bird, Gene Gibson.

BOONVILLE: Boonville 48–41 Heritage Hills; Tecumseh 63–46 Cannelton; Tell City 50–40 South Spencer: Boonville 51–44 Castle; Tecumseh 56–55 Tell City; Boonville 58–53 Tecumseh. Officials: Jerry Newsom, Richard Hughes, Ron James, Richard Eynon.

BROWNSBURG: Plainfield 59–52 Cascade: Danville 55–44 Avon; Brownsburg 52–50 Mooresville; Plainfield 41–40 Danville; Plainfield 61–56 Brownsburg. Officials: Tom Knox, Judson Raver, Edward Koors, Don Resler.

CALUMET: Crown Point 55–48 Highland, Munster 73–50 Griffith; Lake Central 82–69 Lake Station Edison; Merrillville 64–48 Calumet; Munster 64—60 Crown Point; Merrillville 74–68 Lake Central; Merrillville 57–50 Munster. Officials: John Lozier, Jeffrey Shelhart, Doug Carl, Larry Jones.

CARMEL: Sheridan 54–49 Hamilton Heights; Hamilton Southeastern 66–59 Westfield; Carmel 46–44 Noblesville; Sheridan 53–38 Hamilton Southeastern; Sheridan 57–39 Carmel. Officials: James Wehsollek, Steven Skiles, Robert Gilmore, Gary Cheesman.

CLAY CITY: Brazil 71–54 North Central (Farmersburg); Sullivan 60–48 Clay City; Union (Dugger) 58–52 Staunton; Brazil 47–39 Sullivan; Brazil 58–38 Union. Officials: Dave Loewenstein, Darrell Eaton, Michael Zehr, Stephen Fisher.

COLUMBIA CITY: Whitko 53–38 Columbia City; Manchester 59–47 Churubusco; Whitko 67–65 Carroll; Whitko 72–66 Manchester. Officials: Frank DeSantis, Russ Radtke, James Kowalski, Dale Blosser.

COLUMBUS: Brown County 77–73 Edinburgh; Columbus East 51–32 Hauser; Columbus North 96–56 Brown County; North 53–49 East. Officials: Bill Wullner, John Lyskowinski, Dale Goodwin, G. R. Honchell.

CONNERSVILLE: Brookville 60–37 Union County; Laurel 77–55 Centerville; Connersville 33–22 Cambridge City Lincoln; Boonville 63–59 Laurel (ot); Connersville 69–35 Brookville. Officials: Joe Gilliland, Roger Holder, Robert Gentry, David Lee.

DEKALB: Eastside 62–54 Hamilton; Leo 58–42 Fremont; Angola 56–28 Howe Military; DeKalb 69–46 Garrett: Leo 54–53 Eastside (ot); DeKalb 50–45 Angola (ot); DeKalb 55–54 Leo.

Officials: Bob Carr, Herb Pruett, Steven Smith, Paul Cox.

EAST CENTRAL: East Central 61–51 South Ripley; Batesville 74–62 Jac-Cen-Del: East Central 63–53 Milan; Batesville 69–53 East Central. Officials: McKee Munk, Glen Clemons, Ronald Mahan, Gary Woodling,

EAST CHICAGO: East Chicago Roosevelt 80–54 East Chicago Washington; Hammond Noll 65–53 Whiting; Roosevelt 38–34 Noll. Officials: Don O'Connor, Charles Redinger, Dan Pfeifer, Robert Storm.

EAST NOBLE: Central Noble 71–60 Prairie Heights: East Noble 70–59 West Noble: Bethany Christian 61–55 Lakeland; Fairfield 52–40 Westview; East Noble 60–53 Central Noble: Fairfield 50–48 Bethany Christian: Fairfield 49—46 East Noble. Officials: Harry Northington, Steve Brown, David Emery, Jerry Christie.

ELKHART: Elkhart Central 86–83 Elkhart Memorial (4ot); Northridge 67–54 Jimtown; Penn 76–43 Concord; Goshen 54–49 North Wood; Central 65–51 Northridge; Penn 80–58 Goshen; Penn 44–42 Central. Officials: Frank Hoagburg, Dave Vendrely, Gaylord Fritz, Larry Hollman.

EVANSVILLE: Bosse 68–54 Memorial; Harrison 68–48 Central; Mater Dei 71–47 Evansville Christian; North 56–55 Reitz; Bosse 87–61 Harrison; North 86–44 Mater Dei; Bosse 85–58 North. Officials: Raymond Norris, Al Christoules, Tom Rohr, Mark Reyher.

FLOYD CENTRAL: Floyd Central 64–51 Borden: Corydon 53–46 Lanesville; Graceland Christian 46–41 South Central (Elizabeth); Floyd Central 59–43 North Harrison: Corydon 63–47 Graceland Christian; Floyd Central 47–40 Corydon. Officials: Ronald Grimes, Gary Leistner, Daniel Henkle, Don Smith, Sr.

FORT WAYNE (#1): New Haven 66–51 Dwenger; South Side 50–39 North Side; Harding 63–58 Concordia (ot); Northrop 60–55 New Haven; South Side 55–47 Harding; Northrop 49–43 South Side. Officials: Mark Masariu, Dick Beck. David Long, Ron Kitts.

FORT WAYNE (#2): Wayne 64–53 Heritage: Snider 80–47 Dwenger; Elmhurst 73–32 Fort Wayne Christian: Woodlan 70–61 Wayne; Elmhurst 71–69 Snider (2ot); Elmhurst 66–64 Woodlan. Officials: Don Nester, Clarence Crain, Paul Hackleman, Lanny Rossman.

FOUNTAIN CENTRAL: Attica 59–56 Covington; Turkey Run 44–43 North Vermillion; Seeger 58–57 Fountain Central; Attica 86–64 Turkey Run; Attica 68–43 Seeger. Officials: Harold Gray, Kenneth Dickman, Mark Hay, Rex Mays.

FRANKFORT: Frankfort 76–62 Tri-Central; Clinton Prairie 60–56 Rossville; Clinton Central 59–46 Tipton: Frankfort 55–49 Clinton Prairie; Clinton Central 73–59 Frankfort. Officials: Jerry Cook. Ron Hosinski, Robert Reed, William Sorukas.

FRANKLIN: Greenwood 67–59 Whiteland; Indian Creek 82–56 Center Grove; Greenwood 65–64 Franklin, Indian Creek 88–57 Greenwood. Officials: Bruce Mayfield, William Amerson, Gary Hawn, James Roberts.

FRANKLIN CENTRAL: Indianapolis Marshall 71–48 Roncalli; Beech Grove 53–41 Franklin Central; Warren Central 47–37 Scecina, Marshall 87–38 Lutheran; Warren Central 63–47 Beech Grove; Marshall 59–55 Warren Central. Officials: Wayne VanSickle, Jim Pitcher. Jerry Middleton, Don Hittle.

GARY: West Side 68–61 Gary Roosevelt; Wallace 89–81 Mann, West Side 70–40 Wirt; Wallace 56–54 West Side. Officials: Dave Avery, Patrick Parks, Ivan Burkle, Craig Martin.

GREENCASTLE: Cloverdale 80–54 North Putnam; Rockville 72–67 Greencastle (ot); South Putnam 62–52 Van Buren; Cloverdale 81–65 Rockville; Cloverdale 58–53 South Putnam.

Tourney Time

Officials: Rick Owens, Tom Crouch, Gene Marsh, Joe Edmonds.

GREENFIELD–CENTRAL: New Palestine 45–43 Eastern Hancock; Mount Vernon 67–64 Greenfield–Central (3ot); Mount Vernon 62–52 New Palestine. Officials: Morris Cohen, Don Criswell, John Tucker, Larry Maxwell.

GREENSBURG: South Decatur 55–35 Morton Memorial; Rushville 66–60 Greensburg; South Decatur 48–47 North Decatur; South Decatur 43–42 Rushville. Officials: Carl March, Phillip Tincher, Greg Fichter, Jack Cummings.

HAMMOND: Morton 59–56 Andrean; Clark 75–50 Gavit; Hammond High 65–49 Morton; Hammond High 59–53 Clark. Officials: Dave Atwell, Louis Harmening, Joe Reed, Thomas Newlin.

HUNTINGTON: Wabash 72–38 White's; Huntington North 50–46 Homestead; Southwood 64–50 Huntington Catholic; Wabash 45–43 Northfield (2ot); North 62–57 Southwood (ot); North 63–40 Wabash. Officials: Stephen White, Paul Crawford, Larry Gilpin, Jim Miller.

INDIANAPOLIS: Broad Ripple 76–39 North Central; Cathedral 56–53 Lawrence North; Tech 68–63 Chatard; Arlington 50–31 Lawrence Central; Broad Ripple 45–44 Cathedral; Tech 58–55 Arlington; Broad Ripple 49–32 Tech. Officials: Bob Marcinek, John Sebben. Robert Graczyk, David Zurcher.

JAY COUNTY: Union City 44–42 Winchester: Randolph Southern 60–50 Monroe Central; Jay County 53–19 Union; Randolph Southern 50–48 Union City (ot); Jay County 35–31 Randolph Southern. Officials: Jay Smith, August Mohri, Tim Smith, Gary Foltz.

JEFFERSONVILLE: New Albany 62–58 Clarksville; Providence 63–57 Jeffersonville; New Albany 71–64 Providence. Officials: Troy Ingram, Tony Watt. Jim Keifer, Dan Moore.

KANKAKEE VALLEY: Rensselaer 60–45 Kouts; Boone Grove 82–55 North Newton; Kankakee Valley 63–46 Lowell; Hanover Central 72–69 Hebron; Boone Grove 88–76 Rensselaer; Kankakee Valley 78–55 Hanover Central: Boone Grove 53–51 Kankakee Valley. Officials: Jerry Larrison, John Stumpf, Frank Bodwell, Clifford Spears.

KOKOMO: Kokomo 88–72 Northwestern; Kokomo Haworth 65–55 Taylor; Western 47–42 Eastern; Haworth 46–45 Kokomo: Western 74–496 Haworth. Officials: Donald Schmidt, Robert Boyle, Mike Winger, Thomas Neuman.

LAFAYETTE: Delphi 59–49 Lafayette Jefferson; West Lafayette 61–60 Carroll; Harrison 75–69 Central Catholic; Delphi 69–49 West Lafayette, Harrison 64–54 Delphi. Officials: Gene Marks, Ralph Cummins, Richard Calloway, Warren Benko.

LEBANON: Zionsville 42–41 Tri-West Hendricks (ot); Lebanon 43–31 Western Boone; Lebanon 47–35 Zionsville. Officials: Richard Cook, Kevin Weinberg, Robert DeBroka, James Reinebold.

LOGANSPORT: North Miami 57–53 Maconaquah; Pioneer 62–49 Caston; Peru 54–53 Cass: Logansport 33–23 North Miami; Pioneer 74–58 Peru; Logansport 66–42 Pioneer. Officials: George Taylor, Michael Wallpe, Douglas Bauman, David Petty.

MADISON: Charlestown 56–53 New Washington, Silver Creek 48–30 Henryville; Madison 60–52 Southwestern; Charlestown 77–61 Madison Shawe; Madison 49–47 Silver Creek, Madison 58–55 Charlestown. Officials: Jimmy Dimitroff, Kenneth Cave, Robert Frye, Phil Vidito.

MARION: Marion 68–44 Elwood, Marion Bennett 77–59 Mississinewa; Oak Hill 71–61 Madison–Grant; Marion 79–63 Marion Bennett; Marion 88–86 Oak Hill (ot). Officials: Jerry Karstens, Robert Gootee, Dan Kunkel, James Anderson.

IHSAA Scores | 1980–1989

MARTINSVILLE: Bloomington North 60–46 Edgewood; Owen Valley 67–52 Eminence; Martinsville 62–55 Monrovia; North 58–37 Owen Valley; North 70–67 Martinsville (3ot). Officials: Keith Combs, Charles Bertram, Charlie Siebe, James Dunlap.

MICHIGAN CITY: LaPorte 53–46 New Prairie; Michigan City Marquette 74–65 Westville; Rogers 70–69 Elston (ot); Marquette 56–52 LaPorte; Rogers 48–47 Marquette. Officials: Nick Sweigart, Tom May, Paul Danko, Mike Waisnora.

MUNCIE: Yorktown 65–59 Cowan; Muncie Southside 57–48 Muncie Northside; Muncie Central 58–49 Muncie Burris; Muncie Southside 58–52 Yorktown; Muncie Southside 33–31 Muncie Central. Officials: Chuck Weinkauf, John Adams, Richard Foxen, Terry Stewart.

NEW CASTLE: Blue River Valley 73–68 Hagerstown; Richmond 85–51 Tri; New Castle 82–47 Knightstown; Northeastern 63–58 Shenandoah; Richmond 87–47 Blue River Valley; New Castle 76–52 Northeastern; New Castle 73–64 Richmond. Officials: Ken Gorrell, Dennis Maude, Jim Oxley, Jerry Petro.

NORTH JUDSON: Oregon–Davis 76–67 Knox: Winamac 69–62 Culver Community; West Central 47–44 North Judson; LaCrosse 60–58 South Central; Oregon-Davis 82–72 Winamac; West Central 52–46 LaCrosse; Oregon-Davis 83–54 West Central. Officials: Ron Beard, Sam Lower, Phil Abernathy, Steve Cherry.

NORTH MONTGOMERY: North Montgomery 63–53 Southmont; Crawfordsville 59–39 McCutcheon; North Montgomery 43–38 Crawfordsville. Officials: Norman Chestnut, Gary Byrer, Michael Short, William Fields.

PAOLI: Springs Valley 52–48 Eastern (Pekin); West Washington 78–71 Salem; Paoli 38–37 Crawford County; Springs Valley 72–45 West Washington; Springs Valley 54–52 Paoli. Officials: Mason Meeks, Charles Hadley, Charles Burchette, Mark Baltz.

PLYMOUTH: Plymouth 54–44 LaVille; Glenn 54–40 Bremen; Argos 90–55 Culver Military Academy; Plymouth 55–48 Glenn; Plymouth 61–56 Argos. Officials: Dick Modricker, William Kachel, William Gebhart, Bill Champion.

PRINCETON: North Posey 72–59 Oakland City Wood; Princeton 66–60 Mount Vernon; Gibson Southern 68–37 New Harmony; Princeton 60–55 North Posey: Princeton 61–44 Gibson Southern. Officials: Steve Welmer, Michael McCarty, Ray Lammlein, Roger McGriff.

SEYMOUR: Scottsburg 65–53 Austin; Jennings County 76–62 Seymour; Brownstown Central 56–33 Crothersville; Jennings County 66–57 Scottsburg; Brownstown Central 78–48 Jennings County. Officials: Temme Patterson, Dennis Thomas, James Reid, Richie Moore.

SHELBYVILLE: Morristown 63–45 Southwestern; Triton Central 74–49 Waldron; Morristown 55–53 Shelbyville; Triton Central 61–54 Morristown. Officials: Mel Botkin, Thomas Dull, Matthew Turner, David Hurst.

SOUTH ADAMS: Southern Wells 53–45 Bluffton; Bellmont 68–56 Adams Central; Norwell 67–53 South Adams; Bellmont 93–80 Southern Wells; Norwell 88–81 Bellmont. Officials: Jerome Fawley, Ryan Estes, Tom Schenkel, Dale Cramer.

SOUTH BEND: Washington 58–47 St. Joseph's; Mishawaka 65–57 Adams; Clay 75–67 Mishawaka Marian; LaSalle 62–59 Riley; Mishawaka 66–61 Washington; LaSalle 72–62 Clay; LaSalle 64–61 Mishawaka. Officials: Mike Bohan, Bob Harvey, Denis Ward, Jesse Lynch.

SOUTH DEARBORN: Lawrenceburg 62–52 South Dearborn: Rising Sun 74–52 Switzerland County; Rising Sun 49–47 Lawrenceburg. Officials: Rudy Williams, Robert Stanley, Kim Baker, Tom Jerles.

Tourney Time

SOUTHPORT: Perry Meridian 49–41 Southport; Indianapolis Attucks 61–45 Decatur Central; Indiana School for the Deaf 51–43 Park Tudor; Manual 75–55 Howe; Perry Meridian 64–54 Attucks: Manual 92–49 Indiana School for the Deaf, Manual 59–58 Perry Meridian, Officials: Norman Hathcoat, James Fairchild, Thomas Urban, Rich Clark.
SOUTHRIDGE: Jasper 55–34 Northeast Dubois; Southridge 67–44 Forest Park; Jasper 48–34 Perry Central; Southridge 63–53 Jasper. Officials: John Evans, Jim Fish, Doug Coddington, Phil Sullivan.
SWITZ CITY CENTRAL: L & M 49–48 Worthington; Central 56–55 Shakamak; Linton-Stockton 52–46 Eastern (Greene Co.); Bloomfield 54–36 L & M; Linton-Stockton 65–61 Central; Bloomfield 68–62 Linton-Stockton (ot). Officials: Don Snedeker, Bill Graham, David Chalk, Robert Beeson,
TERRE HAUTE: West Vigo 81–65 Montezuma; Terre Haute North 62–55 Rosedale; Terre Haute South 64–37 South Vermillion; North 63–55 West Vigo; South 73–49 Terre Haute North. Officials: Robert Kirk, Bill Shobe, Robert Collins, Jack Behme.
TRITON: Wawasee 78–65 Tippecanoe Valley; Warsaw 68–43 Triton; Wawasee 83–49 Rochester: Warsaw 53–50 Wawasee. Officials: Leland Thompson, David Berman, Steven Willett, Pete Deakyne.
VALPARAISO: Wheeler 80–62 River Forest; Hobart 72–43 Washington Twp.; Portage 93–64 Morgan Twp.; Valparaiso 48–36 Chesterton; Wheeler 71–62 Hobart; Valparaiso 48–44 Portage; Valparaiso 52–43 Wheeler. Officials: Richard Freeman, Jon Davenport, Anthony Zappia, Michael DeVault.
VINCENNES: South Knox 64–60 Vincennes Rivet; Vincennes 90–36 North Knox; Vincennes 66–42 South Knox. Officials: Robert Klein, David Pruett, Max Cameron, David Willoughby.
WASHINGTON: Washington 70–45 Loogootee; Barr-Reeve 57–48 Pike Central: Shoals 63–45 North Daviess; Washington 60–46 Washington Catholic; Barr-Reeve 76–39 Shoals; Washington 56–42 Barr-Reeve. Officials: Bob Wolfe, Rex Nichols, William Holzer, Tony Primavera.

1983 REGIONALS

ANDERSON: Western 45–43 Sheridan; Anderson 78–57 Wapahani; Anderson 72–63 Western. Officials: Richard Freeman, Jerry Karstens, Jerome Fawley, Michael DeVault, Frank DeSantis, Don O'Connor.
COLUMBUS: Indian Creek 65–51 Bloomington North; Columbus North 75–68 Triton Central; Indian Creek 63–61 Columbus North. Officials: Robert DeBroka, James Reinebold, Gary Cheesman, Bob Storm, Jerry Cook, Richard Cook.
CONNERSVILLE: Connersville 49–48 Batesville; South Decatur 45–44 Rising Sun; Connersville 63–42 South Decatur. Officials: Leland Thompson, John Evans, Bob Wolfe, Terry Stewart, Mike Bohan, Jimmy Dimitroff.
ELKHART: Warsaw 63–61 Fairfield: Plymouth 55–52 Penn; Plymouth 64–49 Warsaw. Officials: Herb Pruett, Phil Sullivan, Sam Lower, Norman Hathcoat, James Wehsolek, Ron Beard.
EVANSVILLE: Princeton 64–48 Boonville; Evansville Bosse 66–55 Vincennes ; Princeton 82–77 Bosse (4ot). Officials: Dave Avery, Steven Brown, Ron Kitts, Mark Masariu, Larry Jones, John Lozier.
FORT WAYNE: Northrop 67–54 Elmhurst; DeKalb 75–70 Whitko; DeKalb 51–50 Fort

Wayne Northrop. Officials: Thomas May, Craig Martin, Warren Benko, Ronald Carter, Timothy Fogarty, Gene Marks.

FRANKFORT: Lebanon 47–46 Plainfield; North Montgomery 53–47 Clinton Central; Lebanon 59–51 North Montgomery. Officials: Nick Sweigart, Mike Waisnora, David Zurcher, John F. Goss, Jr., Bob Marcinek, Roger DeYoung.

GARY: Gary Wallace 52–50 Merrillville; East Chicago Roosevelt 72–71 Hammond; Wallace 70–68 East Chicago Roosevelt. Officials: Rudy Williams, Rich Clark, Rick Owens, Stephen White, Wayne VanSickle, Troy Ingram.

INDIANAPOLIS: Broad Ripple 77–64 Brebeuf; Marshall 59–57 Manual; Broad Ripple 61–52 Marshall. Officials: Tom Knox, Thomas Neuman, Frank Hoagburg, Paul Cox, Donald Schmidt, Bob Carr.

LAFAYETTE: Benton Central 55–50 Harrison; Attica 57–56 Boone Grove; Benton Central 61–56 Attica. Officials: Dave Atwell, Larry Maxwell, James Fairchild, Carl March, Steven Fisher, Dave Loewenstein.

MARION: Huntington North 59–56 Norwell; Marion 82–64 Logansport; Marion 83–55 Huntington North. Officials: Lanny Rossman, Don Nester, John Adams, Robert Klein, Chuck Weinkauf, Jesse Lynch.

MICHIGAN CITY: Valparaiso 76–58 Oregon–Davis; Michigan City Rogers 76–67 South Bend LaSalle; Valparaiso 34–32 Rogers. Officials: Harry Northington, Dick Modricker, Jerry Christie, Bill Champion, Mike Crouch, Jim Cox.

NEW CASTLE: New Castle 68–56 Muncie Southside; Jay County 43–35 Mount Vernon; New Castle 75–54 Jay County. Officials: Tony Primavera, John Stumpf, Joe Gilliland, Clarence Crain, Clifford Spears, Jerry Larrison.

SEYMOUR: Brownstown Central 51–48 Madison; Floyd Central 61–46 New Albany; Floyd Central 40–35 Brownstown Central. Officials: Robert Kirk, Jack Behme, Temme Patterson, Keith Combs, James Dunlap, Mel Redman.

TERRE HAUTE: Cloverdale 79–76 Bloomfield; Terre Haute South 66–56 Brazil; Cloverdale 57–54 South. Officials: G. R. Honchell, Steve Cherry, Robert Beeson, Don Smith Sr., Don Snedeker, Bill Wullner.

WASHINGTON: Washington 63–53 Southridge; Bedford-North Lawrence 61–50 Springs Valley; Washington 69–64 Bedford-North Lawrence. Officials: Jerry Newsom, Steve Welmer, Richard Eynon, Dan Moore, Ken Gorrell, Jerry Petro.

1983 SEMI–STATES

FORT WAYNE: DeKalb 49–44 Plymouth; Marion 49–47 Valparaiso; Marion 64–63 DeKalb. Officials: Steve Weimer, Jerry Newsom, Bill Wullner, Don Snedeker, Jerry Petro, Ken Gorrell.

INDIANAPOLIS: Connersville 67–45 Indian Creek; New Castle 79–64 Indianapolis Broad Ripple; Connersville 70–57 New Castle. Officials: Bob Carr, Jim Wehsollek, John Lozier, Harry Northington, Richard Cook, Bob Marcinek.

LAFAYETTE: Anderson 74–64 Lebanon; Gary Wallace 70–62 Benton Central; Anderson 70–64 Gary Wallace. Officials: Gene Marks, Roger DeYoung, Frank DeSantis, Don O'Connor, Troy Ingram, Wayne VanSickle.

TERRE HAUTE: Princeton 58–54 Cloverdale; Washington 71–70 Floyd Central; Princeton

Tourney Time

56–54 Washington. Officials: Chuck Weinkauf, Jesse Lynch, Nick Sweigart, Warren Benko, Jim Dimitroff, Jerry Larrison.

1983 FINALS—March 26

INDIANAPOLIS (Market Square Arena): Connersville 62–57 Princeton; Anderson 89–87 Marion (2ot); Connersville 63–62 Anderson. Officials: Richard Cook, Jerry Larrison, Don O'Connor, Jerry Petro, Troy Ingram, Jesse Lynch.

1984 SECTIONALS

ANDERSON: Lapel 46–42 Frankton; Pendleton Heights 67–66 Daleville; Anderson Highland 86–50 Alexandria-Monroe; Anderson 82–73 Anderson Madison Heights; Pendleton 83–61 Lapel; Anderson 63–60 Anderson Highland (ot); Anderson 74–60 Pendleton Heights. Officials: Chuck Weinkauf, John Adams, Richard Foxen, Terry Stewart.

BEDFORD-NORTH LAWRENCE: Bedford-North Lawrence 75–30 Medora; Bloomington South 64–43 Mitchell; Bedford-North Lawrence 50–49 Bloomington South. Officials: Jerry Larrison, John Stumpf, Frank Bodwell, Clifford Spears.

BEN DAVIS: Ben Davis 59–58 Pike (ot); Brebeuf 87–71 Speedway; Indianapolis Washington 68–58 Ritter; Ben Davis 46–42 Northwest; Brebeuf 91–80 Washington; Ben Davis 93–80 Brebeuf. Officials: Wayne VanSickle, Jim Pitcher, Jerry Middleton, Don Hittle.

BLACKFORD: Blackford 87–58 Eastbrook; Delta 56–55 Wapahani (2ot); Blackford 69–54 Wes–Del; Blackford 52–49 Delta. Officials: Leland Thompson, David Berman, Steven Willett, Pete Deakyne.

BOONVILLE: Boonville 57–46 Tecumseh; Heritage Hills 59–47 Cannelton; South Spencer 57–50 Tell City; Boonville 65–49 Castle; Heritage Hills 65–58 South Spencer; Boonville 50–47 Heritage Hills. Officials: Carl March, Phillip Tincher, James Newlin, Greg Fichter.

BROWNSBURG: Mooresville 52–51 Brownsburg (3ot); Danville 57–54 Plainfield; Cascade 46–43 Avon; Mooresville 56–52 Danville; Cascade 68–55 Mooresville. Officials: Rick Owens, Tom Crouch, Gene Marsh, Joe Edmonds.

CALUMET: Calumet 39–30 Lake Station Edison; Merrillville 59–58 Griffith; Lake Central 74–33 Crown Point; Highland 65–53 Munster; Merrillville 68–43 Calumet; Lake Central 80–66 Highland; Lake Central 46–45 Merrillville (ot). Officials: Dick Modricker, William Kachel, William Gebhart, William Champion.

CARMEL: Noblesville 80–39 Sheridan; Carmel 75–57 Hamilton Southeastern; Hamilton Heights 75–59 Westfield; Noblesville 61–54 Carmel; Noblesville 80–52 Hamilton Heights. Officials: Troy Ingram, Jim Keifer, Larry Alsip, Tony Watt.

COLUMBIA CITY: Whitko 91–66 Churubusco; Carroll 66–53 Columbia City; Manchester 73–71 Whitko; Carroll 58–53 Manchester. Officials: Mark Masariu, David Long, Charles Burchette, Ronald Kitts.

COLUMBUS: Columbus East 84–55 Hauser; Edinburgh 55–52 Brown County (ot); Columbus North 76–57 Columbus East; Columbus North 86–58 Edinburgh. Officials: Norman Chestnut, David Bromm, Lowell DePoy, William Fields.

CONNERSVILLE: Connersville 60–52 Union County; Cambridge City Lincoln 52–50

IHSAA Scores | 1980–1989

Laurel; Brookville 62–32 Centerville; Connersville 51–40 Cambridge City Lincoln; Connersville 64–48 Brookville. Officials: Morris Cohen, John Tucker, Thomas Marshall, Larry Maxwell.

EAST CENTRAL: Batesville 70–65 Milan; East Central 72–53 South Ripley; Batesville 67–60 Jac-Cen-Del (ot); East Central 41–39 Batesville. Officials: Ron Ramsey. Jerry Judd, Al Smith, Richard Hughes.

EAST CHICAGO: Hammond Noll 66–46 Whiting; East Chicago Roosevelt 83–69 East Chicago Washington; Noll 63–60 Roosevelt. Officials: Jerome Fawley, Ryan Estes, Tom Schenkel, Dale Cramer.

EAST NOBLE: Westview 70–50 Bethany Christian; Lakeland 66–55 Prairie Heights; East Noble 62–58 Fairfield; West Noble 69–65 Central Noble; Westview 52–49 Lakeland; East Noble 66–64 West Noble; East Noble 51–49 Westview. Officials: George Taylor, Robert Stanley, Kim Baker, Tom Jerles.

ELKHART: Elkhart Central 81–61 Goshen; Elkhart Memorial 82–61 Concord; Penn 81–57 Jimtown; North Wood 38–34 Northridge; Central 60–59 Memorial; Penn 67–60 North Wood; Penn 69–60 Central. Officials: Mike Bohan, Denis Ward, Clark Hamilton, Jesse Lynch.

EVANSVILLE: Central 59–46 Reitz; Bosse 75–60 Harrison; North 65–56 Memorial; Mater Dei 101–55 Christian; Bosse 59–54 Central; Mater Dei 72–51 North; Bosse 93–54 Mater Dei. Officials: Dave Atwell, Lou Harmening, Joe Reed, Thomas Newlin.

FLOYD CENTRAL: Floyd Central 46–43 Corydon Central; Borden 42–40 Graceland Christian; North Harrison 61–41 Lanesville; Floyd Central 67–33 South Central (Elizabeth); North Harrison 51–43 Borden; Floyd Central 65–53 North Harrison. Officials: Robert Kirk, Robert Collins, Marvin Williams, William Shobe.

FORT WAYNE (#1): Woodlan 74–62 North Side; Northrop 103–44 Luers; South Side 50–48 Snider; Woodlan 63–48 New Haven; Northrop 46–45 South Side; Northrop 66–47 Woodlan. Officials: Frank DeSantis, John Goss, Robert Modrowski, Daniel Yagodnik.

FORT WAYNE (#2): Dwenger 93–80 Heritage; Wayne 63–62 Concordia; Elmhurst 92–40 Christian; Dwenger 72–53 Harding; Elmhurst 59–54 Wayne; Elmhurst 59–58 Dwenger. Officials: Joe Gilliland, Robert Gentry, Ed Scahill, Roger Holder.

FOUNTAIN CENTRAL: Covington 67–47 Attica; North Vermillion 59–43 Turkey Run; Fountain Central 69–45 Seeger; Covington 59–57 North Vermillion (2ot); Covington 53–45 Fountain Central. Officials: Warren Benko, Ronald McDougal, Mark Tulchinsky, Richard Calloway.

FRANKFORT: Tipton 48–21 Rossville; Tri-Central 64–54 Clinton Central; Frankfort 66–60 Clinton Prairie; Tri-Central 42–40 Tipton; Frankfort 72–61 Tri-Central. Officials: Ron Beard, Phillip Abernathy, Sam Lower, Steve Cherry.

FRANKLIN CENTRAL: Indianapolis Scecina 54–45 Franklin Central (ot); Marshall 41–40 Roncalli; Warren Central 81–27 Lutheran; Scecina 63–61 Beech Grove (ot); Warren Central 65–57 Marshall; Warren Central 92–60 Scecina. Officials: James Wehsollek, Steven Skiles, Robert Gilmore, Gary Cheesman.

GARRETT: Leo 63–37 Angola; Eastside 86–62 Fremont; Hamilton 57–24 Howe Military; Garrett 53–49 DeKalb; Leo 54–53 Eastside; Garrett 64–42 Hamilton; Garrett 57–50 Leo. Officials: Jim Miller, Paul Crawford, Larry Gilpin, Stephen White.

GARY: West Side 57–42 Wirt; Roosevelt 68–64 Mann; West Side 66–64 Wallace; West Side 67–58 Roosevelt. Officials: Richard Freeman, Jon Davenport, Steve Badylak, Michael DeVault.

Tourney Time

GREENCASTLE: South Putnam 63–46 North Putnam; Greencastle 73–50 Rockville; Van Buren 70–46 Cloverdale; South Putnam 60–59 Greencastle; South Putnam 61–59 Van Buren. Officials: Keith Combs, Charles Bertram, Charles Siebe, James Dunlap.

GREENFIELD–CENTRAL: Greenfield–Central 85–63 Eastern Hancock; New Palestine 42–39 Mount Vernon; Greenfield–Central 60–56 New Palestine. Officials: Dave Avery, Patrick Parks, James Campbell, Ivan Burkle.

GREENSBURG: Greensburg 77–42 North Decatur; South Decatur 52–47 Rushville; Greensburg 93–39 Morton Memorial; Greensburg 65–46 South Decatur. Officials: Rudy Williams, Douglas Bauman, James Robinson, David Petty.

GREENWOOD: Center Grove 64–45 Whiteland; Franklin 69–54 Indian Creek; Center Grove 52–40 Greenwood; Franklin 59–41 Center Grove. Officials: Bob Beeson, Larry Sintz, David Chalk, Mike Wallpe.

HAMMOND: Hammond Clark 55–50 Andrean; Hammond 45–44 Morton (ot); Gavit 56–54 Clark; Hammond 61–49 Gavit. Officials: Richard Cook, Paul Danko, Thomas Templin, Kevin Weinberg.

HUNTINGTON: Huntington North 67–45 Wabash; Southwood 74–50 Northfield; Homestead 78–37 White's; Huntington North 80–41 Huntington Catholic; Homestead 78–61 Southwood; North 60–49 Homestead. Officials: Roger DeYoung, Russ Radtke, Brad Groninger, Dale Blosser.

INDIANAPOLIS: Arlington 74–61 Tech; Cathedral 68–60 Chatard; Lawrence North 62–58 Broad Ripple; North Central 58–50 Lawrence Central; Arlington 64–54 Cathedral; Lawrence North 52–50 North Central; Arlington 64–58 Lawrence North. Officials: Harry Northington, Steven Brown, David Emery, Jerry Christie.

JAY COUNTY: Jay County 64–36 Union (Modoc); Randolph Southern 79–64 Winchester; Union City 56–48 Monroe Central; Jay County 51–48 Randolph Southern; Union City 39–34 Jay County. Officials: Jim Cox, Fred Hamilton, David Raabe, Mike Crouch.

JEFFERSONVILLE: New Albany 71–59 Clarksville; Providence 57–52 Jeffersonville; Providence 68–66 New Albany. Officials: Don Nester, Clarence Crain, Paul Hackleman, Lanny Rossman.

KANKAKEE VALLEY: Boone Grove 60–57 Hebron; North Newton 64–53 Hanover Central; Lowell 64–53 Kouts; Kankakee Valley 51–47 Rensselaer; Boone Grove 80–57 North Newton; Kankakee Valley 57–56 Lowell; Kankakee Valley 58–46 Boone Grove. Officials: Jerry Cook, Ron Hosinski, Dave Petrie, Bill Sorukas.

KOKOMO: Kokomo 42–41 Kokomo Haworth; Western 83–51 Northwestern; Taylor 75–55 Eastern; Kokomo 66–62 Western; Kokomo 65–50 Taylor. Officials: Ron Carter, Larry Nixon, Jack Taylor, Tim Fogarty.

LAFAYETTE: Delphi 80–70 Carroll (Flora); Lafayette Jefferson 60–49 West Lafayette; Harrison 46–43 Central Catholic; Jefferson 64–54 Delphi; Jefferson 44–31 Harrison. Officials: Don O'Connor, Charles Redinger, Dan Pfeifer, Jim Reinebold.

LEBANON: Western Boone 68–64 Tri-West Hendricks; Lebanon 86–35 Zionsville; Lebanon 53–37 Western Boone. Officials: Tom Knox, Judson Raver, Edward Koors, Don Resler.

LOGANSPORT: Logansport 52–33 North Miami; Peru 64–56 Pioneer; Maconaquah 76–75 Caston (4ot); Logansport 57–45 Cass; Peru 50–38 Maconaquah; Logansport 64–52 Peru. Officials: Jerry Karstens, Robert Gootee, Cary Schnick, James Anderson.

MADISON: Henryville 48–46 New Washington; Silver Creek 52–51 Charlestown; Southwestern 58–41 Madison Shawe; Madison 36–34 Henryville; Silver Creek 58–46 Southwestern (Hanover); Madison 55–46 Silver Creek. Officials: Mark Baltz, Terry Magnuson, Mike Davis, Phil Barth.

MARION: Oak Hill 63–56 Mississinewa; Marion 69–57 Marion Bennett; Madison-Grant 67–53 Elwood; Marion 63–58 Oak Hill; Marion 82–53 Madison-Grant. Officials: Roger Pflughaupt, Bob Wasson, Steve Bird, Gene Gibson.

MARTINSVILLE: Edgewood 99–59 Eminence; Martinsville 63–51 Monrovia; Bloomington North 73–63 Owen Valley; Martinsville 63–54 Edgewood; Bloomington North 44–35 Martinsville. Officials: Harold Gray, Mark Hay, Dan Kunkel, Kenneth Dickman.

MICHIGAN CITY: Michigan City Marquette 55–50 Westville; Rogers 108–67 New Prairie; Elston 69–51 LaPorte; Rogers 81–49 Marquette; Rogers 96–61 Elston. Officials: Bob Carr, Herb Pruett, Steve Smith, Paul Cox.

MUNCIE: Southside 70–43 Burris; Yorktown 91–48 Cowan; Northside 60–53 Central; Southside 51–48 Yorktown (ot); Northside 41–39 Southside (ot). Officials: Ken Gorrell, Dennis Maude, Robert Anderson, Jerry Petro.

NEW CASTLE: New Castle 95–55 Hagerstown; Knightstown 53–41 Blue River Valley; Northeastern 69–53 Tri; Richmond 65–42 Shenandoah; New Castle 86–43 Knightstown; Richmond 61–41 Northeastern; New Castle 56–54 Richmond. Officials: Bill Wullner, John Lyskowinski, Dale Goodwin, G. R. Honchell.

NORTH JUDSON: Winamac 79–53 West Central; Culver 66–50 Knox; North Judson 58–44 LaCrosse; Oregon-Davis 61–43 South Central (Union Mills); Winamac 60–43 Culver; Oregon-Davis 73–59 North Judson; Winamac 56–51 Oregon-Davis. Officials: John Lozier, Jeff Shelhart, Doug Carl, Larry Jones.

NORTH MONTGOMERY: Southmont 56–55 McCutcheon; North Montgomery 48–46 Crawfordsville (ot); North Montgomery 69–64 Southmont. Officials: Dave Loewenstein, Michael Zehr, Mark Mason, Steven Fisher.

PAOLI: Crawford County 51–48 Paoli; West Washington 59–54 Orleans (ot); Springs Valley 51–49 Salem; Crawford County 43–41 Eastern (Pekin); West Washington 80–75 Springs Valley; Crawford County 60–55 West Washington. Officials: Raymond Norris, Ronald James, Jerry Taylor, Tom Rohr.

PLYMOUTH: Plymouth 66–46 Bremen; Argos 55–53 Culver Military Academy; Glenn 57–43 LaVille; Plymouth 75–49 Argos; Plymouth 65–50 Glenn. Officials: Jay Smith, August Mohri, Tim Smith, Gary Foltz.

PRINCETON: Oakland City Wood 54–38 Gibson Southern; Princeton 103–53 New Harmony; North Posey 71–70 Mount Vernon (ot); Princeton 68–60 Oakland City Wood; Princeton 57–52 North Posey (ot). Officials: Bruce Mayfield, William Amerson, Gary Hawn, Don Smith, Sr.

SEYMOUR: Brownstown Central 43–39 Austin; Seymour 50–48 Jennings County; Crothersville 50–47 Scottsburg; Brownstown Central 47–45 Seymour; Brownstown Central 53–45 Crothersville. Officials: Melvin Redman, Robert Davis, Richard Kay, William Nimnicht.

SHELBYVILLE: Shelbyville 67–45 Morristown; Triton Central 52–49 Waldron; Shelbyville 87–41 Southwestern (Shelbyville); Shelbyville 57–40 Triton Central. Officials: Norman Hathcoat, Tom Urban, Lynn Perdue, Rich Clark.

Tourney Time

SOUTH ADAMS: Adams Central 65–49 South Adams; Bellmont 67–64 Norwell; Southern Wells 87–70 Bluffton; Belmont 62–44 Adams Central; Bellmont 80–68 Southern Wells. Officials: Bob Wolfe, Rex Nichols, William Holzer, Tony Primavera.

SOUTH BEND: Adams 63–62 Riley (2ot); St. Joseph's 79–58 Mishawaka; LaSalle 62–46 Mishawaka Marian; Clay 69–51 Washington; Adams 61–49 St. Joseph's; Clay 57–56 LaSalle; Adams 53–47 Clay. Officials: Frank Hoagburg, Gaylord Fritz, Al Christoules, Dave Vendrely.

SOUTH DEARBORN: Rising Sun 55–52 South Dearborn; Switzerland County 71–46 Lawrenceburg; Rising Sun 58–43 Switzerland County. Officials: Melvin Botkin, Thomas Dull, Tony Bierschbach, David Hurst.

SOUTHPORT: Indianapolis Attucks 47–31 Park Tudor; Perry Meridian 69–67 Southport (ot); Howe 84–48 School for the Deaf; Manual 56–55 Decatur Central; Perry Meridian 63–52 Attucks; Howe 59–53 Manual; Perry Meridian 56–47 Howe. Officials: Ronald Grimes, Gary Leistner, Daniel Henkle, James Roberts.

SOUTHRIDGE: Forest Park 53–44 Perry Central; Southridge 46–41 Jasper; Northeast Dubois 61–55 Forest Park (ot); Northeast Dubois 49–36 Southridge. Officials: Steve Weimer, Michael McCarty, Ed Roush, Roger McGriff.

SOUTH VERMILLION: Brazil 51–47 Montezuma (2ot); Rosedale 43–41 Clay City; Staunton 52–47 South Vermillion; Rosedale 59–50 Brazil; Rosedale 68–49 Staunton. Officials: Temme Patterson, Dennis Thomas, James Reid, Richie Moore.

SWITZ CITY CENTRAL: Eastern (Greene Co.) 75–46 Switz City Central; Bloomfield 37–26 Shakamak; Linton-Stockton 67–48 Worthington; L & M 72–63 Eastern; Bloomfield 59–51 Linton-Stockton; L & M 69–34 Bloomfield. Officials: Phil Sullivan, Jim Fish, Doug Coddington, John Evans.

TERRE HAUTE: Terre Haute South 84–49 Union (Dugger); Terre Haute North 91–65 West Vigo; North Central (Farmersburg) 73–60 Sullivan; Terre Haute South 69–58 North; South 108–84 North Central. Officials: Mike Waisnora, Mike Reece, Dan Amrhein, Tom May.

TRI–COUNTY: North White 53–48 Frontier; South Newton 48–45 Twin Lakes; Tri-County 58–57 Benton Central; North White 60–59 South Newton; North White 50–48 Tri-County. Officials: Jimmy Dimitroff, Robert Frye, Kenneth Miller, Phil Vidito.

TRITON: Triton 64–55 Tippecanoe Valley; Warsaw 63–53 Wawasee; Triton 75–51 Rochester; Warsaw 82–57 Triton. Officials: Bob Marcinek, John Sebben, Robert Graczyk, David Zurcher.

VALPARAISO: Hobart 58–54 Morgan Twp.; Wheeler 73–64 Washington Twp.; Chesterton 64–42 River Forest; Valparaiso 57–41 Portage; Hobart 62–49 Wheeler; Valparaiso 33–26 Chesterton; Valparaiso 51–32 Hobart. Officials: Donald Schmidt, Mike Winger, Ed Christoffel, Thomas Neuman.

VINCENNES: Vincennes 78–38 North Knox; South Knox 73–64 Vincennes Rivet; Vincennes 69–33 South Knox. Officials: McKee Munk, Glen Clemons, Ronald Mahan, Gary Woodling.

WASHINGTON: Pike Central 48–22 Shoals; Washington Catholic 75–67 North Daviess; Barr-Reeve 68–51 Washington; Loogootee 50–33 Pike Central; Barr-Reeve 37–31 Washington Catholic; Loogootee 45–39 Barr-Reeve. Officials: Robert Klein, David Pruett, Max Cameron, David Willoughby.

IHSAA Scores | 1980–1989

1984 REGIONALS

ANDERSON: Anderson 71–61 Blackford; Noblesville 62–60 Kokomo (ot); Anderson 64–52 Noblesville. Officials: Lanny Rossman, Phil Vidito, John Adams, Don Nester, Timothy Fogarty, Jesse Lynch.

COLUMBUS: Shelbyville 58–45 Bloomington North; Columbus North 67–66 Franklin; Columbus North 46–39 Shelbyville. Officials: Tony Watt, Tom May, Tom Rohr, Raymond Norris, Clifford Spears, Jerry Larrison.

CONNERSVILLE: Greensburg 62–51 Rising Sun; Connersville 58–49 East Central; Greensburg 43–42 Connersville. Officials: David Atwell, Larry Maxwell, Carl March, Ronald Grimes, Melvin Redman, David Loewenstein.

ELKHART: Plymouth 54–34 East Noble; Warsaw 69–53 Penn; Warsaw 67–59 Plymouth. Officials: Dave Avery, Mark Baltz, Ron Kitts, Mark Masariu, Larry Jones, Jimmy Dimitroff.

EVANSVILLE: Vincennes 43–38 Princeton; Evansville Bosse 83–56 Boonville; Vincennes 61–60 Bosse. Officials: Steve Welmer, Thomas Newlin, Gary Woodling, Glenn Clemons, Ken Gorrell, Jerry Petro.

FORT WAYNE: Elmhurst 60–58 (ot); Garrett 59–51 Carroll; Elmhurst 76–56 Garrett. Officials: Harry Northington, Dick Modricker, Bill Champion, Rex Nichols, Mike Crouch, Jim Cox.

FRANKFORT: Frankfort 92–57 Cascade; Lebanon 61–55 North Montgomery; Lebanon 62–57 Frankfort. Officials: G. R. Honchell, Don Smith, Sr., Steve Cherry, McKee Munk, Robert Beeson, Bill Wullner.

GARY: Lake Central 67–66 Hammond; Hammond Noll 53–39 Gary West Side; Lake Central 69–65 Noll. Officials: Tom Knox, Albert Christoules, Frank Hoagburg, Paul Cox, Donald Schmidt, Richard Cook.

INDIANAPOLIS: Ben Davis 73–58 Indianapolis Arlington; Perry Meridian 63–59 Warren Central; Perry Meridian 45–43 Ben Davis. Officials: Mike Waisnora, Dan Kunkel, Ivan Burkle, Mark Hay, John Lozier, Roger DeYoung.

LAFAYETTE: Covington 50–44 Kankakee Valley (ot); Lafayette Jefferson 68–49 North White; Lafayette Jefferson 69–56 Covington. Officials: Rudy Williams, Rich Clark, Steve White, Paul Crawford, Wayne VanSickle, Troy Ingram.

MARION: Marion 62–41 Logansport; Belmont 72–57 Huntington North; Marion 75–67 Bellmont. Officials: Patrick Parks, Gary Cheesman, Dale Cramer, Jay Smith, Jerry Cook, Bob Carr.

MICHIGAN CITY: Valparaiso 60–34 South Bend Adams; Michigan City Rogers 101–79 Winamac; Rogers 70–57 Valparaiso. Officials: Herb Pruett, David Long, Norman Hathcoat, Roger Holder, James Wehsollek, Ron Beard.

NEW CASTLE: Muncie Northside 73–43 Union City; New Castle 66–52 Greenfield Central; New Castle 43–39 Muncie Northside. Officials: William Sorukas, Jerry Karstens, Russ Radtke, Harold Gray, Frank DeSantis, Don O'Connor.

SEYMOUR: Clarksville Providence 48–46 Brownstown Central; Floyd Central 64–46 Madison; Floyd Central 63–50 Providence. Officials: Bob Wolfe, Michael Wallpe, John Evans, Terry Stewart, Bob Marcinek, Mike Bohan.

TERRE HAUTE: South Putnam 48–47 Rosedale; Terre Haute South 64–56 L & M; South 75–50 South Putnam. Officials: Roger McGriff, Robert Kirk, William Nimnicht, Keith Combs,

Tourney Time

James Dunlap, Stephen Fisher.
WASHINGTON: Northeast Dubois 61–50 Bedford–North Lawrence; Loogootee 43–41 Crawford County; Northeast Dubois 46–42 Loogootee. Officials: Chuck Weinkauf, Temme Patterson, Joe Gilliland, Douglas Coddington, Warren Benko, Tony Primavera.

1984 SEMI-STATES

FORT WAYNE: Michigan City Rogers 88–80 Marion; Warsaw 83–75 Fort Wayne Elmhurst; Warsaw 75–73 Michigan City Rogers. Officials: Bob Marcinek, Tim Fogarty, Thomas May, James Wehsollek, Chuck Weinkauf, Roger DeYoung.
INDIANAPOLIS: Columbus North 61–48 Greensburg; New Castle 74–73 Perry Meridian (ot); New Castle 60–59 Columbus North. Officials: Jesse Lynch, Dave Avery, Ken Gorrell, Troy Ingram, James Dunlap, Melvin Redman.
LAFAYETTE: Lake Central 60–59 Anderson; Lebanon 61–55 Lafayette Jefferson; Lake Central 67–53 Lebanon. Officials: Mike Bohan, Donald Schmidt, Tom Knox, Ron Beard, Jerry Petro, Don O'Connor.
TERRE HAUTE: Vincennes 56–44 Northeast Dubois; Floyd Central 70–63 Terre Haute South; Vincennes 89–76 Floyd Central. Officials: Wayne VanSickle, Bob Carr, Clifford Spears, Richard Cook, Frank DeSantis, Steve Welmer.

1984 FINALS—March 24

INDIANAPOLIS (Market Square Arena): Vincennes 64–56 Lake Central; Warsaw 78–74 New Castle; Warsaw 59–56 Vincennes. Officials: Troy Ingram, Chuck Weinkauf, Mike Bohan, Steve Welmer, Roger DeYoung, Melvin Redman.

1985 SECTIONALS

ANDERSON: Anderson Highland 69–56 Lapel; Daleville 66–59 Pendleton Heights; Anderson Madison Heights 67–61 Alexandria, Anderson 54–53 Frankton (ot); Daleville 75–65 Anderson Highland; Anderson 74–69 Madison Heights; Daleville 84–77 Anderson. Officials: Stephen White, Raymond Norris, Kim Baker, Al Christoules.
BEN DAVIS: Pike 77–55 Indianapolis Ritter; Ben Davis 76–48 Speedway; Northwest 66–60 Brebeuf; Pike 73–46 Washington; Ben Davis 64–46 Northwest; Ben Davis 75–54 Pike. Officials: Steve Cherry, Denis Ward, Donald Hopkins, Phil Barth.
BOONVILLE: Heritage Hills 62–28 Evansville Day School; Boonville 81–60 Tell City; Cannelton 62–60 Castle; South Spencer 60–53 Tecumseh; Heritage Hills 59–56 Boonville; Cannelton 48–46 South Spencer (2ot); Heritage Hills 48–40 Cannelton. Officials: Kenneth Gorrell, William Amerson, James Newlin, Gary Hawn.
BROWNSBURG: Plainfield 60–49 Mooresville; Cascade 63–48 Avon; Brownsburg 66–54 Danville; Plainfield 56–48 Cascade; Plainfield 59–57 Brownsburg. Officials: Phil Abernathy, Douglas Bauman, David Trietsch, Sam Lower.
CALUMET: Crown Point 69–55 Calumet; Munster 54–52 Merrillville; Lake Central 76–40 Griffith; Highland 66–52 Lake Station Edison; Crown Point 63–37 Munster; Lake Central 65–51

IHSAA Scores | 1980–1989

Highland, Crown Point 59–52 Lake Central. Officials: Tim Fogarty, Ron James, Steve Badylak, Jerry Taylor.

CARMEL: Westfield 46–45 Hamilton Southeastern; Noblesville 54–47 Carmel; Hamilton Heights 81–62 Sheridan; Noblesville 78–58 Westfield; Noblesville 76–39 Hamilton Heights. Officials: Lanny Rossman, Robert Frye, Paul Hackleman, Michael McCarty.

CENTRAL (SWITZ CITY): Linton-Stockton 49–45 Shakamak; Bloomfield 78–47 Central; L &M 110–58 Eastern (Greene Co.); Linton-Stockton 79–41 Worthington; L & M 26–13 Bloomfield; L & M 37–24 Linton–Stockton. Officials: Don Nester, Robert Klein, Max Cameron, Tony Primavera.

CLAY CITY: Sullivan 73–72 North Central (Farmersburg); Union (Dugger) 73–45 Clay City; Union 39–37 Sullivan. Officials: John Evans, Daniel Henkle, William Fields, Rex Nichols.

COLUMBIA CITY: Whitko 66–53 Fort Wayne Blackhawk Christian; Carroll 50–47 Manchester; Columbia City 57–50 Churubusco; Carroll 80–60 Whitko; Carroll 58–54 Columbia City. Officials: Gary Cheesman, Joe Edmonds, Thomas Dul, Tom Crouch.

COLUMBUS: Columbus North 68–45 Edinburgh; Columbus East 65–50 Hauser; North 80–41 Brown County, East 85–58 North. Officials: Rudy Williams, Ronald McDougal, James Oxley, Phil Sullivan.

CONNERSVILLE: Laurel 50–49 Brookville, Connersville 57–44 Union County; Connersville 52–29 Laurel. Officials: Paul Cox, Jerry Middleton, James Robinson, Gene Marsh.

CRAWFORD COUNTY: Crawford County 49–46 Eastern (Pekin); North Harrison 58–46 Corydon; Lanesville 64–44 South Central; North Harrison 41–39 Crawford County; North Harrison 57–55 Lanesville (ot). Officials: Richie Moore, Norman Chestnut, Mark Logel, Dave Loewenstein.

DEKALB: DeKalb 82–35 Eastside; Leo 65–44 Hamilton; Angola 64–56 Garrett; Fremont 62–40 Howe Military; DeKalb 73–65 Leo; Angola 71–51 Fremont; Angola 63–60 DeKalb (ot). Officials: Michael DeVault, Kevin Weinberg, Robert Boyle, Dale Blosser.

EAST CENTRAL: Jac-Cen-Del 60–53 South Ripley (ot); East Central 58–47 Batesville; Milan 53–51 Jac-Cen-Del; Milan 67–62 East Central. Officials: Bob Beeson, Jim Keifer, Jim Pitcher, Dale Goodwin.

EAST CHICAGO: East Chicago Roosevelt 61–41 Whiting; East Chicago Washington 61–47 Hammond Noll; Washington 62–60 Roosevelt. Officials: Roger DeYoung, Jerry Christie, Terry Weldy, Russ Radtke.

EAST NOBLE: Lakeland 67–62 West Noble; Prairie Heights 58–53 Bethany Christian; Fairfield 68–59 Westview (ot); East Noble 90–42 Central Noble; Lakeland 51–48 Prairie Heights; East Noble 63–58 Fairfield; East Noble 60–46 Lakeland. Officials: Richard Freeman, Dan Amrhein, Doug Cook, Dale Cramer.

ELKHART: Goshen 61–54 Penn; Elkhart Central 75–63 North Wood; Elkhart Memorial 84–64 Jimtown; Concord 57–51 Northridge; Central 66–48 Goshen; Concord 77–65 Memorial; Concord 76–72 Central (ot). Officials: Mike Crouch, William Kachel, Mark Hyman, Mike Burchette.

EVANSVILLE: Bosse 64–61 Central (ot); Harrison 95–58 Evansville Christian; Reitz 78–60 Mater Dei; Memorial 62–46 North; Bosse 77–64 Harrison; Memorial 51–50 Reitz; Bosse 64–61 Memorial. Officials: Larry Maxwell, Thomas Marshall, Charlie Siebe, John Lyskowinski.

FORT WAYNE (#1): Harding 66–60 Luers; South Side 81–40 Christian; Dwenger 74–69

551

Tourney Time

North Side; Harding 56–53 Elmhurst; South Side 73–59 Dwenger; Harding 48–47 South Side (ot). Officials: Chuck Weinkauf, Terrance Magnuson, Ryan Estes, Mark Baltz.

FORT WAYNE(#2): Snider 69–60 Woodlan; Northrop 50–34 Concordia; Wayne 72–55 Heritage; Snider 51–47 New Haven; Northrop 86–48 Wayne; Northrop 59–46 Fort Wayne Snider. Officials: Ron Beard, Mel Botkin, Gene Huston, Thomas Urban.

FOUNTAIN CENTRAL: Fountain Central 71–65 North Vermillion (ot); Covington 57–48 Seeger; Attica 97–67 Turkey Run; Covington 52–46 Fountain Central; Covington 90–82 Attica. Officials: Ivan Burkle, Robert Anderson, Thomas Templin, Ron Ransom.

FRANKFORT: Tipton 51–48 Rossville; Clinton Prairie 73–52 Clinton Central; Frankfort 69–54 Tri Central; Clinton Prairie 59–57 Tipton; Frankfort 72–37 Clinton Prairie. Officials: Larry Jones, David Berman, Raymond Hopper, Ronald Kitts.

FRANKLIN CENTRAL: Warren Central 63–48 Franklin Central; Indianapolis Marshall 53–51 Roncalli; Scecina 71–37 Lutheran; Warren Central 75–49 Beech Grove; Marshall 66–63 Scecina; Warren Central 72–64 Marshall. Officials: Dave Avery, David Hurst, Michael Fawcett, Jack Taylor.

GARY: Gary Roosevelt 57–55 Wallace (ot); Wirt 75–70 Mann; Roosevelt 57–52 West Side; Roosevelt 52–48 Wirt. Officials: John Lozier, Robert Modrowski, Rick Scott, Mark Masariu.

GREENCASTLE: Greencastle 73–43 North Putnam; South Putnam 46–42 Cloverdale; Owen Valley 64–45 Rockville; Greencastle 63–62 South Putnam; Owen Valley 72–70 Greencastle. Officials: Jimmy Dimitroff, Lou Harmening, Phillip Tincher, Ronald Grimes.

GREENFIELD-CENTRAL: Greenfield-Central 44–38 New Palestine; Mount Vernon 57–45 Eastern Hancock; Mount Vernon 61–51 Greenfield-Central. Officials: Jerry Larrison, Patrick Parks, Joseph Pinnick, Pete Deakyne.

GREENSBURG: Rushville 73–70 Greensburg; South Decatur 68–45 North Decatur; Rushville 56–55 South Decatur. Officials: Jerry Petro, Gary Woodling, James Roberts, Jim Roush.

HAMMOND: Hammond High 62–56 Andrean; Gavit 86–61 Clark; 54–52 Morton; Gavit 65–52 Hammond High. Officials: Larry Nixon, Thomas Newlin, Joe Reed, Tom Rohr.

HUNTINGTON: Homestead 84–71 Northfield; White's 72–59 Wabash; Huntington North 108–53 Huntington Catholic; Homestead 60–59 Southwood; Huntington North 101–44 White's; Huntington North 64–52 Homestead. Officials: Frank DeSantis, James Reinebold, Mark Tulchinsky, Jon Davenport.

INDIANAPOLIS: Lawrence Central 65–60 Broad Ripple; Chatard 57–50 Arlington; Cathedral 52–49 North Central ; Lawrence North 85–49 Tech; Chatard 65–56 Lawrence Central; Lawrence North 61–59 Cathedral; Lawrence North 73–58 Chatard. Officials: Troy Ingram, Robert Stanley, Al Smith, Don Hittle

JAY COUNTY: Jay County 66–43 Wes–Del; Delta 58–47 Eastbrook; Blackford 50–48 Wapahani (3ot); Delta 48–34 Jay County; Delta 53–51 Blackford. Officials: Don Resler, Edward Koors, Bob Wasson, Dave Vendrely.

JEFFERSONVILLE: Jeffersonville 57–45 Clarksville; Floyd Central 85–60 Providence; Floyd Central 53–50 Jeffersonville. Officials: G. R. Honchell, Phil Vidito, Walter Bishop, Steve Welmer.

KANKAKEE VALLEY: Boone Grove 67–57 Hanover Central; Kankakee Valley 87–57 Kouts; Hebron 67–53 North Newton; Lowell 70–57 Rensselaer; Kankakee Valley 74–45 Boone Grove; Lowell 71–61 Hebron; Kankakee Valley 64–59 Lowell (ot). Officials: Richard Cook, Jerry

Karstens, Mike Spann, Jay Smith.

KOKOMO: Kokomo 62–54 Western; Taylor 51–39 Northwestern; Maconaquah 75–60 Eastern (Greentown); Kokomo 61–58 Taylor; Kokomo 52–50 Maconaquah. Officials: Judson Raver, Roger Pflughaupt, Steve Bird, Clark Hamilton.

LAFAYETTE: Central Catholic 78–70 Carroll (Flora); Harrison (West Lafayette) 71–57 Delphi; Lafayette Jefferson 75–54 West Lafayette; Harrison 65–62 Central Catholic; Jefferson 67–63 Harrison Officials: Jim Wehsollek, David Long, Fred Hamilton, Harry Northington.

LEBANON: Lebanon 66–52 Western Boone; Zionsville 52–50 Tri-West Hendricks; Lebanon 64–50 Zionsville. Officials: Richard Modricker, Steven Willett, David Gentile, Bob Wolfe.

LOGANSPORT: Peru 71–58 Cass; Logansport 56–50 Pioneer; North Miami 53–51 Caston; Peru 53–50 Logansport; Peru 59–48 North Miami. Officials: Warren Benko, Robert Gootee, Jeffrey Hull, Mike Waisnora.

MADISON: Austin 74–60 Madison Shawe; Madison 62–46 Scottsburg; New Washington 52–50 Southwestern; Austin 52–49 Madison; Austin 61–48 New Washington. Officials: Roger Holder, Larry Alsip, Bob Harvey, Morris Cohen.

MARION: Mississinewa 63–31 Marion Bennett; Marion 81–53 Elwood; Madison Grant 56–53 Oak Hill (ot); Marion 68–52 Mississinewa; Marion 83–55 Madison Grant. Officials: William Sorukas, Tom Neuman, Mike Winger, August Mohri.

MARTINSVILLE: Edgewood 73–61 Monrovia; Bloomington South 94–32 Eminence; Bloomington North 55–51 Martinsville; South 83–48 Edgewood; South 24–19 North (ot). Officials: John Stumpf, Bob Gentry, Tony Bierschbach, John Adams.

MICHIGAN CITY: LaPorte 81–58 New Prairie; Michigan City Rogers 92–57 Michigan City Marquette; Michigan City Elston 81–45 Westville; Rogers 83–75 LaPorte; Rogers 88–60 Elston. Officials: Don O'Connor, Dan Pfieffer, Ed Christoffel, Tim Smith.

MUNCIE: Southside 51–43 Burris; Northside 55–31 Cowan; Yorktown 38–37 Central; Southside 63–34 Muncie; Southside 44–43 Yorktown. Officials: Wayne Van Sickle, Paul Crawford, Michael Davis, Rick Owens.

NEW ALBANY: Charlestown 60–56 Henryville; Silver Creek 67–45 Borden; New Albany 70–50 Graceland Christian; Silver Creek 58–54 Charlestown; New Albany 59–51 Silver Creek. Officials: Joe Gilliland, Ed Scahill, Bill Holzer, Jesse Lynch.

NEW CASTLE: New Castle 110–51 Monroe Central; Blue River Valley 69–28 Morton Memorial; Knightstown 51–45 Shenandoah; Union 78–58 Tri; New Castle 69–32 Blue River; Knightstown 52–46 Union; New Castle 74–48 Knightstown. Officials: Tom Knox, Gaylord Fritz, David Estes, Frank Hoagburg.

NORTH JUDSON: West Central 52–49 Winamac; Oregon-Davis 73–69 North Judson; Knox 67–50 South Central; Culver 68–47 LaCross; Oregon-Davis 59–55 West Central; Culver 65–61 Knox; Culver 48–47 Oregon–Davis. Officials: Thomas May, Paul Danko, Stephen Laughlin, John Goss.

NORTH MONTGOMERY: Crawfordsville 67–50 North Montgomery; Southmont 71–69 McCutcheon; Crawfordsville 66–62 Southmont. Officials: Bill Champion, Steve Brown, Mike Reece, Jim Fish.

PAOLI: Salem 60–45 Paoli; Mitchell 51–50 Orleans; Springs Valley 72–66 West Washington; Salem 70–62 Mitchell; Salem 57–55 Springs Valley (ot). Officials: James Dunlap, Charles Bertram, David Stewart, Michael Zehr.

Tourney Time

PLYMOUTH: Plymouth 57–44 Culver Military; Glenn 81–54 Argos; LaVille 49–43 Bremen; Glenn 73–66 Plymouth; LaVille 57–52 Glenn. Officials: Bob Marcinek, Cary Schnick, Douglas Carl, Daniel Yagodnik.

PRINCETON: North Posey 70–57 Gibson Southern; New Harmony 71–70 Oakland City Wood; Princeton 57–54 Mount Vernon; New Harmony 67–65 North Posey; Princeton 63–59 New Harmony. Officials: Clifford Spears, Dave Atwell, David Kavanaugh, Dan Kunkel.

RICHMOND: Cambridge City Lincoln 62–48 Northeastern; Richmond 59–33 Winchester, Centerville 70–69 Hagerstown; Union City 58–46 Randolph Southern; Richmond 80–58 Cambridge City Lincoln; Union City 74–61 Centerville; Richmond 68–61 Union City. Officials: Norman Hathcoat, Steve Smith, Larry Gilpin, Tony Watt.

SEYMOUR: Crothersville 50–48 Seymour Brownstown Central 78–21 Medora; Bedford-North Lawrence 55–54 Jennings County; Brownstown Central 54–47 Crothersville; Bedford-North Lawrence 70–56 Brownstown Central. Officials: Bill Wullner, Dennis Maude, Larry Sintz, Leland Thompson.

SHELBYVILLE: Shelbyville 66–42 Morristown; Waldron 38–37 Southwestern; Shelbyville 59–54 Triton Central; Shelbyville 59–48 Waldron. Officials: Clarence Crain, Greg Fichter, John Tucker, Carl March.

SOUTH ADAMS: Belmont 102–66 Bluffton; South Adams 64–46 Adams Central; Norwell 64–58 Southern Wells; Belmont 84–59 South Adams; Bellmont 80–64 Norwell. Officials: Jerry Cook, Ron Hosinski, Fred Perry, Jerome Fawley.

SOUTH BEND: LaSalle 67–63 Adams (ot); Riley 73–56 Mishawaka Marian; Clay 81–65 Washington; Mishawaka 66–62 St. Joseph's; Riley 73–64 LaSalle; Clay 62–35 Mishawaka; Clay 74–46 South Bend Riley. Officials: Jim Cox, Tom Schenkel, Steve Godfroy, Dave Raabe.

SOUTH DEARBORN: South Dearborn 59–46 Lawrenceburg; Switzerland County 61–48 Rising Sun; South Dearborn 66–52 Switzerland County. Officials: Roger McGriff, Glen Clemons, Lowell DePoy, Don Smith.

SOUTHPORT: Indianapolis Howe 58–44 Attucks (ot); Manual 98–52 School for the Deaf; Perry Meridian 52–44 Decatur Central; Southport 74–53 Park Tudor; Manual 67–59 Howe; Southport 50–48 Perry Meridian; Southport 56–54 Manual. Officials: Bob Carr, George Taylor, Robert Gilmore, Brad Groninger.

HUNTINGBURG: Southridge 73–45 Northeast Dubois; Forest Park 46–42 Jasper; Southridge 51–47 Perry Central; Southridge 57–37 Forest Park. Officials: Melvin Redman, Robert Kirk, Robert Davis, McKee Munk.

TERRE HAUTE: Northview 67–50 West Vigo; South Vermillion 61–49 Rosedale; Terre Haute North 87–62 Montezuma; Terre Haute South 56–44 Northview; North 64–47 South Vermillion; South 51–50 North. Officials: Temme Patterson, Keith Combs, Rich Kay, Mark Mason.

TRI–COUNTY: Twin Lakes 65–51 Frontier; North White 54–42 Tri–County; South Newton 64–62 Benton Central; North White 60–49 Twin Lakes; South Newton 55–54 North White. Officials: Jeff Shelhart, Jim Campbell, Bruce Klonowski, Kenneth Dickman.

TRITON: Triton 57–52 Rochester; Warsaw 61–53 Tippecanoe Valley; Wawasee 59–45 Triton; Warsaw 64–56 Wawasee. Officials: Nick Sweigart, Richard Calloway, Robert Graczyk, James Lee Anderson.

VALPARAISO: Valparaiso 65–53 Washington Twp.; Hobart 59–52 River Forest; Chesterton 65–42 Wheeler; Portage 59–48 Morgan Twp.; Chesterton 53–42 Portage; Valparaiso 43–36

Hobart; Valparaiso 61–31 Chesterton. Officials: Ron Carter, David Emery, David Vice, Mark Hay.

VINCENNES: Vincennes 56–55 Vincennes Rivet; South Knox 58–55 North Knox (ot); Vincennes 44–37 South Knox. Officials: Stephen Fisher, Bob Collins, James Reid, Gary Leistner.

WASHINGTON: Barr-Reeve 49–34 Shoals; Washington Catholic 68–52 Pike Central; Loogootee 57–40 Washington; Barr-Reeve 62–25 North Daviess; Washington Catholic 65–59 Loogootee; Washington Catholic 46–41 Barr-Reeve. Officials: Bruce Mayfield, Marvin Williams, David Bromm, Michael Wallpe.

WHITELAND: Center Grove 70–69 Indian Creek (ot); Franklin 64–38 Greenwood; Center Grove 78–43 Whiteland; Center Grove 56–52 Franklin. Officials: Mike Bohan, Herb Pruett, David Pruett, Doug Coddington.

1985 REGIONALS

ANDERSON: Kokomo 47–46 Delta; Noblesville 75–57 Daleville; Kokomo 53–52 Noblesville. Officials: Ron Carter, David Raabe, Jeffrey Shelhart, Dave Vendrely, Wayne VanSickle, Bob Beeson.

COLUMBUS: Center Grove 55–52 Shelbyville; Bloomington South 79–69 Columbus East; Bloomington South 71–50 Center Grove. Officials: Tom Rohr, Larry Nixon, Steve Cherry, Jerry Taylor, Bill Wullner, Jerry Larrison.

ELKHART: LaVille 65–53 Concord; Warsaw 61–52 East Noble; Warsaw 72–57 LaVille. Officials: Frank Hoagburg, Judson Raver, Tom Knox, Gary Cheesman, Frank DeSantis, Dick Modricker.

EVANSVILLE: Evansville Bosse 60–48 Heritage Hills; Princeton 76–65 Vincennes; Bosse 81–63 Princeton. Officials: Ed Roush, Don Smith, McKee Munk, Roger McGriff, Steve Weimer, Steve Fisher.

FORT WAYNE: Carroll 76–72 Angola (ot); Northrop 63–52 Harding; Northrop 59–58 Carroll. Officials: William Sorukas, Mark Masariu, Ricky Owens, Jerome Fawley, Kenneth Gorrell, Paul Cox.

FRANKFORT: Lebanon 64–43 Crawfordsville; Frankfort 83–63 Plainfield; Frankfort 72–60 Lebanon. Officials: Tim Smith, Phil Sullivan, Mike Crouch, Tony Watt, Richard Cook, Norman Hathcoat.

GARY: Gary Roosevelt 62–61 Hammond Gavit (2ot); East Chicago Washington 57–55 Crown Point; Washington 69–67 Roosevelt. Officials: Clarence Crain, Dave Avery, Ivan Burkle, William Champion, Don O'Connor, Jerry Cook

INDIANAPOLIS: Ben Davis 75–69 Warren Central; Lawrence North 77–71 Southport; Lawrence North 81–76 Ben Davis. Officials: Bruce Mayfield, John Lyskowinski, Phil Abernathy, Thomas Urban, Ron Beard, Jim Wehsollek.

LAFAYETTE: Lafayette Jefferson 55–40 Covington; Kankakee Valley 66–55 South Newton; Jefferson 66–62 Kankakee Valley. Officials: Larry Jones, Jesse Lynch, Rex Nichols, Michael McCarty, Roger DeYoung, John Lozier.

MARION: Marion 69–62 Huntington North; Bellmont 90–60 Peru; Marion 87–78 Bellmont. Officials: G. R. Honchell, Roger Holder, John Stumpf, John Adams, Troy Ingram, Steve White.

MICHIGAN CITY: South Bend Clay 66–38 Culver; Michigan City Rogers 70–64 Valparaiso;

Tourney Time

Rogers 78–73 Clay. Officials: Warren Benko, Bob Marcinek, Richard Freeman, John Goss, Jim Cox, Bob Carr.

NEW CASTLE: Muncie Southside 62–38 Mount Vernon; New Castle 78–65 Rushville; Muncie Southside 64–57 New Castle. Officials: Don Resler, Gene Marsh, Michael DeVault, Mark Baltz, Joe Gilliland, Clifford Spears.

RICHMOND: Connersville 59–52 South Dearborn; Richmond 84–60 Milan; Richmond 65–47 Connersville. Officials: Chuck Weinkauf, John Evans, Pete Deakyne, Harry Northington, Jerry Petro, Rudy Williams.

SEYMOUR: Austin 64–62 Floyd Central; Bedford-North Lawrence 65–56 New Albany; Austin 59–58 Bedford-North Lawrence. Officials: Richie Moore, Ronald Grimes, Temme Patterson, Mark Mason, James Dunlap, Melvin Redmond.

TERRE HAUTE: L & M 82–75 Terre Haute South; Owen Valley 83–76 Union (Dugger); L & M 61–56 Owen Valley. Officials: Tom May, Nick Sweigart, Al Christoules, Lanny Rossman, Mike Bohan, Tim Fogarty.

WASHINGTON: North Harrison 70–67 Salem; Southridge 65–60 Washington Catholic; Southridge 51–48 North Harrison. Officials: Larry Maxwell, Doug Coddington, Gary Hawn, Carl March, Don Nester, Jimmy Dimitroff.

1985 SEMI–STATES

EVANSVILLE: Southridge 79–59 Austin; L & M 76–71 Evansville Bosse; Southridge 72–54 L. & M. Officials: Joe Gilliland, Jerry Larrison, Bill Wullner, Jim Wehsollek, Jerry Petro, Bob Beeson.

FORT WAYNE: Michigan City Rogers 60–59 Fort Wayne Northrop; Marion 70–65 Warsaw; Marion 83–72 Rogers. Officials: Nick Sweigart, Stephen White, Ron Beard: Mike Bohan, Steve Welmer, Norman Hathcoat.

INDIANAPOUS): Richmond 67–61 Bloomington South (ot); Muncie Southside 63–60 Lawrence North; Richmond 78–61 Muncie Southside. Officials: Richard Cook, Don O'Connor, Roger DeYoung, Frank DeSantis, Ken Gorrell, Tim Fogarty.

LAFAYETTE: Lafayette Jefferson 86–62 Frankfort; East Chicago Washington 69–67 Kokomo; Washington 87–68 Jefferson. Officials: Wayne VanSickle, Jimmy Dimitroff, Don Nester, Dick Modricker, Troy Ingram, Jim Cox.

1985 FINALS—March 23

INDIANAPOLIS (Market Square Arena): Richmond 85–79 East Chicago Washington; Marion 76–52 Southridge; Marion 74–67 Richmond. Officials: Jim Cox, Tim Fogarty, Norman Hathcoat, Jerry Petro, Kenneth Gorrell, Steve Welmer.

1986 SECTIONALS

ANDERSON: Anderson 82–57 Alexandria–Monroe; Anderson Highland 62–60 Anderson Madison Heights; Daleville 49–41 Lapel; Pendleton Heights 50–47 Frankton; Anderson 83–74 Anderson Highland; Pendleton Heights 64–53 Daleville; Anderson 51–49 Pendleton Heights.

IHSAA Scores | 1980–1989

Officials: John Evans, William Holzer, Douglas Carl, Clarence Crain.

BEN DAVIS: Pike 54–35 Brebeuf; Ben Davis 87–61 Indianapolis Washington; Speedway 66–55 Ritter; Pike 66–47 Northwest; Ben Davis 69–64 Speedway; Ben Davis 55–52 Pike. Officials: Tony Watt, Robert Gilmore, Larry Alsip, Dale Goodwin.

BLACKFORD: Wes–Del 59–56 Jay County; Delta 56–38 Eastbrook; Blackford 67–53 Wapahani; Wes–Del 59–53 Delta; Wes–Del 64–61 Blackford. Officials: Don Resler, Mike Winger, Thomas Neuman, Donald Schmidt.

BOONVILLE: Castle 59–39 Evansville Day School; Boonville 59–31 South Spencer; Heritage Hills 41–19 Cannelton; Ted City 71–63 Tecumseh; Boonville 66–44 Castle; Heritage Hills 64–62 Ted City; Heritage Hills 57–53 Boonville. Officials: Stephen Fisher, Michael Zehr, David Kavanaugh, David Bromm.

BROWNSBURG: Plainfield 57–46 Avon; Mooresville 67–56 Cascade; Danville 52–51 Brownsburg; Plainfield 74–53 Mooresville; Plainfield 62–51 Danville. Officials: Roger Holder, David Estes, Michael Smith, Bob Wolfe.

CALUMET: Calumet 71–63 Lake Station Edison; Lake Central 53–52 Griffith; Highland 46–45 Munster; Crown Point 52–50 Merrillville; Calumet 50–47 Lake Central; Crown Point 71–67 Highland; Crown Point 66–58 Calumet. Officials: Roger DeYoung, Thomas Templin, James Reinebold, Jay Smith.

CARMEL: Westfield 68–57 Hamilton Southeastern; Sheridan 64–57 Hamilton Heights; Noblesville 58–53 Carmel; Sheridan 81–74 Westfield; Noblesville 94–60 Sheridan. Officials: Paul Cox, Jerry Middleton, Mark Hyman, Brad Groninger.

CENTRAL (SWITZ CITY): Linton-Stockton 52–48 Shakamak; Bloomfield 71–46 Eastern (Greene Co.); Central 67–62 L & M; Linton-Stockton 55–37 Worthington; Bloomfield 72–48 Central; Bloomfield 61–59 Linton-Stockton (2ot). Officials: Jesse Lynch, Ed Scahill, Walter Bishop, Jr., Robert Klein.

COLUMBIA CITY: Columbia City 65–56 Fort Wayne Blackhawk Christian; Churubusco 52–50 Manchester; Whitko 37–36 Carroll (Fort Wayne); Churubusco 60–58 Columbia City (ot); Whitko 48–43 Churubusco. Officials: Jerome Fawley, Jeffrey Hull, Bruce Klonowski, William Sorukas.

COLUMBUS: Columbus East 63–39 Hauser, Columbus North 56–48 Edinburgh; East 75–51 Brown County; East 64–57 North. Officials: Rex Nichols, Steve Willett, John Lyskowinski, Don Smith.

CONNERSVILLE: Union County 86–76 Laurel; Connersville 69–48 Brookville; Connersville 64–45 Union County. Officials: Jerry Larrison, Frank Bodwell, Jim Keifer, Phil Vidito.

CRAWFORD COUNTY: Corydon Central 55–50 South Central (Elizabeth); Eastern (Pekin) 53–46 Lanesville; North Harrison 61–41 Crawford County; Corydon Central 47–43 Eastern (Pekin); North Harrison 60–29 Corydon Central. Officials: Gary Woodling, William Amerson, David Hevron, McKee Munk

EAST CENTRAL: East Central 71–62 South Ripley, Batesville 63–46 Milan; East Central 77–50 Jac-Cen-Del; East Central 53–49 Batesville. Officials: Stephen White, Michael Davis, Jerry Wallace, Paul Crawford.

EAST CHICAGO: Whiting 59–56 East Chicago Washington; East Chicago Roosevelt 53–43 Hammond Noll; Roosevelt 68–45 Whiting. Officials: Jerry Cook, Dale Blosser, Michael Spann, Dale Cramer.

Tourney Time

EAST NOBLE: West Noble 50–47 Lakeland; Westview 51–37 Bethany Christian; East Noble 63–43 Fairfield; Prairie Heights 75–59 Central Noble; Westview 62–50 West Noble; East Noble 55–46 Prairie Heights; Westview 61–52 East Noble. Officials: Frank Hoagburg, Gaylord Fritz, Jerry Stieglitz, Robert Boyle.

ELKHART: Concord 57–50 Jimtown; Northridge 53–52 North Wood; Goshen 66–45 Penn; Elkhart Central 73–56 Elkhart Memorial; Concord 73–55 Northridge; Goshen 55–49 Central (3ot); Concord 48–47 Goshen. Officials: Tom Knox, Clark Hamilton, David Petrie, Judson Raver.

EVANSVILLE: Bosse 156–30 Christian; Mater Dei 63–49 Harrison; Reitz 68–59 North; Memorial 66–52 Central; Bosse 71–52 Mater Dei; Memorial 57–55 Reitz; Memorial 58–57 Evansville Bosse (ot). Officials: Gary Hawn, Glen Clemons, Lowell DePoy, James Roberts.

FLOYD CENTRAL: Silver Creek 59–57 Henryville; Floyd Central 62–42 Borden; Charlestown 60–57 Graceland Christian; Floyd Central 68–61 Silver Creek (ot); Floyd Central 37–35 Charlestown (ot). Officials: Jerry Petro, Ronald McDougal, Jim Flanagan, Dennis Maude.

FORT WAYNE (#1): Elmhurst 50–49 Wayne; Heritage 69–55 Christian; Northrop 67–41 South Side; Elmhurst 54–43 North Side; Northrop 66–44 Heritage; Northrop 59–45 Elmhurst. Officials: David Raabe, Ryan Estes, Dave Vendrely, Ron Kitts.

FORT WAYNE (#2): Harding 66–58 Luers; Woodlan 57–51 Concordia; Dwenger 83–65 New Haven; Snider 46–44 Harding; Woodlan 83–65 Dwenger; Woodlan 59–56 Snider. Officials: Jim Cox, Mike Burchette, Tom Crouch, Thomas Dull.

FOUNTAIN CENTRAL: Covington 72–40 Fountain Central; Seeger 66–59 Turkey Run; Attica 64–63 North Vermilion; Covington 76–58 Seeger; Attica 54–51 Covington. Officials: Ron Carter, Paul Danko, Steve Badylak, Mark Hay.

FRANKFORT: Clinton Central 63–61 Frankfort (ot); Tipton 69–61 Rossville; Tri-Central 53–52 Clinton Prairie; Tipton 72–51 Clinton Central; Tipton 73–60 Tri-Central. Officials: Mike Bohan, Richard Foxen, Lou Harmening, Bob Anderson.

FRANKLIN: Indian Creek 82–60 Greenwood; Center Grove 62–45 Whiteland; Indian Creek 72–63 Franklin; Center Grove 55–49 Indian Creek. Officials: Bill Wullner, David Chalk, Ronald Mahan, G. R. Honchell.

FRANKLIN CENTRAL: Indianapolis Scecina 59–50 Beech Grove; Marshall 77–46 Lutheran, Warren Central 47–37 Franklin Central; Scecina 61–51 Roncalli; Warren Central 68–57 Marshall; Warren Central 69–58 Scecina. Officials: Rick Owens, Larry Sintz, Joe Edmonds, Gene Marsh.

GARRETT: Garrett 58–49 Leo; Angola 61–59 Eastside; DeKalb 85–45 Howe Military; Hamilton 82–64 Fremont; Garrett 51–46 Angola; DeKalb 79–61 Hamilton; Garrett 69–59 DeKalb. Officials: Mike Crouch, Dave Long, Dennis Jackson, Tom Schenkel.

GARY: Wirt 60–51 West Side; Wallace 57–55 Gary Roosevelt (2ot); Wirt 44–43 Mann; Wallace 70–52 Wirt. Officials: Richard Cook, Jerry Karstens, Phil Marsh, Russ Radtke.

GREENCASTLE: Owen Valley 53–30 Cloverdale; South Putnam 72–56 Rockville; North Putnam 74–65 Greencastle; South Putnam 55–54 Owen Valley; South Putnam 75–66 North Putnam. Officials: Lanny Rossman, Ron Ramsey, Scott Robison, John Adams.

GREENFFIELD CENTRAL: Greenfield–Central 61–32 Eastern Hancock; Mount Vernon (Fortville) 57–56 New Palestine (ot); Mount Vernon (Fortville) 45–43 Greenfield Central. Officials: Chuck Weinkauf, Terrance Magnuson, Mark Medley, John Stumpf.

GREENSBURG: Greensburg 64–38 South Decatur; North Decatur 68–60 Rushville;

IHSAA Scores | 1980–1989

Greensburg 87–60 North Decatur. Officials: Steve Cherry, Don Hopkins, Jack Taylor, Norman Hathcoat.

HAMMOND: Hammond Gavit 53–51 Hammond High; Andrean 72–59 Morton; Gavit 63–52 Clark; Andrean 56–49 Gavit. Officials: Don O'Connor, Terry Weldy. Fred Mohri, Richard Calloway.

HUNTINGTON: Northfield 79–52 White's; Huntington North 72–58 Southwood; Homestead 83–45 Wabash; North 70–59 Northfield; North 63–47 Homestead. Officials: Larry Jones, Kevin Weinberg, David Emery, Rick Scott.

INDIANAPOLIS: Broad Ripple 86–48 Lawrence Central; Cathedral 58–44 Arlington; Lawrence Central 87–58 Tech; North Central (Indianapolis) 51–50 Chatard; Broad Ripple 62–56 Cathedral; North Central 76–59 Lawrence North; Broad Ripple 87–80 North Central (ot). Officials: Thomas Urban, Fred Hamilton, Gene Huston, Phil Abernathy.

JEFFERSONVILLE: Jeffersonville 51–47 Providence; Clarksville 57–56 New Albany, Clarksville 47–46 Jeffersonville (2ot). Officials: Ken Gorrell, Don Hinkle, Ron Pritchett, Ed Roush.

KANKAKEE VALLEY: Kankakee Valley 59–58 Boone Grove (ot); Hanover Central 81–55 Rensselaer; North Newton 58–54 Kouts; Hebron 76–75 Lowell; Hanover Central 66–65 Kankakee Valley; Hebron 65–49 North Newton; Hanover Central 77–57 Hebron. Officials: Tom May, Dan Yagodnik, Ron James, Mike Waisnora.

KOKOMO: Taylor 60–46 Eastern (Greentown); Western 98–78 Maconaquah; Kokomo 61–51 Northwestern; Western 68–57 Taylor; Kokomo 68–58 Western. Officials: Jeff Shelhart, Raymond Hopper, David Triestsch, Dick Modricker.

LAFAYETTE: Central Catholic 75–50 Carroll (Flora); Lafayette Jefferson 90–56 West Lafayette; Delphi 59–57 Harrison (West Lafayette); Jefferson 74–67 Central Catholic; Jefferson 86–56 Delphi. Officials: Joe Gilliland, David Lee, Jack Kopp, Leland Thompson.

LEBANON: Zionsville 64–43 Western Boone; Tri-West Hendricks 56–51 Lebanon; Zionsville 63–54 Tri-West. Officials: Pete Deakyne, Mike Fawcett, William Kachel, Patrick Parks.

LOGANSPORT: Peru 79–45 North Miami; Logansport 62–48 Pioneer, Cass 68–64 Caston; Logansport 56–53 Peru; Logansport 50–39 Cass. Officials: Timothy Fogarty, Brian Weidner, Joe Oyler, Tony Primavera.

MADISON: Scottsburg 68–67 Madison Shawe; Southwestern (Hanover) 54–50 Madison; Austin 56–46 New Washington; Scottsburg 75–56 Southwestern; Austin 60–58 Scottsburg (6ot). Officials: Roger McGriff, Richard Hughes, Urban Keithley, Michael McCarty.

MARION: Marion 96–73 Madison-Grant; Oak Hill 73–46 Marion Bennett; Mississinewa 51–49 Elwood; Marion 66–48 Oak Hill; Marion 71–59 Mississinewa. Officials: Bob Carr, Roger Pflughaupt, Bob Wasson, Mel Botkin.

MARTINSVILLE: Bloomington North 70–53 Edgewood; Bloomington South 86–56 Monrovia; Martinsville 72–52 Eminence; South 77–56 North; South 48–38 Martinsville. Officials: Tom Rohr, David Hurst, Max Cameron, Joe Reed.

MICHIGAN CITY: New Prairie 85–48 Westville; Michigan City Rogers 85–54 Michigan City Marquette; LaPorte 63–62 Michigan City Elston; Rogers 85–59 New Prairie; Rogers 84–82 LaPorte. Officials: Bob Marcinek, Robert Gootee, Mark McCammon, John Goss.

MUNCIE: Northside 82–62 Cowan; Southside 52–49 Muncie Burris; Yorktown 46–45 Muncie Central; Northside 49–48 Southside; Yorktown 52–48 Northside, Officials: James

559

Wehsollek, Larry Gilpin, David Gentile, Sam Lower.

NEW CASTLE: Knightstown 54–53 Shenandoah; New Castle 83–54 Blue River Valley; Union (Modoc) 54–32 Morton Memorial; Tri 63–53 Monroe Central; New Castle 62–55 Knightstown; Tri 54–52 Union (Modoc); New Castle 71–48 Tri. Officials: Gary Cheesman, Douglas Bauman, Steve Godfroy, Jerry Christie.

NORTH JUDSON: South Central (Union Mills) 54–46 Knox; North Judson 71–45 Culver Community; LaCrosse 55–53 Winamac; Oregon-Davis 60–56 West Central; North Judson 79–68 South Central; LaCrosse 57–56 Oregon-Davis; North Judson 89–69 LaCrosse. Officials: Nick Sweigart, Ivan Burkle, Rich Spay, Jerry Taylor.

NORTH MONTGOMERY: North Montgomery 69–59 Crawfordsville; McCutcheon 87–65 Southmont, McCutcheon 57–52 North Montgomery. Officials: Cliff Spears, John Tucker, Dan Breneman, Mike Wallpe.

PAOLI: Springs Valley 53–50 Orleans; Mitchell 64–48 West Washington; Salem 41–36 Paoli; Springs Valley 64–55 Mitchell; Springs Valley 74–58 Salem. Officials: Melvin Redman, Keith Combs, Robert Collins, William Nimnicht.

PLYMOUTH: Plymouth 64–62 Bremen; LaVille 57–50 Argos; Culver Military 62–60 Glenn (2ot); LaVille 60–59 Plymouth, LaVille 56–36 Culver Military. Officials: Bill Champion, Mark Tulchinsky, Duffey Ainsworth, Steven Brown.

PRINCETON: North Posey 49–38 Mount Vernon; Princeton 57–51 New Harmony; Oakland City Wood 57–48 Gibson Southern; North Posey 43–41 Princeton, Wood 55–52 North Posey. Officials James Dunlap, Raymond Norris, Mark Logel, Gary Leistner.

RICHMOND: Winchester 46–44 Cambridge City Lincoln; Richmond 82–50 Northeastern; Randolph Southern 64–56 Hagerstown; Centerville 78–75 Union City; Richmond 84–58 Winchester; Randolph Southern 72–68 Centerville; Richmond 79–56 Randolph Southern. Officials: Ron Beard, George Taylor, Mike Padfield, Rudy Williams.

SEYMOUR: Brownstown Central 60–51 Seymour; Bedford-North Lawrence 65–26 Medora; Jennings County 79–60 Crothersville; Bedford-North Lawrence 52–50 Brownstown Central; Jennings County 81–61 Bedford-North Lawrence. Officials: Don Nester, Joseph Pinnick, Raymond Tebbe, Robert Frye.

SHELBYVILLE: Triton Central 69–46 Waldron; Shelbyville 76–37 Morristown; Triton Central 52–42 Southwestern (Shelbyville); Shelbyville 81–48 Triton Central. Officials: Bob Beeson, Robert Stanley, Mike Alford, Herb Pruett.

SOUTH ADAMS: Southern Wells 83–60 Adams Central; Bellmont 87–82 Norwell; South Adams 70–46 Bluffton; Bellmont 104–74 Southern Wells; South Adams 74–73 Bellmont Officials: Mark Masariu, James Robinson, Bob Dedaker, Harry Northington.

SOUTH BEND: Clay 68–53 LaSalle; Adams 55–48 Washington; Mishawaka 59–54 St. Joseph's; Mishawaka Marian 48–47 Riley; Adams 75–51 Clay; Mishawaka 68–60 Mishawaka Marian; Mishawaka 59–45 Adams. Officials: Frank DeSantis, Jon Davenport, Ed Christoffel, Tim Smith.

SOUTH DEARBORN: South Dearborn 53–49 Lawrenceburg; Switzerland County 60–51 Rising Sun; South Dearborn 52–45 Switzerland County. Officials: Troy Ingram, Don Hittle, Jim Pitcher, Kim Baker.

SOUTHPORT: Park Tudor 65–49 School for the Deaf; Indianapolis Howe 73–58 Perry Meridian; Manual 67–66 Southport (ot); Decatur Central 59–44 Attucks; Howe 67–45 Park Tudor; Manual 63–55 Decatur Central (ot); Howe 67–61 Manual. Officials: Mark Baltz, Tony

Bierschbach, Rick Granger, Bob Harvey.

SOUTHRIDGE: Northeast Dubois 64–56 Forest Park; Jasper 49–44 Perry Central; Southridge 74–51 Northeast Dubois; Southridge 55–53 Jasper. Officials: Temme Patterson, Robert Kirk, Robert Davis, Richie Moore.

SOUTH VERMILLION: Rosedale 54–53 Montezuma; South Vermillion 57–43 West Vigo; Northview 69–43 Rosedale, South Vermillion 61–59 Northview. Officials: Larry Maxwell, Rich Kay, Brad Farmer, Denis Ward.

TERRE HAUTE: Terre Haute South 63–61 Sullivan (ot); North Central (Farmersburg) 64–43 Clay City; Terre Haute North 60–50 Union (Dugger); South 78–60 North Central (Farmersburg); North 56–48 South (ot). Officials: Doug Coddington, Jim Fish, Tom Marshall, Dave Atwell.

TRI–COUNTY: Tri–County 58–50 South Newton; Twin Lakes 62–48 North White; Benton Central 82–62 Frontier; Twin Lakes 65–49 Tri–County; Twin Lakes 69–59 Benton Central. Officials: Larry Nixon, Robert Gentry, David Vice, Fred Perry.

TRITON: Rochester 58–57 Tippecanoe Valley, Wawasee 67–31 Triton; Warsaw 87–45 Rochester; Warsaw 62–51 Wawasee. Officials: John Lozier, Ron Hosinski, James Campbell, Ken Dickman.

VALPARAISO: Morgan Twp.75–48 Washington Twp.; Valparaiso 55–29 Chesterton; Portage 55–53 Wheeler; Hobart 70–59 River Forest; Valparaiso 53–45 Morgan Twp.; Hobart 52–47 Portage; Valparaiso 54–42 Hobart. Officials: Bob Modrowski, James Anderson, David Pruett, Warren Benko.

VINCENNES: Vincennes Rivet 55–38 North Knox; Vincennes 75–57 South Knox; Vincennes 65–58 Vincennes Rivet. Officials: Ronald Grimes, James Newlin, Paul Wahl, Carl March.

WASHINGTON: Shoals 58–47 Washington; Loogootee 67–56 Pike Central; Barr-Reeve 52–48 Washington Catholic; Shoals 54–51 North Daviess; Loogootee 48–47 Barr-Reeve; Loogootee 54–48 Shoals. Officials: Dan Kunkel, John Crapo, Stan Ames, Thomas Newlin.

1986 REGIONALS

ANDERSON: Anderson 69–60 Kokomo; Noblesville 77–47 Wes-Del; Anderson 57–55 Noblesville. Officials: Don Resler, Denis Ward, Thomas Newlin, Doug Coddington, Bill Champion, Tim Fogarty.

COLUMBUS: Bloomington South 80–65 Center Grove; Shelbyville 82–50 Columbus East; Shelbyville 70–50 South. Officials: Rex Nichols, Pete Deakyne, David Atwell, Gary Hawn, Chuck Weinkauf, Mike Bohan.

ELKHART: Concord 49–45 LaVille; Warsaw 46–37 Westview; Concord 57–55 Warsaw (ot). Officials: Russ Radtke, Tom Schenkel, David Raabe, Frank Hoagburg, Richard Cook, Roger DeYoung.

EVANSVILLE: Vincennes 52–50 Heritage Hills; Evansville Memorial 57–42 Oakland City Wood; Memorial 53–51 Vincennes. Officials: Dan Kunkel, Joe Reed, David Bromm, Ronald Grimes, Don Nester, Jesse Lynch.

FORT WAYNE: Garrett 64–62 Woodlan; Fort Wayne Northrop 66–41 Whitko; Northrop 57–36 Garrett. Officials: Leland Thompson, Bob Wolfe, Clarence Crain, James Wehsollek, Gary Cheesman, Jerry Cook.

FRANKFORT: McCutcheon 62–60 Zionsville; Plainfield 59–47 Tipton; Plainfield 56–47

Tourney Time

McCutcheon. Officials: John Adams, John Evans, Lanny Rossman, Joe Gilliland, Stephen White, Bob Carr.

GARY: Crown Point 63–62 East Chicago Roosevelt (ot); Gary Wallace 70–68 Andrean; Wallace 67–56 Crown Point. Officials: Jerome Fawley, Tim Smith, Jay Smith, Tony Primavera, Ron Carter, Frank DeSantis.

INDIANAPOLIS: Warren Central 66–64 Ben Davis; Indianapolis Broad Ripple 69–59 Howe; Warren Central 78–70 Broad Ripple. Officials: G. R. Honchell, Kim A. Baker, Bob Beeson, Tony Watt, Bill Wullner, Troy Ingram.

LAFAYETTE: Twin Lakes 60–54 Attica; Lafayette Jefferson 89–56 Hanover Central; Jefferson 56–54 Twin Lakes. Officials: Warren Benko, Mike Waisnora, Robert Modrowski, Thomas May, Bob Marcinek, Nick Sweigart.

MARION: Huntington North 72–54 South Adams; Marion 85–64 Logansport; Marion 57–54 Huntington North. Officials: Herb Pruett, Rudy Williams, Thomas Knox, Thomas Urban, Jerry Larrison, Ron Beard.

MICHIGAN CITY: Mishawaka 55–54 North Judson; Michigan City Rogers 65–53 Valparaiso; Rogers 95–85 Mishawaka. Officials: Ken Dickman, Jeffrey Shelhart, Ivan Burkle, Dick Modricker, Larry Jones, Don O'Connor.

NEW CASTLE: New Castle 61–48 Yorktown; Greensburg 66–63 Mount Vernon; New Castle 68–66 Greensburg. Officials: Robert Klein, Bob Harvey, Ronald Kitts, Mike Crouch, John Lozier, Jim Cox.

RICHMOND: South Dearborn 47–44 East Central (ot); Connersville 69–68 Richmond (2ot); Connersville 61–40 South Dearborn. Officials: Robert Frye, Paul Cox, Norman Hathcoat, Rick Owens, Mark Masariu, Steve Cherry.

SEYMOUR: Jennings County 73–63 Clarksville; Floyd Central 70–54 Austin; Floyd Central 70–63 Jennings County. Officials: Mark Baltz, Roger Holder, Roger McGriff, Mike McCarty, Larry Maxwell, Stephen Fisher.

TERRE HAUTE: Terre Haute North 54–43 South Vermillion; Bloomfield 67–58 South Putnam; Bloomfield 57–44 North. Officials: Clifford Spears, Gary Leistner, William Nimnicht, Temme Patterson, James Dunlap, Melvin Redman.

WASHINGTON: Southridge 71–60 Springs Valley; Loogootee 64–48 North Harrison; Southridge 59–46 Loogootee. Officials: Larry Nixon, Jerry Taylor, Don Smith, Tom Rohr, Ken Gorrell, Jerry Petro.

1986 SEMI—STATES

FORT WAYNE: Marion 79–72 Fort Wayne Northrop; Michigan City Rogers 108–82 Concord; Marion 83–82 Rogers. Officials: Jesse Lynch, John Lozier, Stephen White, Mark Masariu, Bob Carr, Troy Ingram.

INDIANAPOLIS: Warren Central 58–48 Connersville; Shelbyville 74–67 New Castle; Shelbyville 73–65 Warren Central. Officials: Ron Beard, Jim Cox, Stephen Fisher, Larry Jones, Melvin Redman, James Dunlap.

LAFAYETTE: Anderson 66–57 Lafayette Jefferson; Gary Wallace 56–49 Plainfield; Anderson 72–71 Gary Wallace. Officials: Gary Cheesman, Frank DeSantis, Jerry Larrison, Jerry Petro, Don O'Connor, Jerry Cook

TERRE HAUTE: Evansville Memorial 61–48 Bloomfield; Southridge 69–57 Floyd Central; Southridge 60–52 Memorial. Officials: Bill Wullner, Nick Sweigart, Steve Cherry, Tim Fogarty, Roger DeYoung, Mike Bohan.

1986 FINALS—March 29
INDIANAPOLIS (Market Square Arena): Anderson 70–69 Shelbyville; Marion 63–54 Southridge; Marion 75–56 Anderson. Officials: Bob Carr, Melvin Redman, Don O'Connor, James Dunlap, Roger DeYoung, Jerry Cook.

1987 SECTIONALS
ANDERSON: Alexandria 59–53 Daleville; Anderson Madison Heights 54–52 Anderson Highland; Pendleton Heights 70–60 Lapel; Anderson 59–48 Frankton; Madison Heights 80–68 Alexandria; Pendleton Heights 67–62 Anderson; Madison Heights 43–42 Pendleton Heights. Officials: Troy Ingram, Ronald Kitts, Mark Medley, G. R. Honchell.

BEN DAVIS: Pike 65–55 Indianapolis Northwest; Brebeuf 43–41 Speedway; Ben Davis 71–52 Ritter; Pike 71–52 Washington; Ben Davis 51–40 Brebeuf; Pike 56–39 Ben Davis. Officials: James Wehsollek, Joe Edmonds, Dennis Jackson, Phil Abernathy.

BOONVILLE: Tell City 63–62 Cannelton; Castle 72–45 Evansville Day School; Tecumseh 57–51 Heritage Hills; South Spencer 55–49 Boonville; Castle 58–47 Tell City; Tecumseh 61–39 South Spencer; Castle 71–59 Tecumseh. Officials: Gary Woodling, James Roberts, John Lyskowinski, McKee Munk, Melvin Redman.

BROWNSBURG: Plainfield 62–46 Brownsburg; Avon 73–56 Cascade; Mooresville 58–54 Danville; Plainfield 72–54 Avon; Plainfield 67–52 Mooresville. Officials: Roger McGriff, Stephen Laughlin, Jim Flanagan, David Hurst.

CALUMET: Merrillville 45–43 Highland; Griffith 51–48 Lake Station Edison; Crown Point 72–61 Lake Central; Munster 70–58 Calumet; Merrillville 71–50 Griffith; Crown Point 68–65 Munster; Merrillville 50–49 Crown Point. Officials: Bob Marcinek, Kevin Weinberg, Russ Teal, Russ Radtke.

CARMEL: Carmel 88–71 Hamilton Southeastern; Noblesville 72–44 Hamilton Heights; Sheridan 51–48 Westfield (ot); Carmel 54–52 Noblesville; Carmel 48–37 Sheridan. Officials: Mark Masariu, Morris Cohen, Tom Walters, Phil Vidito.

CENTRAL (SWITZ CITY): Bloomfield 39–33 Shakamak; Central (Switz City) 74–49 Worthington-Jefferson; Linton-Stockton 58–56 (ot) Eastern (Bloomfield); Bloomfield 60–41 L & M; Linton-Stockton 51–50 Central; Bloomfield 39–37 Linton-Stockton. Officials: Doug Coddington, Ronald James, Jeff Culp, Brad Farmer.

CLAY CITY: Union (Dugger) 63–48 North Central (Farmersburg); Sullivan 73–45 Clay City; Sullivan 71–56 Union (Dugger). Officials: John Adams, Ronald McDougal, William Holzer, Ray Tebbe.

COLUMBIA CITY: Carroll (Fort Wayne) 67–54 Churubusco; Manchester 85–46 Fort Wayne Blackhawk Christian; Whitko 69–51 Columbia City; Manchester 65–60 Carroll (Fort Wayne); Whitko 70–56 Manchester. Officials: Tom Knox, Robert Boyle, Gaylord Fritz, William Kachel.

COLUMBUS: Brown County 82–80 Columbus East; Edinburgh 26–16 Hauser; Columbus

Tourney Time

North 91–62 Brown County; North 63–52 Edinburgh. Officials: Clifford Spears, Tony Bierschbach, Lowell DePoy, Larry Gilpin.

CONNERSVILLE: Union County 44–42 (ot) Laurel; Connersville 68–34 Brookville; Connersville 57–38 Union County. Officials: Rick Owens, Scott Robison Rick Granger, Ed Roush.

CRAWFORD COUNTY: North Harrison 57–42 Crawford County; Lanesville 68–61 Eastern (Pekin); Corydon Central 81–32 South Central (Elizabeth); North Harrison 60–59 Lanesville; North Harrison 51–46 Corydon Central. Officials: James Dunlap, Mike Smith, Jim Ralston, Keith Combs.

DEKALB: DeKalb 64–49 Eastside; Hamilton 36–34 Garrett; Leo 67–40 Howe Military; Fremont 56–48 Angola; DeKalb 52–50 Hamilton; Leo 55–47 Fremont; DeKalb 69–60 Leo. Officials: Frank DeSantis, Bruce Klonowski, Fred Mohri, Tim Smith.

EAST CENTRAL: East Central 60–44 South Ripley; Jac-Cen-Del 70–59 Milan; East Central 56–52 Batesville; East Central 43–42 Jac-Cen-Del. Officials: Lanny Rossman, Gene Marsh, Robert Stanley, George Taylor.

EAST CHICAGO: Hammond Clark 52–42 Whiting; East Chicago Central 64–60 Hammond Noll; Central 82–48 Clark. Officials: Nick Sweigart, Dan Amrhein, Phillip Marsh, Jerry Karstens.

EAST NOBLE: Lakeland 73–56 Central Noble; East Noble 55–53 Bethany Christian; Westview 76–61 West Noble; Prairie Heights 65–52 Fairfield; East Noble 53–50 Lakeland; Westview 59–49 Prairie Heights; Westview 61–45 East Noble. Officials: Jerry Fawley, Jeffrey Hull, Mark McCammon, Jon Davenport.

ELKHART: Central 64–52 Jimtown; Concord 79–54 Northridge; Penn 54–45 Goshen; Memorial 65–47 North Wood; Concord 68–64 Central; Penn 56–52 Memorial; Penn 68–66 Concord (ot). Officials: Frank Hoagburg, Ed Christoffel, Jerry Stieglitz, Donald Schmidt.

EVANSVILLE: Harrison 65–61 Central; Reitz 57–56 Maier Dei; Memorial 70–52 North; Harrison 54–45 Bosse; Memorial 64–52 Reitz; Memorial 52–50 Harrison (ot). Officials: Gary Leistner, Paul Wahl, Don Etienne, Michael Zehr.

FORT WAYNE (#1): Northrop 67–42 Heritage; Snider 57–33 Christian; Harding 59–42 North Side; Northrop 48–44 South Side; Snider 50–46 Harding; Northrop 54–52 Snider. Officials: John Evans, Mike Alford, Doug Bauman, Bob Harvey.

FORT WAYNE (#2): Dwenger 76–64 New Haven; Concordia 63–61 Woodlan; Elmhurst 55–50 Luers; Dwenger 49–47 Wayne; Elmhurst 65–61 Concordia; Elmhurst 62–60 Dwenger. Officials: Jerry Cook, Doug Cook, Mike Spann, Gary Cheesman.

FOUNTAIN CENTRAL: Covington 64–57 Seeger, Fountain Central 79–69 Attica; North Vermillion 90–70 Turkey Run; Covington 70–43 Fountain Central; North Vermilion 58–50 Covington. Officials: Bill Champion, James Robinson, Mark Hyman, Steven Brown.

FRANKFORT: Rossville 48–38 Clinton Prairie; Tipton 74–69 Tri-Central; Frankfort 57–49 Clinton Central; Rossville 75–66 Tipton; Frankfort 60–58 Rossville (ot). Officials: Norman Hathcoat, David Willoughby, Kent Smith, Jim Fish.

FRANKLIN CENTRAL: Indianapolis Scecina 62–34 Lutheran, Roncalli 55–54 Franklin Central; Warren Central 76–37 Beech Grove; Roncalli 46–42 Scecina; Warren Central 67–59 Roncalli. Officials: Thomas Urban, Mike Padfield, Bob Dedaker, Mel Botkin.

GARY: Wirt 71–51 West Side; Roosevelt 89–64 Mann; Wallace 73–68 Wirt (2ot); Roosevelt

53–52 Wallace. Officials: Don O'Connor, James Anderson, Duffey Ainsworth, William Sorukas.

GREENCASTLE: Rockville 86–59 Cloverdale; Owen Valley 62–51 North Putnam; South Putnam 74–73 Greencastle; Rockville 62–48 Owen Valley; Rockville 78–61 South Putnam. Officials: Joe Gilliland, Joseph Pinick, Doug Hudson, Leland Thompson.

GREENFIELD CENTRAL: Greenfield Central 55–51 Eastern Hancock; Mount Vernon (Fortville) 69–49 New Palestine; Mount Vernon (Fortville) 94–62 Greenfield Central. Officials: Bob Beeson, Mike Davis, Larry Sintz, John Stumpf.

GREENSBURG: Rushville 63–60 South Decatur; Greensburg 65–58 North Decatur; Rushville 72–69 Greensburg (ot). Officials: Chuck Weinkauf, Keith Fields, Rick Shirk, Ed Scahill.

GREENWOOD: Indian Creek 65–63 Franklin; Center Grove 59–46 Whiteland; Indian Creek 57–56 Greenwood; Indian Creek 62–61 Center Grove (2ot). Officials: Dan Kunkel, John Tucker, Joe Stafford, Dave Atwell.

HAMMOND: Hammond High 70–60 Gavit; Gary Andrean 80–53 Morton; Hammond High 57–55 Andrean. Officials: Roger DeYoung, Robert Modrowski, Paul Danko, Jay Smith.

HUNTINGTON: Huntington North 69–57 Southwood; Homestead 91–23 White's; Northfield 72–63 Wabash; North 58–53 Homestead; Northfield 54–52 North (ot). Officials: Judson Raver, Don Resler, Mike Howell, Mike Winger.

INDIANAPOLIS: Lawrence Central 91–57 Broad Ripple; North Central 63–56 Cathedral; Lawrence North 67–47 Arlington; Tech 57–53 Chatard; North Central 47–42 Lawrence Central; Lawrence North 68–59 Tech; Lawrence North 69–55 North Central. Officials: Bob Carr, David Berman, Tony Ortman, Michael Wallpe.

JAY COUNTY: Wapahani 63–54 Wes-Del; Jay County 74–62 Blackford; Delta 62–44 Eastbrook; Jay County 51–34 Wapahani; Jay County 51–47 Delta. Officials: David Raabe, Don Hittle, Roger Pflughaupt, Clark Hamilton.

JEFFERSONVILLE: Jeffersonville 106–96 Clarksville; Floyd Central 61–51 Providence; Jeffersonville 74–72 Floyd Central. Officials: Mike McCarty, David Chalk, Charles Meyer, Don Smith.

KANKAKEE VALLEY: North Newton 79–76 Hanover Central; Kouts 60–58 Boone Grove; Hebron 57–52 Kankakee Valley–, Lowell 50–47 Rensselaer; Kouts 79–71 North Newton; Lowell 61–54 Hebron; Kouts 56–54 Lowell. Officials: Jerry Taylor, Brian Weidner, Joe Oyler, Dick Modricker, Larry Nixon, Larry Parker.

KOKOMO: Maconaquah 58–46 Eastern (Greentown); Kokomo 48–46 Western; Northwestern 56–40 Taylor; Kokomo 64–61 Maconaquah; Kokomo 46–34 Northwestern. Officials: Bob Klein, Walter Bishop, David Stewart, Jack Taylor.

LAFAYETTE: Central Catholic 49–30 Carroll ; Lafayette Jefferson 69–51 Harrison; West Lafayette 69–60 Delphi; Catholic 62–55 Jefferson; Catholic 62–52 West Lafayette. Officials: Roger Holder, David Estes, Steven Smith, Bob Wolfe.

LEBANON: Lebanon 41–40 Tri–West Hendricks; Zionsville 62–61 Western Boone; Lebanon 70–53 Zionsville. Officials: Larry Nixon, Steve Badylak, Ron McGriff, Rich Kay.

LOGANSPORT: Peru 70–63 North Miami; Logansport 61–55 Cass (ot); Caston 59–53 Pioneer; Peru 70–55 Logansport; Peru 66–44 Caston. Officials: Mike Crouch, Fred Hamilton, Thomas Dull, Michael Burchette.

MADISON: Madison Shawe 79–78 Scottsburg; New Washington 70–57 Austin; Southwestern (Hanover) 50–48 Madison; Shawe 61–59 New Washington; Southwestern 67–63 Madison Shawe. Officials: Denis Ward, Mark Campbell, David Lee, Terry Magnuson.

Tourney Time

MARION: Marion 81–57 Elwood; Mississinewa 69–52 Madison–Grant; Oak Hill 71–48 Marion Bennett, Marion 66–48 Mississinewa; Marion 96–60 Oak Hill. Officials: Mark Baltz, Dale Goodwin, Dave Vendrely, Joe Reed.

MARTINSVILLE: Martinsville 53–52 Monrovia; Bloomington South 60–18 Eminence; Edgewood 59–49 Bloomington North; South 70–59 Martinsville; South 50–46 Edgewood. Officials: Don Nester, Dennis Maude, Michael Short, Bob Anderson.

MICHIGAN CITY: Elston 67–36 Marquette; Rogers 93–59 Westville; New Prairie 78–70 LaPorte; Rogers 71–69 Elston; Rogers 92–65 New Prairie. Officials: Tom May, R.J. Graczyk, Randy Coplen, Richard Calloway.

MUNCIE: Southside 57–56 Central (ot); Burris 57–49 Cowan; Northside 51–48 Yorktown; Southside 64–41 Burris; Southside 55–53 Northside. Officials: Jim Cox, TomCrouch, Gene Huston, David Long.

NEW ALBANY: Silver Creek 62–52 Henryville; New Albany 74–58 Borden; Graceland Christian 66–57 Charlestown; New Albany 71–60 Silver Creek; New Albany 81–71 Graceland Christian. Officials: Ronald Grimes, David Hevron, Ronald Pritchett, Carl March.

NEW CASTLE: Shenandoah 59–55 New Castle; Monroe Central 68–61 Blue River Valley; Knightstown 84–50 Tri; Union (Modoc) 78–54 Morton Memorial; Shenandoah 55–41 Monroe Central; Knightstown 82–61 Union (Modoc); Knightstown 56–53 Shenandoah. Officials: Rudy Williams, Rich Spay, Al Smith, Mike Fawcett.

NORTH JUDSON: Oregon-Davis 61–42 Winamac; North Judson 66–58 Culver Community; LaCrosse 61–59 South Central (Union Mills); West Central 62–42 Knox; Oregon-Davis 76–52 North Judson; West Central 89–66 LaCrosse, West Central 61–59 Oregon-Davis. Officials: Mike Waisnora, Tom Templin, Mike Martin, Rick Scott.

NORTH MONTGOMERY: McCutcheon 72–57 Southmont; Crawfordsville 57–41 North Montgomery; McCutcheon 47–44 Crawfordsville Officials: Ron Carter, Tom Newlin, James Campbell, Dan Yagodnik.

PAOLI: Orleans 76–64 West Washington; Mitchell 56–54 Salem (2ot); Springs Valley 41–40 Paoli; Mitchell 55–50 Orleans; Mitchell 68–62 Springs Valley. Officials: Larry Maxwell; David Bromm, Bill Gardner, Rex Nichols.

PLYMOUTH: Argos 44–41 LaVille (ot); Glenn 73–56 Culver Military Academy; Bremen 55–47 Plymouth; Glenn 48–41 Argos; Bremen 70–56 Glenn. Officials: Larry Jones, Steve Godfroy, David Emery, Mark Hay.

PRINCETON: North Posey 60–35 New Harmony; Princeton 55–40 Mount Vernon; Oakland City Wood 67–63 Gibson Southern (ot); Princeton 60–58 North Posey; Oakland City Wood 51–49 Princeton (ot). Officials: Tom Rohr, John Crapo, Stan Ames, Raymond Norris.

RICHMOND: Richmond 84–60 Northeastern; Randolph Southern 53–45 Union City; Cambridge City Lincoln 66–59 Centerville; Winchester 69–58 Hagerstown; Richmond 75–48 Randolph Southern; Winchester 70–53 Cambridge City Lincoln; Richmond 78–52 Winchester. Officials: Patrick Parks, Donald Hopkins, Dan Breneman, Sam Lower.

SEYMOUR: Crothersville 57–56 Brownstown Central; Jennings County 94–45 Medora; Bedford–North Lawrence 63–60 Seymour; Jennings County 79–45 Crothersville; Bedford-North Lawrence 61–55 Jennings County. Officials: Stephen Fisher, David Kavanaugh, Ronald Kottlowski, James Newlin.

SHELBYVILLE: Shelbyville 49–30 Morristown; Triton Central 67–51 Waldron; Shelbyville

58–46 Southwestern (Shelbyville); Shelbyville 54–53 Triton Central. Officials: Bill Wullner, Jerry Wallace, Jim Pitcher, Clarence Crain.

SOUTH ADAMS: Bellmont 63–42 South Adams; Norwell 80–45 Southern Wells; Adams Central 55–54 Bluffton; Bellmont 69–61 Norwell; Bellmont 98–55 Adams Central. Officials: Paul Cox, Jerry Middleton, Jim Keifer, Brad Groninger.

SOUTH BEND: Washington 64–52 Clay; St. Joseph's 55–54 Mishawaka; LaSalle 67–56 Mishawaka Marian; Riley 72–68 Adams; St. Joseph's 60–54 Washington; Riley 77–57 LaSalle; Riley 75–60 St. Joseph's. Officials: John Lozier, Skip Hopper, Douglas Carl, Kenneth Dickman.

SOUTH DEARBORN: Lawrenceburg 48–45 South Dearborn (ot); Rising Sun 90–46 Switzerland County. Rising Sun 57–40 Lawrenceburg, Officials: Robert Frye, Jack Kopp, Ray Oppel. Paul Crawford.

SOUTHPORT: Decatur Central 51–50 Indianapolis Manual (ot); Howe 56–54 Perry Meridian; Southport 81–35 Park Tudor; Decatur Central 74–52 Indiana School for the Deaf; Southport 70–52 Howe; Southport 60–57 Decatur Central (ot). Officials: Ronald Beard, Larry Alsip, Larry Johnson, Herb Pruett.

SOUTHRIDGE: Northeast Dubois 55–47 Forest Park; Southridge 42–41 Perry Central; Northeast Dubois 49–47 Jasper; Southridge 42–41 Northeast Dubois. Officials: William Nimnicht, Mark Mason, Ronald Mahan, Gary Hawn.

TERRE HAUTE: South 76–74 Northview (2ot); North 86–54 South Vermillion; West Vigo 77–56 Riverton Parke; North 79–69 South; North 68–66 West Vigo. Officials: Mike Bohan, Richard Foxen, Philip Napariu, Steve Willett.

TRI–COUNTY: Twin Lakes 60–48 North White; Benton Central 78–51 South Newton; Tri-County 47–46 Frontier; Benton Central 64–57 Twin Lakes; Benton Central 39–37 Tri-County (3ot). Officials: Dale Cramer, Ron Hosinski, Terry Weldy, Ivan Burkle.

TRITON: Warsaw 59–44 Wawasee; Tippecanoe Valley 54–36 Triton; Warsaw 62–52 Rochester; Tippecanoe Valley 65–56 Warsaw. Officials: Tom Schenkel, Jerry Christie, David Trietsch, Dale Blosser.

VALPARAISO: Chesterton 70–24 Washington Twp.; Valparaiso 49–46 Wheeler; Portage 78–45 River Forest; Morgan Twp.; 57–52 Hobart; Chesterton 55–52 Valparaiso (3ot); Portage 72–62 Morgan Twp.; Chesterton 40–38 Portage. Officials: Richard Cook, Robert Gootee, Jeff Simmons, John Goss.

VINCENNES: Vincennes Rivet 34–32 South Knox; Vincennes 46–44 North Knox; Vincennes 60–53 Rivet. Officials: Mel Redman, Jim Reid, John Schroeder, Robert Davis.

WASHINGTON: Barr-Reeve 41–37 Loogootee; Washington Catholic 37–36 North Daviess; Washington 67–66 Pike Central; Barr-Reeve 57–31 Shoals; Catholic 71–56 Washington; Barr-Reeve 49–47 Catholic (ot). Officials: Temme Patterson, William Amerson, Urban Keithley, Daniel Henkle.

1987 REGIONALS

ANDERSON: Carmel 78–63 Jay County; Anderson Madison Heights 73–67 Kokomo; Carmel 70–68 Madison Heights. Officials: Tom Schenkel, Tom Knox, Jim Cox, Lanny Rossman, Jerry Cook, Mark Baltz.

COLUMBUS: Columbus North 73–66 Indian Creek; Bloomington South 50–49 Shelbyville;

Tourney Time

Bloomington South 82–57 Columbus North. Officials: Joe Gilliland, Ronald Grimes, James Newlin, Mark Masariu, Bob Beeson, Gary Woodling.

ELKHART: Westview 63–61 Bremen; Penn 58–57 Tippecanoe Valley; Penn 69–67 Westview. Officials: John Goss, Kenneth Dickman, Roger DeYoung, Ray Tebbe, Mike Waisnora, Judson Raver.

EVANSVILLE: Memorial 70–63 Castle; Vincennes 59–45 Oakland City Wood; Memorial 54–37 Vincennes. Officials: Tom Rohr, Raymond Norris, Carl March, Brad Farmer, Stephen Fisher, Rich Kay.

FORT WAYNE: Northrop 60–54 Elmhurst Whitko 84–67 DeKalb; Northrop 67–61 Whitko. Officials: Phil Abernathy, Sam Lower, Steve Brown, Dale Blosser, Tom Urban, Mike Crouch.

FRANKFORT: McCutcheon 67–50 Lebanon, Plainfield 69–57 Frankfort; McCutcheon 61–48 Plainfield. Officials: Bob Wolfe, Bob Anderson, Brad Groninger, Rudy Williams, Roger Holder, Dale Cramer.

GARY: Gary Roosevelt 80–59 Merrillville; Hammond 74–63 East Chicago Central; Roosevelt 73–56 Hammond. Officials: Larry Jones, Jon Davenport, Mark Hay, Patrick Parks, Richard Cook, Ron Carter.

INDIANAPOLIS: Warren Central 56–54 Lawrence North (2ot); Pike 62–51 Southport; Pike 60–57 Warren Central. Officials: Dan Kunkel, Jerry Taylor, Larry Nixon, Ivan Burkle, John Lozier, Steve Cherry.

LAFAYETTE: Benton Central 87–57 Kouts; Central Catholic 71–51 North Vermillion; Catholic 63–52 Benton Central. Officials: Clifford Spears, Russell Radtke, Roger McGriff, David Hurst, Frank DeSantis, Thomas May.

MARION: Belmont 62–48 Northfield; Marion 106–69 Peru; Marion 81–70 Bellmont. Officials: Jerome Fawley, Mel Botkin, Rick Owens, Jay Smith, Don O'Connor, John Adams.

MICHGAN CITY: Michigan City Rogers 84–74 South Bend Riley; Chesterton 72–48 West Central; Rogers 79–52 Chesterton. Officials: Tim Smith, Clark Hamilton, Frank Hoagburg, Bill Champion, Bob Marcinek,, Dan Yagodnik.

NEW CASTLE: Rushville 67–53 Knightstown; Mount Vernon (Fortville) 66–62 Muncie Southside; Mount Vernon (Fortville) 77–54 Rushville. Officials: David Raabe, Gary Cheesman, Troy Ingram, Bill Wullner, James Wehsollek, Larry Maxwell.

RICHMOND: Connersville 66–57 East Central; Richmond 73–57 Rising Sun; Richmond 77–63 Connersville. Officials: Leland Thompson, Mike Fawcett, Bob Klein, Herb Pruett, Paul Cox, Bob Carr.

SEYMOUR: Jeffersonville 85–75 Southwestern (Hanover); Bedford-North Lawrence 76–66 New Albany; Bedford-North Lawrence 89–64 Jeffersonville. Officials: Ronald Beard, Michael Wallpe, Mike Burchette, Mike Bohan, James Dunlap, Norman Hathcoat.

TERRE HAUTE: Terre Haute North 75–50 Sullivan; Bloomfield 38–36 Rockville; North 86–65 Bloomfield. Officials: Michael McCarty, Robert Davis, John Evans, Don Nester, Gary Leistner, Temme Patterson.

WASHINGTON: North Harrison 67–54 Southridge; Mitchell 54–50 Barr-Reeve (ot); North Harrison 52–48 Mitchell. Officials: Doug Coddington, Denis Ward, William Nimnicht, Morris Cohen, Melvin Redman, Keith Combs.

1987 SEMI-STATES

EVANSVILLE: Bedford-North Lawrence 70–53 North Harrison; Evansville Memorial 73–71 Terre Haute North; Bedford-North Lawrence 59–51 Memorial Officials: Gary Leistner, Temme Patterson, Larry Maxwell, John Adams, Bob Beeson, Roger Holder.

FORT WAYNE: Penn 75–54 Fort Wayne Northrop; Marion 95–63 Michigan City Rogers; Marion 97–62 Penn. Officials: Paul Cox, Jim Wehsollek, Jerry Cook, Mike Waisnora, Thomas May, Frank DeSantis.

INDIANAPOLIS: Richmond 60–54 Bloomington South; Mount Vernon (Fortville) 63–56 Pike; Richmond 77–67 Mount Vernon. Officials: Thomas Urban. James Dunlap, Ron Carter, Mike Crouch, Richard Cook, Stephen Fisher.

LAFAYETTE: Gary Roosevelt 57–46 McCutcheon; Central Catholic 56–55 Carmel; Roosevelt 66–43 Catholic. Officials: Norm Hathcoat, John Lozier, Bob Marcinek, Bob Carr, Don O'Connor, Melvin Redman.

1987 FINALS—March 28

INDIANAPOLIS (Market Square Arena): Marion 70–61 Bedford-North Lawrence; Richmond 66–60 Gary Roosevelt; Marion 69–56 Richmond. Officials: Melvin Redman, Thomas May, Bob Beeson, Richard Cook, Don O'Connor, Stephen Fisher.

1988 SECTIONALS

ANDERSON: Anderson 66–62 Daleville; Pendleton Heights 61–58 Frankton (ot); Madison Heights 75–69 Highland; Alexandria 82–66 Lapel; Anderson 53–51 Pendleton Heights; Madison Heights 88–61 Alexandria; Madison Heights 65–54 Anderson. Officials: Joe Gilliland, Mark Campbell, Joseph Pinnick, Clarence Crain.

BEN DAVIS: Northwest 66–60 Speedway; Pike 48–43 Brebeuf; Ben Davis 81–67 Ritter; Northwest 79–61 Washington; Ben Davis 69–67 Pike; Ben Davis 80–67 Northwest. Officials: Bob Carr, Jerry Middleton, Dan Breneman, Gary Cheesman, Mike Baas.

BLACKFORD: Jay County 64–54 Blackford; Delta 89–66 Eastbrook; Wapahani 73–43 Wes-Del; Delta 79–74 Jay County; Wapahani 55–48 Delta. Officials: Tom Schenkel, Steve Godfroy, Jerry Alberson, Robert Boyle.

BOONVILLE: Castle 87–48 Cannelton; South Spencer 66–58 Boonville, Heritage Hills 61–57 Tell City; Castle 73–60 Tecumseh; Heritage Hills 57–45 South Spencer; Heritage Hills 56–53 Castle. Officials: Melvin Redman, James Reid, Keith Bagby, Robert Davis.

BROWNSBURG: Brownsburg 79–76 Avon; Mooresville 56–53 Cascade; Plainfield 68–42 Danville; Brownsburg 69–60 Mooresville; Brownsburg 62–61 Plainfield. Officials: Steve Cherry, Mel Botkin, Carl March, Ray Tebbe.

CALUMET: Calumet 74–73 Munster; Highland 59–48 Griffith; Lake Central 64–63 Merrillville; Crown Point 48–41 Lake Station Edison; Highland 77–71 Calumet (ot), Lake Central 74–65 Crown Point; Lake Central 66–63 Highland. Officials: Richard Cook, Richard Calloway, Philip Marsh, Bruce Klonowski.

CARMEL: Sheridan 64–63 Hamilton Heights; Noblesville 78–57 Westfield; Carmel 64–62

Tourney Time

Hamilton Southeastern; Noblesville 69–46 Sheridan; Carmel 67–52 Noblesville. Officials: Don Nester, Steven Willett, Scott Mellinger, David Raabe.

CENTRAL (SWITZ CITY): Bloomfield 45–37 Eastern (Greene Co.); Shakamak 48–46 Central (ot); L&M 62–59 Worthington; Bloomfield 61–44 Linton-Stockton; Shakamak 65–38 L&M; Shakamak 61–59 Bloomfield. Officials: Leland Thompson, Richard Foxen, David Berman, Tom Walters.

COLUMBIA CITY: Whitko 47–44 Churubusco; Manchester 92–59 Fort Wayne Blackhawk; Columbia City 47–44 Carroll (Fort Wayne); Manchester 53–51 Whitko; Manchester 65–53 Columbia City. Officials: Clark Hamilton, Roger Pflughaupt, David Gentile, Donald Schmidt.

COLUMBUS: North 95–65 Brown County; East 57–53 Hauser; North 70–48 Edinburgh; North 87–43 East. Officials: John Evans, James Ralston, Greg McAdams, Philip Napariu.

CONNERSVILLE: Laurel 39–37 Union County, Brookville 56–52 Connersville; Brookville 63–35 Laurel. Officials: Norm Hathcoat, Joe Edmonds, Mike Davis, Kent Smith.

CRAWFORD COUNTY: Corydon 68–32 Lanesville; North Harrison 67–45 Crawford County; Eastern (Pekin) 68–38 South Central; North Harrison 60–52 Corydon; North Harrison 81–56 Eastern (Pekin). Officials: Gary Leistner, James Newlin, Steve Corya, William Nimnicht.

EAST CENTRAL: Batesville 58–41 East Central; South Ripley 65–50 Jac-Cen-Del; Batesville 74–49 Milan; South Ripley 47–38 Batesville. Officials: Rick Owens, Ronald McDougal, Jack Kopp, Mark Medley.

EAST CHICAGO: Hammond Noll 80–47 Whiting; East Chicago Central 57–51 Hammond Clark; Noll 65–43 Central. Officials: John Goss, Jeffery Hull, Al Yelich, Dan Yagodnik.

EAST NOBLE: East Noble 55–41 West Noble; Bethany Christian 50–39 Prairie Heights; Westview 72–67 Central Noble; Fairfield 88–52 Lakeland; East Noble 60–42 Bethany Christian; Fairfield 72–67 Westview (2ot); East Noble 68–65 Fairfield. Officials: Jay Smith, David Emery, Fred Hamilton, Dave Vendrely.

ELKHART: Concord 66–46 North Wood; Central 59–38 Jimtown; Memorial 51–42 Goshen; Penn 60–42 Northridge; Concord 67–52 Central; Penn 61–45 Memorial; Concord 70–45 Penn. Officials: Frank DeSantis, Duffey Ainsworth, Skip Hopper, Mike Winger.

EVANSVILLE: Central 102–63 Day School; Memorial 52–36 Reitz; Mater Dei 49–41 Harrison; Bosse 54–51 North; Central 60–52 Memorial; Mater Dei 56–54 Bosse (ot); Central 55–48 Mater Dei. Officials: James Dunlap, David Hevron, Dennis Espenlaub, John Schroeder.

FLOYD CENTRAL: Floyd Central 67–56 Graceland Christian; Silver Creek 76–71 Charlestown; Henryville 65–39 Borden; Floyd Central 86–51 Silver Creek; Floyd Central 81–58 Henryville. Officials: Keith Combs, Mark Mason, Ron Kottlowski, David Bromm.

FORT WAYNE (#1): Northrop 56–54 North Side; Dwenger 68–55 Luers; Snider 63–52 Harding; New Haven 59–51 Northrop; Dwenger 65–48 Snider; Dwenger 86–78 New Haven. Officials: Kenneth Dickman, Mike Burchette, Gene Huston, David Long.

FORT WAYNE (#2): Elmhurst 72–47 Wayne; South Side 77–59 Woodlan; Concordia 78–35 Heritage; Elmhurst 93–34 Christian; South Side 59–58 Concordia; Elmhurst 70–59 South Side. Officials: Mark Masariu, William Kachel, Mike Padfield, Ronald Kitts.

FOUNTAIN CENTRAL: North Vermillion 69–57 Turkey Run; Fountain Central 54–53 Attica (2ot); Covington 63–53 Seeger; North Vermillion 68–47 Fountain Central; Covington 69–68 North Vermillion. Officials: David Hurst, John Tucker, Joe Reed, Dave Atwell.

FRANKFORT: Rossville 86–67 Clinton Central; Frankfort 59–50 Tri-Central; Tipton 65–46

Clinton Prairie; Rossville 88–75 Frankfort; Tipton 66–56 Rossville. Officials: Dick Modricker, Douglas Hudson, Joseph Stafford, Harry Northington.

FRANKLIN CENTRAL: Franklin Central 74–60 Beech Grove; Indianapolis Scecina 83–70 is Lutheran; Warren Central 53–46 Roncalli; Franklin Central 62–55 Scecina (ot); Warren Central 50–43 Franklin Central. Officials: Paul Cox, Larry Gilpin, J. D. Collins, John Stumpf.

GARRETT: Leo 73–41 Howe Military; Angola 64–48 Hamilton; Eastside 70–65 Fremont; DeKalb 56–51 Garrett; Leo 55–52 Angola; DeKalb 78–70 Eastside; DeKalb 64–59 Leo. Officials: Tim Smith, Russ Teall, Tom Muth, Ed Christoffel.

GARY: Wirt 49–47 Wallace; Roosevelt 86–69 West Side; Wirt 79–55 Mann; Roosevelt 49–38 Wirt. Officials: Roger DeYoung, Jon Davenport, Michael Spann, Dale Cramer.

GREENCASTLE: South Putnam 64–54 North Putnam; Owen Valley 70–55 Cloverdale; Greencastle 67–65 Rockville (ot); South Putnam 70–68 Owen Valley; Greencastle 86–74 South Putnam. Officials: Larry Nixon, John Crapo, Rich Spay, Ed Roush.

GREENFIELD-CENTRAL: Greenfield-Central 85–70 New Palestine; Mt. Vernon (Fortville) 51–48 Eastern Hancock; Greenfield-Central 57–54 Mt. Vernon. Officials: Bill Wullner. Larry Alsip, Mike Alford, David Chalk.

GREENSBURG: North Decatur 62–58 Rushville; Greensburg 68–54 South Decatur; North Decatur 60–58 Greensburg. Officials: Herb Pruett, Gene Marsh, Dale Goodwin, James Roberts.

HAMMOND: Hammond High 67–44 Hammond Gavit; Andrean 76–54 Hammond Morton; Hammond High 84–75 Andrean. Officials: Mike Waisnora, Ron Hosinski, Larry Parker, Jeffrey Simmons.

HUNTINGTON: Homestead 82–49 Southwood; Huntington North 88–68 Wabash; Northfield 83–49 White's; Homestead 51–50 Huntington North; Homestead 52–49 Northfield. Officials: John Lozier, Randy Coplen, Bradley Wilson, Steven Brown.

INDIANAPOLIS: Chatard 79–58 Broad Ripple; Lawrence North 59–55 Tech (ot); North Central 72–48 Arlington; Cathedral 94–83 Lawrence Central; Chatard 66–65 Lawrence North; Cathedral 67–61 North Central; Chatard 71–53 Cathedral. Officials: Mark Baltz, David Lee, Bob Hallgrath, George Taylor, Doug Coddington

JEFFERSONVILLE: Jeffersonville 86–78 New Albany; Clarksville 82–68 Providence; Jeffersonville 100–86 Clarksville. Officials: Lanny Rossman, Jim Flanagan, Norman Chestnut, Robert Frye.

KANKAKEE VALLEY: Hebron 68–45 Boone Grove; Kankakee Valley 76–46 Hanover Central; Lowell 47–45 Kouts; North Newton 73–56 Rensselaer Central; Kankakee Valley 63–49 Hebron; Lowell 80–40 North Newton; Kankakee Valley 77–62 Lowell. Officials: Ron Carter, James Campbell, Terry Bartell, Rick Scott.

KOKOMO: Maconaquah 66–38 Eastern (Greentown); Kokomo 56–44 Western; Northwestern 62–56 Taylor; Kokomo 61–42 Maconaquah; Kokomo 64–30 Northwestern. Officials: James Wehsollek, Douglas Carl, Kenneth Cobb, Dennis Jackson.

LAFAYETTE: West Lafayette 72–52 Delphi; Harrison 52–44 Carroll (Flora); Lafayette Jefferson 76–64 Lafayette Catholic; Harrison 65–49 West Lafayette; Jefferson 62–57 Harrison. Officials: Larry Jones, Jerry Christie, Dave Willoughby, Mike Crouch.

LEBANON: Zionsville 56–48 Western Boone; Lebanon 47–38 Tri-West Hendricks; Lebanon 59–52 Zionsville. Officials: Timothy Fogarty, Bob Dedaker, Walter Bishop, Thomas Newlin.

LOGANSPORT: Peru 61–49 North Miami; Cass 67–47 Pioneer, Logansport 97–51 Caston,

Cass 42–39 Peru; Logansport 64–46 Cass. Officials: Mark Hay, Ivan Burkle, Jerry Wallace, James Robinson.

MADISON: New Washington 75–44 Southwestern (Hanover); Madison 64–55 Scottsburg; Austin 72–55 Madison Shawe; New Washington 79–51 Madison, New Washington 73–47 Austin. Officials: McKee Munk, Ray Oppel, Donald Hopkins Jr., Urban Keithley.

MARION: Marion 72–55 Oak Hill; Mississinewa 65–35 Elwood; Madison Grant 105–62 Marion Bennett; Mississinewa 45–42 Marion; Madison Grant 53–52 Mississinewa (2ot). Officials: Sam Lower, Larry Johnson, Rick Shirk, Bob Harvey.

MARTINSVILLE: Martinsville 75–66 Eminence; Bloomington North 77–67 Monrovia; Bloomington South 64–49 Edgewood; North 81–78 Martinsville; South 69–66 North. Officials: Michael McCarty, Daniel Henkle, Jeffrey Culp, Steven Smith.

MICHIGAN CITY: Rogers 97–54 Westville; LaPorte 97–66 New Prairie; Elston 93–60 Marquette; LaPorte 89–73 Rogers; LaPorte 97–72 Elston. Officials: Dale Blosser, Jerome Fawley, Joe Oyler, Bill Sorukas.

MUNCIE: Central 69–32 Burris; Northside 72–64 Cowan; Southside 58–56 Yorktown; Central 71–53 Northside; Central 66–61 Southside (ot). Officials: Tom Urban, Jack Taylor, Anthony Ortman, Tom Crouch.

NEW CASTLE: Blue River 72–27 Morton Memorial; New Castle 80–49 Union (Modoc); Tri 69–45 Monroe Central; Shenandoah 49–45 Knightstown; New Castle 79–55 Blue River; Tri 70–60 Shenandoah; New Castle 66–40 Tri. Officials: Troy Ingram, Larry Sintz, Jim Keifer, Don Hittle.

NORTH JUDSON: North Judson 68–64 South Central (Union Mills); Oregon-Davis 90–66 Culver Community; LaCrosse 65–54 Knox; Winamac 61–56 West Central; Oregon-Davis 59–54 North Judson; LaCrosse 78–76 Winamac (ot); Oregon-Davis 90–73 LaCrosse. Officials: Bob Marcinek, Kevin Weinberg, Terry Weldy, Bob Modrowski.

NORTH MONTGOMERY: Southmont 54–47 Crawfordsville, McCutcheon 71–54 North Montgomery McCutcheon 60–45 Southmont. Officials: Patrick Parks, Phil Vidito, Ed Scahill, Mike Fawcett.

PAOLI: Salem 70–65 West Washington; Orleans 57–50 Springs Valley, Mitchell 61–33 Paoli; Orleans 51–49 Salem; Mitchell 54–49 Orleans. Officials: Steve Fisher, Bill Amerson, Ron Pritchett, Gary Hawn.

PLYMOUTH: Plymouth 55–46 Glenn; LaVille 44–36 Culver Military Academy; Bremen 74–64 Argos; Plymouth 58–49 LaVille; Bremen 56–50 Plymouth. Officials: Thomas May, Robert Gootee, Robert Graczyk, James Anderson.

PRINCETON: Princeton 88–47 New Harmony; North Posey 87–72 Oakland City; Mt. Vernon 67–64 Gibson Southern (ot); North Posey 45–44 Princeton; Mt. Vernon 57–49 North Posey. Officials: Temme Patterson, David Kavanaugh, Doug Anoskey, Michael Zehr.

RICHMOND: Northeastern 70–62 Hagerstown; Cambridge City 51–47 Centerville; Richmond 89–48 Winchester; Randolph Southern 50–48 Union City (ot); Cambridge City 48–47 Northeastern; Richmond 89–69 Randolph Southern; Richmond 91–45 Cambridge City. Officials: Bob Beeson, Rick Granger, Jim Pitcher, Russ Radtke.

SEYMOUR: Bedford-North Lawrence 72–59 Jennings County; Brownstown Central 100–81 Medora; Seymour 94–63 Crothersville; Bedford-North Lawrence 90–60 Brownstown Central; Bedford-North Lawrence 85–74 Seymour. Officials: Larry Maxwell, Rich Kay, Ron Mahan, Paul Wahl.

SHELBYVILLE: Shelbyville 56–43 Waldron; Morristown 67–38 Southwestern (Shelbyville); Shelbyville 51–40 Triton Central; Shelbyville 51–49 Morristown. Officials: Robert Anderson, Keith Fields, Gary Hamilton, Brad Groninger.

SOUTH ADAMS: Adams Central 67–46 Southern Wells; Norwell 70–58 Bellmont; South Adams 67–47 Bluffton; Norwell 70–56 Adams Central; Norwell 69–60 South Adams. Officials: Frank Hoagburg, Jerry Stieglitz, Gaylord Fritz,Don Resler.

SOUTH BEND: St. Joseph's 71–52 Adams; Mishawaka Marian 55–53 Washington; Mishawaka 80–62 Riley; LaSalle 73–60 Clay; St. Joseph's 58–37 Mishawaka Marian; LaSalle 56–47 Mishawaka; St. Joseph's 61–48 LaSalle. Officials: Don O'Connor, Douglas Cook, Dan VanTreese,Mark Hyman.

SOUTH DEARBORN: Switzerland County 62–58 Rising Sun; Lawrenceburg 78–70 South Dearborn; Switzerland County 65–64 Lawrenceburg. Officials: Roger Holder, Michael Smith, Kenneth Knapp, Rex Nichols.

SOUTHPORT: Perry Meridian 74–53 Indianapolis Howe; Manual 62–49 Park Tudor; Decatur Central 74–40 Indiana School For The Deaf; Southport 55–45 Perry Meridian; Manual 64–61 Decatur Central; Southport 67–62 Manual. Officials: Mike Bohan, Dennis Maude, Al Smith, John Walker,Chuck Weinkauf.

SOUTHRIDGE: Northeast Dubois 64–44 Forest Park, Jasper 48–24 Perry Central; Northeast Dubois 63–48 Southridge; Northeast Dubois 52–39 Jasper.Officials: Gary Woodling, Lowell DePoy, Eric Ballenger,John Lyskowinski.

SOUTH VERMILLION: Northview 79–59 South Vermillion; West Vigo 73–67 Riverton Parke; Northview 67–63 West Vigo. Officials: Bob Wolfe, Terry Magnuson, Rick Normington Jerry Taylor.

TERRE HAUTE: North 46–44 Sullivan; South 86–41 Clay City; Union (Dugger) 69–51 North Central (Farmersburg); South 62–58 North; South 75–60 Union (Dugger). Officials: Bob Klein, Ron McGriff, Haymon Fields, Scott Robinson.

TRI–COUNTY: Benton Central 67–51 Twin Lakes, Frontier 72–52 Benton Central; Tri–County 80–61 North White; Frontier 54–51 Benton Central; Tri–County 58–50 Frontier. Officials: Nick Sweigart, Jerry Karstens, Mark Martin, Paul Danko.

TRITON: Warsaw 61–50 Wawasee; Tippecanoe Valley 69–65 Rochester; Triton 70–66 Warsaw; Tippecanoe Valley 81–52 Triton. Officials: Judson Raver, Tom Dull, Bryan Enterline Tom Knox.

VALPARAISO: Morgan Twp. 84–53 Wheeler; Valparaiso 62–49 River Forest; Hobart 69–50 Washington Twp.; Portage 49–47 Chesterton; Valparaiso 60–53 Morgan Twp.; Portage 75–54 Hobart; Portage 51–46 Valparaiso. Officials: Jerry Cook, Fred Mohri, Brian Weidner, Mark McCannon.

VINCENNES: Vincennes Rivet 64–53 North Knox; Vincennes 44–42 South Knox, Vincennes 55–47 Rivet. Officials: Ray Norris, Brad Farmer, Ron James, Tom Rohr.

WASHINGTON: Shoals 40–39 Pike Central; Washington Catholic 64–56 Barr-Reeve; Washington 50–49 North Daviess; Loogootee 69–34 Shoals; Washington 50–48 Washington Catholic; Loogootee 66–57 Washington. Officials: Ronald Grimes, Louis Harmening, Lester Baugh, Charles Steve Meyer.

WHITELAND: Greenwood 78–58 Indian Creek; Center Grove 64–35 Whiteland; Franklin 76–74 Greenwood (ot); Center Grove 63–55 Franklin. Officials: Clifford Spears, David Estes, Barry Lauber, Stan Ames.

Tourney Time

1988 REGIONALS

ANDERSON: Anderson Madison Heights 60–56 Carmel; Kokomo 49–32 Wapahani; Kokomo 47–45 Madison Heights. Officials: Gary Woodling, Mark Medley, Rick Owens, Mike Winger, Troy Ingram, Tim Smith.

COLUMBUS: Bloomington South 65–64 Columbus North; Shelbyville 54–52 Center Grove (ot); Bloomington South 55–52 Shelbyville. Officials: David Hurst, Paul Wahl, Mike Bohan, John Lyskowinski, Bill Wullner, Bob Carr.

EAST CHICAGO: Hammond 70–67 Lake Central; Hammond Noll 56–51 Gary Roosevelt; Hammond Noll 66–64 Hammond. Officials: Dale Blosser, Dave Atwell, William Sorukas, Bruce Klonowski, Frank DeSantis, Don O'Connor.

ELKHART: Concord 69–58 Tippecanoe Valley; East Noble 54–41 Bremen; Concord 40–34 East Noble. Officials: Tom Schenkel, James Anderson, Mark Hays, Dan Yagodnik, Bob Marcinek, Dick Modricker.

EVANSVILLE: Heritage Hills 55–52 Vincennes; Evansville Central 65–64 Mt. Vernon; Evansville Central 65–64 Heritage Hills. Officials: Clifford Spears, Michael Zehr, Ronald Grimes, McKee Munk, Gary Leistner, Lanny Rossman.

FORT WAYNE: Fort Wayne Dwenger 84–80 Manchester (ot); DeKalb 75–69 Fort Wayne Elmhurst; Dwenger 95–77 DeKalb. Officials: Jay Smith, Harry Northington, Robert Boyle, Tom Crouch, John Lozier, Larry Jones.

FRANKFORT: Brownsburg 58–50 Lebanon; Tipton 63–55 McCutcheon, Brownsburg 93–82 Tipton. Officials: Larry Nixon, Jerry Taylor, John Evans, Nick Sweigart, Roger DeYoung, Mike Crouch.

INDIANAPOLIS: Warren Central 65–64 Indianapolis Chatard; Ben Davis 61–54 Southport; Ben Davis 66–63 Warren Central. Officials: Sam Lower, Tom Rohr, Raymond Norris, Thomas Newlin, Jim Wehsollek, Kenneth Dickman

LAFAYETTE: Lafayette Jefferson 67–51 Covington; Kankakee Valley 78–64 Tri-County; Jefferson 47–45 Kankakee Valley. Officials: Herb Pruett, Douglas Carl, Bob Klein, Kent Smith, Tom May, Mike Waisnora.

MARION: Homestead 73–65 Madison Grant, Norwell 71–61 Logansport; Norwell 68–51 Homestead. Officials: Frank Hoagburg, Steven Brown, Judson Raver, Bob Harvey, Norm Hathcoat, Tim Fogarty.

MICHIGAN CITY: LaPorte 72–64 South Bend St. Joseph's; Portage 74–71 Oregon Davis; Portage 50–49 LaPorte. Officials: Jerry Cook, Don Resler, Clark Hamilton, Ron Kitts, Ron Carter, John Goss.

NEW CASTLE: Muncie Central 84–61 New Castle; Greenfield-Central 56–50 North Decatur; Muncie Central 100–60 Greenfield-Central. Officials: Bob Wolfe, Robert Frye, Leland Thompson, Tom Knox, Mark Masariu, Bob Beeson.

RICHMOND: South Ripley 70–67 Brookville; Richmond 83–57 Switzerland County; Richmond 103–65 South Ripley. Officials: Patrick Parks, Ray Tebbe, Mark Baltz, Doug Coddington, Paul Cox, Don Nester.

SEYMOUR: Jeffersonville 83–77 Floyd Central; Bedford-North Lawrence 73–62 New Washington; Bedford-North Lawrence 91–68 Jeffersonville. Officials: Mike McCarty, William Nimnicht, Temme Patterson, Rex Nichols, Stephen Fisher, Roger Holder.

TERRE HAUTE: Greencastle 70–64 Northview; Shakamak 58–56 Terre Haute South;

Greencastle 56–49 Shakamak. Officials: Thomas Urban, Robert Anderson, Keith Combs, Clarence Crain, Steve Cherry, Melvin Redman.

WASHINGTON: North Harrison 76–69 Northeast Dubois (2ot); Loogootee 59–57 Mitchell; Loogootee 75–62 North Harrison. Officials: Larry Maxwell, John Stumpf, Carl March, Stan Ames, Joe Gilliland, James Dunlap.

1988 SEMI–STATES

FORT WAYNE: Norwell 60–57 Portage; Concord 84–75 Fort Wayne Dwenger; Concord 65–60 Norwell. Officials: Roger Holder, Paul Cox, Norm Hathcoat, Lanny Rossman, Troy Ingram, Mark Masariu.

INDIANAPOLIS: Ben Davis 69–61 Richmond; Muncie Central 73–59 Bloomington South; Muncie Central 74–69 Ben Davis. Officials: James Dunlap, Don O'Connor, John Lozier, Thomas May, Frank DeSantis, Stephen Fisher.

LAFAYETTE: Hammond Noll 58–46 Brownsburg; Kokomo 65–61 Lafayette Jefferson; Noll 53–40 Kokomo. Officials: Jim Wehsollek, Bob Carr, Steve Cherry, Bob Marcinek, Roger DeYoung, Joe Gilliland.

TERRE HAUTE: Bedford-North Lawrence 72–63 Loogootee; Greencastle 69–65 Evansville Central (ot); Bedford-North Lawrence 62–47 Greencastle. Officials: Bill Wullner, Melvin Redman, Tim Fogarty, Nick Sweigart, Ron Carter, Gary Leistner.

1988 FINALS—March 26

INDIANAPOLIS (Market Square Arena): Muncie Central 60–53 Bedford-North Lawrence; Concord 66–50 Hammond Noll; Muncie Central 76–53 Concord. Officials: Ron Carter, Frank DeSantis, Troy Ingram, Joe Gilliland, Roger DeYoung, Mark Masariu.

1989 SECTIONALS

ANDERSON: Daleville 46–43 Frankton; Pendleton Heights 70–53 Lapel; Alexandria Monroe 68–59 Highland; Anderson 88–84 Madison Heights (ot); Pendleton Heights 62–60 Daleville; Alexandria 87–79 Anderson; Alexandria 83–53 Pendleton Heights. Officials: Don Nester, Rick Normington, Mike Bohan, Robert Frye.

BEN DAVIS: Ben Davis 56–55 Speedway; Pike 89–57 Northwest: Ritter 68–55 Washington; Brebeuf 60–48 Ben Davis; Pike 75–51 Ritter; Brebeuf 56–47 Pike (ot). Officials: David Hurst, Bob Harvey, Kenneth Cobb, John Crapo.

BOONVILLE: Boonville 67–57 Tecumseh; Heritage Hills 69–63 Castle; Cannelton 57–54 Tell City; Boonville 66–63 South Spencer; Heritage Hills 84–60 Cannelton; Heritage Hills 79–64 Boonville. Officials: Gary Leistner, Mark Mason, Lowell DePoy, Ronald Mahan.

BROWNSBURG: Cascade 72–44 Plainfield; Brownsburg 75–54 Avon; Mooresville 69–66 Danville (ot); Brownsburg 74–65 Cascade; Mooresville 70–54 Brownsburg. Officials: Leland Thompson, Kent Smith, Joseph Stafford, Ivan Burkle.

CALUMET: Merrillville 82–42 Lake Station Edison; Crown Point 66–62 Highland; Munster 78–70 Calumet; Lake Central 75–61 Griffith; Merrillville 43–42 Crown Point; Munster 81–75

Tourney Time

Lake Central; Munster 61–53 Merrillville. Officials: Mark Hay, Michael Spann, Mark McCammon, Jerry Karstens.

CARMEL: Carmel 79–62 Sheridan; Noblesville 68–32 Westfield; Hamilton Southeastern 76–54 Hamilton Heights; Noblesville 70–55 Carmel: Noblesville 62–51 Hamilton Southeastern. Officials: Rick Owens, Jim Flanagan, Al Smith, Mark Martin.

CENTRAL (SWITZ CITY): Shakamak 58–57 Central (Switz City) (ot); Eastern (Bloomfield) 75–62 Linton–Stockton; Bloomfield 61–43 L&M; Worthington-Jefferson 56–55 Shakamak (ot); Bloomfield 74–57 Eastern (Bloomfield); Bloomfield 61–58 Worthington-Jefferson. Officials: Rex Nicholas, Steve Willett, Michael Baas, Phil Vidito.

CLAY CITY: Union (Dugger) 64–51 North Central (Farmersburg); Sullivan 72–58 Clay City; Union 64–59 Sullivan. Officials: Doug Coddington, David Willoughby, Jerry Wallace, Joe Reed.

COLUMBIA CITY: Manchester 71–56 Carroll (Fort Wayne); Columbia City 52–38 Churubusco; Whitko 80–45 Fort Wayne Blackhawk; Columbia City 57–56 Manchester (ot); Whitko 72–67 Columbia City. Officials: Tom Urban, Bryan Enterline, Michael Alspaugh, Judson Raver.

COLUMBUS: East 71–58 Edinburgh; Hauser 53–50 Brown County; North 98–85 East; North 87–71 Hauser. Officials: Carl March, McKee Munk, Ronald Pritchett, James Newlin.

CONNERSVILLE: Connersville 98–59 Laurel: Union County 86–75 Brookville; Connersville 64–63 Union County. Officials: Herb Pruett, Gene Marsh, Dave Chalk, Mel Botkin.

CRAWFORD COUNTY: South Central 44–43 Lanesville; Corydon Central 78–76 (ot) Eastern (Pekin); North Harrison 61–55 Crawford County; Corydon Central 62–50 South Central; North Harrison 61–55 Corydon Central. Officials: Temme Patterson, Robert Davis, Douglas Anoskey, Rick Granger.

DEKALB: Fremont 52–51 Leo (2ot); DeKalb 62–46 Eastside; Hamilton 49–45 Howe Military; Angola 53–51 Garrett (ot); DeKalb 51–39 Fremont; Angola 62–43 Hamilton; DeKalb 58–47 Angola. Officials: Jay C. Smith, Douglas Bauman, Jerry Alberson and Don Resler.

EAST CENTRAL: Milan 85–70 East Central; Batesville 72–60 Jac-Cen-Del; South Ripley 64–59 Milan, Batesville 75–48 South Ripley. Officials: Tom Crouch, Dale Goodwin, Robert Hallgrath, Jerry Middleton.

EAST CHICAGO: East Chicago Central 87–51 Hammond Clark; Hammond Noll 65–39 Whiting, Central 60–47 Noll. Officials: Mike Waisnora, Russ Teall, Fred Perry, Richard Cook.

EAST NOBLE: Westview 81–44 Central Noble; Bethany Christian 67–62 Lakeland; East Noble 67–49 Prairie Heights; Fairfield 74–44 West Noble; Westview 77–63 Bethany Christian; East Noble 58–57 Fairfield; Westview 64–61 East Noble. Officials: Douglas Carl, Steve Godfroy, David Long, Kevin Weinberg.

ELKHART: Memorial 75–54 Jimtown; Concord 73–61 North Wood; Goshen 54–45 Northridge; Penn 54–51 Central; Memorial 55–50 Concord, Goshen 73–60 Penn; Memorial 44–36 Goshen. Officials: Tim Smith, David Trietsch. Dan VanTreese, Jon Davenport.

EVANSVILLE: Memorial 76–52 Reitz; North 72–54 Day; Bosse 78–71 Harrison; Central 59–39 Mater Dei; Memorial 61–59 North; Bosse 72–45 Central; Memorial 69–63 Bosse. Officials: Gary Hawn, William Amerson, Otis Broughton, David Kavanaugh.

FORT WAYNE (#1): Harding 84–55 Elmhurst; Dwenger 73–52 Snider; Luers 90–77 Northrop; Woodlan 86–74 Harding; Dwenger 80–62 Luers; Dwenger 71–68 Woodlan. Officials: James Wehsollek, Scott Mellinger, Bradley Wilson, Dennis Jackson.

FORT WAYNE (#2): Wayne 70–64 South Side; Concordia 80–77 North Side (ot); New

IHSAA Scores | 1980–1989

Haven 73–62 Heritage; Concordia 73–71 Wayne; Concordia 68–64 New Haven. Officials: Mike Crouch, Mark Hyman, J.D. Collins, David Raabe.

FOUNTAIN CENTRAL: Fountain Central 67–43 Turkey Run; Attica 64–54 Covington; Seeger 63–60 North Vermillion; Fountain Central 49–44 Attica; Fountain Central 59–57 Seeger. Officials: Thomas Newlin, Terry Bartell, Larry Decker, Scott Robison.

FRANKFORT: Rossville 64–44 Clinton Central; Tipton 73–67 Clinton Prairie; Frankfort 57–46 Tri-Central; Tipton 85–71 Rossville; Tipton 71–56 Frankfort. Officials: Larry Nixon, Stan Ames, David Estes, David Lee.

FRANKLIN: Franklin 89–71 Center Grove; Greenwood 68–59 Whiteland; Franklin 92–57 Indian Creek; Franklin 73–62 Greenwood. Officials: Ron Grimes, Haymond Fields, Eric Ballenger, Russ Radtke.

FRANKLIN CENTRAL: Scecina 59–53 Beech Grove; Roncalli 88–50 Lutheran: Franklin Central 69–65 Warren Central (ot); Roncalli 63–45 Scecina; Franklin Central 60–40 Roncalli. Officials: Mark Baltz, Jack Kopp, John Walker, Jim Pitcher.

GARY: Roosevelt 72–71 Mann; Wirt 60–53 West Side; Roosevelt 67–48 Wallace; Wirt 51–49 Gary Roosevelt (ot). Officials: Thomas May, David Emery, Randy Coplen, Paul Danko.

GREENCASTLE: South Putnam 84–59 Cloverdale, Rockville 64–48 North Putnam; Greencastle 87–86 Owen Valley (3ot); South Putnam 82–74 Rockville; South Putnam 93–82 Greencastle. Officials: Ray Tebbe, Ed Scahill, Danny Shields, Terry Magnuson.

GREENFIELD-CENTRAL: Eastern Hancock 67–55 Greenfield-Central, New Palestine 80–79 Mount Vernon (Fortville) (2ot); New Palestine 64–61 Eastern Hancock. Officials: Bob Wolfe, Rick Shirk, Tony Bova, Jerry Christie.

GREENSBURG: Greensburg 67–66 Rushville; North Decatur 81–68 South Decatur. Greensburg 63–45 North Decatur. Officials: Clarence Crain, Larry Alsip, Larry Johnson, Brad Groninger.

HAMMOND: Hammond 79–57 Gavit; Andrean 62–52 Morton; Andrean 64–49 Hammond. Officials: John Goss, Al Yelich, Rich Calloway, Duffy Ainsworth.

HUNTINGTON: Southwood 84–80 Wabash: Northfield 72–43 Homestead; Huntington North 104–33 White's; Northfield 65–53 Southwood; Northfield 52–48 North. Officials: Gary Cheesman, William Kachel, Jon Custer, Tom Dull

INDIANAPOLIS: Broad Ripple 64–63 North Central; Lawrence North 70–63 Chatard; Tech 67–43 Arlington; Cathedral 63–57 Lawrence Central; Lawrence North 90–72 Broad Ripple; Cathedral 61–51 Tech; Lawrence North 79–56 Cathedral. Officials: Steve Cherry, Donald Hopkins, Jim Keifer, Troy Ingram.

JAY COUNTY: Delta 67–62 Jay County; Blackford 67–62 Wes-Del; Eastbrook 59–55 Wapahani; Delta 60–56 Blackford; Delta 67–58 Eastbrook. Officials: Paul Cox, Harry Northington, Thomas Muth, Mike Winger.

JEFFERSONVILLE: Floyd Central 95–89 Jeffersonville; Providence 69–64 Clarksville; Floyd Central 85–51 Providence. Officials: Mike Zehr, Bob Collins. Lester Baugh, Dennis Maude.

KANKAKEE VALLEY: Hebron 72–53 Kouts; Rensselaer 89–60 Hanover Central; Lowell 65–56 North Newton; Kankakee Valley 68–45 Boone Grove; Rensselaer 69–67 Hebron; Lowell 74–62 Kankakee Valley; Lowell 71–51 Rensselaer. Officials: John Lozier, Dan Amrhein, Robert Goatee, Robert Modrowski.

KOKOMO: Kokomo 71–41 Northwestern; Western 60–52 Eastern (Greentown);

Tourney Time

Maconaquah 64–54 Taylor; Kokomo 72–36 Western; Kokomo 64–61 Maconaquah. Officials: Lanny Rossman, Ronald Kitts, Tom Jerles, Frank DeSantis.

LAFAYETTE: West Lafayette 75–63 Delphi; Lafayette Jefferson 71–60 Harrison (West Lafayette); Central Catholic 65–55 Carroll (Flora); West Lafayette 58–50 Jefferson; West Lafayette 58–52 Catholic. Officials: Jerry Taylor, Tom Rohr, Ron Kottlowski, Rick Scott.

LEBANON: Lebanon 61–48 Western Boone; Tri–West Hendricks 65–59 Zionsville; Lebanon 82–64 Tri–West Hendricks. Officials: Tom Schenkel, Steven Smith, Ronald James, James Campbell.

LOGANSPORT: Peru 91–47 Caston, Pioneer 69–57 Cass; Logansport 79–66 North Miami; Peru 72–52 Pioneer; Logansport 55–50 Peru. Officials: Patrick Parks, Gaylord Fritz, Rich Spay, Ed Christoffel.

MADISON: Madison 70–50 Southwestern (Hanover); New Washington 80–63 Austin; Scottsburg 78–42 Madison Shawe; New Washington 81–62 Madison; New Washington 74–57 Scottsburg. Officials: Bill Wullner, Greg McAdams, John Lyskowski, Philip Napariu.

MARION: Madison Grant 72–57 Mississinewa; Marion 102–60 Marion Bennett; Oak Hill 76–66 Elwood; Marion 67–62 Madison Grant; Marion 70–53 Oak Hill. Officials: Robert Boyle, Don Schmidt, Tony Garton, Frank Hoagburg.

MARTINSVILLE: Eminence 70–68 Martinsville; Bloomington North 77–63 Bloomington South; Edgewood 59–46 Monrovia; North 74–60 Eminence; North 53–45 Edgewood. Officials: Bob Klein, Michael Smith, Thomas Ault, David Berman.

MICHIGAN CITY: Westville 79–59 New Prairie; Rogers 89–60 LaPorte; Elston 74–65 Marquette; Rogers 94–61 Westville; Rogers 84–73 Elston. Officials: Jerry Cook, Bruce Klonowski, Fred Mohri, Jeffrey Simmons.

MUNCIE: Burris 66–60 Cowan; Central 65–57 Yorktown; Southside 86–48 Muncie Burris: Southside 59–55 Central. Officials: Jim Cox, Keith Fields, Doug Flatter, Roger Pflughaupt.

NEW ALBANY: Charlestown 50–47 Graceland Christian; New Albany 83–43 Borden; Silver Creek 90–59 Henryville; New Albany 62–53 Charlestown; New Albany 58–53 Silver Creek. Officials: Michael McCarty, Roger McGriff, Jeffrey Culp, Ron McGriff.

NEW CASTLE: Blue River Valley 63–44 Union (Modoc); Tri 66–65 Monroe Central; Shenandoah 60–50 Morton Memorial; New Castle 64–53 Knightstown; Blue River Valley 62–61 Tri; New Castle 78–58 Shenandoah; New Castle 75–56 Blue River Valley. Officials: Roger Holder, Mark Campbell, Rex Blanton, Fred Hamilton.

NORTH JUDSON: Oregon–Davis 71–62 Culver Community; West Central 76–68 Winamac; North Judson 74–59 Knox; LaCrosse 82–60 South Central (Union Mills); West Central 59–57 Oregon–Davis; LaCrosse 74–61 North Judson; LaCrosse 69–46 West Central. Officials: Dick Modricker, Ron Hosinski, Phil Marsh, Dale Cramer.

NORTH MONTGOMERY: Crawfordsville 71–41 Southmont; McCutcheon 65–52 North Montgomery; Crawfordsville 55–53 McCutcheon (ot). Officials: Clifford Spears, Walter Bishop Jr., John Tucker, Kenneth Knapp.

PAOLI: Paoli 60–44 West Washington; Mitchell 63–57 Springs Valley; Salem 62–49 Orleans; Paoli 52–50 Mitchell; Paoli 61–46 Salem. Officials: Bill Nimnicht, Daniel Henkle, Jay Ritter, Brad Farmer.

PLYMOUTH: Bremen 61–46 LaVille; Culver Military 63–53 Argos; Glenn 57–44 Plymouth; Bremen 54–34 Culver Military; Glenn 50–47 Bremen. Officials: William Sorukas,

James Robinson, Terry Weldy, Jerome Fawley.

PRINCETON: Princeton 77–49 North Posey; Mount Vernon 99–45 New Harmony; Gibson Southern 62–43 Oakland City Wood; Princeton 56–54 Mount Vernon; Princeton 58–53 Gibson Southern. Officials: James Dunlap, John Schroeder, Ray Oppel, Paul Wahl.

RICHMOND: Richmond 97–67 Randolph Southern; Northeastern 80–52 Winchester; Union City 88–70 Cambridge City Lincoln; Hagerstown 67–57 Centerville; Richmond 72–55 Northeastern; Union City 76–66 Hagerstown; Richmond 62–52 Union City. Officials: Norman Hathcoat, George Taylor, Anthony Ortman, Robert Anderson.

SEYMOUR: Bedford-North Lawrence 64–30 Crothersville; Seymour 125–52 Medora; Jennings County 78–74 Brownstown Central; Bedford-North Lawrence 77–58 Seymour; Bedford-North Lawrence 92–64 Jennings County. Officials: Gary Woodling, James Roberts, Barry Lauber, Richard Foxen.

SHELBYVILLE: Shelbyville 75–52 Waldron; Triton Central 67–52 Southwestern (Shelbyville); Morristown 56–54 Shelbyville; Triton Central 58–44 Morristown. Officials: Bob Beeson, Don Hittle, Mark Robbins, Rudy Williams.

SOUTH ADAMS: Southern Wells, 68–63 Bluffton (ot); Bellmont 70–55 Norwell; South Adams 87–61 Adams Central; Bellmont 79–51 Southern Wells; South Adams 69–64 Bellmont. Officials: Sam Lower, Mike Burchette, Gene Huston, Tom Knox.

SOUTH BEND: St. Joseph's 71–65 Riley; LaSalle 87–65 Mishawaka; Clay 74–63 Mishawaka Marian; Adams 60–56 Washington; St. Joseph's 66–64 LaSalle; Clay 58–56 Adams; St. Joseph's 65–62 Clay. Officials: Clark Hamilton, David Gentile, Jerry Stieglitz, David Vendrely.

SOUTH DEARBORN: Rising Sun 64–50 Lawrenceburg; South Dearborn 87–58 Switzerland County; Rising Sun 68–50 South Dearborn. Officials: Mark Medley; Michael Alford. Steve Corya, Larry Sintz.

SOUTHPORT: Indianapolis Manual 78–32 Indiana School for the Deaf; Decatur Central 64–63 Perry Meridian; Southport 69–63 Howe; Manual 80–52 Park Tudor; Southport 73–57 Decatur Central; Southport 66–49 Manual. Officials: Bob Carr, Mike Padfield, Brian Osswald, Raymond Norris.

SOUTHRIDGE: Jasper 75–53 Forest Park; Southridge 60–49 Perry Central; Jasper 66–46 Northeast Dubois; Jasper 49–37 Southridge. Officials: Stephen Fisher, Keith Bagby, Michael Quinn, Charles Meyer.

TERRE HAUTE: North 73–58 Riverton Parke; West Vigo 77–72 Northview; South 60–47 South Vermillion; West Vigo 58–57 North; South 84–67 West Vigo. Officials: John Evans, Doug Hudson, Pat Strong, Tom Walters.

TRI–COUNTY: Twin Lakes 60–56 North White; Benton Central 74–63 Tri–County; Frontier 73–54 South Newton; Benton Central 68–61 Twin Lakes; Frontier 77–66 Benton Central. Officials: Bob Marcinek, Ronald McDougal, Patrick Franklin, Skip Hopper.

TRITON: Tippecanoe Valley 64–55 Rochester; Warsaw 83–56 Triton; Tippecanoe Valley 81–64 Wawasee; Warsaw 56–50 Tippecanoe Valley. Officials: Larry Jones, Ken Dickman, Bryce Heller, Jeffrey Hull.

VALPARAISO: Valparaiso 73–26 Wheeler; Portage 52–51 Hobart; River Forest 67–57 Washington Twp.; Chesterton 47–32 Morgan Twp.; Valparaiso 65–47 Portage; Chesterton 72–47 River Forest; Valparaiso 87–59 Chesterton. Officials: Don O'Connor, Dale Blosser, Larry Parker, Jim Anderson.

Tourney Time

VINCENNES: Vincennes Rivet 58–48 North Knox; Vincennes 78–54 South Knox; Vincennes 53–51 Vincennes Rivet. Officials: Mel Redman, Gary Hamilton, David Hevron, David Bromm.
WASHINGTON: Barr-Reeve 65–57 Shoals; Washington 76–66 North Daviess; Washington Catholic 55–45 Pike Central; Loogootee 56–39 Barr-Reeve; Catholic 68–63 Washington; Washington Catholic 63–61 Loogootee. Officials: Larry Maxwell, James Reid, Dennis Espenlaub, James Ralston.

1989 REGIONALS

ANDERSON: Alexandria 81–76 Delta; Kokomo 60–54 Noblesville; Kokomo 47–39 Alexandria.. Officials: Michael McCarty, Thomas Dull, Ray Tebbe, Ed Christoffel, John Lozier, Bill Wullner.
COLUMBUS: Triton Central 65–61 Bloomington North; Columbus North 85–81 Franklin; Triton Central 90–80 Columbus North. Officials: Bob Wolfe, John Crapo, Clifford Spears, James Ralston, John Evans, Temme Patterson.
EAST CHICAGO: Gary Wirt 68–56 Munster; East Chicago Central 79–56 Andrean: Central 61–53 Wirt. Officials: Mark Baltz, Kevin Weinberg; Mark Hay, Jerome Fawley, Richard Modricker, Larry Nixon.
ELKHART: Elkhart Memorial 76–66 Glenn; Westview 94–77 Warsaw; Memorial 92–67 Westview. Officials: Jay Smith, Jeffrey Simmons, Robert Boyle, Richard Cook, Jim Cox, Thomas May.
EVANSVILLE: Evansville Memorial 55–53 Princeton; Vincennes 54–52 Heritage Hills, Evansville Memorial 54–45 Vincennes. Officials: Gary Woodling, David Bromm. Carl March, Joe Reed, Jerry Taylor, Larry Maxwell.
FORT WAYNE: Whitko 49–44 DeKalb (ot); Fort Wayne Concordia 100–81 Fort Wayne Dwenger; Concordia 81–76 Whitko (ot). Officials: Doug Carl, Jon Davenport, William Sorukas, Dale Cramer, Jerry Cook, Rick Owens.
FRANKFORT: Lebanon 52–43 Crawfordsville: Tipton 67–59 Mooresville (ot); Tipton 59–56 Lebanon. Officials: Bob Klein, Gary Cheesman, Clarence Crain; Larry Johnson, Bob Carr, Ron Grimes.
INDIANAPOLIS: Brebeuf 60–46 Franklin Central; Lawrence North 71–61 Southport; Lawrence North 57–54 Brebeuf. Officials: Tom Urban, Russ Radtke, Herb Pruett, Ivan Burkle, Bob Beeson, Tim Smith.
LAFAYETTE: West Lafayette 69–66 Lowell; Frontier 64–59 Fountain Central; West Lafayette 63–53 Frontier. Officials: Bob Marcinek, James Campbell, John Goss, David Raabe, Don O'Connor, Norman Hathcoat.
MARION: Northfield 69–57 South Adams; Marion 64–58 Logansport; Marion 77–65 Northfield. Officials: Mark Medley, Duffey Ainsworth, Clark Hamilton David Vendrely, Paul Cox, Robert Frye.
MICHIGAN CITY: Michigan City Rogers 74–63 Valparaiso; South Bend St. Joseph's 96–59 LaCrosse; St. Joseph's 78–64 Rogers. Officials: Patrick Parks, Rick Scott, Mike Waisnora, Paul Danko, Mike Crouch, Larry Jones.
NEW CASTLE: Muncie Southside 46–42 New Castle: New Palestine 80–69 Greensburg; Southside 86–83 New Palestine (ot). Officials: Tom Schenkel, Mike Winger, Terry Magnuson,

Scott Robison, Steve Cherry, Mike Bohan.
RICHMOND: Batesville 61–55 Rising Sun. Connersville 79–71 Richmond; Connersville 83–72 Batesville. Officials: Roger Holder, Roger Pflughaupt, Tom Crouch, Tom Knox, James Wehsollek, David Hurst.
SEYMOUR: New Washington 71–61 New Albany; Floyd Central 76–72 Bedford-North Lawrence (ot); Floyd Central 80–68 New Washington. Officials: Doug Coddington, David Kavanaugh, Melvin Redman, David Lee, Gary Leistner, James Dunlap.
WASHINGTON: Paoli 62–54 Washington Catholic; North Harrison 73–66 Jasper; Paoli 67–56 North Harrison. Officials: Rex Nichols, Gary Hawn, Thomas Newlin, James Newlin, Don Nester, Leland Thompson.
WEST VIGO: Terre Haute South 83–55 South Putnam; Union (Dugger) 67–59 Bloomfield; Terre Haute South 67–51 Union (Dugger). Officials: Sam Lower, Richard Foxen, Michael Zehr, Philip Napariu, Stephen Fisher, Bill Nimnicht.

1989 SEMI–STATES

EVANSVILLE: Evansville Memorial 65–62 Terre Haute South; Floyd Central 76–51 Paoli; Floyd Central 88–70 Evansville Memorial. Officials: Lanny Rossman. Ron Crimes, James Wehsollek, David Hurst, Bob Carr, Bob Beeson.
INDIANAPOLIS: Lawrence North 82–56 Triton Central; Muncie Southside 82–53 Connersville; Lawrence North 51–37 Muncie Southside. Officials: Don O'Connor, Bill Nimnicht, John Lozier, Temme Patterson, Stephen Fisher, Gary Leistner.
LAFAYETTE: East Chicago Central 55–50 West Lafayette; Kokomo 57–50 Tipton; Kokomo 70–50 Central. Officials: Mike Crouch, Tim Smith, Dick Modricker, Jim Cox, Jerry Cook, Paul Cox.
SOUTH BEND: South Bend St. Joseph's 76–74 Marion (ot); Elkhart Memorial 84–75 Fort Wayne Concordia (ot); St. Joseph's 78–62 Memorial. Officials: Jerry Taylor, Rick Owens, John Evans, Larry Jones, Steve Cherry, Don Nester.

1989 FINALS—March 25

INDIANAPOLIS (Market Square Arena): Kokomo 73–70 Floyd Central; Lawrence North 81–62 South Bend St. Joseph's; Lawrence North 74–57 Kokomo. Officials: Steve Cherry, Jerry Cook, Bob Carr, Paul Cox, Steve Fisher, Gary Leistner.

1990 SECTIONALS

ANDERSON: Elwood 44–43 Frankton; Anderson 84–61 Alexandria; Madison Heights 60–43 Lapel; Highland 55–42 Pendleton Heights; Anderson 67–46 Elwood; Highland 74–71

Tourney Time

Madison Heights; Anderson 62–59 Highland. Officials: Mike Crouch, Richard Foxen, John Walker, Troy Ingram.

BEN DAVIS: Indianapolis Northwest 57–42 Speedway; Pike 86–43 Ben Davis 65–54 Brebeuf; Northwest 55–45 Ritter; Pike 63–55 Ben Davis; Pike 64–44 Northwest; Officials: Norm Hathcoat, Scott Mellinger, Ronald James, Michael Smith.

BLACKFORD: Blackford 53–52 Monroe Central; Delta 50–49 Jay County (3 ot); Wapahani 56–42 Wes–Del; Blackford 66–50 Delta; Wapahani 66–49 Blackford. Officials: Clark Hamilton, Judson Raver, Gaylord Fritz, Frank Hoagburg.

BOONVILLE: Castle 61–59 Boonville; Cannelton 64–62 Tecumseh (2ot); South Spencer 66–54 Tell City; Castle 61–51 Heritage Hills; South Spencer 68–43 Cannelton; Castle 55–52 South Spencer; Officials: Temme Patterson, Michael Quinn, Eric Ballenger, William Amerson.

BROWNSBURG: Brownsburg 55–34 Plainfield; Cascade 74–62 Avon; Mooresville 51–31 Danville; Brownsburg 50–42 Cascade; Brownsburg 62–54 Mooresville. Officials: Mark Baltz, Anthony Bova, Ron Kottlowski, Steven Smith.

CALUMET: Crown Point 65–59 Highland; Merrillville 52–48 Calumet; Lake Central 63–62 Munster; Griffith 66–50 Lake Station Edison; Merrillville 66–45 Crown Point; Lake Central 68–52 Griffith; Merrillville 58–51 Lake Central. Officials: William Sorukas, Ron Hosinski, Michael Alspaugh, Jeffrey Hull.

CARMEL: Noblesville 57–48 Westfield; Carmel 84–61 Sheridan; Hamilton Southeastern 75–59 Hamilton Heights; Noblesville 50–48 Carmel; Noblesville 57– 55 Hamilton Southeastern (ot). Officials: Clarence Crain, Jack Kopp. Larry Alsip, Dennis Maude.

CENTRAL (SWITZ CITY): Shakamak 74–44 Worthington; Linton-Stockton 66–58 L&M (ot); Central 70–59 Eastern (Bloomfield); Shakamak 53–52 Eastern (Bloomfield); Linton-Stockton 50–36 Central; Shakamak 57–55 Linton-Stockton (ot); Officials: David Bromm, David Hevron, Len Glazier, Raymond Norris.

COLUMBIA CITY: Carroll (Ft. Wayne) 76–52 Fort Wayne Blackhawk; Manchester 90–57 Churubusco; Whitko 59–50 Columbia City; Manchester 63–60 Carroll; Whitko 66–59 Manchester; Officials: Jon Davenport, Steve Godfroy, Mark McCammon, Don Resler.

COLUMBUS: Columbus East 72–55 Columbus North; Brown County 62–47 Hauser; East 81–60 Edinburgh; East 91–62 Brown County. Officials: Gary Woodling, Dale Goodwin, Jim Flanagan, Kent Smith.

CONNERSVILLE: Cambridge City Lincoln 46–43 Morton Memorial; Connersville 101–60 Franklin County; Hagerstown 64–59 Union County; Connersville 46–34 Cambridge City Lincoln; Connersville 60–54 Hagerstown; Officials: Rick Owens, Al Smith, Michael Baas, Roger McGriff.

CRAWFORD COUNTY: Eastern (Pekin) 76–70 South Central (Elizabeth); North Harrison 74–50 Lanesville; Crawford County 49–45 Corydon Central; North Harrison 74–63 Eastern (Pekin); North Harrison 77–73 Crawford County; Officials: James Dunlap, Jeffrey Culp, Fred Cooper, Michael Zehr.

EAST CENTRAL: South Ripley 60–46 Milan, Batesville 72–44 Jac-Cen-Del; East Central 41–40 South Ripley (ot); East Central 56–53 Batesville. Officials: Philip Napariu, Anthony Ortman, Jim Keifer, Russell Radtke.

EAST CHICAGO: Hammond Noll 82–53 Whiting; East Chicago Central 120–40 Hammond Clark; Noll 81–77 Central. Officials: Thomas May, Daniel Amrhein, Larry Parker, Jeffrey Simmons.

IHSAA Scores | 1990–1999

EAST NOBLE: East Noble 62–44 Lakeland; Prairie Heights 45–41 Bethany Christian; Westview 64–48 Fairfield; West Noble 78–37 Central Noble; East Noble 65–49 Prairie Heights; West Noble 87–82 Westview (2ot); East Noble 71–60 West Noble. Officials: Tim Smith, Dave Vendrely, Philip Marsh, Bryan Enterline.

ELKHART: Penn 60–53 Memorial; Concord 74–45 Goshen; Central 48–44 North Wood; Northridge 70–57 Jimtown; Concord 76–61 Penn; Central 66–57 Northridge; Concord 85–63 Central. Officials: Scott Robison, Roger Pflughaupt, David Gentile, Thomas Schenkel.

EVANSVILLE: Bosse 60–23 Mater Dei; Harrison 67–64 Memorial; North 46–32 Central; Reitz 74–43 Day School; Bosse 75–65 Harrison; North 47–46 Reitz; Bosse 56–44 North. Officials: Melvin Redman, Paul Wahl, James Roberts, Gary Leistner, Jim Mann.

FLOYD CENTRAL: Henryville 44–37 Borden; Charlestown 86–55 Silver Creek; Floyd Central 52–44 Graceland Christian; Charlestown 79–47 Henryville; Charlestown 65–60 Floyd Central. Officials: Michael McCarty, Lowell DePoy, Walter Bishop Jr., Steven Willett.

FORT WAYNE (#1): Concordia 70–67 Heritage (ot); Woodlan 61–60 South Side; Harding 59–57 Wayne; Concordia 45–42 Snider; Woodlan 69–59 Harding; Woodlan 62–52 Concordia. Officials: Mark Medley, Michael Alford, Michael Spann, Sr., Daniel Breneman.

FORT WAYNE (#2): Luers 77–39 Christian; North Side 69–50 Northrop; Dwenger 58–42 Elmhurst; New Haven 75–61 Luers; North Side 55–47 Dwenger; North Side 56–51 New Haven. Officials: Douglas Carl, Tony Garton, Terry Weldy, Rudy Williams.

FOUNTAIN CENTRAL: Fountain Central 58–44 Covington; Seeger 43–40 North Vermillion; Attica 74–65 Turkey Run; Fountain Central 78–53 Seeger; Fountain Central 71–65 Attica. Officials: Michael Bohan, Clifford Spears, Joe Oyler, Tom Rohr.

FRANKFORT: Clinton Central 43–41 Frankfort; Tipton 100–61 Tri–Central; Rossville 60–59 Clinton Prairie; Tipton 64–50 Clinton Central; Rossville 77–76 Tipton. Officials: Larry Nixon, James Robinson, Tom Walters, Bill Kachel.

FRANKLIN CENTRAL: Warren Central 64–63 Roncalli (ot); Franklin Central 70–52 Indianapolis Scecina; Beech Grove 76–36 Indianapolis Lutheran; Franklin Central 64–55 Warren Central (ot); Franklin Central 64–47 Beech Grove. Officials: Bob Beeson, Mel Botkin, Brad Groninger, Bob Carr.

DEKALB: Eastside 54–46 Garrett; Angola 52–49 Fremont; DeKalb 91–41 Howe Military; Hamilton 54–51 Leo; Eastside 56–52 Angola; DeKalb 67–52 Hamilton; DeKalb 71–59 Eastside. Officials: Mike Winger, Bryce Heller, David Trietsch, Fred Hamilton.

GARY: Gary Roosevelt 93–69 Mann; West Side 78–47 Wirt; Roosevelt 72–47 Wallace; Roosevelt 68–61 West Side. Officials: Mike Waisnora, Albert Yelich, Robert Modrowski, Jim Anderson.

GREENCASTLE: North Putnam 71–64 Owen Valley; Rockville 72–50 Greencastle; South Putnam 61–52 Cloverdale; North Putnam 68–53 Rockville; North Putnam 47–43 South Putnam. Officials: Lanny Rossman, Joseph Stafford; Rich Spay, Rick Normington.

GREENFIELD–CENTRAL: Eastern Hancock 55–30 New Palestine; Mt. Vernon (Fortville) 54–46 Greenfield–Central; Mt. Vernon (Fortville) 69–54 Eastern Hancock. Officials: Tom Urban, Tom Jerles, Patrick Strong, Jim Pitcher.

GREENSBURG: South Decatur 67–62 Rushville; Greensburg 88–77 North Decatur; Greensburg 73–55 South Decatur. Officials: Sam Lower, Mark Robbins, Michael McGriff, Mike Padfield.

GREENWOOD: Greenwood 55–52 Center Grove; Franklin 79–74 Indian Creek; Whiteland

583

Tourney Time

77–69 Greenwood; Franklin 88–77 Whiteland. Officials: Terry Magnuson, Bob Hallgarth, Jerry Wallace, David Berman.

HAMMOND: Andrean 66–52 Hammond Morton; Gavit 82–76 Hammond High; Andrean 57–56 Gavit. Officials: Nick Sweigart, Frank DeSantis, Robert Gootee, Fred Perry.

HUNTINGTON: Northfield 88–57 Southwood; Huntington 57–55 Homestead; Wabash 88–32 White's; Northfield 72–51 Huntington; Northfield 77–48 Wabash. Officials: Dick Modricker, Mike Burchette, Doug Bauman, Ken Dickman.

JEFFERSONVILLE: New Albany 74–63 Providence; Jeffersonville 81–67 Clarksville; New Albany 74–57 Jeffersonville. Officials: William Nimnicht, Barry Lauber, Danny Shields, Doug Coddington.

KANKAKEE VALLEY: Boone Grove 57–45 Kankakee Valley; Lowell 59–40 North Newton; Rensselaer 71–61 Hanover Central; Hebron 92–72 Kouts; Lowell 61–53 Boone Grover; Hebron 65–54 Rensselaer; Hebron 73–50 Lowell. Officials: John Goss, Ed Christoffel, Richard Calloway, Mark Martin.

KOKOMO: Kokomo 85–48 Eastern (Greentown); Western 67–62 Taylor (ot); Northwestern 56–55 Maconaquah; Western 63–52 Kokomo; Western 79–55 Northwestern. Officials: Tom Crouch, J.D. Collins, Rick Granger, Donald Schmidt.

LAFAYETTE: Central Catholic 80–39 Delphi; Lafayette Jefferson 80–45 Carroll (Flora); Harrison 60–40 West Lafayette; Jefferson 80–79 Catholic; Jefferson 81–67 Harrison. Officials: Don Nester, Kenneth Cobb, John Tucker, Bob Wolfe.

LAWRENCE NORTH: Lawrence North 61–53 North Central; Indianapolis Cathedral 50–39 Lawrence Central; Broad Ripple 58–44 Arlington; Tech 61–55 Chatard; Lawrence North 57–44 Cathedral; Tech 85–51 Broad Ripple; Lawrence North 78–60 Tech. Officials: Joe Reed, Ed Roush, Denis Schinderle, Mark Campbell.

LEBANON: Western Boone 65–56 Tri-West Hendricks; Lebanon 99–55 Zionsville; Lebanon 84–60 Western Boone. Officials: David Lee, Larry Johnson, Norman Delph, John Lozier.

LOGANSPORT: Caston 67–63 Peru; Cass 71–45 Pioneer; Logansport 61–53 North Miami; Caston 85–68 Cass; Logansport 76–68 Caston. Officials: Jim Cox, Stan Ames, Mike Fawcett, David Long.

MADISON: Scottsburg 55–49 Southwestern (Hanover); Madison 66–49 Madison Shawe; Austin 64–61 New Washington; Scottsburg 62–48 Madison; Scottsburg 69–65 Austin. Officials: Larry Maxwell, Ron Mahan, Larry Sintz, McKee Munk.

MARION: Mississinewa 83–59 Eastbrook; Oak Hill 80–53 Marion Bennett; Marion 105–66 Madison-Grant; Mississinewa 61–48 Oak Hill; Marion 95–60 Mississinewa. Officials: Gary Cheesman, Gene Huston, Thomas Dull, Harry Northington.

MARTINSVILLE: Bloomington South 82–65 Eminence; Martinsville 93–72 Bloomington North; Edgewood 68–64 Monrovia; Martinsville 70–64 South; Martinsville 82–81 Edgewood. Officials: Robert Frye, Steven Corya, Brad Sellers, Steve Cherry.

MICHIGAN CITY: Marquette 79–68 Westville; Elston 83–56 New Prairie; LaPorte 63–52 Rogers; Elston 109–62 Marquette; LaPorte 76–72 Elston. Officials: Dale Cramer, James Campbell, Edward Malek, Jerome Fawley.

MUNCIE: Burris 81–54 Cowan; Southside 76–60 Daleville; Central 82–68 Yorktown; Southside 75–55 Burris; Central 83–71 Southside. Officials: Roger Holder, Dennis Jackson, Jerry Stieglitz, Tom Knox.

NEW CASTLE: Shenandoah 67–59 Blue River; New Castle 87–26 Union (Modoc); Tri 54–48 Knightstown: New Castle 89–55 Shenandoah; New Castle 74–47 Tri. Officials: Ray Tebbe, Doug Flatter, Rick Shirk, Jerry Middleton.

NORTH JUDSON: North Judson 71–69 Culver Community; South Central (Union Mills) 59–50 West Central; LaCrosse 64–57 Oregon-Davis, Winamac 78–65 Knox; North Judson 85–50 South Central (Union Mills); LaCrosse 83–55 Winamac; North Judson 61–57 LaCrosse (ot). Officials: Larry Jones, Skip Hopper, Rand Coplen, Dale Blosser.

NORTH MONTGOMERY: McCutcheon 67–43 Crawfordsville; Southmont 56–55 North Montgomery; McCutcheon 45–43 Southmont. Officials: John Crapo, David Willoughby, Gary Hamilton, Haymon Fields.

PAOLI: Paoli 48–44 Mitchell; Orleans 77–69 Springs Valley; West Washington 72–69 Salem (2ot); Orleans 49–48 Paoli; West Washington 77–68 Orleans. Officials: Gary Hawn, Robert Davis, Larry Decker, John Lyskowinski.

PLYMOUTH: Bremen 53–38 Glenn; Plymouth 42–37 LaVille; Culver Military 67–60 Argos; Bremen 55–44 Plymouth; Bremen 42–39 Culver Military. Officials: Jay Smith, Brad Wilson, Jerry Karstens, Mark Hyman.

PRINCETON: Gibson Southern 66–54 North Posey; Oakland City Wood 67–64 Princeton (ot); Mt. Vernon 82–35 New Harmony; Wood 73–60 Gibson Southern: Wood 56–54 Mt. Vernon. Officials: Ron Grimes, Douglas Anoskey, Ron Pritchett, Stephen Fisher, Jay Ritter.

RICHMOND: Union City 62–47 Northeastern; Richmond 89–63 Randolph Southern; Winchester 52–51 Centerville; Richmond 84–49 Union City; Richmond 87–43 Winchester. Officials: Bill Wullner, Greg McAdams, Jerry Alberson, Kenneth Knapp.

SEYMOUR: Bedford-North Lawrence 77–55 Brownstown; Jennings County 88–59 Crothersville; Seymour 104–67 Medora; Bedford-North Lawrence 82–48 Jennings County; Bedford-North Lawrence 69–64 Seymour. Officials: David Kavanaugh, Kim Baker, Brad Farmer, Robert Anderson.

SHELBYVILLE: Southwestern (Shelbyville) 65–62 Morristown; Shelbyville 73–70 Triton Central (4ot); Waldron 87–74 Southwestern (Shelbyville); Shelbyville 71–69 Waldron (2ot). Officials: Bob Klein, Herb Pruett, Mike Fox, Paul Cox.

SOUTH ADAMS: South Adams 91–64 Adams Central; Bellmont 57–56 Norwell; Bluffton 60–58 Southern Wells; South Adams 70–66 Bellmont; South Adams 84–61 Bluffton. Officials: Dave Raabe, Keith Fields, Tom Muth, Gene Marsh.

SOUTH BEND: Washington 61–58 Mishawaka Marian (2ot); LaSalle 53–52 Adams; Clay 80–72 Mishawaka; Riley 79–57 St. Joseph's; LaSalle 49–48 Washington; Riley 57–42 Clay; Riley 74–67 LaSalle. Officials: Richard Cook, Paul Danko, Russ Teall, Jerry Cook.

SOUTH DEARBORN: Lawrenceburg 64–58 Rising Sun; South Dearborn 89–63 Switzerland County; South Dearborn 73–58 Lawrenceburg. Officials: Leland Thompson, Rex Blanton, Donald Hopkins, Don Hittle.

SOUTHPORT: Southport 80–46 Park Tudor; Decatur Central 95–44 Indiana School for the Deaf; Indianapolis Manual 68–53 Perry Meridian; Southport 60–48 Howe; Decatur Central 81–72 Manual; Southport 54–44 Decatur Central. Officials: John Evans, Dan VanTreese, Roderick Weiss, Ron McGriff.

SOUTHRIDGE: Southridge 64–60 Perry Central (2ot); Jasper 43–39 Northeast Dubois; Forest Park 66–58 Southridge; Forest Park 55–42 Jasper. Officials: James Newlin, Mark Mason,

Tourney Time

Dennis Espenlaub, Lester Baugh.
SOUTH VERMILLION: Northview 62–61 South Vermillion; West Vigo 102–59 Riverton Parke; West Vigo 69–68 Northview (ot). Officials: Rex Nichols, Phil Vidito, Patrick Franklin, Ed Scahill.
TERRE HAUTE: Union (Dugger) 60–57 Sullivan; North 70–46 Clay City; South 70–50 North Central (Farmersburg); North 60—54 Union (Dugger); North 59–55 South. Officials: Jerry Taylor. Brian Osswald, David Estes, David Hurst.
TRI–COUNTY: Benton Central 86–72 North White; Frontier 73–58 Twin Lakes; South Newton 63–37 Tri–County; Frontier 78–62 Benton Central; South Newton 70–60 Frontier. Officials: Ivan Burkle, Douglas Hudson, Mark Wise, Terry Bartell.
TRITON: Tippecanoe Valley 82–66 Rochester; Warsaw 92–60 Triton; Wawasee 66–65 Tippecanoe Valley; Warsaw 69–44 Wawasee. Officials: Mark Hay, Bob Dedaker, Fred Mohri, Jerry Christie.
VALPARAISO: Portage 59–24 Wheeler; Chesterton 79–49 Washington Twp.; Valparaiso 80–61 River Forest; Morgan Twp. 87–81 Hobart; Chesterton 70–69 Portage; Valparaiso 63–56 Morgan Twp.; Valparaiso 69–51 Chesterton. Officials: Rick Scott, Douglas Cook, Duffey Ainsworth, Bruce Klonowski.
VINCENNES: Vincennes 94–44 Vincennes Rivet; North Knox 48–45 South Knox (ot); Vincennes 70–58 North Knox. Officials: Tom Newlin, Otis Broughton, Jay Ritter, Jim Reid.
WASHINGTON: Loogootee 43–31 Washington Catholic; Washington 53–39 Shoals; Barr-Reeve 66–51 Pike Central; Loogootee 40–25 North Daviess; Washington 57–44 Barr-Reeve; Loogootee 55–41 Washington. Officials: Carl March, Daniel Henkle, Thomas Ault, Keith Bagby.

1990 REGIONALS

ANDERSON: Anderson 94–46 Wapahani; Western 64–58 Noblesville; Anderson 85–69 Western. Officials: Scott Robison, Gene Marsh, Tom Crouch, Frank, Hoagburg, Bob Beeson, Jerry Taylor.
COLUMBUS: Martinsville 94–77 Columbus East; Franklin 67–66 Shelbyville; Martinsville 82–78 Franklin. Officials: James Newlin, Steven Willett, Lanny Rossman David Hurst, Bill Wullner, Carl March.
EAST CHICAGO: Gary Roosevelt 62–48 Merrillville; Hammond Noll 76–66 Andrean; Gary Roosevelt 71–64 Noll. Officials: John Lozier, Dale Cramer, Jon Davenport, Kenneth Dickman, Tim Smith, Richard Cook.
ELKHART CENTRAL: Concord 72–53 Bremen; East Noble 74–65 Warsaw; Concord 62–40 East Noble. Officials: Mike Winger, Don Resler, Clark Hamilton, Bryan Enterline Nick Sweigart, David Raabe.
EVANSVILLE: Bosse 79–55 Vincennes ; Castle 77–75 Oakland City Wood; Evansville Bosse 81–67 Castle. Officials: John Crapo, Raymond Norris, Gary Hawn, John Lyskowinski, Ron Grimes, David Kavanaugh.
FORT WAYNE: Whitko 88–65 DeKalb; Fort Wayne North Side 67–55 Woodlan; Whitko 76–74 North Side. Officials: Dale Blosser, Gary Cheesman, Jeffrey Hull, Bob Klein, Dick Modricker, Rick Scott.

FRANKFORT: Lebanon 77–58 Rossville; Brownsburg 85–44 McCutcheon; Lebanon 62–50 Brownsburg. Officials: Joe Reed, David Berman, Thomas Newlin, Fred Hamilton, Larry Jones, Thomas May.

INDIANAPOLIS: Lawrence North 69–68 Pike; Southport 72–51 Franklin Central; Southport 57–51 Lawrence North. Officials: Sam Lower, Troy Ingram, Mark Medley, Jerry Middleton, Larry Maxwell, Rick Owens.

LAFAYETTE: Fountain Central 77–69 Hebron; Lafayette Jefferson 77–62 South Newton; Jefferson 68–57 Fountain Central. Officials: Mark Baltz, Tom Rohr, Terry Magnuson, Bob Anderson, Mike Waisnora, Mike Crouch.

MARION: Northfield 72–39 Logansport; Marion 80–52 South Adams; Northfield 73–64 Marion. Officials: Mark Hay, Brad Groninger, Ivan Burkle, Kent Smith, Roger Holder, Thomas Urban.

MICHIGAN CITY: South Bend Riley 112–100 Valparaiso; LaPorte 70–55 North Judson; Riley 81–63 LaPorte. Officials: Jay Smith, Bruce Klonowski, John Goss, Jim Anderson, Jim Cox, William Sorukas.

NEW CASTLE: New Castle 60–55 Muncie Central; Mt. Vernon (Fortville) 69–50 Greensburg; New Castle 78–66 Mt. Vernon. Officials: Leland Thompson, Harry Northington, Douglas Carl, Donald Schmidt, Norman Hathcoat, Don Nester.

RICHMOND: Connersville 62–59 South Dearborn; Richmond 62–51 East Central; Richmond 66–63 Connersville. Officials: Clarence Crain, Mike Padfield, David Lee, Rudy Williams, Mike Bohan, Robert Frye.

SEYMOUR: Scottsburg 48–46 New Albany; Bedford-North Lawrence 65–51 Charlestown; Bedford-North Lawrence 78–58 Scottsburg. Officials: Phil Napariu, Mike Smith, Rex Nichols, Keith Bagby, James Dunlap, Ray Tebbe.

TERRE HAUTE: Terre Haute North 73–60 North Putnam; Shakamak 55–50 West Vigo; North 48–36 Shakamak. Officials: David Bromm, James Reid, Larry Nixon, Dennis Maude, Temme Patterson, John Evans.

WASHINGTON: Loogootee 69–53 West Washington; North Harrison 81–75 Forest Park (ot); Loogootee 49–44 North Harrison. Officials: William Nimnicht, McKee Munk, Gary Woodling, Roger McGriff, Melvin Redman and Michael McCarty.

1990 SEMI–STATES

FORT WAYNE: Northfield 81–72 South Bend Riley; Concord 78–60 Whitko; Concord 54–52 Northfield. Officials: Larry Maxwell, Rick Owens, Bob Beeson, Michael McCarty, Bill Wullner, Don Nester.

INDIANAPOLIS: Southport 61–60 Martinsville (ot); New Castle 59–53 Richmond; Southport 82–68 New Castle. Officials: Ron Grimes, Nick Sweigart, Tim Smith, Carl March, James Dunlap, Temme Patterson.

LAFAYETTE: Lafayette Jefferson 78–74 Lebanon; Anderson 84–78 Gary Roosevelt; Anderson 79–75 Lafayette Jefferson. Officials: Bob Klein, Jerry Taylor, Jim Cox, John Evans, Larry Jones, Melvin Redman.

TERRE HAUTE: Bedford-North Lawrence 56–54 Terre Haute North; Evansville Bosse 36–28 Loogootee; Bedford North Lawrence 72–67 Bosse; Officials: Mike Bohan, Tom Urban, Mike Waisnora, Ray Tebbe, Norman Hathcoat, Roger Holder.

Tourney Time

1990 FINALS—March 25
41,046 tickets were sold, a national high school record.
    INDIANAPOLIS (Hoosier Dome): Concord 70–66 Anderson; Bedford-North Lawrence 58–55 Southport; Bedford-North Lawrence 63–60 Concord. Officials: James Dunlap, Roger Holder, Bill Wullner, Larry Jones, Norman Hathcoat, Temme Patterson.

1991 SECTIONALS
    ANDERSON: Frankton 64–59 Madison Heights; Elwood 57–48 Lapel; Highland 75–57 Alexandria; Anderson 66–56 Pendleton Heights; Frankton 57–37 Elwood; Highland 61–58 Anderson; Highland 58–55 Frankton. Officials: John Evans, Tony Bierschbach, Stan Ames, Paul Cox.
    BEN DAVIS: Brebeuf 61–57 Ben Davis (ot); Speedway 62–57 Ritter; Pike 70–52 Washington; Brebeuf 53–41 Northwest; Pike 46–32 Speedway; Brebeuf 67–38 Pike. Officials: Bob Beeson, Phil Vidito, Patrick Franklin, Roger Holder.
    BOONVILLE: South Spencer 51–41 Tecumseh; Castle 65–60 Cannelton; Boonville 64–56 Heritage Hills; South Spencer 46–31 Tell City; Boonville 67–61 Castle; South Spencer 54–52 Boonville. Officials: Bill Nimnicht, James Roberts, McKee Munk, Temme Patterson.
    BROWNSBURG: Brownsburg 88–62 Danville; Cascade 68–67 Plainfield (ot); Avon 63–53 Mooresville; Brownsburg 86–55 Cascade; Brownsburg 84–71 Avon. Officials: Lanny Rossman, Brad Farmer, Sam Berry, Doug Hudson.
    CALUMET: Merrillville 73–50 Lake Station Edison; Calumet 82–59 Highland; Munster 75–74 Griffith (ot); Lake Central 55–49 Crown Point; Merrillville 75–51 Calumet; Lake Central 88–50 Munster; Lake Central 60–54 Merrillville. Officials: Richard Cook, Mark Tulchinsky, Kevin Weinberg, Robert Modrowski.
    CARMEL: Carmel 101–60 Westfield; Noblesville 74–47 Hamilton Heights; Hamilton Southeastern 57–52 Sheridan; Noblesville 55–53 Carmel; Noblesville 58–37 Hamilton Southeastern. Officials: Troy Ingram, Steve Willett, Terry Johnson, Dan VanTreese.
    CLAY CITY: Sullivan 75–52 Union; North Central (Farmersburg) 86–66 Clay City; Sullivan 71–53 North Central. Officials: Don Nester, Anthony Bova, Michael McLean, Haymon Fields.
    COLUMBIA CITY: Columbia City 70–61 Churubusco; Manchester 60–48 Carroll (Ft. Wayne); Whitko 79–53 Fort Wayne Blackhawk; Manchester 57–54 Columbia City; Whitko 76–65 Manchester. Officials: Jim Cox, Bob Dedaker, Olin Roberts, J.D. Collins.
    COLUMBUS: East 108–59 Brown County; North 84–68 Hauser; East 84–48 Edinburgh; North 61–59 East. Officials: Terry Magnuson, Denis Schinderle, Kyle Ingram, John Lyskowinski.
    CONNERSVILLE: Connersville 102–45 Morton Memorial; Union County 79–57 Cambridge City Lincoln; Franklin County 67–64 Hagerstown; Connersville 84–38 Union County; Connersville 50–47 Franklin County, Officials: Mark Medley, Ken Knapp, Jerry Wallace, Bill Wullner.
    CRAWFORD COUNTY: Crawford County 46–43 North Harrison; Lanesville 65–63 South Central (Elizabeth); Eastern (Pekin) 52–48 Corydon Central (2ot); Crawford County 56–55 Lanesville; Eastern (Pekin) 54–43 Crawford County. Officials: Melvin Redman, Steve Meyer, Eric

Ballenger, Gary Woodling..

EAST CENTRAL: South Ripley 62–55 Jac-Cen-Del; East Central 70–60 Batesville; South Ripley 85–57 Milan; East Central 59–44 South Ripley. Officials: Roger McGriff, Michael McGriff, Don Hittle, Donald Hopkins.

EAST CHICAGO: East Chicago Central 82–74 Hammond Noll; Whiting 65–51 Hammond Clark; Central 56–38 Whiting. Officials: Bruce Klonowski, Michael Spann Sr., Philip Marsh, Larry Jones.

EAST NOBLE: Westview 86–51 Central Noble; Bethany Christian 61–46 Prairie Heights; East Noble 61–48 West Noble; Lakeland 75–64 Fairfield; Westview 62–60 Bethany Christian; East Noble 50–40 Lakeland; Westview 64–57 East Noble. Officials: Scott Robison, Ron Hosinski, Dale Zeigler, Don Resler.

ELKHART: Concord 85–24 Jimtown; Memorial 50–44 Central, Goshen 56–37 NorthWood; Penn 60–51 Northridge; Concord 60–54 Memorial; Penn 42–41 Goshen (ot); Concord 59–47 Penn. Officials: Jon Davenport, Michael Alspaugh, Rick Granger, Ed Christoffel.

EVANSVILLE: Central 71–55 Mater Dei; Bosse 59–44 North; Harrison 64–32 Evansville Day; Central 79–54 Reitz; Harrison 69–68 Bosse; Central 68–67 Harrison. Officials: Stephen Fisher, Michael Quinn, David Hevron, James Dunlap.

FORT WAYNE (#1): South Side 72–61 Woodlan; Wayne 59–53 Luers; Harding 46–44 Heritage; South Side 68–59 Dwenger; Harding 64–58 Wayne (ot); South Side 61–53 Harding. Officials: Fred Hamilton, Norm Delph, Dennis Jackson, William Kachel.

FORT WAYNE (#2): North Side 84–61 Northrop; Concordia 51–49 Snider; New Haven 70–42 Christian; Fort Wayne 74–31 Elmhurst; New Haven 66–64 Concordia (ot); New Haven 68–67 North Side (2ot). Officials: Jay Smith, Tom Jerles, Tom Dull, Jerry Alberson.

FOUNTAIN CENTRAL: Fountain Central 83–39 Seeger; Attica 66–55 North Vermillion; Covington 67–49 Turkey Run; Fountain Central 55–30 Attica; Fountain Central 55–43 Covington. Officials: Robert Anderson, Brian Osswald, Rich Spay, Ivan Burkle.

FRANKFORT: Tri–Central 47–42 Tipton (ot); Clinton Central 65–60 Clinton Prairie; Frankfort 68–61 Rossville; Clinton Central 71–53 Tri–Central; Frankfort 63—59 Clinton Central. Officials. Jerry Taylor, Richard Foxen, Mark Withers, Clifford Spears.

FRANKLIN CENTRAL: Indianapolis Scecina 45–43 Roncalli; Franklin Central 62–43 Beech Grove; Warren Central 63–51 Lutheran; Franklin Central 59–57 Scecina (2ot); Warren Central 47–44 Franklin Central. Officials: Mike Padfield, Gary Hamilton, Larry Sintz, Russ Radtke.

GARRETT: Angola 55–47 Eastside; Hamilton 62–56 Garrett; DeKalb 62–58 Howe Military; Leo 58–44 Fremont; Hamilton 70–68 Angola; DeKalb 55–54 Leo; Hamilton 61–58 DeKalb. Officials: Tim Smith, Judson Raver, Thomas Muth, Roger Pflughaupt.

GARY: West Side 47–41 Wirt; Roosevelt 81–44 Mann; West Side 96–67 Wallace; Roosevelt 79–69 West Side. Officials: William Sorukas, Fred Perry, Edward Malek, Dan Amrhein.

GREENCASTLE: Rockville 61–52 Greencastle, North Putnam 65–57 Cloverdale; South Putnam 41–40 Owen Valley; North Putnam 65–51 Rockville; South Putnam 60–58 North Putnam. Officials: David Lee, Joe Reed, David Estes, Steve Smith.

GREENFIELD–CENTRAL: Greenfield-Central 62–55 Eastern Hancock (ot); Mt. Vernon (Fortville) 76–51 New Palestine; Mt. Vernon 76–58 Greenfield-Central. Officials: David Raabe, Rex Blanton, Mark Robbins, Rick Shirk.

GREENSBURG: Greensburg 58–55 North Decatur; South Decatur 63–57 Rushville; South

Tourney Time

Decatur 60–57 Greensburg. Officials: Leland Thompson, Ron Kottlowski, Len Glazier, Ed Scahill.

HAMMOND: Andrean 79–58 Hammond Gavit; Hammond High 50–45 Morton; Andrean 77–68 Hammond High. Officials: Tom May, Mark Wise, Mark McCammon, Jeffery Simmons.

HUNTINGTON: Northfield 83–54 Wabash; Homestead 71–70 Southwood; Huntington North 90–44 White's; Northfield 71–44 Homestead; Northfield 72–61 North. Officials: Mike Winger, Gaylord Fritz, Richard Nelson, Tony Garton.

JAY COUNTY: Monroe Central 51–49 Wapahani; Delta 65–61 Jay County (ot); Blackford 75–60 Wes-Del; Monroe Central 45–39 Delta; Blackford 49–48 Monroe Central. Officials: Frank Hoagburg, Doug Flatter, Gene Marsh, Brian Enterline.

JEFFERSONVILLE: Floyd Central 85–64 Clarksville; Jeffersonville 121–56 Providence; Jeffersonville 79–60 Floyd Central. Officials: James Newlin, Frank Bodwell, Michael Baas, Lester Baugh.

KANKAKEE VALLEY: Rensselaer Central 63–48 Kankakee Valley; Kouts 88–79 Lowell, Hebron 61—42 North Newton; Boone Grove 59–53 Hanover Central; Rensselaer Central 57–55 Kouts; Hebron 80–74 Boone Grove; Rensselaer Central 75–56 Hebron. Officials: Mike Waisnora, Russ Teal, Randy Coplen, Dick Modricker.

KOKOMO: Eastern 72–66 Taylor; Kokomo 71–43 Northwestern; Maconaquah 57–55 Western; Kokomo 87–70 Eastern (Greentown); Kokomo 73–57 Maconaquah. Officials: Mark Baltz, Bob Wolfe, Larry Johnson, Gene Huston.

LAFAYETTE: Carroll (Flora) 83–73 Delphi; West Lafayette 50–48 Central Catholic; Lafayette Jefferson 80–68 Harrison; Carroll 72–69 West Lafayette; Jefferson 79–64 Carroll. Officials: Larry Nixon, Ronald James, Jerry Christie, Terry Bartell.

LAWRENCE NORTH: North Central 49–45 Lawrence Central; Lawrence North 57–56 Indianapolis Broad Ripple; Arlington 60–58 Chatard; Cathedral 54–50 Tech; North Central 61–57 Lawrence North; Arlington 44–42 Cathedral; North Central 66–52 Arlington. Officials: Harry Northington, Jack Kopp, Larry Alsip, Rudy Williams.

LEBANON: Tri West Hendricks 57–45 Zionsville; Western Boone 68–55 Lebanon; Tri West Hendricks 56–55 Western Boone. Officials: Bob Klein, James Campbell, Jack Urbin, Tony Ortman.

LOGANSPORT: Caston 76–65 Peru; Cass 66–59 Logansport; North Miami 94–58 Pioneer; Caston 88–64 Cass; Caston 77–65 North Miami. Officials: Tom Urban, Kenneth Cobb, Brad Wilson, James Robinson.

MADISON: Madison 72–55 Scottsburg; New Washington 85–70 Madison Shawe; Austin 81–71 Southwestern (Hanover); Madison 52–44 New Washington; Madison 50–47 Austin. Officials: Michael McCarty, Ed Roush, Dale Goodwin, Michael Alford.

MARION: Marion 76–48 Madison-Grant; Eastbrook 99–54 Marion Bennett; Oak Hill 63–61 Mississinewa; Marion 66–48 Eastbrook; Marion 81–61 Oak Hill. Officials: Kenneth Dickman, Tom Crouch, Doug Bauman, Tom Schenkel.

MARTINSVILLE: Bloomington North 90–49 Eminence; Bloomington South 67–58 Martinsville; Monrovia 80–71 Edgewood; North 82–62 South; North 70–56 Monrovia. Officials: Ray Tebbe, Kim Baker, Patrick Strong, Norman Hathcoat.

MICHIGAN CITY: LaPorte 82–76 Rogers, New Prairie 75–63 Westville; Elston 74–53 Marquette; LaPorte 101–61 New Prairie; LaPorte 91–74 Elston. Officials: John Goss, Duffey

IHSAA Scores | 1990–1999

Ainsworth, Marvin Davis, Jerry Cook.

MUNCIE: Central 83–57 Cowan; Southside 84–56 Burris; Yorktown 96–66 Daleville; Southside 77–74 Central; Southside 99–59 Yorktown. Officials: Rick Owens, Jim Keifer, Scott Mellinger, Steve Cherry.

NEW ALBANY: Silver Creek 62–54 Borden, New Albany 70–43 Graceland Christian; Charlestown 117–71 Henryville; New Albany 72–50 Silver Creek; New Albany 55–53 Charlestown. Officials: Larry Maxwell, Robert Davis, Brad Sellers, Greg McAdams.

NEW CASTLE: Tri 59–36 Union (Modoc), Blue River Valley 72–66 Knightstown; New Castle 82–78 Shenandoah, Tri 68–48 Blue River Valley, New Castle 69–41 Tri. Officials: Mike Crouch, David Berman, Keith Fields, Douglas Carl.

NORTH JUDSON: North Judson 70–51 Oregon Davis; Winamac 65–51 Culver Community; Knox 83–78 South Central (Union Mills); LaCrosse 65–53 West Central; North Judson 63–59 Winamac; LaCrosse 80–64 Knox; LaCrosse 56–54 North Judson (ot). Officials: Mark Hay, Dave Emery, Dale Ferraro, Rick Scott.

NORTH MONTGOMERY: McCutcheon 74–62 Crawfordsville; Southmont 78–59 North Montgomery; McCutcheon 73–61 Southmont. Officials: Tom Rohr, Joe Stafford, Paul Mills, Kent Smith.

PAOLI: Salem 68–53 Orleans; Springs Valley 61–60 Mitchell (ot); Paoli 48–46 West Washington; Salem 71–67 Springs Valley; Paoli 55–50 Salem. Officials: James Reid, Daniel Henkle, Thomas Ault, Paul Wahl.

PLYMOUTH: Culver Military Academy 57–44 Argos; LaVille 41–37 Bremen; Glenn 69–66 Plymouth; Culver Military 32–29 LaVille; Glenn 51–47 Culver Military.. Officials: Dale Blosser, Jeffrey Hull, Steve Godfroy, Dave Vendrely.

PRINCETON: Oakland City Wood 51–50 Gibson Southern; Mt. Vernon 67–47 New Harmony; Princeton 64–40 North Posey; Mt. Vernon 77–53 Oakland City Wood; Princeton 46–40 Mt. Vernon. Officials: Gary Leistner, Keith Bagby, Darrell Stone, Jay Ritter.

RICHMOND: Randolph Southern 71–65 Centerville; Richmond 87–44 Winchester; Union City 56–49 Northeastern; Richmond 107–40 Randolph Southern; Richmond 92–24 Union City. Officials: Sam Lower, Mark Campbell, Douglas Zook, Dan Breneman.

SEYMOUR: Seymour 88–35 Medora, Jennings County 50–45 Bedford-North Lawrence; Brownstown Central 68–33 Crothersville; Jennings County 66–58 Seymour; Brownstown Central 77–73 Jennings County. Officials: Rex Nichols, Otis Broughton, Al Smith, Doug Coddington.

SHELBYVILLE: Southwestern (Shelbyville) 86–71 Waldron; Shelbyville 72–69 Morristown; Triton Central 70–69 Southwestern (ot); Shelbyville 56–47 Triton Central. Officials: Brad Groninger, Tom Walters, John Kane, John Walker.

SOUTH ADAMS: Southern Wells 60–57 South Adams; Norwell 69–57 Adams Central; Bellmont 70–38 Bluffton; Norwell 64–53 Southern Wells; Bellmont 73–66 Norwell. Officials: Gary Cheesman, Roderick Weiss, Patrick Dumoulin, David Gentile.

SOUTH BEND: Mishawaka 67–61 Adams; St. Joseph's 49–45 Mishawaka Marian; Riley 102–64 LaSalle; Clay 80–49 Washington; St. Joseph's 64–53 Mishawaka; Riley 97–76 Clay; Riley 82–60 St. Joseph's. Officials: Clark Hamilton, Douglas Cook, Dave Trietsch, Albert Yelich.

SOUTH DEARBORN: Lawrenceburg 62–48 Rising Sun, South Dearborn 85–66 Switzerland County; Lawrenceburg 68–65 South Dearborn. Officials: Mike Smith, Jerry Middleton, Kevin Moore, Bob Hallgarth.

Tourney Time

SOUTHPORT: Perry Meridian 54–47 Decatur Central; Park Tudor 75–40 Indiana School for the Deaf; Southport 64–55 Indianapolis Manual; Perry Meridian 60–52 Howe; Southport 55–52 Park Tudor; Southport 57–54 Perry Meridian. Officials: Philip Napariu, Jim Flanagan, Phil Dant, Herb Pruett.
SOUTHRIDGE: Forest Park 67–66 Perry Central; Northeast Dubois 44–41 Jasper; Southridge 73–44 Forest Park; Southridge 47–36 Northeast Dubois. Officials: David Kavanaugh, Ronald Mahan, Lowell DePoy, William Amerson.
TERRE HAUTE SOUTH: Northview 64–54 South Vermillion, West Vigo 78–61 Riverton Parke; Terre Haute South 64–50 Terre Haute North; Northview 75–73 West Vigo; South 67–49 Northview. Officials: Clarence Crain, Mike Fox, Dennis Maude, Ron McGriff.
TRI-COUNTY: Twin Lakes 74–53 Tri–County; Benton Central 39–36 North White; South Newton 56–37 Frontier; Twin Lakes 55–42 Benton Central; Twin Lakes 56–44 South Newton; Officials: Jim Anderson, Mark Hyman, Richard Calloway, Paul Danko.
VALPARAISO: Chesterton 78–28 Washington Twp.; Portage 74–48 Morgan Twp.; Hobart 54–31 Wheeler; Valparaiso 65–55 River Forest; Portage 61–42 Chesterton; Hobart 65–60 Valparaiso; Portage 67–64 Hobart (2ot). Officials: Dale Cramer, Fred Mohri, Tom Behny, Jerome Fawley.
VINCENNES: North Knox 42–39 Vincennes Rivet; Vincennes 69–46 South Knox; Vincennes 49–25 North Knox. Officials: John Crapo, Fred Cooper, Jim Mann, Dennis Espenlaub.
WARSAW: Triton 78–73 Wawasee; Warsaw 66–65 Rochester; Tippecanoe Valley 74–71 Triton; Warsaw 79–76 Tippecanoe Valley. Officials: Donald Schmidt, Bryce Heller, Bob Stambazze, Jerry Stieglitz.
WASHINGTON: Washington 47–39 Shoals; Loogootee 54–44 Barr-Reeve; Washington Catholic 58–40 Pike Central; Loogootee 48–29 Washington; Washington Catholic 54–51 Loogootee. Officials: Ron Grimes, Larry Decker, Chip Sweet, Dan Shields.
WHITELAND: Greenwood 75–64 Whiteland; Franklin 40–38 Indian Creek; Greenwood 38–36 Center Grove; Greenwood 59–44 Franklin. Officials: Robert Frye, Jeff Culp, Michael Lewis, Jim Pitcher.
WHITE RIVER VALLEY: North Daviess 41–39 Shakamak; White River Valley 75–45 Eastern (Bloomfield); Bloomfield 71–46 Linton Stockton; White River Valley 46–45 North Daviess; White River Valley 35–21 Bloomfield. Officials: Carl March, Steve Corya, Walter Bishop, David Hurst.

1991 REGIONALS

ANDERSON: Blackford 60–59 Kokomo; Anderson Highland 64–50 Noblesville; Highland 74–49 Blackford. Officials: Tim Smith, Russ Radtke, Mike Crouch, Tom Schenkel, Roger Pflughaupt, Tom Rohr.
COLUMBUS: Shelbyville 55–48 Columbus North; Bloomington North 60–53 Greenwood; Shelbyville 62–60 Bloomington North. Officials: Stephen Fisher, Terry Bartell, James Reid, Douglas Hudson, Rick Owens, Mark Baltz.
EAST CHCIAGO: Andrean 57–53 Lake Central; Gary Roosevelt 81–80 East Chicago Central (2ot); Roosevelt 86–57 Andrean. Officials: William Sorukas, Jerome Fawley, Jerry Taylor, Jeffrey Simmons, Jay Smith, Clarence Crain.

ELKHART: Glenn 68–62 Warsaw; Concord 70–57 Westview; Concord 65–50 Glenn. Officials: Scott Robison, Dan Amrhein, Ken Dickman, Al Yelich, Jim Cox, Jim Anderson.

EVANSVILLE: Vincennes 64–55 South Spencer; Princeton 56–41 Evansville Central; Vincennes 54–43 Princeton. Officials: Ron Grimes, Lester Baugh, James Newlin, Ron McGriff, Larry Maxwell, Carl March.

FORT WAYNE: Whitko 75–72 Fort Wayne South Side; New Haven 64–53 Hamilton; Whitko 73–72 New Haven. Officials: Jon Davenport, James Robinson, Jerry Cook, Dale Cramer, Tom Urban, Bruce Klonowski.

FRANKFORT: Brownsburg 70–54 Frankfort; McCutcheon 76–48 Tri-West Hendricks; 90–63 McCutcheon. Officials: Mark Medley, J.D. Collins, Michael McCarty, Herb Pruett, John Evans, Mike Waisnora.

LAFAYETTE: Rensselaer Central 91–88 Lafayette Jefferson; Twin Lakes 57–56 Fountain Central; Rensselaer Central 64–62 Twin Lakes. Officials: John Crapo, Rick Scott, Fred Hamilton, William Kachel, John Goss, Sam Lower.

LAWRENCE: Brebeuf 63–45 Warren Central; Southport 59–56 North Central (Indianapolis) Brebeuf 48–44 Southport. Officials: Larry Nixon, Dan VanTreese, Mike Padfield, Tony Ortman, Gary Cheesman, Mark Hay.

MARION: Marion 78–50 Northfield; Caston 77–69 Bellmont; Marion 67–55 Caston. Officials: Mike Winger, Rick Shirk, Michael Smith, David Vendrely, Ray Tebbe, Richard Cook.

MICHIGAN CITY: LaPorte 83–71 LaCrosse; Portage 65–62 South Bend Riley; LaPorte 77–56 Portage. Officials: Harry Northington, Don Hopkins, Frank Hoagburg, Ed Christoffel, Tom May, David Raabe.

NEW CASTLE: Mt. Vernon (Fortville) 57–51 Muncie Southside (ot); South Decatur 68–66 New Castle; Mt. Vernon (Fortville) 55–49 South Decatur. Officials: Jerry Middleton Doug Coddington, Roger McGriff, Greg McAdams, Troy Ingram, Rex Nichols.

RICHMOND: Richmond 67–60 Connersville; East Central 66–56 Lawrenceburg; Richmond 91–45 East Central. Officials: Donald Schmidt, Tony Garton, Clark Hamilton, Bryan Enterline, Lanny Rossman, Brad Groninger

SEYMOUR: Jeffersonville 94–70 Brownstown; New Albany 66–42 Madison; Jeffersonville 84–64 New Albany. Officials: Bob Anderson, Gary Leistner, Bill Nimnicht, Paul Wahl, Bob Beeson, David Kavanaugh.

WASHINGTON: Washington Catholic 54–40 Eastern (Pekin); Paoli 53–50 Southridge (ot); Washington Catholic 74–58 Paoli. Officials: Philip Napariu, Ed Scahill, Bob Klein, Dennis Espenlaub, Don Nester, David Lee.

WEST VIGO: Terre Haute South 59–44 South Putnam; White River Valley 75–58 Sullivan; Terre Haute South 90–76 White River Valley. Officials: Melvin Redman, Steve Cherry, Robert Frye, Kent Smith, Leland Thompson, Terry Magnuson.

1991 SEMI—STATES

EVANSVILLE: Vincennes 76–66 Washington Catholic; Terre Haute South 96–77 Jeffersonville; Terre Haute South 93–87 Vincennes. Officials: John Evans, Mark Baltz, Ray Tebbe, Rex Nichols, Jim Cox, Troy Ingram.

LAFAYETTE: Gary Roosevelt 42–41 Anderson Highland; Brownsburg 75–54 Rensselaer;

Tourney Time

Gary Roosevelt 69–61 Brownsburg. Officials: Lanny Rossman, Brad Groninger, Mike Crouch, Tom Rohr, Rick Owens, Don Nester.

INDIANAPOLIS: Brebeuf 56–46 Shelbyville; Mt. Vernon (Fortville) 75–73 Richmond; Brebeuf 73–58 Mt. Vernon. Officials: Clarence Crain, David Raabe, Gary Cheesman, Carl March, Thomas May, Tom Urban.

SOUTH BEND: Whitko 87–73 LaPorte, Marion 57–49 Concord; Whitko 67–58 Marion. Officials: Leland Thompson, Mark Hay, John Goss, Mike Waisnora, Bob Beeson, Larry Maxwell.

1991 FINALS—March 23

INDIANAPOLIS (Hoosier Dome): Brebeuf 52–39 Terre Haute South, Gary Roosevelt 83–53 Whitko, Gary Roosevelt 51–32 Brebeuf. Officials: Thomas May, Larry Maxwell, Jim Cox, Don Nester, Bob Beeson, Rick Owens.

1992 SECTIONALS

ANDERSON: Madison Heights 52–41 Frankton; Highland 69–59 Alexandria; Anderson 89–34 Elwood; Highland 67–58 Madison Heights; Anderson 53–52 Highland. Officials: Rex Nichols, Patrick Franklin, David Estes, Larry Maxwell.

BEDFORD NORTH LAWRENCE: Bloomington South 79–53 Eastern (Bloomfield); Bloomington North 71–53 Brown County; Bedford North Lawrence 70–61 Edgewood; Bloomington South 60–49 Bloomington North; South 54–51 Bedford North Lawrence. Officials: Terry Magnuson, Gary Woodling, Jay Ritter, McKee Munk.

BEN DAVIS: Ben Davis 70–59 Ritter; Northwest 65–43 Pike; Ben Davis 73–52 Speedway; Ben Davis 73–51 Northwest. Officials: Clarence Crain, Joe Reed, Arnold Freeman Jr., Steven Smith.

BOONVILLE: Gibson Southern 58–55 South Spencer (ot); Heritage Hills 58–46 Tecumseh; Princeton 71–56 Boonville; Heritage Hills 61–47 Gibson Southern; Princeton 71–50 Heritage Hills. Officials: Stephen Fisher, John Lyskowinski, Ronald Pritchett, Charles Meyer.

BROWNSBURG: Danville 50–47 Tri-West Hendricks; Plainfield 99–68 Cascade; Brownsburg 70–50 Avon; Plainfield 78–44 Danville; Brownsburg 82–67 Plainfield. Officials: Ron McGriff, Michael McGriff; Roger McGriff, Dave Berman.

CALUMET: Lake Central 78–61 Calumet; Hammond Morton 66–56 Griffith; Highland 58–46 Munster; Lake Central 60–49 Hammond Morton; Highland 56–44 Lake Central. Officials: Dale Cramer, Mark McCammon, Dale Ferraro, Jim Campbell.

CARMEL: Carmel 76–42 Hamilton Heights; Westfield 55–53 Hamilton Southeastern; Noblesville 80–52 Sheridan; Carmel 81–48 Westfield; Carmel 61–52 Noblesville. Officials: Norman Hathcoat, John Walker, Anthony Bova, Jerry Middleton.

COLUMBIA CITY: 65–56 Churubusco; Whitko 43–40 Columbia City; Tippecanoe Valley 76–50 Central Noble; Manchester 73–69 Whitko; Manchester 64–59 Tippecanoe Valley. Officials: Richard Modricker, Rick Granger, Robert Neff, Dave Vendrely.

COLUMBUS: Southwestern (Shelbyville) 59–52 Edinburgh; Columbus East 77–39 Hauser; Columbus North 57–38 Waldron; Southwestern 46–45 East; North 56–37 Southwestern. Officials: Michael S. Smith, Ron Kottlowski, Walter Bishop Jr., Tom Walters.

CONNERSVILLE: Franklin County 57–54 Hagerstown; Rushville 64–51 Cambridge City; Connersville 53–37 Union County; Rushville 70–58 Franklin County; Connersville 49–44 Rushville. Officials: Roger Holder, Donald Hopkins, Dale Goodwin, Rick Shirk.

CRAWFORD COUNTY: Perry Central 78–65 Crawford County; Tell City 61–55 Cannelton; Corydon 42–40 North Harrison (ot); Perry Central 59–58 Tell City (2ot); Corydon 56–49 Perry Central. Officials: Bill Nimnicht, Mike Quinn, Robert Davis, Fred Cooper and Alan Agee.

EAST CHICAGO: East Chicago Central 100–44 Hammond Clark; Hammond High 72–63 Hammond Gavit (2ot); Hammond Noll 60–59 Whiting; Central 76–60 Hammond High; Central 64–60 Noll. Officials: John Goss, Mark Wise, Steve Kvachkoff, Fred Perry.

EAST NOBLE: West Noble 62–53 East Noble; Lakeland 62–49 Howe Military; Westview 66–64 Prairie Heights; Lakeland 71–58 West Noble; Westview 52–49 Lakeland. Officials: Jerome Fawley, David Gentile, Thomas Muth, William Sorukas.

ELKHART: Mishawaka 61–53 Central; Concord 53–52 Memorial; Penn 49–46 Mishawaka Marian; Concord 66–54 Mishawaka; Penn 52–40 Concord. Officials: Clark Hamilton, Robert Stambazze, Marvin Davis, Bryan Enterline.

EVANSVILLE (#1): Reitz 65–63 North Posey; Central 83–56 New Harmony; Mt. Vernon 62–52 Mater Dei; Central 60–52 Reitz; Central 68–50 Mt. Vernon. Officials: Gary Leistner, Paul Wahl, Darrell Stone, Ron Mahan.

EVANSVILLE (#2): Harrison 46–42 Memorial; Castle 58–41 Bosse; North 75–53 Day School; Harrison 43–39 Castle; Harrison 49–42 North. Officials: David Kavanaugh, Lowell DePoy, Brad Farmer, Eric Ballenger.

FORT WAYNE NORTH SIDE: Northrop 56–49 Concordia; Dwenger 54–50 Snider; North Side 56–55 Carroll; Northrop 72–57 Dwenger; Northside 74–43 Northrop. Officials: Mike Crouch, Steve Godfroy, Jack Urbin, Jim Cox.

FORT WAYNE WAYNE: Wayne 57–34 Fort Wayne Christian; Luers 54–53 Elmhurst; Homestead 61–57 South Side; Wayne 70–56 Luers; Homestead 66–61 Wayne. Officials: David Raabe, Dennis Jackson, Richard Borror, Tom Crouch.

FOUNTAIN CENTRAL: Benton Central 55–46 South Newton; Attica 72–71 Seeger (ot); Fountain Central 74–47 Covington; Benton Central 55–48 Attica; Benton Central 68–57 Fountain Central. Officials: Leland Thompson, Frank Bodwell, Patrick Dumoulin, Denis Schinderle.

FRANKFORT: Clinton Central 78–60 Clinton Prairie; Frankfort 91–68 Tri Central; Rossville 61–53 Tipton; Frankfort 78–68 Clinton Central; Rossville 64–61 Frankfort. Officials: Robert Anderson, Len Glazier, Michael Smith, Brian Osswald.

FRANKLIN CENTRAL: Indianapolis Cathedral 42–40 Franklin Central; Chatard 68–60 Tech; Warren Central 84–82 Arlington (ot); Cathedral 82–59 Chatard; Cathedral 70–38 Warren Central. Officials: Sam Lower, Mark Campbell, Bob Hallgarth, Rick Owens.

FRANKLIN: Roncalli 69–46 Indian Creek; Whiteland 54–53 Franklin; Center Grove 54–43 Greenwood; Whiteland 79–77 Roncalli (3ot); Center Grove 62–55 Whiteland. Officials: Dennis Maude, Rick Normington, Rodney Chamberlain, Haymon Fields.

GARRETT: DeKalb 79–64 Fremont; Hamilton 54–53 Angola; Garrett 50–33 Eastside; Hamilton 56–55 DeKalb; Garrett 56–55 Hamilton. Officials: Frank Hoagburg, Tom Knox, Olin Roberts, Scott Robison.

GARY: Roosevelt 62–26 Mann; West Side 60–55 Wirt; Andrean 71–63 Wallace; West Side 64–50 Roosevelt; West Side 59–58 Andrean (ot). Officials: Jeffrey Hull, Fred Mohri, Michael

Tourney Time

Alspaugh, Bruce Klonowski.

GOSHEN: North Wood 55–51 Fairfield; Goshen 48–32 Bethany Christian; Northridge 57–47 Jimtown; Goshen 66–57 North Wood; Goshen 61–37 Northridge. Officials: Tim Smith, Dave Trietsch, Gaylord Fritz, Jerry Stieglitz.

GREENCASTLE: Greencastle 64–48 Rockville; South Putnam 51–47 North Putnam; Turkey Run 73–61 North Vermillion; Greencastle 42–39 South Putnam; Turkey Run 27–24 Greencastle. Officials: Larry Nixon, John Crapo, Sam Berry, Gary Hamilton.

GREENFIELD–CENTRAL: Mt. Vernon (Fortville) 70–62 Greenfield-Central; Lapel 79–76 New Palestine; Pendleton Heights 89–70 Eastern Hancock; Mt. Vernon 71–60 Lapel (ot); Mt. Vernon 86–52 Pendleton Heights. Officials: Ken Smith, Stan Ames, Larry Alsip, Dan VanTreese.

GREENSBURG: Jac-Cen-Del 72–56 Batesville; North Decatur 69–52 South Decatur; South Ripley 60–57 Greensburg; Jac-Cen-Del 85–70 North Decatur; Jac-Cen-Del 63–46 South Ripley. Officials: Richard Foxen, Michael Lewis, Jack Kopp, Phil Vidito.

HUNTINGTON: Blackford 64–46 Southwood; Northfield 96–43 White's; Huntington North 64–53 Wabash; Northfield 76–65 Blackford; Northfield 58–56 North. Officials: Jay Smith, Brad Wilson, Robert Childers, Mark Hyman.

JAY COUNTY: Monroe Central 72–59 Union City; Wes-Del 79–51 Wapahani; Jay County 66–56 Delta; Monroe Central 61–59 Wes-Del; Jay County 72–56 Monroe Central. Officials: Paul Cox, Thomas Dull, Jim Keifer, Tony Garton.

JEFFERSONVILLE: Charlestown 65–64 Silver Creek (ot); Providence 58–56 Clarksville (ot); Jeffersonville 77–39 Borden; Providence 58–56 Charlestown; Jeffersonville 92–58 Providence. Officials: Michael McCarty, James Reid, Kevin Moore, Ed Roush.

KANKAKEE VALLEY: Lowell 68–63 Kouts; Boone Grove 66–63 Hebron; Kankakee Valley 54–40 North Newton; Lowell 70–42 Boone Grove; Kankakee Valley 81–77 Lowell (2ot). Officials: Mark Hay, Mark Withers, Ron Stevens, Tom May.

KOKOMO: Kokomo 76–42 Taylor; Maconaquah 78–64 Eastern (Greentown); Northwestern 67–57 Western; Kokomo 79–68 Maconaquah; Kokomo 60–42 Northwestern. Officials: Ivan Burkle, Phillip Dant, John Kane, Herb Pruett.

LAFAYETTE: West Lafayette 71–61 Carroll (Flora); McCutcheon 50–46 Harrison; Lafayette Jefferson 70–61 Central Catholic; West Lafayette 58–50 McCutcheon; Jefferson 95–59 West Lafayette. Officials: Ray Tebbe, Patrick Strong, William Terry Johnson, Paul Danko.

LAWRENCE NORTH: North Central 65–31 Lawrence Central; Lawrence North 76–60 Broad Ripple; Park Tudor 73–49 Indiana School for the Deaf; Lawrence North 59–49 North Central; Lawrence North 60–42 Park Tudor. Officials: Robert Frye, Larry Sintz, Rich Spay, James Robinson.

LEBANON: Lebanon 83–74 Southmont; Crawfordsville 71–58 North Montgomery; Zionsville 61–58 Western Boone (ot); Lebanon 54–49 Crawfordsville; Lebanon 77–56 Zionsville. Officials: Ronald James, Kyle Ingram, Michael Dellinger, Lanny Rossman.

LOGANSPORT: Logansport 67–58 North Miami; Pioneer 58–48 Cass; Caston 59–56 Peru (2ot); Logansport 69–54 Pioneer; Caston 66–61 Logansport. Officials: Terry Bartell, Bob Wolfe, Gene Huston, Michael Spann.

MADISON: Southwestern 87–48 Madison Shawe; Madison 89–33 Henryville; Scottsburg 85–84 New Washington; Southwestern (Hanover) 68–66 Madison; Scottsburg 101–80 Southwestern (Hanover). Officials: Phil Napariu, Mike Baas, Greg Taylor, Mike Fox.

MARION: Madison Grant 58–52 Mississinewa; Marion 93–49 Marion Bennett; Oak Hill

71–61 Eastbrook; Marion 90–87 Madison Grant (2ot); Marion 89–84 Oak Hill. Officials: Thomas Urban, Doug Zook, Dale Zeigler, Don Schmidt.

MARTINSVILLE: Owen Valley 75–52 Eminence; Monrovia 80–74 Cloverdale; Mooresville 65–60 Martinsville; Owen Valley 66–58 Monrovia; Mooresville 49–48 Owen Valley. Officials: Mike Padfield, Michael McLean, Mike Bohan, Joseph Stafford.

MERRILLVILLE: Lake Station 61–54 River Forest; Hobart 45–44 Merrillville (ot); Crown Point 76–42 Hanover; Hobart 48–26 Lake Station; Hobart 65–48 Crown Point. Officials: Jeffrey Simmons, Duffey Ainsworth, Tom Behny, Al Yelich.

MICHIGAN CITY: Michigan City Marquette 60–31 New Prairie; Michigan City Elston 62–58 LaPorte; Michigan City Rogers 76–62 Westville; Elston 76–56 Marquette; Elston 68–51 Rogers. Officials: Jon Davenport, Russ Teall, Ron Hosinski, Bryce Heller.

MUNCIE: Burris 71–63 Daleville; Central 76–39 Cowan; Southside 88–53 Yorktown; Central 76–45 Burris; Central 56–48 Muncie Southside. Officials: Russell Radtke, Kenneth Knapp, Jerry Wallace, Keith Fields.

NEW ALBANY: New Albany 77–59 Floyd Central; South Central (Elizabeth) 34–28 Graceland Christian; Eastern (Pekin) 58–40 Lanesville; New Albany 46–38 South Central; New Albany 59–36 Eastern (Pekin). Officials: James Dunlap, Lester Baugh, Jeffrey Culp, Kim Baker.

NEW CASTLE: Knightstown 77–44 Morton Memorial; Blue River 76–69 Shenandoah; New Castle 84–52 Tri; Knightstown 65–47 Blue River; New Castle 69–40 Knightstown. Officials: Gary Cheesman, Kenneth Cobb, Larry Johnson, Gene Marsh.

NEW HAVEN: Woodlan 62–52 Harding; New Haven 66–59 Heritage; Fort Wayne Blackhawk 62–52 Leo; New Haven 68–45 Woodlan; New Haven 55–33 Blackhawk. Officials: Douglas Carl, Jerry Alberson, Doug Flatter, Douglas Bauman.

NORTH JUDSON: Winamac 63–61 South Central (Union Mills); North Judson 52–28 West Central; Knox 102–52 LaCrosse; North Judson 84–70 Winamac; North Judson 83–76 Knox. Officials: Jim Anderson, Doug Cook, Rich Calloway, Dan Amrhein.

PAOLI: Paoli 71–56 Mitchell; Salem 62–59 Springs Valley; Orleans 61–53 West Washington; Paoli 85–59 Salem; Paoli 52–36 Orleans. Officials: Bob Klein, Dennis Espenlaub, Al Smith, Doug Coddington.

PLYMOUTH: Glenn 68–39 Culver Community; Plymouth 69–61 Bremen; LaVille 71–50 Oregon Davis; Plymouth 60–46 Glenn; Plymouth 63–58 LaVille. Officials: Jerry Cook, Bob Dedaker, Jeff Heiliger, Tom Schenkel.

RICHMOND: Winchester 61–43 Union (Modoc); Richmond 91–49 Northeastern; Randolph Southern 43–42 Centerville; Richmond 70–41 Winchester; Richmond 96–45 Randolph Southern. Officials: Brad Groninger, Jim Pitcher, Wayne Hobson, Bob Beeson.

SEYMOUR: Seymour 100–85 Austin; Brownstown 105–53 Medora; Jennings County 70–49 Crothersville; Seymour 80–63 Brownstown; Seymour 83–81 Jennings County (ot). Officials: Bill Wullner, Brad Sellers, Paul Mills, Greg McAdams.

SHELBYVILLE: Beech Grove 89–71 Indianapolis Lutheran; Morristown 65–64 Shelbyville; Scecina 61–50 Triton Central; Beech Grove 87–68 Morristown; Beech Grove 71–69 Scecina. Officials: Troy Ingram, Mark Robbins, Rex Blanton, Scott Mellinger.

SOUTH ADAMS: South Adams 56–42 Bluffton, Bellmont 97–66 Southern Wells; Norwell 64–60 Adams Central; South Adams 82–69 Bellmont; South Adams 63–47 Norwell. Officials: Fred Hamilton, Daniel Breneman, Mel Botkin, William Kachel.

Tourney Time

SOUTH BEND: Washington 71–65 Riley; St. Joseph's 62–59 Clay; Adams 81–62 LaSalle; St. Joseph's 68–60 Washington; St. Joseph's 62–42 Adams. Officials: Larry Jones, Randy Coplen, Edward Malek, Rick Scott.

SOUTH DEARBORN: Lawrenceburg 74–43 South Dearborn; Switzerland County 66–46 Milan; East Central 63–61 Rising Sun (2ot); Lawrenceburg 79–42 Switzerland County; Lawrenceburg 65–57 East Central. Officials: Ed Scahill. Mike Alford, J. Roderick Weiss, Tony Ortman.

SOUTHPORT: Perry Meridian 64–47 Southport; Indianapolis Washington 59–58 Howe (ot); Manual 61–57 Decatur Central; Perry Meridian 77–66 Washington; Manual 46–45 Perry Meridian. Officials: Steve Cherry, Chip Sweet, Richard Hawley, Norm Delph.

SOUTHRIDGE: Jasper 69–46 Oakland City Wood; Forest Park 47–37 Northeast Dubois; Southridge 49–36 Pike Central; Forest Park 63–61 Jasper; Southridge 55–40 Forest Park. Officials: Melvin Redman, James Mann II, Steven Corya, James Roberts.

TERRE HAUTE NORTH: Terre Haute South 81–56 Northview; West Vigo 75–72 Terre Haute North; South Vermillion 64–52 Riverton Parke; South 67–61 West Vigo; South 87–60 South Vermillion. Officials: John Evans, Danny Shields, Tony Bierschbach, Don Nester.

TWIN LAKES: Rensselaer 69–34 Frontier; Twin Lakes 58–52 Tri-County; North White 59–57 Delphi; Twin Lakes 78–75 Rensselaer; Twin Lakes 68–44 North White. Officials: Jerry Taylor, Clifford Spears, Gary Chambers, Harry Northington, Mike Gruver.

VALPARAISO: Chesterton 37–34 Wheeler; Washington Twp. 67–63 Morgan Twp; Portage 57–44 Valparaiso; Chesterton 78–40 Washington Twp.; Portage 59–44 Chesterton. Officials: Mike Waisnora, David Emery, Philip Marsh, Ed Christoffel.

VINCENNES: South Knox 88–50 Vincennes Rivet; North Central 67–57 Sullivan; Vincennes 53–37 North Knox; North Central (Farmersburg) 64–61 South Knox; Lincoln 55–52 North Central (Farmersburg). Officials: Tom Rohr, Keith Bagby, Tom Ault, Ronald Grimes.

WARSAW: Rochester 74–48 Triton; Culver Military 49–38 Argos; Warsaw 79–54 Wawasee; Culver Military 57–48 Rochester; Warsaw 80–39 Culver Military. Officials: Don Resler, Judson Raver, Richard Nelson, Roger Pflughaupt.

WASHINGTON: Barr–Reeve 70–44 Washington; Loogootee 57–32 Shoals; Washington Catholic 69–67 North Daviess; Barr–Reeve 61–60 Loogootee (ot); Barr–Reeve 42–38 Washington Catholic. Officials: Temme Patterson, Dan Henkle, Mike Harder, James Newlin.

WHITE RIVER VALLEY: White River Valley 84–58 Clay City; Bloomfield 81–63 Union (Dugger); Linton-Stockton 68–57 Shakamak; White River Valley 81–57 Bloomfield; White River Valley 78–51 Linton-Stockton. Officials: J. David Lee, Larry Decker, Thomas Leix, Jim Flanagan, Matt Griffith.

1992 REGIONALS

ANDERSON: Anderson 61–59 Jay County; Muncie Central 68–67 Mt. Vernon (Fortville); Anderson 69–60 Muncie Central. Officials: Ivan Burkle, Mark Hyman, Bob Klein, Scott Robison, Troy Ingram, Clark Hamilton.

COLUMBUS: Lawrenceburg 67–62 Beech Grove; Columbus North 70–60 Center Grove; Lawrenceburg, 64–62 Columbus North. Officials: Phil Napariu, Russell Radtke, David Kavanaugh, James Newlin, Gary Leistner, Temme Patterson.

EAST CHICAGO: East Chicago Central 71–49 Highland; Hobart 49–42 Gary West Side;

Central 55–43 Hobart. Officials: Jeffery Hull, Ed Christoffel, Jon Davenport, Rick Scott, Jerry Cook, Jay C. Smith.

ELKHART: Goshen 38–32 Penn; South Bend St. Joseph's 70–47 Westview; South Bend St. Joseph's 56–47 Goshen. Officials: David Raabe, Tom Schenkel, Frank Hoagburg, Dave Vendrely, Jeffrey Simmons, Tim Smith.

EVANSVILLE: Princeton 68–66 Vincennes (2ot), Evansville Central 57–45 Evansville Harrison; Central 59–50 Princeton. Officials: Terry Bartell, Eric Ballenger, Tom Rohr, Gary Hamilton, Rex Nichols, Larry Nixon.

FORT WAYNE: Homestead 77–54 Garrett; Fort Wayne North Side 77–49 New Haven; Fort Wayne North Side 60–39 Homestead. Officials: Brad Groninger, William Kachel, Fred Hamilton, William Sorukas, Steve Cherry and Norman Hathcoat.

FRANKFORT: Brownsburg 80–75 Carmel; Lebanon 72–55 Rossville; Brownsburg 59–53 Lebanon. Officials: Sam Lower, Tony Ortman, Roger Holder, Harry Northington, Robert Frye, Gary Cheesman.

INDIANAPOLIS: Lawrence North 68–41 Manual; Ben Davis 64–56 Cathedral; Ben Davis 75–72 Lawrence North. Officials: Jerry Middleton, Keith Fields, Kent Smith, Gene Marsh, Bill Wullner, Ray Tebbe.

LAFAYETTE: Lafayette Jefferson 97–58 Benton Central; Twin Lakes 41–38 Turkey Run; Jefferson 118–73 Twin Lakes. Officials: J. David Lee, Herb Pruett, Jim Anderson, Dan Amrhein, Mike Waisnora, Tom Urban.

MARION: Kokomo 62–61 South Adams (2ot); Marion 86–51 Caston; Kokomo 52–47 Marion. Officials: Lanny Rossman, Bryan Enterline, Don Resler, Bryce Heller, John Evans, Paul Cox.

MICHIGAN CITY: Michigan City Elston 57–51 Portage; North Judson 59–53 Kankakee Valley; Elston 83–49 North Judson. Officials: Jerome Fawley, James Robinson, Dale Cramer, Bruce Klonowski, John Goss, Richard Modricker.

NEW CASTLE: Jac-Cen-Del 80–70 Connersville; Richmond 84–68 New Castle; Richmond 100–74 Jac-Cen-Del. Officials: Bob Wolfe, Tom Crouch, Leland Thompson, Tony Garton, Mike Crouch, Clarence Crain.

SEYMOUR: Jeffersonville 86–71 Seymour; New Albany 91–88 Scottsburg (ot); Jeffersonville 86–55 New Albany. Officials: Rick Foxen, David Berman, Terry Magnuson, Frederick Cooper, Stephen Fisher, Michael S. Smith.

TERRE HAUTE: Bloomington South 84–77 Terre Haute South; White River Valley 75–54 Mooresville; White River Valley 58–55 South. Officials: Ed Scahill, Mike Padfield, Bill Nimnicht, Dennis Maude, Melvin Redman, James Dunlap.

WARSAW: Warsaw 47–44 Plymouth; Northfield 77–70 Manchester; Warsaw 96–64 Northfield. Officials: Mark Hay, Jerry Stieglitz, Douglas Carl, Al Yelich, Mike Bohan, Larry Jones.

WASHINGTON: Paoli 62–44 Southridge; Corydon Central 66–49 Barr-Reeve; Paoli 69–55 Corydon Central. Officials: Ron McGriff, Phil Vidito, Michael McCarty Brian Osswald, Robert Anderson, Jerry Taylor.

Tourney Time

1992 SEMI-STATES

FORT WAYNE: Warsaw 61–50 South Bend St. Joseph's; Kokomo 53–40 Fort Wayne North Side; Warsaw 46–44 Kokomo. Officials: Robert Anderson, Ray Tebbe, Troy Ingram, Clarence Crain, Mike Waisnora, Jerry Taylor.

LAFAYETTE: Lafayette Jefferson 99–89 East Chicago Central; Michigan City Elston 74–65 Brownsburg; Lafayette Jefferson 82–62 Michigan City Elston. Officials: Robert Frye, Paul Cox, Steve Cherry, Tim Smith, Jerry Cook, John Evans.

INDIANAPOLIS: Ben Davis 96–87 Anderson; Richmond 71–48 Lawrenceburg; Richmond 79–76 Ben Davis. Officials: Jeffrey Simmons, Clark Hamilton, Melvin Redman, Jay C. Smith, Stephen Fisher, Mike Crouch.

TERRE HAUTE: Evansville Central 60–59 White River Valley; Jeffersonville 85–60 Paoli; Jeffersonville 55–52 Evansville Central (ot). Officials: Rex Nichols, Gary Cheesman, John Goss, Tom Urban, Mike Bohan, Gary Leistner.

1992 FINALS—March 28

INDIANAPOLIS (Hoosier Dome): Richmond 94–92 Jeffersonville (ot); Lafayette Jefferson 71–58 Warsaw; Richmond 77–73 Lafayette Jefferson (ot). Officials: Mike Bohan, Jerry Taylor, John Evans, Stephen Fisher Jerry Cook, Mike Waisnora.

1993 SECTIONALS

ANDERSON: Frankton 52–49 Elwood; Anderson 80–60 Alexandria; Highland 64–50 Madison Heights; Anderson 84–50 Frankton; Anderson 55–43 Highland. Officials: Bob Beeson, Tony Ortman, Arnold Freeman Jr., Ivan Burkle.

BEDFORD NORTH LAWRENCE: Edgewood 58–30 Bloomington South; Bedford North Lawrence 51–42 Eastern (Bloomfield); Bloomington North 53–43 Brown County; Edgewood 58–48 Bedford North Lawrence; Edgewood 58–38 Bloomington North. Officials: Rex Nichols, Thomas Leix, Daniel Henkle, John Lyskowinski.

BEN DAVIS: Brebeuf 62–38 Indianapolis Ritter; Pike 54–45 Speedway; Ben Davis 84–44 Northwest; Brebeuf 64–60 Pike; Ben Davis 53–39 Brebeuf. Officials: John Crapo, Mark Campbell, Al Smith, Haymon Fields.

BOONVILLE: South Spencer 64–57 Princeton; Heritage Hills 47–45 Boonville; Gibson Southern 70–67 Tecumseh (ot); South Spencer 77–56 Heritage Hills; South Spencer 52–50 Gibson Southern. Officials: David Kavanaugh, Mark Logel, Ronald Grimes, Jay Alan Ritter.

BROWNSBURG: Plainfield 73–65 Cascade; Tri-West Hendricks 75–59 Danville; Avon 82–81 Plainfield 85–62 Tri-West; Plainfield 100–82 Avon. Officials: Brian Osswald, Stan Ames, Wayne Hobson, Len Glazier.

CALUMET: Calumet 81–64 Lake Central; Munster 55–38 Hammond Morton; Griffith 53–46 Highland; Calumet 66–37 Munster; Calumet 90–64 Griffith. Officials: John Goss, Duffy Ainsworth, Greg Yergler, Steve Kvachkoff.

CARMEL: Sheridan 68–59 Hamilton Heights; Noblesville 55–53 Westfield Washington; Carmel 56–43 Hamilton Southeastern; Noblesville 68–66 Sheridan; Carmel 54–44 Noblesville.

IHSAA Scores | 1990-1999

Officials: Mike Padfield, Doug Zook, Gene Huston, Jerry Northington.

COLUMBIA CITY: Manchester 52-45 Tippecanoe Valley; Whitko 60-46 Columbia City; Churubusco 79-42 Central Noble; Whitko 69-65 Manchester; Whitko 66-59 Churubusco. David Raabe, Dale Zeigler, Thomas Muth, Jerry Cook.

COLUMBUS: Columbus North 49-45 Columbus East; Southwestern (Shelbyville) 71-57 Hauser; Waldron 67-51 Edinburgh; North 70-51 Southwestern (Shelbyville); North 61-53 Waldron. Officials: Bob Klein, Jerry Wallace, Munk McKee, Russell Radtke.

CONNERSVILLE: Rushville 62-34 Hagerstown; Cambridge City 78-52 Connersville; Franklin County 67-38 Union County; Rushville 61-59 Cambridge City (ot); Rushville 58-46 Franklin County. Officials: Steve Cherry, Jack Kopp, Greg Taylor, Keith Fields.

CRAWFORD COUNTY: Tell City 69-60 Cannelton; Crawford County 62-39 Perry Central; Corydon 51-36 North Harrison; Tell City 42-39 Crawford County; Tell City 53-52 Corydon. Officials: Larry Maxwell, Keith Bagby, Ronald Pritchett, Ed Roush.

DEKALB: DeKalb 80-52 Hamilton; Fremont 57-42 Angola; Eastside 63-58 Garrett; Fremont 56-55 DeKalb; Eastside 59-58 Fremont. Officials: Clark Hamilton, Jerry Stieglitz, Rick Granger, Dave Vendrely.

EAST CHICAGO: East Chicago Central 82-46 Hammond High; Noll 71-39 Hammond Clark; Gavit 60-47 Whiting; Central 44-42 Noll; Central 84-49 Gavit. Officials: Jeffrey Hull, Mark McCammon, Michael Brady, Daniel Amrhein.

EAST NOBLE: East Noble 90-48 West Noble; Lakeland 83-78 Prairie Heights; Westview 70-62 Howe Military; East Noble 65-50 Lakeland; East Noble 66-50 Westview. Officials: Tom Garton, Donald Schmidt, Lance Grubbs, Bob Stambazze.

ELKHART: Central 48-35 Mishawaka Marian; Penn 63-48 Mishawaka; Concord 68-45 Memorial; Central 61-43 Penn; Concord 52-50 Central. Officials: Rick Scott, Jack Urbin, Gaylord Fritz, Bryce Heller.

EVANSVILLE CENTRAL: Mater Dei 56-53 Mt. Vernon; Central 75-61 Reitz; North Posey 62-48 New Harmony; Central 69-56 Mater Dei; Central 59-53 North Posey. Officials: Carl March, James Reid, Matt Griffith, Mike Quinn,

EVANSVILLE HARRISON: Memorial 48-45 Harrison; Bosse 73-70 North; Castle 66-37 Day School; Memorial 56-54 Bosse; Memorial 60-57 Castle. Officials: Gary Leistner, James Newlin, Mike Harder, Stephen Fisher.

FORT WAYNE NORTH SIDE: Concordia 62-56 Northrop; Snider 75-56 Dwenger; North Side 39-37 Carroll (Fort Wayne), Concordia 63-61 Snider; North Side 55-52 Concordia. Officials: Doug Carl, Ed Christoffel, Olin Roberts, Richard Borror.

FORT WAYNE WAYNE: Wayne 55-44 Homestead; South Side 112-27 Fort Wayne Christian; Elmhurst 56-43 Luers; South Side 81-68 Wayne; South Side 56-35 Elmhurst. Officials: Mike Crouch, Dan VanTreese, Kirk Robinson, Mark Hyman.

FOUNTAIN CENTRAL: Attica 53-44 South Newton; Benton Central 83-49 Covington; Fountain Central 52-45 Seeger; Attica 63-59 (ot) Benton Central; Attica 57-43 Fountain Central. Officials: Ray Tebbe, Tony Bierschbach, Sam Berry, Clifford Spears.

FRANKFORT: Clinton Central 63-61 Tipton; Clinton Prairie 66-57 Tri-Central; Frankfort 80-71 Rossville (ot); Clinton Prairie 60-55 Clinton Central; Frankfort 65-63 Clinton Prairie. Officials: Michael Fox; Jim Flanagan, John Kane, Bob Wolfe.

FRANKLIN CENTRAL: Indianapolis Chatard 80-77 Warren Central; Franklin Central 52-

Tourney Time

34 Tech; Arlington 56–55 Cathedral; Franklin Central 60–52 Chatard; Franklin Central 69–59 Arlington. Officials: Norm Hathcoat, Larry Alsip, James Keifer, Kenneth Cobb.

GARY: Wallace 70–62 Roosevelt; Wirt 64–60 Andrean; West Side 52–51 Mann; Wallace 70–61 Wirt; West Side 73–71 Wallace. Officials: Jeff Simmons, Phil Marsh, Dale Ferraro, Russ Teall.

GOSHEN: Northridge 35–32 Goshen; North Wood 62–59 Bethany Christian (4ot); Fairfield 48–40 Jimtown; Northridge 68–52 North Wood; Northridge 66–44 Fairfield. Officials: Bryan Enterline, Frank Hoagburg, Ron Gradeless, Michael Alspaugh.

GREENCASTLE: Greencastle 65–43 North Vermillion; Rockville 64–60 North Putnam; South Putnam 32–24 Turkey Run; Greencastle 53–43 Rockville; Greencastle 35–32 South Putnam. Officials: Tom Rohr, Phil Dant, Michael Lewis, Frank Bodwell.

GREENFIELD-CENTRAL: New Palestine 74–49 Eastern Hancock; Pendleton Heights 57–40 Mt. Vernon (Fortville); Greenfield-Central 83–57 Lapel; Pendleton Heights 55–43 New Palestine; Greenfield-Central 54–40 Pendleton Heights. Officials: Troy Ingram, Mel Botkin, David Estes, Kyle Ingram.

GREENSBURG: Jac-Cen-Del 55–52 North Decatur; Batesville 88–49 South Decatur; Greensburg 82–69 South Ripley; Jac-Cen-Del; 80–74 Batesville; Greensburg 68–62 Jac-Cen-Del. Officials: Sam Lower, Steven Smith, Joseph Stafford, Scott Mellinger.

GREENWOOD: Franklin 69–45 Indian Creek; Whiteland 80–60 Roncalli; Greenwood 53–51 Center Grove; Whiteland 74–72 Franklin (ot); Whiteland 77–61 Greenwood. Officials: Lee Thompson, Larry Sintz, Brad Farmer, Chip Sweet.

HUNTINGTON: Blackford 51–41 Wabash; Huntington North 70–53 White's; Northfield 42–38 Southwood; North 47–37 Blackford; North 51–40 Northfield. Officials: Larry Jones, Jerry Alberson, Dennis Jackson, Jon Davenport.

JAY COUNTY: Jay County 62–50 Union City; Wapahani 54–42 Monroe Central; Delta 74–48 Wes–Del; Jay County 42–39 Wapahani; Delta 72–56 Jay County. Officials: Tom Urban, Michael Alford, J. Roderick Weiss, Jerry Middleton.

JEFFERSONVILLE: Jeffersonville 71–42 Clarksville; Borden 58–54 Charlestown; Silver Creek 81–58 Providence; Jeffersonville 115–55 Borden; Jeffersonville 98–65 Silver Creek. Officials: Fred Cooper, Danny Shields, Jeff Culp, Brad Sellers.

KANKAKEE VALLEY: Boone Grove 77–55 North Newton; Hebron 80–65 Kouts; Lowell 58–43 Kankakee Valley; Hebron 84–58 Boone Grove; Lowell 43–39 Hebron. Officials: Dale Cramer, Tom Behny, Mike Gruver, Marvin Davis.

KOKOMO: Kokomo 64–45 Taylor; Northwestern 86–56 Eastern (Greentown); Maconaquah 67–65 Western; Kokomo 61–48 Northwestern; Kokomo 55–47 Maconaquah. Officials: Gary Cheesman, Patrick Franklin, Rodney Chamberlain, Douglas Bauman.

LAFAYETTE: Carroll (Flora) 71–69 Central Catholic; McCutcheon 80–67 Harrison; Lafayette Jefferson 83–38 West Lafayette; McCutcheon 70–64 Carroll (Flora); Jefferson 85–67 McCutcheon. Officials: Mark Baltz, James Campbell, Rick Hawley, Randy Coplen.

LAWRENCE NORTH: Park Tudor 49–48 North Central; Lawrence Central 86–53 School for the Deaf; Lawrence North 68–65 Broad Ripple; Park Tudor 43–42 Lawrence Central; Lawrence North 69–45 Park Tudor. Officials: Michael Smith, Michael McGriff, Robert Hallgarth, Norman Delph.

LEBANON: Lebanon 66–57 Southmont; Crawfordsville 67–63 Western Boone; Zionsville 57–50 North Montgomery; Lebanon 70–64 Crawfordsville; Lebanon 61–59 Zionsville. Officials:

IHSAA Scores | 1990-1999

Clarence Crain, Mark Robbins, Larry Johnson, Dennis Maude.

LOGANSPORT: Caston 77–68 Pioneer; Cass 64–60 North Miami; Logansport 80–40 Peru; Caston 74–70 Cass; Caston 74–71 Logansport (ot). Officials: Mark Hay, Patrick Dumoulin, Michael Dellinger, Mark Withers.

MADISON: Madison 64–51 Southwestern (Hanover); Henryville 76–70 New Washington; Scottsburg 83–56 Madison Shawe; Madison 74–60 Henryville; Scottsburg 71–64 Madison. Officials: Ron McGriff, Gary Woodling, Walter Bishop, Greg McAdams.

MARION: Mississinewa 50–49 Eastbrook; Madison Grant 69–33 Marion Bennett; Marion 69–56 Oak Hill; Mississinewa 88–85 Madison Grant (2ot); Marion 89–69 Mississinewa. Officials. Paul Cox, Rick Shirk, Gary Chambers, Dan Breneman.

MARTINSVILLE: Owen Valley 59–43 Eminence; Mooresville 83–71 Martinsville; Monrovia 56–53 Cloverdale (ot); Mooresville 70–44 Owen Valley; Mooresville 63–44 Monrovia. Officials: Phil Vidito, Ron Kottlowski, Paul Mills, David Berman.

MERRILLVILLE: Crown Point 54–44 Hanover Central; Merrillville 60–48 Hobart; River Forest 54–45 Lake Station; Merrillville 68–49 Crown Point; Merrillville 92–46 River Forest. Officials: Bruce Klonoski, Mike Smith, Steve Homner, Mike Waisnora.

MICHIGAN CITY: LaPorte 80–48 New Prairie; Rogers 51–49 Westville; Elston 78–24 Marquette; Rogers 53–48 LaPorte; Elston 74–53 Rogers. Officials: Jay Smith, Michael Spann, Jeff Heiliger, Bill Sorukas.

MUNCIE: Central 81–57 Yorktown; Burris 67–54 Southside; Daleville 59–57 Cowan (ot); Central 82–69 Burris; Central 80–40 Daleville. Officials: Fred Hamilton, D. Michael McLean, Kevin Moore, Gene Marsh.

NEW ALBANY: Eastern (Pekin) 51–44 South Central (Elizabeth); Floyd Central 99–52 Lanesville; New Albany 73–46 Graceland Christian; Floyd Central 81–48 Eastern (Pekin); New Albany 58–55 Floyd Central. Officials: Temme Patterson, Robert Davis, Lowell DePoy, Tom Walters.

NEW CASTLE: Shenandoah 43–42 Knightstown; Blue River Valley 86–57 Morton Memorial; New Castle 68–48 Tri; Shenandoah 60–59 Blue River Valley; New Castle 85–75 Shenandoah. Officials: Robert Frye, Jim Pitcher, C. Justin Rutledge, Ed Scahill.

NEW HAVEN: New Haven 64–62 Harding; Heritage 66–65 Fort Wayne Blackhawk (2ot); Leo 70–59 Woodlan; New Haven 44–41 Heritage; Leo 61–49 New Haven. Officials: Brad Groninger, Ed Humphrey, Judson Raver, William Kachel.

NORTH JUDSON: North Judson 71–69 LaCrosse; South Central (Union Mills) 52–49 Winamac (ot); Knox 62–55 West Central; North Judson 85–57 South Central (Union Mills); North Judson 74–62 Knox. Officials: Jerry Fawley, Dale Blosser, Ed Malek, Mark Wise.

PAOLI: Paoli 67–43 West Washington; Springs Valley 72–56 Orleans; Salem 51–49 Mitchell (ot); Paoli 71–49 Springs Valley; Paoli 46–43 Salem. Officials: William Nimnicht, Eric Ballenger, Alan Agee and Kim Baker.

PLYMOUTH: Plymouth 50–37 Culver Community; LaVille 74–45 Oregon Davis; Bremen 63–58 Glenn; Plymouth 47–44 LaVille (ot); Bremen 83–66 Plymouth. Officials: Don Resler, David Emery, Curt Yoder, Al Yelich.

RICHMOND: Randolph Southern 67–58 Union (Modoc); Winchester 63–60 Northeastern (ot); Richmond 89–22 Centerville; Winchester 69–52 Randolph Southern; Richmond 66–43 Winchester. Officials: Tom Crouch, Terry Johnson, Dale Goodwin, Denis Schinderle.

Tourney Time

SEYMOUR: Jennings County 115–61 Medora; Brownstown Central 63–60 Seymour (ot); Austin 71–41 Crothersville; Jennings County 83–71 Brownstown Central (2ot); Jennings County 74–68 (ot) Austin. Officials: Terry Magnuson, James Roberts, Mike Baas, Mike Bohan.

SHELBYVILLE: Beech Grove 72–66 Indianapolis Lutheran; Triton Central 57–49 Morristown; Shelbyville 55–22 Scecina; Beech Grove 55–54 Triton Central; Shelbyville 51–49 Beech Grove. Officials: Bill Wullner Kenneth Knapp, Ernie Brewer, Rick Normington.

SOUTH ADAMS: Adams Central 58–54 Bellmont; South Adams 61–56 Southern Wells; Bluffton 47–44 Norwell; South Adams 70–53 Adams Central; South Adams 84–56 Bluffton. Officials: Jim Cox, Doug Flatter, Dave Trietsch, James Robinson.

SOUTH BEND: Clay 74–45 LaSalle; St. Joseph's 78–44 Adams; Riley 62–60 Washington; St. Joseph's 46–45 Clay; St. Joseph's 61–45 Riley. Officials: Tim Smith, Roger Pflughaupt, Robert Neff, Fred Perry.

SOUTH DEARBORN: South Dearborn 69–57 Switzerland County; East Central 43–41 Milan (ot); Lawrence4urg 65–38 Rising Sun; South Dearborn 57–49 East Central; South Dearborn 55–48 Lawrenceburg. Officials: Richard Foxen, Anthony Bova, Steven Corya, Gary Hamilton.

SOUTHPORT: Perry Meridian 73–54 Decatur Central; Southport 50–44 Indianapolis Washington; Howe 61–56 Manual; Southport 46–40 Perry Meridian; Southport 69–45 Howe. Officials: Roger Holder, Larry Decker, Bill Forehand, Patrick Strong.

SOUTHRIDGE: Northeast Dubois 48–41 Southridge (ot); Forest Park 85–80 Jasper; Pike Central 67–56 Oakland City Wood; Forest Park 53–46 Northeast Dubois; Forest Park 46–40 Pike Central. Officials: James Dunlap, Dennis Espenlaub, Darrell Stone, Charles Steven Meyer.

TERRE HAUTE: Northview 57–33 South Vermillion; Terre Haute South 57–51 West Vigo; Terre Haute North 93–43 Riverton Parke; South 68–43 Northview; North 54–49 South. Officials: Robert Anderson, John Walker, Michael Wallpe, Scott Robison, Terry Kreider.

TWIN LAKES: Frontier 52–43 Twin Lakes; Rensselaer 79–62 Delphi; Tri-County 70–61 North White; Rensselaer 81–50 Frontier; Tri-County 71–65. Rensselaer. Officials: Terry Bartell, Brad Wilson, Dale Gurgel, Doug Hudson.

VALPARAISO: Washington Twp. 69–43 Morgan Twp.; Portage 47–45 Wheeler; Valparaiso 79–66 Chesterton; Portage 64–52 Washington Twp.; Valparaiso 43–42 Portage. Officials: Tom May, Richard Nelson, Ron Stevens, Paul Danko.

VINCENNES: North Central (Farmersburg) 56–54 North Knox (ot); Vincennes 82–55 Vincennes Rivet; South Knox 57–54 Sullivan; Lincoln 77–55 North Central (Farmersburg); South Knox 52–48 Lincoln. Officials: Larry Nixon, Ron James, Rick Gentry, Jerry Taylor.

WARSAW: Rochester 61–42 Argos; Warsaw 91–41 Triton; Wawasee 57–29 Culver Military; Warsaw 104–53 Rochester; Warsaw 56–41 Wawasee. Officials: Tom Schenkel, Robert Childers, David Gentile, Steve Godfroy.

WASHINGTON: Washington Catholic 49–48 Loogootee; North Daviess 63–58 Shoals (ot); Barr–Reeve 57–47 Washington; Washington Catholic 69–58 North Daviess; Washington Catholic 52–48 Barr–Reeve. Officials: Mel Redman, Paul Wahl, Alan Deskins, Doug Coddington.

WHITE RIVER VALLEY: Clay City 82–73 Shakamak; White River Valley 95–61 Union (Dugger); Bloomfield 86–60 Linton Stockton; White River Valley 81–46 Clay City; White River Valley 78–59 Bloomfield. Officials: Lanny Rossman, Joe Reed, Dave Hedge, Kent Smith.

1993 REGIONALS

ANDERSON: Delta 60–55 Muncie Central; Anderson 80–56 Greenfield-Central; Anderson 77–52 Delta. Officials: Tom Schenkel, Bob Stambazze, Bob Klein, Steve Godfroy, Robert Anderson, Mark Baltz.

COLUMBUS: Whiteland 69–67 Shelbyville; Columbus North 70–50 South Dearborn; Columbus North 74–64 Whiteland. Officials: Michael Fox, John Lyskowinski, Phil Vidito, Doug Coddington, Clarence Crain, Melvin Redman.

EAST CHICAGO: Gary West Side 65–60 East Chicago Central; Merrillville 92–44 Calumet; Merrillville 74–63 West Side. Officials: Jerome Fawley, Marvin Davis, Mark Hay, William Sorukas, Tim Smith, Jay Smith.

ELKHART: East Noble 55–29 Northridge; South Bend St. Joseph's 49–48 Concord; St. Joseph's 66–55 East Noble. Officials: Tony Garton, Mark Wise, Doug Carl, Dan Amrhein, John Goss, Jim Cox.

EVANSVILLE: South Knox 62–49 Evansville Central; South Spencer 52–47 Evansville Memorial; South Spencer 67–52 South Knox. Officials: Tom Rohr, John Crapo, Carl March, Mike Quinn, Gary Leistner, Larry Maxwell.

FORT WAYNE: Leo 68–67 Fort Wayne North Side (3ot); Fort Wayne South Side 66–40 Eastside; South Side 75–47 Leo. Officials: Dale Cramer, Jerry Middleton, Rick Scott, James Robinson, Paul Cox, Leland Thompson.

FRANKFORT: Carmel 73–66 Plainfield; Frankfort 84–77 Lebanon; Carmel 65–52 Frankfort, Officials: Tom Crouch, Frank Bodwell, David Raabe, Hayman Fields, Mike Crouch, Rex Nichols.

HUNTINGTON: Huntington North 68–43 Whitko; Warsaw 59–54 Bremen; Warsaw 55–54 North. Officials: Mike Padfield, Ivan Burkle, Sam Lower, Harry Northington, Tom Urban, Brad Groninger.

INDIANAPOLIS: Ben Davis 48–43 Franklin Central; Lawrence North 52–51 Southport; Ben Davis 58–48 Lawrence North. Officials: Ron McGriff, Douglas Hudson, Terry Bartell, Russell Radtke, Troy Ingram, Bob Beeson.

LAFAYETTE: Greencastle 73–66 Attica; Lafayette Jefferson 92–82 Tri-County; Jefferson 67–49 Greencastle. Officials: Tom May, Dennis Maude, Len Glazier, William Kachel, Jeff Simmons, Gary Cheesman.

MARION: South Adams 67–47 Caston; Kokomo 50–48 Marion; South Adams 59–52 Kokomo. Officials: Brian Osswald, Norman Delph, Gene Marsh, Scott Mellinger, Norman Hathcoat, Bruce Klonowski.

MICHIGAN CITY: Michigan City Elston 62–61 Valparaiso; Lowell 63–32 North Judson; Elston 54–47 Lowell. Officials: Bryan Enterline, Jon Davenport, Jeffrey Hull, Mark Hyman, Larry Jones, Don Resler.

NEW CASTLE: Greensburg 79–74 Rushville; New Castle 81–78 Richmond; New Castle 92–90 Greensburg (ot). Officials: Fred Hamilton, Greg McAdams, Bill Wullner, Dave Vendrely, Ray Tebbe, Clark Hamilton.

SEYMOUR: New Albany 70–65 Scottsburg (ot); Jeffersonville 63–50 Jennings County; Jeffersonville 74–59 New Albany. Officials: Dave Kavanaugh, Kent Smith, Temme Patterson, Tom Walters, Robert Frye, William Nimnicht.

WASHINGTON: Paoli 42–40 Forest Park; Tell City 76–62 Washington Catholic; Paoli 61–

Tourney Time

33 Tell City. Officials: Roger Holder, Kim Baker, James Dunlap, Steve Meyer, Michael Smith, Terry Magnuson.

WEST VIGO: White River Valley 64–45 Mooresville; Edgewood 36–35 Terre Haute North; White River Valley 60–53 Edgewood. Officials: Richard Foxen, Denis Schinderle, Fred Cooper, Gary Hamilton, Steve Cherry, Larry Nixon.

1993 SEMI-STATES

EVANSVILLE: White River Valley 50–48 Paoli; Jeffersonville 69–51 South Spencer; Jeffersonville 61–59 White River Valley. Officials: Robert Frye, Melvin Redman, Robert Anderson, Terry Magnuson, Ray Tebbe, Clarence Crain.

INDIANAPOLIS: Ben Davis 67–60 Columbus North; Anderson 85–67 New Castle; Ben Davis 71–62 Anderson. Officials: Tom Urban, William Nimnicht, Tim Smith, Larry Nixon, Gary Leistner, Jeffrey Simmons.

LAFAYETTE: Carmel 63–48 Lafayette Jefferson; Merrillville 74–58 Michigan City Elston; Carmel 59–52 Merrillville. Officials: Troy Ingram, Bruce Klonowski, Michael Smith, Brad Groninger, Paul Cox, Norman Hathcoat.

SOUTH BEND: South Bend St. Joseph's 82–72 Fort Wayne South Side; Warsaw 86–71 South Adams; St. Joseph's 52–45 Warsaw. Officials: Larry Jones, Jay Smith, John Goss, Gary Cheesman, Steve Cherry, Mike Crouch.

1993 FINALS—March 27

INDIANAPOLIS (Hoosier Dome): Ben Davis 62–46 Carmel; Jeffersonville 87–74 South Bend St. Joseph's; Jeffersonville 66–61 Ben Davis. Officials: Paul Cox, Michael Crouch, Steve Cherry, Clarence Crain, Gary Leistner, Ray Tebbe.

1994 SECTIONALS

ANDERSON: Anderson 63–57 Highland; Frankton 47–45 Elwood; Alexandria 53–52 Madison Heights; Anderson 54–50 Frankton (ot); Alexandria 60–58 Anderson. Officials: Jim Cox, Wayne Hobson, Doug Flatter, Mike Crouch.

BEDFORD NORTH LAWRENCE: Eastern (Bloomfield) 67–56 Brown County; Bedford North Lawrence 62–45 Bloomington South; Bloomington North 55–49 Edgewood; Bedford North Lawrence 60–48 Eastern (Bloomfield); Bedford North Lawrence 67–59 Bloomington North. Officials: David Kavanaugh, James Roberts, Lowell DePoy, Doug Coddington.

BEN DAVIS: Ben Davis 58–52 Brebeuf; Pike 84–45 Indianapolis Ritter; Northwest 60–59 Speedway (ot); Ben Davis 52–49 Pike (ot); Ben Davis 74–64 Northwest. Officials: Mark Baltz, Joe Reed, Tony Bierschbach, Scott Mellinger.

BOONVILLE: Princeton 94–45 Tecumseh; South Spencer 60–40 Boonville; Gibson Southern 43–42 Heritage Hills; South Spencer 73–59 Princeton; South Spencer 69–47 Gibson Southern. Officials: Steve Fisher, Chip Sweet, Dave Senning, Gary Leistner.

BROWNSBURG: Brownsburg 93–72 Plainfield; Tri-West Hendricks 73–64 Avon; Cascade 64–60 Danville; Brownsburg 71–46 Tri-West Hendricks; Brownsburg 79–42 Cascade. Officials:

William Terry Johnson, Larry Alsip, Richard Foxen, Haymon Fields.

CALUMET: Calumet 67–63 Munster (2ot); Lake Central 55–48 Highland; Griffith 66–55 Hammond Morton; Lake Central 67–54 Calumet; Lake Central 45–43 Griffith (ot). Officials: Tom May, Tom Behny, Tim Holmes, Mark Wise.

CARMEL: Noblesville 71–58 Sheridan; Hamilton Southeastern 52–50 Westfield; Carmel 73–46 Hamilton Heights; Noblesville 49–45 Hamilton Southeastern; Noblesville 44–42 Carmel. Officials: Terry Bartell, Dan Breneman, Jack Kopp, Ed Scahill.

COLUMBIA CITY: Tippecanoe Valley 68–50 Central Noble; Whitko 64–51 Columbia City; Manchester 61–36 Churubusco; Whitko 61–42 Tippecanoe Valley; Manchester 69–58 Whitko, Officials: Doug Carl, Douglas Cook, Steve Elkins, Dave Vendrely.

COLUMBUS: Columbus East 58–53 Southwestern (Shelbyville); Waldron 71–37 Hauser; Columbus North 76–50 Edinburgh; East 94–78 Waldron; North 60–53 East. Officials: Terry Magnuson, Joseph Stafford, Terry Kreider, John Lyskowinski.

CONNERSVILLE: Franklin County 68–44 Union County; Cambridge City Lincoln 57–54 Hagerstown; Connersville 61–51 Rushville; Franklin County 72–58 Cambridge City Lincoln; Connersville 81–68 Franklin County. Officials: Mike Bohan, Mike Padfield, David Bolsega, Ken Knapp, Scott Robison.

CRAWFORD COUNTY: Tell City 66–58 North Harrison; Crawford County 72–47 Perry Central; Corydon Central 80–43 Cannelton; Crawford County 56–49 Tell City; Corydon Central 59–51 Crawford County (ot). Officials: Bill Nimnicht, Rick Gentry, Daniel Henkle, Michael Quinn.

EAST CHICAGO: Hammond High 68–59 Hammond Clark; East Chicago Central 76–35 Whiting; Hammond Gavit 47–46 Hammond Noll; Central 75–53 Hammond High; Central 85–44 d Gavit. Officials: Mike Waisnora, Jerome Fawley, Richard Calloway, Fred Perry.

EAST NOBLE: Westview 69–66 West Noble; Prairie Heights 61–59 Lakeland (ot); East Noble 62–46 Howe Military; Westview 70–53 Prairie Heights; Westview 51–43 East Noble. Officials: Bryan Enterline, Michael Spann, Jerry Alberson, David Gentile.

ELKHART: Concord 58–52 Mishawaka; Penn 64–62 Memorial; Central 58–40 Mishawaka Marian; Penn 57–56 Concord (ot); Central 52–39 Penn. Officials: Larry Jones, Robert Neff, Steve Homner, Jon Davenport.

EVANSVILLE CENTRAL: North Posey 62–58 Mt. Vernon; Evansville Central 84–49 New Harmony; Reitz 83–59 Mater Dei; Central 78–64 North Posey; Central 66–64 Reitz (ot). Officials: James Dunlap, Darrell Stone, Mike Harder, Fred Cooper.

EVANSVILLE HARRISON: Castle 49–43 Evansville Day; Bosse 65–63 Memorial; Harrison 42–37 North; Bosse 52–48 Castle; Bosse 54–51 Harrison. Officials: Carl March, Tim Jellison, Alan Agee, James Reid.

FORT WAYNE NORTH SIDE: Northrop 50–35 Snider; Dwenger 70–45 Concordia; North Side 61–48 Carroll (Fort Wayne); Dwenger 59–58 Northrop (ot); Dwenger 63–61 North Side. Officials: Bill Kachel, Tony Carton, Mark Hyman. Rodney Chamberlain.

FORT WAYNE WAYNE: Fort Wayne Canterbury 89–44 Fort Wayne Christian; Wayne 70–63 South Side; Luers 67–57 Elmhurst; Homestead 66–55 Canterbury; Wayne 60–38 Luers; Wayne 57–45 Homestead. Officials: Fred Hamilton, Olin Roberts, Larry Johnson, Steve Godfroy, Randall Miller, Tom Kenworthy.

FOUNTAIN CENTRAL: Benton Central 83–46 Fountain Central; Attica 49–39 South

Tourney Time

Newton; Seeger 62–59 Covington (ot); Benton Central 71–69 Attica; Benton Central 73–65 Seeger. Officials: Tom Rohr, Stan Ames, Thomas Leix, Jim Flanagan.

FRANKFORT: Frankfort 89–72 Rossville; Tri Central 75–70 Clinton Central; Tipton 61–31 Clinton Prairie; Frankfort 80–51 Tri Central; Frankfort 49–48 Tipton. Officials: Michael Wallpe, Arnold Freeman Jr., Phillip Napariu, Clifford Spears.

FRANKLIN CENTRAL: Warren Central 57–54 Franklin Central; Indianapolis Arlington 54–52 Indianapolis Tech; Cathedral 49–48 Chatard; Arlington 64–62 Warren Central (ot); Cathedral 51–47 Arlington. Officials: Brian Osswald, Steve Smith, Jim Pitcher, Steve Cherry.

GARRETT: Angola 56–35 Hamilton; Eastside 69–64 Fremont; DeKalb 82–32 Garrett; Eastside 62–52 Angola; DeKalb 57–55 Eastside. Officials: Don Resler, Jeff Heiliger, Douglas Bauman, Judson Raver.

GARY: Wallace 47–41 Wirt; Andrean 73–65 West Side; Roosevelt 44–42 Mann; Andrean 55–52 Wallace; Andrean 64–54 Roosevelt. Officials: William Sorukas, Michael Brady, Ed Malek, Dan Amrhein.

GOSHEN: Northwood 79–34 Bethany Christian; Northridge 41–39 Goshen (ot); Fairfield 53–49 Jimtown; North Wood 53–43 Northridge; Fairfield 50–49 North Wood. Officials: Rick Scott, Mark McCammon, Thomas Muth, Russ Teal.

GREENCASTLE: Turkey Run 65–56 North Putnam; Rockville 72–64 Greencastle; South Putnam 54–42 North Vermillion; Rockville 57–41 Turkey Run; South Putnam 57–39 Rockville. Officials: Roger Holder, Sam Berry, John Walker, Len Glazier.

GREENFIELD–CENTRAL: New Palestine 58–41 Lapel; Greenfield-Central 59–45 Eastern Hancock; Pendleton Heights 88–70 Mt. Vernon (Fortville); Greenfield-Central 65–45 New Palestine; Pendleton Heights 74–68 Greenfield-Central. Officials: Rick Owens, Doug Zook, David Barlow, Jerry Middleton.

GREENSBURG: Batesville 72–61 South Decatur; Greensburg 72–63 North Decatur (ot); Jac-Cen-Del 77–70 South Ripley; Batesville 79–62 Greensburg; Batesville 82–62 Jac-Cen-Del. Officials: Bob Beeson, Ernie Brewer, Dale Goodwin, Greg McAdams.

HUNTINGTON: Wabash 79–31 White's; Northfield 64–62 Blackford; Huntington North 66–41 Southwood; Wabash 61–59 Northfield; North 65–55 Wabash. Officials: Dale Cramer, Jack Urbin, Gene Huston, Jerry Stieglitz.

JAY COUNTY: Monroe Central 60–48 Union City; Wapahani 50–48 Delta (2ot); Jay County 63–52 Wes–Del; Wapahani 62–46 Monroe Central; Jay County 52–51 Wapahani (2ot). Officials: Gary Cheesman, Roger Pflughaupt, Gary Chambers, Tony Ortman.

JEFFERSONVILLE: Charlestown 75–59 Providence; Jeffersonville 57–38 Clarksville; Silver Creek 69–50 Borden; Jeffersonville 85–69 Charlestown, Jeffersonville 94–47 Silver Creek. Officials: Ron McGriff, Greg Taylor; Bill Brinkman, Steve Corya.

KANKAKEE VALLEY: Boone Grove 61–59 North Newton; Kankakee Valley 35–27 Lowell; Hebron 76–51 Kouts; Kankakee Valley 73–62 Boone Grove; Hebron 62–53 Kankakee Valley. Officials: John Goss, Michael Alspaugh, Ronald Stevens, Michael Smith.

KOKOMO: Northwestern 54–47 Taylor, Maconaquah 104–54 Eastern (Greentown); Kokomo 47–30 Western; Maconaquah 58–51 Northwestern; Kokomo 75–38 Maconaquah. Officials: Norman Hathcoat, Dennis Jackson, Richard Hawley, Sam Lower.

LAFAYETTE: McCutcheon 68–51 Harrison; Carroll (Flora) 70–62 West Lafayette (ot); Central Catholic 77–61 Lafayette Jefferson; McCutcheon 65–45 Carroll (Flora); McCutcheon

IHSAA Scores | 1990–1999

58–42 Catholic. Officials: Bob Anderson, Ron James, Jerry Wallace, Ray Tebbe.

LAWRENCE NORTH: Park Tudor 77–68 Indiana School for the Deaf; Lawrence North 81–70 Broad Ripple; North Central 54–51 Lawrence Central; Lawrence North 73–58 Park Tudor; Lawrence North 71–58 North Central. Officials: Lanny Rossman, Mark Robbins, John Kane, Gary Hamilton.

LOGANSPORT: Logansport 70–58 Peru; Pioneer 55–45 North Miami; Cass 68–55 Caston; Logansport 52–44 Pioneer; Logansport 60–57 Cass. Officials: James Robinson, Brad Wilson, Gaylord Fritz, Marvin Davis.

MADISON: Madison 76–72 Scottsburg; Southwestern (Hanover) 72–61 Henryville; Madison Shawe 57–55 New Washington; Madison 70–59 Southwestern (Hanover); Madison 88–52 Madison Shawe. Officials: Bob Klein, Kevin Moore, Al Smith, Ed Roush.

MARION: Marion Lakeview Christian 59–56 Eastbrook; Marion 63–60 Mississinewa; Madison Grant 66–47 Oak Hill; Marion 76–51 Lakeview Christian; Marion 65–49 Madison Grant. Officials: Thomas Urban, Ken Cobb, Bill Forehand, Dale Zeigler.

MARTINSVILLE: Mooresville 88–48 Cloverdale; Martinsville 64–46 Owen Valley; Monrovia 61–47 Eminence; Mooresville 56–55 Martinsville; Mooresville 59–47 Monrovia. Officials: Kent Smith, John Crapo, Michael Lewis, Dennis Schinderle.

MERRILLVILLE: Hobart 46–44 Crown Point; Merrillville 58–29 Hanover; River Forest 45–44 Lake Station; Merrillville 49–43 Hobart; Merrillville 70–32 River Forest. Officials: Jeff Simmons, Greg Yergler, Ron Gradeless, Jeff Hull.

MICHIGAN CITY: Elston 86–56 Marquette; Rogers 60–59 New Prairie; LaPorte 86–54 Westville; Elston 77–60 Rogers; Elston 84–59 LaPorte. Officials: Jerry Cook, Dale Gurgel, Gerald Gruver, Russell Radtke.

MUNCIE: Southside 71–45 Cowan; Yorktown 66–65 Burris; Central 89–59 Daleville; Southside 88–58 Yorktown; Central 86–51 South. Officials: Troy Ingram, J. Roderick Weiss, Bob Hallgarth, Keith Fields.

NEW ALBANY: Graceland 54–47 South Central (Elizabeth); Lanesville 65–48 Eastern (Pekin); New Albany 76–67 Floyd Central; Lanesville 66–55 Graceland; New Albany 58–52 Lanesville. Officials: Larry Maxwell, Larry Decker, Kim Baker, Ron Pritchett.

NEW CASTLE: Blue River Valley 66–47 Morton Memorial; Shenandoah 48–43 Tri; New Castle 60–55 Knightstown; Shenandoah 51–49 Blue River Valley (ot); New Castle 69–55 Shenandoah. Officials: Michael S. Smith, Bob Wolfe, Bart Keesling, Michael Alford.

NEW HAVEN: Harding 84–69 Woodlan; Heritage 60–57 New Haven (ot); Leo 63–42 Ft. Wayne Blackhawk; Harding 67–54 Heritage; Leo 69–56 Harding. Officials: David Raabe, Rick Granger, Mel Botkin, Tom Crouch.

NORTH JUDSON: Knox 76–60 LaCrosse; Winamac 54–36 South Central (Union Mills); North Judson 61–59 West Central; Knox 67–64 Winamac (ot); North Judson 81–63 Knox. Officials: Dick Modricker, Kirk Robinson, Lance Grubbs, Steve Kvachkoff.

NORTH MONTGOMERY: Crawfordsville 62–59 Lebanon (ot); North Montgomery 63–57 Zionsville; Southmont 74–55 Western Boone; Crawfordsville 90–78 North Montgomery; Southmont 84–81 Crawfordsville (2ot). Officials: Jerry Taylor, Ron Kottlowski, Michael Furnish, Tony Bova.

PAOLI: Paoli 72–57 Springs Valley; Orleans 71–46 Salem; Mitchell 72–66 West Washington; Paoli 56–34 Orleans; Paoli 74–50 Mitchell. Officials: Keith Bagby, Mike Baas, Dave Hedge, Paul Wahl.

Tourney Time

PLYMOUTH: Glenn 83–64 Culver Community; Bremen 81–69 Oregon Davis; Plymouth 63–48 LaVille; Glenn 66–54 Bremen; Plymouth 53–46 Glenn. Officials: Tim Smith, Richard Nelson, Stan Foreman, Bob Stambazze.

RICHMOND: Northeastern 85–51 Union; Richmond 70–40 Winchester; Randolph Southern 80–54 Centerville; Richmond 57–49 Northeastern; Randolph Southern 54–52 Richmond. Officials: Norm Delph, Rick Shirk, Dan VanTreese, Gene Marsh, Greg Bowman.

SEYMOUR: Brownstown 82–59 Medora; Seymour 65–64 Jennings County; Austin 74–55 Crothersville; Brownstown 71–63 Seymour; Brownstown 64–55 Austin, Officials: Phil Vidito, Patrick Strong, Walter Bishop, Tom Walters.

SHELBYVILLE: Beech Grove 72–52 Morristown; Indianapolis Scecina 63–51 Indianapolis Lutheran; Shelbyville 73–48 Triton Central; Scecina 60–58 Beech Grove (ot); Shelbyville 76–32 Scecina. Officials: Don Nester, Patrick Franklin, Bob Cochran, Dennis Maude.

SOUTH ADAMS: Adams Central 84–62 Bluffton; South Adams 60–58 Norwell (ot); Southern Wells 56–46 Bellmont (ot); Adams Central 47–46 South Adams; Adams Central 60–58 Southern Wells. Officials: Brad Groninger, Bob Childers, Donald Schmidt, Tom Schenkel.

SOUTH BEND: Adams 59–57 Riley; LaSalle 77–53 St. Joseph's; Clay 84–44 Washington; Adams 70–57 LaSalle; Clay 82–38 Adams. Officials: Jay C. Smith, Al Yelich, Paul Danko, Bryce Heller.

SOUTH DEARBORN: East Central 87–51 Milan; Rising Sun 63–59 South Dearborn; Switzerland County 62–58 Lawrenceburg; Rising Sun 70–52 East Central; Switzerland County 54–50 Rising Sun (2ot). Officials: Lee Thompson, Larry Sintz, James Keifer, Michael McGriff.

SOUTHPORT: Southport 56–45 Indianapolis Manual; Indianapolis Howe 65–62 Indianapolis Washington; Perry Meridian 59–54 Decatur Central; Southport 61–55 Howe; Southport 62–50 Perry Meridian. Officials: David Berman, Mark Campbell, Brad Farmer, Michael McLean.

SOUTHRIDGE: Oakland City Wood 72–48 Northeast Dubois; Southridge 51–39 Pike Central; Forest Park 61–51 Jasper; Southridge 44–35 Oakland City Wood; Southridge 46–34 Forest Park. Officials: Mel Redman, Matt Griffith, Alan Deskin, Brad Sellers.

TERRE HAUTE: Terre Haute South 55–48 West Vigo; Terre Haute North 86–36 Riverton Parke; South Vermillion 60–58 Northview (ot); North 60–53 South (ot); North 69–45 South Vermillion. Officials: Robert Frye, Paul Mills, Justin Rutledge, Frank Bodwell.

TWIN LAKES: Twin Lakes 57–48 Frontier; Tri–County 89–46 Delphi; Rensselaer 56–53 North White; Twin Lakes 81–76 Tri–County (ot); Twin Lakes 70–43 Rensselaer. Officials: Larry Nixon, Harry Northington, Michael Dellinger, Patrick Dumoulin.

VALPARAISO: Valparaiso 60–39 Wheeler; Chesterton 54–46 Portage; Washington Twp. 56–53 Morgan Twp.; Valparaiso 91–53 Chesterton; Valparaiso 100–46 Washington Twp. Officials: Bruce Klonowski, Phil Marsh, Fred Scheub, Kevin Weinberg.

VINCENNES: Vincennes Rivet 41–39 South Knox; Sullivan 67–65 North Central (Farmersburg); Vincennes 77–31 North Knox; Sullivan 49–29 Rivet; Lincoln 80–48 Sullivan. Officials: Rex Nichols, Dennis Espenlaub, Robert Walter, Jay Ritter.

WARSAW: Wawasee 82–50 Triton; Warsaw 86–42 Culver Military; Argos 44–42 Rochester; Warsaw 69–56 Wawasee; Warsaw 53–41 Argos, Officials: Mark Hay, Curtis Yoder, Richard Borror, Clark Hamilton.

WASHINGTON: Barr–Reeve 63–56 Washington; Loogootee 73–43 North Daviess; Shoals

61–51 Washington Catholic; Barr–Reeve 64–59 Loogootee; Barr-Reeve 63–53 Shoals. Officials: Ron Grimes, Lester Baugh, Jeff Culp, James Newlin.

WHITELAND: Center Grove 53–45 Roncalli; Greenwood 48–44 Whiteland; Franklin 69–45 Indian Creek; Center Grove 64–60 Greenwood; Center Grove 57–55 Franklin. Officials: Bill Wullner, Rick Normington, Dan Shields, Gary Woodling.

WHITE RIVER VALLEY: Linton-Stockton 49–47 Shakamak; White River Valley 76–64 Clay City; Bloomfield 87–71 Union (Dugger); White River Valley 58–55 Linton-Stockton; Bloomfield 53–43 White River Valley. Officials: Michael Fox, David Estes, Don Corey, Kyle Ingram.

1994 REGIONALS

ANDERSON: Alexandria 57–54 Jay County; Muncie Central 72–48 Pendleton Heights; Muncie Central 52–49 Alexandria. Officials: Bob Beeson, David Berman, Steve Godfroy, Tom Schenkel, Tim Smith, Rick Owens.

COLUMBUS: Shelbyville 84–49 Switzerland County; Columbus North 73–68 Center Grove; Shelbyville 69–55 Columbus North. Officials: Jerry Taylor, William Terry Johnson, Roger Holder, Kyle Ingram, Mike S. Smith, Mike Bohan.

EAST CHICAGO: East Chicago Central 69–54 Lake Central; Andrean 57–54 Merrillville (ot); Central 67–60 Andrean. Officials: William Sorukas, Jon Davenport, Dale Cramer, Michael H. Smith, Larry Jones, Jerry Cook.

ELKHART: South Bend Clay 67–58 Elkhart Central; Westview 54–49 Fairfield; Clay 63–59 Westview. Officials: Bill Kachel, Jerry Stieglitz, Dave Raabe, Fred Perry, Jeff Simmons, Tom May.

EVANSVILLE: Vincennes 75–58 Evansville Bosse; South Spencer 61–50 Evansville Central, South Spencer 38–37 Vincennes (5ot). Officials: Ron McGriff, Gary Woodling, James Newlin, Scott Mellinger, Larry Maxwell, Stephen Fisher.

FORT WAYNE: Fort Wayne Dwenger 58–34 Fort Wayne Wayne; DeKalb 58–54 Leo (ot); Dwenger 91–62 DeKalb. Officials: Fred Hamilton, Sam Lower, James Robinson, Gene Marsh, Troy Ingram, Dick Modricker.

FRANKFORT: Noblesville 67–54 Southmont; Brownsburg 87–83 Frankfort; Brownsburg 78–56 Noblesville. Officials: Kent Smith, Scott Robison, Leland Thompson, Tom Walters, Bob Anderson, Mark Hay.

INDIANAPOLIS: Lawrence North 50–41 Southport; Ben Davis 57–43 Cathedral; Ben Davis 75–46 Lawrence North. Officials: Terry Bartell, Tony Ortman, Bill Wullner, Greg McAdams, Rex Nichols, Carl March.

LAFAYETTE: McCutcheon 65–50 Benton Central; Twin Lakes 41–36 South Putnam; McCutcheon 57–42 Twin Lakes. Officials: Larry Nixon, Michael Wallpe, Frank Bodwell, Mark Wise, Robert Frye, Mike Fox.

MARION: Marion 77–55 Adams Central; Kokomo 43–39 Logansport; Marion 46–45 Kokomo. Officials: Mark Baltz, Clark Hamilton, Norm Delph, Tony Garton, Jay C. Smith, Bruce Klonowski.

MICHIGAN CITY: Hebron 71–69 Michigan City Elston; Valparaiso 71–56 North Judson; Valparaiso 81–68 Hebron. Officials: Rick Scott, Bryce Heller, Phillip Napariu, Dan Amrhein, John Goss, Mike Waisnora.

NEW CASTLE: Connersville 68–59 Randolph Southern; Batesville 81–74 New Castle;

Tourney Time

Batesville 57–56 Connersville. Officials: Brian Osswald, Gary Hamilton. Terry Magnuson, Steve Corya, Don Resler, Jim Cox.

SEYMOUR: New Albany 54–49 Madison; Jeffersonville 86–45 Brownstown; New Albany 53–51 Jeffersonville. Officials: Melvin Redman, Doug Coddington, Keith Bagby, Ed Scahill, Bill Nimnicht, Dave Kavanaugh.

WARSAW: Manchester 72–64 Huntington North; Plymouth 51–43 Warsaw; Manchester 47–44 Plymouth. Officials: Gary Cheesman, Tom Crouch, Douglas Carl, Dave Vendrely, Tom Urban, Bryan Enterline.

WASHINGTON: Paoli 45–38 Corydon; Barr–Reeve 47–45 Southridge; Paoli 54–47 Barr-Reeve. Officials: Phil Vidito, Jay Ritter, Tom Rohr, Kim Baker, James Dunlap, Richard Foxen.

TERRE HAUTE: Terre Haute North 78–67 Bedford North Lawrence; Bloomfield 58–50 Mooresville; Bloomfield 51–45 Terre Haute North (ot). Officials: Bob Klein, Denis Schinderle, Don Nester, James Reid, Norman Hathcoat, Brad Groninger.

1994 SEMI–STATES

FORT WAYNE: Fort Wayne Dwenger 58–55 Marion; South Bend Clay 73–62 Manchester; Clay 61–51 Dwenger. Officials: Robert Frye, Richard Foxen, Tom Urban, Mark Hay, Larry Jones, Michael Smith.

INDIANAPOLIS: Muncie Central 76–66 Shelbyville; Ben Davis 73–61 Batesville; Ben Davis 60–49 Muncie Central. Officials: Bill Nimnicht, Dave Kavanaugh, Jay Smith, Dick Modricker, James Dunlap, Don Resler.

LAFAYETTE: East Chicago Central 75–63 Brownsburg; Valparaiso 73–68 McCutcheon; Valparaiso 83–82 East Chicago Central (4ot). Officials: Larry Maxwell, Bruce Klonowski, Bryan Enterline, Tim Smith, Norman Hathcoat, Rex Nichols.

TERRE HAUTE: Bloomfield 43–37 South Spencer; New Albany 55–38 Paoli; New Albany 66–36 Bloomfield. Officials: Troy Ingram, Jim Cox, Bob Anderson, Brad Groninger, Jeffery Simmons, John Goss.

1994 FINALS—March 26

INDIANAPOLIS (Hoosier Dome): Valparaiso 84–69 Ben Davis; South Bend Clay 61–57 New Albany; South Bend Clay 93–88 Valparaiso (ot). Officials: John Goss, Larry Jones, Norman Hathcoat, Jeffrey Simmons, James Dunlap, Rex Nichols.

1995 SECTIONALS

ANDERSON: Madison Heights 69–67 Elwood; Alexandria 62–52 Anderson; Frankton 57–44 Highland; Alexandria 79–57 Madison Heights; Alexandria 67–66 Frankton. Officials: Don Nester, Scott Robison, Kenneth Knapp, Tom Walters.

BEDFORD NORTH LAWRENCE: Bedford North Lawrence 71–52 Eastern (Greene); Edgewood 50–39 Bloomington South; Bloomington North 69–63 Brown County; Bedford North Lawrence 56—45 Edgewood; Bedford North Lawrence 74–48 Bloomington North. Officials: Leland Thompson, Matt Griffith, Bill Brinkman, Kent Smith.

BEN DAVIS: Ben Davis 65–36 Speedway; Pike 63–45 Brebeuf; Indianapolis Northwest 60–56 Indianapolis Ritter (ot); Ben Davis 82–53 Pike; Ben Davis 85–62 Northwest. Officials: Larry Nixon, Larry Decker, Danny Shields, Michael McGriff.

BOONVILLE: South Spencer 55–39 Princeton; Booneville 56–51 Gibson Southern; Heritage Hills 59–47 Tecumseh; South Spencer 52–39 Boonville; South Spencer 64–52 Heritage Hills. Officials: David Kavanaugh, Mike Harder, Richard Denson, Keith Bagby.

BROWNSBURG: Brownsburg 67–29 Danville; Plainfield 77–70 Avon; Cascade 58–51 Tri-West Hendricks; Brownsburg 102–56 Plainfield; Brownsburg 69–53 Cascade. Officials: Terry Bartell, Len Glazier, Derek Howard, Steven Smith.

CALUMET: Highland 58–57 Lake Central; Hammond Morton 65–63 Munster; Calumet 53–47 Griffith (ot); Highland 77–66 Morton; Highland 59–50 Calumet. Officials: Bruce Klonowski, Steve Homner, John Van Wagner, Michael Alspaugh.

CARMEL: Noblesville 70–65 Westfield; Hamilton Southeastern 68–57 Hamilton Heights; Carmel 76–52 Sheridan; Hamilton Southeastern 66–62 Noblesville; Carmel 60–57 Hamilton Southeastern (ot). Officials: Norman Delph, Patrick Strong, Michael Lewis, Bill Forehand.

COLUMBIA CITY: Whitko 83–46 Churubusco; Manchester 61–46 Central Noble; Columbia City 54–47 Tippecanoe Valley; Manchester 69–50 Whitko; Manchester 52–36 Columbia City. Officials: Tom Crouch, Rick Granger, Rick Shirk, Steve Godfroy.

COLUMBUS: Columbus North 60–54 Edinburgh; Waldron 54–52 Southwestern; Columbus East 57–46 Hauser; North 79–73 Waldron (ot); North 49–48 East (ot). Officials: Haymon Fields, Jim Wolfe, James Roberts, Phil Dant.

CONNERSVILLE: Cambridge City Lincoln 58–48 Union County; Franklin County 61–45 Hagerstown; Connersville 47–41 Rushville; Cambridge City Lincoln 49–47 Franklin County (ot); Connersville 45–38 Lincoln (ot). Officials: Michael Wallpe, Rod Weiss, Greg Taylor, Mark Robbins.

CRAWFORD COUNTY: Corydon 57–46 North Harrison; Tell City 72–58 Cannelton; Crawford County 50–43 Perry Central; Corydon 48–45 Tell City; Crawford County 42–39 Corydon, Officials: Melvin Redman, Robert Walters, Dave Hedge, Jay Ritter.

DEKALB: DeKalb 82–59 Hamilton; Eastside 67–49 Garrett; Angola 82–46 Fremont; DeKalb 86–63 Eastside; DeKalb 78–63 Angola. Officials: Clark Hamilton, Dale Zeigler, Jeff Wilson, Russ Teall.

EAST CHICAGO: Hammond High 91–54 Whiting; Hammond Gavit 66–56 Hammond Noll; East Chicago Central 87–53 Hammond Clark; Hammond High 57–55 Gavit; Central 70–67 Hammond High (ot). Officials: Steve Kvachkoff, Michael Brady, Fred Scheub, Dan Amrhein.

EAST NOBLE: West Noble 81–75 Prairie Heights (2ot); East Noble 55–52 Westview; Lakeland 71–67 Howe Military (ot); East Noble 67–41 West Noble; East Noble 61–51 Lakeland. Officials: Jerry Stieglitz, Brad Wilson, Ted Garton, Olin Roberts.

ELKHART: Concord 45–43 Mishawaka Marian; Elkhart Central 75–39 Mishawaka; Elkhart Memorial 66–55 Penn; Central 66–41 Concord; Central 64–62 Memorial (ot). Officials: Jay C. Smith, Curt Yoder, Don Schmidt, Ed Christoffel.

EVANSVILLE CENTRAL: North Posey 66–45 Mt. Vernon; Reitz 82–44 Mater Dei; Central 83–43 New Harmony; North Posey 64–53 Reitz; Central 71–59 North Posey. Officials: Gary Leistner, Paul Wahl, Mark Hollsapple, Mike Quinn.

EVANSVILLE HARRISON: Harrison 66–59 Bosse; North 75–37 Evansville Day; Castle

Tourney Time

57–44 Memorial; Harrison 48–39 North; Harrison 75–50 Castle. Officials: Stephen Fisher, Alan Deskin, Wayne Patterson, James Newlin.

FORT WAYNE NORTH SIDE: Dwenger 81–59 Northrop; Concordia 62–50 Carroll (Fort Wayne); North Side 70–48 Snider; Dwenger 77–64 Concordia; North Side 76–71 Dwenger. Officials: Jim Cox, Dennis Jackson, Bart Keesling, Richard Borror.

FORT WAYNE WAYNE: Homestead 65–57 Elmhurst; Luers 91–42 Fort Wayne Christian; South Side 71–68 Wayne; Homestead 56–32 Fort Wayne Canterbury; South Side 77–64 Luers; South Side 75–44 Homestead. Officials: David Raabe, Rodney Chamberlain, Gene Huston, Mark Hyman, Mark Tulchinsky, Lon Graft.

FOUNTAIN CENTRAL: South Newton 46–35 Seeger; Benton Central 61–42 Fountain Central; Covington 48–41 Attica; South Newton 70–67 Benton Central (ot); South Newton 60–39 Covington. Officials: Phil Napariu, Justin Rutledge, Sam Perry, Doug Coddington, Steve Egan.

FRANKFORT: Clinton Central 65–63 Rossville; Frankfort 58–55 Tri-Central; Tipton 45–29 Clinton Prairie; Frankfort 77–70 Clinton Central; Frankfort 94–78 Tipton. Officials: Mark Hay, Frank Bodwell, Tony Bova, Mike Padfield.

FRANKLIN: Roncalli 60–52 Center Grove; Franklin 62–45 Indian Creek; Greenwood 47–40 Whiteland; Franklin 94–65 Roncalli; Franklin 77–52 Greenwood. Officials: Denis Schinderle, Wayne Hobson, Ron Kottlowski, Terry Johnson.

FRANKLIN CENTRAL: Indianapolis Tech 62–54 Arlington (ot); Chatard 57–54 Franklin Central; Cathedral 62–54 Warren Central; Chatard 73–68 Tech; Cathedral 50–38 Chatard. Officials: Sam Lower, Tom Leix, Robert Harding, Jerry Middleton.

GARY: West Side 46–42 Wirt; Andrean 73–52 Mann; Roosevelt 87–77 Wallace; Andrean 63–61 West Side; Andrean 72–60 Roosevelt. Officials: Tom May, Tim Holmes, Robert Filipek, Mark Wise.

GOSHEN: North Wood 48–40 Goshen; Fairfield 59–29 Bethany Christian; Jimtown 62–58 Northridge (ot); North Wood 66–59 Fairfield; North Wood 84–56 Jimtown. Officials: Tim Smith, Bob Neff, Roger Pflughaupt, Richard Nelson.

GREENCASTLE: North Putnam 56–51 Turkey Run; North Vermillion 56–44 Greencastle; Rockville 52–50 South Putnam (ot); North Putnam 84–62 North Vermillion; Rockville 68–64 North Putnam (ot). Officials: Gary Hamilton, Chip Sweet, Jim Flanagan, John Crapo.

GREENFIELD-CENTRAL: New Palestine 61–55 Lapel; Greenfield-Central 79–76 Mt. Vernon (Fortville); Pendleton Heights 56–43 Eastern Hancock; Greenfield-Central 59–48 New Palestine; Pendleton Heights 53–51 Greenfield-Central. Officials: Bob Beeson, Bob Hallgarth, Robert Cochran, Kyle Ingram.

GREENSBURG: Batesville 77–55 South Decatur; South Ripley 98–65 Jac-Cen-Del; Greensburg 86–81 North Decatur (2ot); Batesville 78–60 South Ripley; Batesville 65–59 Greensburg. Officials: Robert Frye, Rick Normington, Jerry Wallace, Tony Ortman.

HUNTINGTON: Northfield 73–38 White's; Wabash 46–45 Blackford; Huntington North 64–42 Southwood; Northfield 50–44 Wabash; North 50–36 Northfield. Officials: Doug Carl, Tom Muth, Jerry Alberson, Dave Gentile, Lon Graft.

JAY COUNTY: Wapahani 61–45 Union City; Wes-Del 63–58 Monroe Central; Jay County 48–43 Delta; Wapahani 55–44 Wes-Del; Jay County 58–38 Wapahani. Officials: Rick Owens, Larry Alsip, Greg Reece, Bob Childers.

JEFFERSONVILLE: Jeffersonville 69–60 Silver Creek; Clarksville 70–61 Charlestown; Providence 93–55 Borden; Jeffersonville 66–43 Clarksville; Jeffersonville 92–54 Providence. Officials: Bill Nimnicht, Dan Henkle, Paul Meagher, Brad Sellers, Tim Stroud.

KANKAKEE VALLEY: Kankakee Valley 55–48 Lowell; Hebron 80–57 North Newton; Kouts 77–73 Boone Grove; Hebron 76–66 Kankakee Valley; Kouts 76–53 Hebron. Officials: Russ Radtke, Dale Gurgel, Joe Skvarek, Kirk Robinson.

KOKOMO: Western 72–54 Eastern (Greentown); Kokomo 62–48 Maconaquah; Taylor 67–53 Northwestern; Kokomo 57–44 Western; Kokomo 54–33 Taylor. Officials: Brian Osswald, Patrick Franklin, Mathew Miller, Michael H. Smith, Randall Gwin.

LAFAYETTE: McCutcheon 74–58 Carroll (Flora); Harrison 69–60 Central Catholic; West Lafayette 75–67 Lafayette Jefferson; McCutcheon 70–58 Harrison; McCutcheon 50–44 West Lafayette. Officials: Rick Scott, Larry Jones, Stan Foreman, Stan Ames.

LAWRENCE CENTRAL: Lawrence North 93–49 Park Tudor; Lawrence Central 107–40 Indiana School for the Deaf; North Central (Indianapolis) 89–44 Broad Ripple; Lawrence North 61–55 Lawrence Central (2ot); North Central 70–61 Lawrence North. Officials: Ric Foxen, Bob Wolfe, John Yantiss, Scott Mellinger.

LEBANON: Lebanon 47–35 Western Boone; Zionsville 70–66 Southmont; North Montgomery 57–49 Crawfordsville; Zionsville 56–50 Lebanon; Zionsville 52–50 North Montgomery. Officials: Tom Rohr, David Barlow, Walter Bishop, Ron James.

LOGANSPORT: Peru 86–72 Caston; Cass 84–58 Pioneer; Logansport 98–69 North Miami; Peru 88–66 Cass; Logansport 75–64 Peru. Officials: Gary Cheesman, Rick Hawley, Jon Custer, Pat Dumoulin.

MADISON: Madison 45–44 New Washington; Henryville 93–63 Madison Shawe; Scottsburg 91–58 Southwestern; Madison 72–40 Henryville; Scottsburg 78–53 Madison. Officials: Carl March, Steve Corya, Bill Meyerrose, Kim Baker.

MARION: Madison-Grant 82–73 Mississinewa; Eastbrook 57–56 Oak Hill; Marion 57–40 Marion Lakeview; Madison-Grant 64–51 Eastbrook; Marion 73–69 Madison-Grant. Officials: James Robinson, Dan VanTreese, Mel Botkin, David Vendrely, Bruce Hosier.

MARTINSVILLE: Mooresville 70–44 Cloverdale; Eminence 66–58 Monrovia; Martinsville 70–36 Owen Valley; Mooresville 64–51 Eminence; Martinsville 79–67 Mooresville. Officials: Phil Vidito, Joe Reed, David Estes, David Berman.

MERRILLVILLE: Merrillville 85–42 Hanover Central; Lake Station Edison 57–53 River Forest; Crown Point 48–41 Hobart; Merrillville 77–36 Lake Station Edison; Merrillville 64–37 Crown Point. Officials: Jerry Cook, Tom Behny, Michael Spann, Jeff Simmons, Andy Simpson.

MICHIGAN CITY: LaPorte 60–42 Westville; Michigan City Elston 69–65 New Prairie (ot); Michigan City Rogers 77–61 Marquette; Elston 55–43 LaPorte; Elston 57–40 Rogers. Officials: Mike Waisnora, Kevin Weinberg, Doug Cook, John Goss.

MUNCIE: Daleville 50–45 Yorktown; Southside 78–56 Central; Cowan 75–46 Burris; Southside 98–70 Daleville; Muncie Southside 76–42 Cowan. Officials: Ray Tebbe, Kenneth Cobb, Jim Keifer, Gene Marsh.

NEW ALBANY: South Central (Elizabeth) 59–44 Eastern; New Albany 50–45 Floyd Central; Lanesville 64–42 Graceland Christian; New Albany 80–54 South Central; New Albany 49–36 Lanesville. Officials: Terry Magnuson, Jeffrey Culp, David Moore, Frederick Cooper.

NEW CASTLE: New Castle 73–36 Shenandoah; Tri 47–44 Blue River Valley; Knightstown

Tourney Time

63–57 Morton Memorial; New Castle 94–46 Tri; New Castle 91–41 Knightstown. Officials: Tom Schenkel, John Walker, Ernie Brewer, Larry Sintz.

NEW HAVEN: Harding 66–45 Leo; New Haven 70–49 Heritage, Fort Wayne Blackhawk 54–39 Woodlan; New Haven 73–54 Harding; New Haven 40–39 Blackhawk. Officials: Brad Groninger, Randall Miller, Doug Flatter, Judson Raver.

NORTH JUDSON: North Judson 82–41 Winamac, West Central 64–55 South Central (Union Mills); LaCrosse 46–42 Knox; North Judson 77–52 West Central; North Judson 90–39 LaCrosse. Officials: Al Yelich, Edward Malek, Mike Gruver, William Sorukas.

PAOLI: Paoli 63–54 West Washington; Springs Valley 65–56 Mitchell; Orleans 64–62 Salem; Paoli 59–51 Springs Valley; Orleans 41–36 Paoli. Officials: Bob Klein, Gary Woodling, Gary Wier, Ed Roush.

PLYMOUTH: Bremen 61–51 Culver; Oregon-Davis 63–55 LaVille; Plymouth 76–47 Glenn; Oregon-Davis 60–59 Bremen; Plymouth 67–51 Oregon-Davis. Officials: Bryce Heller, Mark McCammon, Jack Raabe, Gregory Yergler.

RICHMOND: Centerville 67–53 Winchester; Northeastern 55–52 Union (Modoc); Richmond 78–66 Randolph Southern; Northeastern 73–59 Centerville; Richmond 48–43 Northeastern. Officials: Roger Holder, Wayne Chappell, Gary Chambers, Keith Fields.

SEYMOUR: Jennings County 83–78 Brownstown; Austin 61–51 Crothersville; Seymour 61–47 Medora; Jennings County 85–80 Austin; Jennings County 82–57 Seymour. Officials: Michael Smith, David Bolsega, Michael Baas, Greg McAdams.

SHELBYVILLE: Indianapolis Scecina 65–57 Triton Central; Beech Grove 78–57 Morristown; Shelbyville 87–73 Indianapolis Lutheran; Beech Grove 76–62 Scecina; Shelbyville 78–67 Beech Grove. Officials: Mike Bohan, Joe Stafford, Mike Campbell, Ed Scahill.

SOUTH ADAMS: Norwell 47–43 Southern Wells; Bellmont 66–61 Bluffton (ot); South Adams 37–36 Adams Central; Norwell 68–62 Bellmont; Norwell 63–47 South Adams. Officials: Mike Crouch, Dan Breneman, Tom Kenworthy, Fred Hamilton,

SOUTH BEND: St. Joseph's 71–47 Washington; Riley 79–50 Adams; Clay 78–69 LaSalle; Riley 72–62 St. Joseph's; Riley 71–68 South Bend Clay. Officials: Dale Cramer, Jeff Heiliger, Merlin Nice, Jon Davenport.

SOUTH DEARBORN: East Central 80–48 Milan; South Dearborn 72–69 Rising Sun; Switzerland County 72–63 Lawrenceburg; South Dearborn 72–69 East Central; South Dearborn 75–60 Switzerland County. Officials: Troy Ingram, Dale Goodwin, Mike Alford, Kevin Moore.

SOUTHPORT: Indianapolis Washington 78–44 Decatur Central; Perry Meridian 54–51 Indianapolis Howe; Southport 70–40 Indianapolis Manual; Washington 76–38 Perry Meridian; Washington 67–48 Southport. Officials: Mark Baltz, Arnold Freeman Jr., Terry Kreider, Tony Bierschbach.

SOUTHRIDGE: Pike Central 63–55 Northeast Dubois; Jasper 47–36 Oakland City; Southridge 46–45 Forest Park; Jasper 61–51 Pike Central; Jasper 70–51 Southridge. Officials: Larry Maxwell, David Senning, Tom Jellison, Rex Nichols.

TERRE HAUTE: Northview 61–51 Terre Haute South, Terre Haute North 64–59 West Vigo; South Vermillion 71–42 Riverton Parke; North 60–48 Northview; North 88–44 South Vermillion. Officials: Jerry Taylor, Alan Agee, Michael Furnish, Michael Fox.

TWIN LAKES: Frontier 54–50 North White; Twin Lakes 64–62 Tri-County (2ot); Rensselaer 74–63 Delphi; Twin Lakes 86–80 Frontier; Rensselaer 66–61 Twin Lakes. Officials: Richard

Modricker, Jack Urban, Steve Elkins, Marvin Davis.

VALPARAISO: Wheeler 42–35 Chesterton; Valparaiso 61–48 Morgan Twp.; Portage 63–58 Washington Twp.; Valparaiso 55–47 Wheeler; Portage 42–38 Valparaiso. Officials: Jerome Fawley, Ronald Gradeless, Ronald Stevens, Jeffrey Hull.

VINCENNES: Vincennes 72–44 South Knox; Sullivan 51–50 North Knox; Vincennes Rivet 70–47 North Central (Farmersburg); Lincoln 63–51 Sullivan; Lincoln 88–42 Vincennes Rivet. Officials: Ron Grimes, Rick Gentry, Don Corey, James Dunlap.

WARSAW: Rochester 60–48 Argos; Triton 63–59 Culver Military; Wawasee 60–54 Warsaw; Rochester 58–57 Triton; Wawasee 54–39 Rochester. Officials: William Kachel, Dennis Maude, Larry Johnson, Robert Stambazze.

WASHINGTON: Shoals 70–35 Washington Catholic; Washington 53–48 North Daviess; Loogootee 57–49 Barr-Reeve; Washington 62–55 Shoals; Loogootee 73–64 Washington. Officials: Ron McGriff, Darrell Stone, Donald Whitlow, James Reid.

WHITE RIVER VALLEY: Dugger 59–56 Shakamak; White River Valley 47–43 Clay City; Bloomfield 76–51 Linton-Stockton; White River Valley 58–51 Dugger; Bloomfield 67–64 White River Valley. Officials: Bob Anderson, Greg Bowman, Craig Cress, Dennis Espenlaub.

1995 REGIONALS

ANDERSON: Jay County 55–49 Pendleton Heights; Alexandria 63–62 Muncie Southside; Alexandria 66–47 Jay County. Officials: Michael Wallpe, Greg McAdams, Tom Schenkel, Michael H. Smith, Jay C. Smith, Richard Modricker.

COLUMBUS: South Dearborn 85–64 Columbus North; Shelbyville 95–88 Franklin; Shelbyville 83–81 South Dearborn. Officials: Norman Delph, Tony Ortman, Mark Baltz, Mike Quinn, Rick Owens, Bill Nimnicht.

ELKHART: Elkhart Central 52–47 South Bend Riley; North Wood 52–47 East Noble; Central 48–47 North Wood. Officials: Mark Hyman, Mark Wise, Daniel Amrhein, Robert Starnbazze, Mike Waisnora, Tom May.

EVANSVILLE: Evansville Harrison 62–51 Vincennes; South Spencer 67–63 Evansville Central; Harrison 56–52 South Spencer. Officials: Ron McGriff, James Reid, Terry Magnuson, Ed Roush, Stephen Fisher, Gary Leistner.

FORT WAYNE: Fort Wayne North Side 84–75 DeKalb; Fort Wayne South Side 73–59 New Haven; North Side 73–48 South Side. Officials: Doug Carl, Bill Kachel, Tom Crouch, Ed Christoffel, Troy Ingram, Mike Crouch.

FRANKFORT: Frankfort 71–70 Carmel (ot); Brownsburg 86–57 Zionsville; Brownsburg 103–63 Frankfort. Officials: Ed Scahill, Steve Godfroy, Don Nester, Jerry Middleton, Rick Scott, Gary Cheesman.

GARY: Merrillville 62–58 East Chicago Central; Andrean 68–56 Highland; Merrillville 91–85 Andrean. Officials: Bryce Heller, Russ Radtke, Jerome Fawley, Gregory Yergler, Mark Hay, Terry Bartell.

HUNTINGTON: Huntington North 54–46 Wawasee; Plymouth 49–47 Manchester; Plymouth 61–43 Huntington North. Officials: Sam Lower, Gene Marsh, James Robinson, Keith Fields, Bob Anderson, Ray Tebbe.

INDIANAPOLIS: Ben Davis 79–77 Indianapolis Washington; Cathedral 68–49 North

Tourney Time

Central; Ben Davis 67–65 Cathedral. Officials: Bob Klein, William Terry Johnson, Roger Holder, Richard Borror, Bob Beeson, Carl March.

LAFAYETTE: South Newton 60–47 Rockville; McCutcheon 75–53 Rensselaer; McCutcheon 64–48 South Newton. Officials: Dave Raabe, Fred Hamilton, Jim Cox, Kyle Ingram, Bob Frye, Mike Bohan.

MARION: Marion 73–59 Norwell; Kokomo 68–55 Logansport; Kokomo 46–37 Marion (ot). Officials: Jerry Stieglitz, Scott Mellinger, Clark Hamilton, Jon Davenport, Tim Smith, Brad Groninger.

MICHIGAN CITY: North Judson 74–56 Portage; Michigan City Elston 87–69 Kouts; North Judson 84–64 Elston. Officials: Dale Cramer, William Sorukas, Tom Walters, Marvin Davis, Jerry Cook, Bruce Klonowski.

NEW CASTLE: New Castle 77–54 Richmond; Connersville 52–50 Batesville; New Castle 64–54 Connersville. Officials: Lee Thompson, John Crapo, Haymon Fields, Tony Bierschbach, Larry Nixon, Gary Hamilton.

SEYMOUR: New Albany 83–67 Scottsburg; Jeffersonville 68–60 Jennings County; Jeffersonville 63–60 New Albany (2ot). Officials: Michael Fox, Kent Smith, Brian Osswald, Kim Baker, Larry Maxwell, David Kavanaugh.

TERRE HAUTE: Terre Haute North 81–74 Martinsville; Bedford North Lawrence 74–55 Bloomfield; Bedford North Lawrence 42–41 Terre Haute North. Officials: Keith Bagby, Philip Napariu, Phil Vidito, Ron James, Michael S. Smith, Melvin Redman.

WASHINGTON: Jasper 58–44 Orleans; Crawford County 39–37 Loogootee; Crawford County 38–36 Jasper. Officials: Denis Schinderle, Fred Cooper, Doug Coddington, Dennis Espenlaub, Jerry Taylor, Tom Rohr.

1995 SEMI—STATES

EVANSVILLE CENTRAL: Bedford North Lawrence 55–49 Crawford County; Jeffersonville 86–68 Evansville Harrison; Jeffersonville 70–69 Bedford North Lawrence. Officials: Mike Bohan, Brad Groninger, Jerry Taylor, Larry Nixon, Robert Frye, Stephen Fisher.

INDIANAPOLIS: New Castle 81–74 Alexandria; Ben Davis 80–44 Shelbyville; Ben Davis 65–60 New Castle. Officials: Mark Hay, Bill Nimnicht, Jay C. Smith, Mel Redman, Rick Owens, Jerry Cook.

LAFAYETTE: North Judson 71–64 McCutcheon; Merrillville 74–69 Brownsburg; Merrillville 69–54 North Judson. Officials: Mike Waisnora, Tom May, Troy Ingram, Bruce Klonowski, Larry Maxwell, Michael S. Smith.

SOUTH BEND: Elkhart Central 35–34 Kokomo; Plymouth 58–50 Fort Wayne North; Elkhart Central 62–44 Plymouth. Officials: Bob Anderson, Gary Cheesman, Rick Scott, Richard Modricker, Bob Beeson, Tim Smith.

1995 FINALS—March 25

INDIANAPOLIS (RCA Dome): Merrillville 62–49 Elkhart Central; Ben Davis 82–62 Jeffersonville; Ben Davis 58–57 Merrillville. Officials: Bob Frye, Larry Maxwell, Bob Beeson, Tim Smith, Rick Owens, Mike Smith.

1996 SECTIONALS

ANDERSON: Highland 59–58 Elwood (ot); Anderson 89–75 Madison Heights; Alexandria 69–47 Frankton; Anderson 70–61 Highland; Anderson 65–61 Alexandria. Officials: James Robinson, Mark Robbins, Wayne Chappell, Rick Owens.

BEDFORD NORTH LAWRENCE: Bloomington North 53–51 Brown County; Bloomington South 62–50 Edgewood; Bedford North Lawrence 72–52 Eastern (Bloomfield); Bloomington South 52–49 Bloomington North; Bloomington South 53–51 Bedford North Lawrence. Officials: Phil Vidito, Steven Corya, Rex Wallace, Bob Klein.

BEN DAVIS: Indianapolis Northwest 51–49 Brebeuf; Ritter 79–74 Speedway; Ben Davis 62–55 Pike; Ritter 64–59 Northwest; Ben Davis 78–54 Ritter. Officials: Terry Bartell, Kevin Moore, Bob Hallgarth, Mike Padfield.

BOONVILLE: Boonville 69–63 Heritage Hills; Gibson Southern 44–36 Princeton; South Spencer 57–56 Tecumseh; Gibson Southern 60–56 Boonville; South Spencer 50–49 Gibson Southern. Officials: James Dunlap, Dave Senning, Wayne Patterson, Jay Ritter.

BROWNSBURG: Avon 49–44 Brownsburg; Danville 81–57 Tri-West Hendricks; Plainfield 82–60 Cascade; Avon 65–54 Danville; Plainfield 67–61 Avon. Officials: Mark Baltz, Craig Cress, Phil Dant, Frank Bodwell.

CALUMET: Hammond Morton 66–53 Munster; Highland 51–46 Lake Central; Calumet 62–56 Griffith; Morton 73–63 Highland (ot); Calumet 72–69 Morton. Officials: Mark Wise, Tom Behny, Dan Gurgon, Tim Holmes.

CENTER GROVE: Whiteland 65–61 Roncalli; Franklin 45–43 Greenwood; Center Grove 75–41 Indian Creek; Franklin 53–49 Whiteland; Franklin 70–64 Center Grove. Officials: Bob Anderson, Gary Woodling, Jon Custer, David Berman.

COLUMBIA CITY: Manchester 48–34 Central Noble; Columbia City 69–57 Tippecanoe Valley; Whitko 67–36 Churubusco; Manchester 45–41 Columbia City; Whitko 60–53 Manchester. Officials: Fred Hamilton, Donald Schmidt, Dale Zeigler, Dave Gentile.

COLUMBUS: Columbus East 80–50 Waldron; Columbus North 77–40 Edinburgh; Southwestern (Shelbyville) 50–48 Hauser; East 64–58 North; East 73–52 Southwestern (Shelbyville). Officials: Leland Thompson, Danny Shields, Paul Meagher, Tom Walters.

CONNERSVILLE: Franklin County 49–47 Hagerstown; Connersville 54–48 Cambridge City Lincoln; Rushville 55–38 Union County; Connersville 56–45 Franklin County; Connersville 65–49 Rushville. Officials: Roger Holder, Ken Cobb, John Cowan, Ed Scahill.

CRAWFORD COUNTY: Tell City 64–60 Cannelton; Perry Central 59–47 Crawford County; North Harrison 74–51 Corydon Central; Perry Central 73–71 Tell City; North Harrison 71–56 Perry Central. Officials. David Kavanaugh, Paul Wahl, Mike Harder, Dennis Espenlaub.

EAST CHICAGO: East Chicago Central 53–51 Hammond Noll; Hammond Clark 80–36 Whiting; Hammond High 69–44 Hammond Gavit; Central 74–47 Clark; Hammond High 63–51 Central. Officials: John Goss, Jeffrey Hull, Joseph Skvarek, Steve Kvachkoff.

EAST NOBLE: East Noble 66–44 Westview; West Noble 75–68 Prairie Heights; Lakeland 97–40 Howe Military; East Noble 73–47 West Noble; East Noble 66–40 Lakeland. Officials: David Raabe, Thomas Muth, Eric Coburn, Lance Grubbs.

ELKHART: Penn 69–64 Elkhart Memorial; Concord 62–50 Mishawaka Marian; Elkhart Central 55–44 Mishawaka; Penn 62–49 Concord; Penn 58–56 Central. Officials: Clark Hamilton, Kirk Robinson, Stephen Homner, Tim Smith.

Tourney Time

EVANSVILLE CENTRAL: Central 78–58 Mater Dei; Reitz 77–53 New Harmony; Mt. Vernon 64–55 North Posey; Central 78–76 Reitz (ot); Central 72–54 Mt. Vernon. Officials: Carl March, Rick Gentry, Matt Griffith, Alan Agee.

EVANSVILLE NORTH: North 60–46 Evansville Day; Castle 49–43 Harrison (ot); Memorial 67–62 Bosse; North 64–51 Castle; Memorial 53–40 North. Officials: Gary Leistner, Chip Sweet, Nick Matheis. Melvin Redman.

FORT WAYNE NORTH SIDE: Concordia 55–54 North Side; Dwenger 78–57 Carroll (Fort Wayne); Snider 52–51 Northrop; Dwenger 84–66 Concordia; Dwenger 59–54 Snider. Officials: Mike Crouch, Olin Roberts, Lon Graft, Bruce Hosier.

FORT WAYNE WAYNE: South Side 67–42 Elmhurst; Homestead 121–35 Fort Wayne Christian; Canterbury 75–70 Luers; South Side 65–51 Wayne; Canterbury 77–71 Homestead; South Side 103–53 Fort Wayne Canterbury. Officials: Dennis Jackson, Robert Stambazze, Doug Flatter, Randall Miller, Joe Huff, Butch Lehman.

FOUNTAIN CENTRAL: Covington 83–50 Seeger; Benton Central 86–53 Fountain Central; South Newton 47–36 Attica; Benton Central 66–41 Covington; Benton Central 43–30 South Newton. Officials: Ray Tebbe, Terry Kreider, Walter Bishop, Tony Bierschbach.

FRANKFORT: Tri-Central 61–53 Tipton; Clinton Prairie 69–56 Clinton Central; Frankfort 80–79 Rossville; Clinton Prairie 73–67 Tri-Central; Frankfort 79–71 Clinton Prairie. Officials: Michael Smith, Patrick Franklin, Greg Webb, Steve Elkins.

FRANKLIN CENTRAL: Franklin Central 79–70 Indianapolis Tech; Warren Central 68–50 Chatard; Cathedral 64–45 Arlington; Franklin Central 67–53 Warren Central; Franklin Central 45–41 Cathedral. Officials: William Terry Johnson, Mike Furnish, Greg Reece, Bill Forehand.

GARRETT: DeKalb 74–45 Angola; Eastside 47–36 Hamilton; Garrett 68–55 Fremont; DeKalb 65–45 Eastside; DeKalb 90–72 Garrett. Officials: Mark Hyman, Dennis Maude, Ted Garton, Judson Raver.

GARY: Wirt 64–63 Roosevelt (ot); West Side 86–73 Andrean; Wallace 93–82 Mann; West Side 74–68 Wirt; Wallace 79–71 West Side. Officials: Mike Waisnora, Mark Tulchinsky, Ed Malek, Ron Gradeless.

GOSHEN: Northridge 68–33 Bethany Christian; Goshen 60–37 Jimtown; Northwood 72–42 Fairfield; Northridge 42–40 Goshen; Northridge 53–45 Northwood. Officials: Jay Smith, Merlin Nice, Mark McCammon, Robert Childers.

GREENCASTLE: North Putnam 72–70 Turkey Run (ot); Greencastle 59–38 North Vermillion; South Putnam 46–42 Rockville; Greencastle 72–62 North Putnam; Greencastle 57–44 South Putnam. Officials: Don Nester, Bob Wolfe, Paul Mills, Patrick Strong.

GREENFIELD–CENTRAL: New Palestine 74–45 Greenfield-Central; Pendleton Heights 78–27 Lapel; Mt. Vernon 64–52 Eastern Hancock; Pendleton Heights 50–41 New Palestine; Pendleton Heights 64–51 Mt. Vernon. Officials: Tom Urban, Anthony Bova, Larry Alsip, Kent Smith.

GREENSBURG: North Decatur 69–46 Jac-Cen-Del; Batesville 68–50 South Ripley; Greensburg 48–43 South Decatur; Batesville 71–52 North Decatur; Batesville 56–42 Greensburg. Officials: Dan Breneman, John Yantiss, Derek Howard, Gene Huston.

HUNTINGTON: Huntington North 50–36 Wabash; Northfield 114–31 White's; Southwood 73–61 Blackford (ot); North 57–46 Northfield; North 39–30 Southwood. Officials: Tom Crouch, Steve Smith, Joe Huff, Bob Enterline, Jerry Stieghtz.

JAY COUNTY: Delta 84–52 Wes-Del; Jay County 65–40 Monroe Central; Union City 69–

57 Wapahani; Jay County 64–51 Delta; Jay County 82–44 Union City. Officials: Scott Mellinger, Tom Kenworthy, Rod Weiss, Richard Borror.

JEFFERSONVILLE: Silver Creek 57–48 Providence; Charlestown 64–58 Borden; Jeffersonville 73–48 Clarksville; Silver Creek 63–54 Charlestown; Jeffersonville 57–50 Silver Creek. Officials: Kim Baker, Mike Baas, Donald Whitlow, Mike Quinn.

KANKAKEE VALLEY: Boone Grove 65–30 Hebron; Kankakee Valley 56–50 Lowell; Kouts 60–49 North Newton; Kankakee Valley 65–52 Boone Grove; Kouts 78–68 Kankakee Valley. Officials: Marvin Davis, Ronald Stevens, Fred Scheub, Jon Davenport.

KOKOMO: Western 71–70 Maconaquah; Kokomo 81–43 Eastern (Greentown); Taylor 58–55 Northwestern; Kokomo 53–35 Western; Kokomo 60–30 Taylor. Officials: Douglas Carl, Larry Johnson, Shawn Lambert, Rick Hawley.

LAFAYETTE: Central Catholic 75–56 West Lafayette; Lafayette Jefferson 72–46 McCutcheon; Carroll (Flora) 57–53 Harrison (West Lafayette); Jefferson 81–52 Central Catholic; Jefferson 61–50 Carroll (Flora). Officials: Jerry Taylor, Matthew Miller, Len Glazier, Ron James.

LAWRENCE NORTH: Lawrence Central 89–56 Indianapolis Broad Ripple; North Central (Indianapolis) 81–35 Park Tudor; Lawrence North 122–27 Indiana School for the Deaf; North Central 74–64 Lawrence Central (ot); Lawrence North 47–43 North Central (Indianapolis). Officials: Tom Rohr, Justin Rutledge, Brian Humphrey, Gary Hamilton.

LOGANSPORT: Logansport 57–53 Pioneer; Peru 60–43 North Miami; Cass 60–53 Caston; Logansport 80–49 Peru; Logansport 64–39 Cass. Officials: Tom May, Bill Kachel, Mike Gruver, Lawrence Samano.

MADISON: New Washington 77–74 Southwestern (Hanover); Scottsburg 100–50 Henryville; Madison 75–37 Madison Shawe; Scottsburg 97–70 New Washington; Scottsburg 77–67 Madison. Officials: Mike Wallpe, Bill Brinkman, Dave Moore, Ernie Brewer.

MARION: Madison–Grant 65–41 Eastbrook; Marion 56–40 Marion Lakeview Christian; Oak Hill 51–37 Mississinewa; Madison-Grant 71–54 Marion; Madison-Grant 61–57 Oak Hill. Officials: Norm Delph, Jack Urbin, Robert Harding, Rodney Chamberlain.

MARTINSVILLE: Mooresville 63–58 Owen Valley; Martinsville 95–57 Eminence; Monrovia 86–61 Cloverdale; Mooresville 91–73 Martinsville; Monrovia 69–56 Mooresville. Officials: Mike Bohan, Don Corey, Dan Stewart, Larry Sintz.

MERRILLVILLE: River Forest 58–56 Lake Station; Merrillville 79–62 Hanover Central; Crown Point 80–62 Hobart; Merrillville 93–51 River Forest; Merrillville 72–61 Crown Point. Officials: Dan Amrhein, Robert Filipek, Cary Schnick, Greg Yergler.

MICHIGAN CITY: Marquette Catholic 76–74 New Prairie; LaPorte 78–68 Westville; Michigan City 80–60 Marquette; LaPorte 77–66 Michigan City (ot). Officials: Jerome Fawley, Al Yelich, Andy Simpson, Bob Neff.

MUNCIE: Central 63–39 Muncie Burris; Cowan 51–48 Daleville; Southside 67–49 Yorktown; Central 72–61 Cowan; Southside 91–66 Central. Officials: Brian Oswald, David Barlow, David Bolsega, Wayne Hobson.

NEW ALBANY: Lanesville 63–60 Eastern (Pekin); Graceland Christian 66–55 South Central (Elizabeth); New Albany 74–69 Floyd Central; Graceland Christian 70–42 Lanesville; New Albany 76–47 Graceland Christian. Officials: Ed Roush, Ron McGriff, Tim Stroud, Keith Bagby.

NEW CASTLE: Blue River Valley 76–65 Shenandoah; New Castle 121–26 Morton Memorial; Knightstown, 62–59 Tri; New Castle 99–50 Blue River Valley; New Castle 101–56 Knightstown.

Tourney Time

Officials: Jim Cox, Michael McGriff, Mel Botkin, Jim Keifer.

NEW HAVEN: Harding 65–60 Heritage (ot); New Haven 77–58 Fort Wayne Blackhawk; Leo 62–58 Woodlan, New Haven 63–53 Harding; New Haven 70–58 Leo. Officials: Kyle Ingram, Fred Hamilton, Steve Godfroy, Bart Keesling, Tom Schenkel.

NOBLESVILLE: Carmel 69–44 Westfield; Hamilton Heights 63–62 Sheridan; Noblesville 66–62 Hamilton Southeastern; Carmel 71–51 Hamilton Heights; Noblesville 70–67 Carmel. Officials: Philip Napariu, Robert Cochran, Randall Gwin, Tony Ortman.

NORTH JUDSON: LaCrosse 73–70 Knox; Winamac 76–64 West Central; North Judson 71–52 South Central; Winamac 94–55 LaCrosse, North Judson 58–56 Winamac. Officials: Dick Modricker, Russ Teall, Steve Egan, Ed Christoffel.

NORTH MONTGOMERY: North Montgomery 79–57 Crawfordsville; Western Boone 51–49 Southmont; Lebanon 69–51 Zionsville; Western Boone 60–58 North Montgomery; Western Boone 38–37 Lebanon. Officials: Mike Fox, Sam Berry, Mark Curtis, Rick Normington.

PAOLI: West Washington 52–45 Orleans; Mitchell 61–60 Paoli; Salem 55–52 Springs Valley; West Washington 73–52 Mitchell; West Washington 93–67 Salem. Officials: Doug Coddington, Jeff Culp, Tim Jellison, Bob Walters.

PLYMOUTH: Bremen 64–57 LaVille; Culver 49–45 Oregon-Davis; Plymouth 68–49 Glenn; Bremen 66–34 Culver; Plymouth 85–53 Bremen. Officials: Bruce Klonowski, Jeffrey Heiliger, Jeffrey Morrett, Stan Foreman.

RICHMOND: Centerville 85–49 Union (Modoc); Richmond 70–45 Northeastern; Winchester 80–64 Randolph Southern; Richmond 72–60 Centerville; Richmond 58–48 Winchester. Officials: Greg McAdams, Kenny Knapp, Robert Voss, Rick Shirk.

SEYMOUR: Austin 75–57 Medora; Jennings County 75–49 Seymour; Brownstown 75–60 Crothersville; Jennings County 79–62 Austin; Jennings County 76–70 Brownstown. Officials: Terry Magnuson, William Meyerrose, Dave Hedge, Gary Wier.

SHELBYVILLE: Beech Grove 58–57 Morristown, Shelbyville 72–51 Indianapolis Scecina; Triton Central 70–54 Indianapolis Lutheran; Shelbyville 53–50 Beech Grove; Shelbyville 56–49 Triton Central. Officials: Brad Groninger, Mike Alford, Dale Goodwin, Dan VanTreese.

SOUTH ADAMS: Bellmont 59–49 Norwell; Bluffton 42–27 South Adams; Southern Wells 72–70 Adams Central; Bellmont 41–36 Bluffton; Southern Wells 79–74 Bellmont. Officials: Gene Marsh, Jack Raabe, Jeff Wilson, Keith Fields.

SOUTH BEND: Clay 61–39 St. Joseph's; LaSalle 68–53 Riley; Washington 69–55 Adams; Clay 70–59 LaSalle (ot); Clay 76–62 Washington. Officials: Bryce Heller, Douglas Cook, Dale Gurgel, Russell Radtke.

SOUTH DEARBORN: Rising San 80–65 Switzerland County; South Dearborn 94–71 Milan; Lawrenceburg 54–52 East Central; Rising Sun 82–72 South Dearborn; Lawrenceburg 73–55 Rising Sun. Officials: Jerry Middleton; Greg Bowman, Gary Chambers, Greg Taylor.

SOUTHPORT: Decatur Central 54–45 Indianapolis Manual; Southport 62–33 Perry Meridian; Decatur Central 49–44 Southport. Officials: John Walker, Larry Decker, Greg Stolle, Steve Smith.

SOUTHRIDGE: Pike Central 76–54 Forest Park; Jasper 66–61 Southridge; Northeast Dubois 47–32 Oakland City; Jasper 70–47 Pike Central; Jasper 61–43 Northeast Dubois. Officials: Bill Nimnicht, Alan Deskin, Richard Denson, James Newlin.

TERRE HAUTE: South Vermillion 71–46 Riverton Parke; Terre Haute North 71–59 Terre

Haute South; West Vigo 71–33 Northview; North 59–42 South Vermillion; Terre Haute North 55–53 West Vigo. Officials: Larry Nixon, Arnold Freeman, David Estes, Haymon Fields.

TWIN LAKES: Frontier 46–45 Tri–County; North White 65–58 Rensselaer; Delphi 79–71 Twin Lakes (ot); North White 60–59 Frontier (ot); Delphi 57–51 North White. Officials: Rich Scott, Bradley Wilson, John Van Wagner, Patrick Dumoulin.

VALPARAISO: Morgan Twp. 46–45 Wheeler; Portage 28–25 Valparaiso; Chesterton 83–71 Washington Twp.; Portage 69–45 Morgan Twp.; Portage 67–61 Chesterton (ot). Officials: Jeffrey Simmons, Kevin Weinberg, Kevin Mikesell, Richard Nelson.

VINCENNES: Vincennes Rivet 55–50 North Central (Farmersburg); Sullivan 56–32 South Knox; Vincennes 66–43 North Knox; Vincennes Rivet 71–60 Sullivan; Lincoln 77–35 Rivet. Officials: Rex Nichols, Jim Reid, Darrell Stone, Larry Maxwell.

WARSAW: Warsaw 74–42 Wawasee; Triton 58–44 Culver Military; Rochester 75–69 Argos; Warsaw 66–53 Triton; Warsaw 69–44 Rochester. Officials: Larry Jones, Curt Yoder, Michael Spann, Jerry Cook

WASHINGTON: Loogootee 47–42 Barr-Reeve; North Daviess 53–50 Washington (ot); Shoals 63–42 Washington Catholic; Loogootee 62–59 North Daviess; Loogootee 47–43 Shoals. Officials: Frederick Cooper, Mark Holsapple, Ronald Grimes, Joe Reed.

WHITE RIVER VALLEY: White River Valley 27–24 Union (Dugger); Shakamak 57–48 Clay City; Bloomfield 72–38 Linton-Stockton; White River Valley 45–44 Shakamak (ot); White River Valley 51–46 Bloomfield. Officials: Denis Schinderle, Jimmy Wolfe, Joseph Stafford, John Crapo.

1996 REGIONALS

ANDERSON: Jay County 55–48 Pendleton Heights; Anderson 75–66 Muncie Southside; Anderson 52–51 Jay County. Officials: Kim Baker, Rich Borror, William Terry Johnson, Patrick Dumoulin, Ray Tebbe, Tom Rohr.

COLUMBUS: Shelbyville 55–51 Franklin; Lawrenceburg 65–55 Columbus East; Shelbyville 72–52 Lawrenceburg. Officials: Mike Wallpe, Larry Sintz, Phil Vidito, Ed Scahill, Don Nester, Mike Bohan.

EAST CHICAGO: Gary Wallace 73–64 Merrillville; Hammond High 81–71 Calumet; Gary Wallace 68–64 Hammond High. Officials: Bruce Klonowski, Richard Nelson, Dan Amrhein, Jon Davenport, Jay Smith, Jerome Fawley.

ELKHART: East Noble 38–37 Penn; Northridge 59–42 South Bend Clay; East Noble 41–40 Northridge. Officials: David Raabe, Jerry Stieglitz, Dennis Jackson, David Gentile, Thomas May, Jeffrey Simmons.

EVANSVILLE: Evansville Memorial 66–57 Evansville Central; Vincennes 72–55 South Spencer; Lincoln 53–38 Memorial. Officials: Ron Grimes, Dennis Espenlaub, David Kavanaugh, John Crapo, Gary Leistner, James Dunlap.

FORT WAYNE: Fort Wayne Dwenger 72–67 Fort Wayne South Side; DeKalb 77–60 New Haven; Fort Wayne Dwenger 53–49 DeKalb. Officials: Mark Hyman, Tom Schenkel, James Robinson, Bob Neff, Jim Cox, Larry Jones.

FRANKFORT: Noblesville 68–64 Frankfort; Plainfield 77–54 Western Boone; Plainfield 67–65 Noblesville (ot). Officials: Jerry Middleton, Gary Hamilton, Terry Magnuson, Bill Forehand,

Tourney Time

Jerry Taylor, Rick Scott.

INDIANAPOLIS: Lawrence North 59–38 Decatur Central; Ben Davis 62–59 Franklin Central (ot); Ben Davis 42–37 Lawrence North. Officials: Dan Breneman, Greg McAdams, Tom Urban, Tony Ortman, Mike Crouch, Mike Fox.

LAFAYETTE: Benton Central 61–41 Greencastle; Lafayette Jefferson 87–75 Delphi; Jefferson 64–59 Benton Central (ot). Officials: Dennis Schinderle, Tom Walters, Leland Thompson, William Kachel, Mark Wise, Dick Modricker.

MARION: Kokomo 41–32 Logansport; Madison–Grant 88–66 Southern Wells; Kokomo 56–50 Madison–Grant. Officials: Scott Mellinger, Mike Padfield, Tom Crouch, Rodney Chamberlain, Mark Baltz, Michael H. Smith.

MICHIGAN CITY: Portage 52–49 North Judson; LaPorte 71–63 Kouts; Portage 58–52 LaPorte. Officials: Bryce Heller, Ed Christoffel, Marvin Davis, Steve Kvachkoff, Mike Waisnora, John Goss.

NEW CASTLE: New Castle 62–61 Batesville; Richmond 63–53 Connersville; New Castle 67–52 Richmond. Officials: Gene Marsh, Randall Miller, Ed Roush, Ron James, Larry Nixon, Norman Delph.

SEYMOUR: New Albany 84–57 Scottsburg; Jennings County 77–76 Jeffersonville; New Albany 76–68 Jennings County. Officials: Doug Coddington, Steven Smith, Roger Holder, Bob Klein, Bill Nimnicht, Rex Nichols.

TERRE HAUTE: Bloomington South 77–68 White River Valley; Terre Haute North 59–53 Monrovia; Terre Haute North 59–57 Bloomington South (ot). Officials: Thomas Leix, Tony Bierschbach, John Walker, Rick Normington, Terry Bartell, Brad Groninger.

WARSAW: Warsaw 53–37 Huntington North; Plymouth 66–53 Whitko; Warsaw 52–50 Plymouth. Officials: Fred Hamilton, Judson Raver, Clark Hamilton, Doug Carl, Mark Hay, Kyle Ingram.

WASHINGTON: Loogootee 74–56 West Washington; Jasper 91–72 North Harrison, Jasper 64–60 Loogootee. Officials: Carl March, Keith Bagby, Frederick Cooper, Jay Ritter, Robert Anderson, Brian Osswald.

1996 SEMI–STATES

FORT WAYNE: Warsaw 42–41 East Noble; Fort Wayne Dwenger 52–50 Kokomo; Warsaw 74–63 Fort Wayne Dwenger. Officials: Terry Bartell, Brad Groninger, Phil Napariu, Brian Osswald; Bob Anderson, Ray Tebbe.

INDIANAPOLIS: Anderson 55–44 Shelbyville; Ben Davis 84–77 New Castle; Ben Davis 52–47 Anderson. Officials: Gary Leistner, Dick Modricker, Tom May, Jerome Fawley, Jerry Taylor, Bill Nimnicht.

LAFAYETTE: Gary Wallace 94–77 Portage; Lafayette Jefferson 104–99 Plainfield; Lafayette Jefferson 80–65 Gary Wallace. Officials: Larry Nixon, Michael Fox, Jay C. Smith, Mike Bohan, Jim Cox, Mike Crouch.

TERRE HAUTE: Terre Haute North 69–58 Jasper; New Albany 66–53 Vincennes; New Albany 59–55 Terre Haute North. Officials: Mike Waisnora, Mark Baltz, Mark Wise, Rick.Scott, Don Nester, Mark Hay.

IHSAA Scores | 1990–1999

1996 FINALS—March 23
INDIANAPOLIS (RCA Dome): Ben Davis 61–53 Lafayette Jefferson; New Albany 82–65 Warsaw; Ben Davis 57–54 New Albany. Officials: Jim Cox, Mark Hay, Bob Anderson, Don Nester, Bill Nimnicht, Jerry Taylor.

1997 SECTIONALS
ANDERSON: Frankton 66–63 Anderson Madison Heights; Alexandria 74–69 Elwood (ot); Anderson 57–45 Anderson Highland; Frankton 74–65 Alexandria; Anderson 58–47 Frankton. Officials: Gary Hamilton, Greg Reece, Jim Wolfe, Mark Hyman.

BEDFORD NORTH LAWRENCE: Brown County 72–64 Eastern (Bloomfield); Bloomington North 67–55 Edgewood; Bloomington South 73–55 Bedford North Lawrence; Bloomington North 67–44 Brown County; Bloomington North 48–39 Bloomington South (ot). Officials: Doug Coddington, Donald Whitlow, Anthony Bova, Ron McGriff.

BEN DAVIS: Brebeuf 64–46 Speedway; Indianapolis Northwest 52–36 Indianapolis Ritter; Ben Davis 58–44 Pike; Brebeuf 52–45 Northwest; Ben Davis 62–42 Brebeuf. Officials: Larry Nixon, David Bolsega, John Yantiss, Jerry Taylor.

BOONVILLE: South Spencer 67–59 Princeton; Heritage Hills 32–22 Gibson Southern; Boonville 69–51 Tecumseh; Heritage Hills 59–46 South Spencer; Heritage Hills 63–46 Boonville. Officials: Melvin Redman, Mike Harder, Tim Jellison, Bill Nimnicht.

BROWNSBURG: Avon 62–52 Cascade; Brownsburg 47–45 Danville; Plainfield 61–56 Tri-West Hendricks; Brownsburg 55–44 Avon; Brownsburg 67–61 Plainfield (ot). Officials: Leland Thompson, Terry Kreider, Joe Reed, Jack Urbin.

CALUMET: Calumet 63–62 Highland; Griffith 60–58 Hammond Morton; Lake Central 45–38 Munster; Calumet 69–56 Griffith; Lake Central 73–61 Calumet. Officials: Jerome Fawley, Cary Schnick, Doug Greelee, Doug Cook.

COLUMBIA CITY: Manchester 48–46 Whitko; Columbia City 42–41 Churubusco; Tippecanoe Valley 56–35 Central Noble; Columbia City 61–46 Manchester; Tippecanoe Valley 33–32 Columbia City (ot). Officials: Mike Crouch, Rick Granger, Jeff Morrett, Bob Stambazze.

COLUMBUS NORTH: Hauser 78–64 Waldron; Columbus North 50–45 Columbus East; Edinburgh 55–53 Southwestern (Shelbyville); Columbus North 63–58 Hauser; Columbus North 68–34 Edinburgh. Officials: William Terry Johnson, Mike Furnish, Bob Hallgarth, Greg McAdams.

CONNERSVILLE: Hagerstown 70–64 Union County; Connersville 64–46 Rushville; Cambridge City Lincoln 53–45 Franklin County; Connersville 59–44 Hagerstown; Connersville 55–48 Cambridge City Lincoln. Officials: Rick Owens, Larry Alsip, Rod Weiss, Jerry Middleton.

CRAWFORD COUNTY: Perry Central 54–44 Corydon; Tell City 66–62 Cannelton; North Harrison 62–58 Crawford County; Perry Central 54–51 Tell City; Perry Central 77–64 North Harrison. Officials: Gary Wier, Paul Meagher, Richard Denson, Jay Ritter.

DEKALB: DeKalb 70–49 Fremont; Hamilton 87–64 Garrett; Angola 65–52 Eastside; DeKalb 84–56 Hamilton; DeKalb 64–56 Angola. Officials: David Raabe, Thomas Muth, Michael Spann, David Gentile.

EAST CHICAGO: Hammond Gavit 62–51 Hammond Clark; Hammond High 72–67 East

Tourney Time

Chicago Central; Hammond Noll 61–48 Whiting; Hammond High 87–46 Gavit; Hammond High 82–71 Noll (ot). Officials: Mike Waisnora, Tim Holmes, Fred Scheub, Michael H. Smith.

EAST NOBLE: East Noble 41–24 Westview; Lakeland 63–29 Howe Military; West Noble 53–48 Prairie Heights; East Noble 50–36 Lakeland; East Noble 58–31 West Noble. Officials: Clark Hamilton, Lon Graft, Kevin Weinberg, Jerry Stieglitz.

ELKHART: Penn 53–41 Mishawaka Marian; Elkhart Memorial 67–61 Mishawaka; Concord 53–51 Elkhart Central; Penn 89–67 Memorial; Concord 50–46 Penn. Officials: Larry Jones, Gary Chambers, John Van Wagner, Jr., Merlin Nice.

EVANSVILLE CENTRAL: Mt. Vernon 69–67 Mater Dei, Reitz 88–61 Central; North Posey 83–56 New Harmony; Reitz 79–72 Mt. Vernon; Reitz 56–52 North Posey. Officials: Gary Leistner, Michael Quinn, James Stephens, Chip Sweet.

EVANSVILLE NORTH: Castle 58–55 Day School; Bosse 68–61 Harrison; Memorial 69–55 North; Bosse 61–43 Castle; Bosse 44–32 Memorial. Officials: Dave Kavanaugh, Alan Agee, Nick Matheis, James Newlin.

FORT WAYNE NORTH SIDE: Northrop 75–63 Carroll (Fort Wayne); Concordia 70–60 North Side; Dwenger 70–62 Snider (ot); Concordia 93–68 Northrop; Dwenger 58–53 Concordia. Officials: Gene Marsh, William Kachel, Dennis Hepler, Kirk Robinson.

FORT WAYNE WAYNE: South Side 47–43 Elmhurst; Canterbury 78–40 Fort. Wayne Christian; Wayne 61–50 Homestead; South Side 54–45 Luers; Wayne 67–47 Canterbury; South Side 63–62 Wayne. Officials: Tom Urban, Jack Raabe, Dave Stauffer, Steve Godfroy, Ken Weaver, Brett Patrick.

FOUNTAIN CENTRAL: Fountain Central 44–42 South Newton; Attica 50–44 Seeger; Benton Central 46–42 Covington; Fountain Central 45–37 Attica; Benton Central 54–47 Fountain Central. Officials: Bob Klein, Sam Berry, John Cowan, Rick Normington.

FRANKFORT: Rossville 65–57 Clinton Prairie; Frankfort 76–66 Tipton; Tri-Central 68–51 Clinton Central; Frankfort 71–57 Rossville; Frankfort 85–61 Tri-Central. Officials: Thomas Leix, Tony Bierschbach, Kevin Brown, Pat Dumoulin.

FRANKLIN CENTRAL: Franklin Central 65–63 Warren Central (ot); Indianapolis Chatard 76–57 Indianapolis Tech; Cathedral 61–49 Arlington; Franklin Central 61–54 Chatard; Cathedral 44–40 Franklin Central. Officials: Brad Groninger, Larry Johnson, Jeff Albright, Dan Breneman

GARY: Andrean 46–37 Wirt, Wallace 76–61 Mann; West Side 84–74 Roosevelt; Andrean 90–54 Wallace; West Side 74–69 Andrean (ot). Officials: Jeffrey Simmons, Tom Behny, George Forbes, Steve Kvachkoff.

GOSHEN: Goshen 49–41 Jimtown; Northwood 73–57 Bethany Christian; Northridge 59–39 Fairfield, Goshen 56–44 Northwood; Northridge 59–57 Goshen. Officials: Tim Smith, Richard Nelson, Mark Tulchinsky, Lance Grubbs.

GREENCASTLE: North Vermillion 41–37 South Putnam; Greencastle 57–42 North Putnam; Rockville 57–44 Turkey Run, Greencastle 61–34 North Vermillion; Rockville 65–52 Greencastle. Officials: Phil Vidito, Mark, Curts, Michael Eason, Mike Gruver.

GREENFIELD–CENTRAL: New Palestine 72–47 Eastern Hancock; Mt. Vernon (Fortville) 74–61 Lapel; Pendleton Heights 53–50 Greenfield-Central; New Palestine 63–60 Mt. Vernon (Fortville); New Palestine 61–46 Pendleton Heights. Officials: John Crapo, Jim Keifer, Robert Voss, Rick Shirk.

GREENSBURG: Batesville 60–33 South Decatur; Jac-Cen-Del 79–72 South Ripley;

IHSAA Scores | 1990–1999

Greensburg 54–53 North Decatur; Batesville 71–69 Jac-Cen-Del; Batesville 64–54 Greensburg. Officials: Haymon Fields, Wayne Hobson, Bob Martin, Dan VanTreese.

GREENWOOD: Franklin 51–28 Roncalli; Greenwood 53–43 Center Grove; Whiteland 69–60 Indian Creek; Franklin 65–64 Greenwood; Franklin 74–65 Whiteland. Officials: Tom Rohr, Steve Corya, David Hedge, Gene Huston.

HUNTINGTON: Huntington North 32–29 Wabash; Blackford 69–45 White's; Northfield 59–42 Southwood; North 39–37 Blackford; Northfield 50–48 North. Officials: Norman Delph, Donald Schmidt, Ted Garton, Randall Miller.

JAY COUNTY: Wapahani 59–58 Jay County; Union City 47–42 Monroe Central; Delta 96–51 Wes-Del; Wapahani 73–57 Union City; Delta 73–72 Wapahani. Officials: Rodney Chamberlain, Judson Raver, Doug Flatter, Robert Childers.

JEFFERSONVILLE: Clarksville 66–46 Borden; Charlestown 72–70 Silver Creek (ot); Jeffersonville 85–67 Providence; Charlestown 72–57 Clarksville; Charlestown 54–52 Jeffersonville. Officials: Rex Nichols, David Moore, Walter Bishop, Keith Bagby.

KANKAKEE VALLEY: Hebron 47–45 North Newton (ot); Kankakee Valley 50–38 Lowell; Boone Grove 64–46 Kouts; Kankakee Valley 62–36 Hebron; Boone Grove 64–47 Kankakee Valley. Officials: Dick Modricker, Russ Radtke, Joseph Skvarek, Mark Hay.

KOKOMO: Kokomo 65–55 Maconaquah; Taylor 62–54 Eastern (Greentown); Northwestern 58–46 Western; Kokomo 77–43 Taylor; Kokomo 56–40 Northwestern. Officials: Mike Bohan, David Barlow, Ken Cobb, Marvin Davis.

LAFAYETTE: McCutcheon 41–35 Carroll (Flora); Lafayette Jefferson 76–68 West Lafayette; Harrison (West Lafayette) 72–40 Central Catholic; Jefferson 56–54 McCutcheon; Harrison (West Lafayette) 76–62 Jefferson. Officials: Ray Tebbe, Arnold Freeman, Jr., Mike Fawcett, Brad Wilson.

LEBANON: Western Boone 56–48 North Montgomery; Lebanon 70–36 Southmont; Crawfordsville 83–77 Zionsville; Western Boone 66–64 Lebanon; Western Boone 52–38 Crawfordsville. Officials: Phil Dant, David Berman, Scott Mellinger, Mike Baas.

LOGANSPORT: Logansport 17–13 Pioneer; Peru 63–42 North Miami; Cass 48–47 Caston; Peru 44–39 Logansport; Cass 72–68 Peru (ot). Officials: Brian Osswald, Dennis Jackson, Stan Foreman, Brian Lancaster.

MADISON: Scottsburg 67–58 New Washington; Madison 86–56 Henryville; Southwestern (Hanover) 71–53 Madison Shawe; Scottsburg 65–52 Madison; Southwestern (Hanover) 82–81 Scottsburg. Officials: Ed Scahill, William Meyerrose, Dan Kerker, Brian Humphrey.

MARION: Marion 72–55 Oak Hill; Eastbrook 69–32 Marion Lakeview Christian; Madison-Grant 73–50 Mississinewa; Marion 72–47 Eastbrook; Marion 81–75 Madison-Grant. Officials: Rick Scott, Jeff Wilson, Bart Keesling, Mike Padfield.

MARTINSVILLE: Monrovia 75–66 Cloverdale; Mooresville 101–30 Eminence; Martinsville 67–52 Owen Valley; Mooresville 74–53 Monrovia; Mooresville 64–59 Martinsville. Officials: Steve Smith, Justin Rutledge, Gary Woodling, Patrick Strong.

MERRILLVILLE: Merrillville 76–61 River Forest; Crown Point 55–51 Hobart; Lake Station Edison 46–45 Hanover Central (ot); Merrillville 70–55 Crown Point; Merrillville 48–40 Lake Station Edison. Officials: Jerry Cook, Curtis Yoder, Danny Gurgon, Ron Gradeless.

MICHIGAN CITY: Westville 62–59 Marquette Catholic; LaPorte 59–43 Michigan City; New Prairie 61–57 Westville; LaPorte 68–61 New Prairie. Officials: John Goss, Dale Gurgel, Larry Samano, Greg Yergler.

Tourney Time

MUNCIE: Central 94–56 Cowan; Burris 70–64 Daleville (ot); Southside 81–56 Yorktown; Central 92–40 Burris; South Side 78–53 Central. Officials: Mark Baltz, Rick Hawley, Shawn Lambert, Bob Anderson.

NEW ALBANY: Floyd Central 79–61 South Central (Elizabeth); New Albany 90–40 Lanesville; Graceland Christian 44–40 Eastern (Pekin); New Albany 84–74 Floyd Central; New Albany 76–64 Graceland Christian. Officials: Terry Magnuson, Paul Wahl, Dan Stewart, Derek Howard.

NEW CASTLE: Blue River Valley 80–45 Morton Memorial; New Castle 96–61 Tri; Knightstown 65–52 Shenandoah; New Castle 98–63 Blue River Valley; New Castle 68–46 Knightstown. Officials: Michael Wallpe, Larry Sintz, Dale Goodwin, Bruce Hosier.

NEW HAVEN: New Haven 62–52 Fort Wayne Blackhawk; Harding 61–58 Heritage; Woodlan 90–84 Leo; New Haven 60–42 Harding; Woodlan 68–59 New Haven. Officials: Fred Hamilton, Tom Kenworthy, Kent Lundy, Olin Roberts.

NOBLESVILLE: Carmel 67–42 Westfield; Noblesville 82–50 Sheridan; Hamilton Heights 59–41 Hamilton Southeastern; Noblesville 69–62 Carmel; Noblesville 64–53 Hamilton Heights. Officials: Roger Holder, Steve Elkins, Robert Harding, Matthew Miller.

NORTH CENTRAL (Indianapolis): Indianapolis Broad Ripple 73–49 Park Tudor, Lawrence Central 86–36 Indiana School for the Deaf, North Central 68–61 Lawrence North; Lawrence Central 61–57 Broad Ripple; North Central 62–58 Lawrence Central. Officials: James Robinson, Mark Robbins, Joe Huff, Robert Cochran.

NORTH JUDSON: South Central (Union Mills) 62–56 Knox; West Central 77–76 LaCrosse (2ot); Winamac 71–65 North Judson (2ot); West Central 61–54 South Central; Winamac 63–42 West Central. Officials: Mark Wise, Kevin Mikesell, Robert Filipek, Dan Amrhein.

PAOLI: Paoli 55–51 Orleans; Mitchell 59–56 Salem; Springs Valley 43–41 West Washington; Mitchell 49–41 Paoli; Mitchell 49–42 Springs Valley. Officials: Ed Roush, Wayne Patterson, Mark Gines, Bill Brinkman.

PLYMOUTH: Glenn 64–58 Oregon-Davis; Plymouth 64–39 LaVille; Bremen 55–44 Culver Community; Plymouth 90–48 Glenn; Plymouth 72–46 Bremen. Officials: Jay C. Smith, Eric Coburn, Stephen Homner, Butch Lehman.

RICHMOND: Centerville 84–77 Union (Modoc); Winchester 49–42 Richmond; Northeastern 50–45 Randolph Southern (ot); Winchester 65–46 Centerville; Winchester 48–40 Northeastern. Officials: Tony Ortman, Ernie Brewer, Greg Stolle, Tom Crouch.

SEYMOUR: Jennings County 80–44 Austin; Seymour 73–48 Brownstown Central; Medora 59–54 Crothersville; Jennings County 68–59 Seymour; Jennings County 97–53 Medora. Officials: Denis Schinderle, Danny Shields, David Estes, Don Nester.

SHELBYVILLE: Indianapolis Scecina 62–57 Beech Grove; Triton 65–57 Morristown; Indianapolis Lutheran 57–53 Shelbyville; Triton 62–48 Scecina; Triton 76–44 Lutheran. Officials: Kent Smith, Larry Decker, Kenneth Knapp, Patrick Franklin.

SOUTH ADAMS: Bellmont 32–30 South Adams; Bluffton 54–41 Southern Wells, Adams Central 56–52 Norwell, Bellmont 45–35 Bluffton; Bellmont 58–49 Adams Central. Officials: Bill Forehand, Dale Zeigler, Gregg Holloway, Robert Enterline, Jr.

SOUTH BEND: Washington 80–70 Adams; LaSalle 67–65 St. Joseph's; Riley 75–62 Clay; Washington 87–79 LaSalle; Washington 92–80 Riley. Officials: Bob Neff, Andy Simpson, Edward Malek, Ed Christoffel.

SOUTH DEARBORN: Lawrenceburg 75–62 Milan; Rising Sun 57–44 Switzerland County;

East Central 54–50 South Dearborn; Lawrenceburg 76–67 Rising Sun; Lawrenceburg 60–59 East Central. Officials: Michael McGriff, Frank Bodwell, Randall Gwin, Kevin Moore.

SOUTHPORT: Decatur Central 67–55 Perry Meridian; Southport 55–28 Indianapolis Manual; Decatur Central 61–34 Southport. Officials: Michael Fox, Paul Mills, Mel Botkins, Jon Custer.

SOUTHRIDGE: Jasper 37–34 Northeast Dubois; Pike Central 48–30 Forest Park; Southridge 76–53 Oakland City Wood; Pike Central 62–37 Jasper; Pike Central 67–56 Southridge. Officials: James Dunlap, Matt Griffith, Tim Stroud, Don Corey.

TERRE HAUTE: Terre Haute North 57–40 Northview; Terre Haute South 94–55 South Vermillion; West Vigo 52–45 Riverton Parke; South 53–42 North; South 64–61 West Vigo. Officials: Philip Napariu, Joseph Stafford, Rex Wallace, John Walker.

TWIN LAKES: Tri–County 58–55 Frontier; Delphi 68–57 North White; Twin Lakes 55–34 Rensselaer; Delphi 52–50 Tri-County; Twin Lakes 71–64 Delphi. Officials: Terry Bartell, Greg Webb, Mark Sewell, Ron James.

VALPARAISO: Washington Twp.74–60 Chesterton; Valparaiso 65–47 Morgan Twp.; Wheeler 67–63 Portage; Valparaiso 76–45 Washington Twp.; Valparaiso 62–47 Wheeler. Officials: Bruce Klonowski, Steve Egan, Jeff Kincaid, Jon Davenport.

VINCENNES: North Central (Farmersburg) 66–36 Vincennes Rivet; Knox 68–53 Sullivan; Vincennes 47–23 South Knox; North Knox 62–53 North Central (Farmersburg); Lincoln 62–33 North Knox. Officials: Carl March, Dave Senning, Warren Smith, Dennis Espenlaub.

WARSAW: Warsaw 59–43 Argos; Triton 73–54 Rochester, Culver Military 37–34 Wawasee; Warsaw 60–50 Triton; Warsaw 48–45 Culver Military. Officials: Tom Schenkel, Jeff Heiliger, Mark McCammon, Bryce Heller.

WASHINGTON: Barr-Reeve 55–40 Shoals; Loogootee 62–42 Washington Catholic; Washington 23–22 North Daviess; Barr-Reeve 57–54 Loogootee (ot); Barr-Reeve 47–37 Washington. Officials: Maxwell, Alan Deskin, Rick Gentry, Craig Cress.

WHITE RIVER VALLEY: Shakamak 58–47 Clay City; Bloomfield 53–39 Linton-Stockton; Union (Dugger) 78–40 White River Valley; Bloomfield 42–38 Shakamak; Union (Dugger) 65–46 Bloomfield. Officials: Tom Walters, Len Glazier, Steve Morris, Robert Walters.

1997 REGIONALS

ANDERSON: Delta 63–51 New Palestine; Anderson 76–66 Muncie Southside; Delta 56–48 Anderson. Officials: Dave Raabe, Steve Godfroy, Denis Schinderle, Randall Miller, Mike Crouch, Terry Bartell.

COLUMBUS: Franklin 68–65 Triton Central; Columbus North 65–60 Lawrenceburg; Franklin 53–51 Columbus North. Officials: Leland Thompson, Jerry Middleton, John Crapo, Robert Cochran, Larry Nixon, Brian Osswald.

ELKHART: East Noble 41–40 Northridge; South Bend Washington 66–60 Concord; East Noble 57–52 South Bend Washington. Officials: Tom Schenkel, Dan Amrhein, Clark Hamilton, Steve Kvachkoff, Jeffrey Simmons, Norman Delph.

EVANSVILLE: Vincennes 60–56 Heritage Hills; Evansville Bosse 80–72 Evansville Reitz; Vincennes 63–57 Evansville Bosse. Officials: Bob Klein, Derek Howard, Carl March, Bill Brinkman, Rex Nichols, Larry Maxwell.

Tourney Time

FORT WAYNE: DeKalb 69–56 Woodlan; Fort Wayne South Side 65–47 Fort Wayne Dwenger; DeKalb 54–52 Fort Wayne South Side. Officials: Bill Forehand, Bruce Hosier, Jack Urbin, Merlin Nice, Larry Jones, Jerome Fawley.

FRANKFORT: Frankfort 72–58 Western Boone; Noblesville 60–53 Brownsburg; Noblesville 64–63 Frankfort. Officials: Gene Marsh, Dennis Jackson, Ed Roush, Kirk Robinson, Phil Vidito, Rodney Chamberlain.

GARY: Hammond 71–62 Lake Central; Gary West Side 57–56 Merrillville; West Side 68–61 Hammond. Officials: Haymon Fields, John Davenport, Bob Ness, Bryce Heller, Bruce Klonowski, Dick Modricker.

HUNTINGTON: Plymouth 36–32 Warsaw; Northfield 59–44 Tippecanoe Valley; Plymouth 65–55 Northfield. Officials: Tom Walters, Gene Huston, Kent Smith, Mike Padfield; Tom Urban, Brad Groninger.

INDIANAPOLIS: Cathedral 53–45 Ben Davis; North Central 63–60 Decatur Central; Cathedral 66–62 North Central. Officials: Tony Ortman, Rick Shirk, Michael McGriff, Mike Gruver, Philip Napariu, Rick Owens.

LAFAYETTE: Rockville 45–30 Benton Central; Harrison (West Lafayette) 71–57 Twin Lakes; Harrison 96–49 Rockville. Officials: Thomas Leix, Greg Yergler, Michael Fox, Ron McGriff, John Goss, Mark Baltz.

MARION: Bellmont 66–41 Cass; Kokomo 63–50 Marion; Kokomo 59–52 Bellmont. Officials: Stephen Smith, David Gentile, Gary Hamilton, Robert Childers, Jay C. Smith, Tim Smith.

MICHIGAN CITY: LaPorte 57–51 Valparaiso; Winamac 80–49 Boone Grove; LaPorte 84–70 Winamac. Officials: Mark Wise, Marvin Davis, James Robinson, Matthew Miller, Mike Waisnora, Jerry Cook.

NEW CASTLE: New Castle 56–37 Winchester, Batesville 57–39 Connersville; New Castle 61–58 Batesville (ot). Officials: Fred Hamilton, Dan VanTreese, William Terry Johnson, John Walker, Rick Scott, Mike Bohan.

SEYMOUR: Charlestown 54–47 Southwestern (Hanover); New Albany 104–84 Jennings County; New Albany 72–53 Charlestown. Officials: Doug Coddington, Greg McAdams, Michael Wallpe, Don Corey, Gary Leistner, Michael Fox.

SOUTHRIDGE: Pike Central 52–38 Mitchell; Barr-Reeve 71–47 Perry Central; Pike Central 39–37 Barr-Reeve. Officials: Roger Holder, Ron James, Tom Rohr, Chip Sweet, Ray Tebbe, Terry Magnuson.

TERRE HAUTE: Bloomington North 58–48 Terre Haute South; Union (Dugger) 70–57 Mooresville; Bloomington North 62–51 Union (Dugger). Officials: Gary Wier, Dennis Espenlaub, Melvin Redman, Keith Bagby, James Dunlap, David Kavanaugh.

1997 SEMI—STATES

EVANSVILLE: Bloomington North 52–50 Vincennes; New Albany 70–52 Pike Central; Bloomington North 68–59 New Albany. Officials: Philip Napariu, Mike Bohan, Phil Vidito, Brian Osswald, Ray Tebbe, Tom Urban.

FORT WAYNE: DeKalb 76–52 Plymouth, Kokomo 47–36 East Noble; Kokomo 69–46 DeKalb. Officials: John Goss, Dick Modricker, Larry Jones, Terry Magnuson, Mike Waisnora, Jeff Simmons

INDIANAPOLIS: Delta 59–48 Cathedral; Franklin 71–65 New Castle; Delta 61–54 Franklin. Officials: Mike Crouch, David Kavanaugh, Bruce Klonowski, Terry Bartell, Jay C. Smith, Larry Nixon.

LAFAYETTE: LaPorte 75–64 Harrison (West Lafayette); Noblesville 92–78 Gary West Side; LaPorte 69–59 Noblesville. Officials: Rick Scott, Jerome Fawley, James Dunlap, Michael Fox, Gary Leistner, Rex Nichols.

1997 FINALS—March 22

INDIANAPOLIS (RCA Dome): Bloomington North 50–43 Kokomo, Delta 57–56 LaPorte; Bloomington North 75–54 Delta. Officials: Tom Urban, Mike Waisnora, Gary Leistner, Larry Nixon, Jay C. Smith, Ray Tebbe.

Last game of that great Hoosier tradition…one-class basketball, March 22, 1997.

1998

First year of class basketball. The format:

Sixteen sectionals in each of four classes, based on enrollment, 4A the biggest schools, 1A the smallest. Eight two-team regionals in each class. Two four-team semi-states in each class. Four state championship games in one day at the RCA Dome, Indianapolis. This format used from 1998 through 2001. A four-team Tournament of Champions was played the week after the finals in 1998 and 1999. It was discontinued after two years and those results are not being listed.

1998 CLASS 4A SECTIONALS

EAST CHICAGO: Gary Wirt 67–64 Gary Wallace (2ot); Hammond High 85–71 Gary Roosevelt; Gary West Side 55–53 East Chicago Central; Wirt 48–43 Hammond Morton; Hammond High 72–62 West Side; Hammond High 75–72 Wirt. Officials: Greg Yergler, Russ Radtke, Steve Egan, Ronald Gradeless.

MERRILLVILLE: Highland 73–56 Munster, Merrillville 69–49 Lake Central; Crown Point 74–36 Lowell; Merrillville 69–62 Highland; Crown Point 60–49 Merrillville. Officials: Bruce Klonowski, Danny Gurgon, Michael Smith, Jay Smith.

MICHIGAN CITY: Valparaiso 85–64 Hobart; Chesterton 63–57 Michigan City; LaPorte 72–56 Portage; Valparaiso 62–41 Chesterton; LaPorte 55–38 Valparaiso. Officials: Bryce Heller, Dale Gurgel, Kevin Mikesell, Dale Cramer.

PENN: South Bend LaSalle 58–35 Mishawaka; South Bend Adams 67–54 South Bend Riley; South Bend Clay 48–40 Penn; Adams 60–55 LaSalle; Adams 70–65 Clay (ot). Officials: John Goss, Curtis Yoder, Lawrence Samano, Tom Behny.

ELKHART: Warsaw 70–66 Concord (2ot); Goshen 66–65 Elkhart Memorial (ot); Elkhart Central 63–48 Warsaw; Central 62–45 Goshen. Officials: Steve Godfroy, Bob Neff, Stephen Homner, Clark Hamilton.

EAST NOBLE: Fort Wayne Snider 60–57 East Noble; DeKalb 68–60 Fort Wayne Northrop; Columbia City 59–54 Fort Wayne North Side; DeKalb 84–77 Fort Wayne Snider, Columbia City 56–42 DeKalb. Officials: Randall Miller, Ken Weaver, Mark McCammon, Richard Nelson.

MARION: Marion 65–62 Homestead; Fort Wayne Wayne 56–45 Huntington North; Fort

Tourney Time

Wayne South Side 65–50 Jay County; Marion 63–54 Fort Wayne Wayne; Marion 72–40 Fort Wayne South Side. Officials: Norm Delph, Larry Johnson, Tim Filson, Joe Huff.

LAFAYETTE: Harrison (West Lafayette) 51–50 Lafayette Jefferson; Logansport 56–47 McCutcheon; Kokomo 53–51 Harrison; Kokomo 54–39 Logansport. Officials: Jerry Taylor, Ron James, John Cowan, Larry Nixon.

NOBLESVILLE: Indianapolis Broad Ripple 72–64 Hamilton Southeastern; Pike 66–64 Noblesville; North Central (Indianapolis) 69–58 Carmel; Pike 107–65 Broad Ripple; Pike 69–66 North Central. Officials: Robert Anderson, John Walker, Larry Sintz, Ray Tebbe.

NEW CASTLE: Anderson 62–58 New Castle; Connersville 60–56 Muncie Central; Anderson Highland 56–54 Richmond (ot); Anderson 43–41 Connersville; Anderson 41–40 Anderson Highland. Officials: Tom Rohr, Arnold Freeman Jr., Bob Hallgarth, Dennis Jackson.

PERRY MERIDIAN: Perry Meridian 48–44 Indianapolis Manual; Indianapolis Northwest 62–59 Center Grove; Ben Davis 72–58 Decatur Central; Perry Meridian 57–50 Southport; Ben Davis 64–62 Northwest; Ben Davis 55–49 Perry Meridian. Officials: Brian Osswald, Jon Custer, Robert Voss, Dan Van Treese.

TERRE HAUTE: Mooresville 58–32 Terre Haute South; Terre Haute North 61–44 Brownsburg; Avon 49–46 Northview; Mooresville 45–44 North; Mooresville 65–55 Avon. Officials: Mark Baltz, Tony Bierschbach, Mark Curts, David Barlow.

FRANKLIN CENTRAL: Warren Central 74–70 Franklin Central; Lawrence North 68–57 Indianapolis Tech; Lawrence Central 57–54 Indianapolis Arlington; Warren Central 61–59 Lawrence North; Lawrence Central 71–60 Warren Central. Officials: Rodney Chamberlain, Kenneth Knapp, Larry Alsip, Brad Sellers.

COLUMBUS: Bloomington North 60–43 Columbus East; Martinsville 74–71 Columbus North; Bloomington South 72–57 East Central; Bloomington North 62–55 Martinsville; Bloomington North 61–51 Bloomington South. Officials: Leland Thompson, Michael Furnish, Tom Urban, Pat Strong.

SEYMOUR: Jennings County 84–76 Jeffersonville, Bedford North Lawrence 70–55 Floyd Central; New Albany 66–53 Seymour; Jennings County 74–65 Bedford North Lawrence; Jennings County 58–57 New Albany. Officials: Michael Fox, Wayne Hobson, David Bolsega, Steven Smith.

CASTLE: Evansville North 69–64 Evansville Central; Evansville Harrison 74–55 Castle; Evansville North 67–58 Evansville Reitz, Evansville North 68–63 Evansville Harrison. Officials: Dave Kavanaugh, Wayne Patterson, Richard Denson, Alan Deskin.

1998 CLASS 3A SECTIONALS

CALUMET: Griffith 60–53 Calumet; Hammond Gavit 46–39 Hammond Noll; Andrean 85–41 Hammond Clark; Gary Mann 63–61 Griffith (ot); Andrean 77–58 Gavit; Andrean 79–61 Mann. Officials: Steve Kvachkoff, Doug Cook, Andy Simpson, George Forbes.

TWIN LAKES: Benton Central 58–50 West Lafayette (ot); Kankakee Valley 68–65 Rochester; Twin Lakes 41–38 Rensselaer; Benton Central 56–50 Kankakee Valley; Benton Central 70–56 Twin Lakes. Officials: Terry Bartell, Steve Elkins, Joseph Skvarek, Patrick Dumoulin, Ron Day, Ron James.

PLYMOUTH: South Bend Washington 56–54 Culver Military; South Bend St. Joseph's 49–

IHSAA Scores | 1990–1999

42 New Prairie; Plymouth 55–41 Mishawaka Marian; Washington 57–54 St. Joseph's; Plymouth 64–55 Washington. Officials: Dick Modricker, Jack Urbin, John Van Wagner, Lance Grubbs, Mark McCammon.

NORTHWOOD: Lakeland 55–51 Wawasee; Northridge 62–52 West Noble; Angola 69–55 Northwood; Northridge 77–55 Lakeland; Northridge 71–58 Angola. Officials: Larry Jones, Stan Foreman, Cary Schnick, Merlin Nice.

PERU: Whitko 65–55 Tippecanoe Valley; Peru 79–78 Carroll (Fort Wayne); Fort Wayne Concordia 64–55 Fort Wayne Elmhurst; Peru 76–53 Whitko; Peru 89–78 Concordia. Officials: Mark Hay, Bob Childers, Olin Roberts, James Weinberg.

BELLMONT: Harding 71–61 Norwell; New Haven 78–54 Bellmont; Harding 72–62 Fort Wayne Dwenger, Harding 68–53 New Haven. Officials: Dave Raabe, Rod Weiss, Doug Flatter, Jack Raabe.

MUNCIE: Delta 80–78 Muncie Southside (2ot); Yorktown 65–40 Elwood; Mississinewa. 60–47 Blackford; Yorktown 48–47 Delta; Yorktown 81–67 Mississinewa. Officials: Rex Nichols, Rick Normington, Bob Martin, Kirk Robinson, Anthony Bova.

FRANKFORT: Zionsville 69–54 Westfield; Lebanon 86–53 Frankfort; Crawfordsville 81–65 Western; Hamilton Heights 62–49 Zionsville; Lebanon 52–45 Hamilton Heights. Officials: Mike Padfield, Shawn Lambert, Anthony Bova, Kirk Robinson.

PLAINFIELD: Indianapolis Cathedral 57–56 Indianapolis Chatard, Plainfield 75–72 Brebeuf; Danville 72–59 Indianapolis Scecina; Cathedral 59–51 Plainfield; Cathedral 66–38 Danville. Officials: Doug Coddington, Mark Short, Terry Kreider, Jimmy Wolfe.

SHELBYVILLE: Greenfield-Central 56–55 Pendleton Heights; Mt. Vernon (Fortville) 68–65 New Palestine; Rushville 72–62 Shelbyville; Greenfield-Central 77–71 Mt. Vernon (Fortville); Greenfield-Central 61–54 Rushville. Officials: Phil Vidito, Bill Meyerrose, Pat McCallister, Mike Fawcett.

FRANKLIN: Franklin 73–54 Greenwood; Brown County 51–45 Whiteland; Roncalli 57–43 Beech Grove; Franklin 92–63 Brown County; Franklin 67–49 Roncalli. Officials: Bill Forehand, Paul Mills, Phil Dant, Gary Weir.

WEST VIGO: Sullivan 58–39 Edgewood; Owen Valley 66–56 West Vigo; Sullivan 63–60 South Vermillion; Sullivan 67–60 Owen Valley. Officials: Don Nester, David Berman, Walter Bishop, Denis Schinderle.

GREENSBURG: Batesville 51–48 South Dearborn; Madison 70–45 Franklin County; Greensburg 50–47 Batesville; Madison 76–47 Greensburg. Officials: Roger Holder, Kevin Brown, Greg Stolle, Ed Scahill.

SCOTTSBURG: Silver Creek 58–55 Corydon; Scottsburg 87–71 Charlestown; Providence 71–50 Salem; Silver Creek 81–50 North Harrison; Scottsburg 86–69 Providence; Scottsburg 85–73 Silver Creek. Officials: Terry Magnuson, Rex Wallace, John Yantiss, Ed Roush.

WASHINGTON: Vincennes 51–33 Washington; Gibson Southern 36–31 Jasper, Pike Central 73–48 Princeton, Gibson Southern 45–36 Lincoln, Gibson Southern 63–47 Pike Central. Officials: Ron Grimes, Rick Gentry, Tim Stroud, Dennis Espenlaub, James Dunlap.

BOONVILLE: Evansville Memorial 72–62 Boonville; Heritage Hills 80–63 Mt. Vernon; Evansville Bosse 70–52 Tell City; Evansville Memorial 68–62 Heritage Hills; Evansville Bosse 72–71 Evansville Memorial (ot). Officials: Chip Sweet, Alan Agee, Tim Jellison, Paul Wahl, Jim Stephens.

Tourney Time

1998 CLASS 2A SECTIONALS

BOONE GROVE: Boone Grove 53–51 North Newton; Wheeler 63–56 Hanover Central; River Forest 48–35 Lake Station Edison; Boone Grove 56–45 Wheeler, Boone Grove 75–72 River Forest (ot). Officials: Robert A. Filipek, Jon Davenport, Mark Sewell, Mark Wise.

NORTH JUDSON: Bremen 62–58 Knox; North Judson 47–43 Glenn; Winamac 64–57 LaVille; Bremen 60–45 North Judson; Bremen 51–48 Winamac. Officials: Marvin Davis, Fred Scheub, Jeff Kincaid, Mike Waisnora.

WESTVIEW: Central Noble 47–42 Westview, Jimtown 58–56 Prairie Heights (ot); Fairfield 35–33 Churubusco; Jimtown 41–35 Central Noble (ot); Fairfield 33–28 Jimtown. Officials: Tom Schenkel, Dennis Hepler, Michael Emerson, Mark Tulchinsky, Ed Christoffel.

GARRETT: Leo 73–56 Eastside, Heritage 64–60 Fort Wayne Luers; Woodlan 58–48 Garrett; Heritage 57–54 Leo; Heritage 70–64 Woodlan. Officials: Tom Crouch, Rick Granger, Butch Lehman, Dave Stauffer.

MACONAQUAH: Maconaquah 75–61 Manchester, Southwood 58–47 Northfield; Wabash 57–45 North Miami; Maconaquah 68–66 Southwood; Maconaquah 70–54 Wabash. Officials: Mike Crouch, Matt Miller, Lon Graft, Gary Chambers.

CASS: Northwestern 78–56 Cass; Delphi 67–60 Eastern (Greentown); Pioneer 53–51 Taylor, Northwestern 82–47 Delphi; Northwestern 58–48 Pioneer. Officials: Mark Hyman, Kenneth Cobb, James Galt, Fred Hamilton.

SOUTH ADAMS: Madison-Grant 45–42 South Adams; Bluffton 45–36 Adams Central; Eastbrook 65–47 Oak Hill; Bluffton 78–38 Madison-Grant; Eastbrook 55–50 Bluffton (2ot). Officials: Brad Groninger, Rick Shirk, Don Schmidt, Dan Breneman.

ALEXANDRIA: Shenandoah 64–55 Muncie Burris (ot); Alexandria 64–39 Tipton; Frankton 56–55 Shenandoah; Alexandria 63–56 Frankton. Officials: Philip Napariu, Rick Hawley, Jeff Wilson, Gregg Holloway.

NORTH MONTGOMERY: Southmont 51–47 Fountain Central; Western Boone 72–46 Seeger, Southmont 62–44 North Montgomery; Western Boone 63–52 Southmont. Officials: Gary Hamilton, Sam Berry, Michael Stoffers, Jeff Albright.

GREENCASTLE: Monrovia 69–44 Tri-West Hendricks; South Putnam 70–55 Greencastle; North Putnam 54–47 Cascade; Monrovia 71–51 Cloverdale; South Putnam 67–59 North Putnam; Monrovia 60–50 South Putnam. Officials: Kent Smith, Greg Bowman, Don Corey, Tom Leix.

HAGERSTOWN: Hagerstown 70–67 Union County (2ot); Winchester 73–36 Cambridge City Lincoln; Northeastern 67–46 Centerville; Winchester 52–51 Hagerstown; Winchester 50–34 Northeastern. Officials: Greg McAdams, Ernie Brewer, Frank Bodwell, Brian Humphrey.

SPEEDWAY: Eastern Hancock 77–75 Knightstown; Speedway 67–49 Indian Creek; Triton Central 49–43 Indianapolis Ritter; Speedway 57–52 Eastern Hancock; Triton Central 60–56 Speedway. Officials: Haymon Fields, Joe Reed, Robert Harding, Larry Decker.

LAWRENCEBURG: Switzerland County 71–64 North Decatur, Lawrenceburg 54–46 South Decatur, Switzerland Co. 65–61 South Ripley (2ot); Switzerland County 60–49 Lawrenceburg. Officials: Bob Klein, Michael Eason, Randy Gwinn, Mike McGriff.

SOUTHWESTERN (HANOVER): Southwestern (Hanover) 60–39 Clarksville; Crawford County 54–40 Eastern (Pekin); Austin 69–51 Brownstown; Southwestern 45–40 Crawford County; Southwestern 45–42 Austin. Officials: Ron McGriff, Dan Kerker, David Moore, Bill Brinkman.

PAOLI: South Knox 59–58 North Knox (ot); Linton-Stockton 45–39 Eastern (Greene Co.); Paoli 53–43 Mitchell; South Knox 61–51 Linton-Stockton; Paoli 57–38 South Knox. Officials: Paul Meagher, Mark Gines, Warren Smith, Gary Leistner.

SOUTHRIDGE: Evansville Mater Dei 54–51 North Posey; Forest Park 56–45 Oakland City; South Spencer 52–49 Southridge; Evansville Mater Dei 60–52 Perry Central; South Spencer 76–50 Forest Park; South Spencer 69–68 Evansville Mater Dei. Officials: Carl March, Matt Griffith, David Hedge, Donald Whitlow.

1998 CLASS A SECTIONALS

HEBRON: Kouts 46–45 Whiting (ot); Morgan Twp. 72–52 Hebron, LaCrosse 70–55 Washington Twp.; Kouts 72–55 Morgan Twp.; Kouts 78–68 LaCrosse. Officials: Jeffrey Simmons, Kevin Weinberg, Edward Malek, Brian Lancaster.

TRITON: Oregon–Davis 66–43 Culver Community; Triton 48–47 South Central (Union Mills); Michigan City Marquette 71–61 Argos; Oregon-Davis 62–50 Westville; Michigan City Marquette 50–47 Triton; Oregon-Davis 83–67 Michigan City Marquette. Officials: Rick Scott, Ted Garton, Jeff Morrett, Eric Coburn.

FREMONT: Fremont 52–37 Fort Wayne Christian; Fort Wayne Blackhawk 68–40 Fort Wayne Canterbury; Fremont 67–42 Howe Military; Bethany Christian 74–58 Hamilton; Fremont 49–46 Blackhawk; Bethany Christian 58–52 Fremont. Officials: Jerry Stieglitz, Tom Muth, Michael Spann, Dave Gentile.

SOUTHERN WELLS: Tri-Central 72–53 Wes-Del; Marion Lakeview Christian 64–56 Southern Wells; Daleville 65–47 White's; Tri–Central 60–51 Marion Lakeview Christian; Tri-Central 77–73 Daleville (ot). Officials: Rick Owens, Dale Zeigler, John Pfeiffer, Tom Kenworthy.

TRI–COUNTY: Tri-County 68–45 West Central; Caston 70–61 Frontier, South Newton 42–37 North White; Tri-County 68–66 Caston (ot); South Newton 38–35 Tri-County. Officials: James Robinson, Brett Patrick, Neil McCartney, Greg Webb.

SHERIDAN: Rossville 63–61 Clinton Central; Lafayette Central Catholic 86–74 Clinton Prairie; Carroll (Flora) 60–57 Sheridan; Central Catholic 47–41 Rossville; Central Catholic 55–52 Carroll. Officials: William Terry Johnson, Len Glazier, Mel Botkin, Patrick Franklin.

MONROE CENTRAL: Union City 78–76 Union (Modoc) (2ot), Cowan 52–36 Monroe Central; Wapahani 70–40 Randolph Southern; Union City 55–54 Cowan; Wapahani 69–65 Union City. Officials: Robert Cochran, Judson Raver, Kent Lundy, Tony Ortman.

TRI: Lapel 76–63 Indianapolis Lutheran; Blue River Valley 78–54 Tri; Park Tudor 69–28 Indiana School for Deaf, Blue River Valley 71–56 Lapel; Blue River Valley 64–49 Park Tudor. Officials: Gene Marsh, Justin Rutledge, Doug Bauman, Gene Huston.

ATTICA: Attica 53–40 North Vermillion; Turkey Run 59–45 Riverton Parke, Covington 46–44 Rockville (2ot); Attica 59–47 Turkey Run; Covington 59–55 Attica. Officials: Mike Bohan, Mike Gruver, Doug Greenlee, Craig Cress.

WHITE RIVER VALLEY: Union (Dugger) 67–54 Shakamak; Bloomfield 47–36 White River Valley; Clay City 73–57 Eminence; Union (Dugger) 83–69 North Central (Indianapolis); Bloomfield 69–54 Clay City; Bloomfield 72–44 Union (Dugger). Officials: John Crapo, Mike Baas, Scott Arthur, Jay Ritter.

SOUTHWESTERN (SHELBYVILLE): Edinburgh 60–46 Waldron; Southwestern

Tourney Time

(Shelbyville) 77–64 Morton Memorial; Morristown 48–45 Edinburgh; Morristown 53–50 Southwestern . Officials: Tom Walters, Jerry Middleton, Joseph Stafford, Greg Reece.

MILAN: Jac-Cen-Del 94–89 Madison Shawe; Hauser 97–94 Milan; Rising Sun 78–42 Jac-Cen-Del; Rising Sun 103–96 Hauser (3ot). Officials: Michael Wallpe, Michael Alford, Dale Goodwin, Steven Corya.

ORLEANS: Orleans 49–40 West Washington; Springs Valley 69–20 Medora; Orleans 61 –56 Crothersville (ot); Springs Valley 70–66 Orleans (ot). Officials: Larry Maxwell, Frederick Cooper, Danny Shields, Dennis Espenlaub.

HENRYVILLE: New Washington 78–56 South Central (Elizabeth); Lanesville 80–79 Henryville; Graceland Christian 87–54 Borden, New Washington 78–68 Lanesville; Graceland Christian 74–73 New Washington (ot). Officials: Derek Howard, Kevin Moore, Steve Wyrick, Mike Quinn.

NORTH DAVIESS: Shoals 70–54 Vincennes Rivet; Loogootee 61–32 Barr-Reeve; North Daviess 41–30 Washington Catholic; Loogootee 60–44 Shoals; Loogootee 68–51 North Daviess. Officials: Bill Nimnicht, Steve Morris, Nick Matheis, Keith Bagby.

TECUMSEH: Cannelton 66–59 New Harmony; Northeast Dubois 47–43 Tecumseh; Cannelton 70–61 Evansville Day; Cannelton 70–61 Northeast Dubois. Officials: Melvin Redman, Gary Woodling, James Stephens, Mike Harder.

1998 CLASS 4A REGIONALS

EAST CHICAGO: Crown Point 62–56 Hammond. Officials: Marvin Davis, Mark Hay.
MICHIGAN CITY: LaPorte 49–42 South Bend Adams.
Officials: Jeffrey Simmons, Greg Yergler.
WARSAW: Elkhart Central 46–41 Columbia City. Officials: Rick Scott, James Robinson.
KOKOMO: Marion 71–67 Kokomo (ot). Officials: Phillip Napariu, Michael Wallpe.
ANDERSON: Pike 68–65 Anderson. Officials: Bruce Klonowski, Jerry Taylor.
SOUTHPORT: Ben Davis 56–54 Mooresville. Officials: Mike Crouch, Paul Meagher.
COLUMBUS NORTH: Lawrence Central 45–36 Bloomington North.
Officials: Rex Nichols, Greg McAdams.
JEFFERSONVILLE: Jennings County 86–81 Evansville North.
Officials: Terry Magnuson, Derek Howard.

1998 CLASS 3A REGIONALS

TWIN LAKES: Andrean 65–50 Benton Central. Officials: Larry Jones, Mark Hyman.
PLYMOUTH: Plymouth 47–36 Northridge. Officials: Mark Wise, Jerry Stieglitz.
BELLMONT: Peru 84–74 Harding. Officials: Rick Owens, Gene Marsh.
MUNCIE: Yorktown 57–54 Lebanon. Officials: Brian Osswald, Bob Klein.
SHELBYVILLE: Indianapolis Cathedral 64–48 Greenfield-Central.
Officials: William Terry Johnson, Bob Cochran.
FRANKLIN: Sullivan 71–69 Franklin. Officials: Rodney Chamberlain, Gary Hamilton.
MADISON: Madison 68–65 Scottsburg. Officials: Mike Bohan, Don Nester.
VINCENNES: Evansville Bosse 33–31 Gibson Southern.
Officials: Larry Maxwell, John Crapo.

1998 CLASS 2A REGIONALS

NORTH JUDSON: Bremen 47–29 Boone Grove. Officials: Dick Modricker, Steve Godfroy.
GARRETT: Heritage 53–50 Fairfield. Officials: Bryce Heller, Randall Miller.
CASS: Northwestern 80–67 Maconaquah. Officials: Dave Raabe, Mike Padfield.
ALEXANDRIA: Alexandria 63–58 Eastbrook. Officials: Mark Baltz, Robert Anderson.
GREENCASTLE: Western Boone 67–65 Monrovia. Officials: Tom Rohr, Roger Holder.
HAGERSTOWN: Winchester 63–54 Triton Central. Officials: Michael Fox, Tom Walters.
SOUTHWESTERN (HANOVER): Southwestern (Hanover) 78–51 Switzerland County. Officials: Pat Strong, Doug Coddington.
SOUTHRIDGE: Paoli 68–62 South Spencer. Officials: Melvin Redman, Bill Nimnicht.

1998 CLASS A REGIONALS

CULVER COMMUNITY: Kouts 67–56 Oregon-Davis.
Officials: John Goss, Steve Kvachkoff.
SOUTHERN WELLS: Bethany Christian 57–47 Tri-Central.
Officials: Brad Groninger, Bill Forehand.
CLINTON CENTRAL: Central Catholic 60–36 South Newton.
Officials: Terry Bartell, Phil Vidito.
MONROE CENTRAL: Blue River Valley 67–62 Wapahani.
Officials: Tom Schenkel, Tom Crouch.
WHITE RIVER VALLEY: Bloomfield 54–44 Covington.
Officials: Ron McGriff, Leland Thompson.
SOUTHWESTERN (SHELBYVILLE): Morristown 68–51 Rising Sun.
Officials: Norman Delph, Haymon Fields.
SPRINGS VALLEY: Graceland Christian 97–58 Springs Valley.
Officials: David Kavanaugh, Chip Sweet.
LOOGOOTEE: Loogootee 54–39 Cannelton. Officials: Carl March, Ron Grimes.

1998 CLASS 4A SEMI–STATES

LAFAYETTE: Elkhart Central 60–50 LaPorte; Marion 76–63 Crown Point; Marion 76–71 Elkhart Central (ot). Officials: Brian Osswald, Bill Forehand, Mark Baltz, John Crapo, Rex Nichols, Mike Bohan.
BLOOMINGTON: Lawrence Central 60–56 Jennings County; Pike 64–52 Ben Davis; Pike 73–52 Lawrence Central. Officials: Dave Raabe, Ron Grimes, Carl March, Greg McAdams, Rick Scott, Rick Owens.

1998 CLASS 3A SEMI– STATES

MUNCIE: Plymouth 76–73 Peru; Yorktown 60–50 Andrean, Yorktown 47–42 Plymouth. Officials: Terry Magnuson, James Robinson, Kent Smith, Steve Godfroy, Philip Napariu, Larry Maxwell.

Tourney Time

EVANSVILLE: Madison 60–44 Sullivan; Indianapolis Cathedral 70–58 Evansville Bosse; Indianapolis Cathedral 73–49 Madison. Officials: Terry Bartell, Tom Walters, Tom Rohr, Doug Coddington, David Kavanaugh, Norman Delph.

1998 CLASS 2A SEMI STATES

FT. WAYNE: Alexandria 56–54 Bremen; Northwestern 62–47 Heritage; Alexandria 84–72 Northwestern. Officials: Terry Johnson, Gary Hamilton, Phil Vidito, Mike Padfield, Michael Fox, Bruce Klonowski.

INDIANAPOLIS: Paoli 67–54 Winchester, Southwestern (Hanover) 63–46 Western Boone; Southwestern (Hanover) 47–45 Paoli. Officials: Marvin Davis, Roger Holder, Tom Schenkel, Leland Thompson, Mike Crouch, Mel Redman..

1998 CLASS A SEMI STATES

MARION: Central Catholic 67–54 Bethany Christian; Blue River Valley 88–62 Kouts; Central Catholic 69–57 Blue River Valley. Officials: Bryce Heller, Steve Kvachkoff, Dick Modricker, Gene Marsh, Jeff Simmons, Mark Wise.

TERRE HAUTE: Graceland Christian 70–57 Morristown; Bloomfield 70–44 Loogootee; Bloomfield 75–62 Graceland Christian. Officials: Ron McGriff, Greg Yergler, Brad Groninger, Mark Hyman, John Goss, Larry Jones.

1998 FINALS—March 28

INDIANAPOLIS (RCA Dome):
CLASS 4A: Pike 57–54 Marion.
Officials: Dave Kavanaugh, Jeffrey Simmons.
CLASS 3A: Indianapolis Cathedral 72–47 Yorktown.
Officials: Rex Nichols, Rick Scott.
CLASS 2A: Alexandria 57–43 Southwestern (Hanover).
Officials: John Goss, Phil Napariu.
CLASS A: Central Catholic 56–48 Bloomfield.
Officials: Mike Fox, Mike Crouch.

1999 CLASS 4A SECTIONALS

GARY: East Chicago Central 55–44 Hammond Morton; Gary Wirt 75–69 Gary Roosevelt; Gary West Side 62–52 Gary Wallace; West Side 68–54 Wirt; Central 54–51 Hammond High; West Side 59–42 Central. Officials: Steve Kvachkoff, George Forbes, Jeff Kincaid, Robert Filipek.

MERRILLVILLE: Highland 54–45 Lowell; Merrillville 64–51 Lake Central; Merrillville 58–33 Highland; Crown Point 74–47 Munster; Merrillville 64–39 Crown Point. Officials: Tom Behny, Cary Schnick, Mark McCammon, Ron Gradeless.

MICHIGAN CITY: LaPorte 68–61 Portage; Chesterton 67–43 Hobart; LaPorte 67–57

Chesterton; Valparaiso 72–70 Michigan City (2ot); LaPorte 57–42 Valparaiso. Officials: Mike Waisnora, Bob Martin, Joseph Skvarek, John Goss.

PENN: South Bend Clay 57–56 South Bend LaSalle; Penn 57–38 South Bend Riley; Penn 58–49 Clay; South Bend Adams 65–49 Mishawaka; Penn 58–57 Adams. Officials: Jay C. Smith, Butch Lehman, Fred Scheub, Eric Coburn.

ELKHART: Elkhart Memorial 51–39 Concord; Elkhart Central 72–55 Goshen; Warsaw 66–49 Memorial; Central 53–51 Warsaw. Officials: Jerry Stieglitz, Jeffrey Morrett, Mark Sewell, Bob Childers.

DEKALB: DeKalb 51–32 Columbia City; Ft. Wayne North Side 73–52 Ft. Wayne Northrop; North Side 61–55 DeKalb; East Noble 63–47 Ft. Wayne Snider; North Side 55–44 East Noble. Officials: David Raabe, Brett Patrick, Michael Spann, Jack Raabe.

HUNTINGTON: Marion 50–35 Jay County; Huntington North 59–46 Ft. Wayne South Side; North 72–59 Marion; Ft. Wayne Wayne 66–48 Homestead; North 60–54 Wayne. Officials: Tom Urban, Dave Stauffer, Robert Harding, Pat Dumoulin.

LAFAYETTE: Logansport 48–47 Kokomo; Harrison (West Lafayette) 47–38 McCutcheon; Lafayette Jefferson 77–69 Logansport; Harrison 69–55 Jefferson. Officials: Tom Rohr, Greg Bowman, Michael Eason, Patrick Franklin.

NOBLESVILLE: Noblesville 51–35 Hamilton Southeastern; Pike 55–53 Carmel; Noblesville 62–50 Pike; North Central (Indianapolis) 63–57 Indianapolis Broad Ripple; North Central 59–48 Noblesville. Officials: Mike Bohan, Kent Smith, Larry Johnson, Mike Crouch.

NEW CASTLE: Anderson 73–65 Anderson Highland (ot); New Castle 30–29 Muncie Central; New Castle 50–27 Anderson; Richmond 59–50 Connersville; New Castle 65–49 Richmond. Officials: David Barlow, Justin Rutledge, Dan Kerker, John Yantiss.

DECATUR CENTRAL: Indianapolis Northwest 50–44 Indianapolis Manual; Perry Meridian 44–32 Southport; Ben Davis 73–44 Center Grove; Decatur Central 63–58 Northwest; Perry Meridian 55–53 Ben Davis; Perry Meridian 51–43 Decatur Central. Officials: Mike Padfield, Don Corey, Kevin Lewis, Ron James.

TERRE HAUTE: Brownsburg 61–47 Terre Haute South; Avon 59–50 Mooresville; Avon 54–38 Brownsburg; Terre Haute North 71–48 Northview; Terre Haute North 55– 42 Avon. Officials: Robert Anderson, Anthony Bova, John Walker, Mel Redman.

FRANKLIN CENTRAL: Lawrence North 62–49 Warren Central; Lawrence Central 61–55 Indianapolis Tech; Lawrence North 63–54 Lawrence Central; Franklin Central 72–68 Indianapolis Arlington (ot); Lawrence North 67–46 Franklin Central. Officials: Greg McAdams, Joe Reed, Randall Gwin, Rick Shirk.

COLUMBUS: East Central 57–48 Bloomington North (ot); Columbus North 63–55 Columbus East; Columbus North 82–77 East Central; Bloomington South 71–61 Martinsville; Bloomington South 84–58 Columbus North. Officials: Mike Wallpe, Paul Mills, John Cowan, Mark Curts.

SEYMOUR: Jeffersonville 71–50 New Albany; Floyd Central 62–58 Seymour; Jeffersonville 80–70 Floyd Central; Bedford North Lawrence 64–51 Jennings County; Bedford North Lawrence 84–83 Jeffersonville (4ot). Officials: Ray Tebbe, Frank Bodwell, Arnold Freeman, Jr., Bill Brinkman.

EVANSVILLE: Evansville North 83–58 Castle; Evansville Harrison 54–47 Evansville Reitz; North 60–56 Evansville Central; Harrison 61–58 North. Officials: Ron Grimes, Scott Arthur, Matt Griffith, David Kavanaugh,

Tourney Time

1999 CLASS 3A SECTIONALS

CALUMET: Andrean 76–62 Griffith; Hammond Noll 42–38 Hammond Gavit; Gary Mann 68–56 Hammond Clark; Andrean 86–38 Calumet; Gary Mann 66–53 Noll; Andrean 78–54 Mann. Officials: Greg Yergler, Doug Greenlee, Michael Emerson, Rick Nelson.

KANKAKEE VALLEY: Benton Central 54–39 Rensselaer; Kankakee Valley 60–37 Rochester; Kankakee Valley 50–36 Benton Central; West Lafayette 40–38 Twin Lakes; 53–47 Kankakee Valley. Officials: Mark Wise, Doug Cook, Jerome Jajchik, Russ Radtke.

SOUTH BEND: New Prairie 53–49 Culver Military; Plymouth 58–47 South Bend Washington; Plymouth 72–59 New Prairie; Mishawaka Marian 45–35 South Bend St. Joseph's; Plymouth 46–34 Marian. Officials: Bryce Heller, Curtis Yoder, Andy Simpson, Robert Neff.

NORTHWOOD: West Noble 78–62 Northridge; Wawasee 51–48 Lakeland; West Noble 62–53 Wawasee; Angola 55–51 Northwood; Angola 44–42 West Noble. Officials: Tom Schenkel, Ted Garton, Stephen Homner, Jack Urbin.

WHITKO: Peru 111–107 Tippecanoe Valley (2ot); Carroll (Ft. Wayne) 68–50 Whitko; Carroll 88–86 Peru (ot); Ft. Wayne Concordia 74–56 Ft. Wayne Elmhurst; Carroll 63–61 Concordia. Officials: Larry Jones, John Pfeiffer, Jon Davenport, Rick Scott.

NEW HAVEN: Bellmont 64–63 Ft. Wayne Dwenger (ot); Harding 79–51 New Haven; Bellmont 57–55 (2ot) Norwell; Bellmont 65–61 Harding (ot). Officials: Tim Smith, William Kachel, Ken Weaver, Fred Hamilton.

MUNCIE: Yorktown 57–47 Delta; Muncie Southside 78–50 Mississinewa; Southside 52–48 Yorktown; Elwood 58–45 Blackford; Southside 66–51 Elwood. Officials: Mark Baltz, Tony Bierschbach, Bob Hallgarth, Jimmy Wolfe.

FRANKFORT: Zionsville 51–45 Western; Westfield 70–56 Crawfordsville; Lebanon 43–41 Hamilton Heights; Zionsville 57–53 Frankfort; Lebanon 61–46 Westfield; Lebanon 58–45 Zionsville. Officials: James Robinson, Rick Hawley, Tim Filson, Mike Fawcett.

PLAINFIELD: Indianapolis Cathedral 62–50 Danville; Plainfield 98–58 Indianapolis Chatard; Plainfield 66–53 Cathedral; Brebeuf 65–29 Indianapolis Scecina; Plainfield 78–67 Brebeuf. Officials: Terry Magnuson, Kevin Moore, Kenneth Cobb, Shawn Lambert.

SHELBYVILLE: Mt. Vernon (Fortville) 72–62 Greenfield-Central; Pendleton Heights 63–43 New Palestine; Mt. Vernon 62–52 Pendleton Heights; Shelbyville 53–42 Rushville; Mt. Vernon 63–58 Shelbyville. Officials: Rick Owens, Wayne Hobson, Antoinne Wynne, Rex Wallace.

WHITELAND: Roncalli 61–53 Brown County; Greenwood 47–32 Beech Grove; Greenwood 47–45 Roncalli; Franklin 79–59 Whiteland; Franklin 51–48 Greenwood. Officials: Gary Hamilton, Pat Strong, Craig Petree, Steven Corya.

EDGEWOOD: Edgewood 74–46 South Vermillion; Edgewood 55–48 West Vigo; Sullivan 79–47 Owen Valley; Sullivan 64–50 Edgewood. Officials: Chip Sweet, Alan Agee, Andrew Conrad, Gary Wier.

GREENSBURG: Greensburg 61–54 South Dearborn; Madison 73–51 Batesville; Franklin County 66–54 Greensburg; Madison 66–53 Franklin County. Officials: Don Nester, Tom Lynch, Lawrence Guynn, Mike Furnish.

SCOTTSBURG: Corydon 70–51 Providence; Charlestown 90–61 Salem; Scottsburg 82–62 North Harrison; Silver Creek 60–44 Corydon; Charlestown 85–78 Scottsburg; Charlestown 70–69 Silver Creek. Officials: Derek Howard, Steve Wykick, Dan Morgan, Nick Mattheis.

WASHINGTON: Jasper 53–39 Washington; Pike Central 90–79 Princeton; Pike Central 59–

46 Jasper; Gibson Southern 46–40 Vincennes; Gibson Southern 64–53 Pike Central. Officials: Paul Meagher, Donald Whitlow, Darrell Stone, Alan Deskin.

BOONVILLE: Boonville 67–59 Mt. Vernon; Evansville Memorial 58–57 Evansville Bosse; Boonville 61–60 Evansville Memorial; Heritage Hills 64–63 Tell City; Heritage Hills 58–53 Boonville. Officials: Gary Leistner, Fredrick Cooper, James Stephens, Michael Quinn.

1999 CLASS 2A SECTIONALS

NORTH NEWTON: North Newton 116–112 River Forest (2ot); Boone Grove 75–65 Wheeler; Boone Grove 76–59 North Newton; Lake Station Edison 47–46 Hanover Central; Boone Grove 60–41 Edison. Officials: Dick Modricker, Greg Webb, Mike Gurver, Kevin Mikesell.

WINAMAC: Bremen 79–78 Knox (2ot); Winamac 45–37 Glenn; Bremen 62–61 Winamac; North Judson 51–46 LaVille; Bremen 55–43 North Judson. Officials: Mark Hay, Steve Egan, J. Tim Knowland, Gary Chambers.

WESTVIEW: Fairfield 46–27 Jimtown; Westview 71–55 Churubusco; Westview 74–70 Fairfield; Central Noble 44–30 Prairie Heights; Westview 54–39 Central Noble. Officials: Steve Godfroy, Tom Muth, John Van Wagner, Dave Gentile.

GARRETT: Woodlan 51–47 Garrett; Ft. Wayne Luers 54–48 Heritage; Woodlan 61–55 Ft. Wayne Luers; Leo 60–26 Eastside; Leo 61–41 Woodlan. Officials: Kirk Robinson, Judson Raver, Kent Lundy, Randall Miller.

MACONAQUAH: Manchester 55–39 North Miami; Northfield 54–39 Wabash; Northfield 42–41 Manchester (3ot); Maconaquah 66–58 Southwood; Maconaquah 79–62 Northfield. Officials: Dennis Jackson, Douglas Bauman, Norm Sellers, Steve Elkins.

CASS: Taylor 86–47 Delphi; Northwestern 68–48 Cass; Northwestern 45–44 Taylor; Eastern (Greentown) 73–71 Pioneer; Northwestern 80–53 Eastern (Greentown). Officials: Norm Delph, Gene Huston, Ron Day, Gregg Holloway.

SOUTH ADAMS: Oak Hill 81–73 Madison-Grant (ot); Adams Central 60–57 South Adams; Adams Central 64–55 Oak Hill; Bluffton 65–58 Eastbrook; Bluffton 46–43 Adams Central. Officials: Tom Kenworthy, Jeff Wilson, Olin Roberts, Mark Short.

ALEXANDRIA: Alexandria 78–62 Frankton; Tipton 60–47 Muncie Burris; Alexandria 55–47 Shenandoah; Alexandria 79–52 Tipton. Officials: Brian Osswald, Sam Berry, Lon Graft, Mark Hyman.

NORTH MONTGOMERY: Western Boone 65–55 Southmont; Seeger 70–60 Fountain Central; North Montgomery 40–39 Western Boone; North Montgomery 66–54 Seeger. Officials: Dennis Schinderle, Len Glazier, Phil Dant, Kevin Brown.

GREENCASTLE: North Putnam 82–32 Cloverdale; Monrovia 70–59 Cascade, South Putnam 59–40 Greencastle; Tri-West Hendricks 70–55 North Putnam; Monrovia 85–56 South Putnam; Monrovia 60–51 Tri-West Hendricks. Officials: Larry Nixon, Michael Stoffers, Clifford Brooks, Craig Cress.

HAGERSTOWN: Hagerstown 49–48 Northeastern; Winchester 65–47 Cambridge City Lincoln; Winchester 79–61 Hagerstown; Centerville 58–55 Union County; Winchester 75–67 Centerville. Officials: Roger Holder, Ed Scahill, Joe Huff, Dan VanTreese.

SPEEDWAY: Indianapolis Ritter 73–58 Eastern Hancock; Indian Creek 50–45 Triton Central; Ritter 70–65 Indian Creek; Speedway 62–42 Knightstown; Ritter 62–40 Speedway. Officials: Tom Walters, Brian Lancaster, Mel Botkin, John Crapo.

Tourney Time

LAWRENCEBURG: Lawrenceburg 61–54 South Ripley; Switzerland County 82–68 South Decatur; Lawrenceburg 62–44 North Decatur; Switzerland County 55–54 Lawrenceburg. Officials: Tony Ortman, Rod Weiss, Kenneth Knapp, Greg Reece.

SOUTHWESTERN (HANOVER): Southwestern (Hanover) 74–50 Eastern (Pekin); Austin 79–39 Brownstown; Austin 64–45 Southwestern; Crawford County 94–75 Clarksville; Austin 67–61 Crawford County. Officials: Ed Roush, William Meyerrose, Derek Sullivan and Rick Nonnington.

PAOLI: Eastern (Greene Co.) 52–41 South Knox; Paoli 63–48 Mitchell; Paoli 45–44 Eastern; North Knox 75–73 Linton-Stockton; Paoli 80–66 North Knox. Officials: Bill Nimnicht, Gary Woodling, Mark Christman, Paul Wahl.

SOUTHRIDGE: Perry Central 72–62 Southridge; Evansville Mater Dei 64–60 South Spencer; Forest Park 52–45 North Posey; Perry Central 62–40 Oakland City; Evansville Mater Dei 75–67 Forest Park; Mater Dei 62–56 Perry Central. Officials: Keith Bagby, Rick Gentry, Wayne Patterson, Dave Senning.

1999 CLASS A SECTIONALS

KOUTS: Kouts 82–77 Washington Twp.; Morgan Twp. 74–59 Hebron; Morgan Twp. 64–55 Kouts; LaCrosse 44–35 Whiting; Morgan Twp. 58–52 LaCrosse. Officials: Marvin Davis, Dale Cramer, Dennis Hepler, Lawrence Samano.

TRITON: South Central (Union Mills) 86–59 Culver Community; Triton 78–45 Westville; Michigan City Marquette 75–44 Oregon-Davis; Argos 40–37 South Central (Union Mills); Triton 61–48 Marquette. Officials: Lance Grubbs, Ed Christoffel, Russ Baker, Merlin Nice.

FREMONT: Fremont 40–37 Howe Military; Hamilton 46–42 Ft. Wayne Canterbury; Bethany Christian 37–34 Ft. Wayne Blackhawk; Fremont 53–47 Ft. Wayne Christian; Hamilton 67–59 Bethany Christian; Hamilton 59–50 Fremont. Officials: Bruce Klonowski, Kevin Weinberg, James Weinberg, Clark Hamilton.

SOUTHERN WELLS: Wes-Del 64–48 Marion Lakeview Christian; Tri-Central 75–62 Southern Wells; Tri-Central 65–38 Wes-Del; Daleville 84–49 White's; Tri-Central 78–60 Daleville. Officials: Bill Forehand, Doug Flatter, Don Schmidt, Jerry Middleton.

TRI-COUNTY: Caston 60–45 Frontier; North White 69–66 South Newton (ot); Caston 62–40 North White; West Central 68–60 Tri-County; West Central 63–54 Caston. Officials: Jerry Taylor, Matt Miller, Jim Gait, Stan Foreman.

SHERIDAN: Rossville 70–53 Carroll (Flora); Clinton Prairie 78–61 Clinton Central; Rossville 56–53 Clinton Prairie; Central Catholic 62–53 Sheridan; Central Catholic 62–60 Rossville. Officials: Gene Marsh, Robert Voss, Charles Russell, Patrick McCallister.

MONROE CENTRAL: Wapahani 67–45 Cowan; Monroe Central 61–57 Randolph Southern (ot); Wapahani 53–39 Monroe Central; Union (Modoc) 47–45 Union City; Wapahani 80–63 Union (Modoc). Officials: Tom Crouch, Michael Alford, Rick Granger, Greg Stolle.

TRI: Tri 60–47 Indianapolis Lutheran; Park Tudor 63–29 Indiana School for Deaf; Park Tudor 76–51 Tri; Blue River Valley 54–45 Lapel; Blue River Valley 71–49 Park Tudor. Officials: Brad Groninger, Dale Goodwin, Lou Hanson, Jeff Albright.

ATTICA: Attica 70–51 Rockville; Riverton Parke 71–56 Covington; Riverton Parke 81–68 Attica; North Vermillion 65–43 Turkey Run; North Vermillion 54–50 Riverton Parke. Officials:

Terry Bartell, Neil McCartney, Ed Thornburgh, Steve Morris.

WHITE RIVER VALLEY: Shakamak 68–57 North Central (Farmersburg); White River Valley 72–57 Clay City; Union (Dugger) 55–36 Eminence; Bloomfield 56–45 Shakamak White River Valley 68–64 Union (Dugger) (ot); Bloomfield 66–47 White Rivet Valley. Officials: Doug Coddington, Mark Gines, Jay Kellett, David Bolsega.

SOUTHWESTERN (SHELBYVILLE): Southwestern (Shelbyville) 57–54 Edinburgh; Morristown 72–29 Morton Memorial; Southwestern 59–51 Waldron; Southwestern 74–59 Morristown, Officials: William Terry Johnson, Larry Decker, Larry Sintz, Thomas Leix.

MILAN: Rising Sun 73–44 Madison Shawe; Jac-Cen-Del 73–57 Hauser; Milan 53–50 Rising Sun; Milan 62–60 Jac-Cen-Del. Officials: Brian Humphrey, Mike McGriff, Robert Cochran, Steve Smith.

SPRINGS VALLEY: West Washington 64–63 Springs Valley; Orleans 53–38 Crothersville; West Washington 78–29 Medora; Orleans 67–51 West Washington. Officials: James Dunlap, Mike Harder, Gary Weideman and Jay Ritter.

HENRYVILLE: Graceland Christian 63–60 New Washington; Lanesville 79–68 Borden; Graceland Christian 74–57 Lanesville; Henryville 91–76 South Central (Elizabeth); Graceland Christian 63–56 Henryville. Officials: Ron McGriff, David Moore, Brian Heaton, Tim Stroud.

NORTH DAVIESS: Vincennes Rivet 56–53 Washington Catholic; Loogootee 32–29 North Daviess; Loogootee 23–21 Rivet (2ot); Barr–Reeve 60–36 Shoals; BarrReeve 55–36 Loogootee. Officials: Larry Maxwell, Danny Shields, Michiael Shannon, Rex Nichols.

TECUMSEH: Tecumseh 57–37 Northeast Dubois; Cannelton 54–45 New Harmony; Tecumseh 65–43 Evansville Day; Tecumseh 66–42 Cannelton. Officials: Carl March, Tim Jellison, Warren Smith, Dennis Espenlaub.

1999 REGIONALS

ANDERSON:
  Class 4A: North Central (Indianapolis) 78–59 New Castle.
  Officials: Terry Bartell, Derek Howard.
BELLMONT:
  Class 3A: Carroll 53–34 Bellmont. Officials: Marvin Davis, Brad Groninger.
  Class A: Tri–Central 68–44 Hamilton. Officials: Gene Marsh, Tom Crouch.
CLINTON CENTRAL:
  Class A: Central Catholic 56–47 West Central. Officials: Mark Wise, David Barlow.
COLUMBUS:
  Class 4A: Bloomington South 55–50 Lawrence North (ot). Officials: Mark Baltz, Bob Anderson.
  Class 3A: Sullivan 58–54 Franklin (ot). Officials: Don Nester, Denis Schinderle.
GARRETT:
  Class 2A: Westview 70–59 Leo. Officials: Dave Raabe, Steve Godfroy.
GREENCASTLE:
  Class 4A: Terre Haute North 60–50 Perry Meridian. Officials: Robert Cochran, Chip Sweet.
  Class 2A: Monrovia 66–48 North Montgomery. Officials: Norman Delph, Tom Behny.

Tourney Time

JEFFERSONVILLE:
  Class 4A: Evansville Harrison 66–64 Bedford North Lawrence. Officials: Greg McAdams, Gary Leistner.
KANKAKEE VALLEY:
  Class 3A: Andrean 68–59 West Lafayette. Officials: Tim Smith, Jay C. Smith.
  Class 2A: Bremen 54–51 Boone Grove. Officials: Bruce Klonowski ,Lance Grubbs.
MADISON:
  Class 3A: Madison 92–51 Charlestown. Officials: Larry Maxwell, Ed Roush.
  Class 2A: Austin 55–53 Switzerland County. Officials: Ron McGriff, Kent Smith.
MARION:
  Class 4A: Huntington North 69–63 (ot) Harrison (West Lafayette).
  Officials: Brian Osswald, Mike Wallpe.
  Class 2A: Maconaquah 76–67 Northwestern. Officials: Jerry Stieglitz, Bill Forehand.
MICHIGAN CITY:
  Class 4A: Merrillville 60–50 Gary West Side. Officials: Mark Hay, Kirk Robinson.
  Class 4A: Penn 64–55 LaPorte. Officials: Larry Jones, James Robinson.
MUNCIE:
  Class 3A: Muncie Southside 74–59 Lebanon. Officials: Jerry Taylor, Dennis Jackson.
  Class 2A: Alexandria 62–55 Bluffton. Officials: Tom Walters, Roger Holder.
NEW CASTLE:
  Class 2A: Winchester 63–59 Indianapolis Ritter. Officials: Mike Bohan, Ray Tebbe.
  Class A: Blue River Valley 87–66 Wapahani. Officials: William Terry Johnson, Mike Padfield.
PLYMOUTH:
  Class 3A: Angola 59–53 Plymouth. Officials: Steve Kvachkoff, Mike Waisnora.
SHELBYVILLE:
  Class 3A: Plainfield 71–63 Mt. Vernon (Fortville). Officials: Rick Owens, Larry Nixon.
  Class A: Milan 82–55 Southwestern (Shelbyville). Officials: John Crapo, Tony Ortman.
SOUTHRIDGE:
  Class A: Graceland Christian 67–56 Orleans. Officials: Ron Grimes, Paul Meagher.
  Class 2A: Paoli 77–57 Evansville Mater Dei. Officials: Bill Nimnicht, Keith Bagby.
VINCENNES:
  Class 3A: Gibson Southern 45–22 Heritage Hills. Officials: Carl March, Doug Coddington.
  Class A: Tecumseh 44–36 Barr–Reeve. Officials: Terry Magnuson, Tom Rohr.
WARSAW:
  Class 4A: Elkhart Central 79–68 Ft. Wayne North Side. Officials: Dick Modricker, Greg Yergler.
  Class A: Morgan Twp. 48–39 Triton. Officials: Bryce Heller, Tom Schenkel.
WHITE RIVER VALLEY:
  Class A: Bloomfield 67–50 North Vermillion. Officials: Gary Hamilton, James Dunlap.

1999 SEMI-STATES

CLASS 4A

LAFAYETTE: Elkhart Central 83–54 Penn; Merrillville 77–55 Huntington North; Elkhart Central 67–50 Merrillville. Officials: Terry Magnuson, Tony Ortman, Ron McGriff, Norman Delph, Rick Owens, William Terry Johnson.

INDIANAPOLIS: Bloomington South 66–54 Terre Haute North; North Central (Indianapolis) 83–60 Evansville Harrison; North Central 79–73 (ot) Bloomington South. Officials: Dick Modricker, Greg Yegler, Marvin Davis, James Robinson, Mark Wise, Steve Kvachkoff.

CLASS 3A

MUNCIE: Muncie Southside 54–39 Angola; Andrean 66–48 Carroll (Ft. Wayne); Southside 87–70 Andrean. Officials: Michael Wallpe, Tom Crouch, Steve Godfroy, Brian Osswald, Mark Baltz, Mark Hay.

WASHINGTON: Plainfield 88–75 Madison; Gibson Southern 52–40 Sullivan; Plainfield 55–43 Gibson Southern. Officials: Tom Rohr, Roger Holder, Kent Smith, Don Nester, Larry Maxwell, Bob Anderson.

CLASS 2A

MARION: Westview 76–52 Bremen; Alexandria 71–57 Maconaquah; Westview 68–65 Alexandria. Officials: Terry Bartell, Mike Padfield, Gene Marsh, Brad Groninger, Bruce Klonowski, Bryce Heller.

SOUTHRIDGE: Monrovia 75–73 Austin; Paoli 85–77 Winchester (2ot); Paoli 76–73 Monrovia. (2ot). Officials: Carl March, John Crapo, Ron Grimes, Derek Howard, Mike Bohan, Jerry Taylor.

CLASS A

KOKOMO: Lafayette Central Catholic 67–42 Morgan Twp.; Tri-Central 68–57 Blue River Valley; Central Catholic 52–49 Tri-Central. Officials: Robert Cochran, Tom Schenkel, Jerry Stieglitz, Mark Hyman, Larry Jones, Tim Smith.

GREENCASTLE: Tecumseh 57–53 Milan; Bloomfield 51–35 Graceland Christian; Tecumseh 46–44 Bloomfield. Officials: Gary Hamilton, Doug Coddington, Chip Sweet, Bill Forehand, David Raabe, Bill Nimnicht.

1999 FINALS—March 27

INDIANAPOLIS (RCA Dome):

CLASS 4A: North Central (Indianapolis) 79–74 Elkhart Central. Officials: Larry Maxwell, David Raabe.

CLASS 3A: Plainfield 77–64 Muncie Southside. Officials: Larry Jones, Bruce Klonowski.

CLASS 2A: Westview 71–52 Paoli. Officials: Rick Owens, Mark Wise.

CLASS A: Tecumseh 55–43 Lafayette Central Catholic. Officials: Mark Baltz, Mike Bohan.

Tourney Time

2000–2005

2000 CLASS 4A SECTIONALS

EAST CHICAGO: Gary Roosevelt 74–67 Hammond; East Chicago Central 55–51 Highland; Roosevelt 65–61 Central; Munster 70–68 Gary West Side; Munster 62–59 Roosevelt. Officials: Mark Hay, Steve Egan, Mike Emerson, Doug Greenlee.

MERRILLVILLE: Lake Central 62–40 Hobart; Merrillville 58–43 Crown Point; Merrillville 57–38 Lake Central; Gary Wallace 63–41 Lowell; Merrillville 71–67 Wallace. Officials: Marvin Davis, Jim Galt, Tim Filson, John Van Wagner.

MICHIGAN CITY: Portage 81–65 Valparaiso; Michigan City 71–61 South Bend Washington; Michigan City 67–58 Portage; LaPorte 63–54 Chesterton; LaPorte 64–60 Michigan City. Officials: Bryce Heller, Mark Sewell, Butch Lehman, Andy Simpson.

PENN: Penn 34–33 South Bend Adams; Mishawaka 60–57 South Bend LaSalle; Penn 52–31 Mishawaka; South Bend Clay 57–54 South Bend Riley; Penn 69–49 Clay. First two games were at Penn and LaSalle. Officials: Merlin Nice, Bob Neff, Ken Weaver, Mark Wise.

ELKHART: Concord 60–54 Goshen; Elkhart Central 53–46 Elkhart Memorial; Concord 58–53 Central; Warsaw 46–29 East Noble; Warsaw 53–42 Concord. Officials: Tim Smith, Fred Schueb, Cary Schnick, Ronald Gradeless.

FORT WAYNE NORTHROP: Carroll (Fort Wayne) 72–57 Fort Wayne Snider; DeKalb 60–50 Fort Wayne Northrop; Carroll 57–43 DeKalb; Fort Wayne South Side 61–59 Fort Wayne North Side; Fort Wayne South Side 78–66 Carroll.. Officials: Mike Crouch, Douglas Bauman, Jeffrey Morrett, Gregg Holloway.

ANDERSON: Kokomo 62–56 Anderson; Marion 84–70 Homestead; Marion 66–56 Kokomo; Anderson Highland 50–46 Huntington North; Marion 70–56 Highland. First two games were at Anderson and Marion. Officials: Robert Anderson, John Walker, Antoinne Wynne, David Barlow.

LAFAYETTE: Brownsburg 55–54 McCutcheon (ot); Avon 64–50 Harrison (West Lafayette); Avon 85–70 Brownsburg (ot); Lafayette Jefferson 74–46 Logansport; Jefferson 53–47 Avon. First two games were at McCutcheon and Avon. Officials: Brian Osswald, Rich Hawley, Rick Oliver, John Cowan, Shawn Lambert, alternate Andrew Mitchell.

NOBLESVILLE: Pike 103–55 Carmel, North Central (Indianapolis) 55–36 Broad Ripple; Pike 83–55 North Central (Indianapolis); Noblesville 71–54 Hamilton Southeastern; Pike 71–60 Noblesville. Officials: William Terry Johnson, John Yantiss, Justin Rutledge, Jerry Middleton.

NEW CASTLE: New Castle 82–48 Connersville; Muncie Central 65–40 East Central; New Castle 39–38 Muncie Central; Richmond 58–42 Jay County; New Castle 63–50 Richmond. Officials: Ray Tebbe, Wayne Hobson, Clifford Brooks, Michael Eason.

BEN DAVIS: Southport 57–54 Indianapolis Northwest; Perry Meridian 64–61 Ben Davis; Southport 49–47 Perry Meridian; Decatur Central 47–40 Indianapolis Manual; Southport 59–45 Decatur Central. Officials: Michael Wallpe, Michael Stoffers, Joseph Stafford, Brian Humphrey.

WARREN CENTRAL: Franklin Central 85–69 Indianapolis Arlington; Warren Central 57–48 Lawrence North; Warren Central 71–45 Franklin Central; Lawrence Central 54–51 Indianapolis Tech; Warren Central 64–51 Lawrence Central. Officials: Doug Coddington, Greg

Stolle, Kenneth Knapp, Denis Schinderle.

MOORESVILLE: Terre Haute South 76–71 Mooresville; Terre Haute North 49–48 Plainfield; North 53–51 South; Northview 56–55 Martinsville; North 53–40 Northview. First two games were at Terre Haute South and Plainfield. Officials: Chip Sweet, Danny Shields, Gene Huston, Rick Owens.

COLUMBUS: Bloomington South 65–35 Columbus East; Columbus North 51–43 Center Grove; Bloomington South 44–41 Columbus North; Bloomington North 72–37 Greenwood; Bloomington North 74–30 Bloomington South. Officials: Tom Rohr, Jon Custer, Kevin Lewis, David Kavanaugh.

SEYMOUR: Jennings County 55–48 Floyd Central; New Albany 68–67 Bedford North Lawrence (ot); New Albany 62–52 Jennings County; Jeffersonville 79–56 Seymour; Jeffersonville 58–54 New Albany. First two games were at Floyd Central and New Albany. Officials: Rex Nichols, Donald Whitlow, William Meyerrose, Larry Maxwell.

EVANSVILLE HARRISON: Central 79–70 Harrison; North 80–58 Castle; Reitz 61–49 Central; Reitz 78–49 North. Officials: Gary Wier, Paul Wahl, James Stephens, Alan Deskin.

2000 CLASS 3A SECTIONALS

HAMMOND CLARK: Calumet 63–62 Hammond Morton; Griffith 47–32 Hammond Clark; Calumet 51–49 Griffith (ot); Hammond Gavit 63–52 Hammond Noll; Calumet 57–52 Gavit. Officials: Mike Waisnora, George Forbes, Stephen Homner, Tom Behny.

NEW PRAIRIE: New Prairie 73–69 Kankakee Valley; Andrean 68–48 South Bend St. Joseph's; Andrean 69–48 New Prairie; Gary Wirt 72–52 Gary Mann; Andrean 65–53 Gary Wirt. Officials: Greg Yergler, Ron Day, Kevin Mikesell, Curt Yoder.

PLYMOUTH: Plymouth 58–54 Rochester; Tippecanoe Valley 59–46 Mishawaka Marian; Tippecanoe Valley 61–54 Plymouth; Culver Military 68–56 Whitko; Tippecanoe Valley 51–40 Culver Military. Officials: Richard Modricker, Jack Urbin, Mark McCammon, Doug Cook.

FRANKFORT: Frankfort 41–40 Hamilton Heights; West Lafayette 60–43 Benton Central; West Lafayette 79–72 Frankfort (3ot); Western 81–68 Twin Lakes; West Lafayette 69–52 Western. Officials: Gary Hamilton, Len Glazer, Patrick McCallister, Mark Baltz.

NORTHWOOD: Angola 42–39 Lakeland; Northwood 62–48 Wawasee; Northwood 64–50 Angola; Northridge 65–48 West Noble; Northridge 57–51 Northwood. Officials: John Goss, Brett Patrick, James Weinberg, Bruce Klonowski.

FORT WAYNE WAYNE: Fort Wayne Wayne 39–38 Columbia City (ot); Fort Wayne Dwenger 73–48 Fort Wayne Elmhurst; Wayne 54–48 Dwenger; Concordia 68–62 New Haven; Concordia 57–56 Wayne. Officials: Dennis Jackson, Kenneth Cobb, Robert Harding, Randall Miller.

BELLMONT: Mississinewa 59–35 Blackford; Maconaquah 79–68 Bellmont; Maconaquah 76–55 Mississinewa; Peru 95–81 Norwell; Maconaquah 81–78 Peru (ot). First two games were at Blackford and Bellmont. Officials: Jerry Stieglitz, Tom Kenworthy, Ted Garton, Tom Muth.

MUNCIE: Muncie Southside 70–58 Alexandria; Delta 53–52 Yorktown (ot); Delta 61–46 Southside; Pendleton Heights 56–42 Elwood; Pendleton Heights 46–36 Delta. Officials: James Robinson, Steve Elkins, Kent , Dave Raabe.

MT. VERNON (Fortville): Indianapolis Chatard 68–64 Mt. Vernon (Fortville); Indianapolis Cathedral 51–48 Roncalli; Chatard 52–49 Indianapolis Cathedral; Brebeuf 72–44 Beech Grove;

Tourney Time

Brebeuf 63–51 Chatard. Officials: Ed Roush, Rod Weiss, Michael Furnish, Kevin Brown.

SHELBYVILLE: New Palestine 68–50 Rushville; Whiteland 82–79 Franklin; New Palestine 80–62 Whiteland; Shelbyville 63–47 Greenfield-Central; Shelbyville 45–42 New Palestine. Officials: Tom Urban, Mike Fawcett, Dale Goodwin, Greg Reece.

LEBANON: Danville 44–37 Zionsville; Crawfordsville 44–42 Lebanon; Danville 61–39 Crawfordsville; Westfield 63–54 Southmont; Danville 60–45 Westfield. Officials: Jerry Taylor, Arnold Freeman Jr., Grady Smith, Patrick Dumoulin.

GREENCASTLE: Edgewood 59–54 Owen Valley; South Vermillion 66–54 Greencastle; South Vermillion 68–63 Edgewood; Sullivan 65–58 West Vigo; Sullivan 66–60 South Vermillion. Officials: Tom Walters, Edward Thornburgh, Craig Petree, Tony Bierschbach.

GREENSBURG: Scottsburg 91–75 Brown County, Greensburg 55–51 South Dearborn; Scottsburg 53–42 Greensburg; Franklin County 53–45 Madison; Scottsburg 64–62 Franklin County. First two games were at Scottsburg and South Dearborn. Officials: Terry Magnuson, Dave Bolsega, Rex Wallace, Greg Bowman.

NORTH HARRISON: Mitchell 57–50 Salem; Corydon Central 69–49 North Harrison; Mitchell 61–56 Corydon Central; Charlestown 97–75 Providence; Charlestown 67–66 Mitchell. Officials: James Dunlap, Dennis Espenlaub, Steve Meyer, Mike Harder.

WASHINGTON: Vincennes 57–41 Gibson Southern; Jasper 61–59 Washington (ot); Lincoln 70–51 Jasper; Princeton 61–46 Lincoln. Officials: Dave Senning, Tim Stroud, Jim Davis, Don Corey.

BOONVILLE: Boonville 73–49 Evansville Memorial; Evansville Mater Dei 60–52 Mount Vernon; Mater Dei 61–42 Boonville; Evansville Bosse 83–72 Heritage Hills; Mater Dei 86–60 Bosse. Officials: Ron James, Nick Matheis, Kevin Denu, David Moore.

2000 CLASS 2A SECTIONALS

BOONE GROVE: Boone Grove 66–55 Hebron; Lake Station Edison 68–61 River Forest; Boone Grove 90–46 Edison; Wheeler 65–62 Hanover Central; Boone Grove 52–50 Wheeler. Officials: Robert Filipek, Joseph Skvarek, Lawrence Samano, Russell Radtke.

WINAMAC: North White 76–62 North Newton; Knox 38–23 Winamac; Knox 68–57 North White; Rensselaer 66–43 North Judson; Knox 67–51 Rensselaer. Officials: Rick Scott, Norm Sellers, Mike Gruver, Brian Lancaster.

WESTVIEW: Fairfield 64–54 Bremen; LaVille 58–51 Jimtown; Fairfield 74–43 LaVille; Westview 83–63 Glenn; Westview 61–47 Fairfield. Officials: Kirk Robinson, Michael Spann, Kevin Weinberg, Lance Grubbs.

GARRETT: Prairie Heights 49–38 Churubusco; Eastside 72–67 Garrett; Prairie Heights 67–66 Eastside; Central Noble 57–41 Fremont; Central Noble 50–34 Prairie Heights. Officials: Eric Codburn, Russ Baker, John Pfeiffer, Bob Childers.

HARDING: Fort Wayne Luers 69–51 Woodlan; Heritage 65–43 Bluffton; Luers 86–70 Heritage; Harding 63–44 Leo; Harding 66–55 Luers. Officials: Tom Crouch, Doug Flatter, Dan VanTreese, William Kachel.

CASS: Cass 75–52 North Miami; Southwood 68–61 Manchester; Southwood 63–55 Cass; Northfield 73–57 Wabash; Southwood 66–45 Northfield. Officials: Brad Groninger; Dale Cramer, Philip Teusch, Mark Short.

IHSAA Scores | 2000–2005

EASTBROOK: Eastbrook 53–39 Muncie Burris; South Adams 66–64 Frankton; Eastbrook 51–48 South Adams; Oak Hill 64–50 Madison–Grant; Oak Hill 82–71 Eastbrook. First two games were at Eastbrook and Frankton. Officials: Norman Delph, Rich Shirk, Jim Mettler, Joe Huff.

TIPTON: Northwestern 70–48 Eastern (Greentown); Taylor 67–50 Delphi; Taylor 63–53 Northwestern; Tipton 79–64 Carroll (Flora); Taylor 53–30 Tipton. Officials: Mark Hayman, Robert Voss, Robert Plummer, Jimmy Wolfe.

FOUNTAIN CENTRAL: Western Boone 74–59 Covington; Sheridan 48–37 Seeger; Western Boone 67–56 Sheridan; Fountain Central 49–45 North Montgomery; Western Boone 61–42 Fountain Central. Officials: Don Nester, Todd Reel, Andy Conrad, Tim Pharis, Neil McCartney.

SOUTH PUTNAM: North Putnam 70–56 Cloverdale; Cascade 75–60 Tri–West Hendricks; Cascade 65–47 North Putnam; Monrovia 85–74 South Putnam (2ot); Monrovia 76–74 Cascade (ot). Officials: Jay Slater, Jay Kellett, Joe Reed, Larry Nixon.

HAGERSTOWN: Winchester 76–59 Northeastern; Centerville 58–56 Cambridge City Lincoln; Winchester 71–54 Centerville; Shenandoah 81–64 Hagerstown; Winchester 65–51 Shenandoah. Officials: Bill Forehand, Charles Russell, Dan Kerker, Mike Bohan.

SPEEDWAY: Speedway 79–37 Eastern Hancock; Indian Creek 41–40 Triton Central; Indian Creek 47–43 Speedway; Knightstown 70–62 Indianapolis Scecina; Indian Creek 63–55 Knightstown. Officials: Phil Vidito, Steven Wyrick, Tom Simpson, Mark Curts.

LAWRENCEBURG: Lawrenceburg 62–52 South Ripley; North Decatur 62–40 Switzerland County; North Decatur 47–46 Lawrenceburg; Batesville 60–47 Union County; Batesville 41–40 North Decatur. Officials: Ron McGriff, Kevin Moore, Paul Mills, Mike McGriff.

SOUTHWESTERN (Hanover): Eastern (Pekin) 77–65 Clarksville; Silver Creek 54–52 Southwestern (Hanover); Silver Creek 56–35 Eastern (Pekin); Brownstown Central 70–52 Austin; Silver Creek 57–43 Brownstown Central. Officials: Greg McAdams, Frank Bodwell, Brian Heaton, Bill Brinkman.

SOUTHRIDGE: Tell City 74–71 South Spencer; Forest Park 49–40 Southridge; Tell City 73–66 Forest Park; Paoli 71–67 Crawford County; Paoli 73–69 Tell City. Officials: Bill Nimnicht, Mike Quinn, Warren Smith, Monte McKee.

NORTH KNOX: North Knox 88–73 North Posey; Linton-Stockton 82–65 North Central (Farmersburg); North Knox 80–59 Linton-Stockton; South Knox 61–60 Eastern (Greene Co.); North Knox 47–37 South Knox. Officials: John Crapo, Steve Morris, Michiael Shannon, Fred Cooper.

2000 CLASS A SECTIONALS

MICHIGAN CITY MARQUETTE: Kouts 80–45 Westville; Michigan City Marquette 51–44 Morgan Twp.; Marquette 68–65 Kouts (ot); Whiting 63–43 Washington Twp.; Marquette 67–51 Whiting. Officials: Steve Kvachkoff, Jeff Kincaid, Jerome Jajchik, Jon Davenport.

CULVER COMMUNITY: Triton 52–41 Argos; South Central (Union Mills) 50–42 LaCrosse; Triton 58–40 South Central; Oregon-Davis 41–37 Culver Community; Triton 65–46 Oregon-Davis. Officials: Jay Smith, Matthew Miller, Bob Martin, Denny Hepler.

FORT WAYNE BLACKHAWK: Hamilton 53–50 Fort Wayne Canterbury; Fort Wayne Blackhawk 87–31 Fort Wayne Christian; Hamilton 61–48 Blackhawk; Bethany Christian 51–24

Tourney Time

Howe Military; Bethany Christian 69–64 Hamilton. Officials: Steve Godfroy, Jack Raabe, Steve Grocock, Olin Roberts.

SOUTHERN WELLS: Tri–Central 87–32 White's; Adams Central 77–70 Wes-Del; Tri-Central 63–58 Adams Central; Southern Wells 91–35 Marion Lakeview Christian; Southern Wells 63–58 Tri-Central. Officials: Gene Marsh, Judson River, Clark Hamilton, Larry Johnson.

TRI-COUNTY: Pioneer 52–45 Tri-County; South Newton 64–52 Frontier; South Newton 64–59 Pioneer; Caston 44–40 West Central; Caston 44–37 South Newton. Officials: Terry Bartell, Greg Webb, Tim Knowland, Gary Chambers.

CLINTON CENTRAL: Central Catholic 75–51 Rossville; Park Tudor 50–47 Clinton Central; Central Catholic 52–49 Park Tudor; Clinton Prairie 66–57 Indianapolis Ritter; Central Catholic 75–64 Clinton Prairie. Officials: Mike Padfield, Terry Kreider, Lawrence Guynn, Stanton Foreman.

MONROE CENTRAL: Wapahani 66–53 Cowan; Randolph Southern 72–47 Union (Modoc); Randolph Southern 59–51 Wapahani; Monroe Central 56–51 Union City; Monroe Central 38–37 Randolph Southern. Officials: Robert Cochran, Steven Smith, Lon Graft, Dave Stauffer.

TRI: Daleville 95–52 Morton Memorial; Lapel 63–57 Tri; Lapel 77–61 Daleville; Blue River Valley 85–54 Indiana School for the Deaf; Blue River Valley 64–58 Lapel. Officials: Roger Holder, Dan Morgan, Bob Hallgarth, Ed Scahill.

NORTH VERMILLION: Eminence 64–56 Riverton Park; Rockville 50–36 Turkey Run; Rockville 51–50 Eminence; Attica 68–50 North Vermillion; Attica 39–37 Rockville. Officials: Pat Strong, Jeff Albright, Dick Hammond, Thomas Leix.

WHITE RIVER VALLEY: Union (Dugger) 72–51 North Daviess; Bloomfield 49–39 Clay City; Union 68–59 Bloomfield; Shakamak 63–44 White River Valley; Union 72–51 Shakamak. Officials: Ron Grimes, Rick Gentry, Derek Sullivan, Don Stewart.

EDINBURGH: Edinburgh 55–49 Southwestern (Shelbyville); Waldron 47–39 Morristown; Waldron 65–40 Edinburgh; Hauser 100–69 Indianapolis Lutheran; Hauser 63–54 Waldron. Officials: Kent Smith; Thomas Lynch, Jason Ferguson, Steven Corya.

MILAN: Madison Shawe 61–50 South Decatur; Jac-Cen-Del 69–62 Milan; Rising Sun 49–46 Madison Shawe; Jac-Cen-Del 81–68 Rising Sun. Officials: Tom Ortman, Michael Alford, Randall Gwin, Larry Sintz.

ORLEANS: Orleans 59–50 West Washington; Northeast Dubois 75–65 Crothersville; Northeast Dubois 54–33 Orleans; Springs Valley 69–36 Medora; Northeast Dubois 71–46 Springs Valley. Officials: Paul Meagher, Wayne Patterson, Mark Christman, Gary Woodling.

HENRYVILLE: Lanesville 53–41 Borden; Graceland Christian 50–41 Henryville; Graceland Christian 50–46 Lanesville; New Washington 79–74 South Central (Elizabeth); New Washington 59–43 Graceland Christian. Officials: Derek Howard, Scott Arthur, Gary Weideman, Mark Gines.

LOOGOOTEE: Barr–Reeve 66–50 Shoals; Vincennes Rivet 66–44 Washington Catholic; Loogootee 33–31 Barr-Reeve; Loogootee 57–33 Rivet. Officials: Keith Bagby, Tim Jellison, Mike Zehr, Larry Decker.

TECUMSEH: Evansville Day 44–42 Perry Central; Tecumseh 86–48 New Harmony; Tecumseh 61–51 Evansville Day; Oakland City Wood 51–36 Cannelton; Tecumseh 71–39 Wood. Officials: Jay Ritter, Darrell Stone, Joseph Calderazzo, Melvin Redman.

IHSAA Scores | *2000–2005*

2000 CLASS 4A REGIONALS

MERRILLVILLE: Merrillville 73–56 Munster. Officials: Richard Modricker, Rick Scott.
PENN: Penn 70–50 LaPorte. Officials: Michael Waisnora, Gregory Yergler.
FORT WAYNE SOUTH SIDE: Warsaw 45–44 Fort Wayne South Side. Officials: Norman Delph, Steve Godfroy.
LAFAYETTE JEFFERSON: Marion 75–52 Lafayette Jefferson. Officials: Ray Tebbe, Rex Nichols.
NEW CASTLE: New Castle 95–77 Pike. Officials: Jerry Taylor, Terry Bartell.
WARREN CENTRAL: Warren Central 61–46 Southport. Officials: Larry Nixon, Mark Hyman.
BLOOMINGTON NORTH: Bloomington North 60–48 Terre Haute North. Officials: Phil Vidito, Bill Forehand.
SOUTHRIDGE: Jeffersonville 64–40 Evansville Reitz. Officials: Ed Roush, Chip Sweet.

2000 CLASS 3A REGIONALS

ANDREAN: Andrean 83–67 Calumet. Officials: Bryce Heller, Eric Coburn.
WEST LAFAYETTE: Tippecanoe Valley 47–43 West Lafayette. Officials: Robert Anderson, Michael Wallpe.
FORT WAYNE CONCORDIA: Fort Wayne Concordia 48–47 Northridge. Officials: Tom Urban, Merlin Nice.
PENDLETON HEIGHTS: Pendleton Heights 74–64 Maconaquah. Officials: Jay Smith, Pat Strong.
SHELBYVILLE: Brebeuf 64–57 Shelbyville. Officials: Tom Rohr, Robert Cochran.
SULLIVAN: Danville 55–46 Sullivan. Officials: William Terry Johnson, Kent Smith.
CHARLESTOWN: Scottsburg 66–65 Charlestown. Officials: Bill Nimnicht, Jay Ritter.
BOONVILLE: Evansville Mater Dei 79–48 Princeton. Officials: Gary Wier, John Crapo.

2000 CLASS 2A REGIONALS

KNOX: Knox 62–57 Boone Grove. Officials: Tom Crouch, John Goss.
CENTRAL NOBLE: Westview 52–41 Central Noble. Officials: Steve Kvachkoff, Robert Filipek.
SOUTHWOOD: Harding 73–55 Southwood. Officials: Brian Osswald, Michael Crouch.
TAYLOR: Taylor 81–58 Oak Hill. Officials: Gary Hamilton, Brad Groninger.
MONROVIA: Monrovia 75–72 Western Boone (ot). Officials: Roger Holder, Tony Ortman.
GREENWOOD: Winchester 72–56 Indian Creek. Officials: Doug Coddington, Mike Padfield.
SILVER CREEK: Silver Creek 45–43 Batesville. Officials: Derek Howard, Terry Magnuson.
NORTH KNOX: Paoli 69–60 North Knox. Officials: Ron Grimes, Dave Senning.

2000 CLASS A REGIONALS

TRITON: Triton 41–34 Michigan City Marquette. Officials: Marvin Davis, Kirk Robinson.
SOUTHERN WELLS: Southern Wells 38–37 Bethany Christian. Officials: Tim Smith,

651

Dennis Jackson.
CENTRAL CATHOLIC: Central Catholic 55–49 Caston. Officials: Mark Hay, James Robinson.
BLUE RIVER VALLEY: Blue River Valley 74–68 Monroe Central. Officials: Ron McGriff, Jerry Stieglitz.
WHITE RIVER VALLEY: Union (Dugger) 66–61 Attica. Officials: James Dunlap, Keith Bagby.
JAC-CEN-DEL: Jac-Cen-Del 92–72 Hauser. Officials: Tom Walters, Gene Marsh.
NEW WASHINGTON: Northeast Dubois 55–39 New Washington. Officials: Greg McAdams, Don Nester
TECUMSEH: Tecumseh 31–22 Loogootee. Officials: Paul Meagher, Ron James.

2000 CLASS 4A SEMI—STATES

LAFAYETTE JEFFERSON: Marion 72–55 Penn; Warsaw 50–42 Merrillville; Marion 51–38 Warsaw. Officials: Chip Sweet, Terry Magnuson, Tom Walters, James Robinson, Phil Vidito, Jay C. Smith.

INDIANAPOLIS: Jeffersonville 62–53 Warren Central; Bloomington North 64–45 New Castle; Bloomington North 61–59 Jeffersonville. Officials: Greg McAdams, Mike Padfield, Gary Wier, Kirk Robinson, Mark Hay, Mike Waisnora.

2000 CLASS 3A SEMI—STATES

FRANKFORT: Andrean 77–59 Fort Wayne Concordia; Pendleton Heights 53–47 Tippecanoe Valley; Andrean 56–49 Pendleton Heights. Officials: Norman Delph, Mark Hyman, Ron Grimes, Gene Marsh, Jerry Taylor, Ray Tebbe.

WASHINGTON: Brebeuf 62–48 Danville; Evansville Mater Dei 96–63 Scottsburg; Brebeuf 66–63 Mater Dei. Officials: Ron McGriff, Tony Ortman, Michael Wallpe, Steve Godfroy, Brian Osswald, Larry Nixon.

2000 CLASS 2A SEMI—STATES

MARION: Harding 75–47 Knox; Westview 72–60 Taylor; Westview 59–58 Harding. Officials: Derek Howard, Ed Roush, Marvin Davis, Greg Yegerler, Bryce Heller, Tim Smith.

SOUTHRIDGE: Winchester 55–54 Silver Creek; Paoli 63–61 Monrovia; Winchester 84–73 Paoli. Officials: Paul Meagher, Kent Smith, William Terry Johnson, Robert Cochran, Robert Anderson, Tom Urban.

2000 CLASS A SEMI—STATES

KOKOMO: Lafayette Central Catholic 81–65 Southern Wells; Triton 68–59 Blue River Valley; Central Catholic 66–49 Triton. Officials: Tom Rohr, Dennis Jackson, Richard Modricker, Jerry Stieglitz, Gary Hamilton, Steve Kvachkoff.

GREENCASTLE: Union (Dugger) 72–57 Tecumseh; Jac-Cen-Del 69–66 Northeast Dubois; Union (Dugger) 72–59 Jac-Cen-Del. Officials: Doug Coddington, Bill Forehand, James Dunlap, Keith Bagby, Bill Nimnicht, Tom Crouch.

2000 FINALS—March 25
INDIANAPOLIS (Conseco Fieldhouse):
  CLASS 4A: Marion 62–56 Bloomington North. Officials: Bill Nimnicht, Brian Osswald.
  CLASS 3A: Brebeuf 72–56 Andrean. Officials: Bob Anderson, Steve Kvachkoff
  CLASS 2A: Westview 59–53 Winchester. Officials: Jerry Taylor, Gary Hamilton.
  CLASS A: Central Catholic 82–70 Union (Dugger). Officials: Mark Hay, Phil Vidito.

2001 CLASS 4A SECTIONALS
  GARY WEST SIDE: Highland 58–52 Munster; East Chicago Central 57–53 West Side; Central 57–45 Highland; Gary Roosevelt 79–64 Hammond; Central 44–40 Gary Roosevelt. Officials: John Goss, John Skvarek, Stephen Homner, Steve Kvachkoff.
  MERRIVILLE: Lake Central 55–34 Lowell; Merrillville 70–47 Gary Wallace; Merrillville 55–50 Lake Central; Crown Point 73–46 Hobart; Merrillville 59–41 Crown Point. Officials: Bruce Klonowski, Tom Behny, Mike Emerson, Doug Cook.
  MICHIGAN CITY: Portage 79–48 Michigan City; Chesterton 66–57 LaPorte; Portage 67–56 Chesterton; South Bend Washington 68–61 Valparaiso; Portage 81–73 Washington. Officials: Greg Yergler, Ron Gradeless, James Weinberg, Curtis Yoder.
  SOUTH BEND RILEY: LaSalle 64–59 Mishawaka; Adams 51–47 Riley; LaSalle 51–45 Adams; Penn 65–54 Clay; Penn 61–52 LaSalle. First two games were at Mishawaka and Riley. Officials: Eric Coburn, Mark Sewell, Jerome Jajchik, Bob Neff, Tom Dermody, Eric Kim.
  ELKHART: Warsaw 58–50 Elkhart Central; East Noble 44–43 Concord; East Noble 43–40 Warsaw (ot); Goshen 73–62 Elkhart Memorial; East Noble 68–54 Goshen. Officials: Rick Scott, John Pfieffer, Bob Martin, Ron Day.
  FORT WAYNE NORTHROP: Carroll (Fort Wayne) 64–51 DeKalb; Northrop 57–44 North Side; Carroll 72–36 Northrop; Snider 48–47 South Side; Carroll 59–35 Snider. Officials: Gene Marsh, Doug Flatter, Dave Terhune, Randall Miller.
  MARION: Kokomo 72–64 Homestead; Anderson Highland 59–54 Anderson; Kokomo 66–51 Highland; Huntington North 68–61 Marion; North 72–63 Kokomo. First two games were at Kokomo and Anderson. Officials: Tim Smith, Denis Schinderle, Russ Baker, Larry Jones.
  LAYFAYETTE: Harrison (West Lafayette) 59–51 Brownsburg; Jefferson 68–49 Logansport; Jefferson 55–47 Harrison (West Lafayette); McCutcheon 50–48 Avon; McCutcheon 58–47 Jefferson. Officials: Tom Rohr, Terry Kreider, John Cowan, Gary Chambers.
  NORTH CENTRAL (INDIANAPOLIS): North Central (Indianapolis) 67–61 Noblesville; Carmel 67–56 Hamilton Southeastern; North Central 72–66 Carmel; Pike 101–37 Broad Ripple; Pike 82–64 North Central. Officials: Robert Cochran, Steven Wyrick, Randall Gwin, Kevin Chestnut.
  NEW CASTLE: Muncie Central 73–66 New Castle; East Central 61–42 Connersville; Muncie Central 64–41 East Central; Richmond 43–18 Jay County; Muncie Central 69–38 Richmond.

Tourney Time

Officials: Michael Wallpe, Arnold Freeman Jr., Larry Johnson, Steve Smith.

SOUTHPORT: Ben Davis 62–42 Indianapolis Manual; Southport 57–37 Decatur Central; Ben Davis 70–39 Southport; Perry Meridian 67–37 Indianapolis Northwest; Perry Meridian 60–43 Ben Davis. Officials: Tom Walters, Mark Gines, Roger Marley, Brad Groninger.

LAWRENCE CENTRAL: Franklin Central 64–55 Indianapolis Tech; Lawrence North 57–52 Lawrence Central; Lawrence North 53–39 Franklin Central; Warren Central 59–43 Indianapolis Arlington; Lawrence North 57–41 Warren Central. Officials: Tony Ortrnan, Larry Sintz, Dan Kerker, Greg Reece.

TERRE HAUTE SOUTH: Mooresville 64–63 Terre Haute South; Martinsville 73–64 Northview; Martinsville 65–48 Mooresville; Terre Haute North 88–53 Plainfield; Terre Haute North 63–56 Martinsville. Officials: Mark Baltz, Kevin Lewis, Tim Pharis, Patrick McCallister.

COLUMBUS NORTH: Center Grove 59–44 Columbus North; Bloomington North 66–50 Greenwood; Bloomington North 65–63 Center Grove; Bloomington South 64–44 Columbus East; Bloomington North 64–54 Bloomington South. Officials: Rex Nichols, Don Whitlow, Ed Thornburgh, Wayne Hobson.

SEYMOUR: Bedford North Lawrence 68–59 Jennings County; Jeffersonville 72–61 Floyd Central; Bedford North Lawrence 73–67 Jeffersonville (ot); New Albany 65–54 Seymour; Bedford North Lawrence 51–47 New Albany. Officials: Bob Anderson, Derek Sullivan, Mike Armstrong, Monte McKee.

EVANSVILLE NORTH: Harrison 62–42 Central; Castle 56–47 North; Castle 50–47 Reitz; Harrison 53–47 Castle. Officials: David Kavanaugh, Michael Zehr, Michael Grundman, Ron James.

2001 CLASS 3A SECTIONALS

CALUMET: Griffith 63–49 Hammond Morton; Hammond Noll 70–54 Hammond Gavit; Noll 63–57 Griffith; Calumet 80–61 Hammond Clark; Noll 67–51 Calumet. Officials: Mike Waisnora, Fred Scheub, Tim Mills, Kevin Mikesell.

NEW PRAIRIE: New Prairie 48–41 Gary Wirt; Gary Mann 37–30 Kankakee Valley; Gary Mann 60–57 New Prairie; South Bend St. Joseph's 61–51 Andrean; South Bend St. Joseph's 57–47 Gary Mann. Officials: Bryce Heller, Mark Berger, Michael Noojin, Jon Davenport.

PLYMOUTH: Whitko, 65–57 Culver Military; Rochester 60–56 Mishawaka Marian; Whitko 81–58 Rochester; Plymouth 44–39 Tippecanoe Valley; Whitko 63–53 Plymouth. Officials: Lance Grubbs, William Kachel, Cary Schnick, Mark Hay.

FRANKFORT: West Lafayette 51–48 Hamilton Heights; Frankfort 72–62 Western; West Lafayette 59–48 Frankfort; Benton Central 79–66 Twin Lakes; Benton Central 63–52 West Lafayette. Officials: Michael Eason, Dan Ihrie, Rick Oliver, Richard Hammond, Jim Saddler, Don Nester.

NORTHWOOD: Northwood 63–56 Lakeland; Angola 71–59 Wawasee; Northwood 70–59 Angola; Northridge 69–60 West Noble; Northwood 64–54 Northridge. Officials: Jerry Stieglitz, James Mettler, Mark McCammon, Bob Childers.

NEW HAVEN: Fort Wayne Wayne 49–48 Fort Wayne Elmhurst; Fort Wayne Dwenger 74–60 Fort Wayne Concordia; Wayne 48–40 Dwenger; Columbia City 48–23 New Haven; Columbia City 44–35 Wayne. Officials: Tom Crouch, Robert Voss, Bud Wolf, Brett Patrick.

IHSAA Scores | 2000–2005

BLACKFORD: Bellmont 71–63 Blackford. Norwell 95–88 Peru; Bellmont 76–66 Norwell; Maconaquah 90–63 Mississinewa; Bellmont 72–61 Maconaquah. Officials: Tom Urban, David Nagel, Richard Kraus, Mark Short.

MUNCIE: Delta 65–61 Alexandria Monroe; Pendleton Heights 55–52 Elwood; Delta 58–49 Pendleton Heights; Southside 74–43 Yorktown; Southside 63–53 Delta. Officials: Haymon Fields, Brian Heaton, Dan Stewart, Todd Reel.

MT. VERNON (FORTVILLE): Roncalli 64–49 Mt. Vernon (Fortville); Brebeuf Jesuit 69–60 Indianapolis Chatard; Brebeuf Jesuit 80–54 Roncalli; Indianapolis Cathedral 80–77 Beech Grove (ot); Brebeuf Jesuit 69–60 Cathedral. Officials: Thomas Leix, John Yantiss, Doug Pullins, Patrick Dumoulin.

SHELBYVILLE: Franklin 60–49 Whiteland; New Palestine 42–38 Rushville; New Palestine 60–47 Franklin; Shelbyville 54–53 Greenfield–Central; Shelbyville 62–51 New Palestine. Officials: Terry Johnson, Lawrence Guynn, Dale Goodwin, Bill Brinkman.

DANVILLE: Lebanon 61–54 Southmont; Crawfordsville 69–64 Zionsville; Lebanon 60–31 Crawfordsville; Danville 71–55 Westfield; Lebanon 69–59 Danville. Officials: Doug Coddington, Larry Decker, Kenneth Knapp, Don Corey.

SULLIVAN: Sullivan 53–42 Edgewood; West Vigo 50–34 Greencastle; Sullivan 67–60 West Vigo; South Vermillion 68–51 Owen Valley; Sullivan 55–48 South Vermillion. Officials: Larry Nixon, Len Glazier, Mark Curts, Thomas Lynch.

GREENSBURG: Greensburg 83–68 South Dearborn; Scottsburg 67–59 Franklin County; Greensburg 73–57 Scottsburg; Brown County 74–71 Madison. Greensburg 79–59 Brown County. First two games were at South Dearborn and Franklin County. Officials: Derek Howard, Steve Corya, Bob Hallgarth, Phil Vidito, Kevin Henney, Scott West.

CORYDON CENTRAL: Mitchell 90–71 Providence; Salem 69–54 North Harrison; Mitchell 67–56 Salem; Corydon Central 72–41 Charlestown; Corydon Central 65–49 Mitchell. Officials: Gary Leistner, Danny Shields, Fred Cooper, David Moore.

WASHINGTON: Vincennes 90–59 Princeton; Gibson Southern 68–40 Pike Central;Lincoln 52–44 Gibson Southern; Jasper 55–35 Washington; Jasper 71–69 Lincoln (ot). Officials: Chip Sweet, Gary Weideman, Jay Kellett, James Dunlap.

BOONVILLE: Evansville Bosse 59–54 Boonville; Evansville Mater Dei 71–62 Mount Vernon; Mater Dei 61–42 Bosse; Heritage Hills 62–59 Evansville Memorial; Mater Dei 72–59 Heritage Hills. Officials: Mike Quinn, Scott Arthur, Mark Hopper, Jay Slater.

2001 CLASS 2A SECTIONALS

BOONE GROVE: Boone Grove 77–60 Wheeler; River Forest 71–69 Hebron; River Forest 38–35 Boone Grove; Lake Station Edison 60–53 Hanover Central; River Forest 36–31 Edison. Officials: Mark Wise, Dale Cramer, Steve Egan, Tim Filson.

NORTH NEWTON: North Newton 41–37 North Judson; Rensselaer Central 66–62 North White (ot); Rensselaer Central 72–54 North Newton; Winamac 43–41 Knox; Winamac 62–41 Rensselaer Central. Officials: Neil McCartney, Matthew Miller, Al Guillen, Robert Filipek.

WESTVIEW: Westview 53–52 Fairfield; Bremen 74–43 LaVille; Westview 65–54 Bremen (ot); Glenn 51–35 Jimtown; Glenn 57–54 Westview. Officials: Jay C. Smith, Clark Hamilton, James Galt, Judson Raver.

Tourney Time

GARRETT: Eastside 54–47 Prairie Heights; Central Noble 72–68 Churubusco; Central Noble 52–50 Eastside (ot); Fremont 58–55 Garrett; Central Noble 69–53 Fremont. Officials: Kirk Robinson, Jack Raabe, Kevin Weinberg, Steve Godfroy.

BLUFFTON: Harding 48–37 Bluffton; Heritage 75–68 Woodlan (ot); Harding 66–55 Heritage; Leo 70–60 Fort Wayne Luers; Harding 75–52 Leo. Officials: Dennis Jackson, Rod Weiss, Douglas Bauman, Gregg Holloway.

CASS: Cass 30–16 Northfield; Southwood 77–68 North Miami; Cass 52–39 Southwood; Manchester 52–42 Wabash; Cass 46–20 Manchester. Officials: Mike Crouch, Rick Hawley, Dick Russell, David Raabe.

EASTBROOK: Frankton 57–56 Muncie Burris; Madison-Grant 72–58 Eastbrook; Madison-Grant 56–53 Frankton; Oak Hill 77–59 South Adams; Oak Hill 66–61 Madison-Grant. Officials: James Robinson, Jerry Middleton, Lon Graft, Stanton Foreman.

TAYLOR: Tipton 56–38 Eastern (Greentown); Northwestern 53–50 Taylor; Tipton 59–47 Northwestern; Delphi 39–34 Carroll (Flora); Tipton 40–39 Delphi. Officials: Greg Webb, Michael Furnish, Tim Knowland, Jimmy Wolfe.

NORTH MONTGOMERY: Covington 72–57 North Montgomery; Western Boone 60–41 Sheridan; Covington 61–59 Western Boone; Fountain Central 55–43 Seeger; Covington 60–52 Fountain Central. Officials: Kevin Brown, Jason Ferguson, Stewart Casper, Grady Smith.

SOUTH PUTNAM: Cloverdale 57–42 Tri-West Hendricks; South Putnam 67–58 Monrovia; South Putnam 58–33 Cloverdale; Cascade 54–50 North Putnam; Cascade 45–38 South Putnam. Officials: Gary Wier, Steve Morris, J. K. Wieder, Rick Gentry.

HAGERSTOWN: Hagerstown 51–43 Winchester; Shenandoah 79–55 Centerville; Shenandoah 82–62 Hagerstown; Northeastern 77–60 Cambridge City Lincoln; Shenandoah 69–64 Northeastern. Officials: Greg McAdams, William Meyerrose, Dan VanTreese, Rick Shirk.

SPEEDWAY: Eastern Hancock 57–48 Triton Central; Speedway 87–63 Indianapolis Scecina; Speedway 71–53 Eastern Hancock; Indian Creek 75–71 Knightstown; Speedway 71–47 Indian Creek. Officials: Shawn Lambert, Craig Petree, Bob Whikehart, John Crapo.

BATESVILLE: Batesville 72–54 South Ripley; Switzerland County 78–68 North Decatur; Batesville 63–36 Switzerland County; Lawrenceburg 62–45 Union County; Batesville 67–55 Lawrenceburg. Officials: Roger Holder, Brian Humphrey, Tom Simpson, Ed Scahill.

SILVER CREEK: Southwestern (Hanover) 45–28 Brownstown Central; Eastern (Pekin) 68–49 Clarksville; Eastern 43–42 Southwestern; Austin 59–54 Silver Creek; Eastern 55–52 Austin. Officials: Ron McGriff, Paul Wahl, Robert Singelais, Gary Hamilton.

SOUTHRIDGE: Crawford County 62–60 Forest Park; Paoli 67–61 South Spencer; Crawford County 74–69 Paoli; Tell City 49–48 Southridge; Crawford County 65–64 Tell City. Officials: Jay Ritter, Joseph Calderazzo, Darrell Stone, Dennis Espenlaub.

NORTH KNOX: North Knox 78–61 South Knox; Linton-Stockton 66–51 North Central (Farmersburg); North Knox 78–63 Linton-Stockton; Eastern (Bloomfield) 84–63 North Posey; Eastern 75–72 North Knox. Officials: Ron Grimes, Kevin Denu, James Stephens, Alan Deskin.

2001 CLASS A SECTIONALS

KOUTS: Washington Twp. 48–26 Whiting; Kouts 67–46 Michigan City Marquette; Kouts 56–42 Washington Twp.; Morgan Twp. 67–45 Westville; Kouts 65–52 Morgan Twp. Officials:

IHSAA Scores | 2000–2005

Marvin Davis, Jack Urbin, George Forbes, Andy Simpson.

TRITON: South Central (Union Mills) 50–47 Argos; Culver Community 56–40 Oregon-Davis; South Central 62–47 Culver Community; Triton 63–47 LaCrosse; Triton 39–38 South Central. Officials: Merlin Nice, Butch Lehman, Ken Weaver, John Van Wagner.

BETHANY CHRISTIAN: Fort Wayne Blackhawk 78–41 Fort Wayne Christian; Hamilton 87–34 Howe Military; Hamilton 61–52 Blackhawk; Bethany Christian 55–36 Fort Wayne Canterbury; Hamilton 52–49 Bethany Christian. Officials: Norm Sellers, Robert Plummer, Jeff Morrett, Tom Muth.

SOUTHERN WELLS: Tri–Central 69–60 Southern Wells; Adams Central 92–41 White's; Adams Central 75–59 Tri–Central; Wes–Del 65–46 Marion Lakeview Christian; Adams Central 63–48 Wes–Del. Officials: Mark Hyman, Gene Huston, Jeffrey Pequignot, Tom Kenworthy.

TRI–COUNTY: Tri-County 61–50 West Central (ot); Pioneer 74–65 Frontier; Tri-County 40–35 Pioneer; South Newton 27–26 Caston; South Newton 42–37 Tri-County. Officials: Dick Modricker, Steve Elkins, Larry Samano, Russ Radtke.

CLINTON CENTRAL: Indianapolis Ritter 74–62 Clinton Prairie; Park Tudor 66–59 Rossville; Park Tudor 71–47 Indianapolis Ritter; Central Catholic 58–41 Clinton Central; Park Tudor 62–55 Central Catholic. Officials: Kent Smith, Rex Wallace, Robert Harding, Antoine Wynne.

MONROE CENTRAL: Randolph Southern 62–55 Union (Modoc); Cowan 72–69 Monroe Central; Randolph Southern 63–61 Cowan (ot); Union City 67–38 Wapahani; Randolph Southern 50–46 Union City. Officials: Norman Delph, Michael Alford, Philip Teusch, Joe Huff.

BLUE RIVER VALLEY: Lapel 64–59 Indiana School for the Deaf; Blue River Valley 84–38 Morton Memorial; Blue River Valley 82–66 Lapel; Tri 53–44 Daleville; Blue River Valley 67–60 Tri. Officials: Mike Padfield, Michael McGriff, Rusty Melcher, Rick Owens.

ATTICA: Turkey Run 61–58 Rockville; Attica 73–61 Riverton Parke; Attica 92–90 Turkey Run (3ot); North Vermillion 76–67 Eminence; Attica 69–54 North Vermillion. Officials: Mike Bohan, Andy Conrad, Clifford Brooks, Mike Stoffers.

WHITE RIVER VALLEY: Clay City 45–32 Bloomfield; North Daviess 73–40 Union (Dugger); North Daviess 59–46 Clay City; White River Valley 62–58 Shakamak (ot); North Daviess 49–48 White River Valley. Officials: Larry Maxwell, Michiael Shannon, Larry Steimel, Craig Criss.

EDINBURGH: Morristown 65–59 Edinburgh; Hauser 58–55 Southwestern (Shelbyville); Morristown 69–58 Hauser; Waldron 51–43 Indianapolis Lutheran; Waldron 51–40 Morristown. Officials: Pat Strong, Mark Christman, John Bowen, Tony Bierschbach.

MILAN: Milan 81–74 Jac-Cen-Del; South Decatur 81–52 Rising Sun; Milan 80–70 Madison Shawe; Milan 61–52 South Decatur. Officials: Terry Magnuson, John Fox, Kevin Moore, David Bolsega.

WEST WASHINGTON: Northeast Dubois 74–46 Crothersville; West Washington 54–49 Springs Valley; Northeast Dubois 49–45 West Washington; Orleans 75–30 Medora; Northeast Dubois 61–30 Orleans. Officials: Paul Meagher, Tim Jellison, Gary Woodling, Steve Meyer.

HENRYVILLE: Henryville 51–49 Borden; Lanesville 60–48 Graceland Christian; Henryville 68–55 Lanesville; New Washington 73–65 South Central (Elizabeth); New Washington 44–43 Henryville. Officials: Ed Roush, Tim Stroud, Brian German, Dan Morgan.

LOOGOOTEE: Barr-Reeve 54–22 Washington Catholic; Loogootee 60–34 Shoals; Barr-Reeve 52–35 Vincennes Rivet; Loogootee 26–24 Barr–Reeve. Officials: Carl March, Jack Davis, Warren Smith, Dave Senning.

Tourney Time

TECUMSEH: Evansville Day 68–43 New Harmony; Tecumseh 76–47 Cannelton; Tecumseh 38–32 Evansville Day; Oakland City Wood 49–48 Perry Central; Tecumseh 64–42 Wood. Officials: Keith Bagby, Joe Reed, Brad Dishman, Wayne Patterson.

2001 CLASS 4A REGIONALS

EAST CHICAGO: East Chicago Central 47–44 Merrillville. Officials: Marvin Davis, Neil McCartney.
PORTAGE: Penn 51–43 Portage. Officials: Bryce Heller, Steve Godfroy,
EAST NOBLE: Carroll (Fort Wayne) 62–54 East Noble. Officials: Dick Modricker, Greg Yergler.
HUNTINGTON: McCutcheon 77–60 Huntington North. Officials: Merlin Nice, Shawn Lambert.
PIKE: Pike 73–47 Muncie Central. Officials: Larry Nixon, Larry Maxwell,
PERRY MERIDIAN: Lawrence North 58–57 Perry Meridian. Officials: Norman Delph, Kevin Brown.
TERRE HAUTE NORTH: Bloomington North 54–53 Terre Haute North (ot). Officials: Richard Sweet, David Kavanaugh.
BEDFORD NORTH LAWRENCE: Bedford North Lawrence 53–51 Evansville Harrison (ot). Officials: Gary Leistner, Terry Magnuson.

2001 CLASS 3A REGIONALS

HAMMOND BISHOP NOLL: Hammond Bishop Noll 57–53 South Bend St. Joseph's. Officials: John Goss, Bruce Klonowski.
NORTHFIELD: Benton Central 82–61 Whitko. Officials: Jay C. Smith, Jerry Stieglitz.
NORTHWOOD: Columbia City 52–47 Northwood. Officials: Rick Scott, Dennis Jackson.
BELLMONT: Muncie Southside 69–66 Bellmont. Officials: Michael Wallpe, Mark Baltz.
NORTH CENTRAL (Indianapolis): Brebeuf Jesuit 62–54 Shelbyville. Officials: Carl March, Greg McAdams.
LEBANON: Sullivan 71–63 Lebanon. Officials: Tom Rohr, Pat Strong.
GREENSBURG: Corydon Central 73–65 Greensburg. Officials: Ron McGriff, Doug Coddington.
JASPER: Evansville Mater Dei 64–50 Jasper. Officials: Gary Wier, Ron James.

2001 CLASS 2A REGIONALS

RIVER FOREST: River Forest 47–42 Winamac Community. Officials: Mike Waisnora, Eric Coburn.
GLENN: Central Noble 55–48 Glenn. Officials: Mike Crouch, Mike Padfield.
HARDING: Harding 52–28 Cass. Officials: Kirk Robinson, Rick Owens.
OAK HILL: Oak Hill 64–55 Tipton. Officials: Tom Crouch, Thomas Leix.
COVINGTON: Covington 56–40 Cascade. Officials: William Terry Johnson, Don Nester.
SHENANDOAH: Shenandoah 61–59 Speedway. Officials: Roger Holder, Haymon Fields.

BATESVILLE: Batesville 61–49 Eastern (Pekin). Officials: Rex Nichols, Tony Ortman.
CRAWFORD COUNTY: Eastern (Bloomfield) 63–58 Crawford County. Officials: Derek Howard, Michael Quinn.

2001 CLASS A REGIONALS

KOUTS: Kouts 72–43 Triton. Officials: Lance Grubbs, Mark Wise.
GARRETT: Hamilton 83–77 Adams Central (2ot). Officials: Tim Smith, Gene Marsh.
SOUTH NEWTON: Park Tudor 65–47 South Newton. Officials: Tom Walters, Greg Webb.
RANDOLPH SOUTHERN: Blue River Valley 75–65 Randolph Southern. Officials: Tom Urban, Robert Cochran.
NORTH VERMILLION: Attica 58–51 North Daviess. Officials: Tom Walters, Greg Webb.
WALDRON: Milan 50–49 Waldron. Officials: Ron Grimes, Kent Smith.
NORTHEAST DUBOIS: New Washington 60–58 Northeast Dubois. Officials: Keith Bagby, Jay Ritter.
LOOGOOTEE: Loogootee 55–45 Tecumseh. Officials: Paul Meagher, Ed Roush.

2001 CLASS 4A SEMI–STATES

LAFAYETTE JEFFERSON: Carroll (Ft. Wayne) 67–64 McCutcheon (ot); Penn 48–46 East Chicago Central; Penn 57–52 Carroll (ot). Officials: Roger Holder, Ed Roush, Michael Wallpe, Haymon Fields, James Robinson, Rick Scott.

INDIANAPOLIS: Bloomington North 52–49 Lawrence North; Pike 71–53 Bedford North Lawrence; Pike 78–65 Bloomington North. Officials: Greg McAdams, Mark Hyman, Gary Wier, Doug Coddington, Marvin Davis, Tom Urban.

2001 CLASS 3A SEMI–STATES

FRANKFORT: Muncie Southside 64–54 Hammond Bishop Noll; Columbia City 60–43 Benton Central; Muncie Southside 64–53 Columbia City. Officials: Norman Delph, Steve Godfroy, Dennis Jackson, Greg Yergler, Mike Waisnora, John Goss.

WASHINGTON: Evansville Mater Dei 75–59 Sullivan; Brebeuf Jesuit 60–53 Corydon Central; Mater Dei 68–66 Brebeuf. Officials: Chip Sweet, Kent Smith, Keith Bagby, Jay Ritter, Ron McGriff, Rex Nichols.

2001 CLASS 2A SEMI–STATES

HUNTINGTON NORTH: Harding 69–38 River Forest; Oak Hill 60–53 Central Noble; Harding 73–62 Oak Hill. Officials: Merlin Nice, Tony Ortman, Lance Grubbs, Jerry Stieglitz, Bryce Heller, Tom Rohr.

SOUTHRIDGE: Covington 68–61 Shenandoah; Batesville 89–71 Eastern (Bloomfield); Batesville 59–55 Covington. Officials: Ron Grimes, John Crapo, Robert Cochran, Terry Magnuson, Larry Nixon, Paul Meagher.

Tourney Time

2001 CLASS A SEMI-STATES

KOKOMO: Blue River Valley 60–39 Park Tudor; Kouts 78–77 Hamilton; Blue River Valley 72–53 Kouts. Officials: Kirk Robinson, Gene Marsh, Tom Crouch, Mike Padfield, Jay C. Smith, William Terry Johnson.

GREENCASTLE: Loogootee 57–45 New Washington; Attica 81–71 Milan; Attica 64–61 Loogootee (ot). Officials: Derek Howard, Carl March, Gary Leistner, Ron James, Tim Smith, Mike Crouch.

2001 FINALS—March 24

INDIANAPOLIS (Conseco Fieldhouse):
CLASS 4A: Pike 56–42 Penn. Officials: Ron McGriff, Tim R. Smith.
CLASS 3A: Muncie Southside 81–78 Evansville Mater Dei (ot). Officials: Larry Nixon, James Robinson.
CLASS 2A: Harding 73–70 Batesville. Officials: Marvin Davis, Jay C. Smith.
CLASS A: Attica 64–62 Blue River Valley. Officials: Bryce Heller, Mike Waisnora.

2002—New format:

Sixteen sectionals in each of four classes. Four four-team regionals in each class. Two two-team semi-states in each class. Four sites used for semi-states and each had games from two different classes. Four state championship games in one day at Conseco Fieldhouse, Indianapolis.

2002 CLASS 4A SECTIONALS

EAST CHICAGO CENTRAL: Gary West Side 67–53 Munster; Lake Central 69–36 Lowell; West Side 61–39 Lake Central; East Chicago Central 76–73 Gary Wallace; West Side 72–61 Central. Officials: Doug Greenlee, Robert Filipek, Al Guillen, John VanWagner.

VALPARAISO: Valparaiso 22–17 Portage; Merrillville 64–59 Crown Point; Valparaiso 53–52 Merrillville; Chesterton 58–56 Hobart; Valparaiso 46–28 Chesterton. Officials: Andy Simpson, Joseph Skvarek, Jeffrey Morrett, Curtis Yoder.

MICHIGAN CITY: South Bend Washington 81–46 South Bend Riley; South Bend Clay 71–69 LaPorte; Washington 76–66 South Bend Clay; Michigan City 62–60 South Bend Adams;Washington 101–60 Michigan City. First two games were at Washington and Clay. Officials: John Goss, Fred Scheub, George Forbes, Mike Waisnora.

ELKHART: Elkhart Central 64–56 Mishawaka; Concord 60–41 Goshen; Concord 59–47 Central; Elkhart Memorial 57–36 Penn; Memorial 74–69 Concord. Officials: Merlin Nice, Jon Davenport, Ted Garton, Bryce Heller.

DEKALB: Warsaw 62–47 East Noble; Carroll (Fort Wayne) 55–50 Columbia City; Warsaw 64–51 Carroll; DeKalb 64–46 Warsaw. DeKalb 62–50 Warsaw. Officials: David Raabe, Douglas Bauman, Rusty Melcher, Marvin Davis.

FORT WAYNE NORTHROP: Huntington North 76–69 Fort Wayne Snider; Homestead 79–69 Fort Wayne North Side; Homestead 56–50 Huntington North; Fort Wayne South Side

59–51 Fort Wayne Northrop; Homestead 76–53 South Side. Officials: Rick Scott, Robert Plummer, James Mettler, Greg Holloway.

LOGANSPORT: McCutcheon 71–60 Logansport; Lafayette Jefferson 66–44 Marion; Jefferson 63–52 McCutcheon; Harrison (West Lafayette) 64–58 Kokomo; Jefferson 52–33 Harrison. Officials: Kirk Robinson, Kevin Chestnut, Dean Martin, Mike Padfield.

RICHMOND: Muncie Central 69–49 Anderson Highland; Richmond 72–70 Muncie Southside; Richmond 56–48 Muncie Central; Anderson 62–59 New Castle; Anderson 78–73 Richmond. Officials: Phil Vidito, Antoine Wynne, Greg Bowman, Tony Ortman.

CARMEL: Pike 88–66 Indianapolis Broad Ripple; Hamilton Southeastern 57–56 North Central (Indianapolis); Pike 56–36 Hamilton Southeastern; Noblesville 74–56 Carmel; Pike 56–52 Noblesville (ot). Officials: Tom Rohr, Kent Smith, Dan VanTreese, Bill Brinkman.

LAWRENCE NORTH: Lawrence North 63–51 Warren Central; Indianapolis Arlington 100–63 Connersville; Arlington 84–70 Lawrence North; Warren Central 51–43 Indianapolis Cathedral; Arlington 69–63 Warrant Central (ot). Officials: Larry Maxwell, Jerry Middleton. Rod Weiss, James Robinson.

INDIANAPOLIS TECH: Indianapolis Northwest 49–42 Decatur Central; Ben Davis 73–53 Brownsburg; Northwest 105–76 Ben Davis; Avon 78–57 Tech; Avon 51–37 Northwest. Officials: Rex Nichols, Roger Marley, Kenneth Knapp, Larry Nixon.

GREENWOOD: Greenwood 60–55 Indianapolis Manual (ot); Franklin Central 54–51 Southport (ot); Greenwood 51–44 Franklin Central; Perry Meridian 53–48 Center Grove; Greenwood 50–41 Perry Meridian. Officials: Ray Tebbe, Steven Corya, J.K. Wieder, Jimmy Wolfe.

MARTINSVILLE: Northview 80–58 Mooresville; Martinsville 78–72 Plainfield; Martinsville 73–68 Northview; Terre Haute South 46–40 Terre Haute North; Martinsville 64–58 Terre Haute South. Officials: Michael Wallpe, Craig Petree, Rick Oliver, Thomas Lynch.

COLUMBUS NORTH: Bloomington North 73–42 Columbus North; Columbus East 71–65 Bloomington South; Bloomington North 61–46 Columbus East; Franklin 50–40 East Central; Bloomington North 57–54 Franklin. Officials: Gary Wier, Don Nester, Casey Gaynor, Ed Scahill.

SEYMOUR: Jeffersonville 58–50 Seymour; Bedford North Lawrence 66–55 Floyd Central; Bedford North Lawrence 72–57 Jeffersonville; New Albany 61–42 Jennings County; New Albany 56–49 Bedford North Lawrence. Officials: Donald Whitlow, David Bolsega, Dan Stewart, Dan Morgan.

EVANSVILLE REITZ: Castle 79–54 Evansville Central; Evansville Harrison 63–60 Evansville North; Castle 70–67 Evansville Reitz (2ot); Castle 63–54 Harrison. Officials: Rick Gentry, Scott Arthur, John Trotter, Kevin Denu.

2002 CLASS 3A SECTIONALS

HAMMOND CLARK: Hammond 71–66 Hammond Morton; Hammond Noll 40–38 Highland; Noll 60–51 Hammond; Hammond Clark 38–35 Hammond Gavit; Noll 84–56 Clark. Officials: Steve Kvachkoff, Mark Sewell, Cary Schnick, Russell Radtke.

CALUMET: Gary Roosevelt 52–45 Griffith; Gary Mann 68–63 Calumet; Roosevelt 68–56 Mann; Gary Wirt 59–43 Andrean; Roosevelt 60–41 Wirt. Officials: Bruce Klonowski, Mark

Tourney Time

McCammon, Tom Dermody, Tom Behny.

PLYMOUTH: Knox 64–57 Kankakee Valley; Whitko 48–45 Tippecanoe Valley; Whitko 53–46 Knox; Plymouth 61–41 Culver Military; Plymouth 61–44 Whitko. Officials: Richard Modricker, Steve Elkins, Philip Teusch, Thomas Muth.

FRANKFORT: Frankfort 62–51 West Lafayette; Benton Central 78–64 Western; Benton Central 57–46 Frankfort; Twin Lakes 65–53 Northwestern; Benton Central 59–41 Twin Lakes. Officials: Terry Bartell, Andy Conrad, John Fox, Mark Curts.

NORTH WOOD: South Bend St. Joseph's 60–50 Mishawaka Marian; South Bend LaSalle 76–71 North Wood; LaSalle 64–58 St. Joseph's; Northridge 65–56 New Prairie; LaSalle 70–68 Northridge. Officials: Greg Yergler, Dale Cramer, Jeffrey Pequignot, Butch Lehman.

LAKELAND: Lakeland 64–44 West Noble; Leo 64–53 Fort Wayne Concordia; Leo 56–39 Lakeland; Angola 39–34 Fort Wayne Dwenger; Leo 52–41 Angola. Officials: Eric Coburn, Mark Berger, Dave Terhune, Jay C. Smith.

FORT WAYNE WAYNE: Fort Wayne Wayne 63–45 New Haven; Harding 73–72 Elmhurst; Harding 59–48 Wayne; Fort Wayne Luers 64–40 Heritage; Harding 84–39 Luers. Officials: Mike Crouch, Dennis Jackson, Mark Bauman, Jack Urbin.

BLACKFORD: Jay County 79–62 Peru; Blackford 60–58 Maconaquah; Blackford 50–49 Jay County; Bellmont 66–50 Norwell; Bellmont 54–51 Blackford. Officials: Tom Kenworthy, Michael Alford, Mark Hyman, Rick Owens.

YORKTOWN: Mount Vernon (Fortville) 52–42 Yorktown; Delta 57–51 Pendleton Heights; Delta 59–50 Mount Vernon; Alexandria 56–55 Elwood; Delta 62–49 Alexandria. Officials: Gary Hamilton, Terry Kreider, Robert Harding, Haymon Fields.

HAMILTON HEIGHTS: Zionsville 62–41 Hamilton Heights; Lebanon 72–60 Westfield; Lebanon 52–43 Zionsville; Crawfordsville 50–48 Tipton; Lebanon 60–47 Crawfordsville. Officials: Michael Eason, Doug Pullins, Danny Ihrie, Greg Reece.

BEECH GROVE: Beech Grove 72–64 Brebeuf Jesuit (ot); Indianapolis Chatard 54–48 New Palestine; Chatard 55–52 Beech Grove; Roncalli 71–51 Greenfield Central; Chatard 47–43 Roncalli. Officials: Robert Cochran, Len Glazier, Richard Deering, John Yantiss.

GREENSBURG: South Dearborn 61–45 Rushville; Franklin County 75–74 Greensburg (5ot); Franklin County 56–48 South Dearborn; Whiteland 46–39 Shelbyville; Whiteland 68–55 Franklin County. Officials: Mark Baltz, James Saddler, John Cowan, John Bowen.

NORTH HARRISON: Corydon Central 59–56 Scottsburg; Madison 84–83 North Harrison (ot); Corydon Central 72–67 Madison; Providence 61–57 Silver Creek; Corydon Central 68–52 Providence. Officials: Carl March, Gary Weideman, Mike Baas, Kevin Moore.

OWEN VALLEY: Owen Valley 63–55 Danville; Edgewood 72–62 West Vigo; Edgewood 57–44 Owen Valley; Brown County 61–55 Greencastle; Edgewood 51–47 Brown County. Officials: Chip Sweet, Jason Ferguson, Derek Sullivan, Mike Bohan.

WASHINGTON: Pike Central 54–46 Vincennes; Princeton 56–36 Sullivan; Pike Central 56–49 Princeton; Jasper 74–72 Washington; Jasper 66–39 Pike Central. Officials: Ron James, Darrell Stone, Gregory Hayes, Tim Jellison.

BOONVILLE: Evansville Memorial 50–43 Evansville Bosse; Gibson Southern 61–52 Boonville; Gibson Southern 47–32 Memorial; Heritage Hills 73–68 Mount Vernon; Gibson Southern 53–48 Heritage Hills. Officials: David Kavanaugh, Tim Stroud, Joe Reed, Michael Grundman.

2002 CLASS 2A SECTIONALS

WHEELER: Hanover Central 70–51 North Newton; Wheeler 60–48 Lake Station Edison; Wheeler 84–72 Hanover Central; Boone Grove 63–51 Rensselaer; Boone Grove 59–57 Wheeler. Officials: Ron Day, Kevin Mikesell, James Arnett, Norm Sellers.

NORTH JUDSON: Jimtown 51–27 Triton; Bremen 40–35 North Judson; Jimtown 61–45 Bremen; Glenn 67–43 LaVille; Jimtown 60–30 Glenn. Officials: Mark Hay, James Weinberg, Kent Bennington, Denny Hepler.

WESTVIEW: Central Noble 43–38 Eastside; Westview 78–51 Prairie Heights; Westview 65–58 Central Noble; Fairfield 54–52 Fremont; Fairfield 73–70 Westview (2ot). Officials: Lance Grubbs, Steve Godfroy, John Pfeiffer, Tim Smith.

ROCHESTER: Winamac 53–35 Wabash; North Miami 51–41 Rochester; Winamac 60–40 North Miami; Manchester 59–45 Northfield; Winamac 49–32 Manchester. Officials: Tim Knowland, Tim Mills, Lon Graft, Matthew Miller.

WOODLAN: Bluffton 58–52 Garrett; Churubusco 60–48 South Adams; Bluffton 68–57 Churubusco; Woodlan 79–78 Adams Central; Bluffton 65–51 Woodlan. Officials: Tom Crouch, William Kachel, Mike Johnson, Brett Patrick.

TAYLOR: Delphi 54–44 Sheridan; Taylor 46–44 Cass; Taylor 56–30 Delphi; Clinton Central 57–32 Eastern (Greentown); Taylor 56–52 Clinton Central. Officials: Kevin Brown, Edward Thornburgh, Jay Scott, Kevin Lewis.

MISSISSINEWA: Madison–Grant 62–40 Eastbrook; Mississinewa 83–77 Oak Hill; Madison–Grant 57–49 Mississinewa; Muncie Burris 72–54 Frankton; Muncie Burris 62–54 Madison–Grant. Officials: Shawn Lambert, Judson Raver, Rob Jewson, Dick Russell.

HAGERSTOWN: Northeastern 66–44 Cambridge City Lincoln; Centerville 55–54 Winchester; Centerville 66–57 Northeastern; Shenandoah 81–76 Hagerstown; Shenandoah 54–46 Centerville. Officials: Greg McAdams, Tom Simpson, Larry Johnson, Robert Voss.

FOUNTAIN CENTRAL: Covington 36–32 Southmont; North Montgomery 54–36 Seeger; Covington 54–46 North Montgomery; Fountain Central 49–36 Western Boone; Covington 45–43 Fountain Central. Officials: Greg Webb, Arnold Freeman, Jr., Bob Whikehart, Michael Stoffers.

SOUTH PUTNAM: South Vermillion 60–47 Cascade; North Putnam 68–58 Cloverdale; North Putnam 56–51 South Vermillion; Tri–West Hendricks 46–44 South Putnam (ot); North Putnam 85–83 Tri–West Hendricks (3ot). Officials: Neil McCartney, Lawrence Guynn, Tracy Black, Ron McGriff.

INDIAN CREEK: Indianapolis Ritter 46–44 Park Tudor; Speedway 48–44 Indianapolis Scecina; Speedway 66–53 Indianapolis Ritter; Indian Creek 67–66 Monrovia; Speedway 70–48 Indian Creek. Officials: William Terry Johnson, Mark Gines, Donald McCann, Gene Huston.

BATESVILLE: Eastern Hancock 73–48 Union County; Knightstown 61–54 Triton Central; Eastern Hancock 70–62 Knightstown (2ot); Batesville 47–37 North Decatur; Batesville 62–58 Eastern Hancock. Officials: Terry Magnuson, Larry Sintz, Randall Gwin, Rex Wallace.

SOUTHWESTERN (HANOVER): Switzerland County 89–76 South Ripley; Brownstown Central 67–36 Southwestern (Hanover); Brownstown Central 72–60 Switzerland County; Austin 69–58 Lawrenceburg; Austin 68–51 Brownstown Central. Officials: Ron Grimes, Brian Heaton, William Meyerrose, Jack Davis.

PAOLI: Mitchell 53–44 Eastern (Pekin) (ot); Salem 67–45 Charlestown; Mitchell 72–54

Tourney Time

Salem; Paoli 73–49 Clarksville; Paoli 39–35 Mitchell. Officials: Bob Anderson, Mike Armstrong, Robert Singelais, Wayne Patterson.

NORTH KNOX: Eastern (Bloomfield) 59–49 North Posey; Evansville Mater Dei 72–43 South Knox; Mater Dei 50–42 Eastern; North Knox 69–42 Linton-Stockton; Mater Dei 69–58 North Knox. Officials: Don Corey, John Crapo, Warren Smith, Jay Kellett.

SOUTHRIDGE: South Spencer 55–48 Tell City; Crawford County 71–65 Forest Park; Crawford County 62–46 South Spencer; Southridge 58–53 Perry Central; Crawford County 50–46 Southridge. Officials: Keith Bagby, James Dunlap, James Stephens, Alan Deskin.

2002 CLASS A SECTIONALS

WHITING: Michigan City Marquette 62–46 River Forest; Westville 44–40 Whiting; Marquette 67–46 Westville; South Central (Union Mills) 64–46 Washington Twp.; South Central 64–59 Marquette. Officials: Mark Wise, Jeff Rhody, Jeffrey Nix, Ronald Gradeless.

MORGAN TWP.: Kouts 94–45 Oregon–Davis; Morgan Twp. 59–43 LaCrosse; Kouts 74–53 Morgan Twp.; Hebron 69–39 West Central; Kouts 75–68 Hebron. Officials: Tim Filson, Michael Noojin, James Galt, Doug Cook.

HAMILTON: Lakewood Park Christian 74–52 Howe Military; Bethany Christian 79–54 Fort Wayne Christian; Fort Wayne Blackhawk 58–44 Fort Wayne Canterbury; Hamilton 63–50 Lakewood Park Christian; Bethany Christian 68–63 Blackhawk (ot); Bethany Christian 56–47 Hamilton. Officials: Jerry Stieglitz, Bud Wolfe, Russ Baker, Bob Neff.

CASTON: Caston 72–70 Argos; Southwood 72–29 White's; Caston 52–45 Southwood; Pioneer 62–43 Culver Community; Pioneer 45–41 Caston. Officials: Bob Childers, Mark Short, Dennis Aldridge, Gary Chambers.

TRI–COUNTY: Tri–County 65–48 Frontier; Central Catholic 92–50 North White; Central Catholic 66–56 Tri–County; South Newton 71–66 Carroll (Flora); Central Catholic 45–32 South Newton. Officials: Stanton Foreman, Patrick McCallister, Denis Schinderle, Patrick Dumoulin.

TRI–CENTRAL: Lapel 81–30 Indiana School for the Deaf; Rossville 84–68 Tri-Central; Rossville 63–56 Lapel (ot); Clinton Prairie 44–32 Covenant Christian; Rossville 60–52 Clinton Prairie. Officials: Gary Smith, Wayne Hobson, Gene Wethington, Brad Groninger.

SOUTHERN WELLS: Marion Lakeview Christian 49–36 Cowan; Southern Wells 77–47 Wes-Del; Marion Lakeview Christian 64–58 Southern Wells; Wapahani 59–45 Daleville; Marion Lakeview Christian 58–44 Wapahani. Officials: Norman Delph, Doug Flatter, Richard Kraus, Gene Marsh.

MONROE CENTRAL: Union (Modoc) 72–68 Tri (ot); Union City 70–61 Monroe Central; Union City 55–49 Union (Modoc); Blue River Valley 85–53 Randolph Southern; Blue River Valley 53–51 Union City (2ot). Officials: Brian Humphrey, Rick Hawley, Todd Reel, Tim Pharis.

NORTH VERMILLION: Turkey Run 76–63 Eminence; Rockville 70–61 North Vermillion; Rockville 73–69 Turkey Run; Attica 65–57 Riverton Parke; Rockville 62–59 Attica. Officials: Thomas Leix, Stewart Casper, Brian Hole, David Nagel.

SOUTHWESTERN (SHELBYVILLE): Morristown 69–44 Edinburgh; Southwestern (Shelbyville) 69–56 Indianapolis Lutheran; Morristown 43–36 Southwestern (Shelbyville); Morton Memorial 71–70 Waldron (ot); Morristown 51–47 Morton Memorial. Officials: Doug Coddington, Danny Shields, Dan Kerker, Steve Morris.

IHSAA Scores | 2000–2005

WHITE RIVER VALLEY: North Central (Farmersburg) 87–47 Union (Dugger); Shakamak 47–42 Clay City; Shakamak 46–38 North Central; White River Valley 30–27 Bloomfield (ot); White River Valley 32–28 Shakamak. Officials: Derek Howard, Monte McKee, W. Scott Wagner, Mark Hopper.

MILAN: Hauser 75–48 South Decatur; Rising Sun 66–33 Oldenburg Academy; Hauser 67–52 Rising Sun; Milan 68–64 Jac-Cen-Del; Hauser 72–61 Milan. Officials: Ed Roush, Mark Christman, Scott West, Michael McGriff.

LOOGOOTEE: Loogootee 73–43 Shoals; Barr–Reeve 53–27 Vincennes Rivet; Barr-Reeve 54–47 Loogootee; North Daviess 50–30 Washington Catholic; Barr-Reeve 31–29 North Daviess. Officials: Paul Meagher, Steve Meyer, Larry Steimel, Jay Slater.

OAKLAND CITY WOOD: New Harmony 44–42 Oakland City Wood; Evansville Day 45–43 Cannelton; Evansville Day 57–44 New Harmony; Tecumseh 52–46 Northeast Dubois; Tecumseh 64–52 Evansville Day. Officials: Jay Ritter, Dennis Espenlaub, Paul Wahl, R. Brad Dishman.

SPRINGS VALLEY: Springs Valley 60–51 Medora; South Central (Elizabeth) 60–42 Orleans; South Central 81–52 Springs Valley; West Washington 72–70 Lanesville; South Central 53–45 West Washington. Officials: Dave Senning, Larry Decker, Dick Hammond, Joseph Calderazzo.

HENRYVILLE: Madison Shawe 39–35 Crothersville; Henryville 59–32 New Washington; Madison Shawe 68–49 Henryville; Borden 58–51 Graceland Christian; Madison Shawe 48–40 Borden. Officials: David Moore, Michael Zehr, Steven Wyrick, Gary Leistner.

2002 CLASS 4A REGIONALS

MICHIGAN CITY: Gary West 42–39 Valparaiso; South Bend Washington 73–70 Elkhart Memorial; Gary West 70–62 South Bend Washington. Officials: Ron Day, Denny Helper, Norm Sellers, Jack Urbin, Rick Scott, Mark Hay.

MARION: DeKalb 57–48 Anderson; Lafayette Jefferson 64–48 Homestead; DeKalb 65–53 Lafayette Jefferson. Officials: Gary Hamilton, Haymon Fields, Michael Eason, Gene Marsh, Terry Bartell, Greg Yergler.

INDIANAPOLIS: Greenwood 48–44 Avon; Pike 73–63 Indianapolis Arlington; Pike 51–40 Greenwood. Officials: Richard Modricker, Bill Brinkman, Doug Coddington, Rick Owens, Greg McAdams, Tom Crouch.

SEYMOUR: Castle 64–60 New Albany (ot); Martinsville 65–48 Bloomington North; Castle 58–51 Martinsville. Officials: Kevin Brown, Mike Bohan, Grady Smith, Jimmy Wolfe, Mark Baltz, Phil Vidito.

2002 CLASS 3A REGIONALS

KANKAKEE VALLEY: Hammond Noll 55–40 Plymouth; Benton Central 72–65 Gary Roosevelt; Benton Central 55–49 Noll (ot). Officials: Greg Webb, Ronald Gradeless, Lance Grubbs, Curtis Yoder, Mark Wise, Kirk Robinson.

NORTHWOOD: Harding 58–38 Leo; Bellmont 79–61 South Bend LaSalle; Harding 59–53 Bellmont. Officials: Andy Simpson, Tom Behny, Steve Kvachkoff, Russell Radtke, Merlin Nice, Tom Filson.

Tourney Time

SHELBYVILLE: Delta 62–54 Whiteland; Lebanon 51–49 Indianapolis Chatard (ot); Delta 50–39 Lebanon. Officials: Derek Howard, Robert Cochran, Shawn Lambert, Greg Reece, Michael Wallpe, David Moore.

WASHINGTON: Jasper 40–29 Gibson Southern; Edgewood 61–46 Corydon Central; Jasper 66–62 Edgewood. Officials: Donald Whitlow, Dan Morgan, Ron Grimes, Tim Jellison, Tom Rohr, Keith Bagby.

2002 CLASS 2A REGIONALS

TRITON: Jimtown 39–35 Winamac; Boone Grove 47–40 Fairfield; Jimtown 56–48 Boone Grove (ot). Officials: Bob Childers, Patrick Dumoulin, Doug Greenlee, Brett Patrick, John Goss, David Raabe.

MISSISSINEWA: Muncie Burris 82–53 Shenandoah; Bluffton 56–38 Taylor; Bluffton 77–75 Muncie Burris. Officials: Jerry Stieglitz; Matthew Miller, Gary Chambers, Thomas Muth, Ray Tebbe, Bob Anderson.

SPEEDWAY: North Putnam 54–53 Batesville; Speedway 36–33 Covington; Speedway 50–34 North Putnam. Officials: Brian Humphrey, Thomas Lynch. Don Corey, Ed Scahill, William Terry Johnson, Tim Knowland.

SOUTHRIDGE: Austin 51–48 Evansville Mater Dei; Paoli 60–50 Crawford County; Austin 73–64 Paoli. Officials: David Kavanaugh, Wayne Patterson, Ron James, Joseph Calderazzo, Gary Wier, Paul Meagher.

2002 CLASS A REGIONALS

CULVER COMMUNITY: Bethany Christian 66–65 Pioneer; Kouts 68–65 South Central (Union Mills); Bethany Christian 64–59 Kouts. Officials: Norman Delph, Kevin Lewis, Stanton Foreman, Tim Pharis, Eric Coburn, Neil McCartney.

TIPTON: Rossville 66–46 Lakeview Christian; Lafayette Catholic 81–71 Blue River Valley; Rossville 86–73 Lafayette Catholic. Officials: Thomas Leix, Mark Curts, Tom Kentworthy, Tony Ortman, Mike Crouch, Bruce Klonowski.

WHITE RIVER VALLEY: Morristown 62–43 Rockville; White River Valley 80–70 Hauser; White River Valley 59–57 Morristown. Officials: Carl March, Kevin Denu, Rick Gentry, Alan Deskin, Rex Nichols, Larry Maxwell.

LOOGOOTEE: South Central (Elizabeth) 67–49 Madison Shawe; Barr-Reeve 45–33 Tecumseh; Barr-Reeve 60–54 South Central (Elizabeth). Officials: Jay Ritter, Steve Morris, Dave Senning, Michael Stoffers, Chip Sweet, Terry Magnuson.

2002 CLASS 4A SEMI—STATES

INDIANAPOLIS (Hinkle Fieldhouse): Pike 57–55 Castle. Officials: Rex Nichols, Mike Crouch.

LAFAYETTE JEFFERSON: Gary West Side 69–64 DeKalb. Officials: William Terry Johnson, Mark Wise.

IHSAA Scores | 2000–2005

2002 CLASS 3A SEMI-STATES
LAFAYETTE JEFFERSON: Harding 54–45 Benton Central. Officials: Michael Wallpe, Mark Baltz.
SEYMOUR: Delta 65–63 Jasper (3ot). Officials: Greg McAdams, Chip Sweet.

2002 CLASS 2A SEMI-STATES:
HUNTINGTON NORTH: Bluffton 54–36 Jimtown. Officials: Tom Rohr, Eric Coburn.
INDIANAPOLIS (Hinkle Fieldhouse): Speedway 61–56 Austin. Officials: Rick Scott, Terry Bartell.

2002 CLASS A SEMI-STATES:
HUNTINGTON NORTH: Rossville 81–70 Bethany Christian. Officials: John Goss, Merlin Nice.
SEYMOUR: Barr-Reeve 62–57 White River Valley (ot). Officials: Ray Tebbe, Gary Wier.

2002 FINALS—March 23
INDIANAPOLIS (Conseco Fieldhouse):
CLASS 4A: Gary West Side 58–55 Pike. Officials: Ray Tebbe, Tom Rohr.
CLASS 3A: Delta 65–54 Harding. Officials: John Goss, William Terry Johnson.
CLASS 2A: Speedway 62–48 Bluffton. Officials: Greg McAdams, injured, replaced by Terry Bartell; Rex Nichols.
CLASS A: Rossville 79–68 Barr–Reeve. Officials: Rick Scott, Mike Wallpe.

2003 CLASS 4A SECTIONALS
GARY WEST: Lake Central 60–39 Gary West; East Chicago 39–38 Munster; East Chicago 56–55 Lake Central; Lowell 63–50 Gary Wallace; East Chicago 67–49 Lowell. First two games were at Lake Central and Munster. Officials: Mark Wise, George Forbes, Cary Schnick, Jeffrey Nix.
VALPARAISO: Merrillville 61–58 Valparaiso; Chesterton 71–56 Portage; Merrillville 47–46 Chesterton; Crown Point 58–42 Hobart; Merrillville 70–56 Crown Point. Officials: Doug Greenlee, James Arnett, James Galt, Tim Mills.
MICHIGAN CITY: South Bend Adams 70–66 South Bend Washington (2ot); South Bend Riley 70–57 LaPorte; Riley 62–54 Adams; Michigan City 68–65 South Bend Clay; Riley 82–67 Michigan City. First two games were at Washington and Riley. Officials: Andy Simpson, Joseph Skvarek, Jeff Rhody, Mark Berger.
ELKHART: Central 60–41 Memorial; Concord 44–40 Penn; Central 47–44 Concord; Goshen 54–46 Mishawaka (ot); Central 54–51 Goshen. Officials: Norm Sellers, Mark Sewell, Mike Johnson, Ron Day.
WARSAW: Wawasee 49–46 Carroll (Allen Co.); Columbia City 45–42 Warsaw; Columbia City 58–37 Wawasee; DeKalb 45–36 East Noble; DeKalb 55–49 Columbia City (2ot). Officials:

Tourney Time

Bryce Heller, Thomas Muth, Robert Plummer, Bruce Klonowski.

HUNTINGTON: Homestead 60–56 Ft. Wayne South (ot); Ft. Wayne Snider 49–41 Huntington; Homestead 82–64 Snider; Northrop 59–46 North Side; Northrop 69–66 Homestead. Officials: Mike Crouch, Patrick Dumoulin, Mark Bauman, James Robinson.

LAFAYETTE: Kokomo 59–40 Logansport; Marion 60–57 Harrison; Kokomo 62–43 Marion; Jefferson 61–49 McCutcheon; Kokomo 51–46 Jefferson. Officials: Neil McCartney, Tim Pharis, Patrick McCallister, Michael Wallpe.

NEW CASTLE: Richmond 55–45 Anderson Highland; Muncie Central 54–52 Anderson; Central 46–45 Richmond; Muncie Southside 70–50 New Castle; Central 54–50 Southside. Officials: Terry Bartell, Haymon Fields, Wayne Hobson, Doug Coddington.

NOBLESVILLE: Pike 75–56 North Central (Indianapolis); Carmel 67–48 Broad Ripple; Pike 66–52 Carmel; Noblesville 58–57 Hamilton Southeastern; Pike 67–44 Noblesville. Officials: Larry Nixon, Terry Kreider, J. K. Wieder, Jerry Taylor.

INDIANAPOLIS ARLINGTON: Warren Central 56–55 Lawrence Central; Lawrence North 65–18 Connersville; Lawrence North 55–51 Warren Central; Cathedral 55–53 Arlington; Lawrence North 60–37 Cathedral. Officials: Bob Anderson, Bob Whikehart, Tony Bierschbach, Ray Tebbe.

BEN DAVIS: Ben Davis 56–53 Indianapolis Tech; Avon 55–49 Indianapolis Northwest; Ben Davis 58–55 Avon; Brownsburg 73–58 Decatur Central; Ben Davis 65–58 Brownsburg (ot). Officials: Terry Magnuson, Shawn Lambert, Jerry Middleton, Kevin Moore.

PERRY MERIDIAN: Greenwood 57–55 Center Grove (ot); Indianapolis Manual 54–51 Southport; Greenwood 59–41 Manual; Perry Meridian 64–48 Franklin Central; Perry Meridian 72–51 Greenwood. Officials: Gary Hamilton, Don Nester, Rick Hawley, Mike Fawcett.

TERRE HAUTE NORTH: Northview 61–55 South; Mooresville 48–43 Martinsville; Martinsville 56–42 Northview; North 64–54 Plainfield; North 47–39 Martinsville. Officials: David Kavanaugh, Tracy Black, Lawrence Guynn, Jay Slater.

COLUMBUS: East 61–43 East Central; Bloomington South 72–44 Franklin; South 88–78 East; Bloomington North 54–38 Columbus North; Bloomington South 55–51 Bloomington North (ot). Officials: Ron Grimes, Mark Christman, Rex Wallace, Rex Nichols.

SEYMOUR: New Albany 64–44 Seymour; Jennings County 52–51 Bedford-North Lawrence; New Albany 54–42 Jennings County; Jeffersonville 65–40 Floyd Central; New Albany 47–44 Jeffersonville. Officials: Paul Meagher, Steven Wyrick, Timothy Cartwright, Scott Wagner.

CASTLE: Castle 50–48 Evansville Central; Harrison 57–53 Reitz; Castle 59–43 North; Harrison 71–62 Castle. Officials: Gary Wier, Steve Morris, P. J. Pitts, Wayne Patterson.

2003 CLASS 3A SECTIONALS

HAMMOND CLARK: Morton 62–55 Noll; Highland 56–29 Clark; Highland 42–30 Morton; Hammond High 67–27 Gavit; Highland 63–45 Hammond High. Officials: Mike Waisnora, Kevin Mikesell, Mike Emerson, John VanWagner.

CALUMET: Gary Wirt 52–41 Gary Mann; Andrean 87–41 Calumet; Andrean 70–61 Wirt; Gary Roosevelt 59–56 Griffith; Roosevelt 73–54 Andrean. Officials: Greg Yergler, Fred Scheub, Al Guillen, John Goss.

PLYMOUTH: Knox 60–53 Plymouth; Whitko 69–42 Culver Military; Knox 44–39 Whitko;

Tippecanoe Valley 60–58 Kankakee Valley; Knox 49–43 Tippecanoe Valley (2ot). Officials: Jay Smith, Robert Filipek, Dennis Aldridge, Ronald Gradeless.

FRANKFORT: Benton Central 70–60 Twin Lakes; Western 72–70 Frankfort; Western 66–54 Benton Central; West Lafayette 53–51 Northwestern; Western 64–47 West Lafayette. Officials: Phil Vidito, Todd Reel, Dean Martin, Kevin Lewis.

NORTHWOOD: NorthWood 69–51 Mishawaka Marian; New Prairie 78–49 South Bend St. Joseph's; Northridge 71–67 NorthWood (ot); New Prairie 52–51 Northridge. Officials: Tim Filson, Bud Wolf, Jon Davenport, Denny Hepler.

LEO: Ft. Wayne Concordia 74–45 West Noble; Dwenger 65–52 Angola; Concordia 70–56 Dwenger; Lakeland 66–52 Leo; Lakeland 64–48 Concordia. Officials: Tim Smith, Rob Jewson, Jack Raabe, Steve Godfroy.

NEW HAVEN: Ft. Wayne Elmhurst 64–43 Wayne; Harding 59–43 Luers; Elmhurst 76–60 Harding; Heritage 57–44 New Haven; Elmhurst 66–52 Heritage. Officials: Eric Coburn, David Raabe, Dave Terhune, Bob Neff.

BLACKFORD: Norwell 69–63 Maconaquah; Jay County 75–53 Bellmont; Jay County 69–60 Norwell; Peru 77–71 Blackford; Jay County 69–39 Peru. Officials: Michael Eason, Russ Melcher, Richard Kraus, Kevin Chestnut.

YORKTOWN: Pendleton Heights 58–33 Elwood; Delta 51–47 Yorktown; Pendleton Heights 43–26 Delta; Alexandria 49–47 Mt. Vernon (Fortville); Pendleton Heights 52–49 Alexandria. Officials: Jason Ferguson, Robert Cochran, Arnold Freeman, Jr., Rick Owens.

LEBANON: Hamilton Heights 47–45 Tipton; Lebanon 50–34 Zionsville; Hamilton Heights 64–47 Lebanon; Westfield 55–51 Crawfordsville; Hamilton Heights 54–42 Westfield. Officials: Ron McGriff, Larry Johnson, James Saddler, John Yantiss.

GREENFIELD: Indianapolis Roncalli 41–40 New Palestine; Chatard 71–49 Brebeuf; Chatard 41–39 Roncalli; Greenfield–Central 72–41 Beech Grove; Chatard 56–53 Greenfield-Central. Officials: Craig Petree, Greg Reece, Dick Russell, Greg McAdams.

SHELBYVILLE: Rushville 47–44 Greensburg; Shelbyville 53–51 Franklin Co.; Rushville 44–34 Shelbyville (ot); Whiteland 54–44 South Dearborn; Rushville 44–42 Whiteland (ot). Bill Brinkman, Mike Padfield, Edward Thornburgh, Donald McCann.

MADISON: North Harrison 56–49 Silver Creek; Corydon 72–65 Scottsburg; Corydon Central 75–64 North Harrison; Clarksville Providence 66–64 Madison (ot); Corydon Central 58–36 Providence. Officials: David Moore, Tom Simpson, Dan Kerker, Brian Heaton.

GREENCASTLE: Greencastle 70–55 Edgewood; Danville 54–42 Owen Valley; Greencastle 56–49 Danville; Brown County 65–58 West Vigo; Brown County 69–66 Greencastle (2ot). Officials: Jay Kellett, Casey Gaynor, John Cowan, Greg Bowman.

WASHINGTON: Washington 64–36 Pike Central; Vincennes 71–61 Princeton; Vincennes 55–51 Washington; Sullivan 51–49 Jasper; Sullivan 38–37 Vincennes. Officials: Keith Bagby, Larry Decker, Danny Shields, Tom Rohr.

BOONVILLE: Gibson Southern 55–44 Mt. Vernon (Posey Co.); Boonville 50–42 Evansville Bosse; Gibson Southern 55–32 Boonville; Heritage Hills 51–48 Evansville Memorial (3ot); HeritageHills 38–36 Gibson Southern. Officials: Tim Jellison, Brian Patten, Byron Wilkinson, Michael Zehr.

Tourney Time

2003 CLASS 2A SECTIONALS

BOONE GROVE: Wheeler 71–51 Lake Station Edison; North Newton 73–51 Hanover Central; Wheeler 74–45 North Newton; Boone Grove 65–54 Rensselaer Central (ot); Boone Grove69–66 Wheeler. Officials: Mark Hay, Kent Bennington, Steve Tyler, Gary Chambers.

TRITON: Bremen 53–47 Jimtown; Triton 55–50 Glenn; Triton 70–65 Bremen; North Judson 31–30 LaVille; Triton 69–48 North Judson. Officials: Brett Patrick, Tim Knowland, Robert Harding, Kirk Robinson.

WESTVIEW: Prairie Heights 57–53 Eastside; Central Noble 45–40 Westview; Central Noble 65–38 Prairie Heights; Fremont 56–53 Fairfield; Central Noble 57–41 Fremont. Officials: Curtis Yoder, Dale Cramer, Russ Baker, Doug Cook.

WINAMAC: Northfield 37–34 Winamac; Wabash 60–57 Manchester (ot); Northfield 46–38 Wabash; Rochester 70–52 North Miami; Northfield 53–47 Rochester. Officials: Merlin Nice, Mark Hyman, William Kachel, Richard Modricker.

SOUTH ADAMS: Bluffton 55–47 Garrett; Woodlan 54–49 South Adams; Bluffton 71–61 Woodlan; Adams Central 56–48 Churubusco; Bluffton 44–42 Adams Central. Officials: Tony Ortman, Brad Groninger, Doug Flatter, Tom Kenworthy.

CASS: Taylor 50–46 Eastern; Sheridan 61–31 Clinton Central; Sheridan 50–43 Taylor; Cass 35–14 Delphi; Cass 48–34 Sheridan. Officials: Tom Walters, John Pfeiffer, Philip Teusch, Antoine Wynne.

MISSISSINEWA: Eastbrook 65–56 Mississinewa; Muncie Burris 70–57 Madison-Grant; Burris 71–56 Eastbrook; Oak Hill 76–64 Frankton; Burris 91–75 Oak Hill. Officials: Randall Miller, Steve Elkins, James Newbern, Robert Voss.

HAGERSTOWN: Hagerstown 64–49 Northeastern; Shenandoah 46–41 Cambridge City Lincoln; Hagerstown 58–56 Shenandoah; Winchester 58–43 Centerville; Winchester 73–41 Hagerstown. Officials: Pat Strong, Jay Scott, Chad Sievers, Mark Curts.

NORTH MONTGOMERY: Covington 39–36 North Montgomery; Fountain Central 56–39 Southmont; Covington 42–36 Fountain Central; Western Boone 64–48 Seeger; Covington 65–50 Western Boone. Officials: Mark Baltz, Andrew Conrad, Michael DeBoy, Stewart Casper.

SOUTH PUTNAM: South Putnam 46–44 Cloverdale; Cascade 64–53 South Vermillion; South Putnam 58–51 Cascade; Tri-West Hendricks 61–55 North Putnam; South Putnam 62–49 Tri-West. Officials: Scott Arthur, John Bowen, Brian Hole, Dan Morgan.

SPEEDWAY: Indian Creek 59–51 Heritage Christian; Park Tudor 46–44 Monrovia; Ritter 52–40 Speedway; Scecina 60–57 IndianCreek; Ritter 51–49 Park Tudor; Scecina 48–36 Ritter. Officials: Michael Stoffers, Rick Oliver, Rob Couch, Kevin Brown.

TRITON CENTRAL: Eastern Hancock 68–52 North Decatur; Batesville 44–34 Triton Central; Eastern Hancock 49–40 Batesville; Knightstown 58–48 Union County; Eastern Hancocl 75–60 Knightstown. Officials: Thomas Lynch, Kenton Smith, Rod Weiss, Scott West.

SOUTHWESTERN (HANOVER): Austin 74–56 Switzerland County; South Ripley 45–44 Lawrenceburg; Austin 68–50 South Ripley; Brownstown Central 75–41 Southwestern; Brownstown Central 78–66 Austin. Officials: Donald Whitlow, John Fox, Roger Marley, Steve Meyer.

SALEM: Mitchell 56–41 Eastern (Pekin); Paoli 62–46 Clarksville; Mitchell 59–54 Paoli; Salem 85–62 Charlestown; Salem 54–47 Mitchell. Officials: Alan Deskin, Dick Hammond, Mike Baas, Joe Calderazzo.

NORTH KNOX: Eastern (Greene Co.) 61–52 Linton-Stockton; Evansville Mater Dei 79–48 South Knox; Mater Dei 43–42 Eastern; North Knox 69–56 North Posey; Mater Dei 51–48 North Knox. Officials: Dave Senning, Darrell Stone, Brian Holtz, Kevin Denu.

SOUTHRIDGE: Southridge 61–46 Perry Central; Forest Park 76–57 South Spencer; Forest Park 45–38 Southridge; Crawford County 64–49 Tell City; ForestPark 59–45 Crawford County. Officials: Jay Ritter, Warren Smith, Mark Gines, Dennis Espenlaub.

2003 CLASS A SECTIONALS

WHITING: South Central (Union Mills) 57–48 Whiting; Washington Twp. 49–45 River Forest; South Central 56–48 Washington Twp.; Westville 27–23 Michigan City Marquette; South Central 56–48 Westville. Officials: Steve Kvachkoff, Michael Noojin, Marl McCammon, Tom Dermody.

KOUTS: Morgan Twp. 58–48 Hebron; Kouts 94–64 LaCrosse; Morgan Twp. 67–63 Kouts; West Central 43–21 Oregon–Davis; Morgan Twp. 44–37 West Central. Officials: Marvin Davis, Russell Radtke, Tom Behny, Jack Urbin.

FORT WAYNE BLACKHAWK CHRISTIAN: Blackhawk Christian 77–45 Hamilton; Canterbury 49–45 Bethany Christian; Ft. Wayne Christian 71–65 Howe Military; Blackhawk Christian 84–34 Lakewood Park Christian; Canterbury 53–43 Ft. Wayne Christian; Blackhawk Christian 63–39 Centerbury. Officials: Dave Stauffer, James Mettler, Douglas Bauman, Stanton Foreman.

CULVER: Argos 67–62 Southwood; Pioneer 74–14 White's; Argos 68–60 Pioneer; Caston 41–25 Culver; Caston 33–25 Argos (ot). Officials: Lance Grubbs, Steve Egan, Eric Hartman, James Weinberg.

TRI–COUNTY: Carroll (Flora) 62–45 South Newton; Lafayette Central Catholic 46–37 Tri-County; Central Catholic 60–57 Carroll; Frontier 80–41 North White; Central Catholic 58–55 Frontier. Officials: Greg Webb, Matthew Miller, Dennis Jackson, Rick Scott.

TRI–CENTRAL: Clinton Prairie 60–53 Rossville; Covenant Christian 65–55 Indiana School for the Deaf; Clinton Prairie 37–35 Covenant Christian; Tri-Central 67–48 Lapel; Tri-Central 66–60 Clinton Prairie. Officials: Thomas Leix, Gene Huston, Doug Pullins, Norman Delph.

SOUTHERN WELLS: Southern Wells 63–45 Marion Lakeview Christian; Wapahani 44–43 Cowan; Wapahani 66–61 Southern Wells (ot); Wes-Del 59–37 Daleville; Wes-Del 71–44 Wapahani. Officials: Jerry Stieglitz, Judson Raver, Jeffrey Pequignot, Bob Childers.

MONROE CENTRAL: Blue River Valley 58–51 Randolph Southern; Monroe Central 64–41 Tri; Monroe Central 69–53 Blue River; Union City 63–51 Union (Modoc); Monroe Central 61–51 Union City. Officials: Grady Smith, Michael Alford, Randall Gwin, Michael McGriff.

NORTH VERMILLION: Rockville 44–38 Attica; Riverton Parke 41–25 Eminence; Riverton Parke 45–44 Rockville (ot); Turkey Run 58–36 North Vermillion; Riverton Parke 64–58 Turkey Run. Officials: Mark Hopper, Denis Schinderle, Gene Wethington, Mike Bohan.

SOUTHWESTERN (SHELBYVILLE): Southwestern 66–38 Morristown; Edinburgh 55–53 Indianapolis Lutheran; Southwestern 78–36 Edinburgh; Waldron 87–41 Morton Memorial; Southwestern 49–47 Waldron. Officials: David Nagel, Danny Ihrie, Len Glazier, Richard Deering.

CLAY CITY: Clay City 43–29 Shakamak; Bloomfield 60–23 Union (Dugger); Bloomfield 51–46 Clay City (ot); White River Valley 63–54 North Central (Farmersburg); Bloomfield 37–

Tourney Time

31 White River Valley. Officials: Rick Gentry, David Bolsega, Larry Steimel, Don Corey.

MILAN: Rising Sun 69–55 Hauser; Milan 71–62 South Decatur; Milan 49–43 Rising Sun; Jac-Cen-Del 84–71 Oldenburg Academy; Milan 71–46 Jac-Cen-Del. Officials: Derek Howard, Ed Scahill, Larry Sintz, Brian Humphrey.

NORTH DAVIESS: North Daviess 54–41 Shoals; Loogootee 59–45 Washington Catholic; Loogootee 42–33 North Daviess; Vincennes Rivet 40–37 Barr-Reeve; Loogootee 48–42 Rivet (ot). Officials: Ron James, Paul Wahl, Gary Weideman, Gregory Hayes.

TECUMSEH: Tecumseh 61–45 Cannelton; Northeast Dubois 61–40 New Harmony; Tecumseh 38–33 Northeast Dubois; Evansville Day 43–41 OaklandCity Wood; Tecumseh 48–37 Evansville Day. Officials: Michael Quinn, Michael Polley, Josh Turner, Jack Davis.

ORLEANS: West Washington 68–54 Lanesville; South Central (Elizabeth) 67–39 Medora; West Washington 68–55 South Central; Orleans 52–38 Springs Valley; Orleans 68–61 West Washington. Officials: Brad Dishman, Monte McKee, Michiael Shannon, John Trotter.

HENRYVILLE: Henryville 39–31 New Washington; Graceland Christian 55–38 Borden; Henryville 52–44 Graceland Christian; Shawe Memorial (Madison) 59–22 Crothersville; Shawe Memorial 33–32 Henryville. Officials: Carl March, Steve Corya, Robert Singleais, Mike Armstrong.

2003 CLASS 4A REGIONALS

MICHIGAN CITY: South Bend Riley 76–73 Elkhart Central (ot); Merrillville 57–53 East Chicago; Merrillville 69–68 Riley (ot). Officials: Tim Filson, Denny Hepler, Norm Sellers, Ron Day, Eric Coburn, Tim Smith.

MARION: DeKalb 61–43 Ft. Wayne Northrop; Muncie Central 65–57 Kokomo; DeKalb 52–39 Central. Officials: Craig Petree, Norman Delph, Phil Vidito, Gary Chambers, Mark Hay, Randall Miller.

INDIANAPOLIS: Ben Davis 55–49 Perry Meridian; Pike 55–47 Lawrence North; Pike 65–52 Ben Davis. Officials: Derek Howard, Michael McGriff, Terry Magnuson, Rick Owens, Gary Wier, Ron McGriff.

SEYMOUR: New Albany 68–51 Terre Haute North; Evansville Harrison 64–51 Bloomington South; Harrison 61–40 New Albany. Officials: Rick Gentry, Mike Bohan, David Kavanaugh, Brian Heaton, Mark Baltz, Larry Nixon.

2003 CLASS 3A REGIONALS

PLYMOUTH: Knox 69–64 Western; Gary Roosevelt 59–46 Highland; Roosevelt 68–45 Knox. Officials: Steve Kvachkoff, Bob Neff, Andy Simpson, Bruce Klonowski, Mark Wise, Marvin Davis.

NORTHWOOD: Ft. Wayne Elmhurst 69–62 Lakeland; Jay County 59–48 New Prairie; Elmhurst 62–59 Jay County. Officials: Curtis Yoder, Tim Mills, Greg Yergler, James Weinberg, Merlin Nice, Mike Waisnora.

SHELBYVILLE: Rushville 44–40 Pendleton Heights (ot); Indianapolis Chatard 46–38 Hamilton Heights; Chatard 63–41 Rushville. Officials: Tony Ortman, Mark Curts, Bill Brinkman, Kevin Lewis, Ron Grimes, Pat Strong.

WASHINGTON: Heritage Hills 61–50 Sullivan; Corydon Central 59–47 Brown County;

Central 58–56 Heritage Hills. Officials: Michael Stoffers, Greg Bowman, Tim Jellison, John Yantiss, Dave Senning, Donald Whitlow.

2003 CLASS 2A REGIONALS

TRITON: Northfield 46–38 Central Noble; Boone Grove 71–59 Triton (ot); Northfield 59–42 Boone Grove. Officials: Tom Walters, Steve Godfroy, Grady Smith, Stanton Foreman, Jerry Stieglitz, Doug Greenlee.

BLACKFORD: Cass 55–44 Winchester; Muncie Burris 67–60 Bluffton; Cass 63–50 Burris. Officials: Thomas Leix, Kevin Chestnut, Michael Eason, James Robinson, Lance Grubbs, Jay C. Smith.

SPEEDWAY: Covington 43–40 South Putnam; Eastern Hancock 40–37 Indianapolis Scecina; Eastern 52–47 Covington. Officials: Gary Hamilton, Tom Kenworthy, David Nagel, Robert Voss, Greg Webb, Mark Hopper.

SOUTHRIDGE: Evansville Mater Dei 76–51 Salem; Forest Park 70–63 Brownstown Central; Forest Park 70–52 Mater Dei. Officials: Michael Quinn, Michael Zehr, Ron James, Jay Slater, Keith Bagby, Brad Dishman.

2003 CLASS A REGIONALS

CULVER: Ft. Wayne Blackhawk Christian 56–50 South Central (Union Mills); Morgan Twp. 47–37 Caston; Blackhawk Christian 54–46 Morgan Twp. Officials: Dave Stauffer, Ronald Gradeless, Neil McCartney, Kirk Robinson, Mike Crouch, Bryce Heller.

TIPTON: Lafayette Central Catholic 70–56 Tri–Central; Wes-Del 78–75 Monroe Central; Central Catholic 64–46 Wes-Del. Officials: Thomas Lynch, Doug Coddington, Jason Ferguson, Antoine Wynne, Bob Anderson, Brett Patrick.

WHITE RIVER VALLEY: Southwestern (Shelbyville) 55–47 Riverton Parke; Bloomfield 49–30 Milan; Southwestern 49–45 Bloomfield (ot). Scott Arthur, Kevin Brown, Jay Kellett, Kevin Moore, Terry Bartell, Alan Deskin.

LOOGOOTEE: Loogootee 43–40 Tecumseh; Orleans 60–50 Shawe Memorial; Orleans 40–37 Loogootee (3ot). Officials: Carl March, Don Corey, Jay Ritter, Mike Armstrong, Paul Meagher, David Moore.

2003 CLASS 4A SEMI—STATES

LAFAYETTE: DeKalb 66–51 Merrillville. Officials: Mike Crouch, Greg Webb.

SOUTHPORT: Pike 79–56 Evansville Harrison. Officials: Terry Bartell, Mark Hay.

2003 CLASS 3A SEMI—STATES

LAFAYETTE: Ft. Wayne Elmhurst 71–68 Gary Roosevelt. Officials: Mark Baltz, Lance Grubbs.

SEYMOUR: Indianapolis Chatard 60–38 Corydon Central. Officials: Keith Bagby, Paul Meagher.

Tourney Time

2003 CLASS 2A SEMI-STATES
WARSAW: Cass 40–30 Northfield. Officials: Mark Wise, Eric Coburn.
SOUTHPORT: Forest Park 77–69 Eastern Hancock. Officials: Gary Wier, Ron Grimes.

2003 CLASS A SEMI-STATES
WARSAW: Lafayette Central Catholic 74–50 Ft. Wayne Blackhawk Christian. Officials: Merlin Nice, Jerry Stieglitz.
SEYMOUR: Southwestern (Shelbyville) 78–53 Orleans. Officials: Bob Anderson, Dave Senning.

2003 FINALS—March 29
INDIANAPOLIS (Conseco Fieldhouse):
CLASS 4A: Pike 65–52 DeKalb. Officials: Bob Anderson, Merlin Nice.
CLASS 3A: Indianapolis Chatard 78–44 Ft. Wayne Elmhurst. Officials: Gary Wier, Mike Crouch.
CLASS 2A: Cass 57–48 Forest Park. Officials: Mark Baltz, Terry Bartell.
CLASS A: Lafayette Central Catholic 68–64 Southwestern (Shelbyville). Officials: Mark Wise, Keith Bagby.

2004 CLASS 4A SECTIONALS
EAST CHICAGO CENTRAL: Munster 59–54 Gary West Side; Lake Central 70–53 Highland; Lake Central 55–53 Munster; East Chicago Central 65–39 Lowell; East Chicago Central 67–61 Lake Central. First two games played at Munster and Lake Central. Officials: John Goss, Mark Wise, Rolland Thill, Tim Mills.
PORTAGE: Portage 68–62 Merrillville; Crown Point 55–50 Chesterton; Portage 65–49 Crown Point; Valparaiso 62–43 Hobart; Valparaiso 49–39 Portage. Officials: Greg Yergler, Mark McCammon, James Weinberg, Bruce Klonowski.
MICHIGAN CITY: South Bend Clay 71–68 South Bend Washington; South Bend Riley 72–55 Michigan City; Riley 74–67 Clay; LaPorte 59–50 South Bend Adams; LaPorte 96–88 Riley. First two games played at Clay and Riley. Officials: Tim Filson, Jeffrey Nix, Mark Sewell, Chris Yoder.
ELKHART CENTRAL: Mishawaka 65–39 Elkhart Memorial; Penn 44–39 Elkhart Central; Mishawaka 49–47 Penn (ot); Concord 52–43 Goshen; Concord 50–43 Mishawaka. Officials: Bryce Heller, Butch Lehman, Robert Filipek, Bob Neff.
WARSAW: Columbia City 45–43 Warsaw; East Noble 54–38 DeKalb; Columbia City 55–45 Carroll (Ft. Wayne); Columbia City 42–40 East Noble. Officials: Mark Hay, Russ Melcher, Dale Cramer, Doug Cook.
FT. WAYNE NORTHROP: Ft. Wayne Snider 61–55 Ft. Wayne Northrop; Ft. Wayne South Side 67–53 Homestead; South 83–75 Snider; Huntington North 71–56 Ft. Wayne North Sisw; South 60–58 North (ot). Officials: Rick Scott, Dave Stauffer, James Metler, Tim Knowland.
LAFAYETTE JEFFERSON: Harrison 47–42 McCutcheon; Kokomo 45–42 Logansport;

Kokomo 55–50 Harrison (ot); Jefferson 57–45 Marion; Jefferson 46–44 Kokomo (ot). Officials: Tom Rohr, Terry Bartell, John Cowan, Kevin Lewis.

MUNCIE CENTRAL: Richmond 62–56 Anderson; Muncie Central 63–52 Greenfield Central; Muncie Central 83–71 Richmond; Muncie Southside 54–41 Anderson Highland; Muncie Central 66–51 Muncie Southside. Officials: Ray Tebbe, Mark Baltz, Dennis Jackson, Antoine Wynne.

CARMEL: Hamilton Southeastern 79–53 Westfield; Broad Ripple 75–72 Carmel; Southeastern 70–66 Broad Ripple; North Central 70–49 Noblesville; North Central 81–69 Southeastern. Officials: Tom Walters, Craig Petree, Ronald McCann, Denis Schinderle.

WARREN CENTRAL: Warren Central 76–42 Indianapolis Tech; Cathedral 67–62 Lawrence Central; Lawrence North 73–35 Indianapolis Manual; Indianapolis 71–61 Warren Central; Lawrence Central 74–51 Cathedral; LawrenceNorth 61–47 Arlington. Officials: Grady Smith, Lawrence Guynn, Jerry Middleton, Dan Morgan.

CENTER GROVE: Perry Meridian 63–54 Center Grove; Franklin Central 54–43 Greenwood; Decatur Central 71–55 Franklin; Perry Meridian 61–46 Southport; Franklin Central 52–39 Decatur Central; Franklin Central 45–42 Perry Meridian. Officials: Pat Strong, Casey Gaynor, James Saddler, Jason Ferguson.

AVON: Avon 64–56 Zionsville; Pike 71–40 Ben Davis; Pike 58–35 Avon; Indianapolis Northwest 71–61 Brownsburg; Northwest 64–62 Pike. Officials: Rex Nichols, Andy Conrad, Dean Martin, David Nagel.

PLAINFIELD: Terre Haute South 54–53 Terre Haute North; Plainfield 69–49 Mooresville; South 74–68 Plainfield; Northview 56–48 Martinsville; Northview 45–40 South. Officials: Phil Vidito, Gene Huston, Arnold Freeman, Jr., Rex Wallace.

COLUMBUS NORTH: East Central 79–59 Columbus East; Shelbyville 73–71 Columbus North (2ot); East Central 61–47 Shelbyville; Bloomington North 73–66 Bloomington South (ot); North 52–49 East Central. Officials: Ron McGriff, Bob Anderson, Roger Marley, Steve Meyer.

SEYMOUR: Jennings County 58–54 Bedford North Lawrence; Floyd Central 77–71 Jeffersonville; Floyd Central 70–69 Jennings County; New Albany 63–57 Seymour; New Albany 73–65 Floyd Central. Officials: Terry Magnuson, Larry Steimel, Dick Hammond, Gary Wiedeman.

EVANSVILLE CENTRAL: Central 57–49 Castle; Evansville North 63–50 Evansville Harrison; Central 42–38 Evansville Reitz; Central 69–52 North. Officials: Michael Quinn, Paul Wahl, Kevin Christman, Kevin Denu.

2004 CLASS 3A SECTIONALS

CALUMET: Hammond 62–51 Hammond Clark; Calumet 61–53 Hammond Morton; Hammond 68–64 Calumet; Hammond Gavit 63–53 Griffith; Gavit 85–71 Hammond. Officials: Mike Waisnora, Kevin Mikesell, Robert Bishop, Doug Greenlee.

GARY ROOSEVELT: Roosevelt 63–51 Gary Wirt; Gary Wallace 82–74 Kankakee Valley; Roosevelt 82–72 Wallace; Andrean 78–70 Gary Horace Mann; Andrean 78–75 Roosevelt. Official: Andy Simpson, Russell Radtke, Joe Skvarek, Mark Berger.

PLYMOUTH: Knox 63–42 Culver Academy; Plymouth 58–46 New Prairie; Knox 68–65 Plymouth; South Bend St. Joseph's 54–43 Mishawaka Marian; Knox 49–38 St. Joseph's. Officials: Eric Coburn, Merlin Nice, Mike Emerson, Denny Hepler.

Tourney Time

FRANKFORT: Maconaquah 61–51 Frankfort; Western 59–39 West Lafayette; Western 66–57 Maconaquah; Twin Lakes 56–54 Benton Central (ot); Western 71–67 Twin Lakes (ot). Officials: Mike Bohan, Tracy Black, Justin Markley, Greg Bowman.

NORTHWOOD: Northridge 57–44 NorthWood; Angola 73–65 Wawasee; Northridge 56–45 Angola; Lakeland 72–66 West Noble; Northridge 53–49 Lakeland. Officials: Marvin Davis, Justin Shippy, Al Guillen, Steve Godfroy.

FT. WAYNE WAYNE: Tippecanoe Valley 51–49 Whitko; Peru 62–51 Ft. Wayne Wayne; Tippecanoe Valley 46–36 Peru; Ft. Wayne Elmhurst 62–59 Norwell; Elmhurst 55– 49 Tippecanoe Valley. Officials: Robert Cochran, David Raabe, Douglas Bauman, Robert Voss.

NEW HAVEN: Bellmont 50–44 Ft. Wayne Bishop Luers; Ft. Wayne Concordia 61–47 Ft. Wayne Bishop Dwenger; Bellmont 61–55 Concordia; Leo 77–47 New Haven; Bellmont 52–37 Leo. Officials: Norman Delph, William Kachel, Robert Plummer, Randall Miller.

BLACKFORD: Elwood 62–60 Blackford; Jay County 66–60 Tipton; Jay County 43–40 Elwood; Mississinewa 52–50 Delta; Jay County 73–67 Mississinewa. Officials: Michael Wallpe, Greg Reece, Jeffrey Pequignot, Steve Elkins.

LEBANON: Brebeuf 69–58 Western Boone; Lebanon 61–56 Danville (ot); Brebeuf 40–38 Lebanon; Crawfordsville 47–38 Southmont; Brebeuf 56–47 Crawfordsville. Officials: Donald McCann, Wayne Hobson, Edward Thornburgh, Ed Scahill.

WHITELAND: Chatard 57–53 Beech Grove; Roncalli 54–38 Whiteland; Chatard 44–40 Roncalli. Officials: John Bowen, Chad Sievers, Shane Franks, Mark Christman.

NEW CASTLE: Pendleton Heights 39–35 Hamilton Heights; New Castle 55–43 Mt. Vernon (Fortville); Pendleton 44–43 NewCastle; New Palestine 63–54 Yorktown; Pendleton Heights 60–48 New Palestine. Officials: Gary Hamilton, Michael McGriff, Jack Raabe, Doug Coddington.

CONNERSVILLE: Connersville 59–52 South Dearborn; Rushville 63–48 Franklin County; Rushville 61–56 Connersville; Batesville 39–38 Greensburg; Rushville 68–45 Batesville. Officials: Greg McAdams, Michael Alford, Randall Gwin, Kevin Moore.

GREENCASTLE: West Vigo 66–59 Owen Valley; Sullivan 65–59 Brown County; Sullivan 62–40 West Vigo; Greencastle 54–47 Edgewood; Greencastle 62–58 Sullivan. Officials: Jerry Taylor, Patrick McCallister, Richard Deering, Gregory Hayes.

CORYDON CENTRAL: Corydon Central 63–54 Madison (ot); Salem 70–64 Scottsburg; Corydon Central 73–63 Salem; North Harrison 54–39 Silver Creek; Corydon Central 55–49 North Harrison. Officials: Derek Howard, Timothy Cartwright, Dan Carmichael, David Kavanaugh.

WASHINGTON: Vincennes Lincoln 45–27 Gibson Southern; Jasper 70–52 Princeton; Lincoln 52–45 Jasper; Washington 44–36 Pike Central; Lincoln 64–54 Washington. Officials: Dave Senning, Josh Turner, Alan Deskin, John Trotter.

BOONVILLE: Heritage Hills 62–59 Mount Vernon; Boonville 54–42 Evansville Bosse; Heritage Hills 54–53 Boonville; Evansville Mater Dei 69–52 Evansville Memorial; Mater Dei 59–55 Heritage Hills. Officials: Scott Arthur, Micjael Zehr, Gary Wier, Brian Patton.

2004 CLASS 2A SECTIONALS

HAMMOND NOLL: Wheeler 55–48 Boone Grove; Hammond Bishop Noll 76–21 Lake Station Edison; Wheeler 74–55 Hanover Central; Noll 39–37 Wheeler. Officials: Steve Kvachkoff, Jeff Rhody, Michael Noojin, Norm Sellers.

IHSAA Scores | 2000–2005

WESTVIEW: Glenn 58–51 Fairfield; Jimtown 61–18 Bremen; Jimtown 45–28 Glenn; Westview 57–37 LaVille; Jimtown 67–52 Westview. Officials: Lance Grubbs, Mike Johnson, Rich Kraus, Thomas Muth.

NORTH JUDSON: North Judson 57–50 Winamac; Rochester 60–52 North Newton; Rensselaer Central 62–56 North Judson; Rochester 60–49 Rensselaer Central. Officials: Neil McCartney, J. Michael DeBoy, Jon Davenport, Kirk Robinson.

FOUNTAIN CENTRAL: Delphi 73–39 Fountain Central; Sheridan 68–55 Clinton Central; Delphi 44–38 Sheridan; North Montgomery 58–49 Seeger; Delphi 62–57 North Montgomery Officials: Mark Hopper, Mark Curts, Danny Ihrie, Steve Morris.

GARRETT: Fremont 57–51 Churubusco (ot); Eastside 56–40 Prairie Heights; Eastside 55–53 Fremont; Garrett 70–52 Central Noble; Garrett 37–35 Eastside (ot). Officials: Stanton Foreman, James Newburn, Russ Baker, Bud Wolf.

BLUFFTON: Harding 48–32 South Adams; Adams Central 62–54 Heritage; Harding 69–55 Adams Central; Bluffton 58–22 Woodlan; Bluffton 54–44 Harding. Officials: Tony Ortman, Eric Hartman, Rob Jewson, James Robinson.

CASS: North Miami 73–55 Northfield; Cass 37–20 Wabash; Cass 61–46 North Miami; Manchester 44–43 Southwood; Cass 36–11 Manchester. Officials: Thomas Leix, Brad Clauss, Gene Wethington, Kent Bennington.

TAYLOR: Oak Hill 55–53 Eastbrook; Madison–Grant 73–50 Eastern (Greentown); Madison-Grant 72–68 Oak Hill (ot); Taylor 49–43 Northwestern; Taylor 65–63 Madison-Grant. Officials: Stewart Casper, Rick Hawley, Dave Terhune, Shawn Lambert.

ALEXANDRIA: Alexandria 52–42 Wapahani (ot); Knightstown 71–51 Eastern Hancock; Frankton 66–54 Shenandoah; Muncie Burris 53–51 Alexandria; Knightstown 66–39 Frankton; Knightstown 67–63 Burris. Officials: Michael Eason, Todd Reel, Mark Hyman, Tim Pharis.

HAGERSTOWN: Winchester 56–51 Hagerstown; Centerville 58–41 Northeastern; Centerville 71–70 Winchester (2ot); Cambridge City Lincoln 66–60 Union County; Centerville 74–60 Lincoln. Officials: Bill Brinkman, Jason Hornaday, Dan Kerker, Brian Heaton.

TRITON CENTRAL: Park Tudor 50–48 Heritage Christian; Tritpon Central 43–37 Speedway; Indian Creek 63–49 Park Tudor; Triton Central 53–33 Indian Creek. Officials: Thomas Lynch, Jon Regashus, Jason McKinley, Kenton Smith.

MILAN: Milan 56–46 Lawrenceburg; North Decatur 56–48 Southwestern (Hanover); Milan 73–68 North Decatur; South Ripley 68–61 Switzerland County; South Ripley 63–54 Milan. Officials: Scott West, Tom Simpson, Larry Sintz, Brian Humphrey.

SOUTH PUTNAM: Monrovia 66–52 Tri-West Hendricks; Cloverdale 82–75 North Putnam; Cascade 62–48 South Putnam; Monrovia 79–58 South Vermillion; Cascade 79–66 Cloverdale; Cascade 72–66 Monrovia. Officials: Don Corey, Rick Gentry, Len Glazier, Bob Whikehart.

PAOLI: Mitchell 51–47 Eastern Greene; North Knox 41–40 South Knox; North Knox 45–44 Mithell; Paoli 66–44 Linton–Stockton; North Knox 45–40 Paoli. Officials: Donald Whitlow, Michael Polley, Ed Roush, Joseph Calderazzo.

BROWNSTOWN CENTRAL: Eastern (Pekin) 69–51 Clarksville; Brownstown Central 57–40 Austin; Brownstown Central 75–62 Eastern (Pekin); Providence 81–60 Charlestown; Brownstown Central 68–63 Providence. Officials: Ron Grimes, Rob Couch, Rick Oliver, Monte McKee.

SOUTHRIDGE: Crawford County 50–46 South Spencer; Forest Park 60–58 Southridge; Perry Central 62–51 Tell City; North Posey 79–66 Crawford County (ot); Forest Park 85–58

Tourney Time

Perry Central; Forest Park 64–42 North Posey. Officials: Mike Grundman, Keith Bagby, Warren Smith, Jay Ritter.

2004 CLASS A SECTIONALS

MORGAN TOWNSHIP: Morgan Township 61–49 Kouts; Washington Township 51–34 Whiting; Hebron 47–45 LaCrosse; Morgan Township 51–28 River Forest; Washington Township 48–46 Hebron; Morgan Township 60–42 Washington Township. Officials: Ron Day, James Arnett, Steve Egan, Jack Urbin.

TRITON: Triton 57–42 Oregon-Davis; Michigan City Marquette 67–35 South Central; Argos 60–43 Culver Community; Triton 61–41 Westville; Argos 54–45 Marquette; Argos 64–61 Triton. Officials: Jay C. Smith, George Forbes, Fred Scheub, Gary Chambers.

BETHANY CHRISTIAN: Ft. Wayne Canterbury 83–56 Hamilton; Lakewood Park Christian 76–48 Keystone; Bethany Christian 71–44 Howe Military; Ft. Wayne Blackhawk 65–49 Canterbury; Bethany 77–31 Lakewood; Blackhawk 62–46 Bethany. Officials: Jerry Stieglitz, Ronald Gradeless, John VanWagner, Bob Childers.

TRI–COUNTY: Caston 40–29 South Newton; West Central 52–37 Tri-County; West Central 39–38 Caston; Pioneer 69–35 North White; West Central 45–37 Pioneer. Officials: Greg Webb, Steve Tyler, Dennis Aldridge, Patrick Dumoulin.

FRONTIER: Lafayette Central Catholic 73–41 Clinton Prairie; Carroll (Flora) 56–49 Rossville; Central Catholic 76–53 Frontier; Central Catholic 49–41 Carroll. Officials: Larry Nixon, Brian Hole, Jerry Snider, Richard Modricker.

SOUTHERN WELLS: Southern Wells 66–34 White's; Tri-Central 62–43 Wes-Del; Tri-Central 62–41 Southern Wells; Marion Lakeview Christian 74–47 Daleville; Tri-Central 66–44 Lakeview Christian. Officials: Matthew Miller, John Pfeiffer, Philip Teusch, Mark Short.

MONROE CENTRAL: Blue River Valley 43–38 Tri; Union City 71–23 Rndolph Southern; Union (Modoc) 58–51 Cowan; Monroe Central 59–54 Blue River Valley; Union City 75–38 Union; Monroe Central 80–59 Union City. Officials: Kevin Brown, Dick Russell, Mark Bauman, Kevin Chestnut.

LAPEL: Covenant Christian 70–50 Eminence; Indianapolis Lutheran 48–43 Indiana School for the Deaf; Covenant 45–31 Lutheran; Indianapolis Cardinal Ritter 58–55 Lapel; Ritter 79–77 Covenant (2ot). Officials: J. K. Wieder, Terry Kreider, Brad Groninger, Jay Scott.

SOUTHWESTERN (SHELBYVILLE): Morristown 60–52 Edinburgh; Waldron 74–46 Morton Memorial; Waldron 65–46 Morristown; Southwestern 51–50 Hauser; Waldron 62–49 Southwestern. Officials: Mike Fawcett, Steve Corya, Rod Weiss, W. Scott Wagner.

SOUTH DECATUR: Shawe Memorial 68–55 South Decatur; Rising Sun 52–40 Oldenburg Academy; Jac-Cen-Del 56–55 Shawe; Jac-Cen-Del 50–38 Rising Sun. Officials: David Bolsega, Doug Pullins, Dan Van Treese, Mike Baas.

WEST WASHINGTON: Springs Valley 56–51 West Washington; Orleans 66–47 Northeast Dubois; Orleans 35–32 Springs Valley; Crothersville 57–40 Medora; Orleans 45–33 Crothersville. Officials: Paul Meagher, Mark Gines, Robert Singelais, Wayne Patterson.

HENRYVILLE: Lanesville 51–44 Christian Academy; South Central (Elizabeth) 72–49 New Washington; Lanesville 62–60 South Central; Henryville 77–35 Borden; Henryville 55–38 Lanesville. Officials: David Moore, Steven Wyrick, Danny Shields, Mike Armstrong.

NORTH VERMILLION: Covington 62–50 Riverton Parke; Turkey Run 53–49 Rockville; Covington 55–34 Turkey Run; Attica 47–44 North Vermilion; Covington 47–36 Attica. Officials: Michael Stoffers, Barry Nicoson, Don Nester, Jay Kellett.

WHITE RIVER VALLEY: Bloomfield 30–29 Shakamak; Clay City 66–35 Union (Dugger); Bloomfield 45–42 Clay City; White River Valley 79–41 North Central (Farmersburg); White River Valley 32–29 Bloomfield. Officials: Michiael Shannon, Jack Pitts, Michael Gaither, Jay Slater.

LOOGOOTEE: Barr–Reeve 34–32 North Daviess; Loogootee 59–39 Vincennes Rivet; Loogootee 28–24 Barr-Reeve; Washington Catholic 39–27 Shoals; Loogootee 38–16 Washington Catholic. Officials: Carl March, Byron Wilkerson, Larry Decker, Dennis Espenlaub.

OAKLAND CITY WOOD: Oakland City Wood 70–53 Cannelton; Evansville Day 57–55 New Harmony (ot); Tecumseh 55–33 Wood; Tecumseh 62–23 Day. Officials: Brad Dishman, Brian Holtz, Tim Stroud, Ron James.

2004 CLASS 4A REGIONALS

MICHIGAN CITY: LaPorte 68–66 East Chicago Central; Valparaiso 66–54 Concord; Valparaiso 62–55 LaPorte. Officials: Denny Hepler, Bob Neff, Mark Berger, Norm Sellers, Doug Greenlee, Kirk Robinson, Marvin Davis, Jay Smith, Lance Grubbs.

MARION: Columbia City 59–34 Lafayette Jefferson; Ft. Wayne South Side 61–59 Muncie Central; Columbia City 52–37 South Side. Officials: Tom Leix, Robert Voss, Jay Scott, J. K. Weider, Randall Miller, Dave Stauffer, Mark Hay, Phil Vidito, Thomas Lynch.

PIKE (Hinkle Fieldhouse): North Central (Indianapolis) 73–53 Franklin Central; Lawrence North 74–52 Indianapolis Northwest; Lawrence North 66–53 North Central. Officials: Brian Humphrey, Antoinne Wynne, Bob Cochran, David Bolsega, Rex Wallace, Craig Petree, Derek Howard, Greg Webb, David Moore.

SEYMOUR: Bloomington North 64–57 Evansville Central (ot); Northview 79–74 New Albany; Bloomington North 55–48 Northview. Officials: Mike Armstrong, Mark Christman, Mike Baas, Ron McGriff, Joseph Calderazzo, Dan Morgan, Ron Grimes, Ray Tebbe, Scott Arthur.

2004 CLASS 3A REGIONALS

PLYMOUTH: Western 73–67 Andrean; Knox 72–63 Hammond Gavit; Western 60–35 Knox. Officials: Tim Pharis, Gary Chambers, Steve Elkins, Matt Miller, Kent Bennington, Tim Knowland, Steve Kvachkoff, Rick Scott, Bryce Heller.

NORTHWOOD: Ft. Wayne Elmhurst 61–42 Northridge; Bellmont 53–41 Jay County; Bellmont 58–57 Elmhurst (ot). Officials: James Robinson, Russell Radtke, Jack Urbin, Bob Childers, Mike Johnson, Steve Godfroy, Greg Yergler, John Goss, Tim Filson.

NEW CASTLE: Pendleton Heights 40–35 Rushville; Indianapolis Chatard 55–48 Brebeuf; Chatard 51–34 Pendleton Heights. Officials: Kenton Smith, Doug Coddington, Wayne Hobson, Greg McAdams, Brian Heaton, Dave Nagel, Tom Walters, Bill Brinkman, John Bowen.

WASHINGTON: Vincennes Lincoln 73–59 Greencastle; Evansville Mater Dei 79–71 Corydon Central; Mater Dei 50–49 Lincoln. Officials: Mike Shannon, Steve Morris, Jay Kellett, Carl March, John Trotter, Rick Gentry, Larry Nixon, Mark Hopper, Mike Stouffers.

Tourney Time

2004 CLASS 2A REGIONALS

NORTH JUDSON: Delphi 51–40 Rochester; Jimtown 49–46 Hammond Bishop Noll; Jimtown 52–38 Delphi. Officials: Pat Dumoulin, Jeff Rhody, Jeff Nix, Curt Yoder, Bruce Klonowski, Doug Cook, Mike Waisnora, Ron Day, Andy Simpson.

SOUTH ADAMS: Garrett 69–55 Taylor; Bluffton 35–32 Cass; Garrett 42–40 Bluffton. Officials: Norm Delph, Mark Short, Dick Modricker, Shawn Lambert, Thomas Wolf, Bud Wolf, Jerry Stieglitz, Mike Eason, Scott West.

ALEXANDRIA: Triton Central 75–61 Knightstown (ot); Centerville 72–68 South Ripley; Centerville 61–44 Triton Central. Officials: Mike Faucett, Ed Scahill, Rick Hawley, Stu Casper, Greg Reece, Mike McGriff, Grady Smith, Stan Foreman, Kevin Brown.

SOUTHRIDGE: Brownstown Central 83–74 Forest Park; Cascade 70–46 North Knox; Brownstown Central 73–49 Cascade. Officials: Jay Slater, Ron James, Dennis Espenlaub, David Kavanaugh, Jay Ritter, Wayne Patterson, Paul Meagher, Rex Nichols, Brad Dishman.

2004 CLASS A REGIONALS

TRITON: Ft. Wayne Blackhawk Christian 55–54 Morgan Township; West Central 63–48 Argos; Blackhawk Christian 62–60 West Central. Officials: Mike Bohan, Lawrence Guynn, Denis Schinderle, Pat Strong, Tim Mills, Kevin Chestnut, Eric Coburn, Don McCann, Gary Hamilton.

FRANKFORT: Lafayette Central Catholic 79–69 Indianapolis Cardinal Ritter; Tri-Central 96–65 Monroe Central; Tri-Central 64–58 Central Catholic. Officials: Don Corey, Greg Bowman, Andy Conrad, Scott Wagner, Tracy Black, Jason Ferguson, Neil McCartney, Jerry Taylor, Tom Rohr.

EDINBURGH: Henryville 74–50 Jac-Cen-Del; Waldron 44–40 Orleans; Waldron 61–55 Henryville. Officials: Kevin Moore, Steve Meyer, Monte McKee, Kevin Lewis, Bob Whikehart, Mike Polley, Terry Magnuson, Mike Wallpe, Tony Ortman.

WHITE RIVER VALLEY: Tecumseh 40–39 Loogootee; White River Valley 60–44 Covington; White River Valley 51–36 Tecumseh. Officials: Greg Hayes, Mike Zehr, Brian Patton, Dave Senning, Kevin Denu, Gary Weideman, Mike Quinn, Don Whitlow, Mike Grundman.

2004 CLASS 4A SEMI–STATES

LAFAYETTE JEFF: Columbia City 39–34 Valparaiso. Officials: Greg Yergler, Neil McCartney, Ron Day.

BEDFORD–NORTH LAWRENCE: Lawrence North 63–54 Bloomington North. Officials: Mark Hay, Terry Magnuson, Don Whitlow.

2004 CLASS 3A SEMI–STATES

LAFAYETTE JEFF: Bellmont 58–46 Western. Officials: Mike Waisnora, Marvin Davis, Greg Webb.

SEYMOUR: Evansville Mater Dei 55–44 Indianapolis Bishop Chatard. Officials: Ron Grimes, Derek Howard, Bill Brinkman.

2004 CLASS 2A SEMI-STATES
WARSAW: Jimtown 57–45 Garrett. Officials: Eric Coburn, Steve Kvachkoff, Jay Smith.
BEDFORD–NORTH LAWRENCE: Brownstown Central 81–73 Centerville. Officials: Larry Nixon, Mike Quinn, Phil Vidito.

2004 CLASS A SEMI-STATES
WARSAW: Ft. Wayne Blackhawk Christian 64–57 Tri-Central. Officials: Jerry Stieglitz, Tom Walters, Stanton Foreman.
SEYMOUR: Waldron 82–76 White River Valley. Officials: Paul Meagher, Grady Smith, Mike Eason.

2004 FINALS—March 27
INDIANAPOLIS (Conseco Fieldhouse):
  CLASS 4A: Lawrence North 50–29 Columbia City. Officials: Mike Waisnora, Steve Kvachkoff, Eric Coburn.
  CLASS 3A: Evansville Mater Dei 63–45 Bellmont. Officials: Larry Nixon, Terry Magnuson, Tom Walters.
  CLASS 2A: Jimtown 63–59 Brownstown Central. Officials: Marvin Davis, Jerry Stieglitz, Ron Grimes.
  CLASS A: Waldron 69–54 Ft. Wayne Blackhawk Christian. Officials: Mark Hay, Derek Howard, Greg Yergler.

2005 CLASS 4A SECTIONALS
EAST CHICAGO CENTRAL: Highland 64–45 Lowell; Gary West Side 63–55 Lake Central; West Side 64–60 Highland; Munster 62–55 East Chicago Central; West Side 60–40 Munster. First two games played at Lowell and West Side. Officials: Ron Day, Robert Filipek, Michael Noojin, James Arnett.
MERRILLVILLE: Merrillville 52–29 Portage; Valparaiso 80–54 Hobart; Valparaiso 69–52 Merrillville; Crown Point 61–48 Chesterton; Valparaiso 64–36 Crown Point. Officials: Doug Greenlee, Ronald Gradeless, Robert Bishop, Mark Berger.
MICHIGAN CITY: Michigan City 62–59 South Bend Adams; South Bend Clay 53–36 LaPorte; Clay 55–44 Michigan City; South Bend Washington 71–69 South Bend Riley; Clay 75–62 Washington. First two games played at Michigan City and South Bend Clay. Officials: Merlin Nice, Russell Radtke, Mike Emerson, Bruce Klonowski.
ELKHART CENTRAL: Concord 64–46 Elkhart Central; Elkhart Memorial 58–44 Goshen; Concord 53–51 Memorial; Mishawaka 31–30 Penn; Concord 58–48 Mishawaka. Officials: Denny Hepler, Mark Sewell, Jon Davenport, Kirk Robinson.
DEKALB: Warsaw 70–55 East Noble; Columbia City 49–48 Carroll (Ft. Wayne); DeKalb 43–36 Warsaw; DeKalb 36–34 Columbia City. Officials: Bob Childers, Doug Cook, Russell Baker, Dennis Jackson.

Tourney Time

HUNTINGTON NORTH: Ft. Wayne Snider 57–53 Ft. Wayne Northrop; Homestead 68–65 Huntington North; Snider 70–67 Homestead; Ft. Wayne North Side 82–71 Ft. Wayne South Side; North Side 74–67 Snider. Officials: Thomas Leix, Brad Clauss, Mark Bauman, Gary Chambers.

KOKOMO: Marion 71–69 Lafayette Jefferson (ot); Kokomo 75–71 Logansport (ot); Kokomo 57–56 Marion; Harrison (West Lafayette) 63–42 McCutcheon; Kokomo 72–68 Harrison. Officials: Bob Anderson, Steve Godfroy, Robert Plummer, Kevin Lewis.

RICHMOND: Muncie Southside 81–62 Anderson Highland; Muncie Central 79–58 Anderson; Central 70–39 Southside; Richmond 69–46 Greenfield Central; Central 57–51 Richmond. Officials: Tony Ortman, Ed Roush, Andrew Conrad, Greg McAdams.

NOBLESVILLE: Westfield 60–59 Indianapolis Broad Ripple; Carmel 69–40 Hamilton Southeastern; Carmel 65–32 Westfield; North Central (Indianapolis) 57–43 Noblesville; North Central 60–53 Carmel. Officials: Tom Rohr, Mark Short, Sean Malloy, Brian Heaton.

LAWRENCE CENTRAL: Indianapolis Cathedral 50–47 Lawrence Cntral; Lawrence North 65–27 Indianapolis Manual; Indianapolis 63–55 Warren Central; Cathedral 74–49 Indianapolis Tech; Lawrence North 60–45 Arlington; Lawrence North 39–30 Cathedral. Officials: Gary Hamilton, Greg Reece, Rick Hawley, Ron McGriff.

FRANKLIN CENTRAL: Decatur Central 57–50 Perry Meridian; Franklin Central 54–51 Center Grove; Franklin 55–48 Greenwood; Decatur Central 68–52 Southport; Franklin 44–40 Franklin Central; Decatur Central 70–60 Franklin. Officials: Donald McCann, Ronald McCann, Edward Thornburgh, Casey Gaynor.

BEN DAVIS: Indianapolis Northwest 63–60 Zionsville; Ben Davis 60–47 Avon; Northwest 43–40 Ben Davis; Pike 73–46 Brownsburg; Pike 80–48 Northwest. Officials: Michael Stoffers, Tom Walters, James Saddler, Haymon Fields.

NORTHVIEW: Plainfield 54–51 Terre Haute North; Terre Haute South 67–35 Mooresville; South 77–55 Plainfield; Northview 55–53 Martinsville; South 56–38 Northview. Officials: Gary Wier, Larry Nixon, Patrick McCallister, David Kavanaugh.

SHELBYVILLE: Bloomington South 58–30 Bloomington North; Shelbyville 58–53 Columbus North (ot); South 55–35 Shelbyville; East Central 63–61 Columbus East; South 60–46 East Central. Officials: Don Corey, Mark Curts, Rod Weiss, W. Scott Wagner.

SEYMOUR: Seymour 56–55 New Albany; Jeffersonville 73–30 Floyd Central; Seymour 59–58 Jeffersonville; Jennings County 82–78 Bedford North Lawrence; Jennings County 54–52 Seymour. Officials: Paul Meagher, Rick Oliver, John Ripperger, Mike Baas.

EVANSVILLE HARRISON: Evansville Central 59–52 Evansville Reitz; Evansville Harrison 73–62 Evansville North; Castle 72–63 Central (ot); Harrison 61–47 Castle. Officials: Mike Grundman, Mark Christman, Stephen Marx, Scott Arthur.

2005 CLASS 3A SECTIONALS

HAMMOND CLARK: Hammond 72–33 Calumet; Hammond Morton 54–43 Hammond Clark; Hammond 54–40 Morton; Hammond Gavit 58–45 Griffith (ot); Hammond 52–47 Gavit. Officials: John Goss, Kevin Mikesell, Steve Egan, Andy Simpson.

GARY ROOSEVELT: (Games played at Gary West Side): Gary Wallace 107–80 Kankakee Valley; Gary Roosevelt 66–50 Gary Wirt; Andrean 82–56 Wallace; Andrean 84–75 Roosevelt.

IHSAA Scores | 2000–2005

Officials: Mark Wise, Steve Kvachkoff, George Forbes, Norm Sellers.

PLYMOUTH: Knox 45–38 Culver Academy; Mishawaka Marian 51–43 New Prairie; Marian 60–58 Knox; Plymouth 66–56 South Bend St. Joseph's ; Plymouth 63–50 Marian. Officials: Patrick Dumoulin, Rollan Thill, Dennis Aldridge, James Newburn.

FRANKFORT: Frankfort 52–46 Benton Central; Twin Lakes 87–72 Maconaquah; Twin Lakes 67–58 Frankfort; Western 51–42 West Lafayette; Twin Lakes 57–49 Western. Officials: Phil Vidito, Kenton Smith, Matt Knezevich, Arnold Freeman, Jr.

NORTHWOOD: Northridge 51–48 Northwood (ot); Wawasee 69–51 West Noble; Wawasee 67–36 Northridge; Lakeland 58–52 Angola; Wawasee 58–53 Lakeland. Officials: Jay C. Smith, John VanWagner, Jon Hershberger, Thomas Muth.

WHITKO: Peru 64–57 Ft. Wayne Elmhurst; Ft. Wayne Wayne 72–50 Whitko; Peru 56–51 Wayne; Tippecanoe Valley 79–45 Norwell; Tippecanoe Valley 55–39 Peru. Officials: Stanton Foreman, Justin Shippy, Bud Wolf, Eric Hartman.

BELLMONT: Ft. Wayne Bishop Dwenger 70–54 Ft. Wayne Bishop Luers; Bellmont 60–49 Ft. Wayne Concordia; Bellmont 54–46 Ft. Wayne Dwenger; Leo 74–66 New Haven; Bellmont 60–54 Leo. Offiials: Jason Hornaday, Jack Urbin, Dave Terhune, Robert Voss.

BLACKFORD: Jay County 65–54 Elwood; Mississinewa 49–46 Blackford; Jay County 54–41 Mississinewa; Delta 55–50 Tipton; Delta 43–25 Jay County. Officials: Scott West, John Pfeiffer, Rich Kraus, Todd Reel.

DANVILLE: Lebanon 39–38 Crawfordsville; Danville 74–52 Southmont; Danville 57–47 Lebanon; Brebeuf 68–47 Western Boone; Brebeuf 58–42 Danville. Officials: P. J. Pitts, Jason McKinley, Dan Carmichael, Jason Ferguson.

WHITELAND: Indianapolis Howe 72–63 Indianapolis Washington; Indianapolis Roncalli 54–31 Beech Grove; Roncalli 80–49 Howe; Indianapolis Bishop Chatard 55–43 Whiteland; Roncalli 55–39 Chatard. Officials: David Moore, Antoine Wynne, Dick Russell, Wayne Hobson.

NEW CASTLE: New Castle 60–46 Pendleton Heights; Hamilton Heights 61–51 New Palestine; New Castle 67–50 Hamilton Heights; Yorktown 44–41 Mt. Vernon (Fortville); New Castle 52–41 Yorktown. Officials: Rex Nichols, Chad Sievers, Tim Pharis, Stewart Casper.

CONNERSVILLE: Rushville 63–41 South Dearborn; Greensburg 47–45 Franklin County; Rushville 54–47 Greensburg; Connersville 63–56 Batesville; Rushville 51–44 Connersville. Officials: Mike Fawcett, Robert Cochran, Doug Pullins, Pat Strong.

GREENCASTLE: Owen Valley 66–59 West Vigo; Greencastle 57–47 Sullivan; Owen Valley 59–55 Greencastle; Edgewood 53–48 Brown County; Edgewood 80–75 Owen Valley (3ot). Officials: Jerry Taylor, Jon Regashus, Bob Whikehart, Michael Polley.

SALEM: Salem 63–62 Silver Creek; Scottsburg 82–70 Madison; Scottsburg 83–67 Salem; North Harrison 58–52 Corydon Central; Scottsburg 77–59 North Harrison. Officials: Ron James, John Bowen, Larry Steimel, Joseph Calderazzo.

WASHINGTON: Jasper 51–42 Princeton; Vincennes Lincoln 86–39 Pike Central; Lincoln 58–47 Jasper; Washington 70–51 Gibson Southern; Washington 83–60 Lincoln. Officials: Brian Holtz, Steve Morris, Tyler Kumpf, Tim Stroud.

BOONVILLE: Bonville 54–51 Evansville Bosse; Heritage Hills 57–38 Mount Vernon; Boonville 66–56 Heritage Hills (2ot); Evansville Mater Dei 66–55 Evansville Memorial; Mater Dei 47–38 Boonville. Officials: Wayne Patterson, Kevin Christman, Nick Mattheis, Dennis Espenlaub.

Tourney Time

2005 CLASS 2A SECTIONALS

WHEELER: Boone Grove 59–16 Lake Station Edison; Hammond Bishop Noll 52–45 Wheeler; Boone Grove 76–56 Hanover Central; Boone Grove 75–69 Noll (ot). Officials: Tim Filson, Mike Waisnora, Dale Cramer, Butch Lehman.

LAVILLE: Glenn 53–34 Bremen; Fairfield 60–53 Westview; Glenn 64–54 Fairfield; Jimtown 52–37 LaVille; Glenn 45–36 Jimtown. Officials: Brett Patrick, Fred Scheub, Tim Mills, Curtis Yoder.

WINAMAC: Rensselaer Central 52–48 Rochester; North Judson 58–33 Winamac; Rensselaer 55–35 North Newton; Rensselaer 62–48 North Judson. Officials: Greg Webb, Greg Yergler, Ernie Stephens, J. Michael DeBoy.

NORTH MONTGOMERY: Delphi 63–41 Clinton Central; Sheridan 55–39 Fountain Central; Delphi 50–29 Sheridan; North Montgomery 69–60 Seeger; North Montgomery 72–68 Delphi. Officials: Ray Tebbe, Steve Tyler, Don Nester, Tracy Black.

GARRETT: Churubusco 44–35 Eastside; Garrett 59–58 Central Noble (ot); Churubusco 51–32 Garrett; Fremont 54–51 Prairie Heights; Fremont 87–72 Churubusco. Officials: Dick Modricker, Jerry Stieglitz, Lon Graft, David Raabe.

SOUTH ADAMS: Harding 79–49 Woodlan; South Adams 64–42 Adams Central; Harding 58–32 South Adams; Bluffton 43–40 Heritage; Harding 67–44 Bluffton. Officials: Michael Eason, Mike Johnson, Matthew Hans, Michael McGriff.

MANCHESTER: Cass 24–22 North Miami (2ot); Northfield 42–36 Wabash; Northfield 32–27 Cass; Southwood 49–45 Manchester; Northfield 37–35 Southwood. Officials: Shawn Lambert, Eric Coburn, Russ Melcher, Steve Elkins.

TAYLOR: Northwestern 72–57 Taylor; Eastern (Greentown) 71–59 Oak Hill; Northwestern 72–54 Eastern; Eastbrook 55–44 Madison-Grant; Northwestern 85–81 Eastbrook. Officials: J. K. Wieder, Jerry Snider, James Mettler, Matthew Miller.

ALEXANDRIA: Shenandoan 70–39 Muncie Burris; Frankton 70–66 Alexandria; Eastern Hancock 48–37 Wapahani; Knightstown 70–66 Shenandoah; Frankton 69–60 Eastern Hancock; Knightstown 65–57 Frankton. Officials: Kevin Brown, Randall Miller, William Kachel, Ed Scahill.

HAGERSTOWN: Cambridge City Lincoln 57–54 Northeastern; Centerville 77–67 Winchester; Centerville 81–56 Lincoln; Union County 44–34 Hagerstown; Centerville 52–21 Union County. Officials: Grady Smith, Jay Scott, Shane Franks, Rex Wallace.

SPEEDWAY: Park Tudor 68–39 Triton Central; Speedway 52–47 Indian Creek; Speedway 68–39 Park Tudor; Heritage Christian 64–34 Indianapolis Scecina; Heritage Christian 71–63 Speedway. Officials: David Bolsega, Brian Totton, Danny Ihrie, Rob Couch.

LAWRENCEBURG: North Decatur 63–52 Lawrenceburg; South Ripley 56–39 Milan; North Decatur 49–41 South Ripley (ot); Southwestern (Hanover) 58–50 Switzerland County; North Decatur 49–36 Southwestern. Officials: Donald Whitlow, Jeff Gwin, Dan Kerker, Kevin Moore.

SOUTH PUTNAM: Cloverdale 68–46 North Putnam; Monrovia 61–60 Tri-West Hendricks; Cascade 73–53 South Vermillion; Cloverdale 53–52 South Putnam; Cascade 65–54 Monrovia; Cascade 91–67 Cloverdale. Officials: Jay Kellett, Michael Gaither, Kevin Fetterman, John Trotter.

NORTH KNOX: Linton–Stockton 39–34 South Knox; Paoli 58–56 Mitchell; Paoli 66–53 Linton-Stockton; Eastern Greene 49–44 North Knox; Eastern Greens 49–48 Paoli. Officials: Jay Ritter, Gary Weideman, Michiael Shannon, Alan Deskin.

CHARLESTOWN: Eastern (Pekin) 74–63 Charlestown; Brownstown Central 70–47

Clarksville; Austin 60–56 Eastern; Austin 84–71 Brownstown Central. Officials: Kevin Denu, Steven Wyrick, Dick Hammond, Carl March.

SOUTHRIDGE: Southridge 68–49 Tell City; Perry Central 80–49 Crawford County; Forest Park 79–64 South Spencer; Southridge 52–49 North Posey; Forest Park 78–59 Perry Central; Forest Park 61–46 Southridge. Officials: R. Brad Dishman, Larry Decker, Byron Wilkerson, Michael Zehr.

2005 CLASS A SECTIONALS

KOUTS: Washington Township 59–53 Whiting (2ot); Hebron 56–46 River Forest; Kouts 53–48 LaCrosse; Morgan Township 52–44 Washington Township; Hebron 66–65 Kouts; Morgan Township 61–57 Hebron (ot). Officials: Rick Scott, Jeff Rhody, Jeffrey Noffsinger; Kent Bennington.

CULVER COMMUNITY: Argos 54–50 Triton; Westville 65–51 Oregon-Davis; South Central (Union Mills) 78–77 Culver Community; Argos 53–44 Michigan City Marquette; Westville 59–30 South Central; Argos 56–45 Westville. Officials: James Robinson, Jeffrey Nix, Jeff Hughes, Tim Knowland.

HAMILTON: Hamilton 65–35 Lakewood Park Christian; Ft. Wayne Blackhawk Christian 72–42 Ft. Wayne Canterbury; Keystone 72–62 Howe Military (ot); Elkhart Christian Academy 71–53 Bethany Christian; Blackhawk Christian 56–33 Hamilton; Christian Academy 81–40 Keystone; Blackhawk Christian 60–48 Christian Academy. Officials: Bryce Heller, Robert Neff, Jeffrey Pequignot, Dave Stauffer.

TRI-COUNTY: Caston 52–24 North White; Tri-County 61–35 Pioneer; Tri-County 49–38 Caston; West Central 45–43 South Newton; West Central 45–38 Tri-County. Officials: Terry Bartell, Ryan Crabb, Dean Martin, Denis Schinderle.

FRONTIER: Lafayette Central Catholic 62–40 Carroll (Flora); Clinton Prairie 50–41 Rossville; Central Catholic 71–56 Frontier; Central Catholic 66–48 Clinton Prairie. Officials: Neil McCartney, Stacey Minier, John Cowan, Mike Bohan.

SOUTHERN WELLS: Tri-Central 71–52 Marion Lakeview Christian; Wes-Del 77–45 White's; Tri-Central 90–43 Wes-Del; Southern Wells 61–56 Daleville; Tri-Central 75–40 Southern Wells. Officials: Mark Baltz, Rob Jewson, Joe Rondot, Kevin Chestnut.

TRI: Tri 47–42 Blue River Valley; Monroe Central 65–55 Union (Modoc); Union City 55–51 Cowan; Tri 54–38 Randolph Southern; Union City 67–55 Monroe Central; Tri 70–56 Union City. Officials: Dan Morgan, Kerry O'Brien, Randall Gwin, Lawrence Guynn.

LAPEL: Indianapolis Cardinal Ritter 92–56 Indiana School for the Deaf; Lapel 84–57 Covenant Christian; Indianapolis Lutheran 88–30 International; Ritter 81–45 Eminence; Lapel 79–51 Lutheran; Lapel 70–50 Ritter. Officials: Thomas Lynch, Justin Markley, Michael Alford, Derek Howard.

EDINBURGH: Morristown 72–49 Morton Memorial; Hauser 68–44 Edinburgh; Hauser 57–48 Morristown; Southwestern (Shelbyville) 90–62 Waldron; Hauser 61–47 Southwestern. Officials: Jay Slater, Terry Kreider, Jerry Middleton, Doug Coddington.

SOUTH DECATUR: Jac-Cen-Del 50–43 Oldenburg Academy; South Decatur 47–43 Shawe Memorial; Rising Sun 61–57 Jac-Cen-Del; South Decatur 67–54 Rising Sun. Officials: Bill Brinkman, Tom Simpson, Larry Sintz, Brian Humphrey.

SPRINGS VALLEY: Orleans 38–30 West Washington; Springs Valley 59–43 Crothersville;

Tourney Time

Orleans 54–38 Springs Valley; Northeast Dubois 56–39 Medora; Orleans 42–40 Northeast Dubois (ot). Officials: Dave Senning, Warren Smith, Brian Patton, Mike Armstrong.

NEW WASHINGTON: Lanesville 58–48 Restoration Academy; South Central (Elizabeth) 74–41 Christian Academy of Indiana 41; Henryville 55–30 New Washington; Lanesville 37–34 Borden; Henryville 73–57 South Central; Henryville 43–38 Lanesville. Officials: Mark Gines, Roger Marley, Robert Singelais, Steven Corya.

NORTH VERMILLION: Covington 39–35 Attica; Turkey Run 55–51 Rockville; Covington 31–25 Turkey Run; Riverton Parke 57–48 North Vermillion; Covington 45–39 Riverton Parke. Officials: Mark Hopper, Brian Hole, Len Glazier, David Nagel.

WHITE RIVER VALLEY: North Central (Farmersburg) 64–55 Clay City; Bloomfield 54–51 White River Valley; Union (Dugger) 78–40 Holy Cross; Shakamak 59–58 North Central; Bloomfield 49–33 Union; Bloomfield 44–40 Shakamak. Officials: Rick Gentry, Terry Magnuson, Byron Davis, Ron Grimes.

NORTH DAVIESS: Shoals 36–28 Washington Catholic; Barr-Reeve 50–40 Vincennes Rivet; Barr-Reeve 47–45 Shoals; Loogootee 40–34 North Daviess; Loogootee 40–36 Barr-Reeve (2ot). Officials: Keith Bagby, Gregory Hayes, Jason Enrique, Barry Nicoson.

TECUMSEH: Oakland City Wood 62–55 Evansville Day; Tecumseh 49–47 New Harmony; Wood 75–64 Cannelton; Tecumseh 51–42 Wood. Officials: Michael Quinn, Charles Meyer, Paul Wahl, Josh Turner.

2005 CLASS 4A REGIONALS

MICHIGAN CITY: Gary West Side 66–55 Concord; Valparaiso 69–63 South Bend Clay; Gary West Side 57–43 Valparaiso. Officials: Mark Berger, Butch Lehman, Brad Clauss, Norm Sellers, Kirk Robinson, Curt Yoder, Neil McCartney, Jay Smith, Ron Day.

MARION: Kokomo 58–50 DeKalb; Muncie Central 80–52 Ft. Wayne North Side; Muncie Central 68–39 Kokomo. Officials: Donald McCann, Robert Voss, Jay Scott, Mike Fawcett, Kevin Chestnut, Ed Scahill, Phil Vidito, Michael Eason, J. K. Wieder.

PIKE (Hinkle Fieldhouse): Lawrence North 54–46 Pike; North Central (Indianapolis) 74–61 Decatur Central; Lawrence Central 56–42 North Central. Officials: Ron Gradeless, Doug Coddington, Brian Heaton, Don Corey, Denis Schinderle, Todd Reel, Jerry Taylor, Michael Stoffers, Dave Senning.

SEYMOUR: Bloomington South 76–67 Jennings County (ot); Terre Haute South 73–65 Evansville Harrison; Terre Haute South 66–63 Bloomington South. Officials: Michael Zehr, Stewart Casper, Rob Couch, Scott Arthur, Steven Corya, Jason Ferguson, Ray Tebbe, Bob Anderson, Ron James.

2005 CLASS 3A REGIONALS

PLYMOUTH: Twin Lakes 58–56 Andrean; Plymouth 56–36 Hammond; Plymouth 67–56 Twin Lakes. Officials: James Robinson, Steve Elkins, Eric Hartman, Bob Childers, Tim Knowland, James Newburn, Rick Scott, Mark Baltz, Doug Greenlee.

NORTHWOOD: Bellmont 48–46 Delta; Wawasee 73–63 Tippecanor Valley; Wawasee 73–64 Bellmont. Officials: Brett Patrick, Bruce Klonowski, James Arnett, Jeffrey Nix, Jack Urbin,

Thomas Muth, John Goss, Tim Filson, Shawn Lambert.

NEW CASTLE: Roncalli 72–63 Rushville; New Castle 68–46 Brebeuf; Roncalli 58–47 New Castle. Officials: Greg McAdams, Rex Wallace, Michael Gaither, Ron McGriff, Lawrence Guynn, Chad Sievers, Dick Modricker, Dan Morgan, David Moore.

WASHINGTON: Scottsburg 85–77 Evansville Mater Dei; Washington 72–33 Edgewood; Washington 88–68 Scottsburg. Officials: David Kavanaugh, John Trotter, Barry Nicoson, Josh Turner, Steve Morris, Steve Meyer, Rex Nichols, Jay Slater, Gary Weir.

2005 CLASS 2A REGIONALS

NORTH JUDSON: Glenn 58–47 Rensselaer Central; Boone Grove 51–40 North Montgomery; Glenn 46–44 Boone Grove (ot). Officials: Mike Bohan, Fred Scheub, Kent Bennington, Matthew Miller, Gary Chambers, Michael DeBoy, Greg Webb, Jay Kellett, Mark Wise.

BLACKFORD: Northfield 51–49 Fremont; Harding 81–67 Northwestern; Harding 65–31 Northfield. Officials: Pat Strong, Michael McGriff, Tracy Black, Jason Hornaday, Hamon Fields, Arnold Freeman, Tony Ortman, Bill Brinkman, Scott West.

ALEXANDRIA: North Decatur 65–63 Centerville; Knightstown 76–71 Heritage Christian; Knightstown 75–63 North Decatur. Officials: David Bolsega, Dennis Jackson, Dave Stauffer, Kevin Moore, Brian Humphrey, Mark Short, Gary Hamilton, Terry Bartell, P. J. Pitts.

SOUTHRIDGE: Forest Park 61–51 Estern Greene; Austin 70–62 Cascade; Forest Park 79–63 Austin. Officials: Keith Bagby, Steve Wyrick, Carl March, Kevin Denu, Dennis Espenlaub, Roger Marley, Donald Whitlow, Mike Grundman, Jay Ritter.

2005 CLASS A REGIONALS

TRITON: Morgan Township 50–41 Argos; Ft. Wayne Blackhawk Christian 63–48 West Central; Blackhawk Christian 55–43 Morgan Township. Officials: Patrick Dumoulin, David Raabe, Steve Godfroy, Kevin Brown, Randall Miller, Douglas Cook, Stan Foreman, Denny Hepler, Thomas Leix.

FRANKFORT: Lafayette Central Catholic 84–50 Tri; Lapel 79–63 Tri-Central; Lapel 46–44 Central Catholic. Officials: Kevin Lewis, Jon Regashus, Casey Gaynor, Mark Hopper, Wayne Hobson, Steve Tyler, Tom Rohr, Wayne Patterson, Rick Gentry.

FRANKLIN: Hauser 71–61 South Decatur; Henryville 39–37 Orleans; Hauser 71–44 Henryville. Officials: Joseph Calderazzo, David Nagel, Rick Oliver, Mike Armstrong, Terry Kreider, Mark Curts, Thomas Lynch, Grady Smith, Brian Holtz.

LOOGOOTEE: Covington 55–51 Bloomfield; Loogootee 45–34 Tecumseh; Loogootee 49–34 Covington. Officials: Alan Deskin, Michael Polley, Gary Weideman, Tim Stroud, Scott Wagner, Mike Baas, Paul Meagher, Brad Dishman, Michael Quinn.

2005 CLASS 4A SEMI—STATES

LAFAYETTE JEFFERSON: Muncie Central 69–40 Gary West Side. Officials: Tom Rohr, Tim Filson, Stan Foreman.

SOUTHPORT: Lawrence North 71–52 Terre Haute South. Officials: Rick Scott, Neil McCartney, Shawn Lambert.

Tourney Time

2005 CLASS 3A SEMI-STATES
HUNTINGTON NORTH: Plymouth 62–51 Wawasee. Officials: Gary Hamilton, Tony Ortman, Thom Lynch.
SEYMOUR: Washington 51–46 Roncalli. Officials: Ray Tebbe, Brad Dishman, Bill Brinkman.

2005 CLASS 2A SEMI-STATES
HUNTINGTON NORTH: Harding 56–46 Glenn. Officials: Jerry Taylor, Dick Modricker, Denny Hepler.
SOUTHPORT: Forest Park 76–73 Knightstown. Officials: Phil Vidito, Paul Meagher, Jay Slater.

2005 CLASS A SEMI-STATES
LAFAYETTE JEFFERSON: Lapel 60–45 Ft. Wayne Blackhawk Christian. Officials: John Goss, Michael Stoffers, Grady Smith.
SEYMOUR: Loogootee 36–35 Hauser. Officials: Rex Nichols, Don Whitlow, Michael Eason.

2005 FINALS—March 26
INDIANAPOLIS (Conseco Fieldhouse):
CLASS 4A: Lawrence North 63–52 Muncie Central. Officials: John Goss, Ray Tebbe, Paul Meagher.
CLASS 3A: Washington 74–72 Plymouth (ot). Officials: Rex Nichols, Jerry Taylor, Dick Modricker.
CLASS 2A: Forest Park 68–63 Harding. Officials: Rick Scott, Tom Rohr, Tony Ortman.
CLASS A: Lapel 51–40 Loogootee. Officials: Phil Vidito, Gary Hamilton, Neil McCartney.

The Author and Compiler

Bill May, a native of Hagerstown, Indiana, officiated high school basketball for twenty-three years and worked the state finals in 1972, '73, and '74. He graduated from Ball State Teachers College and held management positions with Perfect Circle Corporation (acquired by Dana Corporation), McCall Corporation, and Firestone Tire and Rubber Company. He attends many high school and NCAA Division III games and has attended the Indiana high school finals for fifty-eight consecutive years.

Bill and his wife of forty-nine years, Carolyn, have lived in Richmond for forty-six years, and have two sons: John and wife Denise, who live in Hurricane, West Virginia; and Paul and wife Tami, who live in Raleigh, North Carolina, with their twins, Aaron William and Kylee Nicole.

Books of Interest

You Lose Some, You Lose Some
The Beyond-Belief Screwed-Up Seasons, Gruesome Games, Doomed Dynasties, Failed Favorites, Pitiful Players, and Fouled-Up Franchises in the History of Sports
By Eric Furman and Lou Harry

Sports fans are familiar with tales of triumphant heroes, remarkable willpower, brilliant strategists, and against-all-odds comebacks. History, after all, is written by the winners. This book isn't about them.

Profiling thirty individuals, teams, and even leagues who distinguished themselves by holding tight to the losing end of the stick, Eric Furman and Lou Harry tell their stories in candid, humorous, fact- and stat-filled entries, including

- The Minnesota Vikings' doomed dynasty
- Chris Webber's infamous time-out
- The less-than-Amazin' Mets of 1962
- And Mary Decker, whose hopes of Olympic victory were nipped by the Budd.

Paperback   Price $14.99
ISBN: 1-57860-183-5

Thursday's Game
Notes from a Golfer with Far to Go
By Tom Chiarella

"**Tom Chiarella is the best golf writer you've never heard of—unless you read *Esquire*, *Links*, or *Washington Golf Monthly*...**"
- SportsIllustrated.com

With the keen eye of a regular guy, Tom Chiarella plays courses that most duffers can only dream of—leaving divots, lost balls, and the occasional picture-perfect pin shot in his wake. Tom brings his A-game, complete with a wry sense of humor and a quick "Fore!" whether he's playing in Scotland, Morocco, Pebble Beach, or his favorite par-three in Terre Haute, Indiana.

Join Tom as he spends a few days with roguish pro John Daly, plays a round with actor Billy Crudup, and hits the links with Vegas singer Don Cherry. Regardless of where he is or who he's playing with, Tom keeps his wit in the fairway and his shots in the rough, making for a wonderful armchair companion.

Hardcover   Price $22.99
ISBN: 1-57860-170-3

Books of Interest

Haunted Hoosier Trails
A Guide to Indiana's Famous Folklore Spooky Sites
By Wanda Lou Willis

Indiana has a long tradition of stories about tragic deaths and restless spirits. In *Haunted Hoosier Trails*, folklorist Wanda Lou Willis passes on these local legends, along with modern folk tales that will raise the hair on your head and stoke the fires of your imagination.

Journey with Wanda Lou Willis to Hazelcot, the deserted dream mansion in Whitley County, Indiana; to the forsaken tomb of the riverboat captain along the Ohio River, where to this day boats toot out their homage to avoid the ghost's curse; and to the bridges near Avon, Indiana, where the unexpected happens around Halloween. Do ghosts walk the trails and back roads, highways and byways of the Hoosier Heartland? Find out for yourself!

Paperback   Price $15.95
ISBN: 1-57860-115-0

More Haunted Hoosier Trails
Folklore from Indiana's Spookiest Places
By Wanda Lou Willis

Beloved Indiana folklorist Wanda Lou Willis returns with an all-new collection of hair-raising tales about spooky cemeteries, lonely roads and haunted homes all over Indiana. Local history buffs will relish the informative county histories that begin each chapter, while thrill-and-chill-seekers will eagerly search out these frightening locales.

In *More Haunted Hoosier Trails*, you can:
- Step inside Hannah House in Indianapolis, and you may encounter the ghosts of escaped slaves on the Underground Railroad who perished in a tragic fire.
- Get a lesson in fear at Indiana University in Bloomington, long believed to be among the most haunted campuses in the country.
- Learn about strange happenings and restless spirits in cities, towns and counties all across the state.

The carefully researched and truly scary tales by one of Indiana's most respected folklorists will enthrall even the most skeptical reader. *More Haunted Hoosier Trails* is a terrifyingly good read.

Paperback   Price $14.99
ISBN: 1-57860-182-7

Books of Interest

Indiana Legends
Famous Hoosiers from Johnny Appleseed to David Letterman
4th Edition
By Nelson Price

Famous Hoosiers have played prominent roles in our nation's cultural, military and sports history. Political leaders, entertainers, sports legends, war heroes, inventors, and even notorious criminals—the great nineteenth state has been home to them all. The fourth edition of *Indiana Legends* features more than one hundred sixty famous Hoosiers, with new material and updated profiles. It's a great resource for readers of all ages, students, local historians and all those interested in Indiana achievements.

Notable Hoosiers in *Indiana Legends* include musician John Mellencamp; movie star Vivica A. Fox; Garfield creator Jim Davis; former Indiana Pacers superstar Reggie Miller; World War II Air Force pilot Margaret Ray Ringenberg; and many more.

Prize-winning interviews by Nelson Price contribute contemporary interest to this collection. Famous Indiana illustrations, portraits and photographs add another rich dimension to the stories.

Paperback   Price $24.99
ISBN: 1-57860-186-X

Barney
The Stray Beagle Who Became a TV Star and Stole Our Hearts
By Dick Wolfsie

The greatest Barney moments, told by his faithful human sidekick—a book destined to make dog lovers laugh, cry, and howl at the moon.

When TV Reporter Dick Wolfsie took in the tiny stray beagle shivering on his front step, he had no idea that the dog would become more than just a faithful companion. Barney the Beagle's career in the public eye included three thousand shows, fourteen commercials, and twelve straight years on the air.

If you followed Barney's antics over the years, you'll recognize your favorite Barney stories here, plus more than a few surprises. If you missed Barney on TV, here's your chance to meet an unforgettable beagle who had heart, brains, and moxie to spare.

Paperback   Price $14.99
ISBN: 1-57860-167-3